ISBN 978-0-428-17035-6
PIBN 11305676

TREATISE ON PRACTICE

IN THE COURTS OF COMMON PLEAS OF PENNSYLVANIA.

BY

F. CARROLL BREWSTER, LL.D.

Frederick

SECOND EDITION, REVISED.

IN TWO VOLUMES.

VOL. I.

PHILADELPHIA:

KAY & BROTHER,

LAW BOOKSELLERS, PUBLISHERS AND IMPORTERS.

1896.

PHILADELPHIA:
DORNAN, PRINTER.

INTRODUCTION TO REVISED EDITION.

THIS work is not designed to take the place of a treatise upon Pleading, Evidence, Equity, or any special department of the law save that indicated by the title.

Nor is it proposed to make it a *résumé* of decisions on Practice. This would in effect convert it into a digest.

Some forty years ago Messrs. Troubat and Haly published a small treatise on Practice, containing only a few hundred pages. The desire for large works subsequently expanded the original edition into two huge volumes. This has been of great advantage to the profession. Without underrating its value, the remark may, however, be safely ventured that the instruction needed by the beginner should be very compact and very clear.

It has been my aim simply to assist the tyro. The veteran needs no help, and could far better teach me than receive my instruction.

Since the first edition of this work a number of suggestions and corrections have been made by members of the Bar in various parts of the State, which have been incorporated in the present edition. For all these the author here desires to express his thanks.

In this edition former publications have been revised. The decisions are cited to date.

F. C. B.

CONTENTS.

THE REFERENCES ARE TO THE PAGES.

VOL. I.

PAGE

VOL. II.

TABLE OF STATUTES.

SECTION

1799.

April 11,	§ 1.	3 Sm. 386.	Partition,	1921
April 11,	§ 2.	3 Sm. 387.	Partition,	1922, 2032, 2034, 2039, 2042, 2045
April 11,	§ 3.		Partition,	1925

1802

April 6,		3 Sm. 530.	Justices,	1428, 1608
April 6,	§ 8.	3 Sm. 516.	Landlord and tenant,	1651

1803.

April 2,		4 Sm. 89.	Ejectments,	680, 682
April 2,	§ 2.	4 Sm. 89.	Ejectments,	580, 658

1804.

Jan. 14,	§ 1.	4 Sm. 107.	Justices,	1590
Jan. 14,	§ 2.	4 Sm. 107.	Justices,	1591
March 27,	{ R. S. of U. S. § 905 p. 170. }		Preparation for trial,	2952, 2953
April 3,	§ 6.	4 Sm. 203.	Landlord and tenant,	1651

1805.

March 29,	§ 13.	4 Sm. 242.	At trial,	3024

1806.

Feb. 24,	§ 25.	4 Sm. 276.	Bills of exceptions,	3070, 3071
March 17,		4 Sm. 300.	Mechanics' claims,	200, 206, 245
March 21,		4 Sm. 328.	Statements,	62, 67, 70
March 21,	§ 3.	4 Sm. 328.	Costs,	3104
March 21,	§ 5.	4 Sm. 328.	Costs,	3118
March 21,	§ 6.	4 Sm. 329.	Amendments,	2404
March 21,	§ 8.	4 Sm. 330.	Original writs,	2313
March 21,	§ 9.	4 Sm. 330.	Attorneys,	3502
March 21,	§ 12.	4 Sm. 332.	Ejectments,	581
March 28,	§ 1.	4 Sm. 335.	Partition,	1923
March 28,	§ 2.	4 Sm. 335.	Partition,	1924

1807.

April 7,	§ 1.	4 Sm. 398.	Partition,	1926, 1983, 2005
April 7,	§ 1.	4 Sm. 398.	Original writs,	2286
April 7,	§ 2.	4 Sm. 476.	Original writs,	2296
April 7,	§ 2.	4 Sm. 398.	Partition,	1927, 2005
April 7,	§ 3.	4 Sm. 399.	Original writs,	2289
April 7,	§ 3.	4 Sm. 399.	Partition,	1928, 1983
April 7,	§ 4.	4 Sm. 400.	Partition,	1930, 2012
April 7,	§ 5.	4 Sm. 400.	Partition,	1929
April 7,	§ 4.	4 Sm. 400.	Abatement,	2390
April 13,		4 Sm. 476.	Ejectments,	582
April 13,	§ 2.	4 Sm. 476.	Ejectments,	631
April 13,	§ 4.	4 Sm. 477.	Abatement,	2389
Dec. 4,		4 Sm. 482.	Attachments,	121

				SECTION
May 8,	§ 1.	P. L. 44.	Mortgages,	195
May 8,	§ 2.	P. L. 44.	Mortgages,	195
May 8,	§ 3.	P. L. 44.	Mortgages,	195
May 15,		P. L. 69.	Preparation for trial,	2949
May 16,		P. L. 84.	Mechanics' claims,	203, 204
May 22,		P. L. 105.	Divorce.	811
May 22,		P. L. 111.	Execution,	3144*b*
May 22,		P. L. 100.	Justices.	1409
May 22,		P. L. 112.	Limitations,	3651*b*
May 22,		P. L. 111.	Municipal liens,	376
May 22,		P. L. 114.	Partition,	2042
June 8,	§ 28.	P. L. 345.	Appeals,	3405
June 24,		P. L. 243.	Account render,	330, 341
June 24,		P. L. 212.	Appeals,	3463*nn*
June 24,		P. L. 246.	Execution,	3234
June 24,		P. L. 236.	Negligence,	1874, 1889
June 24,		P. L. 237.	Partition,	2041
June 24,		P. L. 346.	Original writs,	229
June 24,	§ 1.	P. L. 236.	Abatement,	2391
June 24,	§ 1.	P. L. 212.	Appeals,	3463*nn*
June 24,	§ 1.	P: L. 236.	Actions after death,	2216, 2217
June 24,	§ 2.	P. L. 236.	Limitations,	3640
June 24,	§ 2.	P. L. 212.	Appeals,	3463*nn*
June 24,	§ 2.	P. L. 236.	Actions after death,	2216, 2217
June 24,	§ 3.	P. L. 212.	Appeals,	3463*nn*
June 24,	§ 4.	P. L. 212.	Appeals,	3463*nn*
June 24,	§ 5.	P. L. 212.	Appeals,	3463*oo*
June 24,	§ 6.	P. L. 212.	Appeals,	3463*pp*
June 24,	§ 7.	P. L. 212.	Appeals,	3463 *qq*, 3463*rr*
June 24,	§ 8.	P. L. 212.	Appeals,	3463*ss*, 3463*tt*, 3463*uu*
June 24,	§ 9.	P. L. 212.	Appeals,	3463*rr*, 3463*ww*
June 24,	§ 10.	P. L. 212.	Appeals,	3463*xx*, 3463*yy*
June 24,	§ 11.	P. L. 212.	Appeals,	3463*zz*
June 24,	§ 12.	P. L. 212.	Appeals,	3463*aaa*
June 24,	§ 13.	P. L. 212.	Appeals,	3463*bbb*
June 24,	§ 14.	P. L. 212.	Appeals,	3463*ccc*
June 24,	§ 15.	P. L. 212.	Appeals,	3463*ccc*
June 25,		P. L. 308.	Divorce,	746, 750, 799
June 25,		P. L. 282.	Execution,	3165
June 25,		P. L. 283.	Escheats,	1148
June 25,		P. L. 280.	Original writs,	2236
June 25,	§ 1.	P. L. 279.	Depositions,	2489
June 25,	§ 1.	P. L. 300.	Lunatics and drunkards,	3680*a*
June 25,	§ 2.	P. L. 279.	Depositions,	2489
June 25,	§ 2.	P. L. 300.	Lunatics and drunkards,	3680*b*
June 25,	§ 3.	P. L. 279.	Depositions,	2489
June 25,	§ 3.	P. L. 300.	Lunatics and drunkards,	3680*c*
June 25,	§ 4.	P. L. 300.	Lunatics and drunkards,	3680*d*
June 25,	§ 5.	P. L. 300.	Lunatics and drunkards,	3680*e*
June 25,	§ 6.	P. L. 300.	Lunatics and drunkards,	3680*f*
June 25,	§ 7.	P. L. 300.	Lunatics and drunkards,	3680*g*

TABLE OF CASES.

[THE REFERENCES ARE TO THE SECTIONS.]

VOL. I.—E

VOL. I.—K

CHAPTER I.

§ 1. Your services will generally not be invoked until settlement is hopeless. Wherever it is possible, the lawyer should counsel some effort to avoid litigation. Even when it is necessary to sue, and the defendant is not about to leave the jurisdiction, it is best to address him sómewhat in this form:

LAW OFFICE OF A. B.,
No.

To Mr. C. D.,
    (or to C. D., Esq.)

DEAR SIR:

    A claim against you has been placed in my hands for collection by Mr. E. F. If you intend to settle it, I shall be happy to see you at my office to-morrow morning at 9 o'clock. Otherwise, please refer me to your counsel.

                    Very respectfully yours,
                        A. B.

If the claim involve items of account, avoid stating the amount in your letter. I have known a lawyer's mistake in this behalf to embarrass a recovery. Remember here and everywhere that your letter may be read to a jury.

Shun carefully all threats. If necessary to hint at a criminal prosecution, reserve this for a personal interview with the defendant's counsel. If you however write, some form like this may be adopted:

SIR:

    Mr. E. F. has called on me and stated the particulars of his complaint against you. As you are familiar with the details, I need not here repeat them. My purpose in writing is simply to suggest that you see Mr. E. F. or myself as soon as possible.

                    Very respectfully yours.

§ 2. **When parties are brought together,** use all honorable efforts to make them settle. This remark applies not only to the period before suit brought, but to every subsequent stage of the war. Directly after you have gained a half-way victory is a very opportune time to negotiate. Your enemy will be slightly disheartened by your success. Your difficulty here and all through your professional life may not be so much with the adversary as with your client. Write over your doorway, " *Cave Clientem.*" Repeat the words at every interview. As to settlements, you can honorably represent the chances of war, the risks of litigation, the advantages of closing at once, the saving of time, of fees, and costs. When all arguments fail, do not get cross with your client; do not exclaim, as the great Eldon did (when at the bar) to an obstinate litigant: " You infernal fool, if you do not settle I will begin to call you hard names." On the contrary, say to him, " Perhaps you are right. Go home, think it over," etc.

§ 3. **Fees.** No subject is more delicate than the treatment of fees. As a general rule, be at first indifferent to your compensation. If asked, leave the matter with the client. Secure his confidence, his friendship. These may be better to you than gold. In criminal cases you can be more strict. After rendering some service—at the second or third interview you can ask for your fee. Some practitioners feel a delicacy as to speaking upon this subject. A letter can be written in such cases :

DEAR SIR:
If convenient, please send me a check for $, as my retainer in the case we spoke of this morning.
                    Very respectfully yours.

Clients have different habits upon the subject. Some never give it a thought. Bankers, brokers, persons of wealth, as a general rule, expect the lawyer to broach the question. You must feel your way. I would advise if the client be a person of position to wait patiently. More is gained by courtesy than with the sledge-hammer. It is narrated of Colonel Ingersoll that he made no demand for a fee all through the long trials of the Star Route Cases.

As to contingent fees—Chief Justice Sharswood denounced them. But their legality has been sustained by the Supreme Court in *Perry* v. *Dickens*, 105 Pa. St., 83 (1884), and cases cited *Ib.*, 89. I would recommend that they only be accepted where the client would otherwise, as from poverty, be without redress, and that they be accompanied with the fullest proofs and the clearest explanations.

§ 4. Deal with no female client except in the presence of her male relative. Let all receipts state the entire amount collected—thus :

A. B. *v.* C. D.
Received   1887, of E. F., four hundred and thirty dollars, which with seven $\frac{50}{100}$ dollars costs due E. F., and thirty dollars allowed him for his professional services, make four hundred and sixty-seven $\frac{50}{100}$ dollars in full for the amount received in above case, and in full to date.

§ 5. **You should keep a mem. book, a docket, an office directory,** a small book to be called a Trial-List, a receipt-book, and some account-books—such as a cash-book and ledger. In your docket every case should be entered the day you issue a writ or enter an appearance. It should be indexed under names of both plaintiff and defendant.

§ 6. **In your trial-list book** all cases should be entered as soon as at issue, with court, term, number, and names of counsel. At stated periods before the appearance of the Court Trial-Lists you should consult this book and see that every case you wish to try is entered by the clerk on the forthcoming list.

§ 7. **Your cash-book** should contain a record of all receipts and personal expenditures. Do not say : " I can always tell what cash I have on hand." The habit of writing down your expenses will make you ashamed of their amount if they are unwise. Remember Lord Bacon's advice : " It is less dishonorable to abridge petty charges (expenses) than to stoop to petty gettings." Nor should you be seduced by even the possession of property to ignore the counsel of prudence. When Boswell inherited an estate, Dr. Johnson advised : " Begin your new course of life with the least show and the least expense possible. Begin with timorous parsimony. Let it be your first care not to be in any man's debt."

§ 8. **Your mem. book** should contain an entry of all engagements, and every case should in some form of entry be present to your eye from its birth to its death. For instance, when you commence a suit which will require from the opposite party an affidavit of defense, you should enter it on your mem. book as of the day for the judgment. When you enter a rule to plead another note should be made. When at issue mem. it for the Trial-List, and so mem. it on to its grave.

§ 9. **Your receipt-book** should evidence all your payments. When you make a collection, write instantly to the client, and when he calls have the receipt prepared for his signature. Let every voucher contain the words—*in full to date.*

Your office directory should contain the names and addresses of all clients and of all whom you sue.

CHAPTER II.

§ 10. By Summons. Except in cases of Foreign Attachment, Domestic Attachment, or Attachment for Fraud, you commence suit upon promissory notes, due-bills, book accounts, bills of exchange, and in all cases *ex contractu* (save the rare instances hereafter noted), by issuing a summons. To do this you draw a *præcipe* in form like the following:

A. B.
  v. }
C. D.

No. 16 Blank St.
> Sir:
>
> Issue summons in assumpsit returnable *sec. leg.*
>
> E. F.,

To   Plaintiff's Attorney.
    Prothonotary of the Court of Common Pleas.   (Insert date.)
            (State the county.)

The abbreviations *sec. leg.* mean *secundum legum,* according to law.

In *Grier* v. *McGlathery,* 16 W. N., 457 (1885), the *præcipe* was not signed by plaintiff nor by any attorney, but upon D. W. Sellers, Esq., undertaking to direct the plaintiff to sign the *præcipe* as the court might order, the rule to quash the writ was discharged.

Præcipe for summons to be directed to sheriff of another county. Such a writ is authorized by Act April 24, 1857, section 1 (P. L., 318), and Act April 8, 1868 (P. L., 70), Br. Purd., 1060, section 146 n. The first Act permits suit to be brought "in any county where the property insured may be located," and the second Act extends the first to life and accident companies. The process may be directed "to the sheriff of either of the counties in this Commonwealth." See *Quinn* v. *Fidelity Association,* 100 Penna. St., 382 (1882), and Act of May 13, 1889, § 1 (P. L., 198), Br. Purd., 1060, section 145.

In the Court of Common Pleas, No.   , of the County of Philadelphia,

A. B.

v.

Fire Insurance Company.

Of June Term, 1890.

No.

To Prothonotary Common Pleas, Philadelphia County.

SIR:

Issue   summons assumpsit in above case, returnable *sec. leg.*

Writ to be directed to sheriff of Allegheny County.

Plaintiff's Attorney.

(Date.)

§ 11. **Where you sue on behalf of a firm** your *præcipe* should give the names of all the members.   Bear in mind that initials are not names.   Your *præcipe* and other papers should not describe a man as F. Smith.   Give the full name as Francis Smith.   Supposing that you sue a firm for a firm, your precept will be like this :

John Smith and Peter Jones, copartners under the firm of
Smith & Company,

v.

Samuel Robinson and James Johnson, copartners under the firm of
Robinson & Company, No. 425 Blank Street.

It is not necessary to insert the residence of the defendant in the *præcipe,* but it is convenient to do so and may afterwards save difficulty.

§ 12. **If the plaintiffs or defendants were a firm, and have dissolved** partnership before you bring suit, insert the word *late* before the word copartners, so that they will be described as *late copartners under the firm of, etc.*

§ 13. **If one of the firm has died** you state it thus : John Smith, who survived Peter Jones, which said Peter Jones in his lifetime and said John Smith were copartners under the firm of, etc.

You do not name the executor or administrator of the dead partner.   Where one of several defendants dies after suit brought, the plaintiff may bring in the executor or administrator of deceased defendant, and proceed at same time against him and the survivor ; but he cannot be compelled to do this.   *Ashe* v. *Guie,* 97 Pa. St., 493 (1881).

§ 14. **Associations or clubs for social or charitable purposes** and the like are not proper partnerships (*Ib.,* 499).   If you sue an association not incorporated, insert in your *præcipe* the names of all the members, and add, *transacting business as* (give the name of the association).   *McConnell* v. *Bank,* 146 Pa. St., 79 (1892).

If you sue a corporation, write the corporate name as the defendant.

Assumpsit against joint tenants, etc., in oil or gas wells. The Act of May 6, 1891 (P. L., 41), provides that any person performing labor or furnishing materials in drilling or operating oil or gas wells may bring assumpsit against a joint owner, joint tenant, or tenant in common having an interest therein to recover the pro rata share due by such owner, and such interest shall be subject to levy and sale on execution, and such owner paying such pro rata share shall have right of action to the same extent as is given laborers, provided that no such owner shall be required to pay any share of the expenses of operations commenced and carried on without his authority or consent.

§ 15. Do not use the word *please* in any *præcipe*, nor sign *Yours truly.* I have seen such phrases; they are, however, out of place. As an officer of the court, it is your privilege to command the issuing of writs of right.

§ 16. In the large counties the work of the prothonotary's office is performed by clerks; the *præcipe* is in such counties delivered to the writ clerk, who prepares the summons. The seal of the court is affixed and the fee paid at the main desk.

In the sheriff's office original process and writs in the nature of summons are given to the appearance clerk, the service being made by deputies. You should see the deputy in special cases and give him full instructions. Watch every officer at every step. Returns, as a matter of fact, are rarely made on return-day.

§ 17. If there be fifteen days between the teste and return-day of your summons file with your *præcipe* "a concise statement of plaintiff's demand, accompanied by copies of all notes, contracts, book entries, or a particular reference to the records of any court within the county in which the action is brought, if any, upon which the plaintiff's claim is founded, and particular reference to such record or to the record of any deed or mortgage or other instrument of writing recorded in such county, shall be sufficient in lieu of the copy thereof. The statement shall be signed by the plaintiff or his attorney, and in the action of assumpsit shall be replied to by affidavit." These are the words of the Act of May 25, 1887. (P. L , 271.)

When a bill of exchange, promissory note, or other instrument is copied, write before the names of all parties signing, indorsing, accepting, etc., the word (signed), and when there are indorsers write "indorsed" and copy the indorsement.

Copy of assignment of bond. If the suit is upon a bond which has been assigned to plaintiff, the assignment should also be copied.

How to describe plaintiff when assignee. If the instrument sued on is negotiable, *i. e.*, a promissory note, bill of exchange, etc., payable to bearer or order, the suit must be brought in name of holder without describing him as assignee, or without naming any party to his use.

When it does not contain the words "order or bearer," and the plaintiff's title is by assignment, then the suit must always be in the name of the assignor to use of plaintiff. Thus, if the claim were upon a note signed by John Doe, simply promising to pay to Richard Roe $500 without adding the words "order or bearer" after Roe's name, and Roe should write upon its back "I assign this note to A." and sign his name, A. could not issue writ against Doe in his own name, but the *præcipe* should be headed "Richard "Roe to the use of A. *v.* 'John Doe.'" Sometimes, but not often, there are several such assignments.

A. may have transferred it to B., B. to C., C. to D., etc. In such a case it would be "Richard Roe to the use of A., to the use of B., to the use of C., to the use of D. against John Doe." This form is all dispensed with when the words "order or bearer" appear on the face of the note.

No copy of protest necessary. Where the suit is against the indorser, and the note has been protested, the attorney need not file a copy of the protest; he need only say, at the foot of his copy and above his signature, "duly protested for non-payment."

When indorser liable though note not protested. It will, of course, be understood that an indorser will in certain cases be held liable, although the note has not been protested, as when he may have waived protest, or may have been notified in due season of non-payment of the note.

When assignee of bond may sue in his own name. Where the suit is upon a bond and the plaintiff is not the original obligee but holds by assignment, he is permitted by *Act of 28 May*, 1715, *section* 3 (1 *Sm.*, 90), to sue in his own name, provided the assignment shall have been made "under hand and seal before two or more credible witnesses."

If there is such assignment, a copy thereof should be filed with the copy of the bond. If the assignment is not under seal or not in presence of two witnesses, the action would again have to be in the name of the original party to the use of the assignee, as above stated in the case of promissory notes not negotiable.

Separate suits against maker and indorser. It is hardly necessary to add that separate suits may be brought and prosecuted at the same time to judgment and execution against all parties liable on notes and bills of exchange, whether makers, drawers, indorsers, or acceptors; *Tarin* v. *Morris*, 2 Dallas, 115 (1790); *Beebe* v. *West Branch Bank*, 7 W. & S., 375 (1844); and the plaintiff may at the same time be selling the goods of the maker of a note and levying upon the lands of an indorser.

No detail of credits necessary. In filing a copy of a book account it is unnecessary and frequently dangerous to attach a copy of all the credits; good faith, of course, requires that no plaintiff should claim more than is justly due, and whenever there has been a payment the attorney should add at the foot of his copy, and above his signature, as follows: " The defendant is entitled to a credit, or credits, to the sum of   dollars," or " the plaintiff claims upon the above a balance of   dollars." If the attorney undertake to give the items of the credits, his client may be prejudiced if there has been any mistake in dates.

A merchant might give a receipt and enter a credit as of a different date, though both referred to the same payment. The defendant might be dishonorable enough to claim two credits instead of one:

This embarrassment is avoided and full faith observed by giving the defendant a general credit in the copy filed, without reference to dates or items.

Herein, as in all other matters, be particular to comply with every requirement of the law, but be careful not to go one hair's breadth beyond.

Compare all copies carefully. The attorney should be careful to compare the copies he files with the originals, and never trust another with this important part of his duty.

His signature is regarded as his certificate to the correctness of the copy.

A very important case, in which a large amount was involved, was commenced against a man in failing circumstances. The plaintiff and his attorney were very anxious to secure judgment at the earliest possible moment. On the day for entering judgment for want of an affidavit of defense it was discovered that an affidavit of defense had been filed, stating that the defendant had never issued checks like the copies filed. This led to an examination of the copy, which showed that the defendant's name had been entirely omitted, although the paper had been prepared by a very careful gentleman. If you serve a copy of this statement on the defendants " not less than fifteen days before the return-day of the writ, it shall be the duty of the defendant in the action of *assumpsit* to file an affidavit of defense on or before the return-day." (*Section* 4, *Act May* 25, 1887.) The statement may be served independently of the writ, and even before the writ is served. *Roseman* v. *Haydock,* 21 W. N., 121 (1888).

Failing to serve your statement fifteen days before the return-day, you may file it "on or at any time after the return-day, and in the action of *assumpsit* unless the defendant shall file a sufficient affidavit of defense within fifteen days after notice that the said statement has been filed, the plaintiff may move for judgment for want thereof." (*Section* 6, *Act May* 25, 1887.)

The statement can be filed at any time before, or on, or after the return-day ; and you can enter judgment fifteen days after service of the writ and statement, but not before the return-day. *Weigley* v. *Teal,* 23 W. N., 521 (1889).

The Copy of Statement served should set forth the names of the plaintiffs of record, and a copy of the affidavit to the statement. *Wolf* v. *Binder,* 28 W. N., 133 (1891).

§ 18. The following **Rules of Court** have been adopted in Philadelphia :

The plaintiff shall serve a copy of the statement of claim on the defendant or his attorney of record if he has one at least fifteen days before moving for judgment for default, except for want of an appearance.

Such copy may be served by the sheriff with the writ, and his return shall be in lieu of the affidavit otherwise required.

If the defendant resides out of the county and has no attorney of record, the copy may be served on him wherever he may be found by messenger or registered letter.

If the residence of the defendant is unknown and he has no attorney of record, the copy intended for him, to be marked "defendant's copy," may be served by leaving it with the prothonotary, who shall deliver it to the defendant or his attorney on request.

An affidavit of the time, place, and manner of serving such copy shall be filed in all cases, except where service is made by the sheriff.

When the defendant's copy is filed in the prothonotary's office, the reasons for so filing it must be stated in detail in the affidavit.

Plaintiff's statement shall contain a specific averment of facts sufficient to constitute a good cause of action.

Such statement shall be supported by an affidavit of the truth of the matters alleged as the basis of the claim, and shall in all cases, where damages are capable of liquidation, contain an explicit averment of the amount claimed to be justly due.

A copy of the affidavit of defense must be served on the plaintiff or his attorney within forty-eight hours after the filing thereof.

Judgment by default of any kind may be moved before and entered by the prothonotary, who shall assess the damages in all cases in which the amount thereof is set forth with certainty in the statement of claim filed.

These rules were adopted in C. P. 2, 3, and 4 on July 9, 1887, and in C. P. 1 on July 16, 1887.

Under the Act and these rules the statement must be sworn to either by the legal or the use plaintiff: *Schick* v. *Goenner*, 21 W. N., 63 (1888); in tort or trespass as well as in *assumpsit: Krauskopf* v. *Stern*, 21 W. N., 185 (1888), and a bill of particulars may be ordered. *Ibid.* If the statement be amended, the amendment must be sworn to: *Ickenger* v. *R. R.*, 20 W. N., 333 (1887).

An affidavit of defense is necessary in all cases of *assumpsit.* In *Krause* v. *R. R.*, 20 W. N., 111 (1887), C. P. No. 4, of Philadelphia, in a very able opinion of ARNOLD, J., decided :

1. That the Act of 1887 applies to cases brought before its passage.

2. It is constitutional.

3. That a claim cannot be founded upon an implied *promise* to pay damages caused by the negligence of the defendant.

4. Oyer of the writ is not demandable. The writ may be issued in trespass and a statement filed in *assumpsit,* and *vice versa.* The variance is not a good cause of demurrer or plea in abatement.

Affidavit of defense must be filed in answer to statement on appeal cases : *Laufer* v. *Landis,* 23 W. N., 460 (1889).

In Philadelphia County, executors and administrators are required to file affidavit of defense. The Philadelphia Court Rule is as follows :

SEC. 4, b. An affidavit of defense shall be required from executors, administrators, guardians, committees, and others sued in a representative capacity: Provided, that an affidavit by the defendant in said cases, stating that he has made diligent inquiry and has not been able to obtain sufficient information to enable him to set forth particularly the nature and character of the defense, but that he believes there is a just and legal defense, shall be deemed a sufficient compliance with this rule. Adopted March 7, 1893.

Prior to the adoption of this rule it had been held that executors and administrators need not file affidavits of defense : *Wireman* v. *Ins. Co.,* 20 W. N., 299.

In *Brooks* v. *Bank,* 23 W. N., 502 (1889), a statement and affidavit were signed by B., with a scroll after his signature ; the word "cashier" did not appear, nor was there any averment in the affidavit of his official position. The affidavit set up that the statement was insufficient, the court below entered judgment and allowed the word "cashier" to be added. The Supreme Court refused to reverse on such a technicality.

A statement to recover for goods sold and delivered did not aver delivery, but a bill of particulars annexed, sworn to as a copy of book entries and showing a charge, cured the defect. *Hubbard* v. *Tenbrook,* 23 W. N., 351 (1889).

If a statement under the Act of 1887 refer to the record of a suit in another county, it should exhibit a full copy of the record—the rule is otherwise where the record is in the county where the suit is brought. *Campbell* v. *Rwy Co.*, 27 W. N., 79 (1890).

Judgment for want of an affidavit of defense cannot be entered during the pendency of a plea in abatement. *Hummel* v. *Myers*, 26 W. N., 279 (1890).

An action of assumpsit may be brought in the common pleas upon the judgment of a justice of the peace of the State. *Alexander* v. *Arters*, 1 District Rep., 359 (1892).

A suit for damages for the breach of a written contract to convey land is in assumpsit. *Bradley* v. *Potts*, 33 W. N., 570 (1893).

An affidavit of defense is not required in an action for a penalty. *Bartoe* v. *Guckert*, 158 Pa. St., 124 (1893).

An affidavit of defense is required in a suit for damages for breach of a written contract to sell land. *Bradley* v. *Potts*, 2 Dist. Rep., 797 (1893).

Judgment for want of a sufficient affidavit may be entered in a suit upon the bond of an employé if the statement present the facts in a full, clear, and explicit manner, so that the damages can be liquidated and assessed. *Trust Co.* v. *Trust Co.*, 4 Dist. Rep., 381 (1895).

An affidavit of defense must be filed to an action on a replevin bond since the Act of 1887. *McGary* v. *Barr*, 47 Leg. Int., 214 (1890).

Municipal corporations need not file affidavits of defense. Municipal corporations shall not be required to file affidavits of defense in actions of assumpsit. Act of April 26, 1893 (P. L., 26).

§ 19. **The Old Practice.** A perusal of the Act of May 25, 1887, discloses no direct repeal of the old laws requiring the filing of affidavits of defense. They are not inconsistent with the new statute, and the common Pleas has in two Counties held the old affidavit of defense law to be still in force. *Commonwealth* v. *Mc-Cutcheon* (Beaver Co.), 20 W. N., 365 (1887) ; *Bank* v. *McHenry* (Philadelphia Co.), *Ib.*, 366 (1887). But in *Gould* v. *Gage*, 20 W. N., 553, 118 Pa. St., 559 (1888), a copy of note was filed—not signed by plaintiff's counsel. He afterward claimed to treat said copy as a statement under the provisions of the Act of May 25, 1887. The Supreme Court held he was not entitled to judgment (1) because the copy was not a "statement accompanied by" a copy of the note, etc., as required by the Act; (2) it was not signed as required. It would appear to be much easier to proceed under the Act of 1887, and to treat the old laws as repealed. *Newbold* v. *Pennock*, 154 Pa. St., 591 (1893).

Judgment for want of affidavit cannot be entered under a rule of court. In *Marlin* v. *Walters*, 24 W. N., 129 (1889), it was ruled that the Act of 1887 superseded a rule of court. The plaintiff in this case entered judgment, to which he was entitled under a rule of court in Warren County. The court below struck it off. The Supreme Court affirmed the judgment. MITCHELL, J., said : " The act was undoubtedly intended as a step towards uniformity of practice. * * * If the plaintiff wants to hold the defendant to an affidavit immediate on his coming into court, *i. e.,* on the return-day, he must *serve a copy of the statement.* If, however, he chooses to wait till the defendant is in court, as required to be on the return-day, then plaintiff need only *file* his statement and *give notice.* Under this system the defendant is not bound to any unreasonable diligence, nor in any danger of being taken unaware. He knows he must be served either with a copy before the return-day, or with notice after it."

§ 20. Under the old laws affidavits of defense were required in *sci. fas. sur* mortgages, recognizances in error, records, mechanics' claims, suits on records, bills, bonds, notes, instruments of writing for payment of money, bail bonds, and insolvent bonds.

Under the old law affidavits of defense were not required where the book account charged commission for the sale of a house and items of money paid. *Fenn* v. *Early*, 113 Pa. St., 264 (1886).

§ 21. Under the old practice, the following instruments have been held to be within the Affidavit of Defense Law :

Recognizance to dissolve foreign attachment. *Gilser* v. *Dialogue*, 4 W. N., 10 (1877).

Recognizance of bail in error. *Beck* v. *Courtney*, 13 W. N., 302 (1883).

Recognizance entered into in Quarter Sessions to support recognizer's family. *Huber* v.' *Commonwealth*, 11 W. N., 496 (1882).

Recognizance of bail for stay of execution is a record, and requires affidavit of defense without copy of recognizance being filed. *Salter* v. *Griffith*, 7 W. N., 288 (1879).

Book entries containing words understandable only to the trade. *Brown* v. *Dupuy*, 4 W. N., 491 (1877).

Copy of bill, being also copy of book entries, the heading of the bill being surplusage. *Richardson* v. *Snyder*, 6 W. N., 414 (1879).

A bond conditioned for payment of costs in an equity suit, including master's fee. *Kase* v. *Greenough*, 7 W. N., 535 (1879).

An averment filed with copy of a note alleging that the interest agreed upon in the note is permitted by the *lex loci contractu*. *Smith* v. *Heister*, 11 W. N., 353 (1882).

A contract of surety on a lease. *Hohl* v. *Korn*, 2 W. N., 277 (1876).

Exemplification of record of foreign judgment. *Power* v. *Winsor*, 3 W. N., 360 (1877), and so ruled in *Mink* v. *Shaffer*, 23 W. N., 348 (1889).

Mortgage where mortgagor alive and executor of *terre tenant* defends. *Dutill* v. *Sully*, 9 W. N., 573 (1881).

Under the Act of 1887 an affidavit must be filed to a suit on a claim-property bond. *Byrne* v. *Hayden*, 23 W. N., 306 (1889).

Foreign Judgment. If plaintiff file a statement claiming under judgment recovered in another State and attaching a copy of the record, the defendant must file his affidavit or judgment may be entered. *Mink* v. *Shaffer*, 23 W. N., 34 (1889).

In an action on a foreign judgment where the averment is made that the defendant appeared by attorney, an affidavit of defense denying that the attorney who so appeared was authorized, or that said attorney was defendant's regularly retained counsel, is sufficient. *Society* v. *Tyler*, 2 Dist. Rep., 693 (1893).

The statement need not aver that the court had jurisdiction of the subject-matter or of the person of the defendant or the nature of the action. *Mink* v. *Shaffer, supra.* In this case there was no "denial by the defendant of his identity with the defendant in the judgment, or of the plaintiff's identity, or of the authority of the counsel of record to appear for him."

In an action on a foreign judgment, if the record is defectively certified, the court will not give judgment for want of a sufficient affidavit of defense if it suggests the defect in the certificate. *Ensign* v. *Kindred*, 35 W. N., 226 ; 163 Pa. St., 638 (1894), overruling *Mink* v. *Shaffer*, 23 W. N., 348 (1889), upon this point.

An action upon a foreign record may be brought although an appeal is pending in the foreign forum, even if such appeal by the laws of such State is a supersedeas. The supersedeas is only to the execution. *Wood Co.* v. *Berry Co.*, 4 Dist. Rep., 141 (1895).

§ 22. **Under the old practice** the following were held not to be within the Affidavit of Defense Law :

Deed from a third party to defendant, not signed by him, for premises " under and subject to " certain mortgage debts of which the plaintiff was assignee. *Morris* v. *Guier*, 5 W. N., 132 (1878).

A mortgage, not containing a covenant to pay, in an action of debt. *Fidelity Co.* v. *Miller*, 6 W. N., 553 (1879).

Contracts of decedent. *Wright* v. *Cheyney*, 10 Phila., 469 (1873).

Non-negotiable note. *Bell* v. *Sterling*, 12 Phila., 230 (1877).

A policy of insurance. *Morton* v. *Ins. Co.*, 35 Leg. Int., 282 (1878).

Bond of indemnity. *Scott* v. *Loughery*, 6 W. N., 123 (1878).

Contract of suretyship. *Bunting* v. *Allen*, 6 W. N., 157 (1878).

Sci. fa. against widow and heirs to charge real estate. *Stadelman* v. *Trust Co.*, 6 W. N., 134 (1878).

Bond of a lunatic's committee. *Strock* v. *Comm.*, 90 Pa. St., 272 (1879).

Amendment after statutory time for judgment does not put plaintiff in better position for judgment. *Bradley* v. *Dusenberry*, 7 W. N., 146 (1879).

Book entries when debt contracted by a married woman *dum sola*. *Langfeld* v. *McCullough*, 11 W. N., 107 (1881).

A premium note of Mutual Ins. Co., payable at such times and in such amounts as directors may require, together with certificate stating time and amount of assessment. *Ins. Co.* v. *Brierly*, 10 W. N., 45 (1881).

Book entries which are merely mem. do not entitle plaintiff to judgment. *Irish* v. *Ass'n*, 13 W. N., 372 (1883).

Administration bond. *Commonwealth* v. *Pelletier*, 8 W. N., 516 (1880); *Comm.* v. *Colgan*, 19 W. N., 131 (1887).

Since the Act of 1887 it has been decided that an action to recover a penalty under the Act of Congress for taking usurious interest is an action *ex delicto*, and an affidavit of defense is not required. *Osborn* v. *Bank*, 32 W. N., 158 (1893).

It may be proper to remark here that at every stage of every case the practitioner should consult the Digests of Laws, the Digests of Decisions, and the Rules of Court.

§ 23. Taking judgment for want of an appearance and for want of an affidavit of defense. The Act of 1887 does not provide for judgment for want of an appearance—see section 61 of this book.

It enables the plaintiff by filing and serving a concise statement of his demand, accompanied by copy, etc. (or by reference to records, etc., and signed by the plaintiff or his attorney, see sections 61–66), to take judgment if no affidavit of defense or an insufficient affidavit be filed.

The summons requires the entry of an appearance, and the laws permitting judgment by default for want of an appearance are not expressly repealed by the Act of 1887.

It would seem, therefore, that judgments for want of an appearance may still be entered.

Proceeding by Act of 1887 is safer, because in order to take judgment for want of appearance a *narr.* had to be filed under the old law. Now the declaration "shall consist of a concise statement," etc. The pleader must, therefore, file a statement under the Act of 1887 as the first step in his case. The trouble of serving his copy is very slight, and if he get a judgment for want of an affidavit of defense it is much more likely to be a finality. It would be best, therefore, to avoid taking judgment for want of an appearance, and to take the judgment for want of an affidavit of defense.

But lest some special reason might present itself for taking judgment for want of an appearance the following *Note of Decisions* may serve as a guide.

Judgment for want of appearance. Under Act of 1836.

As to Summons. In computing ten days before return-day, return-day itself is not to be counted. Service on October 28—return-day November 7, service is good. *Black* v. *Johns*, 68 Pa. St., 83 (1871), AGNEW, J.

Judgment cannot be entered until fourteen full days after service of writ. Service on October 28, return-day November 7. Judgment entered November 11 held proper. *Ibid.*

Same point, *Assn.* v. *Gardiner* (C. P. No. 1), 2 W. N., 95 (1875).

In case of two returns of *nihil* equivalent to a service, service is presumed to have been made on return-day of *alias* writ. *Faunce* v. *Subers* (C. P. No. 4), 1 W. N., 248 (1875).

As to Declaration (now statement).

Under Act of 1836 *narr.* must be filed before return-day.

Foreman v. *Schricon*, 8 W. & S., 43 (1844).

If *narr.* not filed before return-day, the judgment is irregular.

Dennison v. *Leech*, 9 Pa. St., 164 (1848), Rogers, J.

Black v. *Johns*, 68 Pa. St., 83 (1871), Agnew, J.

Kohler v. *Luckenbaugh*, 84 Pa. St., 258 (1877), Gordon, J., and a rule of court otherwise is invalid.

Vanormer v. *Ford*, 98 Pa. St., 177 (1881), Paxson, J.

But such judgment is irregular, not void, and to a *sci. fa.* thereon a plea of *nul tiel record* will not avail. *Hersch* v. *Groff*, 2 W. & S., 449 (1841).

To take advantage of such irregular judgment the defendant must act promptly. *Kohler* v. *Luckenbaugh*, 84 Pa. St., 258 (1877).

The safe practice is:

1. To file statement with the *præcipe* at least three days before the return-day.

2. See that it conforms strictly to Act of 1887, section 61 of this book. Do not trust to your memory, but look at section 61 and compare your work with the law.

3. Let fifteen days intervene between the service of summons and judgment; and although they have elapsed do not sign judgment until the fourth day after the return-day.

4. Before proceeding look at your Rules of Court.

If no appearance entered, and you are entitled to judgment as above, take it thus : File with prothonotary the following paper :

A. B.
  v.   } C. P.   ,   Term, 188 . No. .
C. D.

And now   on motion of E. F., plaintiff's attorney, judgment against the above-named defendant for want of an appearance.

In Philadelphia the prothonotary enters judgments by default.

Act of April 22, 1889 (P. L., 41), provides :

" That the courts of this Commonwealth may, by rule or standing order, authorize the prothonotary to enter judgment upon *præcipe* for want of an appearance, for want of a declaration or plea, or for want of an affidavit of defense, and to enter judgment thereon with the same effect as if moved for in open court."

If your statement contain a copy of a note, or if the cause of action show a sum certain to be due, the prothonotary can assess your damages on your order. (Section 23.)

But there may be many cases in which proof will be needed to ascertain the amount of damages. In such cases a writ of inquiry of damages is issued.

For the law as to this writ—the *præcipe*, etc.—see chapter entitled *Writ of Inquiry of Damages.*

The judgment for want of affidavit of defense can be entered fifteen days after notice of the filing of the statement, but not until the return-day.

Under the Act of 1887, if the statement be served prior to the return-day and more than fifteen days have intervened between the service of the statement and entry of the judgment, a judgment may be entered if the return-day has passed. *Newbold* v. *Pennock*, 154 Pa. St., 592 (1893).

Whenever entitled to judgment for want of an affidavit of defense, you should examine the docket and inquire of the clerk. Sometimes affidavits are filed and not docketed. If entitled to judgment you can enter it, under the Philadelphia rules, before the prothonotary.

Under the old law, upon every regular day for these judgments, the docket was placed before one of the judges at 11 A. M. The attorney mentioned the number of the case. The judge turned to it, and if satisfied, said "judgment." Under the Act of 1887, you give to the prothonotary a paper indorsed *Judgment for want of affidavit of defense and assessment of plaintiff's damages.*

You can use the following as a form :

A. ⎫
v. ⎬ C. P.   , March Term, 1888, No. 20.
B. ⎭

And now, March 20, 1888, judgment for want of an affidavit of defense. Prothonotary to assess the plaintiff's damages.

To the Prothonotary :

SIR : Assess the plaintiff's damages, *sec. reg.*

C. D.,
pro plff.
March 20, 1888.

The prothonotary assesses the plaintiff's damages as follows :

Amount of note, copy filed	$1000 00
Interest on do. from March 20, 1887, to March 20, 1888 . .	60 00
Protest	1 37½
	$1061 37½

!(The prothonotary signs here.)

Interest is recoverable on coupons in the payment of which default has been made. *Love* v. *R. R. Co.*, 45 Leg. Int., 370 (1888).

You should then order a *fi. fa.* by the following :

A. ⎫
v. ⎬ C. P.   , March Term, 1888, No. 20.
B. ⎭

SIR :

Issue *Fi. Fa.* returnable *sec. leg.*

Real debt, $1061.37½.
Interest from March 20, 1888.

To the Prothonotary C. P.

C. D.,
Plaintiff's Attorney.
March 20, 1888.

The real debt is the amount at which the damages have been assessed. If there be a waiver of the exemption law, note on the writ before handing it to the sheriff "exemption waived."

No execution can issue under the Act of 1887, where judgment for want of a plea has been entered, until damages are assessed. The time within which execution must issue does not run from the entry of judgment. *Walker* v. *Wardell*, 25 W. N., 131 (1889).

Opening judgment. The court will open a judgment for want of an affidavit of defense on satisfactory evidence of the existence of a good defense, if seasonable application be made. *Barbe* v. *Davis*, 1 Miles, 118 (1835). *Martin* v. *Hall*, 1 Phila., 233 (1851). *Nicholson* v. *Fitzpatrick*, 2 Id., 205 (1852).

VOL. I.—2

Lost note. Where judgment is entered in a suit on a promissory note which is lost, the court will control the execution until the defendant is protected either by indemnity from the plaintiff or by the statute of limitations. *Reisinger* v. *Magee,* 158 Pa. St., 280 (1893).

Where some defendants file insufficient affidavits. Where suit is brought against a number of stockholders in an unincorporated bank, and some of the defendants file an insufficient affidavit of defense, and the others do not file any affidavit, the plaintiffs should move for judgment against all of the defendants. If he take judgment only against those filing insufficient affidavits, it will be reversed. *Robinson* v. *Floyd,* 32 W. N., 5 (1893). *Murtland* v. *Floyd,* Id., 6 (1893).

§ 24. It is best to have your papers ready, and if there are other suits against the same defendants, be first with your judgment and levy.

Beneath defendant's name write all places where a levy is to be made. In large counties there is in the sheriff's office an execution clerk. Give the *fi. fa.* to him; ascertain the deputy who is to make the levy; see and instruct him. He should take possession of all personal property belonging to the defendant.

On original writs you pay the sheriff for service. On writs of execution $1 is due in advance in counties of population over 300,000. (Act April 1, 1887, P. L., 15.)

Your client should be notified of the judgment and execution. Where circumstances seem to require extra precaution, a clerk of the plaintiff should accompany the deputy sheriff when the levy is made. A watchman should be placed in charge and your client should watch the watchman. Many articles of value might be spirited away. In counties of over 300,000 a watchman's fee ($2 per day) is a legal cost (Act April 1, 1887, P. L., 16), provided a watchman is necessary. Your client should attend the sale.

If he see fit, he can get the sheriff to employ an auctioneer.

§ 25. When subsequent writs of fi. fa. are issued, the same form of *præcipe* can be used, employing for the second execution the word *alias,* for the third *pluries,* for the fourth 2d *pluries,* etc. You must see to it that the first writ is actually returned before another is ordered.

When defendant becomes entitled, after judgment, to a credit, be sure to give it to him. Note on *præcipe,* and see that prothonotary notes on execution, " Credit defendant, $."

Instead of a *fi. fa.* your client may wish to attach moneys or goods on deposit, or debts due to the defendant. For this purpose an attachment in execution is the appropriate writ. It is treated of in its proper place.

§ 26 · **Should an affidavit of defense be filed**, examine it carefully to see if it is sufficient. If clearly so, you must at once enter a rule to plead. The rules applicable to statements are given in the next chapter.

The following Rules are in force in Philadelphia :

Rules to declare or plead may be entered in the prothonotary's office at any time after the return-day of the writ, and on failure to declare or plead within fifteen days after written notice to do so, served upon the adverse party, or his or her attorney of record, with copy of declaration or statement, the prothonotary shall, on motion in writing, enter a judgment of *non pros.* against the plaintiff for want of a declaration or statement, or judgment against the defendant for want of a plea, or at the request of the plaintiff enter a plea and place the case on the trial-list. Judgments by default may be set aside or opened at the discretion of the court, when deemed necessary for the purposes of justice. But the court or any judge thereof may enlarge the time to declare or plead on cause shown.

Rule to plead :

A.
v. C. P. No. 1, March Term, 1888, No. 200.
B.

To the Prothonotary of the Court of Common Pleas No. 1, of Philadelphia County.

SIR : Enter rule on defendant to plead in fifteen days, or judgment *sec. reg.*

> C. D.,
> Plaintiff's Attorney.
> (Date.)

Serve notice with copy of statement. If no plea filed, write for it. If your adversary after being warned will not plead, you can sign judgment for want of a plea.

ENTERING JUDGMENT FOR WANT OF A PLEA.

A.
v. C. P. No. 1, March Term, 1888, No. 200.
B.

To   Esq.,
           Defendant's Attorney.

DEAR SIR :

Enclosed find copy of statement filed in the above case. Please take notice of a rule on defendant to plead in fifteen days or judgment *sec. reg.*

> Very respectfully yours,   E. F.,
> Plaintiff's Attorney.
> (Date.)

City and County of Philadelphia, *ss.*

                on oath says that on the   day of   he served the original notice whereof the above is a true and correct copy on   Esq., the defendant's attorney, with a copy of the statement filed in this case, personally (or by leaving said notice and statement with an adult in charge of his office).

> Sworn to and subscribed }
> before me,   1888. }

Indorse the above :

> A. }
> v. } C. P. No. 1, March Term, 1888, No. 200.
> B. }

Proof of service on defendant's attorney of statement and of notice of rule to plead.

To the Prothonotary C. P.

SIR : Enter judgment against the above-named defendant for want of a plea *sec. reg.*   E. F.,
                                                              Plaintiff's Attorney.
                                                                      (Date.)

You file this and assess the damages as directed by section 23.

If plea filed. File replication—if necessary. Generally the pleas are non assumpsit, payment, and set-off. The replication to these will be non solvit, no set-off, similiter and issue.

> *Indorsement of Replication.*
>
> A. B. }
> v.   } C. P. No.   ,   Term, 1890, No.
> C. D. }
>
> *Replication.*
>
>   E. F.,
>   pro plff.

Enclose a copy to the defendant's attorney. Where only a similiter is required the replication is gradually falling into disuse. The case being at issue, order it on the trial-list and prepare for trial.

Demanding plea waives affidavit of defense. Where a plea is entered upon the plaintiff's motion he cannot thereafter object to the sufficiency of the affidavit of defense. *Edison Co.* v. *Light Co.*, 32 W. N., 327 (1893).

§ 27. **If you regard the affidavit as insufficient,** do not enter any rule to plead, but take a rule for judgment. This is done by handing to the court clerk

> A. }
> v. } C. P. No. 1, March Term, 1887, No. 200.
> B. }

And now, March 20, 1887, on motion of C. D., Esq., plaintiff's attorney, rule on defendant to show cause why judgment should not be entered for want of a sufficient affidavit of defense. Returnable (here insert the next rule day—generally the succeeding Saturday).

Of this you give notice to the defendant's attorney.

Compelling the filing of a plea bars plaintiff from taking judgment for want of affidavit of defense. *Richards* v. *Mink*, 46 Leg. Int., 138 (1889).

§ 28. **You must then prepare your paper-book for the court.** Judge Mitchell's excellent work on Motions and Rules should be frequently consulted.

The paper-book upon this rule should follow this form :

> A.
> v. } C. P.   , March Term, 1887, No. 200.
> B.

Plaintiff's paper-book *sur* rule for judgment for want of a sufficient affidavit of defense.

STATEMENT AND COPY OF NOTE FILED.

These last words must, of course, be changed according to circumstances. If you filed a copy of a long book account, the court will not care to see all the entries. Copy only the heading, the first item, and give the first and last dates and the amount. If the affidavit raise some special question touching the copy, insert the account at length, or so much as may be necessary to enable a judge to understand the case.

If the copy filed be of many notes or a long bond, the same remarks apply.

You then write

COPY OF AFFIDAVIT OF DEFENSE.

This should be inserted at length. You add

PLAINTIFF'S POINTS,

and state your objections to the affidavit, citing authorities.

§ 29. **The great requisites of a paper-book are:**

1. To give the court all necessary information in the smallest compass.

2. To have it clear and legible. Many of those handed up cannot be read. Blurred press-copies should be put in the wastebasket.

3. The substance of each case cited should be stated from the syllabus.

Do not say, " This point is clearly ruled in," and then cite a score of cases, leaving to the judge the labor of examining the books, and as he finds many of them entirely inapplicable, condemning your laziness or your ignorance.

§ 30. As a sample of a correct method of citation, and as furnishing information as to affidavits held to be insufficient, the following brief may be consulted:

In *Comly* v. *Ryan*, 5 Wh., 263 (1839), the defendant attacked the plaintiff's title to the bill. He swore that after it was due it was held by Douglass, Wood & Co., who, being indebted to defendant, agreed to set off one claim against the other. The District Court of Philadelphia gave judgment, and the Supreme Court affirmed it.

Rogers, J., said:

"It is an essential ingredient in the defense that Wood, Douglass & Co. should have been the owners as well as the holders of the bill."

In *Rising* v. *Patterson*, 5 Wh., 316 (1839), the affidavit was much stronger. The defendant swore that there was a just and legal defense to the claim; that the two bills of exchange sued on were at the time of their maturity owned by the payees, who had subsequently made a certain agreement with defendant, under which defendant had made some payments, and which he was ready to comply with in other respects. The defendant also swore that this agreement was binding on the plaintiffs. He added that "he hoped and expected to prove that the plaintiffs are not the owners of the paper, but that it belongs to the payees, who hope by this action to avoid their contract, entered into as above."

The District Court of Philadelphia gave judgment. The Supreme Court declined hearing Mr. Randall for the defendant in error.

In *Ogden* v. *Offerman*, 2 Miles, 40 (1836), the affidavit disclosed this defense: That defendant had not occupied the premises named in the lease sued upon, and "from information defendant verily believed the plaintiff had occupied the property during a greater portion of the time." This was held to be insufficient as alleging neither ouster, eviction, nor surrender.

In *Dawes* v. *White*, 2 Miles, 140 (1837), the affidavit stated that there was a just and legal defense, the nature and character of which were that the check sued on was given for lottery tickets. It was held to be defective because the tickets might have been sold in another State, where the transaction was not prohibited, and the defendant was required to add that the sale took place in Pennsylvania.

In *Brick* v. *Coster*, 4 W. & S., 494, the action was on a bond, given for purchase-money of land. The deed contained a general warranty. The affidavit stated the existence of adverse outstanding claims prior to the purchase. It was held insufficient in not alleging that the claims were good.

In *Brown* v. *Street*, 6 W. & S., 221 (1843), the maker of the note swore to a full defense as against the payee. He then added: "The plaintiff is a particular and intimate friend of the payee, and deponent believes that the payee is the real plaintiff, who uses the name of the plaintiff to accomplish a recovery. The consideration of said note has totally failed; and if said Aldridge succeeds through the name of Street in obtaining payment of the same from the defendants, the defendants will suffer great injustice."

The District Court gave judgment, and in the Supreme Court Mr. St. George T. Campbell, for defendant in error, was not heard.

Rogers, J., said:

"The plaintiff is the holder of a note which is negotiable; and to put him on proof of consideration as between him and the payee, it must be shown that it was obtained or put into circulation by fraud or undue means. Some fact must be alleged from which we can reasonably infer that the note came into the hands of the holder by fraud or without consideration."

In *Moore* v. *Somerset*, 6 W. & S., 262 (1843), the indorser received a notice, which would have been too late if the parties lived in the same town. The affidavit was clear and full save on this point. The hardship of the defendant's case was that he did not know the maker's address. The court below entered judgment, and, in affirming it, the Supreme Court said :

" But the defendant may have been unable to swear to the place of his (the maker's) residence. Very well. He is bound affirmatively to make out a case of negligence, and must swear to facts enough to constitute it. If he cannot do that, he cannot swear to a defense. In this case every fact sworn to may be true, and yet the plaintiff be entitled to recover. It is said that, as the note is dated at Philadelphia, the presumption is that the drawer resided there also. But a defendant is bound to swear to facts, not presumptions."

In *Bryan* v. *Harrison*, 37 Pa. St., 233 (1860), the affidavit presented a full defense, save that it omitted to aver " that the money for which the suit was brought was deposited with defendant under the illegal ' agreement ' described by defendant." The judgment was affirmed.

Black v. *Halstead*, 39 Pa. St., 64 (1861). The defendant swore to a defense as against the payees, and then added that " he had been informed and had reason to believe, that the note sued upon in this case remained in possession of the payees," etc. It was held that the affidavit was insufficient. The defendant must add that he expects to prove the averments, or set out specially the sources of his information, or the facts upon which his belief rests." So, too, it was held in the same case to be insufficient to state that the plaintiff claimed to have two notes, one of which was a forgery, without adding an averment that the note in suit was not actually given by the defendant.

In *Woods* v. *Watkins*, 37 Pa. St., 458 (1861), the defendant swore that he had carefully examined the notes, that he had no recollection whatever of having signed the same, and that he knew there was no consideration for them. This was held to be insufficient.

In *Blackburn* v. *Ormsby*, 41 Pa. St., 97 (1861), the objection to the affidavit was very technical, but judgment was entered against the defendant. He swore that the plaintiff had agreed to accept a bond and mortgage in full for the claim—that he had the instruments prepared, " and with these documents offered plaintiff to carry out his agreement with him in good faith and to its full extent." But because he did not swear that he " tendered " the papers the court entered judgment, and the Supreme Court affirmed.

In *Anspach* v. *Bast*, 52 Pa. St., 356, the affidavit set up an agreement to take payment of the note out of coal to be mined. It then averred a general stoppage of coal operations, etc.

The Supreme Court held that if there were a defense, still the affidavit was defective in not averring that the mines had been diligently and constantly worked.

In *Peck* v. *Jones*, 70 Pa. St., 83, the defense was set up that a public highway had been opened over the land described in the mortgage in suit.

Sharswood, J., said :

" An affidavit of defense which is required by law or rule of court to set out the nature and character of the same, ought to aver distinctly, either upon knowledge or information and belief, every fact necessary to constitute a defense. Nothing should be left to mere inference. The affidavit in this case does not, for this reason, sustain the contention of the plaintiffs in error.

"It does not allege that the plaintiff below knew, at the time of the contract of sale of the lot, the fact that Bedford Avenue, as laid out in the recorded general plan of the district, passed over it, or that he concealed that fact from the defendants. There is no greater presumption that he knew it than that they knew it."

Bank v. *Gregg*, 79 Pa. St., 384 (1875), was a case in which the affidavit was held to be insufficient. The defendant undertook to deny plaintiff's title to the note, thus, "to the best of deponent's knowledge and belief the plaintiffs were not the owners, but the same was owned by Brady & Co."

The Supreme Court said:

"Its insufficiency is apparent. It does not purport to be made on the affiant's actual personal knowledge, and it is defective in not setting forth the sources of his information, or asserting any expectation of ability to prove the facts alleged." Judgment affirmed.

To a recognizance of bail in error, an affidavit alleging that all the cognizors did not acknowledge to owe and be indebted, and suit having been brought against those bound and those not bound, the deponent is not liable, is insufficient. *Warner* v. *Smith*, 2 W. N., 107 (1876).

On appeal from justice, affidavit alleging want of jurisdiction by the justice and not setting forth facts relied on to establish want of jurisdiction is insufficient. *Williams* v. *Shields* et al., 2 W. N., 176 (1876).

To promissory notes, an affidavit alleging that under a mortgage given as collateral for the notes, plaintiff had caused the mortgaged premises to be sold or converted in some way at a ruinous sacrifice and had bought or obtained possession thereof himself, allowing defendants a credit of but $3200, when the property so wrongfully held and obtained was worth not less than $7000, is vague and insufficient. *Price* et al. v. *Glass*, 2 W. N., 472 (1876).

To a draft on "Ridgway Gibbs, Treasurer, No. 56 South Third Street," and accepted "Ridgway Gibbs, Treas.," an affidavit that defendant accepted draft as treasurer and alleging usury is insufficient. *Gibbs* v. *Union Banking Co.*, 2 W. N., 472 (1876).

To suit on a lease made by plaintiff as agent of certain companies, an affidavit alleging that the property was that of the companies for which he styled himself agent, that prior to the time for which the rent is claimed the defendant gave up the premises, and both plaintiff and his companies, afterward and during the time for which the rent is claimed, entered upon, used, and continue to use the premises, but not alleging directly a surrender and acceptance, is vague and insufficient. *Phila. Fire Exting. Co.* v. *Brainerd, Agent, etc.*, 2 W. N., 473 (1876).

An affidavit alleging payments, but not distinctly alleging them to be on account of the demand in suit, is insufficient. *Selden* v. *Building Asso.*, 2 W. N., 481 (1876).

An affidavit alleging a balance due on a partnership account without alleging a settlement and balance found due is insufficient. *Haines* v. *Rapp*, 2 W. N., 595 (1876).

The copy of note filed contained no words of negotiability. The *narr.* filed contained common counts, and appended thereto a second copy of the note containing words of negotiability. The affidavit alleged want of nego-tiability. *Held,* that second copy corrected the first, and that affidavit was insufficient. *Foster* et al. v. *The Bank,* 2 W. N., 617 (1876).

To copy of note filed by indorsee the maker filed an affidavit alleging failure of consideration, but not stating the cause or reason thereof. As failure was either the fault of the maker or arose from a cause known to him, he should have stated the cause, and affidavit was insufficient. *Bright* v. *Hewitt,* 2 W. N., 626 (1876).

To a bond, an affidavit that the bond was executed at the time that an agent with authority from the plaintiffs represented that certain acts would be done, but not asserting that agent was authorized to make these acts conditions of the bond, is insufficient. *Keffer* et al. v. *Robinson* et al., 2 W. N., 689 (1876).

An affidavit setting off damage received by the failure of plaintiffs to fulfil a contract, which deponent was informed and believed amounted to $3000, but not setting forth damages so as to show that they were the direct and immediate consequences of the alleged breach, is insufficient. *Sitgreaves* v. *Griffiths* et al., 2 W. N., 705 (1876).

To a recognizance of bail, an affidavit impugning the record not on ground of fraud or mistake, but on ground that the obligation was not prop-erly acknowledged, is insufficient. *Furst* v. *Ayers* et al., 2 W. N., 722 (1876).

To a book account which credited defendant with draft, and then charged him with the amount of draft and protest, the entry being, "Cash paid draft returned $300," an affidavit alleging that plaintiff had never paid $300, and that such entry was not within the affidavit of defense law, is insuffi-cient. *Binswanger* v. *Fisher,* 3 W. N., 340 (1877).

An affidavit of set-off not stating item, time, or any other particular to render claim tenable is insufficient. *Loucheim* v. *Becker,* 3 W. N., 449 (1877).

An affidavit setting off unliquidated damages on breach of contract is in-sufficient. *Hopple* v. *Bunting,* 3 W. N., 472 (1877).

An affidavit alleging former recovery and not setting forth the record thereof is insufficient. *Richards* v. *Bisler,* 3 W. N., 485 (1877).

An affidavit alleging fraud and not distinctly setting forth the facts is insufficient. *Matthews* v. *Long,* 3 W. N., 512 (1877).

To *sci. fa. sur* mortgage of $7000, an affidavit alleging that defendant received but $6650, and not alleging usury, injustice, or fraud, is insuffi-cient. *Bruner* v. *Wallace,* 4 W. N., 53 (1877).

To *sci. fa. sur* mortgage, an affidavit alleging an agreement of extension, but not setting forth the agreement to show its items, is insufficient. *Berkey* v. *Whitaker,* 4 W. N., 137 (1877).

To a guarantee of prompt payment indorsed on a promissory note, an affi-davit that defendant received nothing for the guarantee, and that the one to whom the guarantee was made is not named in the writing, is insuffi-cient. *Douglass* v. *Second National Bank,* 4 W. N., 163 (1876).

To a note drawn by "A., executor," to the order of A. personally, an affidavit that payment was not demanded of the maker at maturity, and that notice of its dishonor was not given to the indorser, and that the note was not protested, is insufficient. *Aughenbaugh* v. *Roberts,* 4 W. N., 181 (1876).

To a book account, an affidavit alleging that plaintiff had agreed to accept defendant's notes in settlement, but not alleging tender of the notes, is in-sufficient. *Martien* v. *Woodruff* et al., 4 W. N., 211 (1877).

To a promissory note defendant filed an affidavit alleging that plaintiff held the note as indorsee without consideration and for the purpose of depriving defendant of a set-off against the claim of the payee, viz.: that previous to the giving of the note payee sold a carload of window-shade rollers to defendant; that defendant ordered another load of the same kind and quality, for which note in suit was given; that upon opening said rollers they were very inferior, the difference in value being $134.80, and that the loss sustained by the deponent would far exceed $134.80. *Held*, that affidavit did not show a liability for the quality of the rollers, and was, therefore, insufficient. *Coulston* v. *City National Bank*, 4 W. N., 297 (1877).

To book entries, an affidavit alleging that the entries were in trade terms and abbreviations which were not intelligible, but not alleging that defendant cannot understand them, is insufficient. *Brown* et al. v. *Dupuy* et al., 4 W. N., 491 (1877).

An affidavit alleging that lumber had been deceitfully piled so as to conceal the defects, and concluding, "all of which to the best of defendant's knowledge and belief," is defective because it omits the *scienter* and does not say that defendant "expects to prove," etc. *Boothe* v. *Alexander*, 4 W. N., 492 (1877).

To a claim by withdrawing member for amount paid to a building association, an affidavit alleging that losses have occurred, but not stating that they occurred before the withdrawal, is insufficient. *Building Asso.* v. *Silverman*, 4 W. N., 546 (1877).

To an executory contract for the payment of money, an affidavit alleging that defendant is entitled to have decided by a jury whether plaintiff has performed his part of the contract is insufficient. *Fertig* v. *Maley*, 5 W. N., 133 (1878).

An affidavit denying or amending a written agreement, but which is not clear and full and alleges neither fraud, misrepresentation, nor wrongful suppression of the alleged verbal agreement, is insufficient. *Lehman* v. *Jaquett*, 5 W. N., 183 (1878).

To promissory notes, an affidavit alleging that plaintiff held as collateral for the notes mortgages to the full amount of $30,000, that he had sued out the mortgages and bought in the properties for $17,000, when by proper management plaintiff could have realized much more than he did, is insufficient. *Smith* v. *Bunting*, 5 W. N., 186 (1878).

An affidavit averring information and belief, but not that "deponent expects to be able to prove" the facts alleged, is insufficient. *Hermann* v. *Ramsey*, 5 W. N., 188 (1878).

To an exemplification of a foreign judgment, an affidavit denying the sufficiency of the exemplification, but not denying the debt evidenced, is insufficient. *Hartmann* v. *Mfg. Co.*, 5 W. N., 502 (1878).

To a promissory note, an affidavit that suit was brought in plaintiff's name to prevent deponent from defeating the payment of the note in the hands of a note broker, that plaintiff paid for the note with the money of another, but not distinctly averring that he is not a holder for value, is insufficient. *Lingg* v. *Blummer*, 6 W. N., 459 (1879).

To a promissory note, an affidavit averring that the note was without consideration and that indorsee took it for an antecedent debt (instead of "as collateral security for") is insufficient. *Bardsley* v. *Delp*, 6 W. N., 479 (1879).

A supplemental affidavit may set up a new and different defense, but such a course will subject it to close scrutiny. An affidavit averring verbal statements to modify a written agreement but not averring that the written agreement was signed on the faith of the verbal statements, is insufficient. *Callin* v. *Lukens*, 7 W. N., 28 (1879).

An affidavit averring facts in evidence of a surrender, but not averring a surrender accepted by the landlord, is insufficient. *Brenckmann* v. *Twibill*, 7 W. N., 188 (1879).

An affidavit averring a set-off of damages by breach of warranty as to the amount of goods sold to defendant, but not averring that more than the actual value of the goods was paid before an inventory and examination of the goods were made, is insufficient. *Markley* v. *Stevens*, 7 W. N., 357 (1879).

To suit by indorsee against maker of a note, an affidavit averring that the note was given in New York, that it was usurious, and that under a statute of New York and the decisions thereunder said note was void in the hands of third persons, but not particularizing the statute and the decisions, is insufficient. *Boughton* v. *Bank*, 9 W. N., 519 (1881).

In a suit on a foreign judgment where the record shows the summons was properly served, an affidavit of defense averring the process was not legally served is insufficient; the affidavit must show wherein the service was defective. *Motter* v. *Welty*, 2 Dist. Rep., 39 (1892).

An affidavit of defense in an action for goods sold and delivered is not sufficient which sets forth the agreement of plaintiffs to give defendant the exclusive agency for the sale of the goods, and that they took away the agency without cause and deprived defendant of large profits, and that subsequently the parties agreed to compromise, but did not compromise as agreed. This was a mere accord without satisfaction. *Braum* v. *Keally*, 146 Pa. St., 519 (1892).

An affidavit averring that defendant's signature was obtained by duress, but not setting forth the facts which sustain the allegation, is insufficient. In an agreement of sale it was agreed that if the vendor failed to tender a deed within a stipulated time, he should return the bargain money, and also forfeit $500 to the vendee; an affidavit alleging this $500 to be a penalty, and not liquidated damages, is insufficient. *Matthews* v. *Sharp*, 11 W. N., 319 (1882).

To a recognizance entered into in Quarter Sessions for payment of $4 per week for support of recognizor's family, an affidavit averring that shortly after recognizance was entered defendant returned to his family and contributed all his earnings to their support, but that soon after his return his health failed and he was compelled to abandon his occupation, and from that time has been unable to earn steady wages, is insufficient. *Huber* v. *Commonwealth*, 11 W. N., 496 (1882).

To a recognizance of bail in error, an affidavit averring that the writ was taken to a refusal to set aside an execution, which was a matter of discretion with the court, and not the subject of a writ of error, and that therefore the recognizance was without consideration and void, is insufficient. *Beck* v. *Courtney*, 13 W. N., 302 (1883).

An affidavit averring payment and that defendant is not indebted, but not setting out the facts and details of the payment, is insufficient. *McCracken* v. *Presbyterian Church*, 17 W. N., 45 (1886).

An affidavit averring a limited partnership, but not setting out specifically each compliance with each requirement of the Act, is insufficient. *Conrow* v. *Gravenstine*, 17 W. N., 204 (1886).

An averment in an affidavit that goods charged were excessive in amount is too vague. *Jenkinson* v. *Hilands*, 146 Pa. St., 380 (1892).

An affidavit of defense ought to exhibit a copy of a paper set up as a defense in order that the court may judge of its legal effect. The defendant averred simply that the contractor had not "fully complied with his contract with the city" without furnishing a copy of the contract. The Supreme Court held that the affidavit was insufficient. *Erie* v. *Butler*, 120 Pa. St., 374 (1888), Paxson, J. *Reed* v. *Williard*, 47 Leg. Int., 132 (1890).

An affidavit of defense averred that plaintiffs were sole agents of a firm who were indebted to defendant and who had assigned the amount sued on to defendant by a certain order directed to plaintiffs. The affidavit did not state the plaintiffs accepted the order and was therefore insufficient. *Heckscher* v. *Iron Co.*, 26 W. N., 525 (1890).

An affidavit of defense which refers to an injunction granted by the court of another State is insufficient without attaching a copy of the decree, and injunction. *Kraft* v. *Gingrick*, 2 Dist. Rep., 398 (1893).

If an affidavit of defense refer to the statutes of another State it must attach copies thereof or it is insufficient. *Time Co.* v. *Geiger*, 147 Pa. St., 399 (1892).

In an action to recover for yarn sold and delivered by sample, the affidavit of defense set forth that defendant had suffered great loss by reason of claims made by customers because of the inferior quality of the yarn. The affidavit was insufficient in not alleging the quantity, quality, or market price of the yarn purchased. *Ogden* v. *Beatty*, 26 W. N., 524 (1890).

A suit was brought to recover royalties for the use of two patents. Under the agreement royalties were to be paid until the patents expired or were declared invalid. An affidavit of defense which failed to aver either fact was held insufficient. *Hardwick* v. *Galbraith*, 27 W. N., 573 (1891).

When an affidavit of defense avers the payment of all arrearages on a mutual policy of life insurance, but does not set forth how it was paid, in what amounts, or to whom, it is insufficient. *Solly* v. *Moore*, 1 Dist. Rep., 688 (1892).

An affidavit of defense to a *sci. fa. sur* municipal claim for paving, setting forth that the street had previously been graded and macadamized at the expense of abutting owners, was in good order and needed no repair when the paving was done, is insufficient. It did not aver the city approved the kind or quality of the previous paving. *Phila.* v. *Baker*, 140 Pa. St., 11 (1891).

An affidavit of defense for cigars sold which avers a warranty must set forth whether it is in writing or not and its terms. *Voneiff* v. *Braunreuter*, 1 Dist. Rep., 645 (1892).

An affidavit of defense setting forth that the plaintiff was not entitled to bring an action in Pennsylvania because it was a foreign corporation and had not complied with the Act of April 22, 1874, prohibiting such corporation from doing business in Pennsylvania without known place of business and authorized agents therein, but which failed to aver that plaintiff was doing business in said State, is insufficient. *Campbell Co.* v. *Hering*, 139 Pa. St., 473 (1891).

An affidavit of defense to a foreign judgment which does not allege payment is not sufficient. *Potter* v. *Hartnett*, 28 W. N., 120 (1891).

Where defendant sets up a contract as his defense his affidavit should distinctly aver the authority of one not a party to the suit to make the contract. *Class* v. *Kingsley*, 48 Leg. Int., 364 (1891).

An averment in an affidavit of defense that certain items of credit were omitted from plaintiff's statement, without specifying them, is insufficient. *Baker* v. *Reese*, 30 W. N., 437 (1892).

In a suit for assessments against one insured in a mutual insurance company, the affidavit of defense setting forth merely that the assessment was greatly in excess of the needs of the company is insufficient. *Ins. Co.* v. *Bergstresser*, 1 Dist. Rep., 771 (1892).

In a suit for goods sold and delivered, bought by sample and represented to be as good as the sample, an affidavit of defense should state whether the warranty was express or implied, its terms, and the market value of the goods, with reasonable accuracy. The affidavit must not be general or evasive. *Wile* v. *Ousel*, 1 Dist. Rep., 188 (1891).

In a suit to recover attorney fees an affidavit of defense averring that the original actions were managed unskilfully, but not stating in what such unskilfulness consisted, is not sufficient. *Chain* v. *Hart*, 28 W. N., 317 (1891).

When a statement avers the sum sued for is justly due and the work performed at request of defendant, and a copy of book entries is attached an affidavit of defense averring that such copy is defective, without replying to the other averments in the statement, is insufficient. *Ashman* v. *Weigley*, 29 W. N., 569 (1892)

In suit on an award, if the affidavit of defense does not aver that material errors in the proceeding will be proved by the arbitrators themselves, it is insufficient. *Plank* v. *Mizell*, 1 Dist. Rep., 757 (1892).

Where suit is brought by parties styling themselves " heirs at law " of a decedent, an averment in the affidavit of defense that plaintiffs " are not all the heirs," is insufficient, without naming those omitted. *Bakes* v. *Reese*, 30 W. N., 437 (1892).

In an action for the value of flour sold to defendant an affidavit of defense averring that the flour was of bad quality and that the defendant sustained loss of custom, is insufficient. He must set forth what he was able to sell the flour for, the quantity and value of the flour taken back, and the prices, as well as the reasons for customers refusing to pay. *Marshall* v. *Aber*, 1 Dist. Rep., 770 (1892).

Where a judgment of a magistrate was reversed on certiorari and judgment entered for defendant with costs, this is no bar to a recovery in the Common Pleas on the same cause of action. *Jenkinson* v. *Hilands*, 146 Pa. St., 380 (1892).

An affidavit of defense to a paving claim, which avers that the paving referred to in the claim is not original paving, without stating when or with what material the street was originally paved, is insufficient—so, too, an affidavit which avers fraud and misrepresentation as to the kind of pavement without stating by whom the misrepresentations were made or fraud committed, is insufficient. *Harrisburg* v. *Baptist*, 156 Pa. St., 526 (1893).

An affidavit of defense to an action for rent is insufficient which sets forth that the premises were wholly unfit and uninhabitable and dangerous to life, wherefore they were vacated. *Hollis* v. *Brown*, 159 Pa. St., 539 (1894).

In an action for damages against a telegraph company for failure to send a message, an affidavit of defense is insufficient which avers that the defendant transmitted the message promptly and correctly over its own lines to the terminus thereof and delivered it for transmission to another company, without describing the company or stating the terminus. *Conrad* v. *Telegraph Co.*, 162 Pa. St., 204 (1894).

An affidavit of defense which consists of short, disjointed sentences setting forth no particular or specific facts, but constituting single and unconnected propositions involving conclusions of law, is insufficient. The facts should be specifically and sufficiently detailed to enable the court to say whether they amount to a defense. *Bank* v. *Stadelman*, 153 Pa. St., 634 (1893).

In a suit for rent, if the affidavit of defense admits the rent due, but denies the right of plaintiff to recover pending a contest over a will under which the plaintiff claims the demised premises, the court will make absolute the rule for judgment and order defendant to pay the money into court pending the contest. *Dietrich* v. *Dietrich*, 154 Pa. St., 92 (1893).

In an action on a foreign judgment where the record shows an appearance for defendant, an averment in the affidavit of defense that if such appearance was entered deponent had no knowledge of it, is evasive, inasmuch as it does not deny that defendant authorized such appearance. *Moore* v. *Phillips*, 154 Pa. St., 204 (1893).

An affidavit of defense to an action against the surety on a replevin bond is insufficient which sets up matters disputed in the replevin and settled by verdict. *Cox* v. *Hartranft*, 154 Pa. St., 457 (1893).

Where defendants, through their agent, purchased goods, an affidavit of defense to an action for the purchase money, setting forth that the goods were of inferior quality and that the agent had no authority to purchase goods except of a certain quality, was held to be insufficient, there being no allegation that the plaintiffs knew that the agent's authority was limited. *Williams* v. *Sawyers*, 155 Pa. St., 129 (1893).

An affidavit of defense in a suit on a bill of exchange against the drawee, which sets up that the bill was given in part payment of a certain accommodation draft obtained by fraud, but fails to aver that plaintiffs were not *bona fide* holders for value before maturity, although charging them with notice of the alleged fraud, is insufficient. *Bank* v. *Fitler*, 155 Pa. St., 210 (1893).

In an action against the sureties of an administrator to recover the amount of an award, an affidavit of defense is insufficient which merely avers want of diligence in collection without stating that any notice was given the plaintiff to proceed. *Comm.* v. *Degitz*, 167 Pa. St., 400 (1895).

In an action for the price of an engine, an affidavit of defense which avers that it was not furnished according to representations or as agreed, without averring what the agreement was or the representations were, is insufficient. *Machine Works* v. *Ritter*, 4 Dist. Rep., 474 (1895).

In an action upon a lease for rent, an affidavit of defense is insufficient which sets up a mere representation by the plaintiff's agent as to some future act outside the lease, contrary to its terms, and not averred to be false or fraudulent. *Wilcox* v. *Palmer*, 163 Pa. St., 109 (1894).

An affidavit of defense to a municipal claim for paving, that the defendant had paid for grading a street, and that in paving the grade has been raised, but not averring the higher grade increased the cost of paving, is insufficient. *Oil City* v. *Lay*, 164 Pa. St., 370 (1894).

In an action to recover the cost of paving a footway the affidavit of defense averred that part of the work was not in accordance with the proper grade required by the city, and would have to be taken up and relaid, but did not aver the cost of relaying the pavement. It was adjudged insufficient. *Paving Co.* v. *Young,* 166 Pa. St., 267 (1895).

An affidavit of defense to an action by a foreign corporation to recover a subscription to its stock, is insufficient which merely avers that the plaintiff is a foreign corporation and has not filed a statement in the office of the Secretary of State as required by the Act of 1881. *Iron Co.* v. *Vandervort,* 164 Pa. St., 572 (1894).

§ 31. Items not denied by affidavit of defense shall be taken as admitted.

In *Nellis* v. *Reiter,* 2 W. N., 203 (1875), the plaintiff filed a copy of book entries supported by affidavit. The affidavit of defense set up that the prices were in excess of a parol contract under which the goods had been purchased, but there were no particulars given. The court below (STERRETT, P. J.) admitted the copy filed under exception, and the Supreme Court affirmed because "the defendants filed no denial of the items of the account under the rules of court."

§ 32. The following affidavits have been held sufficient :

In *Christy* v. *Bohlen,* 5 Pa. St., 38 (1846) a *sci. fa.* on a recognizance of bail was issued. An affidavit of defense was filed averring that the plaintiff in the original action issued a *fi. fa* , made a levy, and the sheriff collected enough money to pay debt, interest, and costs. Affidavit was held sufficient, although it was objected that in fact the fund raised by the sheriff had never been paid to the plaintiff, but had been received by the landlord under his claim for rent.

That the defendants named as owners in *sci. fa. sur* claim are minors. *Walker* v. *Morgan,* 2 W. N., 173 (1875).

In *Reamer* v. *Bell,* 79 Pa. St., 292 (1875), the affidavit was held to be sufficient because the defendant swore that he was "informed, verily believed, and expected to be able to prove that the plaintiff had no title to the note sued on." It also disclosed a good defense as against the payee of the note, and that the note had been specially indorsed to R. McCurdy, who was not the plaintiff, and who had not indorsed the note. Upon the face of the paper filed the plaintiff was not the owner of the note.

That deponent is informed, believes, and expects to be able to prove that the judgment sought to be revived has been paid by a sheriff's sale, describing it, but excusing omission of details of payments because deponent was unable after effort to obtain inspection of the sheriff's docket. The judgment was sixteen years old. *Moore* v. *Smith,* 2 W. N., 433 (1876) ; Sharswood, J.

Affidavit upon belief and expectation to prove is enough if defendant do not know the facts. *Reznor* v. *Supplee,* 2 W. N., 401 (1876) ; Woodward, J.

To a promissory note, an affidavit that note had been given as a subscription to a church upon the express condition that the lot on which the building was erected should be conveyed to the church, which condition had not been complied with, and that deponent verily believed and expected to be able to prove that the note had been passed to plaintiff to exclude this defense, is sufficient. *Ib.*

To book entries charged to mining company, a bill of exchange drawn on defendant by Bevan & Wallace, and orders on the defendant drawn by the same firm ; an affidavit alleging that defendant never was and is not now a member of the firm of Bevan & Wallace, which firm purchased the goods sued for ; that he was a member of the mining company, but that the mining company never authorized the purchase of the goods ; that defendant believed that plaintiff had charged the goods to Bevan & Wallace, which firm was indebted to the mining company, is sufficient. *Martien* v. *Manheim*, 3 W. N., 10 (1876).

To *sci. fa. sur* mortgage, an affidavit that defendant had executed the mortgage on the promise that it would not be called in for three years, and that no interest is due, is sufficient. *Lippincott* v. *Whitman*, 3 W. N., 313 (1877).

To suit on a promissory note by indorsee, an affidavit that indorsee had not received the note for value before maturity, but that he held it simply to deprive defendant of the defense of a failure of consideration, and setting forth the facts of the failure of consideration, is sufficient. *Moeck* v. *Littell*, 3 W. N., 341 (1876).

To *sci. fa. sur* judgment, an affidavit that the whole amount of the judgment had been paid by illegal and usurious interest to plaintiff, is sufficient. *Seymour* v. *Hubert*, 3 W. N., 423 (1877).

To *sci. fa. sur* mechanic's lien, an affidavit setting forth that the portion of the street paved had, by its deed of dedication, been reserved for market houses, is sufficient. *Philadelphia* v. *Phila. & Read. R. R.*, 3 W. N., 492 (1877).

To suit on note by indorsee, an affidavit that payee took a note to negotiate for benefit of himself and defendant, but instead of so doing he delivered it to plaintiff as collateral security for a pre-existing debt, and that note in suit is an extension of said note, is sufficient. *Royer* v. *Keystone National Bank*, 4 W. N., 86 (1877).

To contract, an affidavit setting forth details of verbal statements, and that writing was signed on the faith of these verbal statements, is sufficient. *Barclay* v. *Wainwright*, 5 W. N., 162 (1878).

To a suit on a note by a subsequent indorsee against second indorser, an affidavit alleging that plaintiff holds the note sued on for the benefit of first indorser, and that the note really belongs to first indorser, is sufficient. *Oberle* v. *Schmidt* et al., 5 W. N., 225 (1878).

An affidavit alleging set-off of $100 for professional services rendered to plaintiff by defendant as an attorney-at-law in and about the business of the plaintiff within six years last past, is sufficient. *Lawrence* v. *Smedley*, 6 W. N., 42 (1878).

To a book account, an affidavit that goods charged to defendant individually were purchased by a partnership is sufficient. *Dusenbury* v. *Bradley*, 6 W. N., 413 (1879).

To copy of note drawn " to order of Susanna P. Prahl " and indorsed " Mrs. Prahl," defendant filed an affidavit alleging that the amount of the note was due to some one, but, as he expected to prove, due to the personal representative of Susanna P. Prahl ; that he believed the note was not indorsed by her voluntarily, her husband being the indorsee. *Held*, that, as plaintiff had not shown his title to the note, the indorsement differing from the name of payee, judgment could not be given. *Prahl* v. *Smaltz*, 6 W. N., 571 (1879).

An affidavit setting forth an agreement by creditors of defendant with him and with each other to settle for thirty per cent. and in a certain way is sufficient, unless it appear from the agreement that it was to be signed by all the creditors before being of force and effect. *Laird* v. *Campbell*, 8 W. N., 134 (1880).

In suit by indorsee against indorser an affidavit alleging that note was indorsed on the assurance that note would be paid on a mortgage, on which defendant was liable, and stating facts which clearly reveal actual fraud in the obtaining and use of the indorsement, is sufficient. *Smith* v. *Building Association*, 9 W. N., 168 (1880).

To suit on bonds guaranteed by the P. & R. R. R. Co., an affidavit alleging that under its charter and the laws of the Commonwealth the railroad company had no corporate power to make the guarantee, is sufficient. (The guarantee was authorized by private Act, March 20, 1872, of which the court could not take judicial notice.) *Timlow* v. *P. & R. R. R. Co.*, 11 W. N., 218 (1882).

An affidavit specifying misrepresentations made by plaintiff in selling the machine for the price of which suit is brought, and stating that the machine was exhibited to defendant in a dark room without windows, and among other machines, so that defendant was compelled to rely on plaintiff's statements, is sufficient. *Scheffers* v. *Stewart*, 11 W. N., 106 (1881).

To recognizance of bail in error, an affidavit that recognizance was to be given for costs only, that the words, " debt, damages, and," were inserted without defendant's knowledge or consent, and contrary to express understanding and agreement, is sufficient as to debt and damages. *Ecoff* v. *Gillespie*, 13 W. N., 564 (1883). An affidavit that indorsee took the note as collateral security for a pre-existing debt, and setting forth that the note was without consideration, is sufficient. *Carpenter* v. *The Bank*, 15 W. N., 523 (1884).

To suit on a lease for rent, an affidavit alleging an agreement in the lease that lessee might purchase the premises, and that lessee had tendered the purchase-money agreed on, and was now ready to pay it with interest, is sufficient. *Knerr* v. *Bradley*, 16 W. N., 72 (1884).

In suit on bond executed more than twenty years, but containing indorsed receipts dated within twenty years, an affidavit suggesting presumption of payment is sufficient. *Lash* v. *Von Neida*, 16 W. N., 93 (1885).

In suit by indorsee against limited partnership on its note, an affidavit that note was given without consideration for the use of the payee, that it was not authorized by the company, and that the Act of Assembly under which defendant was formed forbids such loaning of credit unless a majority of the members in number and value consent, is sufficient. *Bank* v. *Hardware Co.*, 16 W. N., 104 (1885).

To book account, an affidavit alleging that defendant did not buy the goods on his own credit, but as the agent of his wife, who was conducting business under a deed of trust, and that plaintiff knew thereof, is sufficient. *Noble* v. *Krenzkamp*, 17 W. N., 89 ; 111 Pa. St., 68 (1888).

To a recognizance of bail in error, an affidavit alleging coverture is sufficient. *Warner* v. *Smith*, 2 W. N., 107 (1876).

An affidavit is sufficient which avers fraud in procuring the note sued on, and its particulars, with plaintiff's participation therein. *Gere* v. *Unger*, 24 W. N., 7 (1889).

In *City* v. *McCaffrey*, 25 W. N., 213 (1889), a rule for judgment for want of a sufficient affidavit of defense was taken in a suit on a municipal claim. STERRETT, J.: "Assuming, as we must, in cases such as this, that every material averment of fact in the affidavit of defense is true, we think there is sufficient to entitle the defendant to a jury trial. * * * We are not at liberty to go outside of the case * * * for the purpose of considering extraneous facts, either in support of or against the line of defense disclosed by the affiadvit." The affidavit here alleged that the defendant had a full defense to the whole of the plaintiff's claim, that the liens did not set forth the work with sufficient particularity, nor give a sufficient description of the premises or of the buildings thereon, and that no public street had been opened through the grounds and no damages had been assessed as alleged.

In *Church* v. *Jones*, 25 W. N., 396 (1890), suit was brought in the name of a church to recover certain funds, books, and papers which it was alleged the defendant received as treasurer of the church and on demand refused to deliver to his successor in office. The statement averred that the term for which the defendant was elected as treasurer had expired, that the trustees had elected V. in his place, and that V. made the demand which was refused. The affidavit set forth that V. was not the treasurer and that the trustees had never demanded of the defendant to return the books, etc.; it further averred that the suit was not brought by the corporation church, but by certain seceders. The lower court gave judgment for want of a sufficient affidavit. The Supreme Court reversed. STERRETT, J.: "The rule for judgment must be regarded in the nature of a demurrer to the affidavit * * * every material averment of fact contained therein must be accepted as true; if, therefore, either of those averments contain what, in law or equity, amounts to a substantial defense to the plaintiff's claim, the court erred in entering * * * judgment." * * *

In *Lyon* v. *Langfeld*, 47 Leg. Int., 132 (1890), the affidavit of defense averred that after the debt was contracted $160 was paid on account, and that subsequently a partner of the defendant settled the balance, and that plaintiff admitted to the affiant the debt was fully paid. At the time of making his affidavit the defendant was absent from home and could not furnish details as if at home and with access to his books. *Held*, the affidavit was sufficient.

Fiske v. *Bank*, 25 W. N., 454 (1890). Fiske & Co. wrote to the bank, "We will honor R.'s drafts with bill of lading attached." The bank cashed two of these drafts of R. on Fiske & Co. with bills of lading attached. Fiske & Co. refused to honor the drafts or to receive the merchandise. It was sold, and the bank sued Fiske & Co. for the difference between the proceeds of the sale and the amount of the drafts. *Held*, that an affidavit was sufficient which averred that the drafts were for more than the merchandise was worth, and that it was a custom known to the bank that only two-thirds or three-fourths of the value of the merchandise was advanced on drafts.

An action was brought against a railroad company for not delivering its stock in exchange for the bond and coupons of a second railroad, according to an alleged agreement. The statement set forth the bond, the proceedings on the mortgage securing the bond, the sale of the road to a trustee for the bondholders, and the agreement of the first railroad to assume the duties of trustee and issue *its* stock to the holders. The affidavit of defense averred that the conveyance of the trustee to the first railroad was free and discharged from all trusts whatsoever. *Held*, sufficient. *Landis* v. *R. R.*, 26 W. N., 64 (1890).

In *Amer. Academy of Music* v. *Bert*, 47 Leg. Int., 222 (1890), suit was brought upon a lease to recover a stipulated sum for the privilege of occupying the Academy for dramatic representations upon certain nights. The defendant's affidavit of defense set up that he gave notice nearly three months previous to the engagements of his desire to cancel the lease, that under the custom of the theatrical profession one month's notice was ample, and that plaintiff knew of this custom, as the house was leased for theatrical performances. *Held*, a sufficient affidavit of defense.

When the sufficiency of an affidavit of defense is considered, averments of counsel at the argument, or facts not contained in the record or fairly deducible therefrom, cannot be regarded. *City* v. *McCaffrey*, 47 Leg. Int., 247 (1890).

An affidavit calling attention to the fact that upon the face of the book account the contract had been completed more than six years before suit brought, and that defendant made no new promise, is a sufficient claim of the Statute of Limitations. *Fritz* v. *Hathaway*, 26 W. N., 273 (1890).

When a mechanic's lien has been filed for ranges furnished, an affidavit of defense is sufficient which alleges they were portable stoves physically unconnected with the freehold. *Williams* v. *Bower*, 1 Dist. Rep., 88 (1891).

In an action on a note by an indorsee an affidavit of defense is sufficient which avers duress—failure by lessor to furnish steam, causing defendant damage beyond the amount of the note—and that plaintiff is not a *bona fide* holder, but that lessor brings suit in plaintiff's name. *Devlin* v. *Burns*, 23 Atl. Rep., 375 (1892).

An affidavit of defense to action on a foreign judgment is sufficient which sets forth that plaintiffs agreed that defendant should enter their service and in addition to his wages that the judgment should be discharged, and that he did so enter their service and remained until he left by mutual agreement. *Potter* v. *Hartnett*, 29 W. N., 567 (1892).

Where suit is brought on a promissory note by an indorsee against the maker, the affidavit is sufficient if it aver that the note was obtained by fraudulent representations and that the defendant believes it was transferred to plaintiff without consideration to avoid this defense. *Boomer* v. *Henry*, 2 Dist. Rep., 357 (1893).

Where assumpsit is brought for rent, if the tenant in his affidavit of defense avers a surrender of the lease and an acceptance by the agent of the landlord, it is sufficient. *De Morat* v. *Falkenhagen*, 30 W. N., 39 (1892).

Where an affidavit of defense avers a custom, it should be stated positively and not "on information and belief with expectation of ability to prove;" if made by a dealer to whom the custom is well known, it should be so averred. *Weld* v. *Barker*, 153 Pa. St., 466 (1893).

An affidavit of defense setting up the payment by a third party of a sum of money less than the amount of a judgment, with the understanding that it should be in full satisfaction of the judgment, is sufficient, since such payment by a third party is a valid accord and satisfaction. *Fowler* v. *Smith*, 153 Pa. St., 639 (1893). See *Willing* v. *Peters*, 12 S. & R., 177 (1824); *Tucker* v. *Murray*, 2 Dist. Rep., 497 (1893).

Where suit is brought on a note and the affidavit of defense sets up that the note was given in payment for certain doors, blinds, etc., warranted as to size and without opportunity of inspection, which articles were not as represented, could not be used by defendant, and were sold by him at a loss, the affidavit is sufficient. *Bacon* v. *Scott*, 32 W. N., 194 (1893).

An affidavit of defense to a claim for paving is sufficient if it aver that the street upon which the paving was done is occupied by the tracks of a railway company, which under its charter is required to pay for the paving of streets occupied by its tracks. *Phila.* v. *Market Co.*, 154 Pa. St., 93 (1893); 161 *Id.*, 522 (1894); *City* v. *Bowman*, 36 W. N., 138; 166 Pa. St., 393 (1895).

An affidavit of defense is sufficient which avers, in an action for goods sold and delivered, that the goods were furnished defendants as managers of a business entered upon for the benefit of all parties and as a contribution to the stock of the business by plaintiffs. *Lee* v. *Taylor*, 154 Pa. St., 95 (1893).

An affidavit of defense, which avers that the claim upon which suit is brought is identical with the set-off used by plaintiff in another action between the same parties where the plaintiff was defendant, is sufficient. *R. R. Co.* v. *Davenport*, 154 Pa. St., 111 (1893).

In a suit on a promissory note the affidavit of defense set up that the note was delivered in payment of an annual premium upon a policy upon defendant's life, issued by the plaintiff, and that plaintiff's agent agreed that if defendant lived "till the maturity of the note he would be entitled to a rebate of 30 per cent." *Held*, sufficient. *Ins. Co.* v. *Williams*, 32 W. N., 353 (1893).

An affidavit of defense to an action on a policy for the value of a horse insured, averring that the horse was removed beyond the limits permitted by the policy, is sufficient to prevent judgment. *Reck* v. *Live Stock Co.*, 2 Dist. Rep., 502 (1892); *Ins. Co.* v. *Evans*, 102 Pa. St., 281 (1883).

In an affidavit of defense the established and approved form is either to set forth the facts affirmatively for the court to judge as to their sufficiency, or if affiant cannot state them of his own knowledge: "that he is informed, believes, and expects to be able to prove them," etc. The expression "has abundant reason to believe" is not sufficient. *Newbold* v. *Pennock*, 32 W. N., 370 (1893).

In an action on a promissory note an affidavit of defense is sufficient which sets forth that the note was given in payment of a drug store; that plaintiff had falsely and fraudulently misrepresented the receipts of the business, and in furtherance of his fraud filled the bottles with colored waters; had shown the accumulated receipts of many days as the receipts of a single day, and just before defendant took possession had removed all the costly and useful drugs. *Goodwin* v. *Schott*, 159 Pa. St., 552 (1894).

Where an action is brought to recover money paid for an interest in certain alleged banking concessions, an affidavit of defense is sufficient which avers the concessions were in existence when plaintiff invested, and a trust formed, but the concessions were subsequently revoked, and that all the money invested had been applied to expenses. *Frishmuth* v. *Barker*, 159 Pa. St., 549 (1894).

In an action upon a judgment in another State an affidavit of defense setting forth that defendant was not served with process and did not appear is sufficient. *Price* v. *Harrell*, 34 W. N., 442 (1894); 161 Pa. St., 530 (1894). Overruling *Lance* v. *Dugan*, 22 W. N., 132 (1888); *Wetherill* v. *Stillman*, 65 Pa. St., 105 (1870); and reversing *Stewart* v. *Schaeffer*, 33 W. N., 365 (1893).

In a suit on a foreign judgment an affidavit of defense is sufficient which sets forth there was no personal service on defendant in the foreign jurisdiction. *Wissler* v. *Herr*, 162 Pa. St., 552 (1894).

An affidavit of defense is sufficient which denies the grounds of liability averred in the statement and those which arise by implication from the averments made. The defendant is not obliged to go into a detailed history of such denial. *Barker* v. *Fairchild*, 168 Pa. St., 246, 348 (1895).

In an action to recover the price of a carload of cabbage, an affidavit of defense is sufficient which sets forth the custom of the trade as to shipping and packing, and that plaintiff failed to observe the custom, whereby the cabbage underwent a process of sweating, fermentation, and decay. *Davis* v. *Kœnig*, 165 Pa. St., 347 (1895).

In an action for rent an affidavit of defense is sufficient which sets forth an actual eviction by title paramount. *Friend* v. *Supply Co.*, 165 Pa. St., 652 (1895).

An affidavit of defense is sufficient in an action to recover the price of coal against defendant and others trading as a certain company, which avers the defendant was not a member during the period said coal was sold and delivered, and that plaintiff knew it. *Rhoads* v. *Fitzpatrick*, 166 Pa. St., 294 (1895).

An affidavit of defense to a *sci. fa. sur* municipal claim which denies that the city authorized the work to be done is sufficient. *City* v. *Eyre*, 36 W. N., 216 (1895).

An affidavit of defense, in an action for damage for failure to deliver goods, which avers that plaintiff told defendant in purchasing his goods that a competitor had offered to sell at a certain price, whereby defendant agreed at the figure named to sell the plaintiff, and that said statement was false and maliciously and intentionally made to secure a sale below the market price, is sufficient. *Smith* v. *Smith*, 166 Pa. St., 563 (1895).

An affidavit of defense to an action to recover the price of certain oil delivered, which sets forth a warranty, and that said oil was not furnished as warranted, is sufficient. Where an affidavit of defense sets up a warranty as shown by the correspondence and alleges the goods were not of the quality contracted for, it is sufficient. *Baugh* v. *Mitchell*, 36 W. N., 228 ; 166 Pa. St., 577 (1895).

Believes and expects to prove. An affidavit of defense averring "that deponent is informed and verily believes," to which is added "his expectation of ability to prove," is sufficient. *Lewis* v. *Broadbent*, 21 W. N., 31 (1887).

Affidavit by a stranger. In *Griel* v. *Buckius*, 114 Pa. St., 190 (1886), Mr. Justice PAXSON said : "When a defendant puts in a stranger's affidavit, it must show upon its face sufficient reason why it was not made by the defendant himself; that a real disability existed which prevented him from making it, and the circumstances giving rise to the disability."

An affidavit made by counsel of defendant, without assigning reason why it is not made by defendant, is insufficient. Such a defect may be cured by a supplemental affidavit made by the defendant before judgment entered. *Wilkinson* v. *Brice*, 30 W. N., 30 (1892).

§ 33. It will be noticed that the year is mentioned in connection with each decision. This is important; it assists you; it helps the judge; it shows you have examined the case and have not simply snatched it from a Digest. I learned this habit from David W. Sellers, Esq., and have found it excellent practice.

§ 34. The court may think defendant should be allowed time to file a supplemental affidavit. This will impose on you anew the labor of fresh paper-books and of a notice to your opponent that you will call up the rule. If you succeed, you proceed as if judgment had been entered for want of an affidavit. If your rule be discharged and you have not filed a statement, you file it, with rule to plead, etc. If you have already filed a statement, you simply rule the defendant to plead, as already noted.

As to the form of statement, etc., see that title.

§ 35. **All papers should be neatly indorsed** with:

Number.   Term.   Year.

Name of plff. ⎫
    v.   ⎬ Court.
Name of deft. ⎭

Name of the paper.

Name of counsel.

A prothonotary may refuse to receive a paper unindorsed. Here, as everywhere, a man is known by his works. A slovenly indorsed paper placed upon a record is undying evidence of the pleader's laziness; and it is remarkable that those who have the least business and the most time are in the preparation of their papers the most negligent. Do not sneer at these suggestions and call details trifles. Remember Augustin's grand saying: "*Minima sunt minima, sed magnum esse in minimis bonum est.*" (Trifles are trifles, but to be great in trifles is good.)

§ 36. **If the affidavit admit a part of the claim, you can take** a rule for judgment for the amount admitted.

FORM OF RULE.

A. B.   ⎫
  v.   ⎬ C. P. No.   ,   Term, 1890, No.
C. D.   ⎭

And now (date), on motion of plaintiff rule on defendant to show cause why judgment should not be entered for the amount admitted to be due in the affidavit of defense filed in the above case.

Rule returnable (date) 10 A.M.

Indorsement.

A. B.   ⎫
  v.   ⎬ C. P. No. 1,   Term, 1890, No.
C. D.   ⎭

Rule for judgment for amount admitted in the affidavit of defense.

E. F.,

pro plff.

Hand your rule to the court clerk, notify the other side, and prepare your paper-books. If you obtain judgment, assess your damages.

Plaintiff may take judgment for amount admitted by affidavit of defense, and may proceed for balance. In all cases now pending, or hereafter to be commenced, in the several courts of this Commonwealth in which affidavits of defense have been or may be filed to part of the claim of the plaintiff or plaintiffs, the plaintiff or plaintiffs may take judgment for the amount admitted to be due and have execution for the collection of the same, and the cases shall be proceeded in for the recovery of the balance of the demand of the plaintiff or plaintiffs, if anything more should be justly due to such plaintiff or plaintiffs. Act of May 31, 1893 (P. L., 185).

Under the Act of 1893, two judgments may be entered against a defendant in the same suit : one for the amount admitted to be due in the affidavit of defense, and the other on a verdict of the jury for the balance.

A judgment may be entered against the defendant for the amount admitted, with costs to date, and a judgment may be entered against the plaintiff for subsequent costs on failure to establish his claim to the residue. If the affidavit of defense admits certain items to be due, but avers the payment of a larger sum on account of the indebtedness, and it does not appear to what items the payment was applied, judgment will not be given. *City* v. *Railway Co.*, 33 W. N., 522 ; 2 Dist. Rep., 705 (1893).

The judgment for the amount admitted by the affidavit of defense may be entered by the prothonotary upon the præcipe of plaintiff or his attorney. *Roberts* v. *Sharp*, 33 W. N., 524 (1894).

Judgment cannot be entered for an amount admitted to be due, under the Act of May 31, 1893, where certain amounts claimed by the plaintiff are denied by defendant, even though the court decides the affidavit is insufficient as to such part. *Reilly* v. *Daly*, 159 Pa. St., 606 (1894).

Where judgment is moved for the amount admitted to be due, as to which the affidavit of defense alleges that tender was made before suit, judgment will be entered without costs. *McNicholl* v. *Ins. Co.*, 32 W. N., 472 (1893).

The Act of May 31, 1893, does not apply to causes at issue. *De Morat* v. *Entrekin*, 33 W. N., 160 (1893).

Where the affidavit of defense disputes the entire claim, the court will not inquire as to the insufficiency of the affidavit in part and give judgment for that part, with leave to proceed for the balance. *Meyers* v. *Cochran*, 33 W. N., 250 (1893).

In *Taber* v. *Olmsted*, 158 Pa. St., 351 (1893), by a special order previous to the Act of 1893, judgment was entered for the amount

admitted to be due in the affidavit of defense, without waiver as
to the right to go to a jury on the balance.

In *Stedman* v. *Poterie*, 27 W. N., 270 (1890), and *Blydenstein*
v. *Haseltine*, 140 Pa. St., 120 (1891), judgments for the amounts
admitted were allowed, under the Rules of Court.

Judgment for the amount admitted to be due, under the Act
of 1893, may be entered by the prothonotary on the order of
plaintiff's attorney; and if improperly entered, defendant may
enter a rule to strike it off. *Roberts* v. *Sharp*, 3 Dist. Rep., 136
(1894).

§ 37. You will thus observe that in all cases *ex contractu* you
proceed by summons, file your papers, and press for judgment for
want of an affidavit of defense. Where the paper filed is, in your
judgment, sufficient as a defense, you put the case at issue by
ruling defendant to plead.

§ 38. Cases may occur in which the court refuses judgment,
holding the affidavit of defense sufficient; yet you may prefer to
obtain the opinion of the Supreme Court. This you can do by
excepting and appealing. (See Act April 18, 1874, Br. Purd.,
789, section 11, and Act of May 9, 1889, P. L., 158.) But you
must have a clear case for judgment in order to reverse. *Griffith*
v. *Sitgreaves*, 2 W. N., 707 (1876).

Where a rule for judgment for want of a sufficient affidavit of
defense is discharged in open court, in presence of plaintiff's counsel, the ruling should be then and there excepted to and the court
requested to seal a bill. *Comm.* v. *Fleming*, 157 Pa. St., 644
(1893).

§ 39. By Capias. For breach of promise to marry, actions for
fines, penalties for moneys collected by a public officer, for misconduct, or neglect in office or in any professional employment, your
client can issue a *capias* instead of a summons.

It was decided in the Centennial Cases, *Blanco* v. *Bosch*, 3 W.
N., 171 (1876), that there can be no arrest for debt arising *ex contractu* without a special allocatur founded upon an affidavit bringing the case within the Act of 1842.

§ 40. *Philadelphia rules as to affidavit to hold to bail.*

The following are the Philadelphia rules :

No bail shall be required in actions of trespass *vi et armis*, in actions for
libels, slanderous words, malicious prosecution, conspiracy, or false imprisonment, unless an affidavit of the cause of action be made and filed before
the issuing of the writ.

In all actions of trover and conversion the affidavit to hold to bail shall
set forth the circumstances under which the defendant has possessed himself of the goods, the particulars of which they consist, and the value of

them, and in what manner the defendant has converted them to his own use.

A rule to show cause of action and why the defendant shall not be discharged on common bail must be moved for within six days from the return-day of the process. Such rule may be heard and decided by a single judge at such time and place as he may appoint.

Requirements of affidavit to hold to bail. Whether required by rule of court or not required, as a preliminary to the *capias*, draw plaintiff's affidavit to hold to bail. Put in it all the essential words of a *narr.* from the best precedents of declarations. The affidavits to hold to bail must contain defendant's name; it is not sufficient to name him in the caption and refer to him as " defendant." *Flaherty* v. *Lindsay,* 7 W. N., 79 (1879); *Hower* v. *Bennett,* 4 Dist. Rep., 323 (1895).

Where a capias is served on the wrong person, the proper practice is to take a rule to show cause why he should not be discharged on common bail. *Lisansky* v. *Gerzog,* 2 Dist. Rep., 220 (1892).

In *Diehl* v. *Forthuber,* 16 W. N., 227 (1885), a *capias* was issued for an assault. The affidavit did not state where the assault was made. ARNOLD, J., said: "An affidavit to hold to bail should be drawn with as much precision and fulness in essential matters as a *narr.,* although less formality is required. The place where the offense occurred is as essential in the affidavit as the venue is in a declaration." The rule to discharge on common bail was made absolute.

So, too, in *Trianovski* v. *Kleinschmidt,* 20 W. N., 296 (1887). The affidavit simply charged that the defendant said that deponent was a thief—that he was guilty of the crime of "arson," etc. The defendant took a rule to show cause of action and why he should not be discharged on common bail. The court, per THAYER, P. J., said: "What words were used by the defendant in making those charges? Were they spoken in English or German, or in what language? Were the words 'thief' and 'arson' used? If so, in what connection and with what colloquium?

"It may well be that what the plaintiff imputes to the defendant is only the plaintiff's construction put upon the words used, and that if the very words were given they would not warrant the construction put upon them by the plaintiff. To say that one man said of another that he is a thief is only to sum up the result of the plaintiff's interpretation put upon the words actually used. The defendant is entitled to know what words he is charged with. To state the legal effect of the words used is not sufficient. Nor is it sufficient to say, as the plaintiff says in his affidavit, that the defendant said 'this deponent was a thief.' If the defendant used the words 'this deponent,' it is clear he could not have intended the plaintiff. If he did not, it should be stated what words he used to describe 'this deponent.' The plaintiff should have set forth the words used, or at least the substance of them. Nothing less than that will satisfy the requisites of an affidavit to hold to bail. Such an affidavit, as we have heretofore ruled in *Kasper* v. *Newhouser* (14 W. N., 128), must expressly allege what words were spoken by the defendant. The present affidavit does not do that and is in that respect fatally defective." Rule absolute.

An averment, in an affidavit to hold to bail, that deponent has been informed and believed, is insufficient. *Barnett* v. *Stains*, 20 W. N., 274 (1887). An affidavit to hold to bail in a capias for malicious prosecution, on a charge of receiving stolen goods with the knowledge that they were stolen, which fails to set forth that the plaintiff did not know the goods were stolen, is insufficient, and the defendant will be discharged on common bail. *Aarons* v. *Dunseith*, 1 Dist. Rep., 701 (1891).

Since the Act of June 3, 1887, unless the affidavit aver that slanderous words were spoken by a wife in the presence of her husband, or with his knowledge or consent, the husband, if arrested on a capias for such acts of his wife, will be discharged on common bail. *O'Connor* v. *Welsh*, 29 W. N., 92 (1891).

In *Tucker* v. *Hough*, 24 W. N., 91 (1889), the affidavit to hold to bail set forth that defendant had possessed himself of certain goods belonging to plaintiff while in plaintiff's employ. A list was attached, and plaintiff averred that he had demanded a return of the goods, but delivery had been refused. The affidavit did not allege how defendant came into possession, whether lawfully or otherwise. The defendant was discharged.

FORM OF AFFIDAVIT TO HOLD TO BAIL.

The following form was used in a case for breach of promise of marriage. It is not necessary to remind the practitioner that the facts differ in all cases. This is simply given as a general guide or outline:

A. B. ⎫
  v. ⎬
C. D. ⎭

A. B., having been duly sworn according to law, doth depose and say:
That she is the daughter of E. B., who died   and who in his lifetime was Treasurer of the State of Pennsylvania, Clerk of the Senate, and filled several offices of honor and trust. Deponent was twenty-one years of age on the   day of   , 188 , and has resided since the decease of her father with her mother in the city of Philadelphia. Deponent, when twelve years of age, made the acquaintance of C. D., who

is three years her senior, and from their childhood an intimacy existed between them which enabled said C. D. to set on foot and complete the grievances hereinafter detailed.

Having, by reason of their long acquaintance, gained the friendly feeling of deponent in his favor, the said C. D. some years since commenced paying addresses to deponent, which resulted in a solemn engagement of marriage between him and deponent on the night of Christmas .
Deponent was then and still is unmarried, having at no time formed any engagement with or received the addresses of any other person. After this the said C. D. affianced himself to deponent in the presence of her father, and placed upon her finger an engagement ring. She and he then and there mutually promised to marry each other, and the said C. D., in consideration of deponent's said promise, entered into his said engagement of marriage. From this period his addresses were continued by almost daily visits to deponent's house, and by attentions of the most marked character up to the month of August last. Their intercourse during this period was without any interruption, except that occasioned by absence from the city and a coolness of a few months some years since, resulting from deponent's mother having forbidden the said C. D. to visit the house. All parties, however, having been reconciled, his visits continued as before, and his attentions were exclusive to deponent up to the month of August last as above mentioned.

During the whole of this period, with the exceptions already noticed, the addresses of said C. D. were of the most marked character, he being with deponent constantly, taking her to places of amusement, introducing her to the members of his family, permitting her to receive the visits of no other acquaintances, exchanging miniatures, and presenting her with various articles of jewelry. Whenever necessity required the absence of the said C. D. from the city, he corresponded regularly and frequently with deponent, nor had she at any time reason to suspect his fidelity to their engagement until last winter, when he requested her to let him look at his letters, in order, as he alleged, that he might discover the date of the loss of the "New Era," alluded to in one of them. Deponent complied with the request without any hesitation, but as soon as the said C. D. obtained possession of said letters he burned them. Although deponent was surprised at this act, and grieved at the loss of letters which she had so highly prized, she was induced by his protestation of attachment and excuses for his act to overlook it and to permit a continuance of his addresses as theretofore. A short time, however, sufficed to assure deponent that the destruction of their correspondence had been with a view of finally abandoning their engagement, for in the spring of this year   there was a coolness in the manner of the said C. D. toward deponent, and a cessation in the regularity and frequency of his visits, which occasioned deponent still deeper pain. She remonstrated gently as to this, but was met with no frank explanation of it, nor did she receive any satisfaction, except in evasive answers and still greater coldness. His last visit to deponent was on the   and since that date the said C. D. has ceased all visits to or notice of deponent, except that calculated to aggravate her wrong. He has formally stated that he will never marry deponent or comply with his aforesaid engagement to her; and although she has always been ready and willing to fulfil her contract, he has broken the same, and has refused to give any reason or explanation for this injury. Deponent solemnly protests that his breach of honor toward her has been occasioned by no act of hers, nor has she at any time or under any circumstances given any cause therefor. She has always been pure in her conduct, and so far as she knows or believes unsullied in reputation. She can with truth declare that in this rupture of a solemn engagement she has been wholly free from fault. The deponent cannot estimate her damage by any pecuniary standard; she was informed by the said C. D. that his family was wealthy and that he was possessed of considerable means, having been in business in this city, and it being his intention to enter business again. In that aspect of her case her damages would equal if they did not exceed twenty thousand dollars, but she repeats that, independently of any mere settlement in life or estate which she has lost by reason of defendant's breach of his engagement with her, she has sustained in position and character with her family and social circle and has suffered in wounded feelings a loss which no amount of money can ever pay.   A. B.

Sworn to and subscribed before me,

Notary Public.

Allocatur. When your affidavit is ready, if you wish bail in excess of $500 in Philadelphia, present the affidavit to a judge. Write the words, at its foot or on the back, *"Bail allowed, $———."* The judge fills in the amount and puts his initials to the *allocatur.*

Write your *præcipe for capias ad respondendum :*

A.)
v.   }
B.)

SIR : Issue *capias ad respondendum assumpsit.* Bail $———, specially allowed, ret. *sec. leg.*
C. D.,
Plaintiff's Attorney.

To Prothonotary Common Pleas.

Give the writ to sheriff, with defendant's address.

In actions of libel and slander, special bail will be required only where the plaintiff swears positively to special damages or where the defendant is about to leave the jurisdiction. *Renninger* v. *Dillon,* 2 Dist. Rep., 819 (1893).

§ 41. **You have the right to except to the bail** within twenty days after the return-day, if you regard it as insufficient. You do this by filing the following :

A.)
v.   } C. P.   , March T., 1887, No. 100.
B.)

The plaintiff excepts to the sufficiency of the bail in the above case.
C. D.,
Plaintiff's Attorney.
March 10, 1887.

You file this and serve notice on the sheriff. It is best to serve notice also on defendant's attorney, if any, and on the bail.

Within ten days after this notice the bail must justify, or new bail be given on justification.

To enable you to except, it is the duty of the sheriff taking the bond to give notice, in writing, of the names and residences of the bail. He is liable: (1) If he fail to give the notice; or (2) if, giving notice, the bail be excepted to, rejected, and no new bail given. In this latter event, the plaintiff ought not to proceed against the defendant or against the bail, but rule the sheriff to bring in the defendant, and enforce this rule, if necessary, by attachment; to escape, the sheriff must himself put in good bail or pay the money into court.

§ 42. **The sheriff's general returns to a** *capias ad respondendum* are either *non est inventus* (defendant is not found), C. C. et B. B. *cepi corpus* (I have taken the body) and bail-bond, or C. C. et C. *cepi corpus et committitur* (I have taken the body and he is committed). If the defendant be already in jail, the sheriff delivers a copy to the jailer and another copy to the defendant.

§ 43. **The defendant may enter special bail,** as above stated, any time before final judgment, or before the return of the writ he may deposit with the sheriff the amount of bail demanded. This is paid into court and afterward it is appropriated toward the plaintiff's recovery, and refunded if the plaintiff fail.

The defendant may, in like manner, after the return of the writ, by leave of the court, pay the money into court in discharge of himself from imprisonment or in discharge of his bond.

§ 44. **Should the bail make an assignment for the benefit of his creditors,** or apply for the benefit of the insolvent laws, or give bond for such purpose, or remove from the Commonwealth, or signify an intention to do so, an affidavit of the fact may be made, and the prothonotary may enter a rule as of course on the defendant, on three days' notice to him, to find additional bail; and in case of default a special *capias* issues.

Rules to show cause of action, to quash, etc. The courts have full powers on all writs of *capias* to inquire into the cause of action, to quash the writ, to reduce the bail, to discharge without bail, and to order repayment of the whole or part of any deposit made.

In *Blackiston* v. *Potts*, 2 Miles, 388 (1840), it was decided that the application to quash the *capias* on the ground that the defendant was a freeholder, must be made before the expiration of the fourth day after the return-day.

This decision was cited upon the argument in *Evans* v. *Wright*, C. P. No. 4, June Term, 1895, No. 740 (MS.), but a contrary ruling was made and the motion to quash, although made subsequent to the *quarto die post*, was granted.

The discharge of the defendant on common bail depends alone upon the sufficiency of the affidavit of the plaintiff. *Renninger* v. *Dillon*, 2 Dist. Rep., 819 (1893).

A capias will not be quashed where deceit is averred in the purchase of goods. *Bard* v. *Naylon*, 33 W. N., 251 (1893).

A defendant will be discharged on common bail where defendant's property is sufficient, over and above incumbrances, to satisfy plaintiff's demand. *Logan* v. *O'Neill*, 34 W. N., 281 (1894).

The court will dispose of such a rule either by examination of defendant's title-papers or by affidavits, depositions, and searches. *Ibid.*

If the affidavit to hold to bail is insufficient, the defendant is entitled to a rule on plaintiff to show cause of action and why defendant should not be discharged on common bail. This is of course.

FORM OF RULE:

A. B.
   v.   } C. P. No. 1, Dec. Term, 1893, No.
C. D.

And now (date), on motion of L. M., pro defendant, rule entered on plaintiff to show cause of action and why defendant should not be discharged on common bail. Returnable (date).

File this rule, serve notice, and prepare your paper-books. The latter should contain : (1) Copy of the affidavit to hold to bail ; (2) your argument, with citations, etc.

The bail may surrender the principal at any time, and in order to be relieved must do so within fourteen days after service of writ on them. *Carey* v. *Henry*, 3 Clark, 32 (1845).

§ 45. **Certain freeholders are privileged from arrest** in civil actions, by Act of Assembly, March 20, 1725. Br. Purd., 66, section 47 :

No freeholder inhabiting any part of this province, who hath resided therein for the space of two years, and has fifty acres of land or more in fee-simple, well seated, and twelve acres thereof, or more, well cleared or improved, or hath a dwelling-house worth fifty pounds, current money of America, in some city or township within this province, clear estate, or hath unimproved land to the value of fifty pounds like money, shall be arrested or detained in prison by any writ of arrest or *capias ad respondendum*, in any civil action, unless it be in the king's case or where a fine is or shall be due to the king, his heirs or successors ; or unless they be such freeholders as by the Act are made liable to be arrested.

Provided always, That nothing herein contained shall exempt any person from being arrested, or shall debar any person from taking out writs of arrest, if the plaintiff in every such writ, or somebody for him, doth make appear by affidavit, upon oath or affirmation, which the justice that grants such writ is hereby empowered and required to administer, testifying that the defendant in the same writ named has signified his intentions of going to sea, or of removing out of this province, or lurks in secret places, or conceals himself in his own or other's house; or that the defendant in such writ hath refused or neglected, upon demand, to give either real or personal security for the debt, or refused, without process, to appear and put in special bail to the plaintiff's action for the debt or cause for which he complains; or that the defendant suffered himself to be arrested or judgment to be entered against him, or made over his lands or chattels to others, or suffered them to be attached and made no proper defense to such proceedings; or where the plaintiff can make appear from records, or otherwise, that so much of the defendant's estate is mortgaged, aliened, entailed, or liable to one or more judgments suffered or ordered to be entered against such defendant, so that the value of his fee-simple estate, in possession, clear of those and all other incumbrances, will not, as the deponent believes, be sufficient to satisfy the debt demanded; or that the defendant in such writ hath not been a resident in this province for the space of two years next before the date of the same writ; in all which cases writs of arrest shall be granted and the defendant held to special bail, if the case require it; and the justices that grant the same shall cause all the affidavits they take, as above required, to be filed by the clerk of the court where such writs are returnable.

A plea of freehold cannot be maintained where defendant's real estate is incumbered to nearly its full value. *Logan* v. *O'Neill,* 34 W. N., 281 (1894).

But a person who possesses a freehold of the value of $133⅓ is exempt from arrest, without regard to plaintiff's demand. *Ibid.*

Abolition of imprisonment for debt. Nearly all writs of *capias ad respondendum* disappeared after the Act of July 12, 1842. It abolished imprisonment for debt, except in the following cases :

Actions of tort; actions on fines and penalties; promises to marry ; moneys collected by a public officer ; misconduct or neglect in office or in any professional employment. To this it may be added that " proceedings as for contempt to enforce civil remedies " are excepted from the non-imprisonment Act.

This refers to assignees, executors, and other trustees who are liable to attachment for disobedience of orders to pay, etc.

§ 46. **Females are free from arrest by reason of any debt.**

This merciful provision of our statute law has been benevolently extended in favor of married women, so as to protect them from civil arrest for contracts or torts. *Com.* ex rel. *McDowell* v. *Keeper,* 11 W. N., 341 (1882), and cases cited, *Ibid.,* 342.

SHARSWOOD, C. J., said : " The relator is entitled to be discharged if she is a married woman, whether the action against her sound in tort or contract." *Ibid.*

The Act of June 8, 1893, P. L., 344, called the *Married Persons' Property Act*, contains provisions as to rights and liabilities of married women which the practitioner should notice.

The third section provides, as to the liability of a married woman, that she may

sue and be sued civilly in all respects and in any form of action, and with the same effect and results and consequences, as an unmarried person, but she may not sue her husband, except in a proceeding for divorce, or in a proceeding to protect or recover her separate property, whensoever he may have deserted or separated himself from her without sufficient cause, or may have neglected or refused to support her; nor may he sue her except in a proceeding for divorce, or in a proceeding to protect or recover his separate property whensoever she may have deserted him, or separated herself from him without sufficient cause; nor may she be arrested or imprisoned for her torts.

It may be noted that the Act of June 3, 1887 (P. L., 332), section 2, provided that a married woman could sue and be sued for torts done to or committed by her, in all respects as if she were a *feme sole.*

This Act was repealed by the Act of 1893, *supra.*

After the passage of the Act of 1887, and prior to the Act of 1893, in *Whalen* v. *Gabell,* 20 W. N., 274 (1887), C. P. No. 4 of Philadelphia, quashed a *capias* against a married woman for slander. Opinion by THAYER, P. J. This was affirmed by the Supreme Court, 120 Pa. St., 284 (1888), and in *Vocht* v. *Kuklence,* 21 W. N., 518; 119 Pa. St., 365 (1888), STERRETT, J.

Attachment against Administratrix. The exemption of the female was "for or by reason of any debt contracted." Act February 8, 1819. Re-enacted by Act of June 13, 1836. Br. Purd., 67, § 51. The Orphans' Court of Philadelphia accordingly allowed an attachment against an administratrix for not paying over money. *Klein's Estate,* 1 W. N., 250 (1875).

§ 47. The Warrant of Arrest. In the cases where the Act of 1842 exempts the defendant from imprisonment for debt, the plaintiff may obtain a warrant of arrest. He is also entitled to it after judgment recovered. The cases in which this remedy can be invoked are thus described in the second section of the Act abolishing imprisonment for debt, approved July 12, 1842 (P. L., 1842, page 339).

" In all cases where, by the preceding provisions of this act, a party to a suit cannot be arrested or imprisoned, it shall be lawful for the party who shall have commenced a suit or obtained a judgment in any court of record to apply to any judge of the court in which the suit shall have been brought, for a warrant to arrest the party against whom the suit shall have been commenced, or the judgment shall have been obtained, whereupon the said judge shall require of the said party satisfactory evidence, either by the affidavit of the party making such application or some other person or persons, that there is a debt or demand due to the party making such application from the other party in the suit or judgment, in which affidavit the nature and amount of the indebtedness shall be set forth as near as may be.

" If the demand set forth in the affidavit be such that the party could not, according to the provisions of this Act, be arrested, and if the affidavit shall establish to the satisfaction of the judge one or more of the following particulars, to wit :

" That the party is about to remove any of his property out of the jurisdiction of the court in which such suit is brought, with intent to defraud his creditors ;

" Or, that he has property which he fraudulently conceals ;

" Or, that he has rights in action or some interest in any public or corporate stock, money, or evidence of debt which he unjustly refuses to apply to the payment of any such judgment or judgments which shall have been rendered against him belonging to the complainant ;

" Or, that he has assigned, removed, or disposed of, or is about to dispose of, any of his property with the intent to defraud his creditors ;

" Or, that he fraudulently contracted the debt or incurred the obligation respecting which suit is brought,

" It shall be the duty of said judge to issue a warrant of arrest in the form following, to wit :

"   County, *ss.* The Commonwealth of Pennsylvania to the sheriff or any constable of   county, greeting :

" Whereas, complaint has this day been made before me, on the oath (or affirmation, as the case may be) of (here insert the name of the party making the affidavit), setting forth (here briefly set forth the complaint). These are, therefore, to command you to arrest the said   and bring him (or them, as the case may be) before me at my office in (here insert the residence of the judge) without delay, to be dealt with according to law. And have you there also this precept.

" Witness my hand at   , this   day of   . Judge.

" Which warrant shall be accompanied by a copy of all affidavits presented to the judge upon which the warrant is issued, which shall be certified by such judge, and shall be delivered to the party at the time of serving the warrant by the officer serving the same."

A warrant of arrest will not lie against the officers of a joint-stock company. *Fleishman* v. *Price Co.*, 27 W. N., 312 (1890).

§ 48. **Suit to be first begun. The affidavit for the warrant.** It will thus be noticed that if you have not yet commenced suit, you must, before applying for the warrant, issue a summons. This you do by filling up the *præcipe*, as already stated, and getting the summons from the prothonotary.

You must prepare the affidavit of the plaintiff. If he be

absent from the State, his authorized agent can make the affidavit. It should be after the following form :

A.		In the Court of Common Pleas of	County.
v.		Term, 188 , No.	
B.			

A., the plaintiff above named, having been duly sworn according to law,
doth depose and say—1. That B., the defendant, is now justly and truly
indebted to him in the sum of   dollars, upon (a note whereof
the following is a true copy, or upon a book account for goods sold and delivered by plaintiff to defendant, between the   and the
or as the case may be).

2. That for recovery of said amount suit has been brought by deponent
against said defendant in the Court of Common Pleas of   County,
of   ,   Term, 188 , No.   .

3. That for said debt the said defendant cannot by virtue of the first section of the Act of July 12, 1842, be arrested or imprisoned.

4. That the said defendant (is about to remove, etc., or has property, etc.
—quote the words of the Act).

5. That deponent's reasons for thus stating are as follows : (It is recommended to give in narrative form *why* it is charged that the defendant is
about to remove property, or has property which he fraudulently conceals,
etc., etc.; for though it has been held that the facts need not be set out,
yet it is also stated that probable cause must be shown. I cannot understand how this requirement can be met without stating the facts.)

6. Wherefore deponent makes this his application for a warrant to arrest
the said defendant upon the statements of the preceding affidavit, according
to the Act of Assembly in such case made and provided.

Sworn to and subscribed   }
  before me,   1887.   }

An affidavit in support of a warrant of arrest, which avers a
fraudulent sale by defendant of the goods which had been bought
from plaintiff, and that a note for the balance due was unpaid and
suit had been brought thereon, is sufficient. No specific averment
that a particular sum is due is necessary where suit has been
brought. *Kohlhaus* v. *Veit*, 162 Pa. St., 108 (1894).

Where the debt arose from a contract which was not itself a
fraud, the plaintiff cannot, by rescinding the contract, claim that
the debt was fraudulently incurred. *Robinson* v. *Vogel*, C. P. No. 1,
of Phila., Sept. Term, 1895, No. 578.

A warrant of arrest can only issue in a case where a judgment
has been obtained or suit begun. The allegations in support of
the warrant must be clear and definite, otherwise it will be quashed.
Kohlhaus v. *Veit*, 3 Dist. Rep., 142 (1894).

Where a person is taken on a warrant of arrest, he must be
brought before the judge who issued the warrant. *Morch* v.
Raubitscheck, 33 W. N., 567 (1894).

§ 49. You should prepare the warrant, following the .form

already given. Have ready a copy of your client's affidavit.
Write on back of the copy :

A. *v.* B.   Common Pleas,   Term, 188 , No.   .
Certified copy of affidavit on which warrant of arrest is issued in above case.

Take the three papers to the judge. Upon reading the affidavit
he will, if satisfied, sign the warrant and the certificate of the copy.
You give the warrant and the certified copy of affidavit to the officer, with instructions to hand defendant a certified copy when he
makes the arrest. You should be prepared with proof of the
charge made, for the hearing may be prompt and the proceeding
summary. When the defendant is brought before the judge he
must deny, by counter affidavit, the charge, *Berger* v. *Small*, 39
Pa. St., 302 (1861), otherwise the judge will commit him. If he
answer fully and to the satisfaction of the judge, you have the
right to cross-examine him, the answers being reduced to writing.
You have also the right to sustain your charge by calling witnesses, etc.

For every adjournment a bond should be taken, conditioned for
defendant's appearance.

§ 50. **If the judge conclude to discharge the defendant**, that ends
the proceedings under the warrant.

If he give a contrary judgment, the defendant must stand committed, unless he pay the debt, or if it be in judgment, give security to pay, as per section 9 of the Act of 1842. If the charge be
an intent to remove property fraudulently, etc., the defendant may
give bond, under section 10, that he will not remove, etc., and
will not assign, etc. ; and in all cases the defendant may escape
commitment by giving bond, under section 11 of the Act, that he
will, within thirty days, petition for the benefit of the insolvent
laws, etc.

A warrant of arrest under the Act of 1842, and an attachment
under the Act of 1869, may be issued concurrently, the object of
both being to compel the payment of a debt fraudulently contracted
or payment of which is fraudulently evaded. *Grieb* v. *Kuttner*,
26 W. N., 323 (1890).

§ 51. **Attachment against fraudulent debtors.** For certain
cases of fraud another remedy was provided by the Act of March
17, 1869 (P. L., 1869, page 8). It was amended by the Act of May
24, 1887 (P. L., 1887, page 197), and as amended is in these
words :

" That it shall be the duty of any prothonotary of a court of record in
Pennsylvania to issue an attachment against any defendant or defendants

upon the application of any plaintiff or plaintiffs, upon proof by the affidavit of said plaintiffs or any of them, or of any other person for him, her, or them, that said defendant or defendants are justly indebted to him, her, or them in a sum exceeding one hundred dollars, the nature and amount of such indebtedness being set forth in such affidavit, and that said party defendant is about to move his, her, or their property out of the jurisdiction of the court in which said attachment is applied for, with intent to defraud his, her, or their creditors, or that said party defendant has property, rights in action, or interest in any public or corporate stock, money, or evidences of debt, which he, she, or they fraudulently conceal, or that said party defendant has or have assigned, disposed of, or removed, or is about to assign, dispose of, or remove any such property, money, rights in action, interest in public or corporate stock, or evidence of debt, with the intent to defraud his, her, or their creditors, or that he, she, or they fraudulently contracted the debt or incurred the obligation for which such claim is made. *Provided,* That before such attachment shall issue there shall be executed and filed with the prothonotary of the court or (by) the prothonotary of the county in which such attachment is applied for, a bond to the Commonwealth of Pennsylvania for the use of the parties interested, in a penalty of at least double the amount claimed, with good and sufficient surety, to be approved by one of the judges of the said court, conditioned that if the plaintiff or plaintiffs fail to prosecute such attachment with effect or in case such attachment be quashed, dissolved, or ended, then the plaintiff or plaintiffs shall pay to the defendant or defendants in such attachment all legal costs, fees, and damages, which said party defendant or defendants may sustain by reason of such attachment, and which said bond shall remain in the office of the said prothonotary for the use of any party injured as aforesaid."

§ 52. **Affidavit for attachment against fraudulent debtors.** You are to proceed under this by first preparing the affidavit of the plaintiff, or some one for him. It must set forth :

1. An indebtedness exceeding $100. The language of the Act seems to exclude torts and even unliquidated damages.

2. You must state the nature and amount of the indebtedness.

The debt must be presently due. *Simes* v. *Steadwell,* 12 W. N., 292 (1881); *Coaks* v. *White,* 11 W. N., 271 (1882).

3. Follow the language of the Act in the charge of intended removal, concealment, assignment, or other fraud. But do not charge disjunctively removal *or* concealment.

It has been erroneously supposed that blindly following the words of the law is sufficient. As already suggested, under the Act of 1842, the affidavit for the warrant of arrest ought to state facts in support of the charge. This Attachment Act of 1869-1887 in like manner authorizes process to be issued upon a charge of fraud.

Where the complaint is of an intent, the Act may be followed. *Sharpless* v. *Ziegler,* 92 Pa. St., 467 (1880). See also *Vansant* v. *Lunger,* 15 W. N., 549 (1885).

But where the charge is " that defendant fraudulently contracted the debt," and nothing more in this direction, it is insufficient. *Biddle* v. *Black*, 99 Pa. St., 380 (1882).

The affidavit should set forth specifically the fraudulent acts of the defendant; it should sufficiently describe the kind of property and the time when purchased. Mere insolvency and knowledge of it by the purchaser do not establish fraud. *Ib.*, 382 (Mercur, J.).

An affidavit upon which an attachment issues must set forth specifically the amount of defendant's indebtedness. *Wells* v. *Hogan*, 2 Dist. Rep., 98 (1892).

If an attachment under the Act of 1869 has issued upon an affidavit in the words of the Act, the plaintiff, under a rule to dissolve the attachment, may be permitted to take depositions in support of the affidavit. *Harris* v. *Budd*, 1 Dist. Rep., 83 (1891).

The Fraudulent Debtor's Act does not relate to a fraudulent assignment of real estate. *Kline* v. *O'Donnell*, 1 Dist. Rep., 741 (1891).

An affidavit sur attachment, under the Act of 1869, is a sufficient allegation of debt, if it state the time when the debt was contracted and the particular kind of property for which it was contracted. *Wilson* v. *Shapiro*, 2 Dist. Rep., 367 (1892).

Where a person sells on credit and takes notes for the purchase-money, he cannot issue an attachment under the Act of March 17, 1869, before the maturity of the notes. *Jones* v. *Brown*, 167 Pa. St., 395 (1895).

An attachment under the Act of 1869 does not lie upon a debt not due, unless there have been fraudulent representations made when the debt was contracted which would rescind the contract. *Meyers* v. *Rauch*, 4 Dist. Rep., 333 (1895).

In *Born* v. *Zimmermann*, 8 Phila., 233 (1871), it was ruled that affidavits upon which attachments under the Act of March 17, 1869, are issued, must set forth the facts establishing the complaint. A mere allegation of fraud or fraudulent intent in the words of the Act is not sufficient to sustain such an attachment. PIERCE, J.: " Wherever an intent or a fraud is charged against a party, the particular fact or facts which indicate the intent or fraud should be stated to the court, to enable the court to act intelligently and to inform the adverse party of the particular matters which he is challenged to meet." It was held in *Sharpless* v. *Ziegler* (*supra*) that the court ought not to *quash* the writ.

Moyer v. *Kellog*, 1 W. N., 134 (1875), was a rule to dissolve attachment. The affidavit followed the precise words of the Act. ALLISON, P. J.: " The plaintiff should set out in his affidavit the particular acts of defendant which he expects to prove, on which the attachment is issued." Rule absolute.

Robinson v. *Atkins*, 2 W. N., 111 (1875), was a rule to dissolve attachment under Act of 1869. The affidavit set forth that defendant had made a fraudulent contract since his liability to the plaintiff was incurred. The court refused to allow a supplemental affidavit to be filed, and dissolved the attachment.

An affidavit is insufficient which only avers fraud as to part of the claim. *Wright* v. *Ewen*, 44 Leg. Int., 179 ; 24 W. N., 111 (1889).

Where the affidavit is merely a general allegation of fraud, and an affidavit is filed by defendant, the plaintiff must support his affidavit by deposition ; but if it contain specific charges, the burden of disproving them is on the defendant. *Matthews* v. *Dalsheimer*, 10 W. N., 371 (1881) ; *Bradley* v. *Harker*, 15 W. N., 403 (1884). And the practice has not been altered by *Sharpless* v. *Ziegler* (*supra*).

The Act of March 17, 1869 (P. L., 8), is constitutional. *White* v. *Thielens*, 106 Pa. St., 173 (1884).

And the court may refer disputed facts to a master (*Ibid.*).

An attachment may issue against a corporation except as to real estate, and service may be made as provided by the Act of June 13, 1836, section 41. *Bank* v. *Bank*, 13 W. N., 515 (1883).

§ 53. Bond and præcipe in attachment under Act of 1869. Having prepared the plaintiff's affidavit with care, he signs it and swears to it. You file it with the prothonotary, accompanied by the plaintiff's bond. The first section of the Act of 1869 required the plaintiff's bond to be executed *by the plaintiff* or *by some one on his behalf*. These words are omitted in the Act of 1887. A bond in a proceeding by attachment, under the Act of 1869, executed in the firm name by one member of the plaintiff's firm, is sufficient. *Wilson* v. *Shapiro*, 2 Dist. Rep., 367 (1892). The first law required that the bond should be approved by the prothonotary or by a judge. The Act of 1887 requires the approval of a judge. It also changes the condition of the bond. It must now be " to prosecute the attachment," not to prosecute " the action," with effect. With the affiadvit and bond you file the following *præcipe :*

A.
v. }
B.

To the Prothonotary of the Court of Common Pleas of   County.

SIR : Issue attachment against the above-named defendant as required by the Act of March 17, 1869 (P. L., 1869, page 8), as amended by the Act of May 24, 1887, returnable *sec. leg.* Bail $ (double the debt).

C., pro Plaintiff.
(Date.)

With the writ you must give the sheriff full directions what to seize, where to serve defendant, if in the county, and whom to summon as garnishees.

§ 54. **Service of the writ of attachment.** The writ is to be served and returned as directed by the second and third sections of the Act (P. L., 1869, page 9), in these words :

"Every such attachment shall be made returnable on the first return-day of said court next after the time of issuing thereof, and be served by the sheriff of the proper county, or by some general or special deputy by him made, by attaching so much of the money, stocks, rights in action, evidences of debt, or other property of said party defendant, not exempt by law from sale upon execution, as will be sufficient to pay the debt demanded, with costs ; and shall deliver to said defendant or defendants, or one of them, a copy of said attachment, with an inventory of the property or other thing attached, if said party defendant can be found within the county, and, if not found, then by leaving a copy of the same at his, her, or their residence, with some adult member of the family, where he, she, or they reside ; or, if said party defendant do not reside in the county and cannot be found, then by leaving a copy of said attachment and inventory with the person in whose possession or care said property may be, or in whose hands it may be attached, and in case such money, rights in action, interest in public or corporate stock, evidences of debt, or other property shall be found in the hands or possession of any person, persons, or corporation other than the party defendant, such person, persons, or corporation shall be summoned as a garnishee.

"It shall be the duty of the officer serving such attachment to take the property attached into his possession when the same is capable of manual seizure, and when not, the same shall be bound by such attachment in the hands or possession of such party from whom it is due or owing, or whose duty it is to account for the same, unless the party defendant or some one for him, her, or them, shall enter into a bond, with sufficient surety, to be approved by the court from which said attachment shall issue, or the prothonotary thereof, in double the amount of the debt or demand claimed, conditioned that in the event of the plaintiff or plaintiffs recovering judgment in said attachment, that he, she, or they will pay the debt and costs at the expiration of the stay of execution in sums of like amount given to freeholders, or that he, she, or they will surrender up the said property in as good condition as when attached, to any officer having an execution against said party defendant on any judgment rendered in said attachment in favor of the plaintiff."

Judgment for want of an appearance was entered on return of "nihil habet" at second term. *Artman v. Adams*, 11 W. N., 339 (1882).

§ 55. By the third section, it is made the duty of the sheriff to take the property into his possession when possible to do so.

And it was supposed that his omission in this behalf invalidated the proceedings. But this is not a correct view of the law. In *Jaffrey's Appeal*, 101 Pa. St., 583 (1882), Mr. Justice GORDON said that this third section was only " declarative of the sheriff's responsibility—purely descriptive," etc.

In *Driesbach* v. *Mechanics' National Bank*, 113 Pa. St., 554 (1886), Mr. Justice GREEN gives a very clear exposition of the law, holding :

1. That the service was good which complied simply with the directions of the second section.

2. That " as the defendant bank could not allege the invalidity of the attachment because the money attached was left in its own possession, its voluntary assignee for the benefit of creditors is similarly and equally disabled."

Writs of foreign attachment and of attachment execution are liens from the time of service, while the attachment under the Act of 1869, as between writs of the same kind, is a lien from the time the writ comes into the hands of the sheriff for service. *Underhill* v. *McManus*, 4 Dist. Rep., 404 ; 36 W. N., 552 (1895).

§ 56. **Motions to quash, to dissolve, to show cause of action.** Presuming that the writ has been served, the plaintiff may expect some *motions by the defendant :*

1. To quash the writ.

2. To dissolve the attachment.

And, as in other cases, I see no reason why he should not

3. Move for a rule to show cause of action and why the attachment should not be dissolved.

4. He may give bond and dissolve the attachment.

§ 57. **A motion to quash** must always be founded upon some irregularity which renders the writ a nullity, as in the glaring case of a writ issued without any affidavit, or an affidavit of simple indebtedness alone, omitting all charge of fraud.

It will be noted that, besides attaching property, the sheriff must leave a copy of the writ with the defendant, if found.

When this is done it stands equivalent to service of a summons, and though the attachment be irregular, it is error to quash it and thus displace the case entirely.

Thus it was decided by the Supreme Court, in *Sharpless* v. *Ziegler*, already quoted, 92 Pa. St., 470 (1880), in the opinion of Mr. Justice GORDON, in these words :

" The true intention of the Act is the more obvious in that the Court of Common Pleas, or a judge thereof, may, at any time after the attachment has issued, dissolve it on proper cause shown, whether that cause appear from the face of the original affidavit or from evidence dehors that paper. But in such case where there has been a service, or the defendant resides in the county, the suit proceeds to judgment as upon summons in ordinary cases. In the case in hand, however, the plaintiff was turned out of court by the quashing of his writ, and in this manner an end was put to his case, a result which was equivalent to a final judgment. This action of the court was erroneous, and for this cause the judgment is reversed and a *procedendo* is awarded."

In *Biddle* v. *Black,* already quoted, 99 Pa. St., 382 (1882), the same view was enforced.

Mr. Justice MERCUR said : " The learned judge committed no error in dissolving the attachment. * * * It was error, however, to quash the writ. There had been a personal service on the defendant. While the property was justly released, yet the suit goes on."

Dissolving the attachment is discretionary with the court below, and the action of the court can be reviewed only as to the statutory requirements by *certiorari.* *Wetherald* v. *Shupe,* 109 Pa. St., 389 (1885).

An attachment under the Act of 1869 cannot be quashed on the ground that the bond is insufficient. *Hall* v. *Kintz,* 2 Dist. Rep., 16 (1892).

The question as to fraud cannot be retried before the jury. *Walls* v. *Campbell,* 23 W. N., 506 (1889).

The question of fraud can only be determined by the court on a motion to dissolve the attachment, and if no such motion is made, the allegation of fraud in the affidavit cannot be disputed upon the trial of the case. *Herman* v. *Saller,* 25 W. N., 408 (1889).

§ 58. **As to the general rules governing motions to quash,** the following cases may be cited :

When the motion must be made :

Application to set aside proceedings for irregularity should be made in first instance. Defendant should move to quash an attachment execution immediately upon his appearance ; having pleaded, he is too late. *Poor* v. *Holburn,* 57 Pa. St., 415 (1868) ; Sharswood, J.

Motion to quash must be made before answers are filed. *Schober* v. *Mather,* 49 Pa. St., 21 (1865) ; Read, J.

Defendant may object to process before appearance, but not after he has appeared and pleaded to the action. *Sherer* v. *Easton Bank,* 33 Pa. St., 134 (1859) ; Strong, J.

It is too late to move to quash attachment, under Act of 1869, after affidavit of defense filed. *Lowenstein* v. *Sheetz,* 7 Phila., 361 (1870) ; Allison, P. J.

If the attachment be returnable to any other than the return-day next following its issue, it will be quashed. *Parks* v. *Watts*, 18 W. N., 99 ; 112 Pa. St., 4 (1886).

§ 59. The motion to dissolve the writ may be based upon the insufficiency of plaintiff's affidavit, as that it does not set forth specifically the fraudulent acts, nor sufficiently describe the kind of property, etc. See *Biddle* v. *Black*, 99 Pa. St., 381, already cited. In this case depositions were taken. That course would seem to be open ; and, doubtless, the court would have the power to reduce the bail demanded as a preliminary to dissolving the attachment.

Pending a rule to dissolve an attachment under the Act of 1869, with a stay of all proceedings, judgment was entered for want of an affidavit of defense. *Triebel* v. *High*, 1 Dist. Rep., 385 (1892).

§ 60. If the defendant give the bond, and then succeed in dissolving the attachment, the plaintiff cannot, after obtaining judgment, sue out the bond. This was decided in *Fernau* v. *Butcher*, 113 Pa. St., 292 (1886). A statement of the facts of that case may assist the practitioner. An affidavit was filed averring indebtedness, a portion whereof, it was alleged, had been fraudulently contracted. The plaintiffs filed bond and issued the attachment. The defendants then gave bond, and on the same day filed their affidavit denying the fraud. The court granted a rule to show cause why the attachment should not be dissolved. This rule was made absolute, because the fraud averred was not sufficiently proven. As already stated, the defendants had meanwhile given bond. It declared that if the " plaintiffs in said attachment recover judgment in the same," and if defendants paid * * * or surrendered the property, in as good condition as when attached, to any officer having execution against defendants on any judgment in said attachment in favor of plaintiffs, then the obligation to be void, etc.

After the court made the rule absolute, the plaintiffs proceeded and obtained judgment. Unable to collect it, they sued out the bond ; the court below gave judgment for plaintiffs, and the defendants took their writ of error. The Supreme Court reversed. In the opinion (MERCUR, C. J.) the following guides are given :

" The manifest purpose of the statute was not to supersede the usual forms of action for the recovery of debts. It provides a mode of proceeding only when the debtor has committed or is about to commit some fraudulent act. Then, and then only, does it give a creditor the right to forthwith seize the property of his debtor, and to hold the same as security for the payment of a judgment to be thereafter recovered. Without fraud of the debtor his property cannot be thus seized nor held for the security of the creditor. When seized under the allegation of fraud, its release may be procured either by dissolving the attachment or by giving security conditioned for the payment of the judgment which may be recovered 'in said attachment,' or for the return of the property attached.

"Under the view we take of this case it is not necessary to decide now whether an attachment under this Act will lie when the affidavit charges fraud as applicable to only a part of the debt, for a recovery of which the suit is brought. The writ goes out claiming the whole debt as an entirety. If it can be so used as to obtain possession of property to pay a debt concerning a larger portion of which no fraud is alleged, the whole purpose and spirit of the statute will be perverted.

"The intent of the Act is not to take from an unfortunate but honest debtor his property before judgment rendered against him. If the fraud averred is not sufficiently proved, the attachment falls. When it does fall, the plaintiff loses all the security which he temporarily held thereunder. Whether that security existed by virtue of the writ of attachment alone or by the superadded bond of the defendant and his sureties based thereon, a dissolution of the attachment strikes down the security. Without fraud of the defendants, the plaintiffs were not entitled to demand either form of security. When the attaching power was stricken down, the bond of the defendants fell with it.

"The language in the condition of the bond strengthens the conclusions at which we have arrived. It is to secure the payment of a judgment to be recovered 'in said attachment.' It is based on the fact that the property is held under the attachment, and assumes that it legally may be so held. It promises to surrender the property attached 'to an officer having an execution against said defendants on any judgment rendered in said attachment' in favor of said plaintiffs. The judgment, for the payment of which the obligors bound themselves, was to be one that should be rendered in and by virtue of the attachment, and not one that might be obtained 'as in the case of a summons for debt regularly issued and duly served.' That language does not indicate any enlarged right flowing from the issuing of an attachment and the seizure of the property thereunder. On the contrary, it clearly imports a summons in the usual and ordinary form. When the attachment was dissolved, the suit was stripped of all the properties and incidents applicable to the attachment.

"We think the bond was not intended to cover, and does not cover, the case of a judgment recovered on an ordinary summons for debt."

Nor, on the other hand, if the attachment be not dissolved, can the defendant's bond be sued until the final determination of the action commenced by the attachment. In *Harbert* v. *Gormley*, 115 Pa. St., 237 (1886), it was decided that the plaintiff's bond could not be sued out simply because the attachment was dissolved, and that the defendant must wait until the final judgment in his favor. But *Harbert* v. *Gormley* is no longer law; see Act of 1887 (section 51 of this book).

In suit on a bond required by the Act of May 24, 1887, when an attachment under the Act of March 17, 1869, has been quashed, dissolved, or ended, the damages cover all legal costs, fees, and damage by reason of the attachment. *Com.* v. *Trust Co.*, 35 W. N., 87 (1894); *Berwald* v. *Ray*, 165 Pa. St., 192 (1895).

§ 60 *a*. **Consolidation of actions.** This may be ordered by the court on a rule entered for that purpose, and is intended to save expense.

Where several causes of action, which may be joined, exist, one suit only should be brought.

But such a rule will not be made absolute without the consent of the defendant, if he have good reason for objection. *Groff* v. *Musser*, 3 S. & R., 262 (1817).

If the defendant move to consolidate, he must show the causes of action are such as may be joined in the same statement, that the questions are substantially the same, that no defense can be made, or, if made, is substantially the same in all actions, and the defense should be set forth.

This step should be taken before the affidavit of defense is filed.

§ 60 *b*. *The practice is to* take a rule to show cause why the actions should not be consolidated, supporting the rule by an affidavit setting forth the facts and reasons. The rule should be allowed, with a stay of proceedings, and filed, and notice served on the other side. Prepare your paper-books, and argue the matter on the return of the rule.

§ 60 *c*. *Action can be consolidated* where several suits are brought on protested bills of exchange drawn by defendant, payable to different persons, taken up for the honor of one of the indorsers. *Rumsey* v. *Wynkoop*, 1 Yeates, 5 (1791).

Where a number of suits are brought before a justice on promissory notes, on appeal the actions may be consolidated. *Boyle* v. *Grant*, 18 Pa. St., 163 (1851).

Where municipal claims have been filed against separate portions of the same lot, by the same plaintiff, against the same defendant and for the same work. *City* v. *Tyson*, 9 W. N., 367 (1880); *Beltzhoover* v. *Maple*, 130 Pa. St., 342 (1889).

Wherever the cause of action, the defense, and the parties are the same, the defendant's rule to show cause why the actions should not be consolidated will be made absolute. *Wetherill* v. *Wilson*, 26 W. N., 231 (1890).

So, too, by agreement and amicable action of revival a number of judgments may be consolidated. *Beshler Estate*, 129 Pa. St., 268 (1889).

§ 60 d. *When actions cannot be consolidated.* An action upon a promissory note and an action upon a book account which showed a credit for the note. *Stanley* v. *Garrigues*, 1 W. N., 28 (1874).

Several feigned issues under the Sheriff's Interpleader Act, in which there were a number of different execution creditors and one claimant for the goods levied on in all cases. *Uhler* v. *Selfridge*, 1 W. N., 61 (1874).

Several judgments entered for want of affidavits of defense in suits brought by the same plaintiff on promissory notes made by different makers, against one defendant, liable as indorser on all the notes. *Bank* v. *Hunsicker*, 2 W. N., 381 (1874).

CHAPTER III.

§ 61. The following is the text of an important law upon the subject of forms of action, pleading, etc. :

An Act

Providing for the abolition of the distinctions heretofore existing between actions *ex contractu* and actions *ex delicto*, so far as relates to procedure, and providing for two forms of action and regulating the pleadings thereunder.

SECTION 1. Be it enacted, etc., That, so far as relates to procedure, the distinctions heretofore existing between actions *ex contractu* be abolished, and that all demands heretofore recoverable in debt, assumpsit, or covenant, shall hereafter be sued for and recovered in one form of action to be called an " action of assumpsit."

SEC. 2. That, so far as relates to procedure, the distinctions heretofore existing between actions *ex delicto* be abolished, and that all damages heretofore recoverable in trespass, trover, or trespass on the case, shall hereafter be sued for and recovered in one form of action to be called " an action of trespass."

SEC. 3. The plaintiff's declaration in each of said actions, namely, the action of assumpsit and the action of trespass, shall consist of a concise statement of the plaintiff's demand, as provided by the fifth section of the Act of the 21st day of March, A.D. 1806, which in the action of assumpsit shall be accompanied by copies of all notes, contracts, book entries, or a particular reference to the records of any court within the county in which the action is brought, if any, upon which the plaintiff's claim is founded, and a particular reference to such record, or to the record of any deed or mortgage or other instrument of writing recorded in such county, shall be sufficient in lieu of a copy thereof. The statement shall be signed by the plaintiff or his attorney, and in the action of assumpsit shall be replied to by affidavit.

SEC. 4. The plaintiff shall be at liberty in each of said actions to serve a copy of his statement on the defendants. If such service be made not less than fifteen days before the return-day of the writ, it shall be the duty of the defendant in the action of assumpsit to file an affidavit of defense on or before the return-day.

SEC. 5. In the action of assumpsit judgment may be moved for want of an affidavit of defense, or for want of a sufficient affidavit, for the whole or part of the plaintiff's claim, as the case may be, in accordance with the present practice in actions of debt and assumpsit.

SEC. 6. If the plaintiff shall neglect to serve his statement at least fifteen days before the return-day of his writ, he may file it on, or at any time after, the return-day, and in the action of assumpsit, unless the defendant shall file a sufficient affidavit of defense within fifteen days after notice that the said statement has been filed, the plaintiff may move for judgment for want thereof.

SEC. 7. Special pleading is hereby abolished. In the action of assumpsit, the plea of the general issue shall be "*non assumpsit.*" The defendant in the action of assumpsit shall be at liberty, in addition to the plea of "*non assumpsit,*" to plead payment, set-off, and also the bar of the Statute of Limitations, and no other pleas. The only plea in the action of trespass shall be not guilty. The defendant shall plead to the said actions within fifteen days after the return-day, and in default thereof the court may, on motion, direct the prothonotary to enter the plea of the general issue at any time. The pleadings in all courts to be subject to the rules of the respective courts as to notice of special matter.

SEC. 8. The true intent and meaning of this Act is, that it applies only to the present actions of assumpsit, debt, covenant, trespass, trover, and case, and that all other actions now existing shall remain as heretofore, and are in no way affected by the passage of this Act, and that as to the action herein cited it applies to the procedure only, and the legal rights of the party are not in any way to be affected thereby.

SEC. 9. All laws or parts of laws inconsistent herewith be and the same are hereby repealed.

Approved May 25, 1887. (P. L., 271.)

§ 62. **The Act of March 21, 1806,** commonly called the Statement Act, is in these words:

"In all cases in which a suit is, or may be, brought in any court of record within this Commonwealth, for the recovery of any debt, founded on a verbal promise, book account, note, bond, penal or single bill, or all or any of them, and which, from the amount thereof, may not be cognizable before a justice of the peace, it shall be the duty of the plaintiff, either by himself, his agent, or attorney, to file in the office of the prothonotary a statement of his, her, or their demand, on or before the third day of the term to which the process issued is returnable, particularly specifying the date of the promise, book account, note, bond, penal or single bill, or all or any of them on which the demand is founded, and the whole amount what [which] he, she, or they believe is justly due to him, her, or them from the defendant.

"And it shall be the duty of the defendant, at least twenty days before the next succeeding term to which the process issued is returnable, to file in the office aforesaid, either by himself, his agent, or attorney, a statement of his, her, or their account, if any he or she hath, against the plaintiff's demand, and particularly specifying what he, she, or they believe is justly due from him, her, or them to the plaintiff, and it shall be the duty of the prothonotary to file, without the agency of an attorney, such statement."

Other sections provided for judgments by default, for trial by jury, for costs, etc.

§ 63. It will be perceived that under the Act of 1887 a statement may be filed in all actions of assumpsit and of tort. Under the original Act of 1806 it was held that the statement could not be used in debt on bail bond, for rent under sealed lease, for a legacy, etc. These distinctions seem to be swept away by the Act of 1887, and a statement allowed in all assumpsits and torts.

§ 64. **As to the form required,** it would seem that all technicality is abolished. Instead of a formal declaration, the plaintiff can now in the permitted cases file a plain narrative.

He must state the amount claimed. *Shallcross* v. *Kohl*, 3 W. N., 272 (1877).

In this case the plaintiff filed only a copy of the note. The court struck off his rule to plead.

He must avoid the example of the defendants, who, in *Riddle* v. *Stevens*, 2 S. & R., 537 (1816), introduced scandal into a counter-statement, which the court struck out.

§ 65. Observing these plain rules, the plaintiff may find the Act of 1887 a labor-saving machine. The decisions under the law of 1806 were very liberal.

In *Purviance* v. *Dryden*, 3 S. & R., 402 (1817), it was held that the statement under the Act of March 21, 1806, "is not restricted to any particular form." It was added that there was no error in charging an assumption by the defendant, and another who was not summoned and did not appear. The form adopted in that case was very simple. It was in these words :

"The plaintiff's demand is founded on the assumption of the defendants, Samuel Dryden, Jr., and Samuel Purviance, to pay the said plaintiff the sum of $1000, with interest from the 4th of November, 1806, the said defendants, Samuel Dryden, Jr., and Samuel Purviance, then being indebted to the said Samuel Dryden, Sr., for the like sum of $1000, before that time paid, laid out, and expended to the use of the defendants by the said Samuel Dryden, Sr., at the special instance and request of the said defendants, as well as for the like sum had and received by the defendants to the use of the plaintiffs, $1000. Interest from the 4th of November, 1810."

§ 66. In *Boyd* v. *Gordon*, 6 S. & R., 53 (1820), the statement was as follows :

"On the 20th of June, 1811, the plaintiff sold lumber to the defendant, for which the defendant agreed to pay him $106. The defendant afterward gave a note on John Campbell for the delivery of twelve thousand feet of white pine boards, on the express condition that if the plaintiff should not be able to find Campbell when he went up the Susquehanna, he was to return the said note to the defendant the spring following, and the defendant would pay him the money.

"The plaintiff, after repeated inquiries, being unable to find

Campbell, brings this suit to recover from Boyd the said sum of $106, with interest, agreeably to their contract."

It was contended that the statement "set forth no cause of action, because, as the money was to be paid only after the return of the note, in consequence of Gordon's not being able to find Campbell, the return of the note was a condition precedent, and the statement ought to have contained an allegation to that effect." But the court said (opinion by GIBSON, J.) :

"In a statement it is not necessary the plaintiff should aver performance of precedent conditions, for that is implied by the very act of bringing suit for money that otherwise could not be demandable. *Riddle* v. *Stevens*, 2 S. & R., 537, goes this length. The legislature never intended that a plaintiff should disclose his cause of action in a statement with the same nicety and precision of averment that is necessary in a declaration, for that would do nothing toward effecting the object in view, which was to enable suitors, if they should think proper, to conduct their causes in plain cases without the intervention of counsel. They have, therefore, required the plaintiff to specify only ' the date of the promise, book account, penal, or single bill, and the whole amount that he may believe is justly due.' By what authority shall we exact more?"

§ 67. In *Reed* v. *Pedan*, 8 S. & R., 263 (1822), a judgment entered on a confession was opened, and the defendant let into a defense. The plaintiffs filed the following statement :

"Plaintiffs' demand. On the 6th of February, 1815, defendant gave his bond in due form of law to the plaintiffs in the penalty of $3050, conditioned to pay them $1525 on the 6th day of February, 1816, with lawful interest from the date, which sum of $1525 is demanded in this suit."

After verdict and judgment for plaintiffs, the defendant took a writ of error and assigned that there was no declaration, which was necessary, because the case did not come within the provisions of the Act of March 21, 1806. But the Supreme Court (per DUNCAN, J.) said :

"When the defendant was let into a defense it was unnecessary to file either a declaration or statement, the entering of judgment by the prothonotary being substituted for a declaration and confession of judgment by attorney, by virtue of a warrant of attorney. The issue was to ascertain whether anything, and if anything, what, was due on the judgment. The entry was as precise as any declaration or statement. A further declaration or statement would be unnecessary, and is a mere surplusage. This enabled the defendant to put in any plea adapted to his defense, whether *non est factum* or avoidance of the bond, by showing it to be founded on an illegal act, or failure of the consideration, or payment.

" The statement on which the second error is alleged, if it is not surplusage, is not to be scanned with the minuteness of a special pleader in examining a declaration. Such critical examination would defeat the intention of the legislature, which was to render proceedings in courts of justice so plain and easy that every man would be able to conduct his own suit. All the law requires is such a statement as would give information of the nature of the claim, and enable a defendant to plead a judgment on it in bar of any other action. Now, this statement does give such notice, and contains as much certainty as any declaration would. Whether this mode of conducting judicial business is an improvement, an ease to the people, whether it is less expensive—enables them to conduct their suits without the employment of professional men— or otherwise, different speculations will be indulged, and different opinions formed. One thing is pretty certain, that few choose to confide in their own abilities to commence or defend a suit ; and one other thing is very certain, that it is a fruitful source of writs of error and delay. But with these speculations we have no concern ; it is our duty to give effect to the declared will of the legislature. There is no doubt but that, treating a statement as a declaration, the omission to repeat what had been before stated, ' with lawful interest,' is a defect which a verdict would cure. It is not a defective title, though it may be a title defectively stated."

§ 68. In *Cook* v. *Gilbert*, 8 S. & R., 567 (1822), an amicable action was entered in the Court of Common Pleas of Westmoreland County, by an agreement in writing signed by John Reed, attorney for Gilbert, the plaintiff, and by David Cook and Henry Barton, the defendants, in the presence of two subscribing witnesses. The agreement was headed with an account by the plaintiff against Messrs. Cook & Isott, amounting to $728.45 for goods, as per bill rendered. The agreement was that an amicable action should be entered at August Term, 1819, and that the prothonotary should enter judgment against the defendants for the sum of $728.45 damages, and costs of suit.

In the Supreme Court error was assigned, " That the cause of action was not stated in the agreement."

TILGHMAN, C. J., said :

" The cause of action is sufficiently stated in the account at the head of the agreement. It was an account for goods sold, etc., against Cook & Isott. This account the defendants undertook to pay. They assumed the debt, and agreed to give judgment against themselves for it."

§ 69. In *Schlatter* v. *Etter*, 13 S. & R., 36 (1825), it was ruled that " under the statement law, the plea of payment, with leave to give the special matters in evidence, and notice given and accepted, and evidence without objection at the trial, may be considered as a counter-statement. The plea of payment with leave, to a statement, does not admit any fact not mentioned in the statement; if essential, the plaintiff must prove it."

§ 70. In *Bailey* v. *Bailey*, 14 S. & R., 195 (1826), it was held that " in an action on a promissory note against the administrator of the drawer, a statement filed under the Act of 21st of March, 1806, setting forth a copy of the note and claiming the principal and interest due upon it, is sufficient without averring a promise to pay by either the intestate or the defendant."

Chief Justice TILGHMAN said (page 199): " If instead of a statement the plaintiff had filed a declaration, it is true that, unless there had been a count laying a promise by the defendant, no evidence of her promise could be received. But a statement is widely different from a declaration, and we must look to the Act of Assembly for information on that subject. A statement is the creature of the Act of 21st of March, 1806, the object of which was to dispense with form, so that every man might be his own lawyer."

§ 71. In *Morgan* v. *Bank*, 3 P. & W., 391 (1832), the statement was in these words: " The above-stated action is founded on a promissory note, dated the 7th day of September, 1829, drawn by the aforesaid James Morgan for the sum of $1000, and made payable to the said David and Jacob Bright, or order, at the Farmers' Bank of Reading, without defalcation, sixty days after the date aforesaid, which said David Morgan and Jacob R. Bright, by their indorsement on the said note, transferred the same to the plaintiff, and the plaintiff avers that the whole amount of the said note, together with the interest thereon, is due the plaintiff."

Per Curiam. " It would not be easy to devise a more neat, perspicuous, and complete form of statement than the one which is the subject of this writ of error; and it is not a little strange that exceptions of this stamp should be repeated after the decision of *Boyd* v. *Gordon*, 6 S. & R., 53; *Reed* v. *Pedan*, 8 S. & R., 265; *Buck* v. *Nicholas*, *Ib.*, 316; *Cook* v. *Gilbert*, *Ib.*, 567; and *Bailey* v. *Bailey*, 14 S. & R., 195. We are not aware that anything in the assignment of error calls for further remark. *Judgment affirmed.*"

§ 72. To these cases may be added that in *Camp* v. *Bank*, 10

Watts, 130 (1840), it was ruled that a statement was fatally defective which omitted to aver that the payee of the note sued on had indorsed it to the plaintiff, who sued as indorsee without showing title to the note.

Chief Justice GIBSON, in *Snevely* v. *Jones*, 9 Watts, 436 (1840), laid down the following rules :

" Nothing is indispensable to a statement which has not been made so by the statute which has substituted it for a declaration, and that requires no more to be specified than the date of the contract and the amount supposed to be due by it. The terms must doubtless be set forth in an intelligible manner, for it would not else appear that there is an available cause of action, but performance of conditions precedent, and everything beyond the defendant's engagement to pay, may be omitted. All besides is to be shown by evidence."

§ 73. *If the statement be full and clear*, it will save the pleader all the old troubles as to bills of particulars. It also relieves both parties from the perplexity of demurrers, etc.

In a suit against an executor the statement may join an averment as to the promise by the executor with the promise made by the decedent in his lifetime. *Malin* v. *Bull*, 13 S. & R., 441 (1825). And need not aver assets in the executor's possession. *Ibid.*

Where a vendee agrees to pay the debts of a vendor, a creditor may bring an action of assumpsit against the vendee for such debt. *Quinn* v. *Shafto*, 31 W. N., 502 (1892).

In *Slatteny* v. *R. R. Co.*, 21 W. N., 556 (1888), it was held that a plea in abatement could be filed to a statement.

In *Doriot* v. *Hagemann*, 21 W. N., 556 (1888), the statement averred that plaintiff had expended moneys at the special instance and request of the defendant. It was held that defendant was entitled to notice whether he was to meet an express contract, and a more specific statement was ordered.

Remember :

1. A copy of note, etc., is not enough. You must state that you claim so much money, with interest from such a date upon the note, whereof the following is a true copy, etc. (as the case may be). *Gould* v. *Gage*, 20 W. N., 553 (1888).

2. But you need not repeat in your statement matters which appear in the accompanying copy. *Drake* v. *R. R.*, 21 W. N., 122 (1888).

3. The allegation of damages in trespass may be set forth very much as in a *narr.*, by specifying the special damage, " sickness, pain, medicine," etc., and stating the amount of damages in one

sum, *Schnable* v. *Schmidt*, 21 W. N., 153 (1888), and a bill of particulars may be ordered as under the old *narr*. *Krauskopf* v. *Stern*, 21 W. N., 185 (1888).

A bill of particulars was refused in *Flisher* v. *Allen*, 21 W. N., 509 (1888), an action of tort for damages to plaintiff's building, by negligence of defendant in altering an adjoining house. The items of damage were not given. The statement simply averred that plaintiff had been put to "great cost and expense," to plaintiff's damage five thousand dollars.

It was ruled that if the statement be amended after affidavit of defense filed, the defendant need not file a second affidavit to the amended statement; *Fahlnecker* v. *Harrington*, 21 W. N., 541 (1887); but this was overruled in *Jones* v. *Gordon*, 23 W. N., 302 (1889). A claim for work, etc., is defective if it omit to charge that it was done *for* the defendant. The statement must also aver that the sum claimed is *justly* due. Demurrer sustained for these defects. *Schafer* v. *Brotherhood of Carpenters*, 22 W. N., 312 (1888).

4. The statement must be signed by plaintiff or his attorney (see clause 3, section 61); *Gould* v. *Gage*, 20 W. N., 553 (1888); and in Philadelphia all statements must be sworn to. (See section 18.)

In *Byrne* v. *Hayden*, 23 W. N., 306 (1889), the statement was on a claim property bond, and omitted a copy of the list of goods. The court below gave judgment for want of a sufficient affidavit of defense. The Supreme Court reversed, remarking on the absence of any description of the kind, quality, or value of the goods; STERRETT, J. : "It is necessary that the statement should contain all the ingredients of a complete cause of action averred in clear, express, and unequivocal language." A statement may be amended and may present a cause of action in detinue, although the suit is *assumpsit*. To the amended statement the defendant may be required to file a supplemental affidavit. *Jones* v. *Gordon*, 23 W. N., 302 (1889); WILLIAMS, J.

Where a plaintiff's statement attaches a copy of a lease executed by an agent of the lessor, the facts constituting the agency must be set forth. *Lane* v. *Nelson*, 2 Dist. Rep., 18 (1892).

Where a statement set forth the warranty of a horse, and that by agreement he had been examined and found unsound, and that the defendants received the horse from the purchaser, but refused to return his value notwithstanding their promise to the contrary, an affidavit of defense merely denying the warranty is insufficient. *Terry* v. *Wenderoth*, 29 W. N., 517 (1892).

The statement upon a contract is not defective in not setting forth the contract, if the statement aver that the contract is not within the knowledge of plaintiff and is known to the defendant. *Quinn* v. *Shafto,* 31 W. N., 502 (1892).

In an action upon a lost instrument the statement should set forth that the instrument was actually executed and delivered, and that diligent and thorough search has been made for the paper and it could not be found, and all facts must be averred necessary to prove the case on the trial. *Laubach* v. *Meyers,* 29 W. N., 473 (1892).

The affidavit to a statement cannot be made by an attorney. *Warner* v. *R. R. Co.,* 1 Dist. Rep., 248 (1892).

If the statement contain an explicit averment of the amount due, it need not be set out in the affidavit supporting the statement. *Prince Co.* v. *Linderman,* 2 Dist. Rep., 4 (1892).

Where assumpsit is brought for the value of certain stock for which a note, payable in one year, was taken as part payment, the maker agreeing to assign the stock as collateral for the note, but afterward refusing so to do, the note must be returned before suit, or the statement is demurrable. *Rennyson* v. *Reifsnyder,* 1 Dist. Rep., 758 (1892).

An amendment to a statement after the affidavit of defense is filed, is discretionary with the court. Averments advantageous to the defendant cannot be withdrawn. *Heller* v. *Ins. Co.,* 30 W. N., 545 (1892).

An amendment of the statement may be permitted even after judgment on a plea in bar. *Jones* v. *Linden,* 1 Dist. Rep., 725 (1892).

An amendment to a statement must contain such matters of form or of necessary substance as can be replied to by affidavit. It must not be argumentative. *Wigton* v. *R. R. Co.,* 47 Leg. Int., 4 (1889) (C. P. No. 1, of Phila. Co.).

In *Murdock* v. *Martin,* 25 W. N., 288 (1890), the statement set forth that suit was brought for commissions under a contract, by which the plaintiff received commissions upon goods sold by him, as well as those sold by defendants in certain localities—the nature and extent of his claim, the commissions claimed, and the period of time covered by the contract. A copy of the contract was attached. As to the exact amount due, the plaintiff referred defendants to the entries upon their own books.

CLARK, J. : " Now, it is plain that as the purpose of the legislature was merely to simplify the practice, it was certainly not the intention to require the plaintiff to embrace in his statement what, in the very nature of the particular case, he could not know, and the knowledge of which was wholly within the power of his adversary. * * * Having embraced in his statement all that he could know, he gave the defendant an opportunity * * * to compute the exact amount due. * * * This was all, upon any reasonable application of the requirements of the Act of Assembly and the rule of court to this particular case, that could be demanded."

In this case a nonsuit had been entered by the lower court for want of a sufficiently specific statement of the plaintiff's claim. *Held*, that a writ of error would lie without a prior motion to take off the nonsuit.

In *McGarry* v. *Barr*, 25 W. N., 310 (1890), the plaintiff's statement set forth that the action was founded on a replevin bond, and averred that W. " failed to make good his claim in said suit and to return the property replevied, whereby said bond was forfeited." The statement did not exhibit whether the action of replevin was disposed of or not ; whether any or what judgment had been entered ; whether a return of goods had been adjudged, or whether it had been determined that the rent was in arrears, and for what sum.

WILLIAMS, J. : " The condition of the replevin bond sued on was that the plaintiff should ' make good his claim ' to the property replevied, and make return thereof if it should be so adjudged by the judge of the court out of which the said writ issued, and comply with and satisfy the judgment of said court in the premises, and of the Supreme Court * * * if the case shall be removed. * * *

" The statement ought to show the nature and extent of the plaintiff's demand with such clearness and certainty that in default of an affidavit of defense judgment may be taken and liquidated upon the data which it furnishes. * * * Tried by this rule the plaintiff's statement was insufficient."

In *Kunkel* v. *Dundore*, 47 Leg. Int., 94 (1890), a demurrer was filed to a statement in a stock transaction upon the ground, *inter alia*, that a copy of a contract under which the stock was bought was not incorporated in the statement. The statement made no reference to such contract, but its existence was set forth in an affidavit of defense filed before the demurrer. The demurrer was overruled.

A statement is sufficient if it aver facts which constitute a cause of action, and sets forth a *quantum meruit* with a sufficient particularity. *Stull* v. *Title Co.*, 26 W. N., 97 (1890) ; *Fritz* v. *Hathaway*, 26 W. N., 273 (1890).

Failure to name the defendant in the copy of book entries annexed to the statement is no longer a fatal defect, if the statement aver that the entries were charged against the defendant.

If, however, the original entries name the defendant, a copy omitting his name is not a compliance with the requirement of the statute as to a correct and complete copy. An averment that the book entries were intended as a personal charge against defendant " by virtue of a special agreement," no such agreement being set out, is defective. If the book entries be more than six years old, it is not sufficient to keep the claim alive by averring that the amount became " due and payable " at a subsequent date. The lower court may allow an amendment to a statement, after judgment for want of sufficient affidavit of defense has been reversed because of the insufficiency of the statement. *Ibid.*

A statement of claim in an action of assumpsit to recover damages for delay in transmitting a telegraphic message, set forth that the telegram was sent to purchase certain goods at a certain price, provided they could be shipped on a certain vessel; that relying on transmission of message plaintiffs sold goods to arrive on said vessel; that the message was not delivered until vessel had sailed, whereby plaintiffs were unable to deliver goods. The statement was held to be faulty in not averring that, if the order had been delivered, the goods could have been purchased at the price named, and could have been shipped. *Ferguson* v. *Telegraph Co.*, 151 Pa. St., 211 (1892).

In a suit against a married woman, since the Act of 1887, it is not requisite to aver that the articles furnished were necessaries and that she had contracted for them on the strength of her separate estate, nor that they were used by her in trade. *Harar* v. *Croney*, 32 W. N., 90 (1893).

A title company insured plaintiff's title and referred in the policy to the application describing the tract. The deed was prepared by the company with the same description. The tract was smaller than described. The party insured sued on the policy, annexing a copy of it, but not of the application. The statement was held to be insufficient. *Hankey* v. *Title Co.*, 1 Dist. Rep., 657 (1891).

Where a statement in assumpsit contains both an allegation of breach of duty and an allegation of breach of contract, the court, on a rule for a more specific statement, will direct the averment as to breach of duty to be stricken out. *Hunter* v. *Transportation Co.*, 1 Dist. Rep., 538 (1892).

As to what is a sufficient statement by an architect for services, see *Albright* v. *Snyder*, 1 Dist. Rep., 723 (1891); and by a bank in suit upon an account, see *Schoonover* v. *Banking Co.*, 1 Dist. Rep., 733 (1892).

If a rule of court provide that " all items of book accounts and other claims not specifically traversed or denied under oath or affirmation shall be taken as admitted, and no proof thereof shall be required on the trial," the plaintiff, to take advantage of the rule, must have complied with the rule requiring his statement to be verified by affidavit, and the specification of items of claim to be filed. *McDermott* v. *Woods*, 29 W. N., 407 (1892).

Where an amendment to a statement is allowed on the day of trial and a continuance granted, the plaintiff must pay the costs of term. *Lawrence* v. *R. R.*, 27 W. N., 572 (1891).

Where a written contract has been essentially changed by the parties so as to become a parol contract, the plaintiff need not file a copy of the written contract with his statement. *Malone* v. *R. R. Co.*, 157 Pa. St., 430 (1893).

In a suit upon an ordinary bank-check by one not a party to it, the statement must contain averments as to plaintiff's title—presentment to drawee, neglect or refusal on his part to pay, and the amount justly due. *Bank* v. *Soap Co.*, 161 Pa. St., 134; 34 W. N., 447 (1894).

In the light of the cases cited it is hoped that the following **general suggestions as to preparation of statements** may guide the pleader :

1. *Caption.* Give the Court, Term, No., and venue at the head.

2. *Names.* State the plaintiff's and defendant's full names, remembering that initials are not names. J. Smith, plaintiff; P. Brown, defendant, look awkward. It should be John Smith, Peter Brown, etc.

3. *Corporations.* If a corporation be a party, give the correct name from its charter.

4. *Firms.* If a firm be a party, give full names of all the members.

5. *Copies.* In *assumpsit*, exhibit a copy of the book entries, note, bill, bond, or other instrument sued on.

6. *Time and place.* Let the statement be clear, precise, and full. If merchandise was sold, name the kind. Give all dates. State the place.

7. *Performance.* If you sue upon a contract to do or not to do a certain thing, aver the plaintiff's performance " of all things in said agreement on his part stipulated to be kept and performed," and charge that the defendant did not well and truly perform the same in this, averring breach in the very words of the agreement, and expanding your averment as may be necessary thus—*but on the contrary the said defendant did, etc., or the said defendant wholly omitted and neglected, etc.*

8. *Necessary words.* In actions of *tort* always employ the words applicable to the case.

a. In libel or slander "false, scandalous, malicious, and defamatory."

b. In malicious prosecution "falsely and maliciously and without any reasonable or probable cause." As to the prosecution, aver that plaintiff has been acquitted and discharged, and that the case is wholly ended and determined.

c. In trespass "with force and arms."

9. *Negligence.* In actions for negligence describe the business, position, acts, manner of injury, and all the damages sustained by party injured.

a. If he was a passenger in defendants' cars or boat, state that defendants were common carriers ; that they undertook for a certain price to carry plaintiff from   to   ; that it became and was defendants' duty to carry plaintiff safely and carefully, but that neglecting their duty they carelessly and negligently (did or omitted to do, as the case may be) ; and that thereby (follow with the narrative). Describe all injuries, all expenses, all special damages, with particularity.

b. If the plaintiff was injured on the highway, state that he was lawfully walking or driving, etc. Always charge that it was defendant's duty to conduct himself properly (giving details), and aver his neglect of this duty with particularity. Follow with the result to the plaintiff.

c. As negligence is the omission of some duty, the obligation of the defendant should be averred. Then follow with the statement of his negligence in this   charging that he so carelessly and negligently conducted himself in the premises (that he did or omitted to do, etc.).

d. If for trespass to property, then that the thing injured was the *property* of the plaintiff, and its *value.*

e. Insert the words "*other wrongs to the plaintiff then did,*" under which allegation of *alia enormia,* damages and matters which naturally arise from the act complained of, or cannot with decency be stated, may be given in evidence in aggravation of damages, though not specified in any other part of the statement.

f. The words "*against the peace*" (*contra pacem*).

In other respects it should be a *full* statement of the injuries, in the order in which they were committed, and of all the consequent *damages,* and no allegation should be inserted unless there be a probability of its being proved in evidence.

Precision required. In an action to recover alleged overcharges of freight the statement averred that the sums were in excess of the amounts charged by the defendants to other shippers for like services upon like conditions, under similar circumstances, between the same points and during the same period of time, but it did *not* give the names of the persons in whose favor discriminations were alleged to have been made or the instances in which like services had been rendered at less rates, and for these reasons on demurrer it was held defective. *Struble* v. *Penna. R. R.,* 23 W. N., 197 (1888).

Amendment of statement before affidavit of defense filed, or rule taken for more specific statement. Before the affidavit of defense is filed, or before a demurrer to the statement or a rule for a more specific statement is filed, if you wish to amend your statement, take a rule on the defendant as follows :

A. B. ⎱
  v.   ⎰ C. P. No. 1,   Term, 1890. No.
C. D. ⎰

And now (date) on motion of E. F., pro plaintiff, rule entered on defendant to show cause why the statement in the above case should not be amended. Returnable   at 10 A.M.

Properly indorse your rule and hand to the court clerk. Send notice and a copy of the proposed amendment to the counsel for defendant, or, if no appearance entered, to defendant personally.

Prepare your paper-book in support of your amendment and be prepared to argue.

Usually the amendment is a matter of course. If the court grant you leave to amend, file an *amended statement*.

A. B.
  v. } C. P. No. , Term, 1890. No.
C. D.

AMENDMENT TO STATEMENT.

And now (date), by leave of court first had and obtained, plaintiff amends his statement heretofore filed in the above case as follows (here set forth your amendment or amendments).

This amended statement should be signed, sworn to, and filed, and a copy served on the adversary. *R. R. Co.* v. *Walsh*, 29 W. N., 410 (1892). As to the necessity of filing an additional affidavit, see *Jones* v. *Gordon*, 23 W. N., 302.

A number of Forms of Statements will be found in the Appendix.

CHAPTER IV.

§ 74. **Of the various writs known by this name** there are three by which ordinary suits may be commenced—Foreign Attachments, Domestic Attachments, and Attachments under the Fraudulent Debtor's Act. These last are considered under the chapter on Assumpsits (sections 51 to 60). Attachments against vessels and against convicts are treated of hereafter.

There are also writs which may be called final process—Attachments in Execution and Attachments for Contempt, etc.

§ 75. **Foreign attachment** is used for collection of claims against non-residents of the State who are not in the county at the time of issuing the writ, and who have property in the Commonwealth. It does not lie for speculative damages, nor for torts, save as hereinafter noted. It may be issued not only against such non-residents, but also against any foreign corporation, and under it the property of any defendant may be attached, including debts payable *in futuro* and including interests in the estate of any decedent. But no share of a married woman in the estate of a decedent can be thus attached. (Act July 27, 1842, section 1, P. L., 436.)

Nor will it lie to recover a debt due by the estate of a decedent. *Kane* v. *Coyle*, 20 W. N., 317 (1887).

Nor will it lie against an absconding debtor who has left a place of residence in the State. *Scott* v. *Hilgert*, 14 W. N., 305 (1884).

The form of the writ and the practice thereunder are all set out at length in Brightly's Purdon's Digest, under the title of Foreign Attachment.

A foreign attachment may issue against a foreign corporation doing business in the State. *Pierce* v. *Electric Co.*, 28 W. N., 311 (1891).

The resident of another State cannot, by a writ of foreign attachment, secure a preference over an assignment for the benefit of creditors by a citizen of another State. The only exception to this rule is in favor of citizens of this State. *Long* v. *Girdwood*, 150 Pa. St., 413 (1892).

The Act of May 23, 1887 (P. L., 164), prohibits a citizen of this Commonwealth from assigning his claim for a debt against a resident of the State for the purpose of having it collected by attachment in another State. *Sweeney* v. *Hunter*, 29 W. N., 133 (1890).

A judgment in another State between the same parties and for the same cause of action, is a bar to a foreign attachment instituted here after the bringing of suit in the other State, and before judgment in said suit. If the suit be against partners, the judgment is not a bar to a suit here against those not served. *Victor* v. *Alrams*, 2 Dist. Rep., 781 (1893).

Foreign attachment will lie against a foreign insurance company doing business in Pennsylvania, for a debt due a citizen of New Jersey, who was indebted to plaintiff. *Datz* v. *Chambers*, 3 Dist. Rep., 354 (1894).

Inasmuch as an action in assumpsit lies upon a judgment, *Eby* v. *Burkholder*, 17 S. & R., 9 (1827); *Clippinger* v. *Miller*, 1 P. & W., 64 (1829), the action may be commenced by foreign atachment. *Harter* v. *Harter*, 4 Dist. Rep., 211 (1895).

§ 76. **To issue the writ you may use this** *præcipe:*

A.
  v.
B.

To the Prothonotary of the Court of Common Pleas of   County.

SIR : Issue writ of foreign attachment, assumpsit (or trespass). Returnable, *sec. leg.*   Bail $
And indorse the same with the following directions to the sheriff:
Attach all and singular the goods and chattels, lands and tenements, rights and credits, of the defendant, in whose hands soever they may be, and summon them as garnishees, and especially attach all sums due by
      to said defendant, and all property in his hands belonging to said defendant, and summon him as garnishee.

C. (plff.'s atty.)
(Date.)

Pending a summons foreign attachment may issue. *Stockham* v. *Boyd*, 22 W. N., 118 (1888).

§ 77. In all cases you should have prepared, if possible, before you issue this writ, an **affidavit of cause of action.** If your cause of action be *ex delicto*, the affidavit must be filed before the writ issues. If your client be absent, and no clerk or agent can make the affidavit, then prepare and secure it with all dispatch. You may be ruled to show cause of action, and need the affidavit for that purpose.

You should consult the Digest of Laws and your Rules of Court.

When you give the writ to the sheriff he will require a bond for his protection. You must be ready to satisfy this demand.

Give also to sheriff written directions as to where he will find the property of the defendant, and 'whom he is to summon as garnishees, with their addresses.

An affidavit on which a foreign attachment is grounded stands upon the same footing as an affidavit to hold to bail, and is subject to the same rule, including the principle that it can never be helped by a supplemental or amended affidavit. *Jacobs* v. *Tichenor*, 27 W. N., 35 (1890).

§ 78. **The sheriff takes into his possession** personal property of the defendant, requiring indemnity if defendant's title is disputed. *Shriver* v. *Harbaugh*, 37 Pa. St., 399 (1860). He attaches real estate by serving the tenant or other person in possession, by publication if the property be vacant, and by serving the person liable to pay ground-rent or money to defendant. See Act June 13, 1836, sections 48, 49, which provide :

In the case of personal property the attachment shall be executed as follows, to wit :

The officer to whom such writ shall be directed shall go to the person in whose hands or possession the defendant's goods or effects are supposed to be, and then and there declare, in the presence of one or more credible persons of the neighborhood, that he attaches the said goods or effects.

In the case of real estate the attachment shall be executed as follows :

I. If the attachment be levied on houses, other buildings, or lands, it shall be the duty of the sheriff to leave a copy of the writ with the tenant, or other person in actual possession, holding under the defendant in the attachment, and to summon him as garnishee.

II. If there be no person in actual possession as aforesaid, the sheriff shall publish a copy of the writ, for six weeks, in one newspaper printed in the county, if there be one, otherwise in one newspaper published nearest to the land attached ; and such writ shall also be published in one or more newspapers in the city of Philadelphia or elsewhere, as the court, if in session, or a judge thereof, in vacation, at the time of issuing the same, having reference to the supposed place of residence of the defendant, shall direct.

III. If the attachment be levied on a rent-charge, it shall be the duty of the sheriff to leave a copy of the writ with the owner of the messuage, lot, or land out of which such rent shall issue, or upon which the same shall be charged, or if such owner shall not reside within the county, upon the tenant or other person in possession of such messuage, lot, or land, and in either case to summon such person as garnishee.

IV. In all other cases of incorporeal hereditaments the attachment shall be executed by leaving a copy of the writ with the person or persons who may be liable to the payment of money to the defendant, or who may be charged with or otherwise liable to the defendant in respect of such hereditaments. And if there be no such person, by publication, as directed in the case of houses or lands of which there shall be no person in possession as aforesaid.

Perishable property, such as a shallop, *Oniel* v. *Chew,* 1 Dall., 379 (1788), or cattle, *Magee* v. *Beirne,* 39 Pa. St., 50 (1861), may be sold.

Where a foreign attachment is issued against an undivided interest in personal property, the sheriff should take physical possession of the property itself. The court may then order it to be sold as perishable. *Apreda* v. *Romano,* 24 W. N., 124 (1889). But the order does not protect the sheriff from suit by a third party owning the goods. *Magee* v. *Beirne, supra.* The form of the proceeding to secure sale is given under Domestic Attachments.

Sometimes a mortgage or a judgment is held by a non-resident against a non-resident. In such cases the creditor can issue his foreign attachment summoning the judgment defendant or mortgagor as garnishee, but the garnishee, being out of the jurisdiction, the sheriff may execute the attachment by attaching or levying the same upon the lands liened or incumbered. This operates as a stay of proceedings upon the judgment or mortgage, and on final recovery the attaching plaintiff may, on giving security, be subrogated to the rights of the mortgagee or judgment creditor. (Act of May 8, 1855, section 3, P. L., 532.) This Act is in these words :

" All writs of foreign attachment against defendants who are mortgagees and judgment creditors, whose debtors by judgment or mortgage are non-residents, and cannot be personally served with notice or process as garnishee, shall and may be executed by attaching or levying the same on the lands, tenements, and hereditaments upon which the said judgments or mortgages are liens or incumbrances, in the same manner as such writs may now by law be executed upon the lands and tenements of the defendants therein ; and such writs, after such execution, shall bind the rights and interests of such mortgagees or judgment creditors, and shall operate as a stay of proceedings upon said judgments and mortgages, until said attachments are dissolved or otherwise legally disposed of. And upon a final recovery by the plaintiff in such attachment, it shall be lawful for the courts having jurisdiction to subrogate the plaintiffs in said attachments to the rights of the said mortgagees or judgment creditors, until they shall have received satisfaction of their respective debts : *Provided,* That before such subrogation shall be made, the plaintiff in such attachment shall be required to give the same security that is now by law required to be given before execution is issued upon judgments in foreign attachments."

§ 79. The effect of a service of a foreign attachment is to hold the property or thing attached ; and in case of real estate it binds as against subsequent purchasers, mortgagees, and judgment creditors from the time of the execution of the attachment. The sheriff is required to file with the prothonotary a description of the property attached within five days after the attachment. The prothonotary enters this on his docket, and on his judgment docket he must note the names of parties, date, amount, etc. You should see that this is carefully done.

Where a writ of foreign attachment has been issued and judgment taken for want of an appearance, but such judgment is subsequently stricken off because the declaration was not filed before the return-day of the writ, the lien of the attachment is not postponed to one subsequently issued. *Light Co, v. Manfg. Co.*, 26 W. N., 119 (1890).

§ 80. Having issued and duly served the attachment, the plaintiff should be ready with a full affidavit to show cause of action, if thereto required, and he should file a concise statement of his demand, with copies of all notes, contracts, book entries, and with particular reference to any record of the county upon which the claim is founded. (See Act May 25, 1887, section 3.)

When the terms of the affidavit of cause of action are ambiguous, the attachment will be dissolved. The plaintiff's affidavit of cause of action in substance claimed a commission alleged to have been promised plaintiff for negotiating certain bonds; the performance averred was securing a *loan*, and not a sale of the bonds. The affidavit was held defective, and the attachment dissolved. *Graham v. R. R.*, 25 W. N., 65 (1889).

§ 81. The defendant or the garnishee may apply and obtain at any time during the first term a rule to show cause of action, and why the writ should not be dissolved.

The power of quashing writs is limited to proceedings that are irregular, defective, or improper. *Crawford v. Stewart*, 38 Pa. St., 34 (1860). If it appear on the face of the record that the proceedings are void or grossly irregular, or where it is clearly shown that a valid cause of action does not exist, the court may, on motion of defendant or garnishees, quash the writ. *Steel v. Goodwin*, 113 Pa. St., 288 (1886). Whether the plaintiff's debt is due is a question for a jury. *Ibid.* Where judgment goes against a married woman for necessaries, her share in a decedent's estate may be attached. *Evans v. Cleary*, 23 W. N., 509 (1889). If judgment be obtained against her in another State where it is not necessary to join her husband, she can be sued upon the record in Pennsylvania. *Ibid.* If the record show a judgment over six years old, the Statute of Limitations cannot be set up. *Ibid.*

In a foreign attachment, where a question is raised as to the jurisdiction of the court, a motion to quash is the proper practice. *Webb v. Opera Co.*, 3 Dist. Rep., 825 (1894).

If the share of a married woman in a decedent's estate has been attached in violation of the proviso to the first section, Act July 27, 1842 (Br. Purd., 931, section 13), as was attempted in *Del Valle* v. *Welsh*, Common Pleas No. 4, of Philadelphia County, June Term, 1885, Nos. 238, 239, 240, or if the writ be for any other reason void (residence of the defendant in the State, etc.), it may be quashed. *Keegan* v. *Sutton*, 12 W. N., 292 ; *Lummis* v. *Cozier*, 35 Leg. Int., 262. A motion may also be made to set aside its service. In *Hunter* v. *Clark*, 16 W. N., 558 (1885), it was ruled that the sheriff must make a declaration of the attachment in the presence of credible persons of the neighborhood, and for defect in this particular the service was quashed. To the same effect is *Wanamaker* v. *Stevens*, 43 Leg. Int., 56 (1886). In *Brock* v. *Brock*, 18 W. N., 123 (1885), the return was similarly defective—only a debt was attached, and the rule to set aside the service was discharged. But passing by these applications, the plaintiff should expect a rule to show cause of action. Upon this the affidavit exhibited must be full, and contain not the technicalities, but all the essentials of a declaration. It should declare that the defendant, naming him, was before and at the time of the issuing of the above writ, and still is, justly and truly, indebted to the plaintiff in the sum of   dollars, upon the following cause of action, and then the claim should be carefully set out, with copy of any paper or book entry evidencing the debt.

A motion to quash a writ of foreign attachment regularly issued is addressed to the discretion of the court, and is not reviewable. *Holland* v. *White*, 120 Pa. St., 233 (1888) ; *Hall* v. *Oyster*, 168 *Ib.*, 399 (1895).

In *Graham* v. *R. R.*, 26 W. N., 203 (C. P. No. 3, of Phila. Co.), (1890), the plaintiff issued a writ of foreign attachment, which was dissolved ; upon that day the plaintiff issued another writ for the same cause of action, attaching the same property. FINLETTER, J. : " We do not think this practice should be encouraged ; * * * dissolving an attachment is a determination of the plaintiff's right to hold the property of the defendant for any cause which the plaintiff then had, or could have, and he is presumed to have presented it fully. It is therefore *res adjudicata* as fully as a discharge on common bail or dissolving an attachment under the Act of 1869." Writ dissolved.

When the sheriff's return is defective, he will be allowed to amend it, and a rule to set aside the return discharged. *De Thoneux* v. *Pirnay*, 17 W. N., 284 (1886).

If the sheriff make a false return to a writ of foreign attachment, the plaintiff has his action against the sheriff. *Wright* v. *Darlington*, 108 Pa. St., 373 (1885).

Third Term.

In *Collins* v. *Walker*, 6 W. N., 175 (1878), the writ issued July 26, 1877, returnable the third Monday of September, 1877. Service was accepted by the garnishees. Judgment was entered March 19, 1878, for default of appearance.

§ 82. Should the rule to show cause of action be discharged, the defendant may dissolve the attachment by giving bail absolute in a recognizance of double the amount in controversy, with one or more sufficient sureties conditioned for payment of the debt or damages with interest and costs that may be recovered. The bond of the garnishee is given to the sheriff. *Reis* v. *Junker*, 9 W. N., 296 (1880).

§ 83. This security may be entered without resort, in first instance, to a rule to show cause of action, and it may be given at any time, even after sale of property attached. But in this case the dissolution of the attachment does not divest any interest acquired by the sale by any person not party to the attachment. The proceeds of the sale are paid to the defendant.

If defendant enters bail to dissolve a foreign attachment after judgment by default, the attachment and all proceedings connected therewith fall, and the case proceeds as if commenced by summons. The judgment is *in rem*, and not *in personam*. *Borden* v. *Surety Co.*, 33 W. N., 502 (1894).

A judgment by default in foreign attachment entered before the execution of a bond to dissolve the attachment gives no right to sue upon such bond. *Borden* v. *Surety Co.*, 159 Pa. St., 465 (1894).

§ 84. If the defendant does not wish to give security, or cannot obtain it, he may make deposit, as in case of arrest upon *capias ad respondendum*, and thus dissolve the writ, but the suit stands.

§ 85. The remaining defense is to enter an appearance and contest the claim. The suit then proceeds as if commenced by summons, the attachment still holding its lien. The defendant, if served with notice of filing of statement, must, under section 6, Act May 25, 1887, file his affidavit of defense. See chapter Assumpsits as to rules for judgment, paper-books, etc. If, on trial, defendant have final judgment, the attachment is, of course, dead. If the plaintiff recover, he then goes on by *scire facias* against the garnishee.

§ 86. If the defendant do not quash the writ, set aside its service, or enter an appearance, the plaintiff can take judgment for want of appearance at the third term of the court.

In *Shuster* v. *Bonner*, 7 W. N., 17, the attachment was issued Saturday, September 14, 1878, returnable to the third Monday of that month, to wit, September 16. The sheriff executed the writ on the return-day. The plaintiff entered judgment for want of an appearance, March 19, 1879. Mr. John I. Rodgers, for the defendant, obtained a rule to strike off the judgment, and argued that the defendant was entitled to two full terms. The court so decided, and made the rule absolute.

Where a judgment is obtained in a foreign attachment for want of an appearance, and security is entered, the judgment is dissolved. *Borden* v. *Surety Co.*, 2 Dist. Rep., 245 (1893).

In *Melloy* v. *Deal*, 46 Leg. Int., 100 ; 23 W. N., 289 (1889) ; it was ruled that the statement must be filed before the return-day. (But see Act of 1889, below.) That the judgment must be entered at the third term and not after, and that the statute must be strictly construed.

The Act of June 13, 1836, provides :

" It shall be lawful for plaintiff, at the third term of the court after the execution of the writ aforesaid, if he shall have filed his declaration, to take judgment thereon against the defendant for default of appearance, unless the attachment before that time be dissolved."

This is amended by the Act of May 10, 1889 (P. L., 183) :

" It shall be lawful for the plaintiff, at and after the third term of the court, after the execution of the writ, to take judgment against the defendant for default of appearance, unless the attachment before that time be dissolved : *Provided*, That the said plaintiff, fifteen days prior to the entry of said judgment, shall have filed his declaration."

§ 87. **After taking judgment for want of an appearance**, the plaintiff may enter a rule on the prothonotary to assess the damages, which is done by exhibition of evidence, affidavit of plaintiff or of some other person cognizant of the transaction. (Act of April 9, 1870, section 1, P. L., 60 ; Br. Purd., 933, section 21.)

The form for these proceedings may be as follows :

A.
  v. } In the Court of Common Pleas of   County, to   Term.
B.   No.

And now,   , being the third term after the execution of the above writ, the plaintiff, having filed his declaration, on motion of C., Esq., plaintiff's attorney, judgment is entered against the above-named defendant for default of appearance. Prothonotary to assess the plaintiff's damages.

Indorse,

No.   Term,   Year.

A. ⎫
v. ⎬
B. ⎭
Judgment against defendant, for want of an appearance.

C., Plaintiff's Attorney.

The assessment of damages may be after this form :

A. ⎫ In the Court of Common Pleas of   County,   Term,
v. ⎬   188 , No.
B. ⎭

And now,   , 188 ,
Judgment having been entered against the above-named defendant for
default of appearance, the plaintiff enters a rule for the prothonotary to
assess the plaintiff's damages.

C., Plaintiff's Attorney.

Under the above rule the prothonotary assesses the plaintiff's damages
as follows :

Upon the evidence of D., examined under oath before the prothonotary,
the prothonotary finds that (the defendant signed a promissory note to
order of plaintiff January 1, 1887, at thirty days, for $500. The note was
given in evidence by plaintiff.

Amount thereof	$500 00
Interest from its maturity, February 1, 1887, to this date, six months	15 00
The plaintiff's damages are, therefore, assessed at	$515 00

the sum of five hundred and fifteen dollars, and costs.)

E., Prothonotary.

Indorse,

No.   ,   Term, 188 .

A. ⎫
v. ⎬
B. ⎭
Rule for assessment of plaintiff's damages at $515.

The above form must, of course, be changed according to the
facts. Instead of calling a witness, the plaintiff may produce his
own affidavit. Of all this the prothonotary is in the first instance
the judge, and leaves the responsibility with the plaintiff and the
counsel. If the assessment is unjust, the defendant would be heard
by the court, should he complain by affidavit.

Where judgment in foreign attachment is entered for want of an
appearance, it binds only the property attached. *Smith* v. *Eyre*,
30 W. N., 183 (1892).

§ 88. If, however, an appearance be entered, the plaintiff may
file his statement, serve a copy, and take judgment for want of

affidavit of defense. *Allen* v. *Allen*, 23 W. N., 371 (1889); *Smith*
v. *Sayre*, 26 *Id.*, 314 (1890); *R. R. Co.* v. *Snowden*, 166 Pa. St.,
236 (1895). If no sufficient affidavit of defense be filed, the plaintiff may move for judgment for want thereof. The affidavit filed
being sufficient, the plaintiff now enters a rule on defendant to
plead to plaintiff's statement in the following form :

> A. ⎰ In the Court of Common Pleas No.   , of Philadelphia
>   *v.* ⎱ County, of   Term, 1887, No.
> B.

To the Prothonotary of said Court.

SIR : Enter a rule on the defendant in the above case to plead in fifteen
days, or judgment *sec. reg.*

C.,
Plaintiff's Attorney.
(Date.)

Indorse this,

No.   ,   Term, 1887.

> A. ⎰
>   *v.* ⎱ C. P.
> B.

Rule on defendant to plead.

Hand this to the prothonotary, and serve on defendant's attorney
a copy of the statement and a notice of the rule to plead, in this
form :

> A. ⎰
>   *v.* ⎱ C. P. No.   , Philadelphia County,   Term, 1887, No.
> B.

To D. E., Esq., Defendant's Attorney.

DEAR SIR : Enclosed find copy of statement filed in the above case. Be
good enough to take notice that I have entered a rule on defendant to plead
in fifteen days, or judgment *sec. reg.*

Very respectfully,   F. G.,
Plaintiff's Attorney.
(Date.)

The time allowed for pleading is fixed by the Act of 1887 at
fifteen days. For the practice of taking judgment for want of a
plea, see section 26.

If the statement and the rule to plead be filed at the same time,
the rule may be indorsed on the statement below the word "Statement." But where an appearance is entered, the plaintiff should
notify defendant simply of the filing of the statement and press
for judgment for want of affidavit of defense. The statement
should follow the directions in the Act of May 25, 1887. This
Act and the practice regulating statements will be found noted
under the title "Statements." (Sections 61 to 73.)

Under the Act of May 25, 1887 (P. L., 271), an affidavit of defense is required in an action of assumpsit began by foreign attachment in which the defendant has appeared. *Wing* v. *Bradner*, 162 Pa. St., 72 (1894); *Praun* v. *Miller*, 3 Dist. Rep., 536 (1893).

§ 89. **Where a foreign attachment is executed upon land** which had been demised, reserving rent, the delivery of a copy of the writ to the tenant sequesters the rents due and to fall due. Act of June 13, 1836, section 65, P. L., 584.

On return of the writ and on affidavit of just cause of action, the plaintiff may obtain from the court a writ to the sheriff to collect from tenant rent accrued and to accrue. (*Ib.*, section 66.) A writ of estrepement is also provided by Act of May 8, 1855, section 4, P. L., 563.

Where the plaintiff in a foreign attachment refuses to proceed with his case, although the writ had issued more than a year and no appearance has been entered for defendant, on the application of the garnishee the plaintiff may be forced to proceed or to suffer a *non pros*. *Boyd* v. *Davis*, 1 Dist. Rep., 438 (1892).

§ 90. **If the plaintiff obtain judgment against the defendant,** he may collect it by issuing a *scire facias* against each garnishee not jointly liable. The garnishee may force the plaintiff to proceed. *Finch* v. *Bullock*, 10 Phila., 318 (1875).

A judgment of *non pros*. for want of a service of a copy of interrogatories upon garnishees will be stricken off. *Herst* v. *Beckhaus*, 2 Dist. Rep., 199 (1892).

He may move to strike off the judgment and may, on trial, set up its invalidity. *Melloy* v. *Deal*, 46 Leg. Int., 100; 23 W. N., 289 (1889); STERRETT, J. This writ commands the garnishee to show cause why plaintiff should not have execution of the estate and effects of the defendant attached. The plaintiff here, as in cases of attachment in execution, can file his interrogatories to the garnishee, asking what goods, moneys, etc., he had or has belonging to the defendant; whether he owes or is indebted to defendant, etc.

The following may be used as a form of interrogatories :

A.	In the Court of Common Pleas,
v.	County,
B., Defendant,	Term, 188
and	No.
C., Garnishee.	Foreign Attachment.

INTERROGATORIES TO THE ABOVE-NAMED GARNISHEE.

First. Do you know the defendant named in the above-stated action ?
Second. Have you had any business transactions with the said defendant?
If yea, how did your accounts stand at the time the writ in the above

case was served upon you? Was there or was there not at that time, or has there been since, up to the time of your answering, a balance in your hands in favor of the said defendant? State the amount particularly.

Third. Were you at the time the writ in the above case was served upon you, or have you been at any time since, and when, indebted to the said defendant in any manner whatsoever; or did the said defendant hold any bill, bond, note, account, draft, check, due bill, or other instrument of writing then due or thereafter to become due, upon which you had become in any manner liable? State the character and amount of such indebtedness and when and how the same arose.

Fourth. At the time the writ in the above case was served on you, or at any time since, did the said defendant claim from you any money or property on any account whatsoever? Was there then any debt or demand in suit between you? Answer particularly.

Fifth. Had you in your possession or under your control when the writ in the above case was served upon you, any goods or merchandise, or any property, estate, or effects, whatsoever, real or personal, belonging to the said defendant, or in which the said defendant was in any manner interested? If aye, state the nature, quality, and value thereof.

Sixth. Have any letters been received by you from the defendant, or from anyone, wherein it was alleged, represented, or stated that at the time in the writ in the above case was served upon you, or at any time since, the said defendant had any claim or demand against you whatsoever? Annex copies thereof.

(If any matter require a special interrogatory it can be inserted here.)

Plaintiff's Attorney.

The copy served should have the following notice:

To the Garnishee above named, or   *attorney.*
Please take notice that interrogatories, of which the foregoing is a copy, have been filed in the above-stated case, and that a rule has been entered upon the garnishee in the said case to answer the same within days, or judgment *sec. reg.*

Yours respectfully,
Plaintiff's Attorney.

The interrogatories filed should be indorsed:

No.   Term,   188 .
    A. ⎫
    v. ⎬
    B. ⎭
To the Prothonotary of the Court of Common Pleas,   County.
  SIR: Enter rule on garnishees to answer interrogatories in   days, or judgment *sec. reg.*

C.,
Plaintiff's Attorney.
(Date.)

As above directed, the plaintiff serves a copy of the interrogatories and notice of the rule (filling up the blank as to the days), according to the rule of court.

If no answer be filed, an appearance having been entered, it is usual to write to the attorney in default, reminding him that the rule has expired.

§ 91. **If you cannot secure answers,** you are entitled to a judgment, which you enter thus : at foot of a copy of interrogatories, and of the notice to answer attach affidavit of person who served the same :

A. B., having been duly sworn, according to law, doth depose and say, that on the   day of   , A.D. 188 , he served interrogatories and a notice of rule to answer, whereof the foregoing are true and correct copies, on C. D., Esq., attorney for the garnishees, personally.
Sworn to and subscribed before me,   188 .

This you indorse :

                    No. ,   Term,   Year.
A. ⎫
v. ⎬ C. P.,
B. ⎭
Copy of interrogatories and of rule on garnishee to answer, and proof of service of same.
SIR :
Enter judgment against the garnishees in the above case for want of answers, *sec. reg.*

                                        C.,
                                  Plaintiff's Attorney.
                                        (Date.)

To Prothonotary Common
    Pleas, of   County.

The prothonotary will assess the plaintiff's damages as in cases of judgment for want of affidavit of defense, the solitary item being " amount of judgment against original defendant, $, and interest from date."

You then issue *fi. fa.* against the garnishee, as in other cases, that is, of so much of the debt due by defendant and attached in hands of garnishee as may satisfy the judgment, with interest and costs ; and if the said garnishee refuse or neglect on demand by the sheriff to pay the same, then the same to be levied of the said garnishee, his goods and lands, according to law.

§ 92. **If the garnishee answer insufficiently,** proceed by filing exceptions, thus :

" Plaintiff's exceptions to the insufficient answers of the garnishee in the above case.
" The plaintiff excepts to the answer of said garnishee to the first interrogatory, because the said garnishee has not sufficiently answered so much and such part of the said first interrogatory as is embraced by the following :"

(quote the word or words unanswered), and so with the other answers. *Lanback* v. *Black*, 1 W. N., 314 (1875).

Of these exceptions you send full notice to your opponent and give a mem. to the court clerk to put the case on the proper list. You then prepare your *paper-book* sur *exceptions to the insufficient answers of the garnishee.*

Put this heading beneath the caption of the case, copy in parallel columns the slighted interrogatories, the answers thereto, and the exceptions, or call attention of the court to the parts insufficiently answered. If the exceptions be sustained, ask for an order of court on the garnishee to answer fully within a time named or judgment.

If the answers to interrogatories are not sufficiently certain, more specific answers should be required. If certain facts must be ascertained, the court may direct an issue. *Corr's Appeal*, 157 Pa. St., 133 (1893).

§ 93. **The answer may admit something to be due.** You then take a rule for judgment for the amount admitted to be due.

If funds in the hands of a garnishee are attached by A., and the garnishee receives notice from a subsequent judgment creditor, claiming the fund on the ground that the former judgment was obtained by fraud, the garnishee should pay the money into court. *Stockham* v. *Pancoast*, 1 Dist. Rep., 135 (1892).

Judgment will not be entered on answers to interrogatories unless, by a fair interpretation, they admit an indebtedness to defendant for a specific amount or for a sum sufficient to cover plaintiff's claim. *Tube Co.* v. *Receivers*, 36 W. N., 256 (1895).

§ 94. **The answer may admit the possession of certain personal property,** a ring, merchandise, etc. You then secure a rule " to show cause why judgment should not be entered against the garnishee for the property admitted to be in his possession, and why execution should not be levied on the same." On the return of all rules have a paper-book ready containing copy of the answers.

It is unnecessary to repeat that whenever you get judgment you are entitled to issue execution. The judgment is against the garnishee, " and that the plaintiff have execution of so much of the debt due by defendant and attached in the hands of the garnishee as may satisfy the judgment, with interest and costs ; and if the said garnishee refuse or neglect, on demand by the sheriff, to pay the same, then the same to be levied of the said garnishee, his goods and lands, according to law." *Layman* v. *Beam*, 6 Wh., 186 (1840).

Where, in a foreign attachment proceeding, there is a default by the garnishee in not entering appearance, the subsequent practice is thus stated in *Longwell* v. *Oil City Electric Co.*, 35 W. N., 374; 164 Pa. St., 533 (1894), by Mr. Justice MITCHELL:

1. " The garnishee, failing to appear after service of the attachment, with clause of summons, but no specific attachment of goods or credits, plaintiff will be entitled to a judgment by default. But such judgment will be inter-locutory only, and plaintiff cannot liquidate it, or have execution, without first by writ of inquiry or before the prothonotary as the rules of court or the practice in cases of default may prescribe, establishing his claim by evidence of the garnishee's possession of goods or credits of the defendant; and the measure of his damages will be the value of such goods.

2. " If the attachment is levied upon specific goods, the default may be taken as an admission of the possession of such goods, but the plaintiff must, by writ of appraisement or otherwise, establish their value.

3. " If the attachment is of money, or a debt, and the amount appears in the sheriff's return, the default is an admission of all the requisite facts, and no further evidence or inquiry is necessary.

4. " The proper form of the judgment is for plaintiff against the garnishee, and that the garnishee has in his hands certain goods, effects of credits, to wit (naming them) of the value, etc., or that the garnishee is indebted to the defendant in the sum of, etc.

5. " Plaintiff's measure of damages which determines the amount of the judgment against the garnishee is the value of the goods attached, of course not exceeding the amount of his judgment, interest, and costs against the defendant. The single exception is when the garnishee neglects or refuses to answer interrogatories, in which case by the express terms of section 57 of the Act of 1836, the judgment against him is that he has goods or effects of the defendant sufficient to satisfy the plaintiff's demand, and execution may issue against him as for his own proper debt."

For form of judgment against an executor garnishee, see *Maurer* v. *Kerper*, 102 Pa. St., 447 (1883).

§ 95. **The garnishee having filed full answers** denying indebtedness, etc., if you wish to proceed and test the truth of his answer, you file the following:

A.   C. P.,
v.   No. ,   Term,   year.
B.

SIR:

Enter a rule on the garnishee in the above case to plead in   days, or judgment *sec. reg.*   C.,
                                  Plaintiff's Attorney.
                                     (Date.)

To the Prothonotary of the
   Court of Common Pleas
   of   County.

Notice of this must be served as before. No statement against the garnishee is here required. The *scire facias* stands for a *narr.* If the garnishee does not plead, take judgment for want of a plea, as in section 26. The garnishee can plead *nulla bona* (no goods—

that he has nothing of defendant, and owes him nothing). You can then order the case on the trial-list.

§ 96. **When before the jury** the affirmative rests with you ; your client must prove that the garnishee is indebted to the defendant, or has in his hands some property of the defendant.

The case in this aspect stands exactly as if the defendant in your attachment were plaintiff and were suing the garnishee.

Each party has the same right to except, to move for a new trial, to appeal, etc., as if the suit stood originally in that shape.

§ 97. The following **provisions as to execution** explain themselves :

" After a verdict for the plaintiff on any *scire facias* as aforesaid, it shall be lawful for him to have execution of his judgment in the attachment to be levied of the goods or effects so found in the hands or possession of the garnishee, or of so much of them as shall be sufficient to satisfy his demand, together with legal costs of suit and charges as aforesaid." (Act of June 13, 1836, section 59, P. L., 583.)

" The plaintiff may also, at the same time, have execution against the garnishee upon the judgment obtained against him on the *scire facias*, as in the case of a judgment against him for his proper debt, to be executed if the garnishee shall neglect or refuse, upon the lawful demand of the proper officers, to produce and deliver the goods and effects of the defendant as aforesaid, or to pay the debt or duty attached if the same shall be due and payable." (*Ib.*, section 60.)

" But after judgment, before any execution shall be executed, the plaintiff shall give security by recognizance and sufficient sureties to be approved of by the court or by one of the judges thereof, in vacation, with condition that if the defendant in the attachment shall, within a year and a day next ensuing the date of such recognizance, by himself or attorney, come into court and disprove or avoid the debt recovered against him, or shall discharge the same with costs, in such case the plaintiff shall restore to the defendant the goods or effects or the value thereof attached and condemned as aforesaid, or so much thereof as shall be disproved or discharged, or else that they will do it for him." (*Ib.*, section 61.)

In any such case of foreign attachment and final judgment entered, it shall be lawful for the plaintiff at his option, instead of entering the security as required by the sixty-first section of said Act, to leave the property attached remain unsold for a year and a day after such judgment, and thereafter to proceed to make sale by execution, with the like effect as if such security had been entered." (Act of May 8, 1855, section 2, P. L., 532.)

A counsel fee will be allowed in attachment proceedings, where the garnishee admits in his answer that he has in his possession a sum belonging to the defendant, equal to or less than the amount claimed in the attachment. *Johnson* v. *Smith*, 29 W. N., 477 (1891).

If the garnishee put the defendant to unnecessary expense and delay, and denies possession of property really in his hands, he is not entitled to a counsel fee. *Geist* v. *Hartman*, 29 W. N., 477 (1892).

§ 98. In *Fitch* v. *Ross*, 4 S. & R., 557 (1818), a rule was obtained to set aside the *fi. fa.* because the plaintiffs had not previously given the security required by law to restore the property attached or its value, etc. The statute then in force was the Act of 1705, the fourth section of which was the same in substance as our present Act of 1836, above quoted.

"After judgment obtained the plaintiff shall, before sale and after execution awarded, find security." Under the custom of London, the practice had been to enter the security before taking out execution; and so Mr. Sargeant, in his work on Attachments, had stated the Pennsylvania rule. But our Supreme Court held that the security could well be entered after the execution and before the sale.

In the same case (*Fitch* v. *Ross*, 4 S. & R., 557) it was ruled that the death of the defendant after final judgment did not dissolve the foreign attachment, and that the security could well be given to the representatives of the deceased.

§ 99. In that case the *fi. fa.* was in the common form, and in general terms directed the sheriff to levy on the goods of the defendant. It was, however, levied only on the two houses attached. On a rule to set it aside, the point was pressed that the writ should have recited the attachment and ordered a levy on the property attached. This objection was overruled.

A *fi. fa.*, however, against the garnishee in an attachment execution, which in the usual form commanded a levy upon his goods, etc., was set aside in *Layman* v. *Beam*, 6 Wh., 181 (1840), already cited. The garnishee had not appeared. Judgment was entered against him by default. The writ in the common form was set aside and a new *fi. fa.* ordered in the form already given.

After twenty years, judgment on foreign attachment is presumed to be satisfied. *Biddle* v. *Bank*, 16 W. N., 397 (1885).

§ 100. We now reach the *scire facias ad disprobandum debitum.* This writ is allowed by the mercy of the law. The defendant, it is observed, has not been served with process. He is an absentee. His property has been simply attached. At the third term a judgment has been entered for want of an appearance. By the custom of London, there was no judgment, but after four defaults the garnishees were summoned, who pleaded *nil debent*, and the issue being found against them to ascertain the amount of money, there was an award of execution against the money in their hands. This proves that it is a proceeding *in rem* and not *in personam*. Accordingly it was held, in *Phelps* v. *Holker*, 1 Dall., 261 (1788), that no action would lie on a judgment in foreign attachment. Such, also, is the New York ruling. *Kilburn* v. *Woodworth*, 5 Johns., 37. (See argument of Mr. Binney, 4 S. & R., 561.)

After the delay to which the plaintiff has been already subjected, the law might well allow process to go out and the matter to be finally closed. But lest the defendant may not yet have heard of the proceeding and may be able to disprove the claim, the statute requires that the collection be delayed a year and a day.

Meanwhile, if the plaintiff reap the fruit of his *fi. fa.*, he must give security to restore. Within the time named the defendant may issue the *sci. fa. ad disprobandum debitum*. This is done by filing a *præcipe* for the writ in the form given for other process. The Supreme Court, in *Fitch* v. *Ross* (*supra*), said that "this, like putting in bail, puts the plaintiff to the legal proof of the demand and lets the defendant into a full defense. * * * On the *scire facias* every opportunity is given of a hearing and of a full defense, as if the defendants had entered the special bail."

The defendant then having issued his *sci. fa.*, and having caused it to be served on the plaintiff, the case stands precisely as if the defendant had in the first instance put in bail ; that is, he appears, files his affidavit of defense, if thereto required by any rule of court or statute, files his plea, and the case proceeds to final judgment as if commenced by summons.

If the conclusion be with the plaintiff, he proceeds against the property attached if unsold, or the security is discharged if the money has been received.

On the other hand, if the defendant have final judgment, he would ask to dissolve the attachment or he would sue out the recognizance given by the plaintiff, according to the circumstances.

§ 101. A foreign attachment to meet a peculiar case was provided by the **Act of April 6, 1870.** As the Act of 1869 applies to fraud, this statute of 1870 sought to provide a civil remedy in actions for certain assaults and batteries. The law was passed to meet a special case. A man of some means had been much annoyed by rowdy boys on his pavement. After threatening, he endeavored to frighten them by discharging a pistol. He excused the act by the plea of ignorance as to the weapon being loaded. A boy innocent of blame was injured by the ball. The defendant, after giving bail for his appearance at the criminal court, fled. The recognizance was forfeited. As the injured lad could serve no summons, this Act was passed. The defendant paid a large sum to the plaintiff, and the case ended.   It is not probable that a second claim will be found to meet the peculiar requirements of this statute.   It is in these words :

In all cases of arrest for homicide, or for assault or battery, resulting in great bodily harm to the person assaulted, so that his or her life is thereby imperiled, wherein the person arrested has been or shall be held to bail, and has made or shall make default, whereby his or her recognizance has been or shall be forfeited, and has fled or shall flee the jurisdiction of the court, it shall and may be lawful for the person so injured as aforesaid, his or her executors or administrators, to begin his, her, or their action for damages by filing in the proper court a certified copy of the record in such criminal proceeding, together with an affidavit that the defendant has left or is about to leave the jurisdiction of the court ; whereupon the said court shall award and issue an attachment against all and singular the goods and chattels, lands and tenements, rights and credits, of the defendant or any part thereof within the jurisdiction of the said court, which attachment shall be served and shall have the same effect, and the proceedings thereunder against the defendant and against any garnishee or garnishees shall be the same, as in cases of foreign attachment.

The provisions of this Act shall apply to the city and county of Philadelphia.   (Act of April 6, 1870, P. L., 960.)

§ 102. The remedy of foreign attachment was extended by the **Act of May 23, 1887**, to cases in equity.   The statute is in these words :

AN ACT

To provide for the institution of proceedings in equity by process of foreign attachment

SECTION 1. Be it enacted, etc., That in any case in which a bill in equity may hereafter be filed against a defendant or defendants not residing in the State of Pennsylvania, in which there shall be included a prayer of a decree for the payment of money, it shall be lawful for the plaintiff to cause a writ of foreign attachment to be issued against the real or personal estate of such defendant or defendants in the following form :

County, *ss.*
The Commonwealth of Pennsylvania.
To the sheriff of said county, greeting :   We command that you attach   , late of your county, by all and singular his goods and chattels, lands, and tenements, in whose hands or possession soever the same may be, so that he be and appear before our court of   to be holden at   , in and for the said county, on the   day of   next, there to answer the allegation of a bill in equity filed in the Court of Common Pleas of said county.

Which writ shall be executed by the sheriff in the manner prescribed by law for the service of writs of foreign attachment.

SEC. 2. In case the defendant or defendants, against whose property an attachment has been issued as aforesaid, shall not appear and answer the allegations of the bill at or before the first Monday of the third term next ensuing after the issuing of said attachment, then and in such case the plaintiff shall be at liberty to have a decree *pro confesso* entered against said defendant or defendants, and thereafter to proceed upon the decree so entered *pro confesso* by *scire facias* against the garnishee or garnishees in the same manner as proceedings begun by foreign attachment in actions at law.

Approved May 23, 1887.

§ 103. **The seventeenth section of the Act of June 13, 1836** (P. L., 585), provides for issuing a foreign attachment in all cases where two or more are jointly but not severally liable to suit, if one or more are liable to attachment and others be not liable.

The form of the writ is given in Brightly's Purdon, page 936, section 45. It is a summons as to him or those within the jurisdiction, and a foreign attachment against the others. The plaintiff proceeds under the summons against all it embraces, and so with the attachment. If judgment be entered against the first, execution issues ; if this be not satisfied, it shall be lawful for the plaintiff to levy upon the goods attached. The court has, however, power to award execution, if they see cause, against the goods attached in the first instance, saving to all defendants their respective rights.

If any defendant summoned obtain judgment upon a plea in bar of the whole action, and the plaintiffs do not, within a year and a day, sue out and prosecute a writ of error, the attachment may be dissolved.

In *White and Schnebly's Case*, 10 Watts, 217 (1840), a writ was issued, under the Act of 1836, of summons against White and of attachment against Schnebly (a non-resident). The defendants were partners. The writ was executed May 4, 1838. May 28, 1838, the firm made an assignment of the partnership property.

Under agreement, there was a sale, the money brought into court, and the question of distribution submitted. The court below decided that the attachment took the fund first, and awarded the balance to the assignee.

But the Supreme Court reversed, holding that the attachment did not bind partnership property, but the separate property of the non-resident debtor.

In *Fretz* v. *Johnson*, 15 W. N., 208 (1884), a writ issued in like form against two partners. A rule was taken to quash, on the ground that under the Act the writ could only issue when the defendants are jointly and not severally liable. But the court discharged the rule.

§ 104. When a foreign attachment is issued in any county in this Commonwealth, where the property of a non-resident is situated, after the execution of an assignment in another State, but prior to the recording thereof in the county where the property is found, the attachment has priority over the assignment.　*Steel* v. *Goodwin*, 113 Pa. St., 288 (1886).

A receiver was appointed in another State to take charge of property situate there ; a creditor citizen of that State came into Pennsylvania and issued a foreign attachment.　It was held that the title of the receiver prevented the attachment.　*Bagby* v. *R. R.*, 86 Pa. St., 291 (1878).　A foreign attachment duly served and levied takes precedence of ordinary writs of execution issued a later hour the same day.　*Warner's Appeal*, 13 W. N., 505 (1883).

The Act of June 10, 1881 (P. L., 106), authorizing an interpleader to try the title to property seized under a foreign attachment, is unconstitutional.　*Lumber Co.* v. *Reynolds*, 4 Dist. Rep., 573 (1895).

§ 105. With the forms supplied to meet the different stages of the case, and with general direction as to the same, it will thus be seen, on review of the foregoing chapter, that

The plaintiff's attorney must

Prepare his *præcipe*.

　　See the writ properly indorsed.

　　Give it to sheriff with full directions in writing.

　　Give security to the sheriff.

Prepare affidavit of cause of action.

File statement under Act of 1887.

Take judgment if no appearance entered.

　　Assess damages.

　　Issue *sci. fa.* against garnishee.

　　File interrogatories.

　　Enter rule on garnishee to answer.

　　Enter judgment if no answers filed.

　　File exceptions if answers are insufficient.

　　　　Order these on list.

　　　　Prepare paper-book.

　　If answers sufficient, then plaintiff must

Enter rule on garnishee to plead, or judgment.

When plea obtained, order case on trial-list.

If judgment obtained against garnishee, wait the year and day, or give security and proceed with *fi. fa.*

If defendant appear to the attachment, and plaintiff is entitled to judgment for want of an affidavit of defense, he secures it, otherwise

Plaintiff rules defendant to plead.

Forces the case on to trial.　After judgment

Plaintiff proceeds against the garnishee by *scire facias* and the other steps above noted after the direction to *sci. fa.* the garnishee.

If defendant issue his *sci. fa. ad disprobandum debitum*, the plaintiff must maintain his claim as if defendant had appeared to the attachment.

This imperfect outline shadows the plaintiff's attack.

§ 106. **The defendant may resort to the following steps of resistance.** In proper cases he may

Move to quash the writ, or

Move to set aside the service, or

Rule plaintiff to show cause of action and why the attachment should not be dissolved. Failing in these,

Defendant may give bail, or deposit the money, and dissolve the attachment ; or, without dissolving the attachment,

Defendant may enter an appearance.

He must then file an affidavit of defense, if in danger of judgment, and, when ruled,

Defendant must plead, and prepare for trial.

If the defendant has not entered an appearance, he can still, within the year and a day after judgment, issue his *sci. fa. ad disprobandum debitum*, etc.

§ 107. The object of this chapter is not to give a treatise upon the law of foreign attachments. That would require a literal copy of all the Acts of Assembly and a digest of all the decisions bearing upon this subject. A volume would be required for this purpose. The statutes and decisions are already in the Digests, carefully prepared and well arranged.

§ 108. **Domestic Attachments.** The general law of 1836 (which was an enlargement of the Justice's Act of 1752) established a State bankrupt system, which, in its simplicity, might well be imitated by the National Legislature.

The law provides in its first section thus :

Writs of domestic attachments may be issued by the Courts of Common Pleas of the county in which any debtor, being an inhabitant of this commonwealth, may reside, if such debtor shall have absconded from the place of his usual abode, within the same, or shall have remained absent from this commonwealth, or shall have confined himself in his own house, or concealed himself elsewhere, with design, in either case, to defraud his creditors, and the like proceedings may be had if any debtor, not having become an inhabitant of this commonwealth, shall confine or conceal himself within the county with intent to avoid the service of process and to defraud his creditors. Act of June 13, 1836, section 1, P. L., 606.

§ 109. It will be seen that two classes are made subject to the law.

1. Inhabitants of the commonwealth.

2. Those not inhabitants of the commonwealth.

But the cases vary with each class.

The inhabitant may bring himself within the law,

1. If he abscond from the place of his usual abode.

2. If he remain absent from the commonwealth.

3. If he confine himself in his own house, or

4. Conceal himself elsewhere,

With the design in either case to defraud his creditors.

The person not an inhabitant is only brought within the law, if he

Confine himself within the county, or

Conceal himself within the county

With intent to avoid the service of process and to defraud his creditors.

It will be observed that the Fraudulent Debtor's Act of 1869 (considered in the chapter on Assumpsit) does not refer to any of these personal acts. Herein seems to be the distinction. The Act of 1869 (amended by Act of 1887) applies to removal or assignment or concealment of property and to fraud in contracting the debt. The Domestic Attachment Law can only be invoked where the person absconds, conceals himself, etc.

§ 110. It does not often happen that a man absconds yet remains an inhabitant by leaving a residence. If he have a residence, service of a summons can generally be made there whether the defendant absconds or hides. For these reasons, and because no creditor gains any advantage over other creditors by issuing the writ, a domestic attachment is rarely used. If the defendant be not an inhabitant, and be not in the county, your remedy is by foreign attachment. If he be in the county, you have a better chance by serving a summons, and, if possible, arresting him under the Act of 1842. (See section 47.) But if only a summons could be served, I would prefer that and the chance of a judgment by default followed by execution, to the remedy of domestic attachment.

§ 111. Supposing, however, that this is the best relief presenting itself, you proceed thus:

Prepare your client's affidavit, that " A. B. is justly and truly indebted to him in the sum of   dollars, upon the following cause of action " (here state that defendant signed the note, bond, due bill (give a copy), or that he bought of plaintiff goods—state always the dates and amounts—or borrowed money, etc., etc.). A debt not presently due and payable, if there be in other particulars sufficient ground for the domestic attachment, will support the writ. *McCullough* v. *Grishobber*, 4 W. & S., 201 (1842). Be particular to follow the very words of the statute in describing the defendant's acts. Thus, after stating the debt, cause of action, etc., add :

> And deponent further saith that the said A. B. is an inhabitant of this commonwealth, and resides in this county, and that the said A. B., to wit, on the   day of   in the year of our Lord, 188 , absconded from the place of his usual abode (to wit, his residence, No.   Street, in said county) within said county, with design to defraud the creditors of the said A. B.

If the defendant has done something else denounced· by the law, state it with the conjunction *and*, but never in affidavit or any pleading charge that a man was guilty of this *or* of that.

In Domestic Attachment, the affidavit must " aver the the truth of the facts stated," and the words " is informed and believes " are insufficient. *Sharpless* v. *Ankermiller*, 19 W. N., 88 (1887). It must also aver " an intention on the part of the debtor to abscond," and not merely the " creditor's belief of such intention." *Simons* v. *Hickman*, 24 W. N., 92 (1889).

This affidavit should be made by the plaintiff if he be at hand. The law allows it to be made by " some one in his behalf." It is best in such cases to state plaintiff's sickness or absence, and that the person acting is the wife or duly authorized agent of the plaintiff. Indorse the paper " *Plaintiff's affidavit.*"

Write beneath :

To the Prothonotary of the Court of Common Pleas of   County.
      SIR : Issue writ of domestic attachment, returnable *sec. leg.*

C. D.,
Plaintiff's Attorney.
(Date.)

As the writ is peculiar, I would present the affidavit to a judge of the court and get his initials beneath these words :

" Writ allowed."

§ 112. The prothonotary issues the writ.

In handing it to the sheriff, give him, in writing, full directions, the locality of all known real estate, and of all goods, horses, etc., the names and addresses of all persons having the custody of any goods or effects, or indebted to the defendant. The printed form of the writ does not give any summons for the garnishee. But the subsequent section requires it to be in the writ, and it should be inserted, " and that you summon as garnishees all persons in whose hands any of the defendant's money or other effects may happen to be, to appear before our said court at the day and place above mentioned."

The sheriff attaches all personal property, returns an inventory and appraisement. Real estate is attached by serving the tenant or person in possession, if any, by putting up a copy in some conspicuous place on the realty, filing a description, and causing it to be entered on the docket of the prothonotary. The plaintiff's attorney should see to all these details, and that all persons in possession or indebted are served. The writ should be noted on the judgment index. Other creditors may intervene, perishable goods may be sold, testatum attachments may be sued out with the original or afterward, into any other county where defendant has property. The testatum writs are executed as the originals, with double returns, one to the court of the first county and the other to the court of the county where the testatum is executed. The court of the county into which the testatum is issued has power to make all interlocutory orders for sale, for compelling answers, delivery of property to the trustees, etc. Pending the first attachment, no second writ can issue, except these testatums. Other creditors, as above noted, have their chance by making affidavit of debt and suggesting their names upon the record.

§ 113. On the return of the original attachment, the court appoints three trustees, not being creditors, who must file their affidavit to execute the trust according to the best of their skill and understanding, and give security as directed. Thereupon the officer who has taken possession of money or property under the writ must deliver it to the trustees upon demand and on certificate that they have been duly qualified and given security. The trustees give public notice as directed, requiring all debtors to pay to them and all creditors to present their claims. The estate of the defendant vests in the trustees subject to existing liens, and they can take all books, etc., sue in their own names for all estate, debts, etc. *Bona fide* purchasers for value of the realty, without notice and before attachment executed and entered on the docket, are protected.

Bona fide purchasers for value of the personalty without notice or knowledge of the attachment are also protected. Persons paying the defendant or delivering his property *bona fide*, without notice or knowledge of the attachment, shall not be liable to suit.

The wife and family may retain articles exempt from execution.

§ 114. Powers of trustees. Subject to these restrictions, the trustees have very full powers bestowed upon them. ·

They may summon residents of the county supposed to be in-

debted and others residing in the county, and examine them upon
oath as to the estate of the defendant, secret grants, etc.

They may commit all who refuse to attend or to be sworn or to
make answer, the persons thus committed to be enlarged on giving
bail to appear at the next court to answer under direction of the
court, and to abide all orders made by the court. Persons having
books, papers, effects, etc., may also be committed in like manner
on refusal to deliver when legally required.

The trustees may exhibit interrogatories to garnishees residing
in other counties, and the courts of those counties may compel
answer thereto.

The trustees have the high power to issue warrants to cause to
be broken open in the daytime houses, chambers, shops, stores,
warehouses of the defendant or doors therein, and his trunks or
chests, in which effects, books, or papers relating to his estate shall
be or be reputed to be, and to seize the same. They can recover
property conveyed to wife or children or to any person in trust for
them, or conveyed to any person with intent to defraud creditors.

They can redeem all property pledged.

After the term succeeding that to which the writ was returnable, the trustees can sell the personalty, and after the third term
they can sell the realty, always giving ten days' notice, as in case
of sale under execution. The purchaser can recover in his own
name all property, debts, etc., bought by him. A majority of the
trustees is competent to exercise all the powers above named.

Trustees not liable for a mere error of judgment or a mistake of
law, if acting in good faith and under the advice of counsel. *Bradley's Appeal*, 89 Pa. St., 521 (1879); PAXSON, J.

Trustees in domestic attachment who deposit *bona fide* in a bank
of good standing and repute, the funds in their hands, are not responsible for a loss resulting from a failure of the bank. Common
prudence and good faith are all that are required. *Breneman* v.
Mylin, 2 Dist. Rep., 296 (1892).

§ 115. **Perishable goods** may be sold by order of the court or of
any judge in vacation. Before the appointment of trustees any
creditor can apply for the order, and the sale is by the sheriff.
But the trustees may, with leave as aforesaid, make sale of perishable property.

In *Oniel* v. *Chew*, 1 Dall., 379 (1788), already cited under Foreign Attachment, the defendant's interest being attached in a shallop, Levy, after filing a positive affidavit of the debt, moved at
the first term that the shallop might be sold as a perishable com-
modity ; and the motion was accordingly granted.

§ 116. In *Magee* v. *Beirne*, 39 Pa. St., 50 (1861), a similar order was made for the sale of cattle taken under a foreign attachment. It was also there ruled that :

(1) Under the Pennsylvania statute, foreign attachment is not strictly a proceeding *in rem ;* and, therefore, the final judgment in the attachment, though conclusive as to parties and privies, does not include all the world as to a stranger's ownership in the property.

(2) Where the goods attached are ordered to be sold as perishable or chargeable, the title of the purchaser at such sale is indefeasible and unquestionable, whoever the former owner may have been, if the order and sale were under a proceeding *in rem ;* but the sheriff, as defendant in an action of trespass by the real owner, cannot justify the taking of the goods on the ground that by this peculiar rule of law the title of his vendee was validated.

(3) There is no rule of law which compels the real owner of attached property, on notice of the suit, to intervene and defend *pro interesse suo*, on pain of forfeiting his rights of property or of action.

§ 117 "Perishable" does not only mean property like fruits or other articles which may be destroyed in a short time, but the term includes all effects which, by reason of the cost of retaining them or for any other cause may prove of no value before the term arrives at which other goods can be sold. In this sense liquors are not perishable. In *Henisler* v. *Friedman*, 5 Clark, 147 ; 11 Penna. Law Jour., 355 (1852), the court refused to order a sale of wines, etc. But in that case the application was not made until the arrival of the term at which the trustees could sell without any order. The petition was refused for this reason.

§ 118. **The method of obtaining the order** is to present a positive affidavit of the debt, adding that the sheriff has in his possession, or that the trustees have in their possession, the following (describe the property) ; that the same is perishable, and unless the same is sold it will, by the next term, be of no value (or of very little value, etc.). It is best to add the reason, as, in the case of cattle, the cost of keeping them ; in the case of a small vessel, the wharfage, watchman's fees, etc. The sheriff should take care that he do not sell the property of a stranger.

§ 119. **After six months from the first public notice** have expired the trustees advertise a second time, fixing a time and place to receive proofs of claims, and they then file a report of their accounts and of the sum payable to each creditor.

The prothonotary gives the same public notice of the report as in cases of voluntary assignee's accounts; and at the next term, if exceptions are not presented as required by rules of court, the report may be confirmed and distribution be made. If other moneys come into hand, reports may be made and distributions awarded every three months. In these awards, specialties have no preference; *bona fide* creditors whose claims are not yet due receive a dividend; all claims are subject to set-offs, and the balance, if any, after payment of all just demands, costs, and charges, goes to the defendant or his representatives.

The trustees file the final distribution with the prothonotary of the court in which they were appointed.

§ 120. **The court issuing the attachment may, before final decree, dissolve the writ** on affidavit of defendant denying the allegations on which the attachment was founded. They first grant a rule to show cause upon the creditors suing or prosecuting the writ, and they may at the same time make an order staying all further proceedings by the trustees. If satisfied that defendant was not liable to the attachment, they dissolve the same absolutely or upon terms, and order costs to be paid by the creditors prosecuting the writ or by the defendant. But no such order shall invalidate any lawful sale by the trustees or any payment to them.

§ 121. **The old Act of 1752** conferred a jurisdiction somewhat similar upon justices of the peace where the debt did not exceed £5. This law is still in force, the jurisdiction having been increased to $100. With that alteration and an amendment, caused by Act of December 4, 1807, the Act of August 22, 1752, section 1 (1 Smith, 218), reads as follows:

> If any person shall absent him or herself out of this government, or abscond from his or her usual place of abode, not taking care to satisfy his or her just debts, it shall and may be lawful for any justice of the peace of the county where such person's estate may be found to grant a writ of attachment for any debt not exceeding $100, directed to any constable of the same county, to attach the goods and chattels or other effects of such person, to answer the creditor; but, before granting any such attachment the person or persons requesting the same, or some other credible person or persons for him or them, shall, upon oath or affirmation, declare that the defendant in such attachment is indebted to the plaintiff therein named in a sum not exceeding $100, and that the defendant is and has absconded from the place of his usual abode (for the space of six days), with design to defraud his creditors, as is believed, and that the defendant has not left a clear fee simple estate in lands or tenements within this province sufficient to pay his debts, so far as the plaintiff or deponent knows or believes; which oath or affirmation the justice of the peace that grants such writ is hereby empowered and required to administer; and if any attachment be granted out otherwise, or contrary to the true intent and meaning hereof, the justice of the peace so granting the same shall, for every such offense, forfeit the sum of $100 for the use of him or her that will sue for the same.

The Act of 1752 required, as will be seen, an absconding for six days. But the Act of December 4, 1807, conferring like jurisdiction on the Courts of Common Pleas, did not require an absconding for six days, or for any definite term. The fifteenth section of this Act (December 4, 1807) conferred upon justices like jurisdiction with the courts. For this reason the Supreme Court held, in *Jewel* v. *Howe*, 3 Watts, 149 (1834), that the six days' stipulation was repealed.

§ 122. **After accepting the constable's return,** the justice appoints three honest men to be trustees; they are sworn, and take all goods attached. The justice advertises in public places and in one or more newspapers for all creditors to appear, and if there be a just debt due to any person from the defendant exceeding $100, the justice proceeds no further, but certifies all to the Prothonotary of the County Court of Common Pleas. The court grants one attachment for any creditor. The sheriff attaches lands, goods, etc., and the court proceeds. As to the justice, it is enacted that no second attachment shall bind pending the first. The justice may order that cattle, etc., necessary to be maintained at expense, or perishable goods may be sold by the trustees within ten days, of which six days' notice shall be given by advertisement in the most public place. If no debt exceeding $100 shall appear to be due, the goods attached are appraised, and, at expiration of three months, the debtor not appearing and redeeming them, the justice orders the trustees to sell, giving at least ten days' notice by advertisement in the most public places. The trustees deduct all reasonable charges and pay creditors proving their debts within the three months *pro rata*. They then, within six days of distribution, render a true account to the justice.

§ 123. **Dissolving the attachment.** If application be made within twenty days after the return of the writ, the justice has like power with the Court of Common Pleas to dissolve the attachment.

§ 124. **Attachment of vessels.** The Act of June 13, 1836, subjects ships and vessels of all kinds built, repaired, or fitted within this Commonwealth, to a lien for all debts contracted by the masters or owners thereof for work done or materials found or provided in the building, repairing, fitting, furnishing, or equipping of the same in preference to any other debt due from the owners thereof. (P. L., 1836, page 616, section 1, Brightly's Purdon, 145, section 1.). The doubts as to the validity of such legislation, and perhaps other causes, have tended to reduce the number of proceedings under this Act.

§ 125. **As to the general lien of Admiralty Courts**, it would appear from *People's Ferry Co.* v. *Beers*, 20 Howard (1857), page 393, " that liens on vessels encumber commerce and are discouraged, so that where the owner is present, no lien is acquired by the material-man, nor is any where the vessel is supplied or repaired in the home port. The lien attaches to foreign ships and vessels only in favor of the carpenter who repairs in a case of necessity, and in the absence of the owner." CATRON, J. (402). In that case a libel was filed by builders against the steam ferry-boat " Jefferson." The District Court of the United States for the Southern District of New York sustained the libel. The Circuit Court affirmed, but the Supreme Court of the United States dismissed the libel for want of jurisdiction.

§ 126. In the case of *Roach* v. *Chapman*, 22 Howard, 129 (1859), the claimant sought to sustain the libel in the United States Court under the statute of Kentucky, which gave a lien to builders. The District Court of Louisiana sustained the claim.

The Circuit Court dismissed the libel for want of jurisdiction, and the Supreme Court affirmed the decree, holding that a contract for building a ship or supplying engines, timber, etc., is clearly not a maritime contract; and that local laws can never confer jurisdiction on the courts of the United States.

§ 127. *In re The Moses Taylor*, 4 Wallace, 411 (1886), suit was brought, under the California Acts of 1851 and 1860, against the vessel for not furnishing proper provisions to a passenger from New York to San Francisco. The plaintiff obtained judgment. The Supreme Court of the United States reversed, with direction to dismiss the action for want of jurisdiction. They held (opinion by FIELD, J.) that all State laws conferring admiralty jurisdiction *in rem* are void, the remedy being exclusively in the United States Court. The feature which marks the process as a suit in admiralty was stated in that case to be this, " that the vessel or thing proceeded against *itself* is seized and impleaded as the defendant and is judged and sentenced accordingly." (Page 427.)

§ 128. By section 9, Act of Congress, September 24, 1879, exclusive jurisdiction was given to the District Court of the United States in civil causes of admiralty and maritime jurisdiction. From this it would seem that a State law giving an attachment against a vessel for a cause within the admiralty jurisdiction would be void.

In *The Moses Taylor, supra,* an attempt was made to save the California statute by the points : (1) That the constitutional grant of jurisdiction to the Federal courts was not exclusive; and (2) that the Judiciary Act of 1789 contained a clause saving to suitors a common-law remedy. But both these suggestions were over-ruled.

§ 129. *The Hine* v. *Trevor*, 4 Wallace, 555 (1866), and *The Belfast*, 7 Wallace, 624 (1868), reiterated the doctrine that State statutes attempting to give proceedings *in rem* as remedies for marine torts and contracts are void. The common law actions *in personam* and the process by Attachment in Execution and by *fieri facias* are, of course, untouched by these decisions.

§ 130. Seemingly in conflict with the cases cited is the ruling by the Supreme Court of Pennsylvania in *Scull* v. *Shakespear*, 75 Pa. St., 297 (1874). There the lien against the schooner " Maggie Cain " for materials was sustained. Upon the constitutional point AGNEW, C. J., said : " It is contended that a lien such as this, incurred in the building of a vessel, is not within the jurisdiction of a State court, but falls within the Federal jurisdiction, under the Constitution of the United States, and must be enforced in an Admiralty Court. We do not think so. A contract to build a vessel is a contract to be performed on land, falling within ordinary common law, and belongs to the State jurisdiction. It differs not from a contract to build a wagon or a railroad car, made between citizens of the same State, and cannot be drawn into the Federal courts because the vessel is intended to become a subject of maritime law. Whatever question may arise as to those liens, which the Act of 1836 seeks to enforce against a finished vessel after she has entered her appropriate element, certainly there can be none as to liens upon a vessel for work and materials entering into her construction before she has passed within the dominion of maritime law. Some *dicta* and District Court decisions to the contrary were overruled in *People's Ferry Co.* v. *Beers*, 20 Howard, 393 ; *Roach* v. *Chapman*, 22 *Ib.*, 129."

In *Baizley* v. *Brig Odorilla*, 22 W. N., 300 (1888), it was held that the admiralty did not oust the State jurisdiction of a libel for materials, work, etc., repairing, etc., the brig, although the hull was brought from Wilmington to Philadelphia for the purpose of completing the vessel.

§ 131. In cases where the practitioner proceeds under the law cited he will observe the following suggestions :

(1) *The parties who can file a libel* are carpenters, blacksmiths, mastmakers, boat-builders, blockmakers, ropemakers, sailmakers, riggers, joiners, carvers, plumbers, painters, ship-chandlers, coppersmiths, brass-founders, coopers, venders of sail-cloth, lumber-merchants, steam-engine boiler-makers, venders of copper-sheathing, and all manufacturers of iron.

A vender of copper-sheathing has no lien for " rings and bolts." *Merchant* v. *Odorilla*, 5 W. N., 288 (1878).

(2) *As to other matters:* The ship or vessel must be built, repaired, or fitted within this Commonwealth. The debt must be contracted by the master or owner for work done or materials found or provided in the building, repairing, fitting, furnishing, or equipping the ship or vessel. The lien is preferred to any other debt from the owner. It continues during the time intervening between the contracting of the debt and proceeding on the next voyage. The contractor for building the boat has no lien. *Walker* v. *Anshutz*, 6 W. & S., 519.

Where an intermediate agent—not owner and not master—contracts for work, etc., neither he nor his subordinates have a lien. *Harper* v. *New Brig*, Gilpin, 536.

(3) *The libel is* to be filed in the office of the Common Pleas of the county wherein the cause of action shall arise, or where the ship may be found. All claimants may join in the original libel, or become parties by petition. If there be more than one suit, the claims must be consolidated.

In *Odorilla* v. *Baizley*, 47 Leg. Int., 83 (1889), it was decided that the recovery of a judgment by a sub-contractor against a contractor, *in personam*, for work and materials furnished toward the building of a vessel, does not prevent an attachment against the vessel, under the Act of 1836.

§ 132. **A synopsis of the libel** is given in the case cited from 75 Pa. St., 297.

It should be somewhat in the following form :

A. B., Libellant,

v.

The Schooner called the Eagle, her tackle, apparel, and furniture, whereof C. D. is owner and E. F. is master.

In the Court of Common Pleas (No. 1) of Philadelphia County.

I. A. B., of the city of Philadelphia, carpenter, files this his libel in a cause civil and of contract against the schooner called the Eagle, now within the county of Philadelphia, whereof C. D. is owner and E. F. is master.

II. Libellant claims the sum of   dollars, being a debt contracted by the said master (or owner) for work, to wit : carpenter work (or materials, describing them), done, found, and provided in the building (or repairing, fitting, furnishing or equipping, as the case may be) of the said schooner, the Eagle, in the county of Philadelphia and within this Commonwealth, on the following dates (setting out the dates).

III. On said days the said A. B., the libellant, at the request of the said C. D., owner (or E. F., master), of the said schooner, the Eagle, did the said work (or furnished said materials) at (name the place) in the county and State aforesaid, for building (or repairing, etc.) the said schooner, the Eagle.

IV. For this there is still due to A. B., the libellant, the sum of   dollars, according to a bill of particulars hereto annexed as part hereof.

V. And libellant shows that the said schooner, Eagle, is now lying at (describe the place), in the county of Philadelphia, and that she has not proceeded on a voyage since the said work (or materials) above mentioned was done (or were furnished).

VI. Wherefore the said A. B., the libellant, prays for due process to enforce his rights, and that an attachment may issue against the said schooner, " The Eagle," her tackle, apparel, and furniture, and that the said C. D., owner, and E. F., master, of said schooner, be summoned to answer this libel, and that upon hearing the said schooner, " The Eagle," her tackle, apparel, and furniture, be condemned and sold to pay the amount so due to this libellant and costs. And libellant prays for such relief and redress as the court is competent to give in the premises.

A. B.,
Libellant.

G. H.,
Attorney pro Libellant.

City and County of Philadelphia, *ss.*

A. B., the libellant above named, having been duly sworn according to law, doth depose and say that the facts set forth in the above libel are true and correct.

A. B.

Sworn to and subscribed before }
  me,   1887.   }

Interrogatories may be appended if desired.   The bill of particulars must be attached, charging the vessel as Debtor to the Libellant, giving dates, work (or materials), and amounts.

§ 133. Present the libel to a judge and get him to fix the amount of bail, and to put his initials at the foot of the words :

Allowed bail $

The bail fixed is generally twice the amount of the claim to cover interest and costs.   But if the demand be very large, a small excess will be sufficient.   Write your *præcipe* thus :

A. B., Libellant,   ⎫
                         ⎪
       v.   ⎬
                         ⎪
The Schooner Eagle, her tackle,   ⎪
   apparel, and furniture. C. D., ⎪
   owner, and E. F., master.   ⎭

SIR :

Issue attachment, with clause of summons against C. D. and E. F. Bail $, returnable *sec. leg.*

G. H.,
Attorney pro Libellant.
1887.

To the Prothonotary of the Court
  of Common Pleas (No. 1), Philadelphia County.

§ 134. **The Act of 1836** directs that no attachment can be issued against any vessel actually held by process of a United States court, or sold by its order for any debt contracted previously to such sale.

§ 135. **The writ should be given to the sheriff** with instructions as to locality. He serves the persons named as in other cases. He takes the vessel, her tackle, etc., into his custody, and advertises notice thereof in one newspaper of the county once a week for six weeks, stating the name of the vessel, her port, her last commander, and that she will be sold for payment of debt contracted for (as case may be), unless owner, consignee, commander, or some one in their behalf, appear and pay, or otherwise obtain her discharge within three months. The sheriff must also in the notice require all having claims to file them within three months or be debarred.

§ 136. **If owner, master, or agent shall enter into bond** to the Commonwealth, with sureties approved by a judge of the court issuing the writ conditioned to answer all demands then filed, and to satisfy such of them as shall be recovered, the vessel is discharged. The following is the form of the bond filed in *Scull* v. *Shakspear, supra:*

Know all men by these presents : That we,
master and claimant of the schooner, *Maggie Cain*, principal, and
all of the city of Philadelphia, sureties, are held and firmly bound unto the Commonwealth of Pennsylvania in the penal sum of $12,300 lawful money, to be paid to the said Commonwealth of Pennsylvania, to which payment, well and truly to be made, we and each of us do bind ourselves, our and each of our heirs, executors, and administrators, firmly by these presents. Sealed with our and each of our seals. Dated the tenth of February, A.D. one thousand eight hundred and seventy.

The condition of this obligation is such, that whereas the said schooner Maggie Cain has been attached and held under divers writs of attachment issued out of the District Court, for the City and County of Philadelphia, of December Term, 1869, No. 2095, at the suit of William A. Levering, etc., upon libels and petitions severally filed by said parties in said court, under the provisions of the Act of Assembly of the said Commonwealth, approved the 13th day of June, A.D. one thousand eight hundred and thirty-six, entitled an "Act relating to the Attachment of Vessels," and its Supplements.

Now know ye, that if the said schooner Maggie Cain and the masters and owners thereof shall answer all the demands aforesaid, which shall at this time be filed against the said schooner, and shall fully satisfy all such of said demands, and any of them as shall be proved and recovered against the said vessel, or the owners thereof, under and by virtue of the said foregoing attachment, then this obligation to be void, otherwise to be and remain in full force and virtue.

§ 137. **The Act of 1836** directs that further proceedings shall be according to the admiralty practice. The sheriff's return must set forth the time, place, and manner of service. (11 Additional Rules in Admiralty.)

As the Rules in Admiralty are not generally printed in the Rule Books, such of them as apply to this subject are here inserted:

Rule 10. In all cases where any goods or other things are arrested, if the same are perishable, or are liable to deterioration, decay, or injury, by being detained in custody pending the suit, the court may, upon the application of either party, in its discretion, order the same or so much thereof to be sold as shall be perishable or liable to depreciation, decay, or injury; and the proceeds, or so much thereof as shall be a full security to satisfy in decree, to be brought into court to abide the event of the suit; or the court may, upon the application of the claimant, order a delivery thereof to him, upon a due appraisement, to be had under its direction, either upon the claimant's depositing in court so much money as the court shall order, or upon his 'giving a stipulation, with sureties, in such sum as the court shall direct, to abide by and pay the money awarded by the final decree rendered by the court, or the appellate court, if any appeal intervenes, as the one or the other course shall be ordered by the court.

Rule 11. In like manner where any ship shall be arrested, the same may, upon the application of the claimant, be delivered to him, upon a due appraisement, to be had under the direction of the court, upon the claimant's depositing in court so 'much money as the court shall order, or upon his giving a stipulation, with sureties, as aforesaid; and if the claimant shall decline any such application, then the court may, in its discretion, upon the application of either party, upon due cause shown, order a sale of such ship, and the proceeds thereof to be brought into court, or otherwise disposed of, as it may deem most for the benefit of all concerned.

Rule 23. All libels in instance causes, civil or maritime, shall state the nature of the cause, as, for example, that it is a cause, civil and maritime, of contract or of tort or damage, or of salvage, or of possession, or otherwise, as the case may be; and if the libel be *in rem*, that the property is within the district; and, if *in personam*, the names and occupations and places of residence of the parties. The libel shall also propound and articulate in distinct articles the various allegations of fact upon which the libellant relies in support of his suit, so that the defendant may be enabled to answer distinctly and separately the several matters contained in each article; and it shall conclude with a prayer of due process to enforce his rights, *in rem* or *in personam* (as the case may require), and for such relief and redress as the court is competent to give in the premises. And the libellant may further require the defendant to answer on oath all interrogatories propounded by him touching all and singular the allegations in the libel at the close or conclusion thereof.

Rule 26. In suits *in rem*, the party claiming the property shall verify his claim on oath or solemn affirmation, stating that the claimant by whom or on whose behalf the claim is made is the true and *bona fide* owner and that no other person is the owner thereof. And where the claim is put in by an agent or consignee, he shall also make oath that he is duly authorized thereto by the owner; or if the property be, at the time of the arrest, in the possession of the master of a ship, that he is the lawful bailee thereof for the owner. And, upon putting in such claim, the claimant shall file a stipulation, with sureties, in such sum as the court shall direct, for the payment of all costs and expenses which shall be awarded against him by the final decree of the court, or, upon an appeal, by the appellate court.

Rule 27. In all libels in causes of civil and maritime jurisdiction, whether *in rem* or *in personam*, the answer of the defendant to the allegations in the libel shall be on oath or solemn affirmation, and the answer shall be full and explicit and distinct to each separate article and separate allegation in the libel, in the same order as numbered in the libel, and shall also answer in like manner each interrogatory propounded at the close of the libel.

Rule 28. The libellant may except to the sufficiency, or fulness, or distinctness, or relevancy of the answer to the articles and interrogatories in the libel; and if the court shall adjudge the same exceptions, or any of them, to be good and valid, the court shall order the defendant forthwith, within such time as the court shall direct, to answer the same, and may further order the defendant to pay such costs as the court shall adjudge reasonable.

Rule 29. If the defendant shall omit or refuse to make due answer to the libel upon the return-day of the process, or other day assigned by the court, the court shall pronounce him to be in contumacy and default; and thereupon the libel shall be adjudged to be taken *pro confesso* against him, and the court shall proceed to hear the case ex parte, and adjudge therein as to law and justice shall appertain. But the court may, in its discretion, set aside the default and, upon the application of the defendant, admit him to make answer to the libel, at any time before the final hearing and decree, upon his payment of all the costs of the suit up to the time of granting leave therefor.

Rule 30. In all cases where the defendant answers, but does not answer fully and explicitly and distinctly to all the matters in any article of the libel, and exception is taken thereto by the libellant, and the exception is allowed, the court may, by attachment, compel the defendant to make further answer thereto, or may direct the matter of the exception to be taken *pro confesso* against the defendant, to the full purport and effect of the article to which it purports to answer and as if no answer had been put in thereto.

Rule 31. The defendant may object, by his answer, to answer any allegation or interrogatory contained in the libel, which will expose him to any prosecution or punishment for a crime, or for any penalty or any forfeiture of his property for any penal offense.

Rule 32. The defendant shall have a right to require the personal answer of the libellant upon oath or solemn affirmation to any interrogatories which he may, at the close of his answer, propound to the libellant touching any matters charged in the libel, or touching any matter of defense set up in the answer, subject to the like exception as to matters which shall expose the libellant to any prosecution, or punishment, or forfeiture, as is provided in the thirty-first rule. In default of due answer by the libellant to such interrogatories, the court may adjudge the libellant to be in default, and dismiss the libel, or may compel his answer in the premises by attachment, or take the subject matter of the interrogatory *pro confesso* in favor of the defendant, as the court, in its discretion, shall deem most fit to promote public justice.

Rule 33. Where either the libellant or the defendant is out of the country, or unable, from sickness or other casualty, to make an answer to any interrogatory on oath or solemn affirmation at the proper time, the court may, in its discretion, in furtherance of the due administration of justice, dispense therewith, or may award a commission to take the answer of the defendant when and as soon as it may be practicable.

Rule 34. If any third person shall intervene in any cause of admiralty and maritime jurisdiction *in rem* for his own interest, and he is entitled, according to the cause of admiralty proceedings, to be heard for his own interest therein, he shall propound the matter in suitable allegations, to which, if admitted by the court, the other party or parties in the suit may be required, by order of the court, to make due answer ; and such further proceedings shall be had and decree rendered by the court therein as to law and justice shall appertain. But every such intervenor shall be required, upon filing his allegations, to give a stipulation, with sureties, to abide by the final decree rendered in the cause, and to pay all such costs and expenses and damages as shall be awarded by the court upon the final decree, whether it is rendered in the original or appellate court.

Rule 39. If, in any admiralty suit, the libellant shall not appear and prosecute his suit, according to the course and orders of the court, he shall be deemed in default and contumacy ; and the court may, upon the application of the defendant, pronounce the suit to be deserted, and the same may be dismissed with costs.

Rule 40. The court may, in its discretion, upon the motion of the defendant and the payment of costs, rescind the decree in any suit in which, on account of his contumacy and default, the matter of the libel shall have been decreed against him, and grant a rehearing thereof at any time within ten days after the decree has been entered, the defendant submitting to such further orders and terms in the premises as the court may direct.

Rule 51. When the defendant, in his answer, alleges new facts, these shall be considered as denied by the libellant, and no replication, general or special, shall be allowed. But within such time after the answer is filed as shall be fixed by the District Court, either by general rule or by special order, the libellant may amend his libel so as to confess and avoid, or explain, or add to, the new matters set forth in the answer ; and within such time as may be fixed, in like manner, the defendant shall answer such amendments.

§ 138. From these rules it will be observed that sales may be ordered of the property attached as perishable. The defendant should appear and file a full answer. The plaintiff files no replication. Under the Pennsylvania Act, questions of fact must be tried by a jury and the suit proceeds as to motions for a new trial, Bill of Exceptions, etc., as in other cases. The matters of decrees by default, of exceptions to answers for insufficiency, release of the vessel, and other points, are fully explained in the rules quoted.

The Pennsylvania statute gives the form of the final process. (Act June 13, 1836, section 15.) If the proceeds of sale are not sufficient to pay all liens, distribution is made *pro rata* among all claims filed previously to the decree of sale.

§ 139. In *Shakspear* v. *The Maggie Cain*, 3 W. N., 167 (1876) the vessel had been released from the attachment after the giving of the bond (above referred to), under section 11 of the Act. The libellant obtained a verdict upon which the court entered judgment that he should recover of the said respondents and of Scull, who had intervened as part owner, and his sureties. After affirmance of his judgment, the plaintiff levied a *fi. fa.* upon the personal property of Scull, including the vessel, which had returned to port. A rule was taken to set aside the judgment and execution, upon the ground that the bond filed was substituted for the vessel, and that plaintiff should have proceeded by suit on the bond, and not by *fi. fa.* against the property of Scull. The court (PEIRCE, J.) decided that whilst an action on the bond could have been maintained, and would, perhaps, have been the better mode, yet the judgment and execution were regular.

In the case of *Cain* v. *Shakspear*, 3 W. N., 514 (1877), it was held that "the filing of the bond was an absolute release of the vessel." (Opinion by BIDDLE, J.) This judgment was affirmed by the Supreme Court. *Shakspear* v. *Cain*, 5 W. N., 392 (1878).

This would seem to set that question at rest, and the principle is fully sustained by the authorities cited by Messrs. C. M. Husbands and Henry Flanders, 3 W. N., 515.

§ 140. **The Act of April 20, 1858** (P. L., 363), introduces special provisions as to steamboats and vessels navigating the rivers Allegheny, Monongahela, and Ohio in this State. It declares that such vessels shall be subject to a lien :

I. For wages to employés on board.

II. For all debts contracted by the owner, agent, consignee, master, clerk of such vessels for and on account of work done or materials furnished by boat-builders, engine-builders, boilermakers, lumbermen, boat, store, and provision furnishers, carpenters, blacksmiths, mastmakers, blockmakers, ropemakers, sailmakers, chairmakers, furnituremakers, and venders, riggers, joiners, carvers, plumbers, painters, upholsterers, ship-chandlers, coppersmiths, brass-founders, coopers, and venders of sail-cloth and canvas in the building, repairing, fitting, furnishing, or equipping such ships, steam or other boats or vessels of whatsoever kind, character, or description as hereinbefore specified and enumerated.

III. For all bills, bonds, notes, bills of exchange, or all or any other acknowledgment or obligation of indebtedness for and on account of such ships, steam or other boats or vessels as hereinbefore specified and enumerated, signed and given, or purporting to be signed and given, in the name or for or on account of such ships, steam or other boats or vessels, and owned by any owner or owners, agent, consignee, master, clerk, or clerks of the same, to any of the classes above enumerated, whether the same be signed and given on account of work or labor done, or materials furnished in the building, repairing, fitting, furnishing, equipping, or insuring such ships, steam or other boats or vessels as hereinbefore specified and enumerated : Provided, That the lien of the same shall continue in favor and to the benefit of all and every party or parties whomsoever, into whose hands the same may have passed by transfer, assignment, or otherwise.

IV. For all sums due for wharfage or anchorage of any such ships, steam or other boats or vessels of whatsoever kind, character, or description as hereinbefore specified and enumerated.

V. For all demands or damages accruing from the non-performance or mal-performance of any contract of affreightment, or of any other contract entered into by the owner or owners, agent, consignee, clerk, or clerks of any such ships, steam or other boats or vessels as hereinbefore specified and enumerated, touching the transportation of person or property, or for all damages or for injuries done to the same, in any way or manner by such ships, steam or other boats or vessels as hereinbefore specified and enumerated.

§ 141. The Act gives these claims priority in the order above enumerated ; the liens to have precedence of all other claims, provided that no priority shall obtain between the parties specified in the second class other than as the same shall exist by operation of law.

§ 142. The lien for wages is limited to three months' wages. Suit must be brought within sixty days after the wages shall have become due. The suits for claims other than the first class must be commenced within two years after the last item, or the vessel is discharged. The taking of a note or other writing in settlement does not invalidate the lien, provided the time for which the same be given be within the time allowed for the lien.

The proceedings under this Act (of 1858) are the same as prescribed by the Act of June 13, 1836, already sketched.

§ 143. Attachment against convicts. The seventy-eighth section of the Act of June 13, 1836 (P. L., 568), provides for a writ of attachment against convicts. It is in these words :

A writ of attachment, in the form aforesaid, may be issued against a person under sentence of imprisonment, upon conviction of a crime by a court of competent jurisdiction, and such attachment may be dissolved in the manner hereinbefore provided in the case of a foreign corporation, and not otherwise ; but if, in such case, the term of imprisonment of the defendant shall elapse, or if he shall be otherwise legally discharged therefrom before the money shall be paid, it shall be lawful for him to put in and perfect special bail to the plaintiff's action, and thereupon the security which may have been given by him in lieu of bail shall cease and become void, and any deposit which may have been made as aforesaid shall be restored to him.

§ 144. The " form aforesaid " referred to in this section is the form of foreign attachment already given under that head. It is, therefore, unnecessary to do more here than to refer to the practice under that writ as modified by this section of the law.

CHAPTER V.

§ 145. **Special Proceedings.** All that has been written as to *assumpsits* applies to actions on ground-rent deeds, but the peculiarity of some of the proceedings under this head would seem to require notice.

If covenantor solvent. Where the covenantor is alive and it is expected that an execution against his personalty will be sufficient, the proceedings already sketched will suffice. The same remark applies if the present owner have personal property and the claim be for rent accrued during his ownership.

§ 146. *If covenantor dead.* In most cases it happens that the original covenantor is dead, the present owner of the land may be unknown, or the object may be to pass a title. If for these or other reasons a sale of the premises liable to the rent is contemplated, the proceedings in ordinary *assumpsit* would not apply.

§ 147. *Action of covenant abolished only as to name.* The Act of May 25, 1887 (P. L., 271), expressly declares "That so far as relates to procedure * * * all demands heretofore recoverable in debt, assumpsit, *or covenant* shall hereafter be sued for and recovered in one form of action, to be called an action of *assumpsit."* The summons must not, therefore, be, as heretofore, in covenant, but in *assumpsit.* This does not repeal the various Acts regulating proceedings on ground-rent deeds : April 8, 1840 (P. L., 240), April 25, 1850 (P. L., 571), April 8, 1857 (P. L., 175), etc. The concluding section of the Act of 1887 declares "that as to the action herein recited, it applies to the procedure only, and the legal rights of the party are not in any way to be affected thereby." Assuming then that the old remedies remain under a changed name, we may consider the practical method of collecting arrears of ground-rent.

§ 148. *Ejectment will not lie,* except "where a right of re-entry is expressly reserved by the parties ; and clauses to this effect are common." SERGEANT, J., in *Kenege* v. *Elliott,* 9 Watts, 262 (1840). In *Keating* v. *Williams,* 5 Watts, 382 (1836), a right to re-enter was set up ; but it was under a clause which simply authorized the landlord to hold the property until the arrears were paid by rents he might receive. His claim to continue in possession was disallowed because " the entry was not to revest the fee, he was only to hold until paid his arrears, and then he was to tender the possession and an account. He had tendered no account. There was no proof that two years' rent were in arrear when he entered :" opinion of HUSTON, J. (p. 385).

From these citations we may conclude that ejectment, even in cases where the deed authorized re-entry, would not be a favorite remedy. I never knew it resorted to but once, and then the plaintiff was defeated because he proved no demand upon the day the rent fell due. You will observe the terms of the deed. If there be no clause of re-entry, that ends this question. If you have the power desired, then you will probably decide not to enforce it. Should you, however, conclude to re-enter, observe the following directions : Prepare a formal demand in writing for payment of the exact rent. Let your client go to the premises on the day the rent is due with the deed and two witnesses. He must demand payment. If not paid, he reads the clause of re-entry and declares that under it he takes possession. He must be careful to do all this before sunset. It has been recommended to repeat the demand and the reading three times, and if the lot be vacant, the ringing of a bell when the demand is made has been also suggested. After all this, a record of the transaction must be made and formally witnessed. Nothing is to be gained by this trouble, for a sheriff's sale has many advantages.

§ 149. *Distress will lie* for ground-rent in arrears. "A ground-rent reserved upon a conveyance in fee is, in Pennsylvania, a rent service, and to all rent services the right of distress is incident of common right. The assignee of such right has the same right of distress, there being no reversion in the assignor capable of being retained by him so as to affect the right of distress by the assignee." SERGEANT, J., *Kenege* v. *Elliott*, 9 Watts, 262 (1840). The same principle was affirmed in *Wallace* v. *Harmstead*, 44 Pa. St., 492 (1863). In this case Mrs. Wallace lost hope of recovering, as her claim was defeated by an alteration made in the original ground-rent deeds before her purchase of the ground-rents. It is to be regretted that the able argument in that case of E. Spencer Miller, Esq., was not reported. In the learned opinion of Mr. Justice WOODWARD, we find a treatise upon the subject of ground-rents and feudal and allodial tenures.

The following form may be used for the warrant of distress :

Philadelphia,   18—

Mr. (here state name of the debtor.)

    To (name of the owner of the ground-rent), Dr.

(Date.) To six months' ground-rent due on the premises (short description), $.

(Date.) To six months' ground-rent due on the premises (short description), $. (Give date for each installment.)

   To   , Constable.   Whereas (name of the debtor) is now indebted to me in the above sum for ground-rent due on the premises situate   , you are hereby authorized and empowered to collect the above bill of ground-rent, by distraining the goods and chattels of the said (debtor), or of any person or persons lying and being upon said premises, according to the Act of Assembly in such case made and provided; and to proceed to sell the same according to law, for the best price that can be obtained for the same, returning the overplus, if any, to the said (debtor), after paying the said rent and all legal costs and charges for such distress. Witness my hand and seal this   day of   one thousand eight hundred and

          (Signature of ground-rent landlord.)   [L. S.]

Under this warrant the officer makes his distress by going to the premises and demanding the rent; and, if not paid, he makes beneath his warrant the following entry:

By virtue of the above warrant, I do levy on the following goods, being on the above-described premises, to wit: Together with all and singular the goods and chattels on the premises sufficient to pay the rent and costs.   , Constable. City of Philadelphia, 18—

The officer then fills up a blank like the following, and leaves it on the premises, if possible, with the debtor:

        versus   . By virtue of a Landlord's warrant to me directed and dated   day of   18 , for the sum of   dollars, I do hereby levy on the following goods, being on the premises therein described.   Debt, $ Costs, $

   To wit: . Together with all and singular the goods and chattels on the premises sufficient to pay the rent and costs.

                               Constable.

To

    Take notice that by authority and on behalf of your ground-rent landlord,   I have this day distrained the several goods and chattels specified in the above schedule, on the premises situate No.   Street, in the City of Philadelphia, for the sum of   dollars, ground-rent due to him as aforesaid, and that if you do not pay the said ground-rent or replevy the same goods and chattels according to law, within five days hereafter, I shall, after the expiration of said five days from the date hereof, cause the said goods and chattels to be appraised and sold according to the Act of Assembly in such cases made and provided. Given under my hand the   day of   18 .

Constable of   Ward of said city.

   Office hours,   Office,

§ 150. *Exemption.* The Act of April 9, 1849 (P. L., 533), exempts from distress goods of the debtor to the value of three hundred dollars, wearing apparel of himself and family, and all Bibles and school-books in use. Besides these, are also exempted sewing-machines in use and not kept for hire or sale (Act March 4, 1870, P. L., 35), pianos, melodeons, and organs rented to the tenant, of which the landlord has received notice (Act May 13, 1876, P. L., 171), goods of a deceased tenant, *Mickle's Admr.* v. *Miles,* 1 Grant, 350 (1856), things in the custody of the law, *Pierce* v. *Scott,* 4 W. & S., 344 (1842), and things left with the debtor in the way of trade, such as the goods of a boarder at a boarding-house, *Karnes* v. *McKinney,* 74 Pa. St., 396 (1873). The goods of a stranger in the possession of the tenant not necessary for the latter's business are not exempt. *Page* v. *Middleton,* 118 Pa. St., 546 (1888); see also Chapter XLIV.

Ground-rent deeds generally waive the exemption. But care should be taken to observe the exemption unless so waived. If not waived, the debtor has the right, under the second section of the Act cited, to request the officer to " summon three disinterested and competent persons, who shall be sworn or affirmed to appraise the property which the said debtor may elect to retain   *   *   * and property thus chosen and appraised to the value of $300 shall be exempt."

§ 151. **Proceedings upon distress.** The old Act of March 21, 1772, section 1 (1 Smith, 370), regulates proceedings upon distress. It is in these words :

" When any goods or chattels shall be distrained for any rent reserved and due, upon any demise, lease, or contract whatsoever, and the tenant or owner of the goods so distrained shall not, within five days next after such distress taken, and notice thereof, with the cause of such taking, left at the mansion house or other most notorious place on the premises charged with the rent distrained for, replevy the same with sufficient security to be given to the sheriff, according to law ; then and in such case, after such distress and notice as aforesaid, and expiration of the said five days, the person distraining shall and may, with the sheriff, under-sheriff, or any constable in the city or county where such distress shall be taken (who are hereby required to be aiding and assisting therein), cause the goods and chattels so distrained, to be appraised by two reputable freeholders, who shall have and receive for their trouble the sum of two shillings per diem each, and shall first take the following oath or affirmation : *I, A. B., will well and truly, according to the best of my understanding, appraise the goods and chattels of C D, distrained on for rent by E. F.;* which oath or affirmation such sheriff, under-sheriff, or constable are hereby empowered and required to administer ; and after such appraisement shall or may, after six days' public notice, lawfully sell the goods and chattels so distrained, for the best price that can be gotten for the same, for and toward satisfaction of the rent for which the said goods and chattels shall be distrained, and of the charges of such distress, appraisement, and sale, leaving the overplus, if any, in the hands of the said sheriff, under-sheriff, or constable, for the owner's use."

This Act points out a very simple course. It will be noted that the aid of an officer is required in the appraisement. For this reason the distress may as well be by a constable, although the landlord or his agent can seize the goods. If no replevin be issued, the distress proceeds through appraisement and advertisement to sale, which is, of course, the conclusion of this remedy.

To render a distress complete, a seizure of the property distrained must be made, or the landlord must give notice of his claim for rent, and declare that certain goods, naming them, shall not be removed. *Furbush* v. *Chappell*, 105 Pa. St., 187 (1884).

A party may abandon a distress for arrears of rent and bring covenant. *Howell* v. *Bateson*, 9 W. N., 463 (1881).

He who sets up a claim to goods through sale on distress must prove affirmatively that all the statutory requirements of such sale have been complied with. *Murphy* v. *Chase*, 103 Pa. St., 260 (1883).

While the Act of 1772 requires six days' public notice of sale of goods distrained, yet, if good reason be offered for a reasonable adjournment or postponement, the statutory provision is not transgressed. *Holland* v. *Townsend*, 48 Leg. Int., 6 (1890).

Under the Act of 1772, notice of distress is valid if served the day the distress is made. *Whitton* v. *Milligan*, 32 W. N., 31 (1893).

Under the Act of 1772, the appraisement and notice of sale may be made on the same day. *Id.*

§ 152. *Replevin by tenant.* The tenant may replevy the goods distrained. As this may be regarded as a defense, the proceedings in that direction might be reserved to the portion of this work which treats of Defenses. The tenant, however, being at the outset a plaintiff, it may best preserve the continuity of the subject to introduce here the proceeding by replevin.

The writ of replevin is frequently used to test the title to personal property. It may also be invoked by a tenant against an unjust distress. The form of the *præcipe* is different when a tenant is the plaintiff. It may be worded thus :

A. B.
   v.
C. D. (landlord) and E. F. (constable).
To the Prothonotary of the Court of Common Pleas of   County.
   SIR : Issue replevin for the following :
   (here describe the gooods distrained on).

                         Value of goods $.
       "   Amount of rent claimed $.

Returnable *sec. leg.*

                               G. H.,
                        Plaintiff's Attorney.
                            (Date.)

The form of the writ is worthy of notice.
It reads :

County of Philadelphia, *ss.*
   The Commonwealth of Pennsylvania,
            To the Sheriff of the County of Philadelphia, Greeting.
   If   , plaintiff, make you secure of prosecuting
claim with effect against   , defendant, then WE COMMAND
YOU, that you cause the following-described goods and chattels, to wit :
                         to be replevied and delivered
to the said plaintiff and that you put the said defendant by sureties and
safe pledges, so that   be and appear before our judges, at Philadelphia, at our Court of Common Pleas, No.   , of the County of Philadelphia, there to be held the first Monday of   next, to answer the
said plaintiff of a plea, wherefore the said defendant took the goods and
chattels aforesaid, the property of the said plaintiff, and the same unjustly
detain   against sureties and safe pledges, etc. And have you then
there this writ.
   Witness the Honorable   , President Judge of our said Court,
at Philadelphia, the   day of   , in the year of
our Lord one thousand eight hundred and eighty-

                               Prothonotary.

§ 153. Replevin bond required. It will be noted that the writ
commands the replevying of the goods *if the plaintiff make the
sheriff "secure of prosecuting the claim with effect."* The propriety
of this is obvious, for if a plaintiff could grasp goods under a replevin by simply purchasing a writ, men would soon be spoiled of
their movable property.

Hence the Act of March 21, 1772, section 11, requires a bond
from the plaintiff, and " one responsible person as surety in double
the value of the goods distrained," etc. As the sheriff was ultimately
responsible for the sufficiency of this bond, his liability was invoked
as the excuse for heavy fees. The law was in part altered, so far
as Allegheny County is concerned, by the Act of May 19, 1871
(P. L., 986), which provided that in Allegheny County the sureties

may be justified before the prothonotary, and the sheriff thereby relieved from responsibility. The Act of April 10, 1873 (P. L., 776), contains a like provision for Philadelphia, except that the justification must be before a judge. Both these Acts direct that the justification shall be certified by the prothonotary to the sheriff, and the bond " shall become the property of the successful party in the suit without recourse to the sheriff who may have executed said process or received said bond as indemnity." Notwithstanding these Acts and the Interpleader Statute, the fees are constantly overcharged in the sheriff's office, and the members of the bar should unite to apply the remedy to a mischief which discourages honest litigation and emboldens extortion.

Justification of surety. The rules of court in Philadelphia direct that where a surety is required to be approved by a judge or the prothonotary, the party presenting such surety shall, forty-eight hours before the application, give notice in writing to the opposite party, stating the name of the proposed surety, his residence, occupation, and the property he owns. He shall present to the judge or prothonotary an affidavit signed and sworn to by the surety upon a blank to be furnished by the prothonotary in the following form :

> *v.* Court of Common Pleas No.
> Term, 18 . No. . Surety for . Amount $.
> being about to become surety in the above-entitled case, and being duly
> according to law, deposes and says. 1st. I reside at ,
> and my occupation is . 2d. I am the owner of real estate in
> the County of Philadelphia, as follows : 3d. The value
> of the said real estate is , and the rent . It is assessed for
> the purpose of taxation at the value of , and is so assessed in my
> name. 4th. There are incumbrances against the said real estate,
> as follows : , and there is no other judgment binding the said
> land, or mortgage, ground-rent, or other incumbrance of any kind, except
> those above named. 5th. The title to the said real estate is in my own
> name, and the same is not subject to any trust. 6th. I obtained the said
> real estate in by from , and my deed therefor is
> recorded. 7th. There are judgments against me. 8th. I am not
> surety in any other case, or for any public officer. (Signature of surety.)
> Subscribed and before me, , 188 , ,
> Prothonotary.
> Notice of application for approval of this surety was given to the
> by writing on the day of , 188 . , Attorney for .
> The above-named deponent is approved as surety in the above case.
> , Judge.

If the tenant should insert in the *præcipe* a value below the real value of the goods, the landlord should at once notify the sheriff not to execute the writ and give the sheriff an affidavit of the facts ; if need be, the landlord should present an affidavit to the court and ask for an order that the plaintiff give bond as required by the statute " in double the value of the goods distrained." ·

§ 154. Form of replevin bond—suit on bond. It may be well to note the conditions of a replevin bond. You may have to explain its provisions to the surety. It is generally in this form :

KNOW ALL MEN BY THESE PRESENTS, That we   (sureties) are held and firmly bound unto   , Esq., Sheriff of the City and County of Philadelphia, in the just and full sum of   dollars, lawful money of Pennsylvania, to be paid to the said   , Esq., his certain attorney, executors, administrators, or assigns ; to which payment, well and truly to be made and done, we do bind ourselves and each of us, our heirs, executors, and administrators, and every of them, jointly and severally, firmly by these presents. Sealed with our seals, dated this   day of   , in the year of our Lord one thousand eight hundred and eighty-   . The condition of this obligation is such that whereas the above-bounden   (hereinafter called plaintiff) having obtained a certain writ of re-. plevin, issued out of the Court of Common Pleas, No.   , for the City and County of Philadelphia, as of   Term, 18   , No.   , tested at Philadelphia the   day of   , against a certain   (hereinafter called defendant), of the county aforesaid   , commanding the said sheriff that he should replevy and cause to be delivered to the said. plaintiff   . Now, if the above-bounden plaintiff   shall and will prosecute his suit against the said defendant   with effect, and shall and will make return of the goods, if return of the same shall be adjudged, and shall and will also, from time to time and at all times hereafter, well and sufficiently keep and save harmless and indemnify the above-named sheriff and his officers, and his or their heirs, executors, and administrators, and every of them, of and from all manner of suits, action and actions, cost and charges whatsoever that shall and may accrue to him, or them, by reason of the replevy and delivery aforesaid, that then the above obligation to be void and of none effect, otherwise to be and remain in full force and virtue. Sealed and delivered
    in the presence of us :   [L. S.]
                                                          [L. S.]
                                                          [L. S.]
                                                          [L. S.]

When the plaintiff in replevin is defeated, the defendant is entitled to an assignment of this bond in order to sue it out. *The Assignment* is generally made in this form :

For a valuable consideration I,   , sheriff, etc., the obligee within named, do hereby assign, transfer, and set over the within bond or obligation, and all benefit and advantages to be derived therefrom, to   , executors, administrators, and assigns. Witness my hand and seal this   day of   , A.D. 188 . Sealed and delivered
    in the presence of us :   [L. S.]

If the action be not prosecuted with effect, the plaintiff may sue out the replevin bond, and to support the action it is not essential that damages shall have been assessed or judgment *de retorno habendo* entered. *Bank* v. *Hall*, 107 Pa. St., 583 (1884).

If an action be brought on a replevin bond, the statement should set forth the nature and extent of plaintiff's demand with clearness and certainty. It should show the character of the judgment, and the failure of the obligor to comply with its terms. *McGary* v. *Barr*, 47 Leg. Int., 214 (1890).

§ 155. Claim property bond—form. A defendant in replevin may claim property in the chattels, and if he see fit to do so he is at liberty to give a claim property bond and keep possession of the goods. This bond is generally in the following form :

KNOW ALL MEN BY THESE PRESENTS, That we,   (sureties), hereinafter called obligors, âre held and firmly bound unto   , Esquire, Sheriff of the City and County of Philadelphia, in the just and full sum of   dollars, lawful money of Pennsylvania, to be paid to the said   , Esquire, his certain attorney, executors, administrators, or assigns ; to which payment well and truly to be made and done, we do bind ourselves and each of us, our heirs, executors, and administrators, and every of them, jointly and severally, firmly by these presents.

Sealed with our seals, dated this   day of   , in the year of our Lord one thousand eight hundred and   . The condition of this obligation is such that whereas   (hereinafter called plaintiff) having obtained a certain writ of replevin, issued out of the Court of Common Pleas, No.   , for the City and County of Philadelphia,   Term, 18   , No.   , tested at Philadelphia the   day of   , against   (hereinafter called defendant), of the county aforesaid, commanding the said sheriff that he should replevy and cause to be delivered to said plaintiff   , and whereas the said defendant has claimed property in the said goods and chattels, whereof delivery of the same cannot be made to the said plaintiff. Now, if the above bounden defendant shall and do well and truly deliver up the said goods and chattels to the said plaintiff, if the property thereof shall be adjudged in the said plaintiff, and shall and do well and truly abide by the judgment of the said court in all things relating to the premises, and if the said obligors shall also save and keep harmless and indemnify the said sheriff in the premises, then this obligation to be void and of none effect, otherwise to be and remain in full force and virtue.

Sealed and delivered
  in the presence of us :   [L. S.]
                                                    [L. S.]
                                                    [L. S.]
                                                    [L. S.]

When the defendant has final judgment against him, the plaintiff is entitled to have from the sheriff an assignment of this bond, which is made in the form above prescribed for assignment of the replevin bond to the defendant.

§ 156. Directions to sheriff—entering a replevin bond. Presuming that the tenant had obtained the writ and secured the justification of the surety, the tenant takes from the prothonotary a certificate of the justification and delivers the papers to the sheriff, with directions where to find the goods and where to serve the defendants. Then the replevin bond is signed.

Landlord not to give property bond. In cases of rent, the landlord distraining should not give a property bond, for he does not claim to be the owner of the goods. The sheriff delivers the goods to the plaintiff in replevin, and the distress is at an end.

How landlord proceeds after replevin. It then becomes the interest of the defendant (the landlord) to speed the suit. This he does by entering an appearance and by ruling the plaintiff to declare as follows :

A.
v.   } C. P. No. 1, of Philadelphia County.
B.   Term, 18 , No. .
To the Prothonotary of said Court :
SIR : Enter a rule on the plaintiff in the above case to declare in fifteen days, or judgment *sec. reg.*   C. D.,
                                      Attorney pro Defendant.
                                              (Date.)

This being filed, the plaintiff's attorney should be served with the following notice :

A.
v.   } Common Pleas, No. 1, Philadelphia County.
B.   Term, 18 , No. .
To   , Esq., Attorney pro plaintiff.
SIR : Please take notice of a rule this day entered on the plaintiff to declare in fifteen days, or judgment *sec. reg.*
                          Very respectfully yours,
                                      C. D.,
                                  Attorney for Defendant.
                                              (Date.)

Keep a copy of this and of all notices, and note the time and manner of service. Observe your rules of court as to the time for declaring, etc.

If the plaintiff should not file his *narr.* at the expiration of the fifteen days or prescribed time, write to his attorney, reminding him of the default.

§ 157. **Practice in replevin.** Should you be unable to get the *narr.*, you are at liberty, after the expiration of the time, to sign judgment, thus :

A.
v.   } Common Pleas, No. 1, of Philadelphia County.
B.   Term, 18 , No.

(Here copy the notice, as served on the plaintiff's attorney, signature and all.)   At foot, write :

having been duly sworn according to law doth depose and say that on the   day of   , A.D. 18 , he served the original notice, whereof the above is a true and correct copy, on E. F., Esq., the plaintiff's attorney, personally (or by leaving the same with an adult in charge of his office).

(Signature of the deponent.)

Sworn to and subscribed before me.
(Date.)
(Signature of Prothonotary.)

Indorse this paper,

No.   , Term   ,   Year
Name of parties.
Affidavit of service on plaintiff's attorney of notice of rule to declare and order for judgment.

Write beneath this,

To the Prothonotary of the Court of Common Pleas.
SIR : Enter judgment of *non pros.* against the plaintiff in the above case for want of a narr. *sec. reg.*

C. D.,
Defendant's Attorney.
(Date.)

Upon receipt of this affidavit and order the prothonotary, finding that no *narr.* has been filed, in obedience to the rule to declare, files your paper and enters judgment.

You then get from the prothonotary a mem. of all the costs. You are entitled to the statutory attorney fee. Note this and all the costs, with your claim and interest, and send it to plaintiff's attorney, with request to pay, and stating that if not paid you will proceed. He will probably go into court, say he was sick, or fishing, or making campaign speeches, and get the *non pros.* taken off. If he fail, and you are not paid, you can sue out the replevin bond. If he succeed, the plaintiff must file at once his *narr.*

The form of narr. is generally as follows :

In the Court of Common Pleas of the County of   ,   Term, 18 , No. .
County, *ss.*
Whereas A. B. has been attached to answer C. D. of a plea, wherefore he took the goods and chattels of the said C. D. and unjustly detained the same against gages and pledges, until, etc., and thereupon the said   by   attorney, complains that the said   heretofore, to wit, on the   day of   , in the year of our Lord one thousand eight hundred and   , at the county aforesaid, took the goods and

chattels of the said   , to wit :   of the
value of   dollars, and unjustly detained the same against gages
and pledges, until, etc. Wherefore, the said   says that he has been
injured, and has sustained damages to the value of   dollars, and
therefore he brings suit, etc.

Pledges, etc.

§ 158. Avowry—form of avowry. As landlord, it is your interest to speed the case. Prepare, therefore, with dispatch your
avowry. If your ground-rent landlord made the distress by the
agency of a bailiff, you prepare an avowry and cognizance. The
meaning and form of these papers are given in *Chitty's Pleadings*
and other works. Substantially, the bailiff acknowledges that he
took the goods described in the *narr.*, as the bailiff of the other
defendant, upon a distress for rent due to the landlord, who files in
his avowry an avowal that he distrained for rent due and in arrear.
Where the claim is for ground-rent, the original deed should be set
out by reference to its date and place of record ; trace the title to
avowant ; charge the amount due, etc. This avowry you will
perceive is a declaration, and generally should contain all the essentials of a *narr.* for rent.

The following form, generally used in the ordinary cases between
landlord and tenant, may, with the directions above given, assist you
here :

(Name of tenant) *v.* (name of your client) landlord, and (name of your
constable) Bailiff. In the Court of Common Pleas, No. , for the County
of Philadelphia, of   Term, 18 , No.   .

And the said (defendants) by A. B., their attorney, come and defend the
wrong and injury, when, etc., and the said (name of landlord) in his own
right well avows and the said (name of constable) as bailiff of the said (landlord) well acknowledges the taking of the said goods and chattels in the
declaration mentioned, in the dwelling-house in which they were contained,
at the time of the taking as aforesaid, and that they had a right to, and did
justly take the same, because they say that the said plaintiff for a long
time, to wit, for the space of one year (or as the case may be) next before
and ending on a certain day, to wit, the first day of January, A.D. 1886,
and from thence until, and at the said time when, etc., held and enjoyed
the said dwelling-house in which the said goods and chattels were contained
with the appurtenances, as tenant thereof under the said defendant (landlord) by virtue of a certain ground-rent deed dated   , recorded at the
proper office in Philadelphia, on   in   , wherein C.
conveyed to D. the premises   , reserving thereout a certain
yearly ground-rent of $, and the said D. for himself, his heirs,
executors, administrators, and assigns, covenanted to pay to said C., his
heirs and assigns, the said yearly ground-rent, and being so seised of said
premises, subject to said ground-rent, D. on the   day of
          , by deed recorded the   day of   in
the said office   conveyed said premises, subject to said

ground-rent, to E., and being so seised of said premises subject to said ground-rent, E. (here trace the title to the land subject to ground-rent down to the plaintiff in replevin). And the said C., by whom the ground-rent was originally reserved as aforesaid by deed dated   , recorded in said office on   in   conveyed said ground-rent to F. and his heirs and assigns, and said F., being so the owner of said ground-rent, by deed dated   , recorded in said office on   in conveyed said ground-rent to G., his heirs and assigns (here trace the title of the ground-rent to your client, the avowant). And because the sum of   , the ground-rent aforesaid for the space of   ending on the (here state the dates and amounts) and from thence until, and at the time when, etc., was due and in arrear from the said plaintiff said (name of landlord) the said (landlord) well avows and the said (bailiff) well acknowledges the taking of the said goods and chattels in the said dwelling-house, in which they then were, and that they justly took the same as, for, and in the name of a distress for the said ground-rent, so due and in arrear to the said defendant (landlord) as aforesaid, and which still remains due and unpaid, and this they, the said defendants, are ready to verify, wherefore they pray judgment, and a return of the said goods and chattels together with their costs and charges by them about their defense in this behalf expended according to law in such case made and provided, to be adjudged to them.

A. B.,
Attorney for Defendants.

§ 159. **Rule to plead—assessment of damages on default.** When this is filed, the avowant becomes plaintiff and actor. He should at once enter a rule on the *plaintiff to plead*, following the form above given for the rule to declare and entering judgment as already directed in case of default to file a *narr.*, changing simply "*declare*" to "plead," and "*judgment of non pros.*" to "*judgment for want of a plea.*" (See § 26.)

Notify the enemy to pay your rent, interest, and costs. Here again you can sue out the bond, or if you so prefer you can assess your damages.

Damages are assessed upon judgments by default by the prothonotary if there be anything upon the record to justify his action, as if a plaintiff have filed a copy of a note or a bond or a book account. In these proceedings upon ground-rent I see no reason why the prothonotary could not assess the damages, taking the avowry as his guide. You write an order to him:

A. *v.* B. (Court, Term. No. .)
To the Prothonotary.
    SIR : Assess the avowant's damages in the above case.

C. D.,
Avowant's Attorney.
(Date.)

The Prothonotary assesses the avowant's damages as follows:

Amount of rent due upon ground-rent deed dated,
  Recorded   as set forth in avowry . . . $
Interest . . . .

                   _____
                   $
          (The Prothonotary signs here.)

Upon this you issue *fi. fa.*, thus:

  A. }
   v. } Court, Term, and No.
  B. }
To the Prothonotary.
  SIR : Issue *fi. fa.* against the above-named plaintiff, ret. *sec. leg.*
          Real debt, $
(Here state the total of your claim and the interest included in your as-
sessment, and, as your judgment carries interest, you add),
        Interest from
      (the date of the judgment). $
             E. F.,
          Avowant's Attorney.
            (Date.)

Give the writ to the sheriff, observing directions (§ 24).

§ 160. *If the plaintiff plead to your avowry,* he will probably plead no rent in arrear, and payment. He may add *non est fac- tum.* These ought not to require a special replication. But a continuance has been granted because of a want of such a replica- tion and because, as it was technically urged, the case was not at issue.

Replication. You had better, therefore, reply,

  A. *v.* B. (Court Term. No .)
1. As to the pleas of the plaintiff, whereof said plaintiff hath put himself upon the country, the avowant doth the like.
2. To the plea of payment avowant replies *non solvit* and issue.
             E. F.,
          Avowant's Attorney.
            (Date.)

Indorse this,

A. *v.* B. (Court, Term. No. .) Replication.

You will, perhaps, observe that the plaintiff has *not* put himself upon the country. That is true so far as the letter goes. But the law, which allows lazy pleaders to file short pleas, excuses the omissions of commencements and conclusions. It is presumed that he has added to each issue-plea the words, "And of this the plaintiff puts himself upon the country." Your replication that you do the like is called a similiter, and puts the case at issue. The plea of payment, if written out at length, would conclude, " and this the said plaintiff is ready to verify."

Your replication to it means he did not pay and that you take issue.

§ 161. *If a special plea be filed*, search in *Chitty's Pleadings*, the Digest, and other works, to see how far it is exact in form, and whether you can safely demur. Do not adopt this course unless very sure of your point. The courts give a pleader every opportunity to amend his slips and blunders, and you simply lose time and labor. It is better to reply, taking issue, if possible, and following strictly the directions as to replications, lest you run into the jaws of a demurrer.

§ 162. *If a demurrer be filed*, prepare your paper-book *sur* demurrer for the court. Let it contain a brief of the pleadings down to the demurrer, a copy of the plea or replication demurred to, the reasons assigned in the demurrer, your points and citations. See generally §§ 28, 29.

Aim at clearness and singleness of point. Be sure always to sign your argument—to indorse the paper-book with names of parties —Court, Term, No. . Avowant's Paper-book *sur* Demurrer by to , and indorse your name for avowant.

§ 163. *If the case be put at issue as to facts*, order it at once on the trial-list. Watch each list as it appears. Do not let it be delayed by omission of the clerk, and when for trial notify your client promptly, and prepare thoroughly for the jury. General directions for this branch of your work will be given under the appropriate head.

If the foregoing sketch has fulfilled its object, it has instructed how to collect arrears of ground-rent by distress.

§ 164. **Collection of arrears of ground-rent by suit** was formerly by action of covenant or debt.

The Act of April 25, 1850, section 8 (P. L., 571), allows covenant, although the premises be held by deed-poll or otherwise.

The Act of April 8, 1840 (section 1, P. L., 249), makes two returns of *nihil* equivalent to a service. The Act of April 8, 1857, § 2 (P. L., 175), allows judgment to be entered in Philadelphia as in cases of suits upon mortgages in that county. The Act of May 25, 1887 (*ante*, section 61), abolishes all distinctions between actions *ex contractu* and declares that :

" All demands heretofore recoverable in debt, assumpsit, or covenant shall hereafter be sued for and recovered in one form of action to be called ' an action of assumpsit.' "

You will note that in Philadelphia a copy of the ground-rent deed and assignments need not be filed if all are recorded and you properly refer to them.

Bearing in mind all the statutes you will find compiled, *You sue out the ground-rent* claimed, by a *præcipe* in this form :

A. (your client the present owner of the ground-rent. If he be origi-
v.   nal covenantee, you stop with his name).
B. (the original covenantor).

That you may the better understand your client's rights, and the directions which are given further on, I introduce here a synopsis of a ground-rent deed. It begins in the usual form of a con-.veyance of land, and after the *habendum* the following covenants are introduced :

Yielding and paying therefor and thereout, unto the said   heirs and assigns, the yearly rent or sum of   , lawful money of the United States of America, in   yearly payments on the   day of   in every year hereafter, forever, without any deduction, defalcation, or abatement for any taxes, charges, or assessments whatsoever, to be assessed, as well on the said hereby granted lot   as on the said yearly rent hereby and thereout reserved ; the first payment thereof to be made on the   day of   one thousand eight hundred and   .
And on default of paying the said yearly rent on the day and time and in manner aforesaid, it shall and may be lawful for the said   heirs and assigns, to enter into and upon the said hereby granted premises, or any part thereof, and into the buildings thereon to be erected, and to distrain for the said yearly rent so in arrear and unpaid, without any exemption whatsoever, any law to the contrary thereof in any wise notwithstanding, and to proceed with and sell such distrained goods and effects according to the usual course of distresses for rent charges. But if sufficient distress cannot be found upon the said hereby granted premises to satisfy the said yearly rent in arrear, and the charges of levying the same, then and in such case it shall and may be lawful'for the said   heirs and assigns, into and upon the said hereby granted lot   and all improvements wholly to re-enter, and the same to have again, repossess, and enjoy, as in their first and former estate and title in the same, and as though this indenture had never been made. And the said   heirs, executors, administrators, and assigns, do   covenant, promise, and agree, to and with the said   heirs and assigns, by these presents, that he the   said heirs and assigns, shall and will well and truly pay, or cause to be paid, to the said   heirs and assigns, the aforesaid yearly rent or sum of   lawful money aforesaid on the day   and time   hereinbefore mentioned and appointed for payment thereof, without any deduction, defalcation, or abatement for any taxes, charges, or assessments whatsoever ; it being the express agreement of the said parties that the said   heirs and assigns, shall pay all taxes whatsoever that shall hereafter be laid, levied, or assessed, by virtue of any laws whatever, as well on the said hereby granted lots and buildings thereon   to be erected, as on the said yearly rent now charged thereon. Also, that he the said   heirs or assigns, shall and will within   from the date hereof,

erect and build on the said hereby granted lot to secure the said yearly rent hereby reserved. And further, the said do hereby for heirs, executors, administrators, and assigns, expressly waive, relinquish, and dispense unto the said heirs, executors, administrators, and assigns, all and every provisions and provision in the Act of Assembly of the Commonwealth of Pennsylvania, passed on the ninth day of April, A.D. 1849, entitled "An Act to exempt property to the value of three hundred dollars from levy and sale on execution and distress for rent," so far as the same may exempt the said hereby granted lot and any part thereof, and any buildings or improvements to be erected or placed thereon, from levy and sale, by virtue of any writ of execution that may be issued upon any judgment that may be obtained or entered in any action for the recovery of the rent hereby reserved, or hereby covenanted to be paid, and of any arrears thereof, and of the costs of such action and execution; also any other Act of Assembly now or hereafter to be passed, authorizing any stay of execution upon any judgment until an appraisement of the property shall be made, or upon any other condition whatsoever; so that it shall be lawful for the said heirs, executors, administrators, or assigns, to proceed, by execution, to levy upon and sell the said hereby granted lot of ground, and every part thereof, with the buildings and improvements as aforesaid, in the same manner and to the same extent and to the same effect, to all intents and purposes, as if no such Act of Assembly had been passed: provided always, nevertheless, that if the said heirs or assigns, shall and do at any time pay or cause to be paid to the said heirs or assigns, the sum of lawful money as aforesaid, and the arrearages of the said yearly rent to the time of such payment, then the same shall forever thereafter cease and be extinguished, and the covenant for payment thereof shall become void; and then he the said heirs or assigns, shall and will, at the proper costs and charges in the law of the said grantee heirs or assigns, seal and execute a sufficient release and discharge of the said yearly rent hereby reserved, to the said heirs and assigns, forever, anything hereinbefore contained to the contrary thereof notwithstanding. And the said heirs, executors, and administrators, do covenant, promise, and agree, to and with the said heirs and assigns, by these presents, that he the said heirs and assigns, paying the said yearly rent, or extinguishing the same, and taxes, and performing the covenants and agreements aforesaid, shall and may at all times hereafter forever, freely, peaceably, and quietly have, hold, and enjoy, all and singular the premises hereby granted, with the appurtenances, and receive and take the rents and profits thereof, without any molestation, interruption, or eviction of heirs, or of any other person or persons whomsoever, lawfully claiming or to claim, by, from, or under them, or any of them, or by or with their, or any of their act, means, consent, or procurement. In witness whereof, the said parties to these presents have hereunto interchangeably set their hands and seals the day and year first above written.

Sealed and delivered in the presence of us: [Seal.]
                  [Seal.]

In most cases the original parties to the ground-rent deed have long since died, and the ground-rent has come to your client by purchase through many intermediate hands.

§ 165. *If plaintiff holds the ground-rent at second or third hand,* you entitle your *præcipe* thus :

> A. (the present holder),
> Assignee of B. (the party who sold to your client),
> Assignee of C. (the party who sold to B.),
>> (and so through all the conveyances down to original covenantee).
>
> *v.*
> D. (the original covenantor).

§ 166. *If one of the links of title be through a will,* you describe that holder as " devisee of," etc. To make this perfectly clear—if you sue out the original ground-rent—your client being the party who conveyed the land subject to the ground-rent, the *præcipe* is simply in his name as plaintiff against the original covenantor. You understand that covenantor in this connection means the man who took up the land on ground-rent, and who by the original deed covenanted to pay the rent. Covenantee means the seller of the land, to whom the rent is payable. If there be other names in the chain, each must be stated.

§ 167. *If one of the links of your title be by allotment in partition,* and not by conveyance, the form of the præcipe must be varied to suit that fact. Supposing all of these complications to exist, the following may serve as your guide, adding or omitting as the case may require :

> A. (*your client, present holder of the ground-rent*),
> Assignee of B. (*the grantor of your client*), who was assignee of C. (*the grantor of* B.), who was devisee under the last will and testament of D. (*the owner of the ground-rent preceding* C.), the said D. being the person to whom the ground-rent now sued out was set apart and allotted by decree of the Orphans' Court of Philadelphia County in certain proceedings therein for the partition of the estate of E. to the term of October, A.D. 1885, No. 506, which said E. was the assignee of F. (*original covenantee*).
>
> *v.*
> G. (*original covenantor*).

To the Prothonotary of the Court of Common Pleas of Philadelphia County.

SIR : Issue summons in an action of assumpsit, returnable *sec. leg.*, for recovery of the arrears of ground-rent due by G. on the ground-rent deed between F. and the said G., dated September 1, 1880, recorded September 1, 1880, in the proper office at Philadelphia in Deed Book   , No.   , page   , wherein the said F. conveyed to the said G. the premises (description), reserving thereout the yearly ground-rent of $, payable half-yearly on the   days of   and   to him, the said F., his heirs and assigns, and the said G., in said ground-rent deed, duly covenanted to pay the said ground-rent as therein will more fully

appear. And the said F., to whom said ground-rent was thus payable, duly conveyed and assigned said ground-rent to E., his heirs and assigns, by deed dated   , duly recorded in the aforesaid office on
in Deed Book   , No.   , page   . And the said
E., being seized, *inter alia,* of said ground-rent, died on or about the
day of   , and afterward, under certain proceedings had in the
Orphans' Court of Philadelphia County to   Term   , No.   ,
the said ground-rent and all the right, title, and interest therein of said E.
was duly and legally set apart and allotted to D. on the   day of
          , and the said D. being duly and legally seized of said
ground-rent, afterward, to wit, on the   day of   , died
seized thereof, having first duly made and published his last will and testament, dated the   day of   , which was duly admitted to probate by the Register of Wills of Philadelphia County on the   day of
          , and on said last-mentioned day said will was duly recorded in
the office of said Register in Will Book   , No.   , page   ,
and by said will the said D. duly devised said ground-rent and all his estate
therein to C., and the said C., by deed dated   , and recorded in
the proper office at Philadelphia on the   day of   , in Deed
Book   , No.   , page   , duly conveyed and assigned said ground-rent to B., and the said B., by deed dated   ,
and recorded   , in the proper office at Philadelphia in Deed Book
          , No.   , page   , duly assigned and conveyed said
ground-rent to the plaintiff A., who claims herein to recover arrears of said
ground-rent as per the following

STATEMENT.

Six months' ground-rent under the ground-rent deed between F.
          and G., dated and recorded as above stated, due, $
Six months' ground-rent under the same, due, $
   (*Stating all the arrears.*)
   With interest on each arrear (*this interest you do not calculate until you get
judgment by default or verdict*).

K. L.,
Plaintiff's Attorney.
(Date.)

(Add affidavit when required.)

The statement should refer to the book and page of record and assignments of the ground-rent. *Rudderon* v. *Hodges,* 5 W. N., 567 (1878). It need not contain an abstract of the title. *Cox* v. *Williams,* 39 Leg. Int., 108 (1882).

§ 168. **Where defendant dead.** Frequently these writs are sued out against a person who died many years before. With this your client has nothing to do. He generally has no knowledge of the original covenantor, and only knows as to him from rumor. To hunt him up or follow his assignments would give you great trouble and perhaps endanger your title to be made by this proceeding. Herein you do the living owner no injustice, for, as will be presently seen, he must have full notice and has the broadest opportunity of defense.

Indorse this *præcipe :*

No. ,   Term,   Year,

A. ⎫
v. ⎬
G. ⎭

Præcipe for summons for recovery of ground-rent and plaintiff's statement (and affidavit).

K. L.,
Plaintiff's Attorney.
(Date.)

§ 169. Return to writ.   If the defendant be still the owner of the land, subject to the ground-rent, the summons can be served in the usual manner.   But if there be any trouble about finding him, or any doubt as to the ownership, give the writ to the sheriff, with instruction to return it *nihil habet.*   This means that the defendant *has nothing*—that is, has no residence where he can be served.

The sheriff having so returned the writ, you file another *præcipe :*

A. ⎫
v. ⎬
G. ⎭

To the Prothonotary of the Court of Common Pleas of Philadelphia County.

Sir :   Issue *alias* summons in *assumpsit,* returnable *sec. leg.,* said *alias* being founded on the original writ to   Term,   , No.   .

K. L.,
Plaintiff's Attorney.
(Date.)

You should observe that these writs contain all the recitals of your *præcipe.*

The Act of April 8, 1840, section 1 (P. L., 249), should be studied.   It directs that

" In all actions of covenant hereafter brought in any court of record, upon any covenant for the payment of rent on any ground-rent deed, if the sheriff or other officer, to whom any writ of summons is directed, shall make return of the same with ' nihil ' indorsed thereon, it shall and may be lawful for the plaintiff or plaintiffs to sue out an alias writ of summons, returnable in like manner as other writs of summons ; and thereupon, if the said sheriff or other officer shall make return of said alias writ with ' nihil ' indorsed thereon, the said return of two ' nihils ' shall be in all respects equivalent to actual service of the same, as is now the practice in cases of scire facias on judgments and mortgages : Provided, however, That it shall be the duty of the said sheriff, or other officer, to give notice of the said alias writ by serving a copy thereof on the tenant in possession of the premises, if any, or, if there be no such tenant, by posting a copy of the same on some conspicuous part of the premises, at least ten days previous to the return-day thereof, and also by publication in one or more newspapers, in such manner and for such time as the court, by rule or otherwise, shall direct: And provided, also, That the plaintiff or plaintiffs shall have filed within two weeks after the return-day of the first writ of summons in the office of the prothonotary of the said court a copy of the deed on which the suit is brought."

This last proviso does not apply to Philadelphia. The Act of April 8, 1857, § 2 (P. L., 175), relating to Philadelphia, provides:

In all actions hereafter brought for the recovery of ground-rents in the city and county of Philadelphia, judgment may be entered as in cases of suits upon mortgages in said city and county: Provided, That the plaintiff shall file a statement in said court, referring to the book and page of the recorder's office where the ground-rent deed upon which suit is brought is recorded, and if said ground-rent has been assigned, said plaintiff shall also file a statement, referring in like manner to where said assignment or assignments are recorded, which said recording shall be recited in the præcipe and summons, together with the names of the parties to said deed or deeds, then said plaintiff shall be entitled to judgment without filing copies or a declaration, as in cases of action upon mortgages.

If the defendant is deceased, the proper return is *mortuus est*, not *nihil habet*. *Burr* v. *Dougherty*, 8 W. N., 175 (1880). Judgment in covenant *sur* ground-rent deed taken on two returns of "*nihil*" where covenantor dead. *Bunting's Estate*, 16 W. N., 335 (1885).

§ 170. **Widow and heirs not necessary parties.** It will be observed that the word "covenant" has been used in the previous section. The action is now *assumpsit*. This does not affect the operation of the Act of April 8, 1840, for by the Act of 1887 *assumpsit* is simply substituted for covenant. The vital provisions of the Act of 1840 remain. The proviso requiring the officer to serve the tenant in possession of the premises, if any, and, if there be no tenant, by posting and by publication, secures the rights of the owner of the land. In *Rushton* v. *Lippincott*, 21 W. N., 97 (1888), the Supreme Court decided that the widow and heirs need not be made defendants. Let the sheriff give notice to all you believe have any interest, and state the fact in his return. Omit executors and administrators, for generally personal representatives have no interest in the land. See that the return is in conformity with the Act of April 8, 1840, and the rules of your court.

The case of *Hospital* v. *White*, 2 T. & H. Pr., 32, is cited as requiring a declaration. But the statement you have filed with your *præcipe* is the declaration and all that is necessary.

§ 171. **If no appearance entered and the defendant has been served, you may take judgment for want of an appearance four** days after the return-day if he has been served ten days before return-day ; or if served less than ten days, then the defendant has fourteen full days after return-day to enter an appearance.

In case of two returns of "*nihil*" the defendant has fourteen days after the return-day of the alias writ to enter an appearance, and in default thereof you may take judgment on the fifteenth day.

Under the ruling in *Miner* v. *Graham*, 24 Pa. St., 491 (1855), you are not entitled to take judgment for want of an affidavit of defense under two returns of "*nihil*." Move the prothonotary to enter judgment where so permitted by the rules of court. (See section 18.) Where no rule permits you to move the prothonotary, you should move the court for judgment in the following form :

A. } No.   ,   Term, 18 .
 v. }
B. } Common Pleas, No. 1, of Philadelphia County.

And now,   (date)
On motion of C. D., pro plaintiff, the court enters judgment against the defendant in the above case for want of an appearance *sec. leg.*
The prothonotary to assess the plaintiff's damages.

Indorse the court, term, and number of the case, the title of the suit, and judgment for want of appearance.

You take the docket before the court; the judgment is allowed. You file the paper with the prothonotary, and give him the following order and assessment :

A. }
 v. } No.   ,   Term, 18 .
B. } Common Pleas, No. 1, of Philadelphia County.
SIR :
Assess the plaintiff's damages in the above case *sec. reg.*

                              }   C. D.,
To Prothonotary C. P.   }   Plaintiff's Attorney.
                              }   (Date.)
The prothonotary assesses the plaintiff's damages in the above case as follows :
          (here insert your items and interest to date of assessment).
The plaintiff's damages are assessed at the sum of $.
                              (Signature of Prothonotary.)
                                      (Date.)

This paper you indorse :

A. }
 v. } C. P.   Term, 18 . No. .
B. }
Order for and assessment of plaintiff's damages at $.

The above *forms* apply to all judgments for want of an appearance, and to all assessments, whether the claim be on note, account, ground-rent, or other *assumpsit* or covenant.

The assessment of damages is followed by a *prœcipe* for a *fi. fa.* See the form of this and directions, sections 23, 24, 25.

If appearance be entered and no affidavit of defense be filed, you enter judgment at the proper time for want of an affidavit of defense. (See sections 23, 24.)

If an insufficient affidavit be filed, proceed as indicated in sections 27, 28, 29.

If you cannot obtain judgment by default, as above, enter rule on defendant to plead in the form given at section 88. Serve notice of it. If no plea filed, write for it. If necessary, take judgment, section 26.

If defendant plead, you reply, see section 160.

When case at issue, prepare for trial thoroughly, notify client when case is on list, etc.

When judgment obtained, issue *fi. fa.,* as already indicated, section 159.

§ 172. *Proceedings under fi. fa.* In proceedings for recovery of ground-rent, you generally do not expect to levy upon personal property. If you desire to sell the land, give to the sheriff, with the writ, a copy of the description of the premises taken from the ground-rent deed. If the road has been changed to a street, or the ward or township altered in name, you describe the property according to the then existing facts. At the end of the description you write a recital, thus :

Being the same premises which A., by deed dated⁣   and recorded in the proper office at Philadelphia, in Deed Book⁣   , No.⁣   , page   , conveyed to B., reserving thereout the yearly ground-rent of $⁣   payable to the said A., his heirs, and assigns, forever ; for arrears of which the said premises are now levied upon.

You should also, if the premises be improved, add the following :

NOTE.—On the above-described property there is erected (state the improvements) a three-story brick dwelling, with back buildings, etc., as the case may be.

The sheriff should notify the parties and proceed as directed by Act of June 16, 1836, section 43, and the other statutes in such case made and provided.

The proceedings by inquisition, condemnation, *liberari facias,* etc., are described in the chapter on "Execution.'" It is sufficient here to note that you should watch the sheriff's jury and see that the property is condemned.

§ 173. **Upon the return of the fi. fa. issue a venditioni exponas** —a writ under which the sheriff makes sale of property theretofore levied upon, sometimes though rarely personal property, generally, as here, real estate. This writ you obtain from the prothonotary by giving him the following *præcipe:*

Term, 1888. No.

A. ⎫
v. ⎬
B. ⎭

To the Prothonotary of the Court of Common Pleas, No. 1, of Philadelphia
    County.
    SIR : Issue *ven. ex.* in the above case, returnable *sec. leg.* Real debt, $
                Int. from

C. D.,
Plaintiff's Attorney.
(Date.)

The words *ven. ex.* you will recognize as the abbreviations of *venditioni exponas.* The real debt, as already explained, is the amount at which your damages were assessed. After the words " *int. from* " you write the date of your judgment. The words *sec. leg.* are the abbreviations of *secundum legem* (according to law).

The *venditioni* is to be handed to the sheriff within sufficient time to enable him to advertise, as required by law and the court rules.

Notify your client of the time and place of sale and get his instructions.

See that the advertisements note the improvements, or the sale may be set aside.

Your client should attend the sale or authorize some one to do so, and to bid, if necessary, enough to cover the debt—interest, costs, taxes, probable costs of an audit, etc.—so that your execution will certainly be paid in full.

§ 174. **Ordering fund into court.** If, by any possibility, a claim can come in ahead of you, this must be considered. Your client may desire to continue the ground-rent in force as unextinguished. If so, the purchase should be in the name of a third party ; but it is to be hoped that the property will bring sufficient to pay your arrears, etc. The right of any judgment creditor to order the fund into court is generally recognized. If an auditor be appointed, this entails delay and expense. Should such a step be attempted to your detriment, you should file your client's petition, supported by affidavit setting forth that he is the ground-rent landlord, has recovered judgment, that the property has been sold, that the fund is in court, that an audit will delay payment to your client, subject the fund to diminution for fees of the auditor, etc., wherefore your client prays for leave to take out of court the amount due, etc.

In Philadelphia, where there is no interference, the sheriff, upon production of the deed, etc., generally pays claims of this character.

§ 175. **Sheriff's sales.** You must watch for sheriff's sales of the property of your client's debtors. The newspapers containing sheriff's advertisements should be scanned. If the client be a business man, he should be warned to watch also. Sometimes a debtor cooks up a sale to trip his creditor. Sometimes it is the result of necessity. In either event, your clients should watch their debtors and their movements as far as possible. You cannot be expected to play the *rôle* of detective, but you can carefully note the sheriff's sales.

§ 176. **Discharge of the lien of arrears.** Upon this point and the other matters suggested in the foregoing sections, a portion of the opinion of the Supreme Court, per TRUNKEY, J., in *Foulke* v. *Millard*, 108 Pa. St., 235 (1885), may be of profit.

"Arrears of ground-rent, a lien on the land charged, upon a judicial sale of the land, are to be paid out of the proceeds. The owner of the ground-rent cannot elect to refuse the money and continue the lien. When the sheriff makes the sale, he is bound to appropriate the fund in discharge of the liens in the order of priority, or pay the money into court. *Mather* v. *McMichael*, 13 Pa. St., 301.

"A private sale of the land will not divest liens, and the owner of the ground-rent in some circumstances may prosecute proceedings for collection without actual notice to the subsequent grantee. The latter purchases with knowledge of the charge, and often must protect himself. *Charnley* v. *Hansbury, Ib.*, 16. A sheriff's sale divests the lien of the rent ; no lien is divested by a private sale.

"On April 22, 1880, Clayton sued Neville for the arrears and the summons was returned '*nihil habet.*' In September following an alias summons was issued, which was executed by posting and advertising, and on November 22, 1880, judgment was entered for want of an appearance. After the beginning of the suit and before the entry of judgment, the land was sold by the sheriff, who paid the proceeds into court. The lien of the arrears was divested by that sale. If a sheriff's sale of land, subject to the lien of a judgment, be made pending a *scire facias* for its revival, the lien of the judgment is discharged, and it is of no consequence to the purchaser whether judgment be subsequently entered against the defendant reviving the judgment for its full amount. So, when the land was sold by the sheriff to Millard, the lien for the arrears of ground-rent, the foundation of the action in covenant already existed, and thereafter it could not affect the purchaser. It is not a question of actual payment of the debt on which the second sheriff's sale was founded, but whether its lien was divested by the first. The title of the first purchaser is not vitiated by the decree of the court misappropriating the fund. Had the owner of the ground-rent appeared and made known his right, there would have been no such decree.

"The purchaser at the second sale was as much bound to take notice of the first, and of the then existing liens, as would be a purchaser at a second sheriff's sale upon a judgment that was a lien when the first was consummated. No rent that accrued after the sale to Millard was included in the action of covenant which was begun before. The Act of April 8, 1840, providing for the posting and advertising of the alias summons, has no application. Millard was not a terre-tenant till after the beginning of that suit, and there was no occasion for him to appear and make defense."

§ 177. Extinguishment of ground-rents. This is generally done by a deed of extinguishment, and as a general topic has no place in a book on practice. But judicial proceedings are sometimes necessary to secure an extinguishment, and these proceedings may be best considered at this point.

Whether a ground-rent can be extinguished or whether it be irredeemable is a question to be determined by the covenants in the deed reserving the ground-rent, and by the law. See *Springer* v. *Phillips*, 71 Pa. St., 60 (1872); *Quigley* v. *Trust Co.*, 3 Dist. Rep., 275 (1894); *Palairet* v. *Snyder*, 106 Pa. St., 227 (1884).

By the Act of June 24, 1885 (P. L., 161), no ground-rent can hereafter be created which postpones the time of extinguishment longer than twenty-one years or a life or lives in being; and at any time after the time fixed by the deed, which cannot exceed this limit, the ground-rent may be extinguished by payment of the principal and arrearages of rent. If there be no principal sum fixed, it is determined by capitalizing the rent reserved, at the legal rate of interest in force at the time of the reservation of the ground-rent.

Act Constitutional declaring 21 *years a bar.* The Act of April 27, 1855, section 7 (P. L., 369), provided: "That in all cases where no payment, claim, or demand shall have been made on account of or for any ground-rent, annuity, or other charge upon real estate for twenty-one years, or no declaration or acknowledgment of the existence thereof, shall have been made within that period by the owner of the premises subject to such ground-rent, annuity, or charge, a release or extinguishment thereof shall be presumed, and such ground-rent, annuity, or charge shall thereafter be irrecoverable."

This was declared constitutional in *Biddle* v. *Hooven*, 120 Pa. St., 221 (1888).

§ 178. **Judicial proceedings are necessary when the title of an extinguishable ground-rent has become vested in minors, trustees,** or other persons not competent or not authorized to extinguish the rent. The old Act of February 5, 1821 (7 Sm., 355), provides for proceeding by petition to the Supreme Court or to the Court of Common Pleas. But the Constitution of 1874 took away from the Supreme Court all such original jurisdiction (Article V., section 3), and since the establishment of the present Orphans' Court the case of minors and testamentary trustees would generally arise in the Orphans' Court.

The " Price Act " of April 18, 1853 (P. L., 503), besides many other provisions, contains all the elements of the Act of 1821, and was passed with reference to present jurisdiction. It is thus better to follow the directions of this Act in petitioning for the extinguishment of ground-rents.

§ 179. **Judicial proceedings may also be necessary when the ground-rent sought to be extinguished is subject to the lien of judgments or other claims.** This contingency is provided for only in the city and county of Philadelphia (Act of September 6, 1860, P. L., 840), and the city of Reading (Act of March 22, 1865, P. L., 571). These Acts, which are substantially the same, provide that the person desiring to pay off the ground-rent may apply by petition to the Court of Common Pleas, stating the facts, and praying to be allowed to pay the money required for the extinguishment of the ground-rent into court. The court then makes the order, and, upon the sum being paid into court, orders the person in whom is the title of the ground-rent to extinguish the same, reciting in the deed of extinguishment the court proceedings. Such extinguishment conveys a clear title to the ground-rent, free from any lien or incumbrance of the said judgment or judgments, or other incumbrances, or any of them. The fund in court is distributed through an auditor, the same as if it were the proceeds from a sheriff's sale of real estate.

CHAPTER VI.

HOW TO SUE OUT A MORTGAGE.

§ 180. **Foreclosure proceedings.** In New Jersey and other States the proceedings to foreclose a mortgage by bill in equity are cumbersome and tedious. Records must be searched and care taken to make all persons parties who have an interest.

§ 181. **Practice under Pennsylvania statute.** It must be confessed that the old Pennsylvania statute has many advantages over the bill of foreclosure.

The Act of 1705, section 6 (1 Sm., 59), provides amongst other things that " it shall be lawful at any time after the expiration of twelve months next ensuing the last day when the mortgage-money ought to be paid, or other conditions performed, to sue forth a writ or writs of *scire facias.*"

This writ must recite the substance of the mortgage you are about to collect. It is well, therefore, for this purpose, as well for the general preparation of papers, to understand the precise words of all important documents. A mortgage is commonly given as security for a bond. The bond is usually accompanied by a warrant of attorney to confess judgment.

These instruments, if drawn according to the last requirements, should be in the following form :

BOND.

KNOW ALL MEN BY THESE PRESENTS, THAT   (hereinafter called the obligor)   held and firmly bound unto   (hereinafter called the obligee), in the sum of   lawful money of the United States of America, to be paid to the said obligee   certain attorney, executors, administrators, or assigns : to which payment well and truly to be made,   do bind and oblige   heirs, executors, and administrators,   firmly by these presents. Sealed with seal   dated the   day of   , in the year of our Lord one thousand eight hundred and   . The condition of this obligation is such, that if the above-bounden obligor   heirs, executors, or administrators, or any of them, shall and do well and truly pay, or cause to be paid, unto the above-named obligee   certain attorney, executors, administrators, or assigns, the just sum of   lawful money as aforesaid,   together with interest   payable at the rate of   per cent. per annum. And shall produce to the said obligee or   executors, administrators, or assigns, on or before the day of   of each and every year, receipts for all taxes of the current year assessed upon the mortgaged premises; then the above obligation to be void, or else to be and remain in full force and virtue; provided, however, and it is hereby expressly agreed, that if at any time default shall be made in payment of interest as aforesaid   for the space of   days after any   payment thereof shall fall due,   or in production to the obligee   or   executors, administrators, or assigns, on or before the   day of   of each and every year, of receipts for taxes of the current year upon the premises mortgaged, then and in such case the whole principal debt aforesaid shall, at the option of the said obligee   executors, administrators, or assigns, become due and payable immediately, and payment of said principal debt, and all interest thereon, may be enforced and recovered at once, anything herein contained to the contrary notwithstanding. And provided further, however, and it is hereby expressly agreed, that if at any time hereafter, by reason of any default in payment, either of said principal sum,   at maturity, or of said interest, or in production of said receipts for taxes, within the time specified, a writ of *fieri facias* is properly issued upon the judgment obtained upon this obligation, or by virtue of the warrant of attorney hereto attached, or a writ of *scire facias* is properly issued upon the accompanying indenture of mortgage, an attorney's commission for collection, viz.:   per cent., shall be payable, and shall be recovered in addition to all principal, interest, besides costs of suit.

Sealed and delivered in the presence of us: [Seal.]

WARRANT ACCOMPANYING BOND.

To   , Esq., Attorney of the Court of Common Pleas, at   , in the County of   , in the State of   , or to any other attorney of the said court, or any other court there or elsewhere. Whereas,   in and by a certain obligation, bearing even date herewith, do   stand bound unto in the sum of   lawful money of the United States of America, conditioned for the payment of the just sum of   lawful money as aforesaid, together with interest payable   at the rate of per cent. per annum, and for the production to the obligee or executors, administrators, or assigns, on or before the   day of of each and every year, of receipts for all taxes of the current year assessed upon the premises described in the mortgage accompanying said obligation: Provided, however, and it is thereby expressly agreed, that if at any time default shall be made in payment of interest as aforesaid, for the space of   days after any   payment thereof shall fall due, or in production of the obligee   or   executors, administrators, or assigns, on or before the   day of   of each and every year, of receipts for taxes of the current year assessed upon the premises described in the mortgage accompanying said obligation, then and in such case the whole principal debt aforesaid,   shall, at the option of the said obligee   executors, administrators, or assigns, become due and payable immediately, and payment of said principal debt, and all interest thereon, may be enforced and recovered at once, anything therein contained to the contrary notwithstanding. And provided further, however, and it is thereby expressly agreed, that if at any time thereafter, by reason of any default in payment, either of said principal sum

at maturity, or of said interest, or in production of said receipts for taxes within the time specified, a writ of *fieri facias* is properly issued upon the judgment obtained under such obligation, or by virtue of this warrant, or a writ of *scire facias* is properly issued upon the accompanying indenture of mortgage, an attorney's commission for collection, viz.:   per cent., shall be payable, and shall be recovered in addition to all principal and interest, besides costs of suit.   These are to desire and authorize you, or any of you, to appear for   heirs, executors, or administrators, in the said court or elsewhere, in an action of assumpsit there or elsewhere brought or to be brought against   heirs, executors, or administrators, at the suit of the said obligee   executors, administrators, or assigns, on the said obligation, as of any term or time past, present, or any other subsequent term or time there or elsewhere to be held, and confess judgment thereupon, against   heirs, executors, or administrators, for the sum of   lawful money of the United States of America, debt, besides cost of suit, and an attorney's commission of   per cent. in case payment has to be enforced by process of law as aforesaid, by *non sum informatus, nihil dicit*, or otherwise, as to you shall seem meet : And for your, or any of your so doing, this shall be your sufficient warrant.   And   do hereby, for   heirs, executors, and administrators, remise, release, and forever quit claim unto the said obligee   certain attorney, executors, administrators, and assigns, all and all manner of error and errors, misprisions, misentries, defects, and imperfections whatever, in the entering of the said judgment, or any process or proceedings thereon or thereto, or anywise touching or concerning the same.   In witness whereof,   have hereunto set   hand   and seal   this   day of   , in the year of our Lord one thousand eight hundred and
Sealed and delivered in the presence of us :   [Seal.]

MORTGAGE.

THIS INDENTURE, Made the   day of   , in the year of our Lord one thousand eight hundred and   , between   of the first part and   of the other part.   Whereas, the said   in and by   obligation or writing obligatory under hand and seal duly executed, bearing even date herewith, stand bound unto the said   in the sum of   lawful money of the United States of America, conditioned for the payment of the just sum of   lawful money as aforesaid   together with interest payable   at the rate of   per cent. per annum, without any fraud or further delay ; and together with the delivery to the obligee or   assigns, on or before the   day of   of each and every year, of receipts for all taxes of the current year assessed upon the mortgaged premises.   Provided, however, and it is thereby expressly agreed, that if at any time default shall be made in the payment of interest as aforesaid, for the space of   days after any   payment thereof shall fall due, or in delivery to the obligee or   assigns, on or before the   day of   , of each and every year, of receipts for taxes of the current year upon the premises mortgaged, then and in such case the whole principal debt aforesaid shall, at the option of the said obligee,   executors, administrators, or assigns, become due and payable immediately ; and payment of said principal debt, and all interest thereon, may be enforced and recovered at once, anything therein contained to the contrary notwithstanding. And provided further, however, and it is thereby expressly agreed, that if at any time thereafter, by reason of any default in payment, either of said principal sum at maturity, or of said interest, or in delivery of said receipts for taxes, within the time specified, a writ of *fieri facias* is properly issued upon the judgment obtained upon said obligation, or by virtue of said warrant of attorney, or a writ of *scire facias* is properly issued upon this indenture of mortgage, an attorney's commission for collection, viz.:   per cent. shall be payable, and shall be recovered in addition to all principal, interest, and taxes then due, besides cost of suit, as in and by the said recited obligation and the condition thereof, relation being thereunto had may more fully and at large appear. Now this indenture witnesseth, that the said   as well for and in consideration of the aforesaid debt or principal sum of   and for the better securing the payment of the same, with interest as aforesaid, unto the said   executors, administrators, and assigns, in discharge of the said recited obligation, as for and in consideration of the further sum of one dollar unto   in hand well and truly paid by the said   at and before the sealing and delivery hereof, the receipt whereof is hereby acknowledged,   granted, bargained, sold, aliened, enfeoffed, released, and confirmed, and by these presents   grant, bargain, sell, alien, enfeoff, release, and confirm unto the said heirs and assigns (here follows description of the premises).

Together with all and singular   ways, waters, water-courses, rights, liberties, privileges, improvements, hereditaments, and appurtenances whatsoever thereunto belonging, or in any wise appertaining, and the reversions and remainders, rents, issues, and profits thereof,   . To have and to hold the said   hereditaments and premises hereby granted, or mentioned or intended so to be, with the appurtenances, unto the said   heirs and assigns, to the only proper use and behoof of the said   heirs and assigns forever. Provided always, nevertheless, that if the said   , heirs, executors, administrators, or assigns, do and shall well and truly pay, or cause to be paid, unto the said   , executors, administrators, or assigns, the aforesaid debt or principal sum of ,   , on the   day and time hereinbefore mentioned and appointed for payment of the same, together with interest as aforesaid, and shall, on or before the day of   , of each and every year, deliver to the obligee or assigns, receipts for all taxes of the current year assessed upon the mortgaged premises, without any fraud or further delay, that then, and from thenceforth, as well this present indenture, and the estate hereby granted, as the said recited obligation shall cease, determine, and become void, anything hereinbefore contained to the contrary thereof, in anywise notwithstanding. And provided, also, that it shall and may be lawful for the said   , executors, administrators, or assigns, when and as soon as the principal debt or sum hereby secured shall become due and payable as aforesaid, or in case default shall be made for the space of   days in the payment of interest on the said principal sum, after any   payment thereof shall fall due, or in case there shall be default in delivery to the obligee or   assigns, on or before the day   of each and every year, of such receipts for such taxes of the current year assessed upon the mortgaged premises, to sue out forthwith a writ or writs of *scire facias* upon this indenture of mortgage, and to proceed thereon to judgment and execution for the recovery of the whole of said principal debt and all interest, together with an attorney's commission for collection, viz.:   per cent., besides costs of suit, without further stay, any law, usage, or custom to the contrary notwithstanding. In witness whereof, the said parties to these presents have hereunto interchangeably set their hands and seals. Dated the day and year first above written.

[Seal.]

Sealed and delivered in the presence of us :

On the   day of   , Anno Domini 18   , before me,   , personally appeared the above-named   , and in due form of law acknowledged the above indenture of mortgage to be   act and deed, and desired the same might be recorded as such.
Witness my hand and seal the day and year aforesaid.   [Seal.]

The 18th section of Act of June 1, 1889 (P. L., 427), declares it to be unlawful to require the borrower " to pay the tax imposed thereon (the loan) by the 1st section " of said Act.

§ 182. *To collect by the warrant of attorney.* You can enter judgment, if you see fit, upon the warrant. This you do by taking to the prothonotary the bond and warrant. He tears off and files the warrant, handing you back the bond indorsed with the term and number, and with a memorandum that judgment has been entered. You need for this no motion, no order. Under the Philadelphia rules, if the warrant be over ten years old and less than twenty, you must present an affidavit to a judge, setting forth the due execution of the warrant ; that the money is unpaid and the debtor living. With this you move for leave to enter judgment.

If the warrant be over twenty years old, you should prepare a like affidavit on it, obtain a rule to show cause why judgment should not be entered, and serve notice on the debtor, if within the State. The warrant authorizes you to confess judgment " by *non sum informatus, nihil dicit,* or otherwise." This means that if you prefer to retain the warrant of attorney and to take the trouble of preparing a paper to file in lieu of it, you can do so. Many years ago this was the practice. But in this busy age the short cut is preferred. That you may have the form at hand in case it should be desired, the following is given :

NARR. OR STATEMENT.

In the Court of Common Pleas, No. 1, for the County of Philadelphia.
    Of March Term, 1888. No.
County of Philadelphia, *ss.*
    A. B., of the city of Philadelphia, complains of C. D., also of said city, that the said C. D. owes him the sum of $500, being the condition-money named in a certain bond, duly signed and sealed by said C. D., on the first day of January, A.D. 1887, wherein the said C. D. bound himself, his heirs,

executors, and administrators, in the sum of $1000, to be paid to A. B., upon the condition that if said C. D. paid A. B. the sum of $500, with lawful interest in one year from said date, then the said bond to be void, otherwise to remain in full force, as by the following copy of said bond will more fully appear. (Here copy the bond.) And A. B. avers that C. D. owes him upon said bond the sums set forth in the following

STATEMENT.

To wit: Condition of said bond	$500	00
Interest on ditto, due July 1, 1887	15	00
Interest on ditto, " January 1, 1888	15	00
	$530	00

E. F.,
Plaintiff's Attorney.
(Date.)

And the said C. D. comes and says I am not informed of any defense to the above-stated demand, and acknowledge that I owe the same in manner and form as above declared.
C. D.,
by E. F., his Attorney.

The *nihil dicit* seems to be more appropriate. If adopted, write at foot of statement, thus :

And the said C. D. comes and to the said statement and demand of A. B. saith nothing in bar or to the contrary thereof, and admits that he owes the sums above demanded in manner and form as above declared.
C. D.,
by E. F., his Attorney.

A *cognovit actionem* was formerly used in some cases. It is like the foregoing in substance, differing only in that it sets forth :

The said C. D. comes and acknowledges the action above stated against him, and that he owes the sums above demanded.
E. F., Attorney for C. D.

These papers should be indorsed:

No. Term. Year.
A. B. ⎫
  v.   ⎬ C. P.
C. D. ⎭
Narr. and statement *sur* bond.
Defendant's *nihil dicit* (or *cognovit*).
Judgment for plaintiff, $

§ 183. *Execution.* Bearing in mind the suggestion that it is better to enter the judgment by filing the warrant of attorney, you are now ready to issue execution. This you do by giving to the prothonotary a *præcipe* in the words set out, section 23.

If you levy on personal property, you follow the directions as to defendant's address, fee to sheriff, notice to client, the watchman, etc., section 24.

Levy on the real estate. The chances are that you will levy on the mortgaged premises. If so, copy the description of the property from the mortgage. Give the description to the sheriff with defendant's address, if known, and write on the *fi. fa.*, *Real Estate.* The sheriff serves defendant with notice of the levy, and of the meeting of the jury. They condemn the property. The sheriff so returns, and you then issue a *venditioni exponas* by giving the prothonotary the following :

PRÆCIPE FOR VEN. EX.

A. B. ⎫
   v.   ⎬   C. P.
C. D. ⎭   (Term.   Year.   No.)

SIR :

Issue *ven. ex.* returnable *sec. leg.*

Real debt, $

(Amount of judgment.)

Interest from (Date of judgment).

You do not calculate the interest.

It is left in blank as above until

sale.)

To Prothonotary C. P.   E. F.,

Plaintiff's Attorney.
(Date.)

§ 184. **Sale of Real Estate. Directions before the Sale, at the Sale, etc.** The *venditioni* commands the sheriff to sell the real estate. When you give it to the sheriff see that the improvements are correctly stated, and that there are no errors in description. If a house, etc., on the lot is not mentioned in the mortgage, add to the *venditioni* a description on separate paper, thus : *Note,* on the above-described premises there is erected (a three-story brick dwelling, etc., as the case may be). *See that the advertisements are correct,* and that your client receives notice. He should attend and bid (or authorize some one to do so for him) a sum sufficient to pay his debt, interest, costs, the taxes, and prior claims, if any. To this intent examine the searches, etc., which should accompany the mortgage. *If no searches exist,* make careful search to see if any ground-rent, mortgage, judgment, municipal or mechanic claims, or tax claims be ahead of your claim, and regulate your movements accordingly. If a prior mortgage exist which is the first lien, and as to which there is no defense, you will take the property, if you buy, subject to that mortgage. If there be a judgment ahead of your mortgage, it will have a claim upon the purchase-money in advance of your mortgage.

If you purchase at the sheriff's sale, and represent the first lien, you pay only the costs, and the sheriff, upon exhibition of your searches, etc., will take your receipt and make a special return. (See Act of April 20, 1840, sections 1, 2, 3, P. L., 411.)

If a stranger purchase, the sheriff will generally, upon showing your right, pay you and take your receipt.

If difficulty arise, you must get the sheriff to pay the money into court, and have an auditor appointed. Before him you appear and maintain your claim.

If the sheriff will not pay the fund into court, and will not return the writ, go into court after the return-day and get the following rule :

A. B.   }
   v.   (Court,   Term, 18 , No. .)
C. D.   }

And now   18 . On motion of E. F., plaintiff's attorney, the court grants a rule on the sheriff to return the writ in the above case.

When the writ is returned stating the possession of a fund, you are entitled, as of course, to the following order upon making motion for it :

A. B.   }
   v.   (Court,   Term, 18 , No. .)
C. D.   }

And now   18 . On motion of E. F., plaintiff's attorney, the court grants a rule on the sheriff to pay the money into court.

§ 185. **Proceedings on Rules on Sheriff to Return Writs and to Pay into Court. Attachment against Sheriff.** Obedience to these rules is enforced : 1. Upon serving copies of same personally, if possible ; otherwise, upon a clerk in charge of the office. Have an affidavit of service made and filed. 2. By obtaining a rule for an attachment.

A. B.   }
   v.   (Court,   Term, 18 . No. .)
C. D.   }

And now   18 . On motion of E. F., plaintiff's attorney, the court grants a rule on the sheriff to show cause why an attachment should not issue against him for non-compliance with the rule of (date) ordering said sheriff to

This requires personal service on the sheriff.

Have an affidavit of personal service ready on return of the rule. It need hardly be stated that in all cases you should keep copies of notices served, and note the time and manner of service. Affidavits of service ought to contain another copy of the notice, and beneath it an affidavit of the time and manner of service.

Be careful to keep copies of all papers filed.

§ 185 *a. Form of Auditor's Report:*

In the Court of Common Pleas, No   , for the County of
                    Term, 18 .

A. B. ⎫
  v.   ⎬ No.
C. D. ⎭

To the Honorable the Judges of the said Court:

The undersigned auditor appointed to (insert the purposes of the appointment, following the words of the certificate, for example, *to make a proper distribution of the fund arising from the sale of real estate in the above case of the above named-defendant*), as appears by the certificate hereto attached, marked " A," respectfully reports :

That having first been duly sworn to perform his duties with fidelity the auditor fixed (date) and his office   as the time and place for meeting, and caused notice thereof to be advertised according to the rule of court (and the statute, if so required), and in addition thereto gave written notice of said meeting to the counsel of record of the respective parties.

· A copy of said advertisement and of said written notice is hereto attached marked " B."

At the time and place fixed for said meeting the auditor was attended by (names of parties and counsel, stating for whom the latter appeared).

(If any subsequent meetings were held, the report should so state, giving the dates thereof and those present.)

The fund in this case arose as follows :   (here give a brief history).

The following claims were presented to the auditor :

(Here should follow a short statement of all the claims.   Those which are not contested may be briefly disposed of.   For example :   *A claim presented on behalf of E. F. for* (rent, or as the case may be), *amounting to
was not disputed, and is accordingly allowed.*   Contested claims should be separately considered and reported upon.   The contestant's evidence and the claimant's testimony should be briefly recited and the auditor's conclusions set forth, in favor of or against the claim.)

Upon the testimony submitted to the auditor he reports the following

FINDINGS OF FACT.

(These should be clearly and positively set forth.)

Upon the facts as above found the auditor reports the following

CONCLUSIONS OF LAW.

(These should be supported by any authorities pertinent to the auditor's rulings.)

(Where the fund is insufficient to pay all the claims the auditor need not report specifically as to those not entitled to participate, but may say :   *It is unnecessary to discuss the following* claims, as none of them, if fully established, would be entitled to participate in the distribution of the fund on account of its insufficiency.   They are all subsequent to those above mentioned and are none of them preferred claims, *if such be the fact.*)

The fund is therefore distributed as follows :

(Amount paid into court) . . . . $

Deduct : Prothonotary's costs (separate), cost of audit, advertising searches (separate), auditor's fee, and such costs, if any, as are to be paid before any distribution to creditors, enumerating them separately . . . .

Balance for distribution . . . . . . $

Which is awarded as follows :

To   judgt. . . . . . $

costs . . . . .

$

(And so with each claimant participating. Should there be insufficient to pay in full the last claimant entitled, the balance is awarded to him on account) . . . . . . $

$

(Where demands for feigned issues are presented they should be reported. As to Feigned Issues, see that title.)

(Where the rule of court requires notice to be sent before the filing of the report the fact should be stated. A copy of the notice with acknowledgment of its receipt should be attached. If exceptions are received, this should also be noted, and the exceptions should be reported as overruled or sustained, etc.)

All of which is respectfully submitted.

, Auditor.

§ 186. Sci. Fa. sur Mortgage. Another remedy, and that most generally adopted for the collection of a mortgage, is the writ of *scire facias* under the Act of 1705, already cited.

You will, of course, study this and the other statutes pertinent to this subject.

The Act of April 22, 1863, section 1, authorizes the assignee to sue in his own name or in the name of the mortgagee to the use of such assignee.

The former has been the practice for years.

A mortgage of real estate in two or more counties may be foreclosed in either county, and it is not necessary the real estate should be adjoining tracts. *Bldg. Assn.* v. *Russell*, 36 W. N., 260 (1895).

§ 187. Præcipe for Sci. Fa. and Averment of Default. If your client be the original mortgagee, you head the *præcipe* thus :

A. B.   }
   v.
G. H.   }

But if your client be an assignee, the form changes :

A. B., assignee of C. D.,

and if there be two assignments :

    A. B., assignee of C. D.,
        who was assignee of E. F.
        (and so on through the list back to the mortgagee),
    v.
    G. H. (This is the mortgagor.)

Supposing then that your client is second assignee, the *præcipe* will be :

    A. B., assignee of C. D.,
        who was assignee of E. F.,
    v.
    G. H.

To the Prothonotary of the Court of Common Pleas of Philadelphia County.

SIR : Issue *scire facias* returnable *sec. leg.* *Sur* mortgage by

    G. H.   ⎫ Dated (January 1, 18 .)
     to   ⎬
    E. F.   ⎭ Recorded (January 2, 18 .)

in the office for recording deeds, etc., for the County of Philadelphia in Mortgage Book , page , mortgaging the premises therein described, to secure the payment of a certain bond by G. H. to E. F., dated (January 1, 18) in the penalty of ($2000). Conditioned for the payment of ($1000) in one year from date, with lawful interest, payable half-yearly.

Which said mortgage, and the moneys thereby secured, were by the said E. F. duly assigned to C. D. by assignment dated . Recorded in said office in   book,   No. , page , on the   day of   18 .

And said mortgage, and the moneys thereby secured, were by assignment duly executed by the said C. D. on the   day of , recorded on the   day of   in the said office in   book , No. , page , duly assigned to the plaintiff A. B.

(The Averment of Default is given at § 188.)

Sometimes the mortgage contains a stipulation for the payment of installments, and that if they or the interest or taxes be not paid, the principal shall fall due, although it has not matured. In such cases add to the above præcipe the following averment of default :

And the plaintff avers that the said G. H. made default in payment of the (installment of $ due , and said default has continued for more than   *here follow the words of the mortgage ;* or said G. H. made default in payment of the interest or the taxes stipulated to be paid on the   day of   and has continued such default for the space of   days and upward after such semi-annual payment fell due, *averring as many defaults as have occurred, following the words of the mortgage, adding),* whereby the whole principal debt aforesaid has become due and payable immediately, with interest, *with an attorney's commission* for collection, to wit, five per cent., which is also hereby claimed (these last words to be omitted if the mortgage do not contain a clause allowing a commission), as per the following

STATEMENT.

Condition-money of said mortgage, $
Interest from
(date, but no amount).
Commission, $ I. K.,
              Plaintiff's Attorney.
               (Date.)

 (Add affidavit when required.)

If the *præcipe* for a *sci. fa.* refer to the record of the mortgage,
it is sufficient though it omit an averment that the debt is due.
Rhoads v. *Reed*, 8 Pa. St., 438 (1879). It would be wise for the
practitioner to avoid all such omissions.

§ 188. Frequently the mortgage is due by its original terms
without reference to penal clauses as to interest, taxes, etc. When
that is the case, your averment of default, as above, can readily be
changed to meet the precise facts, thus :

And the plaintiff avers that although the time for the payment of said
condition-moneys hath long since elapsed, yet the said G. H. hath not paid
the said principal or any part thereof, but that there are due to plaintiff
thereon the sums named in the following

STATEMENT.

Condition-money of said mortgage due $
Interest on same from
   (*fill in date, but do not here calculate the interest;*
  that is done when you get judgment).
Commissions at   per cent.   I. K.,
              Plaintiff's Attorney.
               (Date.)

 (Add affidavit when required.)

This paper you indorse :

A. B. ⎱
 v. ⎰ C. P. No.   .   Term, 18 . No. .
G. H. ⎰
Præcipe for *sci. fa. sur* mortgage and averment of default.
              I. K.,
              Plaintiff's Attorney.
               (Date.)

§ 189. Form of Sci. Fa. sur Mortgage. If the prothonotary be
busy, he may expect you to fill the *sci. fa.* Every lawyer should
know how to fill, even to write out writs, if he have no printed
blank. It is said that the great Murat always groomed his mare.
The following is believed to be a good form for a *sci. fa. sur* mortgage, containing the penal clauses as to taxes, commission, etc. No
instruction is required to enable you to fill in the blanks. The

printed words preceding and following each space are sufficient
guides :

County of Philadelphia, *ss.*   The Commonwealth of Pennsylvania to
the Sheriff of the County of Philadelphia, greeting : Whereas, in and by a
certain indenture of mortgage, made the   day of   , in
the year of our Lord one thousand eight hundred and   ' , between
           hereinafter called the mortgagor   of the one part,
and   hereinafter called the mortgagee of the other
part (recorded in the office for recording deeds, etc., for the County of
Philadelphia, in Mortgage-book   , No   , page   , etc., on
the   day of   , A.D. 18), reciting, in substance and
effect, that whereas the mortgagor   aforesaid, in and by a certain obligation or writing obligatory, under   hand and seal duly executed,
bearing even date therewith, stands bound unto the mortgagee aforesaid
in the sum of   lawful money of the United States of America,
conditioned for the payment of the just sum of   lawful money
as aforesaid, together with the interest thereon, payable   , at
the rate of   per cent. per annum, and for the production to the said
obligee   and mortgagee or   executors, administrators, or assigns,
on or before the   day of   . of each and every year, of receipts
for all taxes of the current year assessed upon the mortgaged premises :
Provided, however, and it is thereby expressly agreed, that if, at any time,
default shall be made in payment of interest, as aforesaid, for the space of
           days after any   payment thereof shall fall due, or in such
production, to the obligee   and mortgagee or   executors, administrators, or assigns, on or before the   day of   of each and every
year, of such receipts for such taxes of the current year upon the premises
described and mortgaged, then, and in such case, the whole principal debt
aforesaid shall, at the option of the said obligee   and mortgagee
executors, administrators, or assigns, become due and payable immediately ;
and payment of said principal and all interest thereon may be enforced and
recovered at once, anything contained to the contrary thereof notwithstanding : And provided further, however, and it is thereby expressly agreed,
that if at any time thereafter, by reason of any default in payment, either
of said principal sum at maturity, or of said interest, or in production of
said receipts for taxes, within the time specified, a writ of *fieri facias* is
properly issued upon the judgment obtained upon said obligation, or by
virtue of said warrant of attorney, or a writ of *scire facias* is properly issued
upon the said indenture of mortgage, an attorney's commission for collection, viz. :   per cent. shall be payable, and shall be recovered, in addition to all principal, interest then due, besides costs of suit as in and by
the said recited obligation and the condition thereof, relation being thereunto had, may more fully and at large appear.   And the said
as well for and in consideration of the aforesaid debt or principal sum of
           and for the better securing the payment of the same, with interest,
as aforesaid, unto the mortgagee aforesaid   executors, administrators, and assigns, in discharge of the said recited obligation, as for and in
consideration of the further sum of one dollar, unto   in hand well
and truly paid by the mortgagee aforesaid, at and before the sealing and
delivery thereof (the receipt whereof is thereby acknowledged), granted, bargained, sold, aliened, enfeoffed, released, and confirmed, unto the said

mortgagee aforesaid,   heirs and assigns (description)
together with the appurtenances. To have and to hold the same unto the
mortgagee aforesaid   heirs and assigns, to   and their only
proper use and behoof forever. And, in and by the said indenture, it was
provided, also, that it shall and may be lawful for the mortgagee aforesaid
executors, administrators, or assigns, when and as soon as the principal debt or sum thereby secured shall become due and payable as aforesaid, or in case default shall be made for the space of   days, in the
payment of interest on the said principal sum, after any   payment
thereof shall fall due, or in case there shall be default in the production to
the said obligee and mortgagee or   executors, administrators, or
assigns, on or before the   day of   of each and every year, of
such receipts for such taxes of the current year assessed upon the above-
described mortgaged premises, to sue out forthwith a writ or writs of *scire
facias* upon the said indenture of mortgage, and to proceed thereon to judgment and execution, for the recovery of the whole of said principal debt,
and all interest due thereon, together with an attorney's commission for
collection, viz.:   per cent., besides costs of suit, without further stay,
any law, usage, or custom, to the contrary notwithstanding. And whereas,
we have been given to understand that default has been made in the payment of said interest for more than   days after the same became due
and payable, and the delivery of receipts for taxes on the above-described
premises, at the time above described, whereby the whole principal debt
aforesaid has become due and payable, according to the terms and conditions in the said obligation and indenture contained ; and the said
mortgagee aforesaid praying that a fit remedy in this behalf may be provided, we command you that by good and lawful men of your bailiwick you
make known to the said   mortgagor aforesaid that   be and
appear before our Judges, at Philadelphia, at our Court of Common Pleas,
No.   for the County of Philadelphia, there to be held the first Monday of
next, to show if anything   know or ha to say, why the said
mortgaged premises, with the appurtenances, ought not to be taken in execution and sold, to satisfy the debt and interest aforesaid, if to   it
shall seem expedient. And have you then there the names of those by
whom you shall so make it known to   and this writ. Witness the
Honorable   , President of our said Court, at Philadelphia,
the   day of   , in the year of our Lord one thousand eight hundred and eighty

, Prothonotary.

§ 190. Form of Sci. Fa. sur Building Association Mortgage. If
you have a building association mortgage to collect, the *præcipe*,
etc., will be as above given, but the *sci. fa.* should be in the following form :

County of Philadelphia, *ss.* The Commonwealth of Pennsylvania to the
Sheriff of the County of Philadelphia, greeting : Whereas, in and by a certain indenture of mortgage, made the   day of   in the year of
our Lord one thousand eight hundred and   , between   ,
hereinafter called the mortgagor of the one part, and   , hereinafter called the mortgagee of the other part (recorded in the office for
recording deeds, etc., for the County of Philadelphia, in Mortgage-book

No.   , page   , etc., on the   day of   ,
A.D. 18   ), reciting, in substance and effect, that whereas the said mortgagor in and by a certain obligation or writing obligatory under   hand
and seal duly executed, bearing even date therewith, stands bound unto
the mortgagee aforesaid in the sum of   lawful money of the
United States of America, conditioned for the payment of the just sum of
          lawful money as aforesaid, at any time within   year from
the date thereof, together with lawful interest thereon, and together with
all the fines imposed by the constitution and by-laws of the association
mortgagee aforesaid, and a monthly premium of   payable
monthly, on the   of each and every month thereafter; and
should also well and truly pay, or cause to be paid, for the same, in like
money, unto the mortgagee aforesaid, its successors and assigns, the sum of
          on the said   of each and every month thereafter, as and for
the monthly contribution on   shares of the capital stock of the
association mortgagee aforesaid, then owned by the said mortgagor without any fraud or further delay, and should also deliver to the mortgagee
aforesaid, its successors and assigns, on or before the   day of
of each and every year, receipts for all taxes of the current year assessed
upon the premises hereinafter described and mortgaged : provided, however, and it was thereby expressly agreed, that if, at any time, default
should be made in the payment of the said principal money when due, or
of the said interest, or of the said fines, or of the said monthly premium, or
of the monthly contribution on said shares of stock, for the space of
after any payment thereof shall fall due, or in such delivery to the mortgagee aforesaid, its successors or assigns, on or before the   day of
          of each and every year, of such receipts for such taxes of the
current year upon the premises hereinafter described and mortgaged, or if
the said mortgagor   should not well and truly pay, or cause to be paid, the
          taxes on the said premises when the same should become due and
payable, then and in such case the whole principal debt aforesaid should,
at the option of the mortgagee aforesaid, its successors and assigns, immediately thereupon become due, payable, and recoverable ; and payment of
said principal sum and all interest, and all fines thereon, and monthly premiums due, as well as any contribution on said   shares of stock,
then due, may be enforced and recovered at once, anything hereinbefore
contained to the contrary thereof notwithstanding. And it was therein
further agreed, that if the said moneys, or any part thereof, has to be collected by proceedings at law, then an attorney's collection fee of   per
cent. should be added to the amount so collected, as a part of the costs of
such proceedings. And the said mortgagor for   heirs, executors,
administrators, and assigns, thereby expressly waived and relinquished unto
the mortgagee aforesaid, its successors and assigns, all benefit that might
accrue to   them by virtue of any and every law made or to be made
exempting the premises hereinafter described, or any other premises whatever, from levy and sale under execution, or any part of the proceeds
arising from the sale thereof, from the payment of the moneys thereby
secured, or any part thereof, and the cost of such action or execution ; as in
and by the said above-recited obligation and the condition therof, relation
being thereunto had, may more fully and at large appear. And the said
          mortgagor as aforesaid, as well for and in consideration of the
aforesaid debt or sum of   and for the better securing the payment

of the same, with interest, together with all fines, and together with the monthly premium of   , and together with the monthly contribution of   on the said   shares of stock then owned by the said mortgagor unto the mortgagee aforesaid, its successors and assigns, in discharge of the said recited obligation, as for and in consideration of the further sum of one dollar, unto   in hand well and truly paid by the mortgagee aforesaid, at the time of the execution thereof, the receipt whereof is thereby acknowledged, did grant, bargain, sell, release, and confirm unto the   mortgagee as aforesaid, its successors and assigns (description) together with the appurtenances. To have and to hold the same unto the mortgagee aforesaid, its successors and assigns, to and for its and their only proper use and behoof forever. And it was, in and by the said indenture, provided, that in case of default in the payment of the principal, interest, or fines, and the monthly premium as aforesaid, or any part thereof, or in default of the payment of the monthly contribution on the   shares of stock, as above particularly recited and mentioned, or any part thereof, for the space of   after any payment thereof shall fall due, or if the said mortgagor should not well and truly pay, or cause to be paid, the   taxes on the above-described premises, when the same shall become due and payable, then, and in such case, the whole principal debt aforesaid shall immediately thereupon become due, payable, and recoverable ; and it shall and may be lawful for the mortgagee aforesaid, its successors or assigns, to sue out, forthwith, a writ of *scire facias* upon the said indenture of mortgage, and to proceed at once thereon to recover the principal money thereby secured, and all interest, and all fines, and all monthly premiums thereon, as well as any contribution on said   shares of stock then due, according to law, without further stay, any law or usage to the contrary notwithstanding. And it was thereby agreed that in case the said moneys, or any part thereof, has to be collected by a process of law, an attorney's fee of   per cent. shall be added to and collected as a part of the costs of such proceedings. And the said mortgagor for   heirs , executors, administrators, and assigns, thereby waived and relinquished unto the mortgagee aforesaid, its successors and assigns, all benefit that may accrue to   them by virtue of any and every law made, or to be made, to exempt the said above-described premises from levy and sale under execution, or any part of the proceeds arising from the sale thereof, from the payment of the moneys thereby secured, or any part thereof. And whereas, we have been given to understand that default has been made in the payment of the said interest, fines, and monthly premiums and the monthly contribution on said shares of stock, for more than   after the same became due and payable, and the delivery of receipts for taxes on the above-described premises, whereby the whole principal debt aforesaid has become due and payable, according to the terms and conditions in the said recited obligation and indenture contained. And the said   mortgagee aforesaid praying that a fit remedy in this behalf may be provided, we command you, that by good and lawful men of your bailiwick, you make known to the said   mortgagor aforesaid, that   be and appear before our Judges, at Philadelphia, at our Court of Common Pleas, No.   , for the County of Philadelphia, there to be held the first Monday of   next, to show if anything know or ha   to say why the said mortgaged premises, with the appurtenances, ought not to be taken in execution and sold, to satisfy the

debt, interest, fines, monthly premiums, and monthly contributions aforesaid, if to   it shall seem expedient.   And have you then there the
names of those by whom you shall so make it known to   and this writ.
Witness the Honorable   , president of our said court, at Philadelphia, the   day of,   , in the year of our Lord one thousand eight
hundred and eighty-

                                        , Prothonotary.

§ 191. **After the Sci. Fa. is issued,** the writ is given to the sheriff.
If the defendant be dead, without your knowledge, or living and
absent from the county, or you are not able to ascertain his residence in the county, you direct the sheriff to return it *nihil* and
then issue an alias.   Upon two returns of *nihil*, proceed as if the
writ had been served personally (see § 171).   *Nihil habet* means
nothing he has, or that the defendant has no residence at which the
writ could be left.   Two such returns are sufficient service, though
defendant be dead, and are conclusive evidence that he is alive as
to this suit.

In *Chambers* v. *Carson*, 2 Wh., 365 (1837); *Taylor* v. *Young*,
71 Pa. St., 81 (1872); *Tryon* v. *Munson*, 77 Pa. St., 250 (1874);
it was ruled that it is not necessary, under the Act of 1834, to
join the widows and heirs or devisees in a *sci. fa. sur* mortgage, or
to sue any person save the administrator.

This was followed in 1888 by *Rushton* v. *Lippincott*, 119 Pa.
St., 12; see also *Brown* v. *Wagner*, 23 W. N., 252 (1889).

If the defendant be within the county, give the address to the
sheriff by writing it on the writ, and let the writ be served.

If the mortgagor has sold the property, you may direct the sheriff
to serve also the terre-tenant, and let him so return.   The advantage gained by this is that the terre-tenant is precluded by your
judgment.

If no appearance be entered, you can take judgment for want of
it.   General directions for this have been given in the chapter on
Ground-rents.   (Section 171.)

After the judgment, you assess damages, as also already noted.
(Section 171.)

If appearance be entered and no affidavit of defense be filed, enter
judgment at the proper time for want of an affidavit of defense.
(Section 23.)

If an insufficient affidavit be filed, proceed as indicated, sections
27, 28, 29.

In a proceeding by *sci. fa. sur* mortgage against timber land,
with notice to the terre-tenant who had purchased the timber, an
affidavit of defense by such terre-tenant is sufficient which sets
forth that at the time he bought the timber the owner of the land

obtained the consent of plaintiff to make the sale, and the purchase-money was paid by the terre-tenant to the owner, and by
him to the plaintiff, with full knowledge that it was the proceeds
of the sale of said timber.

McCOLLUM, J.: "The bank's consent to the sale * * *
and its acceptance of the proceeds * * * operated as a release of the timber from the lien of the mortgage * * * and
raised an equity in the purchaser which required that in enforcing the judgment * * * the execution should be confined
* * * to the land." *Collins's Appeal*, 166 Pa. St., 179; 37
W. N., 269 (1895). See *Bank* v. *Perrin*, 172 Pa. St., 15 (1895).

An affidavit of defense to a *sci. fa. sur* mortgage is sufficient
which avers the mortgage, when executed, was delivered in escrow
to the attorney who prepared it; that the mortgage had never
been delivered; that the defendant had never received the loan,
and no interest had ever been demanded or paid. *Morgan* v. *Morgan*, 166 Pa. St., 450 (1895).

If you cannot obtain judgment by default, enter rule on defendant to plead. (See section 88.) Serve notice of the rule. If no
plea be filed, write for it. If necessary, take judgment. (Section 26.)

If defendant plead, he will probably plead payment. He might
plead *non est factum* where the execution of the mortgage is questioned.

File a replication if necessary. (Section 160.)

Order the case on the trial-list, notify your client to prepare,
when the case appears notify him again, and be thoroughly ready.

General directions as to trials will be found at Chapters **XXXIX.**
and **XL.**

After judgment it is not necessary to bring in Executor, etc. After
service on mortgagor and judgment, if the mortgagor die, his personal representatives need not be brought in by *sci. fa.* *Hunsecker*
v. *Thomas*, 89 Pa. St., 154 (1879).

§ 192. **When judgment obtained, issue levari facias.** *Præcipe* for
levari facias:

A. B. ⎫
   v. ⎬ C. P.,   Term, 1888. No .
G. H. ⎭

To the Prothonotary of the Court of Common Pleas of   County.

SIR: Issue *levari facias*, returnable *sec. leg.*

        Real Debt, $
        (Amount of your judgment.)
        Interest from
        (*Do not calculate the interest.*)

                             I. K.,
                    Plaintiff's Attorney.
                        (Date.)

The following is the *form of the levari facias:*

County of Philadelphia, *ss.*

The Commonwealth of Pennsylvania to the Sheriff of the County of Philadelphia, greeting :

We command you, that, without any other writ from us, of the lands and tenements which were of   to wit :

(*here is inserted the description of the property copied from the mortgage*).

Together with the hereditaments and appurtenances in your bailiwick, you cause to be levied as well a certain debt of   dollars and cents, lawful money of the United States of America, with the lawful interest thereof, from the   day of   , A.D. 188 , as also dollars and   cents, like money, for costs ; which said debt, with interest and costs aforesaid,   plaintiff lately, in our Court of Common Pleas, No.   , of the County of Philadelphia, before our Judges, at Philadelphia, to wit, on the   day of   , A.D. 188 , by the consideration of the said Court, recovered to be levied of the said above-described property, with the appurtenances, by the default of the said defendant in not paying the said debt, at the time when the same ought to have been paid, according to the form and effect of an Act of Assembly of the Commonwealth of Pennsylvania, in such case made and provided. And have you those moneys before our Judges, at Philadelphia, at our said ourt of Common Pleas, No.   , there to be held on the first Monday of   next, to render unto the said plaintiff for the debt, interest, and costs aforesaid, whereof the said defendant   convict, as appears of record, etc. And have you then and there this writ. Witness the Honorable   , President Judge of our Court, at Philadelphia, the   day of   in the year of our Lord one thousand eight hundred and eighty-

                                               , Prothonotary.

The following is a form of *sheriff's return to levari facias :*

To the Honorable the Judges of the Court within named. I certify that, in obedience to the within writ, after having given due and legal notice of time and place of sale, by advertisements in the public newspapers and hand-bills put up on the property within described and in the most public places in my bailiwick, I did, on Monday, the   day of   , A.D. 188 , at four o'clock P.M., in the   in the   City and County of Philadelphia, expose the property within described to sale by public vendue or outcry, and sold the same to   being the highest and best bidder and   the best price bid for the same. Which money I have ready before the Judges within named, to render as by the said writ I am commanded.

                    So answers

                                               , Sheriff.

In *Ins. Co.* v. *Fisher,* 4 W. N., 414 (1877), it was decided a levari was good though issued more than five years after judgment. This may be doubted as the law at present.

Proceedings after Levari. Here again see that the description is accurate ; that improvements are mentioned ; that your client has notice of the sale ; that he bids or that some one bids for him, if necessary, to prevent sacrifice.

A sale upon a judgment entered same day that mortgage is recorded discharges the lien of mortgage. *Richey's Appeal*, 22 W. N., 154 (1888).

Observe generally the directions given in this chapter as to proceedings after judgment on the bond. (Sections 184, 185.)

§ 193. **Ejectment.** A third remedy to recover money due upon a mortgage is by action of ejectment. The form of the mortgage already given shows that it is, down to the clause of defeasance, in the shape of an absolute conveyance of the land described. Upon default, therefore, it would seem to be clear that the mortgagee could maintain ejectment. This was, however, denied by the mortgagor, in *Smith* v. *Shuler*, 12 S. & R., 240 (1824). Opinion by TILGHMAN, C. J. The objection to this remedy there urged was that the *Sci. Fa.* Act of 1705, already cited, precluded a recovery—until twelve months after last payment was due, and that all the payments secured by the mortgage in that case had not matured. But the Supreme Court, referring to *Simpson* v. *Ammons*, 1 Binn., 175, held that ejectment would lie upon the first default, but that the mortgagee did not, by thus recovering, extinguish the equity of redemption. The mortgagee, the court said, " upon his entry after judgment, is accountable for the profits, and the mortgagor would be entitled to re-possession on payment or tender of so much of the principal as was due, all arrears of interest, and the costs of suit."

This proceeding, not differing in form from other ejectments, is treated of in Chapter XIV.

§ 194. **Proceedings to Compel Satisfaction of a Mortgage.** There are three contingencies, any one of which may prevent the satisfaction of a mortgage by consent : the amount due may be in doubt or disputed ; the legal holder of the mortgage may be a defunct corporation, or an individual absent from the State, with no attorney to act for him ; the mortgage itself may be lost. All these contingencies are provided for by Acts of Assembly.

§ 195. **When mortgage, incumbrance, and charge on land presumed to be paid, under Act of 1895—Petition—Publication—Practice.**

The Act of May 8, 1895, Section 1 (P. L., 44), provides : That in all cases in which, under any proceeding in any court of record of this Commonwealth, or under any deed, last will and testament, mortgage, dower, recognizance, judgment, decree, or other obligation or instrument, any money has been or may hereafter be charged upon land, payable presently or at a future time, and the period of twenty-one years has elapsed or shall have elapsed after the principal of such incumbrance or charge has become or shall have become due and payable, and no payment has been or shall have been made within said period of twenty-one years on account of such incumbrance or charge by the owner or owners of the land sought to be released and discharged, and no sufficient release, acquittance, or acknowledgment of payment of such incumbrance or charge is of record in the county in which the land is situated, it shall be lawful for the orphans' court of the county in which such land is situated, in cases in which the incumbrance or charge is under a decree of an orphans' court, by last will and testament, dower or recognizance charged by said court, and for the Common Pleas Court of the county in which such land is situated in all other cases, upon petition of the owner or owners of the land, or any part thereof, subject to the incumbrance or charge, setting forth the facts, verified by affidavit, and alleging that no payment of principal or interest has been made within said period of twenty-one years on account of said incumbrance or charge by the present owner or owners, or so far as can be ascertained by his or their predecessors in title, and giving the names of all known parties interested in such incumbrance or charge, their places of residence, if known, and a description of the land subject to the charge and sought to be released and discharged, to direct the sheriff of the county to give notice to all such known parties in the county, whose residences are known, by copy served personally or left at their places of abode, and to all parties out of the county, if any, and to all unknown parties, if any, by public notice published in one or more newspapers published within or nearest the county once a week for four successive weeks, which notice shall briefly state the facts set forth in the petition and require the parties to appear in court on a day designated at least thirty days after the filing of the petition, and service of notice as aforesaid to be made at least twenty days prior to the day designated for appearance, at which time, should any person or persons appear and claim payment for or on account of such incumbrance or charge or any part thereof, the court shall enter a rule on the person or persons so appearing and claiming to commence proper legal proceedings to enforce payment of their claim or claims within thirty days after the entry of such rule, and in default of compliance with such rule, or in the event of a non-appearance of any person to answer the petition, or in the event of the joinder of all parties in interest in such petition, the court, being satisfied of the truth of the allegations of the petition, shall decree and direct that the land subject to the incumbrance or charge or any part thereof sought to be released or discharged shall be released and discharged from the same, and the payment thereof, and that a copy of the petition and decree shall be entered of record in the office of the recorder of deeds of the county, for recording which he shall be entitled to a fee at the rate he is entitled by law to charge for recording deeds, which decree and record shall forever thereafter operate as a release and discharge of the land from the incumbrance of the charge and shall bar all actions brought thereon.

Guardians ad litem may be appointed to protect minors.

SEC. 2. The court in which any proceeding provided for in the first section of this Act shall be commenced shall appoint guardians *ad litem* for any minors who may appear to be interested in the incumbrance or charge on land, if such minors do not appear from the allegations of the petition to have guardians, and service of all notices, rules, orders, and other process shall then be made upon such guardians *ad litem*.

Costs.

SEC. 3. All costs of proceedings had on petitions presented under the provisions of this Act shall be paid by the petitioners : Provided, That the costs of proceedings to enforce claims instituted in response to rules granted under the provisions of this Act shall abide the decision of such proceedings.

This Act supersedes the Act of June 10, 1881 (P. L., 97).

FORM OF PETITION.

In the Court of Common Pleas, No.   , for the County of Philadelphia.
No. ,   Term, 1894.
To the Honorable the Judges of the said Court :
  The petition of A. B. respectfully represents :
  1. That your petitioner is the owner in fee of (here set forth description of realty).
  2. That your petitioner acquired said premises by deed from C. D. on (date), and which deed was duly recorded in the office of the Recorder of Deeds in and for the County of Philadelphia in Deed-book   , No.
     , page   , etc.
  The said C. D. acquired title to said premises by deed from E. F. bearing date the   day of   , 1850, and duly recorded in said office in Deed-book   , No.   ; page   , etc.
  3. That on ·   day of   , 1840, E. F., the then owner of said premises, made, executed, and delivered to P. Q. a certain mortgage in the sum of $, payable in   years and which was duly recorded in Mortgage-book   , No.   , page   , etc., and which said mortgage covers the premises above described.
  4. Your petitioner has been informed and believes that from the
day of   , 1849, during the time said premises were owned by the said E. F. and subsequently by C. D., no demand was ever made for the payment of any interest upon the said mortgage or for the principal thereof, and no such demand has ever been made of your petitioner during his possession of said premises.
  5. That it was not until recent negotiations for the sale of said premises and application for a policy of title insurance in the   Trust Company were made that your petitioner was advised that said mortgage appeared upon the record unsatisfied.
  6. There has never been any assignment of the said mortgage.
  7. That the said P. Q. died in the year 1860, and notwithstanding your petitioner has made diligent search for the representatives of the said P. Q., or parties in interest, he has been unable to ascertain if they are alive or dead or who they are, or where located, and notwithstanding he has made and caused to be made diligent search for the said mortgage it cannot be found.
  The name or names of the holder or holders of the said mortgage, if any, are unknown to your petitioner.
  8. That the period of twenty-one years has elapsed since the principal of said mortgage became due and payable, and no payment has been made within said period of either principal or interest. Wherefore, your petitioner prays your honorable Court to order and direct the Sheriff of Philadelphia County to serve a notice, stating the facts set forth in this petition on the known holder or holders of the said mortgage, if to be found in the said county, and whose residence or residences are known, according

to the Act of Assembly in such case made and provided, and in case
the parties are unknown or the parties aforesaid cannot be found in the said
county, that then the said sheriff shall give public notice as aforesaid in one
or more newspapers published within the said county, once a week for four
successive weeks after the presentation of this petition, requiring said parties
to appear on (date), according to the Act of Assembly in such case made and
provided, and to answer this petition and to show cause why satisfaction
should not be entered on the record of the said mortgage by the Recorder
of Deeds of Philadelphia County.

And your petitioner will ever pray, etc.   A. B.

City and County of Philadelphia, *ss.*

A. B., being duly sworn according to law, deposes and says he is the above-
named petitioner and that the facts set forth in the foregoing petition are
true and correct to the best of his knowledge and belief.

Sworn to and subscribed before me,
this   day of   , 1894.   A. B.,

Notary Public.

Annex to the petition the affidavits of C. D. and whoever else
is familiar with the facts.

Such affidavits should follow the averments of the petition.

DECREE.

And now (date) upon consideration of the foregoing petition and affidavits, and on motion of   , pro petitioner, it is ordered and decreed
that the High Sheriff of Philadelphia County serve a notice upon
            or upon the legal representatives of the said   and upon the
known holder or holders of the mortgage described in the said petition if
they or any of them can be found in the same county, and have known residence, and if said parties are unknown and cannot be found, that he shall
give public notice by advertisement of the facts set forth in the within petition once a week for four successive weeks after the presentation of this
petition in the   and the   , newspapers published in the City
and County of Philadelphia, commanding the said parties to appear before
the said court on   the   day of   , to show cause
why the proper decree should not be granted, and satisfaction of the said
mortgage should not be entered on the record thereof as within prayed.

The usual practice is to grant the decree upon the facts set forth
in the petition and affidavits.

In rare cases it may be necessary to refer the case to a Master
before whom the petitioner must appear, give the requisite testimony, and produce the necessary searches.

When the decree is granted, take to the sheriff a copy of the
decree and the necessary advertisement in duplicate.

FORM OF ADVERTISEMENT.

In the Court of Common Pleas, No   , for the County of Philadelphia.

To P. Q., or his legal representatives or whoever may be the holder or
holders of the mortgage hereinafter mentioned.

Take Notice that on (date) A. B. presented his petition averring he is the owner of all that certain lot or piece of ground (here set forth the description).

That an unsatisfied mortgage upon said premises remains of record in the office of the Recorder of Deeds of Philadelphia County given by E. F. to P. Q. dated   for   years, recorded in said office in Mortgage-book   , No.   , page   , for $, and that the period of twenty-one years has elapsed since the principal of said mortgage became due and payable, and no payment has been made within said period of either principal or interest, and praying for satisfaction thereof.

Whereupon said court ordered that notice of said facts be served by the Sheriff of Philadelphia County on said P. Q. or his legal representatives, or whoever may be the known holder or holders of said mortgage if to be found in said county, and having known residence, and if not, then to give public notice by advertisement requiring them to appear in said court on (date) to answer said petition and to show cause why the proper decree should not be granted, and said mortgage satisfied of record.

U. V.,
Sheriff.
Y. Z.,
Attorney for Petitioner.
(Address.)

To the order of publication the sheriff makes the necessary return. Attach to the original petition and decree, (a) the sheriff's return, and (b) the final decree for approval of the court. Order the case on the current motion-list and hand the papers to the court when the case is called.

FORM OF SHERIFF'S RETURN TO ORDER OF PUBLICATION.

To the Honorable the Judges within named.

I do hereby certify and return that I was unable to find the within-named P. Q. or his legal representatives or the holder or holders of the within-mentioned mortgage in my bailiwick, and that in obedience to an order of court to me directed a notice of the facts set forth in the petition hereto annexed, was advertised once a week for four successive weeks after the presentation of the said petition in the Philadelphia *Inquirer*, a daily newspaper published in the city of Philadelphia, and once a week for four successive weeks in the *Legal Intelligencer*, as will appear by a schedule of said advertisements and affidavits of their publication hereto annexed. So answers

, Sheriff.
(Date.)

To the return are attached the affidavits, of which the following is a *form :*

(Advertisement.)
City and County of Philadelphia, *ss.*

S. T., being duly sworn according to law, deposes and says he is connected with the *Legal Intelligencer*, a weekly newspaper published in the city of Philadelphia, and that an advertisement of which the above is a copy was published in said newspaper once a week for four successive weeks, viz. :

Sworn to and subscribed before me,
this   day of   , 1894. } S. T.

Notary Public.

FORM OF FINAL DECREE.

(Caption.)

And now (date) the Sheriff of Philadelphia County having returned that he was unable to find the said P. Q. or his legal representatives, or the holder or holders of the within-mentioned mortgage in his bailiwick, and that in obedience to the said order of court to the said sheriff directed a notice of the facts set forth in the foregoing petition was advertised once a week for four successive weeks after the presentation of the said petition in the Philadelphia *Inquirer*, a daily newspaper published in the city and county of Philadelphia, and once a week for four successive weeks in the *Legal Intelligencer*, as appeared by a schedule of said advertisements and affidavits of their publication annexed to the return of the said sheriff,

And no person appearing to answer the said petition as aforesaid and the court being satisfied of the truth of the allegations of the said petition, it is, on motion of   , pro petitioner, ordered and decreed that the prayer of said petition be granted and that satisfaction shall be entered by the Recorder of Deeds of Philadelphia County on the record of the mortgage given by E. F. to P. Q., dated   and recorded in the office of the Recorder of Deeds in and for the County of Philadelphia in Mortgage-book   , No.   , page   , for $, upon all that certain (here set forth description) on payment of the costs due relative to the entry of said satisfaction of said mortgage or any proceedings thereon, and upon presentation of a certified copy of the petition and decree in said case to be filed by said Recorder of record. Which said satisfaction so entered and filing of said record shall forever thereafter defeat, release, and discharge said mortgage and shall likewise bar all actions brought or to be brought thereon as fully and effectually to all intents and purposes as if the satisfaction had been entered by the legal holder or holders of the said mortgage.

Take a certified copy of the record to the Recorder of Deeds and he will mark the mortgage satisfied, upon payment of his fees.

§ 196. **When there is any dispute as to the amount due.** The Act of April 3, 1851 (P. L., 871), provided, in this contingency, for an action by the mortgagor, and gave the owner of the premises, when not a mortgagor, no remedy. *Assurance Co.* v. *Powers,* 12 Phila., 377 (1877).

The Act of May 25, 1887 (P. L., 6), provides for both mortgagor and terre-tenant or owner, but requires that the mortgage must have been due at least one year.

Under Act of April 3, 1851 (P. L., 871), the mortgagor applies by petition to the Court of Common Pleas of the county in which the land lies, setting forth the facts, and pays into court the amount *claimed by the mortgagee*, stating, if any, the objections to the mortgagee's claim. Upon the payment into court, a decree is made that satisfaction be entered upon said mortgage. The fund in court is distributed on equitable principles, after hearing.

By Act of May 25, 1887 (P. L., 270), the mortgage must have been due for one year or more. Then either the mortgagor or the owner of the land petitions the Common Pleas of the county in which the land lies, setting forth the premises. The sheriff serves a notice on the proper parties, requiring them to issue a *scire facias* returnable to the next term, together with a statement, duly verified, of the amount claimed to be due. After the *scire facias* issues, the suit proceeds regularly, except that there can be no discontinuance or non-suit without the consent of all parties and the court. If the holder of the mortgage refuses or neglects to issue the *scire facias* for sixty days after the service of notice on him, the petitioner can pay the amount *admitted by him* to be due into court, and upon proof of service of the notice by the sheriff on the legal holder of the mortgage, a decree is made that satisfaction be entered upon the record of the mortgage by the recorder, on payment of costs of satisfaction. Such satisfaction is as effectual as if entered by the legal holder.

§ 197. **When the legal holder is a non-resident or has removed, leaving no duly authorized attorney to act for him.** If the residence of the legal holder be known, this contingency can be met by correspondence, and a power of attorney executed by him. But if his residence abroad be unknown, the Act of June 20, 1883 (P. L., 138), provides a remedy. The owner of the mortgaged premises applies by petition to the Common Pleas of the county in which the land lies, setting forth the premises, the name of the legal holder, his whereabouts, if known; if not known, then stating the facts; that the principal is overdue by expiration of time limited, and not by reason of default in interest. The court makes such order as it thinks best for giving notice of the petition and the time of the hearing to all persons interested. At the hearing so fixed, due proof being made of the truth of the petition, the amount of principal and interest is paid into court, with any other money owing on the mortgage, and a decree is made that the recorder enter satisfaction upon the margin of the record of the mortgage. The petitioner, at his cost, then furnishes the recorder with a certificate, under the hand of the clerk, and the seal of the court, containing a copy of the order of the court and an acknowledgment of the payment into court. The recorder then enters satisfaction.

FORM OF PETITION FOR DECREE OF SATISFACTION ON PAYMENT INTO
·   COURT.

In the Court of Common Pleas, No.   , of Philadelphia County.
   No.   ,   Term, 1894.
To the Honorable the Judges of the said Court.
   The petition of A. B. respectfully represents :
   1. That she is the owner of premises No.   , in the City of Philadelphia, and on the   day of   , 1890, executed and delivered
a certain bond and mortgage thereon for $, payable in
years to C. D., with interest thereon at   per cent., and recorded in the
office of the Recorder of Deeds in and for the County of Philadelphia in
Deed-book   , No.   , page   , etc.
   2. That the principal of the mortgage debt is overdue by expiration of
the time therein limited, viz.: (date), and not by reason of default in the
payment of interest.
   That your petitioner is now ready to pay off the principal of said mortgage.
   3. That the said mortgagee, the present holder of the mortgage, is domiciled in the City of Paris, in the Republic of France, and has left no known
duly authorized attorney in fact to enter satisfaction on the record of such
mortgage on the full payment of the principal and interest, and all proper
legal charges.
   4. That (date) she wrote to C. D. addressed to   , Paris, France,
the present address of said mortgagee, advising him that the time limited
in the mortgage had expired and requesting him to appoint some person to
act as his attorney in fact to receive said principal, interest, and legal
charges, and enter satisfaction upon the record, and tendering him the full
amount to date.
   Although more than   months have elapsed, your petitioner has
received no reply to said letter.
   A copy of said letter is hereto attached, marked " Exhibit A."
   5. That she is securing a new loan on said real estate, and it is necessary
to discharge the said mortgage incumbrance, and your petitioner is greatly
inconvenienced and compelled to pay additional interest because of the indifference and neglect of C. D., all of which as well as of this application
the said C. D. has been duly advised. A copy of said letter is hereto attached, marked " Exhibit B."
   6. Your petitioner is ready and anxious to pay into court the said principal, interest, and costs, as follows :
Principal .   .   .   .$
Interest from   to   .   .
Costs .   .   .   .
   Wherefore she prays your Honorable Court to make an order as to giving
notice of said petition and decree and of the time of the hearing thereof to
the said C. D., the only party in interest, and to show cause why upon payment being made into court of the full amount of the principal, interest, and
all other moneys found to be due and owing on said mortgage, amounting to
$, and upon the production to the Recorder of Deeds of the County
of Philadelphia of the proper certificate thereof from the Prothonotary of
the Courts of Common Pleas of Philadelphia County, the said Recorder
shall not enter full satisfaction upon the margin of the record of such mortgage.   (Signature of A. B.)
   (Affidavit of truth of facts.)
   (" Exhibit A " attached.)   (" Exhibit B " attached.)

DECREE.

And now (date) upon consideration of the foregoing petition and on motion of , pro petitioner, it is ordered and decreed that the said C. D. appear on the day of , 1894, 10 A.M., in person or by attorney, and show cause why the prayer of this petition should not be granted and satisfaction of said mortgage be entered of record.

And it is further ordered that a copy of this petition and decree be sent by mail to C. D., addressed to , Paris, France, and that an abstract of said petition with the decree be advertised once a week for four weeks in the *Public Ledger*, a newspaper published in the City of Philadelphia, and also for the same time in the , a newspaper published in the City of Paris, Republic of France.

At the time set forth in the decree, if no answer be filed, present proof of publication, affidavit of service by mail, and the following :

FORM OF FINAL DECREE.

(Caption.)

And now (date) due proof of service of the copy of the petition and order of (date) by mail on the said C. D. as well as the due proof of the publication thereof having been filed and no answer or objection thereto having been presented, it is on motion of , pro petitioner, ordered and decreed that upon payment being made into court of the full amount of the principal, interest, and all other moneys found to be due and owing on said mortgage, amounting to $, and upon the production to the Recorder of Deeds of the County of Philadelphia of the proper certificate thereof from the Prothonotary of the Courts of Common Pleas of Philadelphia County, the said Recorder of Deeds shall enter full satisfaction upon the margin of the record of such mortgage, which shall forever thereafter discharge, defeat, and release the same, and shall likewise bar all actions brought or to be brought thereupon as fully as if such payment had been made to the lawful owner or owners of such mortgage debt, and as if such owner or owners had entered satisfaction of record.

§ 198. **When, after being paid, the legal holder fails to satisfy the mortgage.** The old Act of March 31, 1823 (8 Sm. Laws, 131), provided for this contingency, when the failure was due to death or to removal from the State, and two years had elapsed. It was extended by Act of April 28, 1868 (P. L., 1151), to satisfaction by defunct corporations in Philadelphia and Montgomery Counties. The recent Act of June 11, 1879 (P. L., 141), is, as to procedure, precisely similar to the old Act of 1823 ; it applies when the legal holder has failed, from any cause whatever, to enter satisfaction, and it extends throughout the State the provisions of the Act of April 28, 1868, as to defunct corporations. It also reduces the time which must elapse, to six months. The older Acts, therefore, will not be considered.

The Act of June 11, 1879 (P. L., 141), provides that where payment has been made of all the money or amount due, and the legal holder has failed from any cause whatever to enter satisfaction, and shall so continue for six months, the mortgagor or the owner of the premises may petition the Court of Common Pleas of the county in which the land lies, setting forth the facts. The court then directs the sheriff to serve a notice stating the matters set forth in the petition on the legal representatives, if to be found in the county. If the parties cannot be found in the county, to give public notice by publication in one or more newspapers published within or nearest to the county, once a week for four weeks successively prior to the then next return-day after the petition has been presented, requiring the said parties to appear at the next term and answer the petition.

At the next term, or any subsequent term, proof of full payment is to be made, and the court decrees that satisfaction shall be entered on the record of the mortgage.

If, on proof of payment, either party shall desire any disputed fact to be tried by a jury, an issue is formed and tried accordingly, and if the jury shall find that the full amount has been paid, then satisfaction shall be entered on the record as aforesaid.

. If the legal holder has been a corporation whose existence has terminated, or is doubtful, the notice is to be served on either the president or the treasurer last in office, if he is to be found in the county; otherwise, by publication as in other cases.

§ 199. **When the mortgage is lost, and payment or satisfaction is refused until the mortgage is produced.** This contingency is provided for only in the counties of Philadelphia, Montgomery, and Lycoming, by Act of April 10, 1849 (P. L., 621), which provides that in such case the mortgagor, mortgagee, or legal holder of mortgage, owner of mortgaged premises, or other person interested, may apply by bill or petition to the Common Pleas of the county in which the land lies, setting forth the facts of the case, with the complaint or grievance. After due notice, given in such manner and for such time as the court may direct, to all persons interested, requiring them to appear in court on a fixed day and answer such bill or petition, the court, at the time fixed, or any subsequent time, sitting as a court of equity, has power to examine into the facts of the case and the complaint or grievance, and to grant such relief and make such order and decree therein as the necessities of the case may in justice and equity require, as fully as if the remedy were in the Act particularly prescribed and set forth.

CHAPTER VII.

§ 200. **As to filing liens.** The Act of June 16, 1836, and other statutes supplementary to the law of March 17, 1806, fastened upon the counties therein named a remedy of very questionable utility. The principle thus recognized has, however, been popular with the masses, and has, from time to time, been extended to various artisans, to contractors, to iron works, to mines and bridges, and to leaseholds in certain cases. Of all these, mention will be made under their appropriate heads. It is not the object of this work to give a treatise upon this subject.

The practitioner will, in this and all other cases, examine carefully the statutes and decisions in the Digests. In this particular matter he should also consult the learned and valuable book of Ovid F. Johnson, Esq., on Mechanics' Lien Law in Pennsylvania.

§ 201. **As to preparing claim.** The claim, the county, the work, the time, being all in your favor, if the lien has not been filed, your first duty is to prepare the claim. To do this you need the names of all members of firms who are to be mentioned as claimants or defendants, an accurate description of the property, the items of the work or materials, etc.

You may be assisted in preparing the paper by the following

FORM OF MECHANIC'S CLAIM.

In the Court of Common Pleas, No.   , for the County of Philadelphia.

E. F.
  v.   Term, 18 .
A. B., owner or reputed owner, } No.
  and C. D., contractor.

E. F., of   , files this his claim for the payment of the sum of   dollars   cents, against all   certain   story   building or lot or piece of ground and curtilage appurtenant thereto, situate on the (here insert a particular description of the lot after the following guide : Situate on the east side of Sixth Street, commencing at the distance of 100 feet north of Chestnut Street, in the city of Philadelphia ; thence extending on the east side of said Sixth Street in a northwardly direction 25 feet, thence eastwardly at right angles with said Sixth Street 100 feet, thence southwardly 25 feet, thence westwardly 100 feet to the place of beginning. Containing in front on Sixth Street 25 feet, and in depth 100 feet. If there be an alley, describe it [adding as the fact may be] whereof said lot has the right of way, water, etc.). The said sum of

dollars   cents being a debt contracted for   at the request
of the said   by the said   continuously within six months
last past, for and toward the erection and construction of, and on the credit
of the said building at the times and in the quantities in the annexed
bill of particulars mentioned, to wit : from the   day of   ,
A. D. 18 , to the   day of   , A. D. 18 , which bill said
claimant prays may be taken and considered as part of this lien against
said building of which the said   then was and now is the owner
or reputed owner , and   contractor for the erection of said building with whom the said contract was made ; and the said   claim
to have a lien on said building and the curtilage appurtenant thereto, for
the amount of   said claim, from the commencement of the building according to the Act of Assembly in such case made and provided.
                                        (Signature of Claimant.)

Annex the account, heading it :

BILL OF PARTICULARS REFERRED TO IN THE FOREGOING CLAIM.

This bill should charge the owner, contractor, and houses somewhat thus :

A. B., owner, and C. D., contractor, for three-story brick dwelling-house,
situate on the east side of Sixth Street, 100 feet north of Chestnut Street,
Philadelphia (as the case may be), to E. F. (claimant), Dr.
(Here must be inserted the dates at which the work was done or the
materials furnished, setting forth the kind of work or materials, etc.)

A subcontractor cannot file a mechanic's claim for a lump sum
with no items as to the articles furnished, nor can a contractor file
such claim unless by the owner's agreement. *Caldwell* v. *Carter*,
153 Pa. St., 310 (1893).

A lien against "all that lot, with the buildings, thereon erected,
situate," etc., but no other reference made to buildings upon which
work was alleged to be done, is an insufficient description. *Dorlan*
v. *Market Co.*, 19 W. N., 87 (1886).

The buildings must be particularly described as to materials,
height, location, etc. A description of the land is not sufficient.
Short v. *Ames*, 121 Pa. St., 530 (1888).

A claim containing a statement of the description of the peculi-
arities of a building and the locality, which points it out with reasonable certainty, is a sufficient compliance with the Act. *Steel Co.*
v. *Refining Co.*, 48 Leg. Int., 25 (1890).

In *Harbach* v. *Kurth*, 25 W. N., 301 (1890), it was decided
that if any interested party is dissatisfied with the description of
premises in a mechanic's lien, he may apply to the court, under the
Act of June 16, 1836, and have the curtilage fixed. Failing to do
this, he cannot, after a sale upon the lien, dispute the amount of the
curtilage.

When a mechanic's claim is filed against the estate of a married woman, it is necessary to aver that the materials were furnished the "contractor with her knowledge and consent and at her request and the request of her husband, for the improvement of her separate estate, within six months last past, for and about the erection and construction and upon the credit of the building hereinafter described." That "she was the owner of the building, and that the materials so furnished were actually applied to the improvement of her separate estate, and were necessary for the use and enjoyment thereof." *Kelly* v. *McGehee*, 26 W. N., 493 (1890). A similar ruling was made in *Wolfe* v. *Oxnard*, 152 Pa. St., 623 (1893). But one month subsequent to this decision the Supreme Court decided, in *Milligan* v. *Phipps*, 31 W. N., 561 (1893), that under the Married Woman's Act of 1887 a mechanic's lien against the estate of a married woman need not aver coverture or that the work for which it was filed was necessary for the preservation and enjoyment of her estate. (See § 240.)

Where a mechanic's claim is filed "for work done and material furnished for and about the erection and construction of a building," it is not necessary to aver that notice has been given. *Stokes* v. *Deakyne*, 2 Dist. Rep., 143 (1892).

§ 202. **Apportioned claims.** If your client has done work or has furnished materials for two or more adjoining buildings erected by the same owner, he can file an

APPORTIONED CLAIM.

In the Court of Common Pleas, No.   , for the City and County of Philadelphia.

E. F.
   v.
A. B., owner, and C. D., contractor.   Term, 18   .
    No.

E. F. claims to have a lien for the payment of the sum of
dollars and   cents against all those   adjoining
story   dwelling-houses or buildings, and the lots of ground and curtilage appurtenant to the same, situate on the   side of   Street, between   Street and   Street, in the   Ward of the city of Philadelphia, commencing at the distance of   feet from
Street, thence extending   feet in a   direction. Said entire lot being
      feet front and   feet deep. The said debt or sum of   dollars
and   cents is the price or value of   by the said claimant
for and about the erection and construction of said adjoining buildings within six months last past, to wit, between the   day of
and the   day of   , 1888, of which said buildings the said
            was and is the owner or reputed owner , and
the contractor and builder at whose instance and request the said
            all of said houses adjoining each other as
aforesaid, having been erected by the same owner. And the said
as a part of this   claim ha annexed a bill of particulars, showing the amount or sum claimed, the kind and amount of

and the time when the same   ·   . And the said claimant   apportion   the said sum of   among the said   buildings,
as follows : Against   No. 1.   The sum of   dollars and   cents
on all that certain   story house   feet   inches in front, and
feet   inches in depth, erected on a lot or piece of ground and curtilage,
situate on the   side of   Street ; commencing at the distance
of   feet   inches from   Street, in the city of Philadelphia,
said lot containing in front on said   Street,   feet
inches, and extending of that width in length or depth   feet
inches.

And against   No. 2.   The sum of   dollars
and   cents on all that certain   story   house   feet
inches in front, and   feet   inches in depth erected on a lot or
piece of ground and curtilage, situate on the   side of
Street ; commencing at the distance of   feet   inches from
          Street, in the city of Philadelphia, said lot containing in
front on said   Street   feet   inches, and extending
of that width in length or depth   feet   inches.

(And so on as to the other properties.)

You attach a bill of particulars as in the preceding form.

Indorse your claim or apportioned claim :

No.   ,   Term, 18   , C. P.   M. L. D. (name of claimant)
v. (name of owner) owner or reputed owner, and (name of contractor), contractor.

Mechanics' Lien Claim
for $

L. M.,
Attorney for Claimant.
(Date.)

The claimant should sign both the claim and the bill of particulars.

§ 203. **Indexing the claim.** It is to be recommended that after
the claim has been filed, you see that the clerk has properly indexed it.

The Act of May 16, 1895 (P. L., 84), requires that *sci. fa. sur*
mechanics' claims shall be entered on the judgment index in the
same manner as *sci. fa. sur* judgments, otherwise such *sci. fa.* shall
not continue the lien for a longer period than five years from the
date of its filing as against any purchaser, mortgagee, or other lien
creditor.

§ 204. **Suing out claims.** Clients sometimes prefer that the
claim, when filed, be suffered to rest. Care should be taken that
this indulgence do not extend beyond five years.

FORM OF PRÆCIPE FOR SCI. FA.

A. B.
    v.   Term. Year.
C. D., owner or reputed owner, and   No.
E. F., contractor.

To the Prothonotary of the Court of Common Pleas, No. 1, of Philadelphia County.

SIR : Issue *scire facias sur* mechanic's claim, returnable *sec. leg.*

                                     G. H.,
                              Plaintiff's Attorney.
                                  (Date.)

The form of the sci. fa. is given in the 15th section of the Act of June 16, 1836 (P. L., 699), and the 16th section of the Act requires that " no such *sci. fa.* shall in any case be issued within fifteen days previous to the return-day of the next term."

Some counties (like Philadelphia) have monthly return-days. These take the place of the term days, and the writ must in such places bear fifteen days between its teste and its return. The Act of May 16, 1895 (P. L., 84), provides that no *sci. fa.* shall continue the lien against a terre-tenant whose deed has been recorded, unless the terre-tenant be so named in the writ or signs an agreement in writing.

Compare the writ with your claim, see that all is accurate, and give it to the sheriff with a written mem. of the residences of defendants.

Service of the writ. This is directed by the 17th section of the Act to be the same as in the case of a summons, but in addition a copy is left with a resident of the building, if occupied ; if not, a copy is to be affixed upon the door or other front part of the building.

Posting is insufficient if the house be occupied.

A return of " served and posted " as to the owner and of " *nihil habet* " as to the contractor is sufficient, under the Act of 1836. *Donahoo* v. *Scott,* 12 Pa. St., 45 (1849), and a return of " service " upon the contractor, and " *nihil habet* and posting " as to the owner, held sufficient; *Shoemaker* v. *Duganne,* 5 W. N., 403 (1877) ; but if there be any person residing in the building, a service by " posting " is insufficient ; a copy must be served upon the occupant. *Bradley* v. *Totten,* 7 W. N., 16 (1879).

After service, you proceed as in the cases already noted. If there be no appearance and the time has expired, you take judgment for want of the appearance (section 171).

So, too, as to judgment for want of affidavit of defense (section 2796) ; or for want of sufficient affidavit of defense (section 27).

The defendant having barred your way thus far, your next step is the rule to plead, with notice of the rule served on your opponent, and judgment for want of the plea, if driven to it (section 26).

After plea, you file a replication, if necessary, and when the cause is at issue you notify your client and order the case on the trial-list.

§ 205. **After trial and final judgment in your favor,** you issue execution by giving to the prothonotary the following

PRÆCIPE FOR LEVARI FACIAS.

A. B. ⎫   C. P.   Term, 18 .
  v.   ⎬   No.   .
C. D. ⎭

To the Prothonotary of the Court of Common Pleas, No. 1, of the City and County of Philadelphia.

SIR: Issue *levari facias* in the above case, returnable *sec. leg.*
Real debt, $
Interest from (date of your judgment).

L. M.,
pro Plaintiff.
(Date.)

The *Levari Facias* is in the following form :

County, *ss.* The Commonwealth of Pennsylvania to the Sheriff of said county, greeting : We command you, that without any other writ from us, of the following described building and lot of ground of A. B., to wit (describing the same according to the record), in your bailiwick, you cause to be levied, as well a certain debt of   , which C. D. lately in our Court of Common Pleas for the county aforesaid, by the consideration of the said court, recovered of the said A. B., to be levied of the said building and lot of ground, as also the interest thereon from the   day of   , A. D.   ; and also the sum of   for the costs which accrued thereon, according to the form and effect of an Act of Assembly of the Commonwealth of Pennsylvania in such case made and provided ; and have you these moneys before our Judges at   at our County Court of Common Pleas, there to be held on the   day of   next, to render unto the said C. D. for his debt, interest, and costs aforesaid, and have you then there this writ, etc.

Witness, etc.

(Seal of the Court.)   Prothonotary.

It is singular that the Act of Assembly which gives this form (June 16, 1836, section 21) refers " to a further sum which E. F. recovered against A. B. ; " and although recovered by E. F., the whole (as well C. D.'s judgment as E. F.'s recovery) is, by this form, to be " rendered unto C. D." I have endeavored to correct this by leaving E. F. out of C. D.'s writ.

Pursue the directions stated, sections 184, 185.

§ 206. **Counties in which Claims may be Filed.** The Act of

June 16, 1836, by its own provision, applies "to all counties to which the Act entitled 'An Act securing to mechanics and others payment for their labors and materials, in erecting any house or other building within the City and County of Philadelphia,' passed the 17th day of March, 1806, and the several supplements thereto, now extends." The Act of 1806 applied only to Philadelphia County at its passage, but prior to the Act of 1836 it had been extended to the following counties:

Allegheny (Act April 13, 1835, P. L., 213), Armstrong (March 30, 1831, P. L., 239), Beaver (April 13, 1835, P. L., 213; March 24, 1818, 7 Sm. L., 119), Bedford (March 30, 1831, P. L., 239), Berks (April 11, 1825, P. L., 162), Bucks (March 7, 1821, P. L., 82), Butler (May 7, 1832, P. L., 539), Cambria (March 30, 1831, P. L., 239), Centre (April 10, 1826, P. L., 345), Chester (May 7, 1832, P. L., 539), Clearfield (April 10, 1826, P. L., 345), Columbia (March 24, 1818, 7 Sm. Laws, 119), Crawford (April 10, 1826, P. L., 345), Cumberland (March 24, 1818, 7 Sm. Laws, 119), Dauphin (March 22, 1817, 6 Sm. Laws, 445), Delaware (March 7, 1821, P. L., 82), Erie (April 11, 1825, P. L., 162), Franklin (March 22, 1817, 6 Sm. Laws, 445), Huntingdon (April 13, 1835, P. L., 213), Indiana (April 10, 1826, P. L., 345), Juniata (April 11, 1835, P. L., 190), Lancaster (March 22, 1817, 6 Sm. Laws, 445), Lebanon (March 22, 1817, 6 Sm. Laws, 445), Luzerne (March 7, 1821, P. L., 82), Lycoming (April 10, 1826, P. L., 345), Mercer (April 13, 1835, P. L., 213), Mifflin (March 7, 1821, P. L., 82), Montgomery (March 22, 1817, 6 Sm. Laws, 445), Northumberland (March 24, 1818, 7 Sm. Laws, 119), Perry (May 7, 1832, P. L., 539), Schuylkill (April 11, 1825, P. L., 162), Somerset (April 11, 1825, P. L., 162), Susquehanna (April 1, 1836, P. L., 695), Tioga (March 30, 1831, P. L., 239), Union (April 16, 1827, P. L., 446), Venango (April 11, 1825, P. L., 162), Warren (April 11, 1835, P. L., 190), Washington (April 13, 1835, P. L., 213), and York (March 22, 1817, 6 Sm. Laws, 445). And the Act of 1836 therefore applied to these counties.

It was extended to Lehigh County by its own section 28 (P. L., 1836, page 696), and it was subsequently extended to the following counties:

Adams (Act April 13, 1846, section 1, P. L., 327), Bradford (Act February 19, 1842, section 1, P. L., 22), Carbon (Act April 26, 1850, section 9, P. L., 612), Clarion (Act April 6, 1841, section 22, P. L., 163), Clinton (Act March 19, 1841, section 14, P. L., 99), Elk (Act April 9, 1849, section 1, P. L., 495), Fayette (Act April 16, 1840, section 8, P. L., 412), Greene (Act March 25, 1842, section 30, P. L., 197), Jefferson (Act April 5, 1843, P. L., 171), McKean (Act April 6, 1841, section 22, P. L., 163), Monroe (Act February 19, 1842, P. L., 22), Northampton (Act March 19, 1844, P. L., 140), Pike (Act March 11, 1846, P. L., 113), Potter (Act April 5, 1843, P. L., 171), Westmoreland (Act April 9, 1849, P. L., 495), Wayne (Act April 16, 1840, section 8, P. L., 412).

In *Parson* v. *Winslow*, 1 Grant, 160 (1854), it was decided, per WOODWARD, J., that when a new county is created out of parts of older counties, all of which have the lien law, that law extends by

implication to the new county without special enactment, and the
Act of 1836 'therefore extends to the counties of

Blair (parts of Huntingdon and Bedford, 1846), Cameron (parts of Clinton,
Elk, McKean, and Potter, 1860), Forest (part of Jefferson, 1848, and Venango, 1866), Fulton (part of Bedford, 1850), Lackawanna (part of Luzerne,
1878), Lawrence (part of Beaver and Mercer, 1850), Montour (part of Columbia, 1850), Snyder (part of Union, 1855), Sullivan (part of Lycoming, 1847),
Wyoming (part of Luzerne, 1842).

The Act of 1836 thus extends throughout the State.

§ 207. Claims for Repairs, Alterations, Additions—Leaseholds.
The Act of May 1, 1861 (P. L., 550), which gives a lien for repairs, alterations, or additions, when the debt is not of less amount
than twenty dollars, applied only to Chester, Delaware, and Berks
Counties.

By the Act of May 18, 1887 (P. L., 118), this law was extended
to all the counties of the Commonwealth.

The Act of June 17, 1887 (P. L., 409), which gives a lien on
leaseholds, and on the engine or engines, engine-house, derrick,
tank, building, machinery, wood or iron improvements, oil-wells,
and fixtures, for or about the construction of which on such leasehold labor is performed or furnished, is a general law, and applies
throughout the commonwealth. It also repeals all general laws or
parts of general laws inconsistent therewith.

§ 208. Résumé of the Statutes. It will thus be seen that the
following Acts and their supplements extend throughout the State :

1. Act of June 16, 1836, giving a lien for the payment of all
debts contracted *for work done or material furnished* for or about
the erection or construction of any house or other building.

2. Act of May 1, 1861, giving a lien for the payment of all debts
contracted *for work done and material furnished* for or about *the
repair, alteration of, or addition to* any house or other building.

3. Act of June 17, 1887, giving a lien for the price or value of ` ` ` `
work and labor performed or furnished for or about the construction
of any engine-house, derrick, tank, buildings, machinery, wood or
iron improvement, construction, or erection *upon any leasehold,*
either by written or verbal lease, etc.

It may here be noted that the Act of June 28, 1879 (P. L., 182),
providing for the filing of mechanics' liens in certain cases against
leaseholders for labor in boring, drilling, or mining, and containing a proviso that it shall not apply to counties having more than
20,000 inhabitants, is unconstitutional. *Davis* v. *Clark,* 106 Pa.
St., 377 (1884).

§ 209. The second section of Act of April 9, 1849 (P. L., 495),
which extended the lien law to every fixture in and about iron

works and mines, and to every bridge and building where work is done or material furnished in the construction of such fixture for any corporate body or its contractor, extends to the counties of Allegheny (Act March 1, 1870, P. L., 282), Bradford (Act May 10, 1871, P. L., 675), Columbia and Elk (Act April 9, 1849, P. L., 495), and to Northumberland County (Act May 26, 1871, P. L., 1190).

§ 210. The Act of February 17, 1858 (P. L., 29), giving a lien on improvements, engines, etc., erected by tenants, extended to Allegheny (Act March 21, 1865, P. L., 433), Bradford (Act May 10, 1871, P. L., 668), Carbon (Act April 4, 1868, P. L., 680), Luzerne and Schuylkill (Act February 17, 1858, P. L., 29), Sullivan (Act May 10, 1871, P. L., 668), and Westmoreland (Act March 21, 1865, P. L., 433), and for claims for actual labor by mechanics and laboring men, to Crawford, Erie, Forest, Venango, and Washington Counties (Act June 5, 1874, P. L., 300).

§ 211. The Act of February 27, 1868 (P. L., 212), which extends the lien law to improvements, etc., connected with oil refineries, extends by its own provisions to Allegheny, and as to claims for actual labor done by mechanics and laboring men to Armstrong, Venango, and Warren (Act June 5, 1874, P. L., 300).

§ 212. The Act of April 8, 1868 (P. L., 752), giving a lien on certain property and leaseholds by written lease, extends by its own provision to Venango County, and as to claims for actual labor, to Armstrong, Butler, Clarion, Crawford, and Warren Counties (Act June 5, 1874, P. L., 300).

§ 213. **Against what the claim may be filed.** For work done or materials furnished for or about the erection or construction of any building, or for or about the repair, alteration of, or addition to any building, a claim may be filed against the building, the ground covered by the building, and so much other ground immediately adjacent thereto and belonging in like manner to the owner of such building, as may be necessary for the ordinary and useful purposes of such building. (Act June 16, 1836, P. L., 696; Act May 18, 1887, P. L., 118.)

In *Church* v. *Stettler*, 26 Pa. St., 246 (1856), LEWIS, C. J., said: "No amount of labor or materials furnished for the erection of a building would create a lien if no building should be erected."

If the building, after erection, should be destroyed by accident, before the ground on which it stood passed to the purchaser, the lien would be gone. *Wigton's Appeal*, 28 Pa. St., 161 (1857).

When the building ceases to exist, the lien is gone. *Id.* See *Steel Co.* v. *Mnfg. Co.*, 158 Pa. St., 238 (1893).

Digging cellars and foundations is a part of the construction of

a building, and therefore properly included in a mechanic's lien.
McCristal v. *Cochran*, 147 Pa. St., 225 (1892). Whether a claim
may be filed for the cost of tearing down an old building preparatory to erecting a new one against which the claim is filed has
not been decided. *Id.*

Public buildings belonging to a township or a county—such as
a public school-house, *Patterson* v. *Reform School*, 92 Pa. St., 229
(1879)—are not subject to a claim, because they cannot be taken in
execution (Act April 15, 1834, section 5, P. L., 538); *Wilson* v.
Huntingdon, 7 W. & S., 197 (1844). For the same reason, a claim
cannot be filed against a building of a public corporation necessary
to the enjoyment of its franchises. *Foster* v. *Fowler*, 60 Pa. St., 27
(1868). A church is subject to a claim. *Presbyterian Church* v.
Allison, 10 Pa. St., 413 (1849).

Lumber furnished for the plant of an oil refinery may be the
subject of a lien. *Short* v. *Miller*, 21 W. N., 482; 120 Pa. St.,
470 (1888).

Under the Act of February 17, 1858, a claim can be filed against
a market house and hall erected by a lessee on his leasehold. *Market House* v. *Kearns*, 103 Pa. St., 403 (1884).

A claim may be filed against real estate of a private corporation
transacting a general storage and elevator business. *Storage Co.* v.
Foundry Co., 105 Pa. St., 248 (1888).

§ 214. **How much ground immediately adjacent is subject to a
claim** may be determined in either of two ways: (*a*) The owner
may define in writing, and cause to be entered in a book, to be
kept by the prothonotary, the boundaries, and this is obligatory
on all persons (Act June 16, 1836, section 4, P. L., 696), or (*b*)
in default of such designation, the court, on petition by the owner
or anyone having a lien by mortgage, judgment, or otherwise, or
entitled to a mechanic's lien, shall appoint commissioners to designate the boundaries. Their report, when approved by the court,
is conclusive on all persons. The court may stay a pending execution until such designation is made. (Act June 16, 1836, sections
5–8, P. L., 696.)

§ 215. **If the ground be sold on execution, before the extent of
the lien is ascertained,** distribution is made according to the report
of an auditor appointed to inquire into and report the facts; but
if any of the parties apply therefor, an issue may be directed to
determine disputed facts. (Act June 16, 1836, section 9, P. L.,
696.)

The claim binds no other or greater estate in the ground than
that of the person or persons in possession at the time of com-

mencing the building, and at whose instance the same is erected. (Act April 28, 1840, section 24, P. L., 474.)

§ 216. **Leaseholds—Notice required.** Under Act of June 17, 1887 (P. L., 409), "all persons performing labor or furnishing labor for or about the construction of any engine, house, derrick, tank, buildings, machinery, wood or iron improvement, construction or erection upon any leasehold, either by written or verbal lease, etc., may file a claim against such engine or engines, engine-house, derrick, tank, building, machinery, wood or iron improvement, oil-wells, and fixtures," and the interest of the lessee or tenant in such lease or lot. The owners, contractors, lessee, or tenant cannot remove such property as named in the claim until the claim is paid, or while it is pending and undetermined; provided the claimant issue his *scire facias* within three months. Should removal be attempted, the court may, upon petition, issue an order to the sheriff to seize and hold the property until the claim shall be determined. (Act June 17, 1887, section 5, P. L., 409.)

Under this Act, notice of the intention to file a lien must precede the work. *Strawick* v. *Munhall*, 27 W. N., 195 (1891).

§ 217. **Special Act as to Iron Works, Mines, Bridges, etc.** In Allegheny, Bradford, Columbia, Elk, and Northumberland Counties, the Act of April 9, 1849, section 2 (P. L., 495) (see section 209), extended the Act of 1836 so that a claim may be filed in those counties to include "every fixture in and about iron works and mines, and to every bridge and building where work is done or material furnished in the construction of such fixture, in and about mines or iron works, bridges, or building for any corporate body, or for a contractor in the employment of a corporate body."

§ 218. **Special Act as to Leaseholds.** In Allegheny, Bradford, Carbon, Luzerne, Schuylkill, Sullivan, and Westmoreland Counties, by Act February 17, 1858 (P. L., 29) (see section 210), the claim, under the Act of 1836, may be filed against the interest of a lessee or tenant; and the improvements, engines, pumps, machinery, screens, and fixtures erected, repaired, or put up by mechanics, machinists, and material-men. The same property is subject to lien, in like manner, for actual labor by mechanics and laboring men in Crawford, Erie, Forest, Venango, and Washington Counties. (Act June 5, 1874, P. L., 300.)

§ 219. **Special Act as to Refineries.** In Allegheny County, by Act February 27, 1868 (P. L., 212), the claim may include as property against which it is filed all improvements, engines, pumps, tanks, machinery, and fixtures in or about or in any way connected with or appurtenant to oil or other refineries, and to all tanks for the storage of petroleum, coal, or carbon oil, or the products thereof, whether said tanks be connected with a refinery or otherwise, and on all pumps, machinery, and fixtures connected therewith, whether put up by owners or tenants. If by tenants, then only to the tenant's interest in the land, tanks, etc. The claim to be for doing work or furnishing materials or articles by mechanics, machinists, material-men, and contractors. The same provisions apply only to claims for actual labor done by mechanics and laboring men in Armstrong, Venango, and Warren Counties. (Act June 4, 1874, P. L., 300.)

§ 220. **Special Act as to Leaseholds in Venango County.** By Act April 8, 1868 (P. L., 752), claims may be filed against engines, derricks, tanks, machinery, or wood or iron improvement on land held by written lease and against the leasehold for furnishing material or doing work. The provisions of this Act are similar to, but not the same as, the Act of June 17, 1887 (P. L., 409). As to claims for actual labor done by mechanics and laboring men, this Act of April 8, 1868 (P. L., 752), extends to Armstrong, Butler, Clarion, Crawford, and Warren Counties. (Act June 5, 1874, P. L., 300.)

§ 221. These local Acts contain many provisions peculiar to themselves which cannot be noticed in a general work. They must be consulted in order to learn their details.

§ 222. **By whom the claim may be filed.** *By the architect* who prepares plans and specifications, and who directs and oversees the execution of the work in accordance with the plans; *Bank* v. *Grier*, 35 Pa. St., 423 (1860); but if he simply prepares plans and specifications, and does nothing more, he has no lien; *Price* v. *Kirk*, 90 Pa. St., 47 (1879).

§ 223. *By a principal contractor.* One who contracts with the owner, either for the whole building or for any leading division, such as brickwork or woodwork; the question whether the contract be for a leading division is one for the jury, under proper instructions. *Schenck* v. *Uber*, 81 Pa. St., 31 (1876). Act April 16, 1845, section 5 (P. L., 538). One who merely furnishes lumber is not a "contractor." *Brown* v. *Steele*, 110 Pa. St., 588 (1885).

A contractor does not lose his right to a mechanic's lien because by his contract he is to be paid in kind. *Pierce* v. *Marple*, 30 W. N., 31 (1892).

A contract which provides that the owner should receive the building free of all liens does not prevent the principal contractor from filing a lien for the contract price if unpaid. *Schmid* v. *Im-*

provement Co., 34 W. N., 461 (1894); *Howarth* v. *Church*, 34 W. N., 470 (1894).

§ 224. **Sub-contractors, material-men, and workmen.** All who do work and who furnish materials may file claims, if the work has been done or the materials furnished on the credit of the building and by reason of a contract with either the owner or principal contractor. *Harland* v. *Rand*, 27 Pa. St., 511 (1856); *Schenck* v. *Uber*, 81 *Id.*, 31 (1876); *Steel Co.* v. *Mnfg. Co.*, 33 W. N., 244 (1893). The work must have been done or the materials furnished on the credit of the building; *Barclay* v. *Wainwright*, 86 Pa. St., 191 (1878); and the contract must have been with the owner or principal contractor. A contract with a sub-contractor cannot confer a lien. *Duff* v. *Hoffman*, 63 Pa. St., 191 (1869); *Smith* v. *Stokes*, 10 W. N., 6 (1881). The Act of June 17, 1887 (P. L., 413), to the contrary, was decided unconstitutional. *Iron Works* v. *Oil Co.*, 122 Pa. St., 627; 22 W. N., 435 (1888); *Gearing* v. *Hapgood*, *Id.*, 437 (1888). A sub-contractor who files a lien must comply strictly with the Act of June 16, 1836. *Brown* v. *Myers*, 29 W. N., 393 (1891). A watchman has no lien. *Mc-Grath* v. *Schreiber*, 22 W. N., 312 (1888).

In *Schroeder* v. *Galland*, 26 W. N., 33 (1890), and *Benedict* v. *Hood*, *Id.*, 37 (1890), it was held that where a clause in the contract between the owner and the builder sets forth that the building shall be finished and delivered to the owner " free of all liens and incumbrances," such stipulation is obligatory on all sub-contractors and the latter have no right to lien.

Schroeder v. *Galland* and *Benedict* v. *Hood* were followed by a number of other cases, among which may be mentioned *Tebay* v. *Kirkpatrick*, 29 W. N., 184 (1892); *Lloyd* v. *Krause*, *Id.*, 429 (1892); *Cook* v. *Murphy*, 30 *Id.*, 335 (1892); *Murphy* v. *Ellis*, 1 Dist. Rep., 397 (1892); *Willey* v. *Topping*, 146 Pa. St., 427 (1892); *M'Elroy* v. *Braden*, 152 *Id.*, 78 (1892); *Smith* v. *Levick*, 153 *Id.*, 522; 32 W. N., 79 (1893); *M'Collum* v. *Riale*, 35 W. N., 389 (1884).

In these cases, the ruling in *Schroeder* v. *Galland* and *Benedict* v. *Hood* was substantially re-affirmed; but it was stated that in order to bar the sub-contractor, the clause against liens must be clearly expressed, and that no implication would be sufficient to defeat the sub-contractor's right to file a lien.

In order to meet the decisions in *Schroeder* v. *Galland* and *Benedict* v. *Hood*, the Act of June 8, 1891 (P. L., 225), was passed. It rendered any such contract between the owner and the builder of no effect unless the sub-contractor consented thereto in writing.

In *Waters* v. *Wolf*, 34 W. N., 409, and *McMasters* v. *Normal School, Id.*, 456 (1894), the Act of June 8, 1891 (*supra*), was declared to be unconstitutional.

§ 225. Building contracts containing stipulations against sub-contractors' liens must be recorded and indexed.

The Act of June 26, 1895, § 1 (P. L., 369), provides:

> That no contract for the erection of the whole or any part of any build-ing hereafter made, and no stipulation separately made as part of any such contract, whereby it is sought to deprive or hinder a contractor, sub-con-tractor, material-man, or other person from filing or maintaining a lien, commonly called a mechanic's lien, for work done or material furnished to such building or to any part thereof, shall operate to defeat the right of any sub-contractor, material-man, or other person to file and maintain such a lien, unless such contract(or) or the stipulation shall specifically covenant against such lien by sub-contractor, or other person, and unless said stipu-lation shall be put in writing and signed by the parties thereto prior to the time authority is given to the principal contractor to proceed with said work, and unless said contract or said stipulation shall be filed with the prothonotary of the county where the land lies for record within ten days after its execution.
>
> SEC. 2. The prothonotary shall record such contract or stipulation in the docket provided for mechanics' liens, shall index the same, making the contractor the plaintiff and the owner the defendant, and shall receive for his service the same fee as for filing and recording a mechanic's lien.

§ 226. For what demands claims may be filed. For work done or materials furnished for or about *the erection or construction* of any house or other buildings (Act June 16, 1836, P. L., 696), such as hauling the materials, *Hill* v. *Newman*, 38 Pa. St., 151 (1861), and work done with derricks in hoisting the materials used in construction, *Tizzard* v. *Hughes*, 3 Phila., 261 (1858); work done or materials furnished which go to make up the building, brick, stone, mortar, bricklaying, mason work, door, sash, lumber, hardware, plastering, carpenter work, paint, painting, roofing, and, by express enactment, paperhanging (Act March 24, 1849, P. L., 675), *James* v. *Keller*, 2 Dist. Rep., 165 (1892); plumbing, gas-fitting, and furnishing (Act April 14, 1855, P. L., 238). But this does not include gas-fixtures, *Jarechi* v. *Society*, 79 Pa. St., 403 (1875); the erection of grates and furnaces (Act April 14, 1855, P. L., 238); also work and material for every steam-engine, coal-breaker, or parts thereof, pump gear, hoisting gearing, fix-tures or machinery in and about mills of any kind, iron or coal works, coal mines, and iron mines. (Act April 21, 1856, P. L., 496.) If laying the pavement and brickwork on the building are done under an entire contract, the claim may include the paving, *Yearsley* v. *Flanigen*, 22 Pa. St., 489 (1854), but there can be no lien for work and materials furnished to pave the footway. *Webster* v. *Wakeling*, 2 W. N., 111 (1875); *Paving Co.* v. *Donegan*, 4 Dist. Rep., 243; 36 W. N., 261 (1895); *Edelkamm* v. *Comly*, 1 Dist. Rep., 505 (1892); *contra, Paving Co.* v. *Weir*, 3 Dist. Rep., 32 (1893). In Philadelphia, a lien is given for curbstone for the pavement (Act June 16, 1836, section 20), and for measurement and valuation by any legalized measurer. (Act August 1, 1868, P. L., 1169.) In *Dimmick* v. *Cook Co.*, 19 W. N., 239 (1887), steam-heating apparatus, laundry apparatus, steam pump and pipes, and a large stock or soup kettle furnished to a hotel, as a part of its original construction, were held to be subjects of a claim.

PAXSON, J., clearly stated the legal principle as follows : " This was a large hotel, capable of accommodating two hundred guests. For such a building permanent apparatus for heating, washing, and cooking are as essential as are engines and boilers in a mill. It is true you can eat, wash, and cook without them. So you can grind flour and saw lumber by hand, but the world has outgrown such a mode of doing business, and it is proper that both legislation and judicial decision should keep abreast of the times. A building with only walls and a roof is neither a hotel nor a factory. It is a building, nothing more. When a man constructs a building for a hotel, everything of a permanent character, which will pass as a part of the freehold, and which is reasonably necessary to equip it for the purpose for which it is erected, is a part of such building, and therefore comes within the Act of 1836."

A mechanic's lien for a gasoline machine permanently attached to the freehold was sustained in *Globe Gaslight Co.* v. *Gill*, 1 Dist. Rep., 538 (1892).

A mechanic's claim for machinery may be sustained against a whole manufacturing plant, although the machinery is used in but one building, and the lien is not lost by the destruction of that particular building. *Steel Co.* v. *Mnfg. Co.*, 158 Pa. St., 238 (1893).

Any structure of a substantial and permanent character, independent of the rest of a manufacturing plant of which it is a part, is subject to a mechanic's lien. *Wheeler* v. *Pierce*, 167 Pa. St., 416 (1895).

§ 227. **Work and materials furnished on credit of building need not be actually used.**

Work or materials on which a claim is based must have been furnished for the building and on its credit, *Barclay* v. *Wainwright*, 86 Pa. St., 191 (1878), but it is not necessary that they should have been actually used. *Odd Fellows* v. *Masser*, 24 Pa. St., 507 (1855).

§ 228. **Apportioned Claims.** If the labor has been done or the materials furnished for several *adjoining* buildings belonging to the same owner, there may be filed with the claim an apportionment of the amount among the several buildings, and then each building is subject to its apportioned share. (Act March 30, 1831, P. L., 243 ; Act April 25, 1850, P. L., 576.) If this be not done in the case of such joint claim, the claim is postponed to other lien-creditors. (Act June 16, 1836, P. L., 699.) See *Beitzel* v. *Stair*, 2 Dist. Rep., 337 (1893).

If a joint lien filed for alterations to several adjoining buildings, under the Act of May 1, 1861 (P. L., 550), be not apportioned, it will be postponed to all other lien-creditors. *Bunting's Appeal*, 6 W. N., 12 (1878).

A lien against buildings situated on the same side of the street, but separated by a vacant lot, may be apportioned. *Livezey* v. *Garvin*, 16 W. N., 439 (1885).

An apportioned lien may be filed against separate buildings belonging to the same owner, separated by a carriage-way. *Livezey* v. *Hacker*, 20 W. N., 14 (1886).

If two blocks of houses built under the same contract are divided by merely a *private* way, the right of which belongs to both blocks, there is not such a severance as will prevent an apportionment of the claim among the several houses. *Atkinson* v. *Shoemaker*, 30 W. N., 567 (1892).

A claim which is in effect a joint claim against several blocks of houses, separated by public streets, apportioned first against the blocks and then against the houses composing the blocks, is invalid. *Lucas* v. *Hunter*, 1 Dist. Rep., 165 (1892).

An apportioned claim cannot be filed against blocks of houses on opposite sides of a street. *French* v. *Kaign*, 3 W. N., 495 (1877).

Where two buildings adjoining are separated by a solid brick partition-wall with no internal communication, they form two buildings, and a mechanic's claim against a double brick dwelling, and not apportioned, cannot be sustained. *Roat* v. *Frear*, 167 Pa. St., 614 (1895).

In *Wilson* v. *Forder*, 30 Pa. St., 129 (1858), there was a contract for plastering several houses for a gross sum. No work was done on any except one within six months from the time of filing an apportioned claim. *Held*, that the work on the one did not keep alive the lien as to the others. The work claimed to keep the lien alive was patching, and was performed long after the contract was substantially completed.

The Mechanics' Lien Law recognizes the filing of one lien against several houses and the apportionment of the amount among them. *Liebelt* v. *King*, 21 P. L. J., 144 (1872); *Schultz* v. *Asay*, 2 Pennypacker, 416 (1882); *Millet* v. *Allen*, 3 W. N., 374 (1877).

Where a clear title right exists to file one apportioned lien against certain houses, or separate apportioned liens against each, two apportioned liens may be filed if the same contract and bill of particulars be filed in each. *Brick Co.* v. *Morton*, 2 Dist. Rep., 559 (1893).

As to form of an apportioned claim, see § 202.

§ 229. **Repairs—Alterations—Additions—Notice required.** A claim may be filed for work done or materials furnished for or about the *repair, alteration of, or addition* to any house or other building, provided the debt is not less than twenty dollars. (Act May 18, 1887, P. L., 118.) The Act of May 1, 1861 (P. L., 550), was an extension of the Act of 1836 to repairs, alterations, and additions; and the Act of May 1, 1861, was, by the Act of May 18, 1887, extended throughout the State. The Act of 1887 was declared constitutional in *Smyers* v. *Beam*, 158 Pa. St., 57 (1893).

The claim for repairs, alterations, or additions, under the Act of May 18, 1887, is therefore a part of the Act of 1836, and is governed by the principles already noted (sections 226 to 228).

There are, however, some statutory regulations : (*a*) The claim must be for not less than twenty dollars. (*b*) At the time of furnishing the materials, or performing the work, notice must be given to the owner or the reputed owner of the property, or his or her agent, of the intention to file a lien under the provisions of the Act. If the claim do not aver that notice was given to the owner, as required by the Act, it will be stricken off. *Morrison* v. *Henderson*, 22 W. N., 8 (1888); affirmed in 126 Pa. St., 216 (1889); *Strawick* v. *Munhall*, 27 W. N., 195 (1890); *Kramer* v. *Crump*, 28 W. N., 16 (1891); *Moss* v. *Greenberg*, 3 Dist. Rep., 247 (1894). The requirement of notice extends to all the counties of the State. *Best* v. *Baumgardner*, 122 Pa. St., 17 (1888), GREEN, J. (*c*) No claim can be filed for alterations, repairs, or additions made by a tenant or lessee without the written consent of the owner or reputed owner or his or her duly authorized agent.

A mechanic's claim cannot be filed as for work done to a *new* building, when it appears that such work was merely the addition to and alteration of an old building. *De Wald* v. *Woog*, 158 Pa. S., 497 (1893).

Where the owner of a building so remodelled it that but a small part of the old building was left standing, the new structure was declared an alteration within the meaning of the Act of May 18, 1887 (P. L., 118), requiring notice to the owner of materials furnished or work performed. *Smyers* v. *Beam*, 158 Pa. St., 57 (1893).

§ 230. The Act of August 1, 1868 (P. L., 1168), which applies only to Philadelphia, differs in three particulars from the general law of May 18, 1887 : (*a*) The amount must be not less than fifty dollars ; (*b*) the written consent of the owner or a copy must be filed with the claim or statement ; (*c*) if the property shall have been conveyed to a purchaser before the claim is filed, it is released from the claim. Otherwise, this Act is substantially the same as the general Act of 1887.

In *Thomas* v. *Hinkle*, 24 W. N., 119 (1889), it was *held* that a mechanic's claim filed in Philadelphia against an addition to an old building was subject to the provisions of the Act of August 1, 1868, and created no lien unless filed before the property was conveyed to a third party.

§ 231. **In claims against Leaseholds, notice required.** A claim may be filed for " performing labor or furnishing labor for or about the construction of any engine-house, derrick, tank, buildings, machinery, wood or iron improvement, construction, or erection upon any leasehold, either by written or verbal lease, or for boring, drilling, or mining of any lease or lot as aforesaid, for the development or improvement of the same, whether such labor is or may be done by day, month, or year, or by contract, for the tenant or tenants, lessee or lessees, of such lot, or lease, or parcel of land, or for their use or benefit," " for the price and value of such work and labor," provided " that when the materials were furnished or labor performed by others than the original contractor or contractors, they shall notify the owner or owners, or reputed owners, of the leasehold property, of his or their intention to file a mechanic's lien, and unless such notice be given no such lien shall be filed nor be of any validity." (Act of June 17, 1887, P. L., 409.)

A lien filed under the Act of June 17, 1887, § 1 (P. L., 409), relating to the lien of mechanics, laborers, and others upon leasehold estates, must be preceded by the notice required by the Act. *Strawick* v. *Munhall*, 139 Pa. St., 163 (1891).

§ 232. **Work done and materials furnished included in one claim.** In the counties of Philadelphia and Chester, work performed and materials furnished may be included in the same claim filed. (Act March 24, 1849, section 2, P. L., 675.)

§ 233. **Time for filing.** For work done or materials furnished, for or about the erection or construction, or for or about the repair, alteration of, or addition to any building, the claim must be filed before the expiration of six months after the work shall have been finished or the materials furnished. (Act June 16, 1836, section 14, P. L., 696.)

Six months is also the limit under the Philadelphia Repair Act of August 1, 1868 (P. L., 1168).

One who covenants not to file a lien within six months waives his right. *Scheid* v. *Rapp*, 22 W. N., 438 (1888).

A mechanic's claim under Act of August 1, 1868 (P. L., 1168), filed within six months after completion of work, but after death of debtor, is not entitled to priority over the general debts of decedent. *Hoff's Appeal*, 102 Pa. St., 218 (1883).

Work done to compensate defective performance of a contract for work and material in the construction of a building will not preserve the lien, but work substituted for that called for in the contract may do so. *Harrison* v. *Assn.*, 26 W. N., 84 (1890).

§ 234. Claims on leaseholds and personal property, under Act of June 17, 1887 (P. L., 409), must be filed within thirty days from the time the last work or labor was done.

§ 235. The time begins to run from midnight of the day on which the work has been finished or the material furnished. Thus, materials were furnished December 15th ; the six months began to run at midnight and expired at midnight of June 15th following. A claim filed June 16th was, therefore, too late. *Hall* v. *Dougherty*, 8 W. N., 255 (1880).

§ 236. The limitation begins to run as to each item of the claim from the time of such item. This is the general principle, but the exceptions to it are of more frequent occurrence than the rule itself.

§ 237. The exceptions are: (1) if any of the items of a claim for work done or materials furnished *continuously*, toward the erection of any new building, is *bona fide* within six. months before the filing of the claim, the claim is valid as to all the items. (Act April 14, 1855, section 2, P. L., 238.)

This Act " gives a unity " to items of materials furnished and work done from time to time as if under a contract for the whole. *Hofer's Appeal*, 116 Pa. St., 360 (1887).

A mechanic's claim may be filed within six months from the completion of the work, although some of it may have been done more than six months before the lien filed. *Bartlett* v. *Kingan,* 19 Pa. St., 343 (1852); *Yearsley* v. *Flanigen,* 22 Pa. St., 489 (1854); *Hazzard's Appeal,* 83 Pa. St., 111 (1876); *Brick Co.* v. *Norton,* 2 Dist. Rep., 559 (1893).

The doing or furnishing must be *continuous,* and, therefore, where a building was completed, and shortly afterward an addition not originally contemplated was added, and further work was done on the addition, the two sets of items were not continuous, and the limitation began to run as to the work on the first building from the last item of that work, and not from the last item of the work on the addition. *Diller* v. *Burger,* 68 Pa. St., 432 (1871).

(2) If the items for one building be done or furnished under one entire contract, the limitation begins to run from the date of the last item, in pursuance of the contract. *Parrish's Appeal,* 83 Pa. St., 111 (1876).

But if the items under such a contract are performed on different buildings, the time begins to run, as to each building, from the completion of the work upon that building. *Wilson* v. *Forder,* 30 Pa. St., 129 (1858); *Shannon* v. *Broadbent,* 34 W. N., 466 (1894).

§ 238. If, while work under the contract is being performed, extra work be commenced at the owner's request, and the extra work be finished subsequent to the completion of the contract, the limitation on a claim for both contract and extra work begins to run from the finishing of the extra work. *Rush* v. *Able,* 90 Pa. St., 153 (1879); *Harrison* v. *Assn.,* 26 W. N., 84 (1890).

§ 239. **For what defects claims have been struck off.** A claim can be struck off only for defects apparent on its face. *Miller* v. *Bedford,* 86 Pa. St., 454 (1878).

It has been struck off because filed in a court not having jurisdiction, *Curry* v. *Spunk,* 23 Pa. St., 58 (1854); or because it omitted the owner's name, *Barclay's Appeal,* 11 W. N., 359 (1882); *Steinman* v. *Miller,* 12 W. N., 244 (1882); or the contractor's name, *McCoy's Appeal,* 37 Pa. St., 125 (1860); or because it did not state the nature and character of the work done or the kind of material furnished. *Gray* v. *Dick,* 97 Pa. St., 142 (1881). A claim which names the owner as the " estate of Mary Reece, deceased," is valid. *Reece* v. *Haymaker,* 164 Pa. St., 575 (1894). But a contractor by a special contract with the owner need not thus specify. *Id.* (Act April 16, 1845, P. L., 538.)

It has been stricken off because it omitted to state the amount claimed for each distinct item. *Noll* v. *Swinford,* 2 Pa. St., 187 (1847); or because it did not state that work was done or materials furnished within six months, or because neither upon its face nor by reference to an accompanying paper did it give date or dates to verify the general allegation, *Baptist Church* v. *Trout*, 28 Pa. St., 153 (1857); or because it described the work as done " for and about the erection and construction of the said building *and appurtenance*," *appurtenance* being too indefinite and uncertain. *Barclay's Appeal*, 13 Pa. St., 494 (1850).

A lien which describes as a separate building a department or section of an abattoir plant is defective. *In re Packing Co.*, 4 Dist. Rep., 57 (1894).

In *Iron Works* v. *Oil Co.*, 25 W. N., 63 (1889), the claim was regarded as sufficient in enumerating the several structures, describing their use, dimensions, capacity, and the materials of which each was constructed, and averring that, taken together, the whole constituted an " oil refinery " upon the premises which were described in the lien.

A lien for materials for a gross unitemized sum may be filed where it is confined to an amount made certain by the contract—not otherwise. *Smith* v. *Gilmore*, 34 W. N., 128 (1894).

A sub-contractor's claim will be stricken off, on motion, where there is a lumping charge and the lien does not specify the items of claim for work or materials. *McFarland* v. *Schultz*, 37 W. N., 28; 168 Pa. St., 634 (1895).

A claim has been stricken off where a description of the land was not sufficient, *Short* v. *Ames*, 22 W. N., 354 (1888); or because it was filed against three blocks of buildings belonging to one owner, but separated by streets. *Goepp* v. *Gartiser*, 35 Pa. St., 130 (1860). If the buildings are all upon one lot facing parallel streets, with their yards adjoining in the centre of the lot, *Taylor* v. *Montgomery*, 20 Pa. St., 443 (1853), or if the buildings are separated by private way only. *Kline's Appeal*, 93 Pa. St., 422 (1880).

In a claim for repairs made by a tenant, the copy of lease filed with the claim contained a covenant by the tenant to repair; the claim was struck off. *Boteler* v. *Espew*, 99 Pa. St., 313 (1882).

A claim is not defective because it is filed against one lot which in fact contains four distinct lots. *City* v. *Cadwallader*, 22 W. N., 8 (1887).

A lien filed for materials furnished to a contractor for a temporary erection forming no part of a structure is not good. *Oppenheimer* v. *Morrell*, 118 Pa. St., 189 (1888).

An apportioned claim against houses in different blocks will not be sustained. *Shultz* v. *Asay*, 11 W. N., 195 (1882).

A claim filed as against a new structure, although against an old as well as a new building, the contract attached showing the work to be altering and repairing, will be struck off. *Morrison* v. *Henderson*, 24 W. N., 38 (1889).

It is the right of the owner alone, in a *sci. fa. sur* mechanic's lien, to object to an insufficient description; the contractors may allege that the materials were never furnished for the buildings, or that the charge was excessive, or that the materials had been paid for, but they cannot object to the description of the premises. *Weatheread* v. *Garrett*, 27 W. N., 451 (1891).

If the claim contains one good item, it cannot be stricken off. *McCristal* v. *Cochran*, 147 Pa. St., 225 (1892).

§ 240. **Claims against property of a married woman** have been struck off for not showing on their face that she had an estate in the land, and that the work was done or materials furnished for the improvement of her separate estate, and were so applied, *Shannon* v. *Schultz*, 87 Pa. St., 481 (1878), by her authority and with her consent, *Steinman* v. *Henderson*, 94 Pa. St., 313 (1880), and that it was necessary. *Kuhns* v. *Turney*, 87 Pa. St., 497 (1878).

The Married Persons' Property Acts (June 3, 1887, P. L., 332, and June 8, 1893, P. L., 344) seem to have affected these decisions. The joinder of the husband is no longer necessary. (See § 201.)

These decisions, although some of them prior to the amendment Acts, are of value, as no material amendment can be allowed after the limitation for filing the claim has expired.

In *Schryock* v. *Buckman*, 22 W. N., 289; 121 Pa. St., 248 (1888), it was held that a claim against a woman described as married was fatally defective unless averments were introduced as above required. But if the coverture do not appear, a regular judgment and *levari* will pass a good title to the purchaser at sheriff's sale. (See § 201.)

A contract made by a husband for the improvement of his wife's separate estate, if made with her knowledge and consent, is sufficient to sustain a mechanic's claim filed by a sub-contractor who has furnished materials necessary for the improvement. *Bodey* v. *Thackara*, 28 W. N., 470 (1891); *Bevan* v. *Thackara*, *Id.*, 473; 48 Leg. Int., 439 (1891).

A mechanic's claim averring that materials were furnished to a married woman "at her request" is sufficient. *Duck* v. *O'Rourke*, 19 W. N., 497 (1887).

When the Supreme Court has decided that the claimant is entitled to judgment upon the affidavit of defense filed, the Common Pleas cannot strike off the claim. *Iron Works* v. *Oil Co.*, 25 W. N., 63 (1889).

§ 241. **Amendments of claims** are allowed by Act April 9, 1862,

§ 2 (P. L., 402), by striking out the names of persons who are by mistake included as claimants, owners or reputed owners, contractors, architects, or builders.

The Act of June 11, 1879, § 2 (P. L., 122), provides that the court having jurisdiction in case of any mechanic's claim or lien " is hereby authorized and required, in any stage of the proceedings, to permit amendments conducive to justice and a fair trial upon the merits, including the changing, adding, and striking out the names of claimants and by adding the names of owners and contractors, respectively, whenever it shall appear to such court that the names of the proper parties have been omitted, or that a mistake has been made in the names of such parties, or too many or not enough have been joined in such case : *Provided*, That no amendment so allowed shall have effect or prejudice the rights of *bona fide* purchasers for a valuable consideration without notice, or the rights of other lien creditors, when such purchase has been made, or such other lien would otherwise be prior if such amendment were not made or had not been allowed." The claim may be amended by adding the name of the contractor.   *Coffa* v. *Bldg. Assn.*, 3 Dist. Rep., 566 (1893).

This Act does not limit amendments to the points specified. Under it the right of amendment extends to the form and manner of setting forth the items of the claim, *Snyder* v. *Baer*, 3 Penny., 530 (1883), but no amendment of a material part can be made after the limitation for filing the claim has run. *Knox* v. *Hilty*, 20 W. N., 524 (1888) ; *McFarland* v. *Schultz*, 37 W. N., 28 (1895).

§ 242. **Duration of the lien.**   " The lien of every such debt, for which a claim shall have been filed as aforesaid, shall expire at the end of five years from the day on which such claim shall have been filed, unless the same shall have been revived by *scire facias* in the manner provided by law in case of judgments." (Act June 16, 1836, section 24, P. L, 696.)

It is sufficient if the *scire facias* be issued within five years and duly prosecuted afterward, *Sweeney* v. *McGilligan*, 20 Pa. St., 319 (1853) ; said due prosecution being the securing of a judgment on the *scire facias* within five years after it issues ; and if a judgment be not secured within that time, the lien is lost.   *Hunter* v. *Lanning*, 76 Pa. St., 25 (1874) ; *Phila.* v. *Scott*, 93 Pa. St., 25 (1880).

A *sci. fa.* " to revive the lien " of a mechanic's claim cannot issue. You must issue a *sci. fa.* " to show cause why the claim should not be levied."   Judgment upon the *sci. fa.* may be revived, but there is no writ to revive the lien of the claim.   *Collins* v. *Schock*, 14 W. N., 485 (1884).

A proceeding on a mechanic's claim is not within the meaning of the Act of February 24, 1834, § 34 (P. L., 80), which requires bringing in the personal representatives of a decedent in order to charge the real estate. *Reece* v. *Haymaker*, 164 Pa. St., 575 (1894).

§ 243. **Compelling claimant to proceed.** The Act of June 16, 1836, section 23 (P. L., 696), provides that, if no *scire facias* shall have issued on the claim, it shall be lawful for the owner of the building, or any person interested therein, to apply by petition to the court, setting forth the facts, whereupon the court may grant a rule upon the claimant and other parties interested to appear at a time to be fixed, and, on the return of the rule, may proceed in like manner as if a *scire facias* had been issued by such claimant, and had been duly served and returned. Under this provision the court, on the return of the rule, fixes time within which the claimant shall file his statement and the defendant plead. In *Barton* v. *Morris*, 2 Miles, 109 (1837), the order of the District Court was that if the plaintiff failed to comply with the directions, judgment of *non pros.* should be entered and the claim struck off. When the defendant has set on foot this proceeding the plaintiff cannot suffer a non-suit or go out of court without paying the costs he has put upon the owner. *Seabrook* v. *Swarthmore College*, 65 Pa. St., 74 (1870). (See § 2800.)

§ 244. The Act of August 1, 1868 (P. L., 1169), which applies only to Philadelphia, provides that the owner may move for a rule on the claimant to sue out a writ of *scire facias* to the next monthly return-day, and if the claimant shall not issue the writ in obedience to the rule, the court, on motion, shall strike the lien from the record.

When a rule on claimant to issue *sci. fa.* is made absolute, the writ should be issued to the next return-day to which it could legally issue or the claim will be stricken off. *Suier* v. *Wilbraham*, 22 W. N., 10 (1887). (See § 2801.)

§ 245. **Satisfaction.** The Act of March 17, 1806 (4 Sm. L., 300), applied only to Philadelphia, and authorized a recovery in damages "not exceeding one-half of the debt," upon failure by the claimant, when debt had been satisfied, to enter satisfaction of record within six days after request so to do, and payment of the costs of action, and tender of the office-costs for entering satisfaction.

The Act of April 9, 1849 (P. L., 495), section 2, extends the provisions of the Act of June 16, 1836, and provides that in liens filed for work done and materials furnished about iron works and mines, and to every bridge and building for any corporate body,

the process to obtain satisfaction of any judgment upon such lien
"in any case where by existing laws no lien is given for labor or
materials done or furnished to a corporate body," shall be by writ
of sequestration. This section embraced only Columbia and Elk
Counties, but was extended by Act of March 1, 1870 (P. L., 282),
to Allegheny County, and by Act of May 10, 1871 (P. L., 675),
to Bradford County. As to how far the Act of April 7, 1870
(P. L., 58), curtails the provision under this Act as to sequestration, see *R. R. Co.'s Appeal*, 70 Pa. St., 355 (1872) ; *Bayard's
Appeal*, 72 Pa. St., 453 (1872).

§ 245 *a*. Satisfaction to be entered on request—penalty.

In every case in which the amount of any claims as aforesaid shall be
paid, or otherwise satisfied, it shall be the duty of the claimant, or his legal
representative, at the request of the owner of the building, or of any other
person interested therein, and on payment of the costs, to enter satisfaction
on the record of such claim, in the office of the prothonotary of the court
in which such claim shall have been entered, which shall forever thereafter discharge and release the same. Act of June 16, 1836, § 25 (P. L., 699).

If any person who shall have received satisfaction as aforesaid shall
neglect or refuse to enter satisfaction of such claim as aforesaid within sixty
days after request and payment of the costs of the suit as aforesaid, he shall
forfeit and pay to the party aggrieved any sum not exceeding one-half of
the amount of such claim, to be recovered as debts of like amount are recoverable. Ibid., § 26.

Provided, That nothing in this Act contained shall be construed to
impair or otherwise affect the right of any person to whom any debt may
be due for work done, or materials furnished, to maintain any personal action against the owner of the building, or any other person liable therefor,
to recover the amount of such debt. Ibid., § 27.

§ 245 *b*. Order to satisfy the claim—to mark to use—to satisfy judgment.

(Caption.)

SIR :

Enter satisfaction of claim in the above case.

Signature of Plaintiff.
(Date.)

To Prothonotary C. P.

The claim may be satisfied on the docket without entering a
formal order to satisfy. If the claim has been reduced to a judgment, the form to satisfy the judgment is given at § 3024. Where
a number of *sci. fas.* have been sued out on an apportioned claim,
an order to satisfy the judgment on each *sci. fa.* should be filed.

The judgment may be assigned, and carries with it all the substantial rights of the assignor as fully as if held by him. *Hage-
man's Appeal*, 88 Pa. St., 21 (1878).

If the claim or judgment is marked "to use," the entry may be
made on the docket or a formal order filed.

CHAPTER VIII.

§ 246. **Judgments should be revived every five years**, in order to continue their lien.

§ 247. **When revival not necessary.** The Act of May 19, 1887 (P. L., 132), provides that " Execution may issue upon any judgment of record in any of the courts of this Commonwealth, notwithstanding such judgment may have lost its lien upon real estate, without a previous writ of *scire facias* to revive the same : *Provided, however,* That such execution shall be confined or restricted to the personal property only of the debtor, and that such execution shall not issue after the lapse of twenty years from the maturity of the judgment : *And, provided further,* That at the same time execution is issued, a *scire facias* shall be issued to revive the judgment upon which said execution is issued ; and, in case the defendant or defendants in said writs file an affidavit alleging a just and legal defense against the revival of said judgment, it shall be lawful for the court, or a judge thereof in vacation, to stay the writ of *fieri facias,* by an order preserving the lien thereof, and to order the *scire facias* on the head of the list for trial at the next term for the trial of civil cases."

In *Pierce* v. *Wunder*, 25 W. N., 466 (1890), it was decided that under this Act a *fi. fa.* could issue more than five years after judgment, without renewal, against personal property, but that a levy on real estate and inquisition under it are irregular.

This ruling was at the instance of a stranger to the record. The defendant did not object to the levy. The application to set it aside was made by a railroad company claiming to have purchased the land after the lien of the judgment had expired, and two days before the levy. It has been generally supposed that a claim of title to real estate cannot be settled in this manner.

§ 248. **To preserve a lien on real estate.** You must issue a *sci. fa.* within the term of five years. (Act April 4, 1798, section 2, 2 Sm., 331.) Failing herein, you lose your lien upon the realty both as to other judgments and purchasers.

§ 249. **If lien lost.** The old cases present some curious features. In *Riland* v. *Eckert*, 23 Pa. St., 215 (1854), there were several serious gaps. Suit was brought in the Circuit Court, U. S., against James Wilson. Judgment was recovered April 14, 1800. Nearly thirteen years were allowed to elapse. A *fi.fa.* was issued January 16, 1813, against the administrators of the defendant. Nothing further was done for eighteen years more. Then, in 1831, a *sci. fa.* was issued to revive, and singularly enough, on this dead judgment, " by writing filed judgment by consent was entered to be levied *de terris et de bonis quando acciderint.*" Executions were issued, but no levy made on land until September 21, 1837. The lien of the last judgment was then gone. The land was sold to Eckert. Ejectment was brought under this title against Riland and others who did not claim under Wilson, but who set up : (1) an improvement title ; (2) that the judgment against Wilson's administrator created no lien on the land as against heirs and others, and that Eckert, the purchaser, acquired no title.

The court below decided against the defendants. The Supreme Court affirmed the judgment. The opinion as to the constructive possession under the improvement title is of interest to those who have watched the line of decisions of which this was an outpost. But it has no place here. The point as to the non-joinder of the heirs in the *sci. fa.* was ruled against defendants because they were not the heirs of Wilson and did not claim under them. The levy was held to create a lien because the lien of the judgment was gone at the time of the levy. The opinion of the court on this branch of the case was well expressed by WOODWARD, J. : " The result of legislation and judicial decisions in Pennsylvania touching the liens of judgments and executions on real estate seems to be that where the judgment is a lien there can be no independent lien acquired by execution process thereon ; but where land is seized in execution by virtue of a judgment, which is no lien, the execution becomes a lien on it. This is the ground on which *Packer's Appeal*, 6 Pa. St., 277, and *Jamison's Appeal, Ib.*, 280, are reconciled in *Davis* v. *Ehrman*, 20 Pa. St., 258. In *Todd* v. *McCulloch*, 3 Pa. Rep., 445, it is said to have been established substantially, if not in terms, in *Betz's Appeal*, 1 Pa. Rep., 271, that the lien of a judgment is preserved by an execution only as regards the land levied, a dictum which is not accurate, for since the Act of 1827 the lien of a judgment, according to all the cases, is not continued by an execution levied, but, as is afterward said in the same case, the lien by which lands are bound for more than five years without a *scire facias*, seems to be that which the common law attributes to an execution, rather than the lien of a judgment."

It will be observed that the lien of a judgment in *Riland* v. *Eckert*, just cited, was gone when the land was levied upon. If the lien of the judgment be in force, the execution will not create a lien which will bar judgments entered after the five years from the date of the first judgment. In *Stephen's Appeal*, 38 Pa. St., 15 (1860), THOMPSON, J., thus clearly states and answers the question :

" As was said in *Jamison's Appeal*, 6 Pa. St., 280, ' A judgment and an execution thereon have not, under our Acts of Assembly, distinct and independent liens upon the same land.'

" The question recurs, then : Did the seizure and the extent continue the lien after that of the judgment was gone, it having been made while the judgment was a lien between the parties to it? I think the doctrine of the last-mentioned case and the Act of 1827 will go far to settle this point."

See also *Stauffer* v. *The Commissioners*, 1 Watts, 300 (1832), and *Packer's Appeal*, 6 Pa. St., 277 (1847).

It will thus be seen that if the judgment were more than five years old, the former practice was to issue a *fi. fa.* and *sci. fa.* together, to give a description of the real estate of the defendant to the sheriff and order him to levy thereon, to see that the prothonotary put the *fi. fa.* on the judgment index, and to file with him a description of the land levied on. This is distinctly ruled in *Riland* v. *Eckert*, 23 Pa. St., 215 (1854). WOODWARD, J., said : " Though the lien of the judgment   *   *   had expired before the pluries *fi. fa.* issued, yet a lien was acquired by virtue of the levy made in pursuance of that writ." See also the other cases cited. This seems to be changed by the Act of May 19, 1887 (P. L., 132), and the decision in *Miller* v. *Miller*, 147 Pa. St., 545 (1892). In this case judgment was obtained by A. against B. on May 12, 1885. On July 2, 1890, a *fi. fa.* and *sci. fa.* were issued on said judgment. On July 30, 1890, C. obtained judgment against B. The defendant took a rule to set aside the levy and proceedings under *fi. fa* , so far as they related to real estate. The rule was made absolute and the fund was awarded to C. The Supreme Court affirmed. The only means, therefore, of obtaining execution against the realty, after the five years, is by issuing *sci. fa.* and obtaining judgment. In the meantime, any other judgment entered will take precedence, and any *bona fide* purchaser of the land will take a good title.

It should be noticed that the Act of June 16, 1836, section 1

(P. L., 761), provides that execution on a judgment within a year and a day from the first day of the term at which it was rendered may be issued, and the second section provides that after the expiration of that period execution shall not be issued unless the defendant shall first be warned by writ of *sci. fa.* Then the Act of April 16, 1845, section 4 (P. L., 538), was passed, and provided that execution on a judgment may be issued at any time if the judgment has been revived in five years. The Act of May 19, 1887 (P. L., 132), authorizes the issuing of execution upon a judgment of record after the expiration of the five years without a previous writ of *sci. fa.* to revive; provided (*a*) that such execution be *restrained* to the *personal* property of the debtor; (*b*) that it be issued within twenty years from the maturity of the judgment; (*c*) that a *sci. fa.* to revive be issued simultaneously with it.

§ 250. **If the lien of the judgment be in force.** If the lien of the judgment be in force when the land is levied upon, but expires before the sale, the execution will not create a lien which will precede judgments entered after the five years from the date of the first judgment. *Davis* v. *Ehrman*, 20 Pa. St., 256 (1853); *Stephen's Appeal*, 38 Pa. St., 15 (1860); *Jamison's Appeal*, 6 Pa. St., 280 (1847).

After-acquired lands. Though a judgment is not a lien upon lands of the defendant subsequently acquired, levy may be made upon such lands in the possession of the defendant.

As to several judgments entered before the land was acquired, the first levy takes the fund, without regard to the question of priority of the judgments. *Packer's Appeal*, 6 Pa. St., 277 (1847); *Lea* v. *Hopkins*, 7 Pa. St., 492 (1848).

In Philadelphia County, by the Act of April 20, 1853, section 9 (P. L., 611), after a levy on after-acquired realty, the plaintiff may have the execution certified by the officer making the levy to the prothonotary: whereupon it is to be docketed in the judgment-index, and thenceforth binds the land levied on for five years. Unless the levy be so certified and indexed, there is no lien. The mere docketing and indexing the *fi. fa.* and not indexing the levy on the judgment-index will not suffice. *Appeals of Ross & Ellsbree*, 15 W. N., 217 (1884).

§ 251. **Form of præcipe for sci. fa. to revive :**

A. } In the Court of Common Pleas, No. 1, of Philadelphia County,
v. }   of   Term, 1894, No.   .
B. }

SIR :

Issue *scire facias* to revive the judgment in the above case, returnable *sec. leg.*

To the Prothonotary of said Court.   C.,
                                            Plaintiff's Attorney.
                                                    (Date.)

Where the plaintiff assigns his judgment, it may nevertheless be revived in his name. *Hayes's Appeal,* 35 W. N., 158 (1894).

§ 252. **Avoid amicable revivals ; terre-tenants.** If defendant has aliened land since your judgment, an amicable revival to which the purchaser was not a party would be of no effect. *Baum* v. *Custer,* 22 W. N., 245 (1888). It is best to add on *præcipe* beneath defendant's name the words, " with notice to terre-tenants." Search in recorder's office for conveyances by the defendant. If any deed from him be recorded for the land originally bound by your judgment, then name the grantee as *terre-tenant* in your *præcipe* and *scire facias.* This is required by Act of June 1, 1887 (P. L., 289), which provides that " no proceeding shall be available to continue the lien of said judgment against a terre-tenant whose deed for the land bound by said judgment has been recorded, except by agreement in writing, signed by said terre-tenant and entered on the proper lien docket, or the terre-tenant, or terre-tenants, be named as such in the original *scire facias.*"

The Act of April 16, 1849 (P. L., 664), relating to the revival of judgments, was intended to continue the lien against lands of the debtor by revival against him alone, unless the purchaser or terre-tenant put his deed on record, or was in actual possession, in which case the five years commenced to run in his favor from the date of record of the deed or the time he took possession personally or by his tenant. *Wetmore* v. *Wetmore,* 33 W. N., 11 (1893).

Revival by married woman. If on an amicable *scire facias* a married woman since 1887 revives a judgment given by her prior to 1887, she cannot afterward claim that the original judgment was void. *Lyons v. Burns,* 47 Leg. Int., 222 (1890).

Both parties to sign agreement. An agreement for an amicable *sci. fa.* must be signed by both plaintiff and defendant. *Miller* v. *Miller,* 27 W. N., 23 (1890).

§ 253. **Lien as to decedents.** You must bear in mind that if the defendant die after judgment, your lien on his real estate continues " to bind such estate during the time of five years from his death," * * * " and such judgments shall, during such term, rank according to their priority at the time of such death ; and after the expiration of such term such judgment shall not continue a lien on the real estate of such decedent, as against a *bona fide* purchaser, mortgagee, or other judgment creditor of such decedent, unless revived by *scire facias* or otherwise, according to the laws regulating the revival of judgments." Act of February 24, 1834, section 25 (P. L., 77). (Br. Purd., 593, section 118.)

§ 254. **Revival against representatives of decedents.** Whenever you have choice, do not allow the time to run closely to the expiration of your lien. Proceed a year or two years before the limitation has run.

Revival by representatives of decedents. The Act of June 27, 1883, section 1 (P. L., 163), authorizes " foreign executors or administrators to issue or cause to be issued, in the name of such foreign executor or administrator, *scire facias* within this Commonwealth on all judgments, the lien of which is about expiring and in favor of the testator so represented : *Provided,* That before any further proceedings are had, letters of administration must be granted within this Commonwealth as now provided by law."

§ 255. **To revive against executors or administrators,** write in your *præcipe,* instead of the name of the original defendant, the name of his executor or administrator, thus :

> A.
> *v.*
> C., executor of the last will and testament of B. (or administrator of B., as the case is),

and follow with this variation the form just given.

§ 256. **As to joining widow and heirs of decedent.** The 34th section of the Act of February 24, 1834, directs : " In all actions against the executors or administrators of a decedent who shall have left real estate, where the plaintiff intends to charge such real estate with the payment of his debt, the widow and heirs or devisees, and the guardians of such as are minors, shall be made parties thereto ; and in case such widow and heirs or devisees or their guardians reside out of the county, it shall be competent for the court to direct notice of the writ issued therein to be served by publication or otherwise, as such court may determine by rule of court, and if notice of such writ shall not be served on such widow and heirs or devisees, or their guardians, the judgment obtained in such action shall not be levied or paid out of the real estate of such widow, heirs, or devisees, as shall not have been served with notice of such writ."

Under this statute the question arose in *McMillan* v. *Red,* 4 W. & S., 237 (1842), whether it was necessary to join the widow and heirs as parties in the *sci. fa.* to revive the judgment. The court below decided it was necessary to do so. The Supreme Court reversed. HUSTON, J., dissented.

A previous intimation to this effect had been given one year after the Act of 1834 was passed, in *Warder* v. *Tainter,* 4 Watts, 284.

Chambers v. *Carson,* 2 Wh., 365 (1837); *Taylor* v. *Young*, 71 Pa. St., 81 (1872), and *Tryon* v. *Munson*, 77 Pa. St., 250 (1874), extended the principle of *McMillan* v. *Red* to a mortgage, and directly ruled that under the Act of 1834 it was not necessary to sue the heirs or any person save the administrator.

On the other hand, Judge KENNEDY, in *Warder* v. *Tainter*, 4 Watts, 282, cites, *contra*, several cases of courts of other States. And the English practice seems against our Supreme Court. Judge HUSTON dissented in *McMillan* v. *Red*, and Judge AGNEW dissented in *Taylor* v. *Young*. A *sci. fa.* to revive a judgment recovered against a man in his lifetime should be issued against his personal representatives; it is not necessary to bring in the widow and heirs by a *sci. fa.* against them. *Middleton's Excr.* v. *Middleton*, 106 Pa. St., 252 (1884).

But where there is no judgment in lifetime of debtor, the better practice is to sue the executor first, and, after judgment against him, to issue *sci. fa.* against widow and heirs or devisees. *Colwell* v. *Rockwell*, 11 W. N., 552 (1882). PAXSON, J.

In *Allen* v. *Krips*, 24 W. N., 248 (1889), following the same case in 119 Pa. St., 1 (1888), and *Hope* v. *Marshall*, 96 Pa. St., 395 (1880), it was decided that where judgment was not recovered against the estate of the decedent for more than thirteen years after his death, and a *sci. fa.* issued to bring in the widow and heirs, judgment *de terris* against them in default of appearance was void. " To charge the real estate of a decedent in the hands of his widow and heirs, the latter must be proceeded against within ten years from the death of the decedent."

Making the widows and heirs parties can probably do you no harm, should you deem it safer to do so; and in cases of all suits against decedents the following suggestions may serve you :

§ 257. **Claims against decedent's real estate.** If the defendant has left no will and there is an administrator—a widow and children—you file a suggestion stating the facts. If the case is complicated by a will appointing an executor, who has in turn died, and an administrator *d. b. n. c. t. a.* has been appointed in place of the executor, you state this in your suggestion. An heir or devisee may also have died leaving a will. Trustees may have been appointed. All or any of these matters can be provided for by adapting the following to the facts of your case :

SUGGESTION OF DEFENDANT'S DEATH, AFTER SUIT BROUGHT, FILED TO
CONTINUE LIEN AGAINST REALTY:

A. Lucius Hennershotz, to use of Frank P.
Moody,
v.
Anthony J. Gallagher, defendant, and the Commonwealth Title Insurance and Trust Company, administrators *d. b. n. c. t. a.* of said Anthony J. Gallagher, dec'd.

C. P. No. 1, of Philadelphia County.
June Term, 1878.
No. 648.

And now, February 4, 1888, the plaintiff suggests that the said Anthony J. Gallagher died on or about the 17th day of February, A.D. 1886, seized of certain lands, and leaving a will, wherein and whereby he appointed Augustus B. Gallagher, his son, sole executor, and leaving him surviving the said son, Augustus B. Gallagher, and two daughters, Mary C. Gallagher and Anne E. Gallagher, and as 'to the shares of the said daughters appointed the Philadelphia Trust and Safe Deposit Company trustees. That the said Augustus B. Gallagher died on or about the 25th day of October, A.D. 1886, leaving a will, wherein and whereby he appointed Sarah A. Gallagher sole executrix, legatee, and devisee of him, the said Augustus B. Gallagher, dec'd, and that the Fidelity Insurance, Trust, and Safe Deposit Company have been duly appointed trustees for said Mary C. Gallagher and Anne E. Gallagher, legatees and devisees of Anthony J. Gallagher, dec'd, in the place of said Philadelphia Trust and Safe Deposit Company, who renounced said appointment. And the plaintiff further suggests that letters of administration *de bonis non cum testamento annexo* have been granted upon the estate of the said original defendant, the said Anthony J. Gallagher, to the Commonwealth Title Insurance and Trust Company.

A. B.,
pro Plaintiff.
(Date.)

Indorse with

No., term, year, court, name of parties, etc. Suggestion of defendant's death, of names of children, etc.

You will note that the foregoing suggestion provides not only for the ordinary case of the death of your client's debtor and the substitution of his executor and children, but also and further for the superadded contingencies of the death of the executor and one of the heirs, the appointment of trustees for other heirs, etc.

§ 258. **As to widow.** In the case referred to in the form there was no widow. Should there be a widow, name her, and, in brief, name all the persons who could possibly be affected by your proceeding. In case you have a judgment, then after filing suggestion you give to prothonotary (always adapting the form to the facts) a *præcipe* for *sci. fa.* against executor, etc., *to revive judgment,* thus:

In the Court of Common Pleas, No. 1, of Philadelphia County.
A. Lucius Hennershotz, to use, *v.* The Commonwealth Title Insurance and Trust Company, administrators *d. b. n. c. t. a.* of Anthony J. Gallagher,

dec'd; Sarah A. Gallagher, legatee, devisee, and sole executrix of Augustus B. Gallagher, dec'd; and the Fidelity Insurance, Trust, and Safe Deposit Company, trustee for Mary C. Gallagher and Anne E. Gallagher, legatee and devisee of Anthony J. Gallagher, dec'd; and against the said Mary C. Gallagher and Anne E. Gallagher.

To the Prothonotary of said Court of Common Pleas.

SIR: Issue *scire facias* to revive judgment of A. Lucius Hennershotz against Anthony J. Gallagher, C. P. No. 1, Philadelphia County, to June Term, 1884, No.   , for $ and costs, and to continue lien of same against the real estate of said Anthony J. Gallagher, and why the plaintiff should not have judgment and execution against said lands and said defendants, returnable *sec. leg.*

A. B.,
pro Plaintiff.
(Date.)

Dietrick's Appeal, 107 Pa. St., 178 (1884), Mr. Justice PAXSON:
" In order to continue the lien of a judgment, the original judgment must be correctly recited in the *scire facias;* it must substantially identify the original judgment as to parties, date, and amount."

§ 259. **If no judgment.** If you are proceeding against a decedent to continue the lien of a claim, not in judgment, omit from above *præcipe* the words " to revive judgment," etc., and say, *Sir, Issue scire facias to continue lien of claim in above case against the real estate, etc.*

When sci. fa. issued, hand it to sheriff, giving him the defendant's address, if known, and the names and addresses of all known grantees of land bound by the judgment. It is recommended to hand him also a short description of the lands, taken from the defendant's deeds. These you can find by searching the index in the office of the recorder of deeds.

The subsequent remarks apply solely to the ordinary cases of *sci. fa.* to revive judgment.

If defendant's address unknown, direct sheriff to return *nihil habet.*

Service of sci. fas. must be made on the terre-tenants or persons occupying the real estate bound by the judgment, and on the defendant if he can be found.

Return to sci. fa. See that sheriff makes a full and sufficient return.

If return of nihil made, issue *alias sci. fa.*

Præcipe for alias sci. fa. may be in form already given for the original, inserting the word *alias* before the words *scire facias.*

§ 260. **Proceedings on return of sci. fa.** You proceed as in other cases of *scire facias*. If two returns of *nihil* have been made, they are equivalent to personal service. The presumption is that the defendant is alive, although he may be dead. This was precisely the fact and the ruling in *Warder* v. *Tainter*, 4 Watts, 270 (1835). Charles Tainter (the mortgagor) had died upward of two months before the *sci. fa.* issued. The sheriff returned twice *nihil*, and that there were no terre-tenants in possession. Judgment was entered. The reporter says a *scire facias* issued and the premises were sold. He meant, of course, that the property was sold under *levari facias*. The plaintiff purchased, and got possession. Tainter's heirs brought ejectment, and contended that their ancestor having been dead, the whole proceeding was null. They paid the mortgage-money, interest, taxes, etc., into court, and asked a verdict. They recovered in the Common Pleas; but the Supreme Court reversed. Judge KENNEDY's opinion establishes that two returns of *nihil* are equivalent to a return of *scire feci*, and that nothing can be assigned for error which is contrary to the record.

Two returns of *nihil* are equivalent to a return of *scire feci*. *Tryon* v. *Munson*, 77 Pa. St., 250 (1874).

So in case of mortgage, and the judgment entered cannot be impeached collaterally. *Murray* v. *Weigle*, 118 Pa. St., 159 (1888).

§ 261. The defendant being thus served, you can take **judgment for want of an appearance.** The Act of June 13, 1836, section 33, allows ten days between the service of the summons and the return-day, and section 34 allows ten days between service and judgment by default.

Section 36 of the Act applies the like rules to writs of *scire facias*. In case of two returns of *nihil* judgment may be entered on the fifteenth day after the last return-day. See § 2796.

The form for entering judgment for want of an appearance is given, section 87. You omit the words " being the third term, and plaintiff having filed his declaration." The *scire facias* is always treated as a declaration.

As to time within which *sci. fa.* must issue, see section 275.

As to diligence in prosecuting, see section 276.

As to terre-tenants, sections 276, 277.

If appearance be entered, you can take judgment if no affidavit of defense be filed before the third Saturday after the return-day. See form, section 23.

If insufficient affidavit be interposed, proceed as indicated by section 27.

If sufficient affidavit be filed, enter rule to plead; serve notice. See sections 26, 88.

If plea not filed, write for it. Failing to obtain it, enter judgment for want of plea. See section 26.

Plea. The usual pleas are *null tiel* record and payment.

If nul tiel record pleaded, order the plea on argument list, notify your adversary, and prepare a paper-book. A few lines, stating your judgment and the plea, will suffice. At the time fixed, have in court the docket showing your judgment, and get judgment for the plaintiff on the plea of *nul tiel* record. If there be any mistake in your *sci. fa.,* amend it by moving the court to allow the necessary amendment.

If payment pleaded, reply *non solvit* and issue ; order case on trial-list, and be prepared to maintain the issue before the jury.

In *Whelen* v. *Phillips,* 26 W. N., 363 (1890), a *sci. fa.* was issued on a judgment more than twenty years old. The affidavit of defense set up that the judgment, being older than twenty years, there was a presumption of payment. THAYER, P. J.: " We have always held that an affidavit setting up the Statute of Limitations as a defense was good without it being averred that defendant had not made a new promise. By a parity of reasoning, an affidavit raising a legal presumption of payment is sufficient."

§ 262. **Actions upon Bonds in Error and Sci. Fas. sur recognizance.** In suits upon bonds, the *præcipe,* section 10, will answer. File with *præcipe* your statement—copy of bond and averment of breach. For *sci. fa.,* it is only necessary to note a change in the *præcipe.* You may use the following form :

A. B.	
v.	Court. Term. No.
C. D.	

To the Prothonotary of the Court of Common Pleas, No.　　, Philadelphia County.

SIR : Issue *scire facias sur* recognizance of the above-named C. D., whereof the following is a copy (here copy the recognizance in suit).

After the copy you may add :

of which said recognizance the plaintiff avers the following *breach.* (You then follow the the the condition of the recognizance, inserting the word *not,* as that the said　　*did not* on the　　pay, etc.,) wherefore, there is due to the plaintiff as per following

STATEMENT.

Amount (recite the fact).
Int. from (insert date,
but do not calculate amount).

E. F.,
Plaintiff's Attorney.
(Date.)

Indorse this :

A. B.
   v.   }   Court. Term. No.
C. D.

    Præcipe for *sci. fa.*   or   *Præcipe* for summons.
    Copy of recognizance   Copy of bond
        sued upon and statement.   sued upon and statement.
                                                  E. F.,
                                      Plaintiff's Attorney.
                                               (Date.)

A copy of the whole record need not be filed in suing out a recognizance for stay of execution. *Jones* v. *Raiguel*, 97 Pa. St., 437 (1881).

In *Beck* v. *Courtney*, 13 W. N., 302 (1883), *sci. fa. sur* recognizance was held a sufficient declaration.

Where judgment is entered on a warrant of attorney, no *sci. fa.* is necessary to ascertain damages. The execution is under the control of the court. *Cochlin* v. *Com.*, 11 W. N., 460 (1882).

A justice of the peace alone can issue a *sci. fa.* upon a recognizance of appellant in case of his neglect. *Shivery* v. *Grauer*, 2 Dist. Rep., 388 (1893).

§ 263. **If Commonwealth be the recognizee,** as in the case of the sheriff's recognizance, instead of your client's name write:

       The Commonwealth of Pennsylvania
at the suggestion and to the use of (your client's name)
                    v.
         (name all the recognizors).

Follow above form.

§ 264. **The form of recognizance for sheriffs and coroners** is prescribed by Act April 15, 1834, sections 64, 67 (P. L., 549).

§ 265. **Sheriff's bonds—official bonds.** The same Act, April 15, 1834, gives, in section 65 (P. L., 549), the form of the sheriff's bond.

§ 266. **Actions on official bonds.** The Act of June 14, 1836, section 6 (P. L., 639), directs that :

Every bond and obligation which shall be given to the Commonwealth by any public officer, or by any person appointed under authority of law to execute any public trust ; also, every bond which shall be given by any executor, administrator, guardian, committee, assignee, receiver, or trustee, with intent, in every of the said cases, to secure the faithful execution of the respective offices, employment, or trust, and for the use of all such persons, and bodies politic and corporate, as may be affected by the official acts or neglect of such officer or person, may be sued and prosecuted in the manner following, to wit:

I. The writ shall in such case be issued in the name of the Commonwealth, and the names of the persons by whom the same shall be sued out shall be suggested as plaintiffs therein, and such persons shall be liable for the costs of the suit, in like manner as plaintiffs in other cases.

II. If two or more persons having several interests shall join in suing such writ, it shall be lawful for them to declare separately thereon, and set forth in their declarations, respectively, the breaches of the condition of such bond or obligation, which shall have been made to their particular injury, or they may join in declaration thereon, and afterward, in their replications or otherwise, according to the course of practice in like cases, set forth upon the record the breaches of the condition aforesaid.

III. It shall be lawful for any other person to whom a cause of action shall have accrued on such bond or obligation at any time before judgment, upon a suggestion filed with leave of the court, to be made a party plaintiff in such writ, and thereupon he may declare and set forth the breaches of condition of such bond or obligation to his particular injury as aforesaid.

IV. The obligors in any such bond or obligation may plead performance of the condition thereof, so far as it respects the person by whom such writ was issued, or any of them, and if such fact be confessed or found, such persons shall be debarred of their action upon that writ.

V. If several persons shall join as aforesaid in any such writ, and if issues be taken by them separately from each other against the defendants, it shall be lawful for them to have a separate trial thereof, or, at their election, such issues may be tried at the same time, and if they be issues in fact, by one and the same jury.

VI. The parties to any issue taken as aforesaid shall be liable for the costs of the trial thereof, in like manner as if they only were parties in the proceeding.

VII. If judgment, upon all issues taken as aforesaid, be rendered for the defendants, such judgments, and the pleadings and proceedings upon which they shall be founded, shall not estop, debar, or otherwise affect the action which any other person or body politic or corporate, may at any time have upon such bond, nor shall such judgment debar any action which the said plaintiffs may have therein, for any subsequent breach or cause.

VIII. If final judgment be rendered against the defendants upon any issue taken as aforesaid, such judgment shall be as follows, to wit:

(1) For the Commonwealth, in the amount of such obligation or bond.

(2) For the plaintiff in such issue, in the amount of damages assessed, and for the costs accrued between such plaintiff and the defendants.

IX. The judgment of the Commonwealth as aforesaid shall remain for the satisfaction of all persons entitled to the benefit of the bond or obligation upon which it was rendered, and for all and singular the like uses and purposes; but the said judgment shall not be a lien upon the real estate of the defendants, unless the Commonwealth shall have commenced the action, nor shall execution thereof be had except in the manner hereinafter provided.

X. The judgment for the plaintiff in such issue as aforesaid shall be a lien upon the real estate of the defendants, to the amount thereof, and such plaintiff may have execution thereof, on (or) a writ of *scire facias*, or other action thereon, in like manner as may be had in a case of judgments in other personal actions.

XI. In all cases where the condition of any such bond shall be broken, after a judgment rendered for the Commonwealth as aforesaid, it shall be lawful for the party aggrieved to proceed by writ of *scire facias* upon such judgment suggesting his interest therein, to assess and 'recover the damages which he shall have sustained, in the manner hereinbefore provided in the case of the breach of the condition of a bond taken to secure the performance of a covenant, after a judgment had upon such bond.

XII. Every judgment rendered for the plaintiff in any such writ of *scire facias* shall be of like effect to all intents and purposes, as judgments obtained by plaintiffs in other personal actions.

XIII. It shall be lawful for the sureties in any bond as aforesaid to pay into court, at any time after suit brought thereon as aforesaid, the whole amount of the penalty of the bond, with all costs of suit up to that time, and thereupon they shall be discharged from all further liability by reason thereof; but nothing herein contained shall debar any person of his action or his right of execution against the officer, trustee, or other person for whom such security was given, for any damages which shall not be paid out of such bond.

From this it will appear that the remedy on the bond differs from the suit on the recognizance.

§ 267. If no suit has been brought on the bond, you will be the first plaintiff.

The præcipe in that case will be :

The Commonwealth of Pennsylvania, at the suggestion and *to the use of*
(your client),
v.
(Names of all the obligors.)

To the Prothonotary of the Court of Common Pleas, No. 1, of Philadelphia County.

SIR : Issue summons in *assumpsit* ret. *sec. leg.* upon the

BOND,

whereof the following is a copy : (Here copy bond at length, signatures of obligors, witnesses, justification, recording—everything.) The plaintiff claims to recover upon the said bond the sum of $ (state full amount of your client's damage), with interest from   and costs upon the following

STATEMENT.

(Here state your case. The following may serve simply as a guide :) The plaintiff on the   day of   brought suit in the Court of Common Pleas, No. 2, of Philadelphia County, to   term, No. , against David Jones to recover the amount of a certain note due by said Jones to plaintiff, and the plaintiff afterward recovered a judgment against said Jones for the sum of   dollars, which judgment is still in full force and unpaid. The plaintiff afterward, to wit: issued out of said court a *fieri facias* against said David Jones for the aforesaid sum of $ with interest from   and costs. Said *fi. fa.* was delivered to   , being then and there sheriff of said county (and one of the obligors in the bond now sued upon) for execution according to law. The said writ commanded the said sheriff that of the goods and chattels, lands and tenements of said David Jones, said sheriff should cause to be levied the said sum of $ and interest and costs. And said David Jones then and there had goods and chattels, subject to said execution and on which the said *fi. fa.* could then and there have been levied, sufficient to satisfy the said writ, and on which the plaintiff requested said sheriff to levy. But the said sheriff, his duty neglecting, was guilty of the following *breach* of said bond, in this that he did not, although thereto by the said plaintiff frequently requested, levy upon said goods and chattels, or any part thereof, or on any goods or chattels or lands or tenements of said David Jones, but falsely returned said writ *nulla bona.* Whereby the plaintiff lost the said sum of $ and interest from   and costs now demanded of said obligors on said bond.

A. B.,
Plaintiff's Attorney.
(Date.)

(Affidavit when required.)

Indorse this paper with names of parties, court, term, and No. :

> *Præcipe for summons.*
> *Statement—Copy of bond sued on.*
> *Suggestion of breach—Amount of claim, etc.*

§ 268. If suit has been brought by another party on the official bond, and no judgment has been entered, you proceed by a suggestion somewhat in the following form :

The Comm. of Penna. ⎫
  to the use of A. B. ⎪
       v.   ⎬
  C. D., E. F., G. H. ⎭

To the Honorable the Judges of the Court of Common Pleas, No. 2, of Philadelphia County.

The suggestion and petition of I. K.,

humbly showeth

1. That a suit has been brought in this Honorable Court to Term, 1886, No.   , by the Comm. of Penna. to the use of A. B. upon the official bond of C. D., High Sheriff of said county.

2. That no judgment has yet been entered in said suit.

3. That your petitioner has a just cause of action upon said bond as follows :

(Here set out the complaint of the petitioner.)

Wherefore he prays this Honorable Court that he may be made a party plaintiff, and be allowed to declare by statement, setting forth the breaches of the condition of such bond to his particular injury as aforesaid.

(Signature of Petitioner)
(*or of his counsel*).

—— (name of petitioner) having been duly sworn, according to law, doth depose and say that the facts set forth in the foregoing petition are true.

Sworn to and subscribed before me,

(Signature of Petitioner.)

Indorse this :

Comm. of Pa. to use
of A. B.
  v.   } No.   , Term, Year,
C. D., E. F., G. H.

PETITION OF I. K.

And now,   , on motion of L. M., attorney for I. K., the court
grant a rule to show cause why I. K. should not be made a party plaintiff
in the above case.

Rule returnable   .

Serve a copy of this petition and notice of the rule on the attorneys of the plaintiffs and defendants.   Have a copy of the petition for each judge, and on the return-day have the rule made
absolute.

Give an order to the prothonotary in this form :

Comm. of Pa.
to the use of A. B.
  v.   } Court.   Term, 1886. No.   .
C. D. *et al.*

To the Prothonotary of the Court of Common Pleas, No. 2, of Philadelphia County.

Sir : Enter my appearance for I. K., who has been made a party plaintiff in the above case by order of court.

L. M.,
Attorney for I. K.
(Date.)

§ 269. Then prepare your statement.

The following form may guide you :

Comm. of Pa.
to the use of A. B.
  v.   } Common Pleas, No. 2, of Philadelphia County,
C. D. *et al.*   Term, 1887. No.   .

I. K., who has been made a party plaintiff in the above case, by leave of
the court, files this, his

STATEMENT.

You must here detail your complaint.   The form under the word statement in the *præcipe* already given (section 267) will be a guide.   Facts vary
in every case.   You must set forth clearly the circumstances leading up to
the breach ; showing how your client stood with reference to the sheriff ;
what writ he delivered to the sheriff ; what the sheriff's duty was ; then
aver *the breach ;* that is, how the sheriff defaulted in his duty ; that he did
not levy ; that he did not serve the summons (if that was the neglected
writ), and exactly how the damage arose.   Then you state your client's
loss in dollars.   Let a copy of the bond accompany the statement.   This
. paper you indorse (always writing term,   No.   , year,   , and
names of parties) :

Statement of I. K.
Copy of bond sued on.
Suggestion of breach.
Amount of claim, etc.

(Affidavit when required.)

§ 270. **What to do with summons.** If you have been the original plaintiff, serve summons, with copy of your statement, etc. See sections 17, 18.

If rule of court requires plaintiff's affidavit to the statement, be sure to attach the affidavit.

If there be no appearance, or no affidavit of defense, or an insufficient affidavit, proceed as suggested, sections 26, 27, 28, etc.

§ 271. **If you have filed suggestion as a new plaintiff,** accompany it with your client's affidavit (if so required by rule of court) and serve it and wait for affidavit of defense.

If affidavit of defense be sufficient, enter rule to plead (section 26), and so on to judgment by default or to trial.

§ 272. It only remains to notice the **case of a party whose cause of action accrues after judgment on the bond.** Such a person, as provided by paragraph XI. of the Act quoted, may " proceed by writ of *scire facias* upon such judgment, suggesting his interest therein," etc.

You file a suggestion in the form above indicated, but do not take a rule to become a party plaintiff. In your suggestion be careful to state your full cause of action. Give copy of the bond and show that, as to you, the condition of the bond was broken after judgment rendered for the Commonwealth. Let your client swear to the suggestion. You then order a *sci. fa.* as per form of *præcipe* heretofore given.

Serve with *sci. fa.* a copy of your suggestion, and proceed as in other cases already delineated.

§ 273. **In all proceedings observe :** (1) That your papers conform to the statute, the facts, and the rules of court.

(2) That process and copies are regularly served.

(3) That you secure judgment by default when clearly thereto entitled :

    (a) For want of appearance.

    (b) For want of affidavit of defense.

    (c) For want of sufficient affidavit of defense.

    (d) For want of a plea.

(4) Failing herein, put your case at issue and press for trial.

§ 274. **Verdict a lien.** The Act of March 23, 1877 (P. L., 34), provides that a verdict by a jury in the Common Pleas for any specific sum of money shall be a lien upon the real estate, within the proper county, of the party against whom the verdict may be rendered. Such verdict is entered on the lien docket as judgments are entered.

A motion for a new trial or in arrest of judgment, if overruled, does not affect the lien of the verdict, which dates from the time of its rendition.

§ 275. **Time within which sci. fa. must issue.** The Act of March 26, 1827 (9 Sm. Laws, 303), provides that a judgment shall be a lien for the term of five years from the day of entry or revival thereof. The five years is *exclusive* of the day on which the judgment is entered. *Green's Appeal*, 6 W. & S., 327 (1843), and the *sci. fa.* may issue on the last day of the five years. *Silverthorn* v. *Townsend*, 37 Pa. St., 263 (1860). If the last day be Sunday, the *sci. fa.* can issue on Monday. In *Lutz's Appeal*, 46 Leg. Int., 335, the judgment was entered April 17, 1876. It was decided that the *sci. fa.* which issued Monday, April 18, 1881, preserved the lien. In case of a judgment which has been revived, the five years begin to run not from the return of the *sci. fa.*, but from the judgment of revival. *Cathcart* v. *Potterfield*, 5 Watts, 163 (1836). The Act of 1827 also provides that the *sci. fa.* may be sued out, whether the money be due and payable on the judgment or not, and that no order or rule of court, or any other process or proceeding thereof, shall obviate the necessity of revival in order to continue the lien.

§ 276. **Diligence in prosecuting sci. fa.** The diligence required in prosecuting the *sci. fa.* is that the plaintiff shall within five years from the time of issuing the writ get a judgment of revival on the *scire facias*. *In re Fulton's Estate*, 51 Pa. St., 204 (1865).

Terre-tenants. If the land on which the judgment is a lien belong to some one other than the defendant, such terre-tenant is not precluded by the judgment on the *scire facias* unless he has been made a party to the proceeding. But it is not necessary that a judgment be entered against the terre-tenant; service on him of the *scire facias* is enough. *Day* v. *Willy*, 3 Brewster, 43 (1868). If the terre-tenant be not thus served, he can afterward make any defense which would have been available before, *Mevey's Appeal*, 4 Pa. St., 80 (1846); but if he be served, he is precluded by the judgment on the *sci. fa.* *Blythe* v. *McClintock*, 7 S. & R., 341 (1821).

The provisions of the Act of April 16, 1849 (P. L., 664), relating to revival of judgments, were intended to continue the lien of a judgment against the lands of a debtor, by revival against him alone, unless the vendee or terre-tenant put his deed on record or was in actual possession, in which case the five years ran in his favor from the date of recording the deed or taking possession. *Wetmore* v. *Wetmore*, 155 Pa. St., 507 (1893).

§ 277. **Time of serving terre-tenant.** It is sufficient to serve the terre-tenant at any time within five years from the day of issuing the *scire facias*. *Porter* v. *Hitchcock*, 98 Pa. St., 625 (1881). This service may be either of the *sci. fa.* or of an *alias* thereon, but it is sufficient if the service be made within five years from the day of issuing the *scire facias*.. *Kirby* v. *Cash*, 93 Pa. St., 505 (1880).

§ 278. **Scire facias on judgments transferred to another county.** When a judgment is transferred to another county, the five years begin to run from the time of entry in the new county, and not from the date of the original judgment. *Knauss's Appeal*, 49 Pa. St., 419 (1865).

The Act of May 4, 1852 (P. L., 584), provides that when a new county is erected out of parts of older counties, and judgments originally entered in the older county shall be or shall have been transferred into the new, and such transferred judgments shall be revived by *scire facias* within five years from the last rendition of judgment in the old county, the lien shall be continued irrespective of the judgment in the old county.

§ 279. **Scire facias against soldiers.** The Act of April 11, 1862 (P. L., 484), provided that the plaintiff might issue his *scire facias* against a defendant who is a soldier, but that judgment of revival should not be rendered while the defendant is in actual service, the issuing of the writ being sufficient to continue the lien. This Act provides for notice to the defendant on his discharge, if he return to the county ; and if he do not return to and acquire a residence in the county, for the issuing of an *alias*. Upon the return of *nihil*, the court may render judgment.

CHAPTER IX.

COMMENCEMENT AND PROSECUTION OF ACTIONS FOR ANNUITIES, ON APPRENTICE-DEEDS, BY AND AGAINST ATTORNEYS, FOR AVERAGE, ON AWARDS, BY BAILEES, ON BILLS OF EXCHANGE, ON CALLS, BY AND AGAINST CARRIERS, ON CHARTER-PARTIES, ON CONTRACTS OF SALE, BY FARRIERS, ON FOREIGN JUDGMENTS, FOR FORBEARANCE, FREIGHT, GOOD-WILL, INDEMNITIES, LEGACIES, LOANS, ON PROMISE OF MARRIAGE, FOR NECESSARIES, FOR PARTY-WALLS, PLEDGES, RENT, REWARDS, TOLLS, WARRANTIES, BY WHARFINGERS.

§ 280. These various causes of action are grouped into one chapter, because little need be added as to them in addition to that which has been already noted in the preceding chapters. All of them fall under the head of *assumpsit*, section 61.

Præcipes. The *præcipe* will follow the form and directions already given. Sections 10, 11, 12, 13, 14, etc.

Statements must be filed. Sections 17, 18.

Affidavits of Defense, Rules for Judgment, Putting at Issue, are all explained in Chapters II. and III.

CHAPTER X.

§ 281. **Study the policy.** When a claim against an insurance company to recover the amount of a loss is placed in the hands of an attorney for collection, his first duty is to read the policy carefully. The suggestion may excite a smile, but cases have occurred in which suit has been brought, and trial had, yet the counsel on both sides had neglected to study the policy. Read it then all through, line by line, word by word. Read it a second time, asking yourself, What does this paper require me to do? You will always find that it demands some notice of loss. Generally it binds you to prompt or immediate notice. It exacts particulars, sometimes proofs, sometimes certificates of magistrates, or, in cases of death, affidavits of physicians and others. Take up all these fine-drawn and wearying requisitions, answer each in its very words and to its broadest scope. Let your work be full and prompt. You always lose by sparing labor. The following can be of service only as a very rough guide. Each company has its own forms, and the policies from different offices may vary in their requisitions.

§ 282. **Get from the company its forms and a blank policy.** The companies have printed notices and proofs of loss, etc., and will on application supply blanks. You will prefer their papers because they issue them, and they cannot complain of defects.

As already suggested, be careful to make all the answers, certificates, etc., very full.

If they desire more light, furnish all in your power.

The Act of April 16, 1891 (P. L., 22), provided for a standard form of Fire Policy. The Act was declared unconstitutional in *O'Neill* v. *Insurance Co.*, 166 Pa. St., 72 (1895).

§ 283. **Particulars of loss by fire.** Fire policies, insuring merchandise, furniture, etc., often require particulars of the loss. Your client will perhaps say, and with justice, that it is hard to require details; that it is impossible to furnish them. But leave the company no excuse. If your client's books have not been destroyed, they should assist him; if his receipts are at hand, or his checks, he can work from them. If all are gone, he can remember the names of those who sold the goods to him and can, with their permission, get their clerks or his own assistants to make out the necessary lists. Do everything to secure the desired information, and if, after all, the amounts obtained do not equal the loss, state in the affidavit that he has not been able to collect all the items, but is certain that his loss is at least the sum claimed.

§ 284. **General Requisites of all Notices :** The date and number of the policy.

The amount insured.

The subject insured. (The life of A., or such a house, or stock, or furniture, or vessel, etc.)

The date of the loss.

The amount of the claim.

Where the policy so requires, send with the above a copy of the policy, certificates, affidavits, etc., in exact accordance with the conditions.

Keep a copy of all papers served. Let the copy be compared with the original documents, and let the person who serves be able to swear to the service and to the copy.

It being understood that the claims and notices differ according to the requirements of the policies and circumstances of each case, the following *Form of Claim on a Life Policy* may serve simply as a guide. It is to be made by the person claiming the assurance.

Notice is hereby given to the A. B. Company of the United States that C. D., of Philadelphia, County of Philadelphia, State of Pennsylvania, has died ; that said C. D. was the same person whose life was assured by said company by their policy No.   , dated   , for the sum of dollars ; that all premiums had been duly paid upon said policy ; that the undersigned had a good and valid interest to the amount assured in the life of said deceased ; and, in proof of claim under said policy, answers as follows :

1. Name of deceased, C. D.
2. Residence, 500 North Front Street, Philadelphia.
3. Occupation at date of assurance, minister of the gospel.
4. Occupation since assurance was effected, same.
5. Place and date of birth, Philadelphia, January 1, 1820.
6. Whence is the date of birth derived? From family record, certificate of birth, or otherwise? From his own statement.
7. Place and date of death, Trenton, New Jersey, September 1, 1888.
8. How long had you known deceased? For   years.
9. State all facts regarding cause and circumstances of death. Health failing for about two months prior to death. Serious symptoms from July, 1888, to time of decease.
10. State the precise duration of the last illness of the deceased. As above.

11. Were his habits of life correct, sober, and temperate? Had they always been so? If not, to what extent did he use spirituous liquors? Habits always good; used no spirituous liquors.

12. Refer to the policy and state if to your knowledge and belief the deceased complied with the terms contained therein. He did.

13. In what capacity, or by what title do you claim the assurance? As executor of the last will of C. D., deceased, and legatee of the policy.

14. Had the deceased any other insurance on his life? If so, state in what companies and for what amounts, and the dates of the polices respectively. C. D., to my knowledge, was not insured in any other companies.

Dated at Philadelphia this　　　day of　　　, 1888.

(Claimant's signature and residence.)

STATE OF PENNSYLVANIA,   } ss.
CITY AND COUNTY OF PHILADELPHIA, }

On the　　　day of　　　, 1888, personally appeared before me, the above-named (claimant's name), to me known, and made oath that the foregoing statements by him made are true and full to the best of his knowledge and belief.

G. H.,
[SEAL.]　　　　　　　　　　　　　　　　　　Notary Public.

§ 285. Frequently instructions are printed to this effect:

Each of the within certificates must be sworn to, and the certificate of the County Clerk must, in all cases, be obtained, that the person administering the oath was duly authorized for that purpose.

When a policy is payable to the legal representatives of the insured, the statement must be made by his or her executor or administrator.

When a policy is payable to a named beneficiary of full age, the statement must be made by such beneficiary.

When a policy is payable to a minor, the statement must be made by his or her guardian.

When a policy has been assigned, the original assignment, or a properly authenticated copy thereof, must be presented with proofs of death.

When a policy, payable by its terms to one beneficiary if surviving, has, by the death of such beneficiary, become payable to another, proof of the death of such first beneficiary must be furnished by affidavit of respectable persons well acquainted with such deceased beneficiary.

When a policy is payable to the children in general of a person, or to any other class of persons, whose names are not separately mentioned in the policy, proof must be furnished of how many children there are, or of how many the class consists, and the names and ages of the persons.

When the statement is made by an administrator, executor, or guardian, certified copies of appointment and authority must be furnished.

§ 286. Generally the certificate of an attending physician is required, thus:

1. Name of deceased, C. D.
2. Occupation, minister of the gospel.
3. Residence, 500 North Front Street, Philadelphia.
4. How long had you been acquainted with the deceased? Ten years.
5. Were you his medical attendant or adviser before his last illness? If

so, for what disease, and when? I was his medical attendant in the summer of 1888, for disease of the heart.

6. Was the deceased afflicted with any chronic disease? If so, what disease, and for what period? With disease of the heart for three months.

7. Date of first visit, July 1, 1888.

8. Date of last visit, September 1, 1888.

9. Date of death, September 1, 1888.

10. State the disease of which the deceased died, and any important medical facts connected therewith. Was it complicated by any other disease? If so, by what disease, and for how long? Fatty degeneration of heart with dilatation.

11. Was the deceased strictly temperate? Was death caused proximately or remotely by the use of intoxicating drinks or opium? Strictly temperate. No.

12. Was there any special cause, proximate or remote, for the death, in the habits, occupation, residence, family history, personal constitution, or previous diseases of the deceased? Not to my knowledge.

13. State the age or apparent age of the deceased. Sixty-eight years.

14. Did you see the body of the deceased and was it, of your own knowledge, that of the same person described in the policy of insurance on which the claim is based? Yes.

15. Had the deceased any other medical attendants during last illness? No other.

Dated at   , this   day of   , 1888.

(Signature and address of physician.)

STATE OF NEW YORK, }
CITY AND COUNTY OF NEW YORK, } ss.

On this   day of   , 1888, before me, came the above-named (name of physician), known to me as a physician in regular standing, and made oath that the answers by him to the foregoing questions are true and full, to the best of his knowledge and belief.

J. K.,
Notary Public.

[SEAL.]

STATE OF NEW YORK, }
CITY AND COUNTY OF NEW YORK, } ss.

I,   , clerk of the Court of Common Pleas of said county, said court being a court of record, do hereby certify that (name of notary), whose name is subscribed to the *jurat* of the annexed affidavit and thereon written, was at the time of taking such affidavit a notary public of said State, dwelling in said county, commissioned and sworn and duly authorized to take the same; and, further, that I am well acquainted with the handwriting of such notary public and verily believe the signature to said *jurat* is genuine.

In Testimony Whereof, I have hereunto set my hand and affixed the seal of said county and said court this   day of   , 1888.

J. L.,
Clerk.

[SEAL.]

§ 287.

STATEMENT OF THE UNDERTAKER.

1. Name of deceased, C. D.

2. Residence, 500 North Front Street, Philadelphia, Pa.

3. Did you see and inter the body of said deceased, and do you know that

it was the body of the person described in the accompanying statement of the claimant in this case beyond a doubt? I did; I do.

4. Date of birth. This blank to be filled, if possible, from the family record. Born, Philadelphia, January 1, 1820.

5. Place and date of interment, Woodlands Cemetery, Philadelphia; September 4, 1888.

Dated at Philadelphia this   day of   , 1888.

(Signature and address of undertaker.)

STATE OF PENNSYLVANIA, }
CITY AND COUNTY OF PHILADELPHIA, }

On this   day of   , 1888, personally appeared before me, the above-named (name of undertaker),. to me known, and made oath that the foregoing statements by him made are true and full to the best of his knowledge and belief.

G..H.,

[SEAL.]   Notary Public.

STATE OF PENNSYLVANIA, } ss.
CITY AND COUNTY OF PHILADELPHIA, }

I (name of prothonotary), prothonotary of the Courts of Common Pleas of said county, which are courts of record, having a common seal, being the officer authorized by the laws of the State of Pennsylvania to make the following certificate:

Do certify that (name of notary) before whom the annexed oath or affirmation was made, was at the time of so doing a notary public for the Commonwealth of Pennsylvania, residing in the county of Philadelphia, duly commissioned and qualified to administer oaths and affirmations and to take acknowledgments and proofs of deeds or conveyances for land and tenements in the State of Pennsylvania, and to all whose acts, as such, full faith and credit are and ought to be given, as well in courts of judicature as elsewhere; and that I am well acquainted with the handwriting of the said notary public and verily believe his signature thereto is genuine, and that said oath or affirmation purports to be taken in all respects as required by the laws of the State of Pennsylvania.

In Testimony Whereof, I have hereunto set my hand and affixed the seal of said court this   day of   , in the year of our Lord one thousand eight hundred and eighty-eight.

M. N.,

[SEAL.]   Prothonotary.

§ 288.

STATEMENT OF A FRIEND.

1. Name of deceased, C. D.

2. How long had you known deceased? About ten years.

3. Place and date of death, Trenton, New Jersey, September 1, 1888.

4. Age of deceased at death, sixty-eight years.

5. Have you seen the body of the person deceased, and is it to your knowledge the same person described in the policy on which the claim is based? I have seen the body of deceased and it is the same person described in policy.

6. State all the facts within your knowledge relating to the cause of death. Disease of the heart.

7. Was the deceased in the habit of using spirituous liquors? If so, to what extent, and did it affect his health? Strictly temperate.

Dated at Philadelphia this   day of   , 1888.

(Signature and address of friend.)

STATE OF PENNSYLVANIA, }
CITY AND COUNTY OF PHILADELPHIA, } *ss.*

On this   day of   , 1888, personally appeared before me, the above-named (name of friend), to me known, and made oath that the foregoing statements by him made are true and full to the best of his knowledge and belief.

G. H.,
[SEAL.]   Notary Public.

(Prothonotary's certificate for this notary as before.)

§ 289.

LETTER FROM COUNSEL, ENCLOSING THE PROOFS.

Philadelphia,   , 188 .

To the A. B. Company of the United States.

GENTLEMEN : Enclosed please find the proofs, etc., of the death of C. D., insured in your company by policy dated   , No.

Will you kindly notify me at your earliest convenience :

Whether the inclosed proofs, etc., are in proper form and are all that you require in that behalf.

Very respectfully yours,

(Signature of counsel.)

§ 290. **In fire policies, notice of loss may be served at general office or on agent in ten days, and the proofs within twenty days.** The Act 27 June, 1883, section 1 (P. L., 165), Br. Purd., 1051, section 93, provides : " Where any property shall be destroyed by fire in this Commonwealth, where the same is covered by policies of insurance, either held by the assured or an assignee of the same as collateral security, the conditions of insurance, as to the notice of loss and the furnishing of preliminary proofs, shall be deemed to have been complied with if the assured or the assignee, or either of them, shall furnish the company, at its general office, or to the agent of the company who countersigned the policy or policies of insurance, the notice of loss, within ten days from the date of the fire, and the preliminary proofs within twenty days from the said date : *Provided,* That in case the agent who countersigned the policy or policies of insurance shall have been removed or succeeded by some other agent of the company, after such policy was written, and prior to the date of the fire, then the notice and the preliminary proofs aforesaid may be served on any other agent of the company authorized to effect contracts of insurance and countersign policies of any such insurance companies."

If notice is promptly given of loss in fire insurance, the company cannot protect itself on the ground of insufficient proof, unless they have pointed out the defect in the proofs submitted and called for more specific proofs. *Ins. Co.* v. *Cusick*, 109 Pa. St., 158 (1885); *Ins. Co.* v. *Block, Id.*, 535 (1885); *Thierolf* v. *Ins. Co.*, 110 Pa. St., 87 (1885).

If a policy of insurance require "immediate" notice shall be given the company, the word *immediate* must be construed to mean within a reasonable time under all the facts and circumstances of the case. *Assn.* v. *Smith*, 24 W. N., 33 (1889), PAXSON, C. J. And the same construction is placed upon "as soon as possible" where detailed proof of loss must be submitted. *Ins. Co.* v. *Hazen*, 17 W. N., 249 (1885).

If a policy provide that with proofs of loss, information as to plans, specifications, etc., shall be given, and the company endeavor to adjust the loss by appointing appraisers, such preliminary proofs are waived. *Snowden* v. *Ins. Co.*, 22 W. N., 554 (1888). Or where, upon receiving notice of loss, the company denies all liability, preliminary proofs are waived. *Ins. Co.* v. *Erb*, 17 W. N., 273 (1886).

If a policy of insurance does not provide that there shall be a forfeiture if notice of loss is not given within a prescribed time, the court will not so enforce. *Ins. Co.* v. *Evans*, 102 Pa. St., 281 (1883).

§ 291. **Policies need no seal.** "*Policies of insurance* made or entered into by the company may be made either with or without the seal thereof, and they shall be subscribed by the president or such other officer as may be designated by the directors for that purpose, and attested by the secretary; and when so subscribed and attested shall be obligatory on the company." Act May 1, 1876, section 17 (P. L., 58); Br. Purd., 1046, section 63.

§ 292. **Policies must copy the application, by-laws, etc.** The Act of May 11, 1881, section 1 (P. L., 20); Br. Purd., 1046, section 62, provides that "all life and fire insurance policies upon the lives or property of persons within this Commonwealth, whether issued by companies organized under the laws of this State or by foreign companies doing business therein, which contain any reference to the application of the insured, or the constitution, by-laws, or other rules of the company, either as forming part of the policy or contract between the parties thereto, or having any bearing on said contract, shall contain, or have attached to said policies, correct copies of the application, as signed by the applicant, and the by-laws referred to; and, unless so attached and accompanying the policy, no such application, constitution, or by-laws shall be received in evidence, in any controversy between the parties to, or interested in, the said policy; nor shall such application or by-laws be considered a part of the policy or contract between such"parties." This Act is applicable only where the company offers the policy in evidence. *Title Co.* v. *Ins. Co.*, 47 Leg. Int., 188 (1890).

The Act has been construed according to its terms in *Ins. Co.* v. *Dunham*, 117 Pa. St., 460 (1888); *Ins. Co.* v. *Hallock*, 22 W. N., 151 (1888); and declared constitutional in *Ins. Co.* v. *Musser*, 120 Pa. St., 384 (1888).

Having waited the time required by the policy, and no satisfactory arrangement having been reached, you bring suit. Many policies prescribe a Statute of Limitations for the insurer. Do not delay beyond the time named.

But for the Act of March 14, 1873, the suit would always be in the name of the promisee or covenantee. That Act (P. L., 1873, page 46), Br. Purd., 1048, section 73, directs that *the assignee of policy may sue in his own name.*

It provides that " it shall be lawful for the assignee or assignees of the whole or any part of any policy of life, fire, or marine insurance, his executors or administrators, to bring suit, in the name of the assignee or assignees, for his, her, or their interest in any policy of insurance, against the company issuing the same, upon the happening of the contingency provided against." The *form of action* is *assumpsit. Præcipe for summons,* same as section 10, and follow general directions, section 16, etc.

§ 293. **Suit may be brought in county where property insured is located, and writ may be directed to sheriff of any other county and served by him.** The Act 24th April, 1857, section 1 (P. L., 318), enacts that, "in addition to the remedies now provided by law, it shall be lawful for any person or persons, body politic or corporate, who may have a cause of action against any insurance company incorporated by the legislature of this Commonwealth or against any insurance company that may have an agency established in this Commonwealth, to bring suit in any county where the property insured may be located, and to direct any process to the sheriff of either of the counties in this Commonwealth; and it shall be the duty of said sheriff to execute all process directed to him under the provisions of this Act, upon the president or other chief officer of the company against whom the same issued, as he shall be directed, or upon the agent of any company not incorporated by the legislature of this Commonwealth; and the manner of service and return shall be in the same manner as like process is now by law required to be made, and the same shall be returned to the court issuing the same, and all proceedings upon any suit not under this Act shall be the same as in other cases." See § 10.

By Act of April 8, 1868 (P. L., 70), this Act is extended to life and accident insurance companies. *Shrom* v. *Ins. Co.*, 11 W. N., 530 (1882) ; *Spangler* v. *Aid Society*, 12 *Id.*, 312 (1882). This was extended by the Act April 4, 1873, section 13 (P. L., 20), so that the service might in the case of foreign insurance companies be made upon an agent appointed by the company for that purpose, or on a party designated by the insurance commissioner, or on the insurance commissioner.

The Act of June 20, 1883 (P. L., 134), amends the Act of 1873, as follows :

All writs, rules, orders, notices, or decrees aforesaid, shall be directed to the sheriff, constable, or other officer authorized by law to serve similar writs, of the county wherein the same shall be issued, who is hereby authorized to serve the same on any and every person or persons, body politic or corporate, named in said process with said company, either as plaintiff, defendant or otherwise, or who may be impleaded in said action, suit, or proceeding with said company found in said county, and either before or after the service on the person or persons, body politic or corporate, found in said county aforesaid, as may be directed by the plaintiff or person issuing said process or his attorney, and in the absence of such direction as shall be most convenient, the officer to whom said process may be directed, shall, by writing indorsed on or attached to said process, deputize the sheriff, constable, or other officer of the county where the State agent designated by any company as provided by law to receive service of process for said company may reside, to serve the same on him ; and in default of an agent appointed by the company as aforesaid, then the officer so charged with the service of said process, shall, in like manner, deputize the sheriff, constable, or other officer aforesaid of the county where the agent, if any there be, named by the insurance commissioner may reside, to serve the same on him ; and in default of such agent named by the insurance commissioner as aforesaid, then in like manner to deputize the sheriff, constable, or other officer as aforesaid of the county where office of the insurance commissioner may be located to serve the same upon him, and each and every service so made shall have the same force and effect to all intents and purpose as personal service on said company in the county where said process issued.

Under the Act of April 8, 1868, it was held that suit could be brought against a life insurance company in the county where the insured had his residence. *Quinn* v. *Fidelity Association*, 100 Pa. St., 382 (1882).

A valid service cannot be made upon an agent empowered only to effect insurance, or upon a travelling agent. *Parke* v. *Ins. Co.*, 44 Pa. St., 422 (1863).

Service on foreign insurance companies must be upon the agent appointed for that purpose, at his office. A travelling agent is not such an agent. *Liblong* v. *Ins. Co.*, 82 Pa. St., 413 (1876).

As to time of suing. A policy of insurance provided that suit should not be sustainable unless brought within twelve months after the date of the fire; an action was brought within sixty days of furnishing proofs of loss, but dismissed as premature according to the terms of the policy. A second action instituted after the time provided for in the policy was decided to be too late. *Howard Ins. Co.* v. *Hocking*, 47 Leg. Int., 109 (1889).

§ 294. **Act of 1849. Service on officer, etc., of foreign corporation.** The Act of March 21, 1849, section 3 (P. L., 216), Br. Purd., 938, section 7, provides that in any suit or action against any foreign corporation, " process may be served upon any officer, agent, or engineer of such corporation, either personally or by copy, or by leaving a certified copy at the office, depot, or usual place of business of said corporation, and such service shall be good and valid in law to all intents and purposes."

Act of April 8, 1851, section 6 (P. L., 354), Br. Purd., 428, section 127, directs that " in any case when any insurance company or other corporation shall have an agency or transact any business in any county of this Commonwealth, it shall and may be lawful to institute and commence an action against such insurance company or other corporation in such county, and the original writ may be served upon the president, cashier, agent, chief, or any other clerk, or upon any directors or agents of such company or corporation within such county, and such service shall be good and valid in law, to all intents and purposes."

In *Benwood Iron Works* v. *Hutchinson*, 101 Pa. St., 359 (1882), the sheriff's return was " Served July 27, 1881, by delivering a true and attested copy of the within writ to Alonzo Loring, secretary of the Benwood Iron Works, and by making known to him the contents thereof." The court, quoting this return, said it was sufficient. They referred to *Patton* v. *Ins. Co.*, 1 Phila., 396 (1852), where the return was " Served a true and attested copy of the within writ personally on Alfred Edwards, an agent of the within-named defendants, and made known to him the contents thereof," which was also held valid.

The Supreme Court said " that ruling has been accepted ever since."

The same ruling was made in *Kennard* v. *R. R. Co.*, 1 Phila., 41 (1850), and in *Coxe* v. *R. R. Co.*, 11 W. N., 386 (1882). In the latter case the service was made by leaving a copy with an adult member of the president's family.

But in *Hunt* v. *Assn.*, 17 W. N., 423 (1886), the sheriff's return was "Served June 2, 1885, by giving a true and attested copy of within summons to S. S. Fowler, agent for the within-named Economical Mutual Benefit Association, within this county, and making known to him the contents thereof." Inasmuch as it was not alleged the defendant was a foreign corporation doing business in the county, it was held insufficient.

§ 295. If service be made improperly on officer of a foreign corporation. Should service be made upon an officer of a foreign corporation, when he was casually present, or when said corporation was for other reasons not suable in the courts of this State upon the contract or matter on which the action is founded, a plea to the jurisdiction is the proper remedy, and not a rule to set aside the service. *Benwood Iron Works* v. *Hutchinson*, 101 Pa. St., 359 (1882); *National Bank* v. *Shipbuilding Co.*, 2 Cent. Rep., 56 (1886); *Branson* v. *Machine Co.*, 40 Leg. Int., 5 (1882); *Telephone Co.* v. *Telephone Co.*, 46 *Id.*, 200 (1889).

Service of a summons on a soliciting agent of an insurance company is insufficient. *Connors* v. *Ins. Co.*, 1 Dist. Rep., 720 (1892).

§ 296. The Narr. or Statement. Set out a copy of the policy, aver your client's performance in detail and generally that he did all things required of him, charge the defendant's breach, following in all cases as nearly as may be the language of the instrument.

§ 297.

FORM OF STATEMENT ON A FIRE INSURANCE POLICY.

In the Court of Common Pleas, No.   , of Philadelphia County, of March Term, 1889, No. 200. County of Philadelphia, *ss.*

The plaintiff, A. B., claims of the defendant (name of company) the sum of   dollars, according to a certain policy of insurance, in writing, executed and delivered to the plaintiff by defendant on   at   .
Said policy was delivered in consideration of the sum of   dollars paid by the plaintiff to the defendant on   at   , the receipt whereof was in said policy acknowledged. A copy of said policy is hereto attached and made part hereof.

The plaintiff avers that he has performed all things on his part to be performed, but the defendant has broken its covenants on its part to be performed in this:

That on   at   the premises in said policy of insurance mentioned were destroyed by fire, which did not happen by (here insert any causes, as insurrection, usurped power, etc., provided for by the policy, nor was the building used for the purpose of carrying on any trade denominated hazardous), and that on   at   the plaintiff gave notice to the defendant of the fire and loss, and on   at   did deliver to the defendant a particular account of plaintiff's loss and damage, and also of the value of the premises insured, and when and how the fire originated to the best of plaintiff's knowledge (if policy so required, add: and annexed to said notice was a certificate under the hand and seal of a notary public, stating that he was acquainted with the character and circumstances of the insured, and that, without fraud, he had sustained a loss or damage upon the premises insured, to the sum of   dollars), yet the defendant has not paid to the plaintiff the said sum of money by it insured, nor repaid nor reimbursed him for the loss sustained by the said fire, or any part thereof, although so requested, contrary to the form and effect of the policy of insurance.

E. F.,
Plaintiff's Attorney.
(Date.)

(Plaintiff's affidavit when required.)

§ 298.

FORM OF STATEMENT ON SEA POLICY OF INSURANCE. (LOSS OF GOODS.)

In the Court of Common Pleas, No. 4, of Philadelphia County, of March Term, 1889, No. 200. County of Philadelphia, *ss.*

The plaintiff, A. B., claims of the defendants (name of the company) the sum of   dollars for a loss upon the plaintiff's goods and merchandise insured by the defendants in consideration of the sum of   dollars paid by plaintiff on   at   to defendants, said insurance having been effected by the defendant's policy of insurance, which, in consideration of the aforesaid payment, the defendants on the   day of   1889, executed in due form and delivered to the plaintiff. The following is a true copy of said policy (here copy the policy and all the conditions, articles, etc.). And the plaintiff saith that on the   day of   1889, goods of the plaintiff of the value of five thousand dollars were loaded in (Philadelphia), in and on board the said vessel in said policy mentioned, to be carried therein on the said voyage, and that the plaintiff was then and from thence, until and at the time of the loss, the owner of the said goods so shipped to the value of all the moneys by him caused to be insured thereon, and that the said vessel with his said goods on board set sail from   on her said voyage to   , and whilst proceeding on the voyage, and before her arrival at the place last mentioned (here state the particulars of the loss ; the proximate and not the remote cause should be regarded and the loss be stated as it can be proved). (It must appear to be within the terms of the policy. If the policy covered *capture by enemies* it may be in this form :)
the said vessel with the plaintiff's goods on board was on the high seas, with force and arms and in a hostile manner, captured, seized, and taken by certain enemies of the United States.

(*If by storm*)
the said vessel was, by the perils and dangers of the sea, by tempest and violence of the winds and waves, broken, damaged, and destroyed, and the plaintiff's goods on board of the said ship then and there became and were wholly lost to the plaintiff.

(*If lost by shipwreck*)
the said vessel by the perils of the sea was wrecked and totally lost, whereby the plaintiff's goods on board thereof were wholly destroyed and lost.

(The above may be varied according to the circumstances, as, if the ship became leaky and it was necessary for her to proceed to the nearest port and whilst endeavoring to reach it she was lost by storm ; or if she were lost by striking rocks, foundering, stranding, lost by eating of worms, by collision, fire, in all these and other cases state the fact as it may be, always charging that thereby the plaintiff's goods then and there became and were wholly lost and never did arrive at (the port of destination), of all which the defendants, on   of   1889, at the county aforesaid, had due notice, and were requested to pay him, the said plaintiff, five thousand dollars so by plaintiff insured, and which defendants ought to have paid according to the form of the policy.)   (If the policy required a notice in writing or certificates, aver in the words of the article a full compliance and always add a general averment thus :)

and plaintiff avers that from the time of the issuing of the policy he has fully performed all the stipulations and conditions thereof as required by said policy to be performed by him ; but that defendants have broken the same in this, that (here charge a breach in the language of the conditions binding the defendants, *e. g.*, that the defendants did not, thirty days after the receipt by them of notice of said loss, nor at any time thereafter, pay any part thereof to the plaintiff), and that there is therefore justly due by defendants to plaintiff the sums named in the following

Statement.

Amount of plaintiff's loss under the above policy   .   .   . $5,000 00
Interest from   to   ,   .   _____

E. F.,
Plaintiff's Attorney.

(Plaintiff's affidavit when required.)   (Date.)

§ 299.

FORM OF STATEMENT UPON A LIFE INSURANCE POLICY.

In the Court of Common Pleas, No.   , of Philadelphia County, of March Term, 1889, No. 200. County of Philadelphia, *ss.*

The plaintiff, A. B., claims of the defendant (name of company) the sum of   dollars upon a certain policy of insurance, dated   , with interest thereon from   , justly due and payable to the plaintiff by the defendant, of which claim the following is a

Statement.

A policy of insurance, dated   , was executed and delivered by the defendant to the plaintiff on   at   in consideration of the sum of   dollars paid on that day by plaintiff to defendant. The following is a copy of said policy (here insert copy of policy with all conditions, etc.).

The plaintiff avers that he has always, from the time of the making of the policy of insurance, performed all things on his part to be fulfilled, according to the tenor and effect of that instrument ; that E. F., the party insured for the benefit of A. B., died on   at   whilst the said policy was in force ; and that he, the said plaintiff, furnished the said defendant with good and sufficent proofs of the death of said E. F. ; and that the said E. F., in his lifetime, in all things performed the conditions and covenants stipulated in said instrument ; yet the defendant has not performed its covenants in this, that although so requested it did not, months after such proof had been furnished (follow the condition of the

policy) of the death of E. F., or at any time, pay to the plaintiff the sum
of   dollars, or any part thereof, but has failed so to do.

G. H.,

Plaintiff's Attorney.

(Plaintiff's affidavit when required.)   (Date.)

§ 300. **Policies for benefit of dependent relatives to be exempt from creditors' claims.** "All policies of life insurance, or annuities upon the life of any person, which may hereafter mature and which have been or shall be taken out for the benefit of, or *bona fide* assigned to the wife or children of any relative dependent upon such person, shall be vested in such wife or children or other relative full (free) and clear from all claims of the creditors of such person." Act April 15, 1868, section 1 (P. L., 103); Br. Purd., 1048, section 71.

§ 301. **If policy upon property lost, company may be compelled to furnish a copy.** The Act 4 March, 1850, section 1 (P. L. 126), Br. Purd., 1048, section 74, provides : " Whenever any policy of insurance upon any property, real or personal, granted by any body corporate or politic, shall have been lost or destroyed, such body corporate or politic shall, on proof of the loss or destruction of the same, in the manner hereinafter provided, furnish to the person or persons whose policy has been so lost or destroyed a copy of the same, together with the transfers which have been approved and recorded on the books of such body corporate, if any, which may have been made by the original or any subsequent grantee of such policy, to the person or persons having the same at the time of the loss or destruction thereof; the copy so made to be as effectual for the security and indemnification of the person or persons holding the same as the original, and subject, like it, to the transfer to any person purchasing the property insured.

" Sec. 2. On the application of any person or persons to the Court of Common Pleas of the county in which the property has been insured, setting forth the loss or destruction of the policy of insurance, on oath or affirmation, together with a description of the property, the amount for which it was insured, the person or persons to whom granted, if practicable, together with the *mesne* transfers thereof, the court shall grant a rule on the body corporate or politic which granted such policy of insurance, commanding such body corporate or politic to appear before said court on a day certain, not less than twenty days from the service of said rule, to show cause why a copy of such policy of insurance should not be supplied, in pursuance of the provisions of the first section of this Act; and on the default of such body corporate or politic to ap-

pear and show cause why such copy as aforesaid should not be
supplied, the court shall issue a mandate to such body corporate or
politic to furnish such copy in ten days after the service of the
same; and on the neglect or refusal of such body corporate or
politic to furnish a copy as aforesaid, the court, on due proof of
the service of such mandate, and the neglect or refusal of such
body corporate or politic to furnish such copy, shall direct a judgment to be entered by the prothonotary in favor of the person or
persons making the application, against the said body corporate or
politic, for the sum for which the said policy of insurance was
granted, which said judgment shall stand for the security of the
plaintiff or plaintiffs, for such time as the policy of insurance itself
would have done, and for the like purposes; and the costs of the
proceedings shall be paid by the defendant; and the officers rendering services shall receive the like fees as are now allowed by
law for similar service."

If no appearance entered, see section 23.

If appearance entered, but no affidavit of defense filed, see section 23.

If insufficient affidavit filed, see section 27.

If affidavit of defense be sufficient, enter rule to plead. Section
26.

If no plea filed, see section 26.

When plea filed, reply.

§ 302. The pleas in this, as in all actions of *assumpsit,* may be
non-assumpsit, payment, set-off, and the Statute of Limitations.
Act of May 25, 1887, section 7 (P. L., 272). *Ins. Co.* v. *Reinoehl,*
4 Pa. C. C. Rep., 161 (1887).

To the first you could reply thus:

As to the plea wherein the defendant has put itself on the country the
plaintiff doth the like.

This is called a *similiter,* and it is often expressed by the one
word, "*similiter,*" in the replication.

To the plea of payment you could reply:

And the plaintiff for replication to the plea saith that the said defendant
did not pay the sum in this suit claimed, as in said plea alleged; and of
this the said plaintiff puts himself on the country.

The plaintiff replies briefly, thus:

Non solvit (he did not pay).

To the plea of set-off you reply:

No set-off.

If the plea be the bar of the Statute of Limitations, your replication, where no new matter is to be alleged, will be a traverse or contradiction of the plea. Thus, if the policy were not under seal and contained no special limitation, the Statute of Limitations would be pleaded, as follows:

Non assumpsit infra sex annos (did not promise within six years), or *actio non accrevit infra sex annos* (the action did not accrue within six years),

or both.

To this you would reply, thus:

Assumpsit infra sex annos, or *actio accrevit infra sex annos,*

replying in both forms where both have been pleaded.

See also sections 160, 161, 162.

No further special direction in regard to actions on policies of insurance, in a work on practice, is required. After the case is at issue, it is proceeded in as are other actions of *assumpsit*. See Chapter II.

CHAPTER XI.

§ 303. **Account render** is an action brought to compel the statement and settlement of an account by one who holds or has received money or goods as the agent for another.

It may be argued by some that the old action of account render is within the letter and spirit of the Act of 1887. If so, the proceeding would be by summons in *assumpsit*. The theory upon which the writ in account issued was undoubtedly the implied promise of the defendant to pay whatever sum should be found due. And one of the counts in the printed form used in *assumpsit* was to that effect. But, on the other hand, the Act of May 25, 1887, does not in terms refer to account render. It says, section 61, of this book :

" That so far as relates to procedure the distinctions heretofore existing between actions *ex contractu* be abolished, and that all demands heretofore recoverable in debt, *assumpsit*, or covenant shall hereafter be sued for and recovered in one form of action to be called an ' action of *assumpsit*.' "

The third section of the Act prescribes the filing of a " concise statement of the plaintiff's demand." This would be difficult in most cases of account render, and in some instances it would be impossible.

It is not for a writer upon practice to decide questions untouched by the courts. Referring to them the settlement of the point, should it ever be presented, it is now proposed to aid the attorney in the pursuit of claims against those who are bound to render an account.

It should be borne in mind " that the proceedings in this action being difficult, dilatory, and expensive, it is now seldom used, especially as the party has in general a more beneficial remedy by a special action of *assumpsit*, or an action for money had and received, or, where the matter is of an intricate nature, by resorting to a court of equity." Roberts's Digest (17), citing Bul. N. P., 127 ; 1 Tidd's Pr., 1, and Bac. Abr., tit. Account F., pages 20, 21, where it is said " the action of account is now little used or understood."

Judge ROBERTS, commenting on this, says : " As no court of

chancery exists in Pennsylvania, it is conceived that the action of account would afford in a variety of instances a remedy more convenient and effectual to the parties than those which are substituted for it." He quotes, in support of this view, " the opinion of one of the most profound lawyers and able judges that ever dignified the bench."

§ 304. This comment was written at a time when our courts were without equity powers, and the entire aspect of the case is changed by the Act of October 13, 1840, section 19 (P. L., 1841, 7 ; Br. Purd., 57, section 5). It directs that

" The Supreme Court, the several district Courts, and courts of Pommon Cleas within this Commonwealth shall have all the powers and jurisdiction of courts of chancery in settling partnership accounts, and such other accounts and claims as by the common law and usages of this Commonwealth have heretofore been settled by the action of account render ; and it shall be in the power of the party desirous to commence such action, to proceed either by bill in chancery or at common law, but no bill in chancery shall be entertained unless the counsel filing the same shall certify that, in his opinion, the case is of such a nature that no adequate remedy can be obtained at law, or that the remedy at law will be attended with great additional trouble, inconvenience, or delay."

Though the action of account render is not obsolete (*McLean* v. *Wade*, 53 Pa. St., 146, 1865), it is difficult to understand why it should ever be preferred to the bill in equity, but cases may arise in which the common-law action is desired. The remedy in equity, under the above Act of Assembly, is co-extensive in its scope with the right to maintain account render at common law.' *Adams' Appeal*, 113 Pa. St., 449 (1886) ; *Baugher* v. *Conn*, 1 Pa. C. C. Rep., 184 (1886) ; affirmed in *Baugher's Appeal*, 8 Cent. Rep., 166.

In seeming contradiction of these cases, it is held in *Gloninger* v. *Hazard*, 42 Pa. St., 389 (1862), and in *Appeal of Pittsburgh R. R. Co.*, 99 Pa. St., 77 (1881), citing many other cases, that equity will not take jurisdiction " where the accounts are all on one side and no discovery is sought or required." But it may be observed of this line of cases, that they arise independently of partnership transactions, and that they relate to the proposed substitution of bill in equity for the action of *assumpsit* or covenant, not for account render proper ; damages being sought for breach of contract, rather than an accounting for money received.

§ 305. **The English Statutes** reported by Judge Roberts to be in force in Pennsylvania are :

52 Hen. III., ch. 23, A.D. 1267, which provided that bailiffs who withdraw and have no lands may be attached ;

13 Edw. I., ch. 11, A.D. 1285, which also provided for an arrest ; and

13 Edw. I., ch. 23, A.D. 1285, which gave the writ of account to executors.

It is decided in *Griffith* v. *Willing*, 3 Binney, 317 (1811), that section 27 of the statute of 4 Anne, ch. 16, A.D. 1705, extending account render to tenants in common, has also been adopted in Pennsylvania.

§ 306. **Jurisdiction.** Original jurisdiction in account render is wholly in the Court of Common Pleas. Justices of the peace have no jurisdiction in this action. *Wright* v. *Guy*, 10 S. & R., 227 (1823).

§ 307. **Against whom the action lies.** " The writ of account (*de computo*) lies against one as guardian, bailiff, or receiver, to compel the defendant to exhibit and settle his accounts. It commands him to render a just account to the plaintiff, or to show to the court good cause to the contrary." (Roberts's Dig., 9.) The writ can be issued against a partner, against a tenant in common, by a client against his attorney, by ward against guardian, by *cestui que trust* against trustee, by one joint tenant against the other, *Norris* v. *Gould*, 17 Phila., 318 (1884) ; by a landlord against a tenant who is under contract to pay a proportion of the profit for rent, by principal against factor, and generally wherever one person has received money as the agent of another. *Bredin* v. *Kingland*, 4 Watts, 420 (1835).

§ 308. **By whom the writ may be issued.** " By the ancient common law this remedy was confined to the parties themselves, because they alone were presumed to be privy to the matters of account between them ; and therefore the writ could not be sued out by executors. To this rule, however, there were some exceptions ; for this remedy might be had by the executors of a merchant *per ligem mercatoriam ;* so of the successors of a prior, for the body corporate never dieth ; and the king may maintain an action of account against the executors of any accountant." And by 13 Edward I., ch. 23 (1285), executors shall have a writ of account as the testator might have had if he had lived. (Roberts' Dig., 9.)

§ 309. **Writs for account may be maintained in certain cases by heir of deceased against bailiff of deceased without administering.** In *McLean* v. *Wade*, 53 Pa. St., 146 (1866), Daniel McLean had undertaken, at request of his dying son, to act as agent (or bailiff)

in regard to the estate of his infant granddaughter. He so acted for many years, and on his death the granddaughter sued his executors in account render. They objected, *inter alia*, that McLean had acted as executor *de son tort;* that the Orphans' Court alone had jurisdiction, and that plaintiff could not sue without administering. But the Supreme Court, overruling all the objections, said, as to the last point : " If there be no debts and no distribution needed, and only a solitary heir, administration would seem to be useless." It will be noted that the suit was brought " by the heir, some twenty-six years after the death of her father." It may be maintained by a patentee who has granted another a license to manufacture the patented article for a certain royalty. *Adams' Appeal*, 113 Pa. St., 49 (1886).

Upon the death of a partner, if there be an amount due his representatives and credited on the firm books, account render and not *assumpsit* will lie. *Ferguson* v. *Wright*, 7 Phila., 92 (1868).

If the account had been so far liquidated in any other than a partnership transaction, *assumpsit* and not account render would undoubtedly have been proper. *Brubaker* v. *Robinson*, 3 P. & W., 295 (1831).

In cases where there are no complicated accounts to adjust and but a single transaction took place, *assumpsit* will lie between partners. *Monument Co.* v. *Johnson*, 29 W. N., 117 (1891).

§ 310. **Against whom it does not lie.** " It lieth not against one as a servant, apprentice, comptroller, surveyor, chamberlain, or the like, unless he be charged as bailiff or receiver." ` (Roberts' Dig., 11.)

" A guardian or bailiff cannot be charged as a receiver ; for a receiver shall not be allowed his expenses, but guardians and bailiffs are entitled to an allowance for their trouble and expenses ; yet where they become such of their own wrong, or depart from the authority given to them, they are not entitled to allowance, nor for losses, in consequence of negligence or gross ignorance." (Roberts's Dig., 13.)

§ 311. *It does not lie for mesne profits* in ejectment against the executors of the defendant, a trespasser, who died pending the action of ejectment. *Harker* v. *Whitaker*, 5 Watts, 474 (1836).

It will not lie against a widow who continues to occupy her husband's land after his death, she not having received rent therefor and her interest in his estate not having been set aside to her. *Kelly* v. *Kelly*, 13 Phila., 179 (1879).

Neither account render nor bill in equity for an account will lie against an alleged co-tenant by one out of possession, unless the question of title has been first tried at law. *Frisbee's Appeal*, 88 Pa. St., 144 (1878).

There must be express or implied privity of contract between the parties to maintain account render, and it will not lie by the administrator of a widow to recover her dower from her husband's grantee. *Conklin* v. *Bush*, 8 Pa. St., 514 (1848).

Nor will it lie by one partner against the other to recover a share of losses which have been paid by the plaintiff. *McFadden* v. *Sallada*, 6 Pa. St., 283 (1847); *Thouron* v. *Paul*, 6 Wh., 615 (1841).

Money of the firm must have come into the hands of the partner defendant. *Demmy* v. *Dougherty*, 1 Pears., 236 (1863).

Ordinarily one partner cannot maintain the action jointly against his copartners. For him to do so there must be a joint liability to account. *Portsmouth* v. *Donaldson*, 32 Pa. St., 202 (1858); *Whelen* v. *Watmough*, 15 S. & R., 153 (1826).

Account render cannot be maintained when there has been but a single transaction between the parties not involving complicated or mutual accounts. *Galbreath* v. *Moore*, 2 Watts, 86 (1883); *Wright* v. *Cumpsty*, 41 Pa. St., 102 (1861); *Knerr* v. *Hoffman*, 65 Pa. St., 126 (1870).

§ 312. **Limitation.** The statutory limitation in account render is six years from the time when the right of action accrues, except upon accounts " such as concern the trade of merchandise between merchant and merchant, their factors or servants " (Act of March 27, 1713, section 1 ; 1 Sm., 76), when the six years begin to run from the date of the last item in the mutual accounts.

§ 313. **The Pennsylvania Statutes** are : March 30, 1821, section 1 (7 Sm., 429), which extended the arbitration law to account render.

April 4, 1831, section 1 (P. L., 492), giving the jury power to settle the accounts.

February 24, 1834, section 50 (P. L., 83), authorizing account render against executors for legacies.

October 13, 1840, section 18 (P. L., 1841, 7), empowering the courts to appoint auditors, or to impanel a jury to settle the accounts, to require answers to interrogatories, and to compel production of books, etc.

These last powers come very near to the chancery jurisdiction.

§ 314. **Procedure.** Account render is begun by summons, though in a proper case a writ of foreign attachment may be employed. *Strock* v. *Little*, 45 Pa. St., 416 (1863). *To commence the action,* file the following *Præcipe in account render :*

A. }
v. }
B. }

To the Prothonotary of the Court of Common Pleas of   County.
    SIR : Issue summons in account render, returnable *sec leg.*

C.,
Plaintiff's Attorney.
(Date.)

§ 315. The Summons. See sections 11, 12, 13, 14. After securing the summons, you follow the general directions as to other cases,
section 16.

If a writ of account render is quashed in one court of common
pleas for *defect in form*, this does not bar a new writ issuing from
another court. *Clark v. Ballou*, 1 Dist. Rep., 430 (1892).

§ 316. Filing of Declaration. Have your *narr.* ready and file
it on the return-day.

§ 317. Form of Declaration. Pursuing as nearly as possible the
general directions of the Act of May 25, 1887 (section 61, this
book), let your *narr.* be concise, yet full.

The plaintiff, in his declaration, must take care to charge the defendant properly, as bailiff, receiver, or guardian, according to the
fact. 2 Bull., 277.

§ 318. As to Bailiffs and Receivers. A bailiff hath the charge of
lands, goods, or chattels, to make the best benefit thereof for the
owner.

A receiver is one who has received money, and is to account for
it. A bailiff is answerable for the profits he might have made ; a
receiver for the precise sum or goods only.

§ 319. Allowance to Bailiff, Receiver, and Guardian. A bailiff,
as well as a guardian, is to be allowed his disbursements and reasonable charges ; and a bailiff, receiver, or guardian shall be allowed
whatever is lost by inevitable accident. A receiver is allowed
nothing for his expenses but what was agreed between the parties.

§ 320. As to Narr. against Bailiff and Receiver. In declaring
against one as bailiff, it is unnecessary to state from whom he received the money. But in declaring against one as a receiver, it is
necessary to state by whose hands he received. Co. Litt., 172 *a ;*
3 Keb., 425. However, the omission is only matter of form, and
is aided by the judgment to account. 2 Lev., 126. And it is not
necessary to be particular with regard to the precise time or the
exact amount of the money. *Ibid.*

A bailiff cannot properly be charged as receiver ; nor a receiver
as bailiff, since their accountability and the allowances to be made
them are different. 1 Rol., 119. In uncertain cases, however,

it is the safer practice to charge the defendant both as bailiff and
receiver.

§ 321.

FORM OF STATEMENT IN ACCOUNT RENDER BY AN ADMINISTRATOR
AGAINST BAILIFF OF HIS INTESTATE.

In the Court of Common Pleas, No. 4, of Philadelphia County.
Of March Term, 1889. No.   .

City and County of Philadelphia, *ss.*

The defendant, D., was summoned to answer A., the administrator of the
estate of S., deceased, of a plea that he render an account to said plaintiff,
and thereupon the plaintiff files this his statement and declaration of claim ;
for that the said D., at etc., from etc., to etc., and during the lifetime of said
S. was the bailiff and receiver of the said S., during which time the said D.
received, of the moneys of the said S., at   , from   ,
to   , aforesaid, all the several sums of money mentioned in the
schedule annexed, amounting to   dollars, to merchandise with
and make profits thereof, and to render a reasonable account thereof to the
said S. on demand ; yet the said D., though often requested, never rendered
such reasonable account to the said S. in his lifetime, nor since his decease
to the plaintiff, though requested, but still neglects so to do. Wherefore
the said plaintiff claims of said defendant   dollars damages.

B.,
Plaintiff's Attorney.
(Date.)

(Affidavit of plaintiff where required by rule of court.)
(Attach the schedule of amounts charged against defendant.)

§ 322.

FORM OF STATEMENT, EXECUTOR OF PARTNER AGAINST ONE OF
SURVIVING PARTNERS AS BAILIFF.

In the Court of Common Pleas, No. 4, of Philadelphia County.
Of March Term, 1889. No.   .

City and County of Philadelphia, *ss.*

The defendant, D., was summoned to answer A., executor of the last will
of S., deceased, of a plea that he render an account to said plaintiff, and
thereupon the plaintiff files this his statement and declaration of claim ; for
that whereas the said D. was bailiff to the said S., however and from whatever cause and contract arising, for the common use and benefit of the said
S., the said D., and one W. P., from   , to   , at   , of
certain merchandise of the said S., to wit, of the third part of thirty-eight
tuns of wine (etc.), of the value of   dollars, which merchandise the
said S., the said D., and W. P., in the life of said S., had occupied for their
common use and benefit ; and the same, during the time aforesaid, were intrusted to the hands of the said D., by the assent of the said S. and W. P.,
to merchandise for their common profit ; and the said D. thereof to render
his reasonable account to the said S. when thereto requested ; yet (etc., as
before).

B.,
Plaintiff's Attorney.
(Date.)

(Affidavit where required by rule of court.)

§ 323. In a count similar to this, judgment was attempted to be arrested because the plaintiff had declared against D. as a *general* bailiff, whereas it appeared that he was a *special* one, for it is between merchants and tenants in common, and because the plaintiff had declared for a third part when he ought to have declared for the whole, and because W. P. ought to have been joined. But the objections were overruled; for the plaintiff might sue, though his companion would not; and it may be he committed only his third part to the defendant. *Hackwell* et ux. v. *Eastman*, 2 Cro., 410. So, in *Martin* v. *Crompe*, 1 Ld. Ray., 340 (MSS.), it was *held*, that a surviving partner might properly sue the factor of the partnership in account render without joining the representative of his deceased partner.

§ 324.

FORM OF STATEMENT IN ACCOUNT RENDER BY ONE TENANT IN COMMON AGAINST ANOTHER AS HIS BAILIFF.

(Follow preceding form as to court, term, number, venue, etc., down to the words " for that whereas.")

For that whereas the said D., on, etc., and from thence continually until, etc., was bailiff of the plaintiff for a certain farm, situate, lying, and being, etc., and, during all that time, receiving the issues thereof and whereof the said plaintiff and the said D. were seized undividedly, as tenants in common, viz., the said plaintiff of one undivided moiety thereof, and the said D. of the other moiety, to the common profit of the said plaintiff and the said D., and to render a reasonable account thereof to the plaintiff when thereto requested; yet, though requested, etc. Wherefore (conclude as in preceding form.

B.,

Plaintiff's Attorney.

(Affidavit when required.)   (Date.)

§ 325.

FORM OF STATEMENT AGAINST A BAILIFF FOR NOT RENDERING AN ACCOUNT OF GOODS NOT DELIVERED TO MERCHANDISE WITH.

(Follow first form in account render as to court, term, number, venue, etc., down to words " for that whereas.")

For that whereas the said D. at   had been bailiff to the plaintiff from the   day of   to the   day of   , and during all that time had the care and management of divers goods and chattels of the plaintiff, to wit, one-half of the brig " Snow," with all her tackle, apparel, furniture, and appurtenances, of the value of   dollars; also one-half of the sloop called   , with all her tackle, etc., of the value of   dollars, and also of one-half of the cargo of the said sloop consisting of divers goods and merchandises, to wit,   of the value of   dollars, to merchandise and make profit thereof for the plaintiff; and thereof to render to the plaintiff the said D.'s reasonable account on demand; yet the said D., though requested, has not rendered his reasonable account thereof, but neglects so to do. Wherefore (conclude as in prior form.)

B.,

Plaintiff's Attorney.

(Affidavit when required.)   (Date.)

§ 326.

ANOTHER FORM OF STATEMENT AGAINST A BAILIFF.

(Follow the first form of statements in account render as to court, term, number, venue, etc., down to words) :

For that the said D., at   on   , was bailiff to the plaintiff of twenty pairs of men's shoes,   , all of the value of   dollars, to carry them to the West Indies, the dangers of the sea excepted, and there to merchandise with them to the plaintiff's best profit, and thereof to render the plaintiff his reasonable account, on demand, saving to the said D. one-half of the profits thereof; and the said D. afterward carried the said goods safe to   , in the West Indies ; yet he hath not rendered his reasonable account thereof, though requested, but unjustly neglects so to do.   Wherefore (conclude as in first form).   B.,
                                                                     Plaintiff's Attorney.
(Affidavit of plaintiff when required.)   (Date.)

§ 327.

FORM OF STATEMENT BY CONSIGNOR OF GOODS.

(Follow the first form of statement in account render down to) :

For that the said D. at   , from   to   , was the plaintiff's bailiff, and, in that time, had the care and management of the plaintiff's five hogsheads of molasses, containing   of the value of   dollars, to transport to Philadelphia (the dangers of the seas only excepted), and there to sell the same for the plaintiff's best advantage, and to lay out the proceeds in the following manner, viz.,   and to render to the plaintiff a reasonable account thereof, when thereto required ; and the plaintiff avers that the said D. transported the goods aforesaid safely to said Philadelphia, and there sold the same ; yet, though requested, he hath not rendered his reasonable account thereof, but unjustly neglects so to do. Wherefore (conclude as in first form).   B.,
                                                                     Plaintiff's Attorney.
(Affidavit of plaintiff when required.)   (Date.)

§ 328.

FORM OF STATEMENT AGAINST A BAILIFF OF LANDS WHO COLLECTED FOR COMMON BENEFIT OF HIMSELF AND OTHERS.

(Follow first form down to the words) :

For that the said D. and A. in his lifetime, to wit, on   and from thenceforth until   at   were bailiffs of the said S. in his lifetime, of the several messuages, buildings, parts of buildings, lots and tracts of land, and parcels of real estate, mentioned in the schedule hereto annexed, with the appurtenances, of them the said S., D., and C., now deceased ; and for all that time had the care and management thereof, and received the issues and profits thereof, for the common benefit and profit of the said S., D., and C. during his life, and after his decease, for the common benefit and profit of the said S. and D., and the executors of the testament of the said C., to render a reasonable account thereof to the said S. when they should be thereto required ; yet, (etc., as before.)
                                                                     B.,
                                                                     Plaintiff's Attorney.
(Affidavit when required.   Attach the Schedule.)   (Date.)

Although this form is given in a work of authority, it would be simpler and safer in this and kindred cases of difficulty to proceed by Bill in Equity.

§ 329. **After filing Narr.** If no appearance be entered, you can take judgment for want of an appearance. Section 23.

If appearance be entered, you enter rule to plead. Section 26.

If no plea be filed, you take judgment. Section 26.

If plea be filed admitting liability to Account, or if Judgment is to be entered for want of appearance or plea, you move the court for judgment *quod computet* (that he account), if there be one defendant; *quod computent* (that they account), if more than one defendant.

If the plea admit liability to account, this motion should be placed on the list and will be called up in court.

§ 330. **Judgment quod computet.** The following may be used as a form for entering this judgment:

A.	Common Pleas of	County.
v.	Term, 188 .	No.
B.		

And now   on motion of C., plaintiff's attorney, the court enter judgment against defendant *quod computet* (or against defendants *quod computent*) and refer the case to
            Esq. (or to   &   Esqs.), to state an account *sec. leg.*

Judgment *quod computet* is purely interlocutory; its effect is to compel the rendering of an account, which account is then adjusted by subsequent process. For this purpose the Act of October 13, 1840 (Br. Purd., 56, section 4), already quoted, gives the court the power " to either appoint auditors and proceed according to the practices and usages of the common law, or direct a jury to be impanelled to settle the accounts." The Act of June 24, 1895 (P. L., 243), allows an appeal from the interlocutory decree requiring the defendant to account in an equity case of account.

In most cases it would be very difficult to settle accounts before a jury; and the questions are, therefore, referred to auditors. As one competent person is generally preferred to two or three, one auditor is usually appointed.

In *McLean* v. *Wade*, 53 Pa. St., 146 (1866), the plaintiff entered no formal judgment *quod computent*. But the defendants being liable to such a judgment under the pleadings, the court below allowed the jury to liquidate the amount due. This was assigned for error, but the Supreme Court decided that a " formal judgment of *quod computet* was not indispensable."

It will be observed that the defendants' liability to account was admitted by the pleadings.

§ 331. **After plea filed denying liability to account.** You must, as in other cases, demur to the plea or take issue upon it. Do not demur for an objection which may be avoided by an amendment. Section 161. You take issue by filing a replication. If the plea conclude "to the country," the replication is a *similiter*. Section 160. *If the case be put at issue on the facts*, see section 163. If an issue of law be raised by demurrer, proceed as directed in section 162.

§ 332. **The Auditors.** After the interlocutory judgment to account, auditors are appointed, whose sole business is to adjust the accounts between the parties. For this purpose the parties themselves are admitted as witnesses to their accounts. "It has been decided elsewhere that the report of the auditors, if not objected to by the parties, will be considered as conclusive of the balance struck; but their report may be objected to, either on account of any mistake of the law or any improper admission or rejection of evidence, or because they have taken into consideration matters not submitted to them." (2 Day's Rep., 116.)

But this statement, that the report of the auditors may be objected to "on account of any mistake," etc., does not correctly express the law of Pennsylvania. Nor is the law altogether correctly stated in the following footnote to Brightly's Purdon (57, r).

"The auditors are mere clerks to take and state the accounts between the parties. They have no power to decide any matter of dispute, either in point of fact or law. If the matters offered by either party be disputed by the other, he may either demur or take issue before the auditors. If there be more points of dispute than one, there may be a demurer or an issue on each, which are to be certified by the auditors to the court, and then the matter of law will be decided by the court and the issues of fact by a jury, after which the account will be finally settled by the auditors, according to the result of the trials."

The author of this treatise was of counsel in the cases cited in the footnote, and he has no recollection that the law was laid down by the District Court of Philadelphia as above stated. Be this as it may, the rule as to

§ 333. **Powers of auditors and as to demanding issues, etc.**, were very clearly announced by STRONG, J., in *Little* v. *Stanton*, 32 Pa. St., 299 (1858), in these words : "A report of auditors in an action of account render is totally unlike in effect to a report of auditors in an Orphans' Court. It is not subject to revision by the court upon its merits. The report is final both in fact and in law. True, while the account is pending before the auditors, either party may demand that an issue of fact or of law arising in the case may be sent to the court for decision, and the decision will be binding upon the auditors ; but if either the fact or the law be submitted to the decision of the auditors in the first instance, their adjudication is the end of the controversy. It is not subject to the revision of the court. The court can interfere only where auditors have been guilty of misconduct. This is the law in England, whence we obtained the action of account render, and, with the exception of one or two of our very early cases, it has always been the law in Pennsylvania. Before the year 1807, exceptions to the merits either in fact or in law, of an auditor's report in account render, had been allowed in a very few cases, but this court then determined " that thereafter such an innovation upon the rules of the action would not be tolerated. *Snyder* v. *Caster*, 4 Yeates, 358 ; *Gratz* v. *Phillips*, 3 Binn., 475, and *Moore* v. *Hunter*, reported in a note to the same case. In *Crousillat* v. *McCall*, 5 Binn., 433, the rule is unqualifiedly asserted, and it has ever since been the recognized law of the State. The exceptions which were filed to the auditor's report in this case were therefore a nullity, and should have been disregarded by the court." * * * " It is sufficient to say that the court had no power to reform the auditor's report, no issue of fact or law having been certified to them."

The same ruling was repeated in *Stewart* v. *Bowen*, 49 Pa. St., 245 (1865) ; AGNEW, J. " The auditor made his report, which was excepted to for certain alleged errors, there being no charge of misconduct. But upon an allegation of an error in calculation, the report was recommitted by the court for correction. It came before the auditor, when the defendant insisting upon a rehearing upon certain matters, the plaintiff protested and withdrew. The auditor, although of opinion that he had no power to hear and decide any matter anew, concluded to hear the case and report the facts to the court. He did so, and with his report set up several issues of fact, which the defendant tendered in the rehearing. Upon the return of the report into court the court refused to consider the second report, and gave judgment for the plaintiffs upon the original report. It seems the auditor found no material error of calculation, and so stated in his second report. The defendant now complains, alleging that the court ought to have heard him again, and erred in rejecting his prayer for issues of fact."

" The parties having chosen the action of account render and a reference to an auditor, according to the rules of law in that mode of proceeding, must abide by the remedy thus adopted. It is settled that the adjudication of the auditor in this form of proceeding is the end of controversy, and is not subject to the revision of the court; that the court can interfere only when the auditor has been guilty of misconduct: *Little* v. *Stanton*, 32 Pa. St., 300, Doubtless for an error of calculation merely, the court might recommit the report to the auditor for correction, but not for a rehearing. The plaintiff did not acquiesce, but insisted upon his right to the original report. When the report, therefore, was returned, we see no error in discarding the second report, founded upon the rehearing, and in disregarding a demand for issues not asked for in time. The court was right in entering judgment upon the report as originally made, especially as the auditor found no mere clerical error of computation to correct. We cannot go into the report and make detailed calculations to find out the correctness of this opinion."

§ 334. **Proceedings** before auditors. The auditors are sworn as in other cases. The party required to account should produce his statement. The judgment *quod computet* has settled his liability to account, the question now is as to the amount due to him or by him. He may present an account which shows that the plaintiff is in his debt. Should he fail to exhibit any statement, he may be required, under the Act of October 13, 1840, section 18 (P. L., 7, Br. Purd., 56), already quoted, to answer interrogatories, to produce books, etc. He may also, under Act of May 23, 1887, section 7 (P. L., 160), be called as for cross-examination.

The plaintiff is at liberty to produce a statement charging the defendant according to the plaintiff's view. If no demand be made for a certificate to the court as to questions of law or of fact, the case proceeds before the auditors up to the filing of their report, when "it is final both in fact and in law." 8 Casey, 299 (*supra*). But if either party so desire, "while the account is before the auditor," an issue or issues in law or of fact may be certified to the court.

§ 335.

FORM OF DEMAND FOR AN ISSUE OF LAW.

A.
v.   } In the Court of Common Pleas, No. 4, of Philadelphia County.
B.   March Term, 1889, No. 6.

DEMAND OF DEFENDANT THAT AN ISSUE OF LAW MAY BE SENT TO THE COURT FOR DECISION.

To C. D., Esq., the auditor in the above case.

The demand of the defendant B. for an issue of law respectfully showeth:

That on the   day of   , 1889, this defendant presented to the auditor his account. That he has claimed an allowance for his just and lawful commissions, amounting to   dollars. That the plaintiff has objected to the allowance of said commissions, and has claimed that because (here state the facts relied upon by plaintiff) the defendant has lost and forfeited all claim to commissions, which facts are not disputed; but defendant denies that upon said facts he has forfeited his commissions. Wherefore, the facts being undisputed, the following question of law has arisen, viz. :

Whether upon the facts above stated the defendant has or has not as matter of law forfeited his right to charge his commissions.

The plaintiff contending that, as matter of law upon said facts, the commissions have been forfeited.

And the defendant denying this, and contending that, as matter of law upon said facts, the commissions have not been forfeited.

And the defendant demands that this issue of law be sent to the court for decision.

Signature of defendant.
Signature of his counsel.
(Date.)

Affidavit of defendant that the matters set forth in above demand are true.

Here it will be observed that the defendant admits the facts. No issue of law could arise upon disputed facts. The facts must be admitted or settled before a question of law can arise upon those facts. A case may present, at the same time, a question of law upon certain facts admitted and separate issue as to matters disputed. Thus one or more questions of law and of fact may exist at the same time. Separate issues may be demanded as to each. But in all demands for issues of law there must be no contention as to facts in those particular issues.

Where the facts are disputed and you are not content to leave the question to the decision of the auditor, you must demand an issue.

§ 336.

FORM OF DEMAND FOR AN ISSUE OF FACT.

A.   ⎱
v.   ⎬   Court, Term, No., etc., as above.
B.   ⎰

To C. D., Esq., the auditor in the above case.

The demand of the plaintiff A. for an issue of fact respectfully showeth :

That in the settlement of the account produced by the defendant before the auditor in the above case, the defendant has claimed that he paid to plaintiff the sum of   dollars on   , and in support of said allegation, the defendant has produced a writing purporting to be a receipt from plaintiff to defendant for said sum on said date, and the plaintiff has denied that the defendant paid plaintiff said sum as above claimed by defendant, and plaintiff has further denied that said writing is plaintiff's receipt, and plaintiff has charged that said writing is a forgery. And thereupon a question of fact has arisen, to wit, whether said payment was made and whether said writing is genuine. And the plaintiff further shows that the question thus arising is important and is material to the just determination of the case and to the settlement of said account, and he avers that said payment was not made and that said so-called receipt is a forgery. Wherefore the plaintiff demands that the following issue of fact be certified by the auditor to the court, to wit, did the defendant pay to the plaintiff on the sum of   dollars, and is said so-called receipt genuine ?

And the plaintiff demands that said issue be tried by a jury.

Signature of plaintiff.
Signature of his counsel.

Plaintiff's affidavit that the facts above set forth are true ; that the question whether, etc., is important and material; that the defendant asserts   that the plaintiff denies this assertion ; that the truth is, said payment was not made as alleged by defendant ; and that said so-called receipt is a forgery.

It need hardly be stated that the matters exhibited in the foregoing forms are only imagined, in order to present the proper outlines, and that every demand must present the facts exactly as they have appeared, stating with clearness the precise questions to be referred to the court.

§ 337. **When issues are properly demanded**, the auditor must report them to the court. They are ordered upon the argument list by either counsel. He who orders should notify his adversary. If there is to be a contest, both sides should prepare paper-books, giving the court the history of the case, points, authorities, etc.

§ 338. **Upon demand for issue of fact**, the court will send any material question to a jury. The counsel generally agree upon the framing of the issue; but if they cannot do so, the court directs them. The party taking the affirmative should be made plaintiff, e. g., the defendant who alleged he had made the payment, and that the receipt was genuine, would be plaintiff.

§ 339. **Narr. and plea in feigned issue.** The old form set forth a conversation in which defendant promised plaintiff to pay him $100 if certain things were so ; that is, in the case above suggested the defendant in the account render becomes plaintiff in the feigned issue, and sues the plaintiff in the account render for $100 promised to be paid if the payment claimed before the auditor had been made and if the receipt were genuine. The narr. then, of course, averred that the payment had been made and that the receipt was genuine, wherefore the defendant (in the feigned issue) owed plaintiff (in the feigned issue) the $100 so wagered. The defendant would admit that he made a bet, but deny the matters averred by plaintiff. Thus the cumbersome feigned issue was framed. A simpler method would be the following :

A.
v. } Court, Term, and number.
B.

A feigned issue is hereby stated by the above-named parties under the order of court made .... upon the following question :

Did B. on .... pay A. .... dollars and is the receipt held by B. for said sum genuine ?

B. affirms that he did so pay and that the receipt is genuine.

A. denies this.

The affirmative of the issue is with B. And the issue is to be tried with same effect as if a *Narr.* in feigned issue had been filed setting forth a discourse, wager, etc., and a plea thereto had been filed admitting the wager, but denying plaintiff's averments, all in the usual form.

Signatures of parties.
Signatures of counsel.

§ 340. After issues decided. The parties return to the auditor, who states the account in the light of the results. He should include all matters in account between the parties down to the time of filing his report. *Tutton* v. *Addams*, 45 Pa. St., 67 (1863).

It is not enough for him to state simply the balance he finds due ; he must itemize his report and give the calculations by which he arrives at his decision. *Finney* v. *Harbeson*, 4 Yeates, 514 (1808).

After the auditor states his report, it is filed with the prothonotary of the Common Pleas, and has the effect of a verdict. Judgment may be entered and execution issued upon it as in other cases. For form of *præcipe* for *fi. fa.* and proceedings relative thereto, see sections 23, 24, 25. The statutes concerning stay of execution (Act of June 16, 1836, section 3, P. L., 762 ; Br. Purd. Dig., 829, section 9, *et seq.*) apply to judgments in actions of account render.

§ 341. Error. After final judgment the cause may be removed to the Supreme Court by an appeal. Upon this subject see Br. Purd. Dig., page 787, title Errors and Appeals, and Act of May 9, 1889 (P. L., 158). Follow the statutes carefully. As judgment *quod computet* is not final but interlocutory, the appeal will not issue upon it forthwith, but must await the final judgment on the auditor's finding. *Beitler* v. *Zeigler*, 1 P. & W., 135 (1829), referred to and approved in *Gessell's Appeal*, 84 Pa. St., 238 (1877), on page 240. The Act of June 24, 1895 (P. L., 243), allows an appeal from the interlocutory decree in equity, fixing the liability of the defendant to account. On the other hand, judgment for defendant upon a plea in bar in account render is final, and plaintiff may have his appeal at once.

CHAPTER XII.

§ 342. **Various kinds of municipal claims.** The claims to be here considered are of various kinds—for taxes, benefits assessed, for opening streets, pitching and paving streets and alleys, digging down, filling up, curbing, paving, repairing footways, for introducing water, for culverts, for laying iron pipes, for sewers, and for removing nuisances.

§ 343. **All enforced in the same general way.** All are, however, enforced in the same general way. A claim is filed and a *sci. fa.* issued. The writ is prosecuted as any other *sci. fa.* subject to the provisions specially applicable.

Assumpsit cannot be sustained to recover a municipal assessment for paving. *Phila.* v. *Merklee*, 159 Pa. St., 515 (1894) ; *Phila.* v. *Bradfield*, Id., 517 (1894).

§ 344. **No charge is a lien unless so declared.** In *City* v. *Dickson*, 47 Leg. Int., 83 (1889), it was held that the second section of the Act of May 17, 1887, intended to validate certain municipal assessments, was unconstitutional.

§ 345. **General abstract of legislation.** *Lien in Philadelphia for taxes, rates, and levies.* The Act of February 3, 1824, section 1 (8 Sm., 189 ; P. L., 18), makes all taxes, rates, and levies upon real estate in Philadelphia, together with all additions to, and charges on the said taxes, etc., a lien on the real estate, having priority over and to be satisfied before any recognizance, mortgage, judgment, debt, obligation, or responsibility to which the real estate may become liable after the passing of the Act. This is altered by Act of January 23, 1849. See sections 364, 365.

§ 346. *Collectors to give receipts, etc.* The seventh section required persons collecting registered taxes, etc., to receipt for the same and to certify the payment to the county commissioners within thirty days, under penalty of five dollars.

§ 347. *Water-rents not a lien.* The eighth section applied the lien to all taxes, etc., levied by authority of the city of Philadelphia, or of any corporation in the county of Philadelphia, except that rents for Schuylkill water should not be within the Act.

§ 348. *Liens in Philadelphia for streets, culverts, etc.* The Act of April 23, 1829 (P. L., 301), gave the right to file liens for paving or curbing any street, court, or alley, for laying footways or cartways, and for relaying pavements, curbs, or footways, which liens shall have priority over any recognizance, mortgage judgment debt, or obligation : *Provided*, That no owner shall be required to curb or pave except in front of his property, *and to no greater extent than one-half of the width.*

The Act of April 16, 1840, section 9 (P. L., 412), empowered the authorities in Philadelphia County to file in Common Pleas office all claims " for pitching and paving streets and alleys, for digging down, filling up, and for curbing, paving, and repairing any footway within the same, and also for building culverts and laying down iron pipes; " and all amounts for taxes, rates, and levies assessed by any incorporated district or township.

§ 349. *What the claim was to set forth.* The tenth section of the last-cited Act required that claims should set forth " the name of the owner or reputed owner, and as nearly as may be an accurate description of the real estate against which the same is filed, and where the said estate is situate." The lien was to remain until the claim was paid, and could be sued out as a mechanic's claim by *scire facias*, but no land of a minor was to be sold until after two years from his attaining his majority.

§ 350. *What to be proved on trial in Philadelphia.* The plaintiff was only bound to show that the work was done or the materials furnished and the value. The defendant could only contest these matters or prove payment or release. Act of April 19, 1843, section 1 (P. L., 342).

§ 351. *Lien limited to six months, unless claim filed, and then to five years, unless revived.* The Act of April 16, 1845, section 2 (P. L., 488), declared that none of these claims for work or for materials by the board of health or any municipal corporation " shall be a lien for more than six months, unless the claim for the same shall be filed in the office of the prothonotary of the proper court, nor shall the same continue a lien longer than five years from the time of filing, unless revived by *scire facias* in the manner provided in the case of mechanic's claims."

Where a sheriff's sale is made after work done for municipal improvements, but before claim filed, the lien is discharged. *City* v. *Cox*, 29 W. N., 519 (1892).

§ 352. *The Treasurer of Philadelphia County* was empowered to collect taxes registered in the office of the county commissioners, to employ counsel at five per cent., etc. Act April 16, 1845, section 3 (P. L., 496). This was restrained to collection of State, county, road, and poor taxes by section 7, Act March 11, 1846 (P. L., 115).

The fourth section of the Act of April 16, 1845, authorized suits by the treasurer in the name of the county of Philadelphia before any alderman or justice or court, and upon producing certificate, judgment to be entered unless defendant proved payment.

§ 353. *Two returns of Nihil in tax claims.* The fifth section made two returns of *nihil* equivalent to a service, as in cases of suits upon mortgages. But the tenant (if any) was to be served. If no tenant, a copy of the *alias* writ was to be posted on some conspicuous part of the premises ten days before the return-day ; and publication was to be made (reciting the amount of the tax and the description of the real estate, as set forth in the registry) in one or more newspapers of the city of Philadelphia.

§ 354. *Registered Taxes cease to be liens five years from January first of the year succeeding that in which they became due, unless suit brought and duly proceeded in to Judgment.* Act March 11, 1846, section 1 (P. L., 114). The second section of this Act declared that if claim for taxes exceeded $100 it could be filed in prothonotary's office, and a *sci. fa.* issued, or action of debt to recover a general judgment be proceeded in—the claim was to be *prima facie* evidence—and judgment might be entered for want of affidavit of defense. If property had been conveyed, and deed recorded after assessment of the tax, the present owner was to be served ; and if there were several owners of distinct portions of the premises, the tax was to be apportioned. If any owner be omitted, he may be made a party, and, on proof of service, judgment may be entered by default : *Provided,* That such apportionment should not affect the personal liability of the owner at the time of the assessment for the whole tax, costs, etc.

In Philadelphia, registered taxes cease to be a lien, unless a *sci. fa.* is issued within five years from the first of January next after they become due. *Phila.* v. *Hiester*, 142 Pa. St., 39 (1891) ; *City* v. *Allert*, 29 W. N., 113 (1891); *Phila.* v. *Kates*, 150 Pa. St., 30 (1892) ; *City* v. *Ryers*, 27 W. N., 71 (1890).

§ 355. *Taxes cease to be liens unless recorded in prothonotary's office within two years of assessment, and revived within five years thereafter.* By Act of May 4, 1889 (P. L., 79), it is provided that " No county, city, borough, township, or school tax, levied or assessed, shall remain a lien on real estate for a longer period than two years from the time of such levy or assessment unless the same be entered of record in the prothonotary's office of the proper county in which such real estate is situate ; and no lien so entered therefor, or for any municipal improvement claim, shall remain a lien thereon for a longer period than five years from the date of such entry unless the same be revived and continued by writ of *scire facias* within said period, and duly prosecuted to judgment, as in the case of judgment liens."

§ 356. *Service of sci. fa. in Philadelphia* for taxes, municipal charges, assessments, and expenses of removing nuisances was directed to be by sheriff posting true and attested copy on conspicuous part of premises described, and by publishing brief notice in a daily newspaper in said county twice a week for two weeks before return-day. This service being made, the plaintiffs " may proceed to recover judgments as in suits on mechanics' liens." Act March 11, 1846, section 3 (P. L., 115). See sections 383, 395, 427, 428, 429, 430, 450, and 490 of this book.

§ 357. *All claims in Philadelphia evidence without proof, and the defendant deprived of many defenses.* The fourth section of the Act last cited (P. L., 115), provides : " Such claims may, in suits thereon, be read as evidence of the facts therein set forth ; and no plea alleging non-joinder or mis-joinder of parties ; no plea averring want of notice to remove nuisances ; no plea touching the rates or proportions of contribution among parties jointly interested ; nor any plea touching the question of ownership shall be allowed in any such action."

§ 358. *Sheriff's Hand-bills* to note at foot name of plaintiff and character of claim, or sale may be set aside. *Ibid.*, section 5.

§ 359. *Lien not divested by judicial sale* for so much as the proceeds shall be insufficient to discharge and pay. *Ibid.*, section 6 (P. L., 115).

So regarding lien for taxes. Act April 19, 1883, section 6 (P. L., 11).

§ 360. *Apportionment of Taxes.* The eighth section of the Act of March 11, 1846, authorized the commissioners of Philadelphia County to apportion taxes jointly assessed on separate properties.

§ 361. *The costs of prothonotary and sheriff to be collected from the defendants, and not from the county.* Act March 13, 1847, section 1 (P. L., 340).

§ 362. *Advertisement and Redemption.* In cases of municipal claims in Philadelphia notice must be given once a week in two daily papers for three months before suit brought. One year after sale allowed for redemption on payment of all costs, charges, and twenty per cent. on amount for which property sold. Act January 23, 1849, section 3 (P. L., 686). But the requirement as to advertisement was repealed, and in lieu thereof the city solicitor was required to cause diligent search to be made for the owner or reputed owner of all property named in claims of every kind filed by the city, and to serve him with notice to pay in ten days. Act of March 23, 1866, section 1 (P. L., 303).

§ 363. *The right of redemption was extended to claims for removing nuisances.* Act April 26, 1855, section 1 (P. L., 303). And to two years, with right to compel conveyance by petition and attachment. Act May 13, 1856, section 11 (P. L., 569).

§ 364. *Lien of Philadelphia mortgages* not to be defeated unless the claim duly registered in the proper office prior to the recording of the mortgage. Act of January 23, 1849, section 4 (P. L., 686).

§ 365. *Philadelphia Ground-rents protected.* No such ground-rent to be divested by the sale of the land for non-payment of tax charge or assessment on said real estate ; but ground-rent shall be assessed as a distinct estate, and payment of tax or assessment enforced as in other cases. *Ibid.*, section 5 (P. L., 686).

§ 366. *Universities, Colleges, Academies, and School-houses* were made liable for pitching, paving, and laying pipes for Schuylkill water. Act March 11, 1850, section 4 (P. L., 165). But this was twisted and the privileges of the universities, etc., re-established by Act of April 15, 1850, section 11 (P. L., 469).

§ 367. *When cartway ordered to be paved with cubical blocks.* Where the cartway of a street shall be ordered to be paved with cubical blocks, every owner of the · lot of ground opposite such pavement shall cause the foot pavement to be supported with cut granite curbstones, and in case of neglect or refusal, shall be liable for proceedings as are now authorized in the case of owners neglecting or refusing to curb a footway. Ord. Feb. 12, 1852, section 1.

§ 368. *Receiver of Taxes in Philadelphia.* By Act of February 2, 1854, section 11 (P. L., 29), the receiver of taxes in Philadelphia is to collect all taxes, etc., and certify all taxes and claims : "*Provided*, that if any person against whom such taxes shall have been assessed shall make affidavit that he did not own the premises for which such taxes were assessed at the time they accrued and became a lien thereon, the said taxes shall be collected of the true owner thereof, or by proceedings to sell the premises by execution." (*Ibid.*, page 30.)

Where taxes remain unpaid for one year after they have become delinquent, the receiver of taxes shall procure an accurate description of the real estate on which they are assessed, at the cost of the owner, such cost not to exceed one dollar, and shall file liens, keep the same revived, and proceed to collect them from time to time. Act April 19, 1883, section 6 (P. L., 11).

§ 369. *Tax Sales vest in purchaser good title subject to right of redemption.* *Sales* made in suits instituted by the receiver of taxes or under his directions shall vest in the purchaser a good title subject to the right of redemption, which is limited to two years from the date of acknowledgment of the sheriff's deed upon payment to the purchaser of the amount of his bid with ten per cent. thereon, together with costs, etc. *Ibid.*, section 5.

§ 370. *Lien for Water-pipes.* The ordinance of January 29, 1855, section 3 (41), provides that whenever pipes for the conveyance of water shall have been laid in any square of street or highway, the chief engineer of the water-works shall, within five days thereafter, inform the surveyor of the district, who shall, within ten days thereafter, assess the expense against the owners of ground fronting on said street, in proportion to their respective fronts thereon, and make out duplicate bills therefor, which he shall deliver to the chief engineer of the water-works, who shall take steps to collect the same as therein directed. If the bills be not paid in four months, he shall deliver them, together with a description of the property, to the city solicitor, who shall forthwith file claims for and proceed to collect the same as is practised and allowed by law.

§ 371. *Paving.* Ordinance of May 3, 1855, section 2 (141), provides that whenever the cartways of a public street or portion thereof shall have been paved by authority of councils, the expenses thereof, excluding the expenses of paving at the intersection of public streets, shall be assessed against the several owners of ground fronting the said street, each to the centre thereof and in proportion to their fronts thereon ; if the said assessments shall not be paid after the proceedings therein directed, the city solicitor shall file claims for and proceed to collect the same.

§ 372. *General notice to tax-payers* is directed to be given by the receiver of taxes on the first Mondays of October, November, and December, three times, in three newspapers, to pay the taxes then due ; that if they are not paid by the first day of the following January, interest will be charged thereafter, and that the names of the delinquents will then be published. When so published, they shall be alphabetically arranged for the several wards. Act May 13, 1856, section 8 (P. L., 569).

But this requirement to publish the names of delinquents is to apply to personalty only when its assessed valuation exceeds $100. Act May 13, 1857, section 2 (P. L., 489).

By Act 23 May, 1874, section 5 (P. L., 232), the receiver of taxes in Philadelphia is directed to publish a detailed statement of delinquent tax-payers, giving their names, the amount of tax, and the property upon which it is due, in five daily and two Sunday newspapers, " and in such one newspaper as is now authorized by law to publish advertisements of legal notices, within one week succeeding the fifteenth day of January of each year   *   *   * The same number of times as is now required by law." And the city solicitor shall direct the publication of all municipal liens in the same manner.

§ 373. *Assessors to make return.* The assessors are to return dimensions of each lot with assessments to the city commissioners, and if their return is uncertain, the surveyor of the district shall furnish accurate measurement and precise description. Act May 16, 1857, section 2 (P. L., 549).

§ 374. *Duties of receivers, solicitors, prothonotaries, etc.* The receiver of taxes is to register unpaid taxes annually, and to send to the city solicitor a list of those registered and unpaid in January, every two years succeeding the year for which they were levied, with bills therefor. The city solicitor is to collect them by sale of the real estate on which they are a lien. The controller shall audit the receiver's accounts. Clerk of the Orphans' Court and prothonotary of Common Pleas shall certify to the receiver all real estate sold and confirmed in their courts. Act April 21, 1858, section 2 (P. L., 385). ·

The receiver may sue in the name of the city of Philadelphia. Act April 12, 1859, section 1 (P. L., 543).

§ 375. *Amendments* may be allowed before or at the trial, on notice, under rule of court. If made on trial, continuance may be granted to defendant. Act April 21, 1859, section 9 (P. L., 387).

§ 376. *Further regulations as to tax sales.* All taxes on the same property filed in the same court are to be collected in one suit. Sale to be stayed unless enough bid to pay all in arrear to State and city, or unless city purchased, which they are authorized to do, subject to redemption and the right to redeem to continue until six months' previous notice published as in case of suits for registered taxes ; after period for redemption expired, city to advertise as required in Orphans' Court sales, and sell. Act April 9, 1861, section 5 (P. L., 269).

When property is sold by the sheriff for taxes, if the proceeds be not sufficient to pay taxes and costs, the receiver may either stay the sale or buy the property in behalf of the city and take title thereto. Act April 19, 1883, section 4 (P. L., 11).

The Act of May 22, 1895 (P. L., 111), provides that the lien of all taxes against real estate shall be divested by judicial sale, provided the amount of the purchase-money shall equal the amount of the taxes. The officer having taxes for collection against any land advertised to be sold, or the county commissioners, if the taxes have not been certified for collection, shall give notice to the officers or persons selling such land of the amount of taxes due, and the officer selling such land shall pay said taxes out of the proceeds arising from the sale first after payment of the costs of sale.

§ 377. *Penalties and abatements* in tax cases were fixed by Act of April 17, 1861, section 1 (P. L., 354).

§ 378. *In municipal claims the owner may compel plaintiff to proceed.* Whenever a claim shall be filed in the name of the city of Philadelphia, any person entitled to defend may notify in writing the attorney of record; or use plaintiff, or if no such counsel or person, then the city solicitor, requiring him to issue *sci. fa.* to next monthly return-day, which shall be at least fifteen days from notice. If no writ issued on motion and due proof of notice, the court shall strike claim from record ; Act February 21, 1862, section 1 (P. L., 44) ; or the amount, with sufficient to cover interest and costs, may be paid into court to abide result. Thereupon the claim ceases to be a lien, and shall be stricken from judgment index. *Ibid.*, section 2 (P. L., 44).

§ 379. *Locality Index* to be kept by prothonotaries in Philadelphia for all claims, municipal and private, frontages and distances to be noted, twenty-five cents allowed for each claim indexed, and forty cents for search. Acts March 31, 1864, section 1 (P. L., 171) ; February 16, 1866, section 1 (P. L., 50).

§ 380. *Assessed benefits a lien.* The Act of April 1, 1864 (P. L., 207), section 3, provides that " when the court has confirmed the award of the jury as aforesaid, the solicitor of the city of Philadelphia shall notify the property-owners benefited of the amount assessed against the property of each, and have delivered to them bills for the sums so assessed," and the claim filed by him, after non-payment within thirty days after the delivery of the bill, " shall be a lien against the premises assessed, and shall be collected in the same manner as municipal claims are now by law collected."

§ 381. *As to laying water-pipe before paving.* No district surveyor shall prepare for paving the cartway of a street until a certificate of the chief engineer of the water department that water-pipe has been laid or is not required to be laid, is filed in the survey department. Ord. May 23, 1864, section 1 (122).

§ 382. *Sewer charges a lien.* Sewers or drains may be constructed and the charge recovered as liens for laying water-pipes are now recovered, and with same allowance for corner lots. When owners do not pay, the tenants may pay and hand the receipt to owner as so much cash paid for rent. Act March 27, 1865, section 1 (P. L., 791).

§ 383. *Proceedings required on Sci. Fa.* Writs of *sci. fa.* are to be served by the sheriff by advertising and posting as required before 1866. But before judgment by default the court is to be satisfied by affidavit as to the following matters in reference to the owner or reputed owner :

1. If he has any known residence in the city, that he has been served at least ten days before issuing writ with notice of claim, personally or by serving an adult member of his family at his residence.

2. If he has a residence out of the city, then the affidavit must show that notice prepaid was mailed to the owner at his address at least fifteen days before suit brought.

3. If the address cannot be ascertained, the premises liened must be visited by the deponent, and if occupied by an adult, notice must be served on him and inquiry made for owner ; if premises unoccupied or inquiry fruitless, notice must be affixed to post, tree, fence, or structure. Inquiry must also be made of occupant of nearest dwelling and nearest ward assessor ; if inquiries fruitless, notice must be served upon assessor, who must forthwith report it to board of revision, who shall file it alphabetically according to the wards. If a name of owner be found, he shall be served, his name shall be added to record, and he shall be made a defendant in any suit brought. This Act to apply to all claims to use or otherwise ; all municipal claims to be filed by city solicitor. Five per cent. to be allowed him in lieu of all costs, commissions, etc. Act March 23, 1866, section 2 (P. L., 303).

In the absence of any legal proceedings, the city solicitor cannot collect the five per cent. allowed by the Act of 1866 unless steps are taken to find the owner and to demand payment. *Phila.* v. *Milligan,* 147 Pa. St., 338 (1892).

Under the Acts of 1830 and 1866, ten days' notice of the claim must be served on the registered owner. *City* v. *Fitton,* 27 W. N., 340 (1890).

Where the defendant agrees to the issuing of an amicable *sci. fa. sur* municipal claim, he thereby waives the benefit of the Act of March 23, 1866, requiring notice. *City* v. *Schofield,* 166 Pa. St., 389 (1895).

§ 384. *Application for sewers to be made to surveyors.* All applications for the construction of sewers or drains not exceeding three feet in diameter must be made to the board of surveyors, with a list of the property-owners fronting on the sewers and the dimensions of each front, and when approved by the board and sanctioned by the committee of surveys and regulations, notice shall be given to the chief commissioner of highways, who shall advertise for the construction of the same, and allot the work to the lowest and best bidder giving the requisite security. Ord. May 12, 1866, section 3 (143).

§ 385. *Assessment bills to be taken by contractor as cash, and he may file lien.* The contractor shall accept as cash and collect the assessment bills indorsed by the commissioner of highways. He may use the name of the city of Philadelphia and employ all legal remedies, whether of *lien* or otherwise, to which the city may be competent. *Id.*, section 4 (143).

§ 386. *No sewer shall be constructed when assessment bills insufficient.* City solicitor may file claims for sewers or drains ; but no sewer shall be constructed under this ordinance where the assessment bills are insufficient to pay the cost thereof, until an appropriation to meet the deficiency be made by councils. *Id.*, section 5 (144).

§ 387. *Costs of connection with sewer in Philadelphia, a Lien on Premises connected.* Whenever any lot or premises shall be connected with a sewer, in pursuance of an Act of Assembly or ordinance of the city of Philadelphia, the cost thereof shall be a lien upon the lot or premises, and the lien shall be filed and collected in the same manner as are liens for the said sewer charges or assessments. Act of April 10, 1867, section 1 (P. L., 1111).

§ 388. *Change of street paving.* Upon a petition of a majority of property-owners of a block to have the character of the street paving changed, councils may direct it to be done, and the cost shall be a lien upon all the property fronting on said block. Act April 18, 1867, section 1 (P. L., 1303).

§ 389. *Macadamizing streets in the rural wards.* So much of Acts of Assembly as authorize owners to have streets paved is extended to macadamizing or turnpiking such streets in the rural wards, to be paid for and liens to be filed as in cases of paving streets in said city. This Act shall not apply to any road on which tolls are authorized to be collected. Act March 13, 1868, section 1 (P. L., 316).

§ 390. *Claims against one lot really belonging in parcels to different owners may be apportioned* on affidavit or other proper evidence, so that no more than due proportion shall be charged against the several lots. Upon payment of any part so apportioned, court may direct satisfaction *pro tanto.* The remainder of the lien to be unaffected. Act March 22, 1869, section 1 (P. L., 477).

§ 391. *Notice of city charge for paving.* Notice must be given to property-owners of the amount the city will charge for neglect in paving. Ord. May 7, 1869, section 1 (191).

§ 392. *No street to be paved till sewer constructed.* When application is made for paving, it must be ascertained whether such street require drainage by sewer, and, if so, such street shall not be paved until the necessary sewer shall have been constructed. Res. June 14, 1873 (306).

§ 393. *Award of paving contracts in Philadelphia.*

In Philadelphia, it is enacted by ordinance that, upon application by a majority of property-owners and after ordinance passed for the paving of any street, " it shall be the duty of the chief commissioner to award the contract for the same to a practical paver or pavers regularly engaged in such business, and known to be such : Provided, That security for the same shall be the same as now regulated by Act of Assembly : Provided, That any contractor failing to perform his work in accordance with the terms of his contract shall be deemed a defaulter, and no bid shall thereafter be received from or contract awarded to such defaulting contractor." Ord. Dec. 23, 1874, section 10 (431).

§ 394. *In Philadelphia, the authority to pave* has generally been conferred by ordinance, whereof the following is a form :

"*Resolved by the Select and Common Councils of the city of Philadelphia,* That the Department of Highways be and is hereby authorized and directed to enter into a contract with a competent paver or pavers, who shall be selected by a majority of the owners of property fronting on

·   from   to
                   in the   Ward, for the paving thereof
with rubble pavement ; cost of intersections not to exceed fourteen thousand six hundred and seventy dollars. The conditions of which contract shall be that the contractor or contractors shall collect the cost of said paving from the owners of property fronting on said street, and shall enter into an obligation to the city to keep said street in good repair for three years after the paving is finished."

§ 395. *Non-residents.* Whenever it shall appear by affidavit filed of record that, after diligent search and inquiry, the registered owner of real estate in Philadelphia against whom municipal claim has been filed is a non-resident or cannot be found, the sheriff may post a true and attested copy of *sci. fa.* on a conspicuous part of the premises and shall advertise a brief notice in a daily newspaper in said county twice a week for two weeks before the return-day (sheriff's costs not to exceed three dollars), the posting and publication to be equivalent to personal service on registered owner ; and plaintiff may proceed to judgment for want of appearance or affidavit of defense. The facts set forth in the affidavit as to non-residence to be conclusive. But notice of intended issuance of *sci. fa.* shall be given to all registered or reputed owners as required by Act of March 23, 1866. Act June 10, 1881, section 1 (P. L., 91).

The Act of April 22, 1891 (P. L., 25), provides :

That whenever it shall be made to appear, by affidavit filed of record, that after diligent search and inquiry the registered owner of any real estate against which any municipal claim for taxes has been or may be hereafter filed as a lien by, or in the name of any city or borough in this Commonwealth, are non-residents of such city or borough, or cannot be found therein, it shall and may be lawful for the sheriff to whom any writ of *scire facias* for the collection of any such claim is directed, to proceed to "make known" the same by posting a true and attested copy of said writ on a conspicuous part of the premises therein described, and by publishing a brief notice in a newspaper within said county for two weeks before the return-day (the sheriff's costs for such service not to exceed three dollars in each case), and such posting and publication shall be equivalent in all respects to a personal service of said writ on such registered owner or owners, which posting and publication being made, the plaintiff may proceed to recover judgment in default of an affidavit of defense, and the facts set forth in the said affidavit thereby required to be filed shall be conclusive for the purposes of the case as to the non-residence of the defendant or registered owner : *Provided*, That notice of the intended issuance of such writ of *scire facias* shall be given to all registered or reputed owners of such real estate, in accordance with the Act of Assembly approved March 23, A.D. one thousand eight hundred and sixty-six.

The city or borough solicitor shall appoint one or more persons to serve the notices herein provided for.

§ 396. *As on mechanics' claims, so sci. fa. and lev. fas. may issue on municipal claims.* Act of April 23, 1889 (P. L., 48), provides : " That when a lien for work done or materials furnished by or under the authority of the board of health, or any municipal corporation, shall be authorized to be filed under any general or special Act, and no process is provided for the collection of the debt, charge, or assessment upon which such lien has been or may hereafter be filed, writs of *scire facias* and *levari facias* may be issued thereon, as in the case of mechanics' liens, and the same costs shall be taxed."

§ 397. **Powers conferred upon the city of Philadelphia.** By various Acts of Assembly special authority was given.

§ 398. *As to Nuisances.* The board of health or a committee, having first obtained a warrant founded upon the complaint of two householders, directed to the sheriff of the county of Philadelphia, or his deputy, were authorized to enter and search between sunrise and sunset all houses, stores, cellars, and other enclosures where they may have just cause to suspect any nuisance to exist. Act of January 29, 1818, section 27 (P. L., 58).

§ 399. *Paving footways.* Councils may require unpaved streets, alleys, etc., to be curbed and paved by owners of the ground fronting thereon at their own cost, if one-half of owners apply to councils, but not more than three squares shall be included in one application. Act April 10, 1826, section 1 (P. L., 336).

If the owner neglect, after twenty days' notice, commissioners may pave, curb, repair, etc., and recover by civil suit, or by distress, with twenty per cent. added, the tenant being authorized to pay and defalk from the rent ; and until the same be paid it shall be a lien on the ground. But the owner shall not be required to pave and curb footway of a greater breadth than four feet in front of a lot whereon a dwelling-house is not erected. *Ibid.*, section 2 (P. L., 336).

§ 400. *Paving and Curbing.* The Act of April 23, 1829, section 1 (P. L., 301), authorized councils to pave and curb any private streets, courts, and alleys, both as to footways and cartways, at the expense of the owners of the ground fronting or bordering thereon ; but private streets, courts, or alleys not intended for the passage of carts need not be curbed, and private alleys which shall be enclosed and intended for the sole use of the owner or occupier are not required to be paved.

A municipal claim for curbing along a footway may be filed against a charitable institution. *City* v. *Pa. Hospital*, 28 W. N., 434 (1891).

§ 401. *Grading and curbing.* The Act of April 16, 1838, section 3 (P. L., 626), authorized the councils to grade, pave, repair, curb, and recurb footways or sidewalks, and collect the expenses by suit in the same manner that debts of like amount are by law recoverable.

Where a curb is set by the city without notice to the property-owner, the owner must pay therefor as much as the work would have cost if he had done it, and a municipal lien may be filed for that amount. *Phila.* v. *Meighan*, 159 Pa. St., 495 (1894).

§ 402. *Water-pipe.* The Act of February 2, 1854, section 40 (P. L., 43), authorized councils to charge owners of the ground in front of which the work is done for paving streets—except at intersections—also to charge them for water-pipe, and authorized the filing of liens in the name of the city therefor.

§ 403. *Sewers and drains.* The Act of March 27, 1865, section 1 (P. L., 791), gave councils the power to construct sewers and drains in the streets. As to liens, see section 382.

§ 404. **Property exempt from taxation.** By various Acts of Assembly the following property was exempted from taxation :

Churches, meeting-houses, or other regular places of stated religious worship, with the grounds annexed thereto [burial grounds belonging to religious congregations], universities, colleges, academies, and school-houses belonging to any county, borough, or school district, or incorporated, endowed, erected, or established by the laws of this State, with the ground annexed thereto, court-houses, and jails. The exemption of the ground attached to the foregoing properties shall extend to ten acres of such ground. Lunatic asylums, almshouses, poor-houses [parsonages with five acres of lands attached thereto], houses of refuge, penitentiaries, and asylums, schools, and hospitals supported by State appropriations, charitable institutions supported by voluntary contributions, with the lands attached thereto [the lands and premises of cemetery companies held in trust solely to improve such lands and premises, and whose revenues are devoted to that object, and not to the benefit or profit of the corporators], burial grounds not used or held for private, or corporate, profit, hospitals, universities, colleges, seminaries, academies, associations, and institutions of learning, benevolence, or charity, with the ground thereto annexed and necessary to the occupancy and enjoyment of the same, founded, endowed, and maintained by public or private charity. Property in course of erection which, when complete, will be exempt. Acts April 16, 1838, section 29 (P. L., 525) ; July 2, 1839, section 3 (P. L., 576) ; April 8, 1873 (P. L., 64); May 14, 1874 (P. L., 158) ; June 4, 1879 (P. L., 90). A church property which is rented out and produces income is subject to taxation. *Phila.* v. *Barber,* 160 Pa. St., 123 (1894). Followed in *Library Co.* v. *City,* 161 *Id.,* 155 (1894). A charity which excludes from its benefits any person because he has not a particular relation to some society, church, or other organization, is not a " purely public charity." *Phila.* v. *Masonic Home,* 160 *Id.,* 572 (1894). The Act of April 26, 1893 (P. L., 25), provides that real estate which has ceased to be exempt from taxation shall be subject to a tax for the proportionate part of the year during which its exemption ceased.

By Act of May 14, 1874 (*supra*), it is provided that all property, real and personal, other than that which is in actual use and occupation for the purposes therein enumerated, and from which an income or revenue is derived, shall be subject to taxation, except where exempted by law for State purposes.

Article IX. of the Constitution of Pennsylvania, of 1874, provides as follows :

" SECTION 1. All taxes shall be uniform upon the same class of subjects within the territorial limits of the authority levying the tax, and shall be levied and collected under general laws ; but the General Assembly may, by general laws, exempt from taxation public property used for public purposes, actual places of religious worship, places of burial not used or held for private or corporate profit, and institutions of purely public charity.

" SEC. 2. All laws exempting property from taxation, other than the property above enumerated, shall be void."

§ 405. Injustice of the legislation as to collection of claims. The student of the laws sketched in the foregoing abstract will not fail to observe the monstrous injustice of many of these statutes.

All recognized principles of law and all constitutional requirements as to due process were in some of them quietly and offensively ignored.

Where the owner is absent, and the proceeding is *in rem*, there would seem to be reason in allowing the creditor to serve the property and to advertise.

But though the owner were ever so well known, the Act of 1846 allowed a plaintiff to proceed who simply posted and advertised the writ. He need not have search made for the defendant. He need not serve even a tenant. He could have a writ posted one minute, torn down the next, advertise the *sci. fa.*, and ruin the owner.

This and similar acts of class legislation were secured by the men who have been a curse to every city in this Commonwealth where the unfortunate system of Philadelphia prevails. They are the street jobbers, the highway contractors, who secure contracts, fulfill them only in part, file their liens, and divide fortunes with officials whose power they perpetuate.

A remedy for a portion of this mischief was sought by the draughtsmen of the Act of March 23, 1866.

It was submitted, before being sent to Harrisburg, to Hon. Eli K. Price and others. Since its passage, the wrongs practised under the old system have been in part remedied.

§ 406. Councils of cities of second class may grade, curb, pave, etc. By Act of May 16, 1889 (P. L., 228), it is provided, as to cities of the *second* class, that councils may grade, pave, macadamize, and curb streets, and assess the expenses on properties benefited, provided that no street should be graded, paved, or macadamized except on petition of one-third of property-owners.

. The petition must be accompanied by affidavit of a credible person that signatures are genuine; that the persons are owners of one-third of property fronting thereon.

After councils pass the ordinance, the fact that the petition was signed by one-third shall not be questioned.

Section 17 directs that the board of viewers shall, where the damages exceed the benefits, add the excess to the expense of the construction (grading, etc.), and the amount shall be assessed upon property benefited.

The cost of bridges, culverts, etc., is to be regarded as part of the expense for grading, etc.

Section 20. Sewers may be constructed and costs assessed as in cases of grading, etc.

Section 23. After final approval by councils or the court, in case of appeal of the report of the board of viewers, the plan and report shall be handed to city treasurer, who is directed to give notice to each owner of his assessment, and that a claim will be filed if not paid within thirty days. If not so paid, the city attorney shall file a lien.

Provisions are also made for board sidewalks, paving sidewalks, repairing sidewalks, resetting curbstones, filing lien if owners neglect, and issuing writs of *sci. fa.* and *lev. fa.* The Act of June 14, 1887, is repealed.

§ 407. **Taxes and assessments in cities of third class, liens, etc.** The Act of May 23, 1889 (P. L., 323), providing for the government of cities of the third class, sets forth that taxes and assessments shall be first liens on the land fronting the streets where the improvements are made for six months after the work is completed, and then a specification of lien must be filed, which shall designate the date and amount of assessment, the land assessed, the name of the owner or reputed owner. This extends the lien for ten years, and shall have priority over other liens and incumbrances, and shall not be divested by a judicial sale.

§ 408. **Cities of third class may assess for local improvements.** The Act of May 23, 1889 (P. L., 272), authorizes cities other than of first and second classes to provide by ordinance for assessment of cost of local improvements theretofore made upon abutting property.

The assessments shall be made by three viewers appointed by councils. Notice of the time and place of making said assessment shall be given—and if not paid in sixty days from time assessment is made, may be collected, with interest and five per cent. penalty, in an action of assumpsit.

The assessments may be made payable by installments, and in case of default in payment of an installment, all to be due. The constitutionality of the Act was upheld in *City* v. *Black*, 132 Pa. St., 568 (1890), and *City* v. *Pennell*, 169 *Id.*, 301 (1895).

§ 409. **Constitutional legislation.** The following Acts have been sustained :

The provision in the Act of April 19, 1843 (P. L., 342), that a defendant can " only deny that the work was done or materials furnished, or prove that the price charged was greater than their value, or that the amount claimed has been paid or released," though its force, since the Consolidation Act of February 2, 1854, was doubted by Mr. Justice WILLIAMS, in *Phila.* v. *Edwards*, 78 Pa. St., 62 (1875), has been recognized in *Phila.* v. *Burgin*, 50 Pa. St., 539 (1865) ; in *Phila.* v. *Brooke*, 81 Pa. St., 23 (1876) ; and *Fell* v. *Phila.*, *Ibid.*, 58 (1876). In the last-cited case, however, the operation of the provision would seem to be restrained to those portions of the city which were " within what were the limits of the incorporated districts of the county of Philadelphia when the Act of the 19th of April, 1843, was passed." In the later case of *Craig* v. *Philadelphia*, 89 Pa. St., 265 (1879), the Act is expressly stated to be confined in its operation to those portions of the city. To the same effect is *Pepper* v. *City*, 114 Pa. St., 96 (1886).

§ 410. *Michener* v. *City*, 118 Pa. St., 535 (1888), per PAXSON, J. : " Councils are the sole judges of the necessities of sewers, and their judgment is conclusive. * * * The laws and ordinances authorizing the construction of sewers in the city of Philadelphia are constitutional."

§ 411. Without citing at length from a number of decisions, it may be sufficient to say that all prior to 1870 are collated in the learned dissenting opinion of READ, J. *Hammett* v. *City*, 65 Pa. St., 164 (1870). He cites as cases sustaining assessments, the following : *Pennock* v. *Hoover*, 5 Rawle, 291 (paving) ; *Pennell's Appeal*, 2 Pa. St., 216 (pipes); *Northern Liberties* v. *Swain*, 13 Pa. St., 113 (pipes) ; *Thomas* v. *Northern Liberties*, *Id.*, 117 (paving); *Perry* v. *Brinton*, *Id.*, 202 ; *Pray* v. *Northern Liberties*, 31 Pa. St., 69 (paving) ; *Northern Liberties* v. *St. John's Church*, 13 Pa. St., 104 (pipes) ; *Gault's Appeal*, 33 Pa. St., 94 ; *City* v. *Tryon*, 35 Pa. St., 401 (culvert) ; *Spring Garden* v. *Wistar*, 18 Pa. St., 195 (paving).

In *City* v. *Greble*, 38 Pa. St., 339, it was decided that the city could not enter liens for culverting done within the limits of the *old* city.

In *Lipps* v. *The City*, 38 Pa. St., 503, lot-owners were assessed for a culvert built outside of the boundaries of the old city.

§ 412. **Unconstitutional legislation.** *Hammett* v. *Philadelphia*, 65 Pa. St., 146 (1870), SHARSWOOD, J., has the merit of being the first case in which the Supreme Court restrained the legislative unconstitutional jobbing of the highways in the interest of politicians.

March 23, 1866 (P. L., 299), an Act was approved authorizing the improvement of Broad Street, Philadelphia. This was followed by an ordinance authorizing the laying of the Nicholson pavement.

To the *sci. fa. sur* claim the defendant filed an affidavit of defense setting forth in substance that, prior to 1866, the street had been paved at the expense of the lot-owner, and whilst the street was in good order the city contracted for the work mentioned in the claim. He averred that the Act and the ordinance were unconstitutional. The District Court entered judgment for want of a sufficient affidavit of defense. The Supreme Court reversed—holding that the measure would not be taxation, but confiscation. " Whenever a local assessment upon an individual is not founded upon, and measured by, the extent of his particular benefit, it is *pro tanto* a taking of his private property for public use without any provision for compensation." The Act was therefore held to be unconstitutional. READ and WILLIAMS, JJ., dissenting.

§ 413. *Washington Avenue*, 69 Pa. St., 352 (1871), AGNEW, J. An Act of May 3, 1870 (P. L., 1298), authorized the appointment of commissioners to grade and macadamize Washington Avenue, Allegheny County. They had power to assess lands within from half to three-quarters of a mile of the avenue.

Owners of property not abutting on the avenue filed a bill to restrain the commissioners, upon the ground that the Act was unconstitutional. The Master reported that the plaintiffs would be benefited. The court below awarded an injunction. The commissioners appealed. The Supreme Court held that as the improvement was a general public benefit, the Act was unconstitutional, and the judgment of the lower court was affirmed. In *Ballantine's Appeal*, 5 W. N., 321 (1878), a bridge over a stream at the crossing of a street is held to be a public benefit, the cost of which cannot be assessed against property upon the neighboring thoroughfares.

§ 414. In *Seely* v. *Pittsburg*, 82 Pa. St., 360 (1876), AGNEW, C. J., said : " The cases of frontage cited, so far as discoverable, were of city lots in close juxtaposition." The Acts of April 2, 1870 (P. L., 796), and March 20, 1872 (P. L., 474), were held in this case to be unconstitutional because " The blending of town and country, of city lots and farm lands * * * constitute a group so motley and discordant * * * that the frontage or per foot front rule cannot be applied to it. * * * The Act assumes to make a wide and costly avenue, extending long distances through rural lands, where it is not needed, and to make the cost of the whole the measure of the cost of each owner."

§ 415. To the same effect are *Kaiser* v. *Weise*, 85 Pa. St., 366 (1877); *City* v. *Coal Co.*, 105 Pa. St., 445 (1884), GORDON, J.; *Dickinson* v. *City*, 14 W. N., 367 (1884); *City* v. *Rule*, 93 Pa. St., 15 (1880); *Pittsburgh Appeal*, 118 Pa. St., 458 (1888).

In the last-named case it was ruled, however, that a bill in equity to cancel the lien and enjoin its collection would not be entertained, because the work charged for was actually done, the lien therefor regularly entered and the plaintiff's property greatly increased in value by the improvement. It appeared he had not contributed or offered to contribute to the cost of the benefit received. The Supreme Court held, therefore, that he had no ground for equitable relief, and that he must abide by his legal rights. *Ordered that the bill be dismissed.*

§ 416. *Craig* v. *City*, 89 Pa. St., 265 (1879), WOODWARD, J. (PAXSON, J., dissenting). An Act of April 5, 1870 (P. L., 890), authorized the highway commissioner in Philadelphia to open Market Street and to enter into a contract to curb and pave the same. This was done and a claim filed. On the trial of the *sci. fa.* the defendant offered to prove that the premises were in a rural district, used for farm purposes, were assessed as rural, and that the opening, etc., was not called for save as a public improvement. The plaintiff objected, the objections were sustained by the court below, the verdict and judgment were against the owner. The Supreme Court held that if the facts were as stated in defendant's offers, the evidence was admissible and the Act unconstitutional. The judgment was reversed.

" Where property is rural, there is an absence of power to charge it by the foot front measure of liability." *City* v. *Keith*, 1 Cent. Rep., 898 (1886).

§ 417 Owner not objecting in time to the assessment of rural property is estopped. *Brown* v. *City*, 5 Cent. Rep., 699 (1886); *Pepper* v. *City*, 114 Pa. St., 96 (1886). The owners of property having signed an agreement for the paving of a highway upon which their premises fronted, afterward appeared before councils and protested against such paving being done, and against the assessment of the cost thereof upon them, not upon the ground that the property was rural, but for other reasons. After the passage of the ordinance and the completion of the work, a lien was filed against the property and *sci. fa.* issued thereon. They endeavored to defend, alleging that the property was rural. *Held*, affirming the lower court, that they were estopped from making this defense. See also *Bidwell* v. *City*, 5 W. N., 41 (1878).

§ 418. **The jury must decide whether property is rural. Burden of proof on the owner.** *City* v. *Adams*, 7 Cent. Rep., 195 (1887).

The jury are the sole judges whether property is urban, suburban, or rural. To the same effect is *Lukens* v. *City*, 13 W. N., 86 (1882), which holds that the classification of the board of revision of taxes is not conclusive upon the question whether property is rural. It must be left to the jury to say.

Stewart v. *City*, 4 Cent. Rep., 674 (1886). Land within the city limits is *prima facie* urban. The burden rests with him who endeavors to prove it rural. *Held*, also, by a divided court, that the assessment of property as rural for purposes of general taxation will not estop the city, in a claim for paving, from alleging it to be urban.

§ 419. **Lien is valid if the property be urban when the work is done.** In *Keith* v. *City*, 24 W. N., 115 (1889), it was held that paving done under an ordinance applying the foot front rule to property decided to be rural at the time the ordinance was passed, would support a municipal claim if the property had ceased to be rural when the work was done. Part of the work in question had been done in 1874. Upon lien filed it was decided at the trial that the lot against which the lien had been filed was rural property. Verdict and judgment accordingly for defendant. Four years later other work was done under authority of the same ordinance, upon the street, in front of another portion of the same lot. At the trial, upon *sci. fa. sur* claim therefor, the record of the proceedings upon the former lien was offered in evidence by the defendant. Objected to; objection sustained. Verdict for plaintiff. Upon writ of error judgment upon this verdict was affirmed. "The record was inadmissible for any purpose. Assuming that the defendant's property was of a rural character in 1874, and the record, if received, could establish no more, it does not follow that this was its condition in 1878. Indeed it is alleged, and it would appear to have been proved, that in 1878 very valuable improvements had been made in this vicinity; that a large number of dwelling-houses had recently been erected and were occupied, and that places of business, manufacturing establishments, etc., had been located in the immediate vicinity and were in operation ; in short, that the bounds of the built-up city then embraced this property. The court was right in refusing this record." Per CLARK, J.

§ 420. *City* v. *Savage*, 22 W. N., 3 (1888). The Act of May 23, 1874 (P. L., 230), providing that any city of the third class may become subject to its provisions by ordinance, was held unconstitutional as special legislation, and a municipal claim filed under it was declared void and ordered to be stricken from the record. But this was overruled on re-argument, and the Act was declared constitutional. 23 W. N., 332 (1889).

§ 421. *Appeal of the City of Scranton School District*, 113 Pa. St., 176 (1886), per GREEN, J., declared local and unconstitutional the Act of March 18, 1875 (P. L., 15), providing for the assessment, levy, and collection of taxes in cities of the third class, and providing, further, that no city of the third class should become subject to the Act until it was accepted by ordinance.

The distinction between the two last-cited cases is very narrow.

§ 422. **Act of 1883 unconstitutional.**

By Act of June 27, 1883, section 4 (P. L., 161), it was provided that in cities of the first class the issuing of a *sci. fa.* to collect a municipal claim should have the additional force of a *sci. fa.* to revive the lien, and where it was served by posting and advertising, or otherwise as provided by the law, the prothonotary, on order of plaintiff's attorney, might enter a judgment of revival.

It is satisfactory to note that this Act was declared unconstitutional by Common Pleas, No. 4, of Philadelphia, in a learned opinion of ARNOLD, J. (16 W. N., 331), which was affirmed by the Supreme Court. *City* v. *Pepper*, *City* v. *Church*, *City* v. *Coulston*, 19 W. N., 109 ; 115 Pa. St., 291 (1887). In *City* v. *Coulston*, a re-argument was ordered upon a collateral question, and the judgment was again affirmed. 21 W. N., 71 (1888).

§ 423. *City* v. *Pepper*, 16 W. N., 331 (1885). The following is extracted from the opinion of ARNOLD, J., in this case :

" In regard to this remarkable Act (June 27, 1883, P. L., 161), we would observe that every writ of *scire facias* properly issued and served has the effect of reviving the lien of the claim for five years. * * * The Act is confined to cities of the first class. Whether it is constitutional will be for future consideration, when its advocates will be called upon to reconcile it with article III., section 7, of the Constitution, which declares that the General Assembly shall not pass any local or special law authorizing the creation, extension, or impairing of liens, or providing or changing methods for the collection of debts * * * the rights of persons and property must be secured under general laws in the courts, and must be uniform throughout the State. That part of the Act which in effect says that if a property-owner, sued upon a municipal claim, makes defense and joins issue with his opponent, the attorney òf the opponent may exercise judicial power, and order a judgment to be entered against him, is a piece of one-sided legislation which it will be difficult to sustain * * * That part of the Act which treats of a distinct writ of *sci. fa.* to revive the lien of the claim treats of that which does not exist. There is only one writ of *sci. fa. sur* mechanics' or municipal claims authorized by law—a writ to show cause why the debt should not be levied (Act of June 16, 1836, section 15), and that must be issued within five years from the filing of the claim, otherwise the lien of the debt will expire * * * When judgment is recovered on that writ, the lien of the debt may be revived every five years, as in cases of judgments, * * * but not otherwise, * * * and the lien of the debt cannot be revived by any proceeding apart from the writ to levy it. * * * The effect of the *sci. fa.* to levy the debt, when properly issued and legally served, is to revive the lien for the five years which are allowed by law to enable the plaintiff to recover a judgment; and if he pursues his suit with due diligence, he will have ample time for that purpose. If he does not use due diligence, he will lose his claim. * * *

" The law does not recognize the possibility, when due diligence has been observed, that the plaintiff can fail to obtain a judgment within five years." ·

§ 424. The provision of the *Act of May* 24, 1887 (P. L., 204), dividing the cities of the State into seven classes, was held to be unconstitutional, *Ayars' Appeal*, 122 Pa. St., 266 (1889); hence a municipal lien filed in pursuance of that Act is void, and no judgment on it can be sustained. *Shoemaker* v. *City of Harrisburg*, 122 Pa. St., 285 (1889), STERRETT, J. ; *Berghaus* v. *City of Harrisburg*, 122 Pa. St., 289 (1889), STERRETT, J.

Improvements made under unconstitutional laws declared to be valid. The Act of May 6, 1891 (P. L., 71), provides :

That whenever, heretofore, any city, borough, township, or other municipal division of the State has authorized by any act, ordinance, resolution, or contract passed or made, the grading, paving, macadamizing, or otherwise improving of any street, lane or alley, or any part thereof, or the construction of any sewer or branch or part thereof, and in pursuance of such act, ordinance, resolution, or contract, work or labor has been done or is being done, or material furnished or is being furnished, or private property has been or is being taken, injured, or destroyed, and properties in the neighborhood of any such improvement have been or will be, when completed, peculiarly benefited by the same, but owing to the act or acts of the General Assembly under which any such improvement has been made being declared unconstitutional, or is or are otherwise invalid, or for any reason said properties cannot be assessed with said benefits, as the law, under which they were made or are being made, contemplated, now, by this Act, such improvements are made valid and binding, and any such city, borough, township, or other municipal division of the State is hereby authorized to ascertain, levy, assess, and collect such costs, damages, and expenses in manner as follows :

Petition to be presented.

1. Said city, borough, township, or any municipal division of the State, or any person or persons interested, at any time after such work or labor has been done or materials furnished, or damage done, may present its, her, his, or their petition in any Court of Common Pleas of the proper county, setting forth briefly the improvement and what it is, and what street, lane, or alley has been graded, paved, macadamized, or otherwise improved, or what sewer has been constructed, and also setting forth that the costs, expenses, and damages incurred in such grading, paving, macadamizing, or otherwise improving, or in the construction of such sewer, have not been collected or fully paid to said city, borough, township, or municipal division, and praying the court to appoint three disinterested freeholders to ascertain and determine the costs, damages, and expenses of such grading, paving, macadamizing, or other improvement, or of the construction of such sewer, and the damages done to private property by reason of such grading, paving, and macadamizing or other improvement, or the construction of such sewer, and to fairly and ratably assess the said damages, costs, and expenses upon the property benefited, and to make report thereof to the court.

Notice of petition to be given.

2. Upon the presentation of such petition the court shall direct notice thereof to be given to all parties interested by an advertisement inserted at least three times in two or more newspapers of the proper city, borough, or township, or other municipal division of the State, one of which newspapers may be printed in the German language, and by at least ten hand-bills posted ten days before the hearing in conspicuous places along the line of the improvement and the vicinity thereof, that on a day certain therein to be named, and not less than ten days after the last insertion of the advertisement in the newspapers, the court will pass upon and decide said application, and that any person interested therein may be heard in reference thereto.

Viewers to be appointed.

3. Upon said named day the court shall, unless some good objection is made thereto, appoint three disinterested freeholders as viewers. Any two of said viewers may decide all questions, and in all respects have all the powers, discretion, and jurisdiction of all three viewers, but all three viewers shall act unless in case of sickness or other unavoidable cause.

Viewers to be sworn or affirmed.

4. Upon said appointment being made, said viewers shall be sworn or affirmed by some person authorized to administer oaths, well and truly to perform the duties imposed upon them and true report to make to the court.

To fix time and place to hear the parties.

5. It shall be the duty of said viewers, after being sworn or affirmed, to fix a day and hour and place when and where they will hear all parties in interest, of which meeting notice shall be given by at least three insertions in two newspapers of the proper city, borough or township, or other municipal division, one of which may be printed in the German language, and by at least ten hand-bills posted in conspicuous places along the line of the improvement and in the vicinity thereof; the last of said insertions in the newspapers and the posting of hand-bills shall be at least ten days before the meeting. The viewers shall visit the improvement and personally inspect the same, and also visit and personally inspect the properties in the neighborhood supposed to be damaged or benefited thereby.

And to assess the cost of the improvements.

At the time and place fixed they shall hear all parties interested, with power to adjourn from time to time, and after a full hearing of all parties on all questions before them they shall ascertain and determine the total damages and costs and expenses of such improvement, and these damages and costs and expenses they shall fairly and ratably assess upon the properties benefited, but not in any case to exceed the benefit peculiarly resulting from such improvement. If property peculiarly benefited to the full amount of damages, costs, and expenses cannot be found, the viewers shall find the excess of damages, costs, and expenses. They shall, thereupon, prepare a report, together with a plan of the properties damaged and benefited, and their report shall set forth what the improvement is, whether it be a sewer or grading, paving, macadamizing, or other improvement of a street, lane, or alley, the place and places where it was made, the damages, costs, and expenses of the improvement, the properties in the neighborhood benefited peculiarly by said improvement, and the name or names of the owner or reputed owner of each parcel, the amount of damages allowed in each case, and the amount of benefits assessed against each property, and what amount, if any, of damages, costs, and expenses are not assessed upon property peculiarly benefited thereby.

Notice of report of viewers to be given.

6. Said viewers shall then give notice, by three insertions each in two newspapers in the proper city, borough, or other municipal division, that their report is ready, and on a day certain therein to be named, and not earlier than ten days after the last insertion, that they will present the same to court, and, in the meantime, said report will remain at a place to be designated in said notice, and subject to inspection and exception. If any exceptions are filed, the viewers shall give a hearing on the same, and may, after such hearing, modify their report if equity and justice shall require.

Exceptions to report.

7. On the day named, if no exceptions are. filed, or if exceptions are filed, then upon a subsequent day to be named by them, said viewers shall file their report in the proper Court of Common Pleas, and thereupon said court shall approve the same *nisi*, and within twenty days thereafter any person in interest may file exceptions to any part or the whole of said report. If no objections are filed, the report shall be approved absolutely; but if exceptions are filed, the court shall speedily hear the same, and may, as to right and justice shall appertain, confirm or set aside, change or modify said report, or refer the same back to the same or another board of viewers, or make such other order as to the court shall seem proper. Within thirty days after the final confirmation of said report or the fixing of damages, any party whose property has been taken, injured, or destroyed may appeal from said decision, and, on said appeal, the amount of such damages shall, at the demand of either party, be determined by a jury according to the course of the common law.

After final decree upon report, assessment to be a lien.

8. When the court has made its final decree confirming the said report or fixing the amount of the assessments in each case, the sums thus ascertained as benefits shall, if properly filed as a municipal lien or sued within six months, be a lien upon the property assessed, and shall be due and payable to the treasurer of the proper city, borough, township, or other municipal division within thirty days from the date of the said decree; and the clerk of the proper court, on the making of such decree, shall deliver to said treasurer a certified copy of the decree and report. Said assessments shall bear interest, beginning at the expiration of thirty days from the date of said decree. If not paid within said time, the said treasurer shall deliver the same to the city solicitor or the attorney of said city, borough, township, or other municipal division, who shall proceed to collect the same by an action of assumpsit, or to secure the same by filing a lien therefor under the general laws of the Commonwealth in such case made and provided, and proceeding thereon to collect the same.

Costs to be paid out of treasury of municipality.

9. All the costs of the proceedings, including advertisements, hand-bills, and costs of service, shall be paid by the proper city, borough, township, or other municipal division, and any excess of damages, costs, and expenses, over and above the benefits as determined by the final decree of the court, shall also be paid out of the treasury of the proper city, borough, township, or other municipal division. Where there is no newspaper in the munīci-pal division concerned, notice shall be printed in such county newspapers as exist, not exceeding two.

Proceedings under Act not to apply to work done more than two years prior to passage of Act.

10. Proceedings under this Act shall only include the ascertainment, assessment, levy, and collection of the costs, expenses, and damages and benefits of all improvements completed within two years preceding the date of the approval of this Act, and of those now in process of completion, when and as the same are completed; and power and authority is hereby given to the

different cities, boroughs, townships, and other municipal divisions of the State to complete such improvements now in process of completion; and upon such completion to proceed as aforesaid for the ascertainment, assessment, and collection of the same.

Where assessment in excess of damages, rebate to be made.

11. If, upon any appeal or trial in the case of any person or persons whose property has been taken, injured, or destroyed, the result shall be that the appellant or appellants recovers or recover less damages for property taken, injured, or destroyed, than he or she, or they, was, or were, awarded by the court from which said appeal was, or appeals were, taken, then the court may thereupon order and compel the city, borough, township, or other municipal division to repay to the several property-owners assessed for benefits their ratable proportion of so much of said assessments as were made by reason of said excess of damages.

Right of trial by jury preserved.

12. This Act shall in no event be construed as depriving any person of a right of trial by jury, where such right has been conferred upon him or her by the Constitution of this State, but in any such case such right must be demanded within thirty days from the date of the final decree of the court fixing the matter or thing on which such right of trial by jury is demanded.

Appeal.

13. The decree of the proper Court of Common Pleas shall be binding and conclusive in all cases arising under this Act, except that where any-one appeals and there is a trial, either party thereto or any party interested in any assessment may appeal to the Supreme Court as in other cases, provided said appeal be taken within one year from the final judgment on such a trial, but such appeal shall not be a supersedeas unless taken within thirty days after such judgment.

§ 424 *a*. **Final assessment for municipal improvement to be a lien.** The Act of May 16, 1891 (P. L., 69), provides:

That whenever hereafter there shall be any final assessment made on any property or properties to pay for the costs, expenses, and damages, or either, of any municipal improvements, whether such improvement has been heretofore made, or is now in progress, or shall hereafter be made by any city, borough, township, or other municipal division of the State, the property so assessed shall be subject to a lien for the amount of such assessment, said lien to date from the time of the final confirmation of the report under which said assessment may be made, or a final decree of the court fixing such assessments, and shall if filed within six months from said final assessment or confirmation remain a lien upon said properties until fully paid and satisfied: *Provided*, That a writ of *scire facias* shall be issued to revive the same at the expiration of every period of five years after the lien is filed.

Requirements of lien.

SEC. 2. Any city, borough, township, or other municipal division or corporation of the State entitled to such lien may, within six months from the date of the decree or order finally fixing said assessment, file a lien therefor in the office of the prothonotary of any Court of Common Pleas of the county within which the property lies. Said liens shall state the name of the party claimant, which shall be the city, borough, township, or other municipal division of the State making such improvement, the owner or reputed owner, and a reasonable description of the property, the amount or sum claimed to be due, for what improvement the claim is made, and the time when the assessment was finally confirmed or made.

To be collected by sci. fa.   Proceedings thereon.

SEC. 3. The lien when thus filed shall be proceeded upon for collection by writ of *scire facias*, in accordance with the course of the common law. Said writ of *scire facias* shall be made returnable to the monthly or other return-day in the respective courts, and shall be served upon the owner or reputed owner personally, or by leaving a copy thereof, duly attested, with an adult member of his family at his dwelling-house, at least ten days before the return-day thereof. If the owner of the property cannot be found, or has no dwelling within the county in which the property lies, the sheriff shall thereupon return the said writ *nihil*, and thereupon an *alias scire facias* may issue, which shall be served by notice posted upon the premises, stating the substance of the writ, at least ten days prior to the return-day, and also by advertisement in at least two newspapers published in the county in which the premises are located, and nearest thereto, once a week for three successive weeks.

Such posting and publication shall be equivalent to a service.

Service of writ, appearance, affidavit, etc.

SEC. 4. If the writ shall have been served, and no appearance entered on or before the return-day thereof, the plaintiff therein shall be entitled to judgment after the return-day thereof for the debt, interest, and costs of such lien. If an appearance be entered, the plaintiff shall also be entitled to judgment unless a sufficient affidavit of defense be filed within fifteen days after the return-day. If such affidavit be filed, the cause shall then be proceeded with in accordance with the rules of law and the practice of the courts.

Proceedings after judgment.   Levari facias.

SEC. 5. When final judgment shall have been entered upon such lien the plaintiff therein may have a writ or writs of *levari facias*, and upon the same the sheriff shall cause the said property to be advertised for sale in at least two newspapers of the proper county once a week, for three weeks before the day of sale, and shall also give notice by at least ten hand-bills posted in conspicuous places, and one of which shall be posted upon the property, of the time and place of such sale, and thereupon shall proceed to sell the same. The proceeds of sale shall be distributed in accordance with law.

For what lien may be filed.

SEC. 6. The municipal improvements for which a lien may be filed shall include all improvements heretofore made, or now in progress, or hereafter made, and the assessments or reassessments to be made for the costs, damages, and expenses of grading, paving, macadamizing, or otherwise improving any street, lane, or alley or parts thereof, or the construction of any sewer or the opening, widening, straightening, extending, or laying out of any street, lane, or alley, or parts thereof, or the vacation of the same, or the construction or laying of boardwalks or sidewalks.

Appeal to be sued out within a year.

SEC. 7. Any party aggrieved by any final judgment on any such lien may have an appeal to the Supreme Court of the State as in other cases, the same to be sued out within one year from the entry of such judgment, and not otherwise; but such appeal shall not be a supersedeas unless taken within thirty days after such judgment.

Property-owner may compel plaintiff to proceed.

SEC. 8. Any person owning any property against which a lien shall be filed under this Act may at any time present a petition to the proper court praying that the plaintiff in such lien be compelled to proceed for the collection thereof, and thereupon the court may make such order as the justice of the case shall require.

See § 408.

§ 425. The Act of May 13, 1871 (P. L., 840), which authorized the councils of Pittsburgh to regrade or repave the streets, and to refer to viewers the questions whether the improvement would be of local or general benefit, and what proportion the district benefited should pay, was declared unconstitutional. When property adjacent to a street has borne the charge of the original paving, "it has fully paid for all its local advantages, and it cannot thereafter be charged for maintenance and repairs." *Appeal of Orphan Asylum,* 111 Pa. St., 135 (1885), per GORDON, J. *Hammett* v. *Philada.,* 65 Pa. St., 146 (see section 412), was cited and approved.

This case was followed in *Wistar* v. *City,* 111 Pa. St., 604 (1886), where it was held that a property-owner could not be compelled to pay for a new curb, the old one having been in good order and condition.

§ 426. **Owners of adjoining property must pay for keeping footway in repair.** *Smith* v. *Borough of Kingston,* 120 Pa. St., 357 · (1888).

The General Borough Act of April 3, 1851 (P. L., 320), as amended by the Act of 22 May, 1883 (P. L , 39), gives to boroughs power "to regulate the roads * * * streets * * * and footwalks * * * to survey, lay out, enact, and ordain footwalks * * * to require and direct the grading, curbing, paving, and guttering of the side or footwalks, by the owner or owners of the lots respectively fronting thereon." Under the first of these Acts, the footwalk in front of defendant's property had been duly laid by a former owner. Fourteen years afterward, this walk being in a bad state of decay, defendant, the then present owner, was notified by the borough authorities to repair. Neglecting to do so, repairs, amounting to the laying of a new walk, were made by the borough, and a lien was filed therefor. *Held*, that this lien was good. This case recognizes the distinction between the repaving of a cartway or street and that of a foot or sidewalk. The first is a general benefit, for which the community should pay, while the second is essentially for the good of the adjoining lot-owners, and is properly chargeable to them when such repaving is needed to keep the footway in good order.

§ 427. **Registry Acts, Registration thereunder. Title of purchaser at sheriff's sale.**

Registry Act of Philadelphia. The statute relating to the registration of real estate in the city of Philadelphia enacts :

" That the duty of registering real estate, in the city of Philadelphia, shall hereafter devolve upon the purchaser, devisee by will, the person to whom an allotment in partition shall have been made, or their agent, and they shall be required to present their deeds or title papers at the registry bureau, so that the same may be indorsed, in accordance with the Act of Assembly to which this is supplementary ; and all owners of real estate, in the said city, not registered as by law directed, are required forthwith to do so, and if after three months' notice, by public advertisement in at least five daily papers of said city (two of which shall be German), and a written or printed notice shall have been served on the owner or owners, and they shall fail to have such record made, then, and in that case, they shall be subject to a fine of five dollars for such neglect, and in case the same is neglected for the space of six months, a lien for the accumulated fines and costs shall be filed and collected as municipal claims are now or may hereafter be by law collected ; the said fines to be paid into the city treasury ; and, further, no property so returned shall be subject to sale for taxes or other municipal claims thereafter to accrue as a lien of record thereon, except in the name of the owner as returned, and after recovery by suit and service of the writ on him, made as in case of a summons." Act of March 29, 1867, section 1 (P. L., 600).

§ 428. *Registry Act of Pittsburgh.* The Act relating to the registry of lots in the city of Pittsburgh is, that " it shall be the duty of all owners of houses and lots or tracts of ground to furnish forthwith descriptions of their property to the engineer, to aid him in making up his book of plans ; and whensoever such descriptions shall have been furnished and the certificate of the engineer or his assistant shall be received, no property so returned shall be subject to sale for taxes or other municipal claims thereafter to accrue as lien of record thereon, except in the name of the owner as returned and after recovery by suit and service of the writ on him as in case of a summons, *scire facias*, or other appropriate writ." Act of February 24, 1871, section 4 (P. L., 126).

The plain object of this Act was to prevent real estate of those who had complied with the law from being swept from them without their knowledge by a judicial sale upon a municipal claim.

§ 429. *Registry Act of Allegheny City.* The provision for the registry of real estate in the city of Allegheny is as follows:

"It shall be the duty of all owners of houses and lots or tracts of ground to furnish forthwith descriptions of their property to the engineer, to aid him in making up his books of plans; and whensoever such description shall have been so furnished, and the certificate of the engineer or his assistant shall be received, no property so returned shall be subject to sale for taxes, or other municipal claims thereafter to accrue as a lien of record thereon, except in the name of the owner as returned, and after recovery by suit and service of the writ on him, made as in case of a summons; should this be neglected or omitted, or not be complied with as promptly as may be deemed necessary to insure the early completion of the plans, then, after one month's notice, by public advertisement in the official papers of the city to the owners of real estate in said city not registered, and a written or printed notice shall have been served on the owner or owners or delivered upon the property; should they fail to have such record made, then and in that case they shall be subject to a fine of five dollars for each month of such neglect, dating from the termination of said advertisement; and in case the same be neglected for the space of six months, a lien for the accumulated fines and costs shall be filed and collected as municipal claims are now or may be hereafter by law collected; the said fines to be paid into the city treasury; the notice to parties failing to register property may be given so as to embrace the property of any particular ward or section, or any number of wards, or the city at large, at the discretion of the said city engineer." Act of April 2, 1869, section 4 (P. L., 645).

§ 430. *Construing the Registry Acts in favor of owners*, the Supreme Court (per PAXSON, J.) said:

"The failure to serve the writ [in a municipal claim] according to the Act of Assembly upon a registered owner * * * is something more than an irregularity which may be cured by the judgment.

"Where the owner has been properly served, I apprehend, mere irregularities would be cured, and a purchaser at sheriff's sale would be protected by the judgment. * * * But without such service the court acquires no jurisdiction, the judgment entered on such suit is absolutely void, and the Act of Assembly prohibits a sale of the premises upon any execution issued thereon.

"In the case in hand the plaintiff's deed was registered in compliance with the Act of Assembly. Judgment was taken against him on the *scire facias* upon the return of two '*nihils.*' Neither the *scire facias* nor the *alias* was served upon the plaintiff, nor had he any notice or knowledge thereof. * * *

"There does not appear to have been any attempt to make personal service. The proceeding was *in rem*, and the first writ was returned 'posted' and *nihil* as to the defendant. This return goes upon the theory that an effort had been made to find the defendant and had failed. The *alias* then issued, and it was the duty of the sheriff again to make personal service if within his power, and, if unable to do so, to post the writ upon the premises the second time, thus giving the defendant named therein another chance to learn of the proceeding against his property. The sheriff appears to have done nothing whatever with the second writ. * * * The property should have been posted on this *alias*, as well as upon the original, and the writ should have been so returned. As it stands, there was no legal service." *Ferguson* v. *Quinn*, 23 W. N., 38 (1888).

§ 431. *Sheriff's vendee will not take good title if the sale be made in violation of statutory prohibition. Kern* v. *Simons*, 7 W. N., 359 (1879). A municipal claim was prosecuted to judgment, and the property was sold. The sheriff's vendee brought ejectment. The defendant set up that the proceeding on the claim was void because of non-compliance with the Act of March 29, 1867. It was held in the lower court that the irregularities could not be taken advantage of by the defendant in the ejectment, and that they were cured by the judgment and the sheriff's deed.

But this judgment was reversed in the Supreme Court (*Simons* v. *Kern*, 92 Pa. St., 455, 1880), where it was held, per STERRETT, J., that the failure to serve the registered owner, as required by the Registry Act of 1867, was a fatal defect, which altogether avoided the proceedings, and which was not cured by the sale under the *levari*. "It cannot be doubted that a sale made in direct violation of this statutory prohibition is void. It is not a mere irregularity that would be cured by the acknowledgment of the sheriff's deed."

§ 432. *If property registered, correct name and service required.* A claim of the city for benefits to property arising from the

opening of a certain street was filed eight years after the death of
the owner naming the deceased as " owner or reputed owner," and
adding " whoever may be owner," and describing the premises " in
accordance with the Act of April 1, 1864 * * * of all of
which said owner or reputed owner had notice as required by law."
When the lien was filed the property was registered in the name of
the deceased, but the title had descended to the children, two of
whom were then minors.   The record showed service upon Margaret White, the widow of the decedent, alone ; but she died two
years before the award.   It was held that the record averment
was insufficient and the claim was disallowed.   *White's Estate*, 45
Leg. Int., 394 (1888). The question of the validity of these claims
and of the notices thereof is examined in this case with great learning
and ability by ASHMAN, J.

§ 433. *Where law requires registered owner to be named, omission
to comply is fatal.*   In *Gans* v. *City*, 102 Pa. St., 97 (1883), TRUN-
KEY, J., it was held, that where a law directs that no registered lot
shall be subject to municipal claims " except in the name of the
owner as returned," a claim filed against " unknown owner or reputed owner, or whoever may be owner," the title being registered
in the name of the owner, is a nullity ; and this although the name
of the real owner be afterward suggested of record and the *sci. fa.*
be served on him.   He can plead the plaintiff's failure to comply
with the law, in bar of the claim.

Wolf v. *City*, 105 Pa. St., 25 (1884).   Claim was filed, not against
• the registered owner, but against his vendor.   *Held*, that this was
a good defense to the *sci. fa. sur* claim.

§ 434. *Registered property not liable unless owner served with preliminary notice.   City* v. *Woodward*, 13 W. N., 372 (1883). A registered owner cannot be made liable for the opening of a street, unless he is served with notice of the meeting of the jury of damages.
City v. *Dungan*, 23 W. N., 243 (1889), PAXSON, C. J.   A
claim was filed for the cost of abating a nuisance.   The body of
the claim did not aver notice given to the *registered* owner.   It
was held to be fatally defective, and was stricken off.   The object
of the notice is to enable the owner to remove the nuisance, and
thus avoid the increased expense of having it done by the city.

" The object of the Registry Act was twofold : (*a*) To enable the
city to designate the true owner with reasonable certainty, and (*b*)
to provide for actual notice to such owner of municipal claims
affecting his property."   Judgment affirmed.

Notice to abate a nuisance must be given to the registered owner
when there is one.   *City* v. *Laughlin*, 48 Leg. Int., 265 (1891).

§ 435. *If registered owner not served with preliminary notice, he can defend the sci. fa.* *Hershberger* v. *City*, 115 Pa. St., 78·(1886), CLARK, J. If one can show that he had no notice under the Act of January 6, 1864 (P. L., 1131), though the report of the viewers has been confirmed, he may defend the *scire facias* by proving that the improvement with which he is charged was made upon other ground than that described in the ordinance; and this although the Act March 14, 1872 (Pittsburgh Act), provided "that no assessment for the opening, etc. * * * in the city of Pittsburgh * * * shall be defeated for want of any notice * * * or for any other informality * * * provided that this Act shall not be construed to prevent any defense showing want of authority * * * or any other matter or thing affecting the merits of the claim."

§ 436. *Sheriff's vendee takes title free of defects in claim, irregularity of service, etc. But an owner not named and not served can defend the ejectment by proving claim was paid. Delaney* v. *Gault*, 30 Pa. St., 63 (1858), STRONG, J. A *scire facias* on a municipal claim is a proceeding *in rem*. The Act which provides for the filing of the claim does not require that the claim refer to the Act.

After judgment upon the *scire facias*, it is too late to inquire in any collateral proceeding into the sufficiency of the sheriff's return, or whether service has been properly made, if it be returned.

But one not named as owner, and not served, can defend an ejectment brought by the sheriff's vendee by proving that the claim was in fact paid. *Delaney* v. *Gault, supra.*

McConnell v. *Gates*, 4 Penny., 377 (1884). The sheriff's return showed the writ not to have been posted two weeks before return-day; yet the property having been sold upon the *levari, held*, that the title of the sheriff's vendee could not be attacked in a collateral proceeding.

So the sheriff's vendee takes a good title where the *sci. fa.* is returned "made known by posting and publishing *sec. reg.*" *Douglass* v. *Herold*, 17 Phila., 2 (1877).

Emrick v. *Dicken*, 92 Pa. St., 78 (1879), PAXSON, J. A municipal claim is a proceeding wholly *in rem*, and it involves no personal liability on the part of the owner of the property against which it is filed. Property in Allegheny City was sold as that of an "unknown owner." The owner was known to the municipal authorities. This fact cannot be shown as against a purchaser at sheriff's sale. The irregularity was cured by the fourteenth section of Act April 1, 1870 (P. L., 751), "relative to streets in city of Allegheny."

White v. *Ballentine*, 96 Pa. St., 186 (1880), GORDON, J. Under the Pittsburgh Registry Act of February 24, 1871 (P. L., 126), a purchaser at a sheriff's sale of property liened in the wrong name acquires title as against the true owner unless the property be duly registered before the charge " accrued as a lien of record."

Hering v. *Chambers*, 103 Pa. St., 172 (1883), TRUNKEY, J. The return to the *sci. fa.* failed to show a posting on a *conspicuous* part of the premises, and that the writ was served twice a week for two weeks before return-day. It was held that the purchaser under the *levari* took a good title, and that the defects were irregularities which could not be inquired into in a collateral proceeding.

City v. *Fraley*, 18 W. N., 508 (1886), FINLETTER, P. J. One who has purchased the property from the defendant after claim filed and *sci. fa.* advertised and posted, cannot object to the judgment on the ground that the lot being registered the writ should have been personally served.

Soullier' v. *Kern*, 69 Pa. St., 16 (1871). Judgment upon a *sci. fa. sur* municipal claim, the court having jurisdiction, is conclusive upon the question whether the paving for which the lien has been filed was authorized by the city. Such judgment standing unreversed cannot be impeached collaterally. In ejectment against the sheriff's vendee, the authority to do the paving cannot be inquired into.

§ 437. **Objections to Claims.** *A borough cannot open roads by ordinance.* Borough v. *Gilmore*, 15 W. N., 342 (1884), PAXSON, J. The twenty-seventh section of the Borough Act of 1851 (P. L., 326) provides : " That like proceedings shall be had for the opening * * * of the roads * * * in accordance with this Act as are provided * * * for * * * opening of public roads."

Under this law, a borough cannot by ordinance order the setting back of fences. If they do so, and a fence is removed, the owner can sue in trespass, but he cannot assess his damages under the Act of 1851. The remedy therein provided was intended only for persons aggrieved by any regulation under said Act.

§ 438. *Claim must aver notice.* Borough v. *Gilmore*, 15 W. N., 343 (1884), PAXSON, J. Where the law authorizing municipal action requires a demand upon the owner as a pre-requisite, it must be averred in the claim, and whatever is necessary to confer jurisdiction must be stated, or the claim will be stricken off. The claim in this case did not aver notice, and did not clearly state that the fence removed was within the lines of the street. In the bill annexed to the claim and made part thereof, it was stated to be for

" removing obstructions from defendant's sidewalk in taking down
fence on East Main Street in said borough." This left it doubtful
whether the defendant's sidewalk or the borough street was obstructed. The claim was defective, and was properly stricken off.

In *City* v. *Stevenson*, 6 Pa. C. C. Rep., 287 (1888), a claim was
filed under an ordinance which required prior notice to owner and
default by him. It was held that the lien must specifically aver
such prior notice and default, or it is fatally defective. It cannot
be amended, and the claim was stricken off. But this was reversed
in Supreme Court, 25 W. N., 367, and it was held that the claim
could be amended.

The provision of the ordinance of 1855, that notice shall be
given the property-owner, is simply intended for the internal administration of the city office, and is not intended to give property-
owners a new defense. It is directory, not mandatory. *City* v.
Schofield, 25 W. N., 388 (1890). (C. P. of Phila.)

Where a municipal claim fails to aver notice to the registered
owner, it will be stricken off. *City* v. *Crump*, 1 Dist. Rep., 698
(1890).

§ 439. *Improvement must be in accordance with law. Cost of wall
not allowed.* *Rwy. Co.* v. *City*, 92 Pa. St., 100 (1879), MERCUR,
J. " The city can create a valid municipal lien for improving a
street only when the improvement is made in pursuance of law.
The street must first be duly established. Its width must be fixed,
and the improvement made within its lines, before the expense
thereof can be imposed on the lands of an adjoining owner." The
claim in this case was filed for the cost of a stone wall, which became necessary in consequence of the improvement of Church
Avenue, Allegheny City. The wall was built partly on the street
and partly on defendant's property. The Supreme Court said :
" This wall was built in violation of law," and the whole cost of
it was disallowed.

Macadamizing is an original paving, under the Act of May 23,
1889, which relieves the owners of abutting property from liability
for subsequent paving. *City* v. *Segelbaum*, 151 Pa. St., 172 (1892).

§ 440. *Lien will not lie for work unauthorized by councils.* *City*
v. *Gallagher*, 16 Phila., 15 (1883), per BIDDLE, J. An ordinance authorized the construction of a sewer, termed the " L Street
sewer," upon certain streets. The survey department, without
authority, changed the route of the sewer and prepared plans for
it upon different streets. A contract was made with A. for the
building of the sewer over the new route, and an ordinance was
passed approving the contract with A. " for the construction of the

main sewer on L Street." The ordinance did not purport to change the route of the sewer, nor did it indicate what contract was referred to. *Held*, that the work upon the sewer was unauthorized; that it was not ratified by councils, and that the lien therefor was void. Judgment for defendant.

§ 441. *Claims not allowed against a railroad or land adjoining or on a turnpike.* *City* v. *R. R. Co.*, 33 Pa. St., 41 (1856), LOW-RIE, J. Where municipal authorities pave a road which lies side by side with a railroad, they cannot file a claim against the company. This was followed in *Junc. R. R. Co.* v. *City*, 7 W. N., 87 (1879), reversing the same case, reported under the name of *Holgate* v. *Junction R. R. Co.*, in 35 Leg. Int., 192.

Breed v. *City*, 85 Pa. St., 214 (1877), PAXSON, J. Under the Act of April 1, 1870 (P. L., 751), by which the city of Pittsburgh was authorized to lay out, widen, and extend the streets of the city, and to grade and pave them, a turnpike toll road within its limits cannot be widened at the expense of property-owners.

Borough of Milesburg v. *Green*, 22 W. N., 180 (1888). The Act of May 22, 1883 (P. L., 39), empowered boroughs to pave "lands abutting on and along the sides of turnpike roads." *Held*, that a borough ordinance directing the laying of footwalks *on a turnpike* was *ultra vires* and void, and that a lien filed for such improvement could not be sustained.

§ 442. *Benefits may be assessed against railroad companies.* *In re Berks Street*, 12 W. N., 10 (1882). A jury to assess damages caused by the opening of a street in Philadelphia assessed a part of the benefits arising therefrom against railroad companies owning land near the street. Part of this land was covered by machine-shops, depots, etc., and part by railroad tracks. Exceptions to the report of the jury were dismissed in the lower court. *Held*, that such dismissal was proper. Proceedings affirmed.

§ 443. *Lien for paving vacant space in highway good.* *Slocum* v. *City*, 11 W. N., 167 (1881). *Sci. fa. sur* municipal claim. A paved highway in Philadelphia had in its centre an unpaved space upon which had stood a market-house. Under ordinance, a contract was entered into for the paving of this space, and liens for the expense thereof were filed against the owners of property abutting on the highway opposite. *Held*, that such liens were valid. This was followed in *Alcorn* v. *City*, 17 W. N., 368 (1886).

§ 444. *Claims against lot composed of parts.* *City* v. *Allen*, 21 W. N., 153 (1888). A lien against one lot is good although the lot is composed of two parts, the title to which was acquired by the defendant at different times and from different owners, if the size of the parts show them to be incapable of separate use and that they really form one lot. The facts distinguish this from *Pennell's Appeal*, 2 Pa. St., 216 (1845). In that case the lots were actually separate and distinct. See *City* v. *Cadwallader*, 22 W. N., 8 (1888).

§ 445. *Claim for work upon a highway is good only against land actually abutting thereon.* A municipal claim for work done upon a street is good only against the lots actually fronting thereon. If it be so filed as to include a lot in the rear of one which touches or abuts upon the highway, it is as to such rear lot void, and a sheriff's sale under it passes no title thereto. *Wiler* v. *Griffith*, 45 Leg. Int., 486 (1888).

So, if a railroad running parallel to the highway separate it from a lot, a claim filed against the lot for work done upon the highway cannot be sustained. *City* v. *Eastwick*, 35 Pa. St., 75 (1860).

§ 446. *Claim not good against property specially exempted from taxation.* *Olive Cemetery Co.* v. *The City*, 93 Pa. St., 129 (1880). The charter of a cemetery company provided that the cemetery, "when used as a place of sepulchre, shall be exempt from taxation excepting for State purposes." A sewer was constructed on a street along the line of which was a part of the cemetery. An assessment was charged and a claim filed in due form. Upon case stated disclosing the foregoing facts, it was *held*, reversing the lower court, that the company under its charter was exempt therefrom, and that the lien was invalid.

In *Erie* v. *Church*, 105 Pa. St., 278 (1884), a *sci. fa. sur* municipal lien was issued against a church property for part of the cost of a sewer built in the street upon which the church fronted. The lower court discharged the plaintiff's rule for judgment for want of a sufficient affidavit of defense. The judgment was affirmed.

But in *Church's Appeal*, 165 Pa. St., 475 (1895), following *Northern Liberties* v. *Church*, 13 Pa. St., 104 (1850), it was held that the constitutional exemption relates to taxes proper, and not to special assessments imposed upon property for the payment of local improvements, and in that case a lien for paving in front of a church was sustained. The same distinction was made in *Railroad* v. *Decatur*, 147 U. S., 190 (1892). See also § 404.

§ 447. *Claim filed against an "estate" as owner good.* *City* v. *Wistar*, 10 W. N., 275 (1881). A municipal claim filed against an "estate owner or reputed owner" is valid.

§ 448. *Claim may be filed against heirs of A. as owners.* *Northern Liberties* v. *Coates*, 15 Pa. St., 245 (1850), COULTER, J. A municipal claim filed against the heirs of a deceased owner or reputed owner, or whoever may be owner, and describing the real estate against which it is claimed as a lien, is a sufficient designation of the ownership of the premises. This was followed in the case of *Wistar* v. *City*, 86 Pa. St., 215 (1878), which upheld a claim similarly filed.

§ 449. *Bad quality of water-pipe no defense.* *Swain* v. *The City*, 22 W. N., 120 (1888). It is not competent to show as a defense to a *sci. fa. sur* municipal claim for laying water-pipe that the pipe is second-hand, corroded, and in such condition that it will soon burst, and will require constant repair. The cost of repair or substitution will not fall on the property-owner, but on the city.

§ 450. **Writ and service—Filing of claim and statement— Revival.** *Registered owner must be served and within time as required.* If the registered owner be not served as directed, and within the time required by law, the lien is lost. An acceptance of service by one not a member of the bar, without authority disclosed for his act, is of no effect. *City* v. *Jacobs*, 22 W. N., 348 (1888).

City v. *Laws*, 20 W. N., 63 (1887). The *sci. fa.* had been returned "made known" by posting, advertising, and "*nihil habet*" as to C., the actual and present owner. Service was not made on the registered owner of the property. It was held that the proceeding was defective.

§ 451. *Sci. fa. must be returned strictly as required by law.* *Wistar* v. *City*, 86 Pa. St., 215 (1878), PAXSON, J. If the *sci. fa.* be not returned as posted on a *conspicuous* part of the premises *for two weeks before the return-day* and publication made, as required, *two weeks before the return-day*, the defect is fatal. The italicized words should appear in the return. Their omission is not aided by the averment that this was "agreeably to the Act of Assembly." As to the effect of such defective service after judgment and sale under proceedings on the *sci. fa.*, see *Hering* v. *Chambers*, 103 Pa. St., 172 (1883).

In a *sci. fa. sur* municipal claim, the property-owner, where certain rights are conceded him, either by statute or ordinance, may assert them against the city as legal plaintiff as well as against the contractor to whose use the city sues. *City to use* v. *Jewell's Estate*, 26 W. N., 150 (1890).

Where judgment for want of an appearance was taken in a *sci. fa.* upon a claim for registered taxes, and the sheriff's return was defective, the judgment was stricken off. *Philadelphia* v. *Newkumet*, 1 Dist. Rep., 558 (1892).

§ 452. *Under Act of 1866, search must be made for owner.* This *is indispensable. City* v. *Hanbest,* 15 W. N., 349 (1884), ARNOLD, J. The Act of March 23, 1866, section 1 (P. L., 303), provides that " *before any scire facias* shall be issued, it shall be the duty of the city solicitor to cause diligent search to be made for the owner of the real estate against which the claim may be filed, and serve him or her with a written or printed notice to pay the claim within ten days."

This provision is not directory merely, but indispensable ; the omission to comply with it is fatal, and service of the notice to pay after *sci. fa.* issued will not suffice. The writ was quashed.

City v. *Robbins,* 18 W. N., 39 (1886). A *sci. fa.* to revive and continue lien was set aside where the writ was not signed by the city solicitor—no preliminary notice to pay given, and no return entered.

§ 453. *General averment in claim not evidence of notice. City* v. *Donath,* 9 W. N., 415 (1881), PAXSON, J. An ordinance directed the chief commissioner to notify the owners on a certain street to pave their footways on or before April 1, 1870. A notice in pursuance of this was served on the tenant in possession and a notice to pave was served on defendant, an owner, in 1874, four years too late ; the defendant refused to pave, and the work was done by a contractor with the city. Neither of the notices had been properly served. The city having failed to prove its averment of notice to the owner " agreeably to the Act of Assembly," it was held the claim was not evidence of the service, and that a non-suit was properly entered.

§ 454. *Claim must be filed in time. City* v. *Knowlson,* 92 Pa. St., 116 (1879), GORDON, J. The Act of January 6, 1864 (P. L., 1131), provided that municipal claims should be filed within six months after the completion of the work, and it was ruled that want of compliance with this provision would defeat the lien.

§ 455. *Statement must be filed in time. Borough* v. *Siggins,* 110 Pa. St., 291 (1885). The Act of April 3, 1851 (P. L., 320) (the General Borough Law), provided that claims for paving should be recoverable in the same way as claims under the provisions relative to mechanics' liens, and that the statement should be filed in thirty days after the expense incurred. As the statement was not so filed in this case, the lien was struck off. The claim is not a lien for six months unless it is filed.

§ 456. *Alias sci. fa. to continue the lien preserves the claim for five years. Ketchum* v. *Singerly,* 12 Phila., 189 (1877). The mechanic's claim was filed in 1867. *Sci. fa.* issued in 1868. In 1876 a plea was filed averring that more than five years had elapsed since the issuing of the *sci. fa.* and no judgment had been entered. The replication averred the issuing of an *alias sci. fa.* to revive and continue the lien in 1872, and denied that the lien was gone.

ALLISON, P. J. : " The question is, does the record produced support the replication ? * * * The twenty-fourth section of Act of June 16, 1836, reads : ' The lien of every such debt, for which a claim shall have been filed as aforesaid, shall expire at the end of five years from the day on which such claim shall have been filed, unless the same shall be revived by *sci. fa.* in the manner provided by law in case of judgments ; in which case such lien shall continue in like manner for another period of five years, and so from one such period to another, unless such lien be satisfied, or the same be extinguished by sheriff's sale or otherwise according to law.'

" The plaintiff has now pending his *sci. fa.* to recover the amount of his demand against the property mentioned in the claim, and also a *sci. fa.* issued under the provisions of the twenty-fourth section to continue the lien of the claim as filed for a further period of five years. * * *

" If the twenty-fourth section does not give to him the right thus to continue the lien of his claim as a claim, then further proceedings upon both writs of *sci. fa.* must terminate, as more than five years have elapsed since the day on which the first *sci. fa.* issued, and recovery has not been had, nor has judgment been entered upon the *sci. fa.* last issued. In *Sweeney* v. *McGittigan*, 20 Pa. St., 319, it is decided that the lien of a claim had not expired by reason of five years having elapsed between the filing of the claim and the verdict. The decision of the court is based on section 24, making the proceedings to conform to the law relating to the revival of judgments under which the lien is continued, if *sci. fa.* is issued within the five years and duly prosecuted afterward. * * * The defendants contend that this section (24) confers no power to continue the lien of a claim as such, and that its true interpretation must be held to be a power to continue the lien of a judgment upon a claim, under the fifteenth section of the Act ; but the language of the section does not sustain this construction. It speaks of the lien of the debt for which a claim has been filed ; the rendering contended for would require us to strike out the word debt and insert judgment in its stead, and then to read it that the lien of every such judgment for which a claim has been filed as aforesaid shall expire, but this interpretation cannot be allowed, because no claim had been, nor could it be filed for a judgment, and it is not the judgment which is to expire, but the lien of the debt for which the claim has been filed ; the same, that is the claim, shall be revived by *scire facias* in the manner provided by law in case of judgments. It is not, therefore, the revival of a judgment on a claim, as in case of other judgments, but it is the continuance or revival of a claim, to be reached in the same manner in which a judgment is revived.

" We are of opinion that the record supports the replication, and that the lien of the claim has not been lost." See section 458.

§ 457. *Lien lost unless revived every five years. Collins v. Schoch,* 14 W. N., 485 (1884), ARNOLD, J. " The Act of June 27, 1883, gives a writ of *scire facias* upon a municipal claim, issued within five years, the additional effect of a *scire facias* to revive and continue the lien. * * * The purpose of this Act is to prevent the claim from being lost by reason of the litigation upon it requiring more than five years for its determination, as happened in *City* v. *Scott (supra).* * * *

" When the claim or debt has passed into a judgment, it may be revived for another space of five years, and so on indefinitely until paid. * * * But the first proceeding must be by *scire facias* to levy the debt, and not to revive and continue the lien."

Claim filed March 27, 1879.

Writs of *sci. fa.* to levy claim and revive lien issued March 24, 1884.

Rule for judgment for want of sufficient affidavit of defense discharged.

City v. *Unknown Owner,* 23 W. N., 271 (1888). The *sci. fa.* to revive must issue within five years, and be prosecuted to judgment within five years of issuance. The judgment was entered September 2, 1878. No *sci. fa.* issued until October 30, 1883. The writ was quashed. See also *Silverthorn* v. *Townsend,* 37 Pa. St., 263 (1860), STRONG, J. ; *Lichty* v. *Hochstetler,* 91 Pa. St., 444 (1879), GORDON, J. ; *Kirby* v. *Cash,* 93 Pa. St., 505 (1880), GORDON, J. ; *City* v. *Ward,* 16 W. N., 76 (1885) ; *City* v. *Unknown Owner,* 23 W. N., 371 (1888) ; *Church* v. *City,* 108 Pa. St., 466 (1885), CLARK, J. To preserve a claim, the lien must be revived each term of five years. Judgment on the first *sci. fa. sur* claim was entered October 1, 1877. The *sci. fa.* to revive was not issued until October 4, 1882. The judgment entered on it was reversed. *City* v. *Carr,* 21 W. N., 444 (1888). Judgment on a municipal claim must be obtained within five years from the issue of the original *sci. fa.* The time cannot be extended by the issue of *alias* and *pluries* writs.

The lien of a municipal claim for taxes under the Act of March 11, 1846, is not preserved unless a *sci. fa.* issues *within five years* from the first day of January succeeding the year for which the tax was assessed. *City* v. *Kates*, 30 W. N., 345 (1892).

§ 458. *Issuing sci. fa. to continue lien does not help plaintiff unless claim actually revived in five years. Claim must be revived every five years.* *City* v. *Scott*, 3 W. N., 562 (1877), affirmed in 93 Pa. St., 25 (1880). A *sci. fa.* upon a claim for taxes must be prosecuted to judgment within five years after issuing it, in order to preserve the lien of the claim. The issuing of a *sci. fa.* to continue the lien does not help the plaintiff. The claim was filed March 16, 1871. The *sci. fa.* issued November 1, 1871, returned *nihil*. An *alias* issued November 17, 1871. Served, by posting and publication, October 31, 1876. A *sci. fa.* was issued to revive and continue the lien. Verdict for plaintiff, January 11, 1877. Judgment was arrested below, and this was affirmed in the Supreme Court.

Ketchum v. *Singerly, supra*, section 456, was distinguished on the ground that there the *alias sci. fa.* issued within five years of filing the original claim, while in this case more than that period elapsed between the filing of the claim and the issuance of the writ which was relied on to keep it alive. The court declined to express an opinion whether *Ketchum* v. *Singerly* was well decided.

§ 459. *Affidavit of service of alias sci. fa. not required.* *Wistar* v. *City*, 9 W. N., 98 (1880). *Alias sci. fa sur* municipal claim. An affidavit of service of the original *sci. fa.* under the Act of March 23, 1866, having been filed, judgment was entered by default. This judgment was afterward reversed in the Supreme Court for defects in the service, and the record was remitted. An *alias* was issued, but no second affidavit of service was filed, and judgment by default was again taken. Upon writ of error assigning the omission to file a second affidavit, it was *held* that such second affidavit was not necessary, and that the judgment was good. To the same effect is *City* v. *Hemphill*, 24 W. N., 79 (1889).

§ 460. *Lien not lost because verdict is entered more than five years after claim filed, if the sci. fa. was issued within the five years and was prosecuted diligently.* *Sweeney* v. *McGittigan*, 20 Pa. St., 319 (1853), LOWRIE, J. A mechanic's claim was filed in September, 1845, and *sci. fa.* in December, 1845, and returned " made known " in January, 1846. Verdict, October 28, 1850. *Held*, that the lien of the claim had not expired by reason of five years having elapsed between the filing of the claim and the verdict. LOWRIE, J.: " The Mechanics' Lien Act of 1836, section 24, expressly refers to the law relating to the revival of judgments as an analogy for this proceeding, and under that law the lien is continued if a *scire facias* be issued within the five years, and duly prosecuted afterward."

Cornelius v. *Junior*, 5 Phila., 171 (1863), HARE, J. "A *scire facias* issued within the five years, to establish the right to enforce a mechanic's claim or have execution on a judgment, will revive the lien incidentally and by legal construction, although not purporting to be for the purpose of revival."

§ 461. *Service of sci. fa. must show strict obedience to the law; setting forth that it was done agreeably to the Act is not enough. Upon sci. fa. to revive, two returns of nihil are a sufficient service.* *O'Bryne* v. *City*, 93 Pa. St., 225 (1880), MERCUR, J. This was a *sci. fa.* on a municipal lien for taxes. The writ issued January 19, 1878. The docket showed it to be returnable to the first Monday of February, but no return-day was named in the writ. The sheriff returned the writ, "Made known January 28, 1878, by posting a true and attested copy of the within writ on a conspicuous part of the premises herein described, and by advertising notice for two weeks in, etc., agreeably to Act of Assembly in such case made and provided."

Held, That the return was insufficient, because by no possibility could a service made on January 28 be two weeks before the first Monday of the following February. The judgment for the city was reversed.

City v. *Theis*, 12 W. N., 239 (1882). On a *sci. fa.* to continue the lien of a municipal claim two returns of *nihil*, without posting, are sufficient.

§ 462. **Powers of councils and rights of property-owners.** *When a statute makes councils the judge of any fact, their action conclusive.* *Erie* v. *Bootz*, 72 Pa. St., 196 (1872), SHARSWOOD, J. An Act authorized the councils of Erie to grade, pave, etc., provided that their action must be based upon "the petition of a majority of" property-owners. The second section of the law directed that where the councils should, by ordinance, order the grading, etc., the question whether a majority had petitioned "should cease."

It was held that the action of councils, regularly taken, was conclusive upon the question of the petition being by the majority.

Michener v. *The City*, 118 Pa. St., 535 (1888). To a *sci. fa. sur* municipal claim for an assessment of the cost of a sewer constructed under ordinance enacted according to law, an affidavit of defense was filed alleging that defendant's property was already drained by sewers which answered all its needs, and that the new sewer was neither a private benefit to his property nor a public necessity. A rule for judgment for want of sufficient affidavit of defense was made absolute, and this *judgment affirmed* per PAXSON, J. :

" The plaintiff alleges, however, that his property is not benefited by the sewer. He may or may not be mistaken in this. We cannot say. But this is a species of taxation, and all taxation is presumed to be for the benefit, directly or indirectly, of the tax-payer or his property. Laid as taxes are, under general laws, there will always be cases of apparent individual hardship. * * * It would be intolerable if, in every instance of special taxation, the question of benefits could be thrown into the jury-box. It would introduce into municipal government a novel and dangerous feature. It would substitute for the responsibility of councils, limited though it be, the wholly irresponsible and uncertain actions of jurors."

In *City* v. *Cadwallader*, 20 W. N., 14 (1887), and in *Waln's Heirs* v. *City*, 11 W. N., 314 (1882), the same ruling was made.

§ 463. *Property liable though no application was made to councils to pave.* Spring Garden v. Wistar, 18 Pa. St., 195 (1852), LOW-RIE, J. The seventh section of the Act of March 12, 1830 (P. L., 427), provided " that the commissioners of the District of Spring Garden be and they are hereby authorized to open Broad Street, from the intersection of Callowhill and Broad Streets to the Ridge Road, of the same width as it now is between Vine and Callowhill Streets, and cause the same to be levelled and paved as soon as may be ; the expense and cost of the same to be assessed and paid in like manner and under the same regulations as are now in force and provided for levelling and paving streets within the said district."

The twenty-first section of the Act incorporating the District of Spring Garden, passed March 22, 1813 (P. L., 144), provided that the " commissioners shall have full power and authority, and they are hereby directed, upon the application of a majority of the freeholders holding property on any street * * * surveyed and regulated as aforesaid, within the said district, to pitch and pave the cartway thereof, agreeably to the said regulation : *Provided*, That not more than two squares shall be included in any one application ; and to tax the owners of the lots of ground bounding thereon, to defray the expense thereof, in proportion to their respective fronts therein."

It was held that the owner of a lot was bound to pay his proportion for paving done by virtue of the first-cited Act, although no application had been made by lot-owners for the improvement.

§ 464. *Where majority of property-owners have right to select contractor, no other can file a lien.* Reilley v. City, 60 Pa. St., 467 (1869), WILLIAMS, J. An Act provided that no contract should be made by a head of department for the city, unless for objects

authorized by councils.   By resolution of councils, a department
was authorized to contract for paving, etc., with the condition that
the contractor should be selected by a majority of property-owners
of the front to be paved, the costs of paving, etc., to be collected
from the owners of property in front of which the work should
be done ; on a *sci. fa. sur* lien entered for the paving : *Held*, that
the claimant could not recover unless he proved that he had been
selected by a majority of the owners.   His selection by such majority cannot be inferred from the implied adoption of his work by
the city in allowing him to bring suit in its name.   The contractor
doing the work without such selection was a mere volunteer, and
could not recover either from the city or from the owners.

The department had no authority to enter into a contract unless
with one selected by a majority of the lot-owners, and the contractor is presumed to have had notice of the resolution.   Having
submitted the selection to the lot-holders, the city could not adopt
the work of a paver not chosen by them and oblige them to pay the
cost.

The decision in this case was followed in *City* v. *Stewart*, 1 W.
N., 242 (1873).   *Infra*, section 467.

§ 465. *Contract in violation of ordinance may be ratified by councils.*   But when an ordinance required the paver to be selected by
a majority of property-owners, and he was, in fact, not so selected,
and by subsequent ordinance the contract awarding the work to
him was expressly ratified and approved, his lien for such work
was held good.   *City* v. *Hays*, 93 Pa. St., 72 (1881).

§ 466. *Where statute authorizes paving on application of majority
such application is a pre-requisite to jurisdiction.*   "*Nunquam indebitatus*" *requires plaintiff to prove everything.*   *Pittsburgh* v. *Walter*, 69 Pa. St., 365 (1871), SHARSWOOD, J.   The Act of April 1,
1868, section 11 (P. L., 567), authorized the councils of Pittsburgh to grade if the " majority in interest of the owners whose
property is situated or abuts thereon " make such application, and
to assess the cost and enter a lien against the abutting lots.   *Held*,
that the application was a pre-requisite to give councils jurisdiction
to order the grading.

The plea of *nunquam indebitatus* in such a case requires a plaintiff to prove whatever is necessary to support the assessment ;
though in strictness a defendant ought perhaps to traverse by special pleas all the facts essential to the case of the plaintiff.

§ 467. *Plaintiff must produce the written contract or account for it.*
City v. *Stewart*, 1 W. N., 242 (1873), affirming *Reilley* v. *City*
(*supra*).

Sci. fa. sur municipal claim. An alleged written contract with the owners was not produced by the plaintiff, but he sought to prove that the contractor had been selected by a majority of the owners, by producing certain owners of real estate above and below the square in which the defendant's property was situate, and by asking the contractor whether he had been so selected. The missing contract not being sufficiently accounted for, the offer was excluded. Verdict for defendant. The ruling of the court was assigned for error. *Per curiam*, judgment affirmed.

§ 468. *Where two nominations made (the first not being revoked), commissioners can select.* Long v. O'Rourke, 10 Phila., 129 (1874), per FINLETTER, J. The nomination by property-owners of a second person does not revoke the selection of the first. The commissioners can then select.

§ 469. *Owners may revoke their appointment before contract awarded.* City v. R. R. Co., 12 Phila., 479 (1877). Rule for new trial and motion for judgment on points reserved. *Sci. fa. sur* municipal claim for paving.

Where a city ordinance authorizes the highway department to enter into a contract for paving with a paver selected by a majority of property-owners, it is competent for any of those who have by writing selected a particular paver, to revoke their selection at any time before the contract is awarded to him. In this case plaintiff was selected as paver by forty-nine out of ninety-seven property-holders. Seventeen of them revoked their selection before the contract was awarded to him. Upon securing the contract, he began the work of paving, and upon its completion filed this lien. THAYER, P. J. Rule for new trial discharged and judgment for defendant.

§ 470. *Where law requires notice of assessment, additional notice provided for by ordinance is not indispensable.* Winter v. City, 15 W. N., 329 (1884). By Act of May 1, 1876 (P. L., 94), it is provided that the councils of cities not of the first class, before passing an ordinance authorizing the paving of streets, shall direct their engineer to make an estimate of the total cost of such improvement, together with a map or plan of the property liable to assessment, and shall appoint a board of viewers to value such property and to fix the amount of the owners' liability. This estimate, plan, and schedule must be attached to the ordinance, and must remain on file in the proper office for the benefit of those interested.

The city of Reading passed an ordinance for paving, under this Act, stipulating that, in addition to the above measures, thirty days' notice should be given to lot-owners. It did not appear in this case that such notice was actually given. *Held*, that the giving of the thirty days' notice was a mere matter of grace, that the ordinance was in that respect only directory, and that the owner of property was not released from liability by the omission to give him notice. *Judgment* of the lower court sustaining the lien *affirmed* per GORDON, J., MERCUR, C. J., dissenting.

§ 471. *Laws conferring power to assess must be strictly followed. Provisos are not directory, they are limitations of power.* Commissioners v. *Keith*, 2 Pa. St., 218 (1845). A proviso to an Act conferring power of assessment declared that the curbing should be not less in length than one nor exceeding three squares at one time. ROGERS, J., said : " The proviso is a limitation of power and amounts to a negation of all authority beyond its prescribed and clearly defined limits. It cannot be that the proviso is directory merely." Judgment for the defendant.

Harper's Appeal, 1 Cent. Rep., 585 (1885). When an Act of Assembly requires an estimate of expenses and an ordinance assessing the same prior to the building of a sewer, such ordinance and assessment passed after the sewer has been constructed are null and void. Equity will enjoin the collection of a tax levied thereunder.

§ 472. **Publication. Proof necessary. Requirements and effect of claim.** *If Act require publication, lien cannot be enforced without strict compliance with the law. Where the statute did not name the number of days, but said simply days, this means more than one day.* Olds v. *Erie*, 79 Pa. St., 380 (1875), GORDON, J. The Act of May 1, 1861, section 2 (P. L., 614), empowered the councils of Erie to order a street to be paved, but provided that no ordinance * * * shall be passed until   days' notice of the improvement prayed for has been given in the official paper of the city." Each proceeding of councils in relation to a proposed improvement was published as a news item in the official paper on the day after its occurrence only, but no notice was published by direction of the councils. *Held*, that this was not a compliance with the Act, that " days " meant more than one day, and that reasonable notice was necessary. The judgment below for plaintiff was reversed.

§ 473. *Where advertisement prior to award of contract is required, proof of such advertisement is necessary.* Fell v. *Phila.*, 81 Pa. St., 58 (1876), WOODWARD, J., *overruling the lower Court in 9 Phila.*, 180 (1874). The Act of April 21, 1855 (P. L., 269), provided that no contract for new paving shall be binding in Philadelphia without an ordinance therefor.

An ordinance of December 31, 1862, required, before a paving contract should be awarded, that the applicant should give notice by advertisement, two weeks before the application, of his name, the place and quantity of paving, the names and residences of the signers for his selection, with the request to lot-owners to meet the department at a time named to show cause why the contract should not be awarded. There was no evidence of such advertisement in this case. The agreement with the owners was for a cobble-stone pavement, whereas councils had not conferred authority to lay other than a rubble pavement. The irregularities were held fatal, and judgment was entered for defendant.

§ 474. *Plaintiff must prove publication strictly as required.* *City* v. *Sanger*, 5 W. N., 335 (1878). An ordinance required that notice of the application for the contract should be published for two weeks in two daily papers, setting forth, *inter alia*, the name and residence of each person signing for contractor. To the *sci. fa.* the defendant pleaded that the claimant's notice of his application for the contract had not been published for two weeks, as required by the ordinance.

The claimant, on the trial, offered in evidence a file of the *Bulletin* newspaper to show the advertisement. It did not contain the residences of the property-owners. On objection that the notice had not been published as required by the ordinance, the court excluded the offer. A non-suit was entered. The Supreme Court affirmed.

See, however, *Brientnall* v. *City*, 103 Pa. St., 156 (1883). The opinion of the Supreme Court in that case is very meagre, but it seems to indicate a contrary ruling.

§ 475. *Claim attaches from the time work is begun.* *Norton* v. *Borough*, 43 Leg. Int., 187 (1885). A municipal claim, filed under the General Borough Act of April 3, 1851 (P. L., 320), attaches from the time when the work is begun, and not before. It cannot affect an owner of the property who parts with his title prior to the beginning of the work for which the lien is filed.

§ 476. *Claim need not state the several items.* *Pittsburgh* v. *Cluley*, 66 Pa. St., 449 (1870), AGNEW, J. "A Mechanic's Lien Act furnishes only a general and not a specific analogy and rule of proceeding." A municipal claim need not state the several amounts and kind of material.

§ 477. *Claim need only state one date.* In *City* v. *Wood*, 4 Phila., 156 (1860), ALLISON, J., a motion was made to strike off a lien upon the ground that it did not state when the work was done or the materials furnished, the averment being "for work done, * * * duly assessed, and charged, viz., 1858, March 22."

It was held that this was sufficiently specific, as it meant that the work was done and the assessment was made all on the same day.

§ 478. *Nuisance claims need not state time or amount of labor and materials. City* v. *The Gratz Land Co.*, 38 Pa. St., 359 (1861), STRONG, J. Claims for expenses attending the removal of nuisances, authorized by the Act of April 7, 1830 (P. L., 348), are sufficiently precise, though they do not aver when the work was done or materials furnished.

NOTE.—This does not apply to other municipal claims. The Act of April 16, 1840, and subsequent Acts, assimilated claims for paving, etc., to claims of mechanics and material-men under Act June 16, 1836. "But claims for removal of nuisances were authorized by the Act of April 7, 1830 (P. L., 348), before the Act of 1836 was passed. * * * No Act of Assembly at the time required that the claim should state when the work was done, etc."]

In *City* v. *Van Vrankin*, 39 Leg. Int., 402 (1882), the claim for removing a nuisance did not state the amount of labor and materials. The court refused to strike it off.

Board of Health—Action as to nuisance conclusive—Power to file liens. Under the Act of January 29, 1818, the board of health are empowered to have removed all nuisances which, in their opinion, endanger the health of the citizens of Philadelphia. By a supplement thereto, approved April 7, 1830, it is provided that the expenses attending the removal of any nuisance shall be a lien on the premises from which the nuisance is removed, and the Board of Health are authorized to file a claim therefor, such claims to be recovered in like manner as mechanics' claims.

In *Kennedy* v. *The Board of Health*, 2 Pa. St., 366 (1845), it was decided that the Board have final jurisdiction in determining the question of nuisance, and their action is conclusive.

A municipal claim may be filed for abating a nuisance consisting of a foul privy well. *City* v. *Goudey*, 36 W. N., 246 (1895); *City* v. *Glading, Id.*, 247 (1895).

§ 479. *Precision is necessary. Claim for " conduit gas " invalid, and stricken off after judgment. Amendment refused. Facts must be set forth. Commissioners* v. *Flanigan*, 3 Phila., 458 (1859). Precision in a claim is necessary. The Act of April 21 1858 (P. L., 387), permits amendments before or at the trial, but not where judgment has been obtained. A claim was struck off after judgment on the *sci. fa.*, because it charged for " *conduit gas.*" The Act made the property liable for the expenses of " laying gas-pipes." The court refused leave to amend.

All facts necessary to sustain validity of a claim must be set out, or the claim may be stricken off. But the evidence need not be disclosed, nor need the ordinance under which the work was done be set forth in the claim. *City* v. *Richards*, 23 W. N., 339 (1889); *Schlag* v. *City*, 42 Leg. Int., 354 (1885).

§ 480. *A claim fatally defective may be amended.* *City* v. *Uber*, 1 W. N., 160 (1875). A municipal claim describing the lot as larger than it was may be amended.

Where a lien erroneously recites that notice was given to a person, as owner, who was in fact the agent of the registered owner, and the lien names the registered owner, an amendment setting forth that notice was given to the registered owner will be permitted even after a rule has been entered to strike the lien off. *City* v. *O'Reilly*, 32 W. N., 166 (1889).

City v. *Hower*, 93 Pa. St., 332 (1880), STERRETT, J. The Act of April 21, 1858, section 9 (P. L., 387), provided " that municipal claims for taxes, liens, public assessments, or charges may be amended at any time before or at the trial, on notice given the defendant under rule of court."

Mr. Justice STERRETT : " Such Acts should be liberally construed, and while amendments are not a matter of right, they should be allowed where it can be done without prejudice to intervening rights."

The claim contained no description of the property liened. It had been stricken off, and a motion to amend had been disallowed in the court below. The Supreme Court held that the claim was fatally defective, but allowed the amendment.

Claim may be amended by averring notice to owner to set the curb, etc. *City* v. *Richards*, 23 W. N., 339 (1889).

Amendments to municipal claims should be fortified by affidavit of their truth. *City* v. *Laughlin*, 48 Leg. Int., 265 (1891).

In filing a municipal claim under the Borough Act of April 3, 1851, an averment of demand and refusal before work done by the borough is not necessary; but if plaintiff applies for leave to so amend, such amendment should be allowed. *Borough* v. *R. R. Co.*, 27 W. N., 177 (1891).

A municipal lien can be amended at any time before the Statute of Limitations closes on the claim. *City* v. *Busch*, 35 W. N., 564 (1895).

§ 481. *Claim is prima facie evidence contractor was chosen by majority, where it so avers.* *City* v. *Collum*, 1 W. N., 525 (1875), THAYER, J. A municipal claim stating that a contractor was selected by a majority of those in interest is *prima facie* evidence of that fact. The plaintiff is not bound in the first place to prove that averment. This case is, in the opinion of the court, distinguished from *Reilly* v. *City* (60 Pa. St., 467), because the claim in the latter case contained no averment that the contractor was chosen by the majority, whereas in this case the claim did so aver.

§ 482. *Defect as to absence of dates, waived by pleading.* Howell v. *City*, 38 Pa. St., 471 (1861), WOODWARD, J. " The objection to the lien for want of dates might have been formidable on demurrer or a motion to strike off, but after pleading to the *scire facias* it must be considered as waived."

§ 483. *Substantial compliance with ordinance is sufficient.* Watson v. *City*, 93 Pa. St., 111 (1880), PAXSON, J. The lot described in the claim was angular; there appeared to have been some slight inequalities in the width of the pavement, which varied a few inches from the width required by ordinance. It was held that the owners could not resist the recovery on this ground—the jury having found that there was a substantial compliance with the ordinance.

The claim averred that the requisite notice to pave had been given. This was *prima facie* evidence of the notice.

§ 484. *Averment in claim that work was duly authorized is not proof that owner was notified and was in default.* City v. *Walter*, 39 Leg. Int., 42 (1882). On a trial of a *sci. fa. sur* municipal claim, the authority to do the work must be affirmatively shown either by being recited in the claim, or by evidence *aliunde :* this includes all the steps requisite for the existence of the authority, including notice to the owner and default by him. A mere general averment in the claim that the work was " duly authorized " is not a sufficient averment of such notice and default to make a *prima facie* case, even under the Act March 11, 1846 (P. L., 115), which makes the claim evidence of the " facts therein set forth." MITCHELL, J.

§ 485. **Owner may show work was defectively done. Affidavit of defense should show copy of paper relied on.** *Pepper* v. *City*, 114 Pa. St., 96 (1886), TRUNKEY, J. The power to ordain the paving of streets in Philadelphia is vested in councils. If the contractor's work · is so defectively done as to be worthless, he has no right to recover against the property-owner who can set up this defense, although he is not nominally a party to the contract. Defects which lessen the value of the pavement can be deducted from the contract price. This was followed by the ruling in *Erie* v. *Butler*, 120 Pa. St., 374 (1888), PAXSON, J. In this latter case it was also ruled that an affidavit of defense ought to exhibit a copy of a paper set up as a defense, in order that the court may judge of its legal effect. The defendant averred simply that the contractor had " not fully complied with his contract with the city " without furnishing a copy of the contract. The Supreme Court held that the affidavit was insufficient.

§ 486. **Where money is paid into court, if claimant suffer non-suit, the money is to be paid to defendant. He cannot suffer voluntary non-suit after having been required to issue sci. fa.** *City* v. *McGarry*, 11 W. N., 168 (1881). Where money has been paid into court and plaintiff notified to proceed, if, on the trial, he suffer a non-suit, his claim is gone, and the court may order the fund to be paid to the defendant.

City v. *Sanger*, 8 W. N., 151 (1880). Plaintiff in a *sci. fa.* on a municipal claim, having been required, under the Act of February 21, 1862 (P. L., 44), to proceed, cannot suffer a voluntary non-suit.

§ 487. **Claims bear interest.** Municipal claims bear interest from the time of demand made. *Schenley* v. *Commonwealth*, 36 Pa. St., 29 (1859).

§ 488. **Entry of satisfaction by mistake may be vacated where rights of third parties have not intervened.** *City* v. *Thomas*, 9 W. N., 240 (1880). Where a municipal lien is satisfied by mistake through the negligence of an official, the court has the power to vacate the entry.

City v. *Matchett*, 116 Pa. St., 103 (1887). The city is estopped from enforcing payment of a claim satisfied by mistake, against the purchaser of the property without notice.

§ 489. **Misdescription in receipt for assessment cannot be taken advantage of.** *Wolf* v. *City*, 105 Pa. St., 25 (1884). *Sci. fa. sur* municipal lien. A sewer having been built by virtue of an ordinance and contract thereunder, A., an owner of property upon the street in which it was laid, paid the amount of his assessment to the contractor, and afterward obtained a receipt in due form therefor, in which the location of his property was misdescribed. His deed and a plan of his property were registered. The city retained a bill against his premises as rightly described, but in the name of a former owner. The latter was named as " owner " in a claim filed by the city against the property. After *sci. fa.* issued, A. was suggested as " the present and actual owner." *Held*, reversing the lower court, that these facts constituted a good defense to the *sci. fa.*, and that the receipt for A.'s assessment would not have prevailed against a lien upon the property erroneously described therein.

§ 490. **Preliminary steps.** Every claimant should understand the

importance of two words—Notice and Form.   Frequently the notices are intrusted to careless hands and no proof preserved of the
service.   Worse even than this, no steps are taken to ascertain that
.the notices are properly addressed.   Look at the facts in several of
the cases cited *supra*, especially in *White's Appeal*, 45 Leg. Int.,
394 (1888).   There the owner had carefully registered the property to guard against the very danger which nearly swept it from
his children.   He died in 1871.   The claimant presumably took
no pains to visit the property.   Eight years after the death of the
owner the plaintiff filed his claim against the dead man, and alleged that a notice had been served on Margaret White, who had
also died two years before the assessment.   It is not strange that
he lost his claim.   In cases requiring paving, repairs, removal of
nuisances, opening of streets, etc., notice should be served on the
owner, where it is possible to find him, and proof of the service
carefully made.

Where registry laws exist, the record should be searched, the tax
office visited, the assessor called upon, and inquiry made of the
neighbors.   In these and other ways the true name can be ascertained and service secured.   Judge Ashman's remarks on this subject are very pertinent.   He says, in the case cited :

" The plea of inconvenience, based, as here, on the difficulty of
service, was brought forward in *Simons* v. *Kern*, 37 Leg. Int., 74
(1880), but the Supreme Court said : ' If a remedy be needed, the
power to provide it belongs to the legislature and not to the courts.
Arguments from inconvenience should not be permitted to prevail
against the positive prohibition of the statute.'   The Registry Act
of 1867 (P. L., 600) required owners to return their title papers
to the proper office, that they might be registered, and provided
that ' no property so returned shall be subject to sale for taxes or
other municipal claims thereafter to accrue, as a lien of record
thereon, except in the name of the owner as returned, and after recovery by suit and service of the writ on him made, as in case of a
summons.' "

Note every detail in the Act or ordinance under which you proceed, and be careful that each necessary step has been taken as
therein directed.   See that your claim recites all the facts requisite
to make it valid ; that the averments as to notice, search, etc., be
true, and that all averments be susceptible of ready proof if disputed.   When the claim has been filed and *sci. fa.* issued, do not
rely too confidently upon the industry and knowledge of the sheriff
or his deputy.   Insist that the return to the writ be made in due

form, that it be not vague and general where it ought to be explicit, and that it conform to legal requirements. Rather abandon your *sci. fa.* and issue an *alias*, where time and circumstances will permit, than ignore a defect of which your adversary may take advantage when it is too late to cure the evil, or, at all events, when much useless additional expense has been incurred.

In this connection consult the statutes above cited, especially the Acts of March 23, 1866, and March 29, 1867.

FORMS.

The following forms of notices, of affidavits, and of claims may be found useful.

§ 491.

NOTICE FROM BOARD OF HEALTH FOR IMMEDIATE REMOVAL OF A
NUISANCE.

No.   .   Ward,   .

Health Office, Philadelphia,   188 .

To   owner or occupier of premises situated

You are hereby notified and required to have removed immediately a certain nuisance on the above-described property, arising from a
privy   which nuisance has been declared to have a tendency to endanger and be prejudicial to the public health. On failure to do and perform which, the said nuisance will be removed at your expense, and a lien entered agreeably to the provisions of the Act of Assembly.

By order of the Board of Health.

Chief Clerk.

You will be liable to a penalty not exceeding two hundred dollars, by neglecting or refusing to have the said nuisance immediately removed.

Extract from the Act of Assembly of January 29, 1818, for establishing a Health Office, etc.

SECTION 27. " If the owners or occupiers of the premises on which any nuisance may be found, and the owners of the house to which the said privies are appurtenant shall, on due notice thereof, refuse or neglect to have the same immediately removed, emptied, or corrected, as aforesaid, he, she, or they so refusing or neglecting, shall forfeit and pay, for every such offense, any sum not less than twenty nor more than two hundred dollars, to be recovered and appropriated as by this Act directed."

SECTION VII., Act March 16, 1855.—" Every person in the city or county of Philadelphia, whether owner, agent, or occupant of property, who shall employ or contract with any unlicensed person to clean his or her privy-well, or sink, or who shall receive from any unlicensed person any portion of the contents of a privy-well, or sink, emptied and cleaned within the limits of the jurisdiction of the Board of Health, shall for every such offense forfeit and pay to the Board of Health the sum of twenty-five dollars, to be recovered as debts of like amount are by law recoverable."

§ 492.

NOTICE FROM BOARD OF HEALTH FOR REMOVAL OF A NUISANCE WITHIN
A TIME TO BE NAMED.

No.   Ward,   .
                    Health Office, Philadelphia,   188 .
To   , owner, agent, or occupier of premises situated
    You are hereby notified and required to have removed within
                    days from the date of the service hereof, a certain nuisance
on the above-described property, arising from
                    , which nuisance has been declared to have a tendency to en-
danger and be prejudicial to the public health.   On failure to do and perform which, the said nuisance will be removed at your expense, and a lien
entered agreeably to the provisions of the Act of Assembly.
                    By order of the Board of Health.
    Attest :   Chief Clerk.
                              Clerk.

    This notice to be indorsed with the same Extracts from the Act
of Assembly as in section 491.
    .§ 493.

NOTICE TO REPAIR SIDEWALK, ETC.

                    Bureau of Highways,
          Office, City Hall.   Entrance, Market and Juniper Streets.
No.   Philadelphia,   , 188 .
                    Footway or Sidewalk Notice.
    In accordance with ordinances of Councils, you are hereby notified and
directed to have completed within thirty days from date of this notice the
following :   in front of property situate
on
                    Assistant Commissioner of Highways.
    Served   , 188   , by
    Attention is called to the requirements of city ordinances printed on the
back of this notice.
    Ordinance of April 20, 1874, *page* 150, provides that in no case shall the
city pay for grading more of the street than is contained between the curb
lines (that is the cartway only) without allowance for slope ; and provides
further, that when Councils shall direct the grading of any street the chief
commissioner of highways shall notify the owners of property on each side
to grade the sidewalks within thirty days, and if the owners fail to comply,
that the work shall be done and liens be filed against the property.   Ordinances that direct the grading of any street generally contain a clause requiring property-owners not only to grade, but to curb and pave the sidewalks.
    Ordinance of May 3, 1855, *page* 141, provides that the cartways and foot-
ways of all private streets and the footways of all public streets shall be
graded, curbed, paved, and kept in repair at the expense of the owner of
the ground fronting thereon ; that in front of improved property the sidewalks shall be paved the full width ; that where the cartway is paved the
sidewalks in front of vacant lots shall be paved at least eight feet wide in
streets that are not less than forty feet in width, and five feet wide in

streets less than forty feet in width, and that the balance of the sidewalk not paved shall be graded and covered for a depth of four inches with gravel; that in streets where the cartway is unpaved the sidewalk shall be at least five feet in width, and made of brick, stone, or plank when and as may be directed by the department of highways; that private cartways leading across footways shall be paved with broad, flat stones, hewn and laid close together, or with hard bricks laid edgewise; that whenever Councils shall order the paving of any cartway, or the paving, grading, and curbing of any footway, every owner of ground fronting on such street shall, without delay, at his own cost, cause the footway in front of his ground to be graded, paved with brick or flat stones, and supported with curbstones.

Ordinance of April 5, 1869, *page* 125, provides that in all streets not less than twenty feet in width the curbstones shall not be less than four feet long, twenty inches wide, and five inches thick.

Ordinance of February 12, 1852, *page* 1298, provides that where the cartway is ordered paved with cubical blocks owners of ground opposite shall cause the foot pavement to be supported with cut granite curbstones not less than eight inches in thickness, two feet in depth, and six feet in length.

Ordinance of June 7, 1882, *page* 158, provides that whenever, in the opinion of the chief commissioner of highways, any sidewalk requires paving, repaving, or repairing, or the curbstones require setting or resetting, he shall notify the owners of property fronting the same to do the necessary work within thirty days. In case the owner neglects to comply with said notice, the chief commissioner may have the work done and the bill presented to the owner, and if the owner, for a period of thirty days, neglects to pay such bill, a lien may be entered against the property. That the prices shall not exceed for paving, repaving, or repairing $1.00 per square yard, for curbing $1.25 per lineal foot, and for curb resetting 25 cents per lineal foot.

§ 494.

NOTICE OF MUNICIPAL CLAIM BEFORE PROCEEDING.

The City	Docket p.
v.	Court of Common Pleas No.
	Term, 188 . No.

DEAR SIR:

Please notice that a claim for   amounting to $.
has been filed in the above court and docketed in this office against the lot situated   and that the same is now due, with interest and costs thereon. You are further notified to make payment of the same to the city solicitor within ten days, and that if the same is not paid within said time a writ of *scire facias* will be issued, additional costs incurred, and the property may be sold at sheriff's sale.

Very respectfully, etc.,

City Solicitor.

City Solicitor's office,

No.   .   Street, Philadelphia.

NOTE.—The costs on the *scire facias* amount to   . *Please bring this notice with you.*

§ 495.

AFFIDAVIT OF PERSONAL SERVICE ON OWNER.

The City v.	Court of Common Pleas, No. Term, 18 . No. Municipal Claim.

, having been duly sworn according to law, deposes and says : That   the owner or reputed owner of the lot described in the above claim, and that   ha a known residence in the City of Philadelphia. Deponent further saith that on the   day of   , 18 , he served the original notice (a true and correct copy of which is hereto annexed) upon the said owner or reputed owner of the said lot, by

Sworn to and subscribed before
  me, this   day
  of   188

          Notary Public.

§ 496.

AFFIDAVIT WHERE OWNER IS A NON-RESIDENT.

The City v.	C. P., No. Term, 18 . No. Municipal Claim.

, having been duly sworn according to law, deposes and says : That   is the owner or reputed owner of the premises described in the above claim, and that the said   has no known residence in the city of Philadelphia. Deponent further saith that he made diligent inquiry and search for the said   , as follows : On the day of   , 188 , the premises liened were visited by deponent, and the said premises being occupied by an adult, to wit, by an original notice (a true and correct copy of which is hereto annexed) was then and there served by deponent upon said adult, by handing the same to him personally on the day and year above mentioned ; and inquiry was then and there made by deponent for the said   and deponent having by said inquiry ascertained that the said had no residence in the city of Philadelphia, but that he had a certain residence outside of said city, to wit,   deponent mailed at Philadelphia, postpaid, and directed to said   at his residence, as above stated, a true and correct copy of the notice hereto attached on the   day of   , A.D. 188 , the same being at least fifteen days before suit was brought.

Sworn to and subscribed before
  me, this   day
  of   A.D. 188

          Notary Public.

§ 497.

AFFIDAVIT WHERE OWNER CANNOT BE FOUND AND HIS ADDRESS CANNOT BE ASCERTAINED.

v.	C. P., No. . Term, 188 . No. Municipal Claim.

, having been duly   according to law, deposes and says : That on the   day of   , A.D. 188 , he visited the lot upon which the above claim is a lien, and made diligent search and inquiry for the owner or reputed owner thereof, and for his name and address, but that he was unable to find said owner or reputed owner thereof, or to ascertain the name and address of the said owner or reputed owner thereof. And the inquiry made on said premises for the owner or reputed owner thereof, and for the name and address of the owner or reputed owner thereof being fruitless, deponent served a notice (of which the annexed is a true and correct copy) on said property by affixing the same to   and deponent further, on the same day and year last above mentioned, made inquiry for the reputed owner of said premises of the occupant of the nearest dwelling and of the nearest Ward Assessor, and said inquiries being also fruitless, deponent, on the day and year last above mentioned, served another notice (whereof a true and correct copy is hereto attached) on the said Assessor personally.

            to and subscribed before me, ⎫
    this   day of   , A.D. 188 . ⎬
                                         ⎭
            Notary Public.

§ 498.

AFFIDAVIT OF DILIGENT SEARCH FOR OWNER, ETC.

The City   ⎫   C. P., No. ,   Term, 188 , No.
    v.   ⎬   Municipal Claim.
                       ⎭

            being duly   according to law, deposes and says : That   is the registered owner of the premises against which the above claim is filed. That he has visited said premises and made diligent search and inquiry for said registered owner, and that said owner could not be found in said city, and has no known residence therein.

            to and subscribed before me, ⎫
    this   day of   , A.D. 188 . ⎬
                                         ⎭
            Notary Public.

§ 499.

NOTICE OF ASSESSMENT OF BENEFITS AND CLAIMS FOR BENEFITS ASSESSED.

See Act of April 1, 1864, sections 1, 2, 3. (Br. Purd., 1498, sections 604, 605, 606.)

NOTICE.

In the matter of the opening of   ·   from
to

NOTICE OF ASSESSMENT OF BENEFITS.

                                Philadelphia,   188 .

DEAR SIR :

The jury appointed by the court to assess the damages arising from the opening of   from   to   , and also determine the benefits accruing to property in the vicinity, have assessed as benefits against your property on   the sum of $

There will be a meeting of the Jury on   , 188 , at o'clock   M., at the Law Department, No.   Street.

You are requested to attend personally or by counsel if you have any objection to urge against the benefits assessed upon your property as aforesaid.

Very respectfully,

City Solicitor.

Assistant Solicitor.

§ 500.

CLAIM FOR BENEFITS ASSESSED.

The City of Philadelphia	In the Court of Common Pleas, No.
v.	, for the City and County of Philadelphia, of Term, 188 . No. .
owner, or reputed owner, and registered owner, or whoever may be owner.	

The " City of Philadelphia " hereby files its claims against all that certain lot or piece of ground   situate on the
side of   at the distance of   from the
               side of   in the   Ward of the
City of Philadelphia ; containing in front or breadth on the said
          and extending of that width in length or depth
for   dollars and   cents, being the sum assessed
against said property as above described, in accordance with the Act of Assembly, approved the 1st day of April, 1864, as the benefit occasioned to it
by the opening of   '   street, as found and determined by a
jury of viewers, etc., appointed on the   day of
188 , by the Court of Quarter Sessions of the said City and County, and
the report of which jury was duly confirmed by said Court on the
          day of   , 188 , of all which said registered owner
had due notice as required by law, which sum of
dollars and   cents, together with the lawful interest, is
claimed as a lien against said premises, whoever may be the owner or
owners thereof, agreeably to the several Acts of Assembly in relation
thereto.

City Solicitor.

§ 501.

CLAIM FOR CULVERT.

The City of Philadelphia, to the use of	In the Court of Common Pleas, No.
v.	, for the County of Philadelphia: Term, 18 . No.
owner, or reputed owner, or whoever may be owner.	

The City of Philadelphia to the use of   file this their
claim against   owner or reputed owner , or whoever
may be owner , of all that certain lot or piece of ground

for work done and materials furnished, within six months, last past, in constructing a culvert on　　　　　　　in front of the said lot of ground, and premises, per bill and statement, as follows :　Philadelphia,

To　　　　　of culvert, at $　　　per foot,　　　$
Interest from
Five per cent. (Act March 23, 1856).

$

Amounting to　　　　　　　　　　dollars, for which sum, with interest thereon from the above date, a lien is claimed against the premises above described, whoever may be the owner or owners thereof, the said culvert having been duly petitioned for by owners of property fronting on said street where the culvert was constructed. Which said petition was presented to the Board of Surveyors of the City of Philadelphia, and thereupon the said board, by resolution approved by the Committee on Surveys of City Councils, did direct the said culvert to be constructed. And the cost and expenses of the construction of the said culvert are herein duly assessed and charged at the just value thereof, against the lot of ground and premises above described, agreeably to the several Acts of Assembly of the Commonwealth of Pennsylvania, relating to municipal claims for paving, culverting, etc.

　　　　　　　　　　　　　　　　　　　　　　　City Solicitor.

　　　　　　　　Attorney pro Claimant.

§ 502.

CLAIM FOR WATER-PIPE.

The City of Philadelphia *v.* 　　　　　owner, or reputed owner, and　　　　registered owner, or whoever may be owner.	In the Court of Common Pleas, No. 　, for the City and County of Philadelphia, of Term, 188 . No. .

The " City of Philadelphia " hereby files its claim against all that certain piece or lot or piece of ground　　　　　　　situate on the side of　　　　　　　　　　at a distance of from the　　　　　　side of　　　　　　　in the Ward of the City of Philadelphia ; containing in front or breadth on the said　　　　　　　　　　and extending of that width in length or depth 　　　　　　　　　　for work done and materials furnished by the said city, in laying water-pipe in front of said lot, and duly assessed and charged as follows, to wit :

　　　　　　　　　　　　188
To　　　feet　　　　inches of water-pipe @ $1.00 per foot, $
　　　　　　　　　　dollars,　　　　　　　　cents, which sum, together with the lawful interest, is claimed as a lien against said premises, whoever may be the owner or owners thereof, agreeably to the several Acts of Assembly in relation thereto.

　　　　　　　　　　　　　　　　　　　　　　　City Solicitor.

§ 503.

CLAIM FOR REMOVING NUISANCE.

The City of Philadelphia

v.

registered owner, or reputed owner,
or whoever may be owner.

In the Court of Common Pleas, No.
, in and for the City and County
of Philadelphia, of
Term, 18 . No.

Whereas, the Board of Health of the City of Philadelphia have removed a nuisance from a lot of ground, situate　　　　　　　　　, which nuisance consisted of　　　　　　　　and after due notice to the said
registered owner, or reputed owner,
to remove said nuisance, and non-compliance with said notice on
part, it was removed by the said Board of Health; which said work was done on the　　　　　　　　day of　　　　　　　　eighteen hundred and ninety-　　　　, and in the doing of which, on said day, the said Board of Health incurred and paid　　　　　　　　　dollars and　　　　　cents and expenses thereof—the following being a Bill of Particulars of said expenses, to wit:

Now, the City of Philadelphia files in the said Court this its claim against the said　　　　　　　　　registered owner, or reputed owner, of said lot, and every other person or persons owners thereof, and against the said lot of ground and every part thereof, the sum of
dollars, which said sum was the expense incurred in the removal of said nuisance, and, with lawful interest, is claimed as a lien against said premises, agreeably to the several Acts of Assembly in relation thereto.

City Solicitor.

§ 504.

CLAIM FOR PAVING AND REPAIRING SIDEWALK.

The City of Philadelphia

v.

owner, or reputed
owner, and　　　　　　　registered
owner, or whoever may be owner.

In the Court of Common Pleas,
No. , for the City and County
of Philadelphia, of
Term, 188 , No.

The "City of Philadelphia" hereby files its claim against all that certain lot or piece of ground　　　　　　　　situate on the
side of　　　　　　at the distance of　　　　　　　　from the
side of　　　　　　　in the　　　　　　　Ward
of the City of Philadelphia; containing in front or breadth on the said
　　　　　and extending of that width in length or depth
for work done and materials furnished by the said city, in　　paving and repairing the sidewalk, and　　　setting the curbstone in front of said lot, and duly assessed and charged as follows, to wit:

188 .

To   cubic yards of footway grading, @   cents per yard, $
To   square yards of footway   paving, @   cents per yard, $
To   feet   curbstone   set @   cents per foot, $
To curb regulations $
To measuring charge $

                                                    Total, $

     •   dollars,   cents, which sum, together with the lawful
interest, is claimed as a lien against said premises, whoever may be the
owner or owners thereof, agreeably to the several Acts of Assembly in relation thereto ; the said work having been done by the chief commissioner
of highways of the city of Philadelphia, in pursuance of the directions contained in the ordinance of the Select and Common Councils of the said city
of Philadelphia, approved the seventh day of June, A.D, 1882, after due
notice to the said registered owner.

                                                    City Solicitor.

§ 505.

CLAIM FOR REGISTERED TAXES.

The City of Philadelphia

          v.

                    owner or reputed
owner, or whoever may be owner, and
          registered owner.

In the Court of Common Pleas,
No. , for the City and County
of Philadelphia, of
Term, 188 , No. . M. L. D.

     The city of Philadelphia hereby files a claim against all that certain lot
or piece of ground situate on the   of   in
the   Ward of the city of Philadelphia, at the distance
of
On which is erected   for
city taxes, duly rated and assessed upon said property, and registered for
non-payment according to law, together with the interest and other charges
lawfully done thereon, as follows, to wit :

          City tax for the year 18   .   .   .   . $
          Interest   .   .   .   .   .   .
          City tax for the year 18   .   .   .   .
          Interest   .   .   .   .   .   .
          City tax for the year 18   .   .   .   .
          Interest   .   .   .   .   .   .
          City tax for the year 18   .   .   .   .
          Interest   .   .   .   .   .   .
          City tax for the year 18   .   .   .   .
          Interest   .   .   .   .   .   .
          Commissions and cost .   .   .   .   .

          Altogether being the sum of .   .   .   . $

(dollars and   cents), with interest from the date of .
filing, which is claimed as a lien against said premises, whoever may be the

owner or owners thereof, agreeably to the several Acts of Assembly in relation thereto.

Solicitor for Receiver of Taxes for
the City of Philadelphia.

§ 506.

WHERE OWNER WISHES TO SAVE COSTS HE MAY DO SO IN AN AMICABLE
ACTION.

City of Philadelphia		Docket page
v.	}	C. P., No. , Term, 18 .
		No. . M. L. D.

And now, to wit :   , 188 , it is hereby agreed
between the above-named plaintiff and defendant that an amicable action
of *scire facias* be entered in the above case, with the same effect as if a writ
of *scire facias sur* municipal claim had been issued, returnable on the first
Monday of   and duly returned by the sheriff " made known."

Preliminary notice is waived.

§ 507. *For forms for præcipes,* see sections 204 and 205, omitting
the word *mechanic's.*

For *judgment* for want of appearance, see sections 23, 171, and
383.

For judgment for want of affidavit of defense, see sections 23
and 383 ; or for want of sufficient affidavit of defense, sections 27
and 28.

For *assessment of damages,* see sections 23 and 171.

If you are driven to demanding a plea, see section 204.

The execution is by *levari facias,* as in section 205.

CHAPTER XIII.

THE COMMENCEMENT AND PROSECUTION OF ACTIONS FOR SLAN-
DER, LIBEL, MALICIOUS PROSECUTION, FALSE IMPRISONMENT,
SEDUCTION, CONSPIRACY, CRIM. CON., ENTICING AWAY AP-
PRENTICE, ACTIONS FOR DAMAGES OCCASIONED BY NEGLI-
GENCE, TROVER, TRESPASS VI ET ARMIS, NEGLIGENCE OF
OFFICIALS, AND TORTS GENERALLY.

§ 508. **Consolidation of actions in tort.** The second section of
the Act of May 25, 1887 (section 61 of this book), declares,
" That so far as relates to procedure, the distinctions heretofore
existing between actions *ex delicto* be abolished, and that all damages heretofore recoverable in trespass, trover, or trespass on the
case, shall hereafter be sued for and recovered in one form of action, to be called ' an action of trespass.' "

§ 509. **Advantages of the Act of 1887.** Before the passage of
this Act, the elaboration of the various suits named in the title to
this chapter would have required a volume. Fortunately for the
pleader and client, much labor is saved by the new law. Those
who admire the intricacies of special pleading and the fine-spun distinctions between actions of. trespass *vi et armis* and actions on the
case, may, perhaps, complain of the Act. It probably has its imperfections; but that it confers a blessing upon the attorney and
client can hardly be doubted by any person who will take the
trouble to recall Chitty's capital directions as to the form of the
action. Was the injury committed *with force* or without force?
Was it immediate and direct, or mediate and consequential?
Think of the consolation derived from this warning: " It is
FREQUENTLY DIFFICULT to determine when the injury is to be
considered forcible or not, and when immediate and consequential,
and, therefore, when trespass or case is the proper remedy." (1
Chitty's Pl., 125.) Accordingly the student was assisted by this
author in twenty printed pages of directions and over two hundred
citations, in order to decide in doubtful cases upon the simple question of the form of the writ. The glories of all this uncertainty
are further shown by the decisions of Pennsylvania courts, cited
under the head " *When case lies*," and the citations under the opposite head " *When trespass lies.*"

§ 510. Perhaps no better illustration of the uncertainty of the law could be found than in a comparison of the two cases of *Maher* v. *Ashmead*, 30 Pa. St., 344 (1858), and *Royer* v. *Swazey*, 10 W. N., 432 (1881). In both the plaintiff below had been arrested upon criminal process and had been discharged. In the first suit the injured party brought an action on the case. After several verdicts and new trials, she at last got a judgment below. But the Supreme Court reversed ; because, although the arrest had been made upon a warrant, yet the process did not charge a crime. The action should, therefore, have been trespass. With this before him, the counsel of the plaintiff in the second suit brought trespass *vi et armis*. The words of the warrant are not given in the report. The court below non-suited the plaintiff and the Supreme Court affirmed the judgment, holding that the process, being lawful, the abuse of it was to be redressed by an action on the case. Thus each plaintiff was defeated upon the merest technicality.

§ 511. **Capias in cases of torts.** For all matters treated of in this chapter, a capias can issue where the defendant is a male or an unmarried female, and not a freeholder. The exemption of women from arrest for debt is noted, section 46. In *Vocht* v. *Kuklence*, 119 Pa. St., 365 (1888), and *Whalen* v. *Gabell*, 120 Pa. St., 284 (1888), the exemption of *married* women from arrest upon capias in actions of *tort* is justified. The exemption in *tort* does not extend to *femes sole ; Comm.* ex rel. *McDowell* v. *Keeper*, 11 W. N., 341 (1882) ; *Klein's Est.*, 1 W. N., 250 (1875). The privilege of freeholders is cited, section 45. The essentials of the affidavit to hold to bail and subsequent steps are described, section 40. Your *præcipe* for the capias, instead of *assumpsit*, says " an action of trespass." *Affidavit for capias*, see section 40.

§ 512.

FORM OF AFFIDAVIT TO HOLD TO BAIL IN SLANDER.

A. B. ⎫
   v. ⎬
C. D. ⎭

City and County of Philadelphia, *ss.*

A. B., on oath, says that he has been for many years a salesman, and has resided in Philadelphia upward of   years.

Deponent further saith that C. D., on or about the   day of at Philadelphia, spoke of and concerning deponent in the presence and hearing of a number of persons the following false, scandalous, and malicious words. " He (deponent) set fire to dry goods store in Louisville, Kentucky, and left there without paying his (deponent's) debts. ' Thereby meaning to charge deponent with the crime of arson and with defrauding his creditors. Deponent further saith that both of said charges are untrue, and that he has never been guilty of said offenses, or either of them, or been heretofore suspected of the same. Deponent has sustained, by reason of the grievances above mentioned, loss to an amount exceeding $1000 in business and character.

Sworn to and subscribed before me, }

§ 513. Sometimes it may be important to accompany the plaintiff's affidavit with the affidavit of another person :

A. B. }
   v. }
C. D. }

City and County of Philadelphia, *ss.*

E. F., a resident of the City of Philadelphia, having been duly affirmed according to law, doth depose and say, that during the latter part of
                or the first of this present month, he heard the above-named defendant, C. D., speak of and concerning the plaintiff, A. B., the following words, to wit: "there was a man poisoned me, and his wife is a member of our church;" deponent asked C. D. who he was; C. D., the defendant, replied, "God Almighty knows that I" (said defendant meaning) "have been poisoned by A. B." (the plaintiff meaning).

Deponent further saith that these words were spoken in the presence and hearing of deponent and of a number of persons. Deponent has known plaintiff for some time ; he is a man of family and apparent respectability and integrity.

Affirmed and subscribed before me, }

A. B. }
   v. }
C. D. }

City and County of Philadelphia, *ss.*

A. B., having been duly sworn according to law, doth depose and say that he is now a resident of this county, and has so resided here for seventeen years last past.

Deponent is a man of family, hath always led an upright and honest life, and never been guilty of poisoning, of attempting to murder, or of any crime whatever, nor has deponent ever been suspected of the same until the committing of the grievances hereinafter set forth.

Deponent further saith, that on or about the
               , at this county of Philadelphia, C. D., the defendant, spoke of and concerning deponent, and in the presence and hearing of a number of persons, the following false, scandalous, malicious, and defamatory words, to wit: "A. B." (deponent meaning) "has poisoned me" (defendant meaning), and also that on   at the said county, said C. D., defendant, said to deponent, in the presence and hearing of a number of persons, the following false and scandalous words, to wit: "You" (deponent meaning) "have poisoned me" (defendant meaning), thereby charging deponent with the crime of attempting to kill and murder. Deponent further saith that both of said charges are wholly false, and that defendant knew the same to be untrue. The defendant, C. D., is a man of apparent respectability and means, and one whose position would be calculated to give credit to such a report. Deponent further saith that this slander has been frequently repeated by the defendant, and that it has to a great extent injured deponent's reputation and affected his character.

Deponent verily believes that if defendant is not held to bail he will leave the jurisdiction of this court to avoid service of process.

It is impossible for deponent to fix the amount of his damages exactly, but he estimates the same to be at least the sum of $1000.

Sworn to and subscribed before me, }

§ 514.

AFFIDAVIT TO HOLD TO BAIL, CONSPIRACY TO SLANDER, TO FALSELY ARREST, ETC.

A. B. }
v.
C. D. and E. F. }

City and County of Philadelphia, *ss.*

A. B., having been duly sworn according to law, doth depose and say:

That on the   A. D.,   at the County of Philadelphia, C. D. and E. F. illegally and wrongfully combined and conspired together to injure deponent—to slander him, and to prosecute him, and arrest him falsely and maliciously, and without any reasonable or probable cause whatever. In pursuance of said illegal conspiracy C. D. procured E. F. to go before   Esq., one of the magistrates of the city of Philadelphia (then and there having jurisdiction to issue warrants for misdemeanors, felonies, etc.), and on the day and year aforesaid, at the county aforesaid, falsely and maliciously, and without any reasonable or probable cause, to charge this deponent on oath with having received a large sum of money, and with being about to leave this country with intent to defraud deponent's creditors. On which false charge the said C. D. and E. F. procured from the said magistrate a warrant under his hand and seal for the apprehending of deponent, and on said warrant the said C. D. and E. F. procured deponent to be arrested by his body and taken before said magistrate, and held to bail in the sum of $1000 (to prevent a commitment being issued) for deponent's appearance on the

•   day of   at   o'clock, A.M. And deponent having appeared before said magistrate at said time, and no one having appeared to sustain said prosecution at either hearing, deponent was honorably discharged, and said prosecution is fully ended and determined.

Deponent further saith, that in pursuance of the unlawful combination aforesaid, the said C. D., on or about the   day of   at the county aforesaid, in the presence and hearing of several persons, spoke the following false and scandalous words of and concerning deponent, in substance, to wit: " A. B." (deponent meaning) "is about to leave the country and cheat his creditors," thereby meaning to charge deponent with a design to cheat and defraud his creditors.

Deponent is by occupation a manufacturer of glass, and is largely engaged in that business—to the extent of $50,000 per annum, as nearly as deponent can state the same. His credit and business character are all important to him, and he believes that the wrongs above detailed were committed with the view of injuring him in his aforesaid lawful calling.

The slander above mentioned was repeated by said C. D. to persons with whom deponent was dealing, and had reference to his said business.

Deponent avers that said criminal charge and slander were wholly false, and that both the said C. D. and E. F. knew said charge and slander to be entirely without foundation.

By means of these said grievances deponent has been put to inconvenience, in being compelled to neglect his business; has been obliged to expend money in order to defend said prosecution; has been exposed by the aforesaid arrest; and has sustained in feeling, business, and character damage to a large amount, to wit, to at least the sum of
dollars.

Deponent firmly believes that unless said parties are held to bail they will leave this jurisdiction to avoid suit.

Sworn to and subscribed before me, }

§ 515.

AFFIDAVIT TO HOLD TO BAIL, TRESPASS, BREAKING INTO A DWELLING, ETC.

A. B.
   v.
C. D. and E. F. } •

City and County of Philadelphia, *ss.*

A. B., the plaintiff, having been solemnly affirmed according to law, affirms and says:

That heretofore, to wit, on the   day of   A.D.
   C. D. and E. F., with force and arms, unlawfully broke into and entered the dwelling-house of said A. B., situate and being in the county of Philadelphia; and with force and arms unlawfully broke the door of deponent's said dwelling-house (describe all the acts complained of), and other wrongs to deponent then and there did, whereby deponent hath been greatly injured and otherwise sustained damage, to wit, to the amount of
dollars.

Affirmed and subscribed before me, }

§ 516.

AFFIDAVIT TO HOLD TO BAIL, DECEIT, FRAUD.

A. B.
  v.
C. D. }

City and County of Philadelphia, *ss.*

A. B., having been duly sworn according to law, doth depose and say:

That on the   day of   A.D.
at the city of Philadelphia, C. D. obtained from this deponent
dollars of the moneys of deponent by fraud and false pretenses. On the day and year aforesaid the said C. D. had a certain horse which he knew to be diseased and unsound; and for the purpose of defrauding deponent out of   dollars the said C. D. then and there falsely, fraudulently, knowingly, and deceitfully represented to deponent that said horse was sound; and by means of such deceitful, false, and fraudulent representation deponent was induced to purchase said horse and pay said C. D. therefor the sum of   dollars; whereas, in truth and in fact, the said horse was then and there unsound and diseased, and was so known to be to the said C. D., and by reason of such unsoundness and disease the said horse was useless and of no value, and deponent was injured to the amount of   dollars and upward. The said C. D. is about to leave the city.

Sworn to and subscribed before me, }

§ 517. **Allocatur.** In all cases it must be remembered that the rules of court should be consulted when an *allocatur* is required. Present the affidavit to judge with the words indorsed : *Bail allowed, $* . The judge fixes the amount. Write your *prœcipe* (form, section 40), omitting the word *assumpsit* and inserting " in an action of trespass."

§ 518. **Affidavits to hold to Bail in other cases.** It is unnecessary to multiply forms of affidavits to fit all supposable cases. The attorney can easily prepare an affidavit by consulting the foregoing, by studying the statements, and by using the essential words applicable to the particular case.

In an action of libel for charging the teacher of a school with carelessness in keeping account of money, special damage is sufficiently alleged for the purpose of holding to bail, by an allegation that persons who would otherwise have come to the plaintiff to be taught have been kept away by means of said libel. *Bériac* v. *Wellhoff*, 27 W. N., 53 (1890).

§ 519. **Præcipe for summons in tort.** In all these actions, when begun by summons, your *prœcipe* can follow this form :

A.
 v.
B.

SIR :

Issue summons in an action of trespass, returnable *sec. leg.*

          C.,
        Plaintiff's Attorney.
         (Date.)

To Prothonotary of Common Pleas (state the county).

See sections 10, 11, 12, etc.

§ 520. **After the writ is issued,** note on it the defendant's address ; give to sheriff with directions. See section 16. As to rule to show cause of action and why defendant shall not be discharged on common bail, rule to quash the writ, etc., see § 44.

§ 521. **Statement to be filed in actions of tort.** Instead of the old declaration, you must file a " concise statement," as required by the Act of 1887, § 3. See section 61.

The statement must be signed by the plaintiff or his attorney. A signature to the *jurat* is sufficient. *Tilley* v. *Rowe*, 23 W. N., 491 (1889).

An explicit averment of the amount claimed should be made, but damages in trespass need not always be set out by items. A claim " for pain and suffering, loss of time, medical attendance, and medicines, and for injuries to his (plaintiff's) shoulder and head, in the sum of five thousand dollars," was *held* sufficiently specific under the Act of 1887. *Schnable* v. *Schmidt*, 21 W. N., 153 (1888).

The distinctions between actions in *tort* and those upon contracts is not abolished by the Act. Where negligence is the gist of the action, the plaintiff cannot waive the *tort* and file a statement in *assumpsit*. *Krause* v. *R. R. Co.*, 20 W. N., 111 (1887). But if the statement be in *tort* upon a writ of *assumpsit*, or *vice versa*, the variance cannot be taken advantage of. *Id.*

In deceit a *scienter* must be alleged and proved. *Griswold* v. *Gebbie*, 24 W. N., 72 (1889).

§ 522. **Affidavit to Statement.** This is required in Philadelphia even to statements in *tort*. See Rules of Court, section 18 of this book, and *Krauskopf* v. *Stern*, 21 W. N., 185 (1888).

The affidavit may be made by either the legal or the equitable plaintiff, or by plaintiff's attorney. *Schick* v. *Goenner*, 21 W. N., 63 (1888).

If the affidavit be made by a stranger, cause must be shown why the plaintiff did not swear to the statement. *Tombler* v. *Dinan*, 4 Pa. C. C., 309 (1888). See § 539.

§ 523. **Particularity of Statement and Affidavit required in Philadelphia.** As to this, see section 18 of this book.

§ 524. **Time of filing Statement.** According to the language of the Act, the statement can be filed and served fifteen days before the return-day of the writ, or on the return-day, or at any time thereafter.

In *Weigley* v. *Teal*, 23 W. N., 521 (1889), the Supreme Court held that the statement in *assumpsit* might be filed and served at any time, and that judgment for want of an affidavit of defense could be taken fifteen days afterward, provided that a return-day had intervened. The language of the court in this case is quite general, and it appears applicable also to the action of trespass, and to judgment for want of an appearance. The summons issued October 22, 1888, returnable November 5th. On October 24th the statement was filed and served. On November 14th the plaintiff took a rule for judgment, which was made absolute on November 24th.

" In the present case the judgment was entered more than fifteen days after the return-day and service of the statement. The filing and service before the return-day was certainly as effective as would have been a filing and service on the return-day. To hold otherwise would be sticking in the bark. The Act should be so construed as to effectuate the intention of the legislature. It was never intended that there should be a *hiatus* of fourteen days next preceding the return-day, in which the plaintiff can neither file nor serve his statement of claim." Judgment affirmed, per STER-RETT, J.

§ 525. **No affidavit of defense in torts.** The affidavit of defense required by the statute is in " the action of *assumpsit*; " none is required in trespass.

§ 526. **Essentials of statements in particular actions.** In addition to the suggestions of sections 63–73, it may be proper to note the special requirements of certain cases.

§ 527. *Statements in slander and libel.* Whatever the law of libel may have been in criminal cases, the rule in civil cases has always been that the truth was and is a justification. The *narrs.* in slander and libel have always charged that the words uttered or written were false. Malice, and, in proper cases, special damage, should also be averred. Upon this subject, see *Moore* v. *Rowbotham*, 44 Leg. Int., 264 (1887).

It must be remembered that while the Act of 1887 has dispensed with the need of much of the unnecessary verbiage formerly used, averments essential to the action must still be made.

Pleaders should observe these and other requirements, for although the courts have been liberal, it is easier to avoid a demurrer than to answer it.

§ 528. *Innuendoes.* The innuendo explains the words used, but it cannot change or enlarge their meaning. Whether the innuendo is sustained by the words is generally a question for the jury. Save where the words are actionable in themselves, special damage must be alleged. Spoken words are actionable in themselves when they impute the commission of a punishable offense which involves moral turpitude, or having a loathsome disease likely to exclude the plaintiff from society. Words which are not actionable in themselves become so when they are spoken of a person in his profession, office, or trade, and necessarily or naturally tend to injure him therein. If the words were spoken or written in a foreign language, they should be set out in the original, followed by a translation; and in such case it should be averred in the statement in slander that the words were understood by those who heard them.

The innuendo cannot be shown by the opinion of witnesses as to the impression they took from the language. *Rwy. Co.* v. *McCurdy*, 19 W. N., 163 (1886).

§ 529. *Form of Statement in Libel.* The following may serve as a form in libel. It was filed in a case in which the plaintiff held a public office and had been charged with exacting from his employés a portion of their wages. The pleader will, of course, understand that the facts do not exactly agree in any two cases. The averments here employed must be changed to meet the proofs. The plaintiff may be a professional man, or the libel may not have any reference to his calling.

§ 530.

FORM OF STATEMENT IN LIBEL, THE PLAINTIFF BEING AN OFFICIAL.

A. B.   C. P., No. .
   v.   September Term, 188 .
C. D.   No. .

The plaintiff, A. B., claims of the defendant, C. D., the sum of   , which sum is justly due and payable to the plaintiff by the defendant upon the cause of action whereof the following is a statement :

That at the time of the committing by C. D. of the grievances hereinafter mentioned, plaintiff was and for a long time prior thereto had been a public officer of the city of Philadelphia, to wit   plaintiff was first appointed to the position about   and has held said office to the present time. During this period plaintiff has enjoyed not only the confidence of his official superiors, but the esteem and respect of all who knew him and of the community in general. Plaintiff has never been guilty of (*receiving bribes, of taking money from employés*), or any similar offense ; but has on the contrary always discharged his duties with strict integrity.

And plaintiff further saith that C. D., who resides at No. Street, Philadelphia, well knowing the premises, and intending to injure plaintiff and to deprive him of his good name, and further wickedly intending to cause plaintiff to be removed from his said office, on the   day of   last past, at the city of Philadelphia, did falsely, maliciously, wickedly, and illegally make and publish of and concerning plaintiff and of and concerning plaintiff, as   aforesaid, the following false, scandalous, illegal, defamatory, and malicious writing and libel, in substance as follows : (Here you set out the words of the libel, and state how it was published, whether in a newspaper or otherwise.)

And plaintiff further saith that the charge in said writing (or publication) contained against him is false ; that (here negative the charges of the libel).

And plaintiff further saith that C. D. well knew said charges to be untrue when he made them.

And plaintiff further saith that said letter (or publication) is a false and malicious libel. Plaintiff denies the truth of all charges so injuriously made against him in said

By reason of this libel (or these libels) plaintiff has been brought into reproach, said charges have been widely published, and plaintiff has suffered in character and in feelings to an amount which exceeds five thousand dollars. Wherefore he brings suit.

L. M.,
pro Plaintiff.
(Date.)

(Affidavit.)

Where special damage is alleged to support an action for words not actionable *per se*, the statement should set out the names of parties prevented from dealing with the plaintiff. *Bériac* v. *Wellhoff*, 27 **W. N.**, 96 (1890).

§ 531. *Statements in Slander* should aver that the words were false, scandalous, malicious, and defamatory, and that they were uttered in the presence and hearing of others. See § 539.

§ 532. The following form may be used for a statement :

A. B.	C. P., No. .
v.	September Term, 188 .
C. D.	No. .

The plaintiff, A. B., claims of the defendant, C. D., the sum of   ,
which sum is justly due and payable to the plaintiff by the defendant upon the cause of action whereof the following is a statement :

That the said A. B. is a good, true, honest, and virtuous inhabitant of this Commonwealth, and as such from the time of his nativity hitherto hath demeaned and behaved himself, and from all and all manner of larceny and all such enormous crimes has for the space of his past life until the time of speaking and uttering the false, scandalous, malicious, and defamatory words hereafter mentioned to have been spoken, remained free and unsuspected. And the said A. B. was esteemed and reputed a person of good name, fame, credit, and reputation ; by reason whereof he had gained the love, good will, and esteem of all his neighbors and divers other good people of this Commonwealth. (If the plaintiff has been injured in his trade or calling, add.) And whereas also the said A. B. for a long time past, and before the speaking and uttering the false, scandalous, and defamatory words hereafter mentioned to have been spoken, followed and carried on the lawful art, trade, and business of a (here state the trade, etc.), and by means thereof gained and acquired many large sums of money. Nevertheless, the said C. D. contriving the said A. B. not only to deprive of his good name, fame, and credit aforesaid, and to bring him into scandal and disrepute among his neighbors, but also to subject the said A. B. to prosecution and punishment for larceny, on the   day of
one thousand eight hundred and   at the county aforesaid, to the said A. B. and in his presence and the presence and hearing of others did speak and publish the following false, scandalous, malicious, and defamatory words, to wit : " You " (the said plaintiff meaning) " stole my money ;" thereby meaning and intending to charge the said A. B. with the crime of larceny. (If the slander has been repeated to other persons, you can charge thus—and the said C. D. further, on the   day
of   in the year last aforesaid, at the county aforesaid, in the presence and hearing of other persons, did speak and publish of and concerning the said A. B. other false, scandalous, malicious, and defamatory words, to wit : " He " (the plaintiff meaning) " is a thief ;" thereby meaning and intending the said A. B., plaintiff, to charge with the crime of larceny. (And so in as many different forms as the defendant has repeated the slander the plaintiff is at liberty to charge it.) And the said A. B. in fact saith that he is nowise guilty of the said several larcenies by the said false, scandalous, and defamatory words so injuriously laid to his charge ; by reason whereof the said A. B. has not only been greatly hurt and injured in his good name, fame, and reputation aforesaid, and been brought into disgrace and disrepute among his neighbors and divers other persons, who ever since the speaking and uttering the said several false, scandalous, and

defamatory words so vehemently, suspected him of having been guilty of larceny, and as also being a person meriting punishment, that they have refused to have any communion or conversation with him, but he the said A. B. has been subjected and made liable to prosecution and punishment for the said crime of larceny. (If your client has been injured in his trade or calling, you add—and the said A. B. further in fact saith, that divers persons who used to have dealing and business with him, the said A. B., in his said lawful art, trade, and business, and by means of whom the said A. B. had gained large sums of money, have ever since the speaking and uttering the said several false, scandalous, and defamatory words, refused to have dealings or business with the said A. B.) Whereupon the said A. B. has sustained and claims damages to the value of five thousand dollars, and therefore brings suit.

E. F.,
Attorney pro plaintiff.
(Date.)

(Affidavit.)

§ 533. *Special damages*, such as loss of customers, expulsion from a church or lodge, etc., should be specially set out, with as much particularity as the case permits. For this no form can guide in all cases. Whatever the actual damage may have been, it is always susceptible of precise statement.

§ 534. *Inducement and form of inducement.* Sometimes a statement of particular matter is necessary. Wherever you expect to prove it you should aver it, and if your client know of it, there is no excuse for its omission. This, when put in the statement, should appear before the averment as to the words spoken. The following may explain this suggestion and supply a *form:*

And whereas the said A. B. before the committing of the grievances hereinafter mentioned had bought of one G. H. a large quantity of lumber, to wit (mention quantity), for a certain price, to be paid by the said A. B. to the said G. H., at a certain time not elapsed at the time of the committing of the grievances hereinafter charged,

then, after charging the slander as above stated, in the conclusion of the statement after the averment of general damage you can insert the following :

§ 535.

AVERMENT OF SPECIAL DAMAGE.

And thereby also, afterward and before the time appointed for the payment of the price of said lumber so purchased by plaintiff of G. H., when the said plaintiff requested the said G. H. to deliver said lumber to said plaintiff, the said G. H. wholly refused to deliver the same or any part thereof unless the plaintiff would before such delivery pay the price thereof, and in order to procure the delivery of said lumber the plaintiff was forced to pay and did pay G. H. the sum of   dollars at the city aforesaid on (date). The said refusal of G. H. being by reason of the aforesaid (slander or libel).

§ 536.

AVERMENT OF SPECIAL DAMAGE IN LOSS OF A CUSTOMER.

And thereby also one E. F., who, before and at the time of the committing of the said grievances, had been used and accustomed to deal with and who otherwise would have continued to deal with the said plaintiff in the way of his aforesaid trade and business, hath from thence hitherto wholly neglected and refused so to do.

See *Bériac* v. *Wellhoff*, 27 W. N., 96 (1890).

§ 537.

ANOTHER AVERMENT OF SPECIAL DAMAGE IN LOSS OF CUSTOM, THE PLAINTIFF KEEPING A BATHING-HOUSE.

By reason and by means of the committing the said grievances, and on no other account whatsoever, I. K. and family, L. M., N. O., P. Q., and divers other persons who would otherwise have frequented and bathed in and from the said rooms, with the appurtenances, of the said plaintiff, and paid him certain reward in that behalf, have, on the occasion of the committing of the said grievances by the said defendant, wholly declined and neglected so to do ; and the said plaintiff hath thereby lost and been deprived of divers great gains and profits which might and would have otherwise arisen and accrued to him from the said persons so bathing in the said rooms, with the appurtenances, as aforesaid, and the said plaintiff hath been and is by reason of the committing of the said several grievances, otherwise greatly injured and damnified, to wit, at the city aforesaid, to the damage of the said plaintiff of five thousand dollars.

§ 538.

FORM OF STATEMENT FOR SLANDER OF TITLE OF REAL ESTATE.

A. B.   }   C. P., No.   .
  v.   }   September Term, 188 :
C. D.   }   No.   .

The plaintiff, A. B., claims of the defendant, C. D., the sum of   , which sum is justly due and payable to the plaintiff by the defendant upon the cause of action, whereof the following is a statement :

The said plaintiff, before and at the time of the committing of the grievances by the said defendant hereinafter mentioned, was seized as in fee and in the reversion of and in certain land with the appurtenances, situate, lying, and being on   in the county of   immediately expectant upon the death of one E. F., who was then seized of the same premises in her demesne as of freehold, for the term of her natural life. The said plaintiff before and at the time of the committing the grievances hereinafter mentioned, was desirous of selling his said estate and interest by public auction, and for that purpose the said plaintiff, before and at the time of the committing of the said grievances, to wit, on   at   caused his said estate and interest to be, and the same then and there were put up and exposed to sale by public auction by one G. H., as the auctioneer and agent of the said plaintiff, in order that the same might be then and there sold for the said plaintiff. Yet the said defendant, well knowing the premises, but contriving and falsely and fraudulently intending to injure the said plaintiff and to cause it to be suspected and believed that the said plaintiff had no title, estate, or interest of, in, or to the said land with the appurtenances, and to hinder and prevent the said plaintiff from selling or disposing of his said estate or interest in the same, and to cause and procure the said plaintiff to sustain and be put to divers great expenses attending the said exposure to sale, and to vex, harass, oppress, impoverish, and wholly ruin the said plaintiff, heretofore, to wit, on   aforesaid, at   aforesaid, wrongfully and injuriously, falsely and maliciously caused and procured a certain person, to wit, one W. M., to attend and be present at and upon such exposure to sale of the said plaintiff's estate and interest as aforesaid, and then and there, upon such exposure to sale, and before the said estate and interest had been sold and disposed of, falsely and maliciously caused and procured the said W. M. to assert and represent, and the said W. M. did then and there accordingly, falsely, maliciously, and wickedly say in the presence and hearing of divers persons then and there present at and upon such exposure to sale as aforesaid, of and concerning the said plaintiff, and of and concerning the said G. H., so being such auctioneer as aforesaid, and of and concerning the said land with the appurtenances, and the said plaintiff's estate and the interest therein, that (here set out the words with the appropriate innuendoes). By means of the committing of said several grievances by the said defendant as aforesaid, divers of the said persons who were so present at and upon the said exposure to sale as aforesaid, and who were then and there about to be and become purchasers of the said estate and interest of the said plaintiff, and who might and would otherwise have bid for and purchased the same, especially I. K., who was then and there about to bid for and who would otherwise have purchased the same, were then and there deterred and prevented from bidding for and becoming purchasers of the said estate and interest of the said plaintiff, and then and there, and from thence, have wholly declined to purchase the same, and thereby the said plaintiff was then and there hindered and prevented from selling and disposing of his said estate and interest, and hath thereby not only lost and been deprived of all the advantages and emoluments which he might and would have derived and acquired from the sale thereof, but has been forced and obliged to pay, lay out, and expend divers large sums of money, amounting in the whole to a large sum of money, to wit, the sum of   in and about the said exposure to sale, and   expenses incidental thereto, to wit, at the county aforesaid :

In addition to said sum of .   .   .   . $

the plaintiff claims for loss on sale of said property .   .

Amount of claim .   .   .   . $.

R. S.,

Plaintiff's Attorney.

(Date.)

(Affidavit.)

§ 539.

FORM OF STATEMENT—SLANDER AS TO PLAINTIFF'S SHIP.

A. B.   ⎫   C. P., No. .

  v.   ⎬   September Term, 188 .

C. D.   ⎭   No. .

The plaintiff, A. B., claims of the defendant, C. D., the sum of   , which sum is justly due and payable to the plaintiff by the defendant upon the cause of action, whereof the following is a statement :

Before and at the time of the said defendant committing the grievances hereinafter mentioned, at the city of Philadelphia, the said plaintiff was possessed as of his own property, of a certain ship or vessel called and which said ship or vessel one E. F., before and at the time of the committing the grievances hereinafter mentioned, was about to hire and would (had not such grievances been committed) have hired of the said plaintiff to go and proceed on a certain voyage for certain freight and reward to be therefor paid to the said plaintiff, nevertheless the said defendant, well knowing the premises, but contriving and wrongfully and maliciously intending to injure the said plaintiff, and to induce the said E. F. not to hire the said ship or vessel as aforesaid, and thereby to deprive the said plaintiff of all the profits, emoluments, rewards, and advantages he would have derived and acquired from the said ship or vessel being so hired as aforesaid, heretofore, to wit, on   at the city aforesaid, in a certain discourse which the said defendant then and there had with the said E. F., of and concerning the said ship or vessel, in the presence and hearing of the said E. F., falsely and maliciously spoke and published, of and concerning the said ship or vessel, the false, scandalous, and malicious words following, that is to say (here insert the words, as "When I saw her her keel was hove up eighteen inches in a straight line"), thereby then and there meaning that (here insert the proper innuendo and denial of the words—the following form serves only to illustrate this direction) the keel and floors of said ship were broken at the time when he, the said defendant, had seen the same, whereas in truth and in fact, at no time when he, the said defendant, saw the said ship or vessel, nor when he spoke and published the said slander as aforesaid, her keel was in any place hove up eighteen inches in a straight line, nor was the said ship or vessel in any manner imperfect as the said defendant so asserted and alleged as aforesaid. By means of the speaking and publishing of which said several false, scandalous, and malicious words as aforesaid by the said defendant, the said E. F., giving credit to and believing that the said representations and assertions were true, afterward, to wit,   at the city aforesaid, the said E. F. wholly refused to hire the said ship or vessel as aforesaid, and thereby the said plaintiff lost and was deprived of all the profits, emoluments, rewards, and advantages he would have derived of and from the said ship or vessel having been so hired as aforesaid ; and the said plaintiff hath been also, by means of the speaking and publishing the said several words as aforesaid, otherwise greatly injured and damnified, to wit, at the city of Philadelphia aforesaid, to the amount of five thousand dollars.

G. H.,
Plaintiff's Attorney.
(Date.)

(Affidavit.)

A declaration in slander need not aver to whom or at what place the slander was uttered, nor can a bill of particulars be required. *Thacher* v. *Schaeffer*, 19 W. N., 566 (1887).

The affidavit to a statement in slander, under the Act of 1887, set forth that the facts within the plaintiff's " own knowledge are true and just," and that those "stated upon information are just and true to the best of her knowledge, information, and belief, and she expects to be able to prove the same on the trial of the cause," and it was held sufficient. *Grimley* v. *Receveuve*, 21 W. N., 573 (1888).

§ 540. Malicious Prosecution. The statement should aver that the plaintiff has been a good citizen, and should then set out chronologically the different steps of the prosecution. The defendant, on a certain day, appeared before a magistrate, naming him, who had authority to administer oaths and issue warrants, and to bind defendants over for trial at the criminal court. The substance of the information, of the warrant, the fact of the arrest, of the binding over, of the prosecution of the case in the criminal court by the defendant, the return of a bill of indictment, the trial before the petit jury, the acquittal of the plaintiff, etc., should all be set forth. It should be averred that all of defendant's acts were false, malicious, and without any reasonable or probable cause. It should also be stated that the original prosecution is ended and determined, and that the final judgment was in favor of the plaintiff.

False Imprisonment. This action is akin to malicious prosecution. The gist of the action is the unlawful detention, and malice will be inferred from want of probable cause. *Colter* v. *Lower*, 35 *Ind.*, 285 (1871) ; *McCarthy* v. *De Armit*, 99 Pa. St., 63 (1881) ; *Neall* v. *Hart*, 115 Pa. St., 354 (1886).

§ 541.

FORM OF STATEMENT IN MALICIOUS PROSECUTION.

A. B.   }   C. P., No. .
  v.   }   September Term, 188 .
C. D.   }   No. .

The plaintiff, A. B., claims of the defendant, C. D., the sum of   , which sum is justly due and payable to the plaintiff by the defendant upon the cause of action, whereof the following is a statement :

The said plaintiff now is a good, true, honest, just, and faithful citizen, and as such hath always behaved and conducted himself, and hath not ever been guilty, or until the time of the committing of the several grievances by the said defendant, as hereinafter mentioned, been suspected to have been guilty (of felony), or of any other such crime, by means whereof the said plaintiff, before the committing of the said several grievances by the said defendant, as hereinafter mentioned, had deservedly obtained and acquired the good opinion and credit of all his neighbors and other good citizens at the city of Philadelphia ; yet the said defendant, well knowing the premises, but contriving and maliciously intending to injure the said plaintiff in his aforesaid good name, fame, and credit, and to bring him into public scandal, infamy, and disgrace, and to cause the said plaintiff to be imprisoned for a long space of time, and thereby to impoverish, oppress, and wholly ruin him, heretofore, to wit, on (date of warrant), at the city aforesaid, went and appeared before one E. F., Esq., then and there being one of the magistrates in and for the city and county of Philadelphia, and also to hear and determine divers felonies, trespasses, and other misdemeanors committed in the said county, and to bind over and commit for the same, and then and there, before the said E. F., so being such magistrate as aforesaid, to wit, at the city aforesaid, the said C. D. falsely and maliciously and without any reasonable or probable cause whatsoever, charged the said plaintiff with having [feloniously stolen a certain gold watch of the said defendant], and upon such charge the said defendant falsely and maliciously, and without any reasonable or probable cause whatsoever, caused and procured the said E. F., so being such magistrate as aforesaid, to make and grant his certain warrant, under his hand and seal, for the apprehending and taking of the said plaintiff, and for bringing the said plaintiff before him, the said E. F. (recite the warrant correctly), or some other magistrate for the said county of Philadelphia, to be dealt with according to law for the said supposed offense. And the said defendant, under and by virtue of the said warrant, afterward, to wit, on the day and year last aforesaid, to wit, at the city aforesaid, wrongfully, unlawfully, unjustly, and without any reasonable cause whatsoever, caused and procured the said plaintiff to be arrested by his body, and to be imprisoned, and kept and detained in prison for a long space of time, to wit, for the space of two hours, then next following, and until he, the said defendant, afterward, to wit, on the day and year last aforesaid, at the county aforesaid, falsely and maliciously, and without any reasonable or probable cause whatsoever, caused and procured the said plaintiff to be carried and conveyed in custody before the said E. F., so being such magistrate as aforesaid (if the plaintiff was committed for further examination, then insert this averment), and to be committed by the said magistrate for a further examination to the prison of the said county, and there, to wit, in the said prison, the said defendant then and there, falsely and maliciously, and without any reasonable or probable cause whatsoever, caused and procured the said plaintiff to be imprisoned, and to be kept and detained in prison for a long space of time, to wit, for the space of two days then next following, and until he, the said defendant, afterward, to wit, on   falsely and maliciously, and without any reasonable or probable cause whatsoever, caused and procured the said plaintiff to be carried and conveyed in custody before the said magistrate, to be examined before the said magistrate touching and concerning the said supposed crime. The said magistrate, having heard and considered all that the said defendant could say or allege against the said plaintiff touching and concerning the said supposed offense, then and there, to wit, on the day and year last aforesaid, at the city aforesaid, adjudged and determined that the said plaintiff was not guilty of the said supposed offense, and then and there caused the said plaintiff to be discharged out of custody, fully acquitted and discharged of the said supposed offense ; and the said defendant hath not further prosecuted his said complaint, but hath deserted and abandoned the same, and the said complaint and prosecution are wholly ended and determined, to wit, at the city aforesaid.

(If, instead of having been discharged by the magistrate, the plaintiff was bound over or was committed, you change the above form. State the action of the magistrate, that the plaintiff was compelled to find bail, or that, being unable to find security, he was committed to the county prison. Then aver that at the   sessions of the Court of Oyer and Terminer and Quarter Sessions of the Peace for that county the defendant falsely, maliciously, and without any reasonable or probable cause, prosecuted the plaintiff, and procured an indictment to be preferred against the plaintiff, charging plaintiff with the crime of   ; that afterward the said defendant falsely, maliciously, and without any reasonable or probable cause, prosecuted the said plaintiff upon the said indictment, and the plaintiff having pleaded not guilty the case came on to be tried on before said court and a jury, and thereupon the said jury on rendered a verdict of not guilty and acquitted the plaintiff, and the said plaintiff, by the judgment of the said court, was fully acquitted and discharged of said indictment and of said prosecution, and the said complaint and prosecution are wholly ended and determined, as by the record and proceedings of said court to   Sessions, 1889, number   will more fully appear.) By means of which premises the plaintiff has been and is greatly injured in his credit and reputation, has been brought into disgrace among his neighbors and others, has been suspected of (felony), has suffered great anxiety of mind and pain of body, has been deprived of his liberty for the space of   .   has been obliged to lay out large sums of money, amounting in the whole to   dollars, in and about procuring his discharge from said imprisonment and defending himself in the premises, has been greatly hindered by reason of the premises from transacting his lawful business of   , and by means of the premises the plaintiff has been and is otherwise greatly injured in his credit and circumstances, to the damage of the plaintiff five thousand dollars.

G. H.,
Plaintiff's Attorney.
(Date.)

(Affidavit.)

§ 542. **The action for damages arising from seduction** must be brought by the father of the female seduced, if he be alive.   If the father be dead, the mother may, under Act of April 19, 1843 (Br. Purd., 1909, section 1), maintain the suit.   The criminal prosecution for seduction will not lie unless the female be under twenty-one years of age.   She must also be of good repute, and there must be a promise of marriage.

§ 543. **Damages in seduction.**   The civil remedy is founded exclusively upon the relation of master and servant.   The female is bound to render service to the parent.   She is disabled by reason of sickness, etc., hence arise a loss of service and a right of action. But this once established, the damages are not limited to the value of the service thus lost, and, if the circumstances warrant, they may be exemplary.

In *Phelin* v. *Kenderdine*, 20 Pa. St., 361 (1853), LEWIS, J., quoted with approval the following statement of the law by the Supreme Court of the United States :

" It is a well-established principle of the common law, that, in actions of trespass, and all actions on the case for *torts*, a jury may inflict what are called exemplary, punitive, or vindictive damages upon a defendant, having in view the enormity of his offense rather than the measure of compensation to the plaintiff." *Day* v. *Wood-worth* et al., 13 Howard (U. S.), 371.

Accordingly our Supreme Court has ruled that damages may be given for " all that the plaintiff can feel from the nature of the injury." *Phelin* v. *Kenderdine, supra.*

§ 544. **As to the promise of marriage,** it was ruled in the same case, so far as the promise of marriage tends to show the nature of the injury to the parent, or the means by which it was accomplished, it is proper evidence ; the jury, however, are not to award to the father any part of the damages which belong to the daughter by reason of the breach of the contract of marriage.

§ 545. **English decisions in cases of seduction.** The following are rulings in English cases :

The action lies for debauching an adopted daughter. *Irwin* v. *Dearman,* 11 East, 23.

A parent, in that character merely, cannot support an action for debauching or beating his daughter, which is only sustainable in respect of the supposed loss of service, some slight evidence of which must in general be adduced. *Dean* v. *Peel,* 5 East, 45 ; *Weedon* v. *Timbrell,* 5 T. R., 360.

The daughter is a good witness, *Cock* v. *Wortham,* 2 Stra., 1024 ; though she need not be called as a witness for plaintiff, *Ravill* v. *Satterfit,* Holt, C. N. P., 451. Not calling her, however, renders the plaintiff's case open to observation. The daughter cannot be cross-examined as to illicit intercourse with other men, and evidence of a promise of marriage is not admissible, and the plaintiff cannot call witnesses to the girl's good character unless the defendant has by evidence attacked it, *Dodd* v. *Norris,* 3 Camp., 519 ; *Bamfield* v. *Massey,* 1 Camp., 460. Evidence of mental pain is admissible, *Bedford* v. *McKowl,* 3 Esp., 119 ; and the state and situation of the family may be proved in aggravation of damages, *Id.* It may also be proved in aggravation of damages that the defendant professed to visit the family, and was received as the suitor of the daughter, *Elliott* v. *Nicklin,* 5 Price, 641. The defendant may, in mitigation of damages, adduce any evidence of the improper, negligent, and imprudent conduct of the plaintiff himself ; and where he knew that the defendant was a married man, and allowed his visits in the probabilities of a divorce, Lord Kenyon held the action could not be supported. *Reddie* v. *Scoolt,* Peake's Rep., 240.

§ 546. **Pennsylvania decisions.** In addition to those already cited, it is only necessary to refer to *Hollis* v. *Wells,* 3 Clark, 169 (1845), as supporting *Reddie* v. *Scoolt, supra ; Hoffman* v. *Kem-*

erer, 44 Pa. St., 452 (1863), forbidding the cross-examination prohibited by the English cases ; and *Fernsler* v. *Moyer*, 3 W. & S., 416 (1842), sustaining the right of a guardian to sue.

§ 547.

STATEMENT IN ACTION FOR SEDUCTION.

A. B.   C. P., No. .
  v.   September Term, 188 .
C. D.   No. .

The plaintiff, A. B., claims of the defendant, C. D., the sum of   ,
which sum is justly due and payable to the plaintiff by the defendant upon the cause of action, whereof the following is a statement :

The said defendant, contriving and wrongfully and unjustly intending to injure the said plaintiff, and to deprive him of the service and assistance of E. F., the daughter and servant of the said plaintiff, heretofore, to wit, on and on divers other days and times between that day and the day of bringing this suit, at the county of Philadelphia, debauched and carnally knew the said E. F. then and there, and from thence for a long space of time, to wit, hitherto, being the (daughter and) servant of the said plaintiff, whereby the said E. F. became pregnant and sick with child, and so remained and continued for a long space of time, to wit, for the space of nine months then next following, at the expiration whereof, to wit, on , at the county aforesaid, she, the said E. F., was delivered of the child with which she was so pregnant as aforesaid. By means of which said several premises, she, the said E. F., for a long space of time, to wit, from the day and year first above mentioned hitherto, became and was unable to do or perform the necessary affairs and business of the said plaintiff, so being her (father and) master as aforesaid, and thereby the said plaintiff, during all that time, lost and was deprived of the service of his said (daughter and) servant, to wit, at the county aforesaid ; and, also, by means of the said several premises, the said plaintiff was forced and obliged to and did necessarily pay, lay out, and expend divers sums of money, in the whole amounting to a large sum of money, to wit, the sum of dollars, in and about the nursing and taking care of the said E. F., his said (daughter and) servant, and in and about the delivery of the said child, to wit, at county aforesaid. To the damage of said plaintiff five thousand dollars. Wherefore he brings suit. (If the female were not the daughter of the plaintiff, omit the words " daughter " and " father " throughout ; they are not necessary.)

R. S.,
Plaintiff's Attorney.
(Date.)

(Affidavit.)

§ 548. Action for conspiracy. Where your client has been injured by the unlawful agreement of two or more to inflict damage, followed by an overt act giving effect to the illegal purpose, an action will lie. This was called an action on the case in the nature of a writ of conspiracy. Conspiracy falls within the category of torts, and under the Pennsylvania Act of 1887 the action for it is in trespass.

§ 549. *Special cases in which it was held that the action was maintainable.* When two or more acting in bad faith agree to confine another in a lunatic asylum without just cause, and do so confine him. *Hinchman* v. *Ritchie*, Brightly's Reports, 143 (1849). Where two or more agree to assist a debtor to defraud his creditor, and commit some overt act to the injury of the creditor. *Mott* v. *Danforth*, 6 Watts, 304 (1837); *Penrod* v. *Morrison*, 2 P. & W., 126 (1830). Where two or more maliciously petitioned against the appointment of plaintiff to the position of school teacher. *Vanarsdale* v. *Laverty*, 69 Pa. St., 103 (1871). Where defendants conspired to charge plaintiff, a teacher, with insanity, and did so charge him to his special damage. *Wildee* v. *McKee*, 43 Leg. Int., 307 (1886). There must be proof of a corrupt combination and agreement. *Newall* v. *Jenkins*, 26 Pa. St., 159 (1856); *Kirkpatrick* v. *Lex*, 49 Pa. St., 122 (1865).

It will, of course, be noted that the action will lie in many other cases than those here specially cited. In general, it may be maintained whenever two or more have combined together to do an unlawful act, or a lawful one by unlawful means, and any overt steps have been taken in pursuance of such combination, to the injury of the plaintiff.

When one alone may be sued. One alone may be sued, but it must be alleged that he conspired with some other or others, though it has been held that even these words may be omitted. See cases cited, Oliver's Precedents, 448, and *Laverty* v. *Vanarsdale*, 65 Pa. St., 507 (1870), explained in *Collins* v. *Cronin*, 117 Pa. St., 35 (1887).

§ 550. *Præcipe* in an action for conspiracy is in the form given at §§ 511, 519.

§ 551. *Statement in Conspiracy.* This must, in some respects, follow the form of an indictment for conspiracy. Although the case noted below is liberal to the pleader, it will generally be found safer to allege precisely what the defendants illegally conspired and agreed to do ; how this was to injure the plaintiff ; what they did as overt acts ; and how the plaintiff was damaged.

Haldeman v. *Martin*, 10 Pa. St., 369 (1849), was an action for conspiracy to defame. The counsel for plaintiffs in error (defendants below) argued that the *narr.* was defective in not charging the overt acts ; that the words spoken should have been laid at least in substance ; and that the omission to aver that the reports were maliciously spread was fatal. The Supreme Court, however, affirmed the judgment, and *held*, further, that the plaintiff could prove that she had been deserted by her acquaintances without special averment to that effect in the *narr.*

§ 552. *As to statement of special damage.* GIBSON, C. J. (10 Pa. St., 372) : " The law is settled, that particular damage, where it is a separate and independent part of the cause of action, must be specially laid, but where it is the natural consequence of an injury, actionable without it, it need not be set out ; and what is a more natural consequence of successful defamation than loss of intercourse with friends ? The plaintiff was, therefore, at liberty to prove that she had been deserted by her acquaintances in consequence of the slander, without having alleged the fact in her declaration."

§ 553. *As to setting out the words. As to averring " falsely and maliciously," and as to charging overt acts.* In the same case (10 Pa. St., 372) the court also said :

" The objection to the counts on which the verdict was ultimately entered is not sustained. A conspiracy to do an illegal thing is actionable, if injury proceed from it ; and where the illegal purpose has been executed, it is false and malicious wherever the motive for the conspiracy to execute it was false and malicious. *Ex vi termini* a conspiracy to accuse is evidence of its illegality ; and as the presumption of innocence holds till it is rebutted, it is also evidence of falsity till the contrary be shown. Falsity of the charge in the first instance implies malice ; and where the uttering of the words in which it is made is not the gist of the action, they need not be set out. The act to be done may be stated in general terms, provided it be stated with convenient certainty. In *Hood* v. *Palm,* 8 Pa. St., 237, a declaration in an action for conspiracy to charge the plaintiff with fraud, stated the charge made pursuant to the conspiracy, according to the substance, and not the words of it ; and this, too, without exception by the defendant's counsel."

§ 554.

FORM OF STATEMENT IN CONSPIRACY.

A. B. ⎫   C. P., No. .
   v.   ⎬   September Term, 188 .
C. D. *et al.* ⎭   No. .

The plaintiff, A. B., claims of the defendant, C. D., the sum of   , which sum is justly due and payable to the plaintiff by the defendant upon the cause of action, whereof the following is a statement:

Before and at the time of the committing of the grievances by the defendants as hereinafter charged, the plaintiff followed the lawful occupation of a merchant in said city, and by means of his honesty and fairness in said calling for twenty years past had acquired the confidence of persons who sold to and who bought from him, and of many others. The defendants, well knowing the premises and intending to injure the plaintiff and to ruin

him in his said business, on the first day of November, in the year aforesaid, at the county aforesaid, unlawfully, wickedly, and maliciously conspired and agreed together to injure the plaintiff, to damage him in his
said calling of a merchant, to deprive him of his customers, to defame his
character, and to subject him to great loss. And the said defendants further
unlawfully, wickedly, and maliciously conspired and agreed together, on
the day and year and at the county aforesaid, to effect their aforesaid unlawful, wicked, and malicious purposes by the following unlawful, wicked,
and malicious means, to wit, that they would slander the said plaintiff, that
they would report that he was dishonest, that they would charge him with
being a thief. (Set out all the means by which the conspiracy was to be
effected.) And in pursuance of said illegal, wicked, and malicious conspiracy, combination, and agreement of said defendants, the said defendant
C. D. afterward, to wit, on the day and year and at the county aforesaid, spoke
and uttered, in the presence and hearing of other persons of and concerning the said plaintiff and of and concerning the plaintiff as a merchant as
aforesaid, the following false, scandalous, malicious, and defamatory words,
to wit, " A. B." (the plaintiff meaning) " is a thief," thereby meaning and intending to charge the said plaintiff with the crime of larceny.

And in further pursuance of said illegal, wicked, and malicious conspiracy and agreement of said defendants, the said defendant F. G. afterward
(state what F. G. said or did, following the form).

And the plaintiff saith that he is in nowise guilty of the said crimes so injuriously laid to his charge, and that by reason thereof he has been greatly
hurt in his good name and brought into disgrace among his neighbors and
others, who, ever since the speaking of the said false, scandalous, malicious, and defamatory words, have so suspected him of having been guilty
of larceny that they have refused to have any communion with him, and
the said plaintiff has been made liable to prosecution for said crime of larceny. And the plaintiff further saith that divers persons who used to have
dealings and business with him in his said lawful business and by means
of which he had gained large sums of money, have ever since the speaking
the said several false, scandalous, malicious, and defamatory words refused
to have dealings or business with the said A. B., whereupon the said A. B. hath
sustained and claims damages to the amount of five thousand dollars.

E.,
Attorney for Plaintiff.
(Date.)

(Special damages can be averred according to the circumstances.)
(Affidavit.)

Changing the phraseology to conform to the facts, this precedent
would answer for conspiracies to libel, to maliciously prosecute,
and all other conspiracies to commit torts.

§ 555.

FORM OF STATEMENT IN ACTION FOR CRIM. CON.

A. B.   C. P., No. .
    v.   September Term, 188 .
C. D.   No. .

The plaintiff, A. B., claims of the defendant, C. D., the sum of   ,
which sum is justly due and payable to the plaintiff by the defendant upon
the cause of action, whereof the following is a statement :

The said defendant, contriving and wrongfully, wickedly, and unjustly intending to injure the said plaintiff and to deprive him of the comfort, fellowship, society, aid, and assistance of E. F., the wife of the said plaintiff, and to alienate and destroy her affection for the said plaintiff, heretofore, to wit, on   and on divers other days and times between that day and the day of exhibiting this bill, at the county of Philadelphia, wrongfully, wickedly, and unjustly debauched and carnally knew the said E. F. then and there, and still being the wife of the said plaintiff, and thereby the affection of the said E. F. for the said plaintiff was then and there alienated and destroyed, and also, by means of the premises, the said plaintiff hath from thence hitherto wholly lost and been deprived of the comfort, fellowship, society, aid, and assistance of the said E. F., his said wife, in his domestic affairs, which the said plaintiff during all that time ought to have had, and otherwise might and would have had, to wit, at the county of Philadelphia aforesaid. To the damage of the said plaintiff of   dollars, and therefore he brings his suit, etc.

G. H.,
Attorney pro Plaintiff.
(Date.)

(Affidavit.)

When it may be doubtful whether the criminal conversation can be proved and the defendant has enticed away or harbored the wife, the count may be added, as in the following form, changing " servant," " apprentice," etc., to wife.

§ 556.

FORM OF STATEMENT FOR ENTICING AWAY SERVANT OR APPRENTICE.

A. B.   ⎫   C. P., No. .
    v.   ⎬   September Term, 188 .
C. D.   ⎭   No. .

The plaintiff, A. B., claims of the defendant, C. D., the sum of   , which sum is justly due and payable to the plaintiff by the defendant upon the cause of action, whereof the following is a statement :

Before and at the time of the committing of the several grievances by the said defendant as hereinafter mentioned, one E. F. was, and from thence hitherto hath been and still is, the servant (or apprentice) of the said plaintiff, in his trade or business of a   , which the said plaintiff then exercised and carried on, and still doth exercise and carry on, to wit, at the county of Philadelphia ; yet the said defendant, well knowing the premises, but contriving and wrongfully and unjustly intending to injure, prejudice, and aggrieve the said plaintiff in his aforesaid trade and business, and to deprive him of the services of the said E. F. as such servant (or apprentice) as aforesaid, and of the profits, benefits, and advantages which might and would otherwise have arisen and accrued to him from such service whilst the said E. F. was such servant (or apprentice) of the said plaintiff as aforesaid, to wit, on   at the county aforesaid, unlawfully, wrongfully, and unjustly enticed, persuaded, and procured the said E. F., so then being the servant (or apprentice) of the said plaintiff as aforesaid, to depart from and out of the service of the said plaintiff, by means of which said enticement, persuasion, and procurement, and on no other account whatsoever, the said E. F., so being such servant (or apprentice) as

aforesaid, then and there, to wit, on the day and year aforesaid, at the
county aforesaid, unlawfully, wrongfully, and unjustly, and without license
or consent, and against the will of the said plaintiff, departed from and out
of the service of the said plaintiff, and hath remained and continued absent
from such service for a long space of time, to wit, from thence hitherto,
whereby the said plaintiff hath, for and during all that time, lost and been
deprived of the service of the said E. F. in his aforesaid trade and business,
and of all the profits, benefits, and advantages which might and would have
otherwise arisen and accrued to him from such service, and hath been and
is otherwise greatly injured in his aforesaid trade and business, to wit, at,
etc., (venue) aforesaid, to the damage of the said plaintiff, two thousand
dolars.

G. H.,
Plaintiff's Attorney.
(Date.)

(Affidavit.)

§ 557.

FORM OF STATEMENT FOR HARBORING AN APPRENTICE.

A. B. ⎫ C. P., No. .
  v.   ⎬   September Term, 188 .
C. D. ⎭ No. .

The plaintiff, A. B., claims of the defendant, C. D., the sum of   ,
which sum is justly due and payable to the plaintiff by the defendant upon
the cause of action, whereof the following is a statement :

That one E. F. heretofore, to wit, on the   at the
county aforesaid, then and still being the apprentice of the said plaintiff,
unlawfully, wrongfully, and unjustly, without the license or consent and
against the will of the said plaintiff, departed and went away from and out
of the service of the said plaintiff, and afterward, to wit, on the day and
year aforesaid, there went and came to the said defendant ; yet the said defendant, well knowing the said E. F. to be the apprentice of the said plaintiff, but contriving and wrongfully and unjustly intending to injure the said
plaintiff, and to deprive him of the service of the said E. F., his said " apprentice," and of all the profits, benefits, and advantages which might and
would otherwise have arisen and accrued to him from such service, then
and there, to wit, on the day and year aforesaid, at the county aforesaid,
unlawfully, wrongfully, and unjustly received the said E. F., so then being
the " apprentice " of the said plaintiff as aforesaid, into the service of the
said defendant, and harbored, detained, and kept the said E. F. in his said
service for a long space of time, to wit, from the day and year last aforesaid
hitherto ; whereby the said plaintiff, for and during all that time, lost and
was deprived of the service of the said E. F., and of all the profits, benefits,
and advantages which might and would otherwise have arisen and accrued
to him from such service, to wit, at the county aforesaid, and has been
otherwise greatly damaged to the amount of.   dollars, wherefore
he brings suit.

G. H.,
Plaintiff's Attorney.
(Date.)

(Affidavit.)

§ 558. Action for damages occasioned by negligence. Statements in these cases are more strictly narratives than any other form of pleading. They should describe the party injured, not only by name and occupation, but by his relation to the plaintiff at the time of receiving the injury. For example, if the result has been death and the suit be by the widow and children, A. should be described as the widow of B., the deceased. The children, C., D., and E., should be so named. Their ages should be given. The occupation of the party injured, the place where the injury was received, the cause of the injury, etc., should be stated with reasonable precision. Minute details are not required, but time, place, and pertinent circumstances so far as known should be set forth.

The plaintiff is not required to give a particular statement of the amount claimed for each item of damage, *Mallon* v. *Gay*, 28 W. N., 93 (1891) ; but the statement must set forth the particular acts of negligence on which he relies and the accompanying affidavit must aver the actual damage incurred. *Childs* v. *Pa. R. R. Co.*, 27 W. N., 510 (1891).

The Act of May 8, 1895 (P. L., 54), provides that whenever injury not resulting in death shall be wrongfully inflicted upon the wife, and a right of action thereby accrues to the wife and the husband, the injury shall be redressed in only one suit brought in the names of the husband and wife. The husband or wife may waive his or her right of action, and if after service of a rule to join, either party fails to join within twenty days, such waiver shall be presumed. If both join in the suit, separate verdicts shall be rendered and separate judgments entered and separate executions permitted. This Act applies to pending suits, and upon the application of either party, or on its own motion, the court may consolidate such suits. This repeals the Act of June 11, 1879 (P. L., 129). See *Kelley* v. *Township*, 154 Pa. St., 440 (1893).

§ 559.

FORM OF STATEMENT BY WIDOW AGAINST THE EMPLOYERS OF HER HUSBAND FOR CAUSING HIS DEATH BY DEFECTIVE MACHINERY, ETC.

In the Court of Common Pleas, No. 4, for the County of Philadelphia, of December Term, 18 , No. .

(Caption.)

City and County of Philadelphia, *ss.*

The plaintiff, A., claims of the defendant, the B. Company, a corporation of the State of Pennsylvania duly incorporated, the damages hereinafter demanded, which are justly due and payable to the plaintiff by the defendant upon the cause of action, upon the following statement :

The said plaintiff, A., was at the time of the committing of the grievances hereinafter mentioned the wife of one C., who died under circumstances and from the causes hereinafter mentioned, leaving him surviving his widow, the said plaintiff, but no issue, so that the said plaintiff then was and is now the only person entitled to a share in any sum that may be recovered in this action.

And whereas, also heretofore and at the time of the committing of the grievances hereinafter mentioned, to wit, on the   day of   at the county aforesaid, the said C. was employed at the special instance and request of the said defendant in loading a certain wagon-load of goods and merchandise and in preparing the same to be loaded, and in the course of his employment it became and was the duty of the said C., and at the special instance and request of the said defendant he was obliged to and did use and employ a certain elevator or hoisting apparatus then and there belonging to the said defendant and in its possession and control, and by it furnished to the said C. to be used in and about the employment aforesaid. Whereby it then and there became and was the duty of the said defendant to use due and proper care in and about the premises, and to use and to furnish to the said C. to be used a safe, secure, and proper elevator or hoisting apparatus, in and about the work aforesaid. Yet the said defendant, not regarding its duty in that behalf, did not use due and proper care in and about the premises and did not furnish to the said C. to be used a safe, secure, and proper elevator or hoisting apparatus, as it was its duty to do, but on the contrary wholly neglected so to do, and carelessly and negligently and without the knowledge and consent of the said C. furnished to the said C. to use, such an unsafe, insecure, and improper elevator and hoisting apparatus and appliances that by reason thereof a certain shaft, connected with and necessary for the running of said elevator and by the said defendant so aforesaid furnished during and in the proper and ordinary and careful use thereof by the said C., in the course of his employment as aforesaid, gave way and broke, and fell upon and violently struck the said C., and also by reason thereof the said elevator on which the said C. in the ordinary and proper course of his employment there was, violently fell on the ground, and the said C. was with great force and violence thrown down and upon the boxes, barrels, and merchandise with which the said elevator was loaded, whereby he was then and there greatly hurt and injured, and afterward, to wit, on the day and year aforesaid, at the county aforesaid, by reason thereof died. And the said plaintiff in fact says that by reason of the said premises she, the said plaintiff, has suffered the loss of her husband, who was constantly earning and in receipt of good wages, supporting and providing for the said plaintiff and affording her a comfortable livelihood and maintenance, and that by reason of the death of the said C. as aforesaid the said plaintiff is for all time deprived of her means of support and maintenance from her said husband's earnings and of his society, comfort, benefit, and assistance in her affairs in the relation of husband and wife, which she could and had a right to ask and have and would otherwise have had of the said decedent.

Wherefore the said plaintiff says that by reason of the premises she is injured and has sustained damages to the amount of twenty thousand dollars, and therefore she brings suit.

D.,
Attorney for Plaintiff.
(Date.)

(Affidavit.)

§ 560.

In the Court of Common Pleas, No. 4, for the County of Philadelphia, of December Term, 18   , No.   .

(Caption.)

City and County of Philadelphia, *ss.*

The plaintiff, A., claims of defendant, the B. Company, a corporation of the State of Pennsylvania, duly incorporated, the damages hereinafter demanded, which are justly due and payable to the plaintiff by the defendant upon the cause of action, upon the following statement :

That heretofore, to wit, on the   day of   , in the year of our Lord one thousand eight hundred and eighty-nine, at the county aforesaid, the said defendant was the owner of a certain freight depot, situated on Market Street, between Fifteenth and Sixteenth Streets, in the city of Philadelphia aforesaid, and which the said defendant kept open for the transaction of its business with persons having occasion to visit said depot ; and in said depot the said defendant maintained a certain hatchway for the raising and lowering of an elevator ; and it thereupon became and was the duty of the said defendant to maintain said hatchway in such manner that persons entering said building and transacting business therein with or for said defendant should not be exposed to danger of life or limb by falling into or through said hatchway. Yet said defendant, its said duty in this behalf not regarding on the day and year last aforesaid, at the county aforesaid, did not keep or maintain said hatchway in such manner that persons entering said building and transacting business therein with or for said defendant should not be exposed to danger of life or limb by falling into or through said hatchway, but, on the contrary, and notwithstanding defendant's duty as aforesaid, said defendant negligently, carelessly, and in total disregard of the plaintiff's rights, allowed and permitted said hatchway to be left unguarded and unprotected, thereby imperilling and endangering the plaintiff's life. That by reason of said defendant's negligence, carelessness, and want of proper care and attention as aforesaid, the plaintiff on the said   day of   , in the year of our Lord one thousand eight hundred and eighty-nine, to wit, at the county aforesaid, while in the discharge of his lawful business of a clerk, fell through the said hatchway a distance of ten feet, by means whereof one of the legs of the said plaintiff became and was fractured, bruised, and broken ; and said fall also produced a concussion of the plaintiff's spinal cord, and the said plaintiff was otherwise greatly injured, wounded, and cut, insomuch that the said plaintiff then and there became and was sick, sore, lame, and disordered, and was confined to his bed for a long space of time, to wit, for the space of six weeks next following, during all which time the said plaintiff suffered and underwent great pain, and was hindered and prevented from carrying on, transacting, and proceeding in his lawful and necessary affairs and business by him during that time to be performed and transacted, and thereby lost and was deprived of divers great gains and profits which had been accustomed to arise and accrue, and which otherwise would have continued to arise and accrue to the said plaintiff from the transacting and carrying on of the same, and the said plaintiff has not yet recovered from his said injuries so as to be able to attend regularly and without interruption to his said lawful business of a clerk, and he still suffers pain and disorders of the nerves and head, impairing his business capacity, and by means of said premises the said defendant was forced and obliged to and did then and there pay, lay out, and expend divers large sums of money amounting in the whole to the sum of, to wit, one thousand dollars, in and about the curing and endeavoring to cure the said fractures, bruises, cuts, and wounds, to wit, at the county aforesaid.

To the damage of the said plaintiff five thousand dollars, and therefore he brings suit.

C.,
Plaintiff's Attorney.
(Date.)

(Affidavit.)

§ 561. **Trover.** This action, now a form of trespass, lies for the recovery of damages for the wrongful conversion of personal property. Under the old practice the *narr.* averred a casual loss of the property by plaintiff, a finding by defendant, and a conversion of it by him to his own use. In framing a statement under the Act of 1887, the fictitious allegation of loss and finding should be disregarded save where it describes the facts as they really exist. The statement should contain a clear and succinct recital of the cause of action, embracing the facts that are relevant and that are required to make out the plaintiff's case. It should specify the whole amount claimed as well as the value of the several chattels converted. Such decisions as distinguish this action from trespass and case have lost their importance since the consolidation of all actions *ex delicto ;* but the boundary line between this form of trespass and the action in contract is not always clearly marked. It is sometimes difficult to decide whether a suit should be brought in trover or assumpsit. Stated generally, it may be said that in order to sustain trover there must have been either a tortious taking or a tortious withholding of the property. Refusal to deliver it upon demand will in itself imply a conversion, but the conversion may be shown in many other ways. Any assumption of ownership or control which is inconsistent with the title of the true owner will be sufficient. The reports contain many cases upon this branch of the subject. They will be found in the Digests under the appropriate head. The following will serve to exemplify the distinctions which have been made between this action and those sounding in contract, and to illustrate the cases in which trover may be maintained.

§ 562. **When trover lies.** Either an absolute or a qualified property in the plaintiff will support trover. *Weidensaul* v. *Reynolds,* 49 Pa. St., 73 (1865). A special property with right of immediate possession is enough to sustain the action. *Gill* v. *Weston,* 110

Pa. St., 312 (1885). See *Blakey* v. *Douglass*, 5 Cent. Rep., 274 (1886). An unauthorized sale by an agent is a sufficient conversion to justify trover against him without previous demand. *Etter* v. *Bailey*, 8 Pa. St., 442 (1848). It lies for a refusal to return collateral security for a debt upon tender of the amount due. *McIntire* v. *Blakeley*, 10 Cent. Rep., 925 (1888). If one partner wrongfully transfer firm property to a third party not in the course of business, the other partner may maintain trover against such third party. *Agnew* v. *Johnson*, 17 Pa. St., 373 (1851); *McNair* v. *Wilcox*, 121 Pa. St., 437 (1888).

Where, by agreement between A. and B., it was provided that B. should set up his saw mill on A.'s land, and should cut and saw timber growing thereon, the timber to be divided between them in specified proportions, but to remain the property of A. until division ; *it was held* that B. could maintain an action against a third party, who negligently destroyed or carried away the timber before division. *Haverly* v. *R. R. Co.*, 23 W. N., 439 (1889). Otherwise, if B. were merely the agent for A. *Trout* v. *Kennedy*, 47 Pa. St., 387 (1864). Trover will lie to recover a chattel held under a lease which stipulated that the lessor should execute a bill of sale for it after rent had been paid for a certain period, the lessee having defaulted in the payment of rent and refused to deliver the chattel upon demand. *Wheeler Co.* v. *Heil*, 115 Pa. St., 487 (1887). For a certificate, but not " for a share " of stock. *Neilor* v. *Kelley*, 69 Pa. St., 403 (1871). Against one who hires a horse to go to a specified place by a particular route and who deviates from said route and stops at another place, where the horse is destroyed by an accidental fire. *Brown* v. *Baker*, 15 W. N., 60 (1884). Against one for the conversion by his copartner of chattels which came into the possession of the firm upon partnership account. *Nisbet* v. *Patton*, 4 Rawle, 120 (1833). To recover title-papers of real estate retained by a broker, under claim of lien for charges incurred in an unsuccessful effort to sell the real estate, after demand and refusal to deliver. *Arthur* v. *Sylvester*, 105 Pa. St., 233 (1884). See *Jacoby* v. *Laussatt*, 6 S. & R., 300 (1820). No previous demand is required to sustain trover against a bailee who has wrongfully parted with possession of the thing bailed. *Work* v. *Bennett*, 70 Pa. St., 484 (1872); *Taylor* v. *Lyon*, 12 Cent. Rep., 365 (1888).

§ 563. **Trover will not lie.** To recover bonds delivered upon the understanding that the bailee was to pledge them as security for a loan, he having so pledged them. *Duffield* v. *Miller*, 92 Pa. St., 287 (1879). Nor where the bailee was empowered to use them in his business and replace them. *Borland* v. *Stokes*, 120 Pa. St., 278 (1888). Nor to recover a tenant's portion of the produce of a farm worked on shares, which produce was, by agreement, to remain with defendant (the landlord) until it was divided. *Lehr* v. *Taylor*, 90 Pa. St., 381 (1879). In the absence of such agreement trover could be maintained. *Stafford* v. *Ames*, 9 Pa. St., 343 (1848). It will not lie to recover a debt or damages for breach of contract. *Davis* v. *Thompson*, 12 Cent. Rep., 721 (1888). Nor against one in adverse possession of land to recover chattels which he has severed from the realty. In such case ejectment and suit for *mesne* profits are the proper remedies. *Transit Co.* v. *Weston*, 121 Pa. St., 485 (1888). Trover will not lie where the property has come into the defendant's hands lawfully and with plaintiff's consent until demand and refusal to deliver. *Taylor* v. *Hanlon*, 103 Pa. St., 504 (1883); *Springer* v. *Groom*, 21 W. N., 242 (1887). Otherwise where plaintiff has parted with the possession against his consent. *Springer* v. *Groom* (*supra*). Trover cannot be maintained where the plaintiff has the possession of property to which defendant has title, for an assumption of ownership on the part of defendant by a sale of his title, unaccompanied by actual taking or delivery of possession; the plaintiff must show that the right of property was in him when he commenced the action. *Moorehead* v. *Schofield*, 111 Pa. St., 584 (1886). A tenant in common of a chattel cannot maintain trover against his co-tenant for the detention of the joint property. *Heller* v. *Hufsmith*, 102 Pa. St., 533 (1883). Neglect to comply with a demand by letter for the return of goods is not a conversion of them. *Miller* v. *Smith*, 1 Phila., 173 (1851).

§ 564. *Præcipe and form of statement.* In this, as in all the preceding cases discussed in this chapter, your *præcipe* must be in an action of trespass. The facts vary in each case, and the statement should be adapted to them. The following will serve as a statement, in so far as it correctly recites the cause of action:

In the Court of Common Pleas, No. 4, for the County of Philadelphia,
of December Term, 18 , No. .
(Caption.)
City and County of Philadelphia, *ss.*
The plaintiff, A., claims of the defendant, the B. Company, a corporation of the State of Pennsylvania, duly incorporated, the damages hereinafter demanded, which are justly due and payable to the plaintiff by the defendant upon the cause of action, upon the following statement:
The said plaintiff heretofore, to wit, on the   day of
A.D. 18 , at the city and county of Philadelphia, was lawfully possessed, as of her own property, of certain (here describe particularly the goods as

the case may be) of great value, to wit, of the value of   thousand dollars of lawful money of the United States of America.

And being so possessed, the said plaintiff afterward, to wit, on the day and year first above written, at the city and county of Philadelphia aforesaid, casually lost the said   out of her possession, and the same afterward, to wit, on the day and year first above written, at the city and county aforesaid, came to the possession of the said defendant by finding.

Yet the said defendant, well knowing the said   goods and chattels to be the property of the said plaintiff, and of right to appertain and belong to the plaintiff, but contriving and fraudulently intending, craftily and subtly to deceive and defraud the said plaintiff in this behalf, hath not as yet delivered the said   goods and chattels, or any or either of them, or any part thereof, to the said plaintiff, though often requested so to do, and hath hitherto wholly refused so to do ; and afterward, to wit, on the day and year last aforesaid, at the city and county aforesaid, converted and disposed of the said   goods and chattels, to his own use, to the damage of the said plaintiff thirty thousand dollars.

C.,
Attorney for Plaintiff.
(Date.)

(Affidavit.)

§ 565. **Trespass vi et armis.** Here, again, the *præcipe* is in an " action of trespass."

For trespass of nearly every imaginable kind the books of precedents furnish many forms of *narrs*. These, with little difficulty, can be moulded into statements under the Act of 1887. Indeed it would seem almost impossible to err, when all that is required is a full and clear exhibition of the facts. Time and place must always be mentioned. The words " force and arms " should be introduced.

§ 566. **Actions against officers for negligence.** Where an official bond has been given, you can proceed as indicated, sections 266, 267, 268, 269, etc. The common-law action for negligence may be begun by using the *præcipe* given in this chapter.

§ 567.

FORM OF STATEMENT IN CASE OF NEGLIGENCE.

In the Circuit Court of the United States for the   District of Pennsylvania, April Sessions, 18 , No. .

(Caption.)

District of Pennsylvania, *ss.*

The plaintiff, A., claims of the defendant, the B. Company, a corporation of the State of Pennsylvania, duly incorporated, the damages hereinafter demanded, which are justly due and payable to the plaintiff by the defendant upon the cause of action, upon the following statement :

The defendant before and at the time hereinafter mentioned was and from thence hitherto has been and still is the collector of the customs at the port of Philadelphia, to wit, at the district aforesaid, and as such collector of the customs it was defendant's duty, under the laws of the United States and the practice of the said office of collector of customs, to deliver or cause or permit to be delivered to the owners thereof or to those entitled to the possession thereof, the cargoes of vessels arriving at said port from foreign countries; without said delivery or permission to be delivered given by the defendant, it being unlawful to receive or to take possession of said cargoes.

And whereas, to wit, on the   day of   the bark or vessel "Herald" arrived at said port of Philadelphia, to wit, at the district aforesaid, bearing a cargo consisting of   tons of of great value, to wit, ten thousand dollars, consigned to the plaintiff, in whose name and possession was the bill of lading therefor and who was then and there the owner thereof and entitled to receive from the defendant the possession, thereof, whose duty it was then and there to deliver or cause or permit to be delivered to the plaintiff the said cargo, of all of which said premises the defendant then and there had notice.

Yet the said defendant, not regarding his duty as collector of the customs aforesaid, nor the laws of the United States in such case made and provided, nor the usual and proper practice of the said office of collector of customs, but contriving and fraudulently intending subtly and craftily to defraud and injure the plaintiff in this behalf, did not nor would, though often thereto requested, deliver or cause or permit to be delivered to the plaintiff the said property, the said   the cargo of the said bark or vessel "Herald," but on the contrary thereof, the said defendant, so being such collector as aforesaid, so carelessly and negligently behaved and conducted himself in the premises, that by and through the carelessness, negligence, and default of the said defendant the said cargo aforesaid, so being of the value aforesaid, afterward, to wit, on the day and year aforesaid, became and was wholly lost to the said plaintiff, to the damage of the plaintiff ten thousand dollars, and therefore he brings suit.

C.,
Attorney for Plaintiff.
(Date.)

(Affidavit.)

§ 568. **Other forms in tort.** There exist many variations of the action of trespass which have not been specially noted in this chapter. The greater number of them will be found in that miscellaneous group which was classified under the old practice as trespass on the case. Particular directions as to these will not be needed. As suggested in reference to trespass *vi et armis, narrs.* may without trouble be transformed into statements. All essential averments should be retained. Whenever the damage is mediate or the *tort* was committed without violence, expressed or implied, the phrase "with force and arms" should be omitted.

§ 569. **If no appearance be entered,** your summons having been duly served, you can take judgment by default. See section 23 and proceed as directed by section 573.

§ 570. **If an appearance be filed,** enter a rule to plead, and take judgment, if no plea be filed. See section 26.

§ 571. **Plea.** "Special pleading is hereby abolished. * * * The only plea in the action of trespass shall be 'not guilty.'" Section 7, Act of May 25, 1887. See section 61 of this book.

In *Slatteny* v. *R. R. Co.*, 21 W. N., 556 (1888), it was ruled that a plea in abatement might still be filed. See section 2791 *et seq.*

Special matter under the plea of "not guilty" may be given in evidence, upon such notice as is provided for in the rules of the county courts. In Philadelphia, ten days' notice previous to the day set for trial is required. Section 2782.

§ 572. **When plea filed.** Put case at issue by filing replication. The only replication to the plea of not guilty is *similiter.* Avoid a demurrer, as imposing on you delay and the labor of paper-books. If absolutely driven to it, you must demur. As to demurrers, study some standard work on pleading. The general suggestions of sections 160, 161, 162, may be consulted, remembering that you here are *plaintiff*, not *avowant.*

§ 573. **Assessment of damages.** In Philadelphia the "prothonotary shall assess the damages in all cases in which the amount thereof is set forth with certainty in the statement of claim." Upon judgment by default in cases where you cannot assess damages as before the prothonotary, proceed by a Writ of Inquiry of Damages, as explained in Chapter XV.

§ 574. **Limitation.** By Act of 27 March, 1713, section 18, the period of limitation for persons not under disability is fixed at six years in actions of trespass on the case other than slander, in actions of trespass, and of trespass *quare clausum fregit;* at two years in actions of trespass (to the person), of assault, menace, battery, wounding, or imprisonment; at one year in actions for words.

By Act of 25 April, 1850, section 35 (P. L., 575; Br. Purd., 1215, section 20), the limitation of one year is extended to all cases of slander and libel, whether spoken, written, or printed.

In an action for seduction the Statute of Limitations begins to run from the time of the seduction. *Dunlap* v. *Linton*, 48 Leg. Int., 465 (1891).

§ 575. **Executions in cases of tort.** It is not proposed to give details of executions in each chapter. These are more appropriately considered under a separate chapter.

It is only necessary to say here that in addition to the *fi. fa.* against personalty (form of *præcipe*, section 23, and directions, sections 24, 25), and proceeding against realty (sections 172, 173, 175), you are entitled to issue a *capias ad satisfaciendum.*

The *fi. fa.* and *ca. sa.* may both issue at the same time.

If you so proceed, add to the *præcipe* (section 23) the words "and *ca. sa.*" after the words "*fi. fa.*," so that the command will read:

SIR :

 Issue *fi. fa.* and *ca. sa.* returnable *seg. leg.*
      Real debt $
      Interest from

              C.,
           Plaintiff's Attorney.
             (Date.)

To Prothonotary Common Pleas.

§ 576. You give to the sheriff the defendant's address. The officer demands payment of debt, interest, and costs. If the defendant do not pay, the sheriff then requires of him to point out personal property whereon to levy. If this is not done, the demand is made for real property, and failing here, the body of the defendant is taken into custody. The proceedings after this belong more appropriately to the chapter on Executions. If defendant cannot be found, be careful to have the writ properly returned and sue out the bail bond which was given if you commenced the action by *capias ad respondendum.*

CHAPTER XIV.

No chapter of the law better illustrates the march of improvement than that upon which we now enter. By the old English practice, ejectment was a most cumbersome and ridiculous form.

§ 577. **Description of the old ejectment.** Those who have patience sufficient for the task should recall Blackstone's description of this remedy. He says : "The better to apprehend the contrivance whereby the end was effected, we must recollect that the remedy by ejectment is, in its original, an action brought by one who hath a lease for years, to repair the injury done him by dispossession. In order, therefore, to convert it into a method of trying titles to the freehold, it is first necessary that the claimant do take possession of the lands, to empower him to constitute a lessee for years that may be capable of receiving this injury of dispossession. For it would be an offense, called in our law maintenance * * * to convey a title to another when the grantor is not in possession of the land ; and indeed it was doubted at first whether this occasional possession, taken merely for the purpose of conveying the title, excused the lessor from the legal guilt of maintenance. When, therefore, a person, who has right of entry into lands, determines to acquire that possession which is wrongfully withheld by the present tenant, he makes * * * a formal entry on the premises ; and being so in the possession of the soil, he there, upon the land, seals and delivers a lease for years to some third person or lessee ; and having thus given him entry, leaves him in possession of the premises. This lessee is to stay upon the land till the prior tenant, or he who had the previous possession, enters thereon afresh and ousts him ; or till some other person (either by accident or by agreement beforehand) comes upon the land and turns him out or ejects him. For this injury the lessee is entitled to his action of ejectment against the tenant, or this casual ejector, whichever it was that ousted him, to recover back his term and damages. But where this action is brought against such a casual ejector as is before mentioned, and not against the very tenant in possession, the court will not suffer the tenant to lose his possession without any opportunity to defend it. Where-

fore, it is a standing rule that no plaintiff shall proceed in ejectment to recover land against a casual ejector without notice given
to the tenant in possession (if any there be), and making him a defendant, if he pleases.   And in order to maintain the action, the
plaintiff must, in case of any defense, make out four points before
the court, viz. : *title, lease, entry,* and *ouster.*   First, he must show
a good title in his lessor, which brings the matter of right entirely
before the court ; then, that the lessor, being seized or possessed
by virtue of such title, did make him the *lease* for the present
term ; thirdly, that he, the lessee or plaintiff, did enter or take
possession in consequence of such lease ; and then, lastly, that the
defendant ousted or ejected him.   Whereupon he shall have judgment to recover his term and damages ; and shall, in consequence,
have a *writ of possession,* which the sheriff is to execute by delivering him the undisturbed and peaceable possession of his term.

" To this end, in the proceedings, a lease for a term of years is
stated to have been made by him who claims title to the plaintiff
who brings the action, as by John Rogers to Richard Smith,
which plaintiff ought to be some real person and not merely an
ideal, fictitious one who has no existence, as is frequently though
unwarrantably practised ; it is also stated that Smith, the lessee,
entered ; and that the defendant, William Stiles, who is called the
casual ejector, ousted him, for which ouster he brings this action.
As soon as this action is brought, and the complaint fully stated
in the declaration, Stiles, the *casual ejector* or defendant, sends a
written notice to the tenant in possession of the lands, as George
Saunders, informing him of the action brought by Richard Smith,
and transmitting him a copy of the declaration ; withal assuring
him that he, Stiles, the defendant, has no title at all to the premises, and shall make no defense ; and therefore advising the tenant
to appear in court and defend his own title, otherwise he, the
casual ejector, will suffer judgment to be had against him ; and
thereby the actual tenant, Saunders, will inevitably be turned out
of possession.

On receipt of this friendly caution, if the tenant in possession
does not, within a limited time, apply to the court to be admitted
a defendant in the stead of Stiles, he is supposed to have no right
at all ; and, upon judgment being had against Stiles, the casual
ejector, Saunders, the real tenant will be turned out of possession
by the sheriff.

" But if the tenant in possession applies to be made a defendant,
it is allowed him upon this condition ; that he enter into a rule of
court to confess at the trial of the cause, three of the four requi-

sites for the maintenance of the plaintiff's action, viz. : the *lease* of Rogers the lessor, the *entry* of Smith the plaintiff, and his *ouster* by Saunders himself, now made the defendant instead of Stiles ; which requisites being wholly fictitious, should the defendant put the plaintiff to prove them, he must, of course, be non-suited for want of evidence ; but by such stipulated confession of *lease, entry,* and *ouster,* the trial will now stand upon the merits of the *title* only. This done, the declaration is altered by inserting the name of George Saunders instead of William Stiles, and the cause goes down to trial under the name of Smith (the plaintiff) on the demise of Rogers (the lessor), against Saunders, the new defendant, and therein the lessor of the plaintiff is bound to make out a clear title, otherwise his fictitious lessee cannot obtain judgment to have possession of the land for the term supposed to be granted." Blackstone's Commentaries, Book III., p. 201.

§ 578. It is difficult for those who live and practice in an atmosphere of realities, rather than in a mist of fictions, to grasp all this description of the ancient law, though it is very clearly stated by an able jurist. Whilst the author was on a professional visit to Raleigh, the Chief Justice of the Supreme Court of North Carolina asked him "What would be done in Pennsylvania if the defendant should, on the trial of an ejectment before the jury, insist upon the plaintiff proving the ouster, which had never taken place?"

This, it may well be understood, was a terrific question. The only response that could be made was to refer to the Pennsylvania system as having entirely superseded the obsolete fictions. As to the occurrence of the supposed case under the old practice, reply was made that as the claimant was never permitted to defend save upon condition of admitting the ouster, it was impossible that he could at the trial require his adversary to prove it. Such ruling was made in Pennsylvania in the case of *Wilson* v. *Campbell,* 1 Dallas, 126 (1785). But the Chief Justice said the defendant, when allowed to appear, did not, in fact, confess ; he only entered into a rule to confess this *at the trial.* (So, indeed, Blackstone states it.) And if he broke the rule, and, instead of confessing, required proof of his adversary, the question recurred, What was to be done ? It was admitted to the Chief Justice that this point had never before been considered, and he was in turn asked for his solution of the difficulty. The answer was another illustration of the utter confusion of the old practice. The trial judge was to refer the whole record back to the court, and it punished this recreant defendant as for a contempt. Surely no better illustration

than this anecdote could possibly be furnished of the folly of trying fictions instead of settling real issues.

§ 579. **Pennsylvania statutes.** In place of all the old jargon, it
is refreshing to turn to the Pennsylvania statutes. The first now
in force was passed whilst the old system was in operation. It is
the Act of March 21, 1772 (1 Smith, 372).

Tenants to notify landlords. The eighth section requires tenants
receiving declarations in ejectment to give notice forthwith to their
landlords, under penalty of two years' rent. The ninth section
authorizes the courts to suffer landlords to make themselves defendants.

§ 580. *Estrepements.* The Act of April 2, 1803, section 2 (4
Sm., 89), gave greater effect to the statute of Gloucester for the
prevention of waste pending the ejectment. It authorizes the prothonotary in whose court the suit is pending to issue a writ of
estrepement, upon filing of affidavit of any person knowing the
fact that the tenant or defendant has committed or is committing
waste. The affidavit is to be sworn to before one of the judges
named. (See § 651 *et seq.*)

§ 581. *Form of writ.* The Act of March 21, 1806, created our
present system. The twelfth section (4 Sm., 332), declared that
" all writs of ejectment should be in the form following, and not
otherwise, viz.:

[L. S.]   County, *ss.* The Commonwealth of Pennsylvania : To the
sheriff of said county, Greeting : You are hereby commanded that you
summon A. B. to appear before the judges of the Court of Common Pleas,
in and for said county, to be holden at   on the   day of
          next, then and there to answer to a certain complaint made by
C. D. that he the said A. B. now hath in his actual possession a tract of
land, situate in   township, in the said county, containing
acres or thereabouts, bounded by lands of E. F., G. H., the right of possession or title to which he, the said C. D., saith is in him [or them, as the
case may be] and not in the said A. B., all of which the said C. D. aver-
reth he is prepared to prove before our said court. Hereof fail not. Witness J. B., president [or judge, as the case may be] of our said court at
          , the   day of   , Anno Domini one thousand eight
hundred and   . Attested :

J. M.,
Prothonotary.

§ 582. *Description to be filed, etc.* It also enacted that it shall
be the duty of the plaintiff to file in the prothonotary's office, on
or before the first day of the term to which the process is returnable, " a description of the land, with the number of acres which
he claims and declares that the title is in him. And the defendant
shall enter his defense (if any he hath) for the whole or any part

before the next term, and thereupon issue shall be joined." *Id.*, section 12.

The Act of April 13, 1807 (4 Sm., 476), directed that the ejectment thus provided for in Act of 1806 should give a full and effectual remedy ; that parties having undivided interests may join and recover according to their title ; that minors might sue by guardians ; that defendant might defend upon his own title or title of another ; and that the landlord might be admitted as defendant, and should on the trial admit himself to be in possession.

§ 583. *Statutory requirements as to service of the Summons.* The second section of the Act of 1807 provided, as to the service, that wherever it appeared that others not named in the writ are in possession of the whole or of part of the premises the sheriff shall add their names and serve them, and the prothonotary shall enter them to the action, and they shall be parties.

§ 584. *Judgment for want of Appearance.* In case any defendant does not appear, on motion to the court and an affidavit of officer serving the writ, stating manner of service, the same being deemed by the court agreeable to law, judgment may be entered by default for such part as he is possessed of, a writ of possession may issue, and the action proceed as to other defendants.

§ 585. *Effect of return of served.* The sheriff's return of served on any defendant is evidence of such person being in actual possession of the premises or of part thereof.

§ 586. *Writ not to abate by death.* The third section of same Act declares that no writ shall abate by death of either plaintiff or defendant, but the person next in interest may be substituted.

Where the plaintiff in an ejectment dies, his heirs may be substituted as parties, whether or not they so desire. *Ballantine* v. *Negley*, 158 Pa. St., 475 (1893).

§ 587. *Effect of two verdicts for one party.* The fourth section of the Act makes two verdicts and judgments for one party conclusive.

§ 588. *Plea.* It also directs that the plea shall be "not guilty."

§ 589. *If one plaintiff non-suited.* The Act of March 31, 1823 (P. L., 229), provides that if one of several plaintiffs be non-suited, a verdict and judgment may be entered in favor of the other plaintiff or plaintiffs.

§ 590. *If land has been sold for taxes and no one resides on it.* The Act of March 29, 1824, section 4 (P. L., 168), provides for service of the writ on the purchaser. If he cannot be found, then publication is to be made for sixty days.

§ 591. *If defendant re-enter after judgment against him and habere executed.* The Act of February 1, 1834 (P. L., 26), provides for *alias* and *pluries* writs of *habere*, the application for the writ to be made within three years after the return-day of the preceding writ.

§ 592. *In certain cases, one verdict or a judgment by confession to be conclusive.* By Act of April 21, 1846, section 1 (P. L., 424), where ejectment is brought to enforce payment of purchase-money wherein time becomes of essence in the finding of the jury, or in a judgment by confession by fixing a time for such payment, one verdict and judgment unreversed or judgment by confession shall be conclusive between the parties, and a failure to pay the money within the time so fixed shall be deemed a rescission of the contract, and shall render such judgment absolute.

§ 593. *Personal representatives of deceased creditor claiming purchase-money can sustain ejectment.* Following the Act of 1846 (as to ejectments for purchase-money) the statute of April 9, 1849, section 5 (P. L., 526), permits the executor or administrator to maintain ejectment to enforce payment of purchase-money.

§ 594. *If plaintiff in ejectment sell, the purchaser may be substituted on the record by motion in open court.* Act of April 26, 1850, section 4 (P. L., 591).

§ 595. *In ejectment for unpaid purchase-money where no person resides on the land.* The Act of April 14, 1851, section 11 (P. L., 614), permits service on the purchasers or those claiming under them, and if they cannot be found, the court may grant a rule on them to appear and plead. After publication of this sixty days before the return-day, at least three times in one newspaper of the county, the court may give judgment if no appearance.

§ 596. *If defendant not in the county where the land lies,* the writ may be served on any person in the county having charge or superintendence of the land as agent of the defendant. But the court must be satisfied that defendant has had notice in time, and if defendant be a corporation, this notice must be given to the president or other chief officer. Act April 18, 1853, section 1 (P. L., 467).

§ 597. *The other Acts in force* as to ejectments need not be here noticed at length. An abstract will suffice.

§ 598. *Ejectment Index.* Suit must be entered in this, in order to affect purchaser or mortgagee with notice. (Act April 22, 1856, section 2, P. L., 532.)

§ 599. *All defendants where lands unseated or unoccupied,* if not found in the county, may be served by publication of a rule sixty days before its return, as above noted in ejectment for unpaid purchase-money. Act April 13, 1858 (P. L., 256).

The Act of June 26, 1895 (P. L., 346) (amending the Act of April 13, 1858) provides :

That the provision of the eleventh section of the Act passed the fourteenth day of April, one thousand eight hundred and fifty-one, relative to the service of writs in certain actions of ejectment, shall hereafter extend to all cases where claimants and mortgagees may desire to bring actions of ejectment for any unseated or unoccupied lands within this Commonwealth, whenever the adverse claimant or mortgagor does not reside in the county where such lands are situate, and has no known agent or person having the charge or superintendence of said lands resident within said county : *Provided,* That before any trial or ejectment shall be had in such suit it shall be made to appear to the satisfaction of the court that the defendant has had notice in fact of the suit in time to appear and defend it, and if the defendant be a corporation this notice may be given to the president or other chief officers thereof: *Provided,* That this supplement shall not apply to actions of equitable ejectment against vendees to enforce specific performance of agreements for the sale of land.

§ 600. *Where defendant does not appear and plead by the next term,* or withdraws appearance, if duly served, court may direct plea to be entered. But the writ must be served on party actually claiming title. Act December 5, 1860 (P. L., 1861, 844).

§ 601. *No entry* shall arrest running of statutes, unless followed by suit in a year. Act April 13, 1859, section 1 (P. L., 603).

§ 602. *Counsel fees allowed to successful party in Erie County.* Act April 10, 1867 (P. L., 1115).

§ 603. *Action for trespass or mesne profits* does not abate by death of defendant, but executor or administrator to be substituted. Act April 12, 1869 (P. L., 27).

§ 604. *In trespass quare clausum fregit,* where plea was *liberum tenementum* and an ejectment by same parties or privies upon same title, two judgments for plaintiff or defendant shall be a bar. Act April 6, 1869 (P. L., 16).

§ 605. *Where plaintiff non-suited, or verdict for defendant,* defendant may rule plaintiff to sue out writ of error in one year, and if plaintiff fail so to do, he shall be forever debarred. Thereupon defendant may rule plaintiff to show cause why he should not bring second ejectment in one year ; if no good cause for delay, the rule shall be made absolute, and on expiration of the year the plaintiff be forever barred as to the same title. Act April 3, 1872 (P. L., 33). If you wish to speed the cause, see § 610.

§ 606. *Plaintiff may recover mesne profits to date of trial* if he give notice of his claim fifteen days before trial to defendant or his attorneys, and if claim is not barred by Statute of Limitations. Act May 2, 1876 (P. L., 95).

§ 607. *Plaintiff may sue for mesne profits while ejectment pending*

or after its termination, but he cannot proceed to trial until he recover possession.   Act June 11, 1879 (P. L., 125).

§ 608. The Act of February 23, 1889 (P. L., 8), is almost a
copy of the Act of 1879, just quoted.   It provides:

" That whenever an action for ejectment is pending for the recovery of real estate, the plaintiff or plaintiffs therein, or any person having such right of action, may, as well before as after the
termination of such action of ejectment, institute an action or actions for *mesne* profits against the defendant or defendants in such
action of ejectment, or against any other person or persons who
may be liable to such plaintiff or plaintiffs, or other persons, having such right of action for such profits, but such action or actions
for *mesne* profits shall not be proceeded with to trial until the plaintiff or plaintiffs shall have recovered possession of the real estate in
controversy."

§ 609. *Claimants of land sold by sheriff, county treasurer, or commissioners*, not being the defendants as whose property the land was
sold, and being in possession, may petition the court, and obtain a
rule, on the person holding under such sale, to bring ejectment within
ninety days from the time the rule is made absolute, the rule to be
entered in the docket and also on the ejectment index ; service as
in case of summons ; if party out of county, by sheriff or constable
of his residence ; if residence out of State and unknown, affidavit
to be filed and rule served by publication for four weeks prior to
return-day, in a weekly paper of the county.   If no appearance
within time limited, judgment to be entered and party barred.
Act June 11, 1879 (P. L., 127).   Amended by Act of June 24,
1885 (P. L., 152).

§ 610. *Party in possession after one verdict and judgment*, or
judgment against judgment, may rule adverse party to commence
second or third ejectment within six months, or show cause why
the same cannot be brought.   Rule to be entered in case last tried
and served by sheriff as summons.   If the adverse party reside out
of county, it may be served by sheriff where party resides ; if residence out of State, affidavit of non-residence shall be filed and service made by publication of substance of rule in weekly newspaper
of the county for four weeks, and notice shall be served upon the
non-resident.   If adverse party reside out of State before entering
judgment or making rule absolute, court shall be satisfied as to notice in fact of the rule in time to appear and answer, and if adverse
party be a corporation, the notice may be served upon president or
chief officer.   Act May 21, 1881, section 1 (P. L., 24).

The second section provides that court, after lapse of six months after service, shall enter judgment and make the rule absolute, the judgment to be as final as a second or third verdict and judgment would be.

§ 611. *Any party in possession may rule any claimant to bring ejectment in six months.* The Act of May 25, 1893 (P. L., 131), provides :

That whenever any person not being in possession thereof shall claim an interest in, or title to, real estate, it shall be lawful for any person in possession thereof claiming title to the same, to make application to the Court of Common Pleas of the proper county, whereupon a rule shall be granted upon said person not in possession to bring his or her action of ejectment within six months from the service of such rule upon him or her, or show cause why the same cannot be so brought, which rule may be made returnable to any term, or return-day of such court, and be served and returned as writs of summons are by law served and returned : *Provided, however,* When parties claiming, but not in possession, reside without the county where the land lies and within the Commonwealth, in such case the sheriff of the county in which such writ shall issue shall have power to execute the same, and when parties claiming reside outside of the State it shall be lawful for any person to serve notice of said application on such parties, and upon affidavit and satisfactory proof being made of such service had, the court may proceed as fully and effectually as if the same had been made by the sheriff within the jurisdiction of such court, and shall be entered of record and indexed as actions of ejectment are now indexed in the courts of the Commonwealth.

(This repealed the 1st section of the Act of March 8, 1889, P. L., 10.)

§ 612. *Judgment for want of an appearance against claimant who does not appear, etc.* Whenever a person claiming an interest in or title to such real estate shall have been served and shall fail to appear and show cause why such action cannot be brought within six months after such service, it shall be the duty of the court to enter judgment against the person served and make the rule absolute, which judgment shall be final and conclusive between the parties, their heirs and assigns, and thereafter no action of ejectment for the recovery thereof shall be brought by such person claiming an interest in or title to such real estate, or any person claiming by, from, or under such person : *Provided,* That if the party served shall fail to appear and show cause within the period of six months, as aforesaid, he or she shall not in any event be liable for the costs. Act of March 8, 1889, section 2 (P. L., 10).

This *résumé* of statutes is not intended as a digest of the law upon this subject, but rather as a chronological table of Pennsylvania legislation. It will be seen that the form of the writ, the manner of its service, the time for appearing, the method of intervening, the character of the plea, and many details are provided for.

We now look at the practice in this peculiar and important proceeding.

§ 613. **When it lies.** Ejectment is the favorite remedy for all cases of wrongful holding of lands. It may be employed in proper cases to enforce or defeat a trust, pledge, or sale of realty. A citation of all the decisions on this subject would convert a treatise on practice into a digest. The following summary will be found to cover many of the cases and all of the principles.

§ 614. **Who may maintain ejectment.** It may be brought as a substitute for a bill in equity to enforce a trust or for a specific performance; and is sometimes to be preferred to the remedy in chancery. Where facts are in dispute, a jury is frequently better than a master. The answer in equity may require two witnesses or their equivalent to overcome it. As noted in the chapter upon Mortgages, it will lie in such cases. It can be maintained against a railroad company which has entered without paying or giving bond. Executors holding under devise in trust—tenant in common actually ousted—a vendor or a vendee, mortgagor and mortgagee, trustee and *cestui que trust*, lessor and lessee, may all recover in this action when entitled to possession wrongfully withheld. Bare possession without title will suffice as against a mere intruder.

An infant may bring ejectment in the name of his next friend without the appointment of a guardian. *Heft* v. *McGill*, 3 Pa. St., 256 (1846).

§ 615. *Trustee of a church may sue.* A portion of an unincorporated congregation seceded and formed another organization and took possession of the church property. It was held that the trustees in whom the title was vested could maintain ejectment. *Fernstler* v. *Seibert*, 114 Pa. St., 196 (1886).

§ 616. *Ejectment not to be displaced by bill in equity.* An injunction will not be granted when there is an adequate remedy at law by action of ejectment and writ of estrepement. *Leininger's Appeal*, 106 Pa. St., 398 (1884).

Bill in equity cannot be maintained by one in possession of land to try the legal title thereto, on the ground of avoidance of a multiplicity of suits in trespass. *Washburn's Appeal*, 105 Pa. St., 480 (1884). An ejectment bill will be dismissed for want of jurisdiction. *Richard's Appeal*, 100 Pa. St., 52 (1882); *Duncan* v. *Iron Works*, 26 W. N., 479 (1890).

§ 617. *Subrogation may be enforced in ejectment.* Testator devised two tracts of land to A. and B., respectively, B.'s being of the greater value. By title paramount to that of the devisor, A. recovered in ejectment the land devised to B. *Held*, that B. might maintain ejectment against A. for the tract devised to the latter. *Lewis* v. *Lewis*, 13 Pa. St., 79 (1850).

§ 618. **When ejectment does not lie.** One already in possession cannot sue in ejectment, nor can this remedy be applied to maintain a right of way, nor for an incorporeal hereditament, *e. g.*, to collect a ground-rent, nor upon a judgment for land damages, nor for the land covered by a party-wall, nor for dower before assignment.

It hardly needed express ruling to decide that if evicted from part, the owner may sue for that portion, although he is in possession of the residue. *Buchanan* v. *Hazzard*, 95 Pa. St., 240 (1880).

§ 619. *Committee of lunatic.* Where a man while sane provides for his wife and children a home, and afterward becomes a lunatic, the committee cannot maintain ejectment therefor against the wife. *Shaffer* v. *List*, 114 Pa. St., 486 (1886).

§ 620. *It will not lie to enforce a collateral agreement.* A. transferred land to B. by unconditional deed in fee simple, reciting as a consideration therefor the contemporaneous execution by B. of a bond conditioned for the furnishing to A. of specified articles of maintenance each year. Upon failure by B. to perform the conditions of his bond ; *Held*, that ejectment would not lie to recover the land. *Krebs* v. *Stroub*, 116 Pa. St., 405 (1887).

§ 621. *A widow cannot maintain ejectment to recover the land of her deceased husband. Pringle* v. *Gaw*, 5 S. & R., 534 (1820). This was an action of ejectment brought by the widow and children of one John Pringle against the party in possession.

DUNCAN, J.: "By the common law, it is well established, that if the widow's claim be in the nature of dower, an ejectment will not lie before assignment. * * * She is not seized, until assignment, of an undivided third part. * * * It has been the general understanding in Pennsylvania that a widow cannot support ejectment for her thirds as dower at common law ; and that she cannot for her interest under the intestate laws."

But in *Gourley* v. *Kinley*, 66 Pa. St., 270 (1870), the son of James Kinley, deceased, brought ejectment against his mother, who continued in possession of the land, and it was ruled, somewhat at variance with *Pringle* v. *Gaw*, that the heir, before partition, could not maintain ejectment against the widow in possession.

§ 622. *Vendee cannot maintain ejectment without tender of purchase-money.* A vendee or holder of the equitable title who is out of possession cannot enforce specific performance by ejectment without payment or tender of the purchase-money due. Otherwise, if by the terms of his contract he be entitled to possession without such payment, or if, having been put into possession under his contract, he be ousted by fraud, force, or other illegal means. *Orne* v. *Coal Co.*, 114 Pa. St., 172 (1886).

§ 623. *It will not lie for land held by partners as firm property.* Land held by a firm as partnership property to be used for firm purposes is personalty as among the partners. If one partner sell his interest in the land, and the purchaser in turn sell, he cannot maintain ejectment against his vendee to enforce the payment of purchase-money before a settlement of the partnership accounts. In this case all of the parties were members of the firm which had held the land.

"The law is well settled that when a firm holds land, by deed expressed on its face to be the partnership property of the firm, it is stamped, so far as the partners are concerned, with all the attributes of personalty. It continues to be personalty until the partnership is dissolved, the business of the firm settled, and its debts paid. Until that time, it is held like other assets of the firm, and the extent of each partner's interest therein is to be ascertained on a final settlement. In the meantime, even a judgment against one partner will not be a lien on his interest in the land." Per MERCUR, J., *DuBree* v. *Albert*, 100 Pa. St., 483 (1882).

§ 624.

PRÆCIPE FOR SUMMONS IN EJECTMENT.

A. ⎫
v. ⎬
B. ⎭

To the Prothonotary of the Court of Common Pleas (No. 4), of Philadelphia County.

SIR: Issue summons in ejectment, returnable *sec. leg.*, for the premises whereof the following is a description (here describe the property), the title and right of possession whereof the plaintiff claims is in him.

C. D.,
Plaintiff's Attorney.
(Date.)

Indorse this:

A. ⎫
v. ⎬   Court,   Term, No.
B. ⎭

Præcipe in ejectment and description of land claimed.

C. D.,
Plaintiff's Attorney.

Amendment of a *præcipe* in ejectment which included more land than the plaintiff intended to claim, was allowed in Supreme Court. *Brothers* v. *Mitchell*, 157 Pa. St., 484 (1893).

§ 625. **Description to be filed.** As already noted, the Act of 1806 requires the plaintiff to file, on or before the first day of the term a "description of the land with the number of acres."

§ 626. *Let description be filed with præcipe.* Your *præcipe* should describe the land. Indorse it :

Præcipe in ejectment and description of the land claimed.

§ 627. *Let the description be full.* The decisions are not exactly in accord. In *Hawn* v. *Norris,* 4 Binn., 77 (1811), the description was in these words : "A tract of land situate in Armagh Township in the said county, containing fourteen acres and sixty-three perches or thereabouts, bounded by land of the said John Hawn."

Upon objection to this, the court below said : "The difficulty is as to a *description* of the land. What is the meaning of this ? * * * What is a description under the Act? If the legislature had meant a draft, they would have said so. The word is vague ; but it would seem to mean not a draft, but some convenient notice of the claim, which might inform the defendant what was to be tried. * * * The court think the substance has been complied with."

In the Supreme Court, TILGHMAN, C. J., said : "It is not for us to say that the form prescribed by the Act is insufficient. Indeed the description contains as much certainty as the ancient form of ejectment, and in some respects more ; for the old form did not require that the owners of the adjoining lands should be named." Judgment affirmed.

The same ruling seems to have been adopted in *Lyons* v. *Miller,* 4 S. & R., 279 (1818) ; *Thomas* v. *Kulp, Id.,* 271 (1818) ; *Tryon* v. *Carlin,* 5 Watts, 371 (1836) ; and in *R. R. Co.* v. *Roberts,* 8 W. N., 6 (1879).

But in *Hunt* v. *McFarland,* 38 Pa. St., 69 (1860), a different rule was adopted. The description was "a tract of land in Scott Township, Lawrence County, bounded on the west by George and Jacob McCracken, on the south by James Hunt and Alexander Hunt, east by land of Zachariah Dean, and north by land of plaintiff, containing about sixteen acres, more or less, being part of tract No. 1946, in the second district of donation lands," and the Supreme Court ruled, THOMPSON, J., " we think the verdict too vague and uncertain. It was a general verdict for the land described in the ejectment, with six cents damages. On referring to the writ, it is indescriptive excepting by adjoiners. *No shape or form of the land in dispute is given.* We think a delivery of it could not be made by the sheriff. If the jury had found for the plaintiff by a straight line from the maple to the chestnut corner, as they doubtless intended, it would have been sufficient, for this could have been made certain. But they did not do so. The instructions of the court were right enough, but the finding is too vague to sustain the judgment."

In *Flanigen* v. *The City*, 51 Pa. St., 491 (1866), it was ruled that in a city the description by the number of the house, etc., was sufficient. But that was a confessed judgment in an amicable action.

The safe practice is, undoubtedly, so to describe the land that the sheriff can execute his original and final writs without difficulty and with no extrinsic aid or explanation. If the plaintiff say that the property is in a certain township and has certain adjoiners, and no more, that description might fit two or more tracts in different parts of the township. Besides naming the township—or ward—and county, say on what road—or street—on what side of the road or street, the land is, the distance north, south, east, or west from the nearest intersecting street or road, how it is bounded, and its area—if a city lot, its frontage and depth. Thus :

All that certain lot or piece of land (with the three-story brick dwelling, etc., describe improvements as nearly as may be, thereon erected) situate on the west side of South Sixth Street, in the city of Philadelphia. Beginning at a point fifty feet north from the north side of Chestnut Street, thence extending north on Sixth Street twenty-five feet, and in depth between lines at right angles with Sixth Street sixty feet. Bounded on the north by land of A. B., on the south by land of C. D., on the west by land of E. F., and on the east by Sixth Street aforesaid.

§ 628. **Service of Writ.** Having filed your description and secured the summons in ejectment, you deliver it to the sheriff, paying him his costs and giving him directions as to the service. If the defendant reside on the land, you can mark under his name "on the premises." If he reside elsewhere and in the county, note his address, so that he may be served. Besides this, direct the deputy to serve on the land, and if there be any difficulty as to finding it, let him have full explanations. Remind him to secure the names of all who are "in possession of the whole or of part of the premises," to add their names to the writ, and to serve them. See *Nevins* v. *Manufacturing Co.*, 15 W. N., 344 (1884). In that case the sheriff returned one Griffith as in possession, but he did not add Griffith's name as a defendant. The plaintiff took judgment against Griffith for want of an appearance. The court struck it off, and said the sheriff should have added the name of Griffith as a defendant, and that the sheriff should state "in his return his whole action, including the fact of his having found a person not named in the writ in possession, and that thereupon he had added the name of such person to the writ and served the same upon him." Leave was given to the sheriff to amend his return accordingly, and the name of Griffith was added as a defendant.

§ 629. **Sheriff must return served—Plaintiff must prove defendant was in possession.** In *McIntire* v. *Wing*, 113 Pa. St., 67 (1886), where the sheriff did not serve defendants named in writ, but they appeared and pleaded, the plaintiff was non-suited on the trial because he did not prove that defendants were in possession. The plaintiff relied upon the fact that they appeared and pleaded. The Supreme Court affirmed the judgment, holding that in such a case it was necessary to prove that the defendants "were in possession of the premises."

In *Kulp* v. *Bowen*, 122 Pa. St., 78 (1888), it was ruled that the sheriff's return of service raised but a *prima facie* presumption of possession by defendant, which bound no one. The plaintiff is not estopped thereby from denying defendant's possession in another action.

On the authority of *Mitchell* v. *Bratton*, 5 Watts, 70 (1836), and *Ziegler* v. *Fisher*, 3 Pa. St., 367 (1846), a plaintiff, in order to recover in ejectment, must establish not only his own title, but also the possession of the defendant. *McCanna* v. *Johnston*, 19 Pa. St., 438 (1852).

Under the plea of "not guilty," the defendant can defend as to the whole or any part of the land in controversy. *Ziegler* v. *Fisher*, 3 Pa. St., 365 (1846).

By pleading the general issue, defendant does not admit himself to be in possession of the whole of the land claimed. *Bronson* v. *Lane*, 91 Pa. St., 153 (1879); *Contra: Ulsh* v. *Strode*, 13 Pa. St., 433 (1850); *Hill* v. *Hill*, 43 Pa. St., 521 (1862).

"*Not guilty*," *in ejectment, relieves the defendant from showing possession—the onus is on the plaintiff.* *McCanna* v. *Johnson* (*supra*). LEWIS, J.: * * * "H. M., after joining with McCanna in the plea of not guilty * * * claims a ground of defense arising from the failure of the plaintiff below to prove that M.'s actual possession extended over any part of the land in controversy. Be it so. * * * On the authority of *Mitchell* v. *Bratton* (*supra*) and *Ziegler* v. *Fisher* (*supra*), it seems that * * * a plaintiff, in order to recover in ejectment, must establish not only his own title, but also the possession of the defendant. There was error, therefore, in permitting a recovery against M. without proof of his possession." * * *

Bronson v. *Lane* (*supra*).   In ejectment for the land by A., the sheriff returned the writ as "served" upon the defendants, and the latter pleaded "not guilty," but at the trial proved that what they possessed they rightfully possessed under the grant, and as to the residue disproved possession. SHARSWOOD, C. J.: "We have failed .to discover any evidence sufficient to be submitted to the jury which showed possession by the defendants more than under their deeds they had a right to have. * * * Much stress was laid * * * on the fact that there was no disclaimer by the defendants of right to any part of the surface. * * * Disclaimer is never necessary—it may sometimes be advantageous to defendants as regards costs.

"The plea in ejectment, by the Act of 1807, is 'not guilty.' The defendants proved that whatever they possessed, they did rightfully possess under their grants, and as to the residue disproved possession ; thus the *prima facies* of the sheriff's return was met and rebutted. The plaintiff's claim was for the whole and defendants had a right to a general verdict."

Lowenstein v. *Searfoss*, 26 Atl. Rep., 448 (1893). Ejectment is a possessory action, and, in order to recover, the plaintiff must allege and prove that the defendant was in actual possession of the land at the time of the service of the writ. By the Act of 1807, the sheriff's return of service is made *prima facie* evidence of the fact, but it may be rebutted by other evidence, and, if rebutted, the defendant has made a complete defense, whatever may be his liability to the plaintiff in another form of action.

Whether or not the defendant was in actual possession is a question of fact, and where, upon competent evidence, a jury specially finds that the defendant was not in actual possession, a judgment cannot be entered against him, but he is entitled to judgment for his costs, even though he did not file a disclaimer with his plea.

The sheriff's return to a writ of ejectment was :

"Served the within writ of ejectment by giving a true and attested copy .thereof to L. W. B., defendant, personally, and making known to him the contents thereof on December 27, 1888.   C. B. served as above.   So answers
"G. B. S.,
"Sheriff."

(Affidavit of service.)

It was objected that the return did not show that C. B. had served as deputy sheriff, and that the copy filed was not attested. The return was held sufficient. *Bennethum* v. *Bowers*, 26 W. N., 8 (1890).

The sheriff's return to a writ of *habere facias possessionem*, showing that he had placed the plaintiff in possession, is *prima facie* evidence of possession in a second action wherein the plaintiff in the original suit is defendant. *Haupt* v. *Haupt*, 157 Pa. St., 469 (1893).

§ 630. *If defendant be not in the county*, the Act of April 18, 1853, already quoted, authorizes the service on any person in the county having charge or superintendence of the land as agent of the defendant, and if defendant be a corporation, the notice must be given to the president or other chief officer.

In *Losee* v. *McFarland*, 86 Pa. St., 33 (1877), it was held that service on the defendants, who were tenants about to remove from the premises, bound the landlord under whom they were in possession.

§ 631. *Sheriff to make affidavit of service.* The Act of April 13, 1807, section 2, requires that the officer shall make affidavit "stating the manner in which the said service was made" before judgment by default for want of appearance can be entered.

§ 632. **Defendant not bound to appear first term.** You will observe that the defendant, by the Act of December 5, 1860, has until the second term to appear. No judgment by default can be entered the first term. After your writ has been served, have the affidavit of service made, and note the case on your memorandum book, to see if an appearance be entered. It is supposed by many that it is not necessary to file a *narr.*, but as an objection is here, as often elsewhere, saved by labor, it is recommended to file a *narr.* before the return-day, and to be ready with summons returned and with affidavit of service, to take judgment at the second term if no appearance has been entered. See section 171 of this work, as to judgment for want of appearance. As you cannot take judgment in ejectment for want of an affidavit of defense, the remarks in that section in regard to the advisability of waiving your right to judgment for want of appearance have no place here.

Though the *præcipe* and description have been treated as a *narr.* in many cases, some practitioners prefer to file a *narr.* As already suggested, this would seem to be the better practice. It is especially advisable where you intend to claim *mesné* profits. Even when they are not claimed, the practice of filing a *narr.* has advantages.

The following may be used as a

FORM OF NARR. IN EJECTMENT.

In the Court of Common Pleas, No. 4, of Philadelphia County.
Of March Term, A.D. 1889, No. .
County of Philadelphia, *ss.*

C. D. was summoned to answer A. B. in a plea why with force and arms into all that (here describe the land) in said county, the right of possession

whereof was and is in the said plaintiff, the said defendant on (lay a day before teste of writ) at the county aforesaid, entered and from the said land with the appurtenances, buildings, profits, and privileges aforesaid ejected the plaintiff and committed other outrages upon him to the great damage of the said A. B. and against the peace, etc., whereby he says he has lost in *mesne* profits of said land, which he hereby claims, the sum of .
dollars, and that he is injured and has sustained damage to the value of $20,000, and therefore he brings suit.

E. F.,
Plaintiff's Attorney.
(Date.)

§ 633. **As to claiming mesne profits.** If you recover in the eject- ment, your judgment is conclusive in an action of trespass for the *mesne* profits. The ejectment may involve the same questions of fact for the jury, and a claim not only for the land, but for damages may give hostile jurors margin for compromises. It is therefore sometimes expedient to omit in the ejectment all claim for *mesne* profits. If you conclude to do so, alter the above form and charge *that defendant entered,* etc.

And from the said land with the appurtenances aforesaid ejected the plaintiff against the peace, etc., to the damage of the said A. B., and there- fore he brings suit.

E. F.,
Plaintiff's Attorney.
(Date.)

§ 634. **If you obtain judgment for want of an appearance, you secure possession by issuing an habere.** Give the prothonotary your

PRÆCIPE FOR THE HABERE.

A. B. ⎫   Common Pleas, No. 4, of Philadelphia County.
  v.   ⎬   March Term, 1889. No. .
C. D. ⎭

To the Prothonotary of said court :

SIR : Issue *habere facias possessionem* and *fi. fa.* for costs, returnable *sec. leg.*

E. F.,
Plaintiff's Attorney.
(Date.)

§ 635. **Form of habere facias possessionem.** The writ will be given to you in the following :

FORM OF HABERE.

County of Philadelphia, *ss.* [SEAL] The Commonwealth of Pennsyl- vania to the Sheriff of the County of Philadelphia, greeting : Whereas, plaintiff lately, that is to say, on the day of , A.D. 188 , in our Court of Common Pleas, No. 4, of the County of Philadelphia, before our judges, at Philadelphia, by the consid- eration of the said court, recovered against defendant

late of your county,   Now, therefore, we command you that, justly and without delay, the aforesaid plaintiff possession of and in the tenements aforesaid, with the appurtenances, you cause to have, etc. And how you shall have executed this our writ, make known to our judges, at Philadelphia, at our said Court of Common Pleas, No. 4, there to be held the first Monday of   next. And we also command you, that of the goods and chattels, lands and tenements of the said defendant in your bailiwick, you cause to be levied the sum of
dollars and   cents, which was adjudged to the said plaintiff in our said court, for the damages which he sustained by occasion of the trespass upon the said premises by the said defendant and the ejectment of the said plaintiff therefrom, whereof the said defendant is convict, as appears of record, etc. And have you that money before our said judges, at the day and place aforesaid, to render to the said plaintiff for the damages aforesaid. And have you then and there this writ. Witness the Honorable   , President Judge of our said court, at Philadelphia, the   day of   , in the year of our Lord one thousand eight hundred and eighty-
                                        Prothonotary.

If appearance entered, the plaintiff enters a rule to plead (see section 26), and if no response be made, he enters judgment for want of a plea. (Section 26.) Such judgment cannot be had until the second term, however. *Young* v. *Cooper,* 6 W. N., 43 (1878).

If the case be defended, there may be a disclaimer filed by one or more of the defendants, or an application by the landlord to intervene. We will consider these in order.

§ 636. **A disclaimer** is filed when a person served has no claim or title. In such a case, service of the writ has been made upon a stranger who should not have been served. If a defendant appear and plead "not guilty," he can defend as to all or as to part, and disprove possession as to the residue.

But the correct practice for one who has no claim is not to plead. The plea being prescribed as a method of trying the title, should not be resorted to where there is no claim of title. One who makes no pretense of title must enter his disclaimer early. *Steinmetz* v. *Logan,* 3 Watts, 160 (1834).

§ 637.

FORM OF DISCLAIMER.

A. B.   ⎫   In the Court of Common Pleas, No. 4, of Philadelphia
  v.   ⎬   County. Of March Term, 1889. No. .
C. D.   ⎭

And now C. D., served as defendant in the above-entitled cause (or E. F., returned as served by the sheriff in the above case), comes into court, and in his own proper person files this his

Disclaimer

of all title or claim of title or of possession to the premises described in the
writ in the above case, and to every part thereof.

C. D. (or E. F.),

(Disclaimant's signature.)

G. H., Att'y for

(Date.)

The disclaimant should sign and acknowledge this before a magistrate, judge, or notary.   It should be indorsed :

A. B. ⎫
  v.   ⎬   (Court, Term, and No.)
C. D. ⎭

Disclaimer of C. D. (or E. F.).

Name of Attorney.

Obviously, no man should disclaim who has any title.   The instrument is a very solemn renunciation of all claims.

§ 638. *Disclaimer as to part.*   If part of the land be claimed by
the person served, he can plead, as to it (describing the part), "not
guilty," thus :

And the said C. D., as to the part of the premises named in said writ,
which is embraced in the following

DESCRIPTION :

(Here describe part claimed.)

Pleads Not Guilty.

And as to the residue of said land the said C. D. files this his

Disclaimer

of all title or claim of title or of possession to said last-mentioned premises
and to every part thereof.

(Signature and acknowledgment as above directed.)

§ 639. *If Disclaimant had been actually in possession as claiming
title,* the plaintiff can order the case on the trial-list, and by proving
defendant had first claimed and excluded plaintiff, then by giving
in evidence the sheriff's return and the disclaimer, the plaintiff
would be entitled to a verdict which would give him possession
and costs.   This applies to the case of a defendant who plays fast
and loose.   Ordinarily, the disclaimer is filed by one of several defendants, the rest pleading "not guilty."   Do not treat the disclaimant as not pleading and enter a judgment against him for
want of a plea.   The counsel who did this in *Abrahams* v. *Tripner* afterward discovered his error, and asked the court to strike
off his own judgment.   *Tripner* v. *Abrahams*, 47 Pa. St., 220
(1864).

§ 640. *Where husband disclaims.*   In *Duncan* v. *Sherman*, 121

Pa. St., 520 (1888), the husband was sued alone. He filed a disclaimer. The plaintiff, instead of taking judgment without costs, went to issue. On the trial, the defendant showed that his acts were as agent of his wife. But he did not prove any title in his wife. Under instruction, the jury found for defendant. The Supreme Court reversed. WILLIAMS, J., said : "The plaintiff had the right, when this statement went upon the record, to take judgment against the defendant, and so end the case ; but such judgment, as it must rest upon the disclaimer, would necessarily be at the plaintiff's own cost. * * * But the plaintiff had the right to take issue with the defendant upon the question of his possession, and, if he succeeded in showing that the disclaimer was in this particular untrue, then the action was necessary, and the plaintiff was entitled to a judgment for his costs, as well as for the land described in his writ. * * *

"The plaintiff showed possession, *prima facie*, by the sheriff's return, and followed this by proof that the defendant was upon the land, in the exercise of acts of apparent ownership, from time to time. To this showing the defendant's reply was that he was the agent of his wife, and his acts upon the ground were hers, done under her direction. We think this would have been a sufficient reply if he had shown that his wife had title. His disclaimer was, for the purpose of the trial, an admission of the plaintiff's title upon which, as we have seen, judgment might properly be entered against him, and he could not defend his possession under the title of a stranger after such an admission. But we have held that this rule is subject to an exception in favor of the wife ; because otherwise, as has been well said, she would be worse off than a stranger, as she would be put out of possession, with her husband, without a hearing upon her separate right to the possession. * * * It was necessary to show affirmatively that she did not derive her title from him, but by an honest purchase, with her own separate means, or in such other legal manner as would give her a title good against the pursuing creditor. * * * The defendant having, in effect, admitted the title of the plaintiff by his disclaimer, could not defend his position under his wife without showing a title in her. Until this was shown, the legal presumption was in full force that she was in by virtue of his title."

§ 641. **Intervention by landlord.** Cases may occur in which the landlord is not named in the writ or in the sheriff's return. Whilst the tenant might be assisted by the landlord to defeat the plaintiff's recovery, the law allows the landlord to become a party to the case, and this is the safer course.

The Act of 1772, already noted, requires the tenant to give notice to the landlord, and declares that it shall be lawful for the court to suffer the landlord to make himself a defendant.

§ 642.

LANDLORD'S PETITION TO BECOME A PARTY.

A.
v. } In the Court of Common Pleas, No. 4, of Philadelphia County.
B. }   Of March Term, 1889. No. .

To the Honorable the Judges of said Court:

The petition of C. D. humbly showeth:

That a summons in ejectment has been issued in the above case, which has been returned by the sheriff as served upon B. That by said writ the plaintiff claims to recover possession of (brief description of the land). That no other person has been returned as served by the sheriff except the defendant B. (If the sheriff have served others, state the fact according to the record.) That petitioner is the landlord of the defendant B. for said premises under a lease from petitioner to defendant (in writing, a copy whereof is hereto attached) or made (mention date and the term). That defendant has no interest in, or title to, said land save as petitioner's tenant. That the petitioner is the owner of said land in severalty. Your petitioner desires to appear and to defend. (If he failed to petition at the return of the writ, state the reason for the delay, etc.) He therefore prays the court to suffer him to make himself a defendant, to appear and to plead to said writ and to defend the same.

C. D.

(Affidavit of truth of the facts set forth in the petition.)

Indorse:

A.
v. } Court,   Term,   No. .
B. }

Petition and affidavit of C. D., landlord, to be made party defendant, to appear, to plead, and to defend.

And now   on motion of E. F., attorney pro C. D., the court grant a rule on plaintiff and on defendant to show cause why the prayer of the petition should not be granted, and why the petitioner should not be made a party defendant to appear, to plead to said writ, and to defend the same. Rule returnable   .

§ 643. *If the plaintiff oppose this rule,* he should file his answer, stating his reasons. One objection might be that the petitioner was not the landlord of the defendant—that he was an intruder—that the plaintiff was defendant's landlord, and that the petitioner really claimed adversely to both. This was the case in *Boyer* v. *Smith*, 5 Watts, 55 (1836).

§ 644. *The court must pass upon the application.* The statute 11 Geo. II., ch. 19, s. 13, is similar to the Pennsylvania Act. It was at first held in England that no one could be admitted unless he had been in some degree in possession, as receiving rent. But this was repudiated by Lord Mansfield, Burr. Rep., 1290, and the Act was construed to extend to any person whose title was connected and consistent with the possession of the occupier. This is cited in *McClay* v. *Benedict*, 1 Rawle, 424 (1829), where it was ruled that the admission of a party claiming right to defend in ejectment as landlord, under the ninth section of the Act March 21, 1772, is an act of the court, "whose duty it is to inquire, before making the order, whether the applicant stands in relation of landlord, or whether his claim of title is consistent with the possession of the occupier."

ROGERS, J., said: "The ninth section of the Act March 21, 1772, prescribes that it shall and may be lawful for the court, where an ejectment may be brought, to suffer the landlord to make himself a defendant. * * * It is not a matter of course that a person should be made a co-defendant. * * * The very question in dispute between the parties may be, whether the person claiming to be made a co-defendant is entitled to be landlord or not. * * * Hence it is that the Act has very wisely given the court a control over this matter, as otherwise a stranger to the record might obtain an advantage over the parties to the suit."

In that case, no petition or affidavit was filed and no order of court was obtained. A person calling himself attorney for a landlord appeared and entered a rule of reference. It was held that this was irregular.

§ 645. *No intruder can be heard, and there should be no delay.* To *Boyer* v. *Smith*, 5 Watts, 55 (1836), above cited, may be added the case of *Linderman* v. *Berg*, 12 Pa. St., 301 (1849). That suit was commenced in 1846. In 1848, Stewart, a member of Congress, presented a petition setting forth that he had sold the land to the defendant with warranty, and praying to be substituted as defendant, and for delay on account of his official duties requiring his absence. The court below refused the application. The Supreme Court affirmed.

They held that as the petitioner had no reversionary interest, he was not within the statute. They commented also on the delay, saying: "Where the purpose is delay, it might perhaps be thought that the party had dispensed with his right till the exercise of it would be an abuse of it."

§ 646. *Where relation of landlord and tenant subsists, and no unreasonable delay, the Act is mandatory.* In *Bell* v. *Caldwell*, 107 Pa. St., 46 (1884), the application to intervene was refused. The Supreme Court reversed. CLARK, J., stated the law with great clearness: "The power to be exercised by the courts in this behalf is in the interests of public justice, and although the language of the statute is merely permissive in form, yet as public as well as private interests call for its exercise, it must be considered as mandatory.

"W. Patterson Bell was in the actual possession of the premises at the service of the writ—it should have been served upon him and his name entered upon the record as a defendant. He was then, however, a tenant for years, and his landlord was a party to the action. The tenant's possession was involved in the contest of the title—he had no rights which were not identical with those of his landlord, who was the real and substantial party. The tenant, in such case, might well deem it unnecessary to join in the defense. It was the entry of the non-suit by the plaintiff which developed the duty of W. Patterson Bell to defend. If the defendant had not suffered non-suit, the possession of Joseph Bell might have been vindicated by the exhibition of his co-defendant's title. By a mere juggle of a non-suit it is attempted to exclude all evidence of the title upon which that possession might be defended."

§ 647. **Plea.** The only plea is "not guilty." This puts the case at issue. Order the case on the trial-list. Notify your client. Examine every link of your title. Prepare to prove everything. Order certified copies of all papers, and exemplifications of all records necessary for your case. Examine and cross-examine your client and all his witnesses. Then dive into the defense. Prepare your brief for trial, your brief of title, your brief of the law as to all the points which may arise. If any witness be in bad health or about to depart, secure his deposition. If any be absent, enter rule for a commission. In many counties it is the practice, established and regulated by rule of court, to require the parties to file abstracts of their respective titles before trial. See *Scott* v. *Ames*, 4 Penny., 475 (1884) ; *Ireland* v. *Bagaley*, 21 W. N., 240 (1888).

When ejectment is brought by a purchaser at a sheriff's sale, the defendant in the execution cannot set up title under a lease from a third person *after* judgment under which the land was sold. *Dunlap* v. *Cooke*, 18 Pa. St., 454 (1852).

§ 648. **If you obtain verdict and judgment,** issue *habere* and *fi. fa.*, as already noted above. Where judgment has been entered under an amicable action in ejectment, the sheriff will be ordered to proceed to execute the writ of *habere possessionem*, although a third person intervene claiming the possession. *Kelly* v. *Northrop*, 159 Pa. St., 537 (1894). When possession delivered, sue for *mesne* profits.

§ 649. **Execution for mesne profits.** If the recovery in ejectment include *mesne* profits, execution should be issued for them also. Prepare *præcipe* for *fi. fa.*, and proceed as directed in sections 23, 24, and 25.

A *capias ad satisfaciendum* may also issue in such case. *Hopkinson* v. *Cooper*, 8 Phila., 8 (1871).

§ 650. **Under rule for further process, time begins to run from making rule absolute.** In *Herron* v. *Fetterman*, 14 W. N., 480 (1884), it was held that when proceedings are instituted under the Act of June 11, 1879 (P. L., 127), by the party in possession to compel another to bring ejectment in ninety days or be forever barred, the ninety days begin to run from the time when the rule is made absolute.

"The Act * * * must receive a reasonable construction. It is not the initiation of the proceedings before the court which bars the right to bring ejectment, but it is the judgment of the court on making the rule absolute."

By Act of June 24, 1885 (P. L., 152), the process was amended, and the ninety days made by legislative enactment to run from the making absolute of the rule.

§ 651. **Estrepement.** A few suggestions as to estrepement may not be out of place. There were in England two kinds of writs forbidding waste *pendente placito* (pending the suit): one out of chancery, the other issued by the court where the suit was pending. A guardian was forbidden by Magna Charta to commit waste. The Statute of Marleberge, 52 Henry III., ch. 23, was directed against *fermors* (farmers).

By the common law, the only prohibition was against tenant by courtesy, in dower, and guardians.

§ 652. **The English Statutes in force in Pennsylvania** : 6 *Edward I.*, *ch.* 5 (1278). "It is provided, also, that a man from henceforth shall have a writ of waste in the chancery against him that holdeth by law of England or otherwise, for term of life or for term of years or a woman in dower. And he which shall be attainted of waste shall lease the thing that he hath wasted, and moreover, shall recompense thrice so much as the waste shall be taxed at."

§ 653. 6 *Edward I.*, *ch.* 13 (1278). "It is provided, also, that after such time as a plea shall be moved in the city of London by writ, the tenant shall have no power to make any waste or estrepement of the land in demand (hanging the plea), and if he do the mayor and bailiffs shall cause it to be kept at the suit of the demandant. And the same ordinance and statute shall be observed in other cities, boroughs, and everywhere throughout the realm."

§ 654. *The Statute of* 13 *Edward I.*, *ch.* 14 (1285), provided for a summons in cases of waste in lieu of the prohibition formerly allowed.

§ 655. *The Statute of* 13 *Edward I.*, *ch.* 22 (1285), allowed tenant in common to maintain action for waste against his co-tenant.

§ 656. *The Statute of* 20 *Edward I.* (1292) allowed the heir to sue for waste committed in the lifetime of his ancestor.

§ 657. *The Statute of* 2 *Henry VI.*, *ch.* 5 (1433), provided a remedy by reversioners, with treble damages against tenants for waste committed after the tenants have sublet their estates.

§ 658. **The Pennsylvania Statutes.** *All plaintiffs in ejectments may have the writ.* Act of April 2, 1803, section 2 (4 Sm., 89), already cited, declares that the prothonotary or clerk of the court in which the ejectment shall be depending, upon affidavit filed of plaintiff or other person knowing the fact that the tenant or defendant has committed or is committing waste and destruction of or in the premises, shall issue a writ of estrepement to prevent the same, of course, without motion and in vacation, the affidavit to be sworn to before judge of Supreme Court or in any Court of Common Pleas.

§ 659. *Writ extended to Landlords. Purchasers at Sheriff's Sales. Judgment Creditors and Mortgagees.* The next Act was that of March 29, 1822 (7 Sm., 520). In section 1 it extended the remedy to three classes of persons :

1. Any owner during the lease or after its expiration and due notice to the tenant to leave.

2. Any purchasers at sheriff's or coroner's sale after they have been declared highest bidders.

3. Any mortgagee or judgment creditor after condemnation of land by inquisition, or where land is subject to be sold by a *venditioni* or a *levari.*

These parties may apply to Court of Common Pleas of proper county or to judge in vacation, and in petition and affidavit by them or any credible person charge that tenant or person in possession has committed waste or allows or threatens it, and that it is verily apprehended, in consequence of such threat, that such waste will be committed unless restrained.

The court or judge, in their or his discretion, may order prothonotary to issue estrepement, which shall have same effect as an estrepement issued after ejectment brought.

The second section authorizes the court to dissolve the estrepement or make further order therein.

§ 660. *Quarrying, Mining, etc., are Waste.* The Act of March

27, 1833 (P. L., 99), makes quarrying and mining, and all such acts as will do lasting injury, waste.

But if the working and opening were previous to the ejectment, no estrepement can issue until the next term, or until plaintiff file affidavit that the title or right of possession to the premises or part thereof is in him, and until his attorney shall certify his opinion that the title or right, etc., is vested in plaintiff. The court may dissolve the estrepement on security to plaintiff, or on such other terms as court may deem just.

§ 661. *Remainder-man may have Estrepement.* The Act of April 10, 1848 (P. L., 472), extended the remedy so as to embrace estates and tenants for life, and upon application of remainder-man or his agent. But five days* notice must be given not to commit waste or to desist therefrom ; and upon motion to dissolve the writ, the court must inquire into and determine the extent of the reasonable and necessary use and enjoyment by tenants for life. Such use and enjoyment shall not be restrained.

Persons having contingent interest may sue to prevent waste or for damages for its commission. The Act of June 8, 1891 (P. L., 208), provides :

> That from and after the passage of this Act it shall be lawful for any person or persons having a contingent interest in any real estate in this Commonwealth, and not being in possession of the same, to commence and prosecute any suit or suits at law or in equity to prevent the commission of waste to such real estate, or to recover damages for waste committed or injury done to such real estate, in the same manner and form as they might or could do was such interest vested and the person or persons having such interest in actual possession of the same : *Provided,* That before any suit at law or equity is commenced the said person or persons having such contingent interest shall apply to the Court of Common Pleas of the county where such land or part of the same is situated, for the appointment of some suitable person to take and receive any and all moneys that may be so received in any suit or suits, which person shall, after recovery of judgment and before any money or property passes, give such bond with such sureties as may be approved by said court, and shall hold any and all such moneys received as aforesaid subject to the orders of said court. Such receiver shall receive such compensation for his services as the court may allow.

§ 662. *Mortgagees, after commencing proceedings, may issue the Writ.* The first section of Act of April 22, 1850 (P. L., 549 ; Br. Purd., 2080, section 8), went a step further in favor of mortgagees than the Act of 1822. Under the Act of 1822, the land must be subject to be sold by *levari.* The Act of 1850 extended the remedy to all cases after proceedings instituted to collect the mortgage. No mortgagor to be restrained from reasonable and necessary enjoyment of the land, and the court to have power to modify the writs, to make equitable orders, and to enforce them by attachment.

§ 663. *Creditors of Decedent may have the Writ.* The second section of the Act of April 22, 1850, extends the right to the creditor of a decedent, the personal estate being insufficient to pay just debts.

§ 664. *Timber trees not to be removed.* The third section forbids removal of timber trees, although cut down before issuing of the estrepement, if the removal be injurious to the petitioner ; and all timber so removed may be replevied.

§ 665. *Courts may dissolve, etc.* The Act of May 4, 1852, section 2 (P. L., 584), authorizes the courts to hear parties in a summary way, and dissolve estrepements or make further order.

§ 666. *Plaintiffs in Foreign Attachments may have the Writ.* The Act of May 8, 1855, section 4 (P. L., 533), extends the right to an estrepement to plaintiffs in foreign attachments after execution of the writ.

§ 667. *Security to be entered before Estrepement issues, except where ejectment brought to compel specific performance of contract of sale.* The Act of April 11, 1862 (P. L., 430), is very important, for it extends to estrepement the provisions of the Act of May 6, 1844, requiring security upon injunctions. The Act of May 6, 1844, directs that " no injunctions shall be issued by any court or judge until the party applying for the same shall have given bond, with sufficient sureties, to be approved by said court or judge, conditioned to indemnify the other party for all damages that may be sustained by reason of such injunction."

But this security need not be entered in any action of ejectment brought to compel specific performance of contract for sale of land. Act April 2, 1863 (P. L., 250).

§ 668. *Estrepement may issue pending Writ of Error.* Estrepement allowed in real actions, dower, partition, waste, and ejectment after writ of error issued by defendant. Act April 20, 1869, section 1 (P. L., 76).

By the second section the writ is to issue, of course, upon filing affidavit and bond ; the court may dissolve on defendant giving bond.

§ 669. *Tenant in common of timber land cannot cut or remove timber trees without written consent of all co-tenants.* Act May 4, 1869, section 1 (P. L., 1251). The second section declares no title shall pass by his sale, and the others may sue at law and in equity to recover the timber. The third section allows the estrepement to issue on affidavit, etc., as in ejectments for real estate, upon violation of this Act.

§ 670. *Estrepements where mortgage on leasehold sued out.* The provisions of these Acts still further extended to proceedings on mortgages of leaseholds ; affidavit to be filed, security may be required, court may dissolve, enforce orders by attachments, etc. Act June 2, 1871 (P. L., 290).

§ 671. *President Judges may dissolve Estrepements in vacation* on notice. Act Feb. 18, 1873 (P. L., 35).

§ 672. *Estrepement may issue to prevent production of petroleum* where ejectment pending. Act June 5, 1883 (P. L., 79).

Affidavit and bond are to be filed. § 2.

Writ may be dissolved. § 3.

Receiver may be appointed (if there be an open well) by law judge at chambers unless defendant give bond of indemnity. § 4.

§ 673. *Purchasers of unseated lands sold for taxes by County Treasurer*, on petition and affidavit, may obtain estrepement from court or any judge in vacation. The writ may be dissolved on payment of redemption-money during time allowed by law, and all costs of the estrepement ; the *pro rata* amount of twenty-five per cent., which would have accrued at the time such redemption is made, being only required to be paid. Act June 13, 1883 (P. L., 89).

§ 674. *Estrepement pending tax lien to prevent waste of timber.* When taxes are returned to the commissioners, under section 1 of Act June 2, 1881 (P. L., 45) [said Act does not extend to cities of first, second, and fourth classes], of any county, they may sue out a writ of estrepement to prevent cutting of timber trees on land upon which the taxes are assessed, or the removal therefrom of any timber, bark, lumber, or other article manufactured from said timber. The writ shall be in force until the taxes shall have been paid. It shall be obtained by affidavit, and allowed in the same manner as estrepement pending ejectment, with like proceedings and effect as to service and dissolution. Act May 4, 1889 (P. L., 83).

§ 675. *What acts may be restrained by estrepement.* Clearly all acts which amount to waste may be enjoined. *Vastum* is defined by Blackstone to be "a spoil or destruction, in any corporeal hereditaments, to the prejudice of him that hath the inheritance." Black. Comm., Book II., p. 281.

§ 676. *The legislative definitions* in the Pennsylvania statutes above quoted are as follows :

" Quarrying and mining, and all such other acts as will do lasting injury to the premises." Act March 27, 1833, section 3 (P. L., 99).

"Cutting of timber, extracting coal, stone, gravel, sand, oil, peat, slate, plumbago, clay, iron, and other ores and minerals." Act April 20, 1869, section 1 (P. L., 76).

"The cutting of timber trees." Act May 4, 1869, section 1 (P. L., 1251).

"Production of petroleum from land in controversy in any action of ejectment." Act June 5, 1883, section 1 (P. L., 79).

Every act, therefore, which produces a lasting injury to the land may be subject of complaint.

§ 677. *By decision, it has been held waste* for a tenant to open new mines or quarries upon the land. *Griffin* v. *Fellows*, 81 Pa. St., 114 (1873). But tenant for life may work mines already opened, even to exhaustion. *Neel* v. *Neel*, 19 Pa. St., 323 (1852); *Lynn's Appeal*, 31 Pa. St., 44 (1857); *Westmoreland Coal Co.'s Appeal*, 85 Pa. St., 344 (1877); *Irwin* v. *Covode*, 24 Pa. St., 162 (1854); *Sayers* v. *Hoskinson*, 110 Pa. St., 473 (1885). He may also cut timber required in such mining operations. *Neel* v. *Neal* (*supra*), *Lynn's Appeal* (*supra*). It is waste for tenant for life to remove during his occupancy buildings of a permanent character erected by himself, if the inheritance be thereby injured. *McCullough* v. *Irvine*, 13 Pa. St., 438 (1850). So if a judgment debtor remove a house from his land after levy thereon, and the price realized at the sheriff's sale be thereby lessened, this is waste which will sustain an action by the execution creditor. *Christian* v. *Mills*, 16 W. N., 393 (1885). It is waste for the outgoing tenant of a farm to remove the manure. *Lewis* v. *Jones*, 17 Pa. St., 262 (1851). But it is not waste for defendant in ejectment to harvest the annual crop. *Snyder* v. *Depew*, 1 Lack. L. Rec., 477.

§ 678. *Whether the removal of timber constitutes waste* will depend upon the facts of each case, the value of the timber, the custom of neighboring landholders, etc. *Givens* v. *McCalmont*, 4 Watts, 460 (1835); *McCullough* v. *Irvine*, 13 Pa. St., 438 (1850). Cutting timber to the injury of the inheritance by a vendor, under articles of agreement for sale of the land, is waste. *Smith's Appeal*, 69 Pa. St., 474 (1871). A life tenant may cut timber though the land be valuable for no other purpose. *Williard* v. *Williard*, 56 Pa. St., 119 (1867); *Hastings* v. *Crunckleton*, 3 Yeates, 261 (1801); *Beam* v. *Woolridge*, 3 Pa. C. C., 17 (1887). But wanton or excessive use of timber by the life-tenant will be restrained by estrepement. *Williard* v. *Williard* (*supra*). It is not waste for life-tenant to fell and remove decaying trees which would otherwise become worthless. *Sayers* v. *Hoskinson*, 110 Pa. St., 473 (1885).

§ 679. *Mortgagor of property intended to be used as building lots* will be restrained from digging sand and stone when he is thereby lessening the value of the property and diminishing the security of the mortgagee. *Martin's Appeal*, 3 Montg., 75 (1887). The mortgagor of real estate may continue, after the execution of the mortgage, to cut and sell the timber growing upon the premises, and the mortgagee cannot maintain an action for the value of the timber against the vendee thereof, in the absence of collusion or fraud between the vendee and the mortgagor. *Angier* v. *Agnew*, 98 Pa. St., 587 (1881).

Under the Act of March 29, 1822 (7 Sm., 520), estrepement may issue against a tenant during the continuance of the lease without previous notice to quit. *Heil* v. *Strong*, 44 Pa. St., 264 (1863).

§ 680. *Who can issue Estrepements.*

1. As a general rule, all plaintiffs in ejectment. (Act of April 2, 1803.)

2. Judgment plaintiffs who have levied on and condemned land, and the land is subject to be sold by a *venditioni exponas*. (Act of March 29, 1822.)

3. Mortgagees who have proceeded upon their mortgages. (Act of April 22, 1850.)

4. Any owner during the lease, or after its expiration and notice to leave. (Act of March 29, 1822.)

5. Purchasers at sheriff's sales. (Act of March 29, 1822.)

6. Remainder-men. (6 Edward I., ch. 5, and Act of April 10, 1848.)

7. Creditors of decedent. (Act of April 22, 1850.)

8. Plaintiffs in foreign attachment. (Act of May 8, 1855.)

9. Tenants in common of timber land. (Act of May 4, 1869.)

10. Commissioners to prevent waste of timber when taxes are returned unpaid. (Act May 4, 1889.)

In *Givens* v. *McCalmont*, 4 Watts, 460 (1835), it was held that a mortgagee in possession might be restrained from committing waste.

A devisee of a contingent remainder cannot maintain an action for waste. *Sager* v. *Galloway*, 113 Pa. St., 500 (1886). See Act of 1891, cited at § 661.

§ 681. *To obtain Estrepement.* Plaintiffs in ejectment make affidavit, and where the ejectment is not to enforce specific performance on contract for sale of land, they give bond.

When the ejectment is to enforce such specific performance, estrepement issues of course.

The other parties named in the foregoing summary are not treated of in this chapter.

§ 682.

AFFIDAVIT FOR ESTREPEMENT.

A. B.   In the Court of Common Pleas, No. 4, of Philadelphia
   v.   County. Of March Term, 1889. No. .
C. D.

A. B., the plaintiff in the above case, having been duly sworn according to law, doth depose and say :

That the above action is an ejectment brought for the recovery of (here briefly describe the land) in the county of Philadelphia, and that the writ has been duly served on C. D. and so duly returned.

That deponent is the owner of said premises, and entitled to possession thereof.

That C. D., the defendant, has been for some time past, to wit, since   and still is unlawfully committing waste upon said property and materially injuring and destroying the value of the same in this, that the said defendant has been during the time aforesaid and still is unlawfully (here describe the acts of waste) cutting down and carrying away valuable timber, or quarrying stone, or mining coal or iron ore (etc., as the case may be).

That the said C. D. threatens to continue said illegal acts and to commit other acts of waste.

That the aforesaid acts of said C. D. have already resulted in producing injury to said property and loss and damage to deponent to the amount of at least   dollars.

That if the said C. D. is not restrained, he will continue to commit waste and produce an irreparable loss and injury to deponent.

(Plaintiff's signature.)

Sworn to and subscribed before me,   Judge of Court of Common Pleas, No.   , of the County of Philadelphia.

Under the Act of 1803, this affidavit may be made "by the plaintiff or other person knowing the fact."

If the affidavit be made by another than the plaintiff, the phraseology can easily be changed to conform to the fact.

The Act of March 29, 1822, as to landlords, etc., speaks of a "Petition and affidavit." Where a petition is required, the above form of affidavit can readily be changed to a petition, and an affidavit of the truth of the facts can be added.

§ 683. *Præcipe for Estrepement.* When the writ issues of course, file the above affidavit and the following *præcipe :*

A. B.   ⎫
   v.   ⎬   C. P., No. .
C. D.   ⎭   Term, 189 . No. .

To the Prothonotary of the Court of Common Pleas (No. 4) of Philadelphia County.

SIR : Issue estrepement, *sec. leg.*

E. F.,
Plaintiff's Attorney.
(Date.)

Indorse this :

A. B.   ⎫
   v.   ⎬   Court,   Term,   No.
C. D.   ⎭

Præcipe for estrepement.

The prothonotary then signs and puts the seal of the court to the writ. It is rarely issued, and counsel may be compelled to prepare it. § 684.

FORM OF WRIT OF ESTREPEMENT (IN CASE OF A MORTGAGE).

The Commonwealth of Pennsylvania. To the High Sheriff of the City and County of Philadelphia, and to (name of defendant), greeting : Whereas, By the law of the land no waste or strip ought to be committed in any lands or tenements by any tenant during his possession of premises conveyed to him under and subject to the payment of any mortgage debt, and whereas on the   day of   , A.D. 18 , executed and delivered to   a mortgage upon (description of premises) to secure to the said   the payment of the sum of dollars, with interest thereon, in   years from the date thereof, which mortgage contained a proviso, that in case the interest upon the said principal sum in the mortgage shall not be paid within   days after the same shall become due and payable, that then and in such case, at the option of the mortgagee, the whole principal sum shall become due and payable. That the said interest is more than   days in arrears, and that the principal sum has thereby become due and payable, and that the said mortgage is still unsatisfied, and the premises are subject to be sold by a *levari facias* on said mortgage ; and whereas the said (name of defendant) has become the owner of the premises subject to the payment of the mortgage debt of   dollars with interest thereon, and he is now in the possession and occupancy of said premises ; and whereas, by an Act of Assembly of the Commonwealth of Pennsylvania, it is amongst other things provided that it shall and may be lawful for the prothonotary or clerk of the Court of Common Pleas of the proper county, upon petition to the said court setting forth that the defendant is committing waste, and sworn to by the plaintiff, to issue a writ of estrepement to prevent the same ; and whereas the said   , the plaintiff in this writ, has presented his petition to the Court of Common Pleas, No.   , for the County of Philadelphia, setting forth that the defendant is in possession of the said mortgaged premises, as the owner thereof, and that he has committed and is committing waste and destruction of and in said premises in this, that he is (here set forth the grievances). We, therefore, being willing that the law and statute aforesaid shall be maintained and duly observed, do command you, the said sheriff, that you strictly prohibit and restrain the said (name of defendant)

and his agents, and several employés, from doing or committing the said
waste and destruction of, and in the said premises contrary to the law and
statutes aforesaid. And we command you, the said (name of the defendant), that you do not do or commit or cause to be done or committed any
waste or destruction of or in the said premises, and particularly (here set
forth specifically the matters of grievance). Witness the Honorable
                President Judge of the Court of Common Pleas, No.   , for the
County of Philadelphia, the   day of   , in the
year of our Lord one thousand eight hundred and
                                        (Signature of Prothonotary.)

Indorsement :
No.   ,   Term,   1889.
    A. ⎫
    v. ⎬   C. P. No.
    B. ⎭
                      Estrepement.

§ 685. *Service of Estrepement.* The sheriff should read the original writ to the defendant and give him a true and attested copy.

§ 686. *If writ disobeyed,* file affidavit of service as above and of
the acts of disobedience, obtain a rule on defendant to show cause
why he should not be attached for disobedience of the estrepement,
serve this rule personally, have affidavit of personal service ready ;
if no answer be filed, the court will make the rule absolute. Issue
and serve the attachment.

If defendant file an answer denying the charges against him,
enter a rule to take depositions, prove your client's allegations, and
secure the attachment.

§ 687. After judgment in ejectment, the plaintiff cannot assess his
damages by writ of inquiry, he must sue for mesne profits. The
British Statute, 16 and 17 Chas. II., ch. 8 (Rob. Dig., *42), which
provides in section 4 for a writ of inquiry of the *mesne* profits as
damages by any waste committed after the first judgment in dower
or in *ejectione firmœ*, is not in force in Pennsylvania.

The Act of June 11, 1879, and Act of Feb. 23, 1889, cited at
§§ 607, 608, provide : "That whenever an action of ejectment is
pending for the recovery of real estate, the plaintiff or plaintiffs
therein, or any person having such right of action may, as well
before as after the termination of said ejectment, bring an action or
actions for *mesne* profits against any person or persons, but such
action or actions for *mesne* profits shall not be proceeded with to trial
and judgment until the plaintiff or plaintiffs shall have recovered
possession of the real estate in controversy." In *Warren* v. *Steer,*
118 Pa. St., 529 (1888), PAXSON, J., it was *held* that the Act of
1879 afforded a complete remedy for rents, etc., retained pending a
writ of error, if the judgment below were affirmed.

CHAPTER XV.

§ 688. **When issued.** This writ issued at common law where judgment had been entered by default for damages generally and the damages did not admit of calculation. The writ issued to the sheriff, who, with his jury, assessed the damages. The return merely informed the court, who could in all cases assess the damages.

§ 689. *In Philadelphia,* the rule of the Courts of Common Pleas (section 95 *a*) is in these words :

" Judgment by default of any kind may be moved before and entered by the prothonotary, who shall assess the damages in all cases in which the amount thereof is set forth with certainty in the statement of claim filed."

§ 690. *The old rule of Court of Common Pleas in Philadelphia* was in these words :

" The prothonotary shall ascertain the damages in all cases of judgment by default, where the suit is brought on a promissory note, bill of exchange, or book account. He shall also ascertain the damages in all other cases founded on contract, and sounding in damages, where the defendant does not object. But if the defendant object in these last-mentioned cases, or if the action is founded on a *tort*, the damages shall be ascertained by a jury of inquiry. Notice shall always be given at least four days of the execution of a writ of inquiry of damages."

§ 691. **When writ of inquiry not necessary.** In foreign attachments, the prothonotary may assess the damages. See section 87. The Act of 1870 is very clear. In *Thornton* v. *Bonham*, 2 Pa. St., 102 (1845), it was decided that an assessment by writ of inquiry was necessary ; but this was before the Act of 1870. When the statement is on a note, draft, bill of exchange, book account, I O U, lease, ground-rent deed, bond, mortgage, on any contract, verbal or written, for the payment of money, or when the cause of action exhibited in the statement admits of a ready liquidation of the amount due, the prothonotary can assess the damages.

§ 692. **When the writ is necessary.** But in actions of slander, libel, malicious prosecution, conspiracy, seduction, crim. con., enticing away apprentices, trover, actions for damages from negligence, from trespass *vi et armis*, from breach of marriage promise,

and generally in *torts* and actions sounding in *tort* where witnesses
are to be cross-examined, where the defendant has the right to call
witnesses on the question of damages, in all such cases after judgment by default an inquiry is necessary. The prothonotary cannot summon or swear jurors. The rule of court in Philadelphia,
above quoted, does not extend to these cases.

If a defendant admit liability where the amount of damages
claimed is unliquidated, a writ of inquiry may issue or the damages be assessed by a jury, under the Act of 1722. *Bradly* v. *Potts*,
33 W. N., 570 (1893).

§ 693. *Act of* 1722. The old law of May 22, 1722, section 27
(1 Sm. Laws, 144), is in these words : " The justices who give any
interlocutory judgment shall, at the motion of the plaintiff or his
attorney in the action where such judgment is given, make an order,
in the nature of a writ of inquiry, to charge the jury attending at
the same or next court, after such judgment is given, to inquire of
the damages and costs sustained by the plaintiff in such action,
which inquiry shall be made, and evidence given in open court,
and after the inquest consider thereof, they shall forthwith return
their inquisition, under their hands and seals ; whereupon the court
may proceed to judgment, as upon inquisitions of that kind returned
by the sheriff."

This Act is not obsolete. *Wright* v. *Crane*, 13 S. & R., 447
(1826) ; *Tuttle* v. *Loan Co.*, 6 Wh., 216 (1841). But in counties
where the trial-lists are heavy, it would be a serious interruption
to the regular business to take up questions of the assessment of
damages in cases of slander and other *torts*. The Common Pleas,
especially in Philadelphia County, have often shown extreme reluctance in permitting the assessment of damages in the manner
sanctioned by the Act. Lawyers familiar with the common-law
practice naturally prefer it ; but, as indicated below, the nature
and circumstances of your case will sometimes suggest reasons why
the interests of your client are likely to be better served by proceedings under the statute.

§ 694. **Decisions under the Act of 1722.** Under this Act, the
following rulings have been made. In *Kohler* v. *Luckenbaugh*, 84
Pa. St., 258 (1877), it was held that the Act did not abrogate the
writ of inquiry, but gave the plaintiff his choice under which to
proceed.

In *Bell* v. *Bell*, 9 Watts, 48 (1839), it was decided by Chief
Justice GIBSON that there is nothing in the Act of 1722 to give
a party a bill of exceptions upon the execution of a writ of inquiry of damages. The difference between proceedings by the

court to assess damages in England and our own process, he said, is "that what is discretionary in the English practice is a matter of right in ours. By the twenty-seventh section of the Act of 1722 an order in the nature of a writ of inquiry is substituted for the writ itself, pursuant to which the inquest is taken from a panel of jurors on attendance, instead of being composed of persons selected by the sheriff; but when constituted, it finds not a verdict recorded in the usual way, but an inquisition signed and sealed, on which judgment is given as if it were returned attached to a writ by the sheriff.

§ 695. **No bills of exceptions.** The statute allowing bills of exceptions is restrained in practice to the trial of issues of fact. An assessment of damages under the Act of 1722, not being such an issue, no exceptions may be taken in that proceeding.

§ 696. **Jury trying issues of defendants who plead may assess damages against the others.** In *Ridgely* v. *Dobson*, 3 W. & S., 118 (1842), it was ruled that where two or more are sued, the plaintiff takes judgment by default against those who do not plead ; when the issue is tried as to those who plead, "the verdict ascertains the amount due as well by those who plead as those who suffered judgment, and the execution issues against all."

In *Farley* v. *Hall*, 1 W. N., 115 (1874), a *mandamus* was applied for to compel the judges of the District Court of Philadelphia to make the order directed by the Act of 1722. But the Supreme Court refused the *mandamus*.

This was followed by another application to the District Court of Philadelphia, in *Sully* v. *Baum*, 1 W. N., 115 (1874), for an order under the Act of 1722. The court, in refusing the application, gave the following reason :

"Notwithstanding the expressions of Chief Justice GIBSON, in *Bell* v. *Bell*, which might seem to imply that this order is a matter of right in all cases, yet the uniform practice in this county for many years past has been to confine it to cases where a jury is sworn to try the issue as to some of the defendants, and to assess the damages as to others against whom judgments by default have been taken. All other cases of assessments of damages on interlocutory judgments, where the amount is not capable of liquidation by the prothonotary, are sent in the regular course to the sheriff's inquest. To disturb so long settled a practice would be extremely inconvenient."

§ 697. **Practice under Act of 1722 sometimes adopted. It guards against corruption.** In *McHenry* v. *The Union Pass. Rwy. Co.* (C. P., 3, Philada.), 14 W. N., 404 (1884), upon judgment for want of a plea, a rule was taken to show cause why the court should not make an order in the nature of a writ of inquiry to charge the jury attending the next court to inquire of the damages and costs sustained by the plaintiff in accordance with the Act of May 22, 1722.

The rule was opposed. The court, in an able opinion by LUDLOW, P. J., said : " Undoubtedly where a judgment has been taken by default, the common-law writ of inquiry to ascertain damages issued. As a matter of course, the sheriff alone summons the jury, and he may select the requisite number of jurors as he pleases ; the power is in his hands alone, and the direction and control of the whole proceeding before the jury is apart from and entirely out of the presence of the court. In ordinary cases, this system is admirably adapted to the dispatch of business, and was intended, we take it, to reach a class of cases wherein to assess damages was not a complicated thing, and was not embarrassed by a multitude of questions which would seem to require the control of an officer presumed to be learned in the law, and clothed with supervising power of a law judge of a court of record. * * * We feel we are not at liberty to adopt any other course than the one we are about to pursue. * * * Complaint is made to us of what are called ' excessive and almost prohibitive damages against corporations and even individuals in all accident cases,' and therefore we are asked to sanction the practice said to exist, and to discharge this rule ; to all this we reply, that as a matter of public policy, it is better to trust to the jury taken by lot from the wheel and in attendance in open court, than to place cases of this description in the control of men selected by any one man. At the present time, and with the present sheriff, we have no doubt that the jury would be honestly and fairly selected. That is not the question to be solved ; the law gives the plaintiff the power with which we ought not to interfere, especially as the selection of the jury from the panel in open court is more consistent with our idea of right in cases of this description, and when it is also remembered that a corrective power is lodged with the judges, . and is freely exercised where it is apparent that a jury have rendered a verdict in any just sense ' excessive ' or ' prohibitive.' " Rule absolute.

In *Hamill* v. *Rwy. Co.* (of September Term, 1883, No. 521), an unreported case in Court of Common Pleas, No. 4, of Philadelphia County, judgment by default for want of a plea was entered, and a rule similar to that in *McHenry* v. *Rwy. Co.* (*supra*) was discharged. (March 10, 1884.)

In *McKeown* v. *Rwy. Co.* (C. P. 1, Phila.), 15 W. N., 125 (1884), after judgment for want of a plea, the plaintiff obtained a rule to show cause why the court should not make an order under the Act of 1722. The application was resisted, but the court made the order, holding, however, that it rested within their discretion whether to do so or not.

It may seem strange that there should be any struggle on the part of a defendant who has not cared to plead, as to the precise method in which the damages should be assessed. When it is remembered, however, that upon the writ of inquiry influences may be brought to bear which could not be successfully invoked before the court and the regular panel, the difficulty is solved. Default may be made for the very purpose of compelling plaintiff to take judgment and forcing him to go before a sheriff's jury to have his damages assessed.

§ 698. *The conclusions to be drawn* from the decisions above noted are somewhat conflicting.

1. It would seem that under the Act of 1722 it is the absolute right of a plaintiff to have his damages assessed by the regular panel.

2. But that this right will not be enforced by *mandamus*.

3. That the plaintiff may elect whether to issue the old writ of inquiry or proceed under the Act of 1722.

4. Yet the court may refuse to proceed under the Act of 1722.

The practical suggestion to counsel for plaintiff is to issue the writ of inquiry where he has nothing to fear from the defendant's influence with the sheriff or his jury. He may thus reach a result with more speed and satisfaction. But if there be any fear of corruption, if the defendant be a corporation, and especially a railroad, it is recommended to resort to the regular panel, and to pursue the course marked out in the cases last cited.

§ 699. **Mode of taking judgment by default.** *The form in foreign attachments* is given at section 87.

The assessment of damages in foreign attachments, as already noted, is not by writ of inquiry, but according to the form stated at section 87.

Judgment for want of appearance. Vide section 171.

Judgment for want of a plea. Vide section 26.

§ 700. *Having judgment by default*, if the prothonotary cannot assess the damages, you proceed under Act of 1722, in the form indicated by the cases cited, or you give to the prothonotary the following

A. ⎫
v. ⎬   Court.   Term.   No.
G. ⎭

SIR:

Issue Writ of Inquiry of Damages in the above case, returnable *sec. leg.*

C.,

Plaintiff's Attorney.

(Date.)

To the Prothonotary of the Court of Common Pleas
of   County.

§ 701.

FORM OF WRIT OF INQUIRY.

County of Philadelphia, *ss.*   The Commonwealth of Pennsylvania.

To the sheriff of the County of Philadelphia, greeting :

v.   . Whereas, the said plaintiff heretofore, to wit, in
the term of   , A.D. 18 , came into our Court of Common
Pleas, No. , for the County of Philadelphia, and impleaded the said defendant in a certain plea of   in which the said plaintiff declared
as is hereinafter set forth, and the said defendant made default in not
                  . And the said cause was in such manner proceeded in,
that it was adjudged by our said court that the said plaintiff ought to recover   damages against the said defendant which   sustained by
reason of the premises. But because it is unknown what damages the said
plaintiff ha sustained ; we command you, that, by the oaths or affirmations of twelve honest and lawful men of your bailiwick, you diligently inquire what damages the said plaintiff ha sustained, as well by occasion of
the premises, as for   costs and charges by   about   suit in that
behalf expended. And the inquisition that you shall take thereof, make
manifest before our Judges, at Philadelphia, at our said Court of Common
Pleas, No. , for the County of Philadelphia, there to be held the first Monday of   next, under your seal and the seal of those by whose
oaths or affirmations respectively you shall make that inquisition. And
have you then there the names of those by whom you shall make that
inquisition, and this writ. Witness the Honorable   president of our said court, at Philadelphia, the   day of   ,
in the year of our Lord one thousand eight hundred and eighty-

Prothonotary.

§ 702. After writ issues.

Give it to the sheriff. Ascertain time
and place for executing it. Notify defendant. If an appearance
has been entered, notify his counsel. It is sometimes required by
rule of court to put up a notice in prothonotary's office and in the
sheriff's office.

You can use the following form :

A. ⎫
v. ⎬   Court.   Term.   No.
B. ⎭

To the defendant above named.

Please take notice that a writ of inquiry of damages has been issued in
the above case, and that the same will be executed by   , Esq.,

high sheriff, and the case submitted to a sheriff's jury at (name the place as, at the office of said sheriff, or at the   Hotel on the   side of street near   Street, in the County of   ) on (name the day and time, as on Friday, the thirtieth day of November, A.D. 18 , at 10 o'clock A.M.).   Respectfully,   C.,
Plaintiff's Attorney.
(Date.)

§ 703. **Proof of Serving Notices.** Let your notices be served and posted by some one who can read and who compares the papers before they are served and posted, with a copy kept. Let him make affidavit at foot of the copy of the time and manner of service.

When service is not made personally on a defendant, have it made, if possible, on an adult member of his family at his dwelling-house. Let this be stated in the affidavit. Service on an attorney should be made personally or on an adult in charge of his office.

§ 704. **Time of Service.** In *Moore* v. *Heiss*, 4 Yeates, 261 (1805), and in *Duncan* v. *Lloyd*, 1 Miles, 350 (1836), eight days were required. The old rule of court in Philadelphia, already quoted, required but four days.

Follow the rule of court, if there be a rule on this subject.

§ 705. **At meeting of Sheriff's Jury.** Be prepared to prove your damages. The jury are sworn. If defendant does not appear in person or by counsel, prove the service and the posting of the notices; then state to the sheriff and jury the names of the parties, who your client is, his occupation, etc. Mention the cause of action—the judgment—read your statement or state its substance. Call your witnesses. After they are sworn, examine them as to the items of your damage. You will remember that you are not required to prove your cause of action, but the amount which you are entitled to recover.

It is usual, in cases of accounts, to hand to the jury a calculation of your claim and the interest to date.

Where the suit is in *tort*, this is not done. Your opponent, if present, has the right to call witnesses. Examination, cross-examination, and addresses to the jury are the same as in other cases.

When the parties retire, the jury assess the damages. This is written out and handed to you when you call for it, by the sheriff, or he may prefer to send it to the prothonotary. If you receive it, file it with the prothonotary.

§ 706.

FORM OF INQUISITION UPON WRIT OF INQUIRY.

County of Philadelphia, *ss.* An Inquisition, indented and taken at the city of Philadelphia, in the county aforesaid, this   day of   in

the year of our Lord one thousand eight hundred and
before   High Sheriff of the City and
County aforesaid, by the oaths and affirmations of the jurors whose names
and seals are hereunto annexed, good and lawful men of my bailiwick, who
say, upon their oaths and affirmations, that   Plaintiff   in the writ
to this Inquisition annexed, named, has sustained damages by means of the
premises in the said writ mentioned against   Defendant   to
the amount of   lawful money   , and   costs.

In testimony whereof, as well I, the said sheriff, as the jurors aforesaid, to
this Inquisition, have affixed our hands and seals, the day and year above
mentioned.

                                                        Sheriff. [SEAL]
(Attach twelve seals.)

§ 707. **Exceptions to the Execution of Writ and to the return.**
Either party has the right to except to the execution of the writ
for

(a) *Misconduct of the Sheriff.* Summoning a juror incompetent
to serve, and retaining .him on the panel after challenge and
proof; corruption; refusing to swear the jury; refusal to hear
witnesses, and any other irregularity defeating justice.

(b) *Misconduct of the Jury.* Receiving improper communications
as to the case; corruption, etc.

In general, it may be stated that whatever would vitiate the ordinary verdict of a jury will be good ground for exception here.

I know no better guide upon this point than *Graham & Water-
man on New Trials.*

(c) *Defective return.* Want of signature of sheriff, or signatures
of sufficient number of jurors, etc. The return might be amended
in a proper case.

(d) The plaintiff might complain that the assessment was inadequate, or the defendant might object that the damages were grossly
excessive.

In *Leib* v. *Bolton*, 1 Dall., 82 (1784), a motion was made to set
aside the return of the jury of inquiry on the ground that improper
evidence had been received by them. But there was other evidence, and the court refused the motion. The same ruling was
made where it was alleged the damages were too low. *Bender* v.
Gibson, 4 W. N., 543 (1877). But where the jury have made a
plain mistake of law, and proceeded to try the case upon its merits
rather than ascertain the amount due, the assessment of damages
will be set aside. *Reilly* v. *Union*, 12 W. N., 93 (1882).

§ 708. **Time for excepting.** By analogy, these objections should
be filed within four days after return of the writ. But I would
suggest to file them immediately, and obtain a rule to show cause
why the assessment should not be set aside.

Allegations of facts must be supported at first by affidavit of client or his agent. Subsequently, you must take depositions to sustain your averments.

Upon motion and argument *sur* exceptions, you again follow the practice upon motions for new trial.

§ 709. **If Assessment set aside,** the plaintiff can proceed as before, issuing an *alias* writ of inquiry, etc.

§ 710. **If Assessment stand,** execution can be issued as in other cases. Form of *præcipe* for *fi. fa.*, section 23. Suggestions as to levy, etc., section 24.

§ 711. **Writ of Inquiry cannot be used as substitute for action for mesne profits.** The British Statute, 16 and 17 Chas. II., ch. 8 (Roberts's Digest, *42); which provides, in section 4, for a writ of inquiry of *mesne* profits, as damages by any waste committed after the first judgment in dower, or in *ejectione firmæ*, is not in force in Pennsylvania. The Act of 11 June, 1879 (P. L., 109) provides: "That whenever an action of ejectment is pending for the recovery of real estate, the plaintiff or plaintiffs therein may, as well before as after the termination of said ejectment, bring an action or actions for *mesne* profits against any person or persons, predecessor or predecessors in title of the defendant or defendants in said ejectment, but such action or actions for *mesne* profits shall not be proceeded in to trial and judgment until the plaintiff or plaintiffs shall have recovered the possession of the real estate in controversy."

In *Warren* v. *Steer*, 118 Pa. St., 529 (1888), PAXSON, J., it was held that this Act afforded a complete remedy for rents, etc., retained pending a writ of error, if the judgment below were affirmed.

CHAPTER XVI.

§ 712. Definition. Detinue is the name of an action brought for the recovery in specie of personal chattels. At common law the action was originally thought to lie only where the taking was lawful and the detention wrongful; but later this distinction was abandoned, and in proper cases detinue is held maintainable upon an unlawful detainer, irrespective of the manner in which defendant obtained possession. Shars. Blackstone's Comm., Book III., *151, *152, notes. Incidentally, damages for the detention are recoverable in addition to the chattel itself or its value.

§ 713. Infrequency of use. Under our practice, the action has fallen into almost complete disuse. The superior advantages of replevin, which has been given such extended applicability in this State, and the growing preference for equitable forms of procedure, have tended to make the action of detinue almost obsolete. In England, detinue was formerly decided by wager of law, that is, the defendant in the action, by virtue of his own oath and that of eleven of his neighbors, was permitted to acquit himself of the unlawful act alleged against him as the basis of the suit. This naturally discouraged the use of that form of action, and accordingly it is not often met with in the English reports previous to the abolition of wager of law by Statute 3 and 4 William IV., ch. 42, section 13 (1833).

§ 714. When preferable. In the Southern States, detinue was frequently employed for the recovery of slaves. With us its best use would be in those cases where the chattel in question has some peculiar value to its owner apart from its worth to others, as deeds or title papers, or articles endeared by association; and where replevin or bill in equity may not be desired.

§ 715. Classification. Authorities conflict as to whether this action is one of contract or in *tort*. It has been held, on the one hand, that it may be joined with debt and that it will lie where defendant's possession is entirely contractual; on the other, that the gist of the action is the wrongful detainer, even though such detainer be a violation of contract. 1 Chitty's Pleadings (12 Am. ed.), 121. It is, however, most frequently, and perhaps most properly, classed with actions *ex contractu.*

§ 716. **When it lies.** Detinue may be brought only for the recovery of chattels, not for real property. The goods must be distinguishable from others ; thus, it will lie for money in a bag or for a particular bank note, but not for a sum of money generally. It will lie for a horse or cow, or for definitely ascertained head of cattle, but not for so many cattle not specially described ; for wheat or grain in a certain place, but not for a number of bushels unidentified. Where a contract to deliver a special article is violated by the wrongful refusal so to do, detinue may be brought, but not unless the contract distinguish the articles from all others.

As in replevin and trover, a special property in the plaintiff, as that of a bailee, will support the action ; but he must have right of immediate possession. It cannot be brought, therefore, by one entitled only in reversion. The right to possession must have existed at the impetration of the action. A life-tenant of real estate may maintain detinue for the title papers. It is immaterial whether the plaintiff ever had actual possession.

§ 717. **What constitutes possession.** The person who has possession and who wrongfully detains is the proper defendant ; and the action cannot be maintained against one never in possession. It is indifferent how possession may have been obtained, so that the detention be improper. An executor whose testator has had possession is not liable in detinue unless the possession came to him. If a bailee lose the chattels by accident before demand, the action will not lie against him ; though it is said to be otherwise if he wrongfully deliver to another, or if he induce the plaintiff to bring the action against himself by a false representation that they are in his possession. It will lie against an infant for goods still in his possession, which he has bought and refuses to pay for on the ground of his infancy. Cases cited, 1 Chitty's Pl. (12 Am. ed.), 120–125.

§ 718. **Joinder.** It was permissible, and not unusual, under the old practice, to join a count in detinue with others in debt. Under our Act of 1887, which substitutes assumpsit for debt, and a statement for the former declaration, it might require nice ingenuity to weld the two together. Detinue may not be joined with actions *ex delicto.*

§ 719. **Jurisdiction.** Justices of the peace have no jurisdiction in this action. It must be brought in the Common Pleas. *Sprenkel* v. *Spots* (C. P., York County), 2 Tr. and H. Pr., section 1538, n. 11.

§ 720.

A. B. ⎫
  v.   ⎬
C. D. ⎭

SIR:
   Issue summons in detinue returnable *sec. leg.*

                                      E. F.,
                                 Plaintiff's Attorney.
                                    (Date.)

To Prothonotary of Court of Common Pleas,
    No.   , Philadelphia County.

§ 721. **Service of Summons.** Having received from the prothonotary a summons, note defendant's address (residence) upon it.
The writ of summons will be entitled to a term and number. It
should be in the usual form, directing the sheriff to summon the
defendant to answer plaintiff "in a plea of detinue." It is to be
taken to the sheriff for service (*supra,* section 16), and is to be
served as are writs of summons in other personal actions. See
Act 13 June, 1836, section 2, P. L., 572.

§ 722. **Capias.** The action being regarded as one essentially
sounding in contract, it would usually seem improper to begin it
by *capias;* but the writer is not aware of any Pennsylvania decision directly upon the point. If defendant's possession be actually tortious, it may be justifiable to employ that writ. As to
præcipe for capias, affidavit to hold to bail, etc., see sections 39–
40 *et seq.;* sections 511–512 *et seq.*

§ 723. **Declaration.** Service of the writ of summons being
effected, plaintiff's declaration should be filed. In framing the
declaration, the necessary averments to establish a good cause of
action must be included. The chattels must be described with
sufficient particularity to enable the sheriff, upon final judgment
and execution, to take them into his possession. Papers should
be so described as to distinguish them from all others. *Rementer*
v. *Erwin,* 11 W. N., 194 (1882). And even more particularity is
required than in trover or replevin. It is not essential, however,
to state the date of a deed; nor need the value of each of several
chattels be separately averred, though there should be a total valuation placed upon them all. Right of property or possession in
plaintiff, and defendant's wrongful detainer, are to be alleged.
Where a request for delivery is necessary in order to convert defendant's holding into a wrongful detention, as in the case of a
bailment, such request should be laid. The date and place of
bailment need not be precisely stated. In the case of a bailment,
it is usual to declare upon it; in other cases, a fictitious finding by

defendant is generally alleged, as in the old *narr.* in trover. Both forms may be and often are joined in separate counts.

§ 724. *Form of Declaration.* The following, adapted from Chitty's Pleadings, will serve as models upon which to frame the *narr.:*

UPON A BAILMENT TO BE DELIVERED ON REQUEST.

A. B. ⎫
v. ⎬ In the Court of Common Pleas, No.   , of Philadelphia County,
C. D. ⎭   Term, , No. .

Philadelphia County, *ss.* C. D., late of the county aforesaid, yeoman, was summoned to answer A. B., the plaintiff, of a plea in detinue, and thereupon the said A. B., by E. F., his attorney, complains : For that whereas the said plaintiff heretofore, to wit, on the   day of   , A.D. 18 , at the county aforesaid, delivered to the said defendant certain goods and chattels (or deeds and writings), to wit (here describe them in accordance with above directions), of the said plaintiff, of great value, to wit, of the value of   dollars of lawful money, to be redelivered by the said defendant to the said plaintiff, when he, the said defendant, should be thereunto afterward requested, yet the said defendant, though he was afterward, to wit, on the day and year aforesaid, at the county aforesaid, requested by the said plaintiff so to do, hath not as yet delivered the said goods and chattels (or deeds and writings), or any of them, or any part thereof, to the said plaintiff, but hath hitherto wholly neglected and refused, and still doth neglect and refuse, so to do, and still unjustly detains the same from the said plaintiff, to wit, at the county aforesaid, to the damage of the said plaintiff   dollars. And therefore he brings suit.

E. F.,
Plaintiff's Attorney.
(Date.)

§ 725. *Count upon a supposititious finding.* The following may be added as a second count. Insert it between the words "unjustly detains the same from the said plaintiff, to wit, at the county aforesaid," and the words "to the damage of the said plaintiff :"

And whereas also the said plaintiff heretofore, to wit, on the day and year aforesaid, at the county aforesaid, was lawfully possessed of certain other goods and chattels (or deeds and papers), to wit (describe them), of great value, to wit, of the value of   dollars, of like lawful money, as of his own property, and being so possessed thereof, he, the said plaintiff, afterward, to wit, on the day aforesaid, at the county aforesaid, casually lost the same out of his possession, and the same afterward, on the day and year aforesaid, at the county aforesaid, came to the possession of the said defendant by finding, yet the said defendant, well knowing the said last-mentioned goods and chattels (or deeds and papers) to be the property of the said plaintiff, and of right to belong and appertain to him, hath not as yet delivered the same, or any or either of them, or any part thereof, to the said plaintiff, although afterward, to wit, on the day and year aforesaid, at the county aforesaid, requested by the said plaintiff so to do, but hath hitherto wholly refused so to do, and hath detained, and still doth detain, the same from the plaintiff, to wit, at the county aforesaid.

If it be desired to declare solely upon a fictitious allegation of finding, the foregoing may be employed with such slight alteration as is required, and in that case it should be preceded and followed by the heading and conclusion given in the first form.

§ 726. **Appearance and rule to plead.** If no appearance be entered, having filed your *narr.* before the return-day, you may take judgment four days thereafter, provided it be fourteen days after service of the writ. (See section 23.) If defendant enter an appearance, enter a rule upon him to plead. In regard thereto and taking judgment for want of a plea, see section 26. If judgment go by default, damages are to be assessed by writ of inquiry. (See chapter XV.)

§ 727. **Pleas.** The general issue plea in this action is *non detinet,* that the defendant does not detain the goods specified. It is a disputed question whether defendant may deny plaintiff's property in the goods under this plea, and it would be advisable for him to plead specially if he intend to do so. It is held, however, that he may show plaintiff's title to be fraudulent. *Stratton* v. *Minnis,* 2 Munford (Va.), 329 (1811). But he may not show a lien on the goods under that plea, or that the goods were pawned to him, or that plaintiff, who has declared as administrator, is not rightfully so. All these things, and in strictness almost all defenses, except non-detention, should be pleaded specially. The following is the extended

§ 728.

FORM OF GENERAL ISSUE PLEA.

A. B. ⎫
  v.   ⎬   C. P. No. 1. June Term, 1890. No. .
C. D. ⎭

And the said defendant, by G. H., his attorney, comes and defends the wrong and injury, when, etc., and saith that he doth not detain the said goods and chattels (or deeds and papers) in the said declaration specified, or any part thereof, in manner and form as the said plaintiff hath above thereof complained against him, and of this the said defendant puts himself upon the country, etc.

This is briefly pleaded "*non detinet.*"

Many forms for special pleas are given in Chitty on Pleading (12 Am. ed., vol. 3, 1023 *et seq.*), and other standard authors on pleading. These may easily be adapted to suit the circumstances of particular cases.

§ 729. **Replication and issue.** To the general issue plea, a *similiter* is the only reply necessary. Other pleas should be replied to according to their nature and the matters to be alleged in response to them. If the replication put the suit at issue, order it on the list for trial, as in other cases.

§ 730. **Trial.** At the trial of the cause plaintiff must prove such facts as show a good cause of action in him ; thus he must prove his property, absolute or qualified, in the goods, together with right of possession. He must also show defendant to have been in possession before issuance of the writ. The defendant himself must show the fact if he have been legally dispossessed. Proof of demand by plaintiff is only necessary in those cases where demand is relied upon to convert the detainer into a wrongful one, but the detainer must be shown as to the precise goods described in the declaration. It is not necessary to show in what manner defendant became possessed, nor need the fictitious allegation of finding be sustained by evidence ; such allegation cannot be controverted.

§ 731. **Verdict and Judgment.** The jury should find the value of each chattel separately if the verdict be for plaintiff, together with damages, if any, for the detention. This is to enable the sheriff to levy for the proper amount in money in case the goods or part thereof should not be forthcoming. Where they value only in gross, however, the defect may be remedied by writ of inquiry. It is not necessary for them to put a separate valuation upon each component part of an aggregate whole, as of a flock of sheep, etc. If the chattels have been returned to plaintiff, the jury may still find for him in damages for the detainer. The judgment follows the verdict, and if for plaintiff, it is in form that he recover the goods demanded, or the value thereof if he cannot have the goods, and his damages (for the detention), together with costs of suit.

§ 732. **Execution.** Writ of *fi. fa.* or *capias ad satisfaciendum* is obtained by *præcipe*, as in other cases. See sections 23, 575 ; and Chapter on Executions. The sheriff is commanded to seize the articles detained ; and, in default of them, to levy for their value, with damages and costs, from the goods of the defendant if the writ be a *fi. fa.*, or to take his person if it be a *ca. sa.* The sheriff proceeds as under other executions, following the directions of his writ. See Chapter on Executions.

§ 733. **Appeal and Limitation.** Appeal lies from the judgment in this as in other actions. See the Chapter on Appeals. The period of limitation is six years from the time the right of action accrues. Act of 27 March, 1713 (1 Sm. L., 76).

CHAPTER XVII.

DIVORCE.

§ 734. Preamble of the Divorce Law. It is well, in considering the practice in cases of divorce, to bear in mind the preamble of the Act of March 13, 1815. It is rarely referred to. It is in these words :

WHEREAS, The divine precepts of the Christian religion, the promotion of the best interest of human, happiness, the design of marriage, and the object of parties entering into the marriage state, require that it should continue during their joint lives : Yet, where one of the parties is under a natural or legal incapacity of faithfully discharging the matrimonial vow, or is guilty of acts inconsistent with the sacred contract, the laws of every well-regulated society should give relief to the innocent and injured party.

§ 735. Causes of Divorce. Certain grounds of divorce, as declared by Pennsylvania Statutes, are common to both parties. Others apply simply to the case of the wife being libellant.

§ 736. Common to both husband and wife. *Impotence, second marriage, adultery, desertion.*

That either party at the time of the contract was and still is naturally impotent or incapable of procreation ;

Or that he or she hath knowingly entered into a second marriage, in violation of the previous vow he or she made to the former wife or husband, whose marriage is still subsisting ;

Or that either party shall have committed adultery ;

Or wilful and malicious desertion, and absence from the habitation of the other, without a reasonable cause, for and during the term and space of two years. * * *

In every such case, it shall and may be lawful for the innocent and injured person to obtain a divorce from the bond of matrimony. (Act of March 13, 1815, section 1 ; 6 Sm., 286.)

§ 737. *Incest.*

All marriages within the degree of consanguinity or affinity according to the table established by law are hereby declared void to all intents and purposes ; and it shall and may be lawful for the Courts of Common Pleas of this Commonwealth, or any of them, to grant divorces from the bonds of matrimony in such cases, and the parties shall be subject to the like penalties as are contained in the Act against incest ; but when any of the said marriages shall not have been dissolved during the lifetime of the parties, the unlawfulness of the same shall not be inquired into, after the death of either the husband or wife. (Act of March 13, 1815, section 5 ; 6 Smith, 2.6.)

§ 738. *Desertion.* The Act of April 26, 1850, section 5 (P. L., 591), re-enacts the desertion clause of the Act of 1815, and authorizes the filing of the libel " at any time not less than six months after the cause of divorce shall have taken place," but the final decree cannot be entered until after the two years have expired.

§ 739. *Jurisdiction in desertion and adultery, although parties not domiciled in State.* The sixth section of the same Act confers jurisdiction in desertion and adultery "notwithstanding the parties were at the occurrence of said causes domiciled in any other State ; " Provided, The applicant shall be a citizen of this Commonwealth or reside therein one year. In *Bishop* v. *Bishop,* 30 Pa. St., 412 (1858), jurisdiction was denied where the cause occurred in another *country.* But by supplement of April 22, 1858 (P. L., 451), the jurisdiction is extended to cases in which the cause occurs in any other country.

§ 740. *Fraud, force, coercion, sentence for felony.*

In addition to the cases now provided for by law, it shall be lawful for the Courts of Common Pleas of this Commonwealth to grant divorces in the following cases :

I. Where the alleged marriage was procured by fraud, force, or coercion, and has not been subsequently confirmed by the acts of the injured party.

II. Where either of the parties shall have been convicted of a felony and sentenced by the proper court either to the county prison of the proper county, or to the penitentiary of the proper district, for any term exceeding two years ; Provided, That such application for a divorce be made by the husband or wife of the party so convicted and sentenced. (Act of May 8, 1854, section 1 ; P. L., 644.)

By Act of June 1, 1891 (P. L., 143), the second subdivision of § 1 of Act of May 8, 1854, was amended so as to read as follows :

When either of the parties heretofore has been or hereafter shall be convicted of forgery or any infamous crime, either within or without this State, and sentenced to imprisonment for any term exceeding two years : *Provided,* That such application for a divorce be made by the husband or wife of the party so convicted and sentenced : *And provided further,* In cases where the conviction was had outside this State, that the crime for which it was had be one which by the laws of this State may be punished by imprisonment for two years or more.

This extends the jurisdiction to grant divorces when either party has been convicted of forgery, or of any infamous crime, and sentenced to imprisonment therefor, whether within or without this State.

The Act of June 1, 1891, does not apply to a case where the respondent has been convicted of crime punishable in another State by imprisonment for two years only—although the crime be punishable by imprisonment for more than two years here. *Frantz* v. *Frantz*, 1 Dist. Rep., 241 (1892).

Assault with intent to rape is not an infamous crime in Pennsylvania within the meaning of the divorce law of June 1, 1891. *Wheeler* v. *Wheeler*, 2 Dist. Rep., 567 (1893).

§ 741. *Personal abuse, etc.*

It shall be lawful for the several Courts of Common Pleas in this Commonwealth to entertain jurisdiction of all cases of divorce from the bonds of matrimony for the cause of personal abuse, or for such conduct on the part of either the husband or wife as to render the condition of the other party intolerable and life burdensome, notwithstanding the parties were at the time of the occurring of said causes domiciled in another State : *Provided*, That no application for such divorce shall be made unless the applicant therefor shall be a citizen of this Commonwealth, or shall have resided therein for the term of one year, as provided for by the existing laws of this Commonwealth. (Act of March 9, 1855, section 1 ; P. L., 68.)

The Act of June 8, 1891 (P. L., 247), provided that "A wife forced to return to her domicile in this State by husband's adultery, cruelty, indignity, or desertion in another State or country, might sue here ; but if defendant not served, registered letter must be sent."

This Act was repealed by the Act of June 20, 1893, and was declared unconstitutional in *Burdick* v. *Burdick*, 2 Dist. Rep., 622 (1893).

§ 741 *a. Jurisdiction in Divorce extended to various causes. Former domicile of wife. Service of notice, residence, etc.*

That it shall be lawful for the several Courts of Common Pleas in this Commonwealth to entertain jurisdiction of all cases of divorce from the bonds of matrimony, and from bed and board for the causes of adultery committed by the husband, or wilful and malicious desertion on the part of the husband, and absence from the habitation of the wife without reasonable cause, for and during the term and space of two years, or where any husband shall have, by cruel and barbarous treatment, endangered his wife's life or offered such indignities to her person as to render her condition intolerable and life burdensome, and thereby force her to withdraw from his house and family ; where it shall be shown to the court by any wife that she was formerly a citizen of this Commonwealth, and that having intermarried with a citizen of any other State or any foreign country, she has been compelled to abandon the habitation and domicile of her husband, in such other State or foreign country, by reason of his adultery or wilful and malicious desertion and absence from the habitation of the wife without reasonable cause for and during the space and term of two years, or by cruel and barbarous treatment endangered his wife's life or offered such indignities to her person as to render her condition intolerable and life burdensome, and thereby force her to withdraw from his house and family, and has thereby been forced to return to this Commonwealth in which she had her former domicile : *Provided*, That where, in any such case, personal service of the subpœna cannot be made upon such husband by reason of his non-residence within this Commonwealth, the court, before entering a decree of divorce, shall require proof that in addition to the publication now required by law, that actual or constructive notice of said proceedings has been (given) to such non-resident husband, either by personal service or by registered letter to his last known place of residence, and that a reasonable time has thereby been afforded to him to appear and defend in said suit : *And provided further*, That no application for such divorce shall be made, unless the applicant therefor shall be a citizen of this Commonwealth, or shall have resided therein for the term of one year prior to filing her petition or libel as provided by the laws of this Commonwealth.

§ 741 b. *In desertion, libel may be filed in not less than six months after desertion, but no decree until two years elapse.*

SEC. 2. Where the wife petitions the court for a divorce under the provisions of section first of this Act on the ground of wilful, malicious, and continued desertion by the husband from the habitation of the wife without reasonable cause, it shall be lawful for the wife to make application in such case by petition or libel to the proper court at any time not less than six months after such cause of divorce shall have taken place, but the said court shall not proceed to make a final decree divorcing the said parties from the bonds of matrimony aforesaid until after the expiration of two years from the time at which such desertion took place.

SEC. 3. The proceedings in cases embraced within the provisions of this Act, except so far as they are prescribed by this Act, shall be the same as those prescribed by the Act entitled " An Act concerning divorces," approved the thirteenth day of March, Anno Domini one thousand eight hundred and fifteen, and the several Acts supplementary thereto, with the like right of appeal as is therein given.

SEC. 4. The provisions of this Act shall apply to all suits or proceedings for divorce which may be pending in the courts of this Commonwealth at the time it is approved, and to all subsequent divorce proceedings.

SEC. 5. The Act approved the eighth day of June, Anno Domini one thousand eight hundred and ninety-one, entitled " A further supplement to an Act entitled ' An Act extending the jurisdiction of the courts of this Commonwealth in cases of divorce,' " approved the ninth day of March, Anno Domini one thousand eight hundred and fifty-five, is hereby repealed. Act of June 20, 1893 (P. L., 471).

See *Burdick* v. *Burdick*, 2 Dist. Rep., 622 (1893).

§ 742. *Bigamy.*

In all cases where a supposed or alleged marriage shall have been contracted which is absolutely void by reason of one of the parties thereto having a husband or wife living at the time, the Court of Common Pleas shall have power to decree the said supposed or alleged marriage to be null and void upon the application of an innocent or injured party, and the jurisdiction shall be exercised and proceedings conducted according to the principles and forms which are or shall be prescribed by law for cases of divorce from the bond of matrimony. (Act of April 14, 1859, section 1; P. L., 647.)

§ 743. Causes peculiar to the wife.

When any husband shall have, by cruel and barbarous treatment, endangered his wife's life, or offered such indignities to her person as to render her condition intolerable and life burdensome, and thereby force her to withdraw from his house and family, in every such case it shall and may be lawful for the innocent and injured person to obtain a divorce from the bond of matrimony. (Act of March 13, 1815, section 1; 6 Sm., 286.)

§ 744. *Abandonment, Cruelty, Divorce à mensa, Alimony.*

If any husband shall maliciously either abandon his family or turn his wife out of doors, or by cruel and barbarous treatment endanger her life or offer such indignities to her person as to render her condition intolerable or life burdensome, and thereby force her to withdraw from his house and family, it shall be lawful for the Court of Common Pleas of the respective counties, upon complaint and due proof thereof made in the manner prescribed in the Act to which this is a supplement, to grant the wife a divorce from bed and board, and also to allow her such alimony as her husband's circumstances will admit of, so as the same do not exceed the third part of the annual profit or income of his estate or of his occupation and labor, which shall continue until a reconciliation shall take place or until the husband shall, by his petition or libel, offer to receive and cohabit with her again and to use her as a good husband ought to do, and then, in such case, the court may either suspend the aforesaid sentence or decree, or in case of her refusal to return and cohabit, under the protection of the court, discharge and annul the same according to their discretion ; and if he fail in performing his said offers and engagements, the former sentence or decree may be revived and enforced and the arrears of the alimony ordered to be paid. (Act of February 26, 1817, section 1; 6 Sm., 405.)

§ 745. *Divorce à mensa for Adultery.*

In addition to the several causes mentioned in the Act or Acts to which this is a supplement, for which a married woman may obtain a divorce from the bed and board of her husband, with allowance of alimony, shall be that of adultery, and it shall be lawful for the Court of Common Pleas of the respective counties, upon complaint and due proof thereof, made in the manner prescribed by the said Acts to which this is a supplement, or either of them, to grant the wife a divorce from bed and board; and in addition to the powers now conferred upon the said court by the said Acts, or either of them, to grant alimony and the amount thereof it shall be lawful for the said court to decree to be paid by the said husband, in addition thereto, to his said wife, the one-half of the value of all money and property of every kind whatsoever, which the said husband may have received by, through, or from his said wife, as her individual money and property ; which amount the said court shall inquire into and ascertain, by proper proof, on and at the time of the hearing of the said complaint; which decree the said court shall have power to enforce, suspend, or discharge and annul, in the same manner as the said court may now enforce, suspend, or discharge and annul its decrees under and by virtue of the said Acts or either of them. (Act of April 11, 1862, section 1; P. L., 430.)

§ 746. Cause peculiar to Husband—*Cruelty*.

Where the wife shall have, by cruel and barbarous treatment, rendered the condition of 'her 'husband 'intolerable or life burdensome : *Provided*, That in cases of divorce under this Act, if the application shall be made on the part of the husband, the court granting such divorce shall allow such support or alimony to the wife as her husband's circumstances will admit of, and as the said courts may deem just and proper. (Act May 8, 1854, section 1, III.; P. L., 644.)

The above section, Act of May 8, 1854, as amended by Act of June 25, 1895 (P. L., 309), is as follows : " Where a wife shall have, by cruel and barbarous treatment or indignities to his person, rendered the condition of her husband intolerable or life burdensome : *Provided*, That in case of divorce under this Act, if the application shall be made on the part of the husband, the court granting such divorçe may allow such support or alimony to the wife as her husband's circumstances may admit of, and as said court may deem just and proper." Under the Act of 1854 a divorce may be granted a husband where the wife has been guilty of cruel and barbarous· treatment which renders his condition intolerable or life burdensome, although such acts do not endanger his life. *Barnsdall* v. *Barnsdall*, 171 Pa. St., 625 (1895).

§ 747. **Résumé of the kinds and causes of divorce.** From a review of the statutes cited, it will be noted that two kinds of divorce are allowed. A divorce *a vinculo* may be obtained under certain conditions, by either husband or wife. A divorce *à mensa et thoro, with alimony*, may be obtained by the wife.

§ 748. **The causes common to both** may be classified briefly as impotence—second marriage—adultery—desertion—incest—fraud—force—sentence for felony—personal abuse— bigamy—cruelty. For these, absolute divorces may be decreed.

§ 749. **The causes peculiar to the wife are** abandonment and turning her out of doors. For these, and for adultery, she may sue *à mensa and for alimony*.

Cruelty is not here noted as *a cause peculiar* to the wife, for the husband can also sue her for this reason. (See *supra*, section 746.)

§ 750. **For cruelty, the wife may also have alimony**, whether she be libellant (Act of February 26, 1817, section 1 ; cited *supra*, section 744), or defendant (Act May 8, 1854, section 1, III., amended by Act of June 25, 1895 (P. L., 359) ; *supra*, section 746).

These causes will be considered in their order.

§ 751. **Impotence.** It will be observed that the preamble to the Act of March 13, 1815 (section 734 of this chapter), recites that relief should be given "where one of the parties is under a natural * * * incapacity." Hence the first section states as the leading ground "where either party at the time of the contract was and still is naturally impotent or incapable of procreation."

§ 752. *The impotence must date back to the contract.* If it were the result of subsequent accident or disease, and did not exist at the time of the marriage, it is no ground for divorce.

§ 753. *If impotence existed at date of contract, but was subsequently cured* before the application for divorce, it is no ground for a decree.

§ 754. *Definition of impotence.* This is well defined "want of procreative power, inability to copulate or to beget children, sterility, barrenness."

The statute furnishes an excellent definition in the words "incapable of procreation."

§ 755. *This is recognized elsewhere as ground of divorce.* The ecclesiastical law and the statutes of Arkansas, California, Colorado, Delaware, District of Columbia, Florida, Georgia, Idaho, Illinois, Indiana, Iowa, Kansas, Maine, Maryland, Massachusetts, Michigan, Minnesota, Mississippi, Missouri, Montana, Nebraska, Nevada, New Hampshire, New York, North Carolina, Ohio, Oregon, Rhode Island, Tennessee, Texas, Utah, Washington Territory, West Virginia, Wisconsin, all refer to this as a cause of complaint.

§ 756. *Impotence—Possibility of cure when coupled with—Refusal to submit to operation is no defense.* In a husband's suit for a declaration of nullity of marriage on the ground of his wife's incapacity, it appeared that the parties had cohabited irregularly during two years and eight months after the marriage, but that the respondent had always refused to allow the petitioner to attempt to consummate the marriage, alleging that she was not fit for it, and had no sexual desire. The medical evidence showed that sexual connection with the respondent was impossible, but that she might probably be cured by submitting to an operation which would involve very little risk to her life. She had refused to submit to any operation. *Held*, that the petitioner was entitled to a decree of nullity of marriage. *L.* v. *W.* (*otherwise L.*), 51 Law Jour. Rep. (P. D. & A.), 23; 7 Law Rep. (P. D.), 16 (1882).

§ 757. *Impotence—Unreasonable delay in suing held a bar.* A wife lived with her husband for one year and nine months after the marriage. After a lapse of nine years she again lived with him for five years and six months, and left him in consequence of, amongst other things, his ill treatment. Twenty-seven years after the marriage, and when she was forty-eight years of age she brought a suit for nullity of marriage by reason of his impotence. It was proved that she was *virgo intacta*. *Held*, that she was not entitled to relief. *Reynolds* v. *Reynolds*, 45 Law Jour. Rep. (P. D. & A.), 89 ; 1 Law Rep. (P. D.), 405 (*nom. W., falsely called R.*, v. *R.*) (1876). *Semble*, even though one of the parties is impotent, the marriage cannot be annulled if there has been unreasonable delay in instituting suit. *Ibid.*

§ 758. *Impotence—Delay a bar when coupled with acquiescence, etc.* A decree annulling the marriage was refused where suit was brought on the ground of incurable impotence of the man, and it was shown that considerable time had elapsed since the marriage and the separation, during all of which time the petitioner knew of her husband's infirmity ; that after separation she had vainly but repeatedly requested to be received back by him ; that she had as his wife contracted debts for necessaries which the husband had been compelled to pay, and that she subsequently received an allowance. *H——* v. *C——*, 1 Law Times Rep. (N. S.), 489 (1860).

§ 759. *But delay is not a bar where it is not evidence of insincerity.* Delay is not by itself a ground for refusing a decree of nullity of marriage on the ground of the respondent's impotence. A marriage remained unconsummated after seven years' cohabitation through the impotence of the husband. The wife cohabited with another man, and when her husband discovered her misconduct she instituted a suit for a declaration of nullity of marriage. *Held*, that the petitioner's conduct did not amount to such want of sincerity as to disentitle her to a decree of nullity of marriage. *M. (otherwise D.)* v. *D.*, 54 Law Jour. Rep. (P. D. & A.), 68 (1885).

§ 760. *Impotence—Delay, acquiescence, and proofs balanced— Libel dismissed.* The woman cohabited with her husband from their marriage in November, 1848, till July, 1862 ; she then occupied a separate bed for two or three weeks, and left his house in August, 1862, after disputes about other matters, and did not return to it. In May, 1864, she filed her petition for nullity by reason of his impotence ; he traversed this, and alleged consummation. The report of the inspectors pronounced her to be a virgin and apt, and stated that the man had no apparent imperfection. At the hearing, the petitioner and respondent both gave evidence, and medical men, besides the inspectors, gave evidence on both sides. In the result the court *held*, that the petitioner had failed to prove that the marriage had remained unconsummated by reason of the impotence of the man, and dismissed him from the suit. *L——* v. *H——*, 4 Swab. & T., 115 (1865).

§ 761. *Impotence—Delay and charge sustained only by libellant's testimony—Libel dismissed.* In a suit of nullity, by reason of the impotence of the husband, the evidence of the wife was entirely unsupported by the medical witnesses. The parties had resided together without any complaint by the wife on this matter for eight years, and the separation was then enforced by the husband. The court *held* that the charge was not made out, and dismissed the petition. *Tavernor, falsely called Ditchfield,* v. *Ditchfield,* 35 Law Jour. Rep. (N. S.) (P. & M.), 51 (1866).

§ 762. *On a charge of impotence, the unsupported oath of the libellant is not sufficient.* In a suit of nullity by reason of the husband's impotency, the surgical report stated that the physical appearances of the wife were such that she might have had regular connection with her husband during cohabitation. The wife, during the two years' cohabitation, had not complained to her family on this matter, and had separated from her husband by reason of his alleged violence.

The respondent affirmed on oath that the marriage had been consummated. The court declined to pronounce the marriage invalid on the unsupported oath of the party seeking to be relieved from its obligations. *U——, falsely called J——,* v. *J——,* 37 Law Jour. Rep. (N. S.) (P. & M.), 7 (1867).

§ 763. *Impotence—If wife apta—Non-consummation of marriage ground for decree.* In a suit of nullity of marriage by a woman on the ground of impotence, the court not being satisfied with the evidence at the hearing suspended its decree ; but afterward, on motion, pronounced the marriage null upon affidavits that, since the hearing, the parties had renewed cohabitation for some weeks, and that the marriage had not been consummated. *M—— v. H——,* 34 Law Jour. Rep. (N. S.) (P. M. & A.), 12 (1864).

§ 764. *Decree granted for impotence where, after fourteen years, the wife was pronounced intacta et apta—In such a case onus is on husband.* After a cohabitation of fourteen years, a woman presented a petition in the court for divorce and matrimonial causes for a decree of nullity of marriage, on the ground of the man's impotence.

The report of the inspectors and the medical evidence showed that the woman was *virgo intacta et apta viro,* and that there was no apparent defect or malformation in the man. The court was satisfied that the marriage had never been completely consummated, but was not satisfied that the non-consummation arose from the incapacity of the man, and therefore dismissed the petition. *Held,* by the House of Lords, reversing the decree of the court below

34 Law Jour. Rep. (N. S.) (M. & A.), 81 (1865), that the woman was entitled to a decree; that the marriage was null and void, on the ground that the cohabitation had been for a much more lengthened period than was required to raise the presumption against a husband; and that the onus was thrown upon the respondent either of disproving the facts or of showing, by clear and satisfactory evidence, that the result was attributable to other causes than his own impotency. *Lewis, falsely called Hayward*, v. *Hayward*, 35 Law Jour. Rep. (N. S.) (P. & M.), 105 (1866). Lord Chancellor CHELMSFORD.

§ 765. *Impotence—Where respondent absent, no decree will be granted without examination.* As a general rule, a decree of nullity of marriage on the ground of malformation will not be granted unless the existence of incurable malformation is proved by a medical man who has examined the person of the respondent. In a suit of nullity on the ground of the malformation of the woman, the respondent (who was abroad, and who, in consequence of her address being unknown, had not been personally served) had not been examined by the medical inspectors or other medical men. The court suspended its decree, in order that the petitioner might have an opportunity of procuring such an examination, if the respondent should come to England. *T—— v. M., falsely calling herself C——*, 35 Law Jour. Rep. (N. S.) (P. & M.), 10 (1865).

§ 766. *Impotence—Attachment will lie to enforce order for examination.* In a suit for nullity of marriage by reason of malformation, the respondent refused to comply with the order for inspection. The court declined to issue an attachment against her till after the hearing, but intimated that the attachment would issue forthwith if she attempted to remove out of the jurisdiction. *B—— v. L——, falsely called B——*, 38 Law Jour. Rep. (N. S.) (P. & M.), 35 (1869).

§ 767. *Impotence—Decree granted where wife refused to be examined, and the husband's testimony showed that marriage had not been consummated.* Decree of nullity *nisi* granted, in a case where the wife refused to submit to inspection; on evidence by the husband that during three years he had never been able to consummate the marriage, as his attempts to do so had produced hysteria on the part of the wife. *H—— v. P., falsely called H——*, 3 Law Rep. (P. & M.), 126 (1873).

§ 768. *Impotence—Order for personal examination—Our practice has followed the English rule.* In an action for divorce for impotency, an order was made for personal examination of respondent, whereupon each party selected a physician, the commissioner appointed one, approved all three, and prescribed the regulations. *A. C.* v. *B. C.*, 11 W. N., 479 (1882).

This is the same case in which it was ruled that the libel must aver incurability. The libellant amended. The examination was submitted to. The unanimous report of the physicians was in favor of the respondent. The libel was dismissed.

§ 769. *Libel must charge that impotence is incurable.* A libel charging impotency must distinctly aver that it is incurable. *A. C.* v. *B. C.*, 10 W. N., 569 (1881) (per EWING, P. J.). This case is sometimes cited with names of parties (not here repeated), as reported 29 Pitts. Leg. J. (O. S.), 319.

§ 770. *Impotence—Decree might be refused where both parties of advanced age.* It is uncertain if a divorce for impotence would be decreed if the parties are of advanced age.

Fulmer v. *Fulmer*, 13 Phila. Rep., 166 (1879). In this case, THAYER, P. J., said: "The husband, who is libellant, is in his seventy-third year, and the respondent is sixty. The cause of divorce assigned is *impotentia*, whether *propter ætatem* or *propter aliquod naturale impedimentum*, does not appear. It may be doubted whether we would decree a divorce for such a cause between persons of such ages. The English courts, under similar circumstances and for obvious reasons, have refused to do so. *Briggs* v. *Morgan*, 2 Haggard, 339. A celebrated civilian, in commenting upon the subject, inquires *num matrimonium proprie vocari queat quando elumbis senex vetulam effetam ducit*, and rather considers them as honorary members of the matrimonial state, enjoying a title without an office. Puffendorf, Lib. 6, c. 1, 25 ; Poynter, 123, n. b. Fortunately for us, the defects of the libellant's case relieve us from the necessity of deciding so delicate a question as that which presents itself on the threshold, as well as some others which would inevitably arise in the cause of such an inquiry, such, for example, as the nature of the proofs *ad probandum defectus*, and whether in Pennsylvania as in the ecclesiastical courts of England *jurandæ sint obstetrices ad inspiciendam mulierem*. There is no proof of the charge contained in the libel except the libellant's own statements, and those alone are inadequate. *Winter* v. *Winter*, 7 Phila. Rep., 369. In addition to this the proofs, such as they are, have not been taken in conformity with the rules of court upon this subject." Libel dismissed.

§ 771. *Divorce decreed for impotence, although no malformation or structural defect existed.* A marriage is void if consummation is practically impossible, although there be no malformation or structural defect rendering consummation physically impossible. *G——* v. *G——*, 40 Law Jour. Rep. (N. S.) (P. & M.), 83 (1871).

In this case the wife had been examined by three physicians. They testified that there was no malformation or structural impediment. But it appeared that sexual intercourse was practically impossible, and that her condition was hysterical, etc. The judge ordinary held "that consummation was practically impossible," and therefore granted a decree of nullity.

§ 772. *Impotence—No decree granted after death.* The validity of a marriage cannot be questioned on the ground of impotence after the death of one of the parties to the marriage. *A——* v. *B—— and another,* 1 Law Rep. (P. & D.), 559 (1868).

§ 773. **Second marriage in violation of first—Bigamy.** The next ground is thus stated by the Act of 1815, "that he or she hath knowingly entered into a second marriage in violation of the previous vow he or she made to the former wife or husband, whose marriage is still subsisting."

In *Jeffries* v. *Jeffries* (C. P. of Phila., March Term, 1845, No. 128), an unreported case, Mr. J. Murray Rush, for the respondent, made a very able argument in support of the position, that the wife, who had been guilty of bigamy, could not be sued under this law for a divorce by the second husband, because the second ceremony was a nullity. He therefore urged that the law could not divorce persons who had never been legally married, and that only the first husband could sue. The Act of 1859, authorizing a decree of nullity, had not been passed. The divorce was, however, decreed. The language of the Act of 1815 certainly applies in the case mentioned in favor of either husband. If No. 1 could prove cohabitation with No. 2, he could present a libel for adultery. But without any proof of the parties living together, with the simple evidence that his wife had remarried, the statute authorizes the divorce. In like manner No. 2, before the Act of 1859, would seem to have been within the provisions of the Act of 1815.

The divorce was decreed in *Jeffries* v. *Jeffries,* and for the same ground in *Hyde* v. *Hyde* (C. P. of Phila., December Term, 1860, No. 50). In both of these cases the libellant was the second husband.

In *Thompson* v. *Thompson,* 10 Phila., 131 (1874), the facts were that libellant married respondent July 10, 1868 ; that May 10, 1866, she had married one Ryan, who was still her lawful husband. ALLISON, P. J., said : "A subsisting marriage at the time the second marriage was entered into is a distinct ground for a divorce from the bond of matrimony ; not, as often contended, that as between the contracting parties, it may be treated as absolutely null and void, but that *inter* parties it is a cause for which the Courts of Common Pleas may decree a divorce.   *   *   *

" The courts of this Commonwealth do not permit every party to a void marriage to maintain a suit for nullity of marriage ; he must show *prima facie* at least that he is an innocent and injured party.   In England, either party to a void marriage may ask for a decree of the nullity of the marriage, even though he or she entered into the contract with a knowledge of an existing disability, and it is only where such marriage has been induced by positive fraud that the party practising it will be denied relief.

" The libellant confesses in his testimony that he knew, before and at the time of his marriage with respondent, that she had been twice married, first to one J. D., and afterward to W. R."

There was no proof that 'Ryan was living when the marriage between libellant and respondent took place.   Decree refused.

Where the libel prayed for a decree of nullity upon the ground that respondent had a husband living at the time of her marriage with libellant, her answer, denying " that she knowingly entered into a marriage with libellant in violation of a previous vow," and " so far as she is aware, she had another husband living," and averring adultery of the libellant, was held insufficient and was stricken off, with leave to file a new answer.   *Jordan* v. *Jordan*, 13 W. N., 110 (1883).

A second answer was filed averring that libellant was not unaware of the existence of the first husband, if any there was ; that he had more knowledge on the subject than respondent ; that he had been guilty of adultery, and that respondent had married on false report of her husband's death.   The court refused the issue prayed by respondent, the averments in her answer being immaterial, but refused to strike off the answer.   *Id.* v. *Id.*, 13 W. N., 193 (1883).

§ 774. *Well-founded belief in death.*   Where a woman married a second time during the life of her first husband, but with a well-founded belief in his death, it was held that while exempt from the pains of bigamy, yet her first husband, being in full life, and their marriage not having been annulled, the second marriage was *ipso facto* void and null.   *Thomas* v. *Thomas*, 124 Pa. St., 646 (1889).

A celebrated case arose out of the marriage of Mrs. Carson to Major Smith.   The lady, not having heard from her husband for years, married Major Smith.   Carson returned and ordered Smith out of the house.   Smith shot and killed him.   On the trial, before Judge Rush, Oyer and Terminer of Philadelphia, May, 1816,

Smith set up the defense that Carson had raised his arm to strike him. The jury convicted of murder in the first degree, and the defendant was hanged. In order to intimidate the governor into granting a pardon, a plot was laid to kidnap his child, but it failed. In this case, the words, " rumor of the death *in appearance* well founded," were construed by Judge RUSH thus : " We think it means general report that a man died at a particular town or place; was shipwrecked, or lost his life in some way which the report specifies." Wheeler's Criminal Cases, vol. 2, page 81.

§ 775. *Conviction of bigamy avoids the second marriage.* Conviction of bigamy makes the second marriage void, and under the Act of 1815 the court will not decree a divorce after a conviction of bigamy. *Harrison* v. *Harrison,* 1 Phila., 389 (1852).

This decision was under the Act of 1815. The Act of 1859 had not been passed.

In *Heffner* v. *Heffner,* 23 Pa. St., 104 (1854), it was held that the second marriage during the existence of the first contract is absolutely void.

§ 776. *The Act of 1859 recognizes the nullity of the second marriage, and authorizes the decree. Knowledge or notice immaterial.* The Act of 1859 seems to settle whatever doubts may have existed as to the interpretation of the Act of 1815. The Act of 1859 declares : (1) That the second marriage is absolutely void ; (2) that the court may decree it to be null and void. This differs from the old divorce, for it gives the courts of Pennsylvania the power possessed in England of entering a decree of nullity.

Questions of knowledge or notice of the first marriage must be wholly immaterial where the law declares that the second marriage is absolutely void.

Under the Act of 1859, if either party to a marriage, contract a bigamous marriage with a third party, divorce will be decreed upon proof of such fact without proof of adultery. *Ralston* v. *Ralston,* 2 Dist. Rep., 242 (1893).

Under the terms of the Act of 1859, to decree the nullity of a marriage for bigamy it must be shown : (*a*) That the respondent was married to another when the marriage to libellant took place, and (*b*) that the libellant was an innocent or injured party. *O'Keefe* v. *O'Keefe,* 34 W. N., 531 (1894).

Under the Act of 1859, the court can declare a *supposed* marriage void upon the application of the innocent and injured party. *Heinzman* v. *Heinzman,* 4 Dist. Rep., 225 (1894).

§ 777. **Adultery, definition of.** " The voluntary sexual intercourse of a married person with a person other than the offender's husband or wife." The crime of the married party will be adultery ; if the other be unmarried, his (or her) crime is fornication.

§ 778. *To sustain this charge, positive proof is not required.* A wife's visit with a man to a brothel or to a man at his lodgings may be sufficient proof of adultery.

Lord STOWELL said, in *Loveden* v. *Loveden*, 2 Hagg., 2 (1810), "Adultery is seldom susceptible of proof, except by circumstances which would lead the guarded discretion of a reasonable and just man to a conclusion of guilt."

This was cited and approved by Chief Justice GIBSON, in *Matchin* v. *Matchin*, 6 Pa. St., 332 (1847).

§ 779. *Confession of adultery.* A wife's disclosure of her crime, unless it be full, confidential, reluctant, free from suspicion of collusion and corroborated by circumstances, cannot be admitted in evidence. The confession of her paramour, not being communicated to and confirmed by her, cannot be evidence of the crime. *Matchin* v. *Matchin*, 6 Pa. St., 332 (1847).

§ 780. *Insanity is not a defense.* In the case just cited, Chief Justice GIBSON said that the depositions established that the "wife was actually insane." He added, "but the wife's insanity * * * would not be a defense to a libel for adultery." This was decided in 1847. It is gratifying to find that twenty-seven years after this date the House of Lords made the same ruling. Sir Charles Mordaunt sued Lady Mordaunt for dissolution of marriage on the charge of adultery with Viscount Cole and others. The judge ordinary allowed the defendant's father, Sir Thomas Moncreiffe, to appear as guardian *ad litem.* He set up that Lady Mordaunt was insane when sued. On issue framed to try this question, the jury found for respondent. The judge ordinary stayed the proceedings. The court of appeal affirmed. The libellant then asked that his petition be dismissed, with right to test the question in the House of Lords. The court below was reversed. The opinions of BRETT, J., and KEATING, J., were in favor of the respondent ; KELLY, C. B., DENMAN, B., POLLOCK, B., Lord CHELMSFORD, and Lord HATHERLY, *contra.* *Mordaunt* v. *Moncreiffe*, 43 Law Jour. Rep., 49 (Probate and Divorce Cases) (1874).

§ 781. *Adultery—The evidence must be confined to the specifications.* Evidence of matters and facts and as to other times and places than those mentioned in the specifications is not admissible. *Realf* v. *Realf*, 77 Pa. St., 31 (1874).

Where husband and wife have separated by agreement, adultery by either thereafter and not condoned is ground for divorce. *Gee* v. *Gee*, 2 Dist. Rep., 773 (1893).

§ 782. **Desertion.** The next ground mentioned in the statute is "wilful and malicious desertion and absence from the habitation of the other without reasonable cause for and during the term and space of two years. It is not necessary that the defendant should in the strict sense have left the libellant or the home. Refusal to return with the libellant to the home would be a desertion. As if the two should leave the house together for a walk, for a visit, or for a summer sojourn, and the wife should say "I will not go home; I will never return." This would be a desertion. So, too, if the husband's health or business required a change of residence, it would be the duty of the wife to accompany him. Everything in these cases depends upon the good faith of the libellant and the bad faith of the respondent.

§ 783. *Good faith required of the libellant.* A husband cannot, from mere caprice, compel his wife to remove from the comforts of home, friends, and refinement. *Colvin* v. *Reed*, 55 Pa. St., 380 (1867).

But he has the undoubted right to change his domicile as often as business, comfort, or health requires. *Cutler* v. *Cutler*, 2 Brews., 513 (1868).

Where a husband changes his residence and provides a suitable home for his wife, if she refuses to accompany him without cause, such refusal constitutes a desertion. *Beck* v. *Beck*, 163 Pa. St., 649 (1894).

Where the causes set forth in a divorce are merely to advance a scheme or trick to make out a technical case to sever the bonds of matrimony, the libel will be dismissed; otherwise the libellant would be taking advantage of his own wrong. In an attempt to rescind the contract, chicanery will defeat the party practising it. Thus in *Angier* v. *Angier*, 63 Pa. St., 450 (1870), the libellant broke up housekeeping in the absence of his wife without consultation, and then informed her that he had taken board. The respondent's father had fully answered libellant's excuses as to expense, assuming the responsibility of payment of respondent's expenses, and respondent had offered to return to her husband if he would provide a suitable residence where strangers might not be witnesses to his unkind treatment; this he refused to do. His libel was dismissed. The Supreme Court did not regard his conduct as *bona fide*.

In *Butler* v. *Butler*, 1 Pars. Select Eq. Cas., 344 (1849), Judge KING said: "A husband may, by a course of humiliating insults and annoyances, practised in the various forms which ingenious malice could readily devise, eventually destroy the life or health of his wife, although such conduct may be unaccompanied by violence, positive or threatened. * * * To hold absolutely that if a husband avoids positive or threatened personal violence, the wife has no legal protection against any means short of these, which he may resort to and which may destroy her life or health, is to invite such a system of infliction by the indemnity given the wrongdoer. The more rational application of the doctrine of cruelty is to consider a course of marital unkindness with reference to the effect it must necessarily produce on the life or health of the wife ; and if it has been such as affect or injure either, to regard it as true legal cruelty. * * * If austerity of temper, petulance of manner, rudeness of language, a want of civil attention, occasional sallies of passion *do threaten bodily harm, they do amount to legal cruelty.*"

In *Cattison* v. *Cattison*, 22 Pa. St., 275 (1853), the absence of respondent was justified on the ground of the violent temper and intemperate habits of libellant and his assault upon respondent with a knife, as well as other cruel and barbarous treatment. The divorce was refused on this ground.

In *Edmond's Appeal*, 57 Pa. St., 232 (1868), the facts that bruises were constantly inflicted upon respondent by libellant in fits of temper, and his constant interference with respondent's plans even after separation, rendering her unhappy and ill, were offered as an offset to desertion. The libel was dismissed.

Desertion is an actual abandonment of matrimonial cohabitation with an intent to desert, wilfully and maliciously persisted in, without cause, for two years.

But *separation is not desertion.*

In *Ingersoll* v. *Ingersoll,* 49 Pa. St., 251 (1865), the libel set forth that, in consequence of the neglect of the respondent to provide for his wife, she was compelled to live with her relations. It appeared that for a long time the parties corresponded, but that the respondent had not answered his wife's letters for years. The libellant claimed that she was willing to cohabit with her husband. Her libel was dismissed.

§ 784. *Nor has the husband the right to ask the wife to expatriate herself.* In *Bishop* v. *Bishop*, 30 Pa. St., 412 (1858), the respondent would not follow her husband, the libellant, to America. He had married and settled in England ; subsequently, his health being bad, he endeavored to persuade respondent to go with him to America.

This she refused to do, and he came alone. The libellant returned to England some few years after for his family, but his wife refused to come to America, and retained a portion of the family.

THOMPSON, J. : "Would the facts disclosed justify the court in coming to a conclusion favorable to the complainant ? The woman had for years followed the fortunes of her husband—faithful in everything * * * in the face of a great trial, she fails ! The leaving home and country ; the dangers of a long ocean-voyage ; the privations of a stranger in a strange land, may have overmastered her strongest desire to follow his footsteps further, and determined her to cling to her native country, and does not establish wilful and malicious desertion." The libel was dismissed and decree affirmed. See also *Colvin* v. *Reed*, 55 Pa. St., 380 (1867).

§ 785. *Evidence of desertion. Dailey's Appeal*, 10 W. N., 420 (1881), was a libel by the wife against the husband for desertion. The husband and wife had been living at the residence of his mother. The mother ordered the wife away. She appealed to her husband, who refused to accompany her or to provide another home for her. She thereupon was compelled to return to her former home. The husband ever afterward refused to provide a home for her or to contribute toward her support, and never called to see her except upon one occasion.

The court below directed a verdict for respondent, but the Supreme Court reversed, holding that there was sufficient evidence of a wilful and malicious desertion to go to the jury.

§ 786. *Sentence of husband for desertion in Quarter Sessions is no bar to his libel for divorce.* If a husband offer to receive and provide for his wife, and she refuse, without just cause, for two years, this is a desertion. The fact that the husband, meanwhile, was sentenced in the Quarter Sessions to pay for her support may be considered by the jury, but is not a legal bar. *Bauder's Appeal*, 115 Pa. St., 480 (1887). This is a clearer statement of the law than *Vanleer* v. *Vanleer*, 13. Pa. St., 211, or *Schotte* v. *Schotte*, 8 W. N., 236 (1880).

§ 787. *The excuse for the desertion must be that which would justify an independent proceeding for a divorce by the deserter.* If a wife desert her husband for two years, she cannot defend his libel by saying that his temper was bad, his treatment of her capricious or even wicked. She must show cruelty which endangered her life or some other ground which would support a libel on her part. The reason for this is very obvious. Two wrongs do not make a right. The divorce laws permit adultery to be a bar of adultery. But they are silent as to other offsets. Absence of luxurious diet, hard work, scolding, not allowing the wife to go to church, treating her family coldly, do not justify desertion. "The marital contract is one of a binding and solemn character, and it is no light reason, no slight faults, or incompatibility of temper which will justify one of the parties thereto in rescinding it," *Detrick's Appeal*, 117 Pa. St., 459 (1888), PAXSON, J.; nor the fact that libellant occupied a different bed, and had frequently said that he had respondent's personal property, and that was all he cared about, *Eshback* v. *Eshback*, 23 Pa. St., 343 (1854); nor mere rudeness, reproachful language, disagreeable manners, ebullitions of ill temper, *Gordon* v. *Gordon*, 48 Pa. St., 226 (1864). A mere change of residence by the husband and inability to support the wife are not sufficient grounds for a libel by her. *Bell* v. *Bell*, 11 W. N., 156 (1881).

In *McDermott's Appeal*, 8 W. & S., 252 (1844), it was held that the refusal of a husband to receive his wife was a virtual turning her out of doors.

A respondent is not guilty of wilful and malicious desertion who leaves her husband's house in resentment, but soon after returns and is denied admittance. *Hardie* v. *Hardie*, 162 Pa. St., 227 (1894).

The fact that a wife denies a husband her presence and society and refuses to cook his meals, but does not leave him, does not constitute a desertion. *Smith* v. *Smith*, 4 Dist. Rep., 397 (1895).

In *Sowers* v. *Sowers*, 11 Phila., 213 (1876), the libel averred that respondent had offered indignities to the person of the wife rendering her condition intolerable and life burdensome, and that he had turned her out of doors. Respondent had written a letter refusing to receive his wife, but adding "I cannot refuse you admittance." No effort had been made on the part of the wife to gain admission to respondent's habitation. Divorce refused. This decree was affirmed in the Supreme Court. *Sowers' Appeal*, 89 Pa. St., 173 (1879).

Bealor v. *Hahn*, 47 Leg. Int., 120 (1890). MCCOLLUM, J.: "It is well settled that the reasonable cause which will justify husband and wife in abandoning each other is such as would entitle the party to a divorce. * * * Five witnesses called by the plaintiff speak of the relations and conduct of the husband and wife before their separation. H. C. Gibble, a justice of the peace, to whom Mrs. Hahn applied for a warrant against her husband for desertion, says it was Mrs. Hahn's nature to scold and be cross, and that she admitted to him that she had not treated her husband as she should have done. Charles Hahn, a son of the plaintiff, aged twenty-two years, says that he heard his mother call his father 'a d—d liar,' and on one occasion, while he and his father were at the breakfast-table, she said, 'I might just as well poison you, and then you would both be out of the road;' and that in consequence of this remark he was afraid, and left home two weeks afterward. * * * Samuel Plasterer says that Mrs. Hahn once said to him, 'It is a wonder that Mr. Hahn don't take the horses away; they might get poisoned;' but it does not appear that he mentioned this to plaintiff. Priscilla Long says that Mrs. Hahn was not very pleasant when her husband was present, and that she talked unkindly about him. * * * Abraham Schopp says Mrs. Hahn would talk rough and unpleasant to her husband. * * * This is the substance of the evidence on which the plaintiff relies as his justification for abandoning his wife. It exhibits a state of domestic infelicity, but it does not present a case of cruel and barbarous treatment by the wife of the husband, which renders his condition intolerable and life burdensome. *Gordon* v. *Gordon*, 48 Pa., 226; *Jones* v. *Jones*, 66 Pa., 494. The single so-called threat, testified to by the son, did not alarm the husband; there was no act of violence to his person committed by the wife, and there was no evidence from which an attempt or intent to harm him or his estate could be fairly inferred. * * * Where an unexplained desertion appears, it is presumed to be wilful and malicious, and it lies on him to show reasonable and lawful cause for it. If he cannot justify his abandonment of her by evidence which would entitle him to a divorce, he cannot have the rights of a husband in her estate."

In *Grove's Appeal*, 37 Pa. St., 443 (1860), it appeared that the respondent had turned libellant out of doors and forbidden her the house, and likewise subjected her to degrading abuse in the presence of third parties, as well as personally abusing libellant. It further was shown that on a cold and snowy night she had returned, but with difficulty obtained permission to warm herself at respondent's house, and was allowed to stay but a short time; that on different occasions she offered to return, but he, the respondent, steadily refused to receive her. Divorce decreed.

Such a course of cruel treatment on the part of the husband as endangers life or health, and renders cohabitation unsafe, is a good ground for desertion. *Cattison* v. *Cattison*, 22 Pa. St., 275 (1853); *May* v. *May*, 62 Pa. St., 206 (1869).

To justify a turning out of doors of his wife by a husband, the libellant must show such cruel and barbarous treatment as renders his condition intolerable and life burdensome. *Gordon* v. *Gordon*, 48 Pa. St., 226 (1864).

In *VanDyke* v. *VanDyke*, 26 W. N., 228 (1890), McCollum, J., said: "Incompatibility of temper is not a cause for divorce in Pennsylvania, and we may add that it will not justify an abandonment by the husband or wife of his or her marital obligations and duties. If there is anything settled in the law of divorce, it is that the reasonable cause which will justify a desertion must be such as will authorize a dissolution of the marriage bond. Where a desertion is conceded or appears, and is without sufficient legal reasonable cause, it is presumed to be wilful and malicious, and if persisted in for two years or more will entitle the injured party to a divorce."

§ 788. *Subsequent adultery no offset to desertion.* Adultery by the husband after a separation is no bar to his obtaining a divorce for "wilful and malicious desertion and absence from his habitation without reasonable cause for two years and upward." *Ristine* v. *Ristine*, 4 Rawle, 460 (1834).

§ 789. *Temporary cohabitation is not a bar to complaint for desertion.* *Kennedy* v. *Kennedy*, 87 Ill., 250 (1877). Where a wife, without justification, refused for more than two years to go with her husband to a new home, acquired by him within a mile of the old homestead, which they had conveyed to her brother, and live with him there, it was *held*, that his cohabiting with her on one occasion within the time, at her brother's house, while she still so refused, did not bar him of the right to a decree of divorce.

Jacobs v. *Tobleman*, 36 La., 842 (1884). The fact that a husband who has obtained a judgment of separation from bed and board continues to occupy the same house but a separate apartment from that of his wife, while preparing a new home, to which he moves alone as soon as it is ready, is not a reconciliation within the Louisiana Code, and his right to an absolute divorce in one year from the time when judgment was rendered is not barred thereby.

Guthrie v. *Guthrie*, 26 Mo. App., 566 (1887). The wife having separated from the husband for causes which would entitle her to a divorce, her return to him for the sole purpose of nursing him while he is suffering from a supposed mortal ailment, is not necessarily a condonation of past offenses, even though she remain with him thus for several years.

§ 790. *Offers to return must be* bona fide. *McClurg's Appeal*, 66 Pa. St., 366 (1870), was a libel filed by the wife for desertion and cruelty. The answer denied the desertion and set up offers on the part of the husband to receive and cohabit with the wife. The desertion took place July 1, 1864. The libel was filed February 9, 1867.

There were three letters written to the wife by the husband, one in January, 1865, and one in March, 1865, and one about twenty months after March 8, 1865. The last two of these letters contained offers on the part of the husband to return to his wife.

August 10, 1868, during the pendency of the proceedings, the husband's counsel wrote a formal letter to the wife offering a return, and about a week later the wife called upon the husband relative thereto. The lower court disregarded these letters, because it was evident from them that the offers to return were not *bona fide.* The wife got a decree from bed and board, with alimony. The Supreme Court affirmed.

§ 791. *Separation by agreement is not desertion.* An allowance to the respondent by the libellant for over two years may be evidence of an agreement to separate and a bar to a decree for desertion. *Ralston's Appeal,* 93 Pa. St., 133 (1880).

§ 792. **Incest.** All marriages within the degree of consanguinity or affinity, according to the table established by law, are declared void. The table here referred to is that exhibited in the Act of March 31, 1860, section 39 (P. L., 392). It is as follows : " If any person shall commit incestuous fornication or adultery, or intermarry within the degrees of consanguinity or affinity, according to the following table (established by law), he or she shall, on conviction, be sentenced to pay a fine * * * and to undergo an imprisonment * * * and all such marriages are hereby declared void."

The table of degrees of consanguinity and affinity is as follows :

DEGREES OF CONSANGUINITY.

A man may not marry his mother.
"   "   "   father's sister.
"   "   "   mother's sister.
"   "   "   sister.
"   "   "   daughter.
"   "   "   the daughter of his son or daughter.
A woman may not marry her father.
"   "   "   father's brother.
"   "   "   mother's brother.
"   "   "   brother.
"   "   "   son.
"   "   "   the son of her son or daughter.

DEGREES OF AFFINITY.

A man may not marry his father's wife.
"   "   "   son's wife.
"   "   "   son's daughter.*
"   "   "   wife's daughter.
"   "   "   the daughter of his wife's son or daughter.

---

* This is copied from the Statute Book. A man's granddaughter is not related to him by " affinity." She is named in the above table of con-

A woman may not marry her mother's husband.
    "   "   "   daughter's husband.
    "   "   "   husband's son.
    "   "   "   the son of her husband's son or daughter.

§ 793. *Incest cannot be charged after death.* In *Parker's Appeal*, 44 Pa. St., 309 (1863), an uncle was married to his niece, and on his death his widow was granted letters of administration. The question arose as to her right to administer, and it was decided that such a marriage was voidable under the Act of March 13, 1815, section 5 (P. L., 150), but could not be questioned after the death of either party.

In *Walter's Appeal*, 70 Pa. St., 392 (1872), a man married his daughter-in-law, and upon his death his heirs resisted her claim against the estate on the ground that the marriage was void, but it was held that the Act of 1860 was simply a declaration of the law of 1815 limiting dissolution of incestuous marriages to the life of the party.

§ 794. **Fraud, force, coercion, sentence for felony.** The Act of 1854, granting divorces for these reasons, has been already quoted. " It is settled that fraud which would vitiate any other contract will not have that effect when the marriage has actually been solemnized and consummated." * * *

" The want of chastity on the part of the woman, antenuptial incontinence, even though she may have expressly represented herself as virtuous, forms no ground for avoiding the contract." SHARSWOOD, C. J., *Allen's Appeal*, 99 Pa. St., 199 (1881).

To secure a divorce under the Act of May 8, 1854, on the ground of coercion by threats, the latter must be against life and render libellant liable to bodily harm. Mere representations as to pregnancy are not sufficient. *Todd* v. *Todd*, 149 Pa. St., 60 (1892).

Where the libel averred that the respondent had alleged herself to be pregnant by the libellant, and that such representation was false, it was held to be an insufficient ground for divorce. *Hoffman* v. *Hoffman*, 30 Pa. St., 417 (1858).

§ 795. **Duress.** Where a marriage was celebrated under the fear of imprisonment on the false charge of fornication and bas-

---

sanguinity. If the "son's daughter" is to be excluded under "affinity," why not the "daughter's daughter?" And why should it not be extended to the table below, and under " Affinity " prohibit a woman from marrying her ·son's son or her daughter's son? The line thus criticised is a clear mistake, and the fact that it passed and has been allowed to stand is only another evidence of our loose legislation.

tardy, and an arrest thereunder, such duress will avoid the marriage. *Collins* v. *Collins*, 2 Brews., 515 (1869).

A false statement of the woman that she was pregnant by the man, if not believed by the man, is no ground for divorce. *Todd* v. *Todd*, 24 W. N., 31 (1889).

Threats made against the man by the woman's relations to third persons (there being no constraint or fear at the time of ceremony) are not ground for divorce. *Ibid.*

§ 796. **Personal abuse.** The Statute of 1855 gives both parties the right to apply "for the cause of personal abuse, or for such conduct on the part of either the husband or wife as to render the condition of the other party intolerable and life burdensome."

§ 797. "Cruelty within our statute which entitles a wife to divorce from her husband is actual personal violence or the reasonable apprehension of it; or such a course of treatment as endangers her life or health, and renders cohabitation unsafe." *Butler* v. *Butler*, 1 Pars. Select Eq. Cas., 344 (1849), KING, P. J.

§ 798. **Cruel and barbarous treatment**—*Endangering wife's life —Indignities rendering her condition intolerable, life burdensome, and thereby forcing her to withdraw.* It will be observed that if life be endangered, the wife need not withdraw. But she cannot sue for indignities unless they were so intolerable as to render life burdensome and thereby forced her to withdraw. As long as she remain she cannot sue under this head. Nor can she leave unless the excuse come fully up to the requirement of the law.

In *Richards* v. *Richards*, 1 Grant, 392 (1856); 37 Pa. St., 225 (1860), the wife sought to obtain a divorce on the ground of indignities offered to her person, and the act of twisting libellant's nose by respondent was relied on. The libel was dismissed, the court ruling that such conduct, though unlawful and barbarous, was not sufficient to compel her to withdraw from his house and family. It must be continued treatment, and the indignities must not be provoked by libellant.

In *Mason* v. *Mason*, 25 W. N., 178 (1889), WILLIAMS, J., said: "Bad temper alone is not a ground for divorce, nor is mere drunkenness, or indolence, or thriftlessness, or jealousy; but when to all these is added a course of the most abusive and humiliating treatment, public and repeated charges of adultery and abortion, threats to shoot, to kill, to cut out her heart, to cut her into mince-meat, and the like, accompanied by such unmistakable evidence of his purpose to carry his threats into execution as was offered by drawing a razor, by pushing her off the porch of the house, and by breaking up her home and throwing its contents into the street, it seems very clear to us that the condition of this wife was made intolerable and her life burdensome.

"To deprive her of food and other necessaries of life is an indignity to her person. To assault her with a razor or inflict violence upon her is an indignity to her person. To put her in mortal terror by repeated threats to kill is as truly destructive to health as to administer poison."

A libel in divorce by the wife for cruel and barbarous treatment must contain the averment that by reason of such treatment libellant was forced to withdraw from her husband's house and family. *Dunkel* v. *Dunkel*, 1 Dist. Rep., 684 (1892).

A single offer of indignity will not support a divorce proceeding. A decree is justified when indignities have been practised often enough to be designated as a course of conduct. This does not mean physical indignity alone. All indignities must be borne until they render life burdensome and force the libellant to withdraw from her husband's house. *Brubaker* v. *Brubaker*, 4 Dist. Rep., 186 (1894).

Insanity a defense to libel on ground of cruelty. In an action for divorce on the ground of cruel and barbarous treatment, insanity is a sufficient defense. *Hansell* v. *Hansell*, 3 Dist. Rep., 724 (1894).

§ 799. *Cruelty to husband.* Prior to the Act of June 25, 1895 (P. L., 308), it was decided that a husband could not maintain a libel upon the charge of "indignities to his person, rendering his condition intolerable." He must aver "cruel and barbarous treatment." *Hancock* v. *Hancock*, 13 W. N., 29 (1882). *Powers'* *Appeal*, 120 Pa. St., 320 (1888), PAXSON, J. (See section 746.)

In *Jones* v. *Jones*, 66 Pa. St., 494 (1870), the libel set forth that the respondent had threatened to kill libellant; that she kept poison in the house, threatening his life; that by pounding and by opprobrious epithets she endeavored to vex him; that she cast things off the cooking-stove, compelling the family to withdraw to a wash-house, and otherwise made the husband's condition intolerable and life burdensome. Decree granted.

We pass now from these general matters to the question of—

§ 800. **Jurisdiction**

As to the libellant. The Act of 1815 declares that the libel may be exhibited "to the judges of the Court of Common Pleas of the proper county where the injured party *resides.*" Citizenship and residence for twelve months are, under the statute, made synonymous. But no libellant can sue here if residing out of the State.

The verb is not used in the past, but the present tense. It is not where the libellant *has* resided, but where the libellant resides. It is important to keep in view the distinction between these legislative provisions.

Citizenship and residence required. The Act of 1815 says : "No person shall be entitled to a divorce from the bond of matrimony by virtue of this Act who is not a citizen of this State, and who shall not have resided therein at least one whole year previous to the filing his or her petition or libel."

The Act of May 8, 1854, section 2 (P. L., 644 ; Br. Purd., 684), declares that the word "citizen" shall not be so construed as to exclude "any party who shall for one year have had a *bona fide* residence within this Commonwealth previous to the filing of" the petition.

The personal abuse Act of March 9, 1855, section 1 (P. L., 68 ; Br. Purd., 684), requires that the applicant shall be a citizen, *or* shall have resided for one year within the Commonwealth. A mistake might be made in supposing that a proceeding under this Act could be instituted by a non-resident if a citizen ; or that a resident could sue in some other county than that in which he resides. But—

§ 801. *The libellant must reside in the county where libel filed.* This not only appears from the Act of 1815, above quoted, but it has been expressly ruled in *Sherwood's Appeal*, 17 W. N., 338 (1886) : "The court of the county in which the libellant resides has alone jurisdiction of the libel. She cannot go into another county and sue."

§ 802. *Jurisdiction of the cause.* If the parties have always been domiciled in Pennsylvania, or even if their domicile had at one time been outside of the State, but had been unquestionably changed to Pennsylvania, and a cause of divorce should occur outside of the State, the party preserving the domicile here could undoubtedly sue. For instance, if the parties, having married and resided in this State, one of them should commit adultery in New Jersey, the innocent party could sue in Pennsylvania. The same result would follow if they both left the State upon a pleasure excursion and one should desert the other in the State of New Jersey. The party returning to the Pennsylvania home could file a libel here. But where the common domicile was not in this State, and the cause occurred outside the State, and the defendant is not served within the State, our courts have not jurisdiction.

The Act of June 20, 1893 (*supra*, sections 741a, 741 b), permits a wife to obtain a divorce for adultery, desertion, or cruel treatment, where the wife, having been a citizen, marries a foreigner and is compelled to abandon her foreign domicile; the court, before entering a decree, requires actual or constructive notice to the husband by personal service or registered letter.

In New York, the Court of Appeals has decided very strongly against a service by advertisement. In the case of *People* v. *Baker*, 31 Sickels (76 N. Y.), 78 (1879), it appears that one Baker married Sallie West in Ohio. He came to New York. She sued him in Ohio, where the marriage had taken place, and she obtained a divorce. He thereupon married a woman in New York. He was indicted, sentenced for bigamy, and this was affirmed by the Court of Appeals. They held that a court of another State cannot adjudge the dissolution of the marital relations of a citizen of New York residing there during the proceedings elsewhere, without a voluntary appearance and with no actual notice to him, and this although the marriage was solemnized in such other State. At page 80, it was held that even a personal service in New York would not give jurisdiction to the other State. Judge Folger (at page 87) touches the argument that New York had in former cases allowed a substituted service, and says that this was true until the new code.

O'Dea v. *O'Dea*, 1 Cent. Rep., 785 (1885). "A divorce granted by a court of another State against a person who did not reside within that State, was not served with process therein, and did not voluntarily appear, will not be recognized as valid in the courts of New York."

The husband sued for a divorce upon the ground that a former husband of his wife was living at the time of the marriage. The plaintiff and defendant were married in New York, August 30, 1866. In July, 1844, the defendant had married K. in New York and lived with him until 1860, when she went to Toronto. K. went to Ohio, remained there a year, and in March, 1864, sued the woman for a divorce. A copy of the writ and petition was sent by mail and received by the wife. Depositions were taken in Toronto in support of the petition. She was present. May 24, 1864, the Ohio Court decreed a divorce. She then married this plaintiff, as above stated, in New York, in 1866. He sued for this divorce, alleging the nullity of the Ohio decree, and that she was, notwithstanding that divorce, the wife of K. when she married this plaintiff. Judgment was entered for plaintiff in the lower court, was reversed at the general term, but on appeal to the High Court of Errors and Appeals the last order was reversed and the first judgment affirmed.

These authorities clearly show that New York does not recognize a divorce decreed in another State where the defendant was not within the jurisdiction of that State and was not served within it.

In New York, and in most of the other States, the rule is adhered to that there must be in the courts of the State either jurisdiction of the cause of divorce by events occurring within the State, or jurisdiction of the parties by common domicile, or the service of process upon the respondent within the State, or appearance.

Allison v. *Allison*, 18 W. N., 508 (1886). In this case the parties were married in West Virginia. Libellant resided in Philadelphia in 1875, since which time she had supported herself in that city. The libel filed averred desertion by respondent in 1873, while the parties were living in Maryland. The libel was dismissed for want of jurisdiction.

In *Bishop* v. *Bishop*, 30 Pa. St., 412 (1858), the parties had resided together in England, and then libellant had come to America alone. He returned to England to bring his wife and family with him, but respondent, through fear and love of country, refused to come with him to America, and part of the family remained with her. The libel was dismissed for want of jurisdiction. This was remedied by the Act of April 22, 1858 (P. L., 451), which gives jurisdiction where either party at the occurrence of the cause is domiciled in another State or *country*.

In *Love* v. *Love*, 10 Phila., 453 (1873), the proceedings were entirely *ex parte*. It appeared that respondent resided in St. Louis, Mo., had never been served, and had not appeared.

The court said : " It is clear, then, that actual service upon a non-resident or his or her appearance is necessary to give jurisdiction." The remark here as to " actual service" refers to service upon a non-resident who, at the time of service, is within the State, for an extra-territorial service would be of no validity. *Ralston's Appeal*, 93 Pa. St., 133 (1880).

In *Platt's Appeal*, 80 Pa. St., 501 (1876), it appeared the parties were married in New York, and then removed to Ohio. The husband subsequently came to Philadelphia. At the same time the wife went to Wisconsin ; the husband moved to Michigan six months afterward and obtained a divorce.

The decree was declared nugatory, the respondent not being served with process, and not appearing.

The court has no jurisdiction where the marriage was celebrated in another country in which the respondent has always resided.

The fact that the plaintiff is a citizen of Pennsylvania, and that he has resided therein for one year previous to the filing of the libel, does not confer jurisdiction.

Lokes v. *Lokes*, 14 W. N., 306 (1884). In this case the cause of divorce was desertion. The parties were married in England, and libellant had subsequently come to Philadelphia, but respondent remained in Nottingham, England.

The courts of the State of the domicile have alone jurisdiction. All other process is void.

Comm. v. *Maize*, 23 W. N., 572 (1889). In this case the cause of divorce was desertion. The parties were married and domiciled in Centre County, Pa. In 1886, the husband went to Missouri; in 1887, he filed a libel for divorce from his wife in that State; a service of the subpœna was made upon her by sheriff of Centre County.

A decree *a v. m.* was entered against her in Missouri. The husband then returned to Centre County, married another woman, and refused to support the first wife. On a proceeding against him, the question arose as to the validity of the decree in divorce. The Quarter Sessions of Centre County, in a learned opinion by FURST, P. J., refused to recognize the divorce, and held that the husband was bound to support the first wife.

A divorce cannot be decreed where a desertion occurred in another State of which both parties were then resident, and the respondent has not appeared or been personally served. The court has no jurisdiction. *Burdick* v. *Burdick*, 2 Dist. Rep., 622 (1893); *Davis* v. *Davis*, 2 Dist. Rep., 621 (1893).

In *McCartney* v. *McCartney*, 30 W. N., 132 (1892), a libel was filed for desertion; both parties lived and were married in Ireland; their common domicile was Ireland, and subsequently Scotland, where the desertion took place. The libellant had lived here three years and more, but respondent had never been within the jurisdiction of the court. *Held*, that this court had no jurisdiction.

The wife may apply for the divorce in the county of her actual home, although her husband resides in another county. *Smith* v. *Smith*, 1 Dist. Rep., 550 (1892).

§ 803. **Brief of the Pennsylvania Statutes.** The laws specifying the grounds of divorce have been already cited. Before proceeding to the details of the practice in divorce cases it may be appropriate to furnish an abstract of what the legislature has said upon this subject.

§ 804. *Divorces validated.*

The Act of February 27, 1847, section 1 (P. L., 169; Br. Pur., 683), undertook to validate divorces theretofore granted for adultery committed outside the State, both parties being then non-residents, but the libellant having resided in Pennsylvania for one year.

§ 805. *Desertion libel may be filed in six months.*

The Act of April 26, 1850, section 5 (P. L., 591 ; Br. Pur., 683), authorizes the filing of a libel for desertion six months after the desertion, the final decree not to be entered until two years after the desertion.

§ 806. *Jurisdiction in cases of desertion, adultery, etc., outside the State.*

The same Act gives jurisdiction for desertion and adultery, although the parties were then domiciled in another State. The applicant to be a citizen or a resident for one year.

The Act of April 22, 1858, section 1 (P. L., 450 ; Br. Pur., 685), extends the jurisdiction of the original Act to *all* cases where either party was domiciled outside the State. The applicant must be a citizen or a resident for one year.

§ 807. *Proceedings—Libel in proper county.*

The Act of March 13, 1815, section 2 (6 Sm., 287 ; Br. Pur., 686), directs that the libel must be exhibited by the husband or the wife by her next friend " to the judges of the Court of Common Pleas of the proper county where the injured party resides," thirty days before the next term.

In *Fordham* v. *Fordham*, 15 W. N., 250 (1884), a libel issued August 18, returnable to September 18. *Held*, that it was exhibited " thirty days before the next term," although the last of the thirty days fell on Sunday.

§ 808. *Requirements of libel.*

It must " set forth particularly and specially the causes of complaint." It must, when filed by the wife, be signed by her next friend. *Grissom* v. *Grissom*, 8 W. N., 484 (1880). And she must not sue in the name she bore before marriage. *Howard* v. *Lewis*, 6 Phila., 50 (1865).

§ 809. *Affidavit required.*

An affidavit must accompany the libel. " That the facts contained in said petition or libel are true, to the best of his or her knowledge and belief, and that the said complaint is not made out of levity or by collusion between the said husband and wife, and for the mere purpose of being freed and separated from each other, but in sincerity and truth for the causes mentioned in the said petition or libel."

§ 810. *Statutory form of affidavit must be followed.* An affidavit that the facts set forth in the libel are true is not sufficient. It must be sworn to in the form prescribed by the Act March 13, 1815. *Hoffman* v. *Hoffman*, 30 Pa. St., 417 (1858).

§ 811. *Prior to the Act of 1895, a notary could not administer the oath, and the libel might be demurred to for this reason. Reeves* v. *Reeves*, 12 Phila., 188 (1877) ; *Grissom* v. *Grissom*, 8 W. N., 484 (1880).

In *Garrett* v. *Garrett*, 4 W. N., 240 (1877), Judge BRIGGS was of opinion that the notary could administer the oath. The Act of August 10, 1864, section 2 (P. L., 962; Br. Purd., 1610), was cited as conferring on a notary all the powers of a judge or justice to take affidavits.

The Philadelphia rule requires that the affidavit " shall be made before a magistrate of that county."

The Act of May 22, 1895 (P. L., 105), permits the libel and other papers in a divorce suit to be affirmed or sworn to before a notary public, prothonotary, or clerk of the court.

§ 812. *Subpœna.*

On filing libel and affidavit as above, a subpœna issues signed by one of the judges, commanding the defendant to appear at the next.or any subsequent term. (Act of March 13, 1815, section 2; 6 Sm., 287.)

§ 813. *If subpœna served.*

Upon due proof that the subpœna has been personally served (service cannot be accepted), or that a copy had been given to defendant fifteen days before the return, the court shall make such preparatory rules and orders that the cause may be heard and determined at that term or afterward, and the court may proceed *ex parte* if necessary. (*Ibid.*)

§ 814. *Issues.*

If a matter of fact affirmed by one be denied by the other, and either shall desire it tried by a jury, an issue shall be formed and the same tried accordingly. (*Ibid.*)

§ 815. *Where no issue demanded.*

The court inquires and decides, by examination of witnesses, interrogatories, exhibits, or other legal proofs, had either before or at the hearing. (*Ibid.*)

§ 816. *If subpœna not served.*

If proof shall be made that the party could not be found in said county, an *alias subpœna* shall issue returnable the first day of the next or of any subsequent term. If served personally, the case proceeds as directed upon the original subpœna. If proof be made that the defendant could not be found, the sheriff shall publish notices in one or more newspapers printed within or nearest to the county for four weeks successively prior to the first day of the next term to answer. At which, or at any subsequent term, the same proceedings shall be had as above directed. (Act March 13, 1815, section 3; 6 Sm., 287; Br. Pur., 686.)

§ 817. *Bill of particulars.*

Respondent may at any time after the return-day enter a rule on libellant to furnish a bill of particulars, and if it be not furnished within thirty days after service of notice, a decree of *non pros.* shall be entered. The court may upon cause shown extend the time in which to file a bill of particulars. (Act May 25, 1878, section 1; P. L., 156; Br. Pur., 687.)

This law only enforced a right which had always been recognized.

§ 818. *Decree.*

Courts may dismiss libel, decree a divorce from bonds of matrimony, or that the marriage was null and void. After decree divorcing from bonds or declaring marriage void, all duties, rights, and claims accruing to either in pursuance of the marriage shall cease, and the parties may marry again as if they had never been married. (Act March 13, 1815, section 8; 6 Sm., 288; Br. Pur., 687.)

§ 819. *Costs*

May be awarded to successful party, or an order may be made that each pay his or her costs. (*Id.*, section 12.)

§ 820. *Appeal.*

Within one year after final decree either may appeal, upon entering into recognizance with at least one good surety in double the amount of costs, conditioned to prosecute the appeal with effect. (*Ibid.*, section 13, and Act Feb. 8, 1819, section 1; 7 Sm., 151; Br. Pur., 688.)

§ 821. *Where wife is libellant and is a lunatic.*

The petition and affidavit may be presented by any relative or next friend. The lunacy and the circumstances sufficient to satisfy the court of the truth of the allegation shall be set forth in the petition, and upon hearing of the case the question of the lunacy, with every other matter denied, shall be heard. (Act April 13, 1843, section 8; P. L., 235; Br. Pur., 688.)

§ 822. *Conviction of adultery and sentence.*

The record may be given in evidence on application for divorce. (Act March 13, 1815, section 4; 6 Sm., 288; Br. Pur., 688.)

§ 823. *Second marriage upon rumor of death.*

"If any husband or wife, upon any false rumor, in appearance well founded, of the death of the other (when such other has been absent for the space of two whole years) hath married, or shall marry again, he or she shall not be liable to the pains of adultery; but it shall be in the election of the party remaining unmarried, at his or her return, to insist to have his or her former wife or husband restored, or to have his or her own marriage dissolved, and the other party to remain with the second husband or wife; and in any suit or action instituted for this purpose within six months after such return, the court may and shall sentence and decree accordingly." (*Id.*, section 6; Br. Pur., 688.)

§ 824. *Defenses in adultery.*

In any suit for divorce for the cause of adultery, if the defendant shall allege and prove that plaintiff has been guilty of same crime, or has admitted defendant into conjugal society or embraces after he or she knew of the criminal fact, or, if plaintiff be the husband, that he allowed of his wife's prostitution, or received hire for it, or exposed her to lewd company, whereby she became ensnared to the crime, it shall be a good defense and a perpetual bar. (*Id.*, section 7; Br. Pur., 688.) Under the English Act of 1857, "wilful neglect and misconduct of libellant" may bar his right to a decree. *Starbuck* v. *Starbuck*, 59 Law Jour. Rep. (N. S.) (P. D. & A. Div.), 20 (1889), BUTT, J.

§ 825. *No condonation save in cases of adultery.* It will be observed that this law applies only to suits for divorce on the ground of *adultery.* If the charge be desertion, the plaintiff's adultery is no defense ; nor can there be condonation of cruelty.

§ 826. *Defendant guilty of adultery*

Cannot marry the paramour during life of the injured party. Nothing in the Act to render children born of the wife during coverture illegitimate. (Act March 13, 1815, section 9 ; Br. Pur., 688.)

§ 827. *Divorced adulteress cohabiting openly*

With paramour is declared incapable of alienating any of her lands, and all her deeds and wills are declared void. (*Id.*, section 10 ; Br. Pur., 688.)

§ 828. *Divorce à* mensa.

If any husband shall maliciously either abandon his family, or turn his wife out of doors, or by cruel and barbarous treatment endanger her life, or offer such indignities to her person as to render her condition intolerable or life burdensome, and thereby force her to withdraw from his house and family, it shall be lawful for the Court of Common Pleas of the respective counties, upon complaint and due proof thereof, made in the manner prescribed in the Act to which this is a supplement, to grant the wife a divorce from bed and board, and also to allow her such alimony as her husband's circumstances will admit of, so as the same do not exceed the third part of the annual profits or income of his estate, or of his occupation and labor, which shall continue until a reconciliation shall take place or until the husband shall, by his petition or libel, offer to receive and cohabit with her again, and to use her as a-good husband ought to, and then, in such case, the court may either suspend the aforesaid sentence or decree, or, in case of her refusal to return and cohabit, under the protection of the court, discharge and annul the same according to their discretion, and if he fail in performing his said offers and engagements, the former sentence or decree may be revived and enforced, and the arrears of the alimony ordered to be paid. (Act of February 26, 1817, section 1 ; 6 Sm., 405 ; Br. Pur., 688.)

§ 829. *Final decree for alimony a lien.*

Upon a decree à *mensa et thoro,* and the allowance of alimony shall have been made by any of the Courts of Common Pleas of the respective counties of this Commonwealth, or hereafter may be made, it shall be the duty of the prothonotary of said court to enter the said decree on the judgment-docket of said court, which said decree, when so entered, is hereby declared to be and shall remain a lien on the real estate of such respondent, and (until) the same is satisfied for the full amount that may be due up to the period of such satisfaction. And after such lien shall be so entered, it shall be the duty of the prothonotary of said court, upon affidavit by the libellant, that any payment under said decree, as the same has been made due and payable by the court, is due and unpaid, to issue execution on the written order of the libellant, or her attorney, setting forth the amount so due and unpaid, which shall be directed to and served by the sheriff in like manner as executions upon judgment. And if the court should be of opinion that the said lien is not sufficient for the full or permanent security for payment of said decree, it shall have power and authority, on satisfactory proof being made that the respondent is possessed of sufficient estate, to order a decree and require that security, such as shall be determined and approved by said court, shall be given for the due payment of the said alimony according to the terms of said decree; the said security to be either by a bond, with sufficient sureties, or mortgage on real estate, taken in the name of the Commonwealth, to the use of the party entitled to said alimony, or by the deposit of money, to be invested as the court may deem proper, as may seem to the court sufficient to secure the payment of said alimony, as the same may fall due. (Act April 15, 1845, section 1; P. L., 455; Br. Pur., 689.)

§ 830. *Attachment may issue.*

The said courts may enforce their decrees by attachment, on the return of which they may make such order, either to imprison or discharge the defendant, as the facts of the case may justify. (*Ibid.*, section 2; Br. Pur., 689.)

§ 831. *Divorce* à mensa et thoro *decreed for adultery.*

In addition to the several causes mentioned in the Act or Acts to which this is a supplement, for which a married woman may obtain a divorce from the bed and board of her husband, with allowance of alimony, shall be that of adultery; and it shall be lawful for the Court of Common Pleas of the respective counties, upon complaint and due proof thereof made, in the manner prescribed by the said Acts to which this is a supplement, or either of them, to grant the wife a divorce from bed and board; and in addition to the powers now conferred upon the said court by the said Acts, or either of them, to grant alimony, and the amount thereof, it shall be lawful for the said court to decree to be paid by the said husband, in addition thereto, to his said wife, the one-half of the value of all money and property, of every kind whatsoever, which the said husband may have received by, through, or from his said wife, as her individual money or property, which amount the said court shall inquire into and ascertain, by proper proof, on and at the time of the hearing of the said complaint; which decree the said court shall have the power to enforce, suspend, or discharge, and annul, in the same manner as the said court may now enforce, suspend, or discharge and annul its decrees under and by virtue of the said Acts, or either of them. (Act of April 11, 1862, section 1; P. L., 430; Br. Pur., 689.)

§ 832. *The law discourages suits* à mensa.

They were not mentioned in the original Act of March 13, 1815. The courts of England and of this country have denounced them. See *Sir William Scott's* opinion in *Evans* v. *Evans*, 1 Hag. Con., 35; Macqueen on Husband and Wife, 206; 2 Kent Com., 127.

§ 833. The following rules have been adopted in Philadelphia:

Libels shall be framed in general analogy to bills in equity by setting out the matters relied on distinctly in separate paragraphs, consecutively numbered and containing as follows:

PARAGRAPH 1. (*a*) The names of the parties and the time and place of the marriage.

(*b*) The citizenship and domicile of the parties respectively at the time of marriage and since, including a positive averment that the libellant has been a citizen and resident of the State for one whole year previous to the filing of the libel.

(c) Their present place of actual residence, with details of street, number, etc.

In case the present residence of the respondent be unknown to the libellant, then an explicit averment of that fact shall be made, together with a statement of the respondent's last known residence and the time at which he or she was last known to be there.

. If the marriage shall not have been contracted and the present actual residence of both parties shall not also be within the county of Philadelphia, then a full statement shall be made of the time, place, and circumstances under which the parties, or either of them, became domiciled within the jurisdiction of the court.

§ 834.

Subsequent paragraphs shall contain a succinct statement of the time, place, and circumstances of the alleged cause of divorce ; when more than one cause is alleged, each shall be set forth in a separate paragraph. The final paragraph shall contain a prayer for divorce *a vinculo matrimonii* or *à mensa et thoro*, as the case may be.

§ 835. *Affidavit.*

The affidavit to the libel shall be in the form as required by the Act of Assembly and shall be made before a magistrate of this county. (See § 811, *supra*.)

§ 836. *Rule to answer.*

A rule on the respondent to appear and answer within thirty days after the return-day of the subpœna shall be entered of course by the prothonotary at the time of filing the libel.

§ 837. *Notice to respondent.*

A copy of the libel shall be served upon the respondent with the subpœna. The said copy shall have indorsed upon it a notice to the respondent, as follows :

To A. B.,

the within-named respondent :

You are hereby notified and required, within thirty days from Monday, the   day of   next, to cause an appearance to be entered for you in the Court of Common Pleas, No.   , of the County of Philadelphia, and an answer to be filed to the libel for divorce of which the within is a copy.

NOTE.—You are hereby warned that if you fail to enter an appearance and file an answer as above notified and required, the cause will proceed without you, and you will be liable to have a decree of divorce entered against you in your absence.

C. D.,
Attorney for Libellant.

§ 838. *Service.*

The subpœna, copy of libel, and notice to appear and answer shall be served by the sheriff upon respondents who are within the county at the time of the service.

Where the respondent is not within the county, but is within the State, the sheriff shall deputize the sheriff of the county where the respondent may be found to serve a subpœna, with a copy of the libel and notice to appear and answer; and in such case the sheriff shall make return that the respondent could not be found within the county, and that he did therefore deputize the sheriff of such other county to make the service, and shall attach to his own return the affidavit of the officer making the service.

§ 839. *Affidavit of service of subpœna.*

In all cases the officer making the service shall make an affidavit, stating the time, place, and manner of serving the subpœna, copy of libel, and notice to appear and answer, and also that the person so served by him is the respondent named in the writ, and his means of knowing such fact.

§ 840. *Publication.*

Where the first subpœna is returned that the respondent cannot be found in this county or State, which return shall be made to the first day of the next term, which shall commence not less than thirty days after the filing of the libel, an *alias* subpœna may be issued, returnable to the next or any subsequent regular term. If the second subpœna is returned that the respondent cannot be found in this county or State, the prothonotary shall issue, on the application of the libellant, an order on the sheriff, directing him to publish, once a week for four full weeks successively, in the *Legal Intelligencer* and two daily newspapers of large circulation, notice to the respondent in the following form :

To A. B., late of No.   Street, Philadelphia, Pennsylvania.
Whereas C. B., your (husband or wife, as the case may be) has filed a libel in the Court of Common Pleas, No.   , of Philadelphia County, of Term, No.   , praying a divorce against you, now you are hereby notified and required to appear in said court on or before Monday, the day of   next, to answer the complaint of the said C. B., and in default of such appearance you will be liable to have a divorce granted in your absence.

D. E.,
Sheriff of Philadelphia.

And the sheriff shall make due return of his action therein.

§ 841. *Appearance.*

The counsel for the respondent shall enter his appearance by filing a written order, accompanied by a letter of attorney from the respondent, which shall be duly acknowledged before the prothonotary or judge, justice of the peace, or magistrate of the county, district, or State in which the respondent may reside, or if the respondent be without the United States, then before an officer authorized by the laws of this State to take acknowledgments of deeds, etc., in a foreign country. The said letter shall be attached by the master to his report.

§ 842. *Proceeding* ex parte.

Where service has been duly made either personally or by publication, and the respondent does not appear, or having appeared does not answer within thirty days after the return-day, the libellant may proceed *ex parte*.

§ 843. *Answer.*

The respondent may, at any time within thirty days after the return-day, or afterward with leave of the court, upon cause shown for the delay, demur or answer to the libel, or may demur to part and answer to the rest.

The answer shall be responsive to the libel, and shall be arranged in paragraphs corresponding as to subject-matters as nearly as may be with the paragraphs of the libel; but other new matters relied upon by the respondent may be set forth in subsequent paragraphs.

§ 844. *Replication.*

Where the answer shall not be confined to mere denial of the facts averred in the libel, but shall contain new matters, the libellant may file a replication to such new matters only.

No further pleadings shall be made by either party without special leave of the court.

§ 845. *Rule for bill of particulars.*

The respondent may enter a rule for a bill of particulars under the Act of May 25, 1878, of course, at any time before filing his or her answer, but after answer filed no such rule shall be entered unless specially allowed by the court.

§ 846. *Issue may be framed.*

Should the pleadings raise any issue of fact, relevant and material to the relief sought, which either party may desire to have tried by a jury, an issue shall be framed by the party desiring such trial and presented to the court for approval.

The issue shall not be a feigned issue, but one directly framed on the facts alleged and denied in the pleadings. Such issue and trial shall be of right at any time before the taking of testimony upon the merits of the case shall have actually commenced; but thereafter such trial by jury shall be allowed only in the discretion of the court upon motion and cause shown.

§ 847. *Amendments.*

Amendments of the pleadings may be allowed in the discretion of the court; but no amendment of the libel alleging a cause of divorce of a different nature shall be allowed.

§ 848. *Appointment of a master.*

When a case is ready to be proceeded with either upon answer not demanding a trial by jury, or *ex parte*, a master shall be appointed by the court, upon the motion of either party, which motion shall be made in writing and placed upon the regular current motion list of the court. No suggestion or agreement·from parties or counsel as to the person to be appointed master will be received under any circumstances.

§ 849. *Proceedings before the master—Notice by master of meetings.*

The master shall give ten days' written notice to the counsel of both parties of the time and place of taking testimony. If there shall be no appearance for the respondent, the notice shall be given to him or her personally, if possible ; if not, then by leaving it at his place of residence or by registered letter to the address where the master shall have reason to believe it will be most likely to reach him or her.

§ 850. *Master required to give respondent notice.*

In all cases where there is no return of personal service and no appearance is entered for the respondent, it shall be the duty of the master before proceeding to take the testimony upon the merits of the case, to inform himself, by examination of the libellant and by such other means as he shall deem conducive to the purpose, of the residence and address of the respondent; and thereupon the master shall use every exertion, by personal inquiry within the county or by registered letters outside of the county, and in case of failure by these means, then by advertisement in such newspaper or newspapers as, in the opinion of the master, will be most likely to reach the respondent, once a week for four full weeks, and by any other means available, to give actual notice to the respondent of the application for a divorce, the grounds thereof, the name and address of the master, and the time and place of taking testimony in the cause. *Provided,* That in cases in which the respondent was last known to reside and last heard of in the county of Philadelphia, it shall not be necessary to advertise such notice. Thereafter the master may proceed to take testimony upon the merits of the cause, but he shall not file his report until he is satisfied that all means available have been used to give actual notice to the respondent, and the efforts to that end shall be set forth in his report.

§ 851. *Master's duties.*

The master shall make inquiry of the witnesses and report to the court the ages of the libellant and respondent, and the number, names, ages, and residence of their children, if they have any ; and in cases where the subpœna has not been personally served, or, after publication, no appearance has been entered for the respondent, and the other means of giving actual notice to the respondent' shall have failed, the master shall, if possible, give written notice of the proceedings to such children of the respondent as have attained their majority, or, if there are none, then to the parents, brothers, and sisters or other near relatives of the respondent, requesting them to assist him in giving actual notice to the respondent, and report to the court what efforts he has made to effect such notice, and the result thereof. Where the residence of either or both parties is given as within this county, the master shall, by personal inquiry, satisfy himself and report to the court whether the stated residence is correct and *bona fide*, and the length of time the libellant has resided in this State, and also whether the respondent has ever resided in this State, and if so, when and where. In case the residence of either party is given as in another county of this State, the master shall make such inquiries by letter to the sheriff of such other county.

§ 852. *Examination by master.*

When a case is ready to proceed to the testimony upon the merits, the master shall examine each witness specially and in detail upon all matters set forth in the libel and answer and upon such other matters as may appear to be relevant and material. And it shall be his duty, whether requested by either of the parties or not, to summon and examine such witnesses as he may have reason to believe have knowledge of any matters relevant and material to the just and proper determination of the cause.

Neither party shall be allowed to examine any witness called on his or her behalf until after the master shall have finished his examination of such witness, but after the master's examination of such witness the party calling him may supplement his examination-in-chief, and upon the conclusion of such supplementary examination the opposite party may cross-examine.

§ 853. *Powers of master.*

The master shall have the usual powers of a master in equity, in regard to the detention of witnesses for examination and the general course of the proceedings before him, subject to the directions of the court from time to time upon motion of either party.

When objection is made to the competency or relevancy of testimony, the master shall note the objection, and proceed to take the testimony, subject to the objection.

§ 854. *Minutes of meetings.*

The master shall keep minutes of his meetings, noting the attendance and adjournments, and at whose instance the adjournments are had, and annex the same to his report. If either party shall be of opinion that the other party, or the master, is unnecessarily or unjustly delaying the proceedings or increasing the expense thereof, he may notify the master of his exceptions in that regard, and the master shall note the same in his report for such action of the court as may be adjudged just and proper.

§ 855. *Security for costs.*

The master may, with leave of the court, require security for the payment of his and the prothonotary's costs, and may decline to proceed further until such security shall be entered. No rule for divorce shall be made absolute until all the costs are paid.

§ 856. *Master's report.*

The master shall report his proceedings and the testimony, together with his opinion of the case, and shall append thereto the libel and all subsequent papers filed in the case, with a copy of the docket entries, and shall file the same in the office of the prothonotary.

§ 857. *Final decree, notice, etc.*

When the master's report has been approved by the court a rule may be entered of course on the respondent, to show cause why a decree of divorce should not be granted. All such final rules for divorce shall be returnable to the first Saturday of each month and the third Monday of September, and shall be then heard on a divorce list. Notices of such rules shall be served on the respondent personally, if possible; but if the notice cannot be served on the respondent personally, then it shall be served on his or her counsel of record, if there be one, ten days before the time fixed for hearing the rule.

If the notice cannot be personally served on the respondent, and there is no counsel of record, the libellant shall publish a notice once a week for four full weeks in the *Legal Intelligencer* and one daily newspaper in the city of Philadelphia, and give such other notice by advertisement or otherwise as the court may direct in the particular case in the following form :

To A. B., late of No.   Street, Philadelphia, Pennsylvania.

You are hereby notified that a final rule for divorce has been granted against you at the suit of C. B., your   , which will be heard in the Court of Common Pleas, No.   , on Saturday, the   day of   , on which day you may appear and show cause, if any you have, why such divorce should not be granted against you.

C. D.,
Attorney for Libellant.

§ 858. *Affidavit of service.*

In all cases an affidavit of the time, place, and manner of service shall be filed, and in case of service on the counsel of the respondent, or by publication, the efforts which have been made to serve the respondent personally shall be stated in the affidavit.

§ 859. *Service of notices cannot be by libellant or counsel.*

Service of notices or rules upon the respondent shall not be made by the libellant or the next friend, or the counsel of record.

§ 860. Jurisdiction exclusively in Common Pleas. *Winpenny* v. *Winpenny*, 40 Leg. Int., 232 (1883). The jurisdiction in divorce is vested exclusively in the Courts of Common Pleas, under the Act of 1815.

§ 861. Divorce may be brought by both parties at the same time.

In *Zieger* v. *Zieger*, 14 W. N., 122 (1883), C. P. No. 1, of Phila., a rule was taken to quash the libel. Respondent's affidavit in support of the rule set forth that libellant left him some months before filing her libel, and had since resided in Trenton. The respondent had a suit for divorce pending when the wife filed her libel. BIDDLE, J.: "There is no reason why each party should not bring a separate suit in divorce against the other for different causes of action. The question of the libellant's residence being at issue can be determined on the trial of the cause." Rule discharged.

§ 862. Commencement of proceedings. Before preparing your libel, take the statement of your client. Write it out in detail, ascertain the place and date of marriage, the domicile, the cause of divorce, the names of witnesses, etc. If convenience permit, examine the witnesses with particularity. You will thus have before you the case. Compare it carefully with the foregoing *résumé* of

causes, with the decisions, and with the brief of the statutes ; being
sure of the jurisdiction, that your client is a resident, and that your
case is in all respects within the law, proceed to draft the libel.

§ 863. **Requisites of the libel.** You must, of course, address it
to the proper court. If the libellant be the wife, state her Christian and her married name, and the name of her next friend.
Thus, if she were Ann Jones before she married John Smith, do
not call her Ann Jones by her next friend, etc., but Ann Smith
by her next friend, Peter Johnson. State the date and place of
the marriage, the domicile since marriage, the citizenship of libellant, the libellant's address, and the present address of respondent,
if known. The cause of divorce should be averred with care. The
words of the statute should be followed, but a full description of
the offense should be given.

All that is required by the decisions should be stated. The
prayer should be not only for a subpoena, but also for a decree *a
vinculo* or *à mensa*, as required.

A libel in divorce must state the county in which libellant resides. *Johnson* v. *Johnson*, 3 Dist. Rep., 166 (1893).

§ 864. *Precision required in libel.* Where circumstances are
known, they should be set forth with reasonable precision. The
mere general averment will not suffice. As already shown, a libel
charging impotence should aver that it is incurable. In the able
opinion delivered in that case, *A. C.* v. *B. C.*, 10 W. N., 569
(1881), President Judge ELWELL said upon the general question :

" The second section of our Act of Assembly of March 13, 1815,
regulating proceedings in divorce, directs ' that the libellant shall
set forth particularly and specially the causes of his or her complaint.' It is not always safe pleading to set forth the complaint
in the words of the statute. Every material allegation should be
set out unequivocally ; and if a word or phrase has different
meanings, it should appear either directly or by the context in
what sense the pleader uses it. Adultery is a ground for divorce,
but it is necessary either to specify the paramour or state that he is
unknown. That the marriage was procured by ' fraud, force, and
coercion' is ground for divorce, but it is not sufficient to set forth
in the libel that the marriage was so procured. The circumstances
must be particularly set forth. *Hoffman* v. *Hoffman*, 30 Pa. St.,
417. Pleadings should be so accurate and unequivocal that when
they are required to be verified by oath, a conviction for perjury
might follow a false oath."

In *Schlicter* v. *Schlicter*, 10 Phila., 11 (1873), a libel averring "indignities to the person," but not alleging "cruel and barbarous treatment," was stricken off for want of jurisdiction.

A libel in divorce must set forth that an actual marriage had been contracted and celebrated. *Brinckle* v. *Brinckle*, 10 Phila., 1 (1873).

A libel stating adultery as the ground of divorce, and that it had been committed with E. P. and other lewd women unknown, should be supplemented by written notice before trial, without demand as to the times and places and attendant circumstances. If the names of paramours be unknown, it should be so alleged. *Garrat* v. *Garrat*, 4 Yeates, 244 (1805).

If a libel set forth generally the causes of the libellant's complaint, though unaccompanied by the particulars of time, place, etc., it is sufficient to satisfy the requirements of the Act of Assembly, and if respondent require anything more specific, he or she should demand of the libellant a specification of the particulars. *Breinig* v. *Breinig*, 26 Pa. St., 161 (1856); *Hancock's Appeal*, 64 Pa. St., 470 (1870); *Realf* v. *Realf*, 77 Pa. St., 31 (1874).

A libel must state when the desertion began. It is not sufficient to say that there has been a desertion for more than two years. *Raff* v. *Raff*, 25 W. N., 155 (1889).

§ 865. *General complaint sufficient—Respondent must demand specifications—Names, dates, places, can be demanded—"Divers persons unknown" sufficient—But libellant must be confined to his specifications.* The questions as to sufficiency of specifications and the evidence admissible thereunder were carefully considered in *Realf* v. *Realf*, 77 Pa. St., 33 (1874). The following opinion of the court was delivered by GORDON, J.:

"In *Hancock's Appeal*, 64 Pa. St., 470, as well as in the case of *Breinig* v. *Breinig*, 26 Pa. St., 161, it was held that if the libel sets forth generally the causes of the libellant's complaint, though unaccompanied by the particulars of time, place, etc., it is sufficient to satisfy the requirements of the Act of Assembly, and if the respondent requires anything more specific, he or she should demand of the libellant a specification of the particulars intended to be proved. That which is wanting in the petition may thus be supplied, and the respondent fully informed of what he or she may be called upon to meet. This rule is so obviously just and proper that courts should not hesitate to enforce it strictly. In the case in hand, the libellant was required to file a specification setting forth, *inter alia*, the names of the persons with whom the alleged adultery was committed, together with the dates and places.

"In answer to this, the libellant specified the commission of adultery by the respondent with one Daniel Neil, in the months of February, March, and April, 1872, and that on divers occasions in August and September, 1871, she visited a house of ill-fame in Virgin Alley, in the city of Pittsburgh, for the purpose of committing adultery with divers persons unknown to the petitioner.

"We hold these specifications to have been sufficient, and had the proof agreed with the allegations, the decree of divorce would have been well founded. Such, however, was not the case. The witness who testified to the improper intimacy between Neil and Mrs. Realf was proved, in the language of the witnesses, to have been 'soft-witted or crazy,' and besides this, Neil denied all improper intimacy with the respondent. So the house alleged to have been a bawdy-house, and which Mrs. Realf frequented, was not proved to be such, or at least not with sufficient clearness to make out the complainant's cause.

"The court, however, permitted the libellant to go out of his specifications, and prove intimacy with other men, and at other times than those set forth, and in this manner to carry his case with the jury. This was a violation of the wholesome rule above referred to, and for this cause the proceedings must be reversed.

§ 866. **Prayer for decree—Other requisites for a libel.**

A libel must pray for a decree of divorce. Grissom v. *Grissom,* 8 W. N., 484 (1880). In this case, the libel prayed that a subpœna might issue, etc., but it did not pray for a decree for a divorce. It was not signed by the next friend and was not sworn to before a judge or justice, but before a notary. A demurrer on all these grounds was sustained. A libel averring that the marriage was procured by fraud, force, and coercion, without stating any particulars, is defective. *Shriver* v. *Shriver,* 8 W. N., 144 (1879).

Examine the decisions noted in the preceding part of this chapter.

§ 867. *Libel must be signed.* Let libellant sign the libel and the affidavit. If libellant be the wife, the next friend must also sign.

§ 868. *Affidavit to libel.* Follow the words of the statute. See *Hoffman* v. *Hoffman,* 30 Pa. St., 417 (1858), *supra.*

In Philadelphia, the affidavit may be taken before a magistrate or notary public.

§ 869. *Indorsement on libel.* Follow here the rule of court already quoted.

§ 870. *Allocatur.* Indorse also on libel these words : "Subpœna in divorce *a v. m.* (or *à mensa et thoro*) allowed. Returnable *sec. leg.*" Hand to judge for his initials.

§ 871. *Defective libel may be attacked by demurrer or rule for particulars.* In *Shellenburger* v. *Shellenburger*, 6 Pa. C. C. Rep., 287 (1888), the libel did not as fully set forth, as required by the rule of court, the time and circumstances of the libellant's acquiring her residence in Philadelphia County. A motion to quash was made.

THAYER, P. J.: "This is no ground to quash; the omission should be reached by a demurrer or a rule for particulars; but as the defect is admitted, leave is granted to amend without further rule."

§ 872.

GENERAL FORM OF LIBEL.

In the Court of Common Pleas, No. , for the County of Philadelphia, of Term, 18 , No. .
Between ', libellant, and , respondent.
To the Honorable the Judges of the said Court:

The libellant complains and says:

1. That the libellant and respondent were lawfully joined in marriage on the day of , in the year of our Lord one thousand eight hundred and , at , in the State of , and from and after that time they lived together and cohabited in the relation of husband and wife.

2. That at the time said marriage was contracted the libellant was a citizen of the State of , and resided at , in said State; and the respondent was a citizen of the State of , and resided at , in said State; that immediately after their said marriage the said libellant and respondent resided together at , in the State of , and have since resided at . That the present residence of the libellant is at No. Street, in the , in the State of Pennsylvania, and that has been a citizen of the State of Pennsylvania, and hath resided therein for the period of one whole year previous to the filing of this libel; and that the present residence of the respondent is

3. And the libellant avers that, in violation of marriage vow and of the laws of this Commonwealth, the said , the respondent (here describe the cause particularly, giving dates, places, and circumstances).

4. Wherefore the libellant prays that a subpoena may issue, directed to the said the respondent, commanding to appear before your Honorable Court, on Monday, the day of next, A.D. 18 , to answer this libel and complaint; and also, that a decree may be made by your Honorable Court divorcing , the said libellant, from the bonds of matrimony between and the said respondent, as if they had never been married, or as if the said were naturally dead.

(Signature of Libellant),
(and of next friend where the wife is Libellant).

§ 873.

FORM OF AFFIDAVIT.

STATE OF PENNSYLVANIA, ⎰ ss.
COUNTY OF PHILADELPHIA, ⎱

The above named being duly according to law, says that the statements contained in the above libel are true, to the best

of   knowledge, information, and belief; and that the said complaint is not made out of levity, or by collusion between   and
the said respondent   for the mere purpose of being freed and
separated from each other, but in sincerity and truth, for the causes mentioned in the said libel.

              and subscribed ⎱   (Signature of Libellant.)
before me, the   ⎰
day of   18

§ 874.

FORM OF INDORSEMENT FOR LIBEL.

(Indorse the libel thus :)

No. 100.   March Term, 1889.

A. B. (By her next friend—if the case be so) ⎱
  v.   ⎰
C. B.

Libel in Divorce *a v. m.* (or *à mensa et thoro*, as the case may be).

⌐ Let subpœna in divorce *a v. m.* (or *à mensa et thoro*) issue, returnable *sec. leg.*

              (Here the judge places his initials.)

To   the within-named respondent :

You are hereby notified and required, within thirty days from Monday,
the   day of   next, A.D. 18   , to cause an appearance to be entered for you in the Court of Common Pleas, No.   , of
the County of Philadelphia, and an answer to be filed to the libel for divorce, of which the within is a copy.

NOTE.—You are hereby warned that if you fail to enter an appearance
and file an answer as above notified and required, the cause will proceed
without you, and you will be liable to have a decree of divorce entered
against you in your absence.

              Attorney for Libellant.

§ 875.

FORM OF LIBEL FOR DESERTION.

Between   ⎤   In the Court of Common Pleas, No.
       Libellant   ⎬   for the County of
and   ⎥   of   Term, 188
   Respondent.   ⎦   No.

To the Honorable the Judges of the said Court :

The libellant complains and says :

I. (*a*) That the libellant,   , and th e respondent,
were lawfully joined in marriage on the   day of
in the year of our Lord one thousand eight hundred and   ,
at (here state place of marriage particularly), and from and after that time
they lived together and cohabited as husband and wife until the desertion
of libellant by the respondent as hereinafter stated.

(*b*) That at the time of said marriage the libellant and respondent were
both citizens of the State of Pennsylvania and were both domiciled in Philadelphia in said State, and.they so continued their domicile until the desertion of libellant by respondent as hereinafter charged. After their said marriage the said libellant and respondent resided together at   , in the
city of Philadelphia, in said State of Pennsylvania, and thereafter at
              in said city, and that the libellant has been a citizen and

resident of the State of Pennsylvania for one (1) whole year and for many years previous to the filing of this libel.

(c) That the present place of actual residence of the libellant is at   , in the city of Philadelphia and State of Pennsylvania, and that the present residence of the respondent is unknown to the libellant, but   believes and avers that the said respondent is at present a resident of   . Respondent's last known residence was   , and the time at which   was last known to be there was during the months of

II. And the libellant avers that in violation of respondent's marriage vow and of the laws of this Commonwealth the said   , the respondent, in the year of our Lord one thousand eight hundred and eighty-   (here state place), wilfully and maliciously and without a reasonable cause deserted libellant and absented   from   habitation, and has continued in said desertion during the term and space of two (2) years and upward, to wit, from the date of said wilful and malicious desertion,   , thence hitherto. Wherefore the libellant prays that a subpœna may issue directed to the said   , the respondent, commanding   to appear before your Honorable Court on   to answer this libel and complaint; and also that a decree may be given by your Honorable Court for the divorcing and separating   from the said libellant's society, fellowship, and company in all time to come, and   , the said libellant, from the marriage bond aforesaid, as if they had never been married, or as if   , the said   , were naturally dead.

(Signature, and if by a woman the signature of her next friend.)

STATE OF PENNSYLVANIA, } ss.
COUNTY OF PHILADELPHIA, }

The above-named   being duly sworn according to law, deposes and says: That the facts contained in the above libel are true to the best of   knowledge and belief; and that the said complaint is not made out of levity, or by collusion between   and the said respondent,   , for the mere purpose of being freed and separated from each other, but in sincerity and truth for the causes mentioned in the said petition or libel.

Sworn to and subscribed before me, }
    this   day of   , A.D. 188 . }   (Signature of Libellant.)

(Indorse as in preceding form.)

A libel in divorce for desertion averring "an alleged or supposed marriage" will be dismissed. *Connor* v. *Connor*, 1 Dist. Rep., 358 (1891).

§ 876.

FORM OF LIBEL—ABANDONMENT—CRUELTY—PRAYING DIVORCE À MENSA AND ALIMONY.

(Follow the caption in preceding form.)

To the Honorable the Judges of said Court:

The libellant complains and says:

I. (a) That the libellant,   , and respondent,   , were lawfully joined in marriage on the   day of   , in the year of our Lord one thousand eight hundred and   , at (here set forth the place of marriage particularly), and from and after that time they lived and cohabited together until the desertion and abandonment wilfully, maliciously, and knowingly of libellant by respondent and of the family of said respondent as hereinafter set forth.

(*b*) Follow the preceding form as to residences.

(*c*) Follow the preceding form as to residences.

II. And the libellant avers that in violation of respondent's marriage vow and the laws of this Commonwealth, the respondent, on the   day of   , in the year of our Lord one thousand eight hundred and   , at the county aforesaid, did maliciously abandon said libellant and the family of said libellant; and, further, that on the day of   , in the year of our Lord one thousand eight hundred and   , at the county aforesaid, the said respondent did by cruel and barbarous treatment endanger libellant's life.

Wherefore your libellant prays your Honorable Court that a subpœna shall issue from said court directed to the said (name of respondent), commanding him to appear before your Honorable Court on (date or next term of court) to answer this libel, and also that a decree may be given by your Honorable Court granting this libellant a divorce from bed and board, and also allowing such alimony as the said respondent's circumstances will admit of, so the same does not exceed the third part of the annual profit or income of his estate or of his occupation and labor.

And the libellant as in duty bound will ever pray, etc.

(Signature of Libellant.)

Following the affidavit in the preceding form.

Let indorsement follow the first form, changing the words " Libel in Divorce *a v. m.*" to " Libel in Divorce *à mensa et thoro* and alimony."

§ 877.

FORM OF LIBEL FOR ADULTERY.

(Use the caption in the first form.)

To the Honorable the Judges of the said Court :

The libellant complains and says :

I. (*a*). That the libellant,   , and respondent,   , were lawfully joined in marriage on the   day of   , in the year of our Lord one thousand eight hundred and   , at (here set forth the place of marriage particularly), and from and after that time they lived and cohabited together.

Though by the laws of God, as well as by their mutual vows and faith plighted to each other, they were reciprocally bound to that constancy and uniform regard which ought to be inseparable from the marriage state, yet so it is, that the said respondent hath committed adultery as hereinafter set forth.

(*b*) Follow the form as to residences.

(*c*) Follow the form as to residences.

II. And the libellant avers that in violation of respondent's marriage vow and of the laws of this Commonwealth, the respondent, on the   day of   , in the year of our Lord one thousand eight hundred and   , at the county aforesaid, and on divers other days and times since, and at the county aforesaid, committed adultery with divers persons to your libellant unknown, and your libellant charges and avers that since the (above date) at the county aforesaid, the said respondent hath given herself up to adulterous practices and hath been living and still doth live a life of prostitution; the names of the different persons, however, with whom she has had illicit intercourse being unknown to your libellant and he being by reason of his ignorance of said names wholly unable to state the same.

(If names, dates, and places known, set them out.)

Following the first form as to the prayer of libel, affidavit, and indorsement.

§ 878.

FORM OF LIBEL FOR BIGAMY.

(Follow the caption in the form.)

To the Honorable the Judges of the said Court:

The libellant complains and says:

I. (*a*) That the libellant,   , and the respondent,   , were joined in marriage on the   day of   , in the year of our Lord one thousand eight hundred and   , at (here state place of marriage with particularity), and from and after that time they lived together and cohabited as husband and wife, until the discovery by your libellant that the respondent had been lawfully joined in marriage with   , who is still living, as hereinafter stated.

(*b*) Follow paragraph *b* in the preceding form as to residences, etc.

(*c*) Follow paragraph *c* in the preceding form as to residences, etc.

II. And the libellant avers that in violation of the laws of this Commonwealth the said respondent was lawfully joined in marriage with   , on the   day of   , in the year of our Lord one thousand eight hundred and   (the place where the marriage was celebrated), and from that time until shortly before the said marriage with libellant lived and cohabited with the said   , who is yet alive, and has never been divorced from the bonds of matrimony entered into with the said   , but now is the true husband of the said   . That the said respondent, in violation of her said marriage vow made to the said   , her true and lawful husband, knowingly entered into a second marriage with your libellant on the said   day of   , in the year of our Lord one thousand eight hundred and   , as more particularly above set forth.

Follow the prayer, affidavit, and indorsement in first form.

§ 879.

FORM OF LIBEL FOR CRUELTY.

In the Court of Common Pleas, No.   , for the County of Philadelphia, of   Term, 1889, No.   .

Between   , by her next friend, libellant, and   , respondent.

To the Honorable the Judges of the said Court:

The libellant complains and says:

I. That the libellant and respondent were lawfully joined in marriage on the   day of   , in the year of our Lord one thousand eight hundred and   , at   Street, Philadelphia, in the State of Pennsylvania, and from and after that time they lived together and cohabited in the relation of husband and wife.

II. That at the time said marriage was contracted the libellant was a citizen of the State of Pennsylvania aforesaid, and resided at   .

Locust Street, Philadelphia, in said State; and the respondent was a citizen of the State of Pennsylvania, and resided at   .   Street, Phila-

delphia, in said State; that immediately after said marriage the said libellant and respondent resided together at   Street, Philadelphia, in the State of Pennsylvania, and have since resided at No.
Street, Philadelphia, from , till , and at   ,
   , Pennsylvania from , till .

That the present residence of the libellant is at No.   Street, in the city of Philadelphia, in the State of Pennsylvania, and that she has been a citizen of the State of Pennsylvania and hath resided therein for the period of one whole year previous to the filing of this libel; and that the present residence of the respondent is   , Pennsylvania.

III. And the libellant avers that, in violation of his marriage vow and of the laws of this Commonwealth, the said   , the respondent, hath offered such indignities to the person of libellant as to render her condition intolerable and life a burden, thereby compelling her to withdraw from his home and family.

Such conduct began about one year after their said marriage as aforesaid, and continued until   . During this time respondent continually subjected libellant to gross indignities, treating her in the presence of other persons with a great deal of disrespect, using insulting, vile, indecent, and threatening language, reviling her with oaths and profanity, calling her indecent and opprobrious names, making lewd proposals to her serving-woman in her presence and hearing, and using personal violence to her. His drunkenness has been continued and habitual. He has ordered her from his house frequently, and on the   day of , 18 , he ordered her from the house again and struck her in the face with his fist.

By reason of which treatment she has been kept in bodily fear and trepidation, her condition rendered intolerable, her life made burdensome, and she has been compelled to withdraw from respondent's house and family.

IV. Wherefore the libellant prays that a subpœna may issue, directed to the said   , the respondent, commanding him to appear before your Honorable Court, on Monday, the day of next, A. D.
  , to answer this libel and complaint; and also that a decree may be made by your Honorable Court divorcing her, the said libellant, from the bonds of matrimony between her and the said respondent.

(Signatures of Libellant and of next friend.)

STATE OF PENNSYLVANIA, }
COUNTY OF PHILADELPHIA, } *ss.*

The above-named   , being duly sworn according to law, says that the statements contained in the above libel are true to the best of her knowledge, information, and belief; and that the said complaint is not made out of levity, or by collusion between her and the said respondent   for the mere purpose of being freed and separated from each other, but in sincerity and truth, for the causes mentioned in the said libel.

(Signature of Libellant.)

Sworn to and subscribed before me, }
 the   day }
 of }

(Indorse as in first form.)

§ 880. The subpœna is issued by the prothonotary.

FORM OF SUBPŒNA IN DIVORCE.

County of Philadelphia, *ss.*

The Commonwealth of Pennsylvania, to   greeting :

Whereas,   did on the   day of   , A.D. 18 ,
prefer   petition or libel to our judges of our Court of Common Pleas,
No. , for the County of Philadelphia, praying, for the causes therein set
forth, that   might be divorced from the bonds of matrimony entered into with you ; we do therefore command you, the said   ,
that setting aside all business and excuses whatsoever, you be and appear
in your proper person, before our judges, at Philadelphia, at our said Court
of Common Pleas, No. , there to be held for the County of Philadelphia,
on the   Monday of   next to answer the said petition
or libel, and show cause, if any you have, why the said   your
            should not be divorced from the bonds of matrimony, agree-
ably to the Act of the General Assembly in such case made and provided.
And hereof fail not, under the penalty of having the said petition heard
and a decree of divorce granted against you in your absence.

Witness the Honorable   , president of our said court, at Philadelphia, this   day of   , in the year of our Lord one thousand
eight hundred and eighty-nine.

                                                            Prothonotary.

§ 881. *Service of subpœna.* Where the rule of court requires (as
in Philadelphia) a service by the sheriff, it must be obeyed. Hand
to the deputy sheriff the subpœna and two copies of the libel, the
affidavit, the indorsement on the libel, etc. Give the deputy particular instructions as to the residence, etc., of the defendant. Direct
him to read the original subpœna, and to hand the defendant a copy
of the subpœna, and a copy of the libel, affidavit, and indorsements.
Let him make return under oath, indorsed upon the original subpœna, as follows :

§ 882. *Affidavit of service.*

A. B., having been duly sworn according to law, doth depose and say
that he is a deputy sheriff of the county of Philadelphia, that on the
            day of   , A.D. 1890, he personally served upon   ,
the person known by the deponent to be the respondent within named, this
original subpœna in divorce by reading the same to her and by leaving
with her a true and attested copy thereof. Deponent further handed to
her at the same time a true copy of the libel, the affidavit, and the indorsement thereon, as per the paper hereto attached.

                                        (Signature of Deputy Sheriff.)

                So answers

                                        (Signature of Sheriff.)

Sworn to and subscribed before me,

·   § 883. **If respondent be not in the county, but be in the State.**
Service may be made by the sheriff of the county where the respondent may be found within the State. (See the rule of court,
section 838.)

Fillman's Appeal, 99 Pa. St., 286 (1882). A subpœna in divorce may be served by the sheriff of another county than that in which the proceedings were instituted. No special order for such service need be made by the court of original jurisdiction.

§ 884. *Extra-territorial service illegal.* The Act of March 13, 1815, cannot be construed to give a court of Pennsylvania extra-territorial power to bring within its jurisdiction the person of a citizen and resident of another State. *Ralston's Appeal,* 93 Pa. St., 133 (1880).

The words " wherever found " do not authorize a service outside the State. *Id.*

See also on this point *Love* v. *Love,* 10 Phila., 453 (1873) ; *Comm.* v. *Maize,* 23 W. N., 572 (1889) ; *Briggs* v. *Briggs,* 1 Dist. Rep., 780 (1892), and the cases cited in section 802.

§ 885. *Where court rules do not require service by sheriff, anyone can serve the writ.* The Act of March 13, 1815 (P. L., 12), prescribes the mode of serving a subpœna in divorce. It requires that it shall be served personally on the said party, wherever found, or that a copy shall be given to him or her, fifteen days before the return of the same.

There is nothing in the Act, either by its express terms or by a necessary implication, which requires a service by the sheriff.

The subpœna is not directed to him, but to the respondent, and it may be served by anyone. *Fillman's Appeal,* 11 W. N., 195 (1882). In Philadelphia, the rule of court requires that service shall be made by the sheriff upon respondent, within the county at time of service.

§ 886. *If defendant not found,* you get the sheriff to return " *Non est inventus* " (he (or she) is not found).

So answers

(Signature of Sheriff.)

You then file with prothonotary
§ 887.

PRÆCIPE FOR ALIAS SUBPŒNA.

A. ⎱
  v.　⎬　　Court.　　Term,　　. No.
B. ⎰

SIR :

Issue *alias* subpœna in divorce, returnable *sec. leg.*　　　C. D.,
Libellant's Attorney.
(Date.)

To the Prothonotary of the Court of Common Pleas
of　　　　　County.

§ 888. *If alias subpœna returned non est inventus,* you give prothonotary

PRÆCIPE FOR ORDER OF PUBLICATION.

A. ⎫
v. ⎬   Court.   Term,   . No.   .
B. ⎭

SIR :

Issue order of publication in the above case.   C. D.,
Libellant's Attorney.
(Date.)

To the Prothonotary of the Court of Common Pleas
of the county of   .

The Act of 1815 directs that the sheriff shall publish this " in one or more newspapers printed within or nearest to the said county, for four weeks successively prior to the first day of the next term," etc.

§ 889.

FORM OF ORDER OF PUBLICATION.

County of Philadelphia, *ss.*   [SEAL]

The Commonwealth of Pennsylvania to the Sheriff of the County of Philadelphia, greeting :

We command you that by publication, once a week for four full weeks successively, in the *Legal Intelligencer* and two daily newspapers of large circulation published in your bailiwick, you notify   , late of your county, to be and appear in our Court of Common Pleas, No.   , for the county of Philadelphia, on the first Monday of   next, then and there to show cause, if any   has, why   should not be divorced from the bonds of matrimony entered into with   , according to the prayer of petition or libel filed in said court. And have you then there this order, and make your return how you have executed the same. Witness the Honorable   , president of our said court, at Philadelphia, the   day of   , in the year of our Lord one thousand eight hundred and ninety-one.

                                Prothonotary.

In Philadelphia, the publication, in addition to being made in two daily newspapers of large circulation, must be inserted once a week for four full weeks successively in the *Legal Intelligencer.*

The form of the notice is given in the rules of court (section 840).

§ 890. *Return to order of publication.* The sheriff inserts the advertisements and makes his return to the order :

Published as within commanded the notice whereof the following is a true copy (here insert copy of advertisement) in two daily newspapers of large circulation in the city of Philadelphia, to wit,   and   , also in the *Legal Intelligencer,* published in said city, once a week for four full weeks successively. *Non est inventus* as to defendant.

            So answers

                                   Sheriff.

on oath says that he is a deputy sheriff of the county of Philadelphia, and that the above return is true.

Sworn to and subscribed before }
  me,   }

I find nothing requiring that this order be returned on oath ;
but the whole proceeding seems to be so under the ban of suspicion
that I recommend the greatest particularity.

§ 891. *No acceptance of service.* To this end, let not the subpœna
or the alias, or any rule to answer or other notice or paper, be accepted. Your client's case may be ever so just, the defendant may
be ever so base, the court will be quick to grasp at the slightest
circumstance as evidence of collusion.

§ 892. *If defendant be in prison.* If defendant be under sentence, he cannot be served without leave of the court imposing the
sentence. In *Finley* v. *Finley,* the opinion of the Court of Common Pleas, Philadelphia County, was delivered by PEIRCE, J. It
is reported in the *Legal Gazette* of June 7, 1872. " The evidence
in this case makes out clearly a cause for divorce on behalf of the
libellant. But the trouble is that the respondent has been in prison
from and before the commencement of the proceeding, and is still
in prison. The libellant says, in her testimony, ' under the arrest
in January last, the respondent has been convicted in the Quarter
Sessions of this county of an assault and battery upon me, and was
sentenced to prison for eight months.' A person who is in prison
under execution or conviction can scarcely be said to be in such a
condition, though served with process whilst in custody, that it can
be said of him he has had his day in court.

" By the English law, as stated in 1 Tidd's Practice, 306, neither
the plaintiff nor a third person can charge a prisoner with a civil
action, when he is in custody of the marshal, or in any other custody on a criminal account, without leave of the court or judge.

" In *Crackall* v. *Thompson,* 1 Salkeld's Reports, 354, the defendant, pending an action against him in B. R., was taken upon a
warrant in a criminal matter and committed to the compter, and
afterward was there charged with an extent for the Queen. And
he was brought up at the suit of the plaintiff in the action in order
to be declared against in custody of the marshal. It was held that
one so arrested cannot be charged at the suit of a subject in any
action without leave of the court, yet the Queen may charge him ;
and the defendant was remanded.

" That it may be done with leave of the court, seems to be that
process being served under the sanction of the court, the court will
see that no injustice is suffered by the prisoner by reason of his
being in prison.

"In this case, no leave of the court was asked to charge the respondent with this proceeding, and for this reason it might be avoided by him. But of this we give no opinion. We cannot, however, suffer the matter to be further proceeded with until the respondent is out of prison, and personal notice is given to him of any further proceeding in the case; or until he is proceeded against with leave of the court. The proper practice in such a case is to apply to the court for leave to proceed against the party in custody, and then the court will make such orders in the case as will protect the rights of the prisoner; and if necessary will bring him into court on a writ of *habeas corpus* for that purpose. Further proceeding in this case is suspended until the respondent is out of prison and personal notice served on him; or until he is further proceeded against with leave of the court."

§ 893. **Appearance.** In Philadelphia, thirty days are allowed after the return-day (if the writ be served) for entering an appearance. If the writ be returned *non est inventus*, the same time (thirty days) is allowed after the advertisement. The appearance must be by written order accompanied by a letter of attorney duly acknowledged. The following forms may be used:

A. B. ⎱
  v.   ⎰ In the Court of Common Pleas of
C. B.   County, of   Term, 189 . No. .

To the Prothonotary of said Court:

SIR: Enter my appearance for the defendant in the above case.

                             E. F.,
                           Defendant's Attorney.
                               (Date.)

A. B. ⎱
  v.   ⎰ In the Court of Common Pleas of
C. B.   County, of   Term, 189 . No. .

Know all men that I, C. B., the defendant in the above case, have constituted and appointed, and hereby do constitute and appoint E. F. as my attorney, to appear for me in the above case, and to do all things which an attorney may lawfully do in the premises.

Witness my hand and seal, at   this   day of
A.D. 1890.   [SEAL]

Before me (the prothonotary, judge, justice of the peace, or magistrate of the county, district, or State in which the respondent may reside, or, if the respondent be without the United States, then before an ambassador, minister plenipotentiary, charge d'affaires, consul or vice-consul of the United States, commissioner in chancery of the foreign country, notary public of the foreign country), personally appeared the above-named defendant, C. B., and in due form of law acknowledged the foregoing power of attorney to be (his or her) act and deed.

Witness my hand and seal of office, at   this   day of
A. D. 1891.

§ 894. *Appearance on a power of attorney good, though writ not
served.* If appearance be entered on a power of attorney, it is good
although the writ was not served. This does not furnish presumption of collusion as when service is accepted. *Renz* v. *Renz*, 22
W. N., 226 (1888).

§ 895. *If no appearance* be entered within the time required,
the libellant can proceed *ex parte*. The manner of doing this is
prescribed in Philadelphia by the rule of court. A motion is
made in the following form :

A. B.   } In the Court of Common Pleas of the County of
     v. }   of   Term, 1891. No. .
C. B.   }

And now   , 1891, the libellant's attorney moves the court to
appoint a master in the above case, the defendant not having appeared, as
required by law.

This motion might be made by the libellant or the defendant if
the case had proceeded to the filing of an answer, and neither party
had demanded an issue. In that case it would read :

And now   , 1891, an answer having been filed, and neither
party having demanded a jury trial, the   moves the court to appoint
a master.

The motion must be handed to the court clerk, and he places it
on the current-motion list, which is called the next Saturday. If
there be an appearance, notice should be given to the opposite counsel of the motion, and that it will be called on the day named.

If the party moving is entitled to the appointment, it follows as
a matter of course, and the court names some person as master,
thus :

And now   , 1891,   Esq., is appointed master in the
above case.

§ 896. *If appearance, but no answer.* In this connection it may
be proper to add that the same forms are observed where an appearance has been regularly entered, but the defendant is in default
for not filing an answer.

§ 897. *No decree* pro confesso *can be entered.* It is clear, from
the statute already quoted, that the only remedy against a party in
default is to proceed *ex parte*. You cannot take judgment for want
of an appearance or answer.

Kilborn v. *Field*, 78 Pa. St., 194 (1875), SHARSWOOD, J.
There can be no decree *pro confesso* upon a libel for divorce. If
either party will not attend, the court shall inquire and decide *ex
parte* by the examination of witnesses or interrogatories, exhibits,
or other legal proof had either before or at the hearing.

§ 898. *If appearance be entered*, the Philadelphia rules require a demurrer or answer to be filed within thirty days after the return-day. They are silent as to any rule to answer. The indorsement required on the libel is a rule to answer. In counties where no such indorsement is directed, a rule to answer might be necessary. Where required, the following may be used :

§ 899.

RULE TO ANSWER.

A. B. }
  v.   } In the Court of Common Pleas, of   County,
C. B. }   Term, 1891. No. .

To the Prothonotary of said Court :

SIR : Enter rule on respondent to demur, or answer *sec. reg.*

(Signature of Libellant's Attorney.)
(Date.)

Indorse :

A. B. }
  v.   } C. P. No. ,   Term, 1891.
C. B. }

Rule to answer.

(Name of counsel.)
(Date.)

§ 900.

NOTICE OF RULE TO ANSWER.

A. B. }
  v.   } Common Pleas of   County,   Term, 1891. No. .
C. B. }

To   , Esq.,
       Attorney for Respondent.

DEAR SIR : Please notice a rule in the above case on respondent to demur, or answer *sec. reg.*

Very respectfully yours,
(Signature of Libellant's Attorney.)
(Date.)

Keep a copy. If no answer filed, write to your opponent, reminding him that the rule has expired. If defendant continue in default, proceed as above indicated, first filing affidavit of service of notice, etc.

§ 901. **If a demurrer be filed**, it will, of course, be grounded upon some real or supposed defect in the libel. If the precautions given in this chapter as to the framing of the libel, etc., have been observed, the demurrer will simply delay the case.

Either party can order the demurrer on the next appropriate list. The party pressing the case should always have paper-books ready. Usually both parties prepare a paper-book. It should contain a copy of the libel and of the demurrer. Then follow the points stated and the authorities. Counsel ordering the demurrer on the list should notify his adversary. If the demurrer appear to be well taken—

§ 902. Libellant can amend if no new cause of action set up. If the libel by a husband on the ground of cruelty omit the words " cruel and barbarous treatment," it may be amended, because no new cause of action is introduced. *Hancock* v. *Hancock*, 13 W. N., 29 (1882).

Amendment may be allowed if it does not set up a cause of a different nature. In this case amendment was allowed of other acts tending to prove adultery. *Perkins* v. *Perkins*, 16 W. N., 48 (1885).

§ 903. *In Philadelphia, not allowed if new cause assigned.* But an amendment cannot be allowed which sets up an entirely new cause of action. *Matthews* v. *Matthews*, 6 W. N., 147 (1878).

Allowed elsewhere. The cases in which an amendment setting up a new cause of action was refused have been, with few exceptions, those originating in Philadelphia County, where the rule of court expressly forbids such amendment. There is no reason why, under certain restrictions, a proper amendment should not be allowed, particularly where the respondent has not filed an answer. The Supreme Court, in *Powers' Appeal*, 120 Pa. St., 320 (1888), intimated that an amendment of this nature might be made in the lower court, although refusing it in the Supreme Court for other reasons.

The subject is elaborately and ably discussed in the opinion of EWING, P. J., Court of Common Pleas, No. 2, of Allegheny County, in the case of *Clayburgh* v. *Clayburgh*, 15 W. N., 365 (1884). " The original libel filed in this case alleges ' cruel and barbarous treatment, rendering the condition of libellant intolerable and life burdensome.' The respondent was served personally and filed an answer. He demands a jury trial. The libellant now asks leave to amend her libel by adding, as an additional ground for divorce, a charge of adultery. Respondent by his counsel objects to the allowance of the amendment, arguing that the court has no power to permit an amendment adding a new cause of action, and cites *Matthews* v. *Matthews* 6 W. N., 147. Libellant's counsel cites, *contra*, *Toone* v. *Toone*, 10 Phila., 174. Has the court power to allow the amendment ?

" In *Matthews* v. *Matthews, supra*, President Judge THAYER, of Common Pleas, No. 4, of Philadelphia, decides the question in the negative, saying the case ' is too plain for argument,' and then he goes on to show that such a case is not covered by our statutes of amendment. If a proceeding in divorce is an action at common law, the reasoning would be satisfactory and the conclusion correct.

In *Grove's Appeal*, 37 Pa. St., 446, in sustaining an amendment to a libel, the learned Judge, in delivering the opinion, says : ' It presents no new cause of action,' inferentially intimating that in such a case the decision might be different. But no such question was before the court. It is but a remark *currente calamo*, without considering whether the case was at common law or in equity.

" In *Toone* v. *Toone, supra*, Judge Paxson, then of the Common Pleas, decides the question in favor of allowing such amendment, saying that ' the power of the court to permit amendments in a divorce case does not depend on the statutes of amendment ; that they refer to common law actions, not to a proceeding in equity ; and that divorce is in the nature of a proceeding in equity.'

" In this position we find on examination that he is fully sustained by the history of the action and by the authorities. Chancellor Kent, in speaking of divorce proceedings, calls it ' this newly created branch of equity jurisprudence.' The jurisdiction is conferred by statute ; but in this and other States where not otherwise regulated by statute, the proceeding is regulated by equity practice, and by the rules and practice prevailing in the ecclesiastical courts. It adopts largely in its practice as its common law the law of the English ecclesiastical courts. * * * So far as we have been able to examine the cases, the ecclesiastical courts, by their inherent power as courts of equity, exercised the power of permitting amendments in such cases. The courts of probate and divorce, their successors, exercise the same power. In *Cartledge* v. *Cartledge*, reported in the *Jurist*, of June 7, 1862, page 493, a wife filed her petition for divorce on account of cruelty. She subsequently applied to amend by adding a charge of adultery, and by altering the prayer from that of a ' judicial separation ' to that of a ' dissolution of marriage.' She was allowed to amend. * * * In *Parkinson* v. *Parkinson*, 2 Law Rep., P. & D., 27, the wife had petitioned for a dissolution of marriage on the ground of the husband's adultery, coupled with a charge of desertion. On hearing, the court held adultery not to be proven. Subsequently, it appearing to the satisfaction of the court that she had not understood that the acts committed amounted to a legal cruelty, she was permitted to amend by adding a charge of cruelty. In both these cases the libellant was required to serve the respondent with the amended bill. In *Errissman* v. *Errissman*, 25 Ill., 136, a supplemental bill charging adultery was allowed.

" There is no good reason why an amendment charging an additional cause of action should not be allowable in the discretion of the court. It does not seek a new result or decree. It may save time and expense. If it cannot be allowed, there is no good reason why a second libel should not be filed, and the two cases proceed at the same time. If this were an ordinary equity suit, there would be no question as to the power of the court to allow the amendment."

Amendment allowed, a copy of the amended bill to be served on respondent, who was to have thirty days thereafter to answer. See *A.* v. *B.*, 2 Dist. Rep., 394 (1892).

In *Heilbron* v. *Heilbron*, 33 W. N., 240; 158 Pa. St., 297 (1893), where the libel was formally defective in averring too much, yet showed a good cause of action, an amendment striking out the surplusage was allowed.

§ 904. *Amendment allowed after examiner appointed.* A libel may be amended even after it is referred to an examiner, if he has not entered upon the performance of his duties, and no hardship will be imposed upon respondent. *Toone* v. *Toone*, 10 Phila., 174 (1874).

§ 905. *Amendment allowed after testimony commenced before commissioner.* Where a rule of court required that the answer contain a demand for an issue in a divorce suit, an amendment will be allowed even after testimony has been taken before a commissioner. *Magill's Appeal*, 59 Pa. St., 430 (1868).

§ 906. *When amendment cannot be allowed.* After filing of examiner's report. *Pierie* v. *Pierie*, 7 Phila., 405 (1870).

§ 907. *An amendment refused in Supreme Court.* An amendment changing the cause of action, requiring a different line of proof for its support, might be allowed below, but will be refused in the Supreme Court. *Powers' Appeal*, 120 Pa. St., 320 (1888).

§ 908. *Amendment allowed adding affidavit before justice.* In *Cumpston* v. *Cumpston*, 4 W. N., 184 (1877), after answer filed, the libel was amended by adding an affidavit before a justice of the peace, *nunc pro tunc.*

§ 909. *Amendment of writ allowed.* In *Long* v. *Long*, 1 Pa. C. C. Rep., 572 (1886), the libel prayed for a divorce *à mensa et thoro.* By mistake of the prothonotary, the subpœna read as if the prayer had been for a divorce *a v. m.*

On motion, after service of the subpœna and an appearance for respondent, the subpœna was amended. (C. P. No. 2, of Philadelphia.)

§ 910. **Demand for bill of particulars.** The Act of May 25, 1878, allowing this has been already cited, section 817. If the libel do not give full information, the defendant may demand a bill of particulars. This is done in Philadelphia by entering a rule for a bill, and the rule of court declares that "it shall be of course at any time before filing answer; but after answer no such rule shall be entered unless specially allowed by the court."

The Act of May 25, 1878, already cited, allows the entry of the rule at any time after the return-day.

§ 911.

FORM OF RULE FOR PARTICULARS.

A. B.
v.
C. B.
In the Court of Common Pleas of   County.
Term, 1891. No. .

And now   , 1891, the respondent enters a rule on libellant to furnish a bill of particulars within thirty days after service of notice, or *non pros. sec. leg.*

E. F.,
Respondent's Attorney.
(Date.)

Serve notice of this, keep copy, and if the bill be not furnished or time be not extended a decree of *non pros.* can be entered.

§ 912. *Bill of particulars should be full.* In *Butler* v. *Butler*, 1 Pars. Select Equity Cases, 329 (1849), Judge KING stated that the respondent, who had filed an answer to the libel, defending her desertion because of the libellant's cruelty, should have been required to furnish to libellant a specification of "the times, places, and circumstances" of the alleged cruelties. The Divorce Statute exacts that the libel set forth the causes of complaint, "particularly and specially."

§ 913. *Names of witnesses required.* In *Brinckle* v. *Brinckle*, 10 Phila., 144 (1874), already cited, the libellant was ordered "to furnish the names, residences, and occupations of her witnesses."

She alleged a marriage which the defendant denied. He could not possibly meet her case without knowing the names of the proposed witnesses. Under the old rules, if a proceeding were in default of an answer, the libellant was compelled to serve a notice on the respondent of the time and place of taking the testimony, and of the names, etc., of the witnesses.

§ 914. *Names of witnesses not required.* In *Mullison* v. *Mullison*, 13 W. N., 314 (1883) (C. P. No. 3, of Philadelphia), a rule on respondent to show cause why she should not furnish a list of her witnesses to libellant was discharged.

§ 915. *Bill of particulars ordered in action for crim. con.* In *Tilton* v. *Beecher*, 59 N. Y., 177 (1874) (opinion by RAPALLO, J.), an action was brought for criminal conversation. The complaint set forth that the alleged offenses were committed "on the 10th of October, 1868, and on divers other days and times after that day and before the commencement of this action "—thus covering a period of very nearly six years. A motion was made for a bill of particulars, which was denied in the City Court of Brooklyn, but this was reversed on appeal, and the bill of particulars granted.

§ 916. *Time for asking particulars.* It was said in *Bartol* v. *Bartol*, 18 W. N., 8 (1886), that the proper time to ask for particulars is after issue is framed. But it is very clear that no man can be required to answer without a specification and upon a loose general charge.

§ 917. *Particularity required.* The specification should state time and place. *Lord* v. *Lord*, 16 W. N., 496 (1885).

§ 918. *On application of libellant, a bill of particulars may be ordered as to cruelty charged in defendant's answer.* In *Butler* v. *Butler*, 1 Pars. Select Eq. Cas., 329 (1849), the answer of respondent set forth that by reason of the cruel and barbarous treatment of the libellant she was forced to absent herself from cohabitation, and thus sought to justify her desertion. The court held that the libellant might demand from respondent a written specification of the charges by which the general allegations were to be supported, with the times, places, and circumstances of their occurrence, as far as these could be reasonably and practically given. Judge KING said : " When it is clearly shown that the withdrawal of a wife or husband from mutual cohabitation has been the result of an agreement, or has received the subsequent approbation of the other, the continuity of absence under such circumstances is not a wilful and malicious desertion."

§ 919. *Form for bill of particulars.*

A. B. by her next friend E. F. } C. P. No. 1.　June Term,
　　　　　v.　　　　　　　　　　　　
　　　　C. B.　　　　　　　　　} No.　　　　In Divorce.

BILL OF PARTICULARS.

Libellant applies for a divorce on the ground that the respondent has offered such indignities to her person as to render her condition intolerable and life a burden, thereby compelling her to withdraw from his home and family.

Such conduct began about the end of the year　　　, and continued until
　　　　　. During this time respondent continually subjected libellant to gross indignities, treating her in the presence of other persons with great disrespect, using insulting, vile, indecent, and threatening language, reviling her with oaths and profanity, calling her indecent and opprobrious names, making lewd proposals to her serving-woman in her presence and hearing, and using personal violence to her. His drunkenness has been continued and habitual. He has ordered her from his house frequently,

and on the   day of   , he ordered her from his house
again, and struck her in the face with his fist and attempted to shoot
, a servant, who came to her assistance.

(Signature of Counsel.)
Attorney for Libellant.

This was sent by very able counsel. It seems, however, to be
very general. It would be safer to be more precise.

§ 920. **Costs, counsel fees, alimony.** Before treating of the answer in divorce, it may be proper to notice certain preliminary
questions as to security for costs, order for alimony, counsel fees,
etc.

§ 921. *Security for costs* may be ordered on affidavit of respondent that he has a defense to the libel, that libellant and her
next friend are both non-residents, and have no property in the
State. *McElhinney* v. *McElhinney*, 13 W. N., 194 (1883).

§ 922. *Respondent need not give security in Philadelphia for
certain costs.* A respondent will not, in the first instance, be required to give security for costs of master and prothonotary. *Calhoun* v. *Calhoun*, 18 W. N., 428 (1886).

§ 923. *Alimony and expenses allowed to wife in discretion of court.*
A wife, in a divorce proceeding, is entitled to necessary expenses
where she has no separate support. *Melizet* v. *Melizet*, 1 Pars. Eq.
Cas., 77 (1843); *Graves* v. *Cole*, 19 Pa. St., 171 (1852). Even
though evidence be offered of a previously subsisting marriage.
Kline v. *Kline*, 1 Phila., 383 (1852).

This is a matter, however, within the discretion of the court, both
as to amount and duration, and is not subject to review. *Waldron*
v. *Waldron*, 55 Pa. St., 231 (1866).

§ 924. *General principle on which alimony is allowed.* On the
question of alimony, the law makes a plain difference between a
husband and a wife plaintiff. The court shall, on granting a
divorce, allow such support or alimony to the wife as her husband's circumstances will admit. The duty of maintenance, once
assumed by him, is not to be released and thrown upon the public
without a good reason. *Miles* v. *Miles*, 76 Pa. St., 357 (1874).

Alimony will be granted whether the wife be petitioner or respondent. *Smith* v. *Smith*, 1 Dist. Rep., 550 (1892).

If libellant is a minor and the libel is filed by the father as next
friend, the libellant is liable for counsel fee and alimony. Failure
to pay will be enforced by attachment. *West* v. *West*, 1 Dist.
Rep., 699 (1890).

In a proper case, where a decree of divorce has been set aside
because of want of notice to the respondent, the court will grant

alimony, counsel fee, and expenses to the wife, the respondent. *Quelin* v. *Quelin*, 1 Dist. Rep., 677 (1889).

After a libel is dismissed, order for alimony is no longer of force. *Heilbron* v. *Heilbron*, 158 Pa. St., 297 (1893).

An order of the Quarter Sessions requiring a husband to pay for support does not prevent the Common Pleas from decreeing alimony. *Id.*

§ 925. *Alimony cannot be ordered until after return-day.* No order can be made until return of the writ and appearance. *Jones* v. *Jones*, 16 W. N., 259 (1885).

§ 926. *Alimony and counsel fees will be refused to a respondent leading an immoral life.* In *Thompson* v. *Thompson*, 10 Phila., 135 (1874), ALLISON, P. J., said :

" A rule for alimony and counsel fees was heard more than a year ago. It was resisted upon the ground that respondent was living with a man other than her husband ; that they kept house together, and that she thus had means of support which rendered an order such as she prayed the court to make unnecessary. The depositions taken in resistance of the application established the allegations of the libellant, and the order was refused. There has been nothing shown since that hearing to change the case as it then stood before the court. The defense of the respondent rests upon technical grounds alone ; her standing before the court is wholly void of merit, and her conduct in every respect is such as to take from her all claim to a favorable consideration."

§ 927. *Alimony not allowed where wife has income.* Where the income of the wife is sufficient for her support, the necessity upon which arose the practice of giving the wife alimony does not exist. *Toole* v. *Toole*, 1 W. N., 96 (1874).

§ 928. *Alimony allowed though charge of adultery not denied.* In *Brooks* v. *Brooks*, 18 W. N., 115 (1886), the Court of Common Pleas, No. 3, of Philadelphia, granted alimony and counsel fees to the wife, although it was sworn by her husband and uncontradicted by the wife, that she was living in adultery.

Alimony refused where the respondent is guilty of adultery. Alimony will not be granted where respondent is shown to be guilty of adultery. *Kratz* v. *Kratz*, 1 Dist. Rep., 699 (1892).

§ 929. *Counsel fees allowed though charge was conviction of a felony, etc.* *Miller* v. *Miller*, 5 Pa. C. C. Rep., 592 (1887).

In *Sutton* v. *Sutton*, 26 W. N., 398 (1890), the answer denied the charge of adultery averred in the libel ; the court refused to go into the merits on a rule for alimony, and made the rule absolute.

§ 930. *Alimony and counsel fees refused to a wife supported by husband.* Counsel fees and alimony will be refused to a wife living in her husband's house. *Gleason* v. *Gleason,* 12 W. N., 408 (1882).

Refused where she declines to live in a suitable home provided by him. Where the depositions on a rule for alimony show that the respondent has refused to live in a suitable and proper home provided for her by her husband, alimony will be refused. *O'Hara* v. *O'Hara,* 2 Dist. Rep., 452 (1893).

§ 931. *Order for counsel fees suspends rule for bill of particulars.* If an order be made for the payment of counsel fees, the respondent cannot, whilst the order is not complied with, *non pros.* the libellant for not sending bill of particulars. *Jones* v. *Jones,* 23 W. N., 370 (1888).

§ 932. *Master's fee not allowed until report filed.* Counsel fees may be allowed, but an order will not be made to pay master's fee and costs until the report be filed. *Davidson* v. *Davidson,* 18 W. N., 63 (1886).

§ 933. *Counsel fees allowed to destitute wife.* "It has been the uniform practice to allow a wife destitute of a separate estate, who is either suing or defending a cause of divorce, such reasonable sum as will enable her to carry it on." *Breinig* v. *Breinig,* 26 Pa. St., 165 (1856); *Powers' Appeal,* 120 Pa. St., 328 (1888).

§ 934. *Certified order for fees must be personally served.* An attachment cannot issue for non-payment of counsel fees unless a certified copy of the order of court be personally served on respondent. *Waltram* v. *Waltram,* 19 W. N., 181 (1886).

How decree for alimony enforced. To enforce a decree of alimony a *fi. fa.* may be issued, and if that is not sufficient the decree may then be enforced by attachment. *Elmer* v. *Elmer,* 30 W. N., 383 (1892). See § 939.

§ 935.

FORM OF AFFIDAVIT FOR ALIMONY AND COUNSEL FEES.

A. B. ⎫
  v. ⎬ Common Pleas, Term, 1890. No. .
C. B. ⎭

C. B., having been duly sworn according to law, doth depose and say that she is the wife of the libellant above named and the respondent in this case, and that she has a just, true, and full defense to the same. That she has never given herself up to adulterous practices, as the said libellant has in his said libel alleged, nor has she ever committed adultery. Deponent further saith that she is by reason of the conduct of libellant in poor and destitute circumstances, and that she will be compelled, on account of her situation, to lay out large sums of money in defending this suit, in procuring her counsel and securing her testimony. That libellant is worth (here state libellant's circumstances). And she therefore prays your honors to make such order for the payment of a sum to her by the libellant as will support and maintain her properly pending these proceedings and allow her to pay her counsel and defend herself from the said suit.

Sworn to and subscribed before me, this }
          day of   , A. D. 18   . }

(Signature of Respondent.)

§ 936. Indorse this :

A. B. }
  v.   } Common Pleas,   Term, 1890. No. .
C. B. }

AFFIDAVIT OF RESPONDENT.

And now   , 1890, on motion of E. F., respondent's attorney, the court grant a rule on libellant to show cause why an order should not be made for alimony *pendente lite* and for counsel fees. Rule returnable   .

Send notice of this rule to libellant's attorney.

Sometimes counsel can agree upon the proper order.   When this is impossible the libellant should present his affidavit denying the respondent's averments as to libellant's circumstances and as to respondent's poverty.

§ 937.

FORM OF ANSWER TO RULE FOR ALIMONY AND COUNSEL FEES.

A. B. }
  v.   } Common Pleas,   Term, 1890. No. .
C. B. }

A. B., the libellant, in answer to the rule granted in this case, to show cause why an order should not be made for payment of alimony *pendente lite* and for counsel fees, saith :

1. That he is prepared to prove the charges in his said libel contained.

2. That it is not true as in respondent's affidavit stated that respondent is poor or destitute ; on the contrary, the truth is (here set out the facts as they may be, for example, that respondent has been for some time past and now is the owner of the premises   , that she is receiving a rent therefrom of at least $ per annum, or that respondent has received from libellant the following sums, etc.).

It may be that the libellant can add :

3. The respondent has been since and now is living with another man, who supports her.

State all facts which constitute an answer.

(Signature of Libellant.)

Sworn to and subscribed before me,

Generally depositions are taken on both sides.   This is done under a rule.

§ 938.

FORM OF RULE TO TAKE DEPOSITIONS.

A. B. } In the Court of Common Pleas
  v.   }
C. B. }   of   County,   Term, 1890. No. .

And now,   , on motion of   , attorney for
the court grant a rule to take depositions, *sur* rule for alimony and counsel

fees, on behalf of   , before any alderman, justice of the peace, or notary (sometimes commissioner is added), on   , notice to   .

This is cheaper and simpler than to refer to an examiner.

The officer to take the depositions is consulted, a time fixed, and a notice served.

It is more courteous to see the opposite counsel and agree upon the time. Then send him formal notice, that he may advise his client. When depositions have been closed on both sides, the rule is ordered upon the next list, and notice given to the opposite attorney.

Paper-books should be prepared for the court, stating the case, the rule, the points in favor of or against it, an abstract of the testimony relied on, the 'authorities to be cited, etc.

If alimony is allowed, it is gauged by the social position, circumstances, etc., of the parties, from five dollars to twenty dollars per week.

The counsel fee is generally thirty-five dollars. In troublesome cases much higher.

§ 939. *Attachment may issue to enforce payment of alimony and counsel fees.* An attachment will issue where the rule for alimony and counsel fees has not been obeyed. *Ormsby* v. *Ormsby*, 1 Phila., 578 (1855); *Mann* v. *Mann*, 7 W. N., 507 (1879); *Groves' Appeal*, 68 Pa. St., 143 (1871).

Where libellant fails to pay alimony awarded to the respondent, an attachment will be granted to enforce payment. *Wallen* v. *Wallen*, 1 Dist. Rep., 684 (1891). See § 934.

§ 940.

FORM OF PETITION FOR ATTACHMENT.

To the Honorable the Judges of the Court of Common Pleas for the County of   :   .

The petition of   , wife of   , of the county aforesaid, respectfully showeth :

That she filed in this Honorable Court, on the   day of   , A. D. 18 , a petition praying that the   be ordered to pay your petitioner alimony *pendente lite* and her counsel fees.

And your petitioner further showeth that this Honorable Court did, on the   day of   , in the year of our Lord one thousand eight hundred and   , order and decree that the said   should pay to your petitioner the sum of   dollars for each and every week from the   day of   , in the year aforesaid, and so continue to pay said sum for each and every week thereafter until otherwise decreed by this Honorable Court, and that he should also pay the sum of   dollars for counsel fees.

And your petitioner further showeth that said   has not paid to your petitioner the sum of   dollars for each and every week since the   day of   aforesaid, but owes, and is indebted to your petitioner in the sum of　　　　　dollars, being in arrear to said amount of the alimony allowed as aforesaid, on the　　　　　day of　　　, A. D. 18 , and that he has not paid said counsel fees, thereby holding the order of this Honorable Court in contempt.

Your petitioner therefore prays that an attachment may issue out of this Honorable Court to compel obedience to said order and decree. And your petitioner will ever pray, etc.

(Signature of Petitioner.)

　　　　　　　　, being duly　　　　　according to law, doth depose and say that the facts set forth in the above petition are true.

(Signature of Petitioner.)

　　　　　and subscribed before me,　⎫
this　　　day of　　　, A.D. 1889. ⎬
　　　　　　　　　　　　　　　　⎭

Indorsement :

No. . Term, 18 .

A. B. ⎫
　v.　⎬　C. P.
C. B. ⎭

Petition of　　　for Attachment.
(Name of Attorney.)
Pro Petitioner.

1890, March　　. Petition filed and the court grant a rule on　　　, to show cause why an attachment should not issue against him to enforce the order made by the court　　, A. D. 18 . Rule returnable　　　.

Care should be taken to serve a certified copy of this rule personally. A copy should be kept and affidavit of personal service be made.

If no answer be filed or excuse be made, the rule will be made absolute. The prothonotary will issue the attachment. Give it to the sheriff with defendant's address.

§ 941. **If answer be filed to libel,** it must be responsive to the libel and must follow it in paragraphic numbers as nearly as may be. New matters relied on may be set forth in subsequent paragraphs. Herein the pleader should carefully consult the forms, the decisions heretofore noted in this chapter, and all the authorities. The following may serve as a guide :

§ 942.

FORM OF ANSWER DENYING THE MARRIAGE.

The answer of　　　　　, respondent, to the　　　　　libel of　　　　　, libellant, as amended by amendment thereto, filed on the twelfth day of March, A. D. 1874.

This respondent, saving and reserving to himself all and all manner of benefit and advantage of exception to the many untruths, uncertainties, and imperfections in the said amended libel and the said amendments contained, for answer thereto, or to so much thereof as this respondent is advised is necessary or material for him to make answer unto, answereth and saith : (1) *That it is not true* as in said amendment to libel alleged, that in the month of January, A. D. 1857, a marriage was contracted and celebrated between the said libellant and this respondent, and this respondent avers that no such marriage was contracted and celebrated, as falsely therein alleged, and that the said libellant is not his wife. (2) And this respondent, further answering, says that it is not true that from and after the last-mentioned date until the date of the pretended grievances as in the said amended libel mentioned, he lived and cohabited with the said libellant as his wife; and he denies that she was so known and reputed by all of the said libellant's or this respondent's neighbors and acquaintances. (3) And this respondent, further answering, says that the pretended narrative in said amended libel contained, as far as the libellant seeks thereby to establish the existence of a marriage between herself and the respondent, is wholly untrue; but, inasmuch as the said libellant is not this respondent's wife, he is advised that it is not necessary or material for him to make a particular and detailed answer thereto; *and further answering, he says that inasmuch as the said libellant is not his wife, he could not and did not desert her.* All which matters and things this respondent is ready to aver, maintain, and prove as this Honorable Court may direct, and prays to be hence dismissed with costs.

(Signature of Respondent.)

on oath says that the facts set forth in the above answer are true and correct.
Sworn to and subscribed before me, }
1891. }

§ 943.

FORM OF ANSWER (BY WIFE DENYING DESERTION).

In the Court of Common Pleas, for the County of
To the Honorable the Judges of the said Court:
The answer of   to the libel of   , No.   ,   Term, 18 .
This respondent, saving to herself all manner of benefit and advantage of exception to the manifold untruths, uncertainties, and imperfections in the libel contained, for answer thereto, or to so much thereof as this respondent is advised it is in any manner material for her to make answer to, answers and says:

I. (a) That true it is that the said (name of libellant) was lawfully joined in marriage with the respondent on the   day   , in the year of our Lord one thousand eight hundred and   , at
        , and that from and after that time they lived together and cohabited as husband and wife. Yet this respondent doth expressly deny the charge of having maliciously and wilfully deserted and absented herself from the said   , as is stated in the libel of the said
        . But this respondent doth aver that she at all times has been ready and willing to discharge all her marital duties with love and tenderness and continues so at this time.

(b) The respondent admits the allegations contained in paragraph b of the libel. (This is when the residences, etc., have been truly set out. If the libel be not correct, the answer should state the truth.)

(c) The respondent admits the allegations contained in paragraph c of the libel. (The same remark applies here as noted above.)

II. The respondent further avers from the date of the marriage this respondent was compelled to remain at the home of her parents and was supported entirely by them, the said libellant never paying one cent toward

the support and maintenance of respondent. That finding she could obtain from him no support she was compelled on the   **day of**
, A. D. 18 , to apply to the Guardians of the Poor, who issued a warrant for his arrest; that he then wanted this respondent to accompany him to the home of his mother, where he resided. To this she assented, and on the   day of   , A. D. 18 , went to live with him.

That the mother of the libellant immediately commenced to treat respondent with rudeness, and insulted her time and time again. When respondent appealed to libellant to save her from insult his reply was that she might expect to be insulted as long as she remained in the house.

Finding this would not drive respondent away, the libellant refused even to speak to her, passing her by at all times without.the least notice, though she was unconscious of having even in the slightest particular offended him.

Finally, by the cruelty of libellant, this respondent was compelled to return to the home of her parents, where she still resides. On the
day of   , A.D. 18 , the libellant, making no provision for her support, this respondent applied to the Guardians of the Poor, a prosecution was commenced against him, which was settled by the libellant giving a bond to the city of Philadelphia conditioned for her support and maintenance.

All of which this respondent is willing to maintain, and she prays that this may be inquired of by the county, etc.

                                            (Signature of Respondent.)

, the above-named respondent, being duly
according to law, deposes and says the facts set forth in the foregoing answer are true.

                and subscribed before me, ⎫
this   day of   , A. D. 18 . ⎬   (Signature of Respondent.)
                                            ⎭

Indorsement :
No.   Term, 18 .

A. B. ⎫
  v.   ⎬   C. P.
C. B. ⎭

                    Answer.

                Attorney pro Respondent.

§ 944. *Answer* nunc pro tunc *cannot be filed where examiner has held meetings.* In *Schneider* v. *Schneider*, 9 W. N., 253 (1880) (C. P. No. 3, of Philadelphia), the court refused to allow an answer to be filed *nunc pro tunc*, notwithstanding the respondent swore that he could not afford to employ counsel until after the examiner had held a meeting, and that he now desired to oppose the libel.

§ 945. *Answer cannot be filed after examiner's report is in.* In *Newbold's Appeal*, 2 W. N., 472 (1876), a rule demanding an issue and a rule to allow respondent to file a substituted answer were deemed too late after filing of examiner's report and a rule for divorce.

Leave to file an answer *nunc pro tunc* will not be granted where the divorce proceedings have been regular. Such relief can be obtained only where the party can show :

1. That the application is made without unreasonable delay.

2. That it is based upon surprise, haste, ignorance, or mistake.

3. That unless relief be given, positive injury and injustice would be done.

4. That no right has accrued to the other side which it would be inequitable or unjust to disturb. *Shay* v. *Shay*, 9 Phila., 521 (1872), FINLETTER, J.

§ 946. **If plea and demurrer filed together, the demurrer is overruled.** In equity a plea and demurrer cannot be put in at the same time to the same matter, hence where a plea and demurrer were filed to a libel in divorce the plea overruled the demurrer. *Ewing* v. *Ewing*, 2 Phila., 371 (1857).

§ 947. **Replication.** Where the answer sets up new matter, a replication as to it may be filed.

§ 948. **Either party can demand a jury trial.** The demand for issue must be made in reasonable time. *Gillardon* v. *Gillardon*, 16 W. N., 457 (1885).

§ 949. *Demand for jury trial too late after report filed.* In *Allison* v. *Allison*, 46 Pa. St., 321 (1863), a libel was filed for divorce from bed and board with alimony. The answer was filed concluding with a verification and not to the country, and without asking an issue. An application for an issue was made, but not until after the report of the commissioners, and when the final decree was about to be made. The issue was refused by the court.

THOMPSON J.: " The party had a right to an issue to try disputed facts, but he was bound to exercise his right reasonably and with vigilance."

§ 950. *After examiner appointed a prompt demand may secure jury trial.* In *Derringer* v. *Derringer*, 8 Phila., 269 (1871), the answer contained no demand for issue. On June 19, 1871, the master was appointed, and on June 30, 1871, a petition and demand for a jury trial was filed. The court held that under the ruling in *Allison* v. *Allison* the demand was not too late.

In *Fougeray* v. *Fougeray*, 5 W. N., 38 (1877) (C. P. No. 2, Philada.), a rule to withdraw the case from an examiner and to allow an issue to be framed was made absolute upon payment of examiner's costs.

§ 951. *If no jury trial demanded.* If neither party demand a jury trial, the case goes to a master on application of either side.

§ 952. **Framing issues.** *If a jury trial be demanded*, the party so desiring should frame the issue, present it to the opposite side,

and then to the court.   In Philadelphia the rule directs that it shall
not be in the form of a feigned issue, but directly on the facts.
Winpenny v. *Winpenny*, 40 Leg. Int., 232 (1883).

A jury trial is of right at any time before taking of testimony
has been commenced, but thereafter only in the discretion of the
court upon motion and cause shown.

In counties where a different rule prevails the feigned issue may
still be preferred.   The following may serve as a

§ 953. *Form of feigned issue.*

FORM OF DECLARATION.

COUNTY OF PHILADELPHIA, *ss.*

(Name of defendant), late of the said county, was summoned to answer
(name of libellant) of a plea of trespass on the case, etc., whereupon the
said (name of libellant), by her attorney, complains that heretofore, to wit,
on the   day of   ·   , A. D. 1888, at the county aforesaid, a certain discourse was had and moved by and between the said (name of libellant) and the said (name of defendant), wherein a certain question then and
there arose, to wit: whether the said (name of defendant) has from the
month of   , A. D.   , wilfully and maliciously deserted and
abandoned his family, and in that discourse the said (name of libellant)
then and there asserted and affirmed that from the month of   ,
A. D.   , the said (name of defendant) has wilfully and maliciously
deserted his family, which said assertion and affirmation the said (name of
defendant) then and there denied and then and there asserted the contrary
thereof, and thereupon, afterward, to wit, on the day and year first above
mentioned, as aforesaid, at the county aforesaid, in consideration that the
said (name of libellant), at the special instance and request of the said
(name of defendant), had then and there paid him the sum of $500, lawful
money, he, the said (name of defendant), undertook and then and there
faithfully promised the said (name of plaintiff) to pay her the sum of $1000,
like lawful money, if from the month of   , A. D. 18   , he, the said
(name of defendant), had wilfully and maliciously deserted and abandoned
his family.   And the said (name of plaintiff), in fact, says that from the
month of   , A. D. 18   , he, the said (name of defendant), has wilfully
and maliciously deserted and abandoned his family.   Whereof, the said
(name of defendant), afterward, to wit, on the day and year first above mentioned, at the county aforesaid, had notice ; whereby the said (name of defendant), then and there became liable to pay and ought to have paid to
the said (name of plaintiff) the sum of $1000.

And whereas, also, heretofore, to wit, on the day and year first above mentioned, as aforesaid, at the county aforesaid, a certain other discourse was
had and moved between the said (name of plaintiff) and the said (name of
defendant), wherein a certain other question then and there arose, to wit,
whether the said (name of defendant) did on or about the first day of
          , A. D. 18   , wilfully and maliciously turn her, the said (name of
plaintiff) out of doors ; and in that discourse the said (name of plaintiff)
then and there asserted and affirmed that on or about the first day of
          , A. D.   , the said (name of defendant) did wilfully and mali-
ciously turn her, the said (name of plaintiff), out of doors ; which said

affirmation and assertion the said (name of defendant) then and there denied, and then and there asserted the contrary thereof, and thereupon, afterward, to wit, on the day and year first above mentioned, at the county aforesaid, in consideration that the said (name of plaintiff), at the special instance and request of the said (name of defendant), had then and there paid him the sum of $500 in lawful money, he, the said (name of defendant), undertook, and then and there faithfully promised the said (name of plaintiff) to pay her $1000 if on or about the _____ day of _____ , A. D. _____ , he, the said (name of defendant) did wilfully and maliciously turn her, the said (name of plaintiff), out of doors ; whereof, he, the said (name of defendant), afterward, to wit, on the day and year first above mentioned, at the county aforesaid, had notice, whereby the said (name of defendant) then and there became liable to pay and ought to have paid to her, the said (name of plaintiff), $1000. Nevertheless the said (name of defendant), not regarding his said personal promises, has not paid to the said (name of plaintiff) the said several sums of money or any part thereof, but the same to pay has hitherto wholly refused and still doth refuse to the damage of the said (name of plaintiff) $10,000.

(Signature of Counsel)
for plaintiff.

§ 954.

FORM OF PLEAS.

And the said defendant, protesting that he is not bound to plead to the said declaration in feigned issue, and reserving to himself all, and all manner of objections thereto, and to the orders made on this respondent for pleas in this behalf, comes and saith that the said plaintiff ought not to have and maintain her aforesaid action against him, because he saith :

I. That from the month of _____ , A. D. _____ he, the said defendant, has not wilfully and maliciously deserted and abandoned his family in manner and form as in the plaintiff's first count mentioned, and of this he puts himself upon the country.

II. And for a further plea in this behalf, the said defendant comes and saith that on or about the _____ day of _____ , A. D. _____ , the said defendant did not wilfully and maliciously turn the said plaintiff out of doors, in manner and form as in the plaintiff's second count mentioned, and of this he puts himself upon the country.

(Signature of Counsel)
for defendant.

§ 955.

FORM OF SIMILITER.

And the said plaintiff, as to the pleas of the said defendant by him above pleaded, and whereof he hath put himself upon the country, doth the like.

(Signature of Counsel)
for plaintiff.

This form can readily be accommodated to any issue, marriage or no marriage, charges and denials of desertion, adultery, cruelty, etc.

§ 956. *Where no feigned issues* be filed, because the rule of court (as in Philadelphia) forbids that practice, the order is framed directly upon the traverses.

§ 957. *Form of order for issues.* The following in such cases could be adopted :

A. B. ⎫
    v. ⎬ In the Court of Common Pleas, of Philadelphia County,
C. B. ⎭   of March Term, 1891. No. 200.

And now   , 1891, it appearing to the court that a jury trial has been demanded by (respondent or by libellant, or by both parties) upon the matters hereinafter stated which have been alleged and denied in the pleadings : *It is ordered,* that the following issues be tried, to wit (here state the issues as, (I.) were the parties married, or (II.) did the defendant wilfully and maliciously desert the libellant, etc., or (III.) did the defendant commit adultery, etc.), as charged in the libel and denied in the answer. And it is further ordered that in said issues the libellant be the plaintiff, and the respondent be defendant.

§ 958. *If the issue be upon an independent matter,* set up in the answer (as condonation, recrimination, etc.), the respondent would have the affirmative and be the plaintiff in such special issues.

§ 959. *Who to prepare the feigned issues or the order.* The party most anxious to dispose of the case prepares the draft of the feigned issues or the order, and sends it to opposite counsel. If agreed to, they go before a judge, who approves, and the paper is filed. If the counsel differ as to form, they must fix a time to appear before a judge, who settles the question. If argument be desired, of course the case is ordered on the appropriate list and notice given. When an issue to try the facts is prayed, it is proper for the court to direct the form of the issue or issues, and to require the other party to join therein. THOMPSON, J., in *Waldron* v. *Waldron,* 55 Pa. St., 234 (1866).

§ 960. *When issues settled,* the case is ordered on the trial-list and takes its course.

If the jury find for the libellant and no motion be made for a new trial, or if made the motion be overruled, pay the jury fee and enter judgment. Take a rule for a final decree, serve notice, etc., as in cases where no issue was entered. See § 976, changing the averment as to the Master's Report to " Judgment having been entered for libellant on the verdict," and see §§ 977–981.

§ 961. **Master—Appointment of—Proceedings before master.** A master (formerly called an examiner, sometimes a commissioner) is needed where the defendant has failed to appear, or where having appeared the defendant fails-to answer, or where an answer has been filed and no jury trial has been demanded by either party. Counsel must see that the record justifies the reference to a master. If defendant has not appeared, let the subpœna, the alias, the order of publication, be all returned,—the subpœnas *non est inventus,*—the order of publication, advertised as directed, see section 889 of this chapter. The motion for appointment should recite the record as justifying the reference.

§ 962.

ORDER FOR APPOINTMENT OF MASTER.

A. B.   ⎱ In the Court of Common Pleas, of Philadelphia County, of
  v.   ⎰
C. B.   Term, 1890. No. .

And now,   , 1890, it appearing to the court (here recite from the record that the original and alias subpœnas have been duly returned *non est inventus,* that the order of publication has been duly obeyed, and that the defendant has not appeared as required by law, or that defendant is in default for not filing an answer *sec. reg.,* or that an answer and replication have been filed, that neither party has demanded a jury trial), the case is on motion of   *.* ., attorney for the   , referred to   , Esq., as master, to take testimony and to report *sec. reg. et sec. leg.*

This motion is by the Philadelphia rules left with the court clerk and it is placed on the regular current list.

The court fills in the name of the master. The attorney notifies the master.

§ 963. *Notice by the master.* The master and counsel should be very particular in proceedings *ex parte.* Where there has been no personal service of the subpœna and no appearance has been entered, the master should inform himself by examining the libellant and by such other means as he shall deem conducive to the purpose, of the residence and address of the respondent ; and the master must use every exertion by personal inquiry within the county or by registered letters outside of the county, and in case of failure by these means then by advertisement in such newspaper or newspapers as in the opinion of the master will be most likely to reach the respondent, once a week for four full weeks, and by any other means available to give actual notice to the respondent of the application for a divorce, the grounds thereof, the name and the address of the master, and the time and place of taking the testimony. The Philadelphia rules add that where the respondent was last known to reside and was last heard of in the county of Philadelphia, it shall not be necessary to advertise such notice. Thereafter the master may proceed to take testimony, but must not file his report until satisfied that all available means have been used to give actual notice to the respondent. The efforts to this end must be set forth in the report. The object of all these directions is to guard against a decree without notice. They do not apply where there has been a personal service or an appearance.

Where there has been a personal service of the subpœna, it is probable that a notice from the master can be served in like manner. Personal service should be made if possible; if not, then the notice should be left at the respondent's residence or sent by registered letter to the address where the master shall have reason to believe it will be most likely to reach the respondent.

If an appearance has been entered, written notice must be given to the counsel appearing. Libellant's attorney should be notified in like manner.

§ 964.

FORM OF NOTICE WHERE PROCEEDING IS EX PARTE.

A. B.
 v. } In the Court of Common Pleas of Philadelphia County, of
C. B.   Term, 1890. No. .

To   , the respondent above-named :

Please take notice that an application for a divorce has been made in the above case, upon the allegation that you (recite the libel, as, have wilfully and maliciously deserted the libellant and absented yourself from   habitation without a reasonable cause for and during the term and space of two years, or that you have committed adultery, etc., as the case may be). By reason of your default in not (entering an appearance, or, in not filing an answer), the case has been referred to me as master. I have fixed   the   day of   , 1890, at   o'clock M., as the time and my office, No.   Street, in the city of Philadelphia, as the place for taking testimony in the cause, when and where you may attend.

                              (Name of Master.)
                              (Address.)

§ 965. *Where no appearance has been entered* this notice (as already noted) must be served personally if possible, and if all available means are exhausted and no service can be made, then it is sent by registered letter, and it is to be advertised, except where the respondent was last known to reside, or was last heard of in the county of Philadelphia.

§ 966. *If an appearance has been entered.* Service upon counsel is sufficient. In such cases the notice need not recite the libel.

§ 967. *Copies of all notices, advertisements, should be kept,* and memorandum made, so that affidavits can be filed.

§ 968. *Before the Master.* The master must (1) preserve and file proofs of inquiry, of service, or of mailing, advertising, etc.

(2) He must inquire of witnesses and report to the court (a) the ages of the parties; (b) number, names, ages, and residences of their children, if any. Where respondent has not been served and has not appeared, the master must give notice to such children as may have attained their majority; if none, then to the parents, brothers, sisters, or other near relatives of respondent, requesting them to assist in giving actual notice.

(3) The master must report his efforts to effect such notice and the result.

(4) Where the residence of either party or of both parties is given, as within the county of Philadelphia, the master must make personal inquiry and report whether this is correct and *bona fide*, and the length of the residence, and whether respondent has ever resided in this State, and when and where. In case a residence of either party is given as in another county, the master shall make such inquiries by letter to the sheriff of such county.

§ 969. *Examination of witnesses, etc., by master.* After all these directions have been complied with, the master is required to examine each witness specially and in detail upon all material matters. And whether requested or not he is to summon and examine such witnesses as he believes have any knowledge of relevant matters.

Neither party can examine until the master is through with the witness.

§ 970. *If objections made,* the master notes them, but takes the testimony subject to the objections.

§ 971. *Minutes* of all meetings, adjournments, exceptions to the master's delay, etc., must be kept.

§ 972. *Security for costs* may with leave of the court be required by the master for payment of costs of master and of prothonotary. Proceedings may be stayed until it is entered. No divorce shall be decreed until all costs are paid.

§ 973. *Master's report.* He reports all his proceedings, the testimony and his opinion, he appends docket entries, and all the papers, and files report with the prothonotary.

§ 974.

FORM OF MASTER'S REPORT.

To the Honorable the Judges of the Court of Common Pleas, No. , for the County of Philadelphia.

In the matter of the petition of   by her next friend, etc., for a divorce *a v. m.* from   (of June Term, . No.).

The master appointed to take the testimony respectfully reports :

That the docket entries and original papers in the case show the respondent was not served personally with the subpœna and no appearance has been entered for him. There were two subpœnas issued, returnable respectively to the   Monday of   and   Monday of   , both of which were returned by the sheriff *non est inventus.* An order of publication was procured, returnable to the   Monday in   , which was duly returned by the sheriff, indorsing on the same his obedience to the same by publishing a notice to the respondent once a week for four weeks in two daily newspapers published in the city of Philadelphia and in the *Legal Intelligencer,* and *non est inventus* as to said respondent. The subpœnas and order were sued out in proper time, and the proceedings were in strict accordance with and fulfillment of the Acts of Assembly and rules of court in such case made and provided.

The reason alleged for the divorce as stated in the libel is the continuous desertion of libellant by the respondent, wilfully and maliciously and without reasonable cause, and the absenting of himself from her habitation from the early part of the month of   , A. D.   , until the date of filing libel, to wit,   .

Upon receiving notice of his appointment the master held a preliminary meeting on   , at the office of   , for the purpose of ascertaining, if possible, the residence of the respondent. The libellant was examined and testified that she did not know where the respondent could be found; that his last known residence to her was   , but that she had heard that he had moved to   . She directed the master to correspond with   , a brother-in-law of the respondent, who resides on   , Philadelphia; Mrs.   , N. J., a sister of respondent;   , and   . The master thereupon sent registered letters to all the above parties and also three registered letters to the respondent himself; one in care of   , one in care of   , and one in care of   . A copy of the letters sent the above-named parties (other than the respondent) is hereto annexed, marked " Exhibit C," and a copy of the notice sent ‚to the respondent is hereto annexed, marked " Exhibit D." The notice to the respondent was in accordance with the rule of court, giving him information of the application for divorce, the grounds thereof, the name and address of the master, and the time and place of taking testimony in the cause. All the above letters and notices were mailed from the Philadelphia postoffice on   . Answers were received from all the parties (other than the respondent), who, with the exception of   , denied knowledge of the residence or address of the respondent. The answer of   (hereto annexed, marked " Exhibit E"), dated   , was as follows:

" I gave Mr.   's address to the postmaster here who had a registered letter for him. He is with   , this city." Thereupon, on December 30, 1887, the master sent a registered letter of request to   , similar to exhibit " C," and a registered notice, similar to exhibit " D," to the respondent in care of   , with directions on the envelope to the postmaster not to deliver the latter to anyone except   personally. Before this notice could have been delivered to respondent the return postal from the registered letter sent him in care of   , was received with the signature of   affixed. Subsequently, the return postal to the notice sent respondent on   , in care of   , but with directions on the envelope as aforesaid, was received with the signature   affixed. These postals, marked " Exhibit A " and " Exhibit B," are hereto annexed. The signatures on the postals were subsequently identified by   , son of respondent, as of the handwriting of his father, the respondent. (*Vide* testimony.) The master therefore reports that personal notice was given to respondent by two registered letters of the application of divorce, the grounds thereof, the name and address of the master, and the time and place of taking testimony in the cause. The first of these notices ought to have been delivered by due course of mail ten days before the first meeting for taking testimony; and both were delivered in ample time for respondent to have replied before the date of last meeting, but no reply or communication from him (save the return postal as aforesaid) has been received by the master.

The master is satisfied, by personal inquiry, and so reports that the residence of libellant as stated in the libel is correct and *bona fide*, and that the libellant has resided in this county and State since her marriage to the present time. The master is also satisfied and so reports, that from the time of his marriage until , 18 , the respondent was a *bona fide* resident of this county and State.

In pursuance of the notice sent respondent, and of written notice given to counsel for libellant, a meeting for the purpose of taking testimony was held at the office of , Philadelphia, on the day of , A. D. 18 , at o'clock in the afternoon, which, after testimony taken, was, on account of the lateness of the hour, adjourned to , 18 , at o'clock in the afternoon. On account of indisposition the master was unable to attend on , and at his request an adjournment was had until , 18 , at o'clock, at which time the final meeting was held at the same place as the first.

The first meeting was attended by and , of counsel for libellant, who also attended in person, and , witnesses for libellant. The last meeting was attended by the same persons, with the exception of . The libellant was examined as to the fact of marriage, residence, and age of herself and husband, the respondent.

and , testified as to the desertion and other matters stated in the libel. The entire examination of the witnesses, with the exception of that of libellant, which educed the testimony given by her and recorded after the letter (*a*) in her written testimony hereto annexed, was made by the master. The testimony so given by her after the letter (*a*) was so marked because the master doubted her competency to testify to the matters therein contained. His report, however, is made without reference to that testimony, and, therefore, for the purpose of this report, it is immaterial whether or not she was a competent witness to testify to such matters. The master therefore reports that the evidence shows:

I. That a marriage was solemnized by the Friends' ceremony between the libellant and respondent, on the day of , A. D. , at No. , in the city of Philadelphia, Pennsylvania, and that from and immediately thereafter the libellant and respondent cohabited together as husband and wife in the city of Philadelphia, until , 18 .

. II. That at the time of said marriage the libellant and respondent were both citizens of the State of Pennsylvania, and resided in the city of Philadelphia; that the libellant has ever since resided in Philadelphia; and that the respondent also resided in said city until , 18 .

III. That the present residence of libellant is No. Street, Philadelphia.

IV. That the libellant was years of age on the day of , A. D. , and the respondent is forty-six years of age this , .

V. That children were born to libellant and respondent, of whom died in infancy. The names of the two living, with their ages and residences, are as follows: , born , now residing at No. , Philadelphia; , born , now residing at No. , Philadelphia.

VI. The master also reports that from inquiries made he is satisfied that the present residence of respondent is   , and that his address there is, care of

VII. From the evidence in the case, hereto annexed, the master also reports that in his opinion the grounds alleged for the application for divorce are well founded. The two witnesses who were examined (other than libellant) both testified that for many years prior to   , the respondent would periodically neglect his family, go off on drinking sprees, and remain absent from home for weeks at a time, no one knowing where he was. That he was frequently losing situations by such conduct, and that the furniture was levied on for rent and seized for board on several occasions, the libellant or her friends having to redeem the same. During this time the libellant conducted herself properly and 'acted toward her husband in a dutiful and affectionate manner, continually living with him and cohabiting with him, when he had a place provided for her, until   . At that time respondent, with his family, were living at   , Philadelphia, when he left on one of his sprees. The goods were levied on for rent; one of the relatives paid the rent, taking the furniture as security; the housekeeping was broken up; and libellant and her son worked for the money with which they subsequently redeemed the furniture. Respondent lived in Philadelphia until   , but neither supported his family nor lived with libellant. In   of that year he obtained some money from his son, on his promise to send money toward the support of his family as soon as he got a position. He went West and has not contributed anything for the support of his family since that date. He occasionally wrote to his son, but never expressed a single desire to return or support his family. For the past   years, however, he has not communicated with his family.

The master, therefore, is of opinion that respondent has wilfully, maliciously, and without a reasonable cause deserted libellant and absented himself from her habitation continuously since   , and recommends that the prayer of the libel be granted, and that a decree be made divorcing and separating him, the said   , respondent, from the society, fellowship, and company of the libellant in all time to come, and her, the said   , from the marriage bond contracted with the said respondent, as if they had never been married, or as if he, the said   , were naturally dead.

Exceptions to master's report. Where the rules of court are silent upon this subject, the equity rules as to masters' reports might be followed.

§ 975. Rule for divorce. When master's report has been filed it should be handed to a judge. If he mark it "approved," the libellant enters a rule for divorce, thus:

§ 976.

FORM OF RULE FOR DIVORCE.

A. B.
   v. } In the Court of Common Pleas of Philadelphia County,
C. B. }   of March Term, 1890. No. .

And now,   , 1890, the master's report in the above case having been approved by the court, on motion of   , libellant's attorney, a rule is granted on respondent to show cause why a divorce *a v. m.* should not be decreed. Rule returnable (in Philadelphia the first Saturday of each month and the third Monday of September).

§ 977. *Service of notice.* The same old formula is here to be repeated. Serve *personally*, where possible ; otherwise on counsel if an appearance has been entered. Ten days' service before the return-day is required in Philadelphia. If no appearance, and notice cannot be served personally, then it must be published once a week for four weeks in the *Legal Intelligencer* and one daily paper of Philadelphia (and additional notice as directed), in the following § 978.

FORM OF NOTICE OF FINAL RULE.

To C. B., late of No.　　　˙　　Street, Philadelphia, Pennsylvania.

You are hereby notified that a final rule for divorce has been granted against you at the suit of A. B., your　　　　　　, which will be heard in the Court of Common Pleas, No.　, on Saturday, the　　　　day of 　　　　, on which day you may appear and show cause, if any you have, why such divorce should not be granted against you.

C. D.,
Attorney for Libellant.

§ 979. *Affidavit of service.*

In all cases an affidavit of the time, place, and manner of service shall be filed, and in case of service on the counsel of the respondent, or by publication, the efforts which have been made to serve the respondent personally shall be stated in the affidavit.

§ 980. *Service.*

Service of notices or rules upon the respondent shall not be made by the libellant or the next friend or the counsel of record.

§ 981. *Notice of rule where respondent is out of the State.* Where respondent has had notice of proceedings, and he resides in a foreign country, it is not necessary under the rules of court to make effort to serve him personally with notice of the last rule. *Baldwin* v. *Baldwin,* 17 W. N., 222 (1886).

It only remains to note a few general matters.

§ 982. **Testimony.** *Parties may testify where personal service made, or appearance entered.*

A husband and wife shall not be competent or permitted to testify against each other, except in those proceedings for divorce in which personal service of the subpœna or of a rule to take depositions has been made upon the opposite party, or in which the opposite party appears and defends, in which case, either may testify fully against the other, and except, also, that in any proceeding for divorce either party may be called merely to prove the fact of marriage. (Act of May 23, 1887, section 5 ; P. L., 159.)

Where notice of the master's meeting had reached the respondent by registered letter, it was held that the libellant might testify to all facts alleged in her libel, although the subpœna had not been served and the respondent had not appeared. *Kolp* v. *Kolp*, 3 Dist. Rep., 1 (1893).

§ 983. **Commissions and rules to take depositions.** Ancient, infirm, and going witnesses may be examined under the rules of court. A rule is granted by a judge, fixing the notice to be given. This order is complied with and the deposition taken. In like manner the court will grant a rule for a commission outside of the State.

A commission may issue, but if the case is before a master interrogatories are to be framed by him after notice of the names of the witnesses and the offers of testimony as to each, both parties having right to file supplemental and cross-interrogatories. *Snowden* v. *Snowden*, 18 W. N., 347 (1886).

In *Gilbert* v. *Gilbert*, 18 W. N., 535 (1886), it was ruled that the parties should prepare the interrogatories.

It is difficult to understand how a master could prepare any but the general interrogatories.

§ 984. **Discontinuance.** It is settled law in Pennsylvania that a discontinuance must be founded on the express or implied leave of the court. In ordinary cases it has been a long-established practice that a plaintiff may, on payment of costs, discontinue his action without formal leave, but in divorce proceedings the discontinuance must be by express leave of court, otherwise it will be stricken off. *Murphy* v. *Murphy*, 8 Phila., 357 (1871).

§ 985. *Discontinuance may be entered, notwithstanding a pending rule for alimony.* In *Clymer* v. *Clymer*, 45 Leg. Int., 379 (1888), leave was given libellant to discontinue, notwithstanding a pending rule for alimony, which had not been diligently prosecuted.

§ 986. **Condonation.** Reconciliation and subsequent cohabitation are not a bar to a divorce for acts of cruelty, violence, and outrage committed before the reconciliation. *Hollister* v. *Hollister*, 6 Pa. St., 449 (1847) ; *Steele* v. *Steele*, 11 W. N., 21 (1881).

Acts of condonation in a divorce for adultery are a bar to a decree ; subsequent acts of adultery will not avoid its effect. *Bronson* v. *Bronson*, 7 Phila., 405 (1870).

§ 987. **Decree vacated.** A decree may be vacated where a divorce was obtained by fraud, though a marriage subsequently took place on the strength of that decree, and issue born. *Allen* v. *Maclellan*, 12 Pa. St., 328 (1849).

In *Smith* v. *Smith*, 3 Phila., 492 (1859), the evidence showed that the respondent at libellant's instigation and with his consent had visited her father's family in Kentucky. That subsequently she had received a letter from him urging separation, and the first knowledge of the divorce proceeding against her was when a certificate of the decree was forwarded to her by libellant. The decree was vacated by the court on the ground of fraud.

After libellant's death a decree was vacated, where the divorce was obtained in respondent's absence and without notice to her, *Boyd's Appeal*, 38 Pa. St., 241 (1861).

A decree will be vacated which was obtained by fraud or imposition and without proper notice to the other party. *Wanamaker* v. *Wanamaker*, 10 Phila., 466 (1873).

A decree in divorce may be vacated if good grounds be shown therefor, though twelve years have passed since it was obtained and libellant is dead. *Fidelity Ins. Co.'s Appeal*, 93 Pa. St., 242 (1880).

A final decree may be vacated where it has been obtained by fraud. *Nickerson* v. *Nickerson*, 13 W. N., 210 (1883). The fraud practised in this case was the obtaining by libellant of a colorable citizenship in this State, hiring a room in a lodging-house, occupying it very rarely (thirteen nights in fourteen months), false statement in the libel as to residence in the State, being in correspondence with his wife, omitting all reference to the proceeding in divorce, false and perjured testimony that respondent had deserted, etc.

§ 988.

FORM OF PETITION BY A HUSBAND TO ANNUL DECREE OF DIVORCE
FROM BED AND BOARD.

(State the names of the parties, court, term, No., etc.)

To the Honorable the Judges of the said Court :

The petition of   , the above named respondent, respectfully showeth :

That he is informed that on   , the   day of   , in the year of our Lord one thousand eight hundred and   , this Honorable Court made a sentence or decree conformably to the prayer of the libellant above named, that your petitioner and the said libellant should be, and they accordingly were, divorced from bed and board.

Your petitioner does not deem it proper for him, at this stage of the proceeding, to deny the allegations contained in the libel, nor to dispute the justice of the sentence pronounced by this Honorable Court, grounded upon the *ex parte* evidence produced to them ; he is informed and advised that the said sentence is absolute, and precludes contradiction on matters of fact.

Your petitioner is well convinced that he and the libellant can live happily together hereafter, and that their doing so will be essential to the comfort, education, and morals of their young children, and he anxiously avails himself of an indulgent provision of the law, and now offers to this Honorable Court to receive and cohabit with the said libellant again, and to use her as a good husband ought to do.

Your petitioner, therefore, prays this Honorable Court to suspend the aforesaid decree, and that in case the said libellant refuses to return and cohabit with your petitioner under the protection of this court, your Honors may discharge and annul the aforesaid sentence or decree.

And for the faithful performance of this offer and engagement on his part your petitioner will, if necessary, give to this Honorable Court such security as in their discretion they may consider the case to require.

(Attach usual affidavit.)

§ 989. *The action on such an application* rests purely in the sound discretion of the court. The petitioner is already convicted upon the record of the charge named in the libel. If he were never served, if any fraud were practised upon him or upon the court, and if he can deny the charges, he ought not to file this petition ; but he should present a very different application, to wit, a motion to vacate the decree.

If he proceed for a suspension under the form just given, and his petition be resisted, the court may require some proofs of his good faith. These he should be ready to show by depositions taken under a rule or reference, and upon notice to the libellant and her attorney.

§ 990. **Appeal.** See chapter on Appeals, § 3393.

When a divorce is decreed, depositions taken by respondent after the decree are no part of the record on appeal. *Elmes* v. *Elmes*, 9 Pa. St., 166 (1848).

A writ of error will not lie to the final decree of the Common Pleas in divorce proceedings. An appeal is the proper remedy. *Miller* v. *Miller*, 3 Binn., 30 (1810), TILGHMAN, C. J.

On appeal the matters of fact will not be re-tried which have been decided by the jury in a lower court. *Andrews* v. *Andrews*, 5 S. & R., 374 (1819).

An appeal will be dismissed if appellant shall not enter a recognizance with at least one good surety conditioned to prosecute the appeal with effect. *Brom* v. *Brom*, 2 Whar., 94 (1837).

On appeal, an affidavit that it is not intended for delay must be filed. *Brentlinger* v. *Brentlinger*, 4 Rawle, 241 (1833).

§ 991. **Costs on final decree.** In *Shoop's Appeal*, 34 Pa. St., 233 (1859), the libellant obtained a divorce *a v. m.*, on the ground of cruel and barbarous treatment by his wife, and alimony was decreed but costs refused.

Brinckle v. *Brinckle* (C. P. Phila., March Term, 1871, No. 32 ; Supreme Court, January Term, 1879, No. 65). The answer denied the averment of marriage. The jury found for respondent. He filed his bill of costs. It was taxed. A decree was entered "that the libel be dismissed with costs." The libellant appealed, and assigned for error this decree. Her counsel argued that "the court will not ordinarily, if it has any discretion in the premises, decree costs against a defeated wife." He cited 2 Bishop on Marriage and Divorce, 365. The Supreme Court affirmed the decree.

CHAPTER XVIII.

§ 992. Definition. Dower is defined to be the provision which the law makes for a widow out of the lands or tenements of her husband, for her support and the nurture of her children. Coke Littleton, 30 *a*; 4 Kent Comm., 35; Washburn Real Property, 146. The legal proceeding by which she enforces her right to such provision is called with us an action of dower, being the English action of dower, *unde nihil habet.*

§ 993. English Statutes. The following Acts of Parliament have been found to be in force in this State. Report of the Judges, Roberts' Digest, 179 (2d. ed.).

Widow shall have dower.

A widow, after the death of her husband, incontinent, and without any difficulty, shall have her marriage and her inheritance which her husband and she held the day of the death of her husband, and she shall tarry in the chief house of her husband by forty days after the death of her husband, within which days her dower shall be assigned her (if it were not assigned her before) or that the house be a castle; or if she depart from the castle, then a competent house shall forthwith be provided for her, in the which she may honestly dwell until her dower be to her assigned, as it is aforesaid; and she shall have, in the meantime, her reasonable estovers of the common; and for her dower shall be assigned unto her the third part of all the lands of her husband which were his during coverture, except she were endowed of less at the church door. No widow shall be distrained to marry herself, nevertheless she shall find surety that she shall not marry without our license and assent (if she held of us), nor without the assent of the lord if she held of another.

9 Henry III., ch. VII. (1225); Magna Charta.

That part only of this statute is in force which provides that a widow shall tarry in the chief house of her husband forty days after her husband's death, within which days her dower shall be assigned her. Report of the Judges.

§ 994. *Damages to be recovered.* By Statute 20 Henry III., ch. I., Statute of Merton (1235), it is provided that when

Widows are deforced of their dowers "and cannot have their dowers or quarantine without plea" * ·* * "they that be convict of such wrongful deforcement shall yield damages to the same widows;" that is to say, the value of the dower from the time of the husband's death until judgment in favor of the widow ;" " and the deforcers nevertheless shall be amerced at the king's pleasure." (Roberts' Digest, 182.)

§ 995. *Dower* unde nihil habet *maintainable though widow have received part of her dower from another.*

In a writ of dower called *unde nihil habet* the writ shall not abate by the exception of the tenant because she hath received her dower of another man before her writ purchased, unless he can show that she hath received part of her dower of himself, and in the same town before the writ purchased. (3 Edw. I., ch. XLIX. (1275), Roberts' Dig., 184.)

§ 996. *Dispossession of the husband by covin or default.* By 13 Ed. I., Stat. 1, ch. IV. (1285), it is provided that if a husband suffer judgment against him by covin, and give up the land to his adversary, the widow shall not thereby be barred of her dower. If the judgment be by default, the defendant (tenant) shall be required to show " that he had right, and hath in the foresaid land, according to the form of the writ that the tenant before purchased against the husband." This Act further provides that in the foregoing and other enumerated cases the reversioner of the land may be vouched to warranty by the defendant, in order that the widow may not be put to several actions for the recovery of her dower, but that it may be awarded her by virtue of a single judgment. It is also enacted by the same statute that if the widow recover her dower against the guardian of the heir, the heir, upon reaching full age, " shall have an action to demand the seisin of his ancestor against such woman." " In like manner the woman shall be aided if the heir or any other do implead her for her dower, or if she lose her dower, by default, in which case the default shall not be so prejudicial to her, but that she shall recover her dower if she have right thereto." The forms of writs for recovery of dower by the widow, and for recovery of land lost by default, were regulated by the Act, and it was provided that the demandant in such case should not be compelled to resort to a writ of right. See the text of the Act, Roberts' Digest, 185.

§ 997. *Admeasurement of dower.* Statute 13 Edw. I., st.1, ch. VII. (1285), provided the writ of admeasurement of dower for the guardian of minor heirs, but to the heirs is reserved the right to admeasure the dower again when they reach full age, upon allegation that the guardian acted collusively. Roberts' Digest, 187.

§ 998. *Dower barred by elopement and adultery.*

If a wife willingly leave her husband, and go away and continue with her avouterer, she shall be barred forever of action to demand her dower that she ought to have of her husband's lands, if she be convict thereupon, except that her husband willingly, and without coercion of the church, reconcile her, and suffer her to dwell with him ; in which case she shall be restored to action. (13 Edw. I., stat. I., ch. XXXIV. (1285), Roberts' Dig. (2d. ed.), 188.)

§ 999. *Widow may bequeath emblements of dower land.*

Widows may bequeath the crop of their ground, as well as their dowers, as of other lands and tenements, saving to the lords of the fee, all such services as be due for their dowers and other tenements. (20 Henry III., ch. II. (1235), Roberts' Digest (2d. ed.), 208.)

§ 1000. *Execution shall not be stayed.* By Statute 16 and 17 Chas. II., ch. VIII. (1664), it is provided that in writs of error brought after verdict in actions of dower or ejectment, execution shall not be stayed unless plaintiff in error be bound that if judgment be affirmed, or the writ of error be non-suit, or discontinued for default, he will pay to the demandant the costs and damages awarded him by the verdict. Roberts' Dig., 40.

§ 1001. **Pennsylvania Statutes.** *Widow's portion.*

The real and personal estate of a decedent, whether male or female, remaining after payment of all just debts and legal charges, which shall not have been sold or disposed of by will, or otherwise limited by marriage settlement, shall be divided and enjoined (enjoyed) as follows, viz. :

I. Where such intestate shall leave a widow and issue, the widow shall be entitled to one-third part of the real estate for the term of her life, and to one-third part of the personal estate absolutely.

II. Where such intestate shall leave a widow and collateral heirs, or other kindred but no issue, the widow shall be entitled to one-half part of the real estate, including the mansion-house and buildings appurtenant thereto, for the term of her life, and to one-half part of the personal estate absolutely. (Act 8 April, 1833, section 1 ; P. L., 315.)

§ 1002. *Upon failure of heirs* or kindred competent to take, the real estate of the intestate shall vest in his widow. Section 10, *Id.*

§ 1003. *To be in lieu of dower.*

The shares of the estate directed by this Act to be allotted to the widow, shall be in lieu and full satisfaction of her dower at common law. (*Id.*, section 15.)

§ 1004. *Bequest or devise to be in lieu of dower.*

A devise or bequest by a husband to his wife of any portion of his estate or property shall be deemed and taken to be in lieu and bar of her dower in the estate of such testator, in like manner as if it were so expressed in the will, unless such testator shall in his will declare otherwise : *Provided,* That nothing herein contained shall deprive the widow of her choice either of dower or of the estate or property so devised or bequeathed. (Act 8 April, 1833, section 11 ; P. L., 319.)

§ 1005. *Widow not taking under the will to have her share of personalty.*

The eleventh section of the Act of 8 April, 1833, entitled " An Act relating to last wills and testaments," shall not be construed to deprive the widow of the testator, in case she elects not to take under the last will and testament of her husband, of her share of the personal estate of her husband under the intestate laws of this Commonwealth, but that the said widow may take her choice, either of the bequest or devise made to her under any last will or testament, or of her share of the personal estate under the intestate laws aforesaid. (Act 11 April, 1848, section 11 ; P. L., 537.)

§ 1006. *Widow not taking under will to have interest in realty as if her husband had died intestate.*

In case any person has died, or shall hereafter die, leaving a widow and last will and testament, and such widow shall elect not to take under the will, in lieu of dower at the common law, as heretofore, she shall be entitled to such interest in the real estate of her deceased husband as the widows of decedents dying intestate are entitled to under the existing laws of this Commonwealth. (Act 20 April, 1869, section 1 ; P. L., 77.)

§ 1007. *Jurisdiction of Orphans' Court.*

The Orphans' Court of the several counties of this Commonwealth, in which the real estate of such decedent is situated, shall have power, on the application of the widow or anyone interested, to award an inquest to make partition of the same, and to decree the allotments thereof made, or in case of refusal to accept to order a sale thereof and secure the interest of the widow and all others interested, in the same manner and with like force and effect as is now provided by law in the partition of the real estate of persons dying intestate. (*Id.*, section 2.)

§ 1008. *The widow may be cited to make election.*

In every case of a devise or bequest to a widow, which, by force of any last will and testament, or by operation of law, will bar such widow of dower, subject to her right of election of dower, or of the property devised or bequeathed, it shall be lawful for the Orphans' Court, on the application of any person interested in the estate of the decedent, to issue a citation at any time after twelve months from the death of the testator, to any such widow, to appear at a certain time, not less than one month thereafter, in the said court, to make her election either to accept such devise or bequest in lieu of dower, or to waive such devise or bequest, and to take her dower of which election a record shall be made, which shall be conclusive on all parties. If the widow shall neglect or refuse to appear upon such citation, then upon due proof to the court of the service thereof, the said neglect or refusal shall be deemed an acceptance of the devise or bequest, and a bar of dower of which a record shall be made, which shall be conclusive on all parties concerned. (Act 29 March, 1832, section 35 ; P: L., 200.)

§ 1009. *How dower to be secured upon partition.*

Should the widow of the decedent be living at the time of the partition she shall not be entitled to payment of the sum at which her purpart or share of the estate shall be valued, but the same, together with interest thereof, shall be and remain charged upon the premises, if the whole be taken by one child or other descendant' of the deceased, or upon the respective shares, if divided as hereinbefore mentioned, and the legal interest thereof shall be annually and regularly paid by the persons to whom such real estate shall be adjudged, their heirs or assigns, holding the same, according to their respective portions, to the said widow during her natural life, in lieu and full satisfaction of her dower at common law, and the same may be recovered by the widow by distress or otherwise, as rents in this Commonwealth are recoverable. On the death of the widow, the said principal sum shall be paid by the children, or other lineal descendants to whom the said real estate shall have been adjudged, their heirs or assigns, holding the premises to the persons thereunto legally entitled. (*Id.*, section 41 ; P. L., 202.)

§ 1010. *In case the property be sold.* By section 43 it is provided that in case the property be sold, the widow's share of the purchase-money shall remain in the hands of the purchaser during her natural life, the interest to be payable to her regularly and annually, and to be recoverable by distress or otherwise, as rents are recoverable, this to be accepted in satisfaction of dower. Upon the death of the widow, the principal sum so retained is to be paid to those legally entitled thereto.

§ 1011. *If the land consist of several parcels,* the court is given authority, by Act of 7 January, 1867, section 1 (P. L., 1367), to charge the widow's share upon one or more of the tracts, the remaining tracts to be discharged, provided that the tract or tracts upon which her share is charged shall, in the opinion of the court, be fully sufficient to secure payment of principal and interest, and provided that the widow and those entitled at her death shall have the same remedies as they had previously to the passage of this law.

§ 1012. *In York and Fayette Counties.* By Act of 13 February, 1867, section 1 (P. L., 160), the Orphans' Courts of York and Fayette Counties are empowered to appoint commissioners or to award an inquest to make partition or valuation of the widow's dower, and to make the necessary decree therein, upon application of the widow, or of her personal representatives after her death.

§ 1013. *Dower of the widow of an intestate co-tenant.* The Act of 24 April, 1843, section 8 (P. L., 360), makes provision and regulates the practice for securing her dower to the widow of one seized of land as co-tenant or in common with others, she being entitled under the intestate law.

§ 1014. *Jurisdiction where lands lie in several counties.*

All the courts of this Commonwealth now having jurisdiction in matters of partition shall have power to entertain suits and proceedings, whether at law or in equity or otherwise, for the partition of real estate, or the recovery of dower or the widow's third or other part, although the lands to be divided or recovered may lie in one or more counties of this Commonwealth. *Provided,* That such proceeding intended to embrace lands in more than one county shall be brought only in the county where a decedent, whose land is to be divided, had his domicile, or where the homestead, or larger part of the estate in value, shall be situated; and service of process may be made by any sheriff, where real estate to be divided shall be situated, or any defendant may be found; and exemplifications of the record may be filed in every county where such real estate may be situated, in such court thereof as shall correspond in character to that of the court in which such proceeding may have taken place, and be received in evidence with the like effect as the records of the court where filed; except that any exemplification of the proceedings in the Supreme Court shall be filed in the District Court, or Court of Common Pleas of the proper county. (Act 20 February, 1854, section 1; P. L., 89.)

§ 1015. *Equitable jurisdiction in Philadelphia.*

The Court of Common Pleas of Philadelphia County shall have all the power and jurisdiction of a court of equity in all cases of dower and partition within the city and county of Philadelphia. (Act 17 March, 1845, section 3; P.'L., 160.)

§ 1016. *Exemption.*

The widow or the children of any decedent dying within this Commonwealth, testate or intestate, may retain either real or personal property belonging to said estate to the value of three hundred dollars, and the same shall not be sold, but suffered to remain for the use of the widow and family, and it shall be the duty of the executor or administrator of such decedent to have the said property appraised in the same manner as is provided in the Act passed the ninth day of April, in the year 1849, entitled " An Act to exempt property to the value of three hundred dollars from levy and sale on execution and distress for rent." *Provided*, That this section shall not affect or impair any liens for the purchase-money of such real estate. And the said appraisement, upon being signed and certified by the appraisers and approved by the Orphans' Court, shall be filed among the records thereof. (Act 14 April, 1851, section 5; P. L., 613.)

By Act of 8 April, 1859, section 1 (P. L., 425), it is provided that the above exemption may be retained out of any bank-notes, money, stocks, judgments, or other indebtedness to the decedent, to be appraised and set apart by the appraisers of the other personal estate.

Act of 27 November, 1865, section 1 (P. L., 1227), provided that real estate may be retained. If the same consist of a single tenement or messuage, and cannot be divided, and the appraisers may have valued it at not more than six hundred dollars, it shall be set apart for the use of the widow or children, conditioned that the person to whom it shall be set apart shall pay the excess of the valuation over three hundred dollars, within one year from the date of confirmation. Provided that if the real estate be refused by the widow and children at the appraisement, the court, on application, may grant an order to sell the same.

By section 2 of this Act it is provided that the real estate, if taken by the widow or children, shall vest absolutely upon payment of the surplus to those entitled. If it be not taken at the appraisement, but be sold, the sum of three hundred dollars of the purchase-money shall be paid to the widow or children entitled thereto, and the balance, after payment of costs and expenses, shall be distributed.

§ 1017. *Action not to abate.*

No action of dower *unde nihil habet* hereafter brought or now pending and undetermined in the courts of this Commonwealth shall abate by reason of the death of the plaintiff therein ; but the same may be prosecuted by the executors or administrators of said plaintiff, who shall be substituted as plaintiffs therein on the record, or suggestion of the death of the plaintiff, to recover the annual value of the said plaintiff's estate in dower, or the rents, issues, and profits thereof from the time of the decease of the husband until the date of the death of the original plaintiff in such action. (Act 14 March, 1865, section 1 ; P. L., 345.)

§ 1018. *Wife of Lunatic may release dower.*

In all cases where deeds conveying titles to real estate, situated within this Commonwealth, have been or shall hereafter be executed by a committee in lunacy, under an order of any court having jurisdiction of the same, it shall be competent for the wife of such lunatic to release or divest her dower right or claim in the nature thereof in such real estate, in the same manner as if she were a widow and not under coverture : *Provided,* That such release shall have been executed prior to a decree declaring that such lunatic had been restored to his reason or sanity. (Act 28 March, 1879, section 1 ; P. L., 13.)

§ 1019. *Equitable Jurisdiction.*

The several Courts of Common Pleas of this Commonwealth shall each have all the power and jurisdiction of a court of equity in all cases of dower and partition, within their respective counties. (Act 7 July, 1885, section 1 ; P. L., 257.)

§ 1020. **Process in real actions.** The Act of 13 June, 1836, sections 79–88, relative to institution, process, and proceedings in real actions generally, is adverted to in the chapter upon Partition in this book. The provisions of those sections will, therefore, not be inserted here.

§ 1021. **Dower at common law.** At common law, the widow's right of dower is an estate for life, to be assigned her in severalty in one-third part of the lands and tenements in which her husband was seized during coverture of an estate of inheritance that might have descended to issue of the widow. Litt., sections 36, 53 ; 2 Bl. Comm., 129, 131.

A widow is not entitled at common law to dower in an estate of remainder vested in her husband and aliened by him during coverture. *Shoemaker* v. *Walker*, 2 S. & R., 554 (1814). Nor where he has a bare equitable title in land so aliened. *Pritts* v. *Richey*, 29 Pa. St., 71 (1857).

A release of "dower at common law" will bar a claim to dower in land aliened by the husband alone during coverture. *Gray* v. *McCune*, 23 Pa. St., 447 (1854).

§ 1022. **At common law, the widow does not share in personalty.** The Act of 8 April, 1833, section 11 (*supra*, section 1004), is construed to vest in a widow declining to take, under her husband's will, the right of dower only at common law. She is excluded thereunder from participation in his personal estate. *Hinnershitz* v. *Bernhard*, 13 Pa. St., 518 (1850). The subsequent Act (11 April, 1848, section 11 ; *supra*, section 1005), entitling her to her share in the personalty, is not applicable where the husband died before its passage. *Id.* See also Act of 20 April, 1869, section 1, P. L., 77 (*supra*, section 1006), substituting her share in the realty under the intestate law for the common law dower theretofore recoverable by a widow not taking under the will.

§ 1023. **Not divested.** Neither sale upon execution against the husband, nor common recovery suffered by him alone, served to divest the wife's dower in a fee tail at common law. *Sharp* v. *Petit*, 1 Yeates, 389 (1794).

§ 1024. **Statutory dower.** The nature and attributes of dower in Pennsylvania have been considerably modified by our statutes. See *supra*. The widow no longer has a right to several possession of the land out of which her dower is secured. Her share in her husband's estate includes a proportion of his personalty. The dower interest varies from a third to a half in quantity, and neither the seisin of the husband nor possibility of inheritance by issue of the widow, in the strict sense of the common law, is a prerequisite of her claim. "Her interest in his lands is in no respect like dower at common law, except that it is only for life." *Gourley* v. *Kinley*, 66 Pa. St., 274 (1870). The right of statutory dower does not extend to land aliened by the husband in his lifetime. The widow's claim to dower therein is at common law. *Borland* v. *Nichols*, 12 Pa. St., 38 (1849). After a sale of an intestate's land in partition in the Orphans' Court, the widow's interest charged upon it is not properly "dower," but is a money charge upon the land. *Vensel's Appeal*, 77 Pa. St., 71 (1874). It is a lien, though not expressly charged on the premises. *Kline* v. *Bowman*, 19 Pa. St., 24 (1852).

§ 1025. **Dower is an estate in the land.** In *Kurtz's Appeal*, 26 Pa. St., 465 (1856), it is held that purchase-money charged upon land to secure dower is a lien, and that a mortgage subsequent to it will therefore be discharged by a judicial sale of the land. But in later cases this doctrine is repudiated, and dower by statute or at common law is recognized to be an interest or estate in the land, and not a mere lien upon it. As such it cannot be discharged by a sheriff's sale. *Ziegler's Appeal*, 35 Pa. St., 173 (1860); *Schall's Appeal*, 40 Pa. St., 170 (1861); *Gourley* v. *Kinley*, 66 Pa. St., 270 (1870); *Diefenderfer* v. *Eshleman*, 113 Pa. St., 305 (1886). In the last-cited case it was held that dower is not discharged by a sale of the land in partition by decree omitting to direct that it shall be secured, in spite of the widow's acceptance of service of a rule to show cause why the land should not be sold. In *Gourley* v. *Kinley* (*supra*), the preceding cases upon this subject are reviewed, and their conflicting doctrines noticed. In *Watterson's Appeal*, 95 Pa. St., 312 (1880), statutory dower is declared to be an estate of freehold in the land vesting in the widow at the instant of her husband's death.

§ 1026. **Widow is a purchaser.** The widow's dower right, either by statute or at common law, is an estate of purchase, and as such is paramount to the title of the heirs. *Bradfords* v. *Kent*, 43 Pa. St., 474 (1862).

General legacies must therefore abate to make up a deficiency caused by a widow's election not to take under the will. *Bard's Estate*, 58 Pa. St., 393 (1868); *Heineman's Appeal*, 92 Pa. St., 95 (1879).

An annuity in lieu of dower is chargeable on the residuary real estate in case of a deficiency of personal assets. If it be charged upon a redeemable ground-rent, which is afterward paid, the annuity should be secured upon the proceeds in the hands of the heirs or devisees. *Conrad's Appeal*, 33 Pa. St., 47 (1859).

§ 1027. **Widow's interest subject to seizure for her debt.** In *Thomas* v. *Simpson*, 3 Pa. St., 60 (1846), it is held that the interest of a widow in her husband's land, either by devise or intestacy, is an estate which is subject to levy and sale under proceedings against her.

It passes to the widow's assignee in bankruptcy, and it cannot be divested as against creditors by her parol declarations without consideration. *Watterson's Appeal*, 95 Pa. St., 312 (1880).

§ 1028. **Subject to lien of decedent's debts.** She is dowable only of what remains after payment of the decedent's debts, whether of record or not. *Directors of the Poor* v. *Royer*, 43 Pa. St., 146 (1862).

§ 1029. **Dower apportionable as to time.** Dower or annuity in lieu thereof is apportionable, and runs to the last day of the widow's life. *Blight* v. *Blight*, 51 Pa. St., 420 (1866).

§ 1030. **Cannot be compelled to apportion.** If the land be amicably apportioned among the heirs, and the widow afterward proceed against the vendee of a tract from one of them, she is entitled to her share of the value of rents and profits thereof, without regard to the valuation of the other land of which her husband died seized. *Heller's Appeal*, 116 Pa. St., 534 (1887).

§ 1031. **Dower does not merge.** In *Fink's Appeal*, 130 Pa. St., 256 (1889), the fee simple of land in which a widow was entitled to dower vested in her, subject to an intermediate dower in the widow of her son. *Held*, that the right of the former as widow was paramount, and that it did not merge in her fee simple; that therefore she was entitled to possession in her character as fee tenant, subject during her lifetime to dower right in the son's widow upon the proportion of the valuation not covered by her own dower.

§ 1032. **Not a rent charge.** A widow's interest charged upon land is not a rent charge, though perhaps in the nature of one. A release by her of part of the land is therefore not a release of all. *Reigert* v. *Ellmaker*, 14 S. & R., 121 (1826); *Jones' Appeal*, 41 Leg. Int., 314 (1884). See *Shaupe* v. *Shaupe*, 12 S. & R., 9 (1824); *McFarland's Estate*, 28 P. L. J., 49 (1880).

§ 1033. **Possession of the husband not requisite.** The widow of one owning a vested remainder of freehold limited after a life-estate is entitled to dower upon the death of the husband, while the life-estate is still unexpired. Legal seisin in the husband is not essential to our statutory right of dower. *Cote's Appeal*, 79 Pa. St., 235 (1875); *Starr's Estate*, 40 Leg. Int., 5 (1882); *Lynch* v. *Lynch*, 25 W. N., 424 (1890); *Bloodgood's Estate*, 47 Leg. Int., 298 (1890).

In *Cote's Appeal* it was pointed out that *Shoemaker* v. *Walker* (*supra*, section 1021) dealt with an expectancy which the husband had aliened. The action, therefore, being for common law dower, want of seisin in the husband was a fatal impediment.

§ 1034. **Does not embrace personalty.** The word "dower" does not include the widow's right in the personal estate of her deceased husband. *Ellmaker* v. *Ellmaker*, 4 Watts, 89 (1835).

§ 1035. **Of what a widow is dowable.** At an early date it was decided that a widow was not entitled to dower in land held by her husband under a warrant, and aliened by him during coverture; such holding being then (1755) regarded as a mere chattel interest. *Dodson* v. *Davis*, 2 Yeates, 168 (1796). But it was held in 1799 that the widow was dowable of land held by improvement right alone. *Kelly* v. *Mahan*, *Id.*, 515.

Property transferred to a man by one *bona fide* believing herself to be his wife is not subject after his death to dower in favor of his real widow. *Heslop* v. *Heslop*, 82 Pa. St., 587 (1876).

Husband's right to dispose of personalty absolute as to wife. While alive, though upon his death-bed, one can dispose of his property as he pleases, even if the result is to deprive the wife of her dower. *Perry* v. *Perry* (C. P. Lackawanna Co.), 3 Common Pleas Reports, 163 (1886).

Where the decedent had assigned securities to himself as trustee on the books of the corporation with which the securities were deposited and registered, and enclosed the securities in an envelope on which he had indorsed that they belonged to him as trustee for his children *eo nomine*, purchased with funds set apart from time to time for their benefit, in which condition they remain till his death ; *held*, that, without actual delivery, this amounted to a gift *inter vivos*, and constituted a valid trust for the children, and that the securities were not part of the decedent's estate which his widow could elect to share under the intestate laws. *Dickerson's Estate*, 43 Leg. Int., 76 (1886).

Where a husband gave his bond for $3500 to his children, payable in five years, and died before that time had expired ; *held*, that the gift was good against the widow. *Schwartz's Estate*, 42 Leg. Int., 16 (1885).

The power of the husband over his personal property by gift *inter vivos* is absolute. *Pringle* v. *Pringle*, 59 Pa. St., 281 (1868). A man's wife and children have no legal right to any part of his goods, and no fraud can be predicated of any act of his to deprive them of the succession.

Ellmaker v. *Ellmaker*, 4 Watts, 89 (1835). A release of dower will not exclude a widow from a share in the personalty. GIBSON, C. J.: "Who so ignorant as not to know that a husband may dispose of his chattels during the coverture, without his wife's consent, and freed of every post-mortem claim by her?"

§ 1036. Language of the Act of April 8, 1833, is general. The language of the statute is general, and extends to all of the real and personal estate of a decedent "remaining after payment of all just debts and legal charges, which shall not have been sold or disposed of by will, or otherwise limited by marriage settlement." (*Supra*, section 1002.)

§ 1037. Partial intestacy. If the husband die intestate as to part of his estate, the widow is entitled to her share in such part, in addition to what is left her in the will. *Carman's Appeal*, 2 Penny., 332 (1882).

§ 1038. Entitled to dower in an estate in fee determinable by

executory devise. Land was devised to A. and B. equally in fee-simple, with survivorship upon the death of either without issue; A. having died without issue, it was held that his widow was entitled to dower in his part of the land. *Evans* v. *Evans*, 9 Pa. St., 190 (1848). So of a similar devise, construed to be a fee-tail with vested remainders over. *Smith's Appeal*, 23 Pa. St., 9 (1854).

A devise in fee, terminable at the death of the tenant without issue, is subject to dower in favor of his widow. *Lovett* v. *Lovett*, 10 Phila., 537 (1875).

§ 1039. In equitable estates. A widow is dowable in an estate held in trust for her husband, *Shoemaker* v. *Walker*, 2 S. & R., 554 (1814); and in an equity of redemption, *Reed* v. *Morrison*, 12 S. & R., 18 (1824); and in an estate, the legal title of which is in another under agreement to convey to the husband, *Evans* v. *Evans*, 29 Pa. St., 277 (1857). But the execution of a deed and delivery to the grantor's agent, with instructions to deliver it to the grantee upon payment of the purchase-money, followed by delivery to the alienee of the grantee after the death of the latter, upon payment of the consideration by the alienee, will not vest such title in the grantee as to give his widow a right of dower in the land. *Junk* v. *Canon*, 34 Pa. St., 286 (1859).

§ 1040. Jurisdiction. If the decedent die in possession, the legal action of dower will not lie. In such case jurisdiction is in the Orphans' Court exclusively. *Thomas* v. *Simpson*, 3 Pa. St., 60 (1846); *Taylor* v. *Birmingham*, 29 Pa. St., 306 (1857); *Mussleman's Appeal*, 65 Pa. St., 480 (1870); *Gourley* v. *Kinley*, 66 Pa. St., 270 (1870); *Tatham* v. *Ramey*, 82 Pa. St., 130 (1876).

The action at law lies if the land be in possession of another claiming adversely, or of one not amenable to Orphans' Court process. *Galbraith* v. *Green*, 13 S. & R., 85 (1824); *Evans* v. *Evans*, 29 Pa. St., 277 (1857); *Gourley* v. *Kinley* (*supra*).

Statutory dower may be recovered in the common-law action. *Evans* v. *Evans*, 29 Pa. St., 277 (1857).

§ 1041. Widow taking against husband's will. A widow electing not to take under her husband's will was formerly held entitled to dower at common law, and therefore she could not recover the same in the Orphans' Court, but was remitted to her legal action. *Bradfords* v. *Kent*, 43 Pa. St., 474 (1862); *Shaffer* v. *Shaffer*, 50 Pa. St., 394 (1865). But by Act of 20 April, 1869 (P. L., 77), *supra*, the Orphans' Courts are given jurisdiction in such cases, and this Act has been held to oust the jurisdiction of the courts of law. *Robin's Appeal*, 1 W. N., 238 (1875); *Lippincott's Estate*, 7 Phila., 504 (1870). The statute expressly enacts that a widow refusing to take under the will "in lieu of dower at common law as heretofore, shall be entitled to such interest in the real estate of her deceased husband as the widows of decedents dying intestate are entitled to under the existing laws of this Commonwealth."

§ 1042. **Widow of tenant in common.** The widow of one seized of land in common with others, independently of statute, is remitted to her action at law. *Brown* v. *Adams*, 2 Whart., 188 (1836); *Evans* v. *Evans*, 9 Pa. St., 190 (1848); *Evans* v. *Evans*, 1 Phila., 113 (1847). But the power in the premises is conferred upon the Orphans' Court in the cases therein provided by Acts of 24 April, 1843, section 8 (P. L., 360), and 13 March, 1847, section 1 (P. L., 319).

§ 1043. **Equitable jurisdiction.** By Act of 7 July, 1885 (P. L., 257, *supra*, section 1019), equitable power is vested in the Courts of Common Pleas "in all cases of dower and partition within their respective counties." Such jurisdiction had theretofore existed in Philadelphia. See Act 17 March, 1845, section 3 (P. L., 160; *supra*, section 1015).

The remarks upon the preferability of the equitable form of action in partition are equally applicable here.

The personal representative of a widow may maintain an action in equity for an account of rents and profits of her dower interest, though dower was not assigned nor proceedings instituted therefor in her lifetime; she having, however, filed in the Orphans' Court her election not to take under the will of her husband. *Paul* v. *Paul*, 36 Pa. St., 270 (1860).

The courts have jurisdiction in equity to award an annuity in lieu of dower, and to charge the same upon particular real estate. *Borland* v. *Murphy*, 4 W. N., 472 (1877); *Murphy* v. *Borland*, 92 Pa. St., 86 (1879). Under such award, the widow may distrain for arrears. *Id.*

The executor of an estate is not a proper party to the bill. *Drum* v. *Wartman*, 6 Phila., 45 (1865).

If the bill allege that defendant holds the land as trustee for plaintiff's former husband, upon denial of such trusteeship an account will not be decreed until plaintiff establish her right. *Heylin* v. *Ashton*, 7 Phila., 464 (1870).

In *Kelso's Appeal*, 102 Pa. St., 7 (1882), equitable jurisdiction was sustained in the case of a widow who filed her bill against the purchaser of her husband's land at the sale thereof by his assignee in bankruptcy.

Equity jurisdiction is upheld in the case of a widow electing to take against the will of her husband in *Merrill's Appeal,* 16 W. N., 491 (1885); *Heller's Appeal,* 116 Pa. St., 534 (1887).

As to the limits of equitable jurisdiction to decree statutory dower to a widow refusing to take under the will, see *McNickle* v. *Henry,* 28 Leg. Int., 44 (1871), and see also later cases cited above.

Equity has jurisdiction of a bill for the cancellation of a post-nuptial deed of settlement at the suit of a widow electing to take against her husband's will. *Campbell's Appeal,* 80 Pa. St., 298 (1876). If the widow first proceed in the Orphan's Court for distribution and the deed be set up by way of defense, the latter court will, however, take jurisdiction of the entire controversy. *Id.*

§ 1044. **Bar of Dower.—***Sale under Mortgage.* Dower is barred by a sheriff's sale of the land upon a mortgage executed in good faith by the husband alone. *Scott* v. *Croasdale,* 1 Yeates, 75 (1791); *Bryar's Appeal,* 111 Pa. St., 81 (1885).

Even if the mortgage be created by the husband after his wilful desertion of his wife. *Duquesne Saving Bank's Appeal,* 96 Pa. St., 298 (1880).

If the husband alien alone, and the title afterward return to him, subject to the wife's inchoate right of dower, such right will be divested by a sale under a mortgage subsequently executed by the husband. *Aull* v. *Bonnell,* 11 W. N., 376 (1882).

By Waiver. By waiver which may be inferred from the widow's conduct. *Deshler* v. *Beery,* 4 Dall., 300 (1804); *Reed* v. *Morrison,* 12 S. & R., 18 (1824).

§ 1045. *By lapse of time.* And by lapse of more than twenty-one years before making claim. *Allen* v. *Getz,* 2 P. & W., 310 (1831). See *infra,* section 1076.

§ 1046. *By a release. Gray* v. *McCune,* 23 Pa. St., 447 (1854).

§ 1047. *By sheriff's sale of husband's title after alienation.* By a sale of his title under a judgment against the husband, though he has previously aliened. *Directors of the Poor* v. *Royer,* 43 Pa. St., 146 (1862). In this case the husband conveyed the land by an absolute deed, the grantee, however, executing a defeasance thereto. The latter afterward conveyed to a third party; and the title of the husband was subsequently sold by the sheriff under execution against him, and was bought by such third party. After the death of the husband his widow brought an action of dower. *Held,* first, that the deed and defeasance constituting only a mortgage, the husband was still seised at the time of the sheriff's sale; but, second, if he be considered to have aliened, a sale of his title under execution against him, after such alienation, would bar his widow's dower.

In *Thomas* v. *Harris*, 43 Pa. St., 231 (1862), a decedent having contracted to sell land, and the vendee in turn agreeing to sell to C., a third party, upon application of the latter the court decreed the administrators of the decedent, one of whom was his widow, to complete the conveyance. They did so, passing their individual rights as well as those of the decedent. Afterward a judgment obtained against the decedent in his lifetime was revived against his administrators and at sheriff's sale his title was purchased by C. *Held*, that the widow was not entitled to dower in the land, both because she had conveyed her dower right by the terms of her deed, and because the sheriff's sale of decedent's title was a sufficient bar; reversing the earlier case of *Shurtz* v. *Thomas*, 8 Pa. St., 359 (1848), in which, under the same facts, the widow had been declared entitled to her dower.

§ 1048. *Sale under order of court.* By a sale of the land by the husband's assignee, for the benefit of creditors, under order of court, by virtue of the Act of 17 February, 1876 (P. L., 4). *Youngs* v. *Hannas*, 1 Pa. C. C. Rep., 579 (1886).

§ 1049. *Sheriff's sale of estate tail.* Sheriff's sale of an estate tail will bar the dower of the tenant's widow, though it will not pass the title of the heirs. *Eliott* v. *Pearsall*, 4 Clark, 157 (1846).

§ 1050. *Divorce.* By a decree of divorce, A V. M., though irregular; the wife having been the libellant, was held to be estopped from setting up such irregularity. *Miltimore* v. *Miltimore*, 40 Pa. St., 151 (1861).

§ 1051. *Deed of separation.* By provision in a deed of separation between husband and wife, founded upon consideration of property transferred to her use, in spite of occasional subsequent visits to the wife and of cohabitation between them in a single instance. *Hitner's Appeal*, 54 Pa. St., 110 (1867).

By contract of separation, whereby each for a valuable consideration, relinquished whatever marital rights either might have in the estate of the other. *Speidel's Appeal*, 107 Pa. St., 18 (1884). See *Ludwig's Appeal*, 101 Pa. St., 535 (1882).

§ 1052. *Mortgage will not merge in ownership to prevent dower being barred.* If the purchaser of land from an assignee in bankruptcy become the owner of a mortgage against it, given by the bankrupt, and procure the sale of the land under the mortgage, himself buying it at the sheriff's sale, the dower right of the bankrupt's widow is thereby divested. In such case the mortgage will not merge in the ownership of the land against the wish and intention of such purchaser. *Bryar's Appeal*, 111 Pa. St., 81 (1885).

§ 1053. *Arrears discharged by sheriff's sale.* A sheriff's sale of land, subject to a recognizance to secure the dower of a widow, discharges arrears already accrued, but not those afterward arising. *Luther* v. *Wagner*, 107 Pa. St., 343 (1884). See *Mentzer* v. *Menor*, 8 Watts, 296 (1839); *Reed* v. *Reed*, 1 W. & S., 235 (1841); *Dickinson* v. *Beyer*, 87 Pa. St., 274 (1878); *Davison's Appeal*, 95 Pa. St., 394 (1880).

§ 1054. *Ratification of infant's release.* By a release in a deed of antenuptial settlement executed by an infant, if it be ratified by her successor in estate after her death. *Whichcote* v. *Lyle*, 28 Pa. St., 73 (1857).

§ 1055. *Sale under testamentary power.* Dower is divested by sale of the land under a testamentary power for the payment of debts. *Mitchell* v. *Mitchell*, 8 Pa. St., 126 (1848).

§ 1056. *Widow's deed as administratrix.* By the widow's deed as administratrix of her husband, under his agreement to sell and order of court, conveying her own right, title, and estate in the land, as well as those of the decedent. *Thomas* v. *Harris*, 43 Pa. St., 231 (1862).

§ 1057. **Dower is not barred**—*Assignment for creditors.* By an assignment made individually by an insolvent debtor for the benefit of his creditors, either voluntary or compulsory. *Keller* v. *Michael*, 2 Yeates, 300 (1798); *Eberle* v. *Fisher*, 13 Pa. St., 526 (1850); *Helfrich* v. *Obermyer*, 15 Pa. St., 113 (1850); *Blackman's Estate*, 6 Phila., 160 (1866).

§ 1058. *Sale by assignee.* Nor by a sale made by his assignee in bankruptcy. *Worcester* v. *Clarke*, 2 Gr., 84 (1853); *Lazeor* v. *Porter*, 87 Pa. St., 513 (1878); *Kelso's Appeal*, 102 Pa. St., 7 (1882).

In the last-cited case the assignee in bankruptcy purported to sell the land " free of all liens and incumbrances," and on the day of sale the wife of the bankrupt disclaimed having any interest therein and promised to assert no claim of title, but it was held, in spite of these circumstances, that her dower was not barred by the sale.

§ 1059. *By the widow's taking her own property.* She is not barred of her dower by taking property belonging to herself which her husband had treated in his will as if it were his own, bequeathing it to her. *Watterson's Appeal*, 95 Pa. St., 312 (1880).

Only her own act of acceptance under the will, or her deed or writing as required by the Statute of Frauds, will divest her dower. *Id.*

§ 1060. *Vague declarations.* Vague declarations by the widow to an intending purchaser from an heir, as that she " wanted nothing " and " there would be no lawsuit," etc., will not work an estoppel which will bar her claim to dower. *Heller's Appeal*, 116 Pa. St., 534 (1887). See *Watterson's Appeal*, 95 Pa. St., 312 (1880).

§ 1061. *Arrears anterior to first lien not discharged by sheriff's sale.* A sheriff's sale of a tract under the second of several mortgages given by an heir of the decedent, or his vendee, will not divest arrears of dower accrued at the time of such sale, the land being sold subject to the first mortgage. *Heller's Appeal, supra; Schall's Appeal*, 40 Pa. St., 170 (1861); *Helfrich* v. *Weaver*, 61 Pa. St., 385 (1869). See *Vandever* v. *Baker*, 13 Pa. St., 121 (1850); *Bailey* v. *Comm.*, 41 Pa. St., 473 (1862); *Wertz's Appeal*, 65 Pa. St., 306 (1870).

§ 1062. *Judgment to secure dower not divested.* A purchaser of land subject to an annuity, in lieu of dower, gave to the widow and heirs a confessed judgment to secure the same, the lien of which was preserved by successive revivals. Dower interest being in arrear the land was sold under process upon the judgment. At the sheriff's sale notice was given that the land was sold subject to the widow's dower. Interest again being in arrear, upon *sci. fa.*, to revive the judgment against the sheriff's vendee; *held*, that the lien of the judgment was not discharged by the sheriff's sale. *Topson* v. *Sipe*, 116 Pa. St., 588 (1887).

§ 1063. *Accrued arrears not discharged by private sale.* Arrears of dower already accrued are not discharged by the private sale of the land, by the husband's assignee, for the benefit of creditors. *Alleman's Appeal*, 15 W. N., 213 (1884).

§ 1064. *Conveyance not properly acknowledged.* Dower is not barred by a conveyance of husband and wife not acknowledged in accordance with statutory requirements. *Kirk* v. *Dean*, 2 Binney, 341 (1810); *Thompson* v. *Morrow*, 5 S. & R., 289 (1819); *Barnet* v. *Barnet*, 15 Id., 72 (1826).

Nor by an agreement of separation in vague and uncertain terms (proven by parol) not sealed or separately acknowledged. *Walsh* v. *Kelly*, 34 Pa. St., 84 (1859).

§ 1065. *Infant's antenuptial release.* In *Shaw* v. *Boyd*, 5 S. & R., 309 (1819), it was decided that a bond executed by an infant engaging to release her dower does not bind her, although she received the consideration after her husband's death from his executors and her second husband used it. When she received the consideration she was still a minor.

GIBSON, J., said:

The fact of the feme having been an infant at the time of the marriage is altogether inoperative, for a jointure derives its efficacy as a bar, not from any supposed contract or assent of the feme, but by the positive provisions of the stat. 27 H. 8, C. 10, S. 6, which makes no distinction as to age. A jointure will, therefore, be available in the case of an infant wherever it would be so in the case of an adult.

An infant's release of dower by way of antenuptial settlement will not bar the claim unless it be properly ratified. *Whichcote* v. *Lyle*, 28 Pa. St., 73 (1856).

§ 1066. *Antenuptial contracts after engagements to marry require good faith. Kline* v. *Kline*, 57 Pa. St., 120 ; *Kline's Estate*, 64 *Id.*, 122 ; *Tiernan* v. *Binns*, 92 *Id.*, 248 ; *Bierer's Appeal, Id.*, 265 ; *Neely's Appeal*, 23 W. N., 336.

Where the provision for the wife is not so out of proportion to the husband's means as to raise a presumption of fraud or concealment, and there is no proof of fraud or concealment, the contract will be enforced, although no disclosure be made of the extent of the husband's estate. *Smith's Appeal*, 115 Pa. St., 319 (1887) ; approved in *Neely's Appeal*, 124 Pa. St., 426 (1889).

If the contract be merely a pretense executed for the purpose of quieting the husband's children, and with a promise to the intended wife that it shall be destroyed ; and if the husband after marriage obtain the contract for the purpose of destroying it and declare it to be null and void ; this may be equivalent to its actual destruction, though it be kept for years. Destruction of the contract by the husband will bind him, and if assented to by the wife after discoverture will conclude her also. *Gangwere's Estate*, 14 Pa. St., 417 (1850).

An antenuptial contract in which the intended wife relinquishes her " claim to all right of dower to, in, or out of the estate " of the husband, will not bar her right in the personalty left by him at his decease. *Ellmaker* v. *Ellmaker*, 4 Watts, 89 (1835).

If the woman be told that the husband has " a large property," and the antenuptial agreement be thereafter executed voluntarily and in good faith, the non-disclosure of the amount of property owned by him will not affect the validity of the contract, though such property be considerable, and though the consideration moving to the woman be but " one dollar and * * * a comfortable support during life, and at her death a decent Christian burial." *Ludwig's Appeal*, 101 Pa. St., 535 (1882); approved in *Neely's Appeal*, 124 Pa. St., 425 (1889).

It is now clearly established that an antenuptial release of dower does not require a consideration to support it. The marriage itself is a sufficient consideration. *Shea's Appeal*, 121 Pa. St., 302 (1888) ; *Tiernan* v. *Binns*, 92 Pa. St., 248 (1879).

Duress cannot be set up because of rudeness on the part of the man or because of mortification experienced by the bride. In *De La Cuesta v. Ins. Co.*, 136 Pa. St., 78 (1890), PAXSON, C. J., said : "In *Neely's Appeal*, 124 Pa. 406, there was an attempt to set aside an antenuptial contract on the ground of duress. After the marriage-day had been fixed, the guests invited and the caterer engaged, the husband produced an antenuptial contract which he required his intended wife to sign. She protested by her tears ; his reply was, 'No contract, no wedding.' We held there was no duress." A party to the contract is not a competent witness after death of the other party. Per WADDELL, J. *Neely's Appeal*, 124 Pa. St., 411 (1889). The widow's petition in the case last cited, in addition to the matters above quoted, charged that the husband " at no time gave her any information as to the value or character of his estate, nor had she any knowledge on the subject * * * that she was greatly disconcerted and distressed, was unable to read the deed understandingly and to realize its full import and effect " (408). The proof was that after signing she became distressed and was frequently found in tears. The change was so marked as to attract the attention of her dressmaker and housekeeper. The court below rejected the testimony of the wife's trustee as incompetent—the husband being deceased—and dismissed the petition. The Supreme Court affirmed, but did not pass upon the question of the competency of the witness.

An intended wife in consideration of an antenuptial agreement released her interest in her husband's estate. It was held that in order to avoid the contract she must show by two witnesses or the equivalent that a fraud was practised upon her in the execution of the paper. *Kesler's Estate*, 29 W. N., 15 (1891).

A wife left her husband and brought suit to cancel her release of dower, alleging fraud. The husband agreed that if she would return and would withdraw the suit he would give her one-third of the estate. She did return and did abandon the suit. After his death she claimed her one-third. *Held* (reversing the court below), that she had no valid cause of action to abandon ; and that an agreement to allow her one-third if she would return was void because she was bound to live with him. (*Ibid.*)

§ 1067. *Post-nuptial release improperly executed.* A post-nuptial release executed during coverture and not joined in by the husband is no bar to the wife's dower. *Ulp v. Campbell*, 19 Pa. St., 361 (1852) ; *Kreiser's Appeal*, 69 Pa. St., 194 (1871) ; *Campbell's Appeal*, 80 Pa. St., 298 (1876).

A post-nuptial settlement which is without definite consideration or is much to the disadvantage of the wife, will be set aside upon slight evidence of fraud, coercion, or concealment on the part of the husband. *Campbell's Appeal, supra.*

§ 1068. *Fraudulent mortgage.* By a mortgage fraudulently given and knowingly accepted for the purpose of defeating dower. *Killinger* v. *Reidenhauer,* 6 S. & R., 531 (1821). In such case, however, the wife's remedy is strictly equitable. At law dower is discharged by a sale under the mortgage. If the title be transferred to an innocent third party for value, he will, it seems, hold free from the dower. *McClurg* v. *Schwartz,* 87 Pa. St., 521 (1878).

§ 1069. *Administrator's deed under order of court.* By deed of decedent's administrator under order of court in fulfillment of his agreement to sell. *Riddlesberger* v. *Mentzer,* 7 Watts, 141 (1838); *Covert* v. *Hertzog,* 4 Pa. St., 145 (1846).

§ 1070. *Dower at common law not barred by acceptance of devise or share under intestate laws.* The acceptance of her share under the intestate law will not bar a widow's claim to dower in land aliened by the husband alone during the coverture. *Lineaweaver* v. *Stoever,* 1 W. & S., 160 (1841). Nor will the acceptance of a devise under his will, though he have conveyed with general warranty. *Borland* v. *Nichols,* 12 Pa. St., 38 (1849).

§ 1071. *Adultery after husband's desertion.* By a decree of divorce obtained by the husband in a foreign court having no jurisdiction, though the wife commit adultery and declared herself married to another man after the husband's desertion of her. *Reel* v. *Elder,* 62 Pa. St., 308 (1869). By a wife's omission to follow her husband who has deserted her and by her subsequent adultery. *Heslop* v. *Heslop,* 82 Pa. St., 537 (1876).

§ 1072. *Desertion by the wife.* By a wife's unjustified desertion of her husband; though her claim to the exemption of $300 allowed by law is thereby barred. *Nye's Appeal,* 126 Pa. St., 341 (1889).

§ 1073. *By judicial sale.* It has been seen that the right of dower is an estate which is not divested by judicial sale of the land except for the debt of the husband or his predecessor in title.

§ 1074. *Election.* At common law a bequest or devise to a wife was held to be cumulative, and not a bar to her claim of dower; she could take both. *Kennedy* v. *Nedrow,* 1 Dall., 415 (1789). See, however, the Act of 8 April, 1833 (*supra,* section 1004), replacing earlier legislation.

But if the devise were absolutely inconsistent with her right of dower, she was limited to one claim, and in such case was put to her election. *Duncan* v. *Duncan,* 2 Yeates, 302 (1798). A devise of lands during widowhood was held a bar to dower, if the

widow elected to take under the will. *Hamilton* v. *Buckwalter,
Id.*, 389 (1798).

§ 1075. *Proof of election.* The burden of proof is with him who
alleges an election upon the part of the widow to take under the
will. *Cox* v. *Rogers* (*infra*).

But if the widow impeach for fraud, a release of dower duly
executed by her several months after her husband's death for a
consideration, and in settlement of contested rights, with full
knowledge of the facts, the burden of proof is upon her.   Mere
inadequacy of consideration under such circumstances does not constitute fraud. *Bierer's Appeal*, 92 Pa. St., 265 (1879).

§ 1076. *Election in pais.* The election may be indicated by acts
in pais, as by acceptance of legacies bequeathed, and agreement inconsistent with the widow's declared intention to take her dower,
Cauffman v. *Cauffman*, 17 S. & R., 16 (1827) ; or by acceptance
of a legacy, and great lapse of time, *Allen* v. *Getz*, 2 P. & W., 310
(1831) ; *Bradfords* v. *Kent*, 43 Pa. St., 474 (1862) ; *Heron* v.
Hoffer, 3 Rawle, 393 (1832) ; *Cox* v. *Rogers*, 77 Pa. St., 160
(1874).   The election need not be filed in the Orphans' Court,
under provision of the Act of Assembly (*supra*, section 1008).
Light v. *Light*, 21 Pa. St., 407 (1853).

§ 1077. *Knowledge of material facts.* And it will be binding
if she knew the material facts and circumstances at the time, though
she was not apprised of her legal rights, in the absence of imposition or unfair advantage, and the choice not being grossly disad-
vantageous to her. *Light* v. *Light* (*supra*).

§ 1078. *Must be clearly indicated.* But an election *in pais* to
take under the will alleged against a widow must be proven by
clear and positive testimony, showing plain and unequivocal acts
of renunciation on her part, under a full knowledge of all the circumstances, and of her rights. See *Light* v. *Light* (*supra*), to the
contrary.   If she make her election without such knowledge, she is
not bound thereby. *Anderson's Appeal*, 36 Pa. St., 476 (1860) ;
Dickinson v. *Dickinson*, 61 Pa. St., 401 (1869) ; *Cox* v. *Rogers*, 77
Pa. St., 160 (1874) ; *Toomey's Appeal*, 2 W. N., 682 (1876) ;
Rhode's Estate, Id., 188 (1875) ; *Bierer's Appeal*, 92 Pa. St., 265
(1879) ; *Elbert* v. *O'Neil*, 102 Pa. St., 303 (1883).   Taking possession of her own property which her husband had bequeathed her,
as if it belonged to him, does not constitute a widow's election
to take under the will. *Watterson's Appeal*, 95 Pa. St., 312
(1880).

§ 1079. *Estoppel.* Acceptance and use for four years, with a
knowledge of her rights, of property bequeathed a widow, will

create an election by way of estoppel. *Norris' Estate*, 27 P. L. J., 234 (1875).

§ 1080. *Election will not cause intestacy as to property devised to the widow.* A widow's election not to take under the will does not cause intestacy as to a share devised her for life, the executors being directed to sell the real estate.

Sullivan v. *Keiffer*, 122 Pa. St., 135 (1888). In this case the testator devised a portion of his real estate to his widow for life, with remainder over. He directed his executor to convert his estate into money. The widow refused to take under the will. The executor sold the real estate as directed. After the death of the widow the remainder-man, who was testator's heir at law, brought suit against the purchaser of the land for the principal sum charged as dower upon it. *Held*, that the statutory dower accepted by the widow ceased at her death, and her election did not work an intestacy in regard thereto or to the portion devised to her in the will, and that the executor's deed passed a fee-simple to the purchaser, subject only to the widow's dower during her lifetime, no charge remaining upon the land after her decease.

§ 1081. *Bound by election.* Having elected and taken under the will, a widow may not remit herself to her dower rights by her subsequent voluntary breach of the condition of her devise, as by her marriage if she hold during widowhood. *Taylor* v. *Birmingham*, 29 Pa. St., 306 (1857).

§ 1082. *Election not to take under the will is a demand for dower rights.* An election not to take under the will, duly filed in the Orphans' Court, is a sufficient demand of her dower rights to enable her executor after her death to proceed in equity for an account of rents and profits. *Paul* v. *Paul*, 36 Pa. St., 270 (1860).

§ 1083. *Notice to Executors.* Written notice given to the husband's executor three months after his death will have the like effect. *Greiner's Appeal*, 103 Pa. St., 89 (1883). The widow's rights vest at once by virtue of such election. *Id.*

§ 1084. **Marshalling.** A devisee or legatee disappointed by the widow's election to take her dower is entitled to have the assets of the estate marshalled for his benefit. *Gallagher's Appeal*, 87 Pa. St., 200 (1878); *Young's Appeal*, 108 Pa. St., 17 (1884).

§ 1085. **Abatement.** If there be not sufficient, after the widow's election, to pay legacies, they must abate. *Heineman's Appeal*, 92 Pa. St., 95 (1879); *Bard's Estate*, 58 Pa. St., 393 (1868). But the bequests under the will to the widow will be sequestered for the benefit of those whose legacies are so diminished. *Id.; Young's Appeal (supra)*; see *Stewart's Appeal*, 110 Pa. St., 410 (1885).

§ 1086. *Right to elect is personal.* The committee of a lunatic widow may not, without the court's sanction, elect not to take under the will. The discretion should be judiciously exercised by the court in view of the circumstances. In the absence of election, the law leans toward the will. *Kennedy* v. *Johnson,* 65 Pa. St., 451 (1870). The right to elect is purely personal. After the widow's death without having exercised it, her representatives cannot make the election. *Crozier's Appeal,* 90 Pa. St., 384 (1879).

§ 1087. *Cannot elect during coverture.* The wife's written assent to the terms of the will at the time of its making, sealed and executed by her, and duly witnessed, being an election during coverture, is void as against her in law and in equity. She is not bound thereby. *Kreiser's Appeal,* 69 Pa. St., 194 (1871). She cannot elect during coverture. *Campbell's Appeal,* 80 Pa. St., 298 (1876).

§ 1088. *May elect at any time within twelve months.* The widow cannot be required to make her election until twelve months after her husband's death. *Anderson's Appeal,* 36 Pa. St., 476 (1860); *Bierer's Appeal,* 92 Pa. St., 265 (1879).

§ 1089. *Election may be revoked.* It is within the discretion of the auditing judge to allow a widow to withdraw her election to take against the will. *Barry's Estate,* 37 Leg. Int., 62 (1880); *Wessel's Estate,* 26 P. L. J., 45 (1878).

§ 1090. *Form of election not to take under the will.* The following may serve as a form of election in case the widow intends to take in opposition to the will :

, the widow of   , deceased, declares that she claims her share of the real and personal property of said decedent against the will of the said   , deceased, and she notifies the executor and all parties interested, of this her claim to said real and personal estate of said decedent.

(Signed)

(Date.)

Notice in the above form may be served upon the executor of the decedent's estate and other interested parties, or in accordance with the terms of the Act (29 March, 1832, *supra,* section 1008), may be filed in the Orphans' Court. It would be best to pursue both courses in most cases. If the widow make no election, she may be cited to do so after twelve months from the death of the testator. Her neglect to make choice will imply acceptance under the will.

§ 1091. **Assignment of dower.** The widow is entitled to dower at once from the time of her husband's death. She may retain temporary possession even if there be a deficiency of assets to pay debts and her dower interest must therefore finally abate. *Price v. Johnson,* 4 Yeates, 526 (1808).

§ 1092. *Widow and heirs cannot maintain ejectment against each other before assignment.* The heirs cannot maintain ejectment against her before assignment of her dower. *Gourley* v. *Kinley,* 66 Pa. St., 270 (1870).

On the other hand, she will not be permitted to enforce her right of dower by ejectment against the heirs. *Bratton* v. *Mitchell,* 7 Watts, 113 (1838).

§ 1093. *Widow cannot be joined.* Nor can she join with the heirs in ejectment against others holding the decedent's lands. Even at common law she is not seised of an undivided third until assignment. *Pringle* v. *Gaw,* 5 S. & R., 536 (1820).

§ 1094. *By metes and bounds.* At common law, however, she is entitled to assignment by metes and bounds. If the husband in his lifetime alien, therefore, upon her recovery in an action of dower, she should be put in possession of her proportionate share of the land in severalty. In such case the finding by the jury of the annual value of the premises is surplusage, but it will not affect the validity of the verdict and judgment. *Shirtz* v. *Shirtz,* 5 Watts, 255 (1836); *Benner* v. *Evans,* 3 P. & W., 454 (1832); *Barnett* v. *Barnett,* 16 S. & R., 51 (1827); *Leineaweaver* v. *Stoever,* 17 *Id.,* 297 (1828).

§ 1095. *Improvements.* In assigning her dower in severalty to a widow, she is not entitled to advantage by reason of improvements placed upon the land by her husband's vendee. Otherwise as to increase in its value from other causes after alienation. *Thompson* v. *Morrow,* 5 S. & R., 289 (1819). Improvements by the vendee may not be set up by way of defense to the action; they respect only the amount. *Warner* v. *Macknett,* 3 Phila., 325 (1859).

§ 1096. *Income may be impounded.* Pending a claim to dower in a trust estate, a proportionate share of the income will be impounded. *Sharp's Estate,* 6 Phila., 389 (1867).

§ 1097. **Parties.** The action should be brought by the widow against the tenant of the freehold. By Act of 8 June, 1893 (P. L., 344), a married woman is empowered to sue in all respects and in any form of action with the same effect as an unmarried person. If she be married again, therefore, it is no longer necessary to join the new husband as a party to the action. If the widow be an infant, she should sue by next friend; if defendant be within age, suit should be brought against his guardian. If he have none, a guardian *ad litem* must be appointed. The laws upon this subject are applicable alike to all real actions, and they are sufficiently considered in the chapter upon Partition. The widow of an intestate tenant in common is entitled to her action at common law against her late husband's co-tenants. *Brown* v. *Adams*, 2 Whart., 188 (1837).

The plaintiff in this and other real actions is known as the demandant.

§ 1098. **Præcipe.** This action, like all others, is begun by *præcipe* to the prothonotary.

FORM OF PRÆCIPE.

A. B. ⎱
  v. ⎰
C. D. ⎰

SIR :

Issue writ of dower *unde nihil habet* commanding C. D. that justly and without delay he render to A. B., widow, who was the wife of J. B., her reasonable dower which falleth to her out of the freehold which was of the said J. B., late her husband, in the city of Philadelphia, whereof she has nothing as she says. Returnable the first Monday of   next.

G. H.,
Attorney pro Demandant.
(Date.)

To Prothonotary C. P., Philadelphia County.

§ 1099.

FORM OF WRIT.

The Commonwealth of Pennsylvania, to the Sheriff of Philadelphia County, Greeting: Command C. D. that justly and without delay he render unto A. B., widow, who was the wife of J. B., now deceased, the reasonable dower which falleth to her of the freehold which was of the said J. B., her late husband, in the city of Philadelphia, whereof she has nothing as she says, and whereof she complains that the said C. D. deforces her ; and unless he shall do so, and if the said A. B. shall give you security for prosecuting her claim with effect, then summon, by good summoners, the aforesaid C. D. that he be and appear before our judges at Philadelphia, at our county Court of Common Pleas, No. 1, there to be held the first Monday of   next, to show wherefore he will not. And have you then there the names of these summoners, and this writ.

Witness the Honorable, etc.

[SEAL]

§ 1100. **Service and return** are treated in the chapter on Partition. By statute (13 June, 1836, section 79 *et seq.*, P. L., 587), the same rules and statutes govern those subjects in all real actions.

§ 1101. **Declaration or Count.** The statement of demandant's cause of action in dower is technically called a count. It is in substance and form a declaration, and the two terms are applied to it indifferently by most writers. It should be filed before return-day in order to take advantage of the default if defendant do not appear. If he have appeared, it may be accompanied by a rule to plead, and a copy thereof and of the count should be served on his attorney.

If it be not sufficiently specific, defendant may require a bill of particulars as in other cases. The premises should be described with enough particularity to enable the sheriff to deliver seisin. "Tenement" is therefore too vague a word. It is not necessary to lay damages. The proportionate part demanded should be specified, as "a third part of" the premises described. If the land lie in several places, a share of those in each may be claimed.

§ 1102.

FORM OF COUNT OR DECLARATION.

A. B. ⎱
v. ⎰
C. D. ⎰

In the Court of Common Pleas, No. 1, of Philadelphia County.
To December Term, 1890. No. 200.
County of Philadelphia, *ss.*

A. B., widow, who was the wife of J. B., deceased, by G. H., her attorney, demands against C. D. the third part (*or as the case may be*) of (*here enumerate and describe the properties*) with the appurtenances, in the city of Philadelphia, in the county of Philadelphia, as the dower of the said A. B. of the endowment of J. B., deceased, heretofore her husband, whereof she has nothing, etc.

G. H.,
Attorney for Demandant.
(Date.)

§ 1103. **Judgment by default.** If defendant do not appear, or if he omit to plead in response to the rule upon him to do so, judgment may be taken for the demandant by default (see sections 23, 26). Such judgment is followed by writ of inquiry of damages, or of *haberi facias seisinam;* obtained by *præcipe;* the latter where demandant is entitled to possession, the writ of inquiry if she may claim only in damages. If she have right to both, she may take out the two writs, in which case they are commonly united in one.

§ 1104. **View.** After count filed, in the English practice in dower, defendant may ask for a view. A view is not of course, however, and is to be granted only upon cause shown by affidavit. The heir was not entitled to a view at common law if the husband died seised; and by Statute of Westminster II. (not reported by the judges to be in force in this State), it is provided that view shall not be granted to the tenant if the land demanded was aliened by the husband to him or his ancestors "where the tenant ought not to be ignorant what land the husband did alien to him or her or to his or her ancestors." If view be demanded in either case, demandant may counterplead, and issue may be taken thereon. If upon issue of law judgment go for demandant, it will be final. While the doctrine of view has been imported into some of the

United States, it has found no lodgement in Pennsylvania. No adjudication upon the subject is to be met with in our reports.

§ 1105. **Pleas.** Certain pleas in abatement are admissible which are peculiar to this action, in addition to those usually recognized. To an action brought against two or more defendants, entire tenancy may be pleaded by one ; defendants proceeded against as tenants in common may plead several tenure, as may persons holding distinct parcels. Joint tenure may be pleaded by one sued separately. Tenancy for years may also be pleaded, as the proper defendant is the tenant of freehold. The usual effect of these pleas, if well founded, is that the demandant conforms her demand to the true facts. Non-tenure is of the nature of a plea in abatement. It is dilatory in character, and must be accompanied by affidavit that it is not for delay, and should be put in at the earliest moment. It will not be entertained after a plea in bar, though it is sometimes considered such, and it may be joined with others in bar. See, upon this plea, *Cosporus* v. *Jones*, 7 Pa. St., 120 (1847) ; *Jones* v. *Patterson*, 12 Pa. St., 149 (1849) ; *Seaton* v. *Jamison*, 7 Watts, 533 (1838). *Ne unques seise que dower,* that the husband was never seised of such an estate in the land as to give to his widow the right of dower, is sometimes spoken of as the general issue, but it is not strictly so, and there is, in fact, no general issue plea in dower. One claiming under the husband cannot properly defend under this plea. It may be put in to part with other pleas as to the residue. Only the fact of seisin by the husband during coverture is put in issue by this plea. Defendant may plead that the husband of the demandant is alive, but not if he claim under the heir. *Ne unques accouple en loyal matrimonie* (that the demandant and her alleged husband were never joined in lawful wedlock), the wife's elopement and adultery, divorce *a vinculis*, antenuptial settlement, or post-nuptial agreement assented to after the husband's death, the acceptance of a testamentary substitute for dower, release, judicial sale barring dower, the Statute of Limitations, or any matter or thing which serves to bar or divest the widow's dower may be put in issue as a defense to the action. How far these pleas may be joined, especially if they be inconsistent, has not been determined in this State. Defendant would probably in analogy to the personal actions be allowed great latitude in that respect.

Tout temps prist, that the defendant has always been and still is ready to render dower, is like a tender in personal action. If that plea be entered promptly, defendant will be discharged from liability for *mesne* profits unless dower were previously demanded by the widow. If she admit the plea, she may take judgment upon it, and issue the appropriate writ of execution, recovering profits only from the commencement of suit, but she may take issue upon the plea by replication, and will be entitled to her profits from the death of her husband if it prove to be ill-founded in fact. The forms *in extenso* for many of these pleas will be found in Chitty's Pleading, vol. 3, 1316 *et seq.* (12 Am. ed.). It would uselessly burden this work to insert them here. Those of them which are technically known by a few of their salient words are often briefly pleaded with us by writing those words only, as " *Ne unques accouple,*" etc.

§ 1106. **Notice of special matter.** It is customary in this State to try issues in dower updn plea of *ne unques seisie que dower*, with notice to demandant of special matter of defense. This course is open to some objections, but it has the sanction of long usage in its favor.

§ 1107. **Replication and Issue.** Defendant's plea, if not demurrable, should be replied to according to its tenor, with a view to producing an issue. If the replication allege new matter, defendant will rejoin, and so on until a distinct question of fact is raised. When the case is at issue, it should be ordered on the list for trial, or upon the argument list if an issue of law be raised by demurrer at any stage of the pleadings.

§ 1108. **Trial.** At the trial of the cause demandant should prove the facts necessary to support the issue as raised by the pleadings. If the husband did not die seised, she cannot give evidence as to the annual value of the land, as she is not concerned therewith. *Barnett* v. *Barnett,* 15 S. & R.; 72 (1826). If *ne unques seisie que dower* be pleaded without special matter, she need not prove marriage or death of the husband, nor need she show seisin by production of the title papers. Nor in dower need the demandant go further back in title than a fee-simple deed to her husband. *Evans* v. *Evans,* 29 Pa. St., 277 (1857). Defendant simply denying demandant's right may not set up title in a stranger. *Id.* But defendant may upon this issue prove want of seisin in the husband. The usual evidences of marriage are admissible under the plea of *ne unques accouple ;* and so seisin of the husband may be shown by the customary incidents thereof, as by receipt of rent or actual possession by him. The land may be identified as that of the husband by parol. Defendant should be shown to be tenant of the freehold.

§ 1109. **Verdict and damages.** In more recent cases it is held that the action at common law will not lie if the husband die seised and in possession. *Gourley* v. *Kinley*, 66 Pa. St., 270 (1870); *Seider* v. *Seider*, 5 Whart., 208 (1839); see section 1040. But under the older practice, the jury, in finding for the demandant, if the husband died seised, were required also to find the date of his death, of what estate he died seised, the annual value of the land, and damages for detention of dower ; and they should award demandant her costs. But omissions therein may be supplied by writ of inquiry. *Benner* v. *Evans*, 3 P. & W., 454 (1832). If the husband have not died seised, neither damages nor costs should be awarded. *Id.; Sharp* v. *Pettit*, 3 Yeates, 38 (1800). Nor should the annual value of the land be found in that case. *Leineweaver* v. *Stoever*, 17 S. & R., 297 (1828) ; *Shirtz* v. *Shirtz*, 5 Watts, 255 (1836). But these findings, though erroneous, will not vitiate the verdict ; they are mere surplusage, *Id.*, and may be remitted by the demandant. *Barnett* v. *Barnett*, 16 S. & R., 51 (1827). Damages for the detention, where he died seised, ran from the time of the husband's death, and consist of net profits, less taxes, improvements, etc. If *tout temps prist* be pleaded, damages run only from date of demand. *Winder* v. *Little*, 1 Yeates, 152 (1792). Tenant of the freehold is liable for the entire damages, though he may have been in possession but a part of the time. *Seaton* v. *Jamison*, 7 Watts, 533 (1838) ; *Lyle* v. *Richards*, 9 S. & R., 322 (1823). But in a proper case such construction would be given to the Statute of Merton, under which damages are so recoverable, as to avoid injustice. *Jones* v. *Patterson*, 12 Pa. St., 149 (1849).

§ 1110. **Execution.** Having entered judgment upon the verdict for demandant, execution by writ of *haberi facias seisinam* is obtained by *præcipe*. Damages are to be levied by writ of *fi. fa.* or *capias*, which may be joined with the writ of seisin ; under the latter the sheriff should proceed to assign her dower to the widow by metes and bounds, by proceedings of inquisition. For the details of the proper steps to be taken by him under this writ, see the opinions of Judge KENNEDY in *Seaton* v. *Jamison*, 7 Watts, 533 (1838), and in *Benner* v. *Evans*, 3 P. & W., 454 (1832). On the return of the writ either party may apply to the court to inquire into the facts involved ; the courts will grant relief necessary to a legal and proper execution, but will not inquire into matters *dehors* the record upon writ of error. *Benner* v. *Evans, supra.* The demandant is entitled to be endowed as of the value of the land at the time of assignment, leaving out the value of improvements made after alienation by the husband. *Shirtz* v. *Shirtz*, 5 Watts, 255 (1836).

§ 1111. **Remedies to enforce payment of arrears of dower.** Arrears and principal of statutory dower may be recovered by action of debt (assumpsit). *Kline* v. *Bowman*, 19 Pa. St., 24 (1852); *Borough* v. *Welsh*, 117 Pa. St., 174 (1887); *De Haven* v. *Bartholomew*, 57 Pa. St., 126 (1868).

Arrears of dower either at common law or by statute may be recovered by distress, even upon the goods of a stranger upon the land. *Murphy* v. *Borland*, 92 Pa. St., 86 (1879); *Baker* v. *Leibert*, 125 Pa. St., 106 (1889). But the representative of the widow may not distrain for arrears accrued after her death. *Henderson* v. *Boyer*, 44 Pa. St., 220 (1863).

If the dower be secured by recognizance, arrears may be collected by *sci. fa.* thereon, or by distress or assumpsit. If the widow bring action on the *sci. fa.*, judgment should be for the arrears due. If it be entered for the principal of the recognizance also, that part of the judgment will be stricken off as surplusage. *Evans* v. *Ross*, 107 Pa. St., 231 (1884); *Good* v. *Good*, 7 Watts, 195 (1838); *Stewart* v. *Martin*, 2 Watts, 200 (1834). If the arrears be not paid when due, they bear interest; *Stewart* v. *Martin, supra*. The action for arrears of the widow's interest is local, and must be brought in the county where the land lies. *Rodney* v. *Washington*, 42 Leg. Int., 160 (1885).

The widow may not distrain separately upon several parcels of land taken by the heir at the valuation subject to her dower interest, and by him divided. She must distrain at once for the whole amount. *Shouffler* v. *Coover*, 1 W. & S., 400 (1841).

She may proceed for her arrears against the alienee of the land by *mesne* conveyances, and she is not barred by lapse of time (*i. e.*, six years). Judgment in such cases is *de terris*, not personal. *Korstein* v. *Bauer*, 4 Penny., 366 (1884); *Dillebaugh's Estate*, 4 Watts, 177 (1835); *De Haven* v. *Bartholomew*, 57 Pa. St., 126 (1868); *Pidcock* v. *Bye*, 3 Rawle, 183 (1831); *Shelley* v. *Shelley*, 8 W. & S., 153 (1844).

A recognizance or mortgage for the purchase-money taken by order of court under the Act of 29 March, 1832, is but collateral to the lien. *De Haven* v. *Bartholomew (supra)*; *Medlor* v. *Aulenbach*, 2 P. & W., 355 (1831).

It will not be discharged by payment of the principal to the obligee in the recognizance, being the administrator of the decedent's estate. Upon the death of the widow the principal should be paid to the heirs. *Hise* v. *Geiger*, 7 W. & S., 273 (1844). See *Unangst* v. *Kraemer*, 8 W. & S., 391 (1845).

§ 1112. **Limitations.** The period of limitation for a claim of dower is twenty-one years. *Allen* v. *Getz*, 2 P. & W., 310 (1831); *Care* v. *Keller*, 77 Pa. St., 487 (1875).

Omission to claim her rights for six years will not operate as a bar either at law or in equity. *Merrill's Appeal,* 16 W. N., 491 (1885).

If the husband alien in his lifetime, the statute does not begin to run against demandant until his death. *Winters* v. *De Turk,* 25 W. N., 511 (1890); *Culler* v. *Motzer,* 13 S. & R., 356 (1825); *Care* v. *Keller,* 77 Pa. St., 487 (1875). But if the husband be disseised in his lifetime, the statute begins to run at once in favor of the adverse holder, and against both husband and wife. *Winters* v. *De Turk (supra).*

See Brews. Equity Prac., Chapter XIII.

CHAPTER XIX.

THE law under which escheats are now regulated is the Act of May 2, 1889.

§ 1113. What property shall escheat.

That from and after the publication of this Act, if any person, who at the time of his death was seised or possessed of any 'real estate or personal estate within this Commonwealth, has died or shall die intestate, without heirs or known kindred, a widow or surviving husband, such estate, of whatsoever kind the same may be, whether legal or equitable, or whether the same was held by the said person in severalty or as tenant in common, co-tenant, joint tenant, or in partnership with any other person or persons, shall escheat to the Commonwealth, subject to all legal demands on the same. (Act of May 2, 1889, section 1; P. L., 66.)

§ 1114. Property on deposit.

That whensoever any money, estate, or effects shall have been, or shall hereafter be paid into, or deposited in the custody of any court of this Commonwealth, or shall be in the custody of any depository, or of any receiver or other officer of said court, and the rightful owner or owners thereof shall have been or shall be unknown for the space of seven years, the same shall escheat to the Commonwealth, subject to all legal demands on the same. (*Ibid.*, section 2.)

§ 1115. Trust property.

That whensoever any trustee or other person is or shall be seised of any property or estate, real or personal, in a fiduciary capacity, and shall file an account of the same in any court of this Commonwealth, and whensoever it shall appear that the *cestui que trust* or beneficial owner of said property or effects, or any part thereof, has been unknown for a period of seven years, and still remains unknown, then and in such case so much of said property or effects as belonged to said unknown *cestui que trust* or beneficial owner shall escheat to the Commonwealth, subject to all legal demands on the same. (*Ibid.*, section 3.)

§ 1116. Escheator to be appointed by the auditor-general.

That whensoever, by information or otherwise, the auditor-general of the Commonwealth shall become aware of the fact that any property, real or personal, hath escheated or is supposed to have escheated to the Commonwealth under the provisions of this Act, he shall appoint, by commis-

sion under his hand and the seal of his office, some suitable person, resident in
the county where he shall have reason to suppose that the escheated property
or the greater part thereof is situate, to act as escheator of said property;
which said escheator shall have the powers and duties and shall be entitled
to the fees and rewards hereafter nominated and specified in this Act.
(*Ibid.*, section 4.)

§ 1117. Jurisdiction.

That the jurisdiction in all cases of escheat under the provisions of this
Act shall be vested in the courts of this Commonwealth, as follows, namely:

Whenever an escheat shall occur or be supposed to occur by reason of
any person dying intestate, without heirs or known kindred, a widow or
surviving husband, the Orphans' Court of the county wherein said decedent
was resident at the time of his death, or in case said decedent was not at
the time of his death resident within this Commonwealth, then the Orphans' Court of the county in which the greater part of his property, real
and personal, shall be situate, shall have jurisdiction.

Whenever an escheat shall occur, or be supposed to occur, of any
property, estate, or effects deposited in the custody of any court, or with
any depository, receiver, or other officer thereof, the owner whereof shall
be unknown, and whenever any escheat shall occur, or be supposed to
occur, of any property, estate, or effects held by any trustee or other person
in a fiduciary capacity, who shall have filed an account thereof in any court
of this Commonwealth, by reason of the fact that the *cestui que trust* or
beneficial owner thereof shall be unknown, then and in such case the court
in which, or in the custody of any depository, receiver, or other officer of
which, said property, estate, or effects may have been or shall be deposited,
whether the same be real or personal, or in which said account has been or
may be duly filed, shall have jurisdiction. (*Ibid.*, section 5.)

§ 1118. When escheator may apply for letters of administration.

That whensoever any escheator shall be duly commissioned by the auditor-general of and concerning any property, real or personal, escheated or
supposed to have escheated by reason of the fact that the person who was
last seised or possessed of the same has died intestate, without heirs or
known kindred, a widow or surviving husband, and no letters of administration have been granted upon the estate of the said decedent, it shall be
the duty of the said escheator to apply to the register of wills of the county
wherein the said decedent was resident at the time of his death, or in case
the said decedent was at the time of his death [not] resident within this
Commonwealth, then to the register of wills of the county in which the
greater part of the property escheated or supposed to have escheated is or
may be situate, for a grant of letters of administration to him, the said
escheator, upon the estate of the said decedent. And the said register of
wills shall, if no next of kin or creditor of said decedent entitled under existing laws to letters of administration shall appear and demand such letters,
forthwith grant the same to said escheator, in like manner and form as
letters of administration are now granted by existing laws, and said escheator shall be entitled in such case to letters of administration, even
though said decedent was not at the time of his death possessed of any
personal property, but was seised of real estate only, situate within this
Commonwealth. (*Ibid.*, section 6.)

§ 1119. Escheator may petition for citation to party in possession of property—Account to be filed, etc.

That whensoever any escheator shall be duly commissioned by the auditor-general of and concerning any property, real or personal, escheated or supposed to have escheated to the Commonwealth under the provisions of this Act, he shall apply, by petition, to the court having jurisdiction in the premises, to hear and determine whether an escheat has occurred or not, and shall, in his petition, set forth the facts of his appointment and the nature and character of the alleged escheat, and shall also state, as far as he conveniently can, the location, character, and amount of the property, real and personal, alleged to have escheated, together with the name and address of the person or persons having the same in his or their possession ; whereupon the said court shall have power to issue a summons or citation, directed to any administrator or executor, depository of the court, receiver, or other officer of the court, to show cause, if any they have, why they should not file a true and accurate account of all and singular the said property alleged to have escheated, as aforesaid ; and if upon sufficient proof, by oath or affirmation, of the service of said summons or citation, no good and valid cause be shown to the contrary, the said court shall proceed to direct said administrator or executor, depository of the court, receiver, or other officer of the court, to file his said account. And in all cases where any real estate has escheated, or is supposed to have escheated, by reason of the death of the person last seised thereof, without heirs or known kindred, the said court shall have power to order the administrator or executor of said person to file a trué and accurate statement of all the real estate whereof said decedent died seised, describing the same by metes and bounds, together with the buildings and improvements thereon erected, as far as he has been able to ascertain the same. And whensoever it shall appear by the account of any executor or administrator, or any receiver or other officer of the court, or of any trustee or other person in a fiduciary capacity, or upon the audit of any such account, that the said receiver or other officer, trustee, or other person has in his possession, or has any knowledge of the existence of any real estate which shall have escheated, or is supposed to have escheated to the Commonwealth, the said court shall have power to order and direct the said administrator or executor, receiver, or other officer, trustee, or other person filing an account as aforesaid, to file a true and accurate statement of all said real estate, describing the same as aforesaid, so far as he has been or shall be able to ascertain the same ; and any and all accounts and statements filed under 'the provisions of this Act shall be verified by oath or affirmation in the customary manner. (*Ibid.*, section 7.)

§ 1120. Proceedings upon audit of account.

That whensoever any proceedings in escheat have been instituted as aforesaid, the court having jurisdiction in the premises shall, upon the filing of any account or statement by any administrator, executor, depository of the court, receiver, or other officer of the court, or of any trustee or other person in a fiduciary capacity of any property or estate, real or personal, escheated or supposed to be escheated, proceed to the audit and adjudication of said account or statement in the same manner as the said court commonly proceeds upon the audit and adjudication of the accounts of executors, administrators, and trustees ; and shall upon said audit proceed to inquire and determine whether there has been any escheat or not, and if so, in what manner and for what cause said escheat has occurred, and also what estate, real or personal, has escheated, and what is the value thereof. And the said court shall, in all cases where any real estate has escheated or is alleged to have escheated, before proceeding finally to hear and determine the question of escheat, order and direct notice of said proceedings to be served upon the person or persons in possession of said real estate, in such form as the court shall direct, and the said court shall have full power and authority to summon any person or persons who shall be at any time alleged to have any knowledge touching any escheat or any interest therein, to appear before it, and said court shall have full power and authority to examine any and all of said persons upon their oaths or affirmations as to any fact or facts, matter or thing touching said escheat, and shall suffer and permit the escheator and all parties claiming to have any interest in said proceedings to appear therein by counsel or otherwise, and to produce and examine such witnesses under oath or affirmation, as they may see fit, touching said escheat, and the said court shall have full power at any stage of said proceedings, when they may think it wise so to do, to make such orders relative to advertisements and notices of the proceedings as shall best serve to inform and advise all parties having an interest, or who may have an interest, in said proceedings of the pendency thereof. (*Ibid.*, section 8.)

§ 1121. Feigned issue may be framed.

That whenever any proceedings in escheat shall have been instituted, or shall be pending in any court of this Commonwealth, and there shall be any disputed fact or facts touching said escheat, then and in that case the said court shall, upon application of the escheator, or any other person interested, or claiming to be interested, in the said proceedings prior to the filing of a finding or adjudication therein, frame an issue or issues to determine said disputed question or questions of facts, which said issue or issues shall be tried in the Court of Common Pleas of the same county in which the proceedings in escheat shall have been instituted, and shall, if necessary, be certified to said court for that purpose. In cases where escheat proceedings are instituted in the Supreme Court, such issue or issues shall be certified to, and shall be tried by, the Court of Common Pleas of such county as the Supreme Court shall designate. Any party to said issue may, upon the trial thereof, except to the ruling of the court upon any point of evidence or of law, which exception shall be noted by the court and filed of record in the cause, and a writ of error to the Supreme Court may thereupon be taken by any party to said issue, with the usual force and effect. And after the determination of such issue, the Court of Common Pleas in which the same shall have been tried shall certify the result thereof to the court in which the said proceedings in escheat have been instituted. (*Ibid.*, section 9.)

§ 1122. Requisites of adjudication.

That every court having jurisdiction in cases of escheat shall, after the determination of each and every case, file of record a finding or adjudication which shall set forth :

I. Whether an escheat hath occurred or not.

II. In what manner and for what cause the said escheat hath occurred, with the full name of the intestate, if any there be, or of the person who was last seised or possessed of the property in question.

III. What estate, real or personal, hath escheated, and what is the value thereof.

IV. Where said estate, real or personal, is situated, and in whose possession the same then is.

And in case the said court shall find that any property, real or personal, hath escheated, the same shall be awarded to the escheator for and on behalf of the Commonwealth. (*Ibid.*, section 10.)

§ 1123. Exceptions to the adjudication or finding.

That whensoever any adjudication or finding in escheat shall have been filed by any court, exceptions may be filed thereto by the escheator or any other party or parties interested in said proceedings, within the same time, and in the same manner, as exceptions are commonly filed in cases of accounts of administrators, executors, and trustees in the court having jurisdiction in the premises. And the court shall proceed to the hearing and determination of said exceptions in like manner as in the cases of exceptions to the accounts of administrators, executors, and trustees, as aforesaid; and if said exceptions are, after hearing, sustained in whole or in part, the court shall forthwith proceed to file an amended adjudication or finding, in accordance with its determination upon such exceptions. But if no such exceptions are filed within the time limited as aforesaid, then the adjudication or finding of escheat shall be deemed to be confirmed absolutely. (*Ibid.*, section 11.)

§ 1124. Appeal to the Supreme Court.

That the Commonwealth, or any person aggrieved or claiming to be aggrieved by a final adjudication or finding in escheat, may appeal from the same to the Supreme Court, provided that any party other than the Commonwealth so appealing shall give bond, with sufficient security to be approved by the court, conditioned to prosecute the appeal with effect, and to pay all costs that may be adjudged against him, and shall make oath or affirmation that the appeal is not intended for delay. No appeal shall be allowed unless the same shall be entered and security given within thirty days after the filing of the amended adjudication or finding, or the absolute confirmation of the original adjudication or finding by the court having jurisdiction in the premises. And in cases where said appeal shall be duly entered and security given within the time above limited, no further proceeding shall be had touching the said escheat until the same be determined by the Supreme Court, and the record be remitted therefrom. (*Ibid.*, section 12.)

§ 1125. Adjudication to be amended, if required, by Supreme Court.

That if, upon any appeal to the Supreme Court, any portion or the whole of any finding or adjudication of escheat shall be reversed or modified, the court in which said escheat proceedings have been instituted shall, immediately upon the remission of the record thereof by the Supreme Court, prepare and file a corrected adjudication or finding in accordance with the determination of the Supreme Court upon said appeal. (*Ibid.*, section 13.)

§ 1126. Bond of escheator.

That from and immediately after the final determination of any escheat proceedings as aforesaid, the escheator shall file, in the court wherein said proceedings in escheat have been instituted, a bond to the Commonwealth, with sufficient security to be approved by the court, conditioned for the

faithful performance by him of his duties as escheator, and also that he will
faithfully account for and pay over to the State treasury the proceeds of all
property, real or personal, found to have escheated, which shall come into
his possession as escheator. (*Ibid.*, section 14.)

§ 1127. Certified copies of final adjudication to be filed.

That from and immediately after the final determination of any escheat
proceedings as aforesaid, the escheator shall cause a duly certified copy of
the final adjudication or finding in escheat, under the seal of the court
filing the same, to be transmitted to the auditor-general, and shall also
cause a copy thereof, duly certified in like manner, to be filed in the Court
of Common Pleas of every county in which any of the real estate escheated
is situate, other than the county in which the proceedings in escheat have
been instituted. (*Ibid.*, section 15.)

§ 1128. Sale of personal property.

That at the expiration of thirty days from and after the filing of the
final finding or adjudication in escheat, or the absolute confirmation of the
same, the person or persons having in their possession any moneys found
to have escheated shall forthwith pay the same to the escheator, upon receiving from him an acquittance and discharge thereof. And if any person or persons shall have in their possession any personal property found
to have escheated, other than moneys, the escheator may forthwith apply
by petition to the court for an order directed to the person or persons
having the same in his possession to sell and dispose of the same, in such
manner and form and upon such advertisements as the court shall direct;
and the court shall thereupon, if no valid cause be shown to the contrary,
order and direct such sale to be made as aforesaid. and shall further order
an account thereof to be duly returned to the court. And upon return of
said sale the court may order and direct such compensation as it may deem
proper to be paid to the person or persons effecting the same; and shall
also order and direct all the expenses of said sale to be deducted from
said proceeds, and shall thereupon further order and direct the residue of
said proceeds to be paid to the escheator, upon the receipt from him of an
acquittance and a discharge therefor. (*Ibid.*, section 16.)

§ 1129. Sale of real estate.

That at the expiration of thirty days from and after the filing of the final
finding or adjudication in escheat, or the absolute confirmation of the same,
the escheator may apply by petition to the court having jurisdiction of the
proceedings in escheat for an order directing the sale of all real estate
found to have escheated, situate in the county where the escheat proceedings have been instituted; and the said court shall thereupon, if no valid
cause be shown to the contrary, order and direct the administrator or executor of the person who has died last seised or possessed of said real estate,
or the receiver or other officer or trustee or person acting in a fiduciary
capacity, having possession of the same, or if for any reason they cannot
act, then some other proper person or persons to sell said real estate in such
manner and form and upon such advertisement as the court shall direct,
and to execute and deliver a good and sufficient deed or deeds to the purchaser thereof: *Provided*, however, that no sale or sales shall be ordered
or made under the provisions of this Act in any case until security, to be
approved by the court, shall be duly entered by the person or persons

ordered and directed to make such sale, in at least double the value of the real estate proposed to be sold, conditioned for the faithful application of the purchase-money according to the decree of the court; which security shall inure to the benefit of all parties interested, and such security being so given, no purchaser of said real estate shall be bound to see to the application of said purchase-money. (*Ibid.*, section 17.)

§ 1130. Of the purchaser's title.

That the title acquired by all purchasers of real estate, sold under and by virtue of the provisions of this Act, shall be absolute and indefeasible for all such estate or estates as shall have been found to have escheated to the Commonwealth. And the sales shall have like effect as to the discharge of mortgages, judgments, liens, or other incumbrances upon the said real estate as sales made by decree of any of the several Orphans' Courts of this Commonwealth for the discharge of the debts of decedents now have, or may hereafter have, in the several counties of this Commonwealth under existing laws. And it shall be the duty of the court to decree the proper application of the purchase-money of said property, with the aid of an auditor, when deemed necessary, to the discharge of the various mortgages, judgments, liens, or other incumbrances upon said real estate. And the said court shall further order and decree that the residue of the proceeds of the said real estate, after the payment of all expenses of sale, and the payment and discharge of said mortgages, judgments, liens, and incumbrances thereon, shall be forthwith paid to the escheator, upon the receipt from him of an acquittance and discharge therefor. (*Ibid.*, section 18.)

§ 1131. Where real estate in another county.

That whenever any real estate, found to have escheated, shall or may be situate in any other county than that in which the proceedings in escheat have been instituted, the escheator may apply by petition to the Court of Common Pleas of said county for an order directing the sale of the property aforesaid, and the said court shall thereupon proceed in the premises in like manner and form as is hereinbefore provided relative to sales of real estate by order of the court having original jurisdiction in escheat proceedings, and said sales shall be made by the same person or persons upon the entry of like security, in like manner and form, and with the same force and effect, and the like proceedings shall be had touching the distribution of the proceeds of said sales: *Provided*, nevertheless, that no court other than that in which the proceedings in escheat have been originally instituted shall have power to make any order touching the sale of escheated real estate, until a duly certified copy of the final finding or adjudication of escheat is filed therein. (*Ibid.*, section 19.)

§ 1132. Prior sales for unpaid taxes not to be invalidated.

That no sale of escheated real estate under the provisions of this Act shall be deemed or taken to invalidate any title previously acquired thereto under a sale thereof for unpaid taxes, or to authorize the purchaser to redeem said real estate in such case. (*Ibid.*, section 20.)

§ 1133. Escheator to account to Commonwealth.

That the escheator shall, immediately after the receipt by him of any moneys escheated to the Commonwealth, or the proceeds of any property, real or personal, escheated to the Commonwealth, account for and pay over into the State treasury the full amount received by him as aforesaid. (*Ibid.*, section 21.)

§ 1134. Traverse by party who has received no notice.

That any person or persons interested, or claiming to be interested, in any property, real or personal, which shall be found to have escheated to the Commonwealth, who have had no actual notice by citation, advertisement, or otherwise of the pendency of any proceedings in escheat, prior to the conclusion of the audit of the account of the person having the escheated property in his possession, and who shall not have subsequently appeared, either in person or by attorney, in said escheat proceedings, may at any time within three years next after the filing of the final adjudication or finding in escheat, or the absolute confirmation thereof, traverse the same under oath or affirmation, by writing filed in the court finding the same, setting forth his, her, or their interest in said property, and in what particular said finding or adjudication is not true and correct, which said traverse shall be tried in the Court of Common Pleas of the same county in which the original proceedings have been instituted, or where the proceedings have been instituted in the Supreme Court, in the Court of Common Pleas of such county as said Supreme Court may designate. And where said escheat proceedings have not been instituted in the Court of Common Pleas, the courts wherein they have been instituted shall certify the finding or adjudication of escheat and the traverse thereof to the proper Court of Common Pleas for trial. And said traverse shall be tried in like manner and form, and with like effect, as traverses of inquisitions in escheat have been heretofore commonly tried under existing laws. And a writ of error shall lie in such case to the Supreme Court at the suit of any traverser or of the Commonwealth. And upon the determination of such traverse, the court trying the same shall, if necessary, certify the final result thereof to the court in which the original proceedings have been instituted, and in case upon the trial of said traverse it shall be found that the property in question, or any part thereof, had not escheated, and that the person or persons filing said traverse are entitled to the same, or any part thereof, then and in such case said person or persons shall be entitled to receive and to have delivered to them possession of all such property, real or personal, as shall not have been sold or paid into the treasury of the Commonwealth, and in case the same has been sold or paid into the treasury of the Commonwealth, to receive back again from the Commonwealth such sum or sums of money as may have been realized from the sale or payment thereof, after deducting all expenses, or a proportionable part of said sum or sums, according as his or their interest shall be made to appear: *Provided*, nevertheless, that if at the time of the institution of the proceedings in escheat as aforesaid any person having any claim to any of the property, real or personal, found to have escheated, shall be insane or a minor, then and in such case said person, whether he has had actual notice of the pendency of the proceedings in escheat or not, may, if he has not appeared in said proceedings by his committee or guardian, or by the attorney of such committee or guardian, at any time within three years after recovering his sound mind and memory, or attaining full age, as the case may be, traverse the said finding or adjudication of escheat in like manner and form, and with like force and effect, as is hereinbefore provided. (*Ibid.*, section 22.)

§ 1135. Courts may enforce all orders, etc.

That the various courts of this Commonwealth having jurisdiction in escheat proceedings shall have full power and authority to enforce all orders and decrees made by them therein, by attachment or other proper process as the case may require. (*Ibid.*, section 23.)

§ 1136. The informer—His compensation.

That any person who shall first inform the auditor-general by writing, signed by such person, in the presence of two subscribing witnesses, that any escheat hath occurred by reason of the fact that any person hath died intestate without heirs or known kindred, a widow, or surviving husband, and who shall procure necessary evidence to substantiate the fact of said escheat, and shall prosecute the right of the Commonwealth to the property escheated with effect, shall be entitled to one-third part of the price which such property, real or personal, shall produce, after all costs of prosecution and charges of sale are deducted therefrom : *Provided*, nevertheless, that before such third part be paid to said person or his representative, he, she, or they shall give bonds to the Commonwealth, with sufficient security, to be approved by the auditor-general, conditioned to refund the same, or any part thereof, as may be, if any claimant to the estate upon which such one-third shall become payable appear within the time hereinbefore limited, touching said estate and traverse the finding or adjudication of escheat, and establish the title to the property, real or personal, found to have escheated as aforesaid. (*Ibid.*, section 24.)

§ 1137. Feigned issue may be framed where conflicting claims to informer's compensation.

That in all cases of dispute where two or more persons shall claim the reward allowed by the preceding section of this Act, in consequence of information given to the auditor-general of an escheat, it shall and may be lawful for such person or persons, or either of them, to petition the court having jurisdiction of the escheat proceedings stating the facts, whereupon the said court may proceed to determine the matter of dispute, and if the case require, it may direct an issue to be framed between the parties to try their right to the reward aforesaid, which shall be paid according to the final determination of said court, or of said issue, as the case may be. (*Ibid.*, section 25.)

§ 1138. Commonwealth barred after twenty-one years.

That whensoever any property hath escheated or shall escheat to the Commonwealth by reason of the death of the owner last seised or possessed thereof, intestate without heirs or known kindred, a widow, or surviving husband, and there have been no proceedings had, as and for an escheat, for the period of twenty-one years after the decease of the said owner, the Commonwealth shall thereafter forever be debarred from claiming the same as escheated, and that whether such period hath already elapsed, or whensoever hereafter it shall have fully elapsed. (*Ibid.*, section 26.)

§ 1139. Fees.

That the fees in cases of escheat shall be as follows : To the escheator, five per centum on all moneys paid into the State treasury from the sales of escheated property, together with all expenses incurred by him for, in and about the prosecution of the escheat and the performance of the duties imposed upon him by this Act. And the fees of the prothonotaries, and the clerks of the several courts, and the sheriffs and witnesses, shall be the same which they are entitled to receive for similar services in the same court. The above fees and expenses shall be paid out of the State treasury by a warrant from the auditor-general in the customary manner. (*Ibid.*, section 27.)

§ 1140. **Repeal.**

That all Acts, or parts thereof, or supplements thereto relative to escheats, inconsistent with or supplied by the provisions of this Act, be and the same are hereby repealed. (*Ibid.*, section 28.)

§ 1141. **Conveyances by aliens or foreign corporations** to citizens of United States or to corporations of Pennsylvania, authorized to hold real estate before any inquisition taken, shall pass the title free of escheat. Act May 8, 1876, section 1 (P. L., 127). See also Acts of April 8, 1881 (P. L., 9); June 6, 1887 (P. L., 350); May 29, 1889 (P. L., 395).

§ 1142. **Attaint, holding by corporations, etc.** Other statutes provide for cases of attaint—purchases by corporations not authorized to hold, etc.

See Acts of September 29, 1787 (2 Sm. L., 431); April 6, 1833 (P. L., 167); April 19, 1844 (P. L., 313); April 26, 1855, sections 5, 9, 14 (P. L., 328); January 9, 1861 (P. L., 2); May 1, 1861 (P. L., 433); June 2, 1887 (P. L., 302).

§ 1143. **As to return of escheated deposits,** see Act of June 4, 1885 (P. L., 73), and § 1148 *infra.*

§ 1144. **Procedure modified by Act of 1889.** Of the following decisions, those made before the passage of the Act of 1889 must be read with the recollection that procedure in escheat is thereby radically modified. They may, however, aid in making clear the law as so altered, and the new methods of practice which will prevail under proceedings in the Orphans' Courts and elsewhere as established by that statute. They are inserted here in the hope that they will at least throw some light upon the subject.

§ 1145. **Land held by alien.** Upon the death of an alien seised of land it escheats to the State without office found ; but the legislature may vest it in the decedent's widow. *Rubeck* v. *Gardner,* 7 Watts, 455 (1838); see Act of May 1, 1861 (P. L., 433).

§ 1146. **Bargain and sale by lunatic will not bar escheat.** A deed of bargain and sale made by a lunatic, who afterward dies without heirs or kindred, will not prevent the escheat of the land to the Commonwealth. Feoffment and livery of seisin by the lunatic would, however, so far divest his seisin as to avoid the escheat at his death. *Estate of Desilver,* 5 Rawle, 111 (1835).

§ 1147. **Partnership** property. Under Act of June 27, 1864, (P. L., 951), if all the members of a partnership die intestate and without known heirs or kindred, the firm property escheats to the Commonwealth. *Comm.* v. *Land Co.*, 57 Pa. St., 102 (1868).

§ 1148. **Unclaimed funds on deposit.** Unclaimed funds in a saving fund society or deposit company are not subject to escheat under the Act of April 17, 1869 (P. L., 71). That Act contains no provisions by which it can be carried into effect, and the methods provided by Act of September 29, 1787 (2 Sm. L., 425), are not applicable to the escheat of moneys held in trust. Under Act of April 26, 1855, section 9 (P. L., 331), the proceedings must be by *quo warranto. West's Appeal,* 64 Pa. St., 186 (1870); *West* v. *Penna. Co., Id.,* 195 (1870).

The Act of June 4, 1885, section 1, as amended by the Act of June 25, 1895 (P. L., 283), is as follows :

SECTION 1. That whenever any bank, savings institution, or loan company, and each and every saving fund society, insurance or trust company, or other company, institution, association, or corporation' shall have escheated any dividend or profit, balance or deposit, or interest thereon to the Commonwealth, under the Act of Assembly, approved the sixth day of March, one thousand eight hundred and forty-seven, entitled " An Act requiring banks and other corporations to give notice of unclaimed dividends, deposits, and balances in certain cases," and the proceeds thereof are in the State treasury in money, the came shall be refunded to such person or persons, or his, her, or their legal representatives upon his, her, or their producing to the Governor or Auditor-General, State Treasurer, and Attorney-General satisfactory proof that he, she, or they are the person or persons, or the legal representative or representatives of the person or persons whose money has been so escheated.

§ 1149. **Estate in remainder.** An interest in remainder cannot be escheated until the expiration of the preceding life-estate ; and the Statute of Limitations does not begin to run against the Commonwealth until then. *Comm.* v. *Naile,* 88 Pa. St., 429 (1879).

§ 1150. **Property held in trust.** A passive trust will not prevent the estate of a decedent from escheating for want of heirs. *Id.*

§ 1151. **Unlawful holding by corporations.** Under the Act forbidding corporations to hold land in this State, unless expressly authorized (26th April, 1855, P. L., 329), such a corporation is not precluded from owning the chief and controlling interest in another corporation which is empowered to hold land. The latter may, in such case, purchase and hold the land free from liability to escheat.

Commonwealth v. *R. R. Co.,* 132 Pa. St., 591 (1890). In this case the Supreme Court recedes from the view taken by it in 1886, in *Commonwealth* v. *R. R. Co.*, 114 Pa. St., 340, in which it ruled that the question whether the arrangement was a mere device to avoid the escheat should have been left to the jury.   Opinion in the later case by PAXSON, C. J.; STERRETT and CLARK, JJ., dissenting.

Only the Commonwealth is empowered to proceed against a corporation to escheat land which it is incompetent to hold.   Such incompetency cannot be set up by a private person as a defense in an action of ejectment.   *Bone* v. *D. and H. Canal Co.*, 18 W. N., 125 (1886).

§ 1152. **Administrator may claim against escheator.**   An administrator holding assets formerly belonging to the decedent may claim that they are his property and no part of the estate.   He may traverse the inquisition.   The Orphans' Court will stay its adjudication pending the trial of the traverse in the Common Pleas.   *Comm.* v. *Crompton*, 26 W. N., 475 (1890) ; *Murray's Estate*, 13 W. N., 552 (1883).

§ 1153. **Commonwealth not bound by partition.**   If the estate of a tenant in common escheat, the Commonwealth is not bound by a partition of the land among the surviving tenants.   It retains its right to its undivided proportion of the land.   *Holmes* v. *Patterson*, 25 Pa. St., 484 (1854).

§ 1154. **Limitation.**   Upon the subject of the bar of the Statute of Limitations, see section 26 of the Act of May 2, 1889, *supra*, section 1138.

§ 1155. **Escheated land cannot be granted by warrant and survey.** After escheat and forfeiture, the Commonwealth cannot grant the escheated land again by warranty and survey.   If it do so, such grant is a nullity, and confers no title.   *Straub* v. *Dimm*, 27 Pa. St., 36 (1856).

§ 1156. **Trial and evidence.**   In regard to practice upon trial of the traverse, and as to admissibility of evidence, see *Comm.* v. *Hoe*, 26 Leg. Int., 124 (1869).   The Commonwealth is not entitled to a second trial after verdict for the traverser.   *Id.*

§ 1157. **Equity will not interfere.**   The proceedings in escheat should not be enjoined in equity where the questions involved may properly be decided upon a traverse.   *Olmsted's Appeal*, 86 Pa. St., 284 (1878).

§ 1158 **Execution set aside.**   After finding of decease without heirs or kindred, execution should not issue against the administrator during the year following the grant of letters to him.   *Comm.* v. *Weart*, 6 W. N., 237 (1878).   Nor after adjudication in the Orphans' Court and award of the balance in his hands, such award being unappealed from. *Comm.* v. *Palmer*, *Id.*, 486 (1879). In each of the above cases a writ of *fi. fa.* was set aside.

§ 1159. **Claim of the informer** is not directly against the escheator for his share of the commission. It is a claim against the State upon the fund coming into its treasury. *Ayre's Estate*, 1 Pearson, 413 (1859).

§ 1159 *a*. **Compensation allowed deputy escheator where proceedings fail by discovery of next of kin.** Where escheat proceedings fail by the discovery of next of kin, reasonable compensation will be allowed deputy escheator and his counsel. *Bryant's Estate*, 4 Dist. Rep., 192 (1895).

CHAPTER XX.

§ 1160. Office of Alderman abolished. By the Constitution of 1874, Article V., section 12, the office of alderman was abolished as to the city of Philadelphia, and in place thereof the office of magistrate, with jurisdiction not exceeding $100, was created for each thirty thousand inhabitants. The Act of June 1, 1891 (P. L., 143), provides that justices of the peace may secure and use a seal to be affixed to official papers.

§ 1161. Jurisdiction of magistrates in criminal cases—Constitutional safeguards. The Constitution of 1874, Article I., section 8, provides :

" The people shall be secure in their persons, houses, papers, and possessions, from unreasonable searches and seizures ; and no warrant to search any place, or to seize any person or things, shall issue without describing them as nearly as may be, nor without probable cause, supported by oath or affirmation, subscribed to by the affiant."

Article I., section 9 :

" In all criminal prosecutions the accused hath a right to be heard by himself and his counsel, to demand the nature and cause of the accusation against him, to meet the witnesses face to face, to have compulsory process for obtaining witnesses in his favor ; and in prosecutions by indictment or information, a speedy public trial by an impartial jury of the vicinage ; he cannot be compelled to give evidence against himself, nor can he be deprived of his life, liberty, or property unless by the judgment of his peers or the law of the land."

Article I., section 13 :

Excessive bail shall not be required, nor excessive fines imposed, nor cruel punishments inflicted.

§ 1162. As to recognizances.

It is the duty of every justice in Philadelphia before whom any recognizance of bail or surety in any criminal or supposed criminal case shall be taken, to set down accurately and at large, in a docket or record for that purpose, the name, place of abode, particularly describing the same, and the occupation or business of such recognizor or surety ; and if he shall not be a housekeeper, the name and place of abode, particularly describing the same, and the occupation or business of the person or persons with whom he resides. Such justices shall make a full and complete return of said recognizance or surety to the proper court, and all and every the sureties so made on his docket or record relating to such recognizance, together with the proceedings of such justice relating to the case. (Act March 30, 1821, section 1 ; 7 Sm., 426.)

If the justice neglect or refuse to comply with the provisions of this Act, such neglect or refusal shall be deemed a misdemeanor in office. (*Id.*, section 4.)

§ 1163. Recognizances to be returned.

The justices shall be required to return to the clerk of the Quarter Sessions all the recognizances entered into before them by any persons charged with the commission of crime, excepting such cases as may be ended at least ten days before the commencement of the session of the court to which they are made returnable. In cases where recognizances are entered into less than ten days before the commencement of the session to which they are made returnable, the said justices are required to return the same in the same manner as if this Act had not been passed. (Act May 8, 1854, section 1 ; P. L., 678.)

§ 1164. Justices may take bail.

When anyone is arrested on a warrant or bail-piece in any criminal case in which a justice of the peace would be allowed to take recognizance of bail for his appearance to answer the offense or crime, the officer making the arrest may take the accused before a justice and have him released on requisite security, and his return, when properly made, shall exonerate him from further liability. (Act February 23, 1870, section 1 ; P. L., 227.)

§ 1165. Criminal complaint to be entered on docket and returned to court.

The Act of June 11, 1885 (P. L., 110), provides that it shall be the duty of justices and committing magistrates, upon complaint being made in criminal cases upon oath or affirmation of any person, to enter such complaint upon their docket, with the name, residence, and occupation, if any, of all defendants, bail, and witnesses, and return to the clerk of the Quarter Sessions a true transcript within five days after the binding over or committal, and any wilful violation of these requirements shall be declared to be a misdemeanor in office.

The elaboration of the criminal jurisdiction of justices has no place in this work. It may be proper, however, to give a few directions upon this subject.

§ 1166. Issuing a warrant.

Never advise the commencement of a criminal proceeding except in a clear case. If satisfied of this, prepare your client's information. Where the magistrate keeps a book for the purpose (the only proper, but oft-neglected practice), write the complaint or get it written in the book. Your client or the witness signs and swears to it ; the warrant is given to the constable with directions as to the service. You, of course, understand :

(1) That the complaint must be made by one cognizant of the facts, and that it must charge a violation of the criminal law.

(2) That it must give the defendant's name, if known, and, if this be unknown, it must state the fact and describe the person.

(3) That the complaint must be under oath or affirmation.

Disregard of these directions may involve serious consequences.

§ 1167. **A warrant issued on suspicion is void.** In *Connor* v. *Comm.*, 3 Binn., 43 (1810), the warrant was set forth at large in the indictment. It was issued without any previous oath or affirmation, because "it appeared to the judge, from *common report*, that there was strong reason to suspect the said Langs of having knowingly uttered, as true and genuine, certain false and forged notes, purporting to be notes of the Farmers' and Mechanics' Bank of Philadelphia, and that he was likely to depart from and quit the county and retreat to parts unknown, before the witnesses could be summoned before the said judge to enable him to issue a warrant on their testimony on oath." It was held that the warrant was illegal, and that the constable was not bound to execute it.

§ 1168. **But a criminal may be arrested without warrant.** In *Wakely* v. *Hart*, 6 Binn., 318 (1814), the plaintiff had been arrested by the constable, assisted by others, upon information that he had stolen a watch. He was taken to jail without a warrant; the watch was found in his possession, and there were other circumstances raising a presumption of guilt.

The defendant sued for false imprisonment, complaining that no warrant had been issued.

Chief Justice TILGHMAN said : " The provision that no warrant shall issue without describing any person or thing as nearly as may be, nor without probable cause, supported by oath or affirmation, only guards against abuse.

" But it is nowhere said that there shall be no arrest without warrant. To have said so would have endangered the safety of society. The felon who is seen to commit murder or robbery must be arrested on the spot or suffered to escape. So, although not seen, yet if known to have committed a felony, and pursued with or without warrant, he may be arrested by any person. These are principles of the common law essential to the welfare of society, and not intended to be altered or impaired by the Constitution."

§ 1169. **Search warrant.** Where your client is pursuing property stolen from him, you can obtain a search warrant if he can swear to the larceny, and that the goods stolen are in a certain place, describing it and the property. You should here be careful to follow the Constitution and the statute.

§ 1170. **Description required in search warrant.** In *Moore* v.

Coxe, 10 W. N., 185 (1881), the search warrant described the goods as "a quantity of jewelry and other personal effects, etc."

The description was considered sufficient, as it indicated the general character of the goods sought for.

But it is recommended to give a full description of the property where practicable to do so.

§ 1171. **Duty of magistrate at hearing.** When the defendant is arrested, the prosecutor and his witnesses are examined. If a case of probable cause is made out, it is the duty of the magistrate to bind over, and if the case be not bailable, to commit.

§ 1172. **Magistrate cannot inquire into credibility of witnesses—That question is for a jury.** In a preliminary hearing before a committing magistrate on a criminal charge, where the offenses charged have been positively sworn to, the credibility of a witness cannot be inquired into. A grand or petit jury must ascertain whether the witness is worthy of belief. *Comm.* v. *Roop*, 15 W. N., 419 (1885).

If the offense be bailable and security be tendered, he should be examined under oath and his answers recorded.

If bound over, and especially if committed, it is the defendant's privilege to apply for a writ of *habeas corpus*. An abstract of the legislation and of decisions on this subject may assist the practitioner.

§ 1173. **Habeas corpus Act.**

If any person shall be committed or detained for any criminal or supposed criminal matter, unless for treason or felony, the species whereof is set forth in the warrant of commitment, in vacation time and out of term, it shall be lawful for the person so committed or detained, or anyone on his or her behalf, to appeal or complain to any judge of the Supreme Court or to the president or associate judge of the Court of Common Pleas for the county within which the person is so committed or detained; and such judge or justice, upon a view of the copy or copies of the warrant or warrants of commitment or detainer, or otherwise, upon oath or affirmation legally made that such copy or copies were denied to be given by the person or persons in whose custody the prisoner is detained, is hereby authorized and required, upon request made in writing by such prisoner, or any person in his or her behalf, attested and subscribed by two witnesses, who were present at the delivery of the same, to award and grant a *habeas corpus*, under the seal of the court, to be directed to the person or persons in whose custody the prisoner is detained, returnable immediately before the said judge or justices; and to the intent, and that no officer, sheriff, jailer, keeper, or other person to whom such writ shall be directed may pretend ignorance of the import thereof, every such writ shall be made in this manner: "*By Act of Assembly, one thousand seven hundred and eighty-five,*" and shall be signed by the judge or justice who awards the same. (Act of February 18, 1785, section 1; 2 Sm., 275; Act of April 13, 1791, section 9; 3 Sm., 30.)

§ 1174. Duty of person receiving the writ of the judge, etc.

Whenever the writ shall be served upon the officer, sheriff, jailer, keeper, or other persons whatsoever to whom the same shall be directed, by being brought to him, or by being left with any of his under officers or deputies, at the jail or place where the prisoner is detained, he or some of his under officers or deputies shall within three days after the service thereof, upon payment or tender of the charges of bringing the said prisoner, to be ascertained by the judge or justice who awarded the writ, and thereon indorsed, not exceeding twelve pence per mile, and upon security given, by his own bond, to pay the charges of carrying him back, if he shall be remanded, and not to escape by the way, make return of such writ and bring or cause to be brought the body of the prisoner unto or before the judge or justice before whom the said writ is made returnable; and in case of his absence, before any other of the judges or justices; and shall certify specifically and fully the true cause or causes of commitment and detainer of the prisoner, and when he was committed, unless the commitment be in any place beyond the distance of twenty miles, and not above one hundred miles, then within ten days, and if beyond the distance of one hundred miles, then within twenty days.

The judge or justice before whom the prisoner shall be brought shall within two days discharge the prisoner from imprisonment, taking his or her recognizance, with one or more surety or sureties, in any sum according to his discretion, having regard to the circumstances of the prisoner and nature of the offense, for his or her appearance at the next Quarter Sessions of the county where the offense was committed, or in such other court where it may be properly cognizable, as the case shall require, and then shall certify the said writ, with the return thereof, and the said recognizances into the court where such appearance is to be made, unless it shall appear to the said judge or justice that the party so committed is detained upon legal process, order, or warrant for such matter or offenses for which by the law the said prisoner is not bailable. And that the judge or justice may, according to the intent and meaning of this Act, be enabled, by investigating the truth of the circumstances of the case, to determine whether according to law the said prisoner ought to be bailed, remanded, or discharged, the return may, before or after it is filed, by leave of the said judge or justice, be amended, and also suggestions made against it, so that thereby material facts may be ascertained. (Act February 18, 1785, section 1; 2 Sm., 275.)

§ 1175. Right to writ in term time.

In term time it shall be lawful for any prisoner in proper manner to move and obtain his or her *habeas corpus* out of the Supreme Court or the Court of Common Pleas for the county in which he or she is imprisoned, whereupon proceedings shall be had as aforesaid. (*Id.*, section 2.)

§ 1176. The two-term law.

If any person shall be committed for treason or felony, and shall not be indicted and tried in the next term after such commitment, it shall be lawful for the judges or justices, and they are required upon the last day of the term, to set at liberty the said prisoner upon bail; unless it shall appear, upon oath or affirmation, that the witnesses for the Commonwealth, mentioning their names, could not then be produced; if such prisoner shall not

be indicted and tried the second term after his or her commitment, unless
the delay happen on the application or with the assent of the defendant, or
upon trial shall be acquitted, he or she shall be discharged from imprisonment. (*Id.*, section 3.)

Provided, that this shall not be construed to discharge from prison any
person guilty of or charged with treason, felony, or other high misdemeanor
in any other State, and who by the confederation ought to be delivered up
to the executive power of such State, nor any person guilty of, or charged
with, a breach or violation of the laws of nations. (*Id.*, section 4.)

Provided, also, that nothing in this Act shall extend to discharge from
prison any person charged with debt or other action, or with process in
any civil cause, but that after discharge for such criminal or supposed
criminal matter, he or she shall be kept in custody, according to law, for
such other suit. (*Id.*, section 5.)

§ 1177. The fifteen-day section.

In order that no person shall
avoid a trial by procuring a removal, so that he or she cannot be
brought back in time, it is enacted that—

No person shall be removed upon *habeas corpus* within fifteen days next
preceding the term of the court, but upon such *habeas corpus* shall be
brought before the judges, who are thereupon to do what to justice shall
appertain. (*Id.*, section 6.)

Provided, that after such court the person detained may have his or her
habeas corpus. (*Id.*, section 7.)

§ 1178. Penalty if judge refuse the writ.

If any judge, being appealed to, upon view of the copy or copies of the
warrant or warrants of commitment, or upon oath or affirmation made that
such copy or copies were denied, shall refuse or neglect to award any writ
of *habeas corpus* by this Act to be granted, he shall forfeit to the prisoner
or party grieved £300. (*Id.*, section 8.)

§ 1179. Penalty for failing to return writ.

If any officer, sheriff, jailer, keeper, or other person to whom such writ
shall be directed, or any of the under officers or deputies, shall refuse or
neglect to make the returns, or to bring the body of the prisoner, according
to the command of the writ, within the respective times, all and every such
officer, sheriff, jailer, keeper, or other person, under officer, or deputy shall be
guilty of a contempt of the court under the seal of which the said writ shall
have issued, and shall also forfeit to the party aggrieved £100 for the first
offense, and £200 for the second offense, and shall be incapable of holding
or executing his office. (*Id.*, section 9.)

§ 1180. Penalty for refusing copy of warrant.

If any officer, sheriff, jailer, keeper, or other person to whom such writ
shall be directed, or any of his under officers or deputies, upon demand
by the prisoner, or some person in his or her behalf, shall refuse to deliver, or within six hours after demand shall not deliver to the prisoner or
person so demanding a true copy or copies of the warrant or warrants of
commitment or detainer of such prisoner, which are required to be delivered, all and every such officer, sheriff, jailer, keeper, or other person, under

officer, or deputy so offending shall for the first offense forfeit to the prisoner or party grieved £100, and for the second offense £200, and shall also be and is hereby made incapable to hold or execute his said office. (*Id.*, section 10.)

§ 1181. Penalty for re-arrest.

And for preventing unjust vexation by reiterated commitments for the same offense : *Be it enacted,* that no person who shall be delivered or set at large upon a *habeas corpus* shall, at any time thereafter, be again committed or imprisoned for the same offense by any person or persons whatsoever other than by the legal order and process of such court wherein he or she shall be bound by recognizance to appear, or other court having jurisdiction of the cause; and if any other person or persons shall knowingly, contrary to this Act, recommit or imprison, or knowingly procure or cause to be recommitted or imprisoned for the same offense, or supposed offense, any person delivered or set at large as aforesaid, or be knowingly aiding or assisting therein, then he or they shall forfeit to the prisoner or party grieved, any pretense of variation in the warrant or warrants of commitment notwithstanding, the sum of £500, to be recovered by the prisoner or party grieved. (*Id.*, section 11.)

§ 1182. Prisoners not to be removed except by writ.

Any person being committed to any prison, or in custody of any officer, sheriff, jailer, keeper, or other person, or his under officer or deputy for any criminal or supposed criminal matter, shall not be removed from the prison or custody into any other prison or custody unless it be by *habeas corpus* or some other legal writ, or where the prisoner is delivered to the constable or other inferior officer to be carried to some common jail, or where any person is sent by any judge or justice having proper authority to some common workhouse or house of correction, or where the prisoner is removed from one place to another within the same county, in order to his or her trial or discharge in due course of law, or in case of sudden fire or infection or other necessity; and if any person or persons shall, after such commitment as aforesaid, make out, sign, countersign, and issue any warrant or warrants for such removal, except as before excepted, then he or they shall forfeit to the prisoner or party grieved £200, to be recovered by the prisoner or party grieved, in manner aforesaid. (*Id.*, section 12.)

§ 1183. Habeas corpus lies in all cases of restraint.

All provisions made for awarding and granting writs of *habeas corpus* and proceeding thereon, in case of commitment or detainer for any criminal or supposed criminal matter, shall extend to all cases where any person, not being committed or detained for any criminal or supposed criminal matter, shall be confined or restrained of his or her liberty under any color or pretense whatsoever; and upon oath or affirmation made by such person so confined or restrained, or by any other person in his or her behalf of any actual confinement or restraint which is not, to the best of the knowledge and belief of the person so applying, by virtue of any commitment or detainer for any criminal or supposed criminal matter, a *habeas corpus* directed to the person or persons so confining or restraining the party shall be awarded and granted, in the same manner as hereinbefore provided, and the court, judge, or justice before whom the party so confined or restrained shall be brought, shall, after the return made, proceed to examine into the facts relating to the case, and into the cause of such confinement or restraint; and thereupon either bail, remand, or discharge the party so brought, as to justice shall appertain. (*Id.*, section 13.)

§ 1184. Duty of party served with writ—Penalty for refusal.

Wherever any writ of *habeas corpus* awarded and granted, either in term time or vacation, for any person so confined or restrained, and without a commitment for any criminal or supposed criminal matter, shall be served upon the person or persons so confining or restraining such party, by being brought to such person or persons, or by being left at the place where the party shall be so confined or restrained, the person or persons so confining or restraining such party shall make return of such writ, and bring, or cause to be brought, the body of such party according to the command thereof, within the respective times limited, and under the provisions of this Act. Every person refusing or neglecting to make return of such writ, or to bring, or cause to be brought, the body of the party according to the command thereof, within the times respectively limited, shall be guilty of a contempt of the court under the seal of which the said writ shall have issued, and shall forfeit for the first offense to the party aggrieved £100, and for the second offense £200. (*Id.*, section 14.)

§ 1185. Limitation of actions.

No person shall be sued, impleaded, molested, or troubled for any offense against this Act unless such person be sued or impleaded for the same within two years after the time wherein the said offense shall have been committed, in case the party grieved shall not then be in prison, or confined or restrained. If so, then within two years after such release. (*Id.*, section 15.)

In or upon any action for any offense against this Act, the defendant or defendants may plead the general issue, and give the special matter in evidence. (*Id.*, section 16.)

§ 1186. Associate judges may issue writ—It may be issued in vacation—Judge may issue subpœnas, etc.

The president and associate judges shall severally have the powers to issue writs of *habeas corpus* in vacation time and out of term, and to give relief as fully as the president of any Court of Common Pleas at present may or can do. (Act April 13, 1791, section 9; 3 Sm., 30.)

This Act was extended to the judges of the Court of Quarter Sessions of the Peace of Philadelphia County by Act April 4, 1837, section 2 (P. L., 378).

The judge or court before whom any writ of *habeas corpus* shall be returnable shall have the power to issue subpœnas and all other process necessary to compel the attendance of witnesses. (Act April 17, 1866, section 1; P. L., 112.)

§ 1187. Costs. The officer making service and the witnesses are allowed the costs and fees as for similar service and attendance before magistrates.

Costs of service and attendance on the part of the Commonwealth shall be paid by the proper county and taxed as costs in the case. (*Id.*, section 2.)

The Court of Common Pleas or any judge before whom any writ of *habeas corpus* shall be heard shall make an order for the payment by the proper county or by the prosecutors in the case of the costs and fees of witnesses. (Act April 14, 1868, section 1; P. L., 98.)

§ 1188. **Who may have the writ.** A writ of *habeas corpus* may issue upon the petition and affidavit of any person who claims the right of custody over the person restrained. *Holsey* v. *Trevillo*, 6 Watts, 402 (1837).

But if issued without the authority of the relator, the writ will be dismissed. *Comm.* v. *Killacky*, 3 Brews., 565 (1869).

A writ of habeas corpus will not be allowed where the relator has given bail. *Comm.* v. *Gill*, 27 W. N., 311 (1890); *Comm.* v. *Sheriff*, 2 Dist. Rep., 321 (1893).

§ 1189. **How the writ is procured.** The party applying is called the petitioner. When the writ has issued he is termed the relator. If detained upon any process, he must secure a copy of it or be able to swear that he has demanded it, and that the copy has been refused. As already noted, the writ lies in all cases of illegal restraint. A parent may use it to obtain the custody of a child. A husband may issue it for his wife. The wife has been allowed to petition as the attorney of her husband. To touch upon all these cases, still more to treat of them, would expand a book on practice into a dissertation upon the writ and require a volume.

§ 1190. **Petition for the writ of habeas corpus—Instructions.** Like all other petitions, these vary according to the facts. The following is perhaps the most common form :

> Commonwealth *ex. rel.* }
>   *v.* }
> The Keeper of the Philadelphia County Prison. }

To the Honorable   , Judge of the Court of Oyer and Terminer and Quarter Sessions of the Peace of the county of   :

The petition of   humbly showeth that he is illegally in the custody of the keeper of the Philadelphia County Prison, and is unlawfully restrained of his liberty upon a charge which will appear upon reference to the subjoined paper and certificate. He therefore humbly prays your Honor to issue a writ of *habeas corpus* for his relief, agreeably to the Act of Assembly of the 18th of February, one thousand seven hundred and eighty-five. And as in duty bound he will ever pray, etc.

> Witnesses,   }
>   }
>   (Signature and date.)

Sometimes the petitioner is in the custody of the sheriff, sometimes of his bail. Where the petition is by a parent for the custody of a child, it is usual to set out the facts. The petition is presented to a judge, indorsed *writ allowed, returnable*   . The judge fills in the blank for the return-day and signs the allowance. You take this to the clerk, who gives you the writ. Keep a copy.

Serve the original on the respondent. On the day named the respondent must produce the body or show good reason for his omission to do so, and he must attach the commitment, etc. In a criminal case, if you are counsel for the relator, you should notify the district attorney, the magistrate, the prosecutor, and all the witnesses of the issuing of the writ and of the time fixed for the hearing.

§ 1190 a. *Where application made for writ of habeas corpus to discharge inmate of penitentiary, notice to be given authorities that may have committed relator.*

That hereafter when application shall be made to any court of this Commonwealth, or a judge thereof, by an inmate of either of the penitentiaries of the State for a writ of *habeas corpus* for the discharge of such inmate, the court or judge directing such writ to issue and before whom the application shall be heard shall, before the hearing of such application and the discharge of any such inmate, have submitted to it or him proof of notice of the intended application to the authority or authorities that may have committed such inmate to the said penitentiary, and it shall not be lawful for such court or judge to order the discharge of such inmate without proof of notice as aforesaid to the authority or authorities. Act of June 6, 1893 (P. L., 828).

§ 1191. *Petition for* habeas corpus—*case of an infant.* The following form was used as a petition for *habeas corpus* by a father against the mother for the custody of an infant child :

To the Honorable   , one of the Judges of the Court of Quarter Sessions of the Peace for the city and county of Philadelphia :

The petition of   and of   by his father and next friend   , humbly showeth :

That the said   is the son of the petitioner   and   his wife. That on the   day of   , A. D. 18 , the said   · unlawfully deserted the home of her said husband   , and at the time of said desertion took away with her the said   , who was at that time upward of   years. That the taking away of the said   was not only without the consent of his father, but against his known wish and in spite of his express prohibition. That the said   has since requested his wife, the said   , to return to his home and to her duty, and thereby restore to him the lawful custody of his said infant son, but the said   has nevertheless refused so to do.

Your petitioners therefore show that the said   is now illegally restrained of his liberty in this city by the said   , and humbly pray your Honor that a writ of *habeas corpus* may be issued, directed to the said   , commanding her forthwith to bring before your Honor the body of the said   , and show cause, if any she hath, why the said   should not be relieved of the said illegal restraint, and why he should not be delivered into the custody of his said father.

And as in duty bound, etc.

> (Signature of son)
> by his father and next friend.
> (Signature of father.)

(Name of father), one of the petitioners, having been duly sworn according to law, doth depose and say that the facts set forth in the foregoing petition are true and correct.

Sworn to and subscribed before me,   (Signed.)
this   day of   , A. D. 18 .

Notary Public.

§ 1192. Return claiming right to custody of a child. The following may serve as outlining the return in such a case.

To the Honorable the Judges in the annexed writ, named:

(Name of respondent), therein named, in obedience thereto, doth certify that she has the body of (name of infant), therein named, before the said judge, at the time and place therein commanded.

That the said (name of infant) is her son and only child; that he was born on the   day of   , A. D. 18 , and that he will not be   years old until the   of   , A. D. 18 ; that he was born at Philadelphia, in the State of Pennsylvania; that from his birth to the present day he has never been separated from her, that she is his guardian by nature and for nurture, and that her care of him is indispensably necessary for his present and future welfare; that he is now in her custody for the proper and necessary purposes of such care and guardianship, and for no other purpose, and in no other manner, and is in no respect restrained of his liberty or detained illegally; that in her care and guardianship the moral and religious education of her said child is, and will be, suitably attended to, and his and her associations are, and will be, exclusively with persons of upright character and moral and religious habits; that her father (name), residing at No.   , in this city, is possessed of ample means to support and educate the said child in a manner befitting his station and suitable to his expectations, and will do so, provided his father (name), shall refuse to do so, or fail to do so when he shall be required so to do by due process of law hereafter to be had.

That the present age of her said child does not admit of his separation from her without the greatest danger to his health, which requires especial care and attention from her; he needs, and for some years to come will need, a mother's nursing care, which no one else can supply.

That the respondent was married to   , the relator, the father of the said child, at Philadelphia, in the State of Pennsylvania, in the month of   , in the year (date). That from that time until about (date) she lived and cohabited with the said (name), her husband, in the said city of Philadelphia, when on or about the (date), when her child was but   old, she was obliged to take her child and leave her husband, and go to the residence of her father, in this city (name), because of the cruel and barbarous treatment of her said husband to her, he committing acts of violence upon her person, and otherwise physically abusing and maltreating her, to which he added a variety of other circumstances, such as abusive and insulting names and opprobrious epithets, which rendered her life burthensome and condition intolerable, and so at that time obliged her to withdraw herself and her child from the house and society of her husband; that this absence continued for about the period of one week, when, because of the intercession and intervention of the friends of her said husband in his behalf, and because of his solemn promise made to herself, and to her father and to her mother, to amend his life, and to treat her with affection, gentleness, and decorum, as a wife should be treated by her husband, she consented to return with her child to him, and she did so return, and from that time to the (date) she lived and resided with him with her child.

That during that time the said relator abstained from acts of actual violence, but he continued repeating and renewing his former course of conduct. toward her; he was abusive, insulting, violent, and subject to paroxysms and gusts of temper that bordered on insanity. In a variety of ways, both by his manner and his general and unbroken course of deportment, conduct, and language toward her, he disappointed all the expectations of sympathy and affection which he promised to her father, her mother, and herself, to bestow upon her and to display toward her when she had consented to return, and did return in (date); that he refused during all this time to cohabit with her, and excluded himself from her company, and constantly treated her with personal indignity in the presence of their servant by many silent and inexpressible acts of slight and affront; that when the servant was gone, and late at night, he would assail her, abuse her, and rail at her, and apply insulting names to her, and boastfully told her at those times that she had no witnesses; and this conduct continued and became worse and worse from day to day, when (date), she made a personal application to a gentleman with whom   is concerned in business, and who had been the interceding friend for (name), when she was prevailed upon to return to him (date), as before stated. She recited to this gentleman the misery of her life, and asked him to interfere, and prevent and correct, if possible, the conduct of her husband, notwithstanding which her husband continued and repeated his former course of violent, abusive, insulting, and cruel and barbarous treatment toward her in an aggravated degree, and offered indignities to the person of your respondent, until finally she became inexpressibly wretched by the conviction that there was to be no mitigation of her sufferings while she continued in his society and under his control, and her condition was intolerable and her life burthensome, when, on the (date), she was compelled and thereby forced to withdraw from his house and family. She emphatically denies, as is asserted by the relator in his petition, that she unlawfully deserted the home of her said husband (name), and she hereby avers and affirms that her withdrawal was lawful and necessary, and that it was not a desertion, and that it was and is her intention to apply to the courts for protection and support by a proceeding in divorce, and that she has withheld those proceedings from a desire to avoid litigation and exposure, and pending an application made by her counsel for her in her behalf, to have her said husband adjust some suitable terms of separation in an amicable way, and to arrange how and when, and as often as he should name, at such reasonable times and places as he should select, he could enjoy the society of their child (name), all of which her counsel in her behalf proposed and submitted to the said relator in writing, and all of which the said relator has refused in writing to entertain or consider. That the said respondent would long before the (date) have withdrawn from the house and family of the relator by reason of his said conduct, but she was restrained and submitted to all his cruelties because of womanly and wifely and motherly reluctance to involve her family, her husband, her child, and herself, and a public exposure of the distressing life she had led and the scenes she had endured. But by force of the ill treatment she has received, and has before this set forth, and by force of all the considerations herein expressed, she is now living separate and apart from her said husband and under the protection of her parents (names of parents), in this city, and with them, and in their house she has resided with her child since the day she left her said husband, and she feels compelled to continue in this state of separation, and to retain the custody of her child. Her said parents have, at her request, considered the causes of this separation, and given it their entire sanction and approval. Under these circumstances, the respondent is advised that she is not required by law, for the purpose of a hearing involving merely the present custody of her infant child, to enter upon the most painful task of detailing the particular causes which have led to this melancholy result of her marriage, but she begs to reserve the privilege of stating and proving them in case of need, with such explanations as may be deemed necessary for her entire justification in the premises.

That she firmly believes that the interests of the said child in every respect in which an impartial person can regard them would be seriously prejudiced by removal from her custody at this time, or for some years to come. She is advised that in consequence of the tender age of her child at this time that the laws and usages of this Commonwealth will not permit her child to be taken from her until his age shall be much more advanced than it is now. The respondent concludes by again throwing herself upon the judgment of the court, upon that part of the return which particularly adverts to the age and circumstances of her child.

Sworn to and subscribed before }   (Signature of Respondent.)
    me, this   day of |
                A. D. 18   .   }
            Notary Public. }

§ 1193.

FORM OF TRAVERSE.

In the matter of   } In the Court of Quarter Sessions of the
    Commonwealth *ex rel.* | Peace of Philadelphia County,
            v. |
                              } Sessions, 18   .   No.   .

And now (date), the return to the writ of *habeas corpus* in this case having been read and filed, the petitioner traverses the same and says :

1. That the said defendant is not the guardian by nature and nurture of the said infant child, and is not entitled to the exclusive possession and custody of the said child.

2. That the said defendant did not lawfully and with sufficient cause, but on the contrary thereof did unlawfully and without sufficient cause, and now does unlawfully and without sufficient cause, absent herself and remain away from the house of the petitioner.

3. That it is untrue that the relator has done and committed the acts alleged by the defendant in the said return to the writ.

4. That the said defendant unlawfully and without sufficient cause has detained, and now detains, the body of the infant child of the relator.

                                        (Signature of Relator.)
(Usual affidavit.)

§ 1194. **Father's right to custody of child.** In the following cases the right of the father to the custody of a minor child was recognized :

Rex v. *Johnson,* 2 Lord Raymond, 1333 (1723); Ex parte *Hopkins,* 3 P. Williams, 152 (1732); *Blissett's Case,* Loft's Rep., 748 (1774); *King* v. *DeManneville,* 5 East R., 221 (1804); Ex parte *McClellan,* 1 Dowling, K. B. P. C. R., 81 (1831); *Ball* v. *Ball,* 2 Simons R. (Ch.), 35 (1827); *Rex* v. *Greenhill,* 4 Ad. & Ellis, 624 (1836); *Regina* v. *Smith,* 16 Eng. L. & Eq. R., 221 (1852); In re *Halliday's Estate,* 17 Eng. L. & Eq. R., 77 (1853); In re *Hakewell,* 22 *Id.,* 395 (1853); In re *Andrews,* 21 Weekly Reporter, 480 (1873); In re *Edwards,* 42 L. J. Q. B., 99 (1873); In re *Agar-Ellis* v. *Lascelles,* 39 L. T. (N. S.), 380; *People* v. *Chegary,* 18 Wendell (N. Y.), 637 (1836); *People* v. ———, 19 *Id.,* 16 (1837); *Mercein* v. *People,* 25 *Id.,* 65 (1840); *Id.* v. *Id.,* 8 Paige (N. Y.), 47 (1839); *Id.* v. *Id.,* 3 Hill (N.Y.), 399 (1842); *Lindsey* v. *Lindsey,* 14 Georgia, 657 (1854); Ex parte *Hewitt,* 11 Richardson (S. C.), 326; *Nichols* v. *Nichols,* 3 Duer (N. Y.), 642 (1854); *People* v. *Humphreys,* 24 Barb. (N. Y.), 521 (1857); Ex parte *Boaz,* 31 Ala., 425 (1858); *People* v. *Olmstead,* 27 Barb. (N. Y.), 9 (1857); *People* v. *Brooks,* 35 *Id.,* 85 (1861); *State* v. *Richardson,* 40 N. H., 272 (1860); *Comm.* v. *Briggs,* 16 Pick., 203; *Johnson* v. *Terry,* 34 Conn., 259 (1867); *Carr* v. *Carr,* 22 Grattan (Va.), 168 (1872); *Comm.* v. *Potter,* 3 Luz. Leg. Reg., 209 (1874); *Fitler* v. *Fitler,* 2 Phila., 348 (1858).

On a *habeas corpus* proceeding where the wife has arbitrarily deserted her husband, the children will be awarded the husband. *Comm.* v. *Davison,* 4 Dist. Rep., 103 (1895).

§ 1195. **Mother's right to custody of child.** In the following cases the mother successfully maintained her claim to the custody of the minor :

Comm. v. *Addicks,* 5 Binney, 520 (1813); *Hart* v. *Hart,* 8 W. N., 156 (1880).

In the former case the decree was changed three years later. *Comm.* v. *Addicks,* 2 S. & R., 174.

§ 1196. **True rule as to custody of child claimed by father and mother.** The rule seems to recognize no arbitrary standard of sex or age, but to refer the whole question to this inquiry : What is best for the true interest of the child ? *Brown's Estate,* 166 Pa. St., 249 (1895).

The court will use its discretion in awarding the custody of a minor child. *Comm.* v. *Wise,* 3 Dist. Rep., 290 (1893).

In cases of dispute as to which parent shall be entitled to the custody and services of the child, the court in its discretion shall decide—regard first being had to the fitness of the parent and the best interest and permanent welfare of the child.   *Comm.* v. *Dugan*, 2 Dist. Rep., 772 (1893).

The Act of June 26, 1895 (P. L., 316), provides that a married woman who is the mother of a minor child and contributes toward its support, maintenance, and education, shall have equal power, control, and authority over her. child, and shall have equal right to its custody and services as now by law possessed by the husband, the father of the child, provided the mother is a fit and proper person.

§ 1197. **The return must be full and explicit.**   Where the body is produced with the original commitment or writ or paper under which the relator is detained, this is a compliance.   But if the body be not produced, the respondent must be careful to make a satisfactory return.   See *Passmore Williamson's Case*, 26 Pa. St., 9 (1855).

To say that the relator is not *now* in respondent's custody is clearly insufficient, for if the relator were in respondent's custody when the writ was served, the fact that he has been placed in some other person's hands after the service of the writ is no excuse for not producing the body.   If it be the fact that the relator "*never* was in the custody or power or possession of the respondent, and never was by him confined or restrained," it is easy so to return. But if the party had at any time been in the power, etc., of the respondent, such a return would be false.   It was upon this finding that Mr. Williamson was committed in the above case.

The decision in *The Queen* v. *Barnardo* (Gossage's Case), Law Jour. Reports (N. S.), vol. 59, p. 345 (Chancery Division, January 24, 27, 1890; Court of Appeal), presented some peculiar facts.   Harry Gossage, a boy of ten years of age, was abandoned by his mother, his father being dead, in September, 1888, and was received into one of Dr. Barnardo's homes for destitute children. November 10, 1888, a proper person applied for a boy to be adopted and taken to Canada.   Gossage was selected, to be taken November 16, 1888.   November 11, a letter was received at the institute expressing a desire to remove the boy to a Catholic home. November 16, 1888, the boy was delivered to the Canadian.   As he was not handed over to the mother, she obtained a rule *nisi* for a *habeas corpus*.   The return to the rule set out the facts at length, averred that the Canadian "was a fit and proper person," "that since November 16, 1888, the said Gossage has not been and is not now in my possession, custody, or power," etc.   MATTHEW,

J., at Chambers, made absolute the rule *nisi* for the *habeas corpus*. The Divisional Court, Lord COLERIDGE, C. J., and BOWEN, L. J., affirmed, and on hearing in the higher court the appeal was dismissed.

Lord ESHER, M. R., said:

" All the arguments in the present case were urged in the case of *Queen* v. *Barnardo*, 58 Law J. Rep., Q. B., 553 (1889) ; Law Rep., 23 Q. B. D., 305 (1889), and the Irish decision, *In re* Matthews, 12 Irish Com. Law Rep., N. S., 233 (1859), was referred to. We came to the conclusion that where a person having the custody of a child parts with the custody of the child to someone else wrongfully—that is to say, without legal authority—so that he cannot give the child back when he is asked for it, the child being then out of his custody, power, and control, a return to that effect is no answer to proceedings to compel the production of the child. It was not necessary for us in that case to determine whether, if it were shown to be absolutely impossible to produce the child—as, for instance, where the child had died—the court would allow a writ of *habeas corpus* to go merely for the purpose of punishment, nor is it necessary to determine that question now. I have, however, no hesitation in saying that if the case could be brought up to that pitch, and it could be shown that however wrongful had been the conduct of the person against whom the proceedings were being taken, it was impossible for him ever to produce the child, then the writ ought not to go. Nevertheless, we came to the conclusion that if the writ issued it would be no answer to the writ for Dr. Barnardo to say, " I have rendered it almost impossible for me to produce the child ; the child is out of my custody, power, or control, and I do not know where it is." We thought that if Dr. Barnardo had produced that state of things by his own illegal act he must take the consequences. We said that he was bound to use every possible effort to get the child back ; that it was not enough for him to merely write letters for that purpose, but that he must advertise abroad, and, if need be, must himself go abroad ; that he must do everything that mortal man can do in order to obey the writ. All this shows that the court will accept nothing as an excuse but an absolutely clear impossibility of obeying the writ. No such impossibility was made out in that case, nor is it made out here. I think, therefore, that if the writ issues, and if the only answer Dr. Barnardo can make to it is that which he has put before us now, his return to the writ will be bad. He must make further and fuller efforts to obey the writ. If he does not produce the child, he does not obey the writ, and if an application is made to the court, the court will have to consider what the consequences are to be."

This decree was affirmed by the House of Lords, July 25, 1892. Law Jour. Reports (N. S.), vol. 61 (Queen's Bench Div.), 728.

The Lord Chancellor (HALSBURY) and Lords HERSCHELL and WATSON suggested that the writ should not be used to punish a party who had even unlawfully parted with the custody before notice of the writ, and that it was a good return to say that the person named was not at the time of issue in the custody or control of the person served.

§ 1198. *If body not produced and return false or insufficient, respondent may be committed.* See *Williamson's Case*, 26 Pa. St., 9 (1855).

§ 1199. *A return to a habeas corpus in a criminal case should show a lawful warrant or commitment—In time of peace, no suspension of the writ is recognized by the courts.* Commonwealth ex rel. *Cozzens* v. *Frink*, 13 Amer. Law. Reg. (O. S.), 700 (1865), *Habeas Corpus* before THOMPSON, J.

In this case the relator, W. B. N. Cozzens, was tried by court-martial for fraud in furnishing supplies by contract to the War Department.

The Department, upon being advised of a conviction, ordered the arrest of the relator by the provost marshal. Daniel Dougherty and F. Carroll Brewster, for the relator; John C. Knox, Judge Advocate-General, for the Provost Marshal.

The return was :

To the Hon. James Thompson, Judge of the Supreme Court of Pennsylvania :

The undersigned, one of the respondents in the within writ, respectfully makes return thereto, that the relator, W. B. N. Cozzens, was on the 29th June inst. arrested by order of the respondent, and is now detained by him as a prisoner under the authority of the President of the United States, and that the other respondents mentioned in said writ are officers and clerks under the command of this respondent ; and further saith not.

H. A. FRINK,
Colonel and Provost Marshal of Philadelphia.

THOMPSON, J. :

" This return is partly in accordance with the Act of Congress of the 3d of March, 1863, section 1, that whenever the privilege of the writ of *habeas corpus* shall be suspended by the President under the authority of the Act, no military or other officer shall be compelled, in answer to any writ of *habeas corpus*, to return the body of any person detained by him by authority of the President, but upon the certificate under oath of the officer that the prisoner is detained under and by authority of the President, further proceedings under the writ shall be suspended by the judge or court having issued it. This section authorizes the President during the present rebellion, whenever and wherever in his judgment the public safety may require it, to suspend the privilege of the writ of *habeas corpus*, and it is provided that said suspension by the President shall remain in force so long as said rebellion shall continue.

" On this return the important question is, whether on the 29th of June last the rebellion continued or not. This is a fact to be judicially determined like any other fact. It is not for the President only by proclamation to determine this. He is not authorized to fix the *status* of the country on this point by the Act of Congress. The power of suspension depends on the fact of rebellion and its continuance. It ceases with the rebellion, and that fact is as much within judicial cognizance as is any fact under which rights exist and are held. As the privilege of the writ of *habeas corpus* is a constitutional right of every citizen, we are bound to observe a strict construction of every Act which threatens to deprive him of it.

"We have here an expression of legislative intent, which is plain that the suspension of the writ is only to continue during the rebellion. When that ceases the right of the President to continue the suspension ceases, and the courts are bound to give to the citizen his rights under the privilege. There is nothing prescribed as to what shall be the evidence of it. It is, therefore, to be ascertained, like any other fact, by evidence appropriate to such a fact.

"There is abundant evidence in the current history of the times that the rebellion no longer continues. We know its organization is entirely destroyed, its armies captured or surrendered, its officers imprisoned or paroled. In addition, we know that our own armies are being as rapidly mustered as possible. The returning soldiers crowd our streets daily, and we cease to look for battles and victories as events as little to be expected as before the rebellion commenced. There is not a single known body of men in arms anywhere under the once well-known organization called the 'Confederate States of America.' It is completely obliterated with all its forces. Civil government has been set up in all the rebellious States but one, and trade opened by the proclamation of the President, with scarcely any restriction. Every fort, navy yard, and port is again under the government and entire control of the United States, and war has ceased everywhere in the land. The time has arrived, therefore, when a return to the enjoyment of civil rights, under civil government, must take place, and when by express limitation the suspension of the *habeas corpus* should cease.

"This being so, the authority of the President, waiving all other considerations at this time, without more, is not a sufficient warrant for the arrest of a citizen.

"'No warrant shall issue' for the arrest of any person 'but upon probable cause, supported by oath or affirmation.' Constitution of the United States.

"'No warrant to search places or to seize any person or thing shall issue without probable cause, supported by oath or affirmation.' Constitution of Pennsylvania.

"There being no oath here charging a crime or offense and a warrant to authorize an arrest, the arrest is therefore unauthorized and the prisoner is entitled to be discharged.

"In this decision no conflict ought to be felt to exist between the civil and military authority.

"It is an important clause of our Bill of Rights 'that the military shall in all cases and at all times be in strict subordination to the civil power;' and it will doubtless be as agreeable to the military authorities that there should be a return to the normal condition of the country, since happily peace reigns, as it is to the civil authority; no other legal condition can possibly exist now. On this return, therefore, I must discharge the prisoner. I can base nothing on the argument that the prisoner is arrested because there has been a trial before a military tribunal about something, of the nature of which I am not informed, and that the presumption of this conviction occasions his arrest. All this is *ultra* the return, and need not be noticed.

"Prisoner discharged."

In Ex parte *Milligan*, 4 Wallace (U. S.), 2 (1866), this Act of Congress was further interpreted by the Supreme Court of the United States, and it was decided that neither the President, nor Congress, nor the judiciary, can disturb one of the safeguards of civil liberty contained in the Constitution, except to suspend the writ of *habeas corpus* in certain prescribed cases.

The suspension of the privilege of the writ does not suspend the writ itself.

The writ issues as a matter of course, and on its return it is the duty of the court to decide if the applicant is denied the right of proceeding further.

§ 1200. **Decisions applicable to the statutes as to the first and second terms**—*Supreme Court will not relieve on habeas corpus fifteen days before the first term, nor during the term.* If the relator has been bound over by the Court of Quarter Sessions during its session to answer a charge of misdemeanor, the Supreme Court will not assume jurisdiction or grant relief on *habeas corpus*. The Quarter Sessions alone have jurisdiction until the end of the term. *Comm.* v. *Sheriff*, 7 W. & S., 108 (1844). In this case it was contended that the *habeas corpus* should issue within fifteen days preceding the term of the Quarter Sessions, in order to give such court jurisdiction, but it was decided that the meaning of the Act was that fifteen days before the commencement of the sessions, and during the sessions, the *habeas corpus* shall be heard and determined before the *judges of that court*. The same ruling was made in *Clark* v. *Comm.*, 123 Pa. St., 555 (1889).

If persons indicted keep State witnesses from testifying, they are not entitled to be discharged under the two-term rule. *Respublica* v. *Arnold*, 3 Yeates, 263 (1801).

§ 1201. *Discharge under two-term law refused where trial was impossible.* A person indicted for abetting in a murder, and *not tried at second term*, cannot be discharged on *habeas corpus* if the principal has absconded, and proceedings to outlawry against the principal commenced without delay, but not finished for lack of time. *Comm.* v. *Sheriff*, 16 S. & R., 304 (1827), Tod, J. Where a prisoner indicted for a misdemeanor moved to quash the indictment at the second term, and the judges held it under advisement, such postponement is equivalent to the prisoner's consent to delay. Ex parte *Walton*, 2 Whart., 501 (1837). The provision for the discharge of prisoners by the third section of the Habeas Corpus Act does not empower the court to discharge a prisoner charged with murder when there has been no session of the Oyer and Terminer at which he could have been tried. *Comm.* v. *Brown*, 11

Phila., 370 (1875), MITCHELL, J. ; *Clark* v. *Comm.*, 29 Pa. St., 129 (1858), WOODWARD, J. In *Comm.* v. *Jailer*, 7 Watts, 366 (1838), a *habeas corpus* was brought for a man committed for horse-stealing. The prisoner was indicted, but at the first term, and obtained a continuance. The case was brought up at the next sessions, but he was found to be laboring under smallpox. Though convalescent, his aspect was so loathsome that he was remanded. Not having been tried in the second term, he claimed to be discharged under the Habeas Corpus Act. The Supreme Court decided that necessity created an exception to the letter of the Act, and his discharge was refused. The statute cannot avail where there has been no *laches* on the part of the prosecuting officer. In this case the array of jurors had been quashed at two successive terms. *Clark* v. *Comm.*, 29 Pa. St., 129 (1858), WOODWARD, J. If a prisoner become a fugitive from justice, he cannot claim the advantage of the two-term rule. *Comm.* v. *Hale*, 36 Leg. Int., 285 (1879) ; *Comm.* v. *Pulte*, 37 Leg. Int., 493 (1880). In *Comm.* v. *Jailer*, 7 Watts, 366 (1838), the court said : "The legislature intended to prevent wilful and oppressive delay, and it is sufficient that there is no color for an imputation of it." *Comm.* v. *Brown*, 11 Phila., 370 (1875), MITCHELL, J.: The word "term" in the Act of February 18, 1785, does not mean a mere period of time in which the court might have sat, but an actual session, available in law and in fact for the trial ; and all circumstances of physical, moral, or legal necessity which prevent trial are exceptions which take a case out of the statute. In *Clark* v. *Comm.*, 29 Pa. St., 129 (1858), Judge WOODWARD said :

"The term, session, or court intended by the Act is a legally constituted and competent term, session, or court. It meant that a prosecutor should not allow two such terms or sessions of the court, at each of which the defendant might be lawfully indicted or tried, to elapse without bringing on the prosecution. * * * The statute was made to restrain the malice and oppression of prosecutors and to relieve wrongful imprisonment."

§ 1202. **Cases in which the writ may be maintained.** A *habeas corpus* proceeding may be had where it clearly appears that the wrong person has been arrested. In doubtful cases it is for a jury to decide. *Respublica* v. *Gaoler*, 2 Yeates, 258 (1797). It may be brought by a parent for the custody of a child when the application is for the best interests of the child. *Comm* v. *Addicks*, 5 Binn., 520 (1813), TILGHMAN, C. J.; *Comm.* v. *Lee*, 2 S. & R., 174 (1815), TILGHMAN, C. J.; *Comm.* v. *Fee*, 6 S. & R., 255 (1820) ; *Comm.* v. *Demot*, 7 Phila., 624 (1870), AGNEW, J.; or by an apprentice whose indenture has been assigned without the consent of his parents; *Comm.* v. *Jones,* 3 S. & R., 158 (1817); or when a ward is detained from his legal guardian. *Comm.* v. *Reed,* 59 Pa. St., 425 (1868), THOMPSON, C. J. *Comm.* v. *Dugan,* 2 Dist. Rep., 772 (1893).

The writ lies where a person is restrained by relatives without lawful authority. *Comm.* v. *Curby,* 8 Phila., 372 (1871), FINLETTER, J.

§ 1203. **Where writ not maintained.** *If record show no jurisdiction, a defendant is entitled to discharge.* Where, prior to the Act of 1842, it appeared the justice of the peace had exceeded his jurisdiction in giving judgment in debt and issuing a warrant, the defendant was discharged on a *habeas corpus.* *Geyger* v. *Stoy,* 1 Dall., 135 (1785).

§ 1204. *Discharged from State arrest where crime was against United States.* In *Comm.* v. *Ketner,* 92 Pa. St., 372 (1880), PAXSON, J., a man was discharged on *habeas corpus* because he was prosecuted in the courts of Pennsylvnaia. for embezzling the funds of a bank organized under the laws of the United States, which offense was neither indictable under the common law nor the law of Pennsylvania.

§ 1205. *A prisoner illegally discharged from workhouse can be re-committed, but cannot be sent to county jail.* Where a prisoner was discharged from the county workhouse, though illegally, it was held that he could not be re-arrested and committed to the county jail upon a warrant to take and hold him to answer the same indictment, upon which, after trial, conviction, and sentence, he was serving a term of imprisonment at the time of such discharge.

It was held, however, that he might have been taken on a bench warrant and returned to the workhouse. *Comm.* v. *Smith,* 11 W. N., 34 (1881), MITCHELL, J.

§ 1206. *Married woman discharged from capias.* A married woman was discharged on *habeas corpus* because a *capias* could not properly issue against her in case of a conversion by herself and husband of personal property during coverture. *Comm.* v. *Keeper,* 9 W. N., 314·(1880); or in case of her breach of contract to invest moneys received by her from plaintiff. *McDowell* v. *Keeper,* 11 W. N., 341 (1882).

§ 1207. *A person kidnapped in New York and brought into Pennsylvania to answer was discharged on request of Governor of New York.* In *Norton's Case,* 15 W. N., 395 (1884) (C. P. of Clearfield County), KREBS, P. J., one Norton, of New York, charged with larceny, embezzlement, and conspiracy in Pennsylvauia, fled to New York.   By artifice he was brought back into Pennsylvania, arrested, and on a *habeas corpus* was remanded to the sheriff.

The Governor of New York then requested his release.   The prisoner was released on a writ of *habeas corpus* upon the grounds of comity, and that the manner of his arrest and the means employed to bring him out of the State of New York were in express violation of the statutes of New York punishing the crime of kidnapping.

§ 1208. *A commitment for contempt must show the nature of the contempt.* If, on the return to a writ of *habeas corpus* issued from the Supreme Court, it be shown that the relator is held under a commitment for contempt from the lower court which does not show the nature of the contempt, the relator will be discharged on the ground of insufficiency of the commitment.   *Comm.* v. *Perkins*, 124 Pa. St., 36 (1889), PAXSON, C. J.

§ 1209. **Cases in which the writ may be refused or will not avail.** The Supreme Court, in *Comm.* v. *Lecky*, 1 Watts, 66 (1832), GIBSON, C. J., decided that they would not discharge a prisoner on a *habeas corpus* from commitment upon a *capias ad satisfaciendum* issued out of the Court of Common Pleas.   This followed the ruling in *Respublica* v. *Keeper*, 2 Yeates, 349 (1798).   The Act of Assembly of 1785 does not oblige a court to grant a *habeas corpus* where the case has been already heard upon the same evidence by another court.   The party has a remedy by *homine replegiando*. Ex parte *Lawrence*, 5 Binn., 304 (1812).   Nor where a person is imprisoned under the sentence of a competent court.   *Comm.* v. *Keeper*, 26 Pa. St., 279 (1856).

A writ of *habeas corpus* was taken out where defendant, a policeman, fatally wounded a person engaged in an attempt to rescue. The court refused to discharge the prisoner, because where death is the result " of even justifiable violence, a jury should pass upon the case." *Comm.* v. *Megary*, 8 Phila., 607 (1871).

If one be arrested for perjury alleged to have been committed in a civil suit to which he was a party, he will be discharged pending its determination.   *Comm.* v. *Davis*, 29 W. N., 500 (1892).

§ 1210. *Habeas corpus not a substitute for writ of error.*   The defendant's remedy upon an erroneous judgment is a writ of error. A *habeas corpus* cannot be made a substitute for such writ. *Comm.* v. *Deacon*, 8 S. & R., 72 (1822) ; *Comm.* v. *Keeper*, 26 Pa. St., 279 (1856).

§ 1211. *A man will not be discharged if guilty of another offense.* In *Comm.* v. *Hickey*, 2 Pars., 317, PARSONS, J. (1843), a man was bound over by an alderman to appear before the Quarter Sessions, charged with having obtained goods under false pretenses. He was surrendered by his bail, when he sued out a *habeas corpus*, and had a full hearing upon all the facts.

The evidence was insufficient to charge the man with the crime, and he was discharged.   •

The principle was here enunciated that if a man be committed for one offense, and it appear he is guilty of another offense, the court will not discharge him on a *habeas corpus*.

§ 1212. *Habeas corpus may be granted by Supreme Court with a certiorari, in warrant of arrest cases, but relator will be remanded if commitment regular.* *Gosline* v. *Place*, 32 Pa. St., 520 (1859), LOWRIE, C. J. The defendant had been taken into custody under a warrant of arrest issued in an action of assumpsit.

Having been committed, he sued out a *certiorari* to the Supreme Court, alleging that the commitment was irregular. Subsequently he applied to the Supreme Court for a *habeas corpus* to admit him to bail, pending the proceedings upon the *certiorari*.

Held, that the court could, during the pendency of the *certiorari*, grant the writ of *habeas corpus* and admit the defendant to bail.

Held, also, that the commitment, reciting the allegations of the affidavit, the arrest, and the hearing, and that after such hearing the judge was satisfied that the plaintiff's demand was on contract and his allegations substantiated, was sufficient.

§ 1213. *A court will not discharge for a contempt in another tribunal having jurisdiction.* A petition for a *habeas corpus* will be denied where a party was convicted of contempt in the District Court of the United States and brought his petition before the Supreme Court of Pennsylvania. *Williamson's Case*, 26 Pa. St., 9 (1855), BLACK, J.

§ 1214. *Habeas corpus may be refused by State judge if relator committed by United States judge or judge of another county.* In *Williamson* v. *Lewis*, 39 Pa. St., 9 (1861), LOWRIE, C. J., it was decided that a single judge of a State Court who refuses to issue a *habeas corpus* in favor of one who stands committed for contempt by a Federal court is not liable to the penalty of the statute, which does not require its issue in such case.

In *Doyle* v. *Comm.*, 107 Pa. St., 20 (1884), it appeared that one Davis had been adjudged guilty of a contempt by the Court of Common Pleas No. 1, of *Allegheny County;* he was arrested, escaped, and was re-arrested in Warren County; a *habeas corpus* was awarded by the Court of Common Pleas of *Warren County*. It was shown that said Davis was committed for contempt, consisting of acts committed in Forest County in his official capacity as receiver appointed by the Common Pleas of said county. He was discharged. The order was reversed on appeal, because one court cannot disregard or set aside the judgment of another court of co-ordinate jurisdiction.

§ 1215. *Where prisoner arrested to be taken to another county or State.* In *Comm.* v. *Taylor,* 11 Phila., 386 (1875), Judge BRIGGS issued a warrant commanding the sheriff to take a person charged with a felony back to the county where the offense was alleged to be committed.

On an application for a *habeas corpus* before the same judge, it was held that he had no power to inquire into the merits of the charge alleged—he was only to be satisfied that the prisoner was the identical person and the process regular.

The Court has no authority in a *habeas corpus* proceeding to compel a resident of Pennsylvania to go into another State and submit himself to the jurisdiction of such foreign tribunal. *Comm.* v. *Sage,* 34 W. N., 225 (1894), reversing 2 Dist. Rep., 553 (1893).

§ 1216. *If probable cause shown, relator must be remanded—He cannot call witnesses.* In *Gerdemann* v. *Comm.,* 11 Phila., 374 (1875), a priest had been indicted for embezzlement as agent for a church. Upon the hearing of the application for a *habeas corpus,* Judge FIN-LETTER decided that if the Commonwealth made out a sufficient case to warrant the court in sustaining a verdict founded thereon, no further proof was necessary ; that the defense could not, upon such hearing, introduce his witnesses, and that such indictment as agent was lawful.

§ 1217. *A sentenced convict fled to Canada, was brought back under extradition treaty, upon other charges was acquitted, but held for first offense.* In re *Miller,* 15 W. N., 551 (1885) (United States Circuit Court, ACHESON, C. J.), one Miller was sentenced for burglary in Pennsylvania. He escaped from imprisonment and fled to Canada. Burglary not being an extradition crime, informations were made in Pennsylvania charging him with robbery and assault with intent to commit murder. He was brought back under extradition proceedings, but the bills of indictment on such crimes were ignored by the grand jury.

Upon a *habeas corpus* he was remanded upon the ground that there was no provision in the extradition treaty guaranteeing to the extradited person the right to leave the demanding country after his acquittal of the offense for which he was surrendered or after his endurance of the punishment therefor.

§ 1218. **As to the penal sections.** The penalty imposed by the eleventh section of the Habeas Corpus Act is limited to recommitments for the *same criminal* offense, and it is not applicable where the defendant was arrested upon civil process. *Hecker* v. *Jarrett,* 1 Binn., 374 (1808), TILGHMAN, C. J., affirmed in 3 Binn., 404 (1811).

In *Schofield* v. *Root,* 12 Phila., 333 (1878), an action was brought for a second arrest of plaintiff on the charge of larceny as bailee after being discharged upon a *habeas corpus* from commitment for the same offense. Upon a motion for judgment for the defendant upon a point reserved, MITCHELL, J., said : "Our Habeas Corpus Act of 1785 is modelled upon the famous Act of 31 Charles II. The history of the law demonstrates clearly that that Act did not originate the writ of *habeas corpus,* but enlarged its scope and efficiency for the special purpose of speedy relief against arbitrary and illegal commitments to prison.   There was an older writ of *habeas corpus ad subjiciendum* at common law, which is still in use for the *purpose of rehearing the testimony taken before magistrates or courts of inferior jurisdiction,* with a view to the reduction of bail or the discharge of the petitioner, should the evidence fail to disclose a *prima facie* case against him.   The Act of 1785 is a highly penal statute which makes no allowance for mistakes or mitigating circumstances.   Its object was to provide a speedy and efficient remedy against commitments not under due authority of law ; it does not contemplate an examination by the judge or court issuing it òf the merits of the case, or of anything beyond the legal regularity of the commitment upon its face."

Judgment for the defendant, upon the ground that the writ under which plaintiff had obtained his discharge was the common law writ, and not the writ under the Act of 1785.

§ 1219. **Costs, when case dismissed, fall on the county.** Where a justice dismisses a criminal charge, whether a felony or a misdemeanor, his fees are imposed on the county. *County* v. *Schock,* 18 W. N., 326 (1886), TRUNKEY, J.

§ 1220. **Proceedings before justices in civil cases.** When you have satisfied yourself, from examination of statutes and decisions, that the justice has jurisdiction, you must issue a summons except in cases of trespass or for the recovery of money collected by a public officer or for official misconduct.   Act of March 20, 1810, section 2 (5 Sm., 162).

In these you have your choice of summons or *capias.*

§ 1221. *Service of summons.*   The summons must be made returnable not more than eight nor less than five days after the date of the summons, if the defendant be resident in the county, and if non-resident, then it is returnable not less than two nor more than four days from the date thereof. Act of March 20, 1810, section 2 (5 Sm., 162); Act of July 12, 1842, section 26 (P. L., 345); and must be served by producing the original summons, and informing the defendant of the contents thereof, or leaving a copy of it at his dwelling-house, in the presence of one or more of his family or neighbors, at least four days before the time of hearing. Act of March 20, 1810, section 2 (5 Sm., 162).

§ 1222. *Hearing.* On the return-day the plaintiff should be present in person, or by his attorney, prepared to prove his claim. When the case is called, the character and amount of the claim are stated. The defendant generally says "the claim is disputed." The plaintiff proves his ·case. The pleadings are all *ore tenus.* Sometimes continuances take place. The defendant is, of course, at liberty to call witnesses and to contest the case. The magistrate gives judgment, and the dissatisfied party may appeal. The following statutes and decisions apply to the various steps of the proceeding.

§ 1223. Jurisdiction in civil cases. §§ 1224–1269.

The question of jurisdiction of a justice of the peace may be raised at any time even in the Supreme Court on appeal. *Gates* v. *Bloom,* 30 W. N., 127 (1892).

§ 1224. *Contracts.*

Justices of the peace shall have jurisdiction of all causes of action arising on contract, express or implied, in all cases where the sum demanded is not over one hundred dollars, except in case of real contract where the title to lands or tenements may come in question, or an action upon a promise of marriage. (Act March 20, 1810, section 1; 5 Sm., 161.)

The jurisdiction was extended to $300 by the Act of July 7, 1879 (*infra*).

§ 1225. *Amicable judgments or reference.*

Justices of the peace shall have cognizance of any matter under the above Act for any sum exceeding (one) hundred dollars, if the parties voluntarily appear before them for that purpose and confess judgment or submit to a reference. (Act March 20, 1810, section 14.)

A justice of the peace has no jurisdiction over $300 unless the parties voluntarily appear before him. *McDonnell* v. *Hodgins,* 4 Dist. Rep., 305 (1894).

§ 1226. *Magistrates' courts, Philadelphia.*

The Act of February 5, 1875, section 1 (P. L., 56), provided for courts not of record of police and civil causes in Philadelphia, with jurisdiction not exceeding one hundred dollars. These are known as "magistrates' courts."

A similar provision was made by the Act of February 1, 1887, section 1

(P. L., 3), increasing the number of magistrate courts in Philadelphia from twenty-four.to twenty-eight.

§ 1227. *Jurisdiction extended to $300.*

Magistrates and justices of the peace shall have concurrent jurisdiction with the Courts of Common Pleas in actions on contract, either express or implied, of trespass (trover and conversion), where the sum demanded does not exceed three hundred dollars, except in cases of real contract, where the title to lands or tenements may come in question, or action upon promise of marriage. (Act July 7, 1879, section 1; P. L., 194.)

This Act does not refer to Philadelphia County, since the jurisdiction of magistrates in that county is controlled by the Constitution of 1874.

§ 1228. *Trover and trespass.*

Justices of the peace have jurisdiction of actions of trover and conversion, and trespass for the recovery of damages for injury committed on real and personal estate in cases where the value of property claimed or the damages sustained shall not exceed one hundred dollars. (Act March 22, 1814, section 1; 6 Sm., 182.)

The process, return, notices, awards, judgments, and appeals, and the proceedings of justices, constables, referees, and courts, and everything necessary to carry this Act into effect, shall be subject to the general law regulating the recovery of debt not exceeding one hundred dollars, which is not specially provided for. (Act March 22, 1814, section 4; 6 Sm., 182.)

Justices of the peace shall have concurrent jurisdiction with the Courts of Common Pleas of all actions of trespass and of trover and conversion wherein the sum demanded does not exceed three hundred dollars, except in cases of real contract where the title to lands or tenements may come in question, or action upon promise of marriage. (Act July 7, 1879, section 1; P. L., 194.)

This latter Act does not apply to proceedings before magistrates in Philadelphia County.

A justice of the peace has no jurisdiction of an action of trespass on the case for maintaining a nuisance. *Helsey* v. *Witmer*, 4 Dist. Rep., 290 (1895); nor of an action for an injury committed by a dog in the absence of its owner. *Henry* v. *Mulherrin*, 1 Dist. Rep., 607 (1891); nor of actions of trespass on the case for consequential damages, under which head are classed negligence cases. *Thilow* v. *Traction Co.*, 4 Dist. Rep., 83 (1895).

A magistrate has jurisdiction of a suit for injuries to personal property to the amount of $100. *Porter* v. *Ice Co.*, 1 Dist. Rep., 725 (1891).

A justice of the peace has jurisdiction of a claim for damages against an employer for a trespass done by an employé of defendant. *Carle* v. *Ice Co.*, 4 Dist. Rep., 289 (1894).

§ 1229. *In cases of rent landlord may be compelled to defalk.*

The powers of justices of the peace shall extend to all cases of rent not exceeding one hundred dollars, so far as to compel the landlord to defalcate or set off the just account of the tenant out of the same, but the landlord may waive further proceedings before the justice and pursue the method of distress in the usual manner for the balance so settled; but if any landlord shall be convicted, after such waiver, in any court of record of distraining for and selling more than to the amount of such balance, and of detaining the surplus in his hands, he shall forfeit to the tenant four times the amount of the sum detained: *Provided*, that no appeal shall lie in the case of rent, but the remedy by replevin shall remain as heretofore. (Act of March 20, 1810, section 20; 5 Sm., 170.)

§ 1230. *Amicable actions.*

Justices shall take cognizance by amicable suit of all causes of action within their jurisdiction. (Act March 22, 1814, section 7; 6 Sm., 183.)

§ 1231. *For penalties, etc.*

The justices of the peace shall have power to hear and determine all actions of debt for penalty, for breach of any ordinance, by-law, or regulation in the same manner and subject to the right of appeal as in case of debts under one hundred dollars, and such action shall be instituted in the corporate name. (Act April 15, 1835, section 7; P. L., 292.)

§ 1232. *When justice may act as coroner.*

Where there is no lawfully appointed coroner, or he is absent from the county, unable to attend, or his office is held more than ten miles distant from the place where the death occurred or the body found, and an inquest over such dead body is required by law to be held, the justice of the peace of the proper county shall have power to select, summon, and compel the attendance of jurors and witnesses, and the inquest shall have force and effect in law.

The proceedings, before fees or costs are allowed, shall be submitted to the Court of Quarter Sessions, which shall adjudge there was reasonable cause for holding said inquest and approve the same. (Act May 27, 1841, section 15; P. L., 404.)

§ 1233. *Debt* sur *judgment of justice of another State.*

The justices of the peace shall have jurisdiction in action of debt not exceeding one hundred dollars, founded on the judgment or judgments of justices of the peace of an adjoining State having similar jurisdiction. It must appear by a copy of the record or docket entry of the proceedings, certified and authenticated, that the original cause of action was such as would have been within the jurisdiction of a justice of the peace by the laws of this Commonwealth. (Act February 27, 1845, section 8; P. L., 73.)

§ 1234. *Defendant may make same defense as to original claim.*

In actions of debt founded on foreign judgments, the plaintiff shall produce on the trial a copy of the record or docket entry of the previous proceedings before a justice, with his affidavit annexed, certifying the same to be a true and full copy of the record, and that the judgment remains in force, and has not, to his knowledge, been vacated, annulled, or satisfied; also the certificate of the clerk of the Court of Common Pleas or clerk of the county where such justice keeps his office, under the hand or seal of the court or county, that the person before whom the proceedings purport to have been had was at the time an acting justice of the peace of such county, duly appointed or elected, and qualified according to law.

Defendant may make the same defense as he originally was entitled to make to the claim or demand. (*Id.*, section 4.)

§ 1235. *Fines.*

Jurisdiction has been conferred on justices of the peace to hear cases for breach of any by-law of a city, borough, town, or corporate body subjecting the offender to a penalty or fine. Suits for their recovery may be maintained, as in case of debts under the sum of one hundred dollars with right of appeal. (Act April 5, 1849, section 7 ; P. L., 410.)

§ 1236. *Jurisdiction against insurance companies.*

Justices of the peace shall have jurisdiction of cases where any person or persons, body politic or corporate, may have a cause of action against any insurance company incorporated by the legislature of this Commonwealth, or any such company having an agency in this Commonwealth, where the property insured may be located, or in cases of live-stock insurance where the owner may reside.

The service and process and all proceedings shall be the same as in other cases. (Act May 13, 1889, section 1 ; P. L., 199.)

§ 1237. *A justice has jurisdiction of a claim by an officer for his fees ; but no action can be maintained until the end of the first suit.*

In *Lyon* v. *McManus*, 4 Binn., 167 (1811), an action was brought against the defendant to recover certain official fees under $100. TILGHMAN, C. J., decided the justice had jurisdiction, on the ground that the officer performs the services under an implied contract to receive payment at the end of the suit ; but inasmuch as the suit wherein the services had been performed was still pending, the action of the lower court in rendering judgment for the defendant was affirmed.

§ 1238. *Justice may decide in trespass unless reference demanded.*

In an action of trespass before a justice, unless the parties request the intervention of referees, the justice may give judgment. *Shoemaker* v. *Barry*, 1 S. & R., 234 (1814).

§ 1239. *Justice has jurisdiction of action against constable for a false return, although the judgment over $100.*

In *Delaney* v. *Brindle*, 15 S. & R., 75 (1826), judgment was obtained before a justice for a sum greater than $100, under the Act of March 20, 1810, authorizing judgments to be entered by justices for more than $100, where the parties voluntarily appear.

Execution having been issued, the constable made a false return.

Held, that the justice had jurisdiction of an action against the constable.

§ 1240. *Justice has jurisdiction of a suit upon an insolvent bond.*

In *Jones* v. *Smith*, 2 P. & W., 462 (1831), a suit was brought before a justice upon an insolvent bond.' The question was raised as to jurisdiction, but it was decided that such suit was properly brought.

§ 1241. *Contract'of bailment.* A justice has jurisdiction of a suit arising from a contract of bailment. *McCahan* v. *Hirst*, 7 Watts, 175 (1838).

§ 1242. *Award.* A justice of the peace has jurisdiction of an action of debt on an award. *Scott* v. *Barnes*, 7 Pa. St., 134 (1847).

§ 1243. *Justice has jurisdiction of claim under agreement to buy a judgment, although the judgment was a lien on land.* In *Helfenstein* v. *Hirst*, 15 Pa. St., 358 (1850), an action was brought before a justice to recover seventy dollars alleged to be due under an agreement to purchase a judgment against a lot of ground.

It was contended that such agreement was within the first section of the Act of March 20, 1810, excluding from the jurisdiction of a justice cases of real contract where the title to lands or tenements may come in question.

The Supreme Court decided that the agreement was not a real contract, but an agreement to buy and sell a judgment, without regard to or stipulation about title, and that the justice had jurisdiction.

§ 1244. *Damages for breach of contract.* A justice has jurisdiction of an action to recover damages under $100 for breach of contract. *Shannon* v. *Madden*, 1 Phila., 254 (1851); *Conn* v. *Stumm*, 31 Pa. St., 14 (1854).

§ 1245. *Justice has jurisdiction of two or more claims though they aggregate more than $100 if each suit be for less than $100.* In *Boyle* v. *Grant*, 18 Pa. St., 162 (1851), a payee of six promissory notes brought suit on each note before a justice. The cases, on appeal to the Common Pleas, were consolidated so as to make one suit and thus diminish the costs.

On appeal from the decision of the Common Pleas, the Supreme Court approved of the course adopted. The justice had jurisdiction though the aggregate amount represented by the notes was more than $100.

§ 1246. *Justice has jurisdiction of action for trespass to land unless defendant make affidavit that title to land comes in question.* *Lauchner* v. *Rex*, 20 Pa. St., 464 (1853), was an action of trespass for injury to real property. The proceedings having been commenced before a justice, the defendant failed to make an affidavit that the title to land *actually* came in question. It was decided that the justice had jurisdiction.

BLACK, C. J.: "By the Act of 1814, jurisdiction is given to jus-

tices in all actions of trespass for injury to real estate, excluding only
those cases in which the title to lands *actually does* come in question, and in order to determine whether the fact be so, the defendant may interpose his oath and stop the proceeding at any time
before the trial.   The statute giving jurisdiction in trespass would
have been utterly nugatory if it had been clogged with the exception of cases in which the title to land *may* come in question, for it
may be so in *every* case of trespass to land, as much as in every action on real contract.   The justice has authority to determine the
cause unless the defendant makes the fact which ousts his jurisdiction appear in the mode pointed out by the Act.   It is too late to
make the objection after the case comes into the Common Pleas
by appeal." See § 1268.

§ 1247. *Jurisdiction is not exceeded if judgment be confessed for
more than* $100.   *Butler* v. *Urch*, 2 Grant, 247 (1858).   A justice
of the peace can exercise no jurisdiction in deciding a controversy
wherein the claim in dispute exceeds $100.   But if the parties
appear before him, with or without summons, and agree upon the
state of the accounts between them, and one confesses judgment in
favor of the other for a sum exceeding $100, he does not exceed
his jurisdiction in entering and enforcing it.

§ 1248. *A justice has jurisdiction of an action against executors
to compel reimbursement of amount paid by devisee of a debt which
should have been paid out of the residue.*   In *Bell* v. *Bell*, 32 Pa.
St., 309 (1858), an action was brought in the Common Pleas against
executors for reimbursement of a sum paid by the plaintiff in exoneration of lands devised to him, which sum was properly chargeable on the residuary estate.

He obtained a verdict for sixty-seven dollars and seventy-five
cents.   The costs were imposed on him.   The Supreme Court, per
LOWRIE, C. J., decided that the suit was within the jurisdiction of
a justice, and that the plaintiff could not recover costs.

§ 1249. *Justice has jurisdiction of trespass against a constable
for unlawfully selling goods.*   If a constable unlawfully sell goods
exempt from sale, an action of trespass will lie against him whereof
the justice has jurisdiction.   *Stamer* v. *Nass*, 3 Grant, 240 (1858).

§ 1250. *If plaintiff only claim the principal of his debt, and it
be under* $100, *the justice has jurisdiction, although the interest, if
claimed, would swell the demand above* $100.   *Evans* v. *Hall*, 45
Pa. St., 235 (1863).   A justice has jurisdiction where the demand
itself or principal of the claim does not exceed $100.   The plain-
tiff need not include any or all the interest, but may remit part
or all and sue for the balance.   This was followed in *Quigley* v.

Quigley, 10 W. N., 388 (1881) ; *Wood* v. *Lovett*, 1 Penny., 51 (1881).

§ 1251. *Justice has jurisdiction on* sci. fa. *to revive a judgment of* $100, *although the interest swells the claim above* $100. A judgment was obtained before a justice in 1862 for $100 and costs. In 1867 a *sci. fa.* to revive was brought before his successor in office, and the amount, with interest and costs on revival, was $132.84. The Common Pleas, on a *certiorari*, held the justice had jurisdiction. *McGarry* v. *Douredoure*, 6 Phila., 332 (1867) ; *Huston* v. *Donnelly*, 8 Phila., 337 (1871).

§ 1252. *If claim has been reduced by payments to less than* $100, *the justice has jurisdiction, but plaintiff cannot confer jurisdiction simply by remitting part of claim.* In *Bower* v. *McCormick*, 73 Pa. St., 427 (1873), AGNEW, J., an action was brought before a justice in trover, and in order to bring the amount alleged to be due plaintiff within the jurisdiction of the justice, twenty-two dollars was remitted. It was decided that jurisdiction could *not* be conferred in this way. This was followed in *Moore* v. *White*, 11 W. N., 206 (1881).

The same ruling was made in *Peter* v. *Schlosser*, 81 Pa. St., 439 (1876), and MERCUR, J., said : " A creditor who has a claim on his debtor exceeding $100 cannot give jurisdiction to a justice by allowing a credit to defendant of a distinct and independent debt, so as to reduce his demand below $100. However large the claim may have been, yet if it has been reduced by *direct payments* to a sum not exceeding $100, the justice has jurisdiction." *Collins* v. *Collins*, 37 Pa. St., 387 (1860).

A justice has jurisdiction of a claim which is reduced below the statutory limit by direct payment, by dealings amounting to payments and by allowing credits for matters, payment for which has been demanded by defendant. *McFarland* v. *O'Neil*, 155 Pa. St., 260 (1893).

§ 1253. *Act enlarging jurisdiction of justices, constitutional.* The Act of July 7, 1879 (P. L., 194), enlarging the jurisdiction of justices, is constitutional. *City* v. *Meyers*, 18 W. N., 329 (1886).

§ 1254. *No jurisdiction in ejectment, replevin, slander—Real contracts, assault, false imprisonment.*

Justices of the peace have no jurisdiction in actions of ejectment, replevin, or slander, actions on real contracts for the sale or conveyance of lands and tenements, actions for damages in personal assault and battery, wounding and maiming, or actions for false imprisonment. (Act March 22, 1814, section 5 ; 6 Sm., 182.)

§ 1255. *If the judgment exceed the jurisdiction of the justice, this is fatal, and judgment can be arrested even after trial on merits.* In

Moore v. *Wait*, 1 Binn., 219 (1807), a justice gave judgment for $104.26. The defendant appealed, pleaded the general issue, and went to trial. A verdict was found for the plaintiff. The judgment was arrested on the ground that the transcript showed the justice had no jurisdiction, and the subsequent proceedings were void.

The Supreme Court affirmed, opinion by TILGHMAN, C. J. Judge BRACKENRIDGE, although not dissenting, said his "mind was not perfectly satisfied that it was not the defendant's duty to plead to the jurisdiction, either before the justice or in the Common Pleas."

§ 1256. *If the amount in controversy exceed the jurisdiction, this is fatal, although the judgment be for less than $100.* In *Collins* v. *Collins*, 37 Pa. St., 387 (1860), an appeal from the judgment of a justice having been taken, the case was dismissed, after trial and verdict, in the Common Pleas, it appearing that the amount in controversy exceeded the jurisdiction of the justice, although the amount of the judgment was less than $100.

§ 1257. *No jurisdiction of suit on judgment in Common Pleas.* A justice has no jurisdiction of a suit brought upon a judgment rendered in the Common Pleas. *No contract* arises on a judgment of a court of record. *Wilson* v. *Long*, 12 S. & R., 58 (1824).

§ 1258. *Nor of debt against sheriff for an escape.* A justice has not jurisdiction where suit in debt is brought against the sheriff for allowing the escape of a prisoner who was imprisoned for a debt less than $100. *Schaffer* v. *McNamee*, 13 S. & R., 44 (1825).

§ 1259. *Nor for penalty for not satisfying a judgment.* A justice of the peace has no jurisdiction in an action of debt for the recovery of a penalty imposed by statute for not entering satisfaction of a judgment. *Zeigler* v. *Gram*, 13 S. & R., 102 (1825).

§ 1260. *Nor of suit on bail-bond of $15,000, although less than $100 claimed.* A justice of the peace has no jurisdiction of a suit on a sheriff's bail-bond in $15,000 where the plaintiff claims less than $100. *Comm.* v. *Reynolds*, 17 S. & R., 367 (1828).

§ 1261. *A justice has no jurisdiction of a suit for balance of purchase-money of land.* In *Sechrist* v. *Connellee*, 3 P. & W., 388 (1832), suit was brought before a justice for the balance of the consideration-money on the sale of a lot of ground. The Supreme Court held the justice had no jurisdiction. Followed in *Packer* v. *Taylor*, 2 Dist. Rep., 443 (1892).

§ 1262. *No jurisdiction for damages for deficit of land conveyed.* A suit was instituted before a justice to recover damages where the quantity of land conveyed was less than the agreement of sale called for. *Held*, that the justice had no jurisdiction. *Lee* v. *Dean*, 3 Rawle, 325 (1832).

§ 1263. *Nor on a constable's bond.* A justice of the peace has no jurisdiction where a suit is brought upon a constable's bond. *Blue v. Comm.*, 4 Watts, 215 (1835).

§ 1264. *Nor of action against another justice for money collected.* A justice has no jurisdiction where suit is brought against another justice for moneys collected by the defendant in his official capacity. The party aggrieved has a remedy by petition to the Common Pleas. *Montgomery* v. *Poorman*, 6 Watts, 384 (1837).

§ 1265. *Nor of suit by one of two joint owners of notes against the other owner for not suing the notes.* A justice has no jurisdiction where suit was brought by the joint owner of promissory notes against another to recover damages for refusing to collect the notes or allow said joint owner to collect them, whereby the claim was lost. There is no color of contract between them. *Mann* v. *Bower*, 8 Watts, 179 (1839).

§ 1266. *Nor of account render.* A justice of the peace has no jurisdiction in account render. *Wright* v. *Guy*, 10 S. & R., 227 (1823) ; *Steffen* v. *Hartzell*, 5 Whar., 448 (1840).

§ 1267. *Nor of action against constable for not paying out of proceeds of execution the rent in arrears.* In *Seitzinger* v. *Steinberger*, 12 Pa. St., 379 (1849), an action was brought against a constable for not paying out of the proceeds of an execution the year's rent in arrear, under Act of June 16, 1836. The single question presented by the record was, whether the justice had jurisdiction. The Supreme Court decided he had not.

§ 1268. *No jurisdiction in trespass where affidavit sets forth that title to land will arise.* *Lauchner* v. *Rex*, 20 Pa. St., 464 (1853), BLACK, C. J.: "The Act of 1810 expressly excepts from the jurisdiction of justices all cases of real contract where the title to lands may come in question. This excludes from their cognizance every suit on a contract concerning or in any way connected with realty, whether it be to enforce payment of purchase-money or to recover back what has been paid by the vendee after rescission of the agreement, or though it be on a note given in consideration of an easement. In all these cases the title to land may come in question, and they can no more be tried by a justice than ejectment, slander, or battery.

"But, by the Act of 1814, jurisdiction is given to justices in all actions of trespass for injury to real estate, excluding only those cases in which the title to lands actually does come in question, and in order to determine whether the fact be so the defendant may interpose his oath and stop the proceedings at any time before trial."

Stevens v. *Sarver*, 29 Leg. Int., 46 (1872). In an action of trover before a justice, if an affidavit be made " that in the above suit the title to land must come in question positively," and one-half of the cost be tendered or paid, the justice must refuse to entertain jurisdiction of the case, or his proceedings will be reversed on *certiorari*.

In a suit before a magistrate, an affidavit setting forth that the title to real estate *may come in question* filed before the hearing, is a bar to the jurisdiction. *Shober* v. *Henry*, 4 Dist. Rep., 506 (1895).

§ 1269. *Nor of action for deceit.* In *Canan* v. *McCamy*, 1 Pennypacker, 397 (1881), the Supreme Court decided an action on the case for deceit could not be brought before a justice.

Nor in actions in forcible entry and detainer. Formerly, by the Statute of 15 Richard II., Chap. II. (A. D. 1391) (Roberts' Digest, No. *284), and the Statute of 8 Henry VI., Chap. IX. (A.D. 1429) (Roberts' Digest, *285), in force in Pennsylvania, a justice had such jurisdiction, but the Act of March 31, 1860, §§ 21–22 (P. L., 390), took the jurisdiction away from the civil side of a justice's court and provided the proceeding should be by indictment only. (See Brightly's Purdon, p. 506 (Note *r*).

§ 1270. **Summons—Warrant of arrest.**

Justices are empowered and required upon complaint to issue a summons if the party complained of be a freeholder; if not, either a summons or warrant of arrest directed to the constable of the township, ward, or district, where the defendant resides or can be found, or to the next constable most convenient to the defendant.

The summons commands him to cause the defendant to appear on a certain day, not more than eight nor less than five days after the date of the summons. (Act March 20, 1810, section 2; 5 Sm., 162.)

No person shall be arrested or imprisoned on any civil process * * * in any suit or proceeding instituted for the recovery of any money due upon any judgment or decree founded upon contract, or due upon any contract, expressed or implied, or for the recovery of any damages for the non-performance of any contract, excepting in proceedings, as for contempt, to enforce civil remedies, action for fines or penalties, or on promises to marry, on moneys collected by any public officer, or for any misconduct or neglect in office, or in any professional employment. (Act July 12, 1842, section 1; P. L., 339.)

§ 1271. *No capias ad respondendum or ad satisfaciendum shall issue in cases of contract except upon satisfactory proof that judgment is for money collected by public officer, or for official misconduct.*

No execution issued on any judgment rendered by any justice upon any demand arising upon contract, express or implied, shall contain a clause authorizing an arrest or imprisonment of the person against whom the same shall issue, unless it shall be proved by the affidavit of the person in whose favor such execution shall issue, or that of some other person, to the satisfaction of the justice, either that such judgment was for the recovery of money collected by any public officer or for official misconduct. (Act July 12, 1842, section 23 ; P. L., 345.)

§ 1272. *Nor shall* capias *or warrant issue except where* capias ad satisfaciendum *could be issued if claim were in judgment.*

No *capias* or warrant of arrest shall issue against any defendant in any case in which, by the provisions of the preceding section, an execution on the judgment recovered could not be issued against the body, and whenever a capias or warrant of arrest in such case shall issue, the like affidavit shall be required as for the issuing of an execution by the provisions of said sections. (*Id.*, section 24.)

§ 1273. *Warrant or capias.* In case of the issuing of a warrant, the defendant shall be commanded to appear forthwith upon the service of the same. In all cases where a warrant or *capias* is issued, it shall be lawful for the proper constable to take bail for the appearance of the defendant, thus :

" We, A. B. and C. D., are held and firmly bound unto E. F., constable of   , or order, in the sum of   , on condition that the said A. B. shall be and appear before G. H., Esquire, justice of the peace in the said township of   , on the day of   , to answer   in a plea   . " Witness our hands the   day of   "   (Act of March 20, 1810, section 2 ; 5 Sm., 162.)

§ 1274. *If defendant do not appear.*

If on the return of the warrant or *capias* the defendant shall not appear and enter bail before the justice, in the nature of special bail, the constable may assign the obligation to the plaintiff, who may sue in his own name as assignee. If the bail taken by the constable is insufficient, the constable shall be liable.

If special bail be entered, the justice may proceed to a final determination of the suit, and after judgment such bail shall be proceeded against by *scire facias* and be liable in the same manner as special bail is liable in Common Pleas cases, and may surrender the principal to jail within ten days after the service of *sci. fa.* in discharge of the bail ; nevertheless the bail to the constable may enter sufficient special bail, or cause it to be entered, at the return of the warrant or *capias*, where the defendant may neglect or refuse to appear, in which case the justice may proceed as if the defendant had appeared. (Act March 20, 1810, section 2 ; 5 Sm., 162.)

§ 1275. *Sci. fa. against bail may be served as summons served.* In *Buchanan* v. *Specht*, 1 Phila., 252 (1851), Judge KING said : " Although the Act does not, in terms, define how a *scire facias* against bail shall be served, yet a *scire facias* is but a summons. * * * We are certainly safe in adopting that mode prescribed by the Act for the service of other writs of summons."

§ 1276. *Summons may fix the hours.*

All summons may designate the hours of day between which the same shall be returnable; if either party fail to appear, the justice shall render judgment or otherwise determine as provided by law. (Act April 26, 1855, section 3; P. L., 304.)

§ 1277. *Summons must not omit Christian name of defendant.*

In *Honser* v. *Jones*, 1 Phila., 394 (1852), a summons was issued against   Jones and judgment entered for plaintiff against Jones.

The omission of the Christian name of defendant in the summons was held a radical and fatal defect. The proceedings were reversed.

§ 1278. *Summons is defective which does not state locality of justice's office.*

"All compulsory appearance before a justice must be by writ containing information sufficiently clear and explicit to give notice *when* and *where* the defendant is commanded to appear. In this case the summons states the day, hour, and the name of the justice, but wholly omits to state where his office is, or that he has any." The process was defective. *Murdy* v. *McCutcheon*, 95 Pa. St., 435 (1880), MERCUR, J.

The summons of a justice should state the ward of the borough in which his office is located—the omission is fatal on *certiorari*. *Ritchie* v. *Peril*, 1 Dist. Rep., 374 (1892).

§ 1279. *Non-residents — Short summons — Return — Service — Capias or warrant of arrest.*

Whenever a plaintiff shall reside out of this Commonwealth he may, upon giving bond with sufficient surety for the payment of all costs which he may become liable to pay, in the event of his failing to recover judgment against the defendant, have a *capias*, or warrant of arrest, if he shall be entitled to such writ, on making the proper affidavit; or a summons which may be made returnable not less than two nor more than four days from the date thereof, which shall be served at least two days before the time of appearance mentioned therein, and if the same shall be returned, personally served, the justice issuing the same may proceed to hear and determine the case. (Act July 12, 1842, section 25; P. L., 345.)

As to service against non-residents, see §§ 1286, 1288.

§ 1280. *Non-residents may have long summons without first entering security for costs.*

In *Osborne* v. *Everitt*, 103 Pa. St., 421 (1883), the plaintiffs were non-residents and did not enter security for costs before the justice—judgment was for the plaintiffs. An appeal was taken, but subsequently, before the appeal was heard, the matter was arbitrated. A rule was taken on plaintiffs to show cause why all proceedings should not be vacated, as no bonds for costs had been filed by the plaintiffs as non-residents at the commencement of the suit. The rule was made absolute, but the judgment was reversed on appeal, and GREEN, J., *held*, that the Act of March 20, 1810, section 2, authorizing suit before a justice by long summons without first giving security for costs, is not repealed by the Act of July 12, 1842, section 25, giving a right to suit by short summons upon security entered.

§ 1281.

FORM OF SUMMONS.

City of Philadelphia, *ss.*

The Commonwealth of Pennsylvania, to any Constable of said city most convenient to the defendant, greeting :

You are hereby commanded to summon A. B. to be and appear on the day of ., A. D. 18 , between the hours of 10 o'clock A.M. and 11 o'clock A. M., before the subscriber (name), magistrate of Court No. , in and for the said city, to answer (name of plaintiff), in a plea of debt or demand " arising from contract either expressed or implied," not exceeding one hundred dollars.

Witness the said magistrate, at his court in the city of Philadelphia, who hath hereunto set his hand and affixed the official seal thereof, the day of , A. D. 1890.

[SEAL] Magistrate of Court No. . (Address.)

§ 1282. *Service of summons.*

Service of summons on defendant shall be by producing the original summons and informing defendant of its contents, or leaving a copy at his dwelling-house in the presence of one or more of his family or neighbors at least four days before the time of hearing. (Act of March 20, 1810, section 2 ; 5 Sm., 162.)

Where suit is brought before a magistrate against an unincorporated association, all the members must be served, else a plea in abatement may be filed. *Rivers* v. *Lodge*, 1 Dist. Rep., 724 (1892).

§ 1283. *When service may be made upon defendant's agent or clerk—Service on a foreign insurance company.*

Where any person is a non-resident of this Commonwealth, and shall engage in business in any county within this State, and is not in the county at the time of the issuing of any writ or process against such person, it shall be lawful for the officer charged with the service thereof to serve any writ of summons or any other *mesne* process in like manner as summons are served, upon the agent or clerk of such defendant at the usual place of business or residence of such agent or clerk, with the same effect as if served upon the principal personally : *Provided,* that before final judgment is entered in any case under this Act, actual notice in writing shall be given to the party defendant of such action and the nature thereof, proof of which notice shall be made by the production of a copy of such notice, and the oath or affirmation of the plaintiff or other person to the service thereof, to the justice before whom such action is pending. (Act April 2, 1856, section 1 ; P. L., 219.)

This was extended by the Act April 21, 1858, section 1 (P. L., 403), which provided that when any person or persons not resident of this Commonwealth shall do business within the State, the officer charged with the execution of writ or process shall serve the same upon any clerk or agent at the usual place of business or residence of the clerk or agent, with like effect as if served personally upon the principal.

In *Culligan* v. *Russell*, 2 W. N., 440 (1876), the service was held to be irregular because the return did not show that the agent was served personally at his place of business or his dwelling.

The Act of June 20, 1883 (P. L., 134), provides the method of making service upon a foreign insurance company doing business in this State. Service of a summons on a soliciting agent at Wilkesbarre by a constable, when the designated general agent for the State upon whom process shall be served resides in Philadelphia, is invalid. *Connors* v. *Ins. Co.*, 1 District Rep., 115 (1892).

§ 1284. *Returns to summons held to be sufficient.* In *Bar* v. *Purcil*, 2 Phila., 259 (1856), the return was "served by leaving a copy of the original summons at the dwelling of the defendant with a member of the family." *Held* sufficient, as it was a substantial compliance with the requirements of the Act.

In *Snyder* v. *Carfrey*, 54 Pa. St., 90 (1867), the constable made the following return of service : Served "personally on defendant, at his dwelling-house, by leaving a copy of the original summons, and making known the contents thereof."

"This was a sufficient service of any summons." WOODWARD, C. J.

Where a summons shows a return "served by copy," the presumption is that the service of the copy was made as required by law. *Sweeney* v. *Girolo*, 32 W. N., 404 (1893).

§ 1285. *Insufficient returns.* In *Comm.* v. *Dalling*, 2 Pars. Select Eq., 285 (1848), the return was "copy of the within served personally, W. Walton, constable."

KING, J.: "Is this such a return as will sustain a judgment by default? * * * This return does not say that the original was produced to the defendant, or that its contents were made known to him. The evils of a loose practice in the service of writs are innumerable, and should be guarded against." The return was held to be defective.

In *Fraily* v. *Sparks*, 2 Pars., 232 (1848), the return of a constable to a summons was "copy of the within left personally with the defendant." It was held insufficient.

In *Lenore* v. *Ingram*, 1 Phila., 519 (1854), the return to the summons was "copy served personally on defendant." The return was defective.

In *Shourds* v. *Way*, 8 Phila., 301 (1870), the service was " by leaving a correct copy of the within summons upon the premises therein described, being the dwelling-house of the therein named lessee or tenant, with herself personally." FINLETTER, J. " The Act of Assembly expressly requires in the case of personal service that the original summons should be produced to the defendant. In *Buchanan* v. *Specht*, 1 Phila., 252, Judge KING, says : ' Unless the officer making such service produce the writ, his acts are *null* and *void*, for without the production of the writ a defendant is not bound to know, nor can he know, that the officer has such writ in his possession.' "

In *Berrill* v. *Flynn*, 8 Phila., 239 (1871), the constable made a return " served personally. by leaving a copy with defendant at his residence and informing him of the contents thereof, December 24, 1870." PAXSON, J.: " The Act of Assembly points out two modes of service, viz.: 1. By producing the original summons to the defendant and informing him of the contents thereof; and, 2, by leaving a copy of it at his dwelling-house in the presence of one or more of his family or neighbors. The first is a personal service ; the second is a service by copy. The return in this case does not conform to either mode. It is true it states that a copy was left with the defendant at his residence. But a copy of what ? We may infer that it was a copy of the original summons, but the return does not say so."

In *City* v. *Cathcart*, 10 Phila., 103 (1873), the return of service to a summons was " served by serving a copy of original summons on defendant." The return, being obscure, was decided to be insufficient.

In a suit against Rosengarten & Brother, the summons was returned by the constable, " served by producing to the defendants the original summons, and made known to them the contents thereof."

It was held to be defective in not setting out the individual names of the firm, and in neglecting to aver that the defendants were individually served. *Wharton* v. *Rosengarten*, 3 W. N., 258 (1876), C. P. No. 1.

The return to service of a summons before a justice of the peace must be under oath, in order to sustain a judgment by default, for want of an appearance. *Hoary* v. *McHale*, 2 Dist. Rep., 686 (1893); *Knoblauch* v. *Hefron*, 3 Id., 765 (1894).

§ 1286. *If the return of the summons exceed the statutory limit between the teste and the return.* A judgment was obtained before a justice against non-residents of a county where an interval of six days had elapsed between the issuing and return of the writ of summons. A transcript was entered in the prothonotary's office, and a writ of execution issued. The judgment was stricken off for want of jurisdiction. *Pantall* v. *Dickey*, 123 Pa. St., 431 (1888). (See § 1288.)

But in *McGuiley* v. *McDonough*, 27 W. N., 340 (1885), it was ruled, if a defendant appears in response to a summons of a justice made returnable beyond the statutory limit, he cures the irregularity.

§ 1287. *In computing the four days, the teste and the return-day cannot both be counted.* Under the Act of 1810, the day of service and day of hearing cannot both be counted in the four days between the issuance and return-day of the summons. *Ferris* v. *Zeidler*, 5 Phila., 529 (1864) ; *Comm.* v. *Richer*, 13 W. N., 143 (1883).

§ 1288. **Attachment in cases of fraud and against non-residents.**

Where no *capias* can issue and defendant shall reside out of the county, he shall be proceeded against by summons or attachment, returnable not less than two nor more than four days from the date thereof, which shall be served two days before the time of appearance. (Act July 12, 1842, section 26 ; P. L., 345.)

§ 1289. *Jurisdiction.* Justices of the peace have no jurisdiction, under the Act of 1842, to issue an attachment against the property of any person not residing within this Commonwealth. *Vansyckel's Appeal*, 13 Pa. St., 128 (1850).

The Act of July 7, 1879, giving justices jurisdiction in demands not exceeding $300, embraces proceedings by attachment against fraudulent debtors, under Act July 12, 1842, section 27. *Jacoby* v. *Shafer*, 105 Pa. St., 610 (1884).

In attachment proceedings under the Act of 1842, the suit should be brought in the name of the principal, not the agent. *Powell* v. *Roderick*, 1 Dist. Rep., 120 (1892).

1290. *Attachments against non-residents—Jurisdiction.* The Act of July 7, 1879 [increasing the jurisdiction of a justice to $300], embraces attachments against non-resident debtors, under the Act of May 8, 1874 (P. L., 123). *Ormsby* v. *Grinolds*, 42 Leg. Int., 415 (1885) ; *Jacoby* v. *Shafer*, 105 Pa. St., 610 (1884) ; *Enfield* v. *Squire*, 3 Dist. Rep., 349 (1894) ; *contra*, *Ross* v. *Miller*, 14 W. N., 253 (1884).

Under this Act, entry of bail by defendant to dissolve the attachment is sufficient to give jurisdiction of the cause. The appearance of defendant is a waiver of objection to the jurisdiction. *Wright* v. *Milligan*, 31 W. N., 469 (1892).

§ 1291. *Affidavit and bond for attachment in cases of fraud.*

It shall be the duty of any justice to issue an attachment on the application of the plaintiff in any case where no *capias* can issue, upon proof by affidavit of the plaintiff or some other person or persons to the satisfaction of the justice, that the defendant is about to remove any of his property from the county, with intent to defraud his creditors, or has assigned, disposed of, or secreted, or is about to assign, dispose of, or secrete any of his property with the like fraudulent intent; and said affidavit shall specify the amount of the plaintiff's claim, or the balance thereof over and above all discounts which the defendant may have against him. Before the attachment shall issue, the plaintiff, or some one in his behalf, shall execute a bond in double the amount of the claim, with good and sufficient security, conditioned that if the plaintiff shall fail to recover a judgment of at least one-half the amount of the claim, he shall pay to the defendant his damages for the wrongful taking of any property over and above an amount sufficient to satisfy the judgment and costs. If the plaintiff fail in his action, he shall pay defendant his legal costs and all damages which he may sustain by reason of said attachment. (Act of July 12, 1842, section 27 ; P. L., 345.)

An affidavit under this Act which sets forth that defendant is indebted to plaintiff and " is about to dispose of his personal property, * * * and depart from this county with intent to defraud his creditors," is sufficient. *Spencer* v. *Bloom*, 30 W. N., 128 (1892).

An affidavit which merely sets forth that the plaintiff has good " reason to believe that the defendant is about to dispose of his personal property, etc.," is insufficient. *Gates* v. *Bloom*, 30 W. N., 127 (1892).

§ 1292. *Lien of attachment.*

No attachment issued under section 27 of Act July 12, 1842, shall remain a lien on the property attached for a longer period than sixty days after the time when the plaintiff might legally have had execution issued on said judgment.

Whenever an appeal shall be taken, the lien on the property attached shall remain for the period of sixty days after final judgment. (Act March 22, 1850, section 1 ; P. L., 233.)

§ 1293. *Affidavit and bond for attachment against non-residents.*

It shall be the duty of any justice to issue an attachment on the application of the plaintiff in any case where no *capias* can issue upon the affidavit of the plaintiff or other person or persons to the satisfaction of the justice, that the defendant is a non-resident, and such affidavit shall set forth the amount of the plaintiff's claim, or the balance thereof, over and above all discounts which the defendant may have against him. Before the attachment shall issue the plaintiff, or some one on his behalf, shall give bond in double the amount of plaintiff's claim, with good security, conditioned that if the plaintiff fail to recover a judgment for at least one-half the amount of his claim, he shall pay to the defendant his damages for the wrongful taking of property over and above the amount sufficient to satisfy the judgment and costs. If the plaintiff fail in his action, he shall pay to the defendant his legal costs and damages which he may sustain by reason of said attachment. (Act May 8, 1874, section 1 ; P. L., 123.)

The following forms are not in print, and you must prepare them for the magistrate :—

§ 1294.

FORM OF PRÆCIPE FOR ATTACHMENT.

A. B. ⎫
   v. ⎬   Before Magistrate, E. F.
C. D. ⎭   Court No. .

SIR :

Issue attachment for debt as above under the Act of May 8, 1874, and attach goods, chattels, rights, and credits of defendant in the hands of G. H., of Philadelphia.

Returnable   , 1890, between   P.M., and   P.M.
To E. F.,   ⎫   (Signature of Counsel.)
        Magistrate. ⎭   Atty. pro A. B.

Present with the *præcipe* an affidavit of the truth of the facts :

§ 1295.

FORM OF AFFIDAVIT.

A. B. ⎫
   v. ⎬   Before Magistrate, E. F.
C. D. ⎭   Court No. .

City and County of Philadelphia, *ss.*

A. B., being duly sworn according to law, deposes and says that the claim upon which this attachment issues is less than $100, that no *capias* can issue, that the defendant, C. D., is a non-resident of this Commonwealth, and that the defendant became the debtor of the plaintiff in the sum of   dollars in manner following, to wit :

(Here set forth the facts of your case specifically and carefully.)

Sworn to and subscribed before me, ⎫
   this   day of   , 1890. ⎬   (Signature of A. B.)
                                        ⎪
[SEAL]   Magistrate Court No. . ⎭

The affidavit must state that defendant is a non-resident, otherwise the attachment will be quashed. *Bollinger* v. *Gallagher*, 29 W. N., 89 (1891).

With the affidavit must be presented a bond.

§ 1296.

FORM OF BOND.

KNOW ALL MEN BY THESE PRESENTS, That we (plaintiff) and (name of surety), of the city of Philadelphia, are jointly and severally held and firmly bound unto the Commonwealth of Pennsylvania in the sum of (double the amount of your demand) dollars, lawful money of the United States of America, to be paid to the said Commonwealth of Pennsylvania, its certain attorney or assigns, to which payment well and truly to be made we do jointly and severally bind ourselves, and the heirs, executors, and administrators of us and each of us, by these presents.

Sealed with our seals, and dated the   day of   , A. D. 1890.

WHEREAS, the said A. B., plaintiff, has applied to E. F., Esq., Magistrate of Court No.   , of the county of Philadelphia, upon proof by affidavit of A. B., for an attachment against C. D., defendant, under Act of Assembly of said Commonwealth, approved May 8, 1874, and the supplements thereto, in such case made and provided. Now the condition of this obligation is such, that if the said plaintiff shall fail to recover a judgment at least of one-half of the amount of his claim, he shall pay to the defendant his damages for the wrongful taking of any property over and above an amount sufficient to satisfy the judgment and costs, and that if the plaintiff shall fail in his action, he shall pay to the defendant his legal costs and damages which he may sustain by reason of said attachment.

Signed, sealed, and delivered in ⎱   (Signature of Plaintiff.) [SEAL]
the presence of   ⎰   (Signature of Surety.)   [SEAL]

In *Hibbs* v. *Blair*, 14 Pa. St., 413 (1850), proceedings under the Act of 1842 were brought, and the justice entered a non-suit because a copy of the attachment was not served on defendant. Action was brought on the bond, which did not contain the words in the proviso of the twenty-seventh section of the Act, "if the plaintiff shall fail in his action." *Held*, notwithstanding the omission, the sureties were liable.

§ 1297.

FORM OF WRIT OF ATTACHMENT.

COMMONWEALTH OF PENNSYLVANIA, ⎱ ss.
   COUNTY OF PHILADELPHIA,   ⎰

To G. H., Constable, greeting :

We command you that you attach C. D., a non-resident of this Commonwealth, by all and singular his goods and chattels, rights and credits, in whose hands and possession soever the same may be, so that he be and appear before the subscriber, E. F., Esq., Magistrate of Court No.   , in and for the county of Philadelphia, at his office (place), in said city, on (date and hours between which he must appear), there to answer A. B. of a plea of debt, and have you then there this writ.

In witness whereof, I have hereunto set my hand and affixed the official seal of the said court, this (date).

          (Signature)
              Magistrate of Court No.   .
       Inventory of goods, etc., attached.
(The constable here sets forth the inventory on the writ.)

You must give the constable particular directions as to the person or persons in possession of the goods alleged to belong to defendant, where he can seize them, and when, etc.

Watch carefully his return, and assist the constable if necessary.

In attachment under the Act of 1842 against money in the hands of a garnishee, the constable must either take the money or demand a bond for its production, under § 29 of the Act. *McNamara* v. *Roderick*, 1 Dist. Rep., 610 (1892).

§ 1298.

By virtue of the within writ of attachment, I attached on (date), at o'clock   M., goods belonging to the said defendant (name), in the hands and possession of L. M., and left with and delivered to said L. M. a true copy of said attachment and inventory of the property attached, the defendant not being found in the county.

So answers

(Signature)

Constable.

§ 1299. *The condition of the attachment bond is broken if non-suit entered because defendant not served.* If an attachment has been levied on property of the defendant and a non-suit entered because defendant was not served with a copy of the attachment, the condition of the bond is broken. *Hibbs* v. *Blair,* 14 Pa. St., 413 (1850).

§ 1300. *Service of attachment in cases of fraud.*

Every attachment shall be served by the constable by attaching so much of the defendant's property not exempt by law from sale upon execution as will be sufficient to pay the debt demanded, and by delivering to the defendant a copy of the said attachment and an inventory of the property attached if he can be found in the county ; if not so to be found, then by leaving a copy of the same at his place of residence with some adult member of his family, or the family where he shall reside ; if he be a non-resident of the county and cannot be found, then by leaving a copy of said attachment and inventory with the person in possession of the property. (Act July 12, 1842, section 28 ; P. L., 345.)

§ 1301. *Service and return of attachment against non-residents.*

Every attachment against non-resident debtors shall be made returnable not less than two nor more than four days from the date thereof, and shall be served by the constable by attaching so much of defendant's property as will pay the demand, and deliver to him a copy of the attachment with an inventory of the property attached if he can be found in the county ; if not so found, then by leaving a copy of the attachment and inventory with the person having possession of the property. (Act May 8, 1874, section 2 ; P. L., 123.)

The attachment cannot issue returnable in more than four days, even though the fourth day falls on a Sunday. *Protzman* v. *Wolff,* 4 Dist. Rep., 473 (1895).

§ 1302. *Choses in action cannot be attached.* An attachment under the Act of 1842 can only affect such goods as are capable of manual seizure by the constable ; choses in action cannot be attached. *Wolbert* v. *Fackler,* 32 Pa. St., 452 (1859). The same ruling has been made under the Act of May 8, 1874. *Mumford* v. *Deyoe,* 4 Dist. Rep., 575 (1895).

§ 1303. *Defendant may give bond (in cases of fraud).*

The constable shall state specifically in his return the manner of service, and it shall be his duty to take the property attached into his possession unless the defendant, or some one in his behalf, shall enter into bond with sufficient surety in the penalty of double the amount of the claim, conditioned that if the plaintiff recover judgment he will pay the debt and costs at the expiration of the stay of execution given by law to freeholders, or that he will surrender the property attached to any officer having an execution against him on any judgment recovered in such attachment. (Act July 12, 1842, section 29; P. L., 345.)

§ 1304. *Defendant may give bond in cases against non-residents.*

The constable shall state specifically in his return how he served the attachment, and it shall be his duty to take the property attached into his possession unless the defendant, or some one in his behalf, shall enter into bond with sufficient surety in double the amount of the plaintiff's claim, conditioned that if plaintiff recover judgment against him he will pay the debt and costs at the expiration of the stay of execution given to freeholders, or that he will surrender the property attached to an officer having an execution against him on a judgment recovered in said attachment. If the attachment be personally served upon defendant at least two days before the return-day, the justice on the return-day shall proceed to hear the same as upon a summons personally served.

If the same shall not have been so served, the justice shall issue a summons, and if the summons be returned personally served, or that the defendant, after diligent inquiry, cannot be found in the county, then the justice shall proceed to hear and determine the cause as upon a summons personally served. (Act May 8, 1874, section 1; P. L., 123.)

The attachment may be dissolved by entry of bail for payment of debt, interest, and costs and a general appearance in the Common Pleas. *Wright* v. *Millikin*, 152 Pa. St., 507 (1893).

§ 1305. *A return to an attachment is defective unless it specify the goods attached.*

In *Wolbert* v. *Fackler*, 32 Pa. St., 453 (1859), the constable who served the attachment returned "attached defendant's goods, etc., in the hands of H. P. W., and served copy and inventory on H. P. W., the person in whose hands the same were found; also served attachment, summons, and inventory on the defendant personally, July 20, 1857."

The return was held defective in not stating specifically what had been attached.

§ 1306. *Proceedings on attachment in cases of fraud.*

If the attachment be returned served personally upon the defendant at least two days before the return-day thereof, the justice shall, on the return-day, proceed to hear and determine the same as upon the return of a summons returned personally served.

If it shall not have been so served, the justice shall issue a summons against the defendant returnable according to law; and if the said summons shall be returned personally served, or by leaving a copy at the residence of the defendant, or that the defendant, after diligent inquiry, cannot be found in the county, then, in any case, the justice shall proceed to hear and determine the cause as in a summons personally served. (Act July 12, 1842, section 30 ; P. L., 345.)

§ 1307. *Judgment on attachment where defendant not served is not conclusive—Execution—Appeal—Exemption.*

A judgment obtained before a justice, in any suit commenced by attachment, when the defendant shall not be personally served and shall not appear, shall be only presumptive evidence of indebtedness in any *scire facias* thereon, and may be disproven by defendant.

Execution shall be levied only upon property seized by virtue of the attachment, nor shall the defendant be debarred of any set-off.

The right of appeal, both as to the original judgment and upon the judgment rendered after the issuing of a *scire facias*, shall be the same as in proceedings upon a summons personally served. No exemption law of this Commonwealth shall be construed to extend to any debtor not a resident thereof. (Act May 8, 1874, section 4 ; P. L., 123.)

§ 1308. *Exemption allowed in attachment under Act of 1842, if original judgment was on contract.* Under attachment proceedings, according to the Act July 12, 1842, section 27, a claim for exemption will be allowed if the original judgment was on a contract. *Waugh* v. *Burkett*, 3 Gr., 319 (1861).

§ 1309. **Domestic attachments before justices.** The statutes and proceedings will be found at §§ 121, 122, 123.

§ 1310.

FORM OF OATH BEFORE ATTACHMENT ISSUES.

A. B. ⎫ Before E. F., Magistrate of Court No. .
  v. ⎬ Domestic attachment in debt for a sum not exceeding $100.
C. D. ⎭

City and County of Philadelphia, *ss.*

A. B., the plaintiff in the above case, being duly sworn according to law, deposes and says that he is resident in said city and county ; that C. D., of said city, is indebted to him on a promissory note for (a sum not exceeding $100); and that the said C. D. is and has absconded and departed from the place of his usual abode in this State (*or* remains absent from the said State, *or* has confined himself in his house, viz. (name the place), *or* has concealed himself elsewhere), with design to defraud his creditors, as is believed; and that the said C. D. has not left a clear fee-simple estate in lands and tenements within this State sufficient to pay his debts, so far as deponent knows or believes.

Sworn to and subscribed before me, ⎫
  this (date).   ⎪
                                    ⎬   (Signature of A. B.)
              Magistrate.   ⎪
§ 1311.   ⎭

FORM OF WRIT OF DOMESTIC ATTACHMENT.

The Commonwealth of Pennsylvania to G. H., Constable in the city of Philadelphia, of Magistrate's Court No. , greeting :

Whereas, A. B., of the city of Philadelphia, hath on his solemn oath declared before E. F., a magistrate of said county, that C. D., of said county, is indebted to him on bond in the sum of $, and that the said C. D. is and has absconded from the place of his usual abode in said county, with design to defraud his creditors, as is believed, and that the said C. D. hath not left a clear fee-simple estate in lands and tenements within this State sufficient to pay his debts, so far as the said A. B. knows or believes ; and the said A. B. has requested the said magistrate to grant a writ of attachment to attach the goods and chattels or other effects of the said C. D. to answer the said A. B.

We command you that you attach C. D. of said city by all and singular his goods and chattels or other effects, in whose hands or possession soever the same may be found within this county, to answer the said A. B., and so that the said C. D. appear before E. F., Esquire, one of the said magistrates in and for said county on (day, date, and hour), at his office, to answer A. B. of a plea of debt not exceeding $100. Hereof fail not.

Witness the hand and official seal of said magistrate (date).

[SEAL]   Magistrate.

§ 1312. *When domestic attachment may be dissolved.* An affidavit in a domestic attachment is not conclusive, and the attachment, on sufficient proof, may be dissolved.

The parties who have issued the process are bound to support it when attacked. *Boyes* v. *Coppinger*, 2 Yeates, 277 (1798).

§ 1313.

FORM OF APPOINTMENT OF FREEHOLDERS AS TRUSTEES.

City and County of Philadelphia, *ss.*

To A. B., and C. D., and L. M., of   County, greeting :

Your are hereby authorized and required to take into your custody all the goods, chattels, and effects of G. H., of said county, mentioned in the schedule hereunto annexed, and attached at the suit of E. F., for which you are to be accountable until the same shall be disposed of according to law.

Given under my hand and official seal (date).

[SEAL]   Magistrate.

A schedule must be annexed according to the constable's return.

§ 1314.

FORM OF CERTIFICATE TO PROTHONOTARY.

Whereas, A. B., of the city of Philadelphia, on the (date), pursuant to the Act of Assembly of August 22, 1752, and its supplements thereto, did obtain of the subscriber, a magistrate of said city and county of Philadelphia, an attachment against C. D., of said city, directed to the constable of   Ward, in said city, and commanding him to attach the said C. D. by all and singular his goods and chattels or other effects, in whose hands or possession the same might be found in said county, to answer the said A. B. in a plea of debt not exceeding $100 ; and whereas, by virtue of said attachment, the said constable did attach certain goods, chattels, and effects of the said C. D. in the hands of E. F., of said city, as by the constable's return more fully appears, which said goods, chattels and effects have been delivered to (names of trustees) until they should be disposed of according to law.

And whereas, in pursuance of my notice for that purpose, the creditors of the said C. D., appearing on (date) at (place), in order to discover and make proof of their demands against the said C. D., and it appearing that there is a just debt due to G. H., one of the said creditors, exceeding the sum of $100, I have proceeded no further but do deliver and certify the said attachment and all proceedings thereon had before me pursuant to the said Act.

Certified under my hand and official seal, at Philadelphia (date).

(Signature of Magistrate.)

To the Prothonotary of the Common Pleas of Philadelphia County.

[SEAL]

§ 1315. *Property only vests in trustees when appointed — Title does not relate back.* Under a domestic attachment before a justice, the property does not vest in the trustees until after their appointment ; there is no relation back to the time when the attachment issued. *McCormick* v. *Miller*, 3 P. & W., 230 (1831).

Such domestic attachment may be executed by a deputy constable. *Id.*

§ 1316.

FORM OF NOTICE TO CREDITORS.

Whereas, in pursuance of the Act of Assembly of this Commonwealth, approved August 22, 1752, and its supplements thereto, an attachment has been granted by E. F., Esq., one of the magistrates in and for the county of Philadelphia, at the instance of A. B. of said county against C. D. of said county, whereon certain goods, chattels, and effects of the said C. D. have been attached, and are now in the custody of (names of trustees) of said county, trustees, until they shall be disposed of according to law. Now, notice is hereby given to all creditors of C. D. to appear (place) (date), then and there to discover and make proof of their demands agreeably to the directions of the said Act.

E. F.,

(Date.)　　　　　　　•　　　　　　　Magistrate.

§ 1317. *Trustees entitled to balance in hands of sheriff.* In a domestic attachment before a justice trustees in due course were appointed ; the absconding debtor's property was sold under an execution. The trustees claimed the residue in the sheriff's hands after satisfaction of the execution. The court decided the trustees should hold the remainder, though no notice had been given the creditors by advertisement. *Ebert* v. *Spangler*, 3 P. & W., 389 (1832).

§ 1318. *No second attachment pending the first.*

When any attachment shall be granted by any justice or any writ of attachment shall issue out of any county court, no second or other attachment or writ of attachment granted or issued by the said justice, or any other justice within the same county, or by the justices of the same county court, against the real or personal estate of the same defendant, or the execution of them or any of them shall bind or affect the right, title, interest, or property of or in the real or personal estate of the defendant within the same county, or any part thereof, while the proceedings on the said first attachment or writ of attachment remain undetermined. (Act August 22, 1752, section 3 ; 1 Sm., 218.)

§ 1319.

FORM OF ORDER TO TRUSTEES TO SELL PERISHABLE GOODS.

Philadelphia County, *ss.*

To (names of trustees) of Philadelphia County, greeting :

Whereas, among other articles attached as the property of C. D., late of Philadelphia county, and now remaining in your custody until further order, there are (perishable goods) which must be maintained at expense and liable to perish ;

You are hereby required to make sale of said (perishable goods) within ten days from this date, first giving public notice thereof at least six days before the sale by advertisement to be set up at the most public places near the place of sale.

Given under my hand and official seal (date).

(Signature of Magistrate),
Magistrate.
(Date.)

[SEAL]

§ 1320.

FORM OF INVENTORY AND APPRAISEMENT.

(Caption of case.)

Inventory and appraisement of the goods and chattels attached as the property of C. D., at the suit of A. B., in the county of Philadelphia, by virtue of the warrant of R. S., Esq., one of the magistrates in and for the county of Philadelphia, made by G. H. and L. M., appraisers, said appraisers being duly appointed and qualified.

(Here follows inventory.)

(Date.)

G. H.,
L. M.,
Appraisers.

§ 1321.

FORM OF ADVERTISEMENT FOR SALE.

Notice is hereby given, that by virtue of an order from E. F., Esquire, a magistrate in and for the county of Philadelphia, there will be exposed to public sale (date and hour), (place), in said county, (here mention articles, following your inventory), attached as the property of C. D., late of said county, at the instance of A. B., in an action of domestic attachment.

For terms of sale and further particulars, apply to

G. H. (address),
L. M. (address),
O. P. (address),
Trustees.

(Date.)

§ 1322. *Report of sale to be made.* The freeholders, within six days next after making sale and distribution as directed, shall render a true account of their proceedings to the justice who granted the attachment, to be kept by him as a record of their proceedings. Act of August 22, 1752, section 6.

§ 1323. Subpœnas may be issued.

It shall and may be lawful for justices to issue subpœnas and other warrants under their respective hands into any county, to summon persons to give evidence in any matter or cause triable by or before them under such pains or penalties as subpœnas or warrants usually are awarded. (Act May 22, 1722, section 8 ; 1 Sm., 138.)

§ 1324. *A fine is the only punishment for not obeying subpœna.* Where a witness is in contempt for not obeying a *subpœna*, he can only be *fined*. *Comm.* v. *Newton*, 1 Gr., 453 (1851).

§ 1325. **Appearance by an attorney is not a compliance with a recognizance requiring the defendant's appearance.** In *Graves* v. *Beckwith*, 3 P. & W., 525 (1832), A. appeared before a justice on a *capias*, and had the case continued upon B.'s entering into a recognizance, conditioned for the appearance of A. at a certain future day. A.'s attorney appeared on the day appointed, but A. did not appear at all. It was held this was not a proper performance of the condition of the recognizance.

§ 1326. Non-suit.

Where the plaintiff does not appear, either in person or by agent, to substantiate his charge, the justice may proceed to give judgment against him by non-suit for the costs, and fifty cents per day for the reasonable costs of defendant for trouble in attending such suit. (Act March 20, 1810, section 6 ; 5 Sm., 165.)

§ 1327. *Plaintiff cannot appeal if a non-suit be entered by reason of his absence.* In *Selfridge* v. *Tilghman*, 1 Phila., 580 (1855), the plaintiff brought suit, had the summons served, but at the time fixed for hearing neither the plaintiff nor his attorney appeared, and a non-suit was entered by the alderman. *Held*, that the plaintiff could not appeal. A non-suit was entered where, by consent of both parties, a hearing before the justice was twice continued, but at the subsequent hearing the plaintiff did not appear. But its only effect was to put an end to the action without concluding the rights of the parties. *Vought* v. *Sober*, 73 Pa. St., 51 (1873).

§ 1328. *Although a justice has no power to enter a compulsory non-suit, yet it has the force of a judgment unless appealed from.* The only judgment a justice can give is a final judgment subject to the right of appeal, but a justice has no power to enter a compulsory non-suit. Such non-suit has, however, the force of a judgment unless appealed from. *Gould* v. *Crawford*, 2 Pa. St., 89 (1845) ; *Lawver* v. *Walls*, 17 Pa. St., 75 (1851).

§ 1329. *The taking off a non-suit and giving judgment for plaintiff by default is irregular.* In *Cosgrove* v. *Scott*, 8 W. N., 28 (1879), a magistrate entered a non-suit upon the defendant, filing an affidavit that the title to lands would come in question ; subsequently he took off the non-suit upon proper notice to all parties and gave judgment for plaintiff by reason of default of appearance of defendant. MITCHELL, J. (C. P. No. 2, of Phila.) : " No such right is vested in magistrates or any courts of inferior jurisdiction. * * * The subsequent effort to retry the case was irregular."

§ 1330. *After non-suit, plaintiff should appeal.* In *Gord* v. *Middleman*, 25 W. N., 556 (1890), the magistrate gave judgment of non-suit against the plaintiff, but subsequently, on petition filed, opened the judgment, reheard the case, and gave judgment in plaintiff's favor. It was decided the proper practice was to appeal from the judgment unless the opposite party consent to a rehearing.

§ 1331. **A justice may strike off a judgment and enter a discontinuance.** *Comm.* v. *Kite*, 5 S. & R., 399 (1819). The plaintiff, in a *scire facias* against bail, was not present when judgment in the plaintiff's favor was entered by the justice, nor did the plaintiff wish the judgment entered. The day the judgment was entered, the justice, at the request of the plaintiff, discontinued the suit. The Supreme Court held that " under the circumstances of the case, the alderman had a right to strike out the entry of the judgment and enter a discontinuance."

§ 1332. *A discontinuance, although accompanied by a confession of judgment for costs, does not bar plaintiff from bringing a second suit.* If a suit is discontinued before a justice and a judgment confessed for costs, inasmuch as a judgment for costs is implied in a discontinuance, the plaintiff is not barred from bringing a subsequent suit. *Gibson* v. *Gibson*, 20 Pa. St., 9 (1852).

In *Blair* v. *McLean*, 25 Pa. St., 77 (1855), it was decided that where parties submit their proofs, the plaintiff may suffer a voluntary non-suit, or discontinue, or withdraw his action, and he may thereafter bring another suit for the same cause of action.

§ 1333. **When bond required for an adjournment.**

A defendant, against whose body by the provisions of this Act an execution cannot be issued by an alderman or justice, in order to obtain an adjournment, shall give a bond or recognizance in the nature of special bail conditioned that no part of the property of the defendant liable to be taken in execution shall be removed, secreted, assigned, or in any way disposed of, except for the necessary support of himself and family, until the plaintiff's demand shall be satisfied or until the expiration of ten days after such plaintiff shall be entitled to have execution issued on the judgment obtained, if plaintiff shall obtain the same. If the condition of such bond or recognizance be broken and an execution be returned unsatisfied in whole or in part, the plaintiff in an action on the bond shall be entitled to recover the value of the property so removed, secreted, or assigned. (Act July 12, 1842, section 33 ; P. L., 347.)

§ 1334. Proceedings before justice on reference.

If the demand shall be more than five dollars and thirty-three cents, and shall not exceed one hundred dollars, and if either party refuse to submit the determination of the cause to the justice, he shall request them to choose referees—one, two, or three each, and mutually to agree upon a third, fifth, or seventh man, all of whom shall be sworn or affirmed,

"Well and truly to try all matters in variance between the parties submitted to them."

And having heard their proofs and allegations, they, or the majority of them, shall make out an award, under their hands, and transmit the same to such justice, who shall thereupon enter judgment for the sum awarded and costs. The judgment, when not exceeding twenty dollars, shall be final and conclusive to both plaintiff and defendant without further appeal.

The referees shall be notified by the justice of their appointment and of the time and place fixed for a hearing. If any person so chosen or notified shall neglect or refuse to serve, he shall, for every such neglect or refusal, unless prevented by sickness or other unavoidable cause, pay two dollars for the use of the poor or supervisors of the road, which fine shall be recovered as other fines are by law recoverable: *Provided*, that an action shall be brought within thirty days after such neglect or refusal. (Act March 20, 1810, section 3; 5 Sm., 162.)

Where there has been an award, the record of the justice of the peace must show: (*a*) There is an action pending; (*b*) that plaintiff's claim exceeds $5.33; (*c*) that the parties, or one of them, refuses to submit to the determination of the justice; (*d*) the selection of arbitrators; (*e*) their award; (*f*) judgment for sum awarded with costs. *Climenson* v. *Climenson*, 163 Pa. St., 451; 35 W. N., 471 (1894).

§ 1335. Proceedings in trover and conversion and in trespass—
Claim not exceeding ten dollars—Judgment for five dollars and thirty-three cents is final. If oath made that title to land involved, suit to be dismissed.

Where the demand before a justice in proceedings in trover and conversion or trespass for damages for injury to real and personal property does not exceed ten dollars, it shall be his duty to proceed to hear and determine the case. If the demand exceed that sum, then on request of either party or his agent three reputable citizens shall be chosen by the parties or their agents as referees, or if they cannot agree, or if only one party or his agent appear, then the justice shall appoint the referees, who shall be sworn or affirmed justly and truly to assess the damages alleged to have been sustained or the value of property in dispute, which they or a majority of them shall have power to assess.

If both parties or their agents do not prefer a reference, the justice shall proceed to hear and determine, and if the sum adjudged do not exceed five dollars and thirty-three cents the same shall be final and conclusive.

If the defendant before the trial of the action make oath or affirmation that the title to lands will come in question, the justice shall dismiss the same, the costs to be divided. If the damages shall not amount to more than one dollar, the plaintiff shall not recover more costs than damages. (Act March 22, 1814, section 2 ; 6 Sm., 182.)

The above provision as to costs is altered by the Act of February 13, 1816, section 1 (*infra*).

No reference can be had unless both parties agree. Act of April 26, 1855, section 1 (*infra*).

§ 1336. *A submission cannot be made to arbitrators of a claim beyond jurisdiction.* In *Brenneman* v. *Greenawalt*, 1 S. & R., 27 (1814), the parties voluntarily appeared before the justice and submitted their cause to the determination of arbitrators, who made an award in favor of the plaintiff for $250.

The judgment was arrested.

TILGHMAN, C. J.: " In the case before us no judgment was confessed, nor was it submitted to the justice to determine for how much the judgment should be entered, but the cause was referred to arbitrators in the usual way. It is, therefore, not within the provisions of the fourteenth section of the Act of March 20, 1810." See also *McKillip* v. *McKillip*, 2 *Id.*, 489 (1816).

§ 1337. *Consent of both required for a reference—This must be docketed.*

No action shall be referred without agreement or express assent of both parties or their agents, which shall be noted by the justice on his docket. (Act April 26, 1855, section 1 ; P. L., 304.)

§ 1338. *If parties refuse to refer.*

If either party or their agents shall refuse to refer, the justice may proceed to hear and examine their proofs and allegations, and thereupon give judgment, either party having the right to appeal within twenty days after judgment. (Act March 20, 1810, section 4 ; 5 Sm., 163.)

§ 1339. *Where parties desire to refer, but cannot agree on referees, they shall strike from seven names suggested by the justice.*

The Act of May 15, 1879, section 1 (P. L., 62), provided that if the parties or their agents shall fail to agree upon the chosen referees, but desire to submit to reference, then the justice shall write down seven names of disinterested citizens, from which list the parties, commencing with the plaintiff, shall strike alternately until three names be left, who shall be the referees.

§ 1340. *Place of absent referee supplied.*

If a referee shall not attend at the time and place fixed for hearing the cause, it shall be the duty of the referee or referees present (where the parties cannot agree on the person or persons to supply the vacancy, or where only one of the parties attends) to appoint proper persons in place of those who may be absent, and the referees thus appointed shall have the same authority as those originally appointed. (Act March 26, 1814, section 1 ; 6 Sm., 206.)

§ 1341. *Referees to be sworn—Shall swear witnesses—May adjourn.*

The referees shall be sworn or affirmed by a justice of the peace, or they may swear and affirm each other ; then any of them shall administer oaths or affirmations to witnesses, and the said referees, or a majority of them, shall have power to adjourn their meetings to any other time or place as often as they may deem proper. (*Id.*, section 2.)

§ 1342. *Justices may issue subpœnas to appear before referees.*

Justices of the peace shall have power to issue subpœnas for witnesses to appear before arbitrators. (Act of June 16, 1836, section 46 ; P. L., 727.)

§ 1343. *When referees impose fine for disorderly conduct, justice shall issue execution.* A justice of the peace, to whom is sent the certificate of arbitrators, authorizing the justice to collect a fine imposed by them for disorderly conduct, shall make a record of it, and issue execution to collect the same in the manner that judgments under one dollar are by law collected, which sum shall be paid to the county treasurer. Act June 16, 1836, section 45 (P. L., 725).

§ 1344. *Referees may decide as to costs in cases of trespass.*

The referees in proceedings in trespass, in addition to their report of damages, have the power to decide and report as to the costs and in what proportion they shall be paid by the parties, on which report judgment shall be entered for the costs and damages, and execution may issue as in other cases. (Act February 13, 1816, section 1 ; 6 Sm., 323.)

§ 1345. *Justice may set aside award for corruption or misconduct.* Justices necessarily possess and have always exercised the power of setting aside awards for corruption or misconduct of the referees, whether the submission be in pursuance of the statutes or by agreement renouncing the right to except or appeal. *Paul* v. *Cunningham,* 9 Pa. St., 106 (1848).

§ 1346. **Pending suit before justice defendant cannot sue before another justice on same contract.** A man against whom a suit is pending before a justice cannot sue the plaintiff before another justice on the same contract. The first suit may be pleaded in bar of the second, although the second was for wages. *Felpel* v. *Hershour,* 24 W. N., 523 (1889).

§ 1347. **Set-off—Penalty for neglecting to set-off—Rehearing on judgment by default.**

A defendant who shall neglect or refuse in any case to set off his demand, and whether founded upon bond, note, penal or single bill, writing obligatory, book account or damages of assumption, against a plaintiff which shall not exceed the sum of one hundred dollars, shall be forever barred from recovering against the party plaintiff by an after-suit. But in case of judgment by default, the defendant, if he has an account to set off against the plaintiff's demand, shall be entitled to a rehearing before the justice within thirty days, on proof either on oath or affirmation of the defendant, or other satisfactory evidence, that defendant was absent when process was served, and did not return before return-day, or was prevented by sickness or other unavoidable cause; the justice shall have power to render judgment for the balance in favor of the plaintiff or defendant. (Act March 20, 1810, section 7; 5 Sm., 163.)

In a suit before a justice, any set-off not exceeding the jurisdiction of the justice must be pleaded or the defendant be forever barred. *Herring* v. *Adams*, 5 W. & S., 459 (1843).

A tenant who omits to claim a set-off against a landlord's claim for rent before a justice, cannot, in replevin, be allowed such set-off. *Walsh* v. *Greenwood*, 2 Dist. Rep., 64 (1892).

§ 1348. *A plaintiff cannot give jurisdiction by allowing a set-off.* *Stroh* v. *Uhrich*, 1 W. & S., 57 (1841), ROGERS, J. One having a demand over $100 cannot give jurisdiction to a justice by allowing a set-off so as to reduce the claim below $100.

§ 1349. *Set-off must be within the jurisdiction.* A set-off cannot be allowed before a justice which is greater than the amount of his jurisdiction. *Holden* v. *Wiggins*, 3 P. & W., 469 (1832); *Milliken* v. *Gardner*, 37 Pa. St., 456 (1860).

§ 1350. *If set-off exceed jurisdiction, it may reduce or destroy plaintiff's claim.* In *Mills* v. *David*, 22 W. N., 515 (1888), it was decided that, in a suit before a justice, a defendant is not allowed to set up a claim as a set-off which exceeds the jurisdiction of the justice, but it may be admitted to reduce or destroy the plaintiff's cause of action.

§ 1351. *After judgment for plaintiff by default, defendant cannot sue for claim he could have used as offset.* Where suit is brought before a justice for a specific amount under a contract and judgment given by default, the defendant cannot bring a subsequent suit for an alleged breach of the contract which he might have set-off in the former suit. *Shoup* v. *Shoup*, 15 Pa. St., 361 (1850).

§ 1352. *The set-off may be upon an independent contract.* Suit was begun before a justice to recover the price of goods sold and delivered. The defendant gave in evidence as a set-off a special contract between him and the plaintiff, by which plaintiff promised to do certain work for the defendant, and did not. The set-off was properly admitted. *Nickle* v. *Baldwin*, 4 W. & S., 290 (1842).

§ 1353. *A judgment may be set-off.* Where A. brings a suit against B., and B. brings an action against A., which separate suits are not forbidden by the Act of March 20, 1810, and judgment is rendered for the respective plaintiffs, on an appeal by one of the parties, the other may, under the plea of set-off, interpose his judgment against the plaintiff's claim, and in such case, though the verdict be for the defendant, plaintiff is entitled to his costs. *Groff* v. *Ressler*, 27 Pa. St., 71 (1856).

§ 1354. *Right to appeal secured by set-off.* The plaintiff sued for four dollars and forty-three cents wages. The defendant claimed a set-off of nineteen dollars as damages arising from plaintiff's negligence. Judgment was entered for the amount of plaintiff's claim and costs. Defendant appealed. A rule to strike off his appeal was discharged. *Rafferty* v. *Clark*, 18 W. N., 378 (1886).

§ 1355. *On appeal, defendant not confined to original set-off.* On an appeal from the judgment of a justice, the defendant is not confined to the matters of set-off relied on before the justice. *Tate* v. *Tate*, 2 Gr., 150 (1858).

§ 1356. *A set-off cannot be made on appeal, of a claim whereof the justice had no jurisdiction.* In *Deihm* v. *Snell*, 21 W. N., 177 (1888), suit was brought before a justice for the balance due upon a note, and judgment entered for fifty-six dollars and eighty-seven cents in favor of the plaintiff. An appeal was taken. On the trial in the Common Pleas, the defendant offered by way of set-off a contract, under seal, relating to real estate. The justice having no jurisdiction of the contract used as a set-off, it was *held* that the Common Pleas could not assume jurisdiction.

§ 1357. **Jury Trials.** *In certain counties, a jury trial may be demanded where claim over fifty dollars.*

In actions before justices where the sum demanded by the plaintiff shall exceed fifty dollars, either the plaintiff or defendant may demand a jury trial.

The justice shall impanel a jury of six, and the mode of procedure shall be the same as provided in Act of May 1, 1861, so far as the latter applies to civil procedure, and the successful party shall be entitled to full costs.

If the defendant demand a jury trial, he shall make and file an affidavit with said justice that he has a just and legal defense to the whole or a part of the plaintiff's claim ; and if to a part, he shall state how much the plaintiff is justly entitled to recover ; and if the plaintiff shall not accept the offer of the defendant, he shall not recover costs if the judgment is for no larger sum than the amount admitted by defendant. (Act February 18, 1869, section 3 ; P. L., 209.)

This Act originally applied only to Erie County, but was extended by the Act February 18, 1870 (P. L., 188), to Venango County ; by the Act February 25, 1870 (P. L., 254), to Lawrence County ; by the Act March 28, 1870 (P. L., 586), to Crawford County ; and by Act February 29, 1872 (P. L., 190), to Warren County.

The Act April 6, 1870 (P. L., 987), applies to jury trials in Mercer County.

§ 1358. *Jury trial may be demanded* in Erie and Warren Counties if defendant claim set-off or payment beyond fifty dollars.

In actions on contracts in Erie County, if the defendant claim a set-off or payment exceeding fifty dollars, either party may demand a trial by jury of six. (Act March 28, 1870, section 1; P. L., 596.)

This Act was extended to Warren County by Act February 29, 1872 (P. L., 190).

§ 1359. *Selection of jurors in above cases.*

The jurors may be selected from the township, borough, or ward where the justice holds office, or from the adjoining townships, boroughs, and wards, in the discretion of the justice, and either party shall have the right to challenge any of the jury for cause before they are sworn. (Act March 28, 1870, section 4.)

§ 1360. *Vacancies in panel* (in above special cases).

Vacancies occurring in the number of jurors by absence, challenge, or other cause shall be supplied by the justice writing down three names for each vacancy, and the parties shall proceed to strike out until the requisite number to fill the vacancies are left. (*Id.*, section 5.)

§ 1361. *Justice shall strike for the party refusing—Jury may be discharged* (applies only to above special cases).

Where either party shall refuse or neglect to strike out the names, the justice shall act for such party.

If the jury be unable to agree upon a verdict and the justice be satisfied of that fact, he shall discharge them after giving notice to the parties, their agents or attorney.

The justice shall fix a time within three days for another jury, which, when chosen, shall be summoned by the constable upon a new *venire* to be issued by the justice, and the new trial shall proceed. (*Id.*, section 6.)

§ 1362. *Appeal in the special cases above noted.*

Prior to 1893 either party had the right of appeal within twenty days, and if the defendant proved to the satisfaction of a judge of the Court of Common Pleas that he had no knowledge of the proceedings before the justice until the time for appeal had expired, and no summons were legally served upon him, the said judge might order a writ of *certiorari* to be issued.

All proceedings were stayed until the determination of the court on the writ of *certiorari*, upon defendant entering into a recognizance with sufficient surety to pay the debt and costs. This section of the Act of March 28, 1870, was repealed by the Act of May 29, 1893 (P. L., 176).

§ 1363. *In Erie County, jury to be judges of law and fact.*

The jury shall be judges of both the law and the facts of the case : *Provided*, the justice shall have power to exclude evidence.

The jury may ask the opinion of the justice upon the law in the presence of the parties or their counsel before verdict rendered. (*Id.*, section 8.)

§ 1364. *Evidence outside the county or State—Depositions.*

Upon affidavit of either party or his agent that a material witness whose testimony is wanted resides out of the county, or is infirm, or for other causes cannot be obtained personally, the cause shall be postponed to obtain the deposition of such witness.

If such cause be postponed at the instance of the defendant, he shall enter into a recognizance with one sufficient surety, covering the amount in demand and costs, conditioned for his appearance on the day fixed.

When the rule for taking depositions is applied for, the party shall file a copy of the interrogatories to be asked the witnesses. Such copy must be served on the other side, who may file additional questions within four days after the receipt of such copy.

The rule and interrogatories shall be certified by the justice before whom the cause is pending, and shall be sufficient authority for the justice named in the rule to take such depositions.

Where the witnesses reside in the county, or in cases where the parties or their agents agree to enter a rule to take depositions, it may be done without filing interrogatories, upon notice given agreeably to the rule, of the time and place appointed for the examination of the witnesses, and testimony so taken shall be read in evidence on the trial before the justice or referees. (Act March 20, 1810, section 8 ; 5 Sm., 166.)

This was extended by the Act March 30, 1829, section 1 (10 Sm., 312), which provided that testimony out of the State shall be obtained in the same manner.

So much of the above section as requires interrogatories to be filed in taking depositions on rules issued by justices is repealed, except so far as it relates to depositions taken without the State. (Act April 11, 1863, section 1 ; P. L., 346.)

§ 1365. Commissions.

Where it is not convenient to take testimony before a justice a commissioner may be named. The justice shall send him a certificate of his appointment with a certified copy of the rule and interrogatories, and he shall have power to administer oaths and affirmations and take the answers of the witnesses. (Act March 30, 1829, section 2 ; 10 Sm., 312.)

§ 1366. *Subpœnas under commissions.*

Subpœnas may be issued by the justice or commissioner to witnesses requiring their attendance at a certain day, hour, and place, under a penalty not exceeding one hundred dollars. (Act February 26, 1831, section 1 ; P. L., 92.)

§ 1367. *Attachment.*

The commissioner or persons duly authorized may, on proof by oath or affirmation of due service of the subpœna, issue an attachment. (*Id.*, section 2.)

§ 1368. *Remedies against recusant witness.*

The party injured by such non-attendance shall be entitled to the same remedies at law as are provided when a subpœna is issued from a court of record. (*Id.*, section 3.)

§ 1369. *Witness refusing to testify.*

If the person subpœnaed shall attend but refuse to testify, he shall be liable to the same proceedings as if he had appeared and refused to testify in a court of record. (*Id.*, section 4.)

§ 1370. Amendments of names.

Justices shall have power in any stage of proceedings before final judgment, on reasonable notice, to grant a hearing and permit amendments by changing or altering the Christian or surname of any party plaintiff or defendant, where it is shown upon due proof that a mistake or omission has been made in the Christian or surname of such party.

If the adverse party be taken by surprise by such amendment, and shall verify the same by oath or affirmation, the justice shall grant a continuance to such future time as he may deem proper, not exceeding five days. (Act May 12, 1887; P. L., 96.)

§ 1371. Judgments. *Justice cannot enter judgment on warrant of attorney.* A judgment cannot be entered upon a warrant of attorney. The proceedings must be by summons or *capias*. *Alberty* v. *Dawson*, 1 Binn., 105 (1804).

§ 1372. *When justice may enter judgment before return-day.* A justice may render judgment before the return of his writ, if the parties voluntarily appear and the case be heard. *Buckmyer* v. *Dubbs*, 5 Binn., 29 (1812).

§ 1373. *Judgment to be entered within ten days after hearing.*

It shall be the duty of justices of the peace to render judgment within ten days after all the evidence shall have been heard. (Act March 22, 1877, section 1; P. L., 13.)

§ 1374. *Judgments before justices for want of affidavit of defense in cases outside of Philadelphia.*

On any contract for the payment of money, either express or implied, if the plaintiff shall file before the summons issues an affidavit, stating the amount he verily believes due from the defendant, together with a copy of the book-entries or instrument of writing upon which the action is brought, or if the claims are not in writing, if the plaintiff shall file an affidavit setting forth a full and detailed statement of the same, it shall be the duty of the justice to make a copy and duly certify such affidavit and deliver it to the constable. Which certified copy shall be served at the time and in the manner that service of summons is made, and judgment shall be rendered in favor of the plaintiff, unless the defendant at or before the time at which the summons is made returnable shall have filed an affidavit of defense setting forth fully the nature and character of the same.

Such affidavit may be made by an agent cognizant of the facts constituting the cause of action or defense or other matters set forth.

This Act in no way impairs or abridges the right of appeal or proceedings by *certiorari*.

This Act shall not apply to magistrates in cities of the first class. (Act July 7, 1879, section 2; P. L., 194.)

§ 1375. *Judgment by default—If defendant do not appear, if he be freeholder, no execution for twenty days.*

Where defendant does not appear upon summons on the day appointed, the justice may, on due proof, by oath or affirmation of the service of the summons, give judgment by default against the defendant, allowing twenty days for an appeal, if defendant be a freeholder ; if defendant be not a freeholder, the justice may issue execution. If defendant within twenty days after such judgment shall enter bail and pay costs on execution, he shall be entitled to an appeal or stay of execution, as though bail had been entered at the time of rendering such judgment. (Act March 20, 1810, section 6 ; 5 Sm., 165.)

Where a defendant has appeared and a case is adjourned, a judgment subsequently entered in the absence of defendant is not a judgment by default within the meaning of the sixth section of the Act of March 20, 1810. *Baker v. Richart*, 2 Dist. Rep., 195 (1892).

A magistrate in Philadelphia County cannot enter judgment for plaintiff upon a sworn statement of account of goods sold and delivered. The proof of a claim must be given by oral testimony under oath—otherwise the judgment will be reversed on *certiorari. Sauter* v. *Carroll*, 1 Dist. Rep., 122 (1892).

§ 1376. *Judgment final if not over five dollars and thirty-three cents.*

If the parties appear before the justice either in person or by agents, the justice shall proceed to hear their proofs and allegations ; and if the demand shall not exceed five dollars and thirty-three cents, shall give judgment, which shall be final. (Act March 20, 1810, section 3 ; 5 Sm., 162.)

§ 1377. **Confession of Judgment.** *Amicable reference or confession of judgment.*

A justice may take cognizance of any matter for a sum exceeding one hundred dollars if the parties voluntarily appear before him to confess judgment or submit it to him as referee, but no execution shall issue before the expiration of one year from the date of such judgment if the party defendant be a freeholder or shall have entered special bail. (Act March 20, 1810, section 14 ; 5 Sm., 161.)

§ 1378. *A confession of judgment must be at office of justice.* A justice must have an office or court for administering justice. If judgment be confessed in an amicable action before him, in order to give it validity upon his docket it must be before *him at his office. King* v. *King*, 1 P. & W., 15 (1829).

§ 1379. *Where judgment over $100 is confessed, record must show personal appearance of defendant.* Where judgment is confessed in an amicable action for a sum *exceeding* $100, it must appear upon the record that the parties appeared *in person* before the justice and confessed the judgment. *Camp* v. *Wood*, 10 W., 118 (1840).

§ 1380. *Judgment over* $100 *good if confessed by defendant in person.* A judgment confessed before a justice of the peace voluntarily in an amicable action for more than $100 is good.

The plaintiff need not appear *in person* if represented by an agent or attorney, and the defendant appear personally. *Truitt Bros.* v. *Ludwig,* 25 Pa. St., 145 (1855).

§ 1381. *Justice is judge of authority of agent of defendant.* Where judgment is confessed before a justice by an agent of the defendant, the justice is the judge of the authority of the agent. *Barber* v. *Chandler,* 17 Pa. St., 48 (1851).

§ 1382. *If an agent confess judgment against a defendant, the defendant can appeal.* In *Rowen* v. *King,* 25 Pa. St., 410 (1855), judgment was confessed by an agent of the defendant, from which judgment the defendant appealed. His appeal was struck off, but was reinstated by the Supreme Court. BLACK, J.: " Every person against whom a justice of the peace renders judgment is entitled to an appeal. When the judgment is confessed by the defendant in person, it is evidence that the debt is just. But no admission of a debt by another can be strong enough to preclude the party from showing that it was made in ignorance of his rights."

§ 1383. *Decision of Common Pleas on* certiorari *is final.* Where judgment has been confessed in an amicable action before a justice for a sum exceeding $100, and the case is affirmed on *certiorari* to the Common Pleas, the Supreme Court cannot review their decision, on writ of error. *Borland* v. *Ealy,* 43 Pa. St., 111 (1862).

§ 1384. *Where just cause to believe a confessed judgment fraudulent, justice to send transcript to prothonotary.*

Where judgment has been confessed before a justice and it afterward appear by due proof on oath or affirmation that there is just cause to believe such judgment was confessed to defraud creditors, it shall be the duty of the justice to transmit a certified transcript of his proceedings to the prothonotary, who shall file the same for adjudication of the Court of Common Pleas, whose judgment thereon shall be final. (Act March 20, 1810, section 14; 5 Sm., 161.)

§ 1385. *Where justice sends transcript to C. P. of a confessed judgment upon allegation of fraud, the court orders a feigned issue or opens the judgment.* Under the fourteenth section of Act March 20, 1810, a justice has the power to enter judgment by confession for a sum exceeding $100.

If, however, the creditors of the defendant shall make oath that there is just cause to believe such judgment was confessed with intent to defraud creditors, the justice shall transmit a transcript of his judgment to the prothonotary, and the adjudication of the Common Pleas thereon shall be final.

The practice under this Act has been either to order a feigned issue or to present a proper affidavit to open the judgment and permit the creditor or creditors to plead, whereon the verdict and judgment are final. HUSTON, J., in *Coates* v. *Roberts*, 4 Rawle, 110 (1833).

§ 1386. *A judgment confessed bars a subsequent action for same debt.* In *Powell* v. *Shank*, 3 W., 235 (1834), an award of arbitrators was for $300, but, in lieu of the award, judgment was entered by the justice by mutual consent for $240. This being a judgment by confession, the Supreme Court *held*, that it was a bar to a subsequent action for the same debt.

§ 1387. **Opening Judgments.** *Justice may, with consent of parties, open judgment.*

Before an appeal is made the justice may, with the consent of both parties or their agents, open his judgment and give them another hearing. (Act March 20, 1810, section 4; 5 Sm., 163.)

§ 1388. *When judgment may be opened.* A judgment may be opened at the instance of the appellant. The justice must notify the adverse party to appear before him on some day certain within twenty days from the rendition of the judgment; and if such adverse party appear and consent thereto, it shall be in the power of the justice to open the judgment and give them another hearing. Act of March 20, 1810, section 4; or where a defendant, within thirty days, on proof made, shows that he was absent when the process was served, and did not return before the return-day of such process, or that he was prevented by sickness or other unavoidable cause. *Nippes* v. *Kirk*, 8 Phila., 299 (1871); *Long* v. *Caffrey, Id.*, 548 (1871); *Stockdale* v. *Campbell*, 1 Phila., 520 (1860).

Where a judgment is opened before a justice and new judgment for a larger amount is entered, without notice to defendant, the proceedings are void. *Carlin* v. *Holland*, 1 Dist. Rep., 174 (1892).

Any defendant against whom a judgment shall have been rendered where the attachment or summons shall not have been personally served, may, within thirty days after judgment, apply to the justice for a hearing of the matter, and such defendant, or some one in his behalf, shall make affidavit setting forth that he has a just defense to the whole or part of the plaintiff's demand; it shall be the duty of the justice to open judgment and give notice to the plaintiff of the time when he will hear the parties within four to eight days. (Act July 12, 1842, section 31; P. L., 345.)

§ 1389. *When it is duty of justice to open judgment.* The Act of July 12, 1842, section 31, makes it the duty of an alderman who has entered judgment by default to open the judgment and rehear the case upon affidavit of defense, in part or in whole, made by defendant or some person for him. This Act has exclusive reference to attachments and summonses issued under the several provisions of the Act, and does not apply to suits instituted under the Act of 1810. *Whitehead* v. *Gillespy*, 1 Phila., 515 (1854).

§ 1390. *A judgment confessed should not be opened on mere allegation of mistake.* In *Green* v. *Leymer*, 3 Watts, 381 (1834), judgment was confessed before a justice for a sum exceeding $100. Subsequently the defendant represented to the justice that there had been a mistake, and upon notice being given to the other side, and no appearance, the justice opened the judgment and reduced its amount.

This practice was condemned by the Supreme Court as not within the province of the justice.

§ 1391. *If defendant do not appeal, the Common Pleas cannot open the judgment entered on the transcript.* In *Lacock* v. *White*, 19 Pa. St., 495 (1852), an action was brought before a justice and judgment given in favor of plaintiff. No appeal was taken. In due course the transcript was filed in the Common Pleas. Upon affidavit and on application the judgment was opened by the Common Pleas, and defendant let into a defense. BLACK, C. J.: "This was originally a *judgment before a justice* from which there never was an appeal. * * * The plaintiff entered and filed a transcript * * * as a lien on defendant's lands. The point was made whether the Common Pleas had jurisdiction. * * * The sum of our opinion is, that the re-trial of a case like this is anomalous and illegal. The whole matter being conclusively settled by another tribunal, the court had no authority to hear it again."

§ 1392. *Satisfaction to be entered under penalty.*

Any person who shall not in thirty days after written notice of the payment of any judgment with costs in his favor, either by himself or his agents, enter satisfaction on the docket, shall be subject to a penalty of one-fourth the amount of the debt paid for the use of the party aggrieved, except where one of the defendants shall, by writing filed within fifteen days after payment, forbid the plaintiff to do so. (Act March 20, 1810, section 15; 5 Sm., 169.)

This penalty shall be sued and recovered before any justice as debts of similar amount are sued for and recovered. (Act April 4, 1831, section 1; P. L., 458.)

In *Cunningham* v. *McCue*, 31 Pa. St., 470 (1858), an action of debt was brought to recover a penalty for neglecting to enter satisfaction on a judgment.

The question arose as to service of notice to enter satisfaction which had been served on defendant by leaving a copy with his wife, at his residence.

This was held to be a good service.

§ 1393. **Summary Convictions.** *Records* of summary convictions are scrutinized by the courts, as this mode of proceeding is in derogation of the common law, and operates to the exclusion of trial by jury.

In many cases the manner of proceeding is pointed out in the Act of Assembly or ordinance.

Where proceedings are instituted for the recovery of fines for the violation of an ordinance, they are not technically summary convictions, but in the nature of civil suits, and the record need not set forth the evidence at length.

§ 1394. *Jurisdiction.* Justices have power to hear and determine all actions of debt for penalty, breach of any ordinance, by-law, or regulation of such city, township, or borough in the same manner and subject to the right of appeal as debts under $100, and such actions shall be instituted in the corporate name of such city, borough, or township. Act of April 15, 1835, section 7 (P. L., 292); Act of April 5, 1849, section 7 (P. L., 410).

§ 1395. *Directions as to proceedings.* A learned opinion was delivered by HARDING, P. J., Luzerne County, in *Comm.* v. *Davenger*, 30 Leg. Int., 321 (1873): "Justices of the peace are clothed with summary powers in proceedings to recover forfeitures under penal Acts of Assembly; and also with powers partaking somewhat of a summary character for the recovery of penalties or fines for violations of municipal ordinances. * * *

"Where a statute creating an offense provides that the person so offending, on conviction thereof before a justice * * * shall pay a fine, to be recovered as debts of like amount are by law recoverable by any person who may sue for the same, the proceeding should be by summons in debt, in the name of the Commonwealth for the use of the party suing, followed by a judgment for the penalty, if the evidence establishes the guilt of the accused.

"But where a statute imposes a penalty, and gives authority to justices of the peace to take cognizance of its violation, without prescribing a method or form for the prosecution, the proceeding may be instituted either by summons in debt, in the name of the Commonwealth, for such uses as the particular statute may direct, for the penalty, or by a warrant of arrest, at the discretion of the justice.

"This doctrine does not apply where the statute creating an offense provides at the same time a specific mode of prosecution; and where the alleged offender is a citizen or well-known inhabitant, the use of a summons is all that would be necessary ; but where he is an irresponsible or transient person, resort may properly be had to a warrant of arrest.

"Actions of this character must be founded on an information containing the day of the taking of it, the place where it was taken, the name of the informer, the name and official designation of the magistrate before whom it is taken, the name of the offender, together with an exact description of the offense, and also the time of its alleged commission—not the exact day, perhaps, but a point of time should be indicated so that the prosecution shall appear to have been instituted within the limitation of the particular statute.

"Strictly speaking, such proceedings are criminal prosecutions, being nothing less than methods of punishment for a public crime or offense. They are summary convictions. Again, proceedings for the recovery of fines for the violation of borough or city ordinances are not summary proceedings. On the contrary, 'they are of a civil nature, and must be regulated and decided by rules applicable to civil suits ; though being penal in their character, some of the principles relative to summary proceedings are applicable to them.' They should not be instituted, in the name of the Commonwealth, but where the whole penalty goes to the city or borough, the corporate name of such city or borough should be used as plaintiff. If, however, the whole penalty be given to any person who may sue for it, then the corporate name of the city or borough, as the case may be, to the use of the informer, naming him, should appear as plaintiff ; but where the action is *qui tam*, one portion of the penalty going to the informer and the other to the city or borough, the informer should be named as plaintiff, suing for himself as well as for the city or borough. Further, it is vitally essential in these cases that the record of a conviction or judgment against a defendant should exhibit jurisdiction of the subject-matter on the part of the magistrate, a specification of the ordinance violated, and the imposition of a penalty conforming exactly to the fine covered by the ordinance. It must also show either that the defendant confessed the charge or that evidence was adduced to support it ; that witnesses were sworn or affirmed ; that the commission of the offense was within the city or borough enacting the ordinance ; and that judgment was duly entered."

A suit to recover a fine for violation of a borough ordinance should be brought in the corporate name. *Speakman* v. *Speakman*, 1 Dist. Rep., 119 (1892).

§ 1396.

County of , ss.

The information and complaint of A. B., of (place), made and exhibited before E. F., Esq., justice of the peace of , and the said A. B., being duly sworn according to law, deposes and says (here state the offense specially, following the statute or ordinance and the facts as to time, place, etc.), contrary to the statute (or ordinance) in such case made and provided, whereby C. D. according to said statute forfeits the sum of $.

Whereupon A. B. prays that the said C. D. may be summoned to answer the premises before the said justice.

Sworn to and subscribed before me,
(date).

$\left.\begin{array}{c}\\\\\\\end{array}\right\}$ A. B.

Justice of the Peace
for .

The complaint or information must be definite as to substance, time, and place of offense charged. If the defendant appear and go to trial without objection, the irregularity is waived. *Comm.* v. *Burkhart*, 23 Pa. St., 521 (1854).

§ 1397. *How proceedings commenced.* The proceedings may be commenced by summons or *capias.*

Where a person is a freeholder or well-known inhabitant not likely to flee, the better course is to proceed by summons, unless otherwise directed by statute.

The directions as to summons in a civil case are given § 1270 *et seq.*

§ 1398. *In whose name proceeding to be brought.* Where a *certiorari* in summary proceedings was directed to a burgess, the proceedings having been commenced in the name of the Commonwealth, the Supreme Court held that the *certiorari* might be amended. *Reid* v. *Wood*, 102 Pa. St., 312 (1883). If an ordinance prescribe that penalties for the breach of its terms shall be recovered at the suit of the city, an action cannot be maintained by a private person without the city's authorization. *City* v. *Strawbridge*, 4 W. N., 215 (1877). Where an Act of Assembly directs a penalty to be recovered by any person suing for the same, a common informer may sue in his own name. *Megargell* v. *Coal Co.*, 8 W. & S., 342 (1845). See also § 1395.

§ 1399.

County of . ss.

Be it remembered, that on the (date), in said county, A. B. personally appeared before me, a justice in and for , and made complaint and information before me that (here set forth the complaint) contrary to the form of the in such case made and provided, which is as follows (here set forth ordinance or statute).

Whereupon the said C. D. was duly summoned to appear and answer said complaint, and on (date) he appeared before me and declared (here state what C. D. declared), and G. H., of (place), under oath did say (here state the evidence of any witness or witnesses who appeared).

Therefore, it manifestly appearing to me, upon careful examination of the truth of the charges contained in said complaint, that C. D. is guilty of the offense charged against him in said complaint, I, the aforesaid and subscribing justice, do adjudge the said C. D. to forfeit and pay for the same the sum of , with costs of suit to be distributed (here set forth the manner of division) according to law, and in default of such payment, or of goods to satisfy said fine, the said C. D. shall be committed to the county prison, to wit (place) for (time as prescribed by statute, ordinance, etc.).

Given under my hand and official seal (date).

[*Office*] [SEAL]   Magistrate.

§ 1400. *Appeal in summary conviction.*

In all cases of summary conviction in this Commonwealth, or of judgment in suit for a penalty, before a magistrate or court not of record, either party may appeal to such court of record as may be prescribed by law, upon allowance of the appellate court or judge thereof, upon cause shown. (Constitution of 1874, Art. V., section 14.)

In all cases of summary conviction in this Commonwealth before a magistrate or court not of record, either party may, within five days after such conviction, appeal to the Court of Quarter Sessions of the county in which such magistrate shall reside or court not of record shall be held, upon allowance of the said Court of Quarter Sessions or any judge thereof, upon cause shown; and either party may also appeal from the judgment of a magistrate or a court not of record, in a suit for a penalty, to the Court of Common Pleas of the county in which said judgment shall be rendered, upon allowance of said court or any judge thereof, upon cause shown: *Provided*, that all appeals from summary conviction and judgment for penalties shall be upon such terms as to payment of costs and entering bail as the court or judge allowing the appeal shall direct. (Act of April 17, 1876, section 1; P. L., 29.)

The Act of February 5, 1875, section 13; P. L., 56, allowed appeals in cases of summary convictions before magistrates in Philadelphia. Its provisions are supplied by the Act of 1876 (*supra*).

In suits for penalties before a magistrate, an appeal may be had on special allowance upon cause shown, though the amount involved is less than $5.33. *Borough* v. *Lifter*, 4 Dist. Rep., 230 (1895).

§ 1401. *In civil cases.*

FORM OF AFFIDAVIT ON APPEAL.

| Commonwealth of Pennsylvania *ex rel.* E. F. *v.* C. D. | Before , Magistrate of Court No. . Judgment obtained (date) for a penalty of $. |

County of   , *ss.*

C. D., the above-named defendant, being duly sworn according to law, doth depose and say that the appeal taken in the above case is not for the purpose of delay, but that if the proceedings appealed from are not removed, he will be required to pay more money than is justly due.

Sworn to and subscribed before me,
   this   day of   ,18 .
Witness my hand and official seal
   of said court, the day and year   C. D.
   above written.

      Magistrate of Court, No. .
   [SEAL]

§ 1402.

FORM OF BAIL ON APPEAL.

I hold myself indebted to the plaintiff in the sum of fifty dollars, conditioned for all costs that have accrued or may accrue in this case up to the final determination of this suit, and that the defendant will prosecute his appeal with effect.

G. H.,
(Residence.)

§ 1403.

FORM OF TRANSCRIPT.

Transcript from the Docket of L. M., Magistrate of Court No.

Commonwealth of Pennsylvania *ex rel.* E. S. *v.* J. M. Residence, Business,	For a Penalty. Summons issued (date). Returnable between the hours of 3 o'clock P.M. and 3.30 o'clock P.M. W. R., Constable. Returned on oath (date). Served on defendant by leaving the copy of the original summons at the defendant's dwelling-house with an adult member of the family and made known the contents thereof.

And now (date), 3 o'clock P.M., parties appear. Messrs. D. and C. appear for the plaintiff, and F. C. appears for the defendant. Plaintiff claims $100 as a penalty for a violation of sections 1 and 8 of an Act of Assembly approved the   day of   , A. D. 18 , entitled "An Act (here set forth title), which are as follows (here set forth sections). Defendant pleads not guilty, and also that the Act under which this suit is brought is unconstitutional, being contrary to the Constitution of the State of Pennsylvania and the United States. C. W. sworn and examined for the plaintiff (here set forth the evidence at length). After hearing the parties, their proofs and allegations, judgment publicly rendered for plaintiff for a penalty of $100 and costs (date). Defendant files his affidavit and appeals.

City of Philadelphia, *ss.*

I hereby certify the above to be a correct transcript from my docket.

Witness my hand and official seal of said court, the   day of   , 18 .
[SEAL]   Magistrate of Court No. .

To this transcript add the affidavit and bail entered for appeal.

The appellant then obtains this from the justice and indorses the transcript :

No. . Term, 1890.

A. B. ⎫
   v.   ⎬   C. P.   , No.   -
C. D. ⎭

Transcript and Appeal from Magistrate.

And now (date), on motion of F. C., attorney *pro* defendant, and on cause being shown, the court allow an appeal in the case on the costs already paid and on the bond already given.

                       (Initials of Judge.)

Take this to a judge and have approved, then file with the prothonotary. In summary convictions for a fine, an appeal can only be taken upon allowance by the court upon cause shown. *Board* v. *Decker*, 3 Dist. Rep., 362 (1893); *Board* v. *Dairy Co.*, 3 Dist. Rep., 363 (1893); *Comm.* **v.** *Eichenberg*, 140 Pa. St., 158 (1891).

An appeal from the judgment of a magistrate for a penalty may be allowed *nunc pro tunc* in the discretion of the court. *Comm.* v. *Riser*, 147 Pa. St., 342 (1892).

For further instructions see § 1481 *et seq.*

§ 1404. *Requisites of record or transcript.* The record should set forth :

   a. The jurisdiction.

   b. Information or charge against the defendant.

   c. A summons or notice of the information, in order that defendant may appear and make his defense, or an arrest.

   d. The appearance or non-appearance of defendant.

   e. The section of the Act or ordinance violated, quoting its language or the substance thereof, showing that the offense is within such Act or ordinance, and unlawful.

   f. The confession or defense of defendant.

   g. The evidence, which in civil cases need not be set forth *in extenso.* When the proceeding is according to the common law, the substance of the evidence only need be stated, and that the witnesses were sworn or affirmed.

   h. That the offense was committed within the city enacting the ordinance, if such be the case.

   i. The judgment or conviction, and that the fine conforms to the ordinance or Act.

Everything requisite to support the conviction must appear on the record. (See Form of Record, section 1399.)

In a suit for a penalty under an ordinance which forbids a railroad company from running trains across streets without erecting gates and providing watchman, the record must show across what streets the trains ran, without complying with the ordinance. *Borough* v. *Canal Co.*, 1 Dist. Rep., 701 (1892).

In a suit for a penalty, under an ordinance, the record must set forth the ordinance, and the penalty imposed. *Comm.* v. *Hill*, 3 Dist. Rep., 216 (1893) ; *Pittsburg* v. *Madden*, 3 Dist. Rep., 771 (1893).

§ 1405. *Certiorari.* The party convicted has the right to remove the record in a summary conviction into the proper court.

The conviction is either affirmed or quashed in the superior court.

The notes of testimony are not a part of the record on *certiorari.* *Comm.* v. *Gipner*, 118 Pa. St., 379 (1888).

In a suit for a penalty, the particular offense with which defendant is charged and the cause of action must be distinctly set forth. In such case it is not necessary that the evidence should be returned as a part of the record on *certiorari.* *Hess* v. *Monier*, 1 Dist. Rep., 606 (1892).

If defendant convicted before a magistrate and sentenced, voluntarily pays fine and costs, the Common Pleas on *certiorari* cannot, on reversing, order restitution. *Comm.* v. *Gipner*, 118 Pa. St., 379 (1888).

See *Certiorari*, § 1407 *et seq.*

§ 1406. *No appeal to the Supreme Court.* No writ of error lies to the judgment of the Common Pleas on a *certiorari* to a justice of the peace in a suit by a borough to recover a penalty for breach of an ordinance. *Borough* v. *Wadlinger*, 48 Leg. Int., 384 (1891).

The judgment of the Common Pleas reversing the proceedings before a justice, on a *certiorari* in an action to recover a penalty, cannot be reviewed by the Supreme Court. *City* v. *Wadlinger*, 142 Pa. St., 308 (1891) ; *Foster* v. *Erie, Id.*, 407 (1891) ; see *Comm.* v. *Burkhart*, 23 Pa. St., 521 (1854).

All appellate proceedings in the Supreme Court are now taken by an appeal. (See Chapter XLVI.)

§ 1407. Certiorari. *Affidavit required before* certiorari *issues—Writ and service.*

No judge of any court within this Commonwealth shall allow any writ of *certiorari* to remove the proceedings had in any trial before a justice of the peace until the party applying for such writ shall declare, on oath or affirmation before such judge, that it is not for the purpose of delay, but that in the opinion of the party applying for the same the cause of action was not cognizable before a justice, or that the proceedings proposed to be removed are, to the best of his knowledge, unjust and illegal, and if not removed will oblige the said applicant to pay more money, or to receive less from his opponent than is justly due ; a copy of which affidavit shall be filed in the prothonotary's office : *Provided*, that no judgment shall be set aside in pursuance of a writ of *certiorari* unless the same is issued within twenty days after judgment was rendered, and served within five days thereafter.; and no execution shall be set aside in pursuance of the writ aforesaid unless the said writ is issued and served within twenty days after the execution issued. (Act of March 20, 1810, section 21 ; 5 Sm., 172.)

§ 1408.

OATH OR AFFIRMATION TO BE ADMINISTERED BY PROTHONOTARY.

The prothonotaries of the several Courts of Common Pleas are hereby respectively authorized and empowered to administer the oath or affirmation required by the twenty-first section of the Act to which this is a supplement, to be taken on the issuing of any writ of *certiorari*. Which oath or affirmation so administered shall have the same force and effect as if administered by a judge of any of the said courts. (Act February 3, 1817, section 1 ; 6 Sm., 398.) ·

§ 1409. *Bail upon issuing writ.* In *Clark* v. *McCormack*, 2 Phila., 68 (1857), the question arose as to the taking of bail upon issuing writs of *certiorari*.

ALLISON, J.: "It certainly has the authority of a long and uniform practice to support it. * * * The Act of March 21, 1810, is silent upon the subject of bail ; the only prerequisites to the allowance of the writ is an oath or affirmation that it is not for the purpose of delay, etc. * * * · If the writ of *certiorari* is in substance a writ of error, * * * we think it follows, by necessary implication, that the legislature in granting the writ confers, at the same time, all the powers necessary to make the writ effective as a writ of error, and that as the issuing of the *certiorari* is a ministerial act to be performed by the prothonotary or clerk of the court, he has the authority * * * to take the recognizance which *must be entered* to make the writ of value to the purchaser. The right to take bail in such cases might, perhaps, be fairly inferred from the second section of the Act of the 27th of March, 1853, * * * which says, ' whenever an appeal is entered in the Supreme Court, or a *certiorari* is sued out to remove the proceedings of a justice * * * to the Court of Common Pleas, the party, his agent or attorney, may take and enter into the required affidavit and recognizance."

The Act of May 22, 1895 (P. L., 100), provides that on taking a *certiorari* from the judgment of a justice of the peace, the affidavit may be filed and recognizance entered into before the justice *or* prothonotary.

§ 1410. *Bail on* certiorari *in landlord and tenant proceedings.* Under the Act of 1865, a landlord and tenant proceeding under the Act of December 14, 1863, is subject to removal by *certiorari*, but a recognizance for debt, interest, and costs is defective—it should be for rent then due, as well as rent to become due between the issuing of the *certiorari* and the final decision of the court. *Hutchinson* v. *Vanscriver*, 6 Phila., 39 (1865).

A similar ruling was made in *Clapp* v. *Senneff*, 7 Phila., 214 (1869).

§ 1411. *Justice shall prepare transcript—Judgment not to be reversed for want of formality.*

In all cases either party shall have the privilege of removing the cause by writ of *certiorari* from before any justice, whose duty it shall be to certify the whole proceeding had before him by sending the original precepts, a copy of the judgment, and execution or executions, if any be issued: *Provided,* always, that the proceedings of a justice of the peace shall not be set aside or reversed on *certiorari* for want of formality in the same, if it shall appear on the face thereof that the defendant confessed a judgment for any sum within the jurisdiction of a justice, or that a precept issued in the name of the Commonwealth of Pennsylvania, requiring the defendant to appear before the justice on some day certain, or directing the constable to bring the defendant or defendants forthwith before him, * * * and that the said constable having served the said precept, judgment was rendered on the day fixed in the precept or on some other day, to which the cause was postponed by the justice with the knowledge of the parties.

And no execution issued by a justice shall be set aside for informality, if it shall appear on the face of the same that it issued in the name of the Commonwealth of Pennsylvania, after the expiration of the proper period of time, and for the sum for which judgment had been rendered, together with interest thereon, and costs, and a day mentioned on which return is to be made by the constable, and that the cause of action shall have been cognizable before a justice of the peace; and the judgment of the Court of Common Pleas shall be final on all proceedings removed as aforesaid by the said court, and no writ of error shall issue thereon. (Act of March 20, 1810, section 22; 5 Sm., 172.)

§ 1412. *No* allocatur *required.*

No special allowance of a writ of *certiorari* to a justice of the peace shall be held requisite to the maintenance of such writ. (Act April 26, 1855, section 2; P. L., 304.)

In *McGinnis* v. *Vernon*, 67 Pa. St., 152 (1870), THOMPSON, C. J., said: "There is no constitutional requirement that judges of the Common Pleas must allow writs of *certiorari* to justices of the peace. Section 8 of Article V. of the Constitution gives them the power to do so, but the Act of 26 April, 1855, dispenses with the necessity for doing it, and this Act, operating as a remedy merely, is beyond doubt constitutional."

§ 1413. *When judgment will be reversed.* Where there is a defect in the record as, *e. g.*, that judgment was rendered by default before a justice without process being properly served, then the judgment will be reversed on *certiorari*. *Fraily* v. *Sparks*, 2 Pars., 232 (1848).

If judgment has been recovered before a justice and transferred to the docket of a justice of another county, *certiorari* is the proper proceeding to set aside the proceedings of the latter if the record of the original judgment exhibits a want of jurisdiction. It is never too late to attack a judgment void for want of jurisdiction. *Adams* v. *Hill*, 29 Leg. Int., 126 (1872).

Where the record of a justice does not show the appearance of plaintiff or his agent, or that any evidence was offered in support of his demand, a judgment for plaintiff will be reversed. This does not apply to judgments by default. *Young* v. *Abbey*, 1 Dist. Rep., 43 (1891).

The judgment of a justice will not be reversed on *ceritorari* where no evidence is shown on the record in support of plaintiff's claim, if it appears that letters of the defendant, duly proved, were offered and admitted in evidence. *Rupp* v. *Labows*, 2 Dist. Rep., 340 (1893).

§ 1414. *Certiorari a supersedeas in landlord and tenant proceedings.*

In every proceeding or suit brought in the city of Philadelphia * * * by landlords to recover possession of property leased for a term of years, or from year to year, in which a *certiorari* is now allowed, the said *certiorari* shall be a *supersedeas* and the execution upon the judgment * * * shall be suspended until the final determination of the *certiorari* by the court out of which the same issues ; and the said court, if the said determination shall be made adversely to the party at whose instance the writ of *certiorari* has issued, shall proceed to issue a writ of possession directed to the sheriff of Philadelphia County, directing him to deliver actual possession of the premises to the lessor, and also to levy the costs on the defendant in the same manner that costs are now by law levied and collected on other writs of execution : *Provided*, that the said *certiorari* shall be issued within ten days from the date of the judgment rendered in said proceedings, and upon oath of the party applying for the same, to be administered by the prothonotary of the Court of Common Pleas, that it is not for the purpose of delay, but that the proceedings proposed to be removed are, to the best of his knowledge and belief, unjust and illegal, and will oblige him to pay more money than is justly due, a copy of which affidavit shall be filed in the prothonotary's office : *And provided further*, that the party applying for the same shall give security for payment of all costs that have accrued or may accrue, and of the rent which has already or may become due up to the time of the final determination of said *certiorari*, in event of the same being determined against him. (Act of March 24, 1865, section 1 ; P. L., 750.)

§ 1415. *Certiorari cannot be issued out of Supreme Court.*

No writ of *certiorari* issued by or out of the Supreme Court, to any justice in any civil suit or action, shall be available to remove the proceedings had before such justice. (Act March 20, 1810, section 24 ; 5 Sm., 172.)

A *certiorari* will not lie from the Supreme Court to a justice to remove proceedings relating to stray cattle, under the Act of April 13, 1807. *Frick* v. *Patton*, 2 Rawle, 20 (1829).

§ 1416. *Except in proceedings under a sheriff's sale to recover possession.* The Supreme Court has jurisdiction, both before and since the Constitution of 1874, to issue writs of *certiorari* to justices in proceedings by the purchaser at a sheriff's sale to recover possession of property purchased. *Bauer* v. *Angeny*, 100 Pa. St., 429 (1882).

§ 1417. *Certiorari will not issue to review a case settled.* If a defendant voluntarily pay the fine and costs imposed upon him by a justice, the case is at an end, and the Common Pleas cannot review the judgment on a *certiorari* subsequently issued. *Comm.* v. *Gipner*, 20 W. N., 500 (1887).

§ 1418. *When writ will issue.though twenty days have expired.* As a rule, a writ of *certiorari* must be moved within twenty days after judgment rendered, and served within five days thereafter; but if the record fail to exhibit on its face that the justice acted within the scope of his authority, his whole proceedings will be held to be *coram non judice.* Where the jurisdiction does not appear from the record itself, or where the record shows the entry of a judgment by default preceded by a failure of service of summons, or a service not in substantial conformity with the Act, the court will review and reverse the proceedings of the justice, though more than twenty days had elapsed before the *certiorari* was taken. *Paine* v. *Godshall*, 29 Leg. Int., 12 (1872) (C. P. of Luzerne County).

In *Stedman* v. *Bradford*, 3 Phila., 258 (1858), Judge ALLISON said : "Where judgment is given against a defendant without service of a summons, and without notice to him of any kind, a *certiorari* will be allowed if applied for within a reasonable time, which we have held to be, as a general rule, within twenty days after he first had knowledge of a judgment being entered against him, thus making our practice conform to the twenty days allowed by law for an appeal or *certiorari.*

In *Kelly* v. *March*, 15 W. N., 30 (1884), the record showed no appearance by the defendant, and the summons was not served in accordance with the Act of Assembly. On a *sci. fa.* to revive the judgment, a *certiorari* issued from the Common Pleas, and although ten years had elapsed, as the record failed to show jurisdiction, the judgment was reversed.

On *certiorari*, if the summons was improperly served, the judgment will be reversed. *Mfg. Co.* v. *Lewis*, 2 Dist. Rep., 34 (1892).

§ 1419. *Certiorari in cases of penalty may issue after twenty days.* If a proceeding be brought to recover a penalty imposed by ordinance, the *certiorari* need not be issued within twenty days, as in civil actions. *Caughey* v. *Mayor*, 12 S. & R., 53 (1824) ; *Pittsburg* v. *Madden*, 3 Dist. Rep., 771 (1893).

§ 1420. *Entering appeal bars subsequent issue of* certiorari, *and* vice versa. In *City* v. *Kendrick*, 1 Brews., 406 (1867), the practice as to bringing both an appeal and *certiorari* was well defined by the court : " If both remedies were allowed and both prosecuted to final judgment, there might be a judgment for plaintiff in the one and for the defendant in the other proceeding.

" A condition of contradictions would thus be presented well calculated to bring the law into reproach.

" To preserve its symmetry and the congruity of its results, we have concluded, where an appeal is not a mere nullity, that the entry thereof shall be ground for quashing a *certiorari* subsequently issued, and that a *certiorari* regularly issued and served shall in like manner bar an appeal."

A similar ruling was made in *Ward* v. *Harligan*, 1 W. N., 72 (1874).

A party cannot take both an appeal and *certiorari* concurrently from the judgment of a justice of the peace. *Wilcox* v. *Borough*, 2 Dist. Rep., 721 (1892).

§ 1421. *Ineffectual appeal will not quash* certiorari. An ineffectual attempt to take an appeal is no bar to taking a *certiorari*. *Comm.* v. *Feigle*, 2 Phila., 215 (1856).

§ 1422. *If defendant take* certiorari, *no notice to plaintiff required.* Where a defendant takes a *certiorari* to the judgment of a magistrate, he need not notify the plaintiff. *Walker* v. *Hopple*, 16 W. N., 495 (1885).

§ 1423. *Common Pleas cannot direct feigned issue on disputed facts.* Where there are disputed facts arising on a *certiorari*, the Common Pleas cannot direct a feigned issue.

The better practice is, that the parties shall agree on an amicable action before the justice, subject to an appeal, or that the matter shall be heard on a *sci. fa.*, or that it shall be determined as to the facts on affidavits. *Pool* v. *Morgan*, 10 W., 53 (1840).

§ 1424. *Parol evidence in the Common Pleas on* certiorari. On *certiorari* from the Common Pleas, the court can inquire into matters not appearing on the record, but on writ of error no parol evidence can be received. *Buckmeyer* v. *Dubs*, 5 Binn., 29 (1812).

Parol evidence is admissible in the Common Pleas to establish want of jurisdiction, partiality, corruption, extortion, refusal to hear testimony, or the fact that judgment was given on the oath of the party alone.

These exceptions to the rule, that on *certiorari* nothing but the record is brought up, relate to the conduct of the magistrate ; none extend so far as to admit evidence of the conduct of the party. *Road Commissioners* v. *Fickniger*, 51 Pa. St., 51 (1865) ; *Fisher* v. *Nyce*, 60 Pa. St., 109 (1869) ; *McMullin* v. *Orr*, 8 Phila., 342 (1871).

On a *certiorari* to the judgment of a justice, parol evidence is inadmissible to establish coverture of defendant where the record of the justice is silent. *Myers* v. *Stauffer*, 22 W. N., 412 (1888) (C. P. of Beaver County). *Contra*, *Graham* v. *James*, 13 W. N., 279 (1883) (C. P. of Schuylkill County).

On a *certiorari* to determine whether a justice has exceeded his jurisdiction, the aid of affidavits may be invoked. *Burginhofen* v. *Martin*, 3 Yeates, 479 (1803).

Where matters are not shown by the record, the court will receive depositions as to them. *Jones* v. *Pettit*, 4 W. N., 14 (1877).

§ 1425. *On writ of error, depositions not a part of the record.* Where a landlord and tenant proceeding is brought by *certiorari* into the Common Pleas and a writ of error is taken to the judgment, the Supreme Court cannot notice matters not appearing on the record, although proved by depositions in the Common Pleas to have occurred before the justice. *McMillan* v. *Graham*, 4 Pa. St., 140 (1846) ; *Bedford* v. *Kelly*, 61 Pa. St., 491 (1869) ; *Wistar* v. *Ollis*, 77 Pa. St., 291 (1875).

§ 1426. *Decision of the Common Pleas final.* The judgment of the Common Pleas on *certiorari* in a suit under the $100 law of March 20, 1810, is final ; the Supreme Court cannot review the decision. *Borland* v. *Ealy*, 43 Pa. St., 111 (1862) ; *Castor* v. *Cloud*, 2 W. N., 252 (1875) ; *Jacobs* v. *Ellis*, 156 Pa. St., 253 (1893). This includes proceedings in trespass. *Cozens* v. *Dewees*, 2 S. & R., 112 (1815). If the proceedings of a justice under the Act of July 7, 1879, have been reviewed on *certiorari* in the Common Pleas, no writ of error lies therefrom.

The Act of 1879 simply enlarges the jurisdiction of a justice. *Penna. Co.* v. *Stoughton*, 106 Pa. St., 458 (1884) ; *Palmer* v. *Lacock*, 107 Pa. St., 346 (1884). See also § 1406.

§ 1427. *Decision of a mayor's court final.* A *certiorari* does not lie to the Supreme Court from the judgment of a mayor of Philadelphia who has jurisdiction conferred upon him by ordinance coextensive with the powers of a justice. *Spicer* v. *Rees*, 5 Rawle, 119 (1835).

§ 1428. *Writ of error in certain cases.* Cases which do not come within the provisions of the $100 law, but are brought into the Common Pleas on *certiorari* according to the common law, may be reviewed on writ of error. *Comm.* v. *Burkhart*, 23 Pa. St., 522 (1854).

Proceedings under the Landlord and Tenant Act reviewed on *certiorari* in the Common Pleas may be further reviewed on writ of error. *Clark* v. *Yeat*, 4 Binn., 185 (1811).

Where proceedings are brought under the Act of April 6, 1802, to obtain possession of land purchased at a sheriff's sale, and the suit is taken by *certiorari* to the Common Pleas, the proper remedy for the correction of errors is by writ of error ; a *certiorari* to the Supreme Court may be quashed. *Cooke* v. *Reinhart*, 1 Rawle, 321 (1829).

The Act of 1810, which makes the decision of the Common Pleas final on a *certiorari*, does not apply to cases which arise under a special statute giving justices extraordinary jurisdiction. *Zimmerly* v. *Road Commissioners*, 25 Pa. St., 134 (1855).

A *certiorari* will lie from the Supreme Court to remove a proceeding under the Road Laws brought into the Common Pleas on *certiorari* to a justice. *Comm.* v. *Betts*, 76 Pa. St., 465 (1874).

§ 1429. *When record is to be remitted and when not remitted to the justice.* When a case is removed to the Common Pleas on *certiorari*, and the plaintiff suffers a non-suit, the record must be remitted to the justice before defendant can have execution. *Welker* v. *Welker*, 3 P. & W., 21 (1831).

If the judgment is affirmed in a landlord and tenant proceeding, *a writ of habere facias possessionem* may issue from the Common Pleas. *Essler* v. *Johnson*, 25 Pa. St., 350 (1885).

If the judgment be reversed, the record should not be remitted. *Elton* v. *Stokes*, 39 Leg. Int., 159 (1882).

§ 1430. *Costs.*

In all cases where the proceedings of a justice of the peace shall be removed by *certiorari* at the instance of the plaintiff, and the same be set aside by the court, and on the second trial being had before the same, or any other justice, if judgment shall not be obtained for a sum equal to or greater than the original judgment which was set aside by the court, he shall pay all costs accrued on the second trial before the justice of the peace, as well as those which accrued at the court before whom the proceedings have been set aside, including any fees which the defendant may have given any attorney, not exceeding four dollars, in such trial, together with fifty cents per day to the said defendant while attending on the said court in defense of the proceedings of the said justice. Where the proceedings of any justice shall be removed at the instance of the defendant, and be set aside by the court, and it shall appear that he attended the trial before the justice, or had legal notice to attend the same, and on a final trial being had as aforesaid, the plaintiff shall obtain judgment for a sum equal to or greater than the original judgment which was set aside by the court, he shall pay all costs accrued on the second trial before the justice, as well as those which accrued at the court before whom the proceedings have been set aside, including any fees which the plaintiff may have given to any attorney, not exceeding four dollars, to defend the proceedings of the justice, together with fifty cents per day while attending at court on the same, which costs shall be recovered before any justice of the peace in the same manner as sums of similar amount are recoverable ; and in such cases the legal stay of execution shall be counted from the date of the original judgment rendered by the justice. And the court shall, at the term to which the proceedings of the justices are returnable,in pursuance of writs of *certiorari* determine and decide thereon. (Act of March 20, 1810, section 25 ; 5 Sm., 172.)

The right to costs on a proceeding by *certiorari* depends on the relative amount recovered or abated by the subsequent judgment. *Atkinson* v. *Crossland*, 4 Watts, 451 (1835).

The judgment of the Common Pleas on *certiorari* is final as to costs. *Silvergood* v. *Storrick*, 1 Watts, 532 (1833).

Where the Common Pleas reverses the judgment of a justice of the peace on *certiorari*, no judgment for costs can be entered. *Alexander* v. *Figley*, 2 Dist. Rep., 167 (1892) ; *Metz* v. *Ebersole*, 3 Dist. Rep., 672 (1894).

§ 1431. *Præcipe and affidavit for certiorari to a magistrate or justice.*

A. B.
  v.   } Common Pleas,   Term, 1890. No. .
C. D. }

Sir :

Issue writ of *certiorari* in the above case to   , Esq., Magistrate of Court No.   , or (justice of the peace, as the case may be).

Returnable *sec. leg.*

To   , Prothonotary of Common Pleas.   Attorney for Defendant.
                                                                        (Date.)

City and County of Philadelphia, *ss.*

      , the defendant in the above case and applicant for the above writ of *certiorari*, having been duly sworn according to law, deposes and says that said writ is not for the purpose of delay, but that in the defendant's opinion the cause of action was not cognizable before a magistrate (or that the proceedings proposed to be removed are, to the best of his knowledge, unjust and illegal, and if not removed, will oblige the said applicant to pay more money than is justly due).

Sworn to and subscribed before }   (Signature.)
  me, this   day of   , 1890. }

§ 1432.

FORM OF CERTIORARI TO A MAGISTRATE OR JUSTICE.

City and County of Philadelphia, *ss.*

The Commonwealth of Pennsylvania to   , Magistrate of Court No.   (or justice of the peace), greeting :

We being willing, for certain causes, to be certified of a certain plea, etc., between   plaintiff , and   defendant , before you depending, do command you, that the plea aforesaid, with all things touching the same, before our judges of our Court of Common Pleas, No.   ', at Philadelphia, there to be held the   Monday of   next, so full and entire as before you they now remain, you certify and send, together with this writ: that we may further cause to be done thereupon that which of right and according to the laws and Constitution of this Commonwealth ought.

Witness the Honorable   , President of our said court, at Philadelphia, the   day of   , in the year of our Lord one thousand eight hundred and eighty-   .

Prothonotary.

§ 1433. *Return to certiorari.*

To the Honorable the Judges within named :

The plea within mentioned, with all things touching the same so full and entire as before me they remain, I hereby respectfully certify and send, as within I am commanded, together with this writ.

Magistrate of Court No.   (or Justice).

§1434. *Exceptions.* The following rules are in force in Philadelphia :

In all cases of *certiorari*, the particular exceptions intended to be insisted on must be filed two days before the first argument-day, and in default thereof, the judgment below shall be affirmed of course ; the assignment of general errors is insufficient and void. (Rule XIV., section 41.)

It shall be the duty of the party suing out a writ of *certiorari* to cause the record to be returned two days before the first argument-day, in default of which the *certiorari* shall be dismissed. Rules on magistrates to return writs of *certiorari*, directed to them in due season, will be granted, if applied for, on the regular motion-days. (*Ibid.*, section 42.)

§ 1435. *Directions as to steps to be pursued after obtaining* certiorari. Take the writ to the magistrate, serve it upon him, and ask when you can call for the record. Pay his fees. If he says he will send it to the prothonotary, watch the docket, and if the record be not returned in due season, prepare at once an affidavit of the service of the writ and of the default in not returning it. On this secure and serve notice of a rule on the magistrate to return the writ. When record returned, file exceptions and prepare paperbook of   *sur* exceptions. Let it contain :

(1) Copy of transcript.

(2) Your exceptions.

(3) Your points and authorities.

§ 1436. *If material part of record not returned.* File affidavit of service of writ on magistrate, add that a certain material part of the record, viz.,   , has not been returned, move for a rule on the magistrate to show cause why he should not return as part of the record   . Serve notice of this.

§ 1437. *Service of rules.* Notice of these rules should be served personally and a copy kept, so that if necessary obedience may be enforced by filing affidavit of personal service.

§ 1438. Execution. *Stay of execution.*

Where the defendant is a freeholder or enters bail, and the judgment rendered shall be above five dollars and thirty-three cents and not exceeding twenty dollars, there shall be a stay of execution for three months ; and where the judgment shall be above twenty dollars and not exceeding sixty dollars, there shall be a stay of six months ; and where the judgment shall be above sixty dollars and not exceeding one hundred, there shall be a stay of execution for nine months. (Act March 20, 1810, section 9 ; 5 Sm., 166.)

This was amended by the Act June 24, 1885 (P. L., 159), which provided that if the defendant be a freeholder or enters bail absolute with one or more sufficient sureties, and the judgment be above sixty dollars and not exceeding $300, there shall be a stay of execution for nine months.

These Acts do not apply to judgments obtained for wages for manual labor.

§ 1439. *Stay of execution—Bail absolute.*

Bail in all cases where bail is now required for stay of execution shall be bail absolute, with one or more sufficient sureties in double the amount of the debt or damages, interest, and costs recovered, conditioned for the payment thereof in event of the defendant's failure to pay the same at the expiration of the stay of execution. (Act March 20, 1845, section 1 ; P. L., 188.)

§ 1440. *Bail paying—Judgment to be marked to his use.*

Where a judgment * * * shall be paid by a person who has entered bail for stay of execution or otherwise, such judgment shall remain for the use of such person, and may be prosecuted in the name of plaintiff for the recovery of the amount. (Act of April 23, 1829, section 1 ; 10 Sm., 466.)

§ 1441. *Proceeding against special bail without stay of execution.*

In cases of commitment, where special bail is entered, where no appeal shall be made from the justice and the special bail do not surrender the body of the defendant * * * on or before the return-day of the *scire facias* issued by the justice against such bail, and cannot show sufficient cause why he should be exonerated, the justice shall enter judgment and issue execution without stay against him for the same. (Act March 20, 1810, section 5 ; 5 Sm., 162.)

§ 1442.

FORM OF SUGGESTION AND PLEA OF FREEHOLD.

A. B. ⎫
   v.   ⎬   Before E. F., Magistrate of Court No.   .
C. D. ⎭

(Date.) Judgment against defendant for (here briefly state suit), for $.
And now (date), C. D., the defendant, gives the magistrate notice that he is

possessed of an estate of fee-simple within said county, situate (here briefly describe as by the Street and No. of the house), worth more than the amount of above judgment, viz., $, clear of all incumbrances, wherefore he prays that execution of said judgment may stay for   months from (date).

(Signature of C. D.)

City and County of Philadelphia, *ss.*

C. D., being duly sworn according to law, deposes and says that the statements contained in the above suggestion and plea are true.

Sworn to and subscribed before me, }
  this (date).   Magistrate. }

In *Stiles* v. *Powers*, 1 Ash., 407 (1830), it was decided that the best practice was to claim the right of freehold before execution, but that this privilege might be claimed after execution issued, on payment of costs.

§ 1443. *Freehold must be unincumbered.* The defendant against whom two judgments have been recovered the same day cannot suggest freehold for stay of execution, because the lien of either judgment is an incumbrance as against the other, and defendant must show a freehold clear of all incumbrances. *Bank* v. *Crawford*, 2 W. N., 371 (1875).

A similar ruling was made in *Jenks* v. *Grace*, 1 W. N., (1874); *Clippinger* v. *Creps*, 2 Watts, 45 (1833).

§ 1444. *Form of Recognizance for Stay of Execution* used by the magistrates in Philadelphia:

Defendant asks for stay of execution. I hold myself as absolute security in the sum of $, for the payment of the above judgment, with interest and costs of suit.

A. B.,
(Address.)
(Date.)

§ 1445. *Insufficient recognizance.* In *Caldwell* v. *Brindle*, 11 Pa. St., 293 (1849), judgment was obtained before a justice for certain debt and costs. In order to obtain a stay of execution the ·defendant entered into a recognizance :

"July 10, 1843, W. B. enters special bail, etc., for stay of execution, etc., according to law."

No penalty or condition was attached to the terms of the recognizance, nor was the sum set forth ; it was held insufficient to hold the surety.

§ 1446. *Defendant entitled to enter stay of execution until execution issues.* Where an execution has not issued, even though twenty days have expired, a defendant is entitled to enter special bail to obtain stay of execution. *Mann* v. *Alberti*, 2 Binn., 195 (1809).

If security for stay of execution be entered subsequent to security on appeal, the former operates as a discharge of the latter. *Roup* v. *Waldhouer*, 12 S. & R., 24 (1824).

§ 1447. *Where stay of execution is waived—Rehearing.*

In all bonds, bills, or notes, wherein, by a special provision in writing for that purpose, is waived the stay of execution given by this Act, any justice may on application to him made, after such bond, bill, or note becomes due, issue a summons * * * and proceed to hear and determine the same as in other cases ; and on judgment being rendered in favor of the plaintiff, he shall or may issue execution thereon, without stay ; nevertheless, that in case of judgment by default, the defendant may, at any time within twenty days thereafter, be entitled to a rehearing or appeal, * * * although execution may have issued. (Act of March 20, 1810, section 13 ; P. L., 168.)

§ 1448. *Justice shall proceed if appeal not filed.*

Where an appeal is taken * * * and appellant neglects or refuses to file the same in prothonotary's office of the proper county according to law, it shall and may be lawful for the justice * * * to issue execution * * * at the instance and request of the appellee, or proceed by *scire facias* against the bail. (Act April 1, 1823, section 5 ; 8 Sm., 176.)

§ 1449. *Defendant may pay before execution—Justice refusing to pay money received is guilty of misdemeanor.*

Every justice of the peace rendering judgment as aforesaid shall receive the amount of the judgment, if offered by the defendant or his agent, before execution, and pay the same over to the plaintiff or his agent when required. * * * And if the said justice shall neglect or refuse to pay over, on demand, the money so received to the plaintiff or his agent, such neglect or refusal shall be a misdemeanor in office. (Act March 20, 1810, section 11 ; 5 Sm., 167.)

§ 1450. *Execution—Constable's duty—Execution against executors.*

If the amount of the judgment is not paid to the justice as aforesaid, he shall grant execution, if required by the plaintiff or his agent, thereupon, if for a sum not exceeding five dollars and thirty-three cents, forthwith, and for any further sum, after the time limited for the stay of the same. Which execution shall be directed to the constable of the ward, district, or township where the defendant resides, or the next constable most convenient to the defendant, commanding him to levy the debt or demand and costs on the defendant's goods and chattels ; and by virtue thereof shall, within the space of twenty days next following, expose the same to sale, by public vendue, having given due notice of the same by at least three advertisements, put up at the most public places in his township, ward, or district, returning the surplus, if any, to the defendant * * * Or, in case no goods or chattels can be found and the defendant be possessed of lands or tenements, the plaintiff may * * * proceed by a transcript to the prothonotary aforesaid. *Provided,* that executions against executors or administrators shall only be for the assets of the deceased. (*Id.,* section 12.)

The lien of a constable's levy continues only twenty days. *Page* v. *Gardner*, 1 Dist. Rep., 539 (1891).

§ 1451.

FORM OF EXECUTION IN DEBT.

City of Philadelphia, *ss.*

The Commonwealth of Pennsylvania to any constable of said city most convenient to the defendant, greeting:

Whereas, A. B., of said city, on the   day of   , A. D. 1891, obtained judgment before   , magistrate of Court No.   , in and for the said city, against C. D., of said city, for the sum of   dollars and   cents, together with   dollars and   cents, costs, which judgment remains unsatisfied: Therefore, we command you that you levy the said debt and the interest thereon, with the said costs, on the goods and chattels of the said defendant, and indorse hereon, or on a schedule to be hereunto annexed, a list of the same, and within twenty days from the date hereof expose the same to sale, by public vendue, you having given due notice thereof by three or more advertisements, put up at the most public places in said city, and returning the overplus, if any, of the said sale to the said defendant; and of your proceeding herein, together with this execution, make return to our said court within twenty days from the date hereof, to wit, on or before the   day of   , 1891.

Witness my hand and official seal of said court, the   day of Anno Domini 1891.

(Office.)   Magistrate of Court No.   .

§ 1452. *Execution on judgment where defendant not personally served.* No execution issued on a judgment (where defendant is not personally served in a suit commenced by attachment) shall be levied upon other property than such as was seised under the attachment; nor shall the defendant in such case be barred of any set-off which he may have against the plaintiff. Act July 12, 1842, section 32 (P. L., 345).

§ 1453. *Execution on a certified transcript of justice of another county.* A justice of one county may issue execution upon a certified transcript of judgment of a justice of another county. A mis-recital in the body of the execution does not render it void. *Keeler* v. *Neal*, 2 Watts, 424 (1834).

The following statute is the authority for the above decision:

If the party defendant shall not reside in the county where a judgment is had against him before a justice of the peace, the person in possession of the docket in which such judgment may be entered, on application to him made by the plaintiff or his agent, shall make out, certify, and deliver to such applicant a transcript thereof, * * * for the recovery of the amount thereof, with costs, before any justice of the peace in any county where the defendant may reside or can be found, as in cases originally brought before him, and the stay of execution shall be counted from the original entry. (Act of March 20, 1810, section 17; 5 Sm., 169.)

A justice cannot issue execution on the judgment rendered by another justice of the same county, who is then in commission. *Hallowell* v. *Williams*, 4 Pa. St., 339 (1846).

§ 1454. *Capias ad satisfaciendum, when allowed.*

No execution issued on any judgment rendered by an alderman or justice of the peace, upon any demand arising upon contract, express or implied, shall contain a clause authorizing an arrest or imprisonment of the person against whom the same shall issue, unless it shall be proved by the affidavit of the person in whose favor such execution shall issue, or that of some other person, to the satisfaction of the alderman or justice of the peace, either that such judgment was for the recovery of money collected by any public officer, or for official misconduct. (Act of July 12, 1842, section 23 ; P. L., 345.)

§ 1455.

FORM OF EXECUTION AND COMMITMENT.

City of Philadelphia, *ss.*

The Commonwealth of Pennsylvania to any constable of said city most convenient to the defendant, greeting :

Whereas, A. B., of said city   , on the   day of   ,
A. D. 1891, obtained judgment before   , Magistrate of Court No.   ,
for the said city, against C. D., of said city, for the sum of   dollars
and   cents, together with   dollars and   cents, costs, which
judgment remains unsatisfied : Therefore, we command you that you levy the said debt and the interest thereon, with the said costs, on the goods and chattels of the said C. D., and indorse hereon, or on a schedule to be hereto annexed, a list of the same, and within twenty days from the date hereof expose the same to sale, by public vendue, you having given due notice thereof by three or more advertisements, put up at the most public places in said city, and returning the overplus, if any, of the said sale to the said C. D. And for want of sufficient distress, that you take the body of the said debtor into custody, and him convey to the debtor's apartment of the said city, there to be kept by the sheriff or keeper thereof until the debt, interest, and costs aforesaid shall be fully paid. And of your proceedings herein, together with this execution, make return to our said magistrate, within twenty days from the date hereof, to wit, on or before the   day of   , 1891.

Witness our said magistrate at Court No.   , who has hereunto set his hand and the official seal of the said court, the   day of   ,
A. D. 1891.

(Office.)   Magistrate of Court No.   .

§ 1456. *Effect of entering an appeal.* The lien of an execution is destroyed by an appeal to the Common Pleas, and where defendant's goods are sold under a subsequent execution, the first execution creditor cannot come upon the fund for payment. *Cope's Appeal*, 39 Pa. St., 284 (1861). Where an appeal has not been perfected, a magistrate may issue execution at his own risk. *Setterly* v. *Yearsley*, 1 Phila., 517 (1854). A similar ruling was made in

Hevron's Appeal, 29 Pa. St., 240 (1857). Where, after entering bail, an appeal is neglected, a *certiorari* will not avail to set aside an execution subsequently issued. *Jones* v. *Canal Co.,* 10 Phila., 570 (1874).

§ 1457. *Right to recall execution.* A justice has power to recall an execution issued by him, and such order exonerates the constable. *Shuman* v. *Pfoutz,* 1 P. & W., 61 (1829). A similar ruling was made in *Ludwig* v. *Britton,* 3 W. & S., 447 (1842).

In *O'Donnell* v. *Mullin,* 27 Pa. St., 202 (1856), BLACK, J., said : "If a justice of the peace issues execution on a judgment within the time allowed for an appeal, and the appeal is taken afterward, it is the duty of the justice to revoke the execution.

"When the justice notifies the constable that an appeal has been entered and the execution superseded, the constable is bound to return the execution and proceed no further upon it.

"If a constable persists in selling the defendant's property under an execution thus superseded, he is a trespasser as much as if he had no process at all in his hands."

In *Patterson* v. *Pieronnet,* 7 Watts, 337 (1838), an execution was issued immediately upon the judgment of the justice, certain personal property was sold, and the proceeds paid over. It was held that it was then too late to enter bail for stay of execution, although the twenty days had not expired.

If a constable levy upon property under a regular judgment, he must proceed with the execution unless advised by the justice that it is stayed or superseded. *Kramer* v. *Wellendorf,* 20 W. N., 331 (1887).

§ 1458. *Sale must be by levy and advertisement and by public vendue.* A constable's sale without levy or advertisement is illegal. *Ward* v. *Taylor,* 1 Pa. St., 238 (1845).

Personal property sold by a constable in an execution must be by public vendue, and a sale to the plaintiff, no person but the constable being present, is invalid. *Ricketts* v. *Unangst,* 15 Pa. St., 90 (1850).

§ 1459.

FORM OF HANDBILL.
Constable's Sale.

To be sold at public vendue, on , the day of , at o'clock, in the noon, at the house of C. D., (address) Street. To wit: Bedsteads, beds and bedding, bureaus, sofas, lounges, looking-glasses, chairs, tables, queensware, carpets, oil cloths, etc. Together with all and singular the goods and chattels on the premises (place). Seized (under a judgment in an action of debt) as the property of C. D., and to be sold by

(Office.)

Court No. .

Constable,

Ward.

§ 1460. *Constable's return.* The return to an execution must be made by the constable on or before return-day. *Bachman* v. *Fenstermacher,* 112 Pa. St., 331 (1886).

The return of the constable indorsed on the execution should be so worded as to be in form to enter on the docket of the justice. Every return should be signed by him as constable, and dated.

§ 1461. **Exemption.** The Act of April 9, 1849, section 1 (P. L., 533), provides that in any execution upon a judgment obtained upon contract, and distress for rent,

Property to the value of $300, exclusive of all wearing apparel, * * * and all Bibles and school-books * * * shall be exempt from levy and sale on execution, or by distress for rent.

The Act of April 17, 1869, section 1 (P. L., 69), exempts sewing-machines belonging to seamstresses.

The Act of May 13, 1876, section 1 (P. L., 171), exempts pianos, melodeons, and organs, leased or hired. See also § 3160 *et seq.*

The constable shall, if requested by the debtor, summon three disinterested and competent persons, who shall be sworn or affirmed to appraise the property which the debtor shall elect to retain. The constable may administer the oath or affirmation to the appraisers.

Where the defendant before the justice claims the benefit of the exemption law, and it is disallowed, the proper practice is to take an appeal on *certiorari.* *Borland* v. *Spitz,* 153 Pa. St., 590 (1893).

§ 1462.

FORM OF NOTICE CLAIMING BENEFIT OF EXEMPTION LAWS.

A. B. |
  v.   ⊢   Before Magistrate E. F.   Court No.   .
C. D. |

Please take notice that the goods levied upon by you in the above case are exempt from levy and sale, and that I claim the benefit of the exemption law. You are hereby requested to appraise the same and to proceed according to law.

Respectfully,
(Name of Defendant or his Attorney.)
(Date.)

To G. H., Esq., Constable.

§ 1463. *Waiving exemption laws.* . The defendant may waive the benefit of the exemption laws in execution on a judgment for debt. *Case* v. *Dunmore,* 23 Pa. St., 93 (1854); *Bowman* v. *Smiley,* 31 Pa. St., 225 (1858); *Smiley* v. *Bowman,* 3 Grant, 132 (1861).

§ 1464. **Attachment executions.** Justices may issue attachment executions. Act of April 15, 1845, section 1 (P. L., 459).

Any alderman or justice of the peace before whom any judgment remains unsatisfied and an execution has been returned "no goods," may, on the application of the plaintiff and his compliance with the requisitions of the Act to which this is a supplement, issue an attachment in the nature of an execution as therein provided, to levy upon stock, debts, and deposits of money belonging or due to the defendant, in satisfaction of said judgment. (*Id.*, section 2.)

The said writ of attachment may be issued, returnable in not less than four nor more than eight days, and shall be served in the manner pointed out for the service of a summons, upon the debtor, depository, bailee, pawnee, or other persons having property of the defendant in his hands, made liable to attachment. * * * And on or before the return-day of said writ the plaintiff may file with the magistrate interrogatories in writing, addressed to the person summoned as garnishee, in regard to the property and effects of the defendant alleged to be in his hands at the time of the service of said writ, a copy of the same, with a rule to answer, shall be served upon said garnishee personally, to answer under oath or affirmation all such interrogatories as the magistrate shall deem proper and pertinent within eight days after the same shall be served. (*Id.*, section 3.)

§ 1465.

FORM OF ATTACHMENT SUR JUDGMENT.

City of Philadelphia, *ss.*

The Commonwealth of Pennsylvania to any constable of said city most convenient to the defendant, greeting :

We command you that you attach C. D., by all and singular his goods and chattels, rights and credits, in whose hands or possession soever the same may be, so that he be and appear before the subscriber, Magistrate of Court No.   , in and for the said city, on the   day of   , A. D. 1890, at   o'clock in the forenoon, to answer A. B., and also that you make known to E. F. that he be and appear before our said magistrate, on and at the said day and hour to show if anything they, the said defendant and the said garnishee, or either of them, have or has or know, to say why a certain judgment obtained before our said magistrate, on the   day of   , A. D. 1890, against the said C. D., by the said A. B., in the sum of   dollars, besides costs of suit, which judgment remains unsatisfied, shall not be levied of the effects of the said defendant in the hands of the said E. F., and have you then there this writ.

Witness our said magistrate, who has hereunto set his hand and affixed the official seal of said court, the   day of   , A. D. 1890.

(Office.)

[SEAL]   Magistrate of Court No.   .

§ 1466. *Jurisdiction in $300.* The statute extending the jurisdiction of justices to $300 embraces proceedings by attachment execution. *Kuhn* v. *Bank*, 20 W. N., 230 (1887).

§ 1467. *Attachment execution may issue on a certified transcript.* An attachment execution may issue on a judgment entered on a certified transcript from another county. *Bartman* v. *Ensminger*, 14 W. N., 530 (1884).

§ 1468. *Attachment execution cannot issue against wages, etc., nor legacies.* An attachment execution cannot issue against the wages of labor and salaries, even though the defendant agrees to waive such privilege conferred by the Act of April 15, 1845. *Firmstone* v. *Mack*, 49 Pa. St., 392 (1865).

An attachment execution cannot be issued by a justice against a legacy or other interest in the estate of a decedent. *Messinger* v. *Mantz*, 22 W. N., 107 (1888).

§ 1469. *General directions as to proceeding by attachment.* In *Masters* v. *Turner*, 10 Phila., 482 (1872), HARDING, P. J., said: " Jurisdiction by attachment in the nature of an execution was given to * * * justices * * * by the Act of April 15, 1846. How is this jurisdiction to be exercised ? After judgment has been obtained against a defendant, and a return of ' no goods ' had upon an execution issued thereon, debts due to him, deposits of money made by him, stocks, or other personal property belonging to him and not exempt by law from levy and sale, may be attached. His debtor, depositary, bailee, pawnee, or other person having such effects of the defendant in his hands may be summoned as a garnishee ; and after interrogatories have been filed, and a rule had upon him to answer, and a copy, both of the interrogatories and the rule, has been served as the law directs, if the garnishee shall be in default, or if it shall appear by his answers, or be shown by the proofs on hearing, that he owes the defendant a debt, or has in his hands property belonging to the defendant equal to or less in amount or value than the plaintiff's judgment, then judgment should be specially entered that the plaintiff have execution for such sum, naming it, in the hands of the garnishee ; and that, if the garnishee refuse or neglect, on demand made by the constable, to pay the same, then it should be levied of the garnishee's goods and chattels, as in case of a judgment against him for his own proper debt ; and, further, that he be thereupon discharged as against the defendant of the sum so attached and levied.

" If, however, the debt due by the garnishee to the defendant, or the value of the property thus attached be greater than the plaintiff's judgment, in that case the special judgment of the justice should be that the plaintiff have execution of so much thereof, naming the amount, as will satisfy the plaintiff's judgment against the defendant, with interest and costs. The further entry should follow, as in the former instance, relating to a refusal to pay on the part of the garnishee, and also that relating to a discharge, as against the defendant, for the sum so attached and levied.

" With respect to the cost of the attachment proceeding, the plaintiff is not entitled to have execution therefor against the garnishee, except when there has been a recovery against the latter for a sum greater than that admitted by his answers to be due from him to the defendant, or when he has been in default, or contests his indebtedness to the defendant. In either of these events, the costs of the proceeding may be imposed on him, no matter whether the debt due from him to the defendant, or the value of the property belonging to the defendant and in the hands of the garnishee, be greater or less than the amount of the plaintiff's judgment against the defendant. Where the garnishee by his answers admits his indebtedness to the defendant, or that he has property in his hands belonging to the latter, and surrenders it, no liability for the costs of the attachment proceeding ensues as against him. * * * Again, the execution against the garnishee should formally recite the judgment and contain a command to the constable in substantial conformity therewith: The further command should also be inserted that in event of a levy and sale of the goods and chattels of the garnishee agreeably to law, if the proceeds thereof should exceed the amount for which the execution issued, the overplus, less the costs of sale, should be returned to the garnishee. A plaintiff has no right to demand or receive from a constable anything more than the sum to be collected under the command of the writ, even though his judgment against the original defendant be greater than that against the garnishee."

Neither in attachment execution before a justice nor on appeal is the garnishee entitled to have a fee taxed as costs. *Deerwester* v. *Hook*, 1 Dist. Rep., 406 (1892).

§ 1470.

FORM OF INTERROGATORIES TO GARNISHEE AND RULE TO ANSWER.

A. B., plaintiff,
   v.
C. D., defendant,
and E. F., garnishee. } Before G. H., Magistrate of Court No. . Attachment on judgment.

And now, this   day of   , A. D. 1890, on motion of L. M., attorney *pro* plaintiff, rule issued on garnishee, returnable same date as the attachment, to answer the interrogatories filed in the above case. If not answered in eight days, judgment will be rendered, according to the Act of Assembly in such case made and provided.

Witness our said magistrate and the official seal of said court, this day of   , A. D. 1890.

Magistrate of Court No. .

A. B.
   v.
C. D., defendant,
and E. F., garnishee. } Before G. H., Magistrate of Court No. . Attachment on judgment. Interrogatories to be answered by garnishee in writing. [Filed]

First. Do you know the defendant, of whom you are the garnishee in the above writ of attachment?

Second. Have you had commercial or other transactions with the said defendant at the time of the service of the above writ of attachment upon you? If yea, what was the nature of the transactions and state of your accounts with the said defendant at the time of the service of the writ of attachment upon you?

Third. Was there, or was there not, a balance in your hands in favor of said defendant at the time of the service of the said writ of attachment upon you? If yea, state the amount particularly.

Fourth. Had you in your possession any goods, merchandise, moneys, rights, credits, or effects of any nature whatsoever, belonging to the said defendant, at the time of the service of the said writ of attachment upon you? If yea, state the amount of said money and the nature of the rights and credits, and the nature and quantity of said goods, merchandise, and effects.

Fifth. (Here state any additional interrogatories.)

(Here state on whom, when, and how served.)

Sworn to and subscribed before me, this   day of   , A. D. 1890.

Magistrate of Court No.   .

Office,   Street.

If the garnishee in the attachment execution in his answer denies indebtedness to the defendant as principal, but admits dealings with him as agent, judgment will not be entered.   The plaintiff may require, notwithstanding the answers of the garnishee, the issue to be tried before the justice.   *Houpt* v. *Lewis*, 2 Kulp (Luzerne Co.), 337 (1882).

§ 1471. *Return.*   In an attachment execution, *non est inventus* is not a proper return as to the defendant.   *Hains* v. *Viereck*, 2 Phila., 40 (1856).

It is the defendant's money or property which is to be taken by the attachment, and of which he ought to have notice.

§ 1472. *Judgment against garnishee.*

If the garnishee neglect or refuse to answer within eight days (unless for cause shown his time is extended), he shall be adjudged to have in his possession property of the defendant equal in value to plaintiff's demand, and judgment may be rendered by default against said garnishee for the amount of the same with costs.   (Act of April 15, 1845, section 4; P. L., 459.)

If the garnishee admits that there is in his possession or control property of the defendant liable to attachment, then said magistrate may enter judgment specially to be levied out of said effects, or so much as may be necessary to pay the debts and costs.

Provided, that the wages of laborers or the salary of any person in public or private employment shall not be liable to attachment in the hands of the employer.   (*Id.,* section 5.)

§ 1473. *Appeal from judgments upon attachment execution.*

The plaintiff, the defendant, or the garnishee in the attachment may appeal from the judgment of the alderman or justice of the peace to the next term of the Court of Common Pleas, on complying with the provisions of the laws regulating appeals in other cases.   (*Ibid.,* section 6.)

Where the defendant, subsequent to judgment, assigns for the benefit of creditors, and an attachment execution issues, the assignee may take an appeal. *Bletz* v. *Haldeman*, 26 Pa. St., 403 (1856).

In proceedings by attachment execution before a justice of the peace, under the Act of April 15, 1845 (P. L., 459), a writ of *certiorari* to the Common Pleas and subsequent appeal to the Supreme Court may be taken. *Strouse* v. *Lawrence*, 160 Pa. St., 421 ; 34 W. N., 230 (1894).

§ 1474. *Exemption laws.* In attachment execution issued by a justice, a debtor may claim the benefit of the exemption law, and is in time if he makes such claim on the return-day of the attachment. *Kuhn* v. *Bank*, 20 W. N., 230 (1887).

§ 1475. **Filing of transcripts—Liens—Execution thereon—Freeholders.**

The prothonotaries of the respective counties shall enter on their dockets transcripts of judgments obtained before justices of the peace of their proper counties without the agency of an attorney * * * which transcripts the justices shall deliver to any person who may apply for the same, and which judgments from the time of such entries on the prothonotary's docket shall bind the real estate of the defendants ; but no *fieri facias* shall be issued by any prothonotary until a certificate shall be first produced to him from the justice before whom the original judgment was entered, stating therein that an execution had issued to the proper constable as directed by this Act, and a return thereon that no goods could be found sufficient to satisfy said demand. * * * And no judgment * * * shall deprive any person of his or her right as a freeholder longer or for any greater time than such judgment shall remain unsatisfied. (Act March 20, 1810, section 10 ; 5 Sm., 166.)

The Act of June 24, 1885 (P. L., 160), provides that where the transcript of a judgment obtained before a justice has been filed in the prothonotary' office, such judgment

shall thereafter be and have all the force and effect of a judgment originally obtained in the Court of Common Pleas of said county : *Provided*, that before any execution shall be issued in the Court of Common Pleas on such transcript, the city recorder, magistrate, justice of the peace, or alderman before whom such judgment shall have been obtained, shall first certify that an execution has been issued on said judgment, and the constable to whom the same was directed has made return that no goods could be found sufficient to satisfy said demand.

The entry of a justice's transcript can only be made in the county where the original judgment was obtained. *Bowman* v. *Silvers*, 1 Dist. Rep., 762 (1892).

A judgment entered in the Common Pleas on a transcript of a justice of the peace filed as a lien cannot be disturbed on a rule to open—the Common Pleas has no jurisdiction. *Lacock* v. *White*,

19 Pa. St., 495 (1852) ; *Littster* v. *Littster*, 151 Pa. St., 474 (1892). But a judgment entered in the Common Pleas on a transcript from a justice, which on its face is invalid, may be stricken off on motion. *Rice* v. *Foy*, 2 Dist. Rep., 333 (1893) ; see *Cockley* v. *Rehn*, 2 Dist. Rep., 331 (1892).

§ 1476. *Where the judgment before the justice amounts to $100 and upward, execution by the justice is not a necessary preliminary to issuing* fi. fa. *from the Common Pleas.* The Act of May 9, 1889 (P. L., 176), provides :

That where a judgment has been obtained before a justice of the peace to the amount of one hundred dollars and upward, it shall and may be lawful for the plaintiff in such judgment, upon filing a transcript thereof in the Court of Common Pleas of the county in which the judgment was obtained, to have execution thereof in said court without first having an execution issued by the justice and a return of *nulla bona* by a constable. This shall not be construed to affect the right of the defendant in such judgment to supersede the same, by the entry of bail, an appeal, or *certiorari*.

§ 1477. *Where the judgment against a married woman is void, the transcript may be stricken off.* Where judgment has been taken against a man and his wife before a justice by default of appearance, and a transcript filed for the purpose of lien, the judgment, being void as to the wife, may be stricken off. *Brown* v. *McKinney*, 25 W. N., 76 (1889).

§ 1478. *Appeal within twenty days supersedes the lien obtained by filing transcript.* Where an appeal is taken within the twenty days, a transcript filed as a lien against real estate is of no force. *Myers* v. *Bott*, 10 W. N., 259 (1881).

The transcript will be stricken off, on motion, where an appeal is taken. *Rubinsky* v. *Patrick*, 2 Dist. Rep., 695 (1893).

§ 1479. *Where judgment obtained and one of two plaintiffs dies, the survivor may issue execution without* sci. fa. If one plaintiff dies after judgment in a suit before a justice, the survivor may have execution without *scire facias ;* suggesting the death of his co-plaintiff on the record or reciting it in the writ is sufficient. *Berryhill* v. *Wells*, 5 Binn., 56 (1812).

§ 1480. *After five years, judgment must be revived.*

No execution shall be issued on a judgment rendered before a justice of the peace after five years from the rendition of such judgment, unless the same shall have been revived by *scire facias* or amicable confession. (Act May 5, 1854, section 1 ; P. L., 581.)

An execution by a justice upon a judgment more than five years old, without a previous warning by *scire facias*, is irregular. *Bannan* v. *Rathbone*, 3 Grant, 259 (1858).

It will be noted that the ruling in *Heebner* v. *Chave*, 5 Pa. St.,

115 (1847), to the contrary, was previous to the above statute of 1854. (See sections 251 and 252 of this book as to revival of judgments.)

The Act of May 5, 1854, which provides that no execution shall issue on a judgment of a justice after five years unless revived by *sci. fa.*, is not repealed by the Act of June 24, 1885, relating to the filing of a transcript of the judgment in the Common Pleas and to the issuing of execution thereon. Construing the two Acts together, execution must issue within five years, and during that time a transcript can be filed in the Common Pleas, and if there be a return of "*nulla bona*," either before or after filing the transcript, the latter has all the force of a judgment obtained in the Common Pleas. But if five years have elapsed, a *sci. fa.* to revive must issue from the justice of the peace, and after the judgment on the *sci. fa.* there must be a return of "*nulla bona*" within the next five years, before execution can issue from the Common Pleas. While the Act of May 9, 1889 (P. L., 176), dispenses with execution before a justice on judgments of $100 or upward, it does not do away with a *sci. fa.* to revive after five years. *Smith* v. *Wehrly*, 157 Pa. St., 407 (1893); *Printing Co.* v. *Wehrly, Id.*, 415 (1893).

§ 1481. **Appeal.** *The right of appeal favored.* The cases show that the right of appeal has at all times been favored by the courts of Pennsylvania, and that general words in a statute are sufficient to secure it. Nothing short of a plain intention to deprive a suitor of the right will avail in those cases in which the contrary interpretation is sought to be established.

The decisions relating to appeals are so numerous that the effort has been made to present settled questions of practice only, and to collate such mooted points as properly belong to this treatise without discussing them at length.

§ 1482. *When allowed—Judgment of justice for five dollars and thirty-three cents, or of referee for twenty dollars, conclusive.*

If the parties appear before the justice, either in person or by agent, the justice shall proceed to hear their proofs and allegations, and if the demand shall not exceed five dollars and thirty-three cents, shall give judgment, as to right and justice may belong, which judgment shall be final; but if the demand or sum in controversy shall be more than that sum, and shall not exceed one hundred dollars, and either party shall refuse to submit the determination of the cause to the justice, he shall in that case request them to choose arbitrators, * * * and on having heard their proofs and allegations, they, or a majority of them, shall make out an award under their hands, and transmit the same to such justice, who shall thereupon enter judgment for the sum awarded, * * * which judgment so obtained, when not exceeding twenty dollars, shall be final and conclusive to both plaintiff and defendant without further appeal. (Act of March 20, 1810, section 3; 5 Sm., 162.)

§ 1483. *In case of refusal to refer, judgment of justice can be appealed.*

If either party or their agents shall refuse to refer, the justice may proceed to hear and examine their proofs and allegations and thereupon give judgment publicly as to him of right may appear to belong; either party having the right to appeal within twenty days after judgment being given, either by the justice alone, or on award of referees when such award shall exceed the sum of twenty dollars. (*Id.*, section 4.)

§ 1484. *Defendant can appeal where appeal allowed plaintiff.*

The right of appeal from judgment of aldermen and justices of the peace, and from their judgments on awards of referees, is hereby extended to defendants in all cases wherein, by existing laws, the right of appeal is enjoyed by the plaintiffs. (Act of March 20, 1845, section 3; P. L., 189.)

This Act was construed according to its terms in *Priestly* v. *Ross*, 11 Pa. St., 410 (1849).

§ 1485. *Justice to give judgment within ten days from final hearing.*

It shall be the duty of justices of the peace and aldermen of this Commonwealth to render judgment in any cause or causes pending before them within a period of ten days after all the evidence in such causes shall have been heard. (Act of March 22, 1877, section 1; P. L., 13.)

If defendant has no notice that judgment has been entered, the time to appeal begins to run from the expiration of the ten days. *Haines* v. *Townsend*, 1 Chest. Co. Rep., 146; *Imler* v. *Houser*, 2 Del. Co. Rep., 132.

§ 1486. *Appeal in trespass and trover if judgment exceed five dollars and thirty-three cents—Where award exceeds twenty dollars.*

In proceedings in trespass and trover before a justice either party shall have the right of appealing where the judgment shall exceed five dollars and thirty-three cents, and where judgment given on the award of referees exceeds twenty dollars. (Act March 22, 1814, section 3; 6 Sm., 182.)

This Act received a careful construction in the case of *Cook* v. *Dunkle*, 25 Pa. St., 340 (1855), KNOX, J. :

"John G. Dunkle brought an action of trespass against John Cook and Jeremiah McDonald before a justice of the peace. The plaintiff's claim, as set forth on the docket of the justice, was for twenty-five dollars damages for the destruction of his sheep by the defendants' dog; referees were chosen, who awarded in favor of the plaintiff eleven dollars, and judgment was entered upon the award. The defendants appealed to the Court of Common Pleas, where their appeal was dismissed for the reason that the case was not appealable. To reinstate the appeal this writ of error was taken. The third section of the Act of 22 March, 1814, gives to either party the right to an appeal where the judgment given by a justice or an alderman alone exceeds five dollars and thirty-three cents, or where, entered on award of referees, it exceeds twenty dollars in an action of trespass or trover.

" The literal reading of this section would give to either party the right to appeal where the judgment entered upon an award of referees exceeded twenty dollars, and not otherwise. Thus, if the plaintiff's demand was for $100, and the judgment was for one dollar, the letter of the statute would not give him the right of appeal; but if his demand was for twenty-five dollars and his judgment for twenty-four dollars, standing upon the letter alone, his right to an appeal could not have been questioned. Whilst in no case could the defendant appeal if the judgment entered upon the award does not exceed twenty dollars. The injustice of such a statutory provision was so manifest, and its inconsistency so obvious, that the legislative intent was sought for beyond a literal•reading. It was clear that the intention of the legislature was to preserve the right of appeal where the adjudication had been substantially against the party in a sum exceeding twenty dollars by referees or five dollars and thirty-three cents by the justice or alderman alone, and to carry out this intention it was decided by this court, soon after the passage of the Act of 1814, that where the plaintiff's claim exceeded five dollars and thirty-three cents and the judgment of an alderman was for the defendant, the plaintiff had the right of appeal (*Stewart* v. *Keemle*, 4 S. & R., 72); but where the plaintiff's claim in trover was for fifty dollars damages and the referees awarded in his favor eleven dollars, it was held that the defendant could not appeal. *Ulrich* v. *Sarkey*, 6 S. & R., 285. All of the subsequent cases, either under the Act of 1814 or that of 1810, have been in accordance with the principle above stated, that is to say, if the judgment is through the intervention of referees, and the plaintiff's demand, as set forth on the docket, has been reduced more than twenty dollars, he is entitled to an appeal, although the judgment may be for less than that sum. If the judgment is for more than twenty dollars, the defendant can appeal, but where it is for less he cannot, except in cases under the Act of 1810, where a *bona fide* set-off has been made, and the amount which is adjudged against the party, including the set-off, is greater than twenty dollars. *Stoy* v. *Yost*, 12 S. & R., 385; *Soop* v. *Coates*, *I d.*, 388; *Klingensmith* v. *Nole*, 3 P. R., 120; *McCloskey* v. *McConnel*, 9 Watts, 17; *Downey* v. *Ferry*, 2 Watts, 304.

" So stood the law until the passage of the Act of 20 March, 1845, which provided ' that the right of appeal from judgments of aldermen and justices of the peace, and from their judgments on awards of referees, should be extended to defendants in all cases wherein, by existing laws, the right of appeal is enjoyed by plaintiffs.' Under this Act it was held, in *Priestly* v. *Ross*, 11 Pa. St., 410, that where a plaintiff, in an action of trespass, obtained judgment before an alderman for five dollars upon a claim of damages of twenty-five dollars, either the plaintiff or defendant was entitled to an appeal. This Act gives to the defendant an appeal where the plaintiff may have one, but it does not extend the plaintiff's right, and there is no case to be found in our reports where the plaintiff has been allowed an appeal from a judgment entered by a justice of the peace or an alderman, upon an award of referees, unless he has lost, taking his demand as the standard of his rights, more than twenty dollars. In the case under consideration, as the judgment was for eleven dollars, the defendants had no right to appeal, unless they derived their right from the Act of 1845, and as the plaintiff's demand was only reduced fourteen dollars he could not have appealed, and consequently the Act of March 20, 1845, has no bearing upon the case."

§ 1487. *Appeal allowed in attachment under Act of* 1842. Under the Attachment Act of July 12, 1842, section 34, the right of appeal is given to the parties.

§ 1488. *In summary convictions and penalties either party may appeal upon allowance and cause shown.*

In cases of summary conviction in this Commonwealth or of judgment in suit for a penalty before a magistrate or court not of record, either party may appeal to such court of record as may be prescribed by law upon allowance of the appellate court or judge thereof, upon cause shown. (Constitution of 1874, Art. V., section 14.)

An appeal from the judgment of a magistrate or a court not of record, in a suit for a penalty, may be taken upon allowance of the Court of Common Pleas or any judge thereof, upon cause shown : *Provided,* that all appeals shall be upon such terms as to the payment of costs and entering bail as the court or judge allowing the appeal shall direct. (Act April 17, 1876, section 1 ; P. L., 29.)

§ 1489. *On appeal all defects and irregularities before judgment waived.* · By taking an appeal, one waives any defect before judgment which otherwise would have been fatal. *Jones* v. *Canal Co.*, 10 Phila., 570 (1874).

Such irregularities as occurred in the proceedings before a justice are cured on appeal. *Kuhn* v. *Bank*, 20 W. N., 230 (1887).

§ 1490. *The sum in controversy regulates the appeal.* The sum in controversy and not the judgment regulates the right to an appeal. The amount in dispute may, with sufficient certainty, be ascertained by the oath of the justice or other competent authority. *Soop* v. *Coates*, 12 S. & R., 388 (1825) ; *Klinginsmith* v. *Nole*, 3 P. & W., 119 (1831) ; *Downs* v. *Ferry*, 2 W., 304 (1834) ; *McCloskey* v. *McConnell*, 9 W., 17 (1839) ; *Priestly* v. *Ross*, 11 Pa. St., 410 (1849).

§ 1491. *When an appeal lies.* If judgment be given against two defendants, one of them may appeal though the other comes into court and dissents. *Gallagher* v. *Jackson*, 1 S. & R., 492 (1815). An appeal will lie from a judgment upon a *scire facias* on a judgment of justice. *Guilky* v. *Gillingham*, 3 S. & R., 93 (1817); *Watson* v. *Wehrly*, 2 Dist. Rep., 530 (1892). An appeal lies from the judgment of a justice in an action for a penalty incurred by neglecting to serve notice under Arbitration Act of 1810. *Rogers* v. *Bennett*, 16 S. & R., 243 (1827). An appeal may be taken by either party from judgment on a *scire facias* against a constable to recover the amount of an execution. *Sott* v. *Kelso*, 4 W. & S., 278 (1842). Appeal lies from a judgment of non-suit by a justice. He has no power to non-suit unless plaintiff fails to appeal. *Lawver* v. *Walls*, 17 Pa. St., 75 (1851). If a judgment be confessed by mistake or by fraud and the wronged party discovers such fact, he has the right of appeal. *Rowen* v. *King*, 25 Pa. St., 409 (1855). An appeal lies from the judgment of a justice where part of the demand passed upon by the justice was not within his jurisdiction. *Bunce* v. *Stanford*, 27 Pa. St., 265 (1856).

An agent may appeal. *Jones* v. *Canal Co.*, 10 Phila., 570 (1874).

§ 1492. *When appeal does not lie.* If the justice had not jurisdiction, Common Pleas have none on appeal. *Moore* v. *Wait*, 1 Binney, 219 (1807); *Owen* v. *Shelhamer*, 3 *Id.*, 45 (1810); *Wright* v. *Guy*, 10 S. & R., 227 (1823); *Bergman* v. *Roberts*, 61 Pa. St., 497 (1869).

If it does not appear from record that security was entered, appeal does not lie. *Guilky* v. *Gillingham*, 3 S. & R., 93 (1817). No appeal can be allowed where a controversy, the amount of which is more than $100, is submitted to the justice. *Morrison* v. *Weaver*, 4 S. & R., 190 (1818). Nor where an award of referees is less than twenty dollars, unless the plaintiff's claim, set forth upon the records of the justice, exceeds that sum. *Bayard* v. *Hawk*, 3 P. & W., 174 (1831); *Cook* v. *Dunkle*, 25 Pa. St., 340 (1855). (See section 1486.) Nor where the claim is not set forth on the justice's docket. *Walter* v. *Bechtol*, 5 Rawle, 228 (1835). Nor where judgment of justice is less than five dollars and thirty-three cents, and no cross-demand appears to have reduced the amount claimed. *Ellis* v. *Brewster*, 6 Watts, 277 (1837); *Mack* v. *Thayer*, 2 Phila., 291 (1857). Nor where execution has issued and the judgment against one not a freeholder has been satisfied from the proceeds of the sale. *Patterson* v. *Peironnet*, 7 W., 337 (1838). Nor where defendant has allowed twenty days to elapse before taking a rule to show cause why the judgment should not be opened, which rule is dismissed. *Russel* v. *Smith*, 1 Phila., 425 (1853). Where the appeal does not lie, acquiescence of appellee cannot confer jurisdiction. *Morrison* v. *Weaver*, 4 S. & R., 190 (1818); *Stoy* v. *Yost*, 12 S. & R., 385 (1825).

§ 1492 a. *Waiver of appeal must be in writing.* Where a party waives the right of appeal, and agrees to be bound by the decision of the justice, he is estopped from appealing. *Pritchard* v. *Denton*, 8 Watt., 371 (1839).

A waiver of appeal in a lease is binding, and judgment by a magistrate on such lease cannot be appealed from. *Lippincott* v. *Cooper*, 19 W. N., 130 (1886).

In a suit before a justice on a note waiving the right of appeal, even though the defendant denied the signature, there can be no appeal. *Cawley* v. *Bohan*, 120 Pa. St., 295 (1888).

In this case the defendant did not deny under oath his signature, and the question as to the execution of the note was not raised in a legal manner. There was a mere verbal denial by the defendant, whereupon the plaintiff obtained a continuance and subsequently proved that the defendant had signed the note.

Where parties agree to waive the right of appeal, such waiver must be in writing, made before the justice and a part of the record. *Dawson* v. *Condy*, 7 S. & R., 366 (1821).

On appeal from a justice in a suit upon a lease containing a waiver of appeal, a rule to strike off the appeal filed more than a year after the appeal is too late. *Kenney* v. *Ralph*, 1 Dist. Rep., 720 (1892).

§ 1493. **Affidavit on appeal.** *In Philadelphia County.*

In all cases in which judgment shall have been rendered for plaintiff by any alderman in the city of Philadelphia, no appeal shall be allowed unless the defendant shall make oath or affirmation, to be filed in the cause, that the same is not intended for delay merely. (Act of May 1, 1861, section 1; P. L., 535.)

This provision is superseded by the Act of 1865 :

In appeals by defendants in the city of Philadelphia, the defendant, or some one acting in his behalf, having knowledge of the facts of the case, shall file an affidavit with the justice, setting forth that the appeal is not for the purpose of delay, but that if the proceedings appealed from are not removed he or the defendant will be required to pay more money or receive less than is justly due, which affidavit shall be attached to the transcript by the alderman to be filed in the court to which the appeal is taken. (Act March 27, 1865, section 1; P. I., 794.)

§ 1494. *In Allegheny County.*

No appeal from the judgment of an alderman or justice of the peace in the county of Allegheny shall be allowed unless the appellant, or some person acting in his behalf having knowledge of the facts of the case, shall file with the alderman or justice an affidavit, setting forth that the appeal taken is not for the purpose of delay, but that if the proceedings appealed from are not removed the appellant will be required to pay more money or receive less than is justly due, which affidavit shall be attached to the transcript by the alderman or justice, to be filed with the appeal. (Act of May 18, 1871, section 1; P. L., 938.)

§ 1495. *In Lancaster and Dauphin Counties.*

In Lancaster County no appeal shall be allowed unless appellant, or his agent or attorney, shall make oath or affirmation, to be filed in the cause, that he has reason to believe that injustice has been done him, and that the same is not intended for delay merely, and pay all costs accrued, unless appellant make oath that he or she is unable to pay said costs. (Act March 2, 1868; P. L., 256.)

This Act does not apply to non-residents. (*Ibid.*)

The Act of February 23, 1870 (P. L., 221), makes a similar provision for Dauphin County.

§ 1496. *Regulations as to appeals in Cameron, Venango, Erie, Columbia, and Luzerne Counties.* The Act of March 26, 1868 (P. L., 495), provides :

That no appeal shall be allowed in Cameron County unless the party his or their agent or attorney, shall give bail for costs, comply with other requirements, and make an oath or affirmation that such appeal is not taken or entered for the purpose of delay, but in good faith, and because he or they verily believe that injustice has been done to him or them, and that he or they have a just and legal defense to the plaintiff's demand, or is entitled to more than the amount of the judgment, which oath or affirmation shall be filed and annexed to the transcript.

This was extended to Venango County by Act of March 11, 1870 (P. L., 397), and by the Act of April 5, 1870 (P. L., 931).

The Act of March 11, 1870, was extended to Erie and Columbia Counties by Act of March 23, 1872 (P. L., 524).

The Act of February 28, 1870 (P. L., 269), contains similar provisions as to Luzerne County.

§ 1497. *Affidavit required in landlord and tenant proceedings.* In taking an appeal from a landlord and tenant proceeding, an affidavit that the appeal is not taken for delay must be filed. *Carter* v. *Hess,* 3 W. N., 325 (1877).

§ 1498. *Guardian may appeal without affidavit or security.*

A guardian shall be allowed to appeal from the judgment of a justice or an award of arbitrators without being required to make the usual affidavit and without giving surety or paying costs. (Act March 27, 1833, section 1; P. L., 99.)

§ 1499. *Affidavit in suits for wages.*

In all cases in which judgment shall have been rendered by any justice of the peace or alderman in this Commonwealth for wages of manual labor, before the defendant shall be entitled to an appeal from the judgment of the justice or alderman, he or his agent or attorney shall make oath or affirmation that the appeal is not intended for the purpose of delay, but that he believes that injustice has been done him, which affidavit shall be attached to and sent up with the transcript of appeal. And the said defendant shall be required to give good and sufficient bail (for) the payment of the debt and costs to be paid when finally adjudged to be due the plaintiff by the court, in all cases of labor. (Act of April 20, 1876, section 1; P. L., 43.)

An appellant from the judgment of a justice for wages of manual labor must make the affidavit that the appeal is not for the purpose of delay, but because he firmly believes injustice has been done. *Flegal* v. *Dottera,* 1 Dist. Rep., 190 (1892).

§ 1500. *Executor or administrator need not file affidavit.* This Act does not apply to an executor or administrator sued in his representative capacity for wages for manual labor. *Koontz's Admr.* v. *Howsare,* 100 Pa. St., 506 (1882).

An executor or administrator against whom a judgment is recovered before a justice of the peace, may appeal to the Common Pleas without filing an affidavit and entering the security prescribed by the Act of April 20, 1876, section 1 (P. L., 43). *Ibid.*

§ 1501. *When affidavit filed.* Under the Act of May 1, 1861, the affidavit must be filed when appeal entered, not after the expiration of twenty days. *Mountney* v. *McFarland,* 7 Phila., 392 (1870).

§ 1502.

FORM OF AFFIDAVIT ON APPEAL.

A. B.
v.
C. D.
} Before E. F., Magistrate of Court No. .
Judgment obtained .

City of Philadelphia, *ss.*

C. D., the above-named defendant, being duly (sworn or affirmed) according to law, deposes and says that the appeal taken in the above case is not for the purpose of delay, but that if the proceedings appealed from are not removed, he will be required to pay more money than is justly due.

and subscribed before me, this day of , A. D. 1890.
Witness my hand and official seal of said court, the day and year above written.
E. F., Magistrate of Court No. .
[SEAL]
} C. D.

§ 1503. **Bail or Recognizance on Appeal.** *Bail for appeal to be absolute in double amount of costs.*

The bail required by law in cases of appeal shall be bail absolute in double the probable amount of costs accrued and likely to accrue, with one or more sufficient sureties conditioned for the payment of all costs accrued or that may be legally recovered. (Act March 20, 1845, section 1; P. L., 188.)

Depositing money with a justice is not a compliance with the Act requiring a recognizance. *Power Co.* v. *Hutchinson,* 3 Dist. Rep., 658 (1894).

In an appeal from the judgment of a justice of the peace in *forma pauperis,* the party appealing must give security for costs. *Davi-son* v. *Suit Co.,* 4 Dist. Rep., 237 (1895).

One who appeals from the judgment of a justice of the peace must enter bail even though he file an affidavit of his inability to pay costs. *Iams* v. *Hall,* 4 Dist. Rep., 259 (1895).

§ 1504. *All (except municipal) corporations to give bail on appeal or writ of error for debt, interest, and costs.*

Any corporation except a municipal corporation on appeal or writ of error shall give bail absolute for the payment of debt, interest, and costs. (Act of March 15, 1847, section 1; P. L., 361.)

A corporation (not municipal) must give absolute security for debt, interests, and costs, on appeal. *Turnpike Co.* v. *Naglee,* 9 S. & R., 227 (1823); *Young* v. *Colvin,* 168 Pa. St., 449 (1895).

Municipal corporations are privileged to appeal without entering security. *King* v. *District,* 1 Phila., 402 (1852).

The condition of a recognizance to be given under the Act of 1847 by a corporation does not provide for the appearance of the party appealing at the next term of court to prosecute his appeal with effect. *Shivery* v. *Grauer,* 2 Dist. Rep., 387 (1893).

§ 1505. *In trespass.* The security required when defendant appeals from judgment of a justice in trespass must be double the amount recovered. *Langs* v. *Galbraith,* 1 S. & R., 491 (1815).

§ 1506. *In wage cases.* The Act of April 20, 1876, section 1 (section 1499), requires security for payment of debt and costs.

§ 1507. *Attorney may become security without leave of court.* The rule of court prohibiting an attorney from becoming security unless by leave of the court does not apply to security entered before a magistrate on appeal. *Gardy* v. *Moffit,* 14 W. N., 438 (1884). See *Laughlin* v. *Prigg,* 3 Dist. Rep., 418 (1894).

The better practice is for the attorney not to become security.

§ 1508. *Recognizance must be for a certain amount.* The sum of money should be written in the recognizance, for it cannot be supplied by reference to the debt and costs at the date of the entry of the bond, nor will the court assume that the bond had been taken in double the amount. *Caldwell* v. *Brindle,* 11 Pa. St., 293 (1849).

§ 1509. *Sufficient recognizances.*

" June 4, defendant appeals. I, F. S., having been duly sworn and justified, and bound as absolute bail in the sum of twenty dollars, or such sum as may be necessary to pay all costs that have or may accrue in this case in prosecuting this appeal." *Seidenstriker* v. *Buffum,* 14 Pa. St., 159 (1850).

" M. becomes bound in the sum of thirty-five dollars on condition that the defendant shall appear at the next Court of Common Pleas to prosecute his appeal with effect." *Murray* v. *Haslett,* 19 Pa. St., 356 (1852).

PRACTICE IN PENNSYLVANIA.

"I become bail absolute in this case conditioned for the payment of all costs that have accrued, and all costs that may accrue in case the said judgment be affirmed, and also for all rent that has accrued and may accrue up to the time of final judgment."—A. A. H. *Hardy* v. *Watts*, 22 Pa. St., 33 (1853).

"It being by consent of plaintiff's attorney—bail to be taken in the sum of $250—G. H. for bail, he having justified. * * * Whereupon, said G. H. was recognized in the sum of $250 as bail in said suit, according to Act of Assembly, etc., etc." *Harvey* v. *Beach*, 38 Pa. St., 500 (1861).

"A. B. goes security in the sum of fifty dollars for the prosecution of this suit to effect." *Rhey* v. *Baird*, 51 Pa. St., 85 (1865).

§ 1510. *Insufficient recognizances.* The following recognizances were held insufficient :

"J. W. bound in a sum certain to cover all costs that plaintiff will prosecute this appeal with effect." *Williamson* v. *Mitchel*, 1 P. & W., 9 (1829).

A recognizance on appeal from an award before a justice conditioned to pay costs

"With one dollar per day for every day lost by defendant in attending to such appeal." *Shuff* v. *Morgan*, 7 Pa. St., 125 (1847).

"Defendant gives bail, which is entered on the docket, for the sum of $100 ; J. W. B., bail." *Meeker* v. *Brackney*, 35 Pa. St., 276 (1860).

§ 1511. *If transcript not filed and recognizance defective.* Where the transcript has *not* been filed with the prothonotary, but bail has been entered before the justice, the other side may except to bail before the justice, and serve a notice of the rule to justify on the attorney of appellant. *Cummings* v. *Forsman*, 6 Pa. St., 194 (1847).

§ 1512. *If transcript filed, rule appellant to perfect recognizance.* Where a recognizance on appeal is defective, the proper course is to rule appellant to perfect his bail within a specified period, or in default thereof that the appeal be quashed. *Means* v. *Trout*, 16 S. & R., 349 (1827) ; *Burgess* v. *Jackson*, 2 P. & W., 431 (1831) ; *Bream* v. *Spangler*, 1 W. & S., 378 (1841) ; *Adams* v. *Null*, 5 W. & S., 363 (1843) ; *Koenig* v. *Bauer*, 57 Pa. St., 168 (1868) ; *Redheffer* v. *Fitler*, 7 Phila., 338 (1870) ; *Hummer* v. *School District*, 10 Phila., 494 (1874).

The perfected recognizance must then be filed *nunc pro tunc.* *Adams* v. *Null* (*supra*).

§ 1513. *Negligent appellee waives rights under a defective recognizance.* If appellee is negligent in availing himself of a defective recognizance, he waives his right. *Cavence* v. *Butler*, 6 Binn., 52 (1813) ; *Cochran* v. *Parker*, 6 S. & R., 549 (1821) ; *Shank* v. *Warfel*, 14 *Id.*, 205 (1826) ; *Wiedner* v. *Matthews*, 11 Pa. St., 336 (1849).

§ 1514.

FORM OF SECURITY ON APPEAL.

A. B. ⎫
   v.   ⎬   Before E. F., Magistrate of Court No.   .
C. D. ⎭   Judgment obtained

City of Philadelphia, *ss.*

1890, defendant files his affidavit and appéals.

I hold myself indebted to the plaintiff in the sum of   dollars, conditioned for all costs that have or may accrue in this case up to the final determination of this suit, and that the defendant will prosecute his appeal with effect.

(Name of Surety)
(Address.)

§ 1515. **Transcript.** *Docket to be kept—All to be certified on appeal.*

All proceedings before a justice shall be entered at large by him in a docket or book kept for that purpose, in which he shall state the evidence upon which the plaintiff's demand may be founded, whether upon bond, note, penal or single bill, writing obligatory, book-debt, damages or assumption, or whatever it may be.

The whole proceeding shall be certified to the prothonotary of the proper county on appeal, who shall enter the same on his docket, and the suit shall then be subject to the same rules as other actions ; the costs before the justice shall await the event of the suit. (Act March 20, 1810, section 4 ; 5 Sm., 164.)

§ 1516. *Conclusiveness of record.* In *Hazelett* v. *Ford*, 10 Watts, 101 (1840), Chief Justice GIBSON said of a justice and his docket : " He is the judge of a court, which, deriving its jurisdiction from statutory grants, proceeds in most things according to the substance contained in the forms of the common law, and whose docket, as to things adjudicated by him, has the conclusiveness of a record."

§ 1517. *What the docket should set forth as to appearance, process, service, demand, etc.* It should set forth legal service of process, the appearance or default of the defendant, and the presence of plaintiff or a representative, as well as the kind of evidence adduced to support the claim. *Northern Liberties* v. *O'Neil*, 1 Phila., 427 (1853) ; *McCale* v. *Kulp*, 8 Phila., 636 (1871) ; *Paine* v. *Godshall*, 29 Leg. Int., 12 (1872).

In distraint *damage feasant*, the affidavit upon which the action is based and the public notice required by the statute are part of the record, and may be given in evidence in an action of trover for the subject of the distraint. *Miller* v. *Knapp*, 47 Leg. Int., 309 (1890).

It should set forth that the summons was legally served and returned on oath. *Sloan* v. *McKinstry*, 18 Pa. St., 120 (1851). In cases of the non-appearance of the defendant, it should set forth how the process was served. *Fraily* v. *Sparks*, 2 Pars., 232 (1848). The record must show that the justice had jurisdiction. *Kelly* v. *March*, 15 W. N., 30 (1884). In cases of summary proceedings, the jurisdiction must affirmatively appear on the docket. *Graver* v. *Fehr*, 89 Pa. St., 460 (1879). The justice's record should set forth generally the plaintiff's demand, and that it does not exceed $100. *M'Entire* v. *M'Elduff*, 1 S. & R., 19 (1814). Similar rulings were made in *Kirk* v. *Aechternacht*, 1 Phila., 426 (1853) ; *McCale* v. *Kulp*, 8 Phila., 636 (1871) ; *Paine* v. *Godshall*, 29 Leg. Int., 12 (1872) ; *Maxwell* v. *Perkins*, 93 Pa. St., 255 (1880). It should set forth with reasonable certainty how the cause of action arose. *Moore* v. *R. R.*, 11 Phila., 348 (1876). It is not essential that the defendant should have the amount of his claim *entered upon the justice's docket*. A statement made in writing by the plaintiff containing not only the amount of his claim, but the nature of it, is equivalent to an entry of the amount of his claim by the justice on his docket. *Klinginsmith* v. *Nole*, 3 P. & W., 119 (1831). Where judgment is rendered upon the mere production of defendant's promissory note, the record should state that defendant was the *maker* of it. *Leonore* v. *Ingram*, 1 Phila., 519 (1854). If judgment be given against a married woman in an action against husband and wife, the record must show that the debt was contracted by the wife for necessaries for the support of her family. *Gould* v. *McFall*, 111 Pa. St., 66 (1885). Similar rulings were made in *Hartzell* v. *Osborne*, 15 W. N., 142 (1884) ; *Brown* v. *McKinney*, 47 Leg. Int., 49 (1889). In an action before a justice under a city ordinance, the record must show such ordinance ; the court will not take judicial notice of it. *City* v. *Cohen*, 13 W. N., 468 (1883). A similar ruling had been made in *Manayunk* v. *Davis*, 2 Pars., 289 (1851).

A record is fatally defective which does not show upon what day the plaintiff entered his appearance, and judgment was obtained ; *Gwinner* v. *Brendt*, 2 Dist. Rep., 50 (1892) ; or which fails to show that the plaintiff appeared at the time named in the summons and offered the evidence of his claim. *Eilenberger* v. *Bush, Id.* (1892). Where both plaintiff and defendant appear before a justice of the peace, the record, to support a judgment for plaintiff, must show that he offered evidence. *Chambers* v. *Reynolds*, 2 Dist. Rep., 402 (1893). In a suit against a foreign insurance company before a justice of the peace, where the process is served outside of the county, the record should show : (a) That the defendant is a foreign insurance company ; (b) that the summons issued to a constable of the county in which the justice resides; (c) that such constable, by writing indorsed on or attached to the summons, authorized the constable of the county where the State agent of defendant resides to serve the process; (d) that the person upon whom the process was served was the duly designated State agent to receive service of process. *Life Ins. Co.* v. *Cook*, 3 Dist. Rep., 625 (1894).

§ 1518. *Where a judgment is tendered, the record should show the tender.* Where a tender of judgment is made either on the trial of the case or before an appeal, the record should show notice to the plaintiff or his agent of the offer. *Driesback* v. *Morris*, 94 Pa. St., 22 (1880). A similar ruling was made in *Seibert* v. *Kline*, 1 Pa. St., 38 (1845).

§ 1519. *In civil cases, evidence at length need not be set forth.* A justice in ordinary civil cases is not bound to set forth the evidence at large on his docket, but only the kind of evidence produced to support the claim, showing the nature of the contract and the jurisdiction of the justice. *Jones* v. *Evans.* 1 Browne, 207 (1810); *Mulvary* v. *Miller, Id.*, 339 (1811).

§ 1520. *In cases of penalties, evidence must appear at length. Comm.* v. *Cane*, 2 Parsons, 265 (1847). *Certiorari* to justice of the peace. Defendant was charged with disturbing a religious meeting, and convicted. Defendant excepted to the record, *inter alia*, because the nature of the disturbance was not specifically stated. PARSONS, J. :

" It is a well-settled principle that where an Act of Assembly simply imposes a penalty, and gives authority to justices of the peace to take cognizance of the violation thereof, and prescribes no method or form for the prosecution, the conviction must be in accordance with the rules of the common law, and the whole record must show that the proceedings have been conducted, in all respects, according to the course of the common law. * * * There is no fixed and definite charge in the information of the offense, nor is there anything like a regular specific information ; this is indispensably necessary : Paley on Convictions, 58-66, * * * and the rule seems to be this, that the information must contain a complete statement of the offense, with all its qualities, for the evidence subsequently stated can only support the charge, but can by no means extend or supply what is wanting in it.

"Another defect apparent upon the face of the record is that the magistrate has not set out the evidence at length. This he was bound to do : 4 Burr., 2064, and Paley in his Treatise on Convictions * * * has stated the rule of law correctly in these words : ' As the record of conviction is intended to exhibit an exact account of the magistrate's proceedings and to show that the judgment has been legal and regular, it is most natural that the facts should be fitly disclosed, in order that the judgment upon them may be well founded." * * *

" Lord MANSFIELD laid it down as an undoubted maxim that in a conviction the evidence must be set out in order that the superior court may judge of it: 1 Burr., 1163. And so strict is the rule, that it was held in the case of *Rex* v. *Thompson*, 2 T. Rep., 18, that it is the duty of the magistrates in all cases to state the whole of the evidence and not merely the result of it. In the case of *Rex* v. *Serrt*, 7 T. Rep., 152, and *Rex* v. *Clark*, 8 T. Rep., 220, it would seem to be the better opinion that all the evidence should be stated, not only that of the prosecution, but also that of the defendant. He should not state merely the result of the evidence, but the evidence itself."

Proceedings reversed.

Comm. v. *Nesbit*, 34 Pa. St., 398 (1859). *Certiorari* to Mayor of Pittsburg.

Information against defendant for performing labor on Sunday, contrary to Acts of 1794 and 1855. Defendant was ordered to pay a fine of twenty-five dollars. It was assigned for error: 1. That the mayor did not set out on the record the testimony taken by him in the case; 2. That the particular offense was not explicitly set out.

LOWRIE, C. J. :

" * * * It is essential that a summary conviction shall contain a finding that a special act has been performed by the defendant, and that it shall describe or define it in such a way as to individuate it and show that it falls within an unlawful class of acts. Without this, a judgment that the law has been violated goes for nothing. * * * When the record contains no definite facts, but only a legal conclusion from unrecorded facts, the superior court cannot, without compelling a return of the evidence, or taking testimony of what it was, decide whether the legal conclusion, that is, the conviction of the offense, is right or wrong. In such a case, for the safety of the citizen, they usually reverse the conviction, simply because no act appears upon it that justifies the judgment."

A similar ruling was made in *Comm.* v. *Richer*, 13 W. N., 142 (1883).

In a suit before a justice of the peace for a penalty under an ordinance, the record must show definitely the nature of the charge, the ordinance making the act penal, and the penalty provided, and the conviction *followed by the fine.* It should also contain the evidence, or the substance of it, upon which the judgment is founded. *Wilcox* v. *Borough*, 2 Dist. Rep., 721 (1892).

§ 1521. *On* certiorari, *the evidence is no part of the record.* The evidence forms no part of the record upon a *certiorari*. *Comm.* v. *Gipner*, 20 W. N., 500 (1887).

§ 1522. *An agreement to discontinue should appear on docket.* In *Cope* v. *Risk*, 21 Pa. St., 66 (1853), Mr. Justice LEWIS said:

" Where a suit before a justice * * * is terminated by any act or agreement of the parties which amounts, directly or indirectly, to a discontinuance of the action, it is a part of the official duty of the justice to enter such act or agreement upon his docket, and the docket entry is evidence of the same."

§ 1523. *The record should set forth the day of judgment.* If, however, the day of appearance is mentioned, and the judgment then set forth generally, the court will presume it was entered upon the date of the appearance. *Buckmyer* v. *Dubs*, 5 Binn., 29 (1812).

If a justice enters on his record judgment by default, the record should state the hour of the day the plaintiff took judgment. *Lindsay* v. *Sweeny*, 6 Phila., 3Q9 (1867) ; *contra*, *Fronheiser* v. *Werner*, 3 Dist. Rep., 515 (1894) (C. P. Carbon Co.). The transcript must show that the defendant failed to appear at the hour named in the summons. *Smith* v. *Fetherston*, 10 Phila., 306 (1875).

§ 1524. *Waiver of appeal should be docketed.* If judgment be given on a note which contains a waiver of appeal, such waiver should be noted on the docket. It cannot be shown by parol testimony. *Foss* v. *Bogan*, 92 Pa. St., 296 (1879).

§ 1525. *The record should show that security was entered.* On appeal, it must appear from the record that security was given. *Guilky* v. *Gillingham*, 3 S. & R., 93 (1817).

§ 1526. *A transcript cannot be amended by a certificate of facts* within the recollection of a justice relative to the judgment rendered by him. *Boylan* v. *Hays*, 7 Watts, 509 (1838).

If an offer to confess judgment do not appear on the justice's docket, a certificate of such fact is no part of the transcript. *Clements* v. *Gilbert*, 12 Pa. St., 255 (1849).

§ 1527. *When defective transcript waived.* If the transcript of a justice be defective, and yet defendant on the appeal appear and proceed with the trial without raising objection, the defect is waived. *Weidenhamer* v. *Bertle*, 103 Pa. St., 448 (1883).

§ 1528. *The right to amend transcript is vested in the Common Pleas.* Where a transcript does not conform to the justice's docket, which is alleged to be erroneous, and an application is made for leave to amend the docket by the transcript, the decision of the Common Pleas upon the question of the amendment is final. *Caldwell* v. *Thompson*, 1 Rawle, 370 (1829). If a justice commit a mistake in making up his transcript, the court will on motion allow the transcript to be amended. *Kearney* v. *Pennock*, 2 Dist. Rep., 32 (1892).

§ 1529.

FORM OF TRANSCRIPT.

Transcript from the docket of   Magistrate of Court No.   .

A. B.
v.
C. D.

⎱ Summons issued (date, etc.), A. D. 1890. Returnable (date,
    etc.), A. D. 1890. Between the hours of 10 o'clock   M.
    and 11 o'clock M. (Name) constable. Returned on oath
    (date), A. D. 1890. Served on defendant by (here state
    mode of service).

(Here insert record of proceedings to be faithfully transcribed from the docket of the justice or magistrate.)

City of Philadelphia, *ss.*

I hereby certify the above to be a correct transcript from my docket.

Witness my hand and official seal of said court, the   day of 1890.

                     (Name), Magistrate of Court No.   .

§ 1530. *Transcript must be delivered on demand.*

The justice on demand by either plaintiff or defendant shall make out a copy of his proceedings at large, and deliver the same duly certified by him to the party requiring the same.

If he refuse so to do after demand made, it 'shall be deemed a misdemeanor in office. (Act March 20, 1810, section 23 ; 5 Sm., 164.)

The indictment against the justice should state a previous tender of the legal fee. *Wilson* v. *Comm.,* 10 S. & R., 373.

§ 1531. **Record of another County.** *If defendant reside in a county other than where the judgment was obtained, justice may certify the record, etc.*

If the defendant does not reside in the county where judgment is obtained against him, application may be made by the plaintiff or his agent to the person in possession of the docket in which such judgment may be entered, who shall make out, certify, and deliver a transcript of all proceedings and deliver all evidence in his possession for the recovery of the amount thereof, with costs, before the justice of any county where the defendant may reside or can be found, as in cases originally brought before him, and the stay of execution shall be counted from the original entry. (Act March 20, 1810, section 17 ; 5 Sm., 169.)

A justice of the peace to whom a transcript from another county has been handed, may issue thereon a *sci. fa.* to revive, and on the judgment thus obtained issue an execution. *Stewart* v. *Eisenhower,* 4 Dist. Rep., 565 (1895).

§ 1532. **Appellant to file the transcript on or before first day of next term**—*Cause to be decided on merits*—*Proceedings when executor shall plead no assets.*

If the appellant within twenty days after judgment enter bail for an appeal, he shall file the transcript of the record in the prothonotary's office on or before the first day of the next term of the Court of Common Pleas after entering bail.

On appeal, the cause shall be decided on its merits, and no deficiency of form or substance in the record or proceedings, nor any mistake in the form or name of the action, shall prejudice either party.

If any executor or administrator shall declare after judgment against him before a justice that he has not sufficient assets to satisfy the judgment, the justice shall forthwith transmit the record to the prothonotary of the Common Pleas to be entered on his docket, and the court shall adjudge and decree thereon, and appoint auditors to ascertain and apportion the assets. (Act March 20, 1810, section 4 ; 5 Sm., 164.)

§ 1533. *When to be filed in Philadelphia County.*

All appeals from alderman * * * shall be filed in the Court of Common Pleas of the city and county of Philadelphia on or before the monthly return-day in said court next ensuing the date of the entry of the judgment before the alderman, instead of to the first day of the next term, as heretofore. (Act of May 1, 1861, section 1 ; P. L., 535.)

§ 1534. *In Allegheny County.*

All appeals as aforesaid shall be filed in the Court of Common Pleas of the county of Allegheny on or before the monthly or term return-day in said court next ensuing the date of the entry of the judgment before the alderman or justice, instead of to the first day of the next term, as heretofore : *Provided*, that if the appellant shall perfect his appeal by bail and affidavit as aforesaid, within twenty days after the entry of the judgment as aforesaid, such appeal shall be effectual in case he shall file the transcript of the record of the alderman or justice and the affidavit as aforesaid, on or before the next return-day of said court thereafter. (Act of May 18, 1871, section 2 ; P. L., 939.)

§ 1535. *In Delaware County.*

All appeals shall be filed on or before the next return-day after the taking thereof if twenty days shall have elapsed, and if not, then on or before the next return-day thereafter. (Act of April 9, 1862 ; P. L., 347.)

This Act gives at least twenty days in which to file the appeal after it is taken, *i. e.*, until the next monthly return-day ; but if at that time twenty days shall not have elapsed from the time the appeal was perfected, the appellant is allowed until the next monthly return-day to file it in the prothonotary's office. *Machine Co.* v. *Rice*, 1 Del. Co. Rep., 63.

§ 1536. **Practice as to perfecting and filing appeal.** In *Long* v. *McCormick*, 1 W. N., 134 (1874), it was said " the practice directing the appeal to be filed to the return-day next ensuing the entry of judgment has always been to allow the defendant twenty days after judgment in which to perfect his appeal, and to file his appeal before the return-day next after the expiration of the twenty days."

If, however, the appeal be taken before the expiration of the twenty days, the transcript must be filed before the next return-day following the date of the appeal. *Smith* v. *Walker, Id.,* 415 (1875).

If the appeal is taken in twenty days, it need not be entered on the docket in the prothonotary's office within that time; the appeal is properly entered any time before return-day. *Beale* v. *Dougherty,* 3 Binn., 432 (1811).

§ 1537. *Computing the time within which appeal must be entered. Sleck* v. *King,* 3 Pa. St., 211 (1846). If judgment be given against defendant by default, and he afterward in due time has the justice fix a day for a hearing to show cause why the judgment should not be opened, and said judgment is confirmed, the time to appeal runs from the final decision and not from the original judgment.

In computing the time from which an appeal may be taken, the judgment-day is not included. In *Thomas* v. *Assn.,* 3 Phila., 425 (1859), Judge ALLISON said: " In *Agnew* v. *City,* 2 Phila., 340, this court, following the lead of *Thomas* v. *Afflick,* 16 Pa. St., 14, held that the day on which a judgment is entered is to be included in the computation of time for an appeal. *Thomas* v. *Afflick* expressly overruled *Gosweiler's Estate,* 3 Penn., 200, the court saying the rule of computation is to include the first and to exclude the last day. Upon the strength of a decision which we were bound to regard as an authority controlling us, the appeal in *Agnew* v. *City* was stricken off, because, counting the day on which judgment was entered, it was one day too late. *Barbier* v. *Chandler,* 17 Pa. St., 49, followed shortly after *Thomas* v. *Afflick,* and reannounced the same rule, in which case the court held the day of issuing, and also of return, were both to be counted in a summons issued by a justice of the peace. These two cases overthrew the law as it had previously been settled. *Sims* v. *Hampton,* 1 S. & R., 411 ; *Brown* v. *Brown,* 3 S. & R., 496 ; 3 Pa. Rep., 200. And it is but reasonable to suppose that the new rule thus settled by solemn adjudication was to be considered the established law of the land ; but in *Cromelien* v. *Brink,* 29 Pa. St., 524, we have the *last* opinion of the Supreme Court upon the point, which declares *Thomas* v. *Afflick* and *Barbier* v. *Chandler* were erroneously decided, and restores the old rule, excluding the first and including the last day. *Cromelien* v. *Brink,* therefore, requires us to say that *Agnew* v. *City* is no longer to be regarded as of authority in this court, and that the appeal in this case must be allowed."

If the twentieth day fall on Good Friday, the appeal may be perfected on the next succeeding secular day. *Linville* v. *Dalsam,* 5 W. N., 528 (1878).

Where an appeal is taken on a return-day, the party has until the next succeeding return-day to file it. *Dwire* v. *Weber*, 1 W. N., 64 (1874).

In Philadelphia County there are two return-days in September, but the filing of appeals is only to the next monthly return-day. *Hartranft* v. *Clarke*, 4 W. N., 543 (1877).

§ 1538. *Filing appeals* nunc pro tunc. Filing appeals *nunc pro tunc* is allowed only on good cause shown, as where a defendant has exercised due diligence and has been prevented from taking his appeal by absence from the county or sickness of the alderman, or by refusal of the latter to take bail or give defendant transcript : *Kear* v. *Rodgers*, 9 Phila., 525 (1872) ; *Nutz* v. *Barton, Id.*, 526 (1872) ; *Haines* v. *Hillary, Id.*, 526 (1872), or where the delay is due to a mistake or misapprehension of the party appealing. *Mc-Nulty* v. *McCarty*, 4 W. N., 478 (1877).

The appellant must not be guilty of neglect, or such right will be denied. *Hibbs* v. *Stines*, 8 Phila., 236 (1871).

Where an appeal was not filed in proper time, through the oversight of counsel, a rule to allow the appeal to be filed *nunc pro tunc* was granted. *Woods* v. *Brolasky*, 2 W. N., 198 (1875).

Where a party is misled by a magistrate as to taking an appeal, the appeal will be allowed *nunc pro tunc*. *Snyder* v. *Snyder*, 7 Phila., 391 (1870) ; *Kelly* v. *Gilmore*, 1 W. N., 73 (1874) ; *Moore* v. *Krier*, 2 W. N., 724 (1876) ; *Devine* v. *Boyle*, 4 W. N., 139 (1877).

But the misconduct of the magistrate must be official. Where defendant appeals, and the justice promises to file the transcript before the next term in the Common Pleas and neglects to do so, and the defendant subsequently files the appeal himself, the appeal will be stricken off. *Houk* v. *Knop*, 2 Watts, 72 (1833).

A similar ruling was made where the justice promised to make out and deliver the transcript to defendant's attorney, and made it out, but failed to deliver it as promised. *Sherwood* v. *M'Kinney*, 5 Whar., 435 (1840).

Ignorance of the law is no ground for allowing an appeal *nunc pro tunc*. *Uhler* v. *Ketcherra*, 1 W. N., 3 (1874) ; *Hepperd* v. *Van Horn*, 2 W. N., 67 (1876).

Where a transcript sur appeal has not been filed within the time required by the Act by reason of the neglect of the attorney, the court cannot permit it to be filed *nunc pro tunc*. *Ward* v. *Letzkus*, 31 W. N., 412 (1893).

Where an appeal is not properly perfected, and the fault is that of the appellant and not of counsel, the court will not interfere. *Uhler* v. *Ketcherra*, 1 W. N., 3 (1874).

A rule for leave to file an appeal *nunc pro tunc* is too late if execution has issued. *Dobson* v. *Fell*, 14 W. N., 456 (1884).

The Common Pleas, in its discretion, will allow an appeal after twenty days *nunc pro tunc*. *Rwy. Co.* v. *Boyle*, 29 W. N., 20 (1891).

§ 1539. *Rule to file an appeal* nunc pro tunc. As soon as you discover that your client has omitted to file his appeal, if the excuse be sufficient, prepare his affidavit of all the facts and present it to a judge, with the following rule indorsed :

A. B.   }
  v.   Common Pleas, No. .   Term, 1890. No. .
C. D. }

And now (date), on motion of E. F., plaintiff's (or defendant's) attorney, the court grant a rule to show cause why an appeal *nunc pro tunc* should not be filed in the above case.

Returnable (date), 10 A.M. Proceedings to stay.

Having obtained your allocatur, hand your papers to the court clerk, obtain from him a certificate of the granting of the rule, serve it upon the magistrate or justice, and notify the other side. Depositions should then be taken in order to establish your client's right to file his appeal *nunc pro tunc*. The rule is then argued.

§ 1540. **Quashing appeals.** If there be any defect or irregularity on the face of the record of the appeal, you should take a rule to show cause why the appeal should not be quashed. The following form may assist you :

A. B.   }
  v.   Common Pleas, No. .   Term, 1890. No. .
C. D. }

And now (date), on motion of E. F., attorney pro (defendant), the court grant a rule on (plaintiff) to show cause why the appeal in the above case should not be quashed, for the following reasons (state them).

Rule returnable (date), 10 A.M.

INDORSEMENT.

A. B.   }
  v.   Common Pleas, No. .   Term, 1890. No. .
C. D. }

Rule to show cause why appeal should not be quashed.

E. F.,
Attorney pro Defendant.

As this is a rule of course, you do not need the signature of a judge, nor need the rule be supported by affidavit.

Hand the rule to the court clerk ; notify the counsel on the other side, prepare your paper-books, and be ready to argue the case on the next current motion-list.

Where the Common Pleas grant a rule to amend an appeal by

filing an amended transcript, if the amended transcript be still defective, the appeal will be quashed. *Miles* v. *Tanner*, 3 P. & W., 95 (1831).

In *Carothers* v. *Cummings*, 63 Pa. St., 199 (1869), judgment was recovered before a magistrate in favor of plaintiff, and after the twenty days had expired defendant appealed. In due time the defendant entered a *non pros.* for want of a *narr.*, and three weeks subsequently the plaintiff moved to quash the appeal because not entered in proper time. The lower court discharged the rule to quash. The Supreme Court said : " We think the judgment of *non pros.* was not valid, and we think it should be reversed. This will leave the case in court, and, unless the court shall reconsider it, its decision on the motion to quash the case must go on to trial and to final judgment, when the failure to quash can be taken advantage of there. We do not mean to decide that the appeal is not good—matters of which we have no knowledge may possibly exist to render it good. We speak only by the record ; as that stands, the case was not in a situation to authorize the defendant to enter the *non pros.*

" Judgment of *non pros.* reversed and ordered to be stricken off, the case to stand to be proceeded in as if no such entry had been made."

The reporter states that the writ of error was taken to the order discharging the rule to quash. Judge THOMPSON says, in his opinion, that it was taken to the judgment of *non pros.*, and the decision supports his assertion.

§ 1541. *Waiver of right to quash by acquiescence.* A party waives his right to quash by acquiescence in an appeal, and this may be inferred from delay as well as other acts, *Canal Co.* v. *Loftus*, 71 Pa. St., 420 (1872) ; *e. g.*, if the defendant having appealed, the plaintiff files his statement before moving to quash. *Sleck* v. *King*, 3 Pa. St., 211 (1846). See also *Greenawalt* v. *Shannon*, 8 Pa. St., 465 (1848) ; *Hoffman* v. *Dawson*, 1 Jones, 280 (1849), where the motion to quash was denied because the award of arbitrators had been filed before the motion was made.

§ 1542. **Writ of error to dismissal of appeal.** If the appeal be dismissed, a writ of error lies. *Beale* v. *Dougherty*, 3 Binn., 432 (1811).

§ 1543. **Rule to strike off appeal.** If appeal be not filed within the prescribed time, the opposite party may enter a rule to show cause why the appeal should not be stricken off.

Proceed as under section 1540, relating to quashing appeals.

Unless the defendant is unavoidably prevented from entering his appeal before return-day, the appeal will be stricken off. *Wilson* v. *Hathaway*, 8 Phila., 235 (1871).

Where the appeal is defective, yet no injury is done to the other party's rights, the party may perfect his appeal. *Wormelsdorf* v. *Heifner*, 104 Pa. St., 1 (1883).

§ 1544. **If plaintiff appeal, he shall give defendant written notice.** The Philadelphia rule (Rule V., section 6 *a*) is as follows :

" In all cases of appeal by the plaintiff from the judgment of a magistrate the plaintiff shall serve a written notice of the appeal upon the defendant, stating the court, term, and number of the suit, and file an affidavit of such service ten days before taking a judgment by default." This was literally construed in *Howard* v. *Achuff*, 19 W. N., 334 (1887). Judgment for want of 'an appearance cannot be taken in a suit appealed from a magistrate. The first judgment by default would be for want of an affidavit of defense, to obtain which judgment you must comply with the above rule and prove service of your statement.

§ 1545. **Judgment by default on appeal.** The Philadelphia rule (Rule V., section 6) is as follows :

" In all cases of appeal by defendant from judgment of a magistrate where, on the calling of the case for trial, defendant does not appear to prosecute his appeal, and the plaintiff is 'present and ready for trial, the court may, on motion of plaintiff's attorney, affirm the judgment of the magistrate : *Provided*, that when there shall have been an award of arbitrators filed upon such appeal, judgment of affirmance of such award shall be entered, and when the award shall have been for a sum of money, the judgment shall be for that sum, together with the interest thereon from the day of filing the award, or the day named in the report."

Where a defendant appeals from the judgment of a magistrate, and in the Common Pleas the defendant does not appear and the judgment of the magistrate is affirmed, the defendant cannot, on a writ of error, object to the pleadings in the Common Pleas. *Elkinton* v. *Fennimore*, 13 Pa. St., 173 (1850).

§ 1546. **Pleadings on appeal.** When the appeal has been filed, the plaintiff's counsel must file his statement and serve a copy upon the defendant or his attorney. In Philadelphia, the subsequent steps are regulated by rule of court.

The rule in Philadelphia County (section 126 *e*) is as follows :

" In all cases of appeal from judgments of magistrates the pleadings and procedure shall be the same as in like causes commenced in court."

This rule was adopted subsequent to the Act of 1887. It would therefore seem clear that after the appeal has been filed the proceedings are under the Act of 1887.

In some of the county courts a leaning has been made toward the old practice of filing a *narr.* or a copy of the instrument sued on. In the absence of any decision by the Supreme Court upon this point, the better practice seems to be to file your statement in all cases and proceed under the Act of 1887.

A court rule providing that on an appeal from a justice an appearance shall be entered for appellee within a specified time is without force. *Jones* v. *Brown*, 1 Dist. Rep., 675 (1883).

If the plaintiff has appealed and is entitled to judgment for want of an affidavit of defense, before taking such judgment he must serve a notice of his appeal and of the statement upon defendant, as required by rule of court, section 1544.

If the defendant take a *certiorari*, he need not notify the plaintiff. *Walker* v. *Hopple*, 16 W. N., 495 (1885).

§ 1547. **Cause of action continues the same on appeal.** While the appeal and the proceedings in the Common Pleas as to the pleadings are *de novo*, the *cause* of action must continue the same. If the substance of the demand be identical with the proceedings before the justice, the plaintiff may join in his *narr.* a count in trover and conversion, the suit before the justice being upon a contract of bailment. *M'Cahan* v. *Hirst*, 7 Watts, 179 (1838). If the cause of action be the same, though there be a variance in the description of the instrument sued on, it is no ground for reversal on writ of error. *Bechtol* v. *Cobaugh*, 10 S. & R., 122 (1823). In *Esher* v. *Flagler*, 17 S. & R., 141 (1827), the suit before the justice was in trespass, but on appeal the declaration was in assumpsit. The Supreme Court held, where the declaration and the transcript agree in substance, variances in form would be disregarded. In *Kraft* v. *Gilchrist*, 31 Pa. St., 470 (1858), an action of debt was brought before the justice, and on appeal the plaintiff was allowed to declare in trover. In *Steckel* v. *Weber*, 20 Pa. St., 435 (1853), LEWIS, J., said : " Where the parties have voluntarily tried an action of tort under pleadings applicable only to actions on contracts, it is a waiver of all objections to the form of the action, and also to any variance between the form of the proceeding before the justice and that tried on appeal in the Common Pleas."

An action of debt was commenced before a justice and appealed to the Common Pleas. The form of action should have been in tort, but the court charged that under the evidence in the case the action of debt might be sustained. There was no formal *narr.* filed. The Supreme Court held that the case having been tried on its merits, the form of action had prejudiced neither party. *Weiler* v. *Kershner*, 109 Pa. St., 219 (1885).

§ 1548. **The demand, on appeal, cannot be increased.** While it is true that on appeal from the judgment of a justice, the proceedings are *de novo*, it is well settled that the demand cannot be increased beyond the limit of the justice's jurisdiction, except so far as to embrace the interest which has accrued since the institution of suit.

It is not competent for the plaintiff to cure the defect by remitting part of the verdict, or for the court to determine that $100 was the proper amount of damages for which judgment should be entered. *Linton* v. *Vogle*, 1 Pennypacker, 275 (1881). A similar ruling was made in *Schlecht* v. *Restein*, 3 W. N., 95 (1876). *Contra, Darrah* v. *Warnock*, 1 P. & W., 21 (1829), where the plaintiff was allowed to remit the excess at the bar of the Supreme Court.

Under the old practice, the parties on appeal could go to trial without pleadings. *Cunningham* v. *McCue*, 31 Pa. St., 469 (1858).

§ 1549. **When statement must be filed, and judgment of non pros.** In Philadelphia County, the plaintiff has *twelve months from the return-day* to which the appeal was entered in which to file his *narr.* or statement, and not twelve months from the *first day of the term* in which the appeal is entered. *Ellis* v. *Pennington*, 2 W. N., 29 (1875).

The Philadelphia rule is as follows :

"Unless a declaration be filed within twelve months from the return-day * * * to which an appeal is entered, a *non pros.* shall be entered by the prothonotary as a matter of course, unless the parties otherwise agree in writing filed, or the court, upon cause shown, shall extend the time."

In *Simons* v. *Kutz*, 1 W. N., 553 (1874), the defendant took an appeal. It was held that he should give notice to the plaintiff to elect to file a declaration, or to treat the transcript as such before a judgment of *non pros.* is entered. But the contrary was decided in *Ellis* v. *Pennington*, 2 W. N., 29 ; *Paris* v. *Hein*, 6 *Id.*, 124 ; *Snyder* v. *Hensel*, 7 *Id.*, 280.

Where plaintiff, by writing filed, elects to treat his transcript as a *narr.*, but does not notify defendant, judgment of *non pros.* is void. *Govett* v. *Wiley*, 13 W. N., 98 (1883).

A *non pros.* suffered because of change of counsel, was taken off in *Whittaker* v. *Van Arsdalen*, 2 W. N., 98 (1875).

In *Ellis* v. *Donaghy*, 6 W. N., 541 (1879), a *non pros.* was entered more than a year after the action was commenced. On the same day a *narr.* and a rule to plead were filed. The plaintiff swore that at the time his *narr.* was filed there was no judgment of *non pros.* entered on the docket. The *non pros.* was stricken off.

§ 1550. **What should be averred in the statement.** The declaration or statement should bring the case within the jurisdiction of the justice. It has been ruled that the plaintiff may lay his damages at a sum over $100, but that on the trial the evidence must show jurisdiction by the magistrate.

Under the later cases of *Linton* v. *Vogle*, 1 Penny., 275 (1881) ; *Miller* v. *Boyd*, 12 W. N., 353 (1882) ; *Rech* v. *Clemm*, 13 *Id.*, 46 (1883), the declaration should bring the case within the jurisdiction of the justice, and this is the better practice.

Under the old mode of pleading, the *narr.* containing the common counts in assumpsit could lay the damages at $1000 if they were restricted by the bill of particulars filed, showing the claim to be within the justice's jurisdiction.

On appeal in trover neither party is bound by the amount of damages recovered before the justice. *Miller* v. *Crisswell*, 3 Pa. St., 449 (1846).

For the general rules concerning statements, etc., see the Chapters on Assumpsit and on Statements.

For forms of Statements, see the Appendix.

§ 1551. **Amendment on appeals from justices.** Act of 20 March, 1810, section 4 (5 Sm., 164), provided that

"Upon any such appeal from the decision, determination, or order of justices of the peace to the Court of Common Pleas * * * in any county, the cause shall be decided in such court on its facts and merits only ; and no deficiency of form or substance in the record or proceedings returned, nor any mistake in the form or name of the action, shall prejudice either party in the court to which the appeal shall be made."

In *Graham* v. *Vandalore*, 2 Watts, 131 (1833), suit was brought in the name of A., agent for B., against G. In the Common Pleas the action was brought in the name of B. *Held*, that the variance was immaterial.

Where a justice makes an error in the name of a firm as plaintiffs, an amendment will be allowed on appeal. *Bratton* v. *Seymour*, 4 W., 329 (1835).

Action brought before justice in name of treasurer of corporation ; on appeal names of trustees may be substituted. *Comfort* v. *Leland*, 3 Wharton, 81 (1837).

Where a suit is not set out by justice with technical precision, it is the duty of the court, on appeal, to put it in form, and the name of an omitted partner as defendant may be introduced on the record before the jury is sworn. ROGERS, J.: "If we were to hold justices to strict technical rules, it would greatly impair the usefulness of this tribunal, and for this reason we have been very liberal in the allowance of amendments. *Johnston* v. *Fessler*, 7 W., 48 (1838).

In *Megargell* v. *Coal Co.*, 8 W. & S., 342 (1845), it was held that if one sues for a penalty as a common informer, an amendment to the declaration that he sues as well for himself as for the treasurer of the county may be permitted.

On an appeal, the names of the parties may be transposed and changed to adapt the legal form to the merits. *Giffen* v. *Township*, 4 W. & S., 327 (1842); *Eysler* v. *Rineman*, 11 Pa. St., 147 (1849).

A suit before a justice was brought by "A." On appeal, this was amended to "A. and B., late trading as A.," to the use of A. *Gue* v. *Kline*, 13 Pa. St., 60 (1850).

A suit before a justice was brought by "A. and B., trading as B. & Co." v. S. & Co." On appeal, leave was obtained by plaintiff to amend by adding the name of "C., trustee of S. & Co.," defendant. *Seitz* v. *Buffam*, 14 Pa. St., 69 (1850).

In *Kelly* v. *Eichman*, 3 Whar., 419 (1838), an action of assumpsit was brought before the justice in the names of A. and B. (for the use of A.), plaintiffs, against C.

On appeal, it was sought to amend by striking out B., as the contract was with A. The amendment was not allowed. A similar ruling had been made in *Stehley* v. *Harp*, 5 S. & R., 544 (1819).

The court may permit an amendment to the statement at any time during the progress of the cause.

§ 1552. **The judgment of a justice cannot be attacked collaterally except for collusion.** The plaintiff may compel the production of the justice's docket; but, unless this is done, the transcript has the same force as the original and imports absolute verity. *Baird* v. *Campbell*, 4 W. & S., 192 (1842).

§ 1553. *Set-off.* The defendant may offer as a set-off the transcript of a judgment obtained by him against the plaintiff. *O'Neil* v. *Whitecar*, 1 Phila., 446 (1854).

In *Cook* v. *Shirley*, 4 W. N., 560 (1877), it was decided that defendant, on appeal, may plead a set-off, although he made no such claim before the magistrate. A similar ruling was made in *Tate* v. *Tate*, 2 Grant, 150 (1858).

If a justice has not jurisdiction of a demand sought to be used as a set-off, then the Common Pleas, on appeal, cannot entertain the set-off. The form is changed by the appeal, but the cause of action remains the same. *Walden* v. *Berry*, 48 Pa. St., 456 (1865); *Deihm* v. *Snell*, 119 Pa. St., 317 (1888).

A similar ruling was made in *Holden* v. *Wiggins*, 3 P. & W., 469 (1832). See § 1347 *et seq.*

§ 1554. **Cases in which the judgment of a justice bars a subsequent proceedings for the same cause of action.** Where judgment against a plaintiff is rendered by a justice, and plaintiff appeals and discon_ tinues, the judgment before the justice is a bar to any other suit for the same cause of action. *Rose* v. *Turnpike Company*, 3 Watts, 46 (1834).

If a justice erroneously renders judgment against the plaintiff for want of jurisdiction, and the judgment is not appealed from, it is binding on the plaintiff and a bar to another suit for the same cause of action before another justice. *Kase* v. *Best*, 15 Pa. St., 101 (1850).

Where a justice decides in proceedings under the Act of April 3, 1830, that there is no rent in arrear, and that the relation of land_ lord and tenant does not exist, his judgment, unreversed and unappealed from, is a bar to any subsequent proceedings brought for the same purpose before another justice. *Marsteller* v. *Marsteller*, 25 W. N., 421 (1890).

If the plaintiff obtain judgment before a justice, and subsequently appeals to the Common Pleas and afterward discontinues, he cannot proceed upon the judgment given by the justice. *Felton* v. *Weyman*, 10 Pa. St., 70 (1848).

§ 1555. **Voluntary non-suit not a bar.** If the plaintiff, on appeal, suffers a voluntary non-suit on account of lack of jurisdiction of the justice, this does not bar a subsequent action in the Common Pleas. *Township* v. *Gardner*, 16 W. N., 348 (1885). A similar ruling was made where the plaintiff abandoned his first action before the justice. *McCulloch* v. *Logan*, 3 W. N., 88 (1876).

§ 1556. **Costs.** *Plaintiff may lose costs if he sue in Common Pleas when a justice has jurisdiction.*

If suit be brought for any debt or debts, demand or demands in any other manner than is directed by this Act, and the verdict or judgment, exclusive of costs, shall not amount to more than one hundred dollars, unless an affidavit be filed in the prothonotary's office before the issuing of the writ of summons or *capias*, setting forth that he, she, or they did truly believe the debt due or damages sustained exceeded the sum of one hundred dollars, the costs in such suit shall not be recovered. (Act March 20, 1810, section 26 ; 5 Sm., 161.)

In *Graban* v. *Hirshfield*, 47 Leg. Int., 278 (1890), an action was brought in the Common Pleas for $140 for rent ; the plaintiff, however, claimed only thirty dollars before the jury, as he had relet the premises to another tenant soon after the defendant's removal.

GORDON, J.: " The sums received by the plaintiff from the re-letting certainly stand in no better position than direct payments on account of the claim, and a reduction below the jurisdictional amount from payments has been frequently held to bar costs."

Judgment without costs.

The usual practice under this Act is to file your *præcipe* with an affidavit that the debt or damage exceeds $100, as follows :

A. B.   C. P. No. .
    v.   Term, 1896.
C. D.   No. .
SIR :
Issue summons assumpsit, returnable *sec. leg.*

E. F.,
Atty. for Plaintiff.
(Date.)

To Prothonotary C. P.

City and County of Philadelphia, *ss.*

A. B., the above-named plaintiff, being duly sworn according to law, deposes and says that he truly believes that the debt due him by the defendant above named (or the damage sustained by him) for the recovery of which this suit is brought, exceeds the sum of one hundred dollars.

Sworn to and subscribed before me, }
  this   day of   , 1896. }
                             A. B.

§ 1557. *If less than $100 recovered in Common Pleas by reason of set-off.* If less than $100 is recovered in the Common Pleas on a suit by reason of a set-off, the plaintiff shall have his costs. *Spear* v. *Jamieson*, 2 S. & R., 530 (1816); *Sadler* v. *Slobaugh*, 3 *Id.*, 388 (1817); *Bartram* v. *McKee*, 1 W., 39 (1832); *Munich* v. *Id.*, 38 Pa. St., 378 (1859).

If, however, it do not appear that the plaintiff's claim was reduced because of a set-off, costs will be imposed on plaintiff. *Stewart* v. *Mitchel*, 13 S. & R., 287 (1825); *Rogers* v. *Ratcliffe*, 23 Pa. St., 184 (1854); *Iron Co.* v. *Rhule*, 53 Pa. St., 93 (1866).

§ 1558. *Notice of special matter will bring set-off on record.* Where no affidavit has been filed, under the plea of payment, the plaintiff should take a rule on defendant to give notice of special matter, in order to bring the defense on the record and qualify the plea by showing whether set-off or direct payment was the defense. *Iron Co.* v. *Rhule*, 53 Pa. St., 93 (1866).

§ 1559. *Costs on appeal to abide the event of the suit.*

Costs on appeal * * * from the judgment of justices * * * shall abide the event of the suit, and be paid by the unsuccessful party, as in other cases : *Provided*, that if the plaintiff be the appellant, he shall pay all costs which may accrue on the appeal if, in the event of the suit, he shall not recover a greater sum or a more favorable judgment than was rendered by the justice. (Act April 9, 1833, section 1; P. L., 480.)

The statute of 22 and 23 Car. II., c. 9, which provides that if the jury find the damages in certain suits to be under the value of 40 *s.*, the plaintiff shall not recover more costs of suit than the damages so found shall amount to, although in force in Pennsylvania, only refers to suits originally brought in the Common Pleas. Judgments before justices are governed by the Acts of March 22, 1814, and April 9, 1833, which latter Act provides that the costs on appeal shall abide the result of the suit and be paid by the unsuccessful party. *Knappenberger* v. *Roth*, 32 W. N., 181 (1893), following *King* v. *Boyler*, 31 Pa. St., 424 (1858).

§ 1560. *Costs in trespass and trover.* The provision that costs, on appeal, shall abide the result of the suit and be paid by the unsuccesful party, includes appeal in trespass and trover. *King* v. *Boyles*, 31 Pa. St., 424 (1858).

In this case the plaintiff obtained a judgment for thirty-five dollars before a justice. The defendant appealed. The case was tried by arbitrators, who found·that there was no cause of action. The Common Pleas awarded the plaintiff ten cents. *Held*, that he was entitled to full costs.

§ 1561. *In the following cases plaintiff entitled to costs.* If the plaintiff recover the same amount on appeal as before the justice, he is entitled to costs. *Dearth* v. *Laughlin*, 16 S. & R., 296 (1827); *Johnston* v. *Perkins*, 1 P. & W., 23 (1829); see *Barker* v. *Mc-Creary*, 66 Pa. St., 162 (1870).

If plaintiff appeal from a judgment against him, and recovers, he is entitled to a judgment with full costs. *Adams* v. *M'Ilheny*, 1 Watts, 53 (1832).

If, upon appeal, the plaintiff recovers a more favorable judgment than before the justice, though there is an intermediate award of arbitrators for a greater amount than the judgment, he is entitled to costs. *Newhouse* v. *Kelly*, 5 Watts, 508 (1836).

In case the defendant appeal and succeeds in reducing the plaintiff's judgment, plaintiff is nevertheless entitled to costs. *Lindsay* v. *Corah*, 7 Watts, 235 (1838).

If a defendant appeals from an award in favor of the plaintiff, and the plaintiff recovers more than the award, but less than such amount with interest, he is allowed costs. *Haines* v. *Moorhead*, 2 Pa. St., 65 (1845).

§ 1562. *When defendant entitled to costs.* Where separate suits are brought before a justice, and one of the defendants appeals, and on the trial, under the plea of set-off, interposes his judgment before the justice and obtains a verdict in his favor, he is not entitled to his costs. *Groff* v. *Ressler's Admr.*, 27 Pa. St., 71 (1856).

If plaintiff recovers the same amount on an award of arbitrators in the Common Pleas as before the justice, and defendant appeals therefrom and plaintiff is non-suited, the defendant is entitled to costs. *Flick* v. *Boucher*, 16 S. & R., 373 (1827).

If judgment before a justice is given in favor of defendant in a certain amount, and he appeal and recover a verdict of like amount, he is entitled to costs. *Holman* v. *Fesler*, 7 W. & S., 313 (1844).

If, on appeal from the judgment of a justice in favor of defendant, the matter is submitted to arbitrators, who find for plaintiff, and defendant appeals therefrom and obtains a verdict, the costs are imposed on plaintiff. *Addison* v. *Hampson*, 6 Pa. St., 463 (1847).

If defendant obtains judgment before a justice and on plaintiff's appeal the award of arbitrators is "no cause of action," neither party is entitled to costs. *Hoffman* v. *Slosson*, 2 W. & S., 36 (1841).

§ 1563. *Costs where defendant offers to confess judgment for an admitted amount.*

If the defendant on the trial of the cause or before an appeal is taken shall offer to give the plaintiff a judgment for the amount which the defendant shall admit to be due (which offer it shall be the duty of the justice * * * to enter on the record), and if the plaintiff or his agent shall not accept such offer, then and in that case, if the defendant shall appeal, the plaintiff shall pay all the costs which shall accrue on the appeal, if he shall not in the event of the suit recover a greater amount than that for which the defendant offered to give a judgment, and in both cases the defendant's bill shall be taxed and paid by the plaintiff in the same manner as if a judgment had been rendered in court for the defendant. (Act April 9, 1833, section 1; P. L., 480.)

To exempt a defendant from the payment of costs if he intends to rely on the ground of a tender, he should plead the tender before the justice, have it entered on the docket, offer to pay and produce the money before the plaintiff, and on the appeal put in the plea of tender of the money. *Seibert* v. *Kline*, 1 Pa. St., 38 (1845).

In order to escape liability for costs the defendant must tender the amount of the debt, with interest and costs. *McDowell* v. *Glass*, 4 Watts, 389 (1835).

A tender of a sum certain implies that interest is to be added. *Park* v. *Sweeny*, 39 Pa. St., 111 (1861).

An offer to confess judgment for the proper amount should accompany the tender. *Dickerson* v. *Anderson*, 4 Whar., 78 (1838).

§ 1564. *Judgment confessed by agent.* In an action before a justice, an offer to confess judgment can be made by an agent of defendant. *Randall* v. *Wait*, 48 Pa. St., 127 (1864).

§ 1565. *Recovery of sum less than offer.* If, after plaintiff has had judgment rendered in his favor before a justice, defendant makes an offer to confess judgment for a less amount, which offer is rejected, and plaintiff, on the appeal, recovers a less sum than the offer, the defendant is entitled to costs. *Magill* v. *Tomer*, 6 W., 494 (1837).

Where such offer is made at the hearing, and plaintiff, on appeal, recovers less than the offer, the defendant is entitled to costs. *Gardner* v. *Davis*, 15 Pa. St., 41 (1850).

§ 1566. *If judgment increased in Common Pleas.* If the justice give judgment for a smaller amount than the offer, and plaintiff, on appeal, recovers more than the judgment, but less than the offer, the plaintiff is entitled to costs. *McMaster* v. *Rupp*, 22 Pa. St., 298 (1853).

§ 1567. *Judgment cannot be tendered after appeal.* An offer to confess judgment after an appeal is taken is too late. *Bogart* v. *Rathbone*, 1 Pa. St., 188 (1845).

§ 1568. *Counsel fee.* In *Shuey* v. *Bitner*, 3 W. & S., 275 (1842), ROGERS, J., said : " It seems to have been the practice in some counties, under the Act of the 20th of March, 1810, to charge a counsel fee of four dollars in addition to a judgment fee, and fifty cents per day for every day the party attended on the appeal. Without deciding on the propriety of this construction, we are of opinion that since the Act of 1833 there is no foundation for any such practice. * * * The costs are made to bide the event of the suit without regard to the amount recovered, or whether the judgment may or may not be more favorable to the party entering the appeal."

§ 1569. *Constable's fee and mileage.* Where a constable serves a number of writs at the request of a single plaintiff against a number of defendants, he may recover, in addition to his fee for service, mileage in each case at six cents per mile. *McGee* v. *Dillon*, 103 Pa. St., 433 (1883).

§ 1570. *Costs to be paid before delivery of transcript—Act of 1893 regulating costs.*

Justices of the peace for the counties of Centre, Blair, Lehigh, Clinton, Schuylkill, Allegheny, Indiana, Northampton, Luzerne, Lebanon, Berks, Perry, Mifflin, and York may demand and receive from the appellant and from the plaintiff desiring a transcript for entering in the Common Pleas, or other transcripts, in any case tried before them, before giving a transcript of appeal or other transcript, all costs that may have accrued in the said action : *Provided,* that payment of costs in the first instance by the appellant or plaintiff shall not debar him of the right to receive the same from the appellee or defendant in the same manner and to the same extent as provided in the Act of April 9, 1833 : *And provided further,* that any party to suits shall have the right to appeal and demand transcripts without said payment of costs upon making and filing an affidavit with the justice of his inability to pay such costs. (Act of March 2, 1868, section 1 ; P. L., 257.)

The Act of June 24, 1885, extends these provisions throughout the State, and is as follows :

In all cases of appeal from the judgment of an alderman or a justice of the peace, the said alderman or justice shall be entitled to demand and receive from the appellant the costs in the case before the making and delivery of the transcripts for said appeal ; and if the appellant shall finally recover judgment in the case appealed, he shall be entitled to receive and collect from the adverse party the costs so as aforesaid paid on appeal. (Act of June 24, 1885, section 1; P. L., 159.)

Alderman and justices of the peace shall have the same right to demand and receive the costs as aforesaid before issuing a transcript of a judgment recovered before them for entry in the Court of Common Pleas, or other purpose ; and the party paying the same shall be entitled to recover them from the party legally liable to pay the same : *Provided, however,* that any party to a suit before an alderman or justice of the peace shall have the right to appeal and demand and receive transcripts without payment of costs as hereinbefore provided, on their making and filing with the alderman or justice of the peace an affidavit that they are unable through poverty to pay said costs. (*Id.*, section 2; P. L., 159.)

On taking an appeal from a justice of the peace, the party appealing must pay all costs accrued before he shall be entitled to receive his transcript. *Sunday* v. *Snayberger,* 4 Dist. Rep., 296 (1895).

The Act of May 23, 1893 (P. L., 117), regulating and establishing the fees to be charged by justices of the peace, aldermen, magistrates, and constables, so far as it relates to persons who come into office subsequent to the passage of the Act, is constitutional. *Cornell* v. *Beaver Co.,* 3 Dist. Rep., 783 (1894). It repeals the Act of April 2, 1868 (P. L., 3), *Fraim* v. *Lancaster,* 171 Pa. St., 436 (1895).

§ 1571. *Act of* 1885 *applies to Philadelphia.* The Act of June 24, 1885, requiring costs to be prepaid on appeals, applies to cases before magistrates in Philadelphia. *Kelly* v. *Royal,* 46 Leg. Int., 108 (1889).

§ 1572. **Dockets of Justices.** *When justice to deliver his docket, etc.—Executors of justice—If justice interested—If he abscond.*

Where a justice resigns, or is removed from office, or removes from his proper district or county, it shall be his duty to deliver his docket, with all the notes, bonds, and other papers in his possession concerning any judgment or suit entered thereon, to the neighboring justice of the district.

In cases of death, absconding, voluntary or compulsory absence of a justice from his proper place of abode, such duty shall devolve on his legal representatives.

The justice to whom the docket is delivered shall proceed in the same manner and with like effect as the original justice might have done.

If such justice shall be interested in the suit or judgment, such suit or judgment shall be proceeded in by another justice of the proper county, to whom a transcript shall be furnished, as well as the original docket, if required.

If the justice shall abscond or depart from the district without delivering his docket and papers to some justice, it shall be the duty of the person in whose possession the same may be left or found to make a delivery thereof as aforesaid, under the penalty of one hundred dollars.

If the said docket and papers shall not be left in the particular custody of any person, it shall be the duty of any disinterested justice to take possession thereof, and the like proceedings shall be had upon the suits and judgments contained in the said docket as provided for when the docket is properly delivered. (Act February 20, 1833, section 1; P. L., 52.)

§ 1573. *Temporary absence of justice.*

In case of the temporary absence of any justice, it shall be lawful for him, previous to his departure, to deposit his docket and all papers connected with any judgment rendered by him with the nearest justice in the district, who is authorized to issue executions as if the judgments had been originally rendered by him. (Act February 20, 1833, section 2; P. L., 52.)

§ 1574. *On expiration of term, docket to be delivered.*

Every justice elected under this Act shall, on the expiration of his term of office, deliver over his docket and like papers to whomever is elected and commissioned to succeed him. (Act June 21, 1839, section 10; P. L., 379.)

This Act was extended by the Act April 21, 1846, section 6 (P. L., 434), which provided:

That the foregoing Act shall be deemed and construed to extend to all cases of succession in office, whether by death, resignation, removal, or otherwise. In case of the decease of any justice, the delivery shall be made by his legal representative to the person who may be elected to succeed him.

§ 1575. *Proceedings to enforce delivery.* If the term of office of the justice has expired, and he do not deliver his docket to his successor, he cannot be compelled to do so by an order of court upon petition and rule to show cause. *In re Baker*, 44 Pa. St., 440 (1863).

§ 1576. *Removal of justice out of district.*

Every person who has been a justice and has removed or shall remove out of the district for which he was commissioned, shall, upon demand made by any person, deliver, or cause to be delivered, his dockets and all official records to the nearest justice.

If any person shall fail, for twenty days, to comply with the provisions of this section, he shall forfeit and pay one hundred dollars, to be recovered by action of debt for the use of any person who may sue for the same.

He may be compelled to deliver such docket and records by a decree and attachment issued from the Common Pleas or any judge thereof in vacation on application being made therefor by any person. Said court or any judge thereof in vacation shall have power to enforce a delivery of such docket and records against any person in possession of the same, and being about to remove out of the State, without making the delivery thereof; and the same proceedings are authorized to compel the delivery of justice's docket in the hands of any other person who has removed, or may remove, or be about to remove, out of the proper district where such dockets belong. (Act April 21, 1846, section 4; P. L., 434.)

§ 1577. *Lost or destroyed dockets.*

Where dockets shall have been destroyed or lost, it shall be lawful for any person or persons interested in any action pending or judgment had, and who desire to have the same supplied, to apply to such justice, or their successors in office, or to any justice in any county in which the defendant or defendants in such proceedings may reside, by petition setting forth the proceedings to be supplied and verified by affidavit; whereupon the justice shall issue a precept, in the nature of a writ of summons, which shall be served as in other cases requiring the defendant in such action or judgment, or his representatives, to appear before such justice on a day certain to be named in said writ, not less than five nor more than eight days from the issuing thereof, and show cause why the prayer of the petitioner should not be granted.

In all cases where the facts set forth in such petition shall be denied, it shall be the duty of such justice to hear the parties and receive testimony as in other cases, as well his own testimony upon affidavit as the testimony of others. Upon the hearing thereof, if the said justice shall be of opinion that the facts alleged in such petition are true, or in case such facts be not denied, he shall order the said proceedings be supplied, and thereupon enter the same upon his docket; which said entries shall have the same force and effect as if the original record had not been lost or destroyed, and either party may have his remedy by appeal or *certiorari*. (Act April 30, 1850, section 1; P. L., 640; and Act of June 11, 1879; P. L., 151.)

§ 1578. *Civil and Criminal docket to be kept—Fees to be noted—All costs, fines, etc., to be entered in a day-book.*

Each magistrate in Philadelphia shall keep a civil and criminal docket in which shall be entered daily all proceedings of said court, and it shall be the duty of the magistrate receiving any costs, fees, fines, penalties, or other moneys to note the same in the margin of the proper docket opposite to the entry of the case in respect to which the same is received, with date and name of person from whom received. Said docket shall be open to proper inspection.

Each magistrate shall also keep a day-book in which he shall enter all costs, fees, fines, and penalties collected by him, with date and the person from whom and purpose for which received, and the time and manner in which the same is disposed of. (Act February 5, 1875, section 11; P. L., 56.)

§ 1579. Suits against Justices. *Notice.*

No writ shall be sued out against, nor any copy of any process shall be served on, any justice for anything done by him in the execution of his office until notice in writing of such intended writ or process shall have been delivered to him or left at the usual place of his abode by the party or his attorney or agent who intends to sue or cause the same to be sued out or served, at least thirty days before suing out or service of the same.

Such notice shall clearly and explicitly set forth the cause of action which the party claims to have against the justice. On the back of which notice shall be indorsed the name of such attorney or agent, together with the place of his abode. (Act March 21, 1772, section 1; 1 Sm., 364.)

In computing the thirty days, the first day, or day of service, is included; the last day is excluded. *Thomas* v. *Afflick*, 16 Pa. St., 14 (1851). See, however, Act of June 20, 1883 (P. L., 136). § 1580.

FORM OF NOTICE.

(Date.)

To L. M., Justice of the Peace for   County.

SIR : According to the provision of the Act of Assembly, approved March 21, 1772, section 1 (1 Sm., 364), you are hereby notified that if you do not tender sufficient amends within thirty days from above date, I will bring an action against you in the Court of Common Pleas in and for the county of   for the following causes : (here set forth your grievances) by reason of all which illegal and oppressive conduct I have sustained material injury and damage.

Very respectfully yours,

A. B.

§ 1581. *Indorsement of notice.*

A. B.
v.
L. M., Justice of the Peace.
Notice.
E. F.
(Address).
Attorney pro A. B.
(Date).

§ 1582. *Requisites of notice.* The notice should indicate the cause of action with reasonable precision.

It should identify the injury complained of and sought to be redressed.

It should set forth the name of the attorney or agent, with the place of his abode, on the indorsement of the notice. The residence of the attorney need not be in the county where the justice has his office.

If the name of the attorney be not so indorsed, the plaintiff must give his place of abode.

Two or more penalties may be included in the same notice.

If the proposed suit be for taking illegal fees, the notice should state for what act or service the fee was charged, what the legal fee, if any, was, the excess of the illegal over the legal fee, etc.

In an action against a justice of the peace to recover a penalty, under the Act of 1772, for taking illegal fees, the notice must set forth clearly and explicitly the cause of action and should refer to the statute or claim a penalty. *McClelland* v. *Semmens*, 1 Dist. Rep., 356 (1892).

The Act of May 23, 1893 (P. L., 117), repeals the Act of February 3, 1865 (P. L., 92), and inasmuch as it makes no provision for a penalty against a justice of the peace for taking illegal fees, the only remedy is by indictment. *Schultzman* v. *McCarthy*, 5 Dist. Rep., 10 (1895). See § 1595.

§ 1583. *What the notice need not state.* The notice need not state the kind of writ upon which suit will be commenced nor the kind of action.

§ 1584. *Declaration.* The declaration must conform to the notice when suit is instituted in the Common Pleas. *Apple* v. *Rambo*, 13 Pa. St., 9 (1849).

§ 1585. *Amends may be tendered.*

Any justice within thirty days after notice given may tender amends to the party complaining or his agent or attorney.

If it be not accepted, such justice may plead such tender in bar to any action brought against him grounded on such writ or process, together with the plea of not guilty, and any other plea with leave of the court.

If upon issue joined the jury shall find the amends tendered to have been sufficient, then they shall give a verdict for defendant, and in such case, if the plaintiff is non-suited or discontinues his action, or in case judgment shall be given for defendant upon demurrer, such justice shall be entitled to the costs as if he had pleaded the general issue only.

If the jury find no amends were tendered, or that the same were insufficient and against the defendant on other plea or pleas, then they shall give verdict for the plaintiff and such damages as they shall think proper, which he shall recover with costs. (Act of March 21, 1772, section 2; 1 Sm., 364.)

Where an Act gives a penalty to the party aggrieved no sum of money short of the penalty could be sufficient amends. *Lowrie* v. *Verner*, 3 Watts, 318 (1834).

§ 1586. *Amends may be paid into court.*

If the justice shall neglect to tender amends or tender insufficient amends, before the action is brought, he may, by leave of court, at any time before issue joined, pay into court such sum of money as he shall see fit; whereupon such proceedings, orders, and judgments shall be made by such court as in other actions where defendant pays money into court. (Act of March 21, 1772, section 4; 1 Sm., 364.)

§ 1587. *Plaintiff must prove notice was given to justice.*

A plaintiff shall not recover a verdict against a justice unless it is proved upon the trial that notice was given as aforesaid; in default thereof, such justice shall recover a verdict and costs as aforesaid. (*Id.*, section 3.)

Proof may be made by producing the witness who served the notice and having him state, under oath, his mode of service.

The plaintiff cannot prove service by a witness who heard the notice read in defendant's presence, unless he can identify the paper and specify the day. *Minor* v. *Neal*, 1 Pa. St., 403 (1845).

§ 1588. *Plaintiff's evidence limited to the facts in notice.*

No evidence shall be permitted to be given by plaintiff except such as is contained in the notice. (*Id.*, section 5.)

§ 1589. *Limitation in suits against justice or constable.*

No action shall be brought against any justice for anything done in the execution of his office, or against any constable, or other officer, or persons acting as aforesaid, unless commenced within six months after the Act committed. (*Id.*, section 7.)

§ 1590. *Complaints against justices.*

On complaint made in writing, signed by at least twenty of the taxable inhabitants of any township or county, against any justice residing therein, the chief justice or any other of the justices of the Supreme Court, or the president or any associate judge of any of the Courts of Common Pleas, shall issue process to any constable commanding him to summon the said justice so complained of to appear before him on some certain day, which shall not be more than ten nor less than five days from the date of such process, and also to issue compulsory process to compel the attendance, as well of the witnesses named by the complainants as those whom such justice shall require in his behalf. On the day appointed for hearing the said judge shall proceed to examine, on oath or affirmation, all such witnesses as may appear, and shall fairly, carefully, and impartially write down all depositions, cross-examinations, and interrogatories as aforesaid taken, and shall thereupon seal up and transmit the same to the secretary of the Commonwealth, who shall lay them before the legislature. (Act January 14, 1804, section 1; 4 Sm., 107.)

§ 1591. *How costs of complaint against justice to be paid.*

The judge shall transmit a certified schedule or list of the names of the witnesses and the time they respectively attended, together with the account of the costs upon each process served by the constable, to the commissioners of the county; and the expense of such attendance and service, together with all necessary expenses arising under the provisions of this Act, shall be paid out of the moneys raised for the use of the proper county in which such justice resides, upon warrants drawn by the commissioners of the county upon the county treasurer. (*Id.*, section 2.)

§ 1592. *Proceedings against a justice who collects a judgment and refuses to pay over.*

Where a justice shall receive the amount of a judgment rendered by him, or any part thereof, and shall refuse to pay the same over to the plaintiff or his agent or the person to whom it is owing, such refusal shall be a misdemeanor in office.

Besides the remedy for such misdemeanor, the party may petition the Court of Common Pleas of the proper county where the justice resides, setting forth the refusal of the justice to pay over the moneys by him collected. The court shall take immediate order therein, by directing a notice to issue, directed to the justice, returnable forthwith or at such certain day as will suit the convenience of the court, setting forth the contents of the petition.

On the return of the said notice and due proof of the service thereof, if the said justice appears in pursuance of the notice and admits the facts set forth in the petition, or shall neglect or refuse to appear, in either case the court shall enter judgment for the amount so retained by the justice, with interest from the receipt thereof and four dollars to the party aggrieved, besides costs.

Should the facts be disputed by the justice, the court shall, upon his appearance, form an issue, and judgment entered on the verdict of the jury shall be final and conclusive, and execution shall issue forthwith without stay of execution. The court shall decree as to the costs of such issue as to right and justice shall appertain. (Act March 28, 1820, section 8 ; 7 Sm., 310.)

§ 1593. Justices shall give bonds.

Justices and aldermen shall give bond before entering upon the performance of their duties in not less than $500, nor more than $3000, as the Court of Common Pleas or one of the judges thereof in vacation may direct, with one or more sufficient securities, unless the person elected be possessed of a sufficient freehold estate.

Said bond shall be in the name of the Commonwealth, with conditions for the faithful application of all moneys that come into his hands officially. No surety shall be liable unless proceedings be commenced within eight years from the date of the bond, according to the Act of June 14, 1836, relating to Official Bonds. (Act of June 21, 1839, section 6 ; P. L., 378.)

§ 1594. Magistrate's bonds in Philadelphia—Liability of sureties, etc.

A bond shall be given by a magistrate in Philadelphia County with two or more sufficient sureties, who shall be freeholders and approved by one of the judges of the Court of Common Pleas, which bond shall be taken by the prothonotary in the name of the Commonwealth, with conditions for faithful performance of his duties and proper application of all moneys that shall come into his hands as such magistrate. Such bond shall be held in trust for the benefit of all persons who may sustain injury from said magistrate in his official capacity. Said sureties shall not be liable unless proceedings be commenced within six years from the time such causes of action shall accrue. Such bond shall forthwith be recorded in the office for recording of deeds. Copies of such bond, certified by the recorder, shall be good evidence in any action brought against the obligors in the same manner as the original would be. (Act February 5, 1875, section 7 ; P. L., 56.)

§ 1595. Remedies against justice who retains money in his official capacity.

If a justice refuse to pay over moneys received by him in his official capacity, there are two remedies :

First, your proceeding may be by petition to the Court of Common Pleas—citation and hearing—with a jury trial, if demanded, to try an issue of fact ; or,

Second, by proceeding in assumpsit on the justice's bond, as in cases of official bonds.

If a justice of the peace charge fees illegally, under the Act of 1868, the remedy is by indictment. The penal Act of 1814 does not apply. *Irons* v. *Allen*, 169 Pa. St., 633 (1895). See § 1582.

§ 1596. Actions against Constables. *Duties of constables—As to levy.*

When a justice issues execution it shall be directed to the constable of the ward, district, or township where the defendant resides, or the next constable most convenient to the defendant, commanding him to levy the debt and costs on the defendant's goods and chattels.

The constable shall within twenty days next following expose the personalty for sale by public vendue, having given due notice by at least three advertisements put up at the most public places in his township, ward, or district. (Act of March 20, 1810, section 11 ; 5 Sm., 167.)

No action can be maintained against a constable if he refuse to take an execution, he not being a constable " of the ward, district, or township where the defendant resides, or the next constable most convenient to the defendant." *Comm.* v. *Lentz*, 106 Pa. St., 643 (1884).

If the execution be directed to ——, constable, the constable is not *bound* to execute it, although he is *justified* in so doing.

It would have been more proper to direct the writ to the constable by name, or to the constable of the district generally. *Paul* v. *Vankirk*, 6 Binn., 124 (1813), TILGHMAN, C. J.

The constable must make return to the execution *in writing* within twenty days, unless he can show sufficient reason for the delay. *Keller* v. *Clarke*, 6 W. & S., 534 (1843).

§ 1597. *As to details of Execution.* The constable shall indorse the goods or chattels levied upon, and the time of such levy, on the execution or schedule thereto annexed. The constable is empowered to take a bail-bond, for the sufficiency of which he is responsible. Act of March 20, 1810, section 18 (5 Sm., 167) ; Act of March 28, 1820, section 4 (7 Sm., 309).

§ 1598. *Constable to make out his bill for fees, charges, etc.*

When the constable shall collect or receive the debt, interest, and costs, or any part thereof, in any execution, it shall be his duty to make out and deliver to the defendant a bill of particulars of his fees and charges, together with a receipt signed by him, if said fees, etc., are paid. (Act of March 28, 1820, section 3 ; 7 Sm., 309.)

§ 1599. *When constable shall perform duties of coroner.*

In suits in which the sheriff of the county is interested as a party, where no coroner can serve, it is the duty of the constable to perform the duties of coroner as to service of process, etc. (Act of April 22, 1850, section 19 ; P. L., 553.)

§ 1600. **Actions for False Returns.** *When constable makes false returns or fails to produce plaintiff's receipt.*

If the constable make a false return or does not produce plaintiff's receipt on return-day, or make such other return as may be deemed sufficient by the justice, the justice shall issue a summons to be served by a constable, or other fit person or supervisor, who shall execute the same, commanding the constable to appear before him on some certain day, not exceeding eight days from date, and then and there show cause why an execution should not issue against him for the amount of the first execution.

If the constable neglects to appear, or does not show sufficient cause why the execution should not issue against him, then the justice shall enter judgment against such constable for the amount of the first execution, with costs, without stay of execution, which execution shall be directed to any constable, or other fit person or supervisor, whose duty it shall be to execute the same. This shall in no way impair the proceeding with regard to insolvent debtors, and their discharge on full surrender of their property. (Act March 20, 1810, section 12 ; 5 Sm., 167.)

This Act was strictly interpreted in *Bachman* v. *Fenstermacher*, 112 Pa. St., 331 (1886).

§ 1601. *When constable shall refuse to make return of writ, etc.*

Where the justice issues a summons, warrant of arrest, or execution in any civil suit against any constable for any debt or demand alleged to be due by him in his private capacity, such process shall be directed to any other constable in the city or county in which the justice shall reside, and if such constable shall refuse or neglect to make return of the same, or, having collected the money, refuse or neglect to pay over or account for the same, he shall be proceeded against as in the twelfth section of the Act of March 20, 1810. (Act of March 28, 1820, section 1 ; 7 Sm., 308.)

§ 1602. *When constable refuses to pay overplus money.*

If a constable or his deputy refuse or neglect to pay to defendant the overplus money he may have received upon any execution, proceedings may be instituted against him as in cases of false return. (Act of March 28, 1820, section 2 ; 7 Sm., 308.)

§ 1603. *Liability of constable refusing adequate security.* Goods were levied upon by a constable ; there was a dispute as to their liability ; the plaintiff tendered adequate security ; the constable refused to proceed unless certain designated security was given. It was *held*, that the constable should have proceeded. *Meeker* v. *Sutton*, 2 Phila., 288 (1857).

§ 1604. *Proceedings against constable.* If a constable is guilty of official misconduct, suit may be brought against him and his surety on his official bond in the Common Pleas or the party injured may proceed against the constable alone before a justice, and afterward.

against his surety, as prescribed in section 19 of the Act of March 20, 1810. *Palmer* v. *Comm.*, 6 S. & R., 244 (1820).

§ 1605. **Mandamus may issue to a magistrate to compel issuing of a summons.** The Common Pleas will issue a mandamus to compel a magistrate to issue a summons against a constable for unlawful delay in serving and returning a writ. *Comm.* v. *Smith*, 3 W. N., 95 (1876).

§ 1606. **Mode of proceedings against constable.**

No action shall be brought against any constable * * * or any person acting by his order and in his aid, for anything done in obedience to any warrant under the hand and seal of any justice of the peace until demand has been made, or left at the usual place of his abode, by the party or parties intending to bring such action, or by his, her, or their attorney or agent, in writing, signed by the party demanding the same, of the perusal and copy of such warrant, duly certified under his hand, and the same has been neglected or refused for the space of six days after such demand; and in case, after such demand and compliance therewith, by showing the said warrant, and giving a copy thereof, certified as aforesaid to the party demanding the same, any action shall be brought against such constable, or other person or persons acting in his aid, for any such cause as aforesaid, without making such justice or justices who signed or sealed the said warrant defendant or defendants, on producing and proving such warrant at the trial of such action, the jury shall give their verdict for the defendant or defendants, notwithstanding any defect or defects of jurisdiction. * * * If the action be brought jointly against such justice * * * and such constable * * * on proof of such warrant, the jury shall find for such constable, * * * notwithstanding such defect or jurisdiction. * * * If the verdict shall be against the justice * * * the plaintiff or plaintiffs shall recover, his * * * costs to be taxed * * * as to include such costs as plaintiff or plaintiffs are liable to pay to such defendant or defendants for whom such verdict shall be found. * * *

Provided always, that where the plaintiff in such action * * * * shall obtain a verdict, * * * the justices before whom the cause shall be tried shall, in open court, certify on the back of the record that the injury for which such action was brought was wilfully and maliciously committed, the plaintiff shall be entitled to have and receive double costs of suit.

Provided always, that no action shall be brought against any justice * * * for anything done in the execution of his office, or against any constable * * * unless commenced within six months after the Act committed. (Act of March 21, 1772, section 6; 1 Sm., 365.)

No action can be brought against a constable until demand has been made upon the officer and the same has been neglected or refused for six days. *Ream's Appeal*, 157 Pa. St., 444 (1893): *Comm.* v. *Warfel*, 33 W. N., 357 (1893).

§ 1607. **Proceeding against bail.** Where a constable neglects or refuses to perform his duty, if judgment be first obtained against him and nothing can be recovered, the justice is authorized to issue a *scire facias* and proceed against his sureties.　Act of March 20, 1810, section 19 (5 Sm., 170).

§ 1608. Proceedings to Recover Possession of Lands by Purchasers at Sheriff's Sale.　*Legislation.*　It was long considered that on an execution and sale of lands, the sheriff could not give possession to the purchaser, conformably to the English practice, as is more fully set forth in the elaborate and learned opinion in *Pennsylvania* v. *Kirkpatrick* et al., reported in Addison's Reports, 193 (1794).

The initial Act of the legislature on this subject was passed on April 6, 1802 (3 Sm., 530), and its supplement, March 14, 1814 (6 Sm., 133).

The provisions of these Acts found a later substitute in the Act of June 16, 1836 (P. L., 780), which resembles very closely its predecessors, and the decisions therefore under the former Acts relate in all essential respects to the Act of 1836.

Schuylkill County is specially provided for in the Act of May 13, 1871 (P. L., 820), which contains clauses similar to the Act of 1836, but provides in place of a hearing before two justices that the petition shall be presented to the Court of Common Pleas or a judge thereof in vacation, and in place of a jury assessing the damages, this responsibility is cast upon said court or judge.

The Act of May 13, 1871, providing the mode of proceeding in Schuylkill County, has no application to leasehold estates.　*Seltzer* v. *Robbins*, 18 W. N., 113 (1886).

§ 1609. *Purchaser at sheriff's sale to give notice to party in possession.*

Whenever lands or tenements shall be sold by virtue of any execution, * * * the purchaser of such estate may, after the acknowledgment of a deed therefor to him by the sheriff, give notice to the defendant as whose property the same shall have been sold, or to the persons in possession of such estate under him, by title derived from him subsequently to the judgment under which the same were sold, and require him, or them, to surrender the possession thereof to him within three months from the date of such notice.　(Act June 16, 1836, section 105 ; P. L., 780.)

§ 1610.

FORM OF NOTICE OF SHERIFF'S SALE, REQUIRING TENANT TO QUIT THE
PREMISES.

A. B.　　|
　 v.　　}　　Common Pleas No.　　, Term, 1890.　No.　.
C. D.　　|　　　　　　Philadelphia (date).

To G. H.,

　SIR :　Please take notice that, by virtue of a writ of　　　　issued in the above-entitled case, E. F., Esq., High Sheriff (or coroner), of the county of Philadelphia, did on the first day of   , 1890, expose to sale the following property (here describe fully from the deed).

At the said sale I became the purchaser of said premises, and the said sheriff (or coroner), on   , acknowledged a deed to me for said premises.

You are the defendant as whose property the said premises were sold and are in possession thereof (or you were and are in possession of said premises under the defendant in said execution by title derived from him subsequently to the judgment under which said property was sold).

I therefore give you notice and require you to surrender the possession of the said premises to me within three months from the date of this notice or I shall proceed according to law.

Very respectfully,
(Signature of Purchaser.)

§ 1611. *Purchaser may present petition to recover possession.*

If the defendant or any person in possession under him shall refuse or neglect to comply with the notice and requisition of the purchaser as aforesaid, such purchaser, or his heirs or assigns, may apply by petition to any justice of the peace, alderman, or magistrate of the city, town, borough, or county where such real estate may be, setting forth :

1. That he purchased the premises at a sheriff's or coroner's sale.

2. That the person in possession at the time of such application is the defendant as whose property such real estate was sold, or that he came into possession thereof under him.

3. That such person in possession had notice as aforesaid of such sale, and was required to give up such estate three months previous to such application. (Act of June 16, 1836, section 106 ; Act of May 24, 1878, section 1 ; P. L., 134.)

The complaint must set forth all the facts necessary to give the justice jurisdiction.

§ 1612.

FORM OF PETITION BY PURCHASER TO OBTAIN POSSESSION.

To   Esq.,
    Magistrate of Court No.   , of Philadelphia County.

The complaint of A. B. respectfully represents :

That he is the owner of all that certain (here recite description of real estate briefly).

That your petitioner purchased the said premises at a sheriff's (or coroner's) sale on the   day of   , A. D. 1890, and that a sheriff's (or coroner's) deed therefor to your petitioner, bearing date the   day of   , A. D. 1890, was duly acknowledged in open court by the sheriff (or coroner) of said county, and duly entered among the records thereof.

That the person in possession of the above-described premises at the time of this application is C. D., who was the defendant in the execution as whose property such real estate was sold (or is C. D., who was at the time of said sale and now is in possession of said premises, under the defendant in the execution under which the property was so sold, by title derived from said defendant subsequently to the judgment under which said property was so sold). That said C. D., on the (date) had notice from your petitioner,

in writing, of said sheriff's sale, and was on said   day of   ,
1890, and three months previous to this application, duly required, by
notice in writing, personally served upon him by your petitioner, to remove
from and leave the said premises and to surrender the possession thereof to
your petitioner. Notwithstanding which the said C. D. has refused and
neglected, and still doth refuse and neglect, to comply with said notice and
requisition of your petitioner.

That your petitioner prays that a warrant in the nature of a summons,
directed to the sheriff of said county, be issued commanding him to summon
a jury of six men of his bailiwick to appear before you   , Esq.,
Magistrate of Court No.   ,   , at a time and place to be specified,
within not less than three nor more than eight days next after the issuing
thereof, and also to summon the said   , at the same time to appear
before you and said jury, to show cause, if any   has, why delivery of
possession of said premises should not be forthwith given to the petitioner.

(Name of Complainant.)

A. B., the above-named petitioner, being duly sworn according to law,
deposes and says that the facts set forth in the foregoing petition are true
and correct.

Sworn to and subscribed before me,)
  (date).   }
             · Magistrate.)   (Name of Complainant.)

§ 1613. *Justice shall direct precept to sheriff to summon jury and party in possession.*

If the application as aforesaid shall be verified by the oath or affirmation
of the petitioner, or if probable cause to believe the facts therein set forth
be otherwise shown, the said justice, alderman, or magistrate is hereby enjoined or required forthwith to issue his warrant, in the nature of a summons, directed to the sheriff of the county, commanding him to summon a
jury of six men of his bailiwick to appear before said justice or magistrate,
at a time and place to be specified, within not less than three nor more than
eight days next after the issuing thereof, and also to summon the defendant, or person in possession at the same time, to appear before him and
the said jury, to show cause, if any he has, why the delivery of the possession of such lands or tenements should not be forthwith given to the petitioner. (Act of June 16, 1836, section 107, as amended by Act of May 24,
1878, section 2; P. L., 134.)

§ 1614.

FORM OF WARRANT.

COMMONWEALTH OF PENNSYLVANIA,)
   COUNTY OF PHILADELPHIA,   } ss.

To the Sheriff of the County of Philadelphia, greeting :

Whereas I have been informed by the petition of A. B. that he has purchased at a sheriff's sale a certain messuage or tenement and lot of ground
situate (here describe premises), and that a deed for the said premises to
the said A. B. was duly acknowledged by the sheriff (or coroner) on the
(date), and that the said C. D. is now in possession of said premises, and
has had notice of said sale requiring him to give up possession of said
premises three months before the application of the said petitioner; that

the said C. D. has refused, and still doth refuse, to comply with the terms of said notice according to law.

Therefore I command you that you summon a jury of six men of your bailiwick to appear before the undersigned, Magistrate of Court No. , of said county, on the (date and hour), to inquire of such matters as shall be submitted to them in the premises, and also that you summon C. D., of said county, to appear before the said magistrate at his office   , in the city of Philadelphia, at the time named, to show cause, if any he has, why delivery of possession of the said estate should not be forthwith given to the purchaser.

Witness the hand and official seal of the said magistrate.

(Date.)

[SEAL]   (Address.)   Magistrate of Court No. .

§ 1615. *Sheriff must select jury.* If a precept be issued to the sheriff, commanding him to summon a jury, the sheriff cannot select a jury from a list prepared by his deputy. *Pa. R. R. Co. v. Heister*, 8 Pa. St., 445 (1848).

The selection of a jury, being a judicial act, must be performed by the sheriff, and not by his deputy. *McMullen v. Orr*, 8 Phila., 342 (1871).

§ 1616.

FORM OF RETURN OF THE SHERIFF.

I hereby certify and return that I have summoned six good and lawful men of my bailiwick, to be and appear at the time and place within named, and that I have also summoned C. D., the defendant (being the tenant in possession of the within-described premises), by giving to him (date) a true and attested copy of the within writ, and making known to him the contents thereof.   So answers, etc.

Sheriff.

L. M., being duly sworn according to law, deposes and says that the facts set forth in the foregoing return are true.

Sworn to and subscribed before me, this ⎫
        (date).   ⎬   L. M.,
                    Deputy Prothy. ⎭   Deputy Sheriff.

Attached to the return is the following:

SHERIFF'S OFFICE, Philadelphia, September   , 1890.

A. B. ⎫ Before Magistrate   , Court No. .
  v.   ⎬ No.   Street,
C. D. ⎭   on (day and date), at   M.
                                    Jurors (names).
                                            Sheriff.

§ 1617. **Who may Recover Possession.** *A purchaser may recover the interest of the debtor.* A purchaser at a judicial sale has a right to recover the interest the debtor has at the time of sale. If a naked possession only, he succeeds to that right. *Knox v. Herod*, 2 Pa. St., 27 (1845). ·

§ 1618. *A purchaser of land belonging to railroad company subject to servitude.* A purchaser at a sheriff's sale of land belonging to a railroad company, which land is subject to the servitude of their right of way, has a right to the possession of the land, subject to the servitude of the company. *Rwy. Co.* v. *Keenan*, 56 Pa. St., 198 (1867).

§ 1619. *Purchasers of real estate under Orphans' Court sale.*

Purchasers of real estate sold under orders of the Orphans' Court shall, after the confirmation of the sale and execution and acknowledgment of the deed, have a right to proceed to obtain possession of the purchased premises in the same manner as now provided in relation to purchasers at sheriff's sales. (Act April 9, 1849, section 16; P. L., 527.)

This Act applies to Orphans' Court sales in partition.

§ 1620. *Purchaser under a lev. fa. in a mechanic's claim suit.* Where one purchases a property at a sheriff's sale under a *lev. fa.* on a judgment on a mechanic's claim, he may avail himself of the benefit of the Act of June 16, 1836, to recover possession of the premises. *Walridge's Appeal*, 95 Pa. St., 466 (1880).

§ 1621. *Purchaser of interest of tenant at will.* If the defendant in the execution holds as a tenant at will of another, his interest being purchasable, the purchaser at a sheriff's sale is entitled to possession. This decision is under the Act of March 13, 1871 (P. L., 820), relating to Schuylkill County, but it is applicable in principle to the Act of 1836. *Gerber* v. *Hartwig*, 11 W. N., 197 (1881).

§ 1622. **If defendant do not appear, proof of service of warrant must be made.**

If, at the time and place appointed for the hearing of the parties, the defendant or person in possession as aforesaid shall fail to appear, the said justice shall require proof, by oath or affirmation, of the due service of such warrant upon him, and of the manner of such service : *Provided*, that such service shall have been made three days before the return. (Act of June 16, 1836, section 108.)

§ 1623. **If defendant appear, the justice to make inquiry as to title and notice.**

If the defendant, or other person in possession under him as aforesaid, shall be duly summoned as aforesaid, or he shall appear, the said justice and jury shall proceed to inquire :

1. Whether the petitioner, or those under whom he claims, has or have become the purchaser of such real estate at a sheriff's or coroner's sale, as aforesaid; and a sheriff's or coroner's deed for the same, duly acknowledged and certified, shall be full and conclusive evidence of that fact before such justice and jury.

2. Whether the person in possession of such real estate was the defendant in the execution under which such real estate was sold, or came into the possession thereof under him, as aforesaid.

3. Whether the person so in possession has had three months' notice of such sale previous to such application. (*Id.*, section 109.)

§ 1624. **If party in possession claim title under person other than defendant in execution, justice shall summon said person, etc.**

If the person in possession of the premises shall make oath or affirmation before the justice that he does not hold the same under said defendant, but under some other person, whom he shall name, the said justice shall forthwith issue a summons to such person, requiring him to appear before him at a certain time therein named, not exceeding thirty days thence following, and, if at such time, the said person shall appear and make oath or affirmation that he verily believes that he is legally entitled to the premises in dispute, and that he does not claim under the said defendant, but by a different title, or that he claims under the said defendant by title derived before the judgment aforesaid, and shall enter into a recognizance with sureties, as aforesaid, in such case also the justice shall forbear to give judgment. (*Id.*, section 115.)

Where the defendant makes affidavit that he does not hold under the execution defendant, but under a third party, the magistrate cannot be compelled by *mandamus* to enter judgment upon the verdict of the jury before summoning such third person. *Comm.* v. *McClintock*, 36 Leg. Int., 412 ; 13 Phila., 26 (1879).

The justice must issue a summons to such party, even though the defendant in possession has filed no recognizance. *Bauer* v. *Angeny*, 12 W. N., 526 (1882).

§ 1625. **Finding of jury as to damages—Justice shall enter judgment for damages assessed and costs.**

In case of a finding for the petitioner as aforesaid, the jury shall assess the damages as they shall think right against such defendant or person in possession for the unjust detention of the premises, and thereupon the said justice shall enter judgment for the damages assessed and reasonable costs, and such judgment shall be final and conclusive to the parties. (Act of June 16, 1836, section 111.)

The inquest should find that A. B. was the defendant whose land was sold ; that he was in possession at the time ; that the purchaser gave notice to him and the tenants, and that such notice was given three months prior to the application to the justice. *Cooke* v. *Reinhart*, 1 Rawle, 317 (1829).

§ 1626.

FORM OF INQUISITION.

A. B.   ⎱
  v.   ⎰
C. D.

Inquisition taken at Magistrate's Court No.   , in the city of Philadelphia, on the (date), before Magistrate (name), and upon the oaths of (names of jurors), six good and lawful men of said county of Philadelphia, who, being duly sworn and charged to inquire of the premises, do say that the said A. B. in the annexed warrant named has become the purchaser of the real estate therein mentioned, to wit (here describe premises), that a sheriff's (or coroner's) deed therefor to A. B. was duly acknowledged (date) in open Court of Common Pleas No. , of said county.

That the said C. D., now in possession of said premises, holds by title derived from E. F., the defendant in the execution under which the same was sold subsequently to the judgment under which the same was sold (or that C. D. now and at said sale in possession is· the defendant as whose property the said premises were sold), that said C. D. after said sale had three months' notice thereof and of the requisition of the said A. B. to surrender the possession of said premises to him previously to the said application, and that the said C. D. has hitherto refused and neglected to comply with the terms of said notice and requisition.

Wherefore the said magistrate does hereby award possession of said premises to the petitioner, and the jury do assess the damages in favor of A. B. and against the said C. D. for the unjust detention of said premises at the sum of   dollars.

In witness whereof, the said magistrate, as well as the aforesaid jury, have to this inquisition set their hands and seals the day and year first above written.

[SEAL]   Magistrate of Court No. .
                                            (Signatures and seals of six Jurors.)

§ 1627. **Judgment of the justice final.** In proceedings by a purchaser at a sheriff's sale to obtain possession, the judgment of the justice is final and conclusive. Where execution has been returned *nulla bona*, a transcript cannot be filed in the Common Pleas and execution issued thereon. *Amos* v. *Stiles*, 1 W. N., 414 (1875).

§ 1628. **No action lies on such record to recover damages and costs.** No action of debt will lie on such a record. *Bodkin* v. *McDonald*, 2 W. N., 586 (1876) ; supporting *Moyer* v. *Kirby*, 14 S. & R., 162 (1826) ; *contra, Gault* v. *McKinley*, 2 Phila., 71 (1856).

§ 1629. **Transcript of judgment cannot be filed.** The judgment under a proceeding by a purchaser at a sheriff's sale to obtain possession is not within the meaning of the Act of March 20, 1810, section 10, authorizing transcripts of judgments of justices to be entered on the docket of the Common Pleas. *Bodkin* v. *McDonald*, 2 W. N., 478 (1876).

§ 1630. **Justice to issue warrant to deliver possession.**

The said justice shall thereupon issue his warrant, directed to the sheriff, commanding him forthwith to deliver to the petitioner, his heirs or assigns, full possession of such lands or tenements, and to levy the costs taxed by the said justice and the damages assessed by the jury, as aforesaid. (Act of June 16, 1836, section 112.)

§ 1631.

FORM OF WARRANT OF POSSESSION.

City and County of Philadelphia, *ss.*

The Commonwealth of Pennsylvania to the Sheriff of the County of Philadelphia, greeting:

Whereas, due proof has been made before E. F., Esq., a magistrate of

the city of Philadelphia, and six good and lawful men of the same city and county aforesaid, summoned for that purpose, that A. B., of said city, had purchased at sheriff's sale all that certain messuage and lot or piece of ground situate (here describe property) ; that the said A. B., the purchaser at said sale, did, on the   day of   , 1891, give notice to the said C. D., defendant in the execution in possession of said premises (or as case may be) of the said sale, and did require him to surrender up the possession of the said premises to A. B., the said purchaser, within three months after the date of such notice, and the said C. D. has hitherto refused, and doth still refuse to comply therewith. All of which premises being duly found by the said magistrate and jury, according to the form of the Act of General Assembly in such case made and provided. Therefore, I command you, the said sheriff, forthwith to deliver to the said A. B. full possession of the premises aforesaid : And you are also commanded that of the goods and chattels of the said C. D. in your bailiwick you cause to be levied as well the sum of   dollars, which to the said A. B. was awarded by said jury as damages sustained by the unjust detention of the premises as
dollars for costs and charges by A. B. in and about said case and in that behalf expended. Whereof the said C. D. aforesaid is convict. Hereof fail not .

Witness the said magistrate at the city aforesaid, the   day of
in the year of our Lord one thousand eight hundred and ninety-one.

[SEAL]   Magistrate.

§ 1632. **Stay of proceedings.** When the complainant has made it appear that he is the vendee at the sheriff's sale or grantee of such vendee, and that he has given three months' notice to quit, and that the respondent is the defendant in the execution or in possession under such defendant by title subsequent to the judgment, such complainant is entitled to recover possession.

But if the respondent alleges on oath that he does not claim under the defendant, but by adverse title, or that he claims by the same title, but by a transfer of it previous to judgment, the justice should stay the proceedings until the truth of the respondent's allegation can be determined.

In *Lenon* v. *McCall*, 3 S. & R., 102 (1817), TILGHMAN, C. J., said : " The person in possession may stay the proceedings of the justices on making oath that he claims under the defendant in the execution by title derived before the judgment, provided security be given."

The oath is sufficient if it contains a positive averment of title being derived before the judgment.

If the oath and recognizance are offered before judgment is rendered, that is sufficient.

§ 1633. **If party in possession shall make affidavit and file bond, judgment stayed.**

If the person in possession of the premises shall make oath or affirmation before the justices :

1. That he has not come into possession and does not claim to hold the same, under the defendant in the execution, but in his own right ; or;

2. That he has come into possession under the title derived to him from the said defendant before the judgment under which the execution and sale took place, and shall become bound in a recognizance, with one or more sufficient sureties, in the manner hereinafter provided, the said justice shall forbear to give the judgment aforesaid. (Act of June 16, 1836, section 114.)

§ 1634. *Affidavit of defendant and its requisites.* Under the Act of June 16, 1836, the right of the plaintiff to recover can only be denied upon affidavit and proof.

1. That the person in possession has not come into possession and does not claim to hold the same under the defendant in the execution, but in his own right ; or,

2. That he has come into possession under the title derived to him from the said defendant before the judgment under which the execution and sale took place ; or,

3. That he holds under a third person, who claims in his own right, and not under the defendant, or claims under the defendant, by title derived before the judgment.

The affidavit must strictly comply with the terms of the Act. *Bank* v. *Cowperthwaite*, 10 W. N., 532 (1881).

In *Elton* v. *Stokes*, 12 W. N., 240 (1882), it was decided that the affidavit need not set forth the title to the premises by the person in possession *in extenso*, and is sufficient if it conform to the words of the Act and do not specify when the title commenced in possession.

The tenant in possession cannot have a stay of proceedings if his affidavit avers that he holds possession of a part of the premises under the defendant in the execution. *Hawk* v. *Stouch*, 5 S. & R., 157 (1819).

In a proceeding under the Act of April 9, 1849, section 16, by a purchaser at an Orphans' Court sale to recover possession, the tenant filed an affidavit that she claimed the premises in her own right as tenant in fee by title and possession derived prior to the sale. The affidavit was held insufficient. *Hennegan* v. *Williams*, 4 W. N., 458 (1877).

A tenant cannot controvert the title of his landlord or defend the possession against him or anyone claiming title under him. The purchaser at the sheriff's sale succeeds to all the title and rights of the defendant in the judgment under which the premises were sold. *Wilson* v. *Hubbell*, 1 Penny., 413.

§ 1635.

FORM OF AFFIDAVIT PRESCRIBED BY STATUTE.

The oath or affirmation which shall be administered to such claimant shall be in the following form, to wit:

I do (swear or affirm) that I verily believe that I am legally entitled to hold the premises in dispute against the petitioner; that I do not claim the same by, from, or under the defendant, as whose property the same were sold, (or, as the case may be) that I do not claim the same by, from, or under the defendant, as whose property the same were sold, by title derived to me subsequently to the rendition of the judgment under which the same were sold, but by a different title, etc. (Act of June 16, 1836, section 116.)

§ 1636.

FORM OF AFFIDAVIT.

A. B. ⎫ Before E. F., Magistrate of Court No. .
  v.   ⎬ On the petition of A. B., purchaser at a sheriff sale of a cer-
C. D. ⎭ tain tract of land, to recover possession thereof from C. D.
City and County of Philadelphia, *ss.*

C. D., being duly sworn according to law, deposes and says that he is legally entitled to hold the premises in dispute against the petitioner; that he did not come into possession of the premises situate (here briefly describe premises) and does not claim to hold the same under the defendant in the execution, by virtue of which the same were sold as aforesaid, but in his own right [or that he came into possession of the premises situate (here briefly describe premises) under title derived to him from the defendant in the execution before the judgment under which the execution was issued and the sale took place or that he did not come into possession of the premises situate (here briefly describe premises) by title by, from, or under the defendant in the execution, as whose property the same was sold, but by title derived previously to the rendition of judgment under which said premises were sold by deed of conveyance from (here set forth your title)].

Sworn to and subscribed before me, ⎫
  this (date). ⎬
  ⎭
    Notary Public or Magistrate. ⎭
  [SEAL]

§ 1637. Requisites of bond.

The recognizance aforesaid shall be taken in a sum fully sufficient to cover and secure, as well the value of the rents and mesne profits of such lands or tenements, which may have accrued, and which may be expected to accrue, before the final decision of the said claim, as all costs and damages, with condition that he shall appear at the next Court of Common Pleas having jurisdiction and then and there plead to any declaration in ejectment which may be filed against him, and thereupon proceed to trial in due course of practice, and in case he shall fail therein, that he will deliver up the said premises to the purchaser, and to pay him the full value of the rents or mesne profits of the premises accrued from the time of the purchase. (Act of June 16, 1836, section 117.)

§ 1638.

FORM OF RECOGNIZANCE.

KNOW ALL MEN BY THESE PRESENTS, that we, C. D., E. D., F. D., are held and firmly bound unto A. B. in the sum of   dollars, lawful money of the United States of America, to be paid to the said A. B., his heirs, executors, or administrators, to which payment well and truly to be

made we bind ourselves and each of us, our and each of our heirs, executors, or administrators, jointly and severally by these presents.

Sealed with our seals this   day of   , A. D. 1890.

Now the condition of this obligation is such that if the above bounden C.
D. shall appear at the next Court of Common Pleas having jurisdiction,
and then and there plead to any declaration in ejectment which may be
filed against him, and thereupon proceed to trial in due course of practice,
and in case he shall fail therein that he will deliver up the said premises
to the purchaser and pay the said A. B. the full value of the rents or
mesne profits of the premises accrued from the time of purchase thereof,
together with all costs and damages, then this obligation to be void; otherwise, to be and remain in full force and virtue.

Signed, sealed, and delivered in the }
  presence of: }   [SEAL]
                            }   [SEAL]
                                 [SEAL]

§ 1639. If facts found against defendant, justice shall make record.

Upon the finding of the facts as aforesaid, the justice shall make a record
thereof, and thereupon he shall award the possession of such real estate to
the petitioner. (Act of June 16, 1836, section 110.)

§ 1640.

FORM OF RECORD.

A. B. }
  v.   }
C. D. }

Be it remembered, the (date)

Before E. F., Magistrate of Court No.   , for the City and County of
Philadelphia:

The petition of A. B., verified under oath thereof, was presented (date)
to said magistrate setting forth, *inter alia*, that the petitioner had purchased
at sheriff's sale a certain lot or piece of ground with the messuage thereon
erected (here describe premises), and that the deed for the same to the petitioner was duly acknowledged by the sheriff of the county of Philadelphia
(date), in open Court of Common Pleas, No. ; that the said C. D., the defendant in said judgment, then and now in possession of said premises,
was duly notified of the sale of said premises to the petitioner, and required
to deliver possession of said premises to A. B. three months previous to said
application. This C. D. has refused, and still doth refuse, to do. That,
therefore, A. B. applied by petition for his remedy agreeably to the Act of
Assembly. That on the (date) a warrant was issued by the said magistrate to the sheriff of the said county commanding him to summon a jury of
six men to appear before the said magistrate, at Court No. , No.
Street, Philadelphia, on the   day of   , 1890, at (hour), to inquire
of the premises, and also to summon the said C. D. to appear before the
said magistrate and jury at the same time and place, and show cause, if any
he had, why delivery of the possession of the said premises should not be
given to the petitioner. And now (date), the said jury having come before
the said magistrate at the time and place in said warrant named, and the
said C. D. having also appeared, and the said jury having been duly sworn,
the said magistrate and jury proceeded to inquire of the premises, and
found that the said A. B. became the purchaser of the real estate, in his

petition mentioned, being the premises particularly above described, at a sheriff's sale, when said premises were sold by virtue of an execution as the property of the said C. D., and that a sheriff's deed therefor was duly acknowledged by the sheriff aforesaid on the   day of   , 1890, and delivered to the said A. B., and that the said C. D. at the time of said sale was, and now is, in possession of said real estate, and is the defendant as whose property the same was sold (or as case may be) and has had notice of said sale and of the requisition of the said A. B. to give up said estate three months previous to his said application, and that the said C. D. has refused and neglected to comply with said notice or requisition to surrender the possession of the said premises to the petitioner. Therefore it is the judgment of the said magistrate that delivery of possession of the said premises be made to the said petitioner, and also the said jury has assessed the sum of   dollars against the said C. D. as damages for the unjust detention of the said premises.*

Whereupon the said magistrate, the same day, does award possession of the said real estate to the said A. B. and enters judgment against the said C. D. for the sum of   dollars as damages aforesaid, and the sum of   dollars as the reasonable costs by said A. B. in said suit expended.

Concerning all these premises, I, the said magistrate, do make this my record.

In witness whereof, I have hereunto set my hand and official seal the day and year aforesaid.

E. F.,
Magistrate of Court No.   .

[SEAL]

If a stay of proceedings is sought, the record may be as in above form down to the asterisk, and then is as follows :

And the said C. D. then and there makes his affidavit that he has not come into possession of the aforesaid real estate and premises, and does not claim to hold the same under the defendant in the execution as whose property the same were sold, but in his own right (or as the case may be, *e. g.*, that he has come into possession of the said real estate and premises under title derived to him from the defendant in the execution as whose property the same were sold, before the judgment under which the said execution and sale took place).

And the said C. D. then and there also becomes bound in a recognizance, with two sufficient sureties taken and acknowledged before me, the said justice, in the sum of   dollars, and with condition (here fill in the condition of the recognizance).

Concerning all which premises, I, the said magistrate, do make this my record.

In witness whereof, I (conclude as above).

If judgment of possession be entered, the defendant should be found to be the defendant named in the execution under which the property was sold, and to have been then and still in possession ; or if the person in possession be not the defendant in the execution, it should be found that he came into possession of said premises under the defendant in the execution, by title derived from said defendant in the execution subsequently to the judgment under which the premises were sold.

§ 1641. Certiorari not a supersedeas.

No *certiorari* which may be issued to remove such proceedings shall be a *supersedeas*, or have any effect to prevent or delay the execution aforesaid, or the delivery of the possession agreeably thereto. (Act of June 16, 1836, section 113.)

This section received interpretation in *Jackson* v. *Gleason,* 6 Phila., 307 (1867).

On *certiorari*, nothing but the record of the proceedings before the magistrate and jury is before the court. *Rwy. Co.* v. *Keenan,* 56 Pa. St., 198 (1867).

§ 1642. Justice shall give judgment when recognizance forfeited.

If such recognizance shall be forfeited, the justice aforesaid shall proceed to give judgment, and cause such real estate to be delivered up to the petitioner, in the manner hereinbefore enjoined and directed. (Act of June 16, 1836, section 118.)

§ 1643. Proceeding in Common Pleas not a new action.

When a person in possession of land sold by the sheriff makes defense before the justice that he did not obtain, and does not claim, the possession of the land under the defendant in the execution, and enters into the recognizance required, and the cause is certified into court, this is equivalent to a removal by *certiorari* to a higher court for trial, and all the proceedings thereafter are a part of the same cause that was begun before the justice, and not a new cause. *Walker* v. *Bush,* 30 Pa. St., 357 (1858).

In *Dean* v. *Connelly,* 6 Pa. St., 246 (1847), Mr. Justice COULTER said :

"The present case discloses a proceeding commenced before two justices of the peace by a purchaser at sheriff's sale, under the provisions of the Act of 1836, to obtain possession of the land purchased by him. The person in possession made the oath prescribed by the statute and the proceeding was transferred to the Common Pleas according to the provisions of the Act. * * * After the proceeding was transferred, * * * a different issue and a new posture of the case was substituted.

"In order to protect the rights of all parties, the statute authorizes the person in possession to make oath that he did not come in, nor claim to hold, under the defendant in the execution, or that he did come into possession under title derived from defendant before the judgment on which the execution and sale took place. The terms of the oath are that I do not claim the same by, from, or under the defendant as whose property the same were sold, by title derived to me subsequently to the rendition of the judgment under which the same were sold, but by a different title. The

person in possession thus becomes the actor in court, asserts the nature of
the title under which he claims, and admits the judgment and sale.

"And part of his recognizance is, that if he fails therein, that is, the
trial, he will deliver up the said premises to the purchaser. The defendant must establish that he claims under a title which governs and over-
rides the one sold by the sheriff, or else he fails; and therefore the judgment, execution, and sale are admitted and are, in fact, part of the process.
If the recognizance is forfeited by the defendant or person in possession,
either on trial or by his not appearing, the justices are then to proceed and
give judgment and cause the real estate to be given up to the purchaser."

§ 1644. **Directions as to suit in Common Pleas.** A stay of proceedings having properly been entered before the justice, promptly
commence your action in the Common Pleas.

This may be done by commencing the action in the ordinary
way as in cases of ejectment. See Chapter XIV., sections 581,
582 *et seq.* In *Wagner* v. *Graham*, 14 W. N., 343 (1884), it was
decided that when the proceedings are commenced in the Common
Pleas, the plaintiff must secure and file the transcript; that the
recognizance required the defendant only to appear and plead.

§ 1645. **The purchaser may claim rents subsequent to delivery
of deed.**

If any lands or tenements shall be sold upon execution, as aforesaid,
which at the time of such sale, or afterward, shall be held or possessed by
a tenant, or lessee, or person holding or claiming to hold the same under
the defendant in such execution, the purchaser of such lands or tenements
shall, upon receiving a deed for the same, as aforesaid, be deemed the landlord of such tenant, lessee, or other person, and shall have the like remedies
to recover any rents or sums accruing subsequently to the acknowledgment
of a deed to him, as aforesaid, whether such accruing rent may have been
paid in advance or not, if paid after the rendition of judgment on which
sale was made, as such defendant might have had if no such sale had been
made. (Act of June 16, 1836, section 119.)

If after notice shall be given of such sale, as aforesaid, such tenant,
lessee, or other person shall pay any rent or sum accruing subsequently to
the acknowledgment of such deed and notice given him, as aforesaid, to
such defendant, such tenant, lessee, or other person so paying shall nevertheless be liable to pay the purchaser. (*Id.*, section 120.)

In *Bank* v. *Wise*, 3 Watts, 400 (1834), KENNEDY, J., said:

"With respect to those who purchase lands at sheriff's or coroner's sales,
which are held and occupied by tenants under leases given by the defendants named in the executions before the date of the liens of the debts or
claims to satisfy which the sales are made, this section is to me plainly
declarative of what the law was before the passage of the Act. But if it was
intended * * * to embrace the case of a sale of land made by a sheriff
or coroner which is occupied by a lessee or tenant holding the same under
a lease made subsequent to the date of the lien of the judgment under
which the sale is made, then it, in language as forcible and as perspicuous

as it was possible to use, makes the purchaser at the sheriff's or coroner's sale the landlord and the occupant of the land his lessee or tenant, giving the purchaser an express right and authority to demand and receive any rents due subsequent to such sale, and forbidding the tenant of the land after notice of the sale to pay any rent so becoming due to the defendant in the execution, under the penalty of having to pay it again to the purchaser ; thus securing to the purchaser at sheriff's or coroner's sale, in such case, a right merely to the reversion, which, without more, would entitle him to all the rent becoming due or payable after the date of his purchase, as an incident to the estate purchased, the same as in the first case, where the tenant of the land holds under a lease made anterior to the date of the lien of the judgment or claim under which the sale was made.

" His remedies by distress or otherwise for the recovery of the rent that shall become due subsequent to the sale shall be the same as that of the defendant named in the execution would have been, provided the sale had never taken place.

" To rent which became due or payable before the sale it is clear that the purchaser can make no claim ; but to the rent which shall become due or payable after that nothing can be made more clear than his right to it."

This decision is supported by *Braddee* v. *Wiley*, 10 Watts, 362 (1840).

§ 1646. **Attornment.** The purchaser may affirm an existing lease and claim the rent payable under it, unless the sale be subsequent to the time named in the lease when the rent is payable in advance ; if he disaffirm the lease and give the tenant notice to quit, he cannot claim anything under the terms of the lease. *Bank* v. *Ege*, 9 Watts, 436 (1840).

Where no time is stipulated for the payment of rent, it is by law payable at the end of the year. The purchaser's title under his judgment being paramount to the lease, he may affirm the lease and avail himself of the legal remedies of the former owner to recover rent.

The accruing rent runs with the land, and cannot be separated from it by the act of the debtor, before it is due, as against the purchaser under the judgment. *Menough's Appeal*, 5 W. & S., 433 (1843).

§ 1647. **Purchaser has like remedies with owner.** Whenever the owner can maintain an action for use and occupation, the same remedy lies in favor of the purchaser at sheriff's sale for any sum accruing after he has received his deed. *Hayden* v. *Patterson*, 51 Pa. St., 261 (1865).

§ 1648. **If proceedings tainted with corruption, etc.** If a cause be so conducted as to justify the charge of partiality, corruption, and extortion, it is a good ground for setting aside the proceedings.

The proper course in such a case is to bring the record up on *certiorari*, and then show sufficient grounds for corruption, partiality, or extortion, by affidavits. The court will go into proofs in order to determine the truth of the charge.

It is one of the exceptions to the general rule that upon *certiorari* nothing but the record is brought up, and this is allowed that justice may be done and suitors may be protected where they would otherwise be defenseless.

CHAPTER XXI.

LANDLORD AND TENANT.

§ 1649. Distress. *Form of distress, etc.* See Chapter V., Ground Rents, section 149.

For replevin by tenant. See *Id.*, sections 152–155.

Remedy by tenant against landlord for excessive distress. Bring action of trespass. *Præcipe*, section 519.

§ 1650. Jurisdiction of justices in cases of rent.

The power of justices of the peace shall extend to all cases of rent not exceeding one hundred dollars, so far as to compel the landlord to defalcate, or set off, the just account of the tenant out of the same, but the landlord may waive further proceedings before the justice, and pursue the method of distress in the usual manner for the balance so settled; but if any landlord shall be convicted, after such waiver, in any court of record, of distraining for and selling more than to the amount of such balance, and of detaining the surplus in his hands, he shall forfeit to the tenant four times the amount of the sum detained: *Provided*, that no appeal shall lie in the case of rent, but the remedy by replevin shall remain as heretofore. (Act of March 20, 1810, section 20; 5 Sm., 170.)

The Act of March 20, 1810, does not allow the tenant to appeal, but gives him a remedy by replevin. Yet the right of the landlord to appeal is not taken away. *Hilke* v. *Eisenbeis*, 104 Pa. St., 514 (1883).

The matter of distress is so extended in its detail that only the important questions of practice before a justice will be noticed.

The duties of constables in this regard are clearly set forth in the statutes.

Outside of Philadelphia, the jurisdiction of a justice in an action to recover for rent due is enlarged by the Act of May 29, 1879, to the amount of three hundred dollars. *Beatty* v. *Rankin*, 139 Pa. St., 358 (1891); *Harvey* v. *Gunzberg*, 148 Pa. St., 294 (1892).

§ 1651. *Right to restrain for arrears of rent.* Where any tenant is in arrears for rent, and his lease has determined or ended, the landlord may, during the continuance of his title and after the determination of the lease, distrain as he might have done if such lease was not ended. Act of May 21, 1772, section 14 (1 Sm., 375).

For taxes. Tenants residing on lands owned by persons not residing in the township are liable for the payment of road taxes, and
such tax may be deducted from the rent or recovered from the
owner in an action of debt. Act of April 6, 1802, section 8 (3
Sm., 516).

In the same manner tenants are liable for all taxes which may
be deducted from the rent or recovered in an action of debt. Act
of April 3, 1804, section 6 (4 Sm., 203).

The Act of April 15, 1834, section 46 (P. L., 518), provides that
the goods and chattels of a tenant shall be liable to distress and sale
for non-payment of taxes assessed upon the property he occupies.

The Act of April 19, 1883, section 1 (P. L., 9), extends the
above Act so that in cities of the first class the distress may not
only be levied upon the tenant's goods, but the personalty of the
owner of the premises, wherever found.

The right to distrain after tenant's death. A landlord cannot distrain the goods of an insolvent deceased lessee on the demised premises—such goods being in the hands of an administrator. The proper
practice is to claim for the rent at the audit of the administrator's
account. *Stahlman's Estate*, 26 P. L. J., 113 (1879). *Gandy* v.
Dickson, 166 Pa. St., 422; 36 W. N., 95 (1895).

§ 1652. *For fraudulent removal.* Where any tenant fraudulently
or clandestinely conveys or carries off or from the premises goods
and chattels with intent to prevent the landlord from distraining,
the landlord may, within thirty days next ensuing, take and seize
such goods or chattels wherever they may be found, as if actually
distrained upon such demised premises. Act of March 21, 1772,
section 5 (1 Sm., 371).

Provided, that before seizure, no *bona fide* sale for a valuable
consideration shall have been made to a person not privy to such
fraud. *Ibid.,* section 6.

In the city of Philadelphia, where any tenant, before rent is due,
shall fraudulently convey or carry off from such demised premises
goods and chattels, with intent to defraud the landlord, said landlord may consider the rent apportioned up to the time of such
fraudulent act, and within thirty days take and seize such goods
as a distress for the rents, apportioned, wherever found, as if distrained upon the demised premises : *Provided,* he shall make oath,
before such seizure, before some judge or justice of the peace, that
he verily believes that said goods and chattels were carried away
for the purpose of defrauding, as aforesaid : *Provided,* that before
such seizure, no *bona fide* sale for a valuable consideration shall have
been consummated with anyone not privy to such fraud.

This is extended to the cities of Pittsburg and Allegheny by the Act of March 29, 1870 (P. L., 669).

§ 1653. *For dower and in insolvency.* The Act of March 29, 1832, section 43 (P. L., 203), provides that in an Orphans' Court sale of realty charged with dower, the share of the widow of the purchase-money shall remain in the purchaser's hands, and the interest thereof shall be annually paid her. If not so paid, then she may recover it by distress.

The Act of March 29, 1832, section 41 (P. L., 202), provides, in a partition sale of realty charged with dower, the widow shall be entitled to interest on her share of the purchase-money in lieu of dower, due annually, and, if not paid, it may be recovered by distress.

The Act of June 16, 1836, section 28 (P. L., 735), provides that a landlord may distrain for one year's rent upon the goods of an insolvent after his discharge.

§ 1654. *When property seized in execution to be liable for rent due not exceeding one year— Writ not to be stayed without landlord's consent.*

The goods and chattels being in or upon any messuage, lands, or tenements, which are or shall be demised for life or years, or otherwise taken by virtue of an execution, and liable to the distress of the landlord, shall be liable for the payment of any sums of money due for rent at the time of taking such goods in execution : *Provided,* that such rent shall not exceed one year's rent. (Act June 16, 1836, section 83; P. L., 777.)

After the sale by the officer of any goods or chattels he shall first pay out of the proceeds of such sale the rent so due, and the surplus thereof, if any, he shall apply toward satisfying the judgment mentioned in such execution : *Provided,* that if the proceeds of the sale shall not be sufficient to pay the landlord and the costs of the execution, the landlord shall be entitled to receive the proceeds after deducting so much for costs as he would be liable to pay in case of a sale under distress. (*Id.,* section 84.)

Whenever any goods or chattels liable to the payment of rent shall be seized in execution, the proceedings upon such execution shall not be stayed by the plaintiff without the consent of the person entitled to such rent in writing. (*Id.,* section 85.)

The form of a warrant and of a distress are given in sections 149, 150.

§ 1655. *Proceedings on a distress* are set forth in section 151.

Where goods not liable owner must replevy if he knows of distress in time. Where a distress includes the goods of others found on the premises, if the owners desire to assert their title, they have their remedy by an action of replevin—otherwise the landlord may sell, and is not afterward liable in a subsequent action of trespass. *Machine Co. v. Spencer,* 29 W. N., 493 (1892).

But if an owner has no knowledge of a distress in time to re-plevy, he may maintain trespass. *Brown* v. *Stackhouse,* 32 W. N., 407 ; 155 Pa. St., 582 (1893).

Landlord knowingly distraining upon goods left for sale is a tres-passer. A landlord who distrains upon goods, knowing them to be the property of another left for sale, on commission, with the tenant, is a trespasser *ab initio,* and liable in damages to the owner in trespass. *Brown* v. *Stackhouse (supra).*

§ 1656.

FORM OF CONSTABLE'S APPRAISEMENT.

A. B. }
   v. } *Sur* distraint for rent. Costs, $.
C. D. }

We, the undersigned, having been summoned by   , constable of the   Ward, to appraise and value the goods and chattels of C. D., the above-named defendant, and having been duly sworn (or affirmed), appraise and value the same as follows, to wit : (here set forth the personal property of C. D., and the appraised value of each item).

We, the undersigned, having been summoned by   , constable of the   Ward, to appraise and value the goods and chattels of C. D., the above-named defendant, do solemnly swear (or affirm) that we will well and truly appraise the same to the best of our knowledge and ability.

Appraisers :

Appraisers sworn before me, this }
   day of   , A. D. 1891. }

E. F.,
G. H.

Magistrate. }

L. M., Constable.

The inventory in distress should be sufficiently full to inform the tenant of the goods distrained, for which he may issue a writ of replevin.

The landlord is not obliged to weigh and measure goods dis-trained. *Richards* v. *McGrath,* 100 Pa. St., 400 (1882).

§ 1657.

FORM OF WAIVER OF APPRAISEMENT.

A. B. }
   v. } *Sur* distraint for rent. Costs, $.
C. D. }

I hereby request G. H., constable of the   Ward, to dispense with the appraisement of the goods and chattels distrained upon by him on premises (place), upon warrant of distress for the above rent, and I do expressly waive the appraisement of said goods and chattels required to be appraised, under Act of Assembly of March 21, 1772, together with all other Acts and laws requiring said goods and chattels to be appraised, and the waiver of said appraisement being for my benefit, I do hereby agree that said goods and chattels may remain upon the premises until said rent and all legal costs are paid, and if the rent and costs are not paid previously to (date), then I agree that the sale of said goods and chattels may take place, on said premises or at any other place selected therefor by said constable, after six days' public notice of sale, the same as if no waiver had taken place. The waiver of appraisement and other proceedings to be without prejudice to the distress, which is to remain in full force, same as if no waiver had been made.

In witness whereof, I have hereunto set my hand and seal this day of   , A. D. 1891.

                                                   C. D.   [SEAL]

Witness present, }
   L. M.   }

§ 1658. **Exemption laws.** The sheriff, constable, or other officer charged with the execution of any warrant for levying upon and selling the * * * personal property of the debtor shall, if requested by the debtor, summon three disinterested and competent persons, who shall be sworn or affirmed, to appraise the property which the debtor may elect to retain, and the property thus chosen and appraised, to the value of $300, shall be exempt from lévy and sale. Act of April 9, 1849, section 2 (P. L., 533).

This right may be waived in writing by the debtor, or if he neglect to notify the officer charged with the execution that he claims the benefit of the $300 law, it will be presumed the privilege has been waived. *Winchester* v. *Costello*, 2 Pars., 279 (1851).

§ 1659.

FORM OF CLAIM FOR EXEMPTION.

A. B.   }   *Sur* distress for rent before Magistrate   , of Court No. .
   v. }   Rent due, $.   Costs,   .   Distress warrant issued and
C. D.   }   directed to L. M., constable.
To L. M., Constable :

DEAR SIR: Please take notice that as to the above distress I claim the benefit of the Act of Assembly, approved the ninth day of April, A. D. 1849, entitled an Act to exempt property to the value of three hundred dollars ($300) from levy and sale on execution and distress for rent, and that I desire an appraisement in compliance with the said Act of all property levied on under said execution, and I hereby request and notify you to appoint appraisers, and to have the same appraised in compliance with the provisions of the said Act, and request that you will notify me of the time and place of holding such appraisement.

Philadelphia (date).   Very respectfully yours,

                                              C. D.,
                                            (Address.)

§ 1660. **What may be distrained.** The landlord may take and seize cattle or stock belonging to the tenant feeding or depasturing upon all or any part of the premises demised—corn, grass, hops, roots, fruit, pulse, or other product growing on any part of the demised premises. Act of March 21, 1772, section 7 (1 Sm., 371).

Goods of a stranger in the possession of the tenant not in the way of trade, and without hire, may be distrained. *Page* v. *Middleton*, 118 Pa. St., 546 (1888).

§ 1661. **What may not be distrained.** Property to the value of $300, exclusive of wearing apparel of tenant and his family, of Bibles and school-books in use are exempt from distress. Act of April 9, 1849, section 1 (P. L., 533).

Goods of a third person placed with a commission merchant on storage in the way of trade.

Goods of an auctioneer on the premises for the purposes of sale.

Goods of a boarder at a boarding-house actually in use.

Goods in the custody of the law under an execution or attachment or replevin.

Cattle received by a tenant to be pastured for hire.

Fixtures attached to the freehold, and which cannot be removed without destroying their character or injuring them.

Goods in possession of a tenant for sale on commission. *Machine Co.* v. *Spencer*, 28 W. N., 287 (1891).

Goods of a third party, to be sold by a tenant under consignment. *Brown* v. *Stackhouse*, 32 W. N., 407 (1893).

Sewing-machines, leased musical instruments, and typewriters. See § 3165.

§ 1662. **Time within which tenant may replevy.** In computing the five days within which the tenant may replevy his goods, the first day upon which the distress is made is excluded, and if the last day fall on Sunday, the tenant has the following day. *McKinney* v. *Reader*, 6 Watts, 34 (1837).

§ 1663. **Right of tenant as to payment of rent.** Where a landlord, at the tenant's request, agrees that he shall pay his rent at the conclusion instead of the beginning of the month, the landlord cannot thereafter compel a tenant to pay the rent other than at the end of the month, on the ground that the terms of the lease provide for payment in advance. *Wilgus* v. *Whitehead*, 89 Pa. St., 131 (1879).

§ 1664. **Proceedings to obtain possession at end of term—Two justices—Freeholders to be appointed and to award possession after proof of legal notice.**

Where any persons having leased to any person or persons any lands or tenements for a term of one or more years, or at will, paying certain rents, and they or their heirs or assigns shall be desirous upon the determination of the lease to have again and repossess their estate, and for that purpose shall demand and require their lessee to remove from the same, if the lessee or tenant shall refuse to comply therewith, in three months after such request it shall be lawful for the lessor or lessors, his or their heirs or assigns, to complain thereof to any two justices where the premises are situate; upon due proof before said justices that the said lessor or lessors had been quietly and peaceably possessed of the lands and tenements so demanded to be delivered up, that he or they demised the same, under certain rents, to the tenant in possession, or some person or persons under whom such tenant claims or came in possession, and that the term for which the same was demised is fully ended; then it shall be the duty of the said two justices to whom complaint shall be made forthwith to issue a warrant in nature of a summons directed to the sheriff of the county, commanding the sheriff to summon twelve substantial freeholders to appear before the said justices within four days next after issuing the said summons, and also to summon the lessee or tenant, or other person claiming or coming into the possession under the said lessee or tenant, at the same time to appear before the said justices and freeholders to show cause, if any he has, why restitution of the possession of the demised premises should not be forthwith made to such lessor or lessors, his or their heirs or assigns. And if, upon hearing the parties, or in case the tenants or other persons claiming or coming into possession under the said lessee or tenant neglect to appear after being summoned, and it shall appear to the said justice and freeholders that the lessor or lessors had been possessed of the lands or tenements in question, that he or they had demised the same for a term of years, or at will, to the person in possession, or some other under whom he or she claims or came into possession, at a certain yearly or other rent, and that the term is fully ended, that demand had been made of the lessee or other person in possession to leave the premises three months before such application to the said justices, then it shall be lawful for the said justices to make a record of such finding by them, the said justices and freeholders, and the said freeholders shall assess such damages as they think right against the tenant or other person in possession for the unjust detention of the demised premises; for which damages and reasonable costs judgment shall be entered by the said justices, which judgment shall be final and conclusive to the parties; and upon which the said justices shall, and they are required to issue their warrant under their hands and seals directed to the sheriff of the county, commanding him forthwith to deliver to the lessor or lessors, his or their heirs or assigns, full possession of the demised premises, and to levy the costs taxed by the justices, and damages so by the freeholders assessed of the goods and chattels of the lessee or tenant, or other person in possession, any law, custom, or usage to the contrary notwithstanding. (Act March 21, 1772, section 12; 1 Sm., 373.)

Where by law two aldermen are now required to hear and determine any matter before them, the same jurisdiction shall be exercised by one magistrate in Philadelphia County. Act of February 5, 1875, section 12 (P. L., 56).

Aldermen and city recorders are justices of the peace within the meaning of the Act of 1772. *Steamship Co.* v. *Haas*, 31 W. N., 79 (1892).

§ 1665. *Act of 1772 not to apply to joint tenants, co-partners, or tenants in common.*

The provisions of the twelfth section of the Act of 1772 shall not be so construed or extended as to enable any landlord or lessor, his heirs or assigns, by the summary mode of proceeding therein prescribed, to dispossess any person claiming to hold such leased or demised premises as joint-tenant, co-partner, or tenant in common with the landlord or person claiming possession : *Provided*, that the tenant or the person in possession, or the person under whom the tenant may claim to hold, shall, upon the return of the warrant in the nature of a summons issued by the two justices of the peace to whom the landlord, lessor, or person claiming possession may have applied, declare on oath or affirmation, to be taken and subscribed before the said justices, that the premises in dispute are holden and claimed by or under a co-joint tenant, co-partner, or tenant in common with the landlord, lessor, or person claiming possession, and that the person making such oath or affirmation doth verily believe that the premises in dispute do not exceed in quantity or value the just proportion of the joint tenant, partner, or tenant in common, by or under whom the premises may be holden or attempted to be holden : *And provided also*, that the tenant or person in possession, or the person under whom the tenant may claim to hold, shall, with one or more sufficient sureties, become bound by recognizance in the sum of one thousand dollars to the lessor or landlord or person claiming possession, his heirs or assigns, to prosecute his claim at the next Court of Common Pleas to be held for the county where the lands shall be. If the claim shall not be prosecuted then, such proceedings shall be had as would have been had if the recognizance had not been entered into. (Act March 22, 1814, section 1; 6 Sm., 176.)

§ 1666. *Jurisdiction.* The landlord is entitled to the provisions of the Act only when a certain rent is clearly and distinctly reserved in the lease. *McGee* v. *Fessler*, 1 Pa. St., 126 (1845).

If the complainant be a residuary legatee of the original lessor, the justice has not jurisdiction. *May* v. *Kendall*, 8 Phila., 244 (1871).

If it is alleged the magistrate has no jurisdiction, the affidavit of the defendant must set forth that the title to the lands and tenements in question is disputed. If the wife of the tenant make such affidavit, it must be shown that she interposes with the consent and authority of the tenant. *Haffner* v. *Hoeckley*, 3 Brews., 253 (1868).

§ 1667. *Notice to quit.* The Act requires three months' notice before the application to the justices. *Rich* v. *Keyser*, 54 Pa. St., 86 (1867).

Where a lease is made for a year, and the tenant is permitted to hold over, agreeably to the custom of Pennsylvania, he becomes tenant from year to year, and he cannot be dispossessed but by a notice given three months previous to the end of the year. *Fahnestock* v. *Faustenauer*, 5 S. & R., 174 (1819).

If a lease provides that the term is to end on a day certain, it is not necessary to give the tenant three months' notice before the expiration of the lease ; where the termination is uncertain, if the landlord wishes to determine the lease, he must give notice three months before the expiration of the year. *Logan* v. *Herron*, 8 S. & R., 459 (1822).

A notice to quit must be expressed in plain and direct language. A notice to surrender possession or pay an increased rent is not sufficient. *Byrne* v. *Funk*, 13 W. N., 503 (1883).

A verbal notice to quit is sufficient, and if it be a written notice, a mistake in it may be corrected at the time of service. A notice signed by an assignee should be signed by him as assignee.

If the tenant has had notice of the assignment, a notice omitting the word "assignee" is not fatal. *Thamm* v. *Hamberg*, 2 Brews., 528 (1868).

A notice to quit to one of two joint tenants is good. *Glenn* v. *Thompson*, 75 Pa. St., 389 (1874).

Notice to quit may be given by a lessor, his heirs or assigns. The notice by the original lessor, even though the property has been conveyed, is sufficient. *Glenn* v. *Thompson*, 75 Pa. St., 389 (1874).

Notice served February 12, 1867, to quit May 12, 1867, is sufficient and good. *McGowen* v. *Sennett*, 1 Brews., 397 (1867).

§ 1668.

FORM OF NOTICE TO TENANT.

SIR :

Being in the possession of a certain messuage or tenement, with the appurtenances, situate (here briefly describe by street, No., etc.), in the city of Philadelphia, which said premises were demised to you by me for a certain term, to wit, from the   day of   , A. D. 18 , until the   day of   , A. D. 18 , and which said term will terminate and expire on the day and year last aforesaid, I hereby give you notice that it is my desire to have again and repossess the said messuage or tenement, with the appurtenances, and I therefore do hereby require you to leave the same upon the expiration of the said hereinbefore mentioned term.

City of Philadelphia (date).

(Signature of Landlord.)

§ 1669. *Complaint.* A complaint signed A. B. per C. D., agent, and followed by the certificate " sworn before us, etc.," and signed by two aldermen, was sufficient in *Gavit* v. *Hall*, 75 Pa. St., 363 (1874).

§ 1670.

FORM OF COMPLAINT.

To E. F. and G. H., Justices of the Peace for the County of   .

The complaint of A. B. most respectfully sets forth, that he is the owner of certain premises, with appurtenances, situate (here briefly describe), and that he was in possession thereof   when he demised the said premises to a certain C. D. for the full term of   years, which said term is fully ended.

The said A. B., being desirous upon the determination of the said term to have again and repossess the said estate, for that purpose did on the day of   , 1890, last past, demand and require the said C. D. to remove from and leave the same, and that the said C. D. has hitherto refused and still doth refuse to comply therewith; that three months having elapsed since the service of the said notice he makes this complaint, that such proceedings may be taken by you as are directed by the Act of Assembly in such case made and provided.

Sworn to and subscribed before me, ⎱
    this   day of   , A. D. 18 . ⎰   A. B.

§ 1671.

FORM OF PRECEPT TO SHERIFF.

County of   , 88.

The Commonwealth of Pennsylvania to the Sheriff of   County, greeting :

Whereas complaint and due proof were this day made before E. F., Esq., and G. H., Esq., justices of the peace in and for the   county, that A. B., of   , on the   day of   , 18 , was quietly and peaceably possessed of premises (here describe briefly), and being so thereof possessed on the same day and year aforesaid, did demise the said premises to C. D., for the term of (number of years) then next ensuing, at the annual rent of   dollars, and that the said C. D., by virtue of the said demise entered into possession of the said demised premises, and held the same during the said term, and is still possessed of the same, and that the said term for which the said premises were demised is fully ended; and the said A. B., being desirous upon the said determination of the said term to have again and repossess the said premises, for that purpose did, on the   day of   , 1890, demand of and require the said C. D. to remove from and leave the same on or before (date), and that the said C. D. has hitherto refused and still doth refuse to comply with the said demand and requisition to remove from and leave the said premises : Therefore we command you that you summon twelve substantial freeholders of your bailiwick, so that they be and appear before our said justices at (place) on   , the   day of   , 1890, at (hour) o'clock in the forenoon of that day, and that you also summon the said C. D., so that he be and appear before our said justices and the said freeholders, at the day and place last aforesaid, to show cause, if any he has, why restitution of the possession of the said demised premises should not be forthwith made to the aforesaid A. B., according to the form and effect of the Act of the General Assembly in such case made and provided. And this you shall in nowise omit. And have you then there this writ.

Witness the said E. F., Esq., and G. H., Esq., at the city of   aforesaid, the   day of   , 1890.

                              E. F.   [SEAL]
                              G. H.   [SEAL]

§ 1672. *Sheriff must summon jury.* In proceedings under the Act of 1772, the sheriff must summon and select the jury ; a deputy cannot. *Armstrong* v. *Novinger*, 8 Pa. St., 412 (1848).

If there be irregularity in summoning the jurors, and the defendants appear before the inquest and are heard on the merits, all irregularity is waived. *Wistar* v. *Ollis*, 77 Pa. St., 291 (1875).

On *certiorari*, the Common Pleas will not hear affidavits as to such irregularity. *Ibid.*

§ 1673. *Service on tenant.* In proceedings under the Act of March 21, 1772, service on the premises on a person in possession claiming to be agent of the lessee is good. *Watts* v. *Fox*, 64 Pa. St., 336 (1870).

§ 1674. *Sheriff's return.* If the sheriff's return to the warrant states he has summoned twelve freeholders without naming them, and the inquisition states their names, the law presumes the inquest consisted of those summoned. If objection be made, it must be done before the inquest at the hearing. *Gavit* v. *Hall*, 75 Pa. St., 363 (1874).

Be careful to see that the return follows the terms of the statute.

§ 1675. *Proceedings at the inquest.* If an inquest cannot agree, they may be discharged and another *venire* issued. *Cunningham* v. *Gardner*, 4 W. & S., 120 (1842).

If the jurors, after being duly sworn, absent themselves or adjourn to another day without the consent of the parties, the justices may discharge them and issue a new precept to the sheriff, directing him to summon a new jury. *White* v. *Arthurs*, 24 Pa. St., 99 (1854).

§ 1676.

FORM OF INQUISITION.

Inquisition taken at (office), in the county of   , on the day of   , in the year one thousand eight hundred and   , before E. F., Esq., and G. H., Esq., two of our justices of the peace, by the oaths of (names of jurors), and the solemn affirmations of (names of jurors), twelve substantial freeholders of the said county, who, upon their oaths and affirmations respectively do say that A. B., on the   day of   , in the year one thousand eight hundred and   , was quietly and peaceably possessed of certain premises (here briefly describe).

And being so thereof possessed on the same day and year last aforesaid did demise the said premises to C. D. for the term of   years then next ensuing, at the   rent of   dollars, and that the said C. D., by virtue of the said demise entered into possession of the said demised premises, and held the same during the said term, and is still possessed of the same, and that the said term for which the said premises were demised is fully ended; and the said A. B. being desirous upon the said determination of the said term to have again and repossess the said premises for that purpose did, on the   day of   , 1890, demand of and require the said C. D. to remove from and leave the same within   , and that the said C. D. has hitherto refused and still doth refuse to comply with the said demand and requisition to remove from and leave the said premises.

And the said freeholders do assess damages against the said C. D. for the unjust detention of the said demised premises at   dollars, besides all costs of suit. Whereupon it is considered by the said E. F. and G. H.

justices aforesaid, that restitution of the said demised premises be made to the said A. B., and that he recover of the said C. D. his damages aforesaid, together with the costs of suit, amounting to   dollars.

In testimony whereof, as well the said justices as the said freeholders have hereunto set their hands and seals the day and year first above written, at   aforesaid.

E. F.   [SEAL]
G. H.   [SEAL]

(Twelve seals.)

§ 1677. *Requisites of the inquisition.* The inquisition should state the term was ended, and leave no necessary facts uncertain. *Fahnestock* v. *Faustenauer*, 5 S. & R., 174 (1819) ; *May* v. *Kendall*, 8 Phila., 244 (1871). If the tenant has waived the three months' notice, the omission of such averment is fatal. *Hutchinson* v. *Potter*, 11 Pa. St., 472 (1849).

§ 1678. *Justice not to give judgment if landlord's title disputed— Party claiming shall make affidavit that he believes he is entitled to premises.*

If the tenant shall allege that the title to the lands and tenements in question is disputed and claimed by some other person or persons, whom he shall name, in virtue of a right or title accrued or happening since the commencement of the lease so made to him, by descent, deed, or from or under the last will of the lessor, and if thereupon the person so claiming shall forthwith or upon a summons, immediately to be issued by the said justices, returnable in six days next following, before them appear, and on oath or affirmation, to be by the said justices administered, declare that he verily believes that he is entitled to the premises in dispute, and shall with one or more sufficient sureties become bound by recognizance in the sum of one hundred pounds to the lessor or lessors, his or their heirs or assigns, to prosecute his claim at the next Court of Common Pleas to be held for the county where the said lands and tenements shall be, then and in such case, and not otherwise, the said justices shall forbear to give the said judgment : *Provided also,* if the said claim shall not be prosecuted according to the true intent and meaning of the said recognizance, it shall be forfeited to the use of the lessor or landlord ; and the justices aforesaid shall proceed to give judgment, and cause the lands and tenements aforesaid to be delivered to him in the manner hereinbefore directed. (Act of March 21, 1772.)

In *Debozear* v. *Butler*, 2 Grant, 417 (1853), LEWIS, J., said : " Where the tenant has acquired the title, after the commencement of the lease, from the lessor himself by descent, deed, or will, the relation of landlord and tenant is at an end, and the summary remedy to obtain possession no longer applies."

Where the tenant does not pretend that he claims the premises by descent, deed, or will, but by an agreement in writing or contract with the landlord, since the commencement of the lease, he must show either a conveyance executed or such an equitable right to one as would sustain a bill for specific performance in a court of chancery.

§ 1679. *Judgment.* The judgment must be that the premises be delivered up by the lessee to the lessor.

A judgment in the alternative for possession or for the amount of rent is fatally irregular. *Evans* v. *Radford*, 2 Phila., 370 (1858).

§ 1680.

FORM OF WRIT OF RESTITUTION.

County of   , *ss.*

The Commonwealth of Pennsylvania to the Sheriff of   County, greeting :

Whereas due proof has been made before E. F., Esq., and G. H., Esq., two of our justices of said county, and twelve substantial freeholders, summoned for that purpose, that (here copy the finding in the inquisition) all which premises being duly found to be true by the said justices and freeholders, according to the form of the Act of General Assembly in such case made and provided : We therefore command you, the said sheriff, forthwith to deliver to the said A. B. full possession of the demised premises aforesaid. And we also command you, that of the goods and chattels of the said C. D. in your bailiwick, you cause to be levied as well the sum of   dollars, which the said justices have awarded for his damages sustained by the unjust detention of the premises, as for the costs and charges by A. B. in and about his suit in that behalf expended, whereof the said C. D. is convict. And hereof fail not.

Witness the said E. F. and G. H., justices as aforesaid, at (place), in the county aforesaid, the   day of   , A. D. one thousand eight hundred and   .

E. F.   [SEAL]
G. H.   [SEAL]

§ 1681.

FORM OF RECORD.

Be it remembered, that on the   day of   , in the year one thousand eight hundred and   , at (place), in the city of   , due proof was made before E. F., Esq., and G. H., Esq., two of our justices of the peace, that A. B., of   , on the   day of   , in the year one thousand eight hundred and   , was quietly and peaceably possessed of premises (here briefly describe by street and number, etc.). And being so thereof possessed on the same day and year last aforesaid, did demise the said premises to C. D. of said city, for the term of (number of years) then next ensuing, at the annual rent of   dollars, and that the said C. D. by virtue of the said demise entered into possession of the said demised premises, and held the same during the said term, and is still possessed of the same, and that the said term for which the said premises were demised is fully ended ; and the said A. B. being desirous upon the said determination of the said term to have again and repossess the said premises for that purpose did, on the   day of   , 1890, demand of and require the said C. D. to remove from and leave the same on or before (date), and that the said C. D. has hitherto refused and still doth refuse to comply with the said demand and requisition to remove from and leave the said premises. Whereupon the said A. B. then, to wit, on the said

day of   , one thousand eight hundred and   , at the city aforesaid,
prayed us, the said justices of the peace, that a due remedy in that behalf
be provided for him according to the form of the Act of the General Assembly of the State of Pennsylvania, in such case made and provided; upon
which proof and complaint the sheriff of the county of   is commanded that he summon twelve substantial freeholders of his bailiwick, so
that they be and appear before us, the said justices, at the (place), on   ,
the   day of   , 1890, at (hour) o'clock in the forenoon of that day,
and that he also summon the said C. D., so that he be and appear before
us, the said justices and the said freeholders, at the day and place last aforesaid, to show cause, if any he has, why restitution of the possession of the
said demised premises should not be forthwith made to the aforesaid A. B.

Afterward, to wit, on the said   day of   , 1890, at the (place),
L. M., Esq., sheriff of the county of   , appears before us the said justices, and returns that by virtue of the said warrant to him directed he had
summoned twelve substantial freeholders, to wit (here set forth names of
freeholders), and had also summoned the said C. D. to be and appear at
this day and place, as by the said warrant he was commanded; and the
said freeholders being called, appear, and are severally sworn and affirmed.
And the said C. D. also appears; and we, the said justices and the aforesaid freeholders, proceed to hear and examine the proofs and allegations
offered by the said parties, and do find that the said A. B., on the
day of   , 18   , was quietly and peaceably possessed of premises (here
briefly describe). And being so thereof possessed on the same day and
year last aforesaid did demise the said premises to the said C. D. for the
term of   years then next ensuing, at the annual rent of
dollars, and that the said C. D., by virtue of the said demise, entered into possession of the said demised premises, and held the same
during the said term, and is still possessed of the same, and that the said
term for which the said premises were demised is fully ended; and the
said A. B. being desirous upon the said determination of the said term to
have again and repossess the said premises, for that purpose did, on the
day of   , 1890, demand of and require the said C. D. to remove
from and leave the same on or before   , and that the said C. D. has
hitherto refused and still doth refuse to comply with the said demand and
requisition to remove from and leave the said premsies. And the said freeholders assess the sum of   dollars for damages of the said A. B., occasioned by the unjust detention of the said premises. Therefore it is considered and adjudged by us, the said justices of the peace, that the said A.
B. shall and do recover possession of the said premises, and have of the
said C. D. as well the said sum of   dollars for his damages aforesaid,
as   dollars, for his reasonable costs by him expended in and about this
suit in his behalf, concerning which the premises aforesaid we do make
this our record.

In testimony whereof, we, the said justices of the peace, to this our record
have set our hands and seals, at the city of   aforesaid, this
day of   , one thousand eight hundred and

E. F.   [SEAL]
G. H.   [SEAL]

§ 1682. *Requisites of record.* The inquisition is a part of the
record. *Buchanan* v. *Baxter,* 67 Pa. St., 348 (1871).

The Act applies only to leases in which a certain rent is distinctly reserved. If this fact do not appear on the record, the inquest will be set aside. *McGee* v. *Fessler*, 1 Pa. St., 126 (1845).

The record, being an inquest of facts, does not require the testimony to be set out. *Bedford* v. *Kelly*, 61 Pa. St., 491 (1869).

§ 1683. Certiorari *may issue, but it is not a* supersedeas. In proceedings under the Act of 1772, the common law writ of *certiorari* may issue, but it is not a *supersedeas*. *De Coursey* v. *Trust Co.*, 81 Pa. St., 217 (1876).

When a *certiorari* is taken under the Act of 1772, and the record of the magistrate brought into the Common Pleas, a rule to take depositions is improper. *Steamship Co.* v. *Haas*, 31 W. N., 79 (1892).

§ 1684. **Justice to deliver possession of premises to landlord when tenant removes without leaving sufficient property for three months' rent or giving security.**

If any lessee for a term of years in the city and county of Philadelphia shall remove from the demised premises without leaving sufficient property thereon to secure the payment of at least three months' rent, or shall refuse to give security for the payment thereof in five days after demand, and shall refuse to deliver up possession of such premises, it shall be lawful for the landlord or lessor to apply to any two justices within said county and make an affidavit or affirmation of the fact, and thereupon the justices shall forthwith issue their precept to any constable of the proper county, commanding him to summon such lessee before such justices on a day certain, not exceeding eight nor less than five days, to answer such complaint, and the justices shall on the day appointed proceed to hear the case ; and if it appear that the lessee has removed without leaving sufficient goods and chattels on the premises, or giving security for the payment of rent, and has refused to deliver up possession of the demised premises, said justices shall enter judgment against such lessee that said premises shall be delivered up to the lessor forthwith, and shall, at the request of the lessor issue a writ of possession directed to said constable, commanding him forthwith to deliver possession of the premises to the lessor, and levy the costs on defendant in the same manner that executions are directed. (Act March 25, 1825, section 2 ; 8 Sm., 411.)

Where by law two aldermen are now required to hear and determine any matter before them, the same jurisdiction shall be exercised by one magistrate. Act of February 5, 1875, section 12 (P. L., 56).

§ 1685.

FORM OF NOTICE TO TENANT TO QUIT.

Philadelphia,   , 1890.
To C. D.

I hereby demand of and require you to give me security for the payment of at least three months' rent within five days from the date hereof or deliver up to me possession of the premises you now hold as tenant under me, said premises being situated (here locate) (you having removed there-from without leaving sufficient property thereon to secure the payment of at least three months' rent), or I shall proceed to obtain possession thereof according to law.

A. B.,
(Address).

If a tenant quits possession of premises and receives notice to give security for rent in five days, he must tender security within that time or suffer for his neglect. *Ward* v. *Wandell*, 10 Pa. St., 98 (1848).

The notice must be signed by the landlord or his authorized agent. *Powell* v. *Campbell*, 2 Phila., 42 (1856).

§ 1686.

FORM OF COMPLAINT.

City of Philadelphia, *ss.*

On the   day of   , 1890, personally appeared A. B. before me, the subscriber, L. M., Magistrate of Court No.   , of the said city, and being duly sworn according to law, saith that he demised the premises situate No.   Street, in said city, for the term of   years, from the   day of   , A. D. 18   , at an annual rent of   dollars to C. D., who removed therefrom on or about   day of   , 18   ; that there are not sufficient goods and chattels on the premises to pay a quarter's rent; that he refuses to give up possession or security for three months' rent, the same having been demanded more than five days previous to the date hereof.

Sworn to and subscribed before me, ⎫
  the day and year aforesaid.   ⎪
            L. M.,   ⎬
    Magistrate of Court No. . ⎪
(Office.)   ⎭

A. B.

The affidavit of plaintiff must show that the premises were de-mised or rented by plaintiff to defendant. *Mund* v. *Vanfleet*, 2 Phila., 41 (1856).

§ 1687.

FORM OF SUMMONS.

City of Philadelphia, *ss.*

The Commonwealth of Pennsylvania to any constable of the said city, greeting:

Whereas, complaint on oath hath been made before me, the subscriber, L. M., Magistrate of Court No.   , of the said city, by A. B., of said city, that he demised the premises situate No.   Street, in said city, for the term of   years, from the   day of   , A. D. 18   , at an annual rent of   dollars to C. D., who removed therefrom on or about the   day of   , 18   ; that there are not goods enough on the premises to secure the payment of at least three months' rent; and the said C. D. refuses to give up possession, or security for three months' rent, the same having been demanded five days previous to the date hereof. You are therefore commanded to summon the said C. D. to be and appear before the said magistrate, at his court, on the   day of   , 1890, at o'clock   M., to answer the complaint of said A. B.

In witness whereof, I have hereunto set my hand and affixed the official seal of the said court, the   day of   , A. D. 1890.

(Office.)   L. M.,
[SEAL]   Magistrate of Court No. .

§ 1688.

FORM OF WRIT OF RESTITUTION.

City of Philadelphia, *ss.*

The Commonwealth of Pennsylvania to any constable of the said city, greeting :

Whereas, proof was made on the   day of   , 18 , before L. M., Magistrate of Court No.   , for said city, that A. B. demised the premises situate No. (place) Street, in said city, for the term of   years, from the   day of   , A. D. 18 , at an annual rent of   dollars per annum, to C. D., who removed therefrom on or about the   day of   , 18 , without leaving sufficient goods and chattels on the premises to pay and satisfy three months' rent. That the said C. D. has refused to give up possession of said premises, or give security for the payment of three months' rent, the same having been demanded five days previous to making this complaint. Therefore we command you forthwith to deliver actual possession of said premises to the lessor. And we also command you that you levy the costs indorsed hereon on the goods and chattels of the said C. D. And of your proceedings herein make return to our magistrate within ten days after the receipt of this writ, to wit, on or before the   day of   , A. D. 18 .

In witness whereof, I have hereunto set my hand and affixed the official seal of the said court, the   day of   , A. D. 18 .

(Office.)   L. M.,
[SEAL]   Magistrate of Court No. .

INDORSEMENT.

Date,
Returnable,
          Writ of Restitution.
          L. & T. Act 1825.
                    A. B.
                    v.
                    C. D.

Rent, $
Costs, $
Total, $

§ 1689.

FORM OF RECORD.

Landlord and Tenant Case before L. M., Magistrate of Court No. .

(Date), 1890, A. B. appears and makes complaint on oath, that he demised the premises situate No.   Street, in the city of Philadelphia, for   term of   years, from the   day of   , A. D. 18 , at an annual rent of   dollars to C. D., who removed therefrom on or about the   day of   , A. D.

18 ; that there are not sufficient goods and chattels on the premises to pay a quarter's rent; that he refuses to give up possession or security for three months' rent, the same having been demanded more than five days previous to the date hereof.

Same day summons issued, returnable   , 18 , at (hour) o'clock M., G. H., constable; returned on oath. Served on defendant by (mode of service). And now (date), 18 , at (hour) o'clock, there appears before me (here note all who appear personally or by counsel).

After hearing the proofs and allegations of said A. B., our said magistrate does find that A. B. demised the premises situate No.
Street, in the city of Philadelphia, for   term of
years, from   day of   , A. D. 18 , at an annual rent of
dollars to C. D., who has removed therefrom; that there are not sufficient goods and chattels on the premises to pay a quarter's rent; that the said C. D. has refused to give up possession of said premises or security for the payment of three months' rent, the same having been demanded at least five days previous to making this complaint. Our said magistrate also finds that the above complaint is in all respects just and true, and enters judgment against the defendant that he shall deliver up possession of the aforesaid premises to the plaintiff. Whereupon a writ of possession issued (date), G. H., constable; returned. Possession given to plaintiff.

City of Philadelphia, ss.

I hereby certify the above to be a correct transcript from my docket. Witness my hand and the official seal of said court, the   day of
, A. D. 1890.

(Office.)   L. M.,
[SEAL]   Magistrate of Court No. .

§ 1690. *Requisites of record.* The record should show that the lessee is not in possession of the premises in dispute. *Freytag* v. *Anderson*, 1 Rawle, 73 (1828).

And that the magistrate finds the complaint to be true or proved before him, and that the lessee was a tenant for a term of years. *Geisenberger* v. *Cerf*, 1 Phila., 17 (1850); *Uber* v. *Hickson*, 6 *Id.*, 132 (1866).

§ 1691. Proceedings to obtain possession in case of non-payment of rent.

In case any lessee for a term of years, or at will, or otherwise, of a messuage, lands, or tenements, upon the demise whereof any rents are or shall be reserved, where the lessee shall neglect or refuse to pay rent reserved as often as the same may grow due according to the terms of the contract, and where there are no goods on the premises adequate to pay the rent in arrear, except such articles as are exempt from levy and sale, it shall and may be lawful for the lessor to give the lessee notice to quit the premises, within fifteen days from the date of the notice; if such notice is given on or after the first day of April and before the 1st of September, and within thirty days from the date thereof, if given on or after the 1st of September and before the first day of April. And if the lessee shall not within the period aforesaid remove from and deliver up the said premises to the said lessor, or pay and satisfy the rent in arrear, it shall be lawful for the lessor to make complaint on oath or affirmation, to any justice, as the case may require; who, on it appearing that the lessor has demised the premises for a term of years or otherwise, whereof any rent has been reserved, that the said rent is in arrear and unpaid, that there is not sufficient goods and chattels on the premises to pay and satisfy the said rent except such as are by law exempted from levy and sale, and that the lessee has, after being notified, refused to remove and redeliver up possession of the premises, shall then issue his precept, reciting substantially the complaint and allegation of the lessor, directed to any constable of the proper county, commanding him to summon the said lessee to appear before the said justice at a day and time to be therein fixed, not less than three nor more than eight days thereafter, to answer the said complaint. And the said justice shall, on the day appointed, or on some other day then to be appointed by the justice, proceed to hear the case, and if it shall appear that the complaint by the lessor is in all particulars just and true, then the justice shall enter judgment against such lessee that the premises shall be delivered up to the lessor, and at the request of the lessor issue a writ of possession, directed to the constable, commanding him forthwith to deliver actual possession of the premises to the lessor, and also to levy the costs on the defendant in the same manner that costs are now by law levied and collected on other writs of execution; and if on the hearing it shall appear that the complaint is vexatious and unfounded, the justice shall dismiss the same with costs to be paid by the lessor. (Act April 3, 1830, section 1; P. L., 187. Act March 22, 1861, section 1; P. L., 181.)

Where by law two aldermen are now required to hear and determine any matter before them, the same jurisdiction shall be exercised by one magistrate. Act of February 5, 1875, section 12 (P. L., 56).

§ 1692. **In Mercer County, tenant who refuses to perform labor may be dispossessed.**

Whenever any person shall be tenant of any house belonging to another in the county of *Mercer*, and occupies the same under an agreement, verbal or written, to perform labor or services for the owner or owners of said house or tenement, in addition to the rent reserved for the use of said house or tenement, whilst he shall occupy the same, and shall, during such occupancy, refuse or neglect to perform such labor or render such service, it shall and may be lawful for such owner or owners, his, her, or their agent or attorney, to dispossess such tenant in the manner provided by the Act of April 3, 1830, section 1, and the Supplements thereto, after giving thirty days' notice to said tenant to surrender possession of the house or tenement in his possession; and on due proof to the justice of neglect of said tenant to perform such labor or render such service according to the agreement, the said justice shall have power to declare the lease by which such house or tenement is held to be void. (Act May 4, 1864, section 1; P. L., 766, Act April 15, 1869, section 1; P. L., 972. Act of April 17, 1869, section 1; P. L., 1126.)

§ 1693. *Jurisdiction.* The Act of 1830 does not authorize proceedings against a tenant for life or in fee under a perpetual lease. *Trimbath* v. *Patterson,* 76 Pa. St., 277 (1874).

If the title to the premises come in dispute, the only remedy is ejectment, and not the proceeding before a justice. *Mohan* v. *Butler*, 17 **W. N.**, 434 (1886).

In such case, an affidavit that the title to lands will come into question need not be filed; an assertion of the fact, sustained by evidence, is sufficient. *Allen* v. *Ash*, 6 Phila., 312 (1867).

The affidavit of a third party, stating that he claims the reversion, is not sufficient to oust the jurisdiction of the magistrate. *Daly* v. *Barrett*, 4 Phila., 350 (1861).

§ 1694.

FORM OF NOTICE TO TENANT TO QUIT.

Philadelphia (date), 1890.

You are hereby notified to quit the premises situate (here locate), which I have leased to you, reserving rent, " or pay and satisfy the rent due and in arrear," being **$**   , which amount was due on the day of   , 18 , and is hereby demanded (you having neglected or refused to pay the amount so reserved, as often as the same has grown due, according to the terms of our contract, and there being no goods on the premises adequate to pay the rent so reserved, except such articles as are exempt from levy and sale by the laws of this Commonwealth), within   days from the date hereof, or I shall proceed against you as the law directs.

Respectfully yours,

To C. D.   'A. B.

The oath and complaint should be made by the lessor. *Hopkins* v. *McClelland*, 8 Phila., 302 (1871).

§ 1695.

FORM OF COMPLAINT.

City of Philadelphia, *ss.*

On the   day of   , Anno Domini 1890, personally appeared A. B., before the subscriber, L. M., Esq., Magistrate of Court No.   , in and for the said city, and being duly sworn according to law saith that he demised the premises situated   Street, in the city of Philadelphia, for   term of   years to   , at an annual rent of   dollars ; that the said rent, to wit, the sum of   dollars, due on the   day of   , A. D. 1890, is in arrear and unpaid, that there are not sufficient goods and chattels on the premises to pay and satisfy the said rent, except such as are by law exempted from levy and sale, and that the said lessee has (after being notified to quit the said premises within   .   days from the date of the said notice, at which time the amount of rent due was demanded), refused to render and deliver up possession of the said premises.

Sworn to and subscribed before me, ⎫
  (date).   ⎬   A. B.
        L. M.,   ⎪
    Magistrate of Court No. . ⎭

§ 1696.

CITY OF PHILADELPHIA,   ⎫
THE COMMONWEALTH OF PENNSYLVANIA, ⎬ *ss.*

Whereas, complaint on oath or affirmation hath been made before L. M., Esq., Magistrate of Court No. , of the said city, by A. B., that A. B. demised a certain tenement, situated (here locate) in the city of Philadelphia, for the term of   years to C. D., at an annual rent of ‛dollars,   , which rent is in arrear and unpaid; that there are not sufficient goods and chattels on the premises to pay and satisfy the said rent except such as are by law exempted from levy and sale; and that the said lessee has, after being notified according to law, refused to remove and deliver up possession of the said premises. You are therefore commanded to summon the said C. D., to be and appear before our said magistrate, at his court (place), in the said city, on the   day of   , 1890, between the hours of   o'clock M. and   o'clock M., to answer the said complaint.

In witness whereof, our said magistrate has hereunto set his hand and the official seal of said court, the   day of   , A. D. 1890.
(Office.)   L. M.,
[SEAL]   Magistrate of Court No. .

§ 1697. *Defense of tenant.* In proceedings under the Act, a tenant may show in defense that the title of the landlord has expired or has been divested by act of law. *Smith* v. *Crosland*, 15 W. N., 211 (1884).

§ 1698. *Inquisition and judgment.* If the inquisition set forth and find to be true the facts set forth in the complaint, thus establishing the magistrate's jurisdiction, that is sufficient. *McKeon* v. *King*, 9 Pa. St., 213 (1848).

The judgment of the justice need not recite the date of the lease, the expiration of the term, or date of the notice. *Kraft* v. *Wolf*, 6 Phila., 310 (1867).

§ 1699. *Rights of tenant upon adverse judgment.* The tenant, upon the determination of the justice favorably to the landlord, may use any one of three methods :

(*a*) He may pay the rent ascertained and costs, and continue in possession.

(*b*) He may appeal, upon giving proper security, and continue in possession.

(*c*) He may permit the landlord to execute his writ of possession and levy his costs, and take a writ of *certiorari* to remedy anything in the form or manner of proceedings not authorized by law.

· The landlord may use his personal remedy for the recovery of the rent, although repossessed of his property.

§ 1700. *Tenant may supersede writ of possession by payment of rent and costs.*

At any time before the writ of possession is actually executed the lessee may supersede and render the said writ of none effect by paying to the constable, for the use of the lessor, the rent actually due and in arrear and the costs; which rent in arrear shall be ascertained and determined by the justice on due and legal proof, and indorsed by him on the said writ of possession, together with the costs of the proceeding. Of all of which doings the constable shall make return to the justice within ten 'days after receiving the writ, and the constable shall be answerable in default of executing the writ according to its lawful requisitions, or in returning the same, in the same manner as to the amount of rent ascertained and determined and costs, as constables are now by law answerable on other writs of execution.

No writ of possession, however, shall be issued by a justice for five days after the rendition of judgment; and if within the said five days the tenant shall give good, sufficient, and absolute security by recognizance for all costs that may have and may accrue, in case the judgment shall be affirmed, and also for all rent that has accrued or may accrue to final judgment, then the tenant shall be entitled to an appeal to the next Court of Common Pleas; which appeal shall then be tried as other suits, but nothing shall prevent the issuing of a *certiorari* with the usual form and effect. (Act April 8, 1830, section 1; P. L., 187.)

§ 1701.

FORM OF WRIT OF RESTITUTION.

City of Philadelphia, *ss.*

The Commonwealth of Pennsylvania, to any constable of the said city most convenient to the defendant, greeting:

Whereas, proof was made on the   day of   , 1890, before L. M., Esq., Magistrate of Court No.   , of the said city, that A. B. rented to C. D. a certain tenement situated No.   , Street, in the city of Philadelphia, for   term of   year to C. D., at an annual rent of   dollars, the rent whereof is in arrears and unpaid; that there is not sufficient goods and chattels on the premises to pay and satisfy the said rent, except such as are by law exempted from levy and sale; and that the said lessee has, after being legally notified, refused to remove and redeliver up possession of the premises, according to the Act of General Assembly in such case made and provided; and whereon the said magistrate, in consideration of the premises, did enter judgment against the said lessee, that said premises should be delivered up to the lessor; and did also ascertain the amount of rent in arrear to be   dollars. Therefore we command you forthwith to deliver actual possession of said premises to the lessor; and we also command you that you levy the costs indorsed hereon on the goods and chattels of the said C. D. And of your proceedings herein make return to the said magistrate within ten days after your receipt 'of this writ, to wit, on or before the   day of   , 1890.

In witness whereof, the said magistrate has hereunto set his hand and official seal of said court, the   day of   , 1890.

L. M.,
Magistrate of Court No.   .

[SEAL]

INDORSEMENT.

Date,
Returnable,
    Writ of restitution.
        A. B.
         v.
        C. D.
Rent, $
Costs, $
Total, $

FORM OF RECORD.

Be it remembered, that on (date) at the city of Philadelphia A. B. appeared and made complaint under oath before me that he was the lessor of premises No.   Street, in said city, and that on (date) he demised said premises for the term of   years to C. D., at an annual rental of   dollars, and that said rent was payable monthly, to wit, the sum of   dollars per month, and that said lessee is in arrears for   months' rent due on   to wit, the sum of $.

That there are not sufficient goods and chattels on the said premises to pay and satisfy said rent, except such as are by law exempted from levy and sale, and that said lessee has, after being notified to quit the said premises within (here follow the Act of 1830) days from the date of said notice at which time the above rent was demanded, refused to render and deliver up possession of the said premises.

On said day summons issued returnable (date) at (hour) directed to G. H., constable of said county, which was returned duly served under oath by (mode of service). And on (date fixed in summons) at (hour) there appeared before me (here state who appeared and names of counsel), and after hearing the proofs and allegations of said parties said magistrate doth find that (date) A. B. demised said premises situate (place) in said city of Philadelphia, for the term of   years, at an annual rental of   dollars, payable monthly to C. D., and that   months' rent is in arrears, viz. : (state number of months) amounting to   dollars, and that there are not sufficient goods and chattels on said premises to pay and satisfy the said rent, except such as are by law exempted from levy and sale, and that said lessee, after having been notified (date) in accordance with the provisions of the Act in such case made and provided, refused to remove and deliver up possession of said premises.

Whereupon the said magistrate finds said complaint to be true in all respects, and enters judgment against (name), the said lessee, that the said premises shall be delivered up to (name), the said lessor, and at the request of said lessor has issued a writ of possession (date) directed to G. H., constable as aforesaid, commanding him to forthwith deliver possession of said premises to said lessor, and also to levy the costs of said action on said defendant.

Whereupon said writ was duly returned, possession given to said plaintiff and lessor.

In testimony whereof, I have hereunto set my hand and official seal to this said record at the city of Philadelphia (date).

(Office.)   L. M.,
[SEAL]   Magistrate of Court No. .

Under the Act of April 3, 1830, the justice must ascertain the rent due and in arrear, and indorse the same on the writ of possession, yet he cannot issue an execution against the tenant to coerce the payment of the sum. *Rubicum* v. *Williams*, 1 Ash., 230 ; *Trimbath* v. *Patterson*, 76 Pa. St., 280 (1874).

§ 1702. *Requisites of record.* The record of a justice must show the term for which the premises were demised ; the omission will be fatal. *Trimbath* v. *Patterson*, 76 Pa. St., 277 (1874) ; *McDermott* v. *McIlwain*, 75 Pa. St., 341 (1874).

§ 1703. *Bail on appeal.* The Act of March 20, 1845, section 1, providing the condition of recognizance on appeal, does not apply to the proceeding and judgment under the Act of April 3, 1830, section 1.

In proceedings under the Act of April 3, 1830, the following recognizance on appeal was held sufficient :

I become bail absolute in this case conditioned for the payment of all costs that have accrued, and all the costs that may accrue in case that the said judgment be affirmed, and also for all rent that has accrued and may accrue up to the time of final judgment. *Hardy* v. *Watts*, 22 Pa. St., 83 (1853).

§ 1704. *Waiver of appeal.* Where a lessee expressly waives all right to an appeal, writ of error, etc., and agrees that a judgment, order, or decree shall be final and conclusive, it is binding on him. *Lippincott* v. *Cooper*, 19 W. N., 130 (1886).

§ 1705. *Writ of possession, if judgment affirmed on appeal, issues from Common Pleas.* When the judgment of the justice is affirmed on appeal, the writ of *habere facias possessionem* properly issues from the Common Pleas. *Essler* v. *Johnson*, 25 Pa., 350 (1855).

§ 1706. *Certiorari from the Common Pleas.* On *certiorari*, the transcript of the record is sufficient if it discloses facts necessary to give jurisdiction, without setting forth those facts in detail. *Maxwell* v. *Perkins*, 93 Pa. St., 255 (1880).

In proceedings under the Act of April 3, 1830, to obtain a *certiorari*, it is not necessary to make the oath prescribed by the Act of March 20, 1810, section 21. *Rubicum* v. *Williams*, 1 Ash., 230.

§ 1707. **Proceedings to obtain possession at end of term.**

Where any person or persons in this State having leased any lands or tenements to any person or persons for a term of one or more years, or at will, shall be desirous, upon the determination of said lease, to have again and repossess such demised premises, having given three months' notice of such intention to his lessee, and said lessee shall refuse to leave and surrender up the said premises at the expiration of said term, in compliance with the terms of said notice, it shall be lawful for such lessor, his agent or attorney, to complain thereof to any justice of the peace where the premises lie, whose duty it shall be to summon the defendant to appear at a day fixed, as in other civil actions; and upon due proof being made, the tenant having notice of the time and place of hearing, that the said lessor was quietly and peaceably possessed of the lands or tenements so required to be surrendered up, and that he demised the same to the tenant in possession or to some other person under whom such tenant claims, and that the term for which the same were demised is fully ended, and that three months' previous notice had been given of his desire to repossess the same; then and in that case, if it shall appear right and proper to the said justice, he shall enter judgment against the said tenant, that he forthwith give up the possession of the said premises to the said lessor, and the said justice shall also give judgment in favor of the lessor and against the lessee or tenant, for such damages as in his opinion the said lessor may have sustained, and for all the costs of the proceeding; and he shall forthwith issue his warrant to any constable in the county, commanding him immediately to deliver to the lessor, his agent or attorney, full possession of the said demised premises and to levy the damages and costs awarded and taxed by the said justice, of the goods and chattels of the lessee or tenant, or other person in possession, any law, custom, or usage to the contrary notwithstanding. *Provided,* that the defendant may, at any time within ten days after the rendition of judgment, appeal to the Court of Common Pleas in the manner provided in the first section of the Act April 3, 1830: *And provided further,* that such appeal shall not be a *supersedeas* to the warrant of possession, but shall be tried in the same manner as actions of ejectment; and if the jury shall find in favor of the tenant, they shall also assess the damages which he shall have sustained by reason of his removal from the premises and for the amount found by the jury, judgment shall be rendered in his favor, with costs of suit, and that he recover possession of the premises, and he shall have the necessary writ or writs of execution to enforce said judgment: *Provided further,* that the tenant may have a writ of *certiorari* to remove the proceedings as in other cases. (Act December 14, 1863, section 1; P. L., 1125.)

The Act of December 14, 1863, is constitutional. *McGregor* v. *Haines,* 6 Phila., 62 (1865); *Haines* v. *Levin,* 51 Pa. St., 412 (1866).

The Act of April 11, 1866, section 1 (P. L., 97), conferred upon aldermen in this Commonwealth the powers and jurisdiction conferred upon justices by the Act of December 15, 1863.

By the Constitution of 1874, Article V., section 12, the office of alderman is abolished in Philadelphia County, and the powers and jurisdiction formerly vested in that officer are conferred upon a magistrate.

§ 1708. *Where owner acquires title through descent or purchase.*

The Act of 1863 was extended by the Act of February 20, 1867, section 1 (P. L., 30), so as to apply to cases in which the owner or owners of the demised premises have acquired title thereto by descent or purchase from the original lessor or lessors.

§ 1709. *No proceedings to be instituted except upon written lease or parol agreement wherein relation of landlord and tenant is estab-*

lished. It was also provided by the Act March 6, 1872, section 1 (P. L., 22) :

That it shall not be lawful to commence or prosecute any proceedings to obtain possession under the Act of December 14, 1863, unless such proceeding shall be founded upon a written lease or contract in writing, or on a parol agreement, in and by which the relation of landlord and tenant is established between the parties, and a certain rent is reserved.

§ 1710. *Jurisdiction.* If it does not appear that a certain rent was reserved in the lease, the justice has not jurisdiction. *Graver* v. *Fehr,* 89 Pa. St., 460 (1879).

§ 1711.

FORM OF NOTICE TO TENANT TO QUIT.

To C. D.,

SIR : You are hereby notified and required to quit, remove from, and deliver up to me possession of the premises situate (here locate), which you now hold as tenant under me, at the end of your current term, to wit, on the   day of   , A. D. 18   , as I desire to have again and repossess the same.

Respectfully yours,

A. B.,
(Address.)

Philadelphia (date), 18 .

§ 1712. *Requisites of notice.* A lease was for one year from March 25, 1868 ; on December 25, 1868, the landlord gave notice to quit. *Held,* the notice was in time. *Duffy* v. *Ogden,* 64 Pa. St., 240 (1870).

If a tenant lets from month to month, even though the lease contain an agreement to surrender possession on thirty days' notice prior to the expiration of the lease, the tenant is entitled to three months' notice before proceedings can be instituted under the Act of 1863. *Gault* v. *Neal,* 6 Phila., 61 (1865). Aside from proceedings under these special Acts, where a tenant holds under a lease from month to month he is entitled to but one month's notice. *Hollis* v. *Burns,* 100 Pa. St., 206 (1882).

Under the Act of December 14, 1863, notice to quit must be to remove upon determination of the lease, and not upon some other date. *Borough* v. *Walters,* 29 W. N., 483 (1892).

The three months' notice required by Act of December 14, 1863, may be waived, but the inquisition must find such fact. *Coal Co.* v. *Androkus,* 2 Dist. Rep., 764 (1892).

§ 1713.

FORM OF COMPLAINT—NO CHANGE OF OWNERSHIP.

CITY OF PHILADELPHIA,   } ss.
THE COMMONWEALTH OF PENNSYLVANIA, }

On the   day of   , A. D. 18   , personally appeared before me, L. M., Magistrate of Court No.   , A. B., who, being duly sworn according to law, doth depose and say that he is the lessor of certain premises, with

the appurtenances, situate (here locate), and was in quiet and peaceable possession thereof on the   day of   , A. D. 18   , on which last-mentioned day he demised said premises to a certain C. D. for the full term of
        year , at a yearly rent of $, which said term is fully ended; that being desirous, upon the determination of said term, to have again and repossess the said premises, for that purpose he did on the   day of
        , A. D. 18   , demand and require the said C.D. to remove from and leave the same, and that the said C. D. has hitherto refused, and still doth refuse to comply therewith; that three months have elapsed since the service of said notice, and that he makes this complaint that such proceedings may be taken as are directed by the Act of Assembly in such case made and provided.

Sworn to and subscribed before me,
    this   day of   , A. D. 18   .
        L. M.,
        Magistrate of Court No.   .

                                                            A. B.

§ 1714.

FORM OF COMPLAINT BY PURCHASER FROM LANDLORD WHO GAVE THE NOTICE.

CITY OF PHILADELPHIA,
THE COMMONWEALTH OF PENNSYLVANIA, } *ss.*

On the   day of   , A. D. 18   , personally appeared before me, the subscriber, L. M., Magistrate of Court No.   , in and for the said city, E. F., who, being duly sworn according to law, doth depose and say that heretofore, to wit,   A. B. was the owner of a certain lot or piece of ground, with the appurtenances, situate (here locate), and was quietly and peaceably in possession thereof on the   day of   , A. D. 18   , on which last-mentioned day he demised said premises to a certain C. D. for the full term of   year , at the yearly rent of   dollars, which said term is fully ended; being desirous upon the determination of the said term to have again and repossess the said premises, for that purpose he, said A. B., did on the   day of   , A. D. 18   , demand and require the said C. D. to remove from and leave the same, and that the said C. D. has hitherto refused, and still doth refuse, to comply therewith; after making the demise aforesaid, to wit, on the   day of   , A. D. 18   , by a deed of conveyance duly made and executed, bearing date the same day and year for the consideration therein mentioned, A. B. did grant, bargain, and sell the premises aforesaid, with the appurtenances, unto E. F., his heirs and assigns, that three months have elapsed since the service of said notice, and that he makes this complaint that such proceedings may be taken as are directed by the Act of Assembly in such case made and provided.

Sworn to and subscribed before me,
    this   day of   , A. D. 18   .
        L. M.,
        Magistrate of Court No.   .

                                                            E. F.

§ 1715.

FORM OF SUMMONS—NO CHANGE OF OWNERSHIP.

City of Philadelphia, *ss.*

The Commonwealth of Pennsylvania to any constable of said city, greeting :

Whereas, it appears to L. M., Magistrate of Court No.   , in and for
the said city, by complaint, on   day of   , A. D. 18   , that A. B.
was on   day of   , A. D. 18   , quietly and peaceably in possession
of a certain messuage or tenement, with the appurtenances, situate (here
locate), and being so thereof possessed, on the same day and year last aforesaid, did demise the said premises to C. D. for the term of   years then
next ensuing, at the yearly rent of   dollars, and that the said C. D.,
by virtue of the said demise, entered into possession of the said demised
premises, and held the same during the said term, and is still possessed of
the same ; and that the said term for which the said premises were demised
is fully ended ; and that said A. B. being desirous, upon the said determination of the said term, to have again and repossess the said premises, for
that purpose did on the   day of   , A. D. 18   , demand of and
require of the said C. D. to remove from and leave the same ; and that the
said C. D. hath hitherto refused ; and still doth refuse, to comply with the
said demand and requisition to remove from and leave the said premises.
You are therefore hereby commanded to summon the said C. D. to be and
appear on the   day of   , A. D. 18   , between the hours of
and   o'clock in the forenoon, at the said court (place), in the city of
Philadelphia, to show cause, if any he has, why restitution of the possession
of the said demised premises should not be forthwith made to the aforesaid
A. B. according to the form and effect of the Act of Assembly in such case
made and provided. And this you shall in nowise omit.
Witness our said magistrate and the official seal of the said court, the
     day of   , A. D. 18   .

(Office.)   L. M.,
[SEAL]   Magistrate of Court No.   .

§ 1716.

FORM OF SUMMONS—NOTICE BEFORE SALE.

City of Philadelphia, ss.
The Commonwealth of Pennsylvania to any constable of said city,
greeting :
Whereas, it appears to L. M., Magistrate of Court No.   , in and for the
said city, by complaint, on   of   , A. D. 18   , that A. B. was on
the   day of   , A. D. 18   , quietly and peaceably in possession of
a certain messuage or tenement, with the appurtenances, situate (here
locate), and being so thereof possessed, on the same day and year last
aforesaid, did demise the said premises to C. D. for the term of   years
then next ensuing, at the yearly rent of   dollars ; and that the said
C. D., by virtue of the said demise, entered into possession of the said
demised premises, and held the same during the said term, and is still
possessed of the same, and that the said term for which the said premises
were demised is fully ended ; and that said A. B. being desirous, upon the
said determination of the said term, to have again and repossess the said
premises, for that purpose did on the   day of   , A. D. 18   ,
demand of and require of the said C. D. to remove from and leave the
same ; and that the said A. B., after making the demise aforesaid, to wit,
on the   day of   , A. D. 18   , by a certain deed of conveyance
duly made and executed, bearing date the same day and year for the consideration therein mentioned, did grant, bargain, and sell the premises
aforesaid, with the appurtenances, unto E. F., his heirs and assigns, and the

said C. D. has hitherto refused, and still doth refuse, to comply with said demand and requisition to remove from and leave the said premises.

You are therefore hereby commanded to summon the said C. D., to be and appear on the   day of   , A. D. 18 , between the hours of   and   o'clock in the forenoon, at the said court (place), in the city of Philadelphia, to show cause, if any he has, why restitution of the possession of the said demised premises should not be forthwith made to the aforesaid E. F., according to the form and effect of the Act of Assembly in such case made and provided. And this you shall in nowise omit.

Witness our said magistrate and the official seal of the said court, the   day of   , A. D. 18 .

(Office.)

[SEAL]

L. M.,

Magistrate of Court No. .

§ 1717.

FORM OF SUMMONS—CHANGE OF OWNERSHIP—SALE BEFORE NOTICE.

City of Philadelphia, *ss.*

The Commonwealth of Pennsylvania to any constable of said city, greeting :

Whereas, it appears to L. M., Magistrate of Court No. , in and for the said city (place), by complaint on   of   , A. D. 1890, that A. B. was on the   day of   , A. D. 18 , quietly and peaceably in possession of a certain messuage or tenement, with the appurtenances, situate (here briefly describe), and being so thereof possessed, on the same day and year last aforesaid, did demise the said premises to C. D. for the term of · · years then next ensuing, at the yearly rent of   dollars ; and that the said C. D., by virtue of the said demise, entered into possession of the said demised premises, and held the same during the said term, and is still possessed of the same, and that the said term for which the said premises were demised is fully ended ; and that said A. B., after making the demise aforesaid, to wit, on the   day of   , A. D. 18 , by a certain deed of conveyance duly made and executed, bearing date the same day and year, for the consideration therein mentioned, did grant, bargain, and sell the premises aforesaid, with appurtenances, unto E. F., his heirs and assigns, and the said E. F. being desirous, upon the said determination of the said term, to have again and repossess the said premises, for that purpose did on the   day of   , A. D. 18 , demand of and require the said C. D. to remove from and leave the same ; and that the said C. D. hath hitherto refused and still doth refuse to comply with the said demand and requisition to remove from and leave the said premises.

You are therefore hereby commanded to summon the said C. D. to be and appear on the   day of   , A. D. 18 , between the hours of   and   o'clock in the forenoon, at the said court (place), in the city of Philadelphia, to show cause, if any he has, why restitution of the possession of the said demised premises should not be forthwith made to the aforesaid E. F., according to the form and effect of the Act of Assembly in such case made and provided. And this you shall in nowise omit.

Witness our said magistrate and the official seal of the said court, the   day of   , A. D. 1890.

(Office.)

[SEAL]

L. M.,

Magistrate of Court No. .

§ 1718.

FORM OF WRIT OF POSSESSION—NO CHANGE OF OWNERSHIP.

City of Philadelphia, *ss.*

The Commonwealth of Pennsylvania to any constable of said city, greeting :

Whereas, due proof has been made before L. M., Magistrate of Court No. , in and for the said city (place), that A. B. did on the day of , A. D. 1890, demise to C. D. a certain house or tenement, with the appurtenances, situate (here briefly describe), for the term of years, at the rent of dollars per annum ; and that the said C. D., by virtue of the said demise, entered into possession of the said premises, and held them during the said term, and is still possessed thereof ; and that the said term is fully ended ; and that the said A. B. being desirous, upon the determination of the said term, to have again and repossess the said premises, for that purpose did on the day of , A. D. 18 , demand of and require of the said C. D. to remove from and leave the same ; and the said C. D. has hitherto refused, and still doth refuse, to comply therewith. All which premises being duly found by our said magistrate, according to the form of the Act of General Assembly in such case made and provided.

You are therefore hereby commanded forthwith to deliver to the said A. B. full possession of the demised premises aforesaid. And you are also commanded, that of the goods and chattels of the said C. D. in your bailiwick you cause to be levied as well the sum of dollars, which the said L. M., justice, as aforesaid, has awarded for the damages sustained by the unjust detention of the premises as dollars, for his costs and charges by him in and about said suit in that behalf expended, whereof the said C. D. is convict. And hereof fail not.

Witness our said magistrate and the official seal of the said court, the day of , A. D. 18 .

(Office.)

[SEAL]

                                         L. M.,

                                   Magistrate of Court No. .

§ 1719.

FORM OF WRIT OF POSSESSION—CHANGE OF OWNERSHIP—NOTICE BEFORE SALE.

City of Philadelphia, *ss.*

The Commonwealth of Pennsylvania to any constable of said city, greeting :

Whereas, due proof has been made before L. M., Magistrate of Court No. , in and for the said city (place), that A. B. did on the day of , A. D. 18 , demise to C. D. a certain house or tenement, with the appurtenances, situate (here briefly describe), for the term of years, at the rent of dollars per annum ; and that the said C. D., by virtue of the said demise, entered into possession of the said premises, and held them during said term, and is still possessed thereof ; and that the said term is fully ended ; and that the said A. B. being desirous, upon the said determination of the said term, to have again and repossess the said premises, for that purpose did on the day of , A. D. 18 , demand of and require the said C. D. to remove from and leave the same ; and that the said A. B., after making the demise aforesaid, to wit, on the day of , A. D. 18 , by a certain deed of conveyance duly made and executed, bearing date the same day and year for the consideration therein mentioned, did grant, bargain, and sell the premises aforesaid, with the appurtenances, unto E. F., his heirs and assigns, and the said C. D. has hitherto refused and still doth refuse, to comply therewith. All which premises being duly found by our said magistrate, he did thereupon enter judgment against the said tenant that he forthwith give up possession of the said premises to the said E. F., and for the sum of   dollars for his damages sustained by the unjust detention of the premises as well as dollars for his costs and charges by C. D. in and about said suit in that behalf expended. Therefore we command you forthwith to deliver actual possession of said premises to the said E. F., his agent or attorney, and to levy the damages and costs awarded of the goods and chattels of the said lessee or tenant or other person in possession, and for so doing this shall be your sufficient warrant.

Witness our said magistrate and the official seal of the said court, the day of   , A. D. 18 .

(Office.)   L. M.,
[SEAL]   Magistrate of Court No. .

§ 1720.

FORM OF WRIT OF RESTITUTION—CHANGE OF OWNERSHIP—SALE BEFORE NOTICE.

City of Philadelphia, ss.

The Commonwealth of Pennsylvania to any constable of said city, greeting:

Whereas, due proof hath been made before L. M., Magistrate of Court No.   , in and for the said city (place), that A. B. did on the   day of   , A. D. 18 , demise to C. D. a certain house or tenement, with the appurtenances, situate (here briefly describe), for the term of   years, at the rent of   dollars per annum ; and that the said C. D., by virtue of the said demise, entered into possession of the said premises and held them during said term, and is still possessed thereof, and that the said term is fully ended ; and that the said A. B. after making the demise aforesaid, to wit, on the   day of   , A. D. 18 , by his certain deed of conveyance duly made and executed, bearing date the same day and year for the consideration therein mentioned, did grant, bargain, and sell the premises aforesaid, with the appurtenances, unto E. F., his heirs and assigns ; and the said E. F. being desirous, upon the said determination of the said term, to have again and repossess the said premises, for that purpose did on the   day of   , A. D. 18 , demand of and require the said C. D. to remove from and leave the same ; and that the said C. D. has hitherto refused, and still doth refuse, to comply therewith. All which premises being duly found by our said magistrate, he did thereupon enter judgment against the said tenant that he forthwith give up possession of the said premises to the said E. F., and for the sum of   dollars for his damages sustained by the unjust detention of the premises, as well as dollars for his costs and charges by him in and about said suit in that behalf expended. Therefore we command you forthwith to deliver actual possession of said premises to the said E. F., his agent or attorney, and to levy the damages and costs awarded of the goods and chattels of the said lessee or tenant or other person in possession, and for so doing this shall be your sufficient warrant.

Witness our said magistrate and the official seal of the said court, the
day of   A. D. 18   .
(Office.)   L. M.,
[SEAL]   Magistrate of Court No.   .

The Act of December 14, 1863, which directs the magistrate to
issue his warrant forthwith to dispossess the tenant, is repealed by
the supplement of March 24, 1865. *Connelly* v. *Arundell,* 6 Phila.,
38 (1865).

§ 1721.

FORM OF RECORD—NO CHANGE OF OWNERSHIP.

Be it remembered, that on the   day of   , in the year of
our Lord one thousand eight hundred and   , at the city of Philadelphia, due proof was made before L. M., Magistrate of Court No.   , in
and for said city, that A. B., on the   day of   , in the
year one thousand eight hundred and   , was quietly and peaceably
possessed of a certain messuage or tenement, with the appurtenances,
situate (here briefly describe), and being so thereof possessed on the same
day and year last aforesaid, did demise the said premises to C. D., for the
term of   years then next ensuing, at the yearly rent of
dollars ; and that the said C. D., by virtue of the said demise, entered into
possession of the said demised premises, and held the same during said
term, and is still possessed of the same, and that the said term for which
the said premises were demised is fully ended ; and that the said A. B.
being desirous, upon the said determination of the said term, to have again
and repossess the said premises, for that purpose did on the
day of   , A. D. 18   , demand of and require the said C. D. to remove
form and leave the same, and that the said C. D. has hitherto refused, and
still does refuse, to comply with the said demand and requisition to remove
from and leave the said premises. Whereupon the said A. B. then, to
wit, on the said   day of   , A. D. 18   , prayed the said magistrate, that a due remedy in that behalf be provided for him, according to
the form of the Act of the General Assembly of the State of Pennsylvania,
in such case made and provided, upon which proof and complaint one of
the constables of the said city was commanded to summon the said C. D.
to be and appear on the   day of   , A. D. 18   , between the
hours of   and   o'clock in the forenoon, before our said
magistrate, at his court in the said city, to show cause, if any he has, why
restitution of the possession of the said demised premises should not be
forthwith made to the aforesaid A. B., on the   day of   , A. D.
18   , and M. N., constable, returned on oath served on defendant by
(mode of service). Afterward, to wit, on the said   day of   ,
A. D. 1890, at (time) o'clock in the forenoon, at the said court, in the said
city (office) (here state if C. D. appeared and evidence in brief. If C. D.
did not appear, so set forth).

After hearing the proofs and allegations offered by the said A. B., our said
magistrate finds that the said A. B., on the   day of   , A. D. 18   ,
was quietly and peaceably possessed of a certain messuage or tenement,
with the appurtenances, situate (here briefly describe), and being so thereof
possessed on the same day and year last aforesaid, did demise the said

premises to the said C. D. for the term of   years then next ensuing, at the yearly rent of   dollars; and that the said C. D., by virtue of the said demise, entered into possession of the said demised premises and held the same during the said term, and is still possessed of the same, and that the said term for which the said premises were demised is fully ended; and that the said A. B. being desirous, upon the said determination of the said term, to have again and repossess the said premises, for that purpose did on the   day of   , A. D. 18 , demand of and require the said C. D. to remove from and leave the same, and that the said C. D. has hitherto refused, and still doth refuse, to comply with the said demand and requisition to remove from and leave the said premises. And our said magistrate doth assess the sum of   dollars for the damages of the said A. B., occasioned by the unjust detention of the said premises. Our said magistrate did thereupon enter judgment against the said tenant that he forthwith give up possession of the said premises to the said lessor, and that the said lessor shall and do recover, and have of the said lessee or tenant as well the said sum of   dollars for his damages aforesaid, as   dollars for his reasonable costs by him expended in and about this suit in his behalf, concerning which the premises aforesaid our said magistrate doth make this his record.

In testimony whereof, our said magistrate to this his record has hereunto set his hand and official seal of the said court, at the city of Philadelphia, this   day of   , one thousand eight hundred and   .

(Office.)   L. M.,
[SEAL]   Magistrate of Court. No .

§ 1722.

FORM OF RECORD—CHANGE OF OWNERSHIP—NOTICE BEFORE SALE.

Be it remembered, that on the   day of   , in the year of our Lord one thousand eight hundred and   , at the city of Philadelphia, due proof was made before L. M., Magistrate of Court No. , in and for said city, that A. B., on the   day of   , in the year of our Lord one thousand eight hundred and   , was quietly and peaceably possessed of a certain messuage or tenement, with appurtenances, situate (here briefly describe), and being so thereof possessed on the same day and year last aforesaid did demise the said premises to C. D., for the term of   years then next ensuing, at the yearly rent of   dollars; and that the said C. D., by virtue of the said demise, entered into possession of the said demised premises, and held the same during said term, and is still possessed of the same, and that the said term for which the said premises were demised is fully ended; and that the said A. B. being desirous, upon the said determination of the said term, to have again and repossess the said premises, for that purpose did on the   day of   , A. D. 18 , demand of and require the said C. D. to remove from and leave the same; and that the said A. B., after making the demise aforesaid, to wit, on the   day of   , A. D. 18 , by a certain deed of conveyance duly made and exe-. cuted, bearing date the same day and year for the consideration therein mentioned, did grant, bargain, and sell the premises aforesaid, with the appurtenances, unto E. F., his heirs and assigns, and the said C. D. has hitherto refused, and still doth refuse, to comply with the said demand and requisition to remove from and leave the said premises. Whereupon the said E. F., then, to wit, on the said   day of   , A. D. 18 , prayed our said magistrate, that a due remedy in that behalf be provided for him according to the form of the Act of the General Assembly of the State of Pennsylvania in such case made and provided, upon which proof and complaint one of the constables of the said city was commanded to summon the said C. D. to be and appear on the   day of   , A. D. 18 , between the hours of   and   o'clock in the forenoon, at our said magistrate's court (place) in the said city, to show cause, if any he has, why restitution of the possession of the said demised premises should not be forthwith made to the aforesaid E. F., and on the   day of   , A. D. 18 , M. N., constable, returned on oath, served on defendant by (mode of service). Afterward, to wit, on the said   day of   , A. D. 18 , at   o'clock in the forenoon, at the court of our said magistrate, in the said city (here state if C. D. appeared, and briefly set forth the evidence. If C. D. did not appear, so set forth). After hearing the proofs and allegations offered by the said A. B., our said magistrate finds that the said A. B., on the   day of   , A. D. 18 , was quietly and peaceably possessed of a certain messuage or tenement, with the appurtenances, situate (here briefly describe), and being so thereof possessed on the same day and year last aforesaid did demise the said premises to C. D. for the term of   year then next ensuing, at the yearly rent of   dollars ; and that the said C. D., by virtue of the said demise, entered into possession of the said demised premises, and held the same during the said term, and is still possessed of the same, and that the said term for which the said premises were demised is fully ended ; and that the said A. B. being desirous upon the said determination of the said term to have again and repossess the said premises, for that purpose did on the   day of   , A. D. 18 , demand of and require the said C. D. to remove from and leave the same ; and that the said A. B., after making the demise aforesaid, to wit, on the   day of   , A. D. 18 , by a certain deed of conveyance duly made and executed, bearing date the same day and year for the consideration therein mentioned, did grant, bargain, and sell the premises aforesaid, with the appurtenances, unto E. F., his heirs and assigns, and the said C. D. has hitherto refused, and does still refuse, to comply with the said demand and requisition to remove from and leave the said premises. And our said magistrate doth assess the sum of   dollars for the damages of the said E. F., occasioned by the unjust detention of the said premises. Our said magistrate did thereupon enter judgment against the said tenant that he forthwith give up possession of the said premises to the said E. F., and that the said E. F. shall and do recover and have of the said lessee or tenant as well the said sum of   dollars for his damages aforesaid, as   dollars for his reasonable costs by him expended about this suit in this behalf, concerning which the premises aforesaid our said magistrate does make this his record.

    In testimony whereof, our said magistrate to this his said record has hereunto set his hand and the official seal of the said court, at the city of Philadelphia, this   day of   , one thousand eight hundred and   .

L. M.,

[SEAL]   Magistrate of Court No.   .

§ 1723.

FORM OF RECORD—CHANGE OF OWNERSHIP—SALE BEFORE NOTICE.

Be it remembered, that on the   day of   , in the year of our Lord one thousand eight hundred and   , at the city of Philadelphia, due proof was made before L. M., Esq., Magistrate of Court No. , in and for said city, that A. B., on the   day of   , in the year one thousand eight hundred and   , was quietly and peaceably possessed of a certain messuage or tenement, with the appurtenances, situate (here briefly describe), and being so thereof possessed on the same day and year last aforesaid did demise the said premises to C. D., for the term of   years then next ensuing, at the yearly rent of   dollars, and that the said C. D., by virtue of the said demise, entered into possession of the said demised premises, and held the same during said term, and is still possessed of the same, and that the said term for which the said premises were demised is fully ended ; and that the said A. B., after making the demise aforesaid, to wit, on the   day of   , A. D. 18 , by a certain deed of conveyance duly made and executed, bearing date the same day and year for the consideration therein mentioned, did grant, bargain, and sell the premises aforesaid, with the appurtenances, unto E. F., his heirs and assigns, and the said E. F. being desirous upon the said determination of the said term to have again and repossess the said premises, for that purpose did on the   day of   , A. D. 18 , demand of and require the said C. D. to remove from and leave the same, and that the said C. D. has hitherto refused, and still doth refuse, to comply with the said demand and requisition to remove from and leave the said premises. Whereupon the said E. F. then, to wit, on the said   day of   , A. D. 18 , prayed our said magistrate that a due remedy in that behalf be provided for him according to the form of the Act of the General Assembly of the State of Pennsylvania in such case made and provided, upon which proof and complaint one of the constables of the said city was commanded to summon the said C. D., to be and appear on the   day of   , A. D. 18 , between the hours of   and   o'clock in the forenoon, at our said magistrate's court, in the said city, to show cause, if any he has, why restitution of the possession of the said demised premises should not be forthwith made to the aforesaid E. F., and on the   day of   , A. D. 18 , M. N., constable, returned on oath, served on defendant by (mode of service). Afterward, to wit, on the said   day of   , A. D. 18 , at   o'clock in the forenoon, at the court of our said magistrate, in the said city (here state if C. D. appeared and the evidence in brief. If C. D. did not appear, so set forth). After hearing the proofs and allegations offered by the said E. F., our said magistrate does find that the said A. B., on the   day of   , A. D. 18 , was quietly and peaceably possessed of a certain messuage or tenement, with the appurtenances, situate (here briefly describe), and being so thereof possessed on the same day and year last aforesaid did demise the said premises to C. D. for the term of   years then next ensuing, at the yearly rent of   dollars, and that the said C. D., by virtue of the said demise, entered into possession of the said demised premises, and held the same during the said term, and is still possessed of the same, and that the said term for which the said premises were demised is fully ended ; and that the said A. B., after making the demise aforesaid, to wit, on the   : day of   ;, A. D. 18 , by a certain deed of conveyance duly made and executed, bearing date the same day and year for the consideration therein mentioned, did grant, bargain, and sell the premises aforesaid, with the appurtenances, unto E. F., his heirs and assigns, and the said E. F. being desirous upon the said determination of the said term to have again and repossess the said premises, for that purpose did on the day of , A. D. 18 , demand of and require the said C. D.' to remove from and leave the same, and that the said C. D. hath hitherto refused, and still doth refuse, to comply with said demand and requisition to remove from and leave the said premises. And our said magistrate doth assess the sum of dollars for the damages of the said E. F., occasioned by the unjust detention of the said premises. Our said magistrate did thereupon enter judgment against the said tenant that he forthwith give up possession of the said premises to the said lessor, and that the said lessor shall and do recover and have of the said lessee or tenant as well the said sum of dollars for his damages aforesaid, as dollars for his reasonable costs by him expended about this suit in this behalf, concerning which the premises aforesaid our said magistrate doth make this his record.

In testimony whereof, our said magistrate to this his record hath hereunto set his hand and the official seal of the said court, at the city of Philadelphia, this day of , one thousand eight hundred and   .

L. M.,

[SEAL]   Magistrate of Court No. .

§ 1724. *Requisites of record.* The record should show that the plaintiff was peaceably possessed of the premises and delivered them to the tenant or some one under whom he claims; that the term is fully ended, and that he gave three months' notice of a desire to repossess himself of the premises. *Givens* v. *Miller*, 62 Pa. St., 133 (1869); *McGinnis* v. *Vernon*, 67 Pa. St., 149 (1870).

The specific facts contained in the complaint must appear. *McGrath* v. *Donally*, 6 Phila., 43 (1865); *Connelly* v. *Arundel*, 6 Phila., 49 (1865).

It must appear that judgment has been entered. *Dickensheets* v. *Hotchkiss*, 6 Phila., 156 (1866).

If the record show that the writ was issued returnable in three days; that six freeholders were assembled and discharged, and a new *venire* was not issued, the defects are fatal. *Horner* v. *Wetherell*, 19 W. N., 197 (1887).

§ 1725. *Appeal and its effect in Philadelphia County.* Under the Act of 1772, if the title to land shall come into question, the process is arrested and the contention removed to court, yet there is no such provision under the Act of 1863, and the only remedy is appeal. *Koontz* v. *Hammond*, 62 Pa. St., 182 (1869).

The Act of June 25, 1869, section 1 (P. L., 1275), provides that the appeal shall be a *supersedeas* of the warrant of possession in the city of Philadelphia, notwithstanding the terms of the Act of 1863.

The provisions of the Acts of May 1, 1861, and March 27, 1865, requiring, on appeal from the judgment of a magistrate, an affidavit that the appeal is not intended for delay, apply to proceedings under the Act of 1863. *Carter* v. *Hess*, 3 W. N., 325 (1877).

Upon appeal to the Common Pleas, if final judgment is entered in favor of the landlord, said judgment should include all rent that has accrued up to the time of the rendition thereof. *Dunmire* v. *Price*, 12 W. N., 179 (1882).

§ 1726. *Certiorari.* Proceedings under the Act of December 14, 1863, are subject to removal by *certiorari* by the Act of March 24, 1865. *Hutchinson* v. *Vanscriver*, 6 Phila., 39 (1865).

§ 1727. **Proceedings in case landlord has lost the evidence of the beginning and conclusion of the term.**

In all cases in the city of Philadelphia where there is a lease or verbal letting of property for a term of years or from year to year, and the landlord, whether the owner at the time of such lease or letting, or by purchase subsequent thereto, has lost the lease or evidence of the beginning and conclusion of the term, or cannot produce proof of the same, it shall be lawful, at any time after the first year, or after the term of years, as the case may be, for the landlord desiring to recover possession of the demised premises to give notice, in writing, to the tenant that he has lost such lease or is unable to make such proof, and requiring the tenant, within thirty days from the time of service of such notice to furnish him in writing with the date at which his term of tenancy commenced, and such notice, if supported by affidavit, shall be evidence of what it sets forth. If the tenant shall furnish in writing the date as required, such writing shall be evidence of the facts contained in it; but if the tenant shall fail or refuse, within thirty days, to comply with the said requirement, the landlord may, at the expiration of that period, give to the tenant three months' notice to quit the premises occupied by him, and shall proceed thereafter in the same manner as is now provided in case of the usual notice to quit at the end of the term : *Provided,* that if the tenant shall make affidavit, within the thirty days, that he is unable to comply with the requirement of the landlord, stating the causes of such inability, the landlord shall give six months' notice to the tenant to remove from the demised premises, upon which he shall proceed as provided in the cases of the three months' notice. (Act February 28, 1865, section 1; P. L., 253.)

The Act applies only to a tenancy created by a lease which contains a definite term and rent. *McMullin* v. *McCreary*, 54 Pa. St., 230 (1867).

§ 1728.

City of Philadelphia (date), 1890.

Take notice that the evidence of the beginning and conclusion of the term for which the premises now occupied by you, situate (here describe briefly), Philadelphia, were leased or rented to you by A. B., is lost, and that I cannot produce proof of the beginning and conclusion of the term of said tenancy aforesaid ; and you are hereby required to furnish me, in writing, with the date at which your term of tenancy commenced, within thirty days from the date you shall have received this notice.

Very respectfully yours,

To Mr. C. D.   A. B.

City of Philadelphia, *ss.*

Before me, the subscriber, L. M., Magistrate of Court No. , in and for said city, personally appeared A. B., above named, who, being duly sworn according to law, doth depose and say that the facts set forth in the above notice are true, to the best of his knowledge and belief.

Sworn to and subscribed before me, ⎫
   this   day of   , ⎬
   A. D. 1890. ⎮
            L. M., ⎮
      Magistrate of Court No. . ⎭

(Office.)

§ 1729.

FORM OF NOTICE TO QUIT.

City of Philadelphia (date), 1890.

On the   day of   , 1890, I gave you notice requiring you to furnish me in writing, within thirty days from the time of the service of the said notice, with the date at which your term of tenancy commenced of the premises now occupied by you, situate (here describe briefly), Philadelphia, and you having made affidavit, within the said thirty days, that you are unable to comply with the requirements therein, you are hereby required to remove from and surrender to me possession of said premises within six months from the time you shall receive this notice.

Yours, etc.,

To Mr. C. D.   A. B.

§ 1730.

FORM OF COMPLAINT.

CITY OF PHILADELPHIA,   ⎫
THE COMMONWEALTH OF PENNSYLVANIA, ⎬ *ss.*

On the   day of   , A. D. 1890, before me, L. M., Magistrate of Court No. , in and for said city, personally came A. B., who, being duly sworn according to law, deposed and said that he is the landlord of a certain three-story brick house, with the appurtenances, situate (here describe by street and No.), that being in possession of and landlord as aforesaid, he rented the same to C. D., as tenant,   at a certain yearly rent of   dollars ; that the said C. D. was in possession thereof on   day of   , A. D. 18 , and for more than one year previous thereto under said agreement   ; that being desirous upon the determination of the said term to have again and repossess the said premises, for that purpose he did on the said day of   , A. D. 18 , give notice in writing, supported by affidavit, to the said C. D., that he had lost the evidence of and was unable to make proof of the beginning and conclusion of said term, and demanded and required the said C. D. to furnish him within thirty days the date, in writing, at which the term of tenancy commenced, and that the said C. D. failed to comply with the terms of said notice within the thirty days aforesaid ; that he did on the   day of   , A. D. 18 , give notice to and require the said C. D. to remove from and leave the said premises in six months, and that the said C. D. hath hitherto refused, and still doth refuse, to comply therewith; that six months have elapsed since the service of said last-mentioned notice, and that he makes this complaint that such proceedings may be taken as are directed by the Act of Assembly in such case made and provided.

Sworn to and subscribed before me, ⎫
   this   day of   , |
   A. D. 1890. .   ⎬   A. B.
           L. M., |
   Magistrate of Court No. . ⎭

The plaintiff is not required to show that the term of the tenant has terminated. *Mooney* v. *Rogers*, 8 Phila., 297 (1871).

§ 1731.

FORM OF SUMMONS.

City of Philadelphia, *ss.*

The Commonwealth of Pennsylvania to any constable of said city, greeting:

Whereas, it appears to L. M., Magistrate of Court No.   , in and for the said city, by complaint on   day of   , A. D. 1890, that A. B. is the landlord of certain premises, with the appurtenances, situate (here briefly describe), Philadelphia, that being in possession of and landlord as aforesaid he rented the same to C. D. as tenant at a certain yearly rent of   dollars, that the said C. D. was in possession thereof on the   day of   , A. D. 18   , and for more than one year previous thereto under said agreement;   that being desirous upon the determination of the said term to have again and repossess the said premises, for that purpose he did on the said   day of   , A. D. 18   , give notice in writing, supported by affidavit, to the said C. D. that he had lost the evidence of, and was unable to make proof of, the beginning and conclusion of said term, and demanded and required the said C. D. to furnish him within thirty days the date, in writing, at which his term of tenancy commenced, and that the said C. D., within thirty days aforesaid, failed to comply with the said requirement. That he did on the   day of   , A. D. 18   , give notice to and require the said C. D. to remove from and leave the same in six months, and that the said C. D. hath hitherto refused, and still doth refuse, to comply therewith to remove from and leave said premises.

You are therefore commanded to summon the said C. D. to be and appear on the   day of   , A. D. 18   , at (hour) o'clock in the forenoon, before the subscriber at his said court (location of office), in the said city, to show cause, if any he has, why restitution of the possession of the said demised premises should not be forthwith made to the aforesaid A. B. according to the form and effect of the Act of Assembly in such case made and provided. And this you will in nowise omit.

Witness our said magistrate and the official seal of the said court, the   day of   , A. D. 1890.

                                   L. M.,

[SEAL]   Magistrate of Court No.   .

§ 1732.

City of Philadelphia, *ss.*

The Commonwealth of Pennsylvania to any constable of said city, greeting :

Whereas, due proof hath been made before L. M., Magistrate of Court No.   , in and for the said city (office), that A. B. was the landlord of certain premises, with the appurtenances, situate (here briefly describe), that being in possession of and landlord as aforesaid he rented the same to C. D. as tenant   at a certain yearly rent of   dollars, that the said C. D. was in possession thereof on the   day of   , A. D. 18   , and for more than one year previous thereto under said agreement ; that being desirous upon the determination of the said term to have and again repossess the said premises, for that purpose he did on the said   day of ·   , A. D. 18   , give notice in writing, supported by affidavit, to the said C. D. that he had lost the evidence of, and was unable to make proof of, the beginning and conclusion of said term, and demanded and required the said C. D. to furnish him within thirty days the date, in writing at which the term of tenancy commenced, and that the said C. D., within thirty days aforesaid, has failed to comply with the said requirement. That he did on the   day of   , A. D. 18   , give notice to and require the said C. D. to remove from and leave the same in six months, and that the said C. D. hath hitherto refused, and still doth refuse, to comply therewith to remove from and leave said premises. All which premises being duly found by our said magistrate, he did thereupon enter judgment against the said tenant, that he forthwith give up the possession of the said premises to the said lessor, and for the sum of   dollars, for damages sustained by the unjust detention of the premises, as well as for costs and charges by A. B. in and about said suit in that behalf expended. Therefore we command you to deliver actual possession of said premises to the lessor, his agent or attorney, and to levy the damages and costs awarded of the goods and chattels of the said lessee or tenant or other person in possession, and for so doing this shall be your sufficient warrant.

Witness our said magistrate and the official seal of the said court, the   day of   , A. D. 18   .

L. M.,

[SEAL]   Magistrate of Court No.   .

§ 1733.

Be it remembered, that on the   day of   , in the year of our Lord one thousand eight hundred and   , at the city of Philadelphia, due proof was made before L. M., Magistrate of Court No.   , in and for the said city, that A. B. on the   day of   , A. D. 18   , was the landlord of certain premises, with the appurtenances, situate (here briefly describe), that being in possession of and landlord as aforesaid he rented the same to C. D. as tenant   at a certain yearly rent of   dollars, that the said C. D. was in possession thereof on the   day of   , A. D. 18   , and for more than one year previous thereto, under said agreement   ; that being desirous upon the determination of the said term to have again and repossess the said premises, for that purpose he did on the said   day of   , A. D. 18 , give notice in writing, supported by affidavit, to the said C. D. that he had lost the evidence of and was unable to make proof of the beginning and conclusion of said term, and demanded and required the said C. D. to furnish him within thirty days the date, in writing, at which the term of tenancy commenced, and that the said C. D., within the thirty days aforesaid, failed to comply with the said requirement. That he did on the   day of   , A. D. 18 , give notice to and require the said C. D. to remove from and leave the same in six months, and that the said C. D. hath hitherto refused, and still doth refuse, to comply therewith to remove from and leave the said premises.

Whereupon the said A. B. then, to wit, on the said   day of   , A. D. 18 , prayed our said magistrate that a due remedy in that behalf be provided for   , according to the form of the Act of Assembly in such case made and provided, upon which proof and complaint one of the constables of the said city was commanded to summon the said C. D. to be and appear on the   day of   , A. D. 18 , at   o'clock in the forenoon, before our said magistrate's court, in said city, to show cause, if any he has, why restitution of the possession of the said demised premises should not be forthwith made to the aforesaid A. B.   On the   day of   , A. D. 18 , M. N., constable, returned on oath served on defendant (here state mode of service.)

Afterward, to wit, on the said   day of   , A. D. 18 , at o'clock in the forenoon, at our said magistrate's court (place), in the said city, C. D. did appear. After hearing the proofs and allegations offered by the said A. B. our said magistrate does find that the said A. B. on the   day of   , A. D. 18 , was the landlord of certain premises, with the appurtenances, situate (here briefly describe), that being in possession of and landlord aforesaid he rented the same to the said C. D. as tenant   at a certain yearly rent of   dollars, that the said C. D. was in possession thereof on the   day of   , A. D. 18 , and for more than one year previous thereto under said agreement   ; that the said A. B. being desirous, upon the determination of the said term, to have again and repossess the said premises, for that purpose   , did on the   day of   , A. D. 18 , give notice in writing, supported by affidavit, to the said C. D. that he had lost the evidence of and was unable to make proof of the beginning and conclusion of said term, and demanded and required the said C. D. to furnish him within thirty days the date, in writing, at which the term of tenancy commenced, and that the said C. D., within the thirty days aforesaid, neglected or failed to comply with the said requirement. That he did on the   day of   , A. D. 18 , give notice to and require the said C. D. to remove from and leave the same in six months, and that the said C. D. hath hitherto refused, and still doth refuse, to comply therewith to remove from and leave said premises. And our said magistrate doth assess the sum of   dollars for the damage of the said A. B., occasioned by the unjust detention of the said premises. Our said magistrate did thereupon enter judgment against the said tenant that he forthwith give up possession of the said premises to the said lessor, and that the said lessor shall and do recover and have of the said lessee or tenant as well the sum of   dollars for the damages aforesaid, as   dollars for his reasonable costs by him expended in and about this suit in this behalf, concerning which the premises aforesaid our said magistrate doth make this his record.

In testimony whereof, our said magistrate to this his record hath hereunto set his hand and the official seal of the said court, in the city of Philadelphia, this   day of   , one thousand eight hundred and ninety.

L. M.,
Magistrate of Court No. .

[SEAL]

The record must show a tenancy for years, or from year to year, and that the first year of the term is ended, else the magistrate has no jurisdiction under it. *McMullin* v. *McCreary*, 54 Pa. St., 233 (1867).

§ 1734. In Philadelphia, certiorari to proceedings against tenant is a supersedeas, except in proceedings under Act of 1772.

In every proceeding brought in Philadelphia under any of the several Acts by landlords to recover possession of property leased for a term of years, or from year to year, in which a *certiorari* is now allowed, the said *certiorari* shall be a *supersedeas,* and the execution shall be suspended until the final determination of the *certiorari* by the court out of which the same issues; and the said court, if the determination shall be against the party at whose instance the *certiorari* has issued, shall proceed to issue a writ of possession directed to the sheriff of the county directing him to deliver actual possession of the premises to the lessor, and to levy the costs on defendant in the manner that costs are now levied and collected on other writs of execution: *Provided,* that the *certiorari* shall be issued within ten days from the date of the judgment rendered and upon oath of the party applying for the same, to be administered by the prothonotary of the Court of Common Pleas, that it is not for the purpose of delay, but that the proceedings proposed to be removed are to the best of his knowledge and belief unjust and illegal, and will oblige him to pay more money than is justly due; a copy of which affidavit shall be filed in the prothonotary's office: *And provided further,* that the party applying for the same shall give security for the payment of all costs that have accrued or may accrue, and of the rent which has already or may become due up to the time of the final determination of said *certiorari* in the event of the same being determined against him. (Act of March 24, 1865, section 1; P. L., 750.)

As to other cases of *certiorari* see Title—Justices.

The *certiorari* is not a *supersedeas* in proceedings under the Act of 1772. *DeCoursey* v. *Trust Co.*, 81 Pa. St., 217 (1876).

CHAPTER XXII.

MANDAMUS.

§ 1735. Constitutional provision.

The jurisdiction of the Supreme Court shall extend over the State, and the judges thereof shall, by virtue of their offices, be justices of oyer and terminer and general jail delivery in the several counties; they shall have original jurisdiction in cases of injunction where a corporation is a party defendant, of *habeas corpus*, of *mandamus to courts of inferior jurisdiction*, and of *quo warranto* as to all officers of the Commonwealth whose jurisdiction extends over the State, but shall not exercise any other original jurisdiction. (Constitution of 1874, Article V., section 3.)

§ 1736. Statutes. *Jurisdiction.* The Acts of June 14, 1836 (P. L., 626); May 25, 1881 (P. L., 32); and June 24, 1885 (P. L., 150), appear to be superseded by the Act of June 8, 1893 (P. L., 345), which provides as follows :

SECTION 1. That the several Courts of Common Pleas shall, within their respective counties, have the power to issue writs of mandamus to all officers and magistrates elected or appointed in or for the respective county, or in or for any township, district, or place within such county, and to all corporations being or having their chief place of business within such county; and the Court of Common Pleas of the county in which the seat of government is or may be located shall have the power, and it shall be required, to issue the writ of mandamus to the Lieutenant-Governor, Secretary of the Commonwealth, Attorney-General, Secretary of Internal Affairs, Superintendent of Public Instruction, State Treasurer, Auditor-General, Insurance Commissioner, and Commissioners of the Sinking Fund.

§ 1737. *Petition to be presented—Alternative writ to be awarded —When peremptory mandamus may issue in first instance.*

SEC. 2. Any person desiring to obtain a writ of mandamus shall present his petition therefor, verified by affidavit, to the judge or judges of the proper court, either in session or at chambers, setting forth the facts upon which he relies for the relief sought, the act or duty whose performance he seeks, his interest in the result, the name of the person or body at whose hands performance is sought, demand or refusal to perform the act or duty, and that the petitioner is without other adequate and specific remedy at law. If such petition presents the substance of a case for mandamus, the court shall direct that such writ issue in the alternative form : *Provided, however,* that if the right to require the performance of the act is clear, and it is apparent that no valid excuse can be given for not performing it, a peremptory mandamus may be awarded in the first instance and directed to issue forthwith.

§ 1738. *Any person beneficially interested may secure the writ.*

SEC. 3. The writ of mandamus may issue upon the application of any person beneficially interested.

§ 1739. *In whose name writ is to be prosecuted—How action to be docketed.*

SEC. 4. When the writ is sought to procure the enforcement of a public duty, the proceeding shall be prosecuted in the name of the Commonwealth on the relation of the Attorney-General: *Provided, however,* that said proceeding in proper cases shall be on the relation of the district-attorney of the proper county: *Provided further,* that when said proceeding is sought to enforce a duty affecting a particular public interest of the State, it shall be on the relation of the officer intrusted with the management of such interest. In all other cases the party procuring the alternative writ shall be plaintiff, the party to whom said writ is directed shall be defendant, and the action shall be docketed as in ordinary cases, namely,

plaintiff, *versus*   , defendant.

§ 1740. *Alternative writs to be in force for three months—Service and return.*

SEC. 5. All writs in the alternative form shall be in force for three months from their date, and may be served by the plaintiff, or anyone by him authorized, or by any sheriff or deputy sheriff in any county of the Commonwealth in which the defendant may be, by giving the defendant personally a copy thereof, attested by the prothonotary of the court awarding the writ. They shall be returnable at such time, not less than five days after the service thereof, as the court may direct.

§ 1741. *Direction and service of alternative writ against municipal corporation.*

SEC. 6. When the writ is sought against a municipal corporation the alternative writ shall be directed to such of the corporate authorities in their official capacity as are concerned in the execution of the thing required, and service thereof upon any of such officers shall be sufficient.

§ 1742. *Direction and service of alternative writ against private corporation—Direction of peremptory writ.*

SEC. 7. When the writ is sought against a private corporation, domestic or foreign, the alternative writ shall be directed against the corporation by name, and also against any particular person or body of persons connected therewith whom it may be sought to coerce, and service thereof upon any officer or agent of the corporation and upon such particular person or chief officer of such body of persons shall be sufficient. The peremptory writ may be directed to the said corporation, or to the person or body of persons who have the power and whose duty it is to do the act required, or to such superior officer as would be expected to execute the order.

§ 1743. *Direction and service of writ against board or body other than a corporation.*

SEC. 8. When the writ is sought against a board or body other than a corporation, it shall be directed to such board or body in their official capacity, and service shall be made upon a majority of the members thereof, unless the board or body was created by law and has a chairman or other presiding officer appointed pursuant to law, in which case service upon him shall be sufficient.

§ 1744. *Third party may defend writ—His rights and liabilities in such case.*

SEC. 9. It shall be lawful for the court, when applied to for the writ, or upon and after the issuing of the first writ on the petition of any person having or claiming a right or interest in the subject matter, other than the person to whom the writ is prayed to be or has issued, setting forth his right or interest in or to the subject matter of the controversy, to authorize in proper cases such person, even though he could not have been made original defendant, to frame the return and conduct the subsequent proceedings at his own expense, or to take such part therein and on such terms as to the court may seem just; and in such cases, if judgment is given for or against the party suing the writ, such judgment shall be given against or for the party to whom the writ shall have been directed, but the court may authorize the person permitted as aforesaid to frame the return and conduct the subsequent proceedings to use the name of the party to whom such writ shall have been directed for recovery of costs and the enforcing of the judgment, and also for the purpose of an appeal to the Supreme Court, with like force and effect as though the party to whom such writ shall have been directed had sought to recover costs and to enforce the judgment or to appeal to the Supreme Court: *Provided, however*, that when, in such cases, judgment is given in favor of the plaintiff, the court may order that damages and costs, or either, adjudged in favor of such party, shall be paid in whole or in part by the person permitted as aforesaid to conduct the proceedings.

§ 1745. *Court may direct notice of papers filed subsequent to the granting of the writ.*

SEC. 10. The court may direct what notice shall be given of all papers filed in the proceeding subsequent to the granting of the alternative writ.

§ 1746. *Motion to supersede or quash the writ—If motion be unsuccessful, return may be filed.*

SEC. 11. Appearance *de bene esse* shall enable the defendant to take advantage of defective service of the alternative writ. The defendant may move to supersede or quash said writ; if he fails, he shall be permitted to file his return as in this Act mentioned, and to proceed as if such motion had not been made.

§ 1747. *Defendant to file his return to writ—In default thereof, judgment to be given against him as in case of insufficient return.*

SEC. 12. The defendant shall file in the office of the prothonotary of the court awarding the alternative writ a return thereto, verified by affidavit, within the time specified in the writ, and in default thereof judgment shall be given against him with the same effect as if he had filed a return and such return had been adjudged insufficient.

§ 1748. *Court may permit correction of uncertain, vague, evasive, or informal return.*

SEC. 13. In such return, certainty to a certain intent in general, and no more, shall be required. If the return is uncertain, vague, or evasive, or informal in any respect, such opportunity may be afforded for the correction thereof, as to the court shall seem just and reasonable.

§ 1749. *Time shall be allowed to make return, plead, etc.*

SEC. 14. The court applied to for the writ shall allow the plaintiff and defendant, respectively, such convenient time to make return, plead, reply, rejoin, or demur as shall be just and reasonable.

§ 1750. *Return may be demurred to or traversed, etc.*

SEC. 15. The plaintiff may demur to the return, or he may plead to or traverse all or any of the material facts therein contained ; the defendant shall reply, take issue, or demur and like proceedings shall be had as in other actions at law.

§ 1751. *If plaintiff recover judgment, he shall have damages and costs.*

SEC. 16. If a verdict is found for the plaintiff and judgment is entered thereon, or if a judgment is given for him upon a demurrer or by *nihil dicit* or for want of an answer by *non sum informatus* or other pleading, he shall recover his damages and costs.

§ 1751 a. *If defendant have judgment, he shall recover costs.*

SEC. 17. If judgment is given for the defendant, he shall recover his costs.

§ 1751 b. *One recovery for false return is a bar to other actions.*

SEC. 18. If damages are recovered against any person making return as aforesaid, such recovery shall debar every other action for making such return.

§ 1751 c. *Costs allowed or refused in the discretion of the Court.*

SEC. 19. The costs of the application for a writ of mandamus, whether such writ is granted or not, also the costs of the writ if issued and obeyed or not prosecuted to judgment as aforesaid, may be given or refused according to the discretion of the court.

§ 1751 d. *Execution for damages and costs.*

SEC. 20. Damages and costs may be levied by execution as in other cases.

§ 1751 e. *How the plaintiff's damages shall be ascertained.*

SEC. 21. Damages sustained by the plaintiff shall be ascertained by the jury trying any issue in fact ; if no such issue is tried, they shall be ascertained by the court in such manner as may be deemed just and reasonable.

§ 1751 f. *After judgment for plaintiff upon alternative writ, peremptory writ to be awarded.*

SEC. 22. Whenever, in accordance with this Act, judgment is given for the plaintiff, the court may award that a peremptory mandamus shall issue

in that behalf, and shall also enter judgment for damages and costs, and
thereupon such peremptory writ of mandamus may be issued accordingly,
at any time after twenty days from the signing of the judgment, and not
before, unless the exigence of the case, in the discretion of the court, requires it, in which event the court may direct that said writ shall issue
forthwith.

§ 1751 g. *Action by public officer for public benefit, not to abate
by termination of his office.*

SEC. 23. When the writ is sought by a public officer in his official capacity
for the public benefit, the action shall not abate by the termination of his
office, but may be prosecuted by his successor.

§ 1751 h. *Death or removal of plaintiff, executor, administrator,
or trustee not to abate the writ.*

SEC. 24. When the writ is sought by an executor, administrator, or
trustee, the death of the plaintiff or his removal from position by resignation or otherwise shall not abate the writ. But the action may be continued by his successor.

§ 1751 i. *Death, resignation, or removal from office of defendant
not to abate suit.*

SEC. 25. The death, resignation, or removal from office by lapse of time
or otherwise, of any defendant, shall not have the effect to abate the suit,
but his successor may be made a party thereto and any peremptory writ
shall be directed against him.

§ 1751 j. *Amendments.*

SEC. 26. Defects in substance in the alternative writ may be taken advantage of at any stage of the proceeding. Amendments may be allowed as
in other civil actions save as hereinafter mentioned.

§ 1751 k. *Direction, service, and return of peremptory writ.*

SEC. 27. The peremptory writ shall be directed to the same person as
the alternative writ, save as herein authorized ; it shall be served in the
same manner as the 'alternative writ, and it shall be made returnable at
such time as to the court awarding it may seem just and reasonable.

§ 1751 l. *Peremptory writ may be superseded or quashed, but cannot be amended.*

SEC. 28. The peremptory writ, though issued, may be superseded or
quashed for such cause as to the court may seem just, but no amendment
thereto shall be allowed.

§ 1751 m. *Appeal from order granting writ or refusing it—Supersedeas.*

SEC. 29. The party aggrieved by the proceedings had in any Court of
Common Pleas upon any writ of mandamus may remove the same at any
time within twenty days after final judgment, order, or decree, or in cases
where the granting of said writ is required by the first section of this Act,
at any time within twenty days after refusal to 'grant said writ, into the
Supreme Court'by appeal as in other actions of law, and such appeal shall

supersede any peremptory writ awarded by the court and also any execution for damages or costs, upon bail to be given as in other civil cases.

§ 1751 n. *Appeal to supersede peremptory writ issued within* 20 *days after judgment.*

SEC. 30. Such appeal shall also supersede any peremptory writ issued within twenty days after final judgment, order, or decree : *Provided, however*, that the *certiorari* in consequence of such appeal be lodged in the office of the prothonotary of the court awarding the writ before the mandate thereof shall have been fully complied with : *Provided further*, that said appeal shall be made returnable forthwith.

§ 1751 o. *Appeal to be returnable forthwith.*

SEC. 31. Every such appeal may be made returnable forthwith, and, if thus made returnable, it shall be heard and decided by the Supreme Court in any district in which it may be in session, as in this Act provided in cases originating in said court ; and if not thus returnable, it shall be heard and decided by said court when in session in the proper district at the term to which it shall have been made returnable.

§ 1751 p. *Cases undecided by Supreme Court before close of its session shall be certified from district to district.*

SEC. 32. The Supreme Court in any district shall exercise, throughout the State, original jurisdiction in the cases authorized by the organic law of the State ; and if not decided before the close of its session in said district, shall cause the same to be certified to and filed for action with the prothonotary of said court in the district within which it shall be next in session, and so to be certified from district to district until finally decided.

§ 1751 q. *Supreme Court shall dispose of issues of fact, enter judgments, etc., and direct how damages and costs shall be recovered.*

SEC. 33. The Supreme Court in such cases shall dispose of all issues of fact arising therein in such manner as may be deemed just and reasonable, and shall enter such judgments, orders, or decrees and in such manner and on such terms as to it may seem proper, and to that end may make all necessary rules and regulations. Damages and costs allowed by this Act and awarded by the Supreme Court shall be recovered in the manner said court may direct.

§ 1752. *Mandamus against county commissioners.* The Act of April 29, 1844 (P. L., 501), requiring county commissioners to collect taxes, etc., contains the following provision, section 43 :

In the event of the commissioners of any county neglecting or refusing to comply with any of the requisitions of this Act, it shall be the duty of the Supreme Court or the Court of Common Pleas of said county on the application of the State Treasurer, whose duty it is hereby made to apply for the same, to award writs of mandamus requiring compliance therewith and enforce obedience thereto.

§ 1753. Definition of mandamus. Mandamus is defined by Bouvier to be a high prerogative writ, usually issuing out of the highest court of general jurisdiction in a State, in the name of the sover-

eignty, directed to any natural person, corporation, or inferior court
of judicature within its jurisdiction, requiring them to do some particular thing therein specified, and which appertains to their office
or duty.   Bouvier's Law Dictionary, Vol. II., 93 (14th ed.).

The modern writ of mandamus, says High (Extraordinary Legal
Remedies, section 1), may be defined as a command issuing from a
common law court of competent jurisdiction, in the name of the
State or sovereign, directed to some corporation, officer, or inferior
court, requiring the performance of a particular duty therein specified, which duty results from the official station of the party to
whom the writ is directed, or from operation of law.

§ 1754. Not a prerogative writ in the United States. In this
country a mandamus cannot, in any strict sense, be termed a prerogative writ.   From the nature of our system of government, the
writ has necessarily been stripped of its prerogative features ; and
the better considered doctrine now is that the writ has, in the
United States, lost its prerogative aspect, having come to be regarded much in the nature of an ordinary action between the parties, and as a writ of right to the extent to which the party aggrieved shows himself entitled to this particular species of relief.
High, Extr. Legal Rem., sections 3 and 4.

While a mandamus is no longer regarded as a high prerogative
writ, but one of right, yet to be entitled to it the specific right
must be clear and indisputable, for the deprivation of which there
is no other specific legal remedy.

When the right depends upon disputed facts, they must be found
by a jury in relator's favor before the writ will issue ; but where
the question is one of law, it will be determined by the court.
Comm. v. *School Directors,* 4 Dist. Rep., 314 (1895).

§ 1755. When mandamus is allowed. It issues only where there
is a clear and specific legal right to be enforced, or a duty which
ought to be and can be performed, and where there is no other
specific and adequate legal remedy.   The person seeking the relief
must show a clear legal right to have the thing sought by it done,
and done in the manner and by the person sought to be coerced.
The writ, if granted, must also be effectual as a remedy, and it
must be within the power of the respondent, as well as be his duty
to do the act in question.   The exercise of the jurisdiction rests
to a considerable extent within the sound discretion of the court,
subject always to the well-settled principles which have been established by the courts or fixed by legislative enactment.   (*Id.*, section 9.)

In *Rex* v. *Barker,* 3 Burrows, 126 (1762), Lord MANSFIELD

stated the general scope of the remedy by mandamus as follows : " Where there is a right to execute an office, perform a service, or exercise a franchise (more especially if it be in a matter of public concern or attended with profit) ; and a person is kept out of possession or dispossessed of such right, and has no other specific legal remedy, this court ought to assist by mandamus." In this case the writ was granted to compel the trustees of a chapel to admit a minister to the performance of his functions, it appearing that he had been duly elected by the congregation.

§ 1756. *Supreme Court has no jurisdiction to mandamus the Governor to commission a justice of the peace.* In *Comm.* v. *Hartranft*, 77 Pa. St., 154 (1874), a petition to the Supreme Court was presented for a mandamus to be directed to the Governor of Pennsylvania, commanding him to issue a commission to the petitioner, a justice of the peace, the petitioner alleging he was duly elected. Petition was refused on the ground that under article V., section 3, of the Constitution, the Supreme Court had no jurisdiction.

§ 1757. *Indictment not such a remedy as will bar mandamus.* Though mandamus will issue only where the petitioner is without other legal remedy, the fact that an indictment will lie for the omission to do a particular act is no objection to the allowance of a mandamus to compel the performance of that act. *Rex* v. *Railway Co.*, 2 Barn. & Alder., 646 (1819) ; *Reg.* v. *Eastern Counties Ry. Co.*, 10 Adol. & Ellis, 531 (1839).

In *Comm.* v. *Johnson*, 2 Binn., 275 (1810), it was ruled that mandamus would lie to compel the supervisors of public roads to pay orders drawn upon them by justices of the peace, who were authorized by Acts of Assembly to draw such orders. The fact that the supervisors were liable to indictment or suit in their individual character for their refusal to pay was held by TILGHMAN, J., no defense to the petition for a mandamus. " It is said that the supervisors may be indicted for neglect of duty. But if they were indicted and convicted, the orders might still be unpaid. It is said also that if they withhold payment without just cause, they are liable to an action. Granting that they are, it must be brought against them in their private capacity ; and there is no form of action against them which, being carried to judgment, will authorize an execution to be levied on the treasury of the Northern Liberties." Rule for mandamus made absolute.

§ 1758. *To prevent the issuing of a mandamus, the remedy must be competent to reach the end intended to be sought by it.* In *Overseers of Porter* v. *Overseers of Jersey Shore*, 82 Pa. St., 275 (1876), upon writ of error to order of the lower court discharging rule for mandamus, it was held that the relief should have been granted to compel the overseers of a township to provide for a pauper who had been adjudged entitled to a settlement in that township, in spite of the fact that a penalty was provided by statute in case of their refusal to do so.   Opinion by AGNEW, C. J.

§ 1759. *It will lie to compel a court of inferior jurisdiction to enter judgment.*   In *Fish* v. *Weatherwax*, 2 Johns. Cases, 215 (1801) (N. Y.), judgment upon a verdict for plaintiff was arrested in the Common Pleas, because of the insufficiency of his declaration ; he thereupon moved that the court enter judgment for defendant in order that he might take his writ of error.   Upon the court's refusal to do so, he applied for a mandamus from the Supreme Court to enforce the entry of judgment by the judges of the lower court. *Held*, that he was entitled to the writ.   Rule for mandamus granted.

§ 1760. *To compel payment of a judge's salary.*   A mandamus is the proper remedy to compel payment of a salary of a judge fixed by law and payable by the treasurer of the State.   *Comm.* v. *Hepburn*, 5 W. & S., 403 (1843).

§ 1761. *To compel Board of Wardens to define low water mark.* In *Tatham* v. *Wardens of Philadelphia*, 2 Phila., 246 (1857), a mandamus was decided to be the proper remedy where the Board of Wardens twice refused to define the low water mark of Windmill Island, on application of an owner who desired to build a wharf.

§ 1762. *County Commissioners may be compelled to provide funds to pay the interest on obligations assumed by the county.*   *Comm.* v. *Commissioners of Allegheny County*, 32 Pa. St., 218 (1858). Alternative mandamus and return.   The county of Allegheny, under authority of an Act of Assembly, having subscribed to the stock of a projected railway company, and issued interest-bearing bonds in payment of its subscription ; *held*, that mandamus would lie at the suit of a bondholder, commanding the county commissioners to make provision for raising money to pay the interest on the said bonds as it accrued.   The return to the alternative mandamus being insufficient, a motion for a peremptory mandamus was granted.

§ 1763. *To compel delinquent corporation to discharge its liability under a subscription to the stock of a railroad company.*   In *Comm.* v. *Perkins*, 43 Pa. St., 401 (1862), a petition was presented for a mandamus to compel respondents (Commissioners of Allegheny County) to levy and collect a tax for the purpose of paying interest on bonds issued in payment of a subscription by the Commissioners of Allegheny County to the capital stock of the Allegheny Valley Railroad. Opinion by READ, J. "A peremptory writ of mandamus awarded."

§ 1764. *To compel a municipal corporation to provide means for payment of interest on its bonds.* Comm. v. *Councils of City of Pittsburgh*, 34 Pa. St., 496 (1859). Alternative mandamus. *Sur* demurrer to return. The alternative mandamus commanded the Select and Common Councils of the city of Pittsburg to assess and levy a tax to provide for the payment of interest upon bonds issued by the said city. The return set up many grounds of defense, but nowhere disputed the salient facts as alleged in the alternative writ. Upon general demurrer, the opinion of the court was delivered per STRONG, J.: "* * * Judgment must be entered upon the demurrer against the defendants, and a peremptory writ awarded."

§ 1765. *To compel a borough to keep streets in repair.* Where a borough is bound to keep its streets in repair, such performance may be compelled by mandamus. *Borough* v. *Comm.*, 34 Pa. St., 293 (1859).

§ 1766. *Previous demand and refusal to perform public duty not essential.* In *Comm.* v. *Commissioners of Allegheny*, 37 Pa. St., 237 (1860), the decisions in the cases cited, sections 1762, 1764, were followed by the Supreme Court, although no demand for payment had been made before the issuance of the mandamus. Opinion by WOODWARD, J.

The doctrine enounced in these cases was reaffirmed in *Comm.* v. *Councils of Pittsburgh*, 88 Pa. St., 66 (1878), in which mandamus was awarded to compel the levy of a tax to pay municipal bonds issued for public improvements. It has also been adopted in many other cases.

§ 1767. *Members of City Councils may be compelled to meet and elect heads of departments.* *Lamb* v. *Lynd*, 44 Pa. St., 336 (1863). Petition of Owen Lamb *et al.*, members of the Common Council of Philadelphia, praying for a mandamus requiring members of Select Council to meet in joint assembly with Common Council on the day of the next stated meeting, and to proceed to the election of certain municipal officers required by the charter of the city to be chosen by Councils. The defendants set up that three persons had been fraudulently retained as members of the Common Council who were not lawful members of that body, and that the majority had fraudulently excluded two persons who ought to be members, for the purpose of obtaining a majority in favor of one political party so as to control the elections that were to be held at the joint meeting. *Held*, per LOWRIE, C. J., that these facts, if true, afforded no ground for members of Select Council to refuse to do their official duty.   Mandamus awarded.

§ 1768. *To compel the issuing of a certificate to a teacher.*   A mandamus will be granted to compel the issuing by the school controllers of a certificate to a teacher duly qualified and elected.   *McManus* v. *Controllers,* 7 Phila., 23 (1868).

§ 1769. *To compel Councils to make an appropriation directed by statute.*   In *Commissioners* v. *City,* 3 Brews., 596 (1869), a mandamus was granted commanding the Councils of Philadelphia to make an appropriation directed by Act of Assembly to the commissioners appointed to build South Street bridge.

§ 1770. In *Assessors of Philadelphia* v. *Commissioners,* 3 Brews., 333 (1869), the question arose as to granting a mandamus where one Act of Assembly forbade the city officers from making a contract without an appropriation therefor; but a later Act authorized and commanded said officers to purchase certain books, papers, and articles, but no appropriation was made for that purpose.   Rule for mandamus made absolute.

§ 1771. *To compel Highway Commissioners to enter into contract for paving directed by Act of Assembly.*   In *Comm.* v. *Dickinson,* 3 Brews., 561 (1869), the Chief Commissioner of Highways of Philadelphia was required by statute to enter into contracts for paving certain streets, application being made for a mandamus to compel him to enter into such contract.   The return set forth that Councils had made no appropriation.   To this return the relators demurred.   Judgment entered on the demurrer in favor of the Commonwealth, and mandamus awarded.   Opinion by Peirce, J.

§ 1772. *Register of Wills may be compelled to perform a ministerial act.*   *Comm.* v. *Bunn,* 71 Pa. St., 405 (1872), *sur* alternative mandamus and return.   The twenty-fifth section, Act March 15, 1832, provided that, "Where any question of kindred or other disputable and difficult matter comes into controversy before any register, he shall, at the request of any person interested, appoint a register's court for the decision thereof."   A controverted question having arisen before the Register of Philadelphia pending a hearing upon caveat to the probate of a will, he was requested by a party in interest to summon a register's court in accordance with the provisions of the Act.   Upon his refusal, a peremptory mandamus was awarded,.   Opinion by Thompson, C. J.

While a mandamus may issue to compel the Register to perform a ministerial or clerical act, yet it will not lie where there is ample remedy by appeal.   *Comm.* v. *Thomas,* 35 W. N., 255 (1894).

§ 1773. *To compel the Register of Wills to certify to the Orphans'*

Court disputed question of kinship. Mandamus will be granted to compel the Register of Wills to certify a question of disputed kinship to the Orphans' Court. *Taylor* v. *Comm.*, 103 Pa. St., 97 (1883).

§ 1774. *Mandamus will lie to restore to membership in a corporation one who has been unlawfully expelled therefrom. Evans* v. *Philadelphia Club*, 50 Pa. St., 107 (1865). E., being a member of respondent organization, a chartered social club, was expelled from the same for an assault upon another member within the club-house. *Held*, upon demurrer to return to the alternative mandamus, that in the absence of specific power to expel for such a cause conferred by charter, a by-law of the corporation was not a sufficient justification for the expulsion. Peremptory mandamus awarded.

§ 1775. *To restore corporator disfranchised without cause.* Where a corporator has been disfranchised without sufficient cause, or irregularly, he may be restored by mandamus. *Comm.* v. *Society*, 15 Pa. St., 251 (1850).

§ 1776. *If the trial, etc., be regular, mandamus will not lie.* If there be a hearing and trial according to a mode prescribed by an association, and there is no allegation of irregularity in the proceedings, the sentence is conclusive on the merits, and cannot be inquired into collaterally, either by mandamus or any other mode. *Comm.* v. *Society*, 8 W. & S., 247 (1844).

§ 1777. *To compel erection of bridge.* The building of a county bridge was duly authorized in 1859. Nothing was done toward its erection until 1867, when a contract was awarded and afterward rescinded. *Held*, that mandamus would lie to enforce its erection. *Commissioners* v. *Comm.*, 72 Pa. St., 24 (1872).

§ 1778. *To compel rebuilding of a bridge.* A mandamus will be awarded, under Act of May 5, 1876, to compel county commissioners to rebuild a bridge where the road leading to and from the bridge is a turnpike, and the bridge has been accidentally destroyed. *Myers* v. *Comm.*, 110 Pa. St., 217 (1885).

§ 1779. *To compel a railway company to sell tickets at its established rate of fare. State* v. *R. R. Co.*, 2 Cent. Rep., 726 (1886). Desiring to purchase a commutation ticket between two points on the line of the A. railroad company, the relator offered at the proper office of the company the price at which such tickets were sold by it to the public. Acting under instruction from the officers of the company, the agent refused to sell the ticket to him, because on a former occasion he had refused to pay his fare when he had forgotten to bring his commutation ticket with him. Upon a rule for a mandamus to compel the sale of the ticket by the company; *held,* that the relator was entitled to the relief sought.   Mandamus awarded.

§ 1780. *To compel school directors to admit colored children to the public schools.*   *Kaine* v. *Commonwealth,* 101 Pa. St., 490 (1882); ·*Comm.* v. *Williamson,* 10 Phila., 490 (C. P., 1873).   In both of these cases it appeared that colored children were refused admittance to the schools which were provided for the white children of the districts in which they lived, separate schools being established for the children of colored parents.   *Held,* that mandamus would lie to compel the admission of the colored children to the district . schools without distinctions founded upon race or color.

"It is asked, may not the school directors and teachers assign the boy to such room and school as may be adapted to his grade and attainments?   Undoubtedly they may.   Their authority and discretion in that respect is not questioned here.   The objection is that their action is not based on any consideration of his qualifications or attainments, but rests on his color alone."   Judgment awarding peremptory mandamus affirmed.   Per MERCUR, J. *Kaine* v. *Comm.* (*supra*).

§ 1781. *To enforce the right of inspection of the books of a private corporation by a stockholder.*   *Comm.* v. *Phœnix Iron Co.,* 105 Pa. St., 111 (1884); *Phœnix Iron Co.* v. *Comm.,* 113 Pa. St., 563 (1886).   A stockholder in the Phœnix Iron Company, a trading corporation, filed his petition alleging, *inter alia,* that he was largely interested in the company; that its business was extensive, prosperous, and profitable; that no dividend had been declared for many years; that the officers in control of the company were members of a partnership with which they had established intimate business relations upon the part of the company, to the prejudice of the company and to their own advantage as individuals and co-partners; that he intended to file a bill in equity to ascertain and enforce his rights as a stockholder; that he was denied the information in regard to the affairs of the company upon which his bill must be predicated; and denied access to the books and papers of the company which contained such information.   He prayed for a rule upon the company respondent, and upon its officers, to show cause why an alternative mandamus should not be issued requiring respondents to permit the relator to inspect the books and papers of the iron company at reasonable times, in so far as it should be necessary in order for him to ascertain the specified matters recited. This rule was granted and after hearing discharged.   *Held* by the Supreme Court to be error.   Judgment reversed.   Alternative mandamus awarded.   Opinion per TRUNKEY, J.

This case again came before the Supreme Court upon writ of error to the judgment of the lower court, sustaining a demurrer to respondent's return to the alternative mandamus. The facts, and the law bearing upon them, were once more carefully analyzed in a learned opinion by CLARK, J. ; the relator was held entitled to his remedy by peremptory mandamus, and the judgment of the lower court awarding the final writ was affirmed. 113 Pa. St., 563 (1886).

Where stockholders desire a copy of the stock-list for the purpose of consulting with and obtaining proxies from other stockholders to be used at a coming election, such right is legal and may be enforced by mandamus. *Comm. v. Phila. & Reading R. R. Co.*, 3 Dist. Rep., 116 (1893).

A mandamus may issue to compel a bank acting as a transfer agent of City and State loans to permit holders to inspect documents relating to said loans. *In re Guarantee Trust Co.*, 3 Dist. Rep., 205 ; 34 W. N., 14 (1894).

§ 1782. *To prevent discrimination by a telephone company. Bell Telephone Co.* v. *Comm.*, 17 W. N., 505 (1886). The petition for alternative mandamus recited that relator was a telegraph company and respondent a telephone company, both being corporations ; that relator had offered respondent the usual price or rental which it charged the public for the use of telephones, and had requested that it furnish an instrument to relator ; that respondent did furnish a telephone to a rival telegraph company, the W. company ; that the request of relator had been refused. Mandamus prayed for accordingly. The return to the alternative writ denied in general terms the allegations of the petition, and set up that respondent was operating by virtue of a license from the N. telephone company ; that it had offered relator to furnish to it a telephone, "except to facilitate its business in the delivery and transmission of messages ; " that the facilities furnished the W. telegraph company were in pursuance of an agreement between that company and the N. telephone company, whereby the latter agreed not to license the use of its telephones to any line competing with the W. telegraph company for such purposes, and whereby it agreed to fully license the said W. company to use telephones procured from it for transmitting telegraphic messages.

Upon demurrer this return was held insufficient, the demurrer was sustained in the Common Pleas, and the judgment of that court was affirmed upon writ of error, the opinion of ARNOLD, J., who decided the case below, being adopted by the Supreme Court.

§ 1783. *To compel the granting of a license to run omnibuses in the streets of a city.* Comm. v. Baldwin, 9 W. N., 233 (C. P., 1880). Petition for mandamus and return. By Act of Assembly and ordinances thereunder, the Chief Commissioner of Highways of Philadelphia was authorized from time to time to grant licenses to the owner or owners to keep and use omnibuses upon the payment of specified annual license fees for each omnibus. The relator, having tendered the proper amount of fees, requested the commissioner to issue a license to him to run a line of omnibuses upon one of the highways, which request was refused. The petition averred these facts and asked for a mandamus to the commissioner to compel the issuance of the proper license. The return set up that the matter lay within the discretion of the commissioner, and that he had exercised his best discretion; it furthermore recited various reasons for his refusal to grant the license. The court, finding the reasons insufficient to justify the refusal, held that the discretion vested in the commissioner was not such an arbitrary one as would authorize him to refuse to license without good ground for his action. Opinion per ALLISON, P. J. Mandamus awarded.

§ 1784. *To compel the sealing of bills of exception.* A writ in the nature of mandamus, under the Statute of Westminster II. (13 Edw. I., chapter 31), sometimes called a writ of *si ita,* will lie from the Supreme Court to the judges of the lower courts, to compel them to seal bills of exception in proper cases. *Reichenbach* v. *Ruddach,* 121 Pa. St., 18 (1888); *Conrow* v. *Schloss,* 55 Pa. St., 28 (1867).

At common law it would not lie in a criminal case under the Statute of Westminster. The right to a bill of exceptions in such case is under the Act of May 19, 1874. *Haines* v. *Comm.,* 99 Pa. St., 410 (1882).

§ 1785. *To compel the granting of licenses to sell liquor at wholesale.* In re Prospect Brewing Co., 127 Pa. St., 523 (1889). Alternative mandamus and return *sur* application for writ of peremptory mandamus from the Supreme Court to require the judges of the Court of Quarter Sessions of Philadelphia, sitting as a license court, to grant a brewer's license to relator. From the petition for alternative mandamus, and the return thereto, it appeared that the relator, a corporation, had applied to the Court of Quarter Sessions for a renewal of his license for one year from June 1, 1889; that no remonstrance or objection to such application had been filed; that after hearing by the said court the application had been refused, because the judges of the license court found "that the said company had conducted its business during the year then expiring in violation of law ; that said company was not a fit person to receive the license applied for ; and that so far as it was possible for a corporation to possess a moral character, it did not possess a good moral character." *Held*, that the return was uncertain, vague, and indefinite ; that under existing laws applicable to Philadelphia the lower court was required to issue the license, upon application, in the absence of objection or remonstrance thereto, and that where such remonstrance or objection was filed, the court could lawfully inquire only whether the applicant was a citizen of the United States, of temperate habits, and good moral character. Peremptory mandamus awarded. Opinion by Chief Justice PAXSON.

A similar application was refused in *Comm.* v. *Wilson*, 25 W. N., 148 (1889), directed to the Quarter Sessions of Jefferson County, on the ground that *Pollard's Case*, 127 Pa. St., 507, and *Prospect Brewing Co.'s Case, Id.*, 523, were decided upon the local laws in force in Allegheny and Philadelphia Counties, which are the "existing laws" embraced in the Act of May 24, 1887, and that Jefferson County came under the general law of May 22, 1867 (P. L., 40).

§ 1786. *To the return judges of an election to compel them to make a proper return of the votes cast. Thompson* v. *Ewing*, 1 Brews., 67 (1862). By Act of Assembly of July 2, 1839, section 43 (P. L., 528), it was provided that citizens of the Commonwealth in the military service of the United States might exercise the right of suffrage at elections held thereafter. At the election held on the second Tuesday in October, 1861, a large vote was polled by soldiers who were with the army engaged in the war of the rebellion. The prothonotary of the Court of Common Pleas of Philadelphia, acting under advice of the court, certified this soldier vote to the return judges, many of whom refused to include it in their returns. *Held*, that mandamus would lie to compel the return judges to compute the votes thus cast. Peremptory mandamus awarded, per LUDLOW, J.

§ 1787. *To compel return judges to sign certificate of election.* A mandamus will be awarded to compel return judges of a senatorial district to sign a certificate of election. It is not within their power to judge or examine what precedes the county returns or to investigate charges of fraud. *Comm.* v. *Emminger*, 74 Pa. St., 479 (1873).

To compel a justice to grant an appeal. A mandamus will issue in a proper case to compel a justice of the peace to grant an appeal. *Minich* v. *Basom*, 2 Dist. Rep., 709 (1893).

The foregoing citations will serve to illustrate the circumstances under which relief by mandamus is permissible, and in some measure to specialize the general language of the definitions. No attempt has been made to give a complete list of the cases in which the use of the writ of mandamus has been upheld.

§ 1788. **When mandamus will not be granted.** *To compel commissioners in bankruptcy to give certificate of conformity.* *Respublica* v. *Clarkson et al.*, 1 Yeates, 46 (1791). Motion and rule for mandamus to compel the commissioners of bankruptcy to issue a certificate to the petitioner or show cause, etc. By the law then in force in relation to the subject, the bankrupt was entitled to receive a certificate from the commissioners on his conforming to the directions prescribed by the Act of Assembly, which certificate was necessary in order that he might be discharged. The commissioners made return that there appeared to them reason to doubt that the petitioner had made a true, full, and perfect disclosure and discovery as required. *Held,* that this return was sufficient. Rule discharged.

§ 1789. *Nor to try the title to an office which is filled by another.* A mandamus was refused against county commissioners who declined to recognize an assessor, the latter having failed to file his copy of affirmation in the commissioner's office, as required by Act of Assembly. *Comm.* v. *County Commissioners*, 6 Wh., 476 (1841). *Quo warranto*, not mandamus, is the proper remedy to try the title to an office which is already occupied, though the latter writ may issue to put the relator in possession when the office is vacant.

§ 1790. *To compel a court of inferior jurisdiction to decide a case in a particular way.* *Comm.* v. *Judges of Common Pleas*, 3 Binn., 273 (1810). Motion in the Supreme Court for rule upon the judges of the Court of Common Pleas of Philadelphia County to show cause why they should not be compelled by mandamus to admit an appeal from the judgment of an alderman, which they, upon motion, had stricken off. Rule refused. "In the case of the *United States* v. *Lawrence*, 3 Dall., 42, it was determined by the Supreme Court of the United States, *clearly* and *unanimously*, after full argument, that, although they might command an inferior judge to *proceed to judgment,* yet they had no power to compel him to *decide* according to the dictates of any judgment but his own. Upon this principle it would be improper for us to issue a mandamus, because the Court of Common Pleas have already decided according to the dictates of their own judgment." Per TILGHMAN, C. J.

Comm. v. *Cochran*, 5 Binn., 87 (1812). The secretary of the land office, acting under direction of a board of property which was clothed by law with judicial power in the premises, refused to issue patents for land sold by the Commonwealth, except upon tender of the interest which that body had decided to be due, the amount of such interest being in dispute. Upon alternative mandamus and return, the Supreme Court refused to interfere with the discretion of the board of property, and denied the prayer for a peremptory mandamus to the secretary to compel the issuance of the patents. Opinion by TILGHMAN, C. J.

Comm. v. *McLaughlin,* 120 Pa. St., 518 (1888). McLaughlin was convicted in the Court of Quarter Sessions of Montgomery County of maintaining a nuisance, to wit, a magazine for explosives, and sentenced to abate the same and to pay a fine. The district attorney, averring that the nuisance had not been abated in accordance with such sentence, moved the said court to order the sheriff to abate it, which motion was denied ; thereupon he applied to the Supreme Court for a mandamus to the judges of the lower court to compel them to make the order. Petition for mandamus refused.

" The court below has acted upon the application of the district attorney, and refused it. If the court had declined to act, there might have been some ground for the application for a mandamus. That the writ will lie from this court to a lower court to compel the performance of a duty is settled law. Thus, if a judge unreasonably delay judgment in a particular case, he may be compelled to do so by mandamus. But it will not lie to compel him to give judgment in a particular way ; it will only require him to act. Hence, when the judge has acted, mandamus will not lie to reverse his action." Per PAXSON, J.

§ 1791. *Nor to compel the granting of a change of venue.* *Petition of Newlin,* 123 Pa. St., 541 (1888). N. having begun suit against the County of Indiana, in the Court of Common Pleas of that county, moved said court for a change of venue on the ground that all the tax-payers residing in the county were interested adversely to him. His motion was refused. Upon petition to the Supreme Court for a mandamus commanding the judge of the lower court to grant the change of venue asked for, *held,* opinion per WILLIAMS, J., that the petition laid no ground for the writ of mandamus.

§ 1792. *Nor to compel the prothonotary of a court to amend a record.* *Comm.* v. *Hultz,* 6 Pa. St., 469 (1847). The Court of Common Pleas of Allegheny County having refused, upon motion, to direct the prothonotary to amend the record in a case which had been tried in that court, a rule for a writ of mandamus to the prothonotary was taken in the said court to effect the same end. This was refused. Upon writ of error, the order refusing the writ was affirmed.

§ 1793. *Nor to compel admission of an attorney.* A writ of mandamus to the Common Pleas, requiring them to admit an attorney, was refused—such admission is a judicial and not a ministerial act. *Comm.* v. *Judges*, 1 S. & R., 187 (1814).

In *Comm.* v. *Judges*, 5 W. & S., 272 (1843), a mandamus was refused to reinstate an attorney stricken from the rolls of the District Court of Philadelphia.

§ 1794. *Nor to compel the issuing of a commission to a superintendent of instruction not fully qualified.* In *Comm.* v. *Wickersham*, 90 Pa. St., 311 (1879), a mandamus directed to the superintendent of public instruction to issue a commission to the relator, who had been elected city superintendent of schools at Scranton, was refused. It appeared the relator had been objected to by a number of citizens, who were also on the board of school control, as not possessing sufficient qualification.

MERCUR, J.: " It is true, by the Act of April 9, 1867, it is provided that serving as county, city, or borough superintendent shall be deemed a sufficient test of qualification, but the Act also provides that if, upon examination of the evidence of competency, it shall not prove to be such as is required, or if objection be made in conformity with the fourth section of the Act of 1865, the superintendent of common schools shall appoint two competent persons, himself being the third, to examine the person elected, and if, upon such examination, his qualifications are found insufficient, the commission shall not issue.   *   *   *   Such objections were made, the committee appointed, and a report made unfavorable to the relator."

§ 1795. *Nor to compel discretionary acts.* In *Comm.* v. *Commissioners*, 5 Binn., 536 (1813), it appeared that the legislature had directed the county commissioners to draw orders upon the county treasurer for the services of a schoolmaster if they approved thereof. The matter being one of discretion with the commissioners, a mandamus was refused where the commissioners had disapproved the bill.

In *Comm.* v. *Mayor*, 5 Watts, 152 (1836), the Select and Common Councils of Lancaster directed the mayor to issue a certificate of loan to a certain member of Councils for special services. This he declined to do. A mandamus was refused.

In *Comm.* v. *Henry*, 49 Pa. St., 530 (1865), the mayor was duly authorized by Councils to execute leases for coal lands belonging to the Girard Estate to such persons as may be accepted by the superintendent. The mayor, in his return to a writ of mandamus to compel him to execute the leases, alleged that improper means had been used to obtain them, and as the city was trustee for the estate, the proposed leasing would be detrimental to the interests of the trust, and was a matter within his sound discretion. Mandamus refused.

§ 1796. *Nor to compel the affixing of a corporate seal to amendments to a charter.* In *Comm.* v. *Trustees*, 6 S. & R., 508 (1821), a writ of mandamus was refused where a majority of an incorporated body sought to compel the trustees of the corporation to affix the seal to certain alterations and amendments to the charter, contrary to their judgment.

§ 1797. *Nor to seat an official if there be doubt as to his election.* A mandamus will be refused where there is doubt as to the validity of an election. *Comm.* v. *Commissioners*, 5 Rawle, 75 (1835).

§ 1798. *Nor to compel exoneration from a school tax alleged to be unjustly assessed.* In *School Directors* v. *Anderson*, 45 Pa. St., 388 (1863), a mandamus was refused to compel school directors to exonerate and discharge the relator from a tax assessed by them against him.

The petitioner averred that he was charged with school taxes upon a mortgage held against a company in which he owned one-half the stock, which was itself taxed, and that the company was insolvent and unable to pay interest on the mortgage.

WOODWARD, J.: "This was an unprecedented application of the writ of mandamus. It is not the ordinary official duty of school directors to exonerate taxes, but rather to levy and collect them. If they were backward in the exercise of this official function, mandamus might be used to stir them up. But when they have set themselves in motion and are proceeding to discharge the duty imposed by law, they are no longer subject to mandamus."

§ 1799. *Nor to compel school directors to erect a school-house.* In re *Application of Citizens of Manheim Township*, 5 Clark, 400 (1855) (C. P. of Lancaster County). Petition by citizens for mandamus to compel the school directors of Manheim Township to erect an additional school-house. Answer of respondents averring that, after consideration of the subject, the board of directors had decided that it was unnecessary and injudicious to erect the school-house asked for, and that the interest of the township did not require the erection of said school-house. By Act of Assembly, the boards of directors were empowered and enjoined to establish a sufficient number of common schools, and to cause suitable buildings to be erected, purchased, or rented for school-houses. Rule for mandamus discharged, per HAYES, J.

§ 1800. *Nor to compel county commissioners to draw orders on the treasury, there being no money applicable to the purpose in the county treasury.* Comm. v. *Price,* 1 Whar., 1 (1835). The Court of Quarter Sessions, confirming an award of damages in favor of certain persons, ordered the amount awarded to be paid out of the county treasury. The county commissioners refused to draw orders on the treasurer in accordance with this direction. A rule for mandamus was obtained from the Supreme Court, to compel them to do so, by one in whose favor the award was made. Upon the commissioners' answer, showing that there were no funds in the treasury which could be applied to the satisfaction of the award, the rule for mandamus was discharged.

§ 1801. *Nor to compel payment of interest on an order on the county treasurer.* In *Comm.* v. *Commissioners,* 4 S. & R., 125 (1818), the court refused a mandamus to the county commissioners to enforce the payment of interest on an order drawn by the commissioners on the county treasurer.

In *Hester's Case,* 2 W. & S., 416 (1841), a mandamus was refused directed to the county commissioners to pay a certain debt for which no suit had been brought. "The established rule of law, which has been constantly recognized and acted on by this court, is that a mandamus will not be granted where there is a specific remedy by action; * * * the party has a remedy by action. He must first sue the county commissioners and recover against them."

§ 1802. *Nor to compel an act by a corporation whose chief place of business is in a county other than that where proceedings are brought.* In *Whitemarsh Township* v. *R. R.,* 8 W. & S., 365 (1845), a petition for mandamus was presented in the Common Pleas of Montgomery County, setting forth that the Philadelphia, Germantown and Norristown Railroad Company occupied part of the bed of a public road in Whitemarsh Township, Montgomery County, Pa., thereby obstructing the free use and passage of the public road; that the company had not made a good and sufficient road for public accommodation alongside of said railroad in place of the part of the public road so occupied by them. The defendants, on this complaint of the supervisors of the township, responded that defendants had their office and chief place of business in Philadelphia, and had no office or chief place of business in Montgomery County, and that under the Act of June 14, 1836, the court had no jurisdiction. Mandamus refused.

§ 1803. *Nor to compel the allowance of an appeal from assessment of taxes after the statutory period.* The assessor of Doylestown returned to the commissioners that he had assessed relator $50,000, to which the commissioners added $25,000. The relator did not take any steps toward an appeal until after the time allowed by the Act.

" To found the application for the mandamus, the law requires that the applicant establish a specific legal right as well as the want of a specific legal remedy."

" The complaint and decision of the commissioners was December 29, 1848, and the petition to the Common Pleas was not presented until February 9, 1849, long after the expiration of the thirty days allowed by the Act. * * * His case, as presented, is not one of *specific legal right.*"

Mandamus to compel allowance of the appeal refused. *James v. Commissioners,* 13 Pa. St., 72 (1850), BURNSIDE, J.

§ 1804. *Nor to compel supervisors to receive certificates of work from non-residents on account of taxes on unseated lands.* In *Comm. v. Supervisors,* 29 Pa. St., 124 (1858), a writ of mandamus directed to the supervisors of a township to compel them to receive certificates of the amount of work done by non-resident owners of unseated lands and allow a credit therefor was refused, upon the ground that the relator had ample remedy by injunction to restrain the county treasurer from selling such land for taxes.

A writ of mandamus cannot issue to compel a mayor and the clerks of council to certify an ordinance under the Act of March 21, 1866 (P. L., 262), where the record shows that the mayor vetoed the ordinance and that councils failed to pass the ordinance over his veto, even though a technical objection may arise as to the exercise of the veto power. *Comm.* v. *Fitler,* 26 W. N., 369 (1890).

§ 1805. *Mandamus not a substitute for* quo warranto. Mandamus is not the regular mode of showing that a new board of directors of a fire association was elected without authority. The proper proceeding to test their official character would be *quo warranto. Assn.* v. *Benseman,* 4 W. N., 1 (1877).

§ 1806. *The Supreme Court refused a mandamus to compel the letting of stalls in a market, referring the relator to the county court.* In *Comm.* v. *Baroux,* 36 Pa. St., 262 (1860), a petition for mandamus was presented, directed to the commissioner of markets in Philadelphia, to compel him to let stalls in the market-houses, even though the farmers brought meat for sale *not raised on their own farms.*

" We cannot allow it. * * * It is in our discretion to refuse it. * * * If there be an adequate remedy in another form or before *another court.* * * * The Common Pleas has all the authority needed for the case, and we must refer the relator to that tribunal."

§ 1807. *Mandamus will not lie to compel performance of an act by unincorporated bodies.* A writ of mandamus cannot issue from the Court of Common Pleas to individuals in their private relations, nor to associations having no chartered powers. *Wolf* v. *Comm.*, 64 Pa. St., 252 (1870).

§ 1808. *Nor to compel opening of a street not on the city's plans.* In *Comm.* v. *Dickinson*, 83 Pa. St., 458 (1877), an alternative mandamus issued to compel the commissioner of highways in Philadelphia to open Volkmar Street, as directed by Act of Assembly. The return denied that such street was on the city plans. Instead of trying the issue of fact and having it determined in the usual way, the relator demurred on the ground that the return contradicted the Act of Assembly. Mandamus refused.

§ 1809. *Nor to compel the satisfaction of a mortgage which had been lost for forty years.* In *Comm.* v. *Lane*, 3 W. N., 546 (1877), a mandamus to have the Recorder of Deeds of Philadelphia County satisfy a mortgage was refused on the grounds that the instrument had been lost forty years before, and that as relator's title was derived from a sale upon the mortgage, there was no cloud on his title.

§ 1810. *Nor at the suit of a private person to compel the performance of a public duty. Councils of Reading* v. *Comm.*, 11 Pa. St., 196 (1849). This was a petition in the Court of Common Pleas for a mandamus to compel the Councils of Reading to keep open a public street which was alleged to be unlawfully obstructed. The petitioners were private citizens. Upon alternative mandamus, return thereto, and demurrer to the return, the lower court sustained the demurrer and awarded a peremptory mandamus. On writ of error, the judgment was reversed. "The nuisance in this case is a public one, and it does not appear from the statement of the relators that they have received any special injury from it to entitle them to any civil remedy whatever. The obstruction of the sidewalk is not more injurious to them than it is to the inhabitants at large; and it would consequently seem that an indictment is exclusively the means to abate it." Per GIBSON, C. J.

Heffner v. *Comm.*, 28 Pa. St., 108 (1857). The town councils of the borough of P., being authorized and required by statute to open a certain alley, were requested by the relator, a private citizen, to do so. He was the owner of real estate which would have been enhanced in value by the opening of the alley. Councils refused to proceed in the matter, whereupon the relator applied for a mandamus. Upon alternative writ, return, and demurrer, the court below entered judgment for plaintiff. *Held*, to be error. "It is manifest that [the relator's] interest, in kind, if not in degree, is common to all the inhabitants of P. * * * It will be soon enough for the courts to interfere to open that alley when those public officers whose duty it is to see that the laws are executed move the courts to action. The law was enacted for the public; and if the public acquiesce in its non-execution, the courts, who are only other agents of the public, have no duty or power in the premises." Per WOODWARD, J. Judgment reversed and judgment for defendants.

In *Comm.* v. *Park*, 9 Phila., 481 (1872), a petition for mandamus was presented by a private citizen to require Councils, under an Act of Assembly placing Occident Avenue upon the public plans, to have it opened, graded, curbed, and paved. Petition dismissed, on the ground that a private citizen must show a right independent of that which he holds in common with the public.

A mill-owner who has lost custom and been placed at a great disadvantage by reason of the absence of approaches to a bridge is not entitled, as a private relator, to a mandamus to compel the erection of such approaches by the borough officers. *Comm.* v. *Westfield*, 1 Dist. Rep., 495 (1891).

§ 1811. *Nor to compel the laying of a water-pipe, no appropriation being made.* In *Comm.* v. *McFadden*, 8 W. N., 454 (1880), a writ of mandamus directed to the chief engineer of the Water Department of Philadelphia, to compel him to lay water-pipe under an ordinance, was refused, no appropriation having been made.

§ 1812. *Nor to compel the payment of a disputed account.* *Comm.* ex rel. *Prison Inspectors* v. *Commissioners*, 16 S. & R., 317 (1827). *Sur* rule in the Supreme Court to show cause why mandamus should not issue to compel respondents to pay an account for keeping certain convicts in the penitentiary. Respondents showed cause that the charges were unreasonable and the account disputed. *Per Curiam:* "A jury alone is competent to determine the propriety of the charges. The remedy in the first instance is by action against the respondents in their corporate capacity, after which a mandamus to enforce the judgment might be altogether proper; but before the merits are determined in the usual way an application like the present is premature." Rule discharged.

§ 1813. *Nor when a remedy by appeal is provided.* *Comm.* v. *Clark*, 6 Phila., 498 (1868). Demurrer to return to alternative mandamus requiring respondents (the Board of Port Wardens of Philadelphia) to show cause why they should not issue a license to

relator, permitting him to extend a wharf into the Delaware River.
By Act of February 7, 1818, it is provided that if the board shall
refuse an application for a license, the applicant may apply by petition to the Court of Quarter Sessions, who shall proceed to summon a jury, etc.   *Held*, per STRONG, J., that the statute provided
an ample remedy for petitioner, and that mandamus would not lie.
Judgment for respondents.

§ 1814. *Nor to compel the transfer of stock upon the books of a
corporation.   Insurance Co. v. Comm.*, 92 Pa. St., 72 (1879).   The
relator having purchased stock in the respondent company at sheriff's sale, requested the secretary to transfer the stock to him on the
corporation books ; upon refusal, he applied for a writ of mandamus
to compel the making of the transfer.   His right to the stock was
not undisputed.   Judgment for the relator was entered in the lower
court, which judgment was reversed upon writ of error.   " At the
threshold the relator is met with the objection that mandamus will
not lie, for the reason that even if his right to the stock be clear,
and the respondents have wrongfully refused to make the transfer,
he has an adequate remedy in an action on the case for damages.
*   *   *   If the courts here were inclined to enlarge the remedy,
it could not be done in a case where the right is disputed, where no
public interest is involved, where no reason is shown for a transfer
of a specific and favorite thing, and where the remedy by action is
fully adequate."   Per TRUNKEY, J.

§ 1815. *Nor to compel the giving of public contracts to the lowest
bidder.   Comm.* v. *Mitchell*, 82 Pa. St., 343 (1876).   By Act of
24 May, 1874 (P. L., 230), it was provided that work and material for public uses should be furnished under contract to be given
to the lowest responsible bidder.   The water committee of Councils
of Pittsburgh having charge of the erection of water-works advertised for sealed proposals for contracts to do the work required, and
awarded the contract to one who was not the lowest bidder.   *Held*,
affirming the judgment of the lower court, that in the absence of
fraud or corruption mandamus would not lie at the suit of the
lowest bidder to compel the awarding of the contract to him, though
he was found by the court to be in every sense " responsible," because : (1) The matter lies within the discretion of the body empowered to award the contract ; and (2) if injury result from the improper award of the contract, such injury is to the public at large
and not to the lowest bidder, who is therefore without legal right
in the premises.

In *Comm.* v. *Guardians*, 13 W. N., 61 (1883), a mandamus to
compel the guardians of the poor to accept relator's bid for supply-

ing milk was refused. BIDDLE, J.: "By their bid they proposed to contract for certain work ; that bid was not accepted. It was a mere proposal that bound neither party, and as it was never consummated by a contract, the city acquired no right against the relators, nor they against the city. They are wanting in a specific remedy only because they have failed to establish a legal right."

These rulings were reaffirmed by the Supreme Court in *Douglass* v. *Comm.*, 108 Pa. St., 559 (1885).

§ 1816. *Nor will mandamus lie to compel city controllers to countersign warrants.* In *Comm.* v. *Lyndall*, 2 Brews., 425 (1867), a mandamus was awarded against the city controller to compel him to countersign a school-teacher's warrant. BREWSTER, J., dissenting.

But this ruling was *reversed* in *Runkle* v. *Comm.*, 97 Pa. St., 328 (1881) ; *Dechert* v. *Comm.*, 113 Pa. St., 229 (1886).

In these cases, city controllers refused to countersign warrants upon the treasury which were presented to them for that purpose, assigning reasons which, though different in the two cases, involved in each the exercise of discretionary powers upon their part. *Held,* that they could not be compelled by mandamus to countersign the warrants.

"The Act of 23d of May, 1874 (P. L., 230), clothes him [the city controller] with judicial powers ; he must not only countersign warrants drawn on the city treasury, but he is also required to pass upon their rectitude, and for this purpose he may not only make personal inquiry, but may require the production of evidence. * * * Upon him also is imposed ' all the duties now enjoined on county auditors by the laws of this State, and he shall scrutinize, audit, and settle all accounts whatever in which the city is concerned.' But the powers of county auditors are as full and complete within their jurisdiction as are the powers of courts. They may issue subpœnas for parties and witnesses, they may compel the production of books and papers, administer oaths, compel the attendance of witnesses, and punish contempts by attachment. With all this judicial and deliberative power the controller of the city of Reading is clothed, and of necessity he must be left free to exercise his own judgment ; but how can he exercise these important functions if he is to be controlled in his judgment by the Court of Common Pleas, or any other court?" Per GORDON, J., 97 Pa. St., 331.

§ 1817. *Nor to aid an immoral or pernicious calling ; e. g., stock gambling.* *Sterrett* v. *Electric Co.*, 44 Leg. Int., 253 (1887) (C. P. of Philadelphia County). Demurrer to return to alternative man-

damus. This petition was filed to compel the corporation respondent to furnish relator a "ticker" or electrical machine used for
the purpose of quoting the price of stocks. From the return it
appeared that at the place where he desired the machine to be furnished him relator was the keeper of a "bucket shop," wherein
gambling or wagering on the price of stocks was the business carried on, and where no legitimate business was transacted. These
facts being admitted by the demurrer, *Held*, per GORDON, J., that
relator was not entitled to the peremptory writ. Mandamus refused. "The writ of mandamus is not of right, but its issue is
for the sound discretion of the court, and it ought never to be
granted where the object sought to be attained is an immoral one,
or of a pernicious or immoral tendency, or against public policy."

§ 1818. *Nor to compel the granting or transfer of retail liquor
licenses.* In re *Raudenbush's Petition*, 120 Pa. St., 328 (1888).
Petition in the Supreme Court for a writ of mandamus to compel
the judges of the Court of Quarter Sessions of Philadelphia to issue
a retail liquor license to petitioner. The petition set forth in substance that petitioner had carried on the business of selling liquor
at retail at his residence for five years theretofore, having been
licensed so to do ; that he presented his petition to the Court of
Quarter Sessions for a renewal of said license, in accordance with
the terms of the Act of May 13, 1887 (P. L., 108) ; that he had
complied strictly with said Act, and possessed all the qualifications
thereby required ; that at the hearing upon his petition for a license
no remonstrance, objection, or evidence against the granting of the
same had been offered ; that afterward such petition or application
was refused by the said judges. By the Act of 1887 above referred
to, the judges of the Court of Quarter Sessions were empowered to
hear petitions of residents in favor of, and remonstrances against,
granting licenses, and were directed to refuse the same "whenever
in the opinion of the said court, having due regard to the number
and character of the petitioners for and against such application,
such license is not necessary for the accommodation of the public
and entertainment of strangers or travellers, or that the applicant
or applicants is or are not fit persons to whom such license should
be granted."

Held, that the discretion vested by this Act in the judges of the
Court of Quarter Sessions could not be controlled by mandamus,
and that the petition must be refused, per PAXSON, J. "The petitioner assumes that he is entitled as a matter of right to a license
upon complying with the provisions of the Act of 1887, in the
absence of any allegation that he is an improper person to be so

licensed. This is the fallacy which underlies his case, as well as the able argument of his learned counsel. He has no such absolute right, nor has any other man in the Commonwealth. * * * The petitioner begs the whole case when he assumes that he has a right to a license because he is a respectable man, has always kept a respectable house, and that no remonstrances have been filed against him. It is an error to suppose that the sole duty of the court is confined to the inquiry whether the applicant is a citizen of the United States and a man of good moral character, etc. Back of all this lies the question, whether the petitioner's house is 'necessary for the accommodation of the public and entertainment of strangers and travellers,' and the plain duty of the Court of Quarter Sessions, under the Act of. Assembly, is to so exercise its discretion as to 'restrain' rather than increase the sale of liquor. * * , * The question is one of public concern ; the petitioner is no party to it in the sense that persons are parties to private litigation."

In re Blumenthal's Petition, 125 Pa. St., 412 (1889). In this case the decision in *Raudenbush's Petition* was quoted and followed, and a petition for a mandamus to compel the judges of the Court of Quarter Sessions to transfer a license to sell liquor was denied, the said judges having refused an application for such transfer. The original licensee in this case died during the term for which his license was granted, and the application for a transfer was made by his widow, who was also devisee of the premises in which liquor was licensed to be sold.

"She was entitled to a héaring, and if she had been denied that, it could be secured to her by mandamus, but there the remedy ends, and the judgment to be pronounced as a result of the hearing is for the Court of Quarter Sessions, not for us. * * * The court below had the power under the Act of 1858 to transfer this license, but it was a matter of discretion, and not reviewable here." Petition dismissed, per PAXSON, C. J.

§ 1819. **Rule to show cause formerly required.** Under the old method of practice, before the alternative writ could go out it was necessary for the relator to take a rule on the respondent to show cause why the mandamus should not issue. This course was pursued in all the earlier cases, and the merits of the entire controversy were often determined upon the return to the preliminary rule. See *Respublica* v. *Clarkson*, 1 Yeates, 46 (1791) ; *Comm.* v. *Johnson*, 2 Binn., 275 (1810) ; *Comm.* v. *Rosseter, Id.*, 360 (1810) ; *Comm.* v. *Cochran*, 5 *Id.*, 87 (1812) ; *Comm.* v. *Commissioners*, 16 S. & R., 317 (1827) ; *Comm.* v. *Commissioners*, 1 Wh., 1 (1835).

§ 1820. *But a preliminary rule is no longer necessary.* By Act of.

June 14, 1836, section 20 (P. L., 626), it was provided that the person or persons who ought to make return to the writ should make his or their return to the first writ of mandamus issued.

Since the passage of that Act the practice has prevailed of issuing the alternative mandamus (which is itself substantially a rule to show cause), upon *ex parte* petition, supported by affidavit, and without putting the relator to his preliminary rule.

"The Act of Assembly very plainly points the course to be pursued when a proper suggestion is filed. If it contain the substance of a case for mandamus, the course is to issue an alternative writ, commanding the defendant to perform the act required, or return his reason for not doing it." *Treasurer of Jefferson Co.* v. *Shannon*, 51 Pa. St., 221 (1865).

In *Keasy* v. *Bricker*, 60 Pa. St., 9 (1868), Mr. Justice AGNEW very ably sets out the steps preceding the issuing of a mandamus. They "are not to be assimilated to a proceeding in equity, with all its attendant pleadings. The ordinary practice is to direct an alternative mandamus to issue when the court is satisfied, on affidavits, that the writ should be issued as a matter of justice and right, to compel the performance of an act or duty, for which otherwise there would be no adequate remedy. This gives the party to whom it is directed an opportunity to do the act or to show good reason at the return of the writ why he should not do it. He does this by making a return to the writ. It is at this point the pleadings in the cause begin. The return may traverse the facts alleged in the writ, or, admitting them, may avoid performance by stating sufficient facts in excuse. The relator may then demur, plead to, or traverse the facts set forth in the return."

See also *Phœnix Iron Co.* v. *Comm.*, 113 Pa. St., 563 (1886), in which the foregoing cases are cited and approved. The Act of June 8, 1893, § 2, dispenses with any preliminary rule and adopts the practice stated in *Keasy* v. *Bricker*, *supra*, § 1737.

Since the Act of 1836, the course of taking the preliminary rule to show cause was sometimes adopted, either because of it being required by rule of court, or because the practitioner preferred it. *McMahon* v. *Association*, 2 Brews., 441 (1868) ; *Comm.* v. *Iron Co.*, 105 Pa. St., 111 (1884) ; *Telegraph Co.* v. *Comm.*, 114 Pa. St., 592 (1886).

A rule to show cause must still be taken before mandamus can issue against the city of Philadelphia upon the award of a road jury. In re *Devereux Street*, 13 Phila., 103 (1879).

§ 1821. *Where defendants appear, and there is no controversy as to facts, the right of relator being clear, a peremptory writ may issue* *in first instance.* In *Comm.* v. *Borough,* 15 W. N., 506 (1884), TRUNKEY, J., said : " The ordinary practice is to direct an alternative mandamus where good cause, *prima facie,* appears, and this gives the parties an opportunity to do the act or show cause at the return of the writ why they should not. * * *

" If the defendants have appeared to a rule or notice of an application for a mandamus, and have been heard, and there is no controversy in respect to the facts, and the right of the relator is clear, a peremptory writ may, in the discretion of the court, be issued in the first instance." Under § 2 of the Act of 1893, above cited, a peremptory writ may be issued in the first instance where the right is clear.

§ 1822. **Writ returnable in a different district.** A writ of mandamus may be issued by the Supreme Court at Pittsburgh and made returnable to the Supreme Court for the Western District. BLACK, J.: "Our jurisdiction is over the whole State. It is not the practice to issue writs beyond the district in which they are made returnable, and that is all that was decided in *Duffy* v. *Turnpike,* 9 S. & R., 59. But no law forbids it. There are cases, and this is one of them, in which the rule of practice ought to be relaxed, though it certainly would not be relaxed if a motion were made to quash the writ in a purely local and private case." *R. R.* v. *Commissioners,* 21 Pa. St., 9 (1852).

§ 1823. **Requisites of suggestion.** The suggestion or petition for the alternative writ should set forth all the facts specifically which, if true, would entitle the relator to the relief sought, and it must show a clear *prima facie* right to the mandamus. All the facts relied upon should be stated so clearly that the respondent may admit or deny them in his return, so that an issue may be framed upon the fundamental averments made by the relator. The suggestion should show that relator has a specific right and is without other adequate remedy, though it is not always necessary to so allege in terms. The act or acts whose performance is sought to be compelled by the mandamus must be clearly and distinctly specified. See High, Extraor. Rem., section 450 *et seq.*

In the case of *Telegraph Co.* v. *Comm.,* 114 Pa. St., 592 (1886), the Supreme Court indicates the degree of precision and certainty which is required in the suggestion for alternative mandamus as well as in the return thereto. Relator, in substance, averred that respondent was a corporation engaged in the business of furnishing telephones for hire ; that it charged the uniform price of eighty-four dollars per year for such hire ; that relator had tendered that sum to respondent and requested that a telephone be furnished to it ; that respondent had refused to comply with this request and had demanded the sum of $150 per year for doing so. Mandamus prayed for accordingly. Respondent's return alleged that its rate for furnishing telephones varied with the distance, cost of erection, etc. ; that it charged $150 per year for telephones at the distance from its office at which relator desired one, and that it had always been ready and willing to furnish one to relator upon being paid that sum, etc. Upon demurrer the lower court held this return uncertain and evasive, and entered judgment for relator, whereupon respondent sued out a writ of error.

"As in considering a demurrer regard must be had to all the pleadings, and not merely that part of them to which the demurrer refers, we must, in order to reach a correct result, review the writ which, of course, follows the petition. * * * It may be admitted that all that is essentially necessary to maintain the writ of mandamus is found in the above statement : that is, that a definite legal right exists in the relators to have the telephone service and a consequent duty on the part of the company to furnish it. There is also in this statement of facts on which the right is made to depend, certainty to a common intent ; that is, they are stated with a precision sufficient to express the right of the one and the duty of the other in such manner that the ordinary mind, disregarding technicalities of pleading, may easily apprehend them. So also, as the want of a specific legal remedy is made to appear from the same source, we may concede that there is enough in the petition to warrant the alternative writ. But on the principles above stated, we are at a loss to discover why the answer was not sufficient. Certainty to a common intent is the rule, and that applies as well to the answer as to the petition, and it is sufficient that the former, without ambiguity or evasion, responds to and denies the assertions of the latter." Judgment reversed. Opinion by GORDON, J.

The relator, in his petition, ought to set forth or refer to the law or ordinance imposing the duty averred by him. *Smith* v. *Comm.*, 41 Pa. St., 335 (1861).

§ 1824. *Form of suggestion.* The following may be used as a form of suggestion, the allegations in each case being carefully adapted to the facts :

§ 1825.

FORM OF SUGGESTION FOR MANDAMUS TO DELIVER BOOKS, ETC., OF A CORPORATION.

Commonwealth *ex relatione*

    v.

Your petitioner respectfully represents that prior to May 4, 1884, was president of the   Company, and as such president had in his possession the books, papers, and other property of said corporation, to wit, the certificate of corporation of the _____ Company; the corporate seal of the _____ Company; the minute book of said corporation; two stock ledgers of said corporation marked respectively G. M. D. " A.," and G. M. D. " B. ;" the stock certificate book; the minute book of _____ Railroad Company; deed from the sheriff of _____ County to _____, for the property of the _____ Railroad Company, and assignment of the same to the _____ Railroad Company; deed of the sheriff of _____ County to _____ for the same property; deed of the sheriff of _____ County to _____, for the property and franchises of the _____ Company, and assignment of the same to the _____ Railroad Company; contract between the _____ Company and _____; deed and releases for right of way to the _____ Railroad Company, the _____ Railroad Company, _____ Company, and the _____ Company, and other books, papers, and effects belonging to said _____ Company; that by decree of this Honorable Court it was adjudged and decreed that _____ was duly elected president of the _____ Railroad, at the stockholders' meeting of said corporation, held under the supervision of a Master appointed by this court, on _____, and adjourned to _____ and thereafter to serve for the ensuing year, yet the said _____ continues to hold and retain possession of said books, papers, and other property of the said _____ Company, and has neglected and refused to deliver the same to your petitioner, although said _____ has been requested so to do; that by reason of the premises and said refusal your petitioner has suffered great damage, and has no specific and legal remedy therefor.

He therefore prays this Honorable Court to issue a writ of mandamus directed to said _____, commanding him, the said _____, to deliver to your petitioner the said books and papers, and other property of the said _____ Company, and he will ever pray.

_____, being duly sworn according to law, deposes and says the facts set forth in the above petition are just and true to the best of his knowledge and belief.

Sworn to and subscribed before me, ⎫
   this _____ day of _____, 18 . ⎬
        Notary Public. ⎭

§ 1826.

FORM OF SUGGESTION FOR MANDAMUS TO COMPEL THE OPENING OF STREETS DULY AUTHORIZED BY ACT OF ASSEMBLY.

In the Court of Common Pleas, in and for the city and county of Philadelphia.

And now, October 1, 1872, comes F. Carroll Brewster, Esq., Attorney-General, into court, and gives the court here to understand and be informed that the Commonwealth of Pennsylvania, by " An Act to authorize the opening and paving of certain portions of Fifteenth, Sixteenth, and Norris Streets," approved May 6, 1872 (P. L., 1163), did (*inter alia*) direct the Chief Commissioner of Highways to open Fifteenth, Sixteenth, and Norris Streets through Monument Cemetery, of which Mahlon H. Dickinson, then and now Chief Commissioner of Highways, had and has notice.

And the court is here further informed that the said streets, before the passage of said Act, had been marked out and through said cemetery, so that the same can be opened easily, and without disturbing any who have been interred therein.

Your relator therefore asks that this court may command the said Mahlon H. Dickinson, as Chief Commissioner of Highways, to open Fifteenth, Sixteenth, and Norris Streets through Monument Cemetery, of the same width as laid out on the existing plans, up to the boundary lines of said cemetery, or the cause why not to show unto your Honors in answer to said command.

F. CARROLL BREWSTER,
Attorney-General.

§ 1827.

FORM OF PETITION FOR A MANDAMUS TO SEAL A BILL OF EXCEPTIONS
IN A CRIMINAL CASE.

Appellants, v. The Commonwealth of Pennsylvania, Appellee.	In the Supreme Court of Pennsylvania for the Eastern District. · Term, 18 . No. .

To the Honorable the Judges of the Supreme Court of the State of Pennsylvania :

The petition of   humbly showeth that they are the appellants in the above-entitled cause, wherein an appeal was specially allowed by your Honorable Court on the   day of   , A. D. 18 , to remove the record and proceedings in the Court of Quarter Sessions of the Peace of the county of Philadelphia, to   sessions, 18 , No. . Your petitioners sought by said appeal to bring before your Honorable Court certain errors committed by the Hon.   , an associate justice of the said Court of Quarter Sessions in the said case, which was tried before him and a jury on the   days of   , A. D. 18 . That during said trial the said judge made the following rulings, all of which are alleged by your petitioners to be errors, and as to all of which the petitioners duly excepted at the time, and the judge at the request of their counsel noted exceptions, to wit (here insert copy of exceptions).

And your petitioners further show that when petitioners' counsel stated their exceptions the learned judge noted the same, and that he has now in his possession the original bills of exceptions ; that, although required so to do, he has not filed the same, and has twice refused to seal the formal copy thereof, prepared and tendered to him for that purpose. And your petitioners attach hereto as part hereof the said bill of exceptions and the charge excepted to, which are marked " Exhibit A."

And your petitioners further show that the right of a suitor to a bill of exceptions is secured by the Statute of 13 Edward I., chapter 31 (1285), reported as in force in this State (Roberts' Digest, 92), that the remedy for the refusal of a judge to seal a bill is provided by that law and is now here prayed.

That the Act of the General Assembly of this Commonwealth, approved May 19, 1874, expressly gives to petitioners the right to a bill of exceptions in these words :

" In the trial of all cases of felonious homicide and in all such other criminal cases as are exclusively triable and punishable in the Courts of Oyer and Terminer and General Jail Delivery, exceptions to any decision

of the court may be made by the defendant, and a bill thereof shall be
sealed in the same manner as is provided and practised in civil cases ; and
the accused, after conviction and sentence, may remove the indictment,
record, and all proceedings to the Supreme Court. In capital offenses a
writ of error or *certiorari* shall stay execution of sentence ; in all other
cases such writs shall not stay or delay execution of sentence or judgment
without the special order of the Supreme Court or a justice thereof for that
purpose ; and in case of such order, the said Supreme Court or justice may
make such order as the case requires, for the custody of the defendant or for
admission to bail. In all other criminal cases exceptions, as aforesaid, may
be taken, and in cases charging the offense of nuisance, or forcible entry
and detainer, or forcible detainer, exceptions to any decision or ruling of
the court may also be taken by the Commonwealth, and writs of error and
certiorari, as hereinbefore provided, may be issued from the Supreme Court
to all criminal courts, when specially allowed by the Supreme Court or any
judge thereof." (P. L., 1874, section 1.)

And your petitioners further show that the said refusals of said learned
judge, the Hon.   , to seal the aforesaid bills of exceptions are to
the grievous and manifest injury of the petitioners and against the statutes
in such case made and provided.

They therefore pray this Honorable Court to award a writ, conformably
to the statute in such case made and provided (13 Edward I., chapter 31),
directed to the said Hon.   , commanding him to appear at a certain
day either to confess or deny the matters herein set forth ; and if he confess
the same, to affix his seal to said exceptions or to so much of the same as
he shall so confess, and your petitioners also pray for such other writ,
relief, and remedies as by law petitioners are entitled to.

And as in duty bound they will ever pray.

(Signatures.)

The petitioners above named, having been duly   according to law,
do depose and say that the facts set forth in the foregoing petition are true
and correct, to the best of their knowledge and belief.

Sworn to and subscribed before me, ⎱
    this   day of   18 . ⎰

          Prothonotary. ⎰
Here attach bills of exceptions as " Exhibit A."

COPY OF INDORSEMENT.

et al., Appellants, *v.* The Commonwealth of Pennsylvania, Appellee,	Supreme Court of Pennsylvania, Term, 18 . No. .

Petition of Appellants to the Supreme Court.

" To award a writ conformably to the statute in such case made and provided, directed to Hon.   , commanding him to appear at a certain
day, either to confess or deny the matters therein set forth ; and if he
confess the same, to affix his seal to said exceptions," and for such other
writ, relief, and remedies as by law petitioners may be entitled to.

§ 1828.

FORM OF PETITION FOR A MANDAMUS TO COMPEL A JUDGE TO SEAL A
BILL OF EXCEPTIONS IN A CIVIL CASE.

A. B. *et al.*, Appellants, ⎫ Supreme Court of Pennsylvania, Eastern District.
　　　v.　　　　　　　　⎬　　　　　Term, 18　, No.　.
C. D., Appellee.　⎭

To the Honorable the Judges of the Supreme Court of the Commonwealth
　of Pennsylvania :

　The petition of　　　　　　　　respectfully represents :

1. That they are appellants in the above-entitled cause, wherein an
appeal was issued on the　　　　　day of　　　　　, A. D. 18　, whereby
your petitioners and the other plaintiffs therein named sought to bring
before this Honorable Court certain errors committed by the Honorable
　　　　　, an associate justice of the Court of Common Pleas for
the county of　　　　　, in a certain cause which was tried before him and
a jury on divers days and times between the　　　　　day of　　　　　and the
　　　　　day of　　　　　, the record and proceedings of said case so
sought to be removed being entitled as of　　　　　Term, 18　, No.　, in
the said Court of Common Pleas for the city and county of　　　　　.

2. That　　　　　, late of the city of　　　　　, died on the　　　　　day of
　　　　　, A. D. 18　, seized and possessed of real estate and premises
　　　　　in the city of　　　　　, producing rental of about　　　　　per
annum, and of personalty consisting chiefly of mortgages, insurance, and
railway securities to the amount of about　　　　　, as far as can at present
be ascertained.

3. That on the　　　　　day of　　　　　, A. D. 18　, there was presented
for probate before　　　　　, Esquire, then register of wills of the county of
　　　　　, a certain writing dated the　　　　　day of　　　　　, A. D. 18　,
by a certain person calling herself　　　　　, and who claimed to be the
widow of the said decedent by virtue of an alleged marriage contracted on
the　　　　　day of　　　　　, 18　, which said writing the said proponent
averred to be the last will and testament of said　　　　　, and by the
terms of which the entire estate, real and personal, of the decedent was
devised and bequeathed to her absolutely, and she was appointed the sole
executrix.

4. That on the said date of the　　　　　day of　　　　　, A. D. 18　, two
certain papers were presented for probate before the said register by　　　　　,
one of your petitioners, one of said writings being dated the　　　　　day of
　　　　　, 18　, and the other of them dated the　　　　　day of　　　　　, 18　,
which first writing said　　　　　averred to be the last will and testament
of the said　　　　　, in which said proponent was named as a legatee in
the sum of $15,000, and the second writing as a codicil to said first writing,
in which said proponent was named as the residuary devisee and legatee of
the entire estate of the decedent after the payment of certain annuities and
legacies therein named, the principal of which amounted in the aggregate
to the sum of about $15,000.

5. That at the said time the said　　　　　objected before the said register
to the probate of the said writing of the date of　　　　　day of　　　　　,
18　, alleged to have been executed by the said　　　　　, and averred
said will was procured by duress, fraud, imposition, and undue influence
exercised over the mind of the said　　　　　, and that at the time the

said writing was alleged to have been executed the said   was not of sound disposing mind, memory, and understanding, and requested that an issue might be directed to the Common Pleas to try by a jury the validity of said writing and the matters of fact which might be objected to.

That (names of defendants), next of kin of   , deceased, also objected before the said register and averred that the said writing of the date of   of   , 18 , was procured by duress, fraud, conspiracy, imposition, and undue influence exercised over the mind of the said   , and that at the time said writing was alleged to have been executed the said   was not of sound disposing mind, memory, and understanding, and requested that an issue might be directed as aforesaid, to try by a jury the validity of said writing and the matters of fact that might be objected to.

6. That the said register proceeded to hear testimony as to the validity of the said writing of the date of the   day of   , 18 , and the argument of counsel thereon, and on the   day of   , 18 , refused to admit said writing to probate as the last will and testament of the said   , deceased, and on the   day of   , 18 , issued his precept to the Court of Common Pleas for the county of   , commanding that an action should be entered upon the record of the said court as of the day of the delivery of his said precept into the office of the prothonotary between the said   , executrix and devisee named in the writing dated the   day of   , 18 , and the said   , legatee and devisee aforesaid, and   , next of kin as aforesaid, with such of the said parties as plaintiffs and defendants as the said court shall order and direct, so that an issue therein might be formed upon the merits of the controversy between the said parties and tried in due course of law according to the practice of the said court in an action commenced by writ, as follows :

(1) Whether or not at the time of the making of the said alleged writing of the date of the   of   , 18 , the said   was of sound disposing mind, memory, and understanding.

(2) Whether or not the said alleged will was made by reason of undue influence exercised over the mind of the said   .

That on the same day the said precept was entered upon the record of the said court as of No. , of   Term, 18 .

7. That it was then so proceeded with in the said court that the said   , executrix and devisee named in the said writing of the   day of   , 18 , should be plaintiff, and the said   , legatee and devisee as aforesaid, and the several above-named parties as cousins, as next of kin of the said   , should be the defendants, and that an action was then entered on the record of the said court in the above form between the said parties to try the issues set forth in the precept of the said register.

8. That on the (date) the pleadings were filed in the said court by the counsel for the respective parties, in which issue was raised and joined upon the matters and things set forth in the said precept of the said register in accordance with the terms and requirements thereof.

9. That on the (date) a jury was called and sworn in the said court to try and determine the issues and questions aforesaid, before the Honorable   , one of the associate justices of the said court ; that said cause was proceeded with under the direction of the said associate justice until (date),

when the said jury rendered their verdict for the said plaintiff on both
issues, upon which verdict judgment was entered on the (date).

During the progress of the trial various exceptions to the ruling of the
court as to the admission and rejection of evidence were taken by   ,
of counsel for defendants.

The court charged the jury (date), when exceptions were taken by
to various parts thereof, and also to the ruling of the court on both plaintiff's and defendants' points, all of which were noted at the time.

10. A few days before the trial it was agreed in writing by all the counsel, both for the plaintiff and defendants, that the testimony of the witnesses and all rulings, and the charge of the court, should be taken by
(name), stenographer, and three copies thereof should be made and furnished by him, as follows :   . In pursuance of this agreement the
testimony of all the witnesses examined at the trial, and all rulings of the
court on the admission and rejection of testimony, and all exceptions were
taken by the stenographer, and copies of the same were furnished under
said agreement to the court and counsel daily as the trial progressed.   The
charge of the court and its rulings on both plaintiff's and defendants'
points, with all exceptions thereto, were taken by the stenographer, and
copies thereof furnished to the court and counsel the day following, so that
in one day after the verdict the court and counsel had full and correct
copies of all testimony, rulings, and matters incident to the cause in accordance with the agreement aforesaid.

11. (Here set forth the presentation of bills of exceptions to the court,
the difficulties attending the same, and final refusal of the judge to seal
said bill of exceptions, including conversations, correspondence, and every
matter incident to the demand and refusal. Set forth the rule of court
relied upon in support of the refusal to seal the bill.)

(In this case it was the rule requiring a copy of the bill of exceptions to
be served on counsel.)

12. And your petitioners respectfully show that the said rule of court
cannot under any reasonable or proper construction be held to have any
application to a case like the present, when by virtue of an agreement as
to the taking of the testimony and charge by a stenographer and the furnishing of copies to the respective parties, the attorney for the successful
party has already in his possession, practically in like manner as if directly
furnished by his adversary, a copy of the bill of exceptions. That the
object of the rule is to prevent a surprise to the party and his attorney, not
to compel the unsuccessful party to the performance of an useless, and, in
cases like the present, involving such a voluminous mass of testimony, an
almost impossible task.

That this agreement in this case under which the testimony and charge
were taken really substituted and took the place of the rule in this case as
to a furnishing of the copy of the bill.

But, even apart from this agreement, the rule must have and receive
such a reasonable construction and application as shall make it not a denial
and obstruction, in such cases as the present, of the right to an appeal
altogether, and that the rule as undertaken to be applied and enforced
against your petitioners would amount not to a regulation, but to a practical denial of the privilege of an appeal and right of appeal given by the
statutes of the Commonwealth.

13. Your petitioners further show that the said refusal of the said

judge, the Honorable   , to seal the aforesaid bill of exceptions is to
the grievous and manifest injury of the petitioners and the plaintiffs in
said appeal, and against the statute in such case made and provided, and
your petitioners and the said appellants being entitled to have the said
several errors of the said judge reviewed and corrected by your Honorable
Court therefore pray :

That your Honorable Court award its writ in conformity with the statute
in such case made and provided, directed to the said Honorable   ,
commanding him to appear at a certain day, either to confess or deny the
matters herein set forth ; and if he confess the same, to affix his seal to the
exceptions aforesaid, and they will ever pray, etc.

(Signatures of Petitioners.)

STATE OF PENNSYLVANIA, } ss.
COUNTY OF   ,

        , being duly sworn according to law, deposes and says the facts
set forth in the foregoing petition are just and true, to the best of his knowledge, information, and belief.

Sworn to and subscribed before me, ⎫
    this   day of   , A. D. 18 . ⎬   (Signature of Petitioner.)
                                        ⎭

[SEAL]   Notary Public.

INDORSEMENT.

No.   .   Term, 18 .
In the Supreme Court of Pennsylvania, Eastern District.
A. B. *et al.*, Appellants, ⎫
    v.   ⎬
C. D.,   Appellees. ⎭

Petition of A. B. *et al.*, appellants, to award a writ conformably to the
statute in such case made and provided, directed to the Honorable   ,
commanding him to appear at a certain day, either to confess or deny the
matters therein set forth ; and if he confess the same, to affix his seal to bill
of exceptions.

(Signatures of Counsel)
pro Petitioners.

Writ allowed returnable.

(Signature of Justice of Supreme Court.)

It will be observed that the facts in the case from which this
form is taken were peculiar. See 121 Pa. St., 18 (1888), and 127
Pa. St., 564 (1889). The writ of error was issued before this petition was presented. The pleader will readily make his petition
conform to the facts of his case. .

§ 1829. **Allowance of writ.** The suggestion or petition having
been sworn to by the relator, have it allowed by the court or a
judge thereof, then take it to the prothonotary, who will issue the
alternative writ.

§ 1830. **Form of writ.** The alternative mandamus should, in
general, follow the language of the petition, and it should command the respondent to do the thing or things prayed for, or show

cause why he should not do so.   This example will show the form
of the writ:

§ 1831.

FORM OF ALTERNATIVE WRIT OF MANDAMUS TO OPEN STREETS DULY
AUTHORIZED BY ACT OF ASSEMBLY.

City and County of Philadelphia, *ss.*

The Commonwealth of Pennsylvania, to Mahlon H. Dickinson, Chief
Commissioner of Highways, greeting :

Whereas, F. Carroll Brewster, Attorney-General, has filed his information in our Court of Common Pleas, setting forth that by an Act to authorize the opening and paving of certain portions of Fifteenth, Sixteenth, and
Norris Streets, approved May 6, 1872 (P. L., 1163), the Chief Commissioner
of Highways is directed to open Fifteenth, Sixteenth, and Norris Streets,
through Monument Cemetery, of which you, the said Mahlon H. Dickinson, have had notice, and that said streets, before the passage of said Act,
had been marked out through said cemetery, so that the same can be
opened easily and without disturbance of any interment.

And whereas, on said information, and according to the prayer thereof,
the said court did order a writ of alternative mandamus should issue as
prayed for ; therefore,

We command you, the said Mahlon H. Dickinson, as Chief Commissioner of Highways, to open Fifteenth, Sixteenth, and Norris Streets,
through Monument Cemetery, of the same width as laid out on the existing
plans up to the boundary lines of said cemetery, or the cause why not you
show, in answer to this writ, on the eleventh day of October, 1872, and
herein fail not.

Witness, the Honorable Joseph Allison, president of our said court, at
Philadelphia, this first day of October, 1871.

GEORGE T. DEISS,
Deputy Prothonotary.

[SEAL]

§ 1832.

FORM OF WRIT ADDRESSED TO A JUDGE TO COMPEL HIM TO SEAL HIS
BILL OF EXCEPTIONS.

Eastern District of Pennsylvania, *ss.*

The Commonwealth of Pennsylvania to   , greeting :

Whereas, by statute, among other things, it is provided that in any suit
before the justices where an exception is taken, if the said justice before
whom the same is taken refuse to allow the same, and the party making
the exceptions puts the same in writing, and requires the justice to put his
seal thereto in testimony of the same, if he refuse so to put his seal, it shall
be affixed as in said statute. is set forth :

And whereas (names of petitioners) have filed their petition before the
justices of the Supreme Court of Pennsylvania, complaining that lately in
a certain case in the Court of Common Pleas, No.   , for the county of
          , as of   Term, 18 , No , before you, the said (name of
judge), between (name of plaintiff) and (names of defendants), various exceptions were taken and alleged to certain rulings and to your charge, and
those exceptions have been put in writing for that you refuse to allow the
same, and have been repeatedly required and prayed to affix your seal to
those exceptions according to the form of the aforesaid statute.   Yet so it

is, that you have objected and still do object and refuse to affix your seal to the aforesaid exceptions, to the grievous injury and manifest prejudice of the said (names of defendants), and they did pray said justices to provide a remedy for them.

And whereas, said petition so filed before the justices of the Supreme Court of Pennsylvania is in words and figures as follows (here insert petition at length).

And because we are desirous that the aforesaid statute be strictly observed, and that justice be done to the said   et al. in the premises, we command you that if so it be, that on or before Saturday, the of   , Anno Domini 18   , you affix your seal to the aforesaid exceptions thus had before you in the aforesaid suit by the aforesaid in writing, according to the form of the statute aforesaid. And herein fail not, under the penalty in such cases pending.

Witness the Honorable   , Doctor of Laws, Chief Justice of our said Supreme Court, at   , this   day of   , in the year of our Lord one thousand eight hundred and   , and of the Commonwealth the one hundred and   .

Prothonotary.

§ 1833. **Mandamus must be directed to the proper parties.** In *Respublica* v. *Commissioners*, 4 Yeates, 181 (1805), a mandamus directed to the commissioners of Philadelphia County to pay the salary of the gaol-keeper, was refused.

It was provided by statute that the inspectors should draw the orders and have them countersigned by the commissioners. It was shown that an arrangement was made between the commissioners and inspectors, whereby the former were allowed to draw the orders.

The court decided the agreement was a mere nullity so far as it contravenes the Act of Assembly. The court must see the law carried into execution, notwithstanding a practice may have prevailed against it.

§ 1834. **If the writ be against corporation officers, the corporation should be a defendant.** A writ of mandamus to compel the officers of a corporation to permit relator to examine their books should make the corporation a party defendant. *Comm.* v. *Coit*, 15 W. N., 270 (1884). See § 1742.

§ 1835. **Service of the writ**—*The original must be handed to defendant.* Service need not be made by the sheriff. The writ should be served by giving the original to the respondent. If there be more than one respondent, copies should be given, and the original shown to each of them, except one, to whom the original must be given. A return to the final writ that defendant was served by leaving a copy with him is not good, and will not support an attachment for disobedience. *Comm.* v. *Brady*, 6 Phila., 121 (1866).

In *Ely* v. *Penn District*, 1 Phila., 18 (1850), it was decided that service of a mandamus upon a township by serving the president and clerk of the board was not sufficient; it should be upon the commissioners.

§ 1836. **Respondent must be given time to comply.** In *Childs* v. *Comm.*, 3 Brews., 194 (1870), the alternative writ issued, and on the same day a peremptory mandamus was awarded. *Held*, to be error. The respondent must be given sufficient time to comply with the requirements of the alternative writ. Per SHARSWOOD, J., quoting section 22, Act of 14 June, 1836 (P. L., 626). See § 1749.

§ 1837. **If no appearance** be entered by the return-day of the writ, prepare and file an affidavit showing that service has been made upon respondent, and stating the date and manner thereof, and enter judgment for want of an appearance. See section 23 of this book.

§ 1838. **No rule on the defendant to demur, plead, or answer is necessary.** The form of the writ requires a return. Defendant may move to quash, and, if unsuccessful, should have his return ready to be filed. If he desire to speed the case, he may rule the plaintiff to demur, etc., to the return.

Commonwealth of Pennsylvania *ex relatione* A. B. *v.* C. D.	Common Pleas, No. 1. March Term, 1890. No. 100.

SIR:

Enter rule on plaintiff to demur, plead, or answer in fifteen days, or judgment *sec. reg.*

> E. F.,
> Attorney for Respondent.
> (Date.)

To Prothonotary, Common Pleas.

Notice and copy of this rule should be served on the attorney who has appeared for relator, and another copy kept. Upon default, the usual reminder should be sent to counsel. If it is disregarded, file affidavit of service and take judgment. See section 26.

§ 1839. **Relator must not move for judgment on the return—** *He must demur, plead, or traverse—This gives defendant opportunity to amend.* In *Adams* v. *Duffield*, 4 Brews., 9 (1863), a petition for mandamus was presented to the Court of Common Pleas, setting forth that relator was elected a member of Common Council in Philadelphia, and his term would not expire till December, 1862; that defendants, members of Common Council, declared his seat vacant previous to that time because he became an officer of the United States.

The defendants responded that by Act of February 2, 1854, section 35, they were empowered to judge of the qualification of their members, and that the Act of April 16, 1838, section 38, forbade the relator to continue to hold the office of councilman after his appointment as a United States officer. The court awarded the mandamus without a demurrer, plea, or traverse of material facts being filed.

The Supreme Court reversed, per LOWRIE, C. J.: "We have no doubt the Common Pleas has jurisdiction by mandamus over municipal as over county and township officers. * * * The defendants had made their return, and according to form prescribed by the statute and insisted on by us, * * * it was then the duty of the relator to demur, plead to, or to traverse all or any of the material facts contained in such return. He did nothing of the kind. He moved to disallow the returns and enter judgment in his favor, and this was done. We cannot sanction this practice, for it leaves it entirely uncertain on what grounds the case was decided. It leaves the defendants uninformed of the nature of the objections to be raised to the return, and takes away their right to amend their return in the regular course of pleading."

§ 1840. **If respondent demur or move to quash,** which he may do if he conceive the suggestion to be irregular or defective upon its face, prepare your paper-book against his motion, and order the case upon the argument-list. See sections 28, 29, in regard to preparation of paper-books.

§ 1841. **If respondent plead** to your suggestion, file a replication where the plea demands one, and put the case on the trial-list when it is properly at issue.

§ 1842. **If answer or return be filed,** you may, in your turn, demur, plead to, or traverse the answer. If it allege facts which are untrue, and which, as stated, constitute a good defense to your petition, deny them by means of a traverse. If the answer be such that further statement of the facts is necessary to put the question in its proper light, embody your new allegations in the form of a plea or traverse. By these means an issue of fact or of law will sooner or later be forced upon your adversary, which must be disposed of respectively before a jury or upon argument in court.

In *Haines* v. *Comm.*, 99 Pa. St., 410 (1882), it was held that the return to a writ under the Statute of Westminster, to compel the sealing of a bill of exceptions in civil or criminal cases, was conclusive, and could not be contravened.

§ 1843. **Return, sufficiency of.** The return to the mandamus must set forth the facts with sufficient certainty. Where a by-law of a society provides that the expulsion of a member must be on *sufficient evidence*, it must appear that proofs were taken and that the charge made by the board was in writing, and signed by them as required by the charter. *Society* v.*Comm.*, 52 Pa. St., 125 (1866).

In the return to an alternative mandamus, the facts upon which the denial of the relator's rights is based must be set forth directly, specifically, and positively. *Comm.* v. *Chittenden*, 2 Dist. Rep., 804 (1893) ; *Comm.* v. *School Directors*, 4 Dist. Rep., 314 (1895).

§ 1844. **Demurrer to Answer.** It will be noticed that many cases are decided upon demurrer to the return or answer ; and upon examination of respondent's reply to the alternative writ it is probable that you will find your opportunity to demur. This will, in general, serve to bring before the court the entire question of your right to the relief sought as well as the sufficiency of the return. Remember, however, that by demurrer you admit all the facts properly alleged by respondent. *Ackerman* v. *Buchman*, 109 Pa. St., 254 (1885). Demurrer will be proper if the return be uncertain, vague, or evasive, or if it be defective in substance, alleging facts which, if true, constitute no bar to your right to mandamus. But defendant is not obliged to traverse facts or answer breaches of duty not assigned in the writ. *R. R. Co.* v. *Comm.*, 120 Pa. St., 537 (1888). The return must, however, distinctly aver facts, not mere inferences or arguments therefrom. *Comm.* v. *Pittsburgh*, 34 Pa. St., 496 (1859) ; *Comm.* v. *Commissioners*, 37 Pa. St., 237 (1860) ; *Comm.* v. *Commissioners, Id.*, 277 (1860). The certainty required in the return is of that degree called "certainty to a common intent in general." The facts must be so clearly stated as to admit of a fair and ready comprehension. Possible objections need not be anticipated. See *Telegraph Co.* v. *Friend*, 114 Pa. St., 592 (1886) ; *Comm.* v. *Commissioners*, 32 Pa. St., 218 (1858) ; *Comm.* v. *Hancock*, 9 Phila., 535 (1872).

Having filed your demurrer, prepare to sustain it upon argument. Order it upon the list and be ready with your paper-book. Judgment in your favor upon the demurrer will be final, not *respondeat ouster*.

§ 1845.

DEMURRER TO THE RETURN TO A MANDAMUS TO OPEN STREETS DULY
AUTHORIZED BY ACT OF ASSEMBLY.

Com. *ex rel.* Attorney-General ⎫
    v.   ⎬ Common Pleas, September, 1872.   No. 209.
Mahlon H. Dickinson.   ⎭

The said relator saith that the said return of Mahlon H. Dickinson, and the matters contained therein, are not sufficient in law to preclude the Commonwealth from having the writ of peremptory mandamus commanding him, the said Mahlon H. Dickinson, as Chief Commissioner of Highways, to forthwith open Fifteenth, Sixteenth, and Norris Streets, through Monument Cemetery, of the same width as laid out on the existing plans, up to the boundary lines of said cemetery, and the following causes of demurrer are specifically assigned:

I. That neither the Act of March 15, 1847, nor of March 12, 1849, disabled the Commonwealth from opening highways on compensation being made for the land taken.

II. That the enactment of May 6, 1872, in said alternative writ of mandamus recited, abrogated any previous law requiring the consent of any citizen of the Commonwealth to the opening of the streets named in said enactment.

III. Because the said return is in other respects uncertain, informal, insufficient, and defective.

Wherefore, for want of a sufficient return, the said relator prays that a peremptory mandamus do issue.

F. CARROLL BREWSTER,
Attorney-General.

§ 1846.

FORM OF ANSWER TO SUGGESTION FOR MANDAMUS TO DELIVER BOOKS, ETC., OF A CORPORATION.

Commonwealth *ex rel.*

v.

} Common Pleas, No. . Term, 18 . No. .

Sur rule to show cause why a writ of mandamus should not issue, etc.

, the respondent, for answer to· the above rule heretofore granted against him on the relation of , says :

1. Respondent is advised and submits to the court, that the said is not the proper and legal custodian of the books and papers or other assets of the Railroad Company specified in his said suggestion, and has no right to demand the same of this respondent or to have the writ of mandamus prayed for. That the only proper parties to such a proceeding are the corporation named in such suggestion and its treasurer or secretary, who alone would be entitled to the custody of the said books and papers if no receiver had been appointed to take and hold the same.

2. And further answering this respondent says : That to Term 18 , in the Court of Common Pleas, No. , for the city and county of Philadelphia, and others filed their certain bill in equity against the same corporation, the Railroad Company, and against this respondent, and others, the directors of said corporation, praying, among other things, for the appointment of a receiver.

And afterward, to wit, on the day of (months before the entry of the decree in favor of said relator referred to in his said suggestion), such proceedings were had in the said bill in equity pending in said Court of Common Pleas, No. , that by the consideration and judgment of said court it was then ordered and decreed that , Esq., be appointed receiver, to take charge of the books and papers, charter, and other assets of the corporation defendant, and the same to preserve under the direction of the said court.

And this respondent was enjoined from intermeddling with the affairs of said corporation or doing any act by which the present *status* of the case or the rights of the parties shall be affected, of which decree respondent was

duly notified, and the same still remains in full force. And respondent
further saith that he contested the said proceedings in the Court of Common Pleas, No.   , and defended the same to the best of his ability; that
said decree was obtained against his objection and in spite of his defense,
and without his consent or collusion.

And respondent is advised that the aforesaid proceedings and decree are
a bar to the claim herein set up by the relator, and that said Court of
Common Pleas, No.   , having obtained jurisdiction over said corporation
and its books and assets and over this respondent upward of a year before
the bill was filed in this court, the respondent cannot be further required
to answer to your Honors in this behalf.

Wherefore respondent asks to be hence dismissed with his reasonable
costs.

, having been duly affirmed according to law, doth affirm and say
that the facts above set forth are true, to the best of his knowledge and
belief.

Affirmed to and subscribed before me, ⎫
    this   day of   , 18 .   ⎬
                                                ⎭

                    Notary Public. ⎭

§ 1847.

FORM OF RETURN TO A MANDAMUS TO OPEN STREETS DULY
AUTHORIZED BY ACT OF ASSEMBLY.

The Commonwealth of Pennsylvania ⎫
    ex rel. F. Carroll Brewster   ⎪
                v.   -   ⎬   Common Pleas,
    Mahlon H. Dickinson,   ⎪ September Term, 1872. No. 209.
Chief Commissioner of Highways. ⎭

The return of Mahlon H. Dickinson, the defendant above named, to the
writ of alternative mandamus, shows to the court:

1. That this defendant is informed, and believes it to be true, that the
Monument Cemetery Company of Philadelphia, the corporation named in
the Act of the General Assembly of the Commonwealth of Pennsylvania,
passed March 15, 1847, and referred to in the Acts of Assembly cited in the
said writ, being advised that the said Act of March 15, 1857, was in some
of its provisions unconstitutional, at a formal and regular meeting of its
corporators, in the year 1847, rejected the whole of the said Act of Assembly, and refused to accept the same.

2. That on the 12th of March, 1849, the said General Assembly passed
an Act entitled "An Act relating to the Monument Cemetery of Philadelphia," which was duly and legally accepted by the said corporation, the
third section of which is in these words, viz.:

"That no streets or roads shall hereafter be opened through the grounds
of the said cemetery company, occupied as a burial ground, except by and
with the consent of the managers thereof."

That this last Act is wholly unrepealed and in full force. That the
streets mentioned in the said writ, if opened as demanded, will pass
through the grounds of the said Monument Cemetery Company, occupied as
a burial ground, and that the managers thereof have not given their consent
thereto.

3. That whilst it is true that there are no interments of human bodies
actually made in the parts of said cemetery grounds which will be occupied

by said streets, if opened as demanded through the same, yet there are such interments in close proximity thereto, and that the opening of said streets as demanded will necessarily destroy to a great extent the privacy and sacredness of said burial ground, and entail very large cost upon the said cemetery company, and that the whole of the ground proposed to be taken by the opening of said streets is occupied by said cemetery company for a burial ground, and for no other purpose.

4. That if the said Act of March 15, 1857, was, prior to its attempted repeal, a valid Act, and part of the charter of the said "The Monument Cemetery Company of Philadelphia," which was originally incorporated by the Commonwealth of Pennsylvania, by Act passed March 19, 1838, then the Act of May 6, 1872, is unconstitutional, so far as it attempted to repeal the third section of the Act of March 15, 1847.

Wherefore the said defendant prays to be hence dismissed with his costs, etc.

(Here insert affidavit.)

§ 1848.

FORM OF ANSWER TO A MANDAMUS TO SEAL A BILL OF EXCEPTIONS IN AN ISSUE DEVISAVIT VEL NON.

et al., Appellants, } In the Supreme Court of Pennsylva-
v. } nia, for the Eastern District.
Appellees. } Of   Term, 18 . No. .

To the Honorable the Judges of said Court:

The answer of   to the writ hereto attached directed to him by the said court on the   day of   , A. D. 18 .

This respondent by protestation, not admitting or allowing any of the matters of the petition of   to be true as they are therein alleged, answering, saith:

That on (date), there was called for trial before this respondent in the Court of Common Pleas, No.   , for the county of Philadelphia, a certain case in which   , executrix mentioned in the last will and testament of   , deceased, was plaintiff, and   et al. (naming them), were defendants, the same being an issue framed in said court on a precept from the Register of Wills of Philadelphia County, to determine whether or not   , deceased, was, at the time of the making of his last will and testament, dated   , 18   , of sound disposing mind, memory, and understanding, and whether or not said will was made by undue influence exercised over the mind of the said   .

That at said trial   , Esq., appeared as counsel for plaintiff, and   , Esq., and   , Esq., appeared as counsel for the various defendants.

That the said Court of Common Pleas, No.   , had not then, and never has had, an official stenographer, nor was there an official stenographer employed in the trial of said cause.

That prior to the trial, for their own convenience, counsel for the respective parties in interest entered into the following agreement:

v. } C. P., No. .   Term 18 . No. .
et al. }

"And now (date), it is hereby agreed between counsel for all the parties in interest that   be employed as stenographer to take the testimony and charge of the court in the above case; that three copies thereof be made, one for the court, one for counsel for plaintiff, and one for counsel for defendants; and that the stenographer be paid out of the funds of the estate of　　　, deceased."

That said agreement was signed by counsel for the various parties in interest, but this respondent was not a party thereto. That it was not intended to, and did not and could not, take the place of the rules of court hereinafter set forth, without the consent of this respondent, which consent was neither asked nor given at any time.

That in point of fact four copies, in all respects alike, were made by the stenographer, one copy of which was given to this respondent, one to counsel for plaintiff, and two to counsel for defendants.

That the copy from time to time given this respondent was alleged to contain the oral testimony given on the trial of the cause and the charge of the court, but it did not contain, as in said petition averred, all the testimony, rulings, charges, and exceptions incident to the case.

That said trial was so proceeded with that on (date), the jury rendered a verdict for the plaintiff on both issues.

That for many years prior to said trial, at that time and always since then, the rules of said Court of Common Pleas, No.　, have provided, *inter alia*, as follows (here insert rules of court).

That the said court had and has power to make said rules, and they are not only reasonable, but are essential to the orderly and proper administration of public justice in courts of law. That said rules have been published from time to time, and are well known to all practitioners in said court, and may be readily and easily known to all litigants. That rules in all essential respects similar to the foregoing are in force in all the Courts of Common Pleas of this Commonwealth, so far as are known to this respondent; and said rules, in *hæc verba*, were in force in your Honor's court, when sitting as a Court of *Nisi Prius*, prior to the adoption of the Constitution of this Commonwealth in 1874, which abolished said Court of *Nisi Prius;* and sections　　　, as above, are conjoined and form rule as at present in force in your Honor's court.

That on (date),　　　, Esq., one of the counsel for the appellants, presented to this respondent a book alleged to be a bill of exceptions, and this respondent was requested to affix his seal thereto; but said alleged bill of exceptions was confessedly incorrect and incomplete, and the request to seal the same was withdrawn by　　　, and at his request the same was marked, in accordance with section　　　of the rules of court aforesaid, as follows: " Presented (date),　　　." No agreement of any kind was made in relation thereto, either by this respondent or by counsel for the appellee, in this respondent's presence or with this respondent's knowledge.

That nothing further was ever done in relation to said alleged bill of exceptions, so far as is known to this respondent, until (date) (here state the facts).

Mr.　　　then stated that counsel for the appellee had examined the alleged bill of exceptions, and had agreed thereto with the single change that the exceptions to the charge of the court should be sealed as exceptions for Mr.　　　, instead of exceptions for defendants as prepared by him, Mr.　　　; and that counsel for the appellee had subsequently agreed to the same thing in the presence of this respondent. This was denied by counsel for the appellee, who asserted that he had had no opportunity to examine said alleged bill of exceptions, and had not examined it, and that he had made no agreement of any kind in relation thereto. Said alleged agreements of counsel not being in writing, this respondent, under the rules of court as aforesaid, was obliged to consider the same as of no validity.

As a matter of fact, no such agreement was made in the presence of this respondent.

Counsel for the appellants then tendered to counsel for the appellee an alleged copy of said alleged bill of exceptions, to be used in the then present sealing of the bill; but counsel for the appellee refused to receive the same for that purpose, because not in compliance with the rules of court aforesaid.

It was admitted at that time by all of the counsel for the appellants then present, to wit,   , that there had been a failure on their part to comply with the rules of court as aforesaid; and counsel for the appelllee insisting upon a compliance therewith, this respondent declined to seal said alleged bill of exceptions.

It was also admitted by counsel for the appellants that they had received during the trial two complete copies of the testimony and charge of the court, in all respects similar to the one received by counsel for the appellee; and it was also stated by them that, with all the force they could put to work, it had taken them all the intervening time from the receipt of the letter of counsel for the appellee as aforesaid, requiring a copy of the bill, until the then present hour, to transform one of said copies into a copy of said alleged bill of exceptions.

Counsel for the appellants admitted that the time for sealing the bill, as provided by the rules of court aforesaid, had expired, and requested this respondent to give them further time than as provided in said rules; but the same was objected to by counsel for the appellee, and this respondent saw no reason why the rules of court could not, and should not, have been complied with, and therefore declined so to do.

No other time was ever mentioned or fixed by counsel for the appellants for sealing of said alleged bill of exceptions, nor was this respondent, at any subsequent time, requested to examine the same or affix his seal thereto,

That as to the other alleged agreements between counsel in said petition set forth, this respondent has no personal knowledge of the same, and they were and are denied by counsel for the appellee, and are not in writing, and must, therefore, under the rules of court as aforesaid, and under rule   of your Honor's court, be considered of no validity.

And this respondent further showeth to your Honors that he had no opportunity to examine such alleged bill of exceptions until after the service of this writ upon him, when there was served upon him a copy of said alleged bill of exceptions, in which copy it is stated, among other things, that certain exceptions, seventeen in number, were taken by the defendants to the charge and rulings of this respondent, which were never taken by them in manner and form as therein set forth, nor were they noted or stated as so taken in the copies furnished by the stenographer as aforesaid. That said alleged bill of exceptions is, in this respect, in precisely the form in which it was on (date), when it was presented to this respondent, as hereinbefore set forth, and he declined to seal the same because it did not correctly recite the facts. And this respondent avers that it is not a true bill of exceptions, and does not state 'the exceptions in manner and form as they were taken upon the trial of the cause.

And this respondent further showeth to your Honors that at the conclusion of the trial of said cause counsel for the appellants had two complete copies of the oral testimony and charge, as taken stenographically, the same in all respects as the single copy furnished counsel for the appellee; and in view thereof it was neither unreasonable nor unjust to them to require of them that they comply with the rules of court as aforesaid. And this respondent respectfully submits to your Honors that said rules of court are, of necessity, applicable to all causes alike, whether the testimony taken be much or little, and howsoever counsel, for their own convenience, obtain copies of the same.

And this respondent further showeth to your Honors that the testimony and charge, as furnished by the stenographer, is confessedly incomplete as a bill of exceptions; so much so that counsel for the appellants averred to 'your respondent, and in said petition it is averred that they had " at once set about preparing such a copy (of the alleged bill of exceptions) on the receipt of Mr.   's notice (as aforesaid), and though hardly possible they had by use and combination of all materials been able only by this moment (date) to prepare the same ;" and this respondent respectfully submits to your Honors that it was unreasonable to ask counsel for the appellee to admit that he had a copy of said alleged bill of exceptions, or to accept that which he had in lieu of the copy to which he was entitled under the rules of court as aforesaid, when, with all the force they could put at work, it took the appellants forty-eight hours to transform a copy in all respects similar to his into an alleged bill of exceptions ; and it is not therefore correctly stated in said petition that counsel for the appellee " has already in his possession, practically in like manner as if directly furnished by his adversary, a copy of the bill of exceptions."

Respondent respectfully submits that an order should be entered by your Honors that this respondent go without day.

(Signature of Respondent.)

Philadelphia County, *ss*.

            , the respondent above named, being duly sworn according to law, deposes and says that the facts set forth in the foregoing answer are just and true, to the best of his knowledge, information, and belief.

Sworn to and subscribed before me, ⎫
  this   day of   , A. D. 1887. ⎬   (Signature of Respondent.)
         Judge, C. P. ⎭

§ 1849. **Bills of exceptions—Return to writ under Statute Westminster II. conclusive.** Upon a petition under the Statute Westminster II. (13 Edw. I., ch. 31) for a writ to the judge of a lower court to compel the sealing of a bill of exceptions, the return of the judge is conclusive. If it be untrue in fact, the relator is left to his remedy by action against the judge for a false return. For this reason greater certainty is required in the return to this writ, certainty to the greatest possible extent ; and the proper method of raising the question of the sufficiency of the return is by filing exceptions to it. *Conrow* v. *Schloss*, 55 Pa. St., 28 (1867); *Haines* v. *Comm.*, 99 Pa. St., 410 (1882).

§ 1850. **Trial.** As already indicated, if an issue of fact be raised at any stage of the proceedings, it must be decided, as in the case of other civil action, before a jury. Order the case on the trial-list, and prepare for trial with its usual incidents of verdict, motion, and rule for a new trial, payment of jury fee, and final judgment.

§ 1851. **Peremptory mandamus.** Any of these roads having been travelled to final judgment in your favor, obtain the writ of peremptory mandamus, which issues of course. It should follow the language of the alternative writ down to the command to show cause, etc. Serve it in the same manner as is required in the case of the alternative mandamus. See section 1835.

§ 1852.

FORM OF PEREMPTORY MANDAMUS.

County of Philadelphia, *ss.*

The Commonwealth of Pennsylvania to (names of respondents), greeting: Whereas (names of relators), lately, that is to say, in the term of , A. D. 18 . , No. , exhibited their petition before the Honorable the Judges of our Court of Common Pleas, No. , for the county of Philadelphia, asking relief touching the matters therein particularly complained of and set forth at length; now therefore, upon due consideration thereof, we do command you (here insert the particular acts and duties to be performed by respondents, as prayed for in your petition).

Witness the Honorable , president of our said court, at Philadelphia, the day of , in the year of our Lord one thousand eight hundred and eighty .

Prothonotary.

§ 1853. **Attachment for contempt.** Where a mandamus is not obeyed, an attachment will issue for contempt. *Comm.* v. *Taylor*, 36 Pa. St., 263 (1860).

Prepare an affidavit showing time and manner of service and averring respondent's neglect or refusal to comply with the mandamus, and take a rule to show cause why the attachment should not issue. The rule being made absolute, get the attachment from the prothonotary and give it to the sheriff for service, with directions as to respondent's address, etc. The sheriff will serve by taking the respondent into custody to await the disposition of the court, which will enforce obedience by process for contempt. See *Comm.* v. *Sheehan*, *81 Pa. St., 132 (1872).

§ 1854.

FORM OF RULE TO SHOW CAUSE WHY AN ATTACHMENT SHOULD NOT ISSUE.

Commonwealth of Pennsylvania *ex rel.*　⎫ Court of Common Pleas,　　, of
　　　　　v.　　　　　　　　　　　　⎬ County. Term, ¦18　. No.　.
　　　A. B. *et al.*　　　　　　　　⎭

And now (date), on consideration of the within affidavit and on motion of　　　　, this court enter a rule on (A. B. *et al.*) to show cause why an attachment should not issue against them for contempt of this court in disobeying the peremptory mandamus issued (date).

Returnable (date).

Get a judge to append his initials.

To this rule the defendant must file an answer. If the court should decide the answer insufficient, an order will be made for the attachment.

§ 1855.

FORM OF ORDER FOR ATTACHMENT.

Commonwealth of Pennsylvania *ex rel.*　⎫ Court of Common Pleas, No.　, of
　　　　　v.　　　　　　　　　　　　⎬ County. Term, 18　. No.　.
　　　C. D. *et al.*　　　　　　　　⎭

And now (date), the answer of the above-named defendants (state official capacity, if any) to the rule granted upon them to show cause why an attachment, as for a contempt, should not be issued against them for disobeying the writ of peremptory mandamus issued against them heretofore, being read, it is judged insufficient as an answer to the rule; and it is decreed that the rule be made absolute; and that an attachment do now issue against (names of defendants), (state official capacity, etc.), and the sheriff of　　　　　County is directed to have them before this court on the first day of　　　.

　　　　　　　　　　　　　　　　　　　(Signature of Judge.)

§ 1856.

FORM OF ATTACHMENT.

STATE OF PENNSYLVANIA,　⎱
COUNTY OF PHILADELPHIA,　⎰ *ss.*

The Commonwealth of Pennsylvania to the sheriff of the said county, greeting :

We command you to attach A. B. so to have him before our Court of Common Pleas, No.　, of said county forthwith, then and there to answer, as well touching a contempt which he, as it is alleged, has committed against us in disobeying the peremptory writ of mandamus issued out of this court (date) as of　　　Term, No.　, as also such other matters as shall be laid to his charge ; and further to abide the orders of our said Court in this behalf. And hereof fail not.

Witness the Honorable　　　, president judge of said court, at Philadelphia, this　　　day of　　　, A. D. one thousand eight hundred and eighty　.

　　　　　　　　　　　　　　　　　　　A. B.,
[SEAL]　　　　　　　　　　　　　　　　　Clerk.

§ 1857. **Damages.** Damages suffered by the relator may be assessed by the jury trying issues of fact, and may be collected by the ordinary process of execution. If the case be decided without the intervention of a jury, relator may have his writ of inquiry of damages. See Chapter XV. upon that head.

Society v. *Comm.*, 31 Pa. St., 86 (1885), LEWIS, C. J. "The Act of 14 June, 1836, gives the right to recover damages in the writ of mandamus as in an action for a false return of such writ."

§ 1858. **Appeal.** From the final judgment of the Court of Common Pleas an appeal will lie to the Supreme Court, as in other actions at law ; but judgment awarding the alternative writ is not final, and an appeal therefrom is premature. *Supervisors* v. *Brodhead*, 7 Cent. Rep., 496 (1887). See sections 1751*m*, 1751*n*, and 1751*o*.

§ 1859. *The pleadings and no extraneous matters are considered by the Supreme Court on appeal.* Those defenses which should be set up in the defendant's return to a writ of alternative mandamus, and which are omitted, cannot be considered on error to the Supreme Court. *Borough* v. *Water Co.*, 97 Pa. St., 554 (1881).

In *Comm.* v. *Dechert*, 16 W. N., 508 (1885), a writ of peremptory mandamus was awarded, directed to the controller of Philadelphia, to countersign a warrant drawn in favor of relator. The respondent took a writ of error, but the relator, fearing that the delay in the Supreme Court would practically be a decision against him, obtained a rule to enforce obedience to the mandamus upon filing a refunding bond, with security, for the repayment of the money if the decision should be reversed.

CHAPTER XXIII.

NEGLIGENCE.

§ 1860. No limitation as to damages for injuries nor as to time within which action shall be brought against corporation, different from other cases.

No Act of the General Assembly shall limit the amount to be recovered for injuries resulting in death, or for injuries to persons or property; and, in case of death from such injuries, the right of action shall survive, and the General Assembly shall prescribe for whose benefit such action shall be prosecuted. No Act shall prescribe any limitations of time within which suits may be brought against corporations for injuries to persons or property, or for other causes, different from those fixed by general laws regulating actions against natural persons; and such Acts now existing are avoided. (Constitution of 1874, article 3, section 21.)

§ 1861. Action shall not abate by death of plaintiff.

No action hereafter brought to recover damages for injuries to the person by negligence or default shall abate by reason of the death of the plaintiff; but the personal representatives of the deceased may be substituted as plaintiff, and prosecute the suit to final judgment and satisfaction. (Act of April 15, 1851, section 18; P. L., 674.)

§ 1862. Widow or personal representatives may maintain action.

Whenever death shall be occasioned by unlawful violence or negligence, and no suit for damages be brought by the party injured during his or her life, the widow of any such deceased, or, if there be no widow, the personal representatives, may maintain an action for and recover damages for the death thus occasioned. (*Ibid.*, section 19.)

§ 1863. Who may bring action.

The persons entitled to recover damages for any injury causing death shall be the husband, widow, children, or parents of the deceased, and no other relative; and the sum recovered shall go to them in the proportion they would take his or her personal estate in case of intestacy, and that without liability to creditors. (Act of April 26, 1855, section 1; P. L., 309.)

§ 1864. When action shall be brought—Declaration.

The declaration shall state who are the parties entitled to such action; the action shall be brought within one year after the death, and not thereafter. (*Ibid.*, section 2.)

§ 1865. **Certain laborers employed on roads, etc., of railroad companies have only rights of employés.**

When any person shall sustain personal injury or loss of life while lawfully engaged or employed on or about the roads, works, depots, and premises of a railroad company, or in or about any train or car therein or thereon, of which company such person is not an employé, the right of action and recovery in all such cases against the company shall be such only as would exist if such person were an employé: *Provided*, that this section shall not apply to passengers. (Act of April 4, 1868, section 1; P. L., 58.)

§ 1866. **Damages.**

In all actions now or hereafter instituted against common carriers, or corporations owning, operating, or using a railroad as a public highway, whereon steam or other motive power is used, to recover for loss and damage sustained, and arising either from personal injuries or loss of life, and for which, by law, such carrier or corporation could be held responsible, only such compensation for loss and damage shall be recovered as the evidence shall clearly prove to have been pecuniarily suffered or sustained, not exceeding in case of personal injury the sum of three thousand dollars, nor in case of loss of life the sum of five thousand dollars. (*Ibid.*, section 2.)

§ 1867. **Article 3, section 21, of the Constitution**—*At first held unavailing as against previous acceptance of the provisions of the Act of April 4, 1868.* Under the constitutional provision, above quoted (Article 3, section 21), it was held in *Pa. R. R. Co.* v. *Langdon*, 92 Pa. St., 21 (1879), per PAXSON, J., that a railroad company accepting by formal resolution of its board of directors that portion of the Act of April 4, 1868 (P. L., 58), which limited the amount recoverable for death caused by the negligence of common carriers, thereby made such Act a part of its charter, which could not be abrogated by the subsequent adoption of the Constitution; that therefore, in spite of the provisions of section 21, Article 3, a company which had so accepted in 1868 could not be held liable in case of death resulting from its negligence in a greater amount than $5000.

§ 1868. *Effect of Article 3, section 21, doubted.* In *Railroad Company* v. *Boyer*, 97 Pa. St., 91 (1881), it was doubted, though not decided, whether the constitutional prohibition repealed the limitation of liability for death under the Act of 1868, and whether that Act applied at all to a railroad company which had not accepted it.

§ 1869. *Limitation of liability held abrogated—Constitution applies equally to accepting and non-accepting corporations. Lewis* v. *Hollahan*, 103 Pa. St., 425 (1883), took more decided ground.

It was therein held that the statutory limitation to $5000 damages
in case of death applied equally to assenting and non-assenting corporations; that the result of non-acceptance by any company was
merely to deprive it of the privilege of indemnity by insurance, as
provided by section 3 of the Act of April 4, 1868, and of the benefit of section 4 of that Act.   Further, that the limitation of liability
contained in said Act was abrogated and repealed by Article 3, section 21, of the Constitution.   The earlier case of *Pa. R. R. Co.* v.
Langdon, supra, was said to be " well decided on other controlling
questions, but we do not see our way clear to follow it as authority
on the precise constitutional question involved in this case.   One
of the questions in that case was as to the effect of acceptance by
the company of the Act of 1868.   In this case that question does
not arise."   Per STERRETT, J.   But in *R. R. Co.* v. *Conway,* 17
W. N., 429 (1886), it was said that *Railroad Co.* v. *Langdon* was
not overruled by *Lewis* v. *Hollahan, supra,* though (per PAXSON,
J.) " some of the reasoning by which it was supported was not
sustained in the later case."   A verdict of over $5000 was sus-
tained, it not having properly appeared at the trial of the cause
that the defendant company had accepted the provisions of the Act
of April 4, 1868.

§ 1870. *Lewis* v. *Hollahan confirmed.   R. R. Co.* v. *Langdon
overruled.*   In *R. R. Co.* v. *Bowers,* 124 Pa. St., 183 (1889), this
vexed question was finally settled.   It was there held doubtful
whether the legislature is empowered to make a binding contract
with corporations limiting their liability for negligence, which it is
beyond the power of a subsequent legislature to repeal or modify ;
and it was explicitly ruled that the limitations of liability contained in the Act of April 4, 1868, were absolutely repealed and
annulled as to accepting or non-accepting corporations by virtue
of the constitutional clause above referred to.   " *Railroad Company*
v. *Langdon,* as was said by our brother STERRETT in *Lewis* v. *Hollahan, supra,* was well decided on other controlling questions, and
upon all of those questions it stands as authority.   To the extent,
however, that it refers to the effect of the present Constitution upon
the Act of 1868, it is now overruled."   Opinion by PAXSON, C. J.
Judgment affirmed upon a verdict for plaintiff of $14,500 (all above
$10,000 remitted), against a carrier which had accepted the Act of
1868, the cause of action being death occasioned by the negligence
of the company defendant.

§ 1871. **Limitation of liability for personal injuries invalid.** The
right to recover damages for personal injuries is not the creature of
statute law.   It is protected wholly and in part by the bill of rights,

and the provision in the Act of April 4, 1868 (P. L., 58), limiting the liability of carriers for such injuries, when caused by their negligence, to $3000 is invalid. *Central Railway* v. *Cook*, 1 W. N., 319 (1875) ; *Passenger Railway* v. *Boudrou*, 92 Pa. St., 475 (1880).

§ 1872. **Special limitations of time for bringing action avoided.** *In re Grape Street*, 103 Pa. St., 121 (1883), section 21, Article 3, of the Constitution was given a broad construction, applying it to· all claims against individuals or corporations without regard to the form of proceedings to enforce the claim. It was held that thereby the limitation of one year prescribed in the general road law of June 13, 1836, section 7, for the commencment of proceedings for assessing damages for the opening of streets was avoided as to damages accrued since the Constitution went into effect. See also *Brower* v. *City*, 26 W. N., 270 (1890).

The special period of limitation of three years, established by Act of April 17, 1866 (P. L., 106), in the cases therein enumerated (for right of way and for use and occupancy), is repealed by *Article 3, section 21*, of the *Constitution of 1874*. *Dowling* v. *R. R. Co.*, 21 W. N., 527 (1888) ; *Seiple* v. *B. & C. V. R. R. Co.*, 129 Pa. St., 425 (1889).

§ 1873. **Limitation under Act of April 26, 1855, not repealed.** But the limitation of one year within which actions must be brought under the Act of 26 April, 1855, is not repealed by this section of the Constitution. *Wasson* v. *Pa. Co.*, 25 P. L. J., 184 (1878) ; *Kashner* v. *R. R. Co.*, 41 Leg. Int., 346 (1884).

§ 1874. **Suit does not abate upon death of wrongdoer.** The provision in the Constitution (Article 3, section 21), that the right of action for injury to persons or property shall survive, means that such right shall survive in favor of the representatives of the person injured, not that it shall survive the death of him who commits the injury. *Moe* v. *Smiley*, 125 Pa. St., 136 (1889). But the Act of June 24, 1895 (P. L., 236), provides that in cases of injuries wrongfully done to the person of another the right of action shall survive against the personal representatives of the wrongdoer.

§ 1875. **Acts of 15 April, 1851, and 26 April, 1855**—*Action thereunder should be brought in name of all surviving children.* Under Acts of 15 April, 1851 (P. L., 674), and 26 April, 1855 (P. L., 309), an action for the death of a father caused by defendant's negligence should be brought in the names of all the children, whether injured by the death or not. The proceeds of the suit are to be divided among them as if under the intestate law, and, though the action is in *tort*, they may recover jointly. *R. R. Co.* v. *Robinson,* 44 Pa. St., 175 (1863).

§ 1876. **If widow survive, action should be brought in her name alone.** If the person killed leave a widow and children, only the former should be made plaintiff, but the children should be named as parties entitled. *R. R. Co.* v. *Decker,* 84 Pa. St., 419 (1877); *Borough* v. *Reinhart,* 41 Leg. Int., 337 (1883).

§ 1877. **Court will not reverse for technical misjoiner after trial on the merits.** If the children be improperly joined as plaintiffs, the Supreme Court will not reverse therefor, after trial on the merits, without objection, and after verdict and judgment against defendant. *R. R. Co.* v. *Conway,* 17 W. N., 429 (1886).

§ 1878. **If decedent leave widow, his parents are not entitled.** If a widow and parents, but no children, survive, the widow alone is entitled to the damages. The parents have no right to any part thereof. *Lehigh Co.* v. *Rupp,* 100 Pa. St., 95 (1882).

§ 1879. **Personal representatives cannot sue for the damages— Widow or relatives have the right.** If the injured person die, the right of action against the wrongdoer for his death survives to his widow, not to his personal representatives. The Act of April 26, 1855, is still the law upon this subject, the legislature having made no further enactment in regard thereto under provision of Article 3, section 21, Constitution of 1874. *Books* v. *Borough of Danville,* 95 Pa. St., 158 (1880).

The Act of April 15, 1851, is modified and altered in this respect by that of April 26, 1855, which confers the right to sue upon the relatives therein mentioned instead of decedent's representatives. *Coakley* v. *R. R. Co.,* 5 Clark, 444 (1858); *R. R. Co.* v. *Zebe,* 33 Pa. St., 318 (1858); *Books* v. *Borough of Danville, supra.* But the earlier Act is not so far repealed as to invalidate proceedings under it before the passage of the later one. *Conroy* v. *R. R. Co.,* 1 Pitts., 440 (1858). A husband suing as administrator of his wife was in that case allowed to amend his *narr.* in accordance with the Act of April 26, 1855, upon the passage of that Act.

§ 1880. **Action lies for death caused by sale of liquor to an intoxicated person.** An action may be maintained by a widow against an innkeeper who has furnished intoxicating liquor to her husband while he was drunk, in consequence of which he fell and received injuries resulting in death. Her right to sue in such case is sustained by Acts of April 15, 1851, sections 18, 19 (P. L., 674), and April 26, 1855, section 1 (P. L., 309), in conjunction with the Act of May 8, 1854 (P. L., 663). *Fink* v. *Garman,* 40 Pa. St., 95 (1861).

§ 1881. **Recovery for death of adult child if the family relation have continued.** Parents may recover for the death of a child over age if the family relation be shown to have continued, and if there be ground for reasonable expectation of pecuniary advantage from him. *R. R. Co.* v. *Adams*, 55 Pa. St., 499 (1867) ; *R. R. Co.* v. *Keller*, 67 Pa. St., 300 (1871).

§ 1882. **The question is for the jury.** It is for the jury to say whether there is such reasonable expectation. *R. R. Co.* v. *Kirk*, 90 Pa. St., 15 (1879).

§ 1883. **No right of action in parents for death of emancipated infant child.** If the child be free by age or emancipation, and live apart from his parents, contributing nothing to their support, they have no right of action for his death. In this case the decedent was an infant nineteen years of age, and married. *Lehigh Co.* v. *Rupp*, 100 Pa. St., 95 (1882).

§ 1884. **Mother cannot recover for injury to minor child.** A mother cannot recover under the Acts for injury (not resulting in death) to her minor son, nor for the expense of medical attendance, etc., incurred in curing him of such injury. *Railway Co.* v. *Stuttler*, 54 Pa. St., 375 (1867). See also *Veon* v. *Creaton*, 27 W. N., 57 (1890), in regard to the "person aggrieved," under Act of May 8, 1854 (P. L., 633), by injuries to a minor son not resulting in his death.

§ 1885. **Father may have an action for injury to infant son.** A father may recover for loss of services of an infant son and for expenses of nursing, etc., if the son be injured by the negligence of another. *R. R. Co.* v. *Kelly*, 31 Pa. St., 372 (1858).

§ 1886. **Mother may recover for death of infant son.** If the minor son of a widow die from his injuries, she may recover against him whose negligence was the cause of it. *R. R. Co.* v. *Bantom*, 54 Pa. St., 495 (1867).

§ 1887. **Mother of a bastard cannot maintain action for his death.** The mother of a bastard has no right of action for negligence resulting in his death. *Harkins* v. *P. & R. R. R. Co.*, 11 W. N., 120 (1881).

§ 1888. **Act of April 26, 1855, is without extra-territorial effect.** The Act of April 26, 1855, has no extra-territorial force. It will not sustain an action by the widow in a Pennsylvania court for an injury committed in New Jersey, resulting in the death of her husband, the law of that State requiring such an action to be brought by the representatives of the decedent for the benefit of the widow and next of kin. *Usher* v. *R. R. Co.*, 126 Pa. St., 206 (1889) ; *Knight* v. *R. R. Co.*, 13 W. N., 251 (1883).

§ 1889. Suit authorized against the representatives of a decedent·wrongdoer. The Acts of April 15, 1851, section 19 (P. L., 674), and April 26, 1855 (P. L., 309), did not authorize a suit against the representatives of one who kills another by violence brought after the death of the wrongdoer. *Moe* v. *Smiley*, 125 Pa. St., 136 (1889). But such action may be maintained under the Act of June 24, 1895 (P. L., 236). See § 1874.

§ 1890. Damages under the Acts of April 15, 1851, and April 26, 1855—*To be measured by pecuniary standard*. Damages for the death of another caused by defendant's negligence are to be estimated by a pecuniary standard. *R. R. Co.* v. *Robinson*, 44 Pa. St., 175 (1863); *R. R. Co.* v. *Zebe*, 33 Pa. St., 318 (1858); *R. R. Co.* v. *Vandever*, 36 Pa. St., 298 (1860); *R. R. Co.* v. *Decker*, 84 Pa. St., 419 (1877).

No mental *solatium* or compensation for the sufferings of the person injured can be allowed the survivors. *R. R. Co.* v. *Zebe, supra;* *R. R. Co.* v. *Butler*, 57 Pa. St., 335 (1868); *R. R. Co.* v. *Vandever*, 36 Pa. St., 298 (1860); *Coakley* v. *R. R. Co.*, 5 Clark, 444 (1858); *Coal Co.* v. *McEnery*, 91 Pa. St., 185 (1879).

§ 1891. Compensation the rule. For negligence without wantonness or malice the damages are merely compensatory. *Lehigh Co.* v. *Rupp*, 100 Pa. St., 95 (1882); *Phila. Traction Co.* v. *Orbann*, 119 Pa. St., 37 (1888); *Collins* v. *Leafy*, 124 Pa. St., 203 (1889).

§ 1892. Probable earnings the true measure of loss by death. The proper measure of pecuniary loss suffered by the death of a father is the amount which the deceased would probably have earned by his intellectual or bodily labor in his business or profession during the residue of his lifetime, and which would have gone for the benefit of those suing, taking into consideration his age, ability, and disposition to labor, and his habits of living and expenditure. Per SHARSWOOD, J., in *R. R. Co.* v. *Butler*, 57 Pa. St., 335 (1868).

§ 1893. Pecuniary damage must be clearly shown. The measure of damage is such compensation only as the evidence shall clearly show to have been pecuniarily suffered by surviving relatives. *R. R. Co.* v. *Decker*, 84 Pa. St., 419 (1877). See *R. R. Co.* v. *Keller*, 67 Pa. St., 300 (1871).

§ 1894. Legal claim upon decedent not essential—*Jury must determine amount*. It is not necessary to sustain the action that the survivors should have had a legal claim upon the person killed. *Id.* The sound sense of the jury must ascertain the pecuniary value from the evidence in the case. *Id.* The damages are such as the court and jury, under all the circumstances, shall consider reasonable. *R. R. Co.* v. *Bantom*, 54 Pa. St., 495 (1867).

§ 1895. **Under Act of 1855 jury should be definitely instructed as to the measure of damage.** Under the Act of April 26, 1855, it is error to allow the jury to apply what standard they may see fit for the measurement of damages. *R. R. Co.* v. *Kelly*, 31 Pa. St., 372 (1858) ; *R. R. Co.* v. *Zebe*, 33 Pa. St., 318 (1858) ; *R. R. Co.* v. *Vandever, Id.*, 298 (1860). See *Collins* v. *Leafy*, 124 Pa. St., 203 (1889).

So it is error to instruct the jury that in measuring the damage "they might also consider the opportunities of acquiring wealth or fortune by change of circumstances in life." *Mansfield Co.* v. *McEnery*, 91 Pa. St., 185 (1879).

But if the idea of mere compensation be fairly expressed in the charge of the court, it is not error that the word "compensation" is omitted. *R. R. Co.* v. *Franz*, 24 W. N., 321 (1889).

§ 1896. **More latitude allowed the jury under Act of 1851.** It would seem to have been proper, however, to allow the jury to find the standard of measurement in a suit by decedent's personal representatives, under Act of April 15, 1851. "The law can furnish no definite measure for damages that are essentially indefinite." Per LOWRIE, J. *R. R. Co.* v. *McCloskey*, 23 Pa. St., 526 (1854).

§ 1897. **Measure of damage in suit for death of minor child.** If the suit be by parents for the death of a minor child, the standard of damage is the pecuniary value of his services during minority, expenses of nursing, medical and funeral expenses, etc. *R. R. Co.* v. *Zebe*, 33 Pa. St., 318 (1858). See *R. R. Co.* v. *Kelly*, 31 Pa. St., 372 (1858) ; *R. R. Co.* v. *Bantom*, 54 Pa. St., 495 (1867).

The standard is the same if the plaintiff be the widowed mother of the deceased minor. *R. R. Co.* v. *Bantom*, *supra*.

§ 1898. **In suit for injury to child, parent should not recover the damages enuring to the person injured.** In estimating the damage to a parent for injury to his minor child, the elements of compensation for which the child himself has a right of action should be excluded from the calculation. *R. R. Co.* v. *Kelly*, 31 Pa. St., 372 (1858).

§ 1899. **Measure of damage for personal injuries.** Damages for injuries resulting from negligence generally include not only the direct expenses incurred by the plaintiff by reason of the injury, but also for the privation and inconvenience he is subjected to, and for the pain and suffering he has already endured, bodily and mentally, and which he is likely to experience, as well as the pecuniary loss he has sustained, and is likely to sustain, during the remainder of his life from his disabled condition. *Scott Township* v. *Montgomery*, 95 Pa. St., 444 (1880).

§ 1900. **Punitive damages.** Exemplary or punitive damages are recoverable where the act of defendant's servant has been committed wilfully and maliciously, or in the absence of actual malice, where it has been committed under circumstances of violence, oppression, outrage, or wanton recklessness. *Coakley* v. *R. R. Co.*, 5 Clark, 444 (1858); *Nagle* v. *Mullison*, 34 Pa. St., 48 (1859); *Phila. Traction Co.* v. *Orbann, supra; R. R. Co.* v. *Lyon*, 123 Pa. St., 140 (1888).

If the injury complained of was caused by the defendant's wilful misconduct, or that entire want of care which would raise a presumption of conscious indifference to consequences, he is liable for exemplary damages. A corporation is so liable for the act of its servant, done within the scope of his authority, under circumstances which would give such right to the plaintiff against the servant were the suit against him. *R. R. Co.* v. *Rosenweig*, 113 Pa. St., 519 (1886). See remarks upon the subject of punitive damages for the recklessness of a servant in *McFadden* v. *Rausch*, 119 Pa. St., 507 (1888); opinion of WLLIAMS, J.

§ 1901. **For enforcement of illegal rule.** Injury occasioned through a corporation's enforcement of an illegal rule which it has adopted may subject such corporation to liability for vindictive damages. *R. R. Co.* v. *Lyons, supra.*

§ 1902. **Jury to decide whether act is malicious or wanton.** If is for the jury to say whether circumstances exist which will warrant punitive damages; but it is error to submit the question without evidence which would fairly justify them in so finding. *Nagle* v. *Mullison, supra; Phila. Traction Co.* v. *Orbann, supra.*

§ 1903. **Evidence of motive admissible.** The motive of defendant is material in determining the question of malice. *R. R. Co.* v. *Lyon*, 123 Pa. St., 140 (1888).

§ 1904. **Act of April 4, 1868**—*In* pari materiâ *with preceding legislation.* The Act of April 4, 1868 (P. L., 58), is in *pari materiâ* with that of April 26, 1855, the two making one system. Its purpose was not to abrogate or limit the earlier Act, but to declare the judicial construction thereof, *i. e.*, that loss by death through negligence is to be measured by a pecuniary standard of value. *R. R. Co.* v. *Keller*, 67 Pa. St., 300 (1871).

§ 1905. *The Act is constitutional.* The provision in the Act of April 4, 1868 (P. L., 58), that the right of action for injury or death to persons employed on or about railroads, etc., shall be only such as would exist if such persons were employés, is constitutional. *Kirby* v. *Pa. R. R. Co.*, 76 Pa. St., 506 (1874).

§ 1906. **Employé of another railroad.** If one railroad company have a right of way over the tracks of another such company, an employé of the latter being upon said tracks in the course of his employment is within the terms of the Act of April 4, 1868; he has no right of action against the first company for injuries received by being struck by its train while so upon the tracks, except such right as its own employé would have. *Mulherrin* v. *R. R. Co.*, 81 Pa. St., 366 (1876).

§ 1907. **One injured while unloading his own goods.** The Act is applicable to one injured while unloading his own goods from the cars of a railroad company, under permission granted by the agent of the company. *Ricard* v. *N. P. R. R. Co.*, 89 Pa. St., 193 (1879).

§ 1908. *Or those of his master.* So it applies to a lad employed by a coal dealer in unloading railroad cars standing upon a siding constructed by the dealer on his own land, the lad being injured through the negligence of the railroad company's servants. *Cummings* v. *R. R. Co.*, 92 Pa. St., 82 (1879). See *Gerard* v. *R. R. Co.*, 12 Phila., 394 (1878).

§ 1909. **Teamster hauling freight for shipper.** A teamster employed by a shipper in hauling freight to the railroad cars, while driving on the public street at the freight station where crossed by the company's tracks at a point practically within its yard, was struck by a moving train and injured. *Held,* that he was within the Act of 1868, and could not recover against the railroad company if his injury resulted from the negligence of its employé. *B. & O. R. R. Co.* v. *Colvin,* 118 Pa. St., 230 (1888).

§ 1910. **Business about the cars in the line of duty.** If the plaintiff be injured in doing an act about the cars of the defendant company which is clearly within the line of his duty, he comes under the terms of the Act, and he can recover only as if he were an employé. *Stone* v. *Pa. R. R. Co.,* 132 Pa. St., 206 (1890).

§ 1911. **Laborer for contractor with the railroad company.** In *Fleming* v. *Pa. R. R. Co.,* 134 Pa. St., 477 (1890), the railroad company defendant had agreed with a firm of contractors who were to construct a bridge upon its route. A workman was employed by the contractors in wheeling bricks between the rails from the brick-pile to the bridge. While so engaged he was struck and killed by a train of the defendant company which was going at a rapid rate of speed, and without warning. In an action by his parents against the company, it was held that he was within the terms of the Act of 1868, and that the court below had therefore properly entered a non-suit. Judgment affirmed.

§ 1912. **Mail agent held not a passenger while travelling in the course of his employment.** A mail agent employed by the United

States Postal Department, while travelling on a railroad in the performance of his duties, is not a passenger within the meaning of the word as used in the proviso to the Act of April 4, 1868. If he be killed by reason of the negligence of an employé of the railroad company, his widow has no right of action against it. *Pa. R. R. Co.* v. *Price,* 96 Pa. St., 256 (1880). Opinion by PAXSON, J.; TRUNKEY, J., dissenting. See also *Bricker* v. *R. R. Co.,* 132 Pa. St., 1 (1890).

§ 1913. **The Act does not apply to one injured while moving cars, not in the course of his employment.** One employed in a mill to haul ashes from one part of the mill-yard to another, across a railway switch in the yard, is not within the Act of April 4, 1868. If in the course of such employment and while moving out of his way empty cars standing upon the switch, he be killed through the negligence of the railroad company's employés, his widow may maintain an action against the company. *Richter* v. *Penna. Co.,* 104 Pa. St., 511 (1883).

Otherwise, if it be part of his duty to shift the cars. *Stone* v. *R. R. Co.,* 132 Pa. St., 206 (1890).

§ 1914. **Nor to newsboy on street passenger car by permission.** A boy selling newspapers by permission upon a street passenger car is not precluded by the Act from recovering against the car company for injuries sustained through the negligence of its employé. *Phila. Traction Co.* v. *Orbann,* 119 Pa. St., 37 (1888).